Book 1 – Ethical and Professional Standards and Quantitative Methods

SCHWESERNOTES™ 2013 CFA LEVEL I BOOK 1: ETHICAL AND
PROFESSIONAL STANDARDS AND QUANTITATIVE METHODS

©2012 Kaplan, Inc. All rights reserved.

Published in 2012 by Kaplan Schweser.

Printed in the United States of America.

ISBN: 978-1-4277-4269-8 / 1-4277-4269-3

PPN: 3200-2844

WELCOME TO THE 2013 SCHWESERNOTES™

Thank you for trusting Kaplan Schweser to help you reach your goals. We are all very pleased to be able to help you prepare for the Level I CFA Exam. In this introduction, I want to explain the resources included with the SchweserNotes, suggest how you can best use Schweser materials to prepare for the exam, and direct you toward other educational resources you will find helpful as you study for the exam.

Besides the SchweserNotes themselves, there are many educational resources available at Schweser.com. Just log in using the individual username and password that you received when you purchased the SchweserNotes.

SchweserNotes™

These consist of five volumes that include complete coverage of all 18 Study Sessions and all Learning Outcome Statements (LOS) with examples, Concept Checkers (multiple-choice questions for every topic review), and Challenge Problems for many topic reviews to help you master the material and check your progress. At the end of each major topic area, we include a Self-test. Self-test questions are created to be exam-like in format and difficulty in order for you to evaluate how well your study of each topic has prepared you for the actual exam.

Practice Questions

To retain what you learn, it is important that you quiz yourself often. We offer CD, download, and online versions of the SchweserPro™ QBank, which contains thousands of Level I practice questions and explanations. Quizzes are available for each LOS, topic, or Study Session. Build your own exams by specifying the topics and the number of questions you choose.

Practice Exams

Schweser offers six full 6-hour practice exams. Practice Exams Volume 1 and Volume 2 each contain three full 240-question exams. These are important tools for gaining the speed and skills you will need to pass the exam. Each book contains answers with full explanations for self-grading and evaluation. By entering your answers at Schweser.com, you can use our Performance Tracker to find out how you have performed compared to other Schweser Level I candidates.

Schweser Library

We have created reference videos, some of which are available to all SchweserNotes purchasers. Schweser Library volumes are typically between 20 and 60 minutes in length and cover such topics as: "CFA Level I Exam Overview," "Calculator Basics," "Code and Standards Overview," and "Time Value of Money." The full Schweser Library is included with our 16-week live or online classes and with our video instruction (online or CDs).

Online Schweser Study Planner

Use your Online Access to tell us when you will start and what days of the week you can study. The online Schweser Study Planner will create a study plan just for you, breaking each study session into daily and weekly tasks to keep you on track and help you monitor your progress through the curriculum.

Additional Resources

Purchasers of the Essential Self-Study or Premium Instruction Packages also receive access to our Instructor-led Office Hours. Office Hours allow you to get your questions about the curriculum answered in real time and to see others' questions (and instructor answers) as well. Office Hours is a text-based live interactive online chat with our team of Level I experts. Archives of previous Office Hours sessions can be sorted by topic or date and are posted shortly after each session.

The Level I CFA exam is a formidable challenge (67 topic reviews and 500+ Learning Outcome Statements), and you must devote considerable time and effort to be properly prepared. There is no shortcut! You must learn the material, know the terminology and techniques, understand the concepts, and be able to answer 240 questions quickly and (at least 70%) correctly. Fifteen to 20 hours per week for 20 weeks is a good estimate of the study time required on average, but some candidates will need more or less time, depending on their individual backgrounds and experience.

To help you master this material and be well prepared for the CFA Exam, we offer several other educational resources, including:

Live Weekly Classroom Programs

We offer weekly classroom programs around the world. Please check Schweser.com for locations, dates, and availability.

16-Week Online Class

Our 16-Week Online Classes are available at New York time (6:30–9:30 pm) or London time (6:00–9:00 pm) beginning in January and August. The approximate schedule for the 16-Week Online Classes (3-hour sessions) is as follows:

Class #	Class #
1 Exam Intro/Quantitative Methods SS2	9 Financial Reporting & Analysis SS10
2 Quantitative Methods SS3	10 Corporate Finance SS11
3 Economics SS4, 5	11 Equity Investments SS13, 14
4 Economics SS5, 6	12 Fixed Income SS15
5 Financial Reporting & Analysis SS7	13 Fixed Income SS16
6 Financial Reporting & Analysis SS8	14 Derivatives SS17
7 Financial Reporting & Analysis SS8, 9	15 Portfolio Management & Alternative Investments SS12, 18
8 Financial Reporting & Analysis SS9	16 Ethical and Professional Standards SS1

Archived classes are available for viewing at any time throughout the season. Candidates enrolled in the 16-Week Online Classes also have full access to supplemental on-demand video instruction in the Schweser Library and an e-mail address to use to send questions to the instructor at any time.

Late Season Review

Whether you use self-study or in-class, online, or video instruction to learn the CFA curriculum, a late-season review and exam practice can make all the difference. Our most complete late-season review course is our residence program in Windsor, Ontario (WindsorWeek) where we cover the entire curriculum over seven days (May 4–10) at all three levels. We also offer 3-Day Exam Workshops in many cities (and online) that combine curriculum review with an equal component of hands-on practice with hundreds of questions and problem-solving techniques. Our Dallas/Fort Worth review program extends to five days (May 13–17). Please visit us at Schweser.com for complete listings and course descriptions for all our late-season review offerings.

Mock Exam and Multimedia Tutorial

On May 18, 2013, and November 23, 2013, the Schweser Mock Exam will be offered live in over 60 cities around the world and as an online exam as well. The optional Multimedia Tutorial provides extended explanations and topic tutorials to get you exam-ready in topic areas where you miss questions on the Mock Exam. Please visit Schweser.com for a listing of cities and locations.

Topic Weighting

In preparing for the exam, you must pay attention to the weights assigned to each topic within the curriculum. The Level I topic weights are as follows:

Topic	Exam Weight
Ethical and Professional Standards	15%
Quantitative Methods	12%
Economics	10%
Financial Reporting and Analysis	20%
Corporate Finance	8%
Portfolio Management	5%
Equity Investments	10%
Fixed Income Investments	12%
Derivatives	5%
Alternative Investments	3%
Total	100%

How to Succeed

There are no shortcuts; depend on the fact that CFA Institute will test you in a way that will reveal how well you know the Level I curriculum. You should begin early and stick to your study plan. You should first read the SchweserNotes and complete the Concept Checkers and Challenge Problems for each topic review. You should prepare for and attend a live class, an online class, or a study group each week. You should take quizzes often using SchweserPro Qbank and go back to review previous topics and Study Sessions as well. At the end of each topic area, you should take the Self-test to check your progress. You should finish the overall curriculum at least four weeks (preferably five weeks) before the Level I exam so that you have sufficient time for Practice Exams and for further review of those topics that you have not yet mastered.

I would like to thank Craig Prochaska, CFA, Content Specialist and Jared Heintz, Lead Editor, for their contributions to producing the 2013 Level I SchweserNotes for the CFA Exam.

Best regards,

Doug Van Eaton

Dr. Douglas Van Eaton, CFA
SVP of CFA Education and Level I Manager

Kaplan Schweser

Reading Assignments and Learning Outcome Statements

The following material is a review of the Ethics and Professional Standards and Quantitative Methods principles designed to address the learning outcome statements set forth by CFA Institute.

STUDY SESSION 1

Reading Assignments

Ethical and Professional Standards and Quantitative Methods, CFA Program Curriculum, Volume 1 (CFA Institute, 2013)

STUDY SESSION 2

Reading Assignments

Ethical and Professional Standards and Quantitative Methods, CFA Program Curriculum, Volume 1 (CFA Institute, 2013)

STUDY SESSION 3

Reading Assignments

Ethical and Professional Standards and Quantitative Methods, CFA Program Curriculum, Volume 1 (CFA Institute, 2013)

LEARNING OUTCOME STATEMENTS (LOS)

STUDY SESSION 1

The topical coverage corresponds with the following CFA Institute assigned reading:

1. **Code of Ethics and Standards of Professional Conduct**
   The candidate should be able to:
   a. describe the structure of the CFA Institute Professional Conduct Program and the process for the enforcement of the Code and Standards. (page 13)
   b. state the six components of the Code of Ethics and the seven Standards of Professional Conduct. (page 14)
   c. explain the ethical responsibilities required by the Code and Standards, including the sub-sections of each Standard. (page 15)

2. **Guidance for Standards I–VII**
   The candidate should be able to:
   a. demonstrate the application of the Code of Ethics and Standards of Professional Conduct to situations involving issues of professional integrity. (page 18)
   b. distinguish between conduct that conforms to the Code and Standards and conduct that violates the Code and Standards. (page 18)
   c. recommend practices and procedures designed to prevent violations of the Code of Ethics and Standards of Professional Conduct. (page 18)

3. **Introduction to the Global Investment Performance Standards (GIPS®)**
   The candidate should be able to:
   a. explain why the GIPS standards were created, what parties the GIPS standards apply to, and who is served by the standards. (page 82)
   b. explain the construction and purpose of composites in performance reporting. (page 83)
   c. explain the requirements for verification. (page 83)

4. **Global Investment Performance Standards (GIPS®)**
   The candidate should be able to:
   a. describe the key features of the GIPS standards and the fundamentals of compliance. (page 84)
   b. describe the scope of the GIPS standards with respect to an investment firm's definition and historical performance record. (page 86)
   c. explain how the GIPS standards are implemented in countries with existing standards for performance reporting and describe the appropriate response when the GIPS standards and local regulations conflict. (page 86)
   d. describe the nine major sections of the GIPS standards. (page 86)

STUDY SESSION 2

5. **The Time Value of Money**
   The candidate should be able to:
   a. interpret interest rates as required rates of return, discount rates, or opportunity costs. (page 100)
   b. explain an interest rate as the sum of a real risk-free rate, and premiums that compensate investors for bearing distinct types of risk. (page 101)
   c. calculate and interpret the effective annual rate, given the stated annual interest rate and the frequency of compounding. (page 101)
   d. solve time value of money problems for different frequencies of compounding. (page 103)
   e. calculate and interpret the future value (FV) and present value (PV) of a single sum of money, an ordinary annuity, an annuity due, a perpetuity (PV only), and a series of unequal cash flows. (page 104)
   f. demonstrate the use of a time line in modeling and solving time value of money problems. (page 118)

6. **Discounted Cash Flow Applications**
   The candidate should be able to:
   a. calculate and interpret the net present value (NPV) and the internal rate of return (IRR) of an investment. (page 138)
   b. contrast the NPV rule to the IRR rule, and identify problems associated with the IRR rule. (page 141)
   c. calculate and interpret a holding period return (total return). (page 143)
   d. calculate and compare the money-weighted and time-weighted rates of return of a portfolio and evaluate the performance of portfolios based on these measures. (page 143)
   e. calculate and interpret the bank discount yield, holding period yield, effective annual yield, and money market yield for U.S. Treasury bills and other money market instruments. (page 147)
   f. convert among holding period yields, money market yields, effective annual yields, and bond equivalent yields. (page 150)

7. **Statistical Concepts and Market Returns**
   The candidate should be able to:
   a. distinguish between descriptive statistics and inferential statistics, between a population and a sample, and among the types of measurement scales. (page 163)
   b. define a parameter, a sample statistic, and a frequency distribution. (page 164)
   c. calculate and interpret relative frequencies and cumulative relative frequencies, given a frequency distribution. (page 166)
   d. describe the properties of a data set presented as a histogram or a frequency polygon. (page 168)
   e. calculate and interpret measures of central tendency, including the population mean, sample mean, arithmetic mean, weighted average or mean, geometric mean, harmonic mean, median, and mode. (page 169)
   f. calculate and interpret quartiles, quintiles, deciles, and percentiles. (page 174)
   g. calculate and interpret 1) a range and a mean absolute deviation and 2) the variance and standard deviation of a population and of a sample. (page 175)

    h. calculate and interpret the proportion of observations falling within a specified number of standard deviations of the mean using Chebyshev's inequality. (page 179)

    i. calculate and interpret the coefficient of variation and the Sharpe ratio. (page 180)

    j. explain skewness and the meaning of a positively or negatively skewed return distribution. (page 182)

    k. describe the relative locations of the mean, median, and mode for a unimodal, nonsymmetrical distribution. (page 183)

    l. explain measures of sample skewness and kurtosis. (page 184)

    m. explain the use of arithmetic and geometric means when analyzing investment returns. (page 186)

8. **Probability Concepts**
The candidate should be able to:

    a. define a random variable, an outcome, an event, mutually exclusive events, and exhaustive events. (page 201)

    b. state the two defining properties of probability and distinguish among empirical, subjective, and a priori probabilities. (page 201)

    c. state the probability of an event in terms of odds for and against the event. (page 202)

    d. distinguish between unconditional and conditional probabilities. (page 203)

    e. explain the multiplication, addition, and total probability rules. (page 203)

    f. calculate and interpret 1) the joint probability of two events, 2) the probability that at least one of two events will occur, given the probability of each and the joint probability of the two events, and 3) a joint probability of any number of independent events. (page 204)

    g. distinguish between dependent and independent events. (page 207)

    h. calculate and interpret an unconditional probability using the total probability rule. (page 208)

    i. explain the use of conditional expectation in investment applications. (page 212)

    j. explain the use of a tree diagram to represent an investment problem. (page 212)

    k. calculate and interpret covariance and correlation. (page 213)

    l. calculate and interpret the expected value, variance, and standard deviation of a random variable and of returns on a portfolio. (page 217)

    m. calculate and interpret covariance given a joint probability function. (page 218)

    n. calculate and interpret an updated probability using Bayes' formula. (page 222)

    o. identify the most appropriate method to solve a particular counting problem, and solve counting problems using the factorial, combination, and permutation notations. (page 224)

STUDY SESSION 3

9. **Common Probability Distributions**
The candidate should be able to:

    a. define a probability distribution and distinguish between discrete and continuous random variables and their probability functions. (page 245)

    b. describe the set of possible outcomes of a specified discrete random variable. (page 245)

    c. interpret a cumulative distribution function. (page 247)

d. calculate and interpret probabilities for a random variable, given its cumulative distribution function. (page 247)

e. define a discrete uniform random variable, a Bernoulli random variable, and a binomial random variable. (page 248)

f. calculate and interpret probabilities given the discrete uniform and the binomial distribution functions. (page 248)

g. construct a binomial tree to describe stock price movement. (page 251)

h. calculate and interpret tracking error. (page 253)

i. define the continuous uniform distribution and calculate and interpret probabilities, given a continuous uniform distribution. (page 253)

j. explain the key properties of the normal distribution. (page 255)

k. distinguish between a univariate and a multivariate distribution, and explain the role of correlation in the multivariate normal distribution. (page 255)

l. determine the probability that a normally distributed random variable lies inside a given interval. (page 256)

m. define the standard normal distribution, explain how to standardize a random variable, and calculate and interpret probabilities using the standard normal distribution. (page 258)

n. define shortfall risk, calculate the safety-first ratio, and select an optimal portfolio using Roy's safety-first criterion. (page 261)

o. explain the relationship between normal and lognormal distributions and why the lognormal distribution is used to model asset prices. (page 263)

p. distinguish between discretely and continuously compounded rates of return, and calculate and interpret a continuously compounded rate of return, given a specific holding period return. (page 264)

q. explain Monte Carlo simulation and describe its major applications and limitations. (page 266)

r. compare Monte Carlo simulation and historical simulation. (page 267)

10. Sampling and Estimation

The candidate should be able to:

a. define simple random sampling and a sampling distribution. (page 280)

b. explain sampling error. (page 280)

c. distinguish between simple random and stratified random sampling. (page 281)

d. distinguish between time-series and cross-sectional data. (page 282)

e. explain the central limit theorem and its importance. (page 282)

f. calculate and interpret the standard error of the sample mean. (page 283)

g. identify and describe desirable properties of an estimator. (page 285)

h. distinguish between a point estimate and a confidence interval estimate of a population parameter. (page 285)

i. describe the properties of Student's t-distribution and calculate and interpret its degrees of freedom. (page 285)

j. calculate and interpret a confidence interval for a population mean, given a normal distribution with 1) a known population variance, 2) an unknown population variance, or 3) an unknown variance and a large sample size. (page 287)

k. describe the issues regarding selection of the appropriate sample size, data-mining bias, sample selection bias, survivorship bias, look-ahead bias, and time-period bias. (page 292)

11. **Hypothesis Testing**
The candidate should be able to:
   a. define a hypothesis, describe the steps of hypothesis testing, describe and interpret the choice of the null and alternative hypotheses, and distinguish between one-tailed and two-tailed tests of hypotheses. (page 303)
   b. explain a test statistic, Type I and Type II errors, a significance level, and how significance levels are used in hypothesis testing. (page 308)
   c. explain a decision rule, the power of a test, and the relation between confidence intervals and hypothesis tests. (page 310)
   d. distinguish between a statistical result and an economically meaningful result. (page 312)
   e. explain and interpret the p-value as it relates to hypothesis testing. (page 313)
   f. identify the appropriate test statistic and interpret the results for a hypothesis test concerning the population mean of both large and small samples when the population is normally or approximately distributed and the variance is 1) known or 2) unknown. (page 314)
   g. identify the appropriate test statistic and interpret the results for a hypothesis test concerning the equality of the population means of two at least approximately normally distributed populations, based on independent random samples with 1) equal or 2) unequal assumed variances. (page 317)
   h. identify the appropriate test statistic and interpret the results for a hypothesis test concerning the mean difference of two normally distributed populations. (page 321)
   i. identify the appropriate test statistic and interpret the results for a hypothesis test concerning 1) the variance of a normally distributed population, and 2) the equality of the variances of two normally distributed populations based on two independent random samples. (page 325)
   j. distinguish between parametric and nonparametric tests and describe the situations in which the use of nonparametric tests may be appropriate. (page 332)

12. **Technical Analysis**
The candidate should be able to:
   a. explain the principles of technical analysis, its applications, and its underlying assumptions. (page 343)
   b. describe the construction of and interpret different types of technical analysis charts. (page 344)
   c. explain the uses of trend, support, resistance lines, and change in polarity. (page 347)
   d. identify and interpret common chart patterns. (page 348)
   e. describe common technical analysis indicators: price-based, momentum oscillators, sentiment, and flow of funds. (page 350)
   f. explain the use of cycles by technical analysts. (page 355)
   g. describe the key tenets of Elliott Wave Theory and the importance of Fibonacci numbers. (page 355)
   h. describe intermarket analysis as it relates to technical analysis and asset allocation. (page 356)

The following is a review of the Ethical and Professional Standards principles designed to address the learning outcome statements set forth by CFA Institute. This topic is also covered in:

CFA INSTITUTE CODE OF ETHICS AND STANDARDS OF PROFESSIONAL CONDUCT GUIDANCE FOR STANDARDS I–VII

Study Session 1

EXAM FOCUS

In addition to reading this review of the ethics material, we strongly recommend that all candidates for the CFA® examination read the *Standards of Practice Handbook 10th Edition* (2010) multiple times. As a Level I CFA candidate, it is your responsibility to comply with the *Code and Standards*. The complete *Code and Standards* are reprinted in Volume 1 of the CFA **Program** Curriculum.

LOS 1.a: Describe the structure of the CFA Institute Professional Conduct Program and the process for the enforcement of the Code and Standards.

CFA® Program Curriculum, Volume 1, page 8

The CFA Institute Professional Conduct Program is covered by the CFA Institute Bylaws and the Rules of Procedure for Proceedings Related to Professional Conduct. The Program is based on the principles of fairness of the process to members and candidates and maintaining the confidentiality of the proceedings. The Disciplinary Review Committee of the CFA Institute Board of Governors has overall responsibility for the Professional Conduct Program and enforcement of the Code and Standards.

The CFA Institute Designated Officer, through the Professional Conduct staff, conducts inquiries related to professional conduct. Several circumstances can prompt such an inquiry:

1. Self-disclosure by members or candidates on their annual Professional Conduct Statements of involvement in civil litigation or a criminal investigation, or that the member or candidate is the subject of a written complaint.

2. Written complaints about a member or candidate's professional conduct that are received by the Professional Conduct staff.

3. Evidence of misconduct by a member or candidate that the Professional Conduct staff received through public sources, such as a media article or broadcast.

4. A report by a CFA exam proctor of a possible violation during the examination.

Once an inquiry has begun, the Professional Conduct staff may request (in writing) an explanation from the subject member or candidate and may: (1) interview the subject member or candidate, (2) interview the complainant or other third parties, and/or (3) collect documents and records relevant to the investigation.

The Designated Officer may decide: (1) that no disciplinary sanctions are appropriate, (2) to issue a cautionary letter, or (3) to discipline the member or candidate. In a case where the Designated Officer finds a violation has occurred and proposes a disciplinary sanction, the member or candidate may accept or reject the sanction. If the member or candidate chooses to reject the sanction, the matter will be referred to a panel of CFA Institute members for a hearing. Sanctions imposed may include condemnation by the member's peers or suspension of candidate's continued participation in the CFA Program.

LOS 1.b: State the six components of the Code of Ethics and the seven Standards of Professional Conduct.

CFA® Program Curriculum, Volume 1, page 14

CODE OF ETHICS

Members of CFA Institute [including Chartered Financial Analyst® (CFA®) charterholders] and candidates for the CFA designation ("Members and Candidates") must:[1]

- Act with integrity, competence, diligence, respect, and in an ethical manner with the public, clients, prospective clients, employers, employees, colleagues in the investment profession, and other participants in the global capital markets.
- Place the integrity of the investment profession and the interests of clients above their own personal interests.
- Use reasonable care and exercise independent professional judgment when conducting investment analysis, making investment recommendations, taking investment actions, and engaging in other professional activities.
- Practice and encourage others to practice in a professional and ethical manner that will reflect credit on themselves and the profession.
- Promote the integrity of, and uphold the rules governing, capital markets.
- Maintain and improve their professional competence and strive to maintain and improve the competence of other investment professionals.

THE STANDARDS OF PROFESSIONAL CONDUCT

I:	Professionalism
II:	Integrity of Capital Markets
III:	Duties to Clients
IV:	Duties to Employers
V:	Investment Analysis, Recommendations, and Actions
VI:	Conflicts of Interest
VII:	Responsibilities as a CFA Institute Member or CFA Candidate

---

LOS 1.c: Explain the ethical responsibilities required by the Code and Standards, including the sub-sections of each Standard.

CFA® Program Curriculum, Volume 1, page 14

STANDARDS OF PROFESSIONAL CONDUCT[2]

I. PROFESSIONALISM

   A. Knowledge of the Law. Members and Candidates must understand and comply with all applicable laws, rules, and regulations (including the CFA Institute *Code of Ethics* and *Standards of Professional Conduct*) of any government, regulatory organization, licensing agency, or professional association governing their professional activities. In the event of conflict, Members and Candidates must comply with the more strict law, rule, or regulation. Members and Candidates must not knowingly participate or assist in any violation of laws, rules, or regulations and must disassociate themselves from any such violation.

   B. Independence and Objectivity. Members and Candidates must use reasonable care and judgment to achieve and maintain independence and objectivity in their professional activities. Members and Candidates must not offer, solicit, or accept any gift, benefit, compensation, or consideration that reasonably could be expected to compromise their own or another's independence and objectivity.

   C. Misrepresentation. Members and Candidates must not knowingly make any misrepresentations relating to investment analysis, recommendations, actions, or other professional activities.

   D. Misconduct. Members and Candidates must not engage in any professional conduct involving dishonesty, fraud, or deceit or commit any act that reflects adversely on their professional reputation, integrity, or competence.

II. INTEGRITY OF CAPITAL MARKETS

   A. Material Nonpublic Information. Members and Candidates who possess material nonpublic information that could affect the value of an investment must not act or cause others to act on the information.

   B. Market Manipulation. Members and Candidates must not engage in practices that distort prices or artificially inflate trading volume with the intent to mislead market participants.

III. DUTIES TO CLIENTS

   A. Loyalty, Prudence, and Care. Members and Candidates have a duty of loyalty to their clients and must act with reasonable care and exercise prudent judgment. Members and Candidates must act for the benefit of their clients and place their clients' interests before their employer's or their own interests.

---

2. Ibid.

B. **Fair Dealing.** Members and Candidates must deal fairly and objectively with all clients when providing investment analysis, making investment recommendations, taking investment action, or engaging in other professional activities.

C. **Suitability.**

1. When Members and Candidates are in an advisory relationship with a client, they must:

   a. Make a reasonable inquiry into a client's or prospective clients' investment experience, risk and return objectives, and financial constraints prior to making any investment recommendation or taking investment action and must reassess and update this information regularly.

   b. Determine that an investment is suitable to the client's financial situation and consistent with the client's written objectives, mandates, and constraints before making an investment recommendation or taking investment action.

   c. Judge the suitability of investments in the context of the client's total portfolio.

2. When Members and Candidates are responsible for managing a portfolio to a specific mandate, strategy, or style, they must make only investment recommendations or take investment actions that are consistent with the stated objectives and constraints of the portfolio.

D. **Performance Presentation.** When communicating investment performance information, Members or Candidates must make reasonable efforts to ensure that it is fair, accurate, and complete.

E. **Preservation of Confidentiality.** Members and Candidates must keep information about current, former, and prospective clients confidential unless:

1. The information concerns illegal activities on the part of the client or prospective client,

2. Disclosure is required by law, or

3. The client or prospective client permits disclosure of the information.

IV. **DUTIES TO EMPLOYERS**

A. **Loyalty.** In matters related to their employment, Members and Candidates must act for the benefit of their employer and not deprive their employer of the advantage of their skills and abilities, divulge confidential information, or otherwise cause harm to their employer.

B. **Additional Compensation Arrangements.** Members and Candidates must not accept gifts, benefits, compensation, or consideration that competes with, or might reasonably be expected to create a conflict of interest with, their employer's interest unless they obtain written consent from all parties involved.

C. **Responsibilities of Supervisors.** Members and Candidates must make reasonable efforts to detect and prevent violations of applicable laws, rules, regulations, and the Code and Standards by anyone subject to their supervision or authority.

V. INVESTMENT ANALYSIS, RECOMMENDATIONS, AND ACTIONS

A. **Diligence and Reasonable Basis.** Members and Candidates must:

1. Exercise diligence, independence, and thoroughness in analyzing investments, making investment recommendations, and taking investment actions.

2. Have a reasonable and adequate basis, supported by appropriate research and investigation, for any investment analysis, recommendation, or action.

B. **Communication with Clients and Prospective Clients.** Members and Candidates must:

1. Disclose to clients and prospective clients the basic format and general principles of the investment processes used to analyze investments, select securities, and construct portfolios and must promptly disclose any changes that might materially affect those processes.

2. Use reasonable judgment in identifying which factors are important to their investment analyses, recommendations, or actions and include those factors in communications with clients and prospective clients.

3. Distinguish between fact and opinion in the presentation of investment analysis and recommendations.

C. **Record Retention.** Members and Candidates must develop and maintain appropriate records to support their investment analysis, recommendations, actions, and other investment-related communications with clients and prospective clients.

VI. CONFLICTS OF INTEREST

A. **Disclosure of Conflicts.** Members and Candidates must make full and fair disclosure of all matters that could reasonably be expected to impair their independence and objectivity or interfere with respective duties to their clients, prospective clients, and employer. Members and Candidates must ensure that such disclosures are prominent, are delivered in plain language, and communicate the relevant information effectively.

B. Priority of Transactions. Investment transactions for clients and employers must have priority over investment transactions in which a Member or Candidate is the beneficial owner.

C. Referral Fees. Members and Candidates must disclose to their employer, clients, and prospective clients, as appropriate, any compensation, consideration, or benefit received from, or paid to, others for the recommendation of products or services.

VII. RESPONSIBILITIES AS A CFA INSTITUTE MEMBER OR CFA CANDIDATE

A. Conduct as Members and Candidates in the CFA Program. Members and Candidates must not engage in any conduct that compromises the reputation or integrity of CFA Institute or the CFA designation or the integrity, validity, or security of the CFA examinations.

B. Reference to CFA Institute, the CFA Designation, and the CFA Program. When referring to CFA Institute, CFA Institute membership, the CFA designation, or candidacy in the CFA Program, Members and Candidates must not misrepresent or exaggerate the meaning or implications of membership in CFA Institute, holding the CFA designation, or candidacy in the CFA Program.

LOS 2.a: Demonstrate the application of the Code of Ethics and Standards of Professional Conduct to situations involving issues of professional integrity.

LOS 2.b: Distinguish between conduct that conforms to the Code and Standards and conduct that violates the Code and Standards.

LOS 2.c: Recommend practices and procedures designed to prevent violations of the Code of Ethics and Standards of Professional Conduct.

CFA® Program Curriculum, Volume 1, page 19

I   Professionalism

I(A)   Knowledge of the Law. Members and Candidates must understand and comply with all applicable laws, rules, and regulations (including the CFA Institute Code of Ethics and Standards of Professional Conduct) of any government, regulatory organization, licensing agency, or professional association governing their professional activities. In the event of conflict, Members and Candidates must comply with the more strict law, rule, or regulation. Members and Candidates must not knowingly participate or assist in and must dissociate from any violation of such laws, rules, or regulations.

Professor's Note: While we use the term "members" in the following, note that all of the Standards apply to candidates as well.

Guidance—Code and Standards vs. Local Law

Members must know the laws and regulations relating to their professional activities in all countries in which they conduct business. Members must comply with applicable laws and regulations relating to their professional activity. Do not violate Code or Standards even if the activity is otherwise legal. Always adhere to the most strict rules and requirements (law or CFA Institute Standards) that apply.

Guidance—Participation or Association With Violations by Others

Members should dissociate, or separate themselves, from any ongoing client or employee activity that is illegal or unethical, even if it involves leaving an employer (an extreme case). While a member may confront the involved individual first, he must approach his supervisor or compliance department. Inaction with continued association may be construed as knowing participation.

Recommended Procedures for Compliance—Members

- Members should have procedures to keep up with changes in applicable laws, rules, and regulations.
- Compliance procedures should be reviewed on an ongoing basis to assure that they address current law, CFAI Standards, and regulations.
- Members should maintain current reference materials for employees to access in order to keep up to date on laws, rules, and regulations.
- Members should seek advice of counsel or their compliance department when in doubt.
- Members should document any violations when they disassociate themselves from prohibited activity and encourage their employers to bring an end to such activity.
- There is no requirement under the Standards to report violations to governmental authorities, but this may be advisable in some circumstances and required by law in others.
- Members are strongly encouraged to report other members' violations of the Code and Standards.

Recommended Procedures for Compliance—Firms

Members should encourage their firms to:

- Develop and/or adopt a code of ethics.
- Make available to employees information that highlights applicable laws and regulations.
- Establish written procedures for reporting suspected violation of laws, regulations, or company policies.

Members who supervise the creation and maintenance of investment services and products should be aware of and comply with the regulations and laws regarding such services and products both in their country of origin and the countries where they will be sold.

Application of Standard I(A) Knowledge of the Law[3]

Example 1:

Michael Allen works for a brokerage firm and is responsible for an underwriting of securities. A company official gives Allen information indicating that the financial statements Allen filed with the regulator overstate the issuer's earnings. Allen seeks the advice of the brokerage firm's general counsel, who states that it would be difficult for the regulator to prove that Allen has been involved in any wrongdoing.

Comment:

Although it is recommended that members and candidates seek the advice of legal counsel, the reliance on such advice does not absolve a member or candidate from the requirement to comply with the law or regulation. Allen should report this situation to his supervisor, seek an independent legal opinion, and determine whether the regulator should be notified of the error.

Example 2:

Kamisha Washington's firm advertises its past performance record by showing the 10-year return of a composite of its client accounts. However, Washington discovers that the composite omits the performance of accounts that have left the firm during the 10-year period and that this omission has led to an inflated performance figure. Washington is asked to use promotional material that includes the erroneous performance number when soliciting business for the firm.

Comment:

Misrepresenting performance is a violation of the Code and Standards. Although she did not calculate the performance herself, Washington would be assisting in violating this standard if she were to use the inflated performance number when soliciting clients. She must dissociate herself from the activity. She can bring the misleading number to the attention of the person responsible for calculating performance, her supervisor, or the compliance department at her firm. If her firm is unwilling to recalculate performance, she must refrain from using the misleading promotional material and should notify the firm of her reasons. If the firm insists that she use the material, she should consider whether her obligation to dissociate from the activity would require her to seek other employment.

Example 3:

An employee of an investment bank is working on an underwriting and finds out the issuer has altered their financial statements to hide operating losses in one division. These misstated data are included in a preliminary prospectus that has already been released.

Comment:

The employee should report the problem to his supervisors. If the firm doesn't get the misstatement fixed, the employee should dissociate from the underwriting and, further, seek legal advice about whether he should undertake additional reporting or other actions.

---

3. Ibid.

Example 4:

Laura Jameson, a U.S. citizen, works for an investment advisor based in the United States and works in a country where investment managers are prohibited from participating in IPOs for their own accounts.

Comment:

Jameson must comply with the strictest requirements among U.S. law (where her firm is based), the CFA Institute Code and Standards, and the laws of the country where she is doing business. In this case that means she must not participate in any IPOs for her personal account.

Example 5:

A junior portfolio manager suspects that a broker responsible for new business from a foreign country is being allocated a portion of the firm's payments for third-party research and suspects that no research is being provided. He believes that the research payments may be inappropriate and unethical.

Comment:

He should follow his firm's procedures for reporting possible unethical behavior and try to get better disclosure of the nature of these payments and any research that is being provided.

I(B)   Independence and Objectivity. Members and Candidates must use reasonable care and judgment to achieve and maintain independence and objectivity in their professional activities. Members and Candidates must not offer, solicit, or accept any gift, benefit, compensation, or consideration that reasonably could be expected to compromise their own or another's independence and objectivity.

Guidance

Do not let the investment process be influenced by any external sources. Modest gifts are permitted. Allocation of shares in oversubscribed IPOs to personal accounts is NOT permitted. Distinguish between gifts from clients and gifts from entities seeking influence to the detriment of the client. Gifts must be disclosed to the member's employer in any case, either prior to acceptance if possible, or subsequently.

Guidance—Investment Banking Relationships

Do not be pressured by sell-side firms to issue favorable research on current or prospective investment-banking clients. It is appropriate to have analysts work with investment bankers in "road shows" only when the conflicts are adequately and effectively managed and disclosed. Be sure there are effective "firewalls" between research/investment management and investment banking activities.

Guidance—Public Companies

Analysts should not be pressured to issue favorable research by the companies they follow. Do not confine research to discussions with company management, but rather use a variety of sources, including suppliers, customers, and competitors.

Guidance—Buy-Side Clients

Buy-side clients may try to pressure sell-side analysts. Portfolio managers may have large positions in a particular security, and a rating downgrade may have an effect on the portfolio performance. As a portfolio manager, there is a responsibility to respect and foster intellectual honesty of sell-side research.

Guidance—Fund Manager Relationships

Members responsible for selecting outside managers should not accept gifts, entertainment, or travel that might be perceived as impairing their objectivity.

Guidance—Credit Rating Agencies

Members employed by credit rating firms should make sure that procedures prevent undue influence by the firm issuing the securities. Members who use credit ratings should be aware of this potential conflict of interest and consider whether independent analysis is warranted.

Guidance—Issuer-Paid Research

Remember that this type of research is fraught with potential conflicts. Analysts' compensation for preparing such research should be limited, and the preference is for a flat fee, without regard to conclusions or the report's recommendations.

Guidance—Travel

Best practice is for analysts to pay for their own commercial travel when attending information events or tours sponsored by the firm being analyzed.

Recommended Procedures for Compliance

- Protect the integrity of opinions—make sure they are unbiased.
- Create a restricted list and distribute only factual information about companies on the list.
- Restrict special cost arrangements—pay for one's own commercial transportation and hotel; limit use of corporate aircraft to cases in which commercial transportation is not available.
- Limit gifts—token items only. Customary, business-related entertainment is okay as long as its purpose is not to influence a member's professional independence or objectivity. Firms should impose clear value limits on gifts.
- Restrict employee investments in equity IPOs and private placements. Require pre-approval of IPO purchases.
- Review procedures—have effective supervisory and review procedures.

- Firms should have formal written policies on independence and objectivity of research.
- Firms should appoint a compliance officer and provide clear procedures for employee reporting of unethical behavior and violations of applicable regulations.

Application of Standard I(B) Independence and Objectivity

Example 1:

Steven Taylor, a mining analyst with Bronson Brokers, is invited by Precision Metals to join a group of his peers in a tour of mining facilities in several western U.S. states. The company arranges for chartered group flights from site to site and for accommodations in Spartan Motels, the only chain with accommodations near the mines, for three nights. Taylor allows Precision Metals to pick up his tab, as do the other analysts, with one exception—John Adams, an employee of a large trust company who insists on following his company's policy and paying for his hotel room himself.

Comment:

The policy of the company where Adams works complies closely with Standard I(B) by avoiding even the appearance of a conflict of interest, but Taylor and the other analysts were not necessarily violating Standard I(B). In general, when allowing companies to pay for travel and/or accommodations under these circumstances, members and candidates must use their judgment, keeping in mind that such arrangements must not impinge on a member or candidate's independence and objectivity. In this example, the trip was strictly for business and Taylor was not accepting irrelevant or lavish hospitality. The itinerary required chartered flights, for which analysts were not expected to pay. The accommodations were modest. These arrangements are not unusual and did not violate Standard I(B) so long as Taylor's independence and objectivity were not compromised. In the final analysis, members and candidates should consider both whether they can remain objective and whether their integrity might be perceived by their clients to have been compromised.

Example 2:

Walter Fritz is an equity analyst with Hilton Brokerage who covers the mining industry. He has concluded that the stock of Metals & Mining is overpriced at its current level, but he is concerned that a negative research report will hurt the good relationship between Metals & Mining and the investment-banking division of his firm. In fact, a senior manager of Hilton Brokerage has just sent him a copy of a proposal his firm has made to Metals & Mining to underwrite a debt offering. Fritz needs to produce a report right away and is concerned about issuing a less-than-favorable rating.

Comment:

Fritz's analysis of Metals & Mining must be objective and based solely on consideration of company fundamentals. Any pressure from other divisions of his firm is inappropriate. This conflict could have been eliminated if, in anticipation of the offering, Hilton Brokerage had placed Metals & Mining on a restricted list for its sales force.

Example 3:

Tom Wayne is the investment manager of the Franklin City Employees Pension Plan. He recently completed a successful search for firms to manage the foreign equity allocation of the plan's diversified portfolio. He followed the plan's standard procedure of seeking presentations from a number of qualified firms and recommended that his board select Penguin Advisors because of its experience, well-defined investment strategy, and performance record, which was compiled and verified in accordance with the CFA Institute Global Investment Performance Standards. Following the plan selection of Penguin, a reporter from the Franklin City Record called to ask if there was any connection between the action and the fact that Penguin was one of the sponsors of an "investment fact-finding trip to Asia" that Wayne made earlier in the year. The trip was one of several conducted by the Pension Investment Academy, which had arranged the itinerary of meetings with economic, government, and corporate officials in major cities in several Asian countries. The Pension Investment Academy obtains support for the cost of these trips from a number of investment managers, including Penguin Advisors; the Academy then pays the travel expenses of the various pension plan managers on the trip and provides all meals and accommodations. The president of Penguin Advisors was one of the travelers on the trip.

Comment:

Although Wayne can probably put to good use the knowledge he gained from the trip in selecting portfolio managers and in other areas of managing the pension plan, his recommendation of Penguin Advisors may be tainted by the possible conflict incurred when he participated in a trip paid for partly by Penguin Advisors and when he was in the daily company of the president of Penguin Advisors. To avoid violating Standard I(B), Wayne's basic expenses for travel and accommodations should have been paid by his employer or the pension plan; contact with the president of Penguin Advisors should have been limited to informational or educational events only; and the trip, the organizer, and the sponsor should have been made a matter of public record. Even if his actions were not in violation of Standard I(B), Wayne should have been sensitive to the public perception of the trip when reported in the newspaper and the extent to which the subjective elements of his decision might have been affected by the familiarity that the daily contact of such a trip would encourage. This advantage would probably not be shared by competing firms.

Example 4:

An analyst in the corporate finance department promises a client that her firm will provide full research coverage of the issuing company after the offering.

Comment:

This is not a violation, but she cannot promise favorable research coverage. Research must be objective and independent.

Example 5:

An employee's boss tells him to assume coverage of a stock and maintain a buy rating.

Comment:

Research opinions and recommendations must be objective and arrived at independently. Following the boss's instructions would be a violation if the analyst determined a buy rating is inappropriate.

Example 6:

A money manager receives a gift of significant value from a client as a reward for good performance over the prior period and informs her employer of the gift.

Comment:

No violation here because the gift is from a client and is not based on performance going forward, but the gift must be disclosed to her employer. If the gift were contingent on future performance, the money manager would have to obtain permission from her employer. The reason for both the disclosure and permission requirements is that the employer must ensure that the money manager does not give advantage to the client giving or offering additional compensation, to the detriment of other clients.

Example 7:

An analyst enters into a contract to write a research report on a company, paid for by that company, for a flat fee plus a bonus based on attracting new investors to the security.

Comment:

This is a violation because the compensation structure makes total compensation depend on the conclusions of the report (a favorable report will attract investors and increase compensation). Accepting the job for a flat fee that does not depend on the report's conclusions or its impact on share price is permitted, with proper disclosure of the fact that the report is funded by the subject company.

Example 8:

A trust manager at a bank selects mutual funds for client accounts based on the profits from "service fees" paid to the bank by the mutual fund sponsor.

Comment:

This is a violation because the trust manager has allowed the fees to affect his objectivity.

Example 9:

An analyst performing sensitivity analysis for a security does not use only scenarios consistent with recent trends and historical norms.

Comment:

This is a good thing and is not a violation.

I(C)   Misrepresentation. Members and Candidates must not knowingly make any misrepresentations relating to investment analysis, recommendations, actions, or other professional activities.

Guidance

Trust is a foundation in the investment profession. Do not make any misrepresentations or give false impressions. This includes oral and electronic communications. Misrepresentations include guaranteeing investment performance and plagiarism. Plagiarism encompasses using someone else's work (reports, forecasts, models, ideas, charts, graphs, and spreadsheet models) without giving them credit. Knowingly omitting information that could affect an investment decision is considered misrepresentation.

Models and analysis developed by others at a member's firm are the property of the firm and can be used without attribution. A report written by another analyst employed by the firm cannot be released as another analyst's work.

Recommended Procedures for Compliance

A good way to avoid misrepresentation is for firms to provide employees who deal with clients or prospects a written list of the firm's available services and a description of the firm's qualifications. Employee qualifications should be accurately presented as well. To avoid plagiarism, maintain records of all materials used to generate reports or other firm products and properly cite sources (quotes and summaries) in work products. Information from recognized financial and statistical reporting services need not be cited.

Members should encourage their firms to establish procedures for verifying marketing claims of third parties whose information the firm provides to clients.

Application of Standard I(C) Misrepresentation

Example 1:

Allison Rogers is a partner in the firm of Rogers and Black, a small firm offering investment advisory services. She assures a prospective client who has just inherited $1 million that "we can perform all the financial and investment services you need." Rogers and Black is well equipped to provide investment advice but, in fact, cannot provide asset allocation assistance or a full array of financial and investment services.

Comment:

Rogers has violated Standard I(C) by orally misrepresenting the services her firm can perform for the prospective client. She must limit herself to describing the range of investment advisory services Rogers and Black can provide and offer to help the client obtain elsewhere the financial and investment services that her firm cannot provide.

Example 2:

Anthony McGuire is an issuer-paid analyst hired by publicly traded companies to electronically promote their stocks. McGuire creates a website that promotes his research efforts as a seemingly independent analyst. McGuire posts a profile and a strong buy recommendation for each company on the website, indicating that the stock is expected to increase in value. He does not disclose the contractual relationships with the companies he covers on his website, in the research reports he issues, or in the statements he makes about the companies on Internet chat rooms.

Comment:

McGuire has violated Standard I(C) because the Internet site and e-mails are misleading to potential investors. Even if the recommendations are valid and supported with thorough research, his omissions regarding the true relationship between himself and the companies he covers constitute a misrepresentation. McGuire has also violated Standard VI(C) by not disclosing the existence of an arrangement with the companies through which he receives compensation in exchange for his services.

Example 3:

Claude Browning, a quantitative analyst for Double Alpha, Inc., returns in great excitement from a seminar. In that seminar, Jack Jorrely, a well-publicized quantitative analyst at a national brokerage firm, discussed one of his new models in great detail, and Browning is intrigued by the new concepts. He proceeds to test this model, making some minor mechanical changes but retaining the concept, until he produces some very positive results. Browning quickly announces to his supervisors at Double Alpha that he has discovered a new model and that clients and prospective clients alike should be informed of this positive finding as ongoing proof of Double Alpha's continuing innovation and ability to add value.

Comment:

Although Browning tested Jorrely's model on his own and even slightly modified it, he must still acknowledge the original source of the idea. Browning can certainly take credit for the final, practical results; he can also support his conclusions with his own test. The credit for the innovative thinking, however, must be awarded to Jorrely.

Example 4:

Paul Ostrowski runs a 2-person investment management firm. Ostrowski's firm subscribes to a service from a large investment research firm that provides research reports that can be repackaged by smaller firms for those firms' clients. Ostrowski's firm distributes these reports to clients as its own work.

Comment:

Ostrowski can rely on third-party research that has a reasonable and adequate basis, but he cannot imply that he is the author of the report. Otherwise, Ostrowski would misrepresent the extent of his work in a way that would mislead the firm's clients or prospective clients.

Example 5:

A member makes an error in preparing marketing materials and misstates the amount of assets his firm has under management.

Comment:

The member must attempt to stop distribution of the erroneous material as soon as the error is known. Simply making the error unintentionally is not a violation, but continuing to distribute material known to contain a significant misstatement of fact would be.

Example 6:

The marketing department states in sales literature that an analyst has received an MBA degree, but he has not. The analyst and other members of the firm have distributed this document for years.

Comment:

The analyst has violated the Standards, as he should have known of this misrepresentation after having distributed and used the materials over a period of years.

Example 7:

A member describes an interest-only collateralized mortgage obligation as guaranteed by the U.S. government because it is a claim against the cash flows of a pool of guaranteed mortgages, although the payment stream and the market value of the security are not guaranteed.

Comment:

This is a violation because of the misrepresentation.

Example 8:

A member describes a bank CD as "guaranteed."

Comment:

This is not a violation as long as the limits of the guarantee provided by the Federal Deposit Insurance Corporation are not exceeded and the nature of the guarantee is clearly explained to clients.

Example 9:

A member uses definitions he found online for such terms as variance and coefficient of variation in preparing marketing material.

Comment:

Even though these are standard terms, using the work of others word-for-word is plagiarism.

Example 10:

A candidate reads about a research paper in a financial publication and includes the information in a research report, citing the original research report but not the financial publication.

Comment:

To the extent that the candidate used information and interpretation from the financial publication without citing it, the candidate is in violation of the Standard. The candidate should either obtain the report and reference it directly or, if he relies solely on the financial publication, should cite both sources.

> I(D)   **Misconduct.** Members and Candidates must not engage in any professional conduct involving dishonesty, fraud, or deceit or commit any act that reflects adversely on their professional reputation, integrity, or competence.

Guidance

CFA Institute discourages unethical behavior in all aspects of members' and candidates' lives. Do not abuse CFA Institute's Professional Conduct Program by seeking enforcement of this Standard to settle personal, political, or other disputes that are not related to professional ethics.

Recommended Procedures for Compliance

Firms are encouraged to adopt these policies and procedures:

- Develop and adopt a code of ethics and make clear that unethical behavior will not be tolerated.
- Give employees a list of potential violations and sanctions, including dismissal.
- Check references of potential employees.

Application of Standard I(D) Misconduct

Example 1:

Simon Sasserman is a trust investment officer at a bank in a small affluent town. He enjoys lunching every day with friends at the country club, where his clients have observed him having numerous drinks. Back at work after lunch, he clearly is intoxicated while making investment decisions. His colleagues make a point of handling any business with Sasserman in the morning because they distrust his judgment after lunch.

Comment:

Sasserman's excessive drinking at lunch and subsequent intoxication at work constitute a violation of Standard I(D) because this conduct has raised questions about his professionalism and competence. His behavior thus reflects poorly on him, his employer, and the investment industry.

Example 2:

Carmen Garcia manages a mutual fund dedicated to socially responsible investing. She is also an environmental activist. As the result of her participation at nonviolent protests, Garcia has been arrested on numerous occasions for trespassing on the property of a large petrochemical plant that is accused of damaging the environment.

Comment:

Generally, Standard I(D) is not meant to cover legal transgressions resulting from acts of civil disobedience in support of personal beliefs because such conduct does not reflect poorly on the member or candidate's professional reputation, integrity, or competence.

Example 3:

A member intentionally includes a receipt that is not in his expenses for a company trip.

Comment:

Because this act involves deceit and fraud and reflects on the member's integrity and honesty, it is a violation.

Example 4:

A member tells a client that he can get her a good deal on a car through his father-in-law, but instead gets her a poor deal and accepts part of the commission on the car purchase.

Comment:

The member has been dishonest and misrepresented the facts of the situation and has, therefore, violated the Standard.

Integrity of Capital Markets

II(A)   Material Nonpublic Information. Members and Candidates who possess material nonpublic information that could affect the value of an investment must not act or cause others to act on the information.

Guidance

Information is "material" if its disclosure would impact the price of a security or if reasonable investors would want the information before making an investment decision. Ambiguous information, as far as its likely effect on price, may not be considered material. Information is "nonpublic" until it has been made available to the marketplace. An analyst conference call is not public disclosure. Selectively disclosing information by corporations creates the potential for insider-trading violations. The prohibition against acting on material nonpublic information extends to mutual funds containing the subject securities as well as related swaps and options contracts.

Guidance—Mosaic Theory

There is no violation when a perceptive analyst reaches an investment conclusion about a corporate action or event through an analysis of public information together with items of nonmaterial nonpublic information.

Recommended Procedures for Compliance

Make reasonable efforts to achieve public dissemination of the information. Encourage firms to adopt procedures to prevent misuse of material nonpublic information. Use a "firewall" within the firm, with elements including:

- Substantial control of relevant interdepartmental communications, through a clearance area such as the compliance or legal department.
- Review employee trades—maintain "watch," "restricted," and "rumor" lists.
- Monitor and restrict proprietary trading while a firm is in possession of material nonpublic information.

Prohibition of all proprietary trading while a firm is in possession of material nonpublic information may be inappropriate because it may send a signal to the market. In these cases, firms should take the contra side of only unsolicited customer trades.

Application of Standard II(A) Material Nonpublic Information

Example 1:

Josephine Walsh is riding an elevator up to her office when she overhears the chief financial officer (CFO) for the Swan Furniture Company tell the president of Swan that he has just calculated the company's earnings for the past quarter, and they have unexpectedly and significantly dropped. The CFO adds that this drop will not be released to the public until next week. Walsh immediately calls her broker and tells him to sell her Swan stock.

Comment:

Walsh has sufficient information to determine that the information is both material and nonpublic. By trading on the inside information, she has violated Standard II(A).

Example 2:

Samuel Peter, an analyst with Scotland and Pierce, Inc., is assisting his firm with a secondary offering for Bright Ideas Lamp Company. Peter participates, via telephone conference call, in a meeting with Scotland and Pierce investment-banking employees and Bright Ideas' CEO. Peter is advised that the company's earnings projections for the next year have significantly dropped. Throughout the telephone conference call, several Scotland and Pierce salespeople and portfolio managers walk in and out of Peter's office, where the telephone call is taking place. As a result, they are aware of the drop in projected earnings for Bright Ideas. Before the conference call is concluded, the salespeople trade the stock of the company on behalf of the firm's clients, and other firm personnel trade the stock in a firm proprietary account and in employee personal accounts.

Comment:

Peter violated Standard II(A) because he failed to prevent the transfer and misuse of material nonpublic information to others in his firm. Peter's firm should have adopted information barriers to prevent the communication of nonpublic information between departments of the firm. The salespeople and portfolio managers who traded on the information have also violated Standard II(A) by trading on inside information.

Example 3:

Elizabeth Levenson is based in Taipei and covers the Taiwanese market for her firm, which is based in Singapore. She is invited to meet the finance director of a manufacturing company, along with the other ten largest shareholders of the company. During the meeting, the finance director states that the company expects its workforce to strike next Friday, which will cripple productivity and distribution. Can Levenson use this information as a basis to change her rating on the company from "buy" to "sell"?

Comment:

Levenson must first determine whether the material information is public. If the company has not made this information public (a small-group forum does not qualify as a method of public dissemination), she cannot use the information according to Standard II(A).

Example 4:

Jagdish Teja is a buy-side analyst covering the furniture industry. Looking for an attractive company to recommend as a buy, he analyzed several furniture makers by studying their financial reports and visiting their operations. He also talked to some designers and retailers to find out which furniture styles are trendy and popular. Although none of the companies that he analyzed turned out to be a clear buy, he discovered that one of them, Swan Furniture Company (SFC), might be in trouble. Swan's extravagant new designs were introduced at substantial costs. Even though these designs initially attracted attention, in the long run, the public is buying more conservative furniture from other makers. Based on that and on P&L analysis, Teja believes that Swan's next-quarter earnings will drop substantially. He then issues a sell recommendation for SFC. Immediately after receiving that recommendation, investment managers start reducing the stock in their portfolios.

Comment:

Information on quarterly earnings figures is material and nonpublic. However, Teja arrived at his conclusion about the earnings drop based on public information and on pieces of nonmaterial nonpublic information (such as opinions of designers and retailers). Therefore, trading based on Teja's correct conclusion is not prohibited by Standard II(A).

Example 5:

A member's dentist, who is an active investor, tells the member that based on his research he believes that Acme, Inc., will be bought out in the near future by a larger firm in the industry. The member investigates and purchases shares of Acme.

Comment:

There is no violation here because the dentist had no inside information but has reached the conclusion on his own. The information here is not material because there is no reason to suspect that an investor would wish to know what the member's dentist thought before investing in shares of Acme.

Example 6:

A member received an advance copy of a stock recommendation that will appear in a widely read national newspaper column the next day and purchases the stock.

Comment:

A recommendation in a widely read newspaper column will likely cause the stock price to rise, so this is material nonpublic information. The member has violated the Standard.

Example 7:

A member is having lunch with a portfolio manager from a mutual fund who is known for his stock-picking ability and often influences market prices when his stock purchases and sales are disclosed. The manager tells the member that he is selling all his shares in Able, Inc., the next day. The member shorts the stock.

Comment:

The fact that the fund will sell its shares of Able is material because news of it will likely cause the shares to fall in price. Because this is also not currently public information, the member has violated the Standard by acting on the information.

Example 8:

A broker who is a member receives the sell order for the Able, Inc., shares from the portfolio manager in the previous example. The broker sells his shares of Able prior to entering the sell order for the fund, but because his personal holdings are small compared to the stock's trading volume, his trade does not affect the price.

Comment:

The broker has acted on material nonpublic information (the fund's sale of shares) and has violated the Standard.

Professor's Note: The member also violated Standard VI(B) Priority of Transactions by front-running the client trade with a trade in his own account. Had the member sold his shares after executing the fund trade, he still would be violating Standard II(A) by acting on his knowledge of the fund trade, which would still not be public information at that point.

Example 9:

A member trades based on information he gets by seeing an advance copy of an article that will be published in an influential magazine next week.

Comment:

This is a violation as this is nonpublic information until the article has been published.

II(B) Market Manipulation. Members and Candidates must not engage in practices that distort prices or artificially inflate trading volume with the intent to mislead market participants.

This Standard applies to transactions that deceive the market by distorting the price-setting mechanism of financial instruments or by securing a controlling position to manipulate the price of a related derivative and/or the asset itself. Spreading false rumors is also prohibited.

Application of Standard II(B) Market Manipulation

Example 1:

Matthew Murphy is an analyst at Divisadero Securities & Co., which has a significant number of hedge funds among its most important brokerage clients. Two trading days before the publication of the quarter-end report, Murphy alerts his sales force that he is about to issue a research report on Wirewolf Semiconductor, which will include his opinion that:

- Quarterly revenues are likely to fall short of management's guidance.
- Earnings will be as much as 5 cents per share (or more than 10%) below consensus.
- Wirewolf's highly respected chief financial officer may be about to join another company.

Knowing that Wirewolf had already entered its declared quarter-end "quiet period" before reporting earnings (and thus would be reluctant to respond to rumors, etc.), Murphy times the release of his research report specifically to sensationalize the negative aspects of the message to create significant downward pressure on Wirewolf's stock to the distinct advantage of Divisadero's hedge fund clients. The report's conclusions are based on speculation, not on fact. The next day, the research report is broadcast to all of Divisadero's clients and to the usual newswire services.

Before Wirewolf's investor relations department can assess its damage on the final trading day of the quarter and refute Murphy's report, its stock opens trading sharply lower, allowing Divisadero's clients to cover their short positions at substantial gains.

Comment:

Murphy violated Standard II(B) by trying to create artificial price volatility designed to have material impact on the price of an issuer's stock. Moreover, by lacking an adequate basis for the recommendation, Murphy also violated Standard V(A).

Example 2:

Sergei Gonchar is the chairman of the ACME Futures Exchange, which seeks to launch a new bond futures contract. In order to convince investors, traders, arbitragers, hedgers, and so on, to use its contract, the exchange attempts to demonstrate that it has the best liquidity. To do so, it enters into agreements with members so that they commit to a substantial minimum trading volume on the new contract over a specific period in exchange for substantial reductions on their regular commissions.

Comment:

Formal liquidity on a market is determined by the obligations set on market makers, but the actual liquidity of a market is better estimated by the actual trading volume and bid-ask spreads. Attempts to mislead participants on the actual liquidity of the market constitute a violation of Standard II(B). In this example, investors have been intentionally misled to believe they chose the most liquid instrument for some specific purpose and could eventually see the actual liquidity of the contract dry up suddenly after the term of the agreement if the "pump-priming" strategy fails. If ACME fully discloses its agreement with members to boost transactions over some initial launch period, it does not violate Standard II(B). ACME's intent is not to harm investors but on the contrary to give them a better service. For that purpose, it may engage in a liquidity-pumping strategy, but it must be disclosed.

Example 3:

A member is seeking to sell a large position in a fairly illiquid stock from a fund he manages. He buys and sells shares of the stock between that fund and another he also manages to create an appearance of activity and stock price appreciation, so that the sale of the whole position will have less market impact and he will realize a better return for the fund's shareholders.

Comment:

The trading activity is meant to mislead market participants and is, therefore, a violation of the Standard. The fact that his fund shareholders gain by this action does not change the fact that it is a violation.

Example 4:

A member posts false information about a firm on internet bulletin boards and stock chat facilities in an attempt to cause the firm's stock to increase in price.

Comment:

This is a violation of the Standard.

III	Duties to Clients

III(A) Loyalty, Prudence, and Care. Members and Candidates have a duty of loyalty to their clients and must act with reasonable care and exercise prudent judgment. Members and Candidates must act for the benefit of their clients and place their clients' interests before their employer's or their own interests.

Guidance

Client interests always come first.

- Exercise the prudence, care, skill, and diligence under the circumstances that a person acting in a like capacity and familiar with such matters would use.
- Manage pools of client assets in accordance with the terms of the governing documents, such as trust documents or investment management agreements.
- Make investment decisions in the context of the total portfolio.
- Vote proxies in an informed and responsible manner. Due to cost benefit considerations, it may not be necessary to vote all proxies.
- Client brokerage, or "soft dollars" or "soft commissions" must be used to benefit the client.
- The "client" may be the investing public as a whole rather than a specific entity or person.

Recommended Procedures of Compliance

Submit to clients, at least quarterly, itemized statements showing all securities in custody and all debits, credits, and transactions.

Encourage firms to address these topics when drafting policies and procedures regarding fiduciary duty:

- Follow applicable rules and laws.
- Establish investment objectives of client. Consider suitability of portfolio relative to client's needs and circumstances, the investment's basic characteristics, or the basic characteristics of the total portfolio.
- Diversify.
- Deal fairly with all clients in regards to investment actions.
- Disclose conflicts.
- Disclose compensation arrangements.
- Vote proxies in the best interest of clients and ultimate beneficiaries.
- Maintain confidentiality.
- Seek best execution.
- Place client interests first.

Application of Standard III(A) Loyalty, Prudence, and Care

Example 1:

First Country Bank serves as trustee for the Miller Company's pension plan. Miller is the target of a hostile takeover attempt by Newton, Inc. In attempting to ward off Newton, Miller's managers persuade Julian Wiley, an investment manager at First Country Bank, to purchase Miller common stock in the open market for the employee pension plan. Miller's officials indicate that such action would be favorably received and would probably result in other accounts being placed with the bank. Although Wiley believes the stock to be overvalued and would not ordinarily buy it, he purchases the stock to support Miller's managers, to maintain the company's good favor, and to realize additional new business. The heavy stock purchases cause Miller's market price to rise to such a level that Newton retracts its takeover bid.

Comment:

Standard III(A) requires that a member or candidate, in evaluating a takeover bid, act prudently and solely in the interests of plan participants and beneficiaries. To meet this requirement, a member or candidate must carefully evaluate the long-term prospects of the company against the short-term prospects presented by the takeover offer and by the ability to invest elsewhere. In this instance, Wiley, acting on behalf of his employer, the trustee, clearly violated Standard III(A) by using the pension plan to perpetuate existing management, perhaps to the detriment of plan participants and the company's shareholders, and to benefit himself. Wiley's responsibilities to the plan participants and beneficiaries should take precedence over any ties to corporate managers and self-interest. A duty exists to examine such a takeover offer on its own merits and to make an independent decision. The guiding principle is the appropriateness of the investment decision to the pension plan, not whether the decision benefits Wiley or the company that hired him.

Example 2:

Emilie Rome is a trust officer for Paget Trust Company. Rome's supervisor is responsible for reviewing Rome's trust account transactions and her monthly reports of personal stock transactions. Rome has been using Nathan Gray, a broker, almost exclusively for trust account brokerage transactions. Where Gray makes a market in stocks, he has been giving Rome a lower price for personal purchases and a higher price for sales than he gives to Rome's trust accounts and other investors.

Comment:

Rome is violating her duty of loyalty to the bank's trust accounts by using Gray for brokerage transactions simply because Gray trades Rome's personal account on favorable terms.

Example 3:

A member uses a broker for client-account trades that has relatively high prices and average research and execution. In return, the broker pays for the rent and other overhead expenses for the member's firm.

Comment:

This is a violation of the Standard because the member used client brokerage for services that do not benefit clients and failed to get the best price and execution for his clients.

Example 4:

In return for receiving account management business from Broker X, a member directs trades to Broker X on the accounts referred to her by Broker X, as well as on other accounts as an incentive to Broker X to send her more account business.

Comment:

This is a violation if Broker X does not offer the best price and execution or if the practice of directing trades to Broker X is not disclosed to clients. The obligation to seek best price and execution is always required unless clients provide a written statement that the member is not to seek best price and execution and that they are aware of the impact of this decision on their accounts.

Example 5:

A member does more trades in client accounts than are necessary to accomplish client goals because she desires to increase her commission income.

Comment:

The member is using client assets (brokerage fees) to benefit herself and has violated the Standard.

III(B)   Fair Dealing. Members and Candidates must deal fairly and objectively with all clients when providing investment analysis, making investment recommendations, taking investment action, or engaging in other professional activities.

Guidance

Do not discriminate against any clients when disseminating recommendations or taking investment action. Fairly does not mean equally. In the normal course of business, there will be differences in the time e-mails, faxes, etc., are received by different clients. Different service levels are okay, but they must not negatively affect or disadvantage any clients. Disclose the different service levels to all clients and prospects, and make premium levels of service available to all who wish to pay for them.

Guidance—Investment Recommendations

Give all clients a fair opportunity to act upon every recommendation. Clients who are unaware of a change in a recommendation should be advised before the order is accepted.

Guidance—Investment Actions

Treat clients fairly in light of their investment objectives and circumstances. Treat both individual and institutional clients in a fair and impartial manner. Members and candidates should not take advantage of their position in the industry to disadvantage clients (e.g., in the context of IPOs).

Recommended Procedures for Compliance

Encourage firms to establish compliance procedures requiring proper dissemination of investment recommendations and fair treatment of all customers and clients. Consider these points when establishing fair dealing compliance procedures:

- Limit the number of people who are aware that a change in recommendation will be made.
- Shorten the time frame between decision and dissemination.
- Publish personnel guidelines for pre-dissemination—have in place guidelines prohibiting personnel who have prior knowledge of a recommendation from discussing it or taking action on the pending recommendation.
- Simultaneous dissemination of new or changed recommendations to all clients who have expressed an interest or for whom an investment is suitable.
- Maintain list of clients and holdings—use to ensure that all holders are treated fairly.
- Develop written trade allocation procedures—ensure fairness to clients, timely and efficient order execution, and accuracy of client positions.
- Disclose trade allocation procedures.
- Establish systematic account review—ensure that no client is given preferred treatment and that investment actions are consistent with the account's objectives.
- Disclose available levels of service.

Application of Standard III(B) Fair Dealing

Example 1:

Bradley Ames, a well-known and respected analyst, follows the computer industry. In the course of his research, he finds that a small, relatively unknown company whose shares are traded over the counter has just signed significant contracts with some of the companies he follows. After a considerable amount of investigation, Ames decides to write a research report on the company and recommend purchase. While the report is being reviewed by the company for factual accuracy, Ames schedules a luncheon with several of his best clients to discuss the company. At the luncheon, he mentions the purchase recommendation scheduled to be sent early the following week to all the firm's clients.

Comment:

Ames violated Standard III(B) by disseminating the purchase recommendation to the clients with whom he had lunch a week before the recommendation was sent to all clients.

Example 2:

Spencer Rivers, president of XYZ Corporation, moves his company's growth-oriented pension fund to a particular bank primarily because of the excellent investment performance achieved by the bank's commingled fund for the prior 5-year period. A few years later, Rivers compares the results of his pension fund with those of the bank's commingled fund. He is startled to learn that, even though the two accounts have the same investment objectives and similar portfolios, his company's pension fund has significantly underperformed the bank's commingled fund. Questioning this result at his next meeting with the pension fund's manager, Rivers is told that, as a matter of policy, when a new security is placed on the recommended list, Morgan Jackson, the pension fund manager, first purchases the security for the commingled account and then purchases it on a pro rata basis for all other pension fund accounts. Similarly, when a sale is recommended, the security is sold first from the commingled account and then sold on a pro rata basis from all other accounts. Rivers also learns that if the bank cannot get enough shares (especially the hot issues) to be meaningful to all the accounts, its policy is to place the new issues only in the commingled account.

Seeing that Rivers is neither satisfied nor pleased by the explanation, Jackson quickly adds that nondiscretionary pension accounts and personal trust accounts have a lower priority on purchase and sale recommendations than discretionary pension fund accounts. Furthermore, Jackson states, the company's pension fund had the opportunity to invest up to 5% in the commingled fund.

Comment:

The bank's policy did not treat all customers fairly, and Jackson violated her duty to her clients by giving priority to the growth-oriented commingled fund over all other funds and to discretionary accounts over nondiscretionary accounts. Jackson must execute orders on a systematic basis that is fair to all clients. In addition, trade allocation procedures should be disclosed to all clients from the beginning. Of course, in this case, disclosure of the bank's policy would not change the fact that the policy is unfair.

Example 3:

A member gets options for his part in an IPO from the subject firm. The IPO is oversubscribed and the member fills his own and other individuals' orders but has to reduce allocations to his institutional clients.

Comment:

The member has violated the Standard. He must disclose to his employer and to his clients that he has accepted options for putting together the IPO. He should not take any shares of a hot IPO for himself and should have distributed his allocated shares of the IPO to all clients in proportion to their original order amounts.

Example 4:

A member is delayed in allocating some trades to client accounts. When she allocates the trades, she puts some positions that have appreciated in a preferred client's account and puts trades that have not done as well in other client accounts.

Comment:

This is a violation of the Standard. The member should have allocated the trades to specific accounts prior to the trades or should have allocated the trades proportionally to suitable accounts in a timely fashion.

Example 5:

Because of minimum lot size restrictions, a portfolio manager allocates the bonds she receives from an oversubscribed bond offering to her clients in a way that is not strictly proportional to their purchase requests.

Comment:

Since she has a reason (minimum lot size) to deviate from a strict pro rata allocation to her clients, there is no violation of Fair Dealing.

III(C) Suitability

1. When Members and Candidates are in an advisory relationship with a client, they must:

   a. Make a reasonable inquiry into a client's or prospective clients' investment experience, risk and return objectives, and financial constraints prior to making any investment recommendation or taking investment action and must reassess and update this information regularly.

   b. Determine that an investment is suitable to the client's financial situation and consistent with the client's written objectives, mandates, and constraints before making an investment recommendation or taking investment action.

   c. Judge the suitability of investments in the context of the client's total portfolio.

2. When Members and Candidates are responsible for managing a portfolio to a specific mandate, strategy, or style, they must make only investment recommendations or take investment actions that are consistent with the stated objectives and constraints of the portfolio.

Guidance

In advisory relationships, be sure to gather client information at the beginning of the relationship, in the form of an investment policy statement (IPS). Consider clients' needs and circumstances and thus their risk tolerance. Consider whether or not the use of leverage is suitable for the client.

©2012 Kaplan, Inc.

If a member is responsible for managing a fund to an index or other stated mandate, be sure investments are consistent with the stated mandate.

Recommended Procedures for Compliance

Members should:

- Put the needs and circumstances of each client and the client's investment objectives into a written IPS for each client.
- Consider the type of client and whether there are separate beneficiaries, investor objectives (return and risk), investor constraints (liquidity needs, expected cash flows, time, tax, and regulatory and legal circumstances), and performance measurement benchmarks.
- Review investor's objectives and constraints periodically to reflect any changes in client circumstances.

Application of Standard III(C) Suitability

Example 1:

Jessica Walters, an investment advisor, suggests to Brian Crosby, a risk-averse client, that covered call options be used in his equity portfolio. The purpose would be to enhance Crosby's income and partially offset any untimely depreciation in value should the stock market or other circumstances affect his holdings unfavorably. Walters educates Crosby about all possible outcomes, including the risk of incurring an added tax liability if a stock rises in price and is called away and, conversely, the risk of his holdings losing protection on the downside if prices drop sharply.

Comment:

When determining suitability of an investment, the primary focus should be on the characteristics of the client's entire portfolio, not on an issue-by-issue analysis. The basic characteristics of the entire portfolio will largely determine whether the investment recommendations are taking client factors into account. Therefore, the most important aspects of a particular investment will be those that will affect the characteristics of the total portfolio. In this case, Walters properly considered the investment in the context of the entire portfolio and thoroughly explained the investment to the client.

Example 2:

Max Gubler, CIO of a property/casualty insurance subsidiary of a large financial conglomerate, wants to better diversify the company's investment portfolio and increase its returns. The company's investment policy statement (IPS) provides for highly liquid investments, such as large caps, governments, and supra-nationals, as well as corporate bonds with a minimum credit rating of AA- and maturity of no more than five years. In a recent presentation, a venture capital group offered very attractive prospective returns on some of their private equity funds providing seed capital. An exit strategy is already contemplated but investors will first have to observe a minimum three-year lock-up period, with a subsequent laddered exit option for a maximum of one third of shares per year. Gubler does not want to miss this opportunity and after an extensive analysis and optimization of this asset class with the company's current portfolio, he invests 4% in this seed fund, leaving the portfolio's total equity exposure still well below its upper limit.

Comment:

Gubler violates Standards III(A) and III(C). His new investment locks up part of the company's assets for at least three and for up to as many as five years and possibly beyond. Since the IPS requires investments in highly liquid investments and describes accepted asset classes, private equity investments with a lock-up period certainly do not qualify. Even without such lock-up periods an asset class with only an occasional, and thus implicitly illiquid, market may not be suitable. Although an IPS typically describes objectives and constraints in great detail, the manager must make every effort to understand the client's business and circumstances. Doing so should also enable the manager to recognize, understand, and discuss with the client other factors that may be or may become material in the investment management process.

Example 3:

A member gives a client account a significant allocation to non-dividend paying high-risk securities even though the client has low risk tolerance and modest return objectives.

Comment:

This is a violation of the Standard.

Example 4:

A member puts a security into a fund she manages that does not fit the mandate of the fund and is not a permitted investment according to the fund's disclosures.

Comment:

This, too, is a violation of the Standard.

Example 5:

A member starts his own money management business but puts all clients in his friend's hedge funds.

Comment:

He has violated the Standards with respect to suitability. He must match client needs and circumstances to the investments he recommends and cannot act like a sales agent for his friend's funds.

III(D) Performance Presentation. When communicating investment performance information, Members or Candidates must make reasonable efforts to ensure that it is fair, accurate, and complete.

Guidance

Members must avoid misstating performance or misleading clients/prospects about investment performance of themselves or their firms, should not misrepresent past performance or reasonably expected performance, and should not state or imply the ability to achieve a rate of return similar to that achieved in the past. For brief presentations, members must make detailed information available on request and indicate that the presentation has offered limited information.

Recommended Procedures for Compliance

Encourage firms to adhere to Global Investment Performance Standards. Obligations under this Standard may also be met by:

- Considering the sophistication of the audience to whom a performance presentation is addressed.
- Presenting performance of weighted composite of similar portfolios rather than a single account.
- Including terminated accounts as part of historical performance and clearly stating when they were terminated.
- Including all appropriate disclosures to fully explain results (e.g., model results included, gross or net of fees, etc.).
- Maintaining data and records used to calculate the performance being presented.

Application of Standard III(D) Performance Presentation

Example 1:

Kyle Taylor of Taylor Trust Company, noting the performance of Taylor's common trust fund for the past two years, states in the brochure sent to his potential clients that "You can expect steady 25% annual compound growth of the value of your investments over the year." Taylor Trust's common trust fund did increase at the rate of 25% per annum for the past year which mirrored the increase of the entire market. The fund, however, never averaged that growth for more than one year, and the average rate of growth of all of its trust accounts for five years was 5% per annum.

Comment:

Taylor's brochure is in violation of Standard III(D). Taylor should have disclosed that the 25% growth occurred in only one year. Additionally, Taylor did not include client accounts other than those in the firm's common trust fund. A general claim of firm performance should take into account the performance of all categories of accounts. Finally, by stating that clients can expect a steady 25% annual compound growth rate, Taylor also violated Standard I(C), which prohibits statements of assurances or guarantees regarding an investment.

Example 2:

Aaron McCoy is vice president and managing partner of the equity investment group of Mastermind Financial Advisors, a new business. Mastermind recruited McCoy because he had a proven six-year track record with G&P Financial. In developing Mastermind's advertising and marketing campaign, McCoy prepared an advertisement that included the equity investment performance he achieved at G&P Financial. The advertisement for Mastermind did not identify the equity performance as being earned while at G&P. The advertisement was distributed to existing clients and prospective clients of Mastermind.

Comment:

McCoy violated Standard III(D) by distributing an advertisement that contained material misrepresentations regarding the historical performance of Mastermind. Standard III(D) requires that members and candidates make every reasonable effort to ensure that performance information is a fair, accurate, and complete representation of an individual or firm's performance. As a general matter, this standard does not prohibit showing past performance of funds managed at a prior firm as part of a performance track record so long as it is accompanied by appropriate disclosures detailing where the performance comes from and the person's specific role in achieving that performance. If McCoy chooses to use his past performance from G&P in Mastermind's advertising, he should make full disclosure as to the source of the historical performance.

Example 3:

A member puts simulated results of an investment strategy in a sales brochure without disclosing that the results are not actual performance numbers.

Comment:

The member has violated the Standard.

Example 4:

In materials for prospective clients, a member uses performance figures for a large-cap growth composite she has created by choosing accounts that have done relatively well and including some accounts with significant mid-cap exposure.

Comment:

This is a violation of the Standard as the member has attempted to mislead clients and has misrepresented her performance.

III(E) Preservation of Confidentiality. Members and Candidates must keep information about current, former, and prospective clients confidential unless:

1. The information concerns illegal activities on the part of the client or prospective client,

2. Disclosure is required by law, or

3. The client or prospective client permits disclosure of the information.

Guidance

If illegal activities by a client are involved, members may have an obligation to report the activities to authorities. The confidentiality Standard extends to former clients as well.

The requirements of this Standard are not intended to prevent Members and Candidates from cooperating with a CFA Institute Professional Conduct Program (PCP) investigation.

Recommended Procedures for Compliance

Members should avoid disclosing information received from a client except to authorized co-workers who are also working for the client. Members should follow firm procedures for storage of electronic data and recommend adoption of such procedures if they are not in place.

Application of Standard III(E) Preservation of Confidentiality

Example 1:

Sarah Connor, a financial analyst employed by Johnson Investment Counselors, Inc., provides investment advice to the trustees of City Medical Center. The trustees have given her a number of internal reports concerning City Medical's needs for physical plant renovation and expansion. They have asked Connor to recommend investments that would generate capital appreciation in endowment funds to meet projected capital expenditures. Connor is approached by a local business man, Thomas Kasey, who is considering a substantial contribution either to City Medical Center or to another local hospital. Kasey wants to find out the building plans of both institutions before making a decision, but he does not want to speak to the trustees.

Comment:

The trustees gave Connor the internal reports so she could advise them on how to manage their endowment funds. Because the information in the reports is clearly both confidential and within the scope of the confidential relationship, Standard III(E) requires that Connor refuse to divulge information to Kasey.

Example 2:

David Bradford manages money for a family-owned real estate development corporation. He also manages the individual portfolios of several of the family members and officers of the corporation, including the chief financial officer (CFO). Based on the financial records from the corporation, as well as some questionable practices of the CFO that he has observed, Bradford believes that the CFO is embezzling money from the corporation and putting it into his personal investment account.

Comment:

Bradford should check with his firm's compliance department as well as outside counsel to determine whether applicable securities regulations require reporting the CFO's financial records.

Example 3:

A member has learned from his client that one of his goals is to give more of his portfolio income to charity. The member tells this to a friend who is on the board of a worthy charity and suggests that he should contact the client about a donation.

Comment:

The member has violated the Standard by disclosing information he has learned from the client in the course of their business relationship.

Example 4:

A member learns that a pension account client is violating the law with respect to charges to the pension fund.

Comment:

The member must bring this to the attention of her supervisor and try to end the illegal activity. Failing this, the member should seek legal advice about any disclosure she should make to legal or regulatory authorities and dissociate herself from any continuing association with the pension account.

IV   Duties to Employers

IV(A)   Loyalty. In matters related to their employment, Members and Candidates must act for the benefit of their employer and not deprive their employer of the advantage of their skills and abilities, divulge confidential information, or otherwise cause harm to their employer.

Guidance

Members must not engage in any activities which would injure the firm, deprive it of profit, or deprive it of the advantage of employees' skills and abilities. Members should always place client interests above interests of their employer but consider the effects of their actions on firm integrity and sustainability. There is no requirement that the employee put employer interests ahead of family and other personal obligations; it is expected that employers and employees will discuss such matters and balance these obligations with work obligations.

Guidance—Employer Responsibility

Members are encouraged to give their employer a copy of the Code and Standards. Employers should not have incentive and compensation systems that encourage unethical behavior.

Guidance—Independent Practice

Independent practice for compensation is allowed if a notification is provided to the employer fully describing all aspects of the services, including compensation, duration, and the nature of the activities *and* if the employer consents to all terms of the proposed independent practice before it begins.

Guidance—Leaving an Employer

Members must continue to act in their employer's best interests until resignation is effective. Activities which may constitute a violation include:

- Misappropriation of trade secrets.
- Misuse of confidential information.
- Soliciting employer's clients prior to leaving.
- Self-dealing.
- Misappropriation of client lists.

Employer records on any medium (e.g., home computer, PDA, cell phone) are the property of the firm.

Once an employee has left a firm, simple knowledge of names and existence of former clients is generally not confidential. There is also no prohibition on the use of experience or knowledge gained while with a former employer.

Guidance—Whistleblowing

There may be isolated cases where a duty to one's employer may be violated in order to protect clients or the integrity of the market, and not for personal gain.

Guidance—Nature of Employment

The applicability of this Standard is based on the nature of the employment—employee versus independent contractor. If Members and Candidates are independent contractors, they still have a duty to abide by the terms of the agreement.

Application of Standard IV(A) Loyalty

Example 1:

James Hightower has been employed by Jason Investment Management Corporation for 15 years. He began as an analyst but assumed increasing responsibilities and is now a senior portfolio manager and a member of the firm's investment policy committee. Hightower has decided to leave Jason Investment and start his own investment management business. He has been careful not to tell any of Jason's clients that he is leaving; he does not want to be accused of breaching his duty to Jason by soliciting Jason's clients before his departure. Hightower is planning to copy and take with him the following documents and information he developed or worked on while at Jason: (1) the client list, with addresses, telephone numbers, and other pertinent client information; (2) client account statements; (3) sample marketing presentations to prospective clients containing Jason's performance record; (4) Jason's recommended list of securities; (5) computer models to determine asset allocations for accounts with different objectives; (6) computer models for stock selection; and (7) personal computer spreadsheets for Hightower's major corporate recommendations which he developed when he was an analyst.

Comment:

Except with the consent of their employer, departing employees may not take employer property, which includes books, records, reports, and other materials, and may not interfere with their employer's business opportunities. Taking any employer records, even those the member or candidate prepared, violates Standard IV(A).

Example 2:

Dennis Elliot has hired Sam Chisolm who previously worked for a competing firm. Chisolm left his former firm after 18 years of employment. When Chisolm begins working for Elliot, he wants to contact his former clients because he knows them well and is certain that many will follow him to his new employer. Is Chisolm in violation of the Standard IV(A) if he contacts his former clients?

Comment:

Because client records are the property of the firm, contacting former clients for any reason through the use of client lists or other information taken from a former employer without permission would be a violation of Standard IV(A). In addition, the nature and extent of the contact with former clients may be governed by the terms of any non-compete agreement signed by the employee and the former employer that covers contact with former clients after employment.

But, simple knowledge of the name and existence of former clients is not confidential information, just as skills or experience that an employee obtains while employed is not "confidential" or "privileged" information. The Code and Standards do not impose a prohibition on the use of experience or knowledge gained at one employer from being used at another employer. The Code and Standards also do not prohibit former employees from contacting clients of their previous firm, absent a non-compete agreement. Members and candidates are free to use public information about their former firm after departing to contact former clients without violating Standard IV(A).

In the absence of a non-compete agreement, as long as Chisolm maintains his duty of loyalty to his employer before joining Elliot's firm, does not take steps to solicit clients until he has left his former firm, and does not make use of material from his former employer without its permission after he has left, he would not be in violation of the Code and Standards.

Example 3:

Several employees are planning to depart their current employer within a few weeks and have been careful to not engage in any activities that would conflict with their duty to their current employer. They have just learned that one of their employer's clients has undertaken a request for proposal (RFP) to review and possibly hire a new investment consultant. The RFP has been sent to the employer and all of its competitors. The group believes that the new entity to be formed would be qualified to respond to the RFP and eligible for the business. The RFP submission period is likely to conclude before the employees' resignations are effective. Is it permissible for the group of departing employees to respond to the RFP under their anticipated new firm?

Comment:

A group of employees responding to an RFP that their employer is also responding to would lead to direct competition between the employees and the employer. Such conduct would violate Standard IV(A) unless the group of employees received permission from their employer as well as the entity sending out the RFP.

Example 4:

A member solicits clients and prospects of his current employer to open accounts at the new firm he will be joining shortly.

Comment:

It is a violation of the Standard to solicit the firm's clients and prospects while he is still employed by the firm.

Example 5:

Two employees discuss joining with others in an employee-led buyout of their employer's emerging markets investment management business.

Comment:

There is no violation here. Their employer can decide how to respond to any buyout offer. If such a buyout takes place, clients should be informed of the nature of the changes in a timely manner.

Example 6:

A member is writing a research report on a company as a contract worker for Employer A (using Employer A's premises and materials) with the understanding that Employer A does not claim exclusive rights to the outcome of her research. As she is finishing the report, she is offered a full-time job by Employer B and sends Employer B a copy of a draft of her report for publication.

Comment:

She has violated the Standard by not giving Employer A the first rights to act on her research. She must also be careful not to take any materials used in preparing the report from Employer A's premises.

Example 7:

A member helps develop software for a firm while acting as an unpaid intern and takes the software, without permission, with her when she takes a full-time job at another firm.

Comment:

She is considered an employee of the firm and has violated the Standard by taking her employer's property without permission.

Example 8:

A member prepares to leave his employer and open his own firm by registering with the SEC, renting an office, and buying office equipment.

Comment:

As long as these preparations have not interfered with the performance of his current job, there has been no violation. The solicitation of firm clients and prospects prior to leaving his employer would, however, be a violation of the Standard.

Example 9:

A member is a full-time employee of an investment management firm and wants to accept a paid position as town mayor without asking his employer's permission.

Comment:

Because the member serving as mayor does not conflict with his employer's business interests, as long as the time commitment does not preclude performing his expected job functions well, there is no violation.

Example 10:

A member who has left one employer uses public sources to get the phone numbers of previous clients and solicits their business for her new employer.

Comment:

As long as there is no agreement in force between the member and his previous employer that prohibits such solicitation, there is no violation of the Standards.

> **IV(B) Additional Compensation Arrangements.** Members and Candidates must not accept gifts, benefits, compensation, or consideration that competes with, or might reasonably be expected to create a conflict of interest with, their employer's interest unless they obtain written consent from all parties involved.

Guidance

Compensation includes direct and indirect compensation from a client and other benefits received from third parties. Written consent from a member's employer includes e-mail communication.

Recommended Procedures for Compliance

Make an immediate written report to employer detailing any proposed compensation and services, if additional to that provided by employer. Details including any performance incentives should be verified by the offering party.

Application of Standard IV(B) Additional Compensation Arrangements

Example 1:

Geoff Whitman, a portfolio analyst for Adams Trust Company, manages the account of Carol Cochran, a client. Whitman is paid a salary by his employer, and Cochran pays the trust company a standard fee based on the market value of assets in her portfolio. Cochran proposes to Whitman that "any year that my portfolio achieves at least a 15% return before taxes, you and your wife can fly to Monaco at my expense and use my condominium during the third week of January." Whitman does not inform his employer of the arrangement and vacations in Monaco the following January as Cochran's guest.

Comment:

Whitman violated Standard IV(B) by failing to inform his employer in writing of this supplemental, contingent compensation arrangement. The nature of the arrangement could have resulted in partiality to Cochran's account, which could have detracted from Whitman's performance with respect to other accounts he handles for Adams Trust. Whitman must obtain the consent of his employer to accept such a supplemental benefit.

Example 2:

A member is on the board of directors of a company whose shares he purchases for client accounts. As a member of the board, he receives the company's product at no charge.

Comment:

Because receiving the company's product constitutes compensation for his service, he is in violation of the Standard if he does not disclose this additional compensation to his employer.

IV(C) Responsibilities of Supervisors. Members and Candidates must make reasonable efforts to detect and prevent violations of applicable laws, rules, regulations, and the Code and Standards by anyone subject to their supervision or authority.

Guidance

Members must take steps to *prevent* employees from violating laws, rules, regulations, or the Code and Standards, as well as make reasonable efforts to *detect* violations. Members with supervisory responsibility should enforce firm policies regarding investment or non-investment behavior (e.g., mandatory vacations) equally.

Guidance—Compliance Procedures

Understand that an adequate compliance system must meet industry standards, regulatory requirements, and the requirements of the Code and Standards. Members with supervisory responsibilities have an obligation to bring an inadequate compliance system to the attention of firm's management and recommend corrective action. While investigating a possible breach of compliance procedures, it is appropriate to limit the suspected employee's activities.

A member or candidate faced with no compliance procedures or with procedures he believes are inadequate must decline supervisory responsibility in writing until adequate procedures are adopted by the firm.

Recommended Procedures for Compliance

A member should recommend that his employer adopt a code of ethics. Employers should not commingle compliance procedures with the firm's code of ethics—this can dilute the goal of reinforcing one's ethical obligations. Members should encourage employers to provide their code of ethics to clients.

Adequate compliance procedures should:

- Be clearly written.
- Be easy to understand.
- Designate a compliance officer with authority clearly defined.
- Have a system of checks and balances.
- Outline the scope of procedures.
- Outline what conduct is permitted.
- Contain procedures for reporting violations and sanctions.

Once the compliance program is instituted, the supervisor should:

- Distribute it to the proper personnel.
- Update it as needed.
- Continually educate staff regarding procedures.
- Issue reminders as necessary.
- Require professional conduct evaluations.
- Review employee actions to monitor compliance and identify violations.
- Enforce procedures once a violation occurs.

If there is a violation, respond promptly and conduct a thorough investigation while placing limitations on the wrongdoer's activities.

Application of Standard IV(C) Responsibilities of Supervisors

Example 1:

Jane Mattock, senior vice president and head of the research department of H&V, Inc., a regional brokerage firm, has decided to change her recommendation for Timber Products from buy to sell. In line with H&V's procedures, she orally advises certain other H&V executives of her proposed actions before the report is prepared for publication. As a result of his conversation with Mattock, Dieter Frampton, one of the executives of H&V accountable to Mattock, immediately sells Timber's stock from his own account and from certain discretionary client accounts. In addition, other personnel inform certain institutional customers of the changed recommendation before it is printed and disseminated to all H&V customers who have received previous Timber reports.

Comment:

Mattock failed to supervise reasonably and adequately the actions of those accountable to her. She did not prevent or establish reasonable procedures designed to prevent dissemination of or trading on the information by those who knew of her changed recommendation. She must ensure that her firm has procedures for reviewing or recording trading in the stock of any corporation that has been the subject of an unpublished change in recommendation. Adequate procedures would have informed the subordinates of their duties and detected sales by Frampton and selected customers.

Example 2:

Deion Miller is the research director for Jamestown Investment Programs. The portfolio managers have become critical of Miller and his staff because the Jamestown portfolios do not include any stock that has been the subject of a merger or tender offer. Georgia Ginn, a member of Miller's staff, tells Miller that she has been studying a local company, Excelsior, Inc., and recommends its purchase. Ginn adds that the company has been widely rumored to be the subject of a merger study by a well-known conglomerate and discussions between them are under way. At Miller's request, Ginn prepares a memo recommending the stock. Miller passes along Ginn's memo to the portfolio managers prior to leaving for vacation, noting that he has not reviewed the memo. As a result of the memo, the portfolio managers buy Excelsior stock immediately. The day Miller returns to the office, Miller learns that Ginn's only sources for the report were her brother, who is an acquisitions analyst with Acme Industries and the "well-known conglomerate" and that the merger discussions were planned but not held.

Comment:

Miller violated Standard IV(C) by not exercising reasonable supervision when he disseminated the memo without checking to ensure that Ginn had a reasonable and adequate basis for her recommendations and that Ginn was not relying on material nonpublic information.

Example 3:

A member responsible for compliance by the firm's trading desk notices a high level of trading activity in a stock that is not on the firm's recommended list. Most of this trading is being done by a trainee, and the member does not investigate this trading.

Comment:

This is a violation of the member's responsibilities as supervisor. She must take steps to monitor the activities of traders in training, as well as investigate the reason for the heavy trading of the security by her firm's trading desk.

V Investment Analysis, Recommendations, and Actions

V(A) Diligence and Reasonable Basis. Members and Candidates must:

1. Exercise diligence, independence, and thoroughness in analyzing investments, making investment recommendations, and taking investment actions.

2. Have a reasonable and adequate basis, supported by appropriate research and investigation, for any investment analysis, recommendation, or action.

Guidance

The application of this Standard depends on the investment philosophy adhered to, members' and candidates' roles in the investment decision-making process, and the resources and support provided by employers. These factors dictate the degree of diligence, thoroughness of research, and the proper level of investigation required.

Guidance—Reasonable Basis

The level of research required to satisfy the requirement for due diligence will differ depending on the product or service offered. A list of some things that should be considered prior to making a recommendation or taking investment action includes:

- A firm's financial results, operating history, and business cycle stage.
- Fees and historical results for a mutual fund.
- Limitations of any quantitative models used.
- A determination of whether peer group comparisons for valuation are appropriate.

Guidance—Using Secondary or Third-Party Research

Members should encourage their firms to adopt a policy for periodic review of the quality of third-party research, if they have not. Examples of criteria to use in judging quality are:

- Review assumptions used.
- Determine how rigorous the analysis was.
- Identify how timely how the research is.
- Evaluate objectivity and independence of the recommendations.

Guidance—Quantitative Research

Members must be able to explain the basic nature of the quantitative research and how it is used to make investment decisions. Members should consider scenarios outside those typically used to assess downside risk and the time horizon of the data used for model evaluation to ensure that both positive and negative cycle results have been considered.

Guidance—External Advisers

Members should make sure their firms have procedures in place to review any external advisers they use or promote to ensure that, among other things, the advisers:

- Have adequate compliance and internal controls.
- Present returns information that is correct.
- Do not deviate from their stated strategies.

Guidance—Group Research and Decision Making

Even if a member does not agree with the independent and objective view of the group, he does not necessarily have to decline to be identified with the report, as long as there is a reasonable and adequate basis.

Recommended Procedures for Compliance

Members should encourage their firms to consider these policies and procedures supporting this Standard:

- Have a policy requiring that research reports and recommendations have a basis that can be substantiated as reasonable and adequate.
- Have detailed, written guidance for proper research and due diligence.
- Have measurable criteria for judging the quality of research, and base analyst compensation on such criteria.
- Have written procedures that provide a minimum acceptable level of scenario testing for computer-based models and include standards for the range of scenarios, model accuracy over time, and a measure of the sensitivity of cash flows to model assumptions and inputs.
- Have a policy for evaluating outside providers of information that addresses the reasonableness and accuracy of the information provided and establishes how often the evaluations should be repeated.
- Adopt a set of standards that provides criteria for evaluating external advisers and states how often a review of external advisers will be performed.

Application of Standard V(A) Diligence and Reasonable Basis

Example 1:

Helen Hawke manages the corporate finance department of Sarkozi Securities, Ltd. The firm is anticipating that the government will soon close a tax loophole that currently allows oil and gas exploration companies to pass on drilling expenses to holders of a certain class of shares. Because market demand for this tax-advantaged class of stock is currently high, Sarkozi convinces several companies to undertake new equity financings at once before the loophole closes. Time is of the essence, but Sarkozi lacks sufficient resources to conduct adequate research on all the prospective issuing companies. Hawke decides to estimate the IPO prices based on the relative size of each company and to justify the pricing later when her staff has time.

Comment:

Sarkozi should have taken on only the work that it could adequately handle. By categorizing the issuers as to general size, Hawke has bypassed researching all the other relevant aspects that should be considered when pricing new issues and thus has not performed sufficient due diligence. Such an omission can result in investors purchasing shares at prices that have no actual basis. Hawke has violated Standard V(A).

Example 2:

A member in the corporate finance department of a securities firm prices IPO shares without doing adequate research because she wants to get them to market quickly.

Comment:

This is a violation of Standard V(A).

Example 3:

A member screens a database of investment managers and sends a recommendation of five of them to a client. Subsequently, but before the client receives the report, one of the recommended firms loses its head of research and several key portfolio managers. The member does not update her report.

Comment:

This is a violation as the member should have notified the client of the change in key personnel at the management firm.

Example 4:

A member writes a report in which she estimates mortgage rates. After reviewing it, a majority of the investment committee vote to change the report to reflect a different interest rate forecast. Must the member dissociate herself from the report?

Comment:

The same facts may give rise to different opinions and as long as the committee has a reasonable and adequate basis for their (differing) opinion, the member is under no obligation to ask that her name be removed from the report or to disassociate from issuing the report.

Example 5:

A member makes a presentation for an offering his firm is underwriting, using maximum production levels as his estimate in order to justify the price of the shares he is recommending for purchase.

Comment:

Using the maximum possible production without acknowledging that this is not the expected level of production (or without presenting a range of possible outcomes and their relative probabilities) does not provide a reasonable basis for the purchase recommendation and is a violation of the Standard.

Example 6:

A member posts buy recommendations in an internet chat room based on "conventional wisdom" and what the public is currently buying.

Comment:

A recommendation that is not based on independent and diligent research into the subject company is a violation of the Standard.

Example 7:

A member is a principal in a small investment firm that bases its securities recommendations on third-party research that it purchases.

Comment:

This is not a violation as long as the member's firm periodically checks the purchased research to determine that it has met, and still meets, the criteria of objectivity and reasonableness required by the Standard.

Example 8:

A member selects an outside advisor for international equities based solely on the fact that the selected firm has the lowest fees for managing the international equities accounts.

Comment:

This is a violation of Standard V(A). The member must consider performance and service, not just fees, in selecting an outside advisor for client accounts.

Example 9:

A member investigates the management, fees, track record, and investment strategy of a hedge fund and recommends it to a client who purchases it. The member accurately discloses the risks involved with the investment in the hedge fund. Soon afterward, the fund reports terrible losses and suspends operations.

Comment:

The bad outcome does not mean there has necessarily been a violation of Standard V(A). A member who has performed reasonable due diligence and disclosed investment risks adequately has complied with the requirements of Standard V(A), regardless of the subsequent outcome.

V(B) Communication with Clients and Prospective Clients. Members and Candidates must:

1. Disclose to clients and prospective clients the basic format and general principles of the investment processes used to analyze investments, select securities, and construct portfolios and must promptly disclose any changes that might materially affect those processes.

2. Use reasonable judgment in identifying which factors are important to their investment analyses, recommendations, or actions and include those factors in communications with clients and prospective clients.

3. Distinguish between fact and opinion in the presentation of investment analysis and recommendations.

Guidance

Proper communication with clients is critical to provide quality financial services. Members must distinguish between opinions and facts and always include the basic characteristics of the security being analyzed in a research report.

Members must illustrate to clients and prospects the investment decision-making process utilized.

All means of communication are included here, not just research reports.

In preparing recommendations for structured securities, allocation strategies, or any other nontraditional investment, members should communicate those risk factors specific to such investments. In all cases, members should communicate the potential gains and losses on the investment clearly in terms of total returns.

When using projections from quantitative models and analysis, members may violate the Standard by not explaining the limitations of the model, which provide a context for judging the uncertainty regarding the estimated investment result.

Recommended Procedures for Compliance

Selection of relevant factors in a report can be a judgment call, so be sure to maintain records indicating the nature of the research, and be able to supply additional information if it is requested by the client or other users of the report.

Application of Standard V(B) Communication with Clients and Prospective Clients

Example 1:

Sarah Williamson, director of marketing for Country Technicians, Inc., is convinced that she has found the perfect formula for increasing Country Technician's income and diversifying its product base. Williamson plans to build on Country Technician's reputation as a leading money manager by marketing an exclusive and expensive investment advice letter to high-net-worth individuals. One hitch in the plan is the complexity of Country Technician's investment system—a combination of technical trading rules (based on historical price and volume fluctuations) and portfolio-construction rules designed to minimize risk. To simplify the newsletter, she decides to include only each week's top-five buy and sell recommendations and to leave out details of the valuation models and the portfolio-structuring scheme.

Comment:

Williamson's plans for the newsletter violate Standard V(B) because she does not intend to include all the relevant factors behind the investment advice. Williamson need not describe the investment system in detail in order to implement the advice effectively, but clients must be informed of Country Technician's basic process and logic. Without understanding the basis for a recommendation, clients cannot possibly understand its limitations or its inherent risks.

Example 2:

Richard Dox is a mining analyst for East Bank Securities. He has just finished his report on Boisy Bay Minerals. Included in his report is his own assessment of the geological extent of mineral reserves likely to be found on the company's land. Dox completed this calculation based on the core samples from the company's latest drilling. According to Dox's calculations, the company has in excess of 500,000 ounces of gold on the property. Dox concludes his research report as follows: "Based on the fact that the company has 500,000 ounces of gold to be mined, I recommend a strong BUY."

Comment:

If Dox issues the report as written, he will violate Standard V(B). His calculation of the total gold reserves for the property is an opinion, not a fact. Opinion must be distinguished from fact in research reports.

Example 3:

May & Associates is an aggressive growth manager that has represented itself since its inception as a specialist at investing in small-capitalization domestic stocks. One of May's selection criteria is a maximum capitalization of $250 million for any given company. After a string of successful years of superior relative performance, May expanded its client base significantly, to the point at which assets under management now exceed $3 billion. For liquidity purposes, May's chief investment officer (CIO) decides to lift the maximum permissible market-cap ceiling to $500 million and change the firm's sales and marketing literature accordingly to inform prospective clients and third-party consultants.

Comment:

Although May's CIO is correct about informing potentially interested parties as to the change in investment process, he must also notify May's existing clients. Among the latter group might be a number of clients who not only retained May as a small-cap manager but also retained mid-cap and large-cap specialists in a multiple-manager approach. Such clients could regard May's change of criteria as a style change that could distort their overall asset allocations.

Example 4:

Rather than lifting the ceiling for its universe from $250 million to $500 million, May & Associates extends its small-cap universe to include a number of non-U.S. companies.

Comment:

Standard V(B) requires that May's CIO advise May's clients of this change because the firm may have been retained by some clients specifically for its prowess at investing in domestic small-cap stocks. Other variations requiring client notification include introducing derivatives to emulate a certain market sector or relaxing various other constraints, such as portfolio beta. In all such cases, members and candidates must disclose changes to all interested parties.

Example 5:

A member sends a report to his investment management firm's clients describing a strategy his firm offers in terms of the high returns it will generate in the event interest rate volatility decreases. The report does not provide details of the strategy because they are deemed proprietary. The report does not consider the possible returns if interest rate volatility actually increases.

Comment:

This is a violation on two counts. The basic nature of the strategy must be disclosed, including the extent to which leverage is used to generate the high returns when volatility falls. Further, the report must include how the strategy will perform if volatility rises, as well as if it falls.

Example 6:

A member's firm changes from its old equity selection model, which is based on price-sales ratios, to a new model based on several factors, including future earnings growth rates, but does not inform clients of this change.

Comment:

This is a violation because members must inform their clients of any significant change in their investment process. Here, the introduction of forecast data on earnings growth can be viewed as a significant change because the old single-variable model was based on reported rather than forecast data.

Example 7:

A member's firm, in response to poor results relative to its stated benchmark, decides to structure portfolios to passively track the benchmark and does not inform clients.

Comment:

This is a significant change in the investment process and must be communicated to clients.

Example 8:

At a firm where individual portfolio managers have been responsible for security selection, a new policy is implemented whereby only stocks on an approved list constructed by the firm's senior managers may be purchased in client accounts. A member who is a portfolio manager does not inform his clients.

Comment:

This is a violation of the Standard because it represents a significant change in the investment process.

Example 9:

A member changes his firm's outside manager of real estate investments and provides information of this change only in the firm's annual report where outside advisers are listed.

Comment:

This is a violation of the Standard. The member should notify clients immediately of such a change in the firm's investment process.

 Professor's Note: Remember, the argument that clients "won't care" about a process change can be turned around to "there's no reason not to disclose the change."

> **V(C)   Record Retention.** Members and Candidates must develop and maintain appropriate records to support their investment analysis, recommendations, actions, and other investment-related communications with clients and prospective clients.

Guidance

Members must maintain research records that support the reasons for the analyst's conclusions and any investment actions taken. Such records are the property of the firm. If no other regulatory standards are in place, CFA Institute recommends at least a 7-year holding period.

A member who changes firms must recreate the analysis documentation supporting her recommendation using publicly available information or information obtained from the company and must not rely on memory or materials created at her previous firm.

Recommended Procedures for Compliance

This record-keeping requirement generally is the firm's responsibility.

Example 1:

One of Nikolas Lindstrom's clients is upset by the negative investment returns in his equity portfolio. The investment policy statement for the client requires that the portfolio manager follow a benchmark-oriented approach. The benchmark for the client included a 35% investment allocation in the technology sector, which the client acknowledged was appropriate. Over the past three years, the portion put into the segment of technology stocks suffered severe losses. The client complains to the investment manager that so much money was allocated to this sector.

Comment:

For Lindstrom, it is important to have appropriate records to show that over the past three years the percentage of technology stocks in the benchmark index was 35%.

Therefore, the amount of money invested in the technology sector was appropriate according to the investment policy statement. Lindstrom should also have the investment policy statement for the client stating that the benchmark was appropriate for the client's investment objectives. He should also have records indicating that the investment had been explained appropriately to the client and that the investment policy statement was updated on a regular basis.

Example 2:

A member bases his research reports on interviews, his own analysis, and industry reports from third parties on his industry and related industries.

Comment:

The member must keep records of all the information that went into the research on which his reports and recommendations are based.

Example 3:

When a member leaves a firm at which he has developed a complex trading model, he takes documentation of the model assumptions and how they were derived over time with him because he will use the model at his new firm.

Comment:

Taking these materials without permission from his previous employer is a violation of his duties to his (previous) employer. While he may use knowledge of the model at the new firm, the member must recreate the supporting documents. The originals are the property of the firm where he worked on developing the model.

VI   Conflicts of Interest

VI(A)   Disclosure of Conflicts. Members and Candidates must make full and fair disclosure of all matters that could reasonably be expected to impair their independence and objectivity or interfere with respective duties to their clients, prospective clients, and employer. Members and Candidates must ensure that such disclosures are prominent, are delivered in plain language, and communicate the relevant information effectively.

Guidance

Members must fully disclose to clients, prospects, and their employers all actual and potential conflicts of interest in order to protect investors and employers. These disclosures must be clearly stated.

Guidance—Disclosure to Clients

The requirement that all potential areas of conflict be disclosed allows clients and prospects to judge motives and potential biases for themselves. Disclosure of broker/dealer market-making activities would be included here. Board service is another area of potential conflict.

The most common conflict which requires disclosure is actual ownership of stock in companies that the member recommends or that clients hold.

Another common source of conflicts of interest is a member's compensation/bonus structure, which can potentially create incentives to take actions that produce immediate gains for the member with little or no concern for longer-term returns for the client. Such conflicts must be disclosed when the member is acting in an advisory capacity and must be updated in the case of significant change in compensation structure.

Guidance—Disclosure of Conflicts to Employers

Members must give the employer enough information to judge the impact of the conflict. Take reasonable steps to avoid conflicts, and report them promptly if they occur.

Recommended Procedures of Compliance

Any special compensation arrangements, bonus programs, commissions, and incentives should be disclosed.

Application of Standard VI(A) Disclosure of Conflicts

Example 1:

Hunter Weiss is a research analyst with Farmington Company, a broker and investment banking firm. Farmington's merger and acquisition department has represented Vimco, a conglomerate, in all of its acquisitions for 20 years. From time to time, Farmington officers sit on the boards of directors of various Vimco subsidiaries. Weiss is writing a research report on Vimco.

Comment:

Weiss must disclose in his research report Farmington's special relationship with Vimco. Broker/dealer management of and participation in public offerings must be disclosed in research reports. Because the position of underwriter to a company presents a special past and potential future relationship with a company that is the subject of investment advice, it threatens the independence and objectivity of the report and must be disclosed.

Example 2:

Samantha Snead, a portfolio manager for Thomas Investment Counsel, Inc., specializes in managing defined-benefit pension plan accounts, all of which are in the accumulative phase and have long-term investment objectives. A year ago, Snead's employer, in an attempt to motivate and retain key investment professionals, introduced a bonus compensation system that rewards portfolio managers on the basis of quarterly performance relative to their peers and certain benchmark indexes. Snead changes her investment strategy and purchases several high-beta stocks for client portfolios in an attempt to improve short-term performance. These purchases are seemingly contrary to the client investment policy statement. Now, an officer of Griffin Corporation, one of Snead's pension fund clients, asks why Griffin Corporation's portfolio seems to be dominated by high-beta stocks of companies that often appear among the most actively traded issues. No change in objective or strategy has been recommended by Snead during the year.

Comment:

Snead violated Standard VI(A) by failing to inform her clients of the changes in her compensation arrangement with her employer that created a conflict of interest. Firms may pay employees on the basis of performance, but pressure by Thomas Investment Counsel to achieve short-term performance goals is in basic conflict with the objectives of Snead's accounts.

Example 3:

Bruce Smith covers East European equities for Marlborough investments, an investment management firm with a strong presence in emerging markets. While on a business trip to Russia, Smith learns that investing in Russian equity directly is difficult but that equity-linked notes that replicate the performance of the underlying Russian equity can be purchased from a New York-based investment bank. Believing that his firm would not be interested in such a security, Smith purchases a note linked to a Russian telecommunications company for his own account without informing Marlborough. A month later, Smith decides that the firm should consider investing in Russian equities using equity-linked notes, and he prepares a write-up on the market that concludes with a recommendation to purchase several of the notes. One note recommended is linked to the same Russian telecom company that Smith holds in his personal account.

Comment:

Smith violated Standard VI(A) by failing to disclose his ownership of the note linked to the Russian telecom company. Smith is required by the standard to disclose the investment opportunity to his employer and look to his company's policies on personal trading to determine whether it was proper for him to purchase the note for his own account. By purchasing the note, Smith may or may not have impaired his ability to make an unbiased and objective assessment of the appropriateness of the derivative instrument for his firm, but Smith's failure to disclose the purchase to his employer impaired his employer's ability to render an opinion regarding whether the ownership of a security constituted a conflict of interest that might have affected future recommendations. Once he recommended the notes to his firm, Smith compounded his problems by not disclosing that he owned the notes in his personal account—a clear conflict of interest.

Example 4:

An investment management partnership sells a significant stake to a firm that is publicly traded. The partnership has added the firm's stock to its recommended list and approved its commercial paper for cash management accounts.

Comment:

Members are required to disclose such a change in firm ownership to all clients. Further, any transactions in client accounts involving the securities of the public firm, and any recommendations concerning the public firm's securities, must include a disclosure of the business relation between it and the partnership.

Example 5:

A member provides clients with research about a company's stock, and his wife inherits a significant amount of stock in the company.

Comment:

The member must disclose this potential conflict to his employer and in any subsequent reports or recommendations he authors. His employer may prudently choose to reassign the stock.

Example 6:

A member's investment banking firm receives a significant number of options as partial compensation for bringing a firm public. The member will profit personally from a portion of these options as well.

Comment:

In any research report on the public firm's securities, the member must disclose the fact that these options exist and include their number and the expiration date(s). Because he will profit personally from these, he must also disclose the extent of his participation in these options.

Example 7:

A member accepts an offer from a stock promoter who will provide additional compensation when the member sells Acme stock to his clients. He does not inform his clients or his employer.

Comment:

The member is in violation of the Standard because he must disclose this additional compensation to those clients to whom he recommends the stock and to his employer. Both have a right to determine for themselves the extent to which this additional compensation might affect the member's objectivity.

Example 8:

A member who is a portfolio manager for a small investment management firm serving individuals accepts a job as a trustee of an endowment fund that has over €1.5 billion in assets and does not disclose this to her employer.

Comment:

This is a significant position that may require a substantial portion of the member's time and may involve decisions on security selection and trading. The member is in violation of the Standard by not disclosing this involvement to her employer and by not discussing it with her employer before accepting the position.

Example 9:

A member replaces his firm's external manager, which has had average results, with a friend's firm.

Comment:

Taking such action without disclosing to his firm that the new manager is a personal friend is a violation of the Standards.

> **VI(B) Priority of Transactions.** Investment transactions for clients and employers must have priority over investment transactions in which a Member or Candidate is the beneficial owner.

Guidance

Client transactions take priority over personal transactions and over transactions made on behalf of the member's firm. Personal transactions include situations where the member is a "beneficial owner." Personal transactions may be undertaken only after clients and the member's employer have had an adequate opportunity to act on a recommendation. Note that family member accounts that are client accounts should be treated just like any client account; they should not be disadvantaged.

Information about pending trades should not be acted on for personal gain. The overriding considerations with respect to personal trades are that they do not disadvantage any clients.

Recommended Procedures for Compliance

All firms should have in place basic procedures that address conflicts created by personal investing. The following areas should be included:

- Limited participation in equity IPOs. Members can avoid these conflicts by not participating in IPOs.
- Restrictions on private placements. Strict limits should be placed on employee acquisition of these securities and proper supervisory procedures should be in place. Participation in these investments raises conflict of interest issues, similar to IPOs.
- Establish blackout/restricted periods. Employees involved in investment decision-making should have blackout periods prior to trading for clients—no "front running" (i.e., purchase or sale of securities in advance of anticipated client or employer purchases and sales). The size of the firm and the type of security should help dictate how severe the blackout requirement should be.
- Reporting requirements. Supervisors should establish reporting procedures, including duplicate trade confirmations, disclosure of personal holdings/beneficial ownership positions, and preclearance procedures.
- Disclosure of policies. When requested, members must fully disclose to investors their firm's personal trading policies.

Members should encourage their firms to adopt such procedures if they have not.

Application of Standard VI(B) Priority of Transactions

Example 1:

Erin Toffler, a portfolio manager at Esposito Investments, manages the retirement account established with the firm by her parents. Whenever IPOs become available, she first allocates shares to all her other clients for whom the investment is appropriate; only then does she place any remaining portion in her parents' account, if the issue is appropriate for them. She has adopted this procedure so that no one can accuse her of favoring her parents.

Comment:

Toffler has breached her duty to her parents by treating them differently from her other accounts simply because of the family relationship. As fee-paying clients of Esposito Investments, Toffler's parents are entitled to the same treatment as any other client of the firm. If Toffler has beneficial ownership in the account, however, and Esposito Investments has preclearance and reporting requirements for personal transactions, she may have to preclear the trades and report the transactions to Esposito.

Example 2:

A brokerage's insurance analyst, Denise Wilson, makes a closed-circuit report to her firm's branches around the country. During the broadcast, she includes negative comments about a major company within the industry. The following day, Wilson's report is printed and distributed to the sales force and public customers. The report recommends that both short-term traders and intermediate investors take profits by selling that company's stocks. Several minutes after the broadcast, Ellen Riley, head of the firm's trading department, closes out a long call position in the stock. Shortly thereafter, Riley establishes a sizable "put" position in the stock. Riley claims she took this action to facilitate anticipated sales by institutional clients.

Comment:

Riley expected that both the stock and option markets would respond to the "sell" recommendation, but she did not give customers an opportunity to buy or sell in the options market before the firm itself did. By taking action before the report was disseminated, Riley's firm could have depressed the price of the "calls" and increased the price of the "puts." The firm could have avoided a conflict of interest if it had waited to trade for its own account until its clients had an opportunity to receive and assimilate Wilson's recommendations. As it is, Riley's actions violated Standard VI(B).

Example 3:

A member who is a research analyst does not recommend a stock to his employer because he wants to purchase it quickly for his personal account.

Comment:

He has violated the priority of transactions by withholding this information from his employer and seeking to profit personally at his employer's expense. The member has likely violated his duty to his employer under Standard IV(A) Loyalty as well.

Example 4:

A member who manages a fund gets hot IPO shares for her husband's account from syndicate firms, even when the fund is unable to get shares.

Comment:

The member has violated the Standard by this action. She must act in the interest of the shareholders of the fund and place allocated shares there first. She must also inform her employer of her participation in these offerings through her beneficial interest in her husband's account(s).

Example 5:

A member allows an employee to continue his duties without having signed a required report of his personal trading activity over the last three months. The employee, a CFA candidate, has been purchasing securities for his own account just before firm buy recommendations have been released.

Comment:

The employee has violated the Standard. The member has also violated Standard IV(C) Responsibilities of Supervisors by allowing the employee to continue in his regular duties.

Example 6:

A member reveals a sell rating on some securities in a broadcast to all of her firm's brokers. The changed rating is sent to clients the next day. Shortly after revealing the change to her firm's brokers and prior to dissemination to clients, she buys puts on the stock for her firm's account.

Comment:

The member did not give clients adequate opportunity to act on the change in recommendation before buying the puts for her firm's account.

VI(C)   Referral Fees. Members and Candidates must disclose to their employer, clients, and prospective clients, as appropriate, any compensation, consideration, or benefit received from, or paid to, others for the recommendation of products or services.

Guidance

Members must inform employers, clients, and prospects of any benefit received for referrals of customers and clients, allowing them to evaluate the full cost of the service as well as any potential impartiality. All types of consideration must be disclosed.

Recommended Procedures for Compliance

Members should encourage their firms to adopt clear procedures regarding compensation for referrals. Firms that do not prohibit such fees should have clear procedures for approval, and members should provide their employers with updates at least quarterly regarding the nature and value of referral compensation received.

Application of Standard VI(C) Referral Fees

Example 1:

Brady Securities, Inc., a broker/dealer, has established a referral arrangement with Lewis Brothers, Ltd., an investment counseling firm. In this arrangement, Brady Securities refers all prospective tax-exempt accounts, including pension, profit-sharing, and endowment accounts, to Lewis Brothers. In return, Lewis Brothers makes available to Brady Securities on a regular basis the security recommendations and reports of its research staff, which registered representatives of Brady Securities use in serving customers. In addition, Lewis Brothers conducts monthly economic and market reviews for Brady Securities personnel and directs all stock commission business generated by referral accounts to Brady Securities.

Willard White, a partner in Lewis Brothers, calculates that the incremental costs involved in functioning as the research department of Brady Securities are US$20,000 annually.

Referrals from Brady Securities last year resulted in fee income of US$200,000 for Lewis Brothers, and directing all stock trades through Brady Securities resulted in additional costs to Lewis Brothers' clients of US$10,000.

Diane Branch, the chief financial officer of Maxwell Inc., contacts White and says that she is seeking an investment manager for Maxwell's profit-sharing plan. She adds, "My friend Harold Hill at Brady Securities recommended your firm without qualification, and that's good enough for me. Do we have a deal?" White accepts the new account but does not disclose his firm's referral arrangement with Brady Securities.

Comment:

White has violated Standard VI(C) by failing to inform the prospective customer of the referral fee payable in services and commissions for an indefinite period to Brady Securities. Such disclosure could have caused Branch to reassess Hill's recommendation and make a more critical evaluation of Lewis Brothers' services.

Example 2:

James Handley works for the Trust Department of Central Trust Bank. He receives compensation for each referral he makes to Central Trust's brokerage and personal financial management department that results in a sale. He refers several of his clients to the personal financial management department but does not disclose the arrangement within Central trust to his clients.

Comment:

Handley has violated Standard VI(C) by not disclosing the referral arrangement at Central Trust Bank to his clients. The Standard does not distinguish between referral fees paid by a third party for referring clients to the third party and internal compensation arrangements paid within the firm to attract new business to a subsidiary. Members and candidates must disclose all such referral fees. Therefore; Handley would be required to disclose, at the time of referral, any referral fee agreement in place between Central Trust Bank's departments. The disclosure should include the nature and the value of the benefit and should be made in writing.

Example 3:

Yeshao Wen is a portfolio manager for a bank. He receives additional monetary compensation from his employer when he is successful in assisting in the sales process and generation of assets under management. The assets in question will be invested in proprietary product offerings such as affiliate company mutual funds.

Comment:

Standard VI(C) is meant to address instances where the investment advice provided by a member or candidate appears to be objective and independent but in fact is influenced by an unseen referral arrangement. It is not meant to cover compensation by employers to employees for generating new business when it would be obvious to potential clients that the employees are "referring" potential clients to the services of their employers.

If Wen is selling the bank's investment management services in general, he does not need to disclose to potential clients that he will receive a bonus for finding new clients and acquiring new assets under management for the bank. Potential clients are likely aware that it would be financially beneficial both to the portfolio manager and the manager's firm for the portfolio manager to sell the services of the firm and attract new clients. Therefore, sales efforts attempting to attract new investment management clients need not disclose this fact.

However, in this example, the assets will be managed in "proprietary product offerings" of the manager's company (for example, an in-house mutual fund) and Wen will receive additional compensation for selling firm products. Some sophisticated investors may realize that it would be financially beneficial to the portfolio manager and the manager's firm if the investor buys the product offerings of the firm. Best practice, however, dictates that the portfolio manager must disclose to clients that he is compensated for referring clients to firm products. Such disclosure will meet the purpose of Standard VI(C), which is to allow investors to determine whether there is any partiality on the part of the portfolio manager when giving investment advice.

Example 4:

An investment consultant conducts an independent and objective analysis of investment managers for a pension fund and selects the best one. Subsequently, the selected advisor makes a payment to the consultant.

Comment:

This is a violation of the Standard. The potential for a payment should have been disclosed to the pension fund. There are very likely regulatory or legal considerations with regard to such payment as well.

VII Responsibilities as a CFA Institute Member or CFA Candidate

VII(A) Conduct as Members and Candidates in the CFA Program. Members and Candidates must not engage in any conduct that compromises the reputation or integrity of CFA Institute or the CFA designation or the integrity, validity, or security of the CFA examinations.

Professor's Note: The Standard is intended to cover conduct such as cheating on the CFA exam or otherwise violating rules of CFA Institute or the CFA program. It is not intended to prevent anyone from expressing any opinions or beliefs concerning CFA Institute or the CFA program.

Members must not engage in any activity that undermines the integrity of the CFA charter. This Standard applies to conduct which includes:

- Cheating on the CFA exam or any exam.
- Revealing anything about either broad or specific topics tested, content of exam questions, or formulas required or not required on the exam.
- Not following rules and policies of the CFA program.
- Giving confidential information on the CFA program to candidates or the public.
- Improperly using the designation to further personal and professional goals.
- Misrepresenting information on the Professional Conduct Statement (PCS) or the CFA Institute Professional Development Program.

Members and candidates are not precluded from expressing their opinions regarding the exam program or CFA Institute but must not reveal confidential information about the CFA program.

Candidates who violate any of the CFA exam policies (calculator, personal belongings, Candidate Pledge) have violated Standard VII(A).

Members who volunteer in the CFA program may not solicit or reveal information about questions considered for or included on a CFA exam, about the grading process, or about scoring of questions.

Application of Standard VII(A) Conduct as Members and Candidates in the CFA Program

Example 1:

Ashlie Hocking is writing Level II of the CFA examination in London. After completing the exam, she immediately attempts to contact her friend in Sydney, Australia, to tip him off to specific questions on the exam.

Comment:

Hocking has violated Standard VII(A) by attempting to give her friend an unfair advantage, thereby compromising the integrity of the CFA examination process.

Example 2:

Jose Ramirez is an investment-relations consultant for several small companies that are seeking greater exposure to investors. He is also the program chair for the CFA Institute society in the city where he works. To the exclusion of other companies, Ramirez only schedules companies that are his clients to make presentations to the society.

Comment:

Ramirez, by using his volunteer position at CFA Institute to benefit himself and his clients, compromises the reputation and integrity of CFA Institute and, thus, violates Standard VII(A).

Example 3:

A member who is an exam grader discusses with friends the guideline answer for and relative candidate performance on a specific question he graded on the CFA exam.

Comment:

He has violated his Grader's Agreement and also the Standard by compromising the integrity of the CFA exam.

Example 4:

A candidate does not stop writing when asked to by the proctor at the CFA exam.

Comment:

By taking additional time compared to other candidates, this candidate has violated the Standard, compromising the integrity of the exam process.

Example 5:

A member who is a volunteer on a CFA Institute committee tells her clients that what she learns through her committee work will allow her to better serve their interests.

Comment:

She has violated the Standard by using her CFA committee position to benefit herself personally and to any extent her 'inside' knowledge has benefited her clients.

Example 6:

A candidate tells another candidate, "I'm sure glad that Bayes' formula was not on the Level I test this year."

Comment:

This is a violation of Standard VII(A). Candidates are not permitted to reveal any formulas required or not required on a CFA exam.

Example 7:

A candidate tells his beloved CFA instructor, "I really appreciate the emphasis that you put on Financial Reporting and Analysis because that was a huge part of the test this year."

Comment:

This is a violation of Standard VII(A). Candidates are not permitted to disclose the relative weighting of topics on the exam.

Example 8:

A candidate tells his mother, "There was an item set on the CFA exam on the Residual Income Model that just kicked my butt."

Comment:

This is a violation of Standard VII(A). Candidates are not permitted to disclose specific topics tested on the exam.

VII(B) Reference to CFA Institute, the CFA Designation, and the CFA Program. When referring to CFA Institute, CFA Institute membership, the CFA designation, or candidacy in the CFA Program, Members and Candidates must not misrepresent or exaggerate the meaning or implications of membership in CFA Institute, holding the CFA designation, or candidacy in the CFA Program.

Guidance

Members must not make promotional promises or guarantees tied to the CFA designation. Do not:

- Over-promise individual competence.
- Over-promise investment results in the future (i.e., higher performance, less risk, etc.).

Guidance—CFA Institute Membership

Members must satisfy these requirements to maintain membership:

- Sign PCS annually.
- Pay CFA Institute membership dues annually.

If they fail to do this, they are no longer active members.

Guidance—Using the CFA Designation

Do not misrepresent or exaggerate the meaning of the designation.

Guidance—Referencing Candidacy in the CFA Program

There is no partial designation. It is acceptable to state that a candidate successfully completed the program in three years, if in fact he did, but claiming superior ability because of this is not permitted.

Guidance—Proper Usage of the CFA Marks

The Chartered Financial Analyst and CFA marks must always be used either after a charterholder's name or as adjectives, but not as nouns, in written and oral communications.

Recommended Procedures for Compliance

Make sure that members' and candidates' firms are aware of the proper references to a member's CFA designation or candidacy, as this is a common error.

Application of Standard VII(B) Reference to CFA Institute, the CFA Designation, and the CFA Program

Example 1:

An advertisement for AZ Investment Advisors states that all the firm's principals are CFA charterholders and all passed the three examinations on their first attempt. The advertisement prominently links this fact to the notion that AZ's mutual funds have achieved superior performance.

Comment:

AZ may state that all principals passed the three examinations on the first try as long as this statement is true and is not linked to performance or does not imply superior ability. Implying that (1) CFA charterholders achieve better investment results and (2) those who pass the exams on the first try may be more successful than those who do not violates Standard VII(B).

Example 2:

Five years after receiving his CFA charter, Louis Vasseur resigns his position as an investment analyst and spends the next two years traveling abroad. Because he is not actively engaged in the investment profession, he does not file a completed Professional Conduct Statement with CFA Institute and does not pay his CFA Institute membership dues. At the conclusion of his travels, Vasseur becomes a self-employed analyst, accepting assignments as an independent contractor. Without reinstating his CFA Institute membership by filing his Professional Conduct Statement and paying his dues, he prints business cards that display "CFA" after his name.

Comment:

Vasseur has violated Standard VII(B) because Vasseur's right to use the CFA designation was suspended when he failed to file his Professional Conduct Statement and stopped paying dues. Therefore, he no longer is able to state or imply that he is an active CFA charterholder. When Vasseur files his Professional Conduct Statement and resumes paying CFA Institute dues to activate his membership, he will be eligible to use the CFA designation upon satisfactory completion of CFA Institute reinstatement procedures.

Example 3:

A member still uses the initials CFA after his name even though his membership has been suspended for not paying dues and for not submitting a personal conduct statement as required.

Comment:

This is a violation of the Standard.

Example 4:

A member puts the CFA logo on his letterhead, his business cards, and the company letterhead.

Comment:

By putting the logo on the company letterhead (rather than the letterhead or business card of an individual who is a CFA charterholder), the member has violated the Standard.

CONCEPT CHECKERS

1. In situations where the laws of a member or candidate's country of residence, the local laws of regions where the member or candidate does business, and the Code and Standards specify different requirements, the member or candidate must abide by:
   A. local law or the Code and Standards, whichever is stricter.
   B. the Code and Standards or his country's laws, whichever are stricter.
   C. the strictest of local law, his country's laws, or the Code and Standards.

2. According to the Standard on independence and objectivity, members and candidates:
   A. may accept gifts or bonuses from clients.
   B. may not accept compensation from an issuer of securities in return for producing research on those securities.
   C. should consider credit ratings issued by recognized agencies to be objective measures of credit quality.

3. Bill Cooper finds a table of historical bond yields on the website of the U.S. Treasury that supports the work he has done in his analysis and includes the table as part of his report without citing the source. Has Cooper violated the Code and Standards?
   A. Yes, because he did not cite the source of the table.
   B. Yes, because he did not verify the accuracy of the information.
   C. No, because the table is from a recognized source of financial or statistical data.

4. Which of the following statements about the Standard on misconduct is *most accurate*?
   A. Misconduct applies only to a member or candidate's professional activities.
   B. Neglecting to perform due diligence when required is an example of misconduct.
   C. A member or candidate commits misconduct by engaging in any illegal activity.

5. Ed Ingus, CFA, visits the headquarters and main plant of Bullitt Company and observes that inventories of unsold goods appear unusually large. From the CFO, he learns that a recent increase in returned items may result in earnings for the current quarter that are below analysts' estimates. Based on his visit, Ingus changes his recommendation on Bullitt to "Sell." Has Ingus violated the Standard concerning material nonpublic information?
   A. Yes.
   B. No, because the information he used is not material.
   C. No, because his actions are consistent with the mosaic theory.

6. Green Brothers, an emerging market fund manager, has two of its subsidiaries simultaneously buy and sell emerging market stocks. In its marketing literature, Green Brothers cites the overall emerging market volume as evidence of the market's liquidity. As a result of its actions, more investors participate in the emerging markets fund. Green Brothers *most likely*:
    A. did not violate the Code and Standards.
    B. violated the Standard regarding market manipulation.
    C. violated the Standard regarding performance presentation.

7. Cobb, Inc., has hired Jude Kasten, CFA, to manage its pension fund. The client(s) to whom Kasten owes a duty of loyalty are:
    A. Cobb's management.
    B. the shareholders of Cobb, Inc.
    C. the beneficiaries of the pension fund.

8. Which of the following actions is *most likely* a violation of the Standard on fair dealing?
    A. A portfolio manager allocates IPO shares to all client accounts, including her brother's fee-based retirement account.
    B. An investment firm routinely begins trading for its own account immediately after announcing recommendation changes to clients.
    C. After releasing a general recommendation to all clients, an analyst calls the firm's largest institutional clients to discuss the recommendation in more detail.

9. The Standard regarding suitability *most likely* requires that:
    A. an advisor must analyze an investment's suitability for the client prior to recommending or acting on the investment.
    B. a member or candidate must decline to carry out an unsolicited transaction that she believes is unsuitable for the client.
    C. when managing a fund to an index, a manager who is evaluating potential investments must consider their suitability for the fund's shareholders.

10. Which of the following is *most likely* a recommended procedure for complying with the Standard on performance presentation?
    A. Exclude terminated accounts from past performance history.
    B. Present the performance of a representative account to show how a composite has performed.
    C. Consider the level of financial knowledge of the audience to whom the performance is presented.

11. The CFA Institute Professional Conduct Program (PCP) has begun an investigation into Chris Jones, a Level II CFA candidate, and a number of his CFA Charterholder colleagues. Jones has access to confidential client records that could be useful in clearing his name and wishes to share this information with the PCP. Which of the following *most accurately* describes Jones's duties with regard to preservation of confidentiality?
    A. Sharing the confidential information with the PCP would violate the Standards.
    B. The Standards encourage, but do not require, that Jones support the PCP investigation into his colleagues.
    C. Jones may share confidential information about former clients with the PCP but may not share confidential information about current clients.

12. Connie Fletcher, CFA, works for a small money management firm that specializes in pension accounts. Recently, a friend asked her to act as an unpaid volunteer manager for the city's street sweep pension fund. As part of the position, the city would grant Fletcher a free parking space in front of her downtown office. Before Fletcher accepts, she should *most appropriately*:
    A. do nothing because this is a volunteer position.
    B. inform her current clients in writing and discuss the offer with her employer.
    C. disclose the details of the volunteer position to her employer and obtain written permission from her employer.

13. Sarah Johnson, a portfolio manager, is offered a bonus directly by a client if Johnson meets certain performance goals. To comply with the Standard that governs additional compensation arrangements, Johnson should:
    A. decline to accept a bonus outside of her compensation from her employer.
    B. disclose this arrangement to her employer in writing and obtain her employer's permission.
    C. disclose this arrangement to her employer only if she actually meets the performance goals and receives the bonus.

14. A member or candidate who has supervisory responsibility:
    A. should place particular emphasis on enforcing investment-related compliance policies.
    B. is responsible for instructing those to whom he has delegated authority about methods to detect and prevent violations of the law and the Code and Standards.
    C. has complied with the Standards if she reports employee violations to upper management and provides a written warning to the employee to cease such activities.

15. Which of the following actions is a *required*, rather than *recommended*, action under the Standard regarding diligence and a reasonable basis for a firm's research recommendations?
    A. Compensate analysts based on a measure of the quality of their research.
    B. Review the assumptions used and evaluate the objectivity of third-party research reports.
    C. Have a policy requiring that research reports and recommendations have a basis that can be substantiated as reasonable and adequate.

16. Claire Marlin, CFA, manages an investment fund specializing in foreign currency trading. Marlin writes a report to investors that describes the basic characteristics of her strategy, which is based on an expected appreciation of the euro relative to other major currencies. Marlin shows the projected returns from the strategy if the euro appreciates less than 5%, between 5% and 10%, or more than 10%, while clearly stating that these forecasts are her opinion. Has Marlin violated the Standard related to communication with clients?
    A. Yes.
    B. No, because she disclosed the basic characteristics of the investment.
    C. No, because she distinguished fact from opinion and discussed how the strategy may perform under a range of scenarios.

17. If regulations do not specify how long to retain the documents that support an analyst's conclusions, the Code and Standards recommend a period of at least:
    A. five years.
    B. seven years.
    C. ten years.

18. Daniel Lyons, CFA, is an analyst who covers several stocks including Horizon Company. Lyons's aunt owns 30,000 shares of Horizon. She informs Lyons that she has created a trust in his name into which she has placed 2,000 shares of Horizon. The trust is structured so that Lyons will not be able to sell the shares until his aunt dies, but may vote the shares. Lyons is due to update his research coverage of Horizon next week. Lyons should *most appropriately*:
    A. update the report as usual because he is not a beneficial owner of the stock.
    B. advise his superiors that he is no longer able to issue research recommendations on Horizon.
    C. disclose the situation to his employer and, if then asked to prepare a report, also disclose his beneficial ownership of the shares in his report.

19. Kate Wilson, CFA, is an equity analyst. Wilson enters two transactions for her personal account. Wilson sells 500 shares of Tibon, Inc., a stock on which her firm currently has a "Buy" recommendation. Wilson buys 200 shares of Hayfield Co. and the following day issues a research report on Hayfield with a "Buy" recommendation. Has Wilson violated the Code and Standards?
    A. No.
    B. Yes, both of her actions violate the Code and Standards.
    C. Yes, but only one of her actions violates the Code and Standards.

20. Hern Investments provides monthly emerging market research to Baker Brokerage in exchange for prospective client referrals and European equity research from Baker. Clients and prospects of Hern are not made aware of the agreement, but clients unanimously rave about the high quality of the research provided by Baker. As a result of the research, many clients with non-discretionary accounts have earned substantial returns on their portfolios. Managers at Hern have also used the research to earn outstanding returns for the firm's discretionary accounts. Hern has *most likely*:
    A. not violated the Code and Standards.
    B. violated the Code and Standards by using third-party research in discretionary accounts.
    C. violated the Code and Standards by failing to disclose the referral agreement with Baker.

21. After writing the CFA Level I exam, Cynthia White goes to internet discussion site *CFA Haven* to express her frustration. White writes, "CFA Institute is not doing a competent job of evaluating candidates because none of the questions in the June exam touched on Alternative Investments." White *most likely* violated the Standard related to conduct as a candidate in the CFA program by:
    A. publicly disputing CFA Institute policies and procedures.
    B. disclosing subject matter covered or not covered on a CFA exam.
    C. participating in an internet forum that is directed toward CFA Program participants.

22. After passing all three levels of the CFA exams on her first attempts and being awarded her CFA Charter, Paula Osgood is promoting her new money management firm by issuing an advertisement. Which of these statements would *most likely* violate the Standard related to use of the CFA designation?
    A. "To earn the right to use the CFA designation, Paula passed three exams covering ethics, financial statement analysis, asset valuation, and portfolio management."
    B. "Paula passed three 6-hour exams on her first attempts and is a member of her local investment analyst society."
    C. "Because of her extensive training, Paula will be able to achieve better investment results than managers who have not been awarded the CFA designation."

ANSWERS – CONCEPT CHECKERS

1. **C** To comply with Standard I(A) Knowledge of the Law, a member must always abide by the strictest applicable law, regulation, or standard.

2. **A** Gifts from clients are acceptable under Standard I(B) Independence and Objectivity, but the Standard requires members and candidates to disclose such gifts to their employers. Standard I(B) allows issuer-paid research as long as the analysis is thorough, independent, unbiased, and has a reasonable and adequate basis for its conclusions, and the compensation from the issuer is disclosed. Members and candidates should consider the potential for conflicts of interest inherent in credit ratings and may need to do independent research to evaluate the soundness of these ratings.

3. **C** According to Standard I(C) Misrepresentation, members and candidates must cite the sources of the information they use in their analysis, unless the information is factual data (as opposed to analysis or opinion) from a recognized financial or statistical reporting service. The U.S. Treasury is one example of a recognized source of factual data.

4. **B** Failing to act when required by one's professional obligations, such as neglecting to perform due diligence related to an investment recommendation, violates Standard I(D) Misconduct. Acts a member commits outside his professional capacity are misconduct if they reflect poorly on the member or candidate's honesty, integrity, or competence (e.g., theft or fraud). Violations of the law that do not reflect on the member or candidate's honesty, integrity, or competence (e.g., an act related to civil disobedience) are not necessarily regarded as misconduct.

5. **A** The statement from the CFO about the current quarter's earnings is material nonpublic information. Ingus violated Standard II(A) Material Nonpublic Information by acting or causing others to act on it.

6. **B** The intent of Green Brothers' actions is to manipulate the appearance of market liquidity in order to attract investment to its own funds. The increased trading activity was not based on market fundamentals or an actual trading strategy to benefit investors. It was merely an attempt to mislead market participants in order to increase assets under Green Brothers' management. The action violates Standard II(B) Market Manipulation.

7. **C** Standard III(A) Loyalty, Prudence, and Care specifies that for the manager of a pension or trust, the duty of loyalty is owed to the beneficiaries, not to the individuals who hired the manager.

8. **B** The firm must give its clients an opportunity to act on recommendation changes. Firms can offer different levels of service to clients as long as this is disclosed to all clients. The largest institutional clients would likely be paying higher fees for a greater level of service. The portfolio manager's brother's account should be treated the same as any other client account.

9. **A**   According to Standard III(C) Suitability, a member or candidate who is in an advisory relationship with a client is responsible for analyzing the suitability of an investment for the client before taking investment action or making a recommendation. A member or candidate who believes an unsolicited trade is unsuitable for the client can either decline to carry it out or ask the client to provide a statement that suitability is not a consideration for this trade. When managing a fund to an index or stated mandate, the manager is responsible for ensuring that potential investments are consistent with the fund's mandate. Suitability for individuals would be a concern for an advisor who recommends the fund to clients, but not for the manager of the fund.

10. **C**   Recommendations stated in Standard III(D) Performance Presentation include considering the sophistication and knowledge of the audience when presenting performance data. Other recommendations are to include terminated accounts in past performance history; to present the performance of a composite as a weighted average of the performance of similar portfolios, rather than using a single representative account; and to maintain the records and data that were used to calculate performance.

11. **B**   Members and candidates are required to cooperate with PCP investigations into their own conduct and encouraged to cooperate with PCP investigations into the conduct of others. Sharing confidential information with the PCP is not a violation of Standard III(E) Preservation of Confidentiality. Any client information shared with the PCP will be kept in strict confidence. Standard III(E) states that members and candidates are required to maintain confidentiality of client records even after the end of the client relationship.

12. **C**   According to Standard IV(A) Loyalty, members and candidates are expected to act for the benefit of their employer and not deprive the employer of their skills. Fletcher is performing work similar to the services that her employer provides. Although the position is a volunteer position, Fletcher will receive compensation in the form of a free parking space. In light of the circumstances, Fletcher must disclose the details of the position to her employer and get written permission before accepting the volunteer position.

13. **B**   Johnson should disclose her additional compensation arrangement in writing to her employer and obtain her employer's written consent before accepting this offer, in accordance with Standard IV(B) Additional Compensation Arrangements.

14. **B**   Members or candidates may delegate supervisory duties to subordinates but remain responsible for instructing them about how to detect and prevent violations. Reporting the violation and warning the employee are not sufficient to comply with Standard IV(C) Responsibilities of Supervisors. The supervisor must also take steps to prevent further violations while she conducts an investigation, such as limiting the employee's activity or increasing her monitoring of the employee. Supervisors should enforce investment-related and non-investment related policies equally.

15. **B**   Standard V(A) Diligence and Reasonable Basis requires analysts who use third-party research to review its assumptions and evaluate the independence and objectivity of the research. The other choices are recommended procedures for compliance with the Standard.

16. **A**   Standard V(B) Communication with Clients and Prospective Clients requires that members and candidates communicate the risk associated with the investment strategy used and how the strategy is expected to perform in a range of scenarios. These scenarios should include those different from the current trend. Marlin should have discussed how her strategy would perform if the euro depreciates instead of appreciating as she expects.

17. B   When no other regulatory guidance applies, Standard V(C) Record Retention recommends that records be maintained for a minimum of seven years.

18. C   Even though the shares are held in trust, Lyons is considered a beneficial owner under Standard VI(A) Disclosure of Conflicts because he has a pecuniary interest in the shares and because has the power to vote the shares. Lyons is obligated to inform his employer of the potential conflict. If Lyons's employer permits him to continue issuing investment recommendations on the company, Lyons must disclose the existence of a potential conflict in his reports.

19. C   Only one of these transactions is a violation. Standard VI(B) Priority of Transactions requires members and candidates to give clients an adequate opportunity to act on a recommendation before trading for accounts in which the member or candidate has a beneficial ownership interest. Members and candidates may trade for their own accounts as long as they do not disadvantage clients, benefit personally from client trades, or violate any regulations that apply. The Standard does not prohibit members and candidates from entering personal transactions that are contrary to what their firms are recommending for clients, as long as the transaction does not violate any of these criteria.

20. C   According to Standard VI(C) Referral Fees, Hern must disclose the referral arrangement between itself and Baker so that potential clients can judge the true cost of Hern's services and assess whether there is any partiality inherent in the recommendation of services.

21. B   Standard VII(A) Conduct as Members and Candidates in the CFA Program prohibits candidates from revealing which portions of the Candidate Body of Knowledge were or were not covered on an exam. Members and candidates are free to disagree with the policies, procedures, or positions taken by the CFA Institute. The Standard does not prohibit participating in CFA Program-related internet blogs, forums, or social networks.

22. C   Standard VII(B) Reference to CFA Institute, the CFA Designation, and the CFA Program prohibits members and candidates from implying superior performance as a result of being a CFA charterholder. Concise factual descriptions of the requirements to obtain the CFA Charter are acceptable. Osgood's statement that she passed the exams on her first attempts is acceptable because it states a fact.

The following is a review of the Ethical and Professional Standards principles designed to address the learning outcome statements set forth by CFA Institute. This topic is also covered in:

INTRODUCTION TO THE GLOBAL INVESTMENT PERFORMANCE STANDARDS (GIPS®)

EXAM FOCUS

The following two topic reviews cover the key features of the Global Investment Performance Standards (GIPS®) as adopted by CFA Institute in 1999 and subsequently updated. Compliance with GIPS is voluntary. For the Level I exam, you are responsible for only the "Introduction to the Global Investment Performance Standards (GIPS®)" and the Preface, Section I, and Section II (through II.0: Fundamentals of Compliance) of the GIPS document. The GIPS document is included in the book of candidate readings for Level I and is also available on the CFA Institute Web site. A helpful glossary of terms is included in the document. Candidates should not underestimate the importance of this material for the exam.

LOS 3.a: Explain why the GIPS standards were created, what parties the GIPS standards apply to, and who is served by the standards.

CFA® Program Curriculum, Volume 1, page 163

In the past, a variety of reporting procedures were misleading at best. Some of these misleading practices included:

- *Representative accounts*—showing a top-performing portfolio as representative of a firm's results.
- *Survivorship bias*—excluding "weak performance" accounts that have been terminated.
- *Varying time periods*—showing performance for selected time periods with outstanding returns.

GIPS are a set of ethical principles based on a standardized, industry-wide approach. Investment firms can *voluntarily* follow GIPS in their presentation of historical investment results to prospective clients. These standards seek to avoid misrepresentations of performance.

GIPS apply to investment management firms and are intended to serve prospective and existing clients of investment firms. GIPS allow clients to more easily compare investment performance among investment firms and have more confidence in reported performance.

Study Session 1

Cross-Reference to CFA Institute Assigned Reading #3 – Introduction to the Global Investment Performance Standards (GIPS®)

LOS 3.b: Explain the construction and purpose of composites in performance reporting.

CFA® Program Curriculum, Volume 1, page 165

A composite is a grouping of individual discretionary portfolios representing a similar investment strategy, objective, or mandate. Examples of possible composites are "Large Capitalization Growth Stocks" and "Investment Grade Domestic Bonds." Reporting on the performance of composites gives clients and prospects information about the firm's success in managing various types of securities or results for various investment styles.

A composite, such as International Equities, must include all portfolios (current and past) that the firm has managed in accordance with this particular strategy. The firm should identify which composite each managed portfolio is to be included in before the portfolio's performance is known. This prevents firms from choosing portfolios to include in a composite in order to create composites with superior returns.

LOS 3.c: Explain the requirements for verification.

CFA® Program Curriculum, Volume 1, page 165

Verification—requirements:

Verification is performed by a third party, not by the firm itself, on a firm-wide basis. This third party verifier must attest that (1) the firm has complied with all GIPS requirements for composite construction on a firm-wide basis and (2) the firm's processes and procedures are established to present performance in accordance with the calculation methodology required by GIPS, the data requirements of GIPS, and in the format required by GIPS.

Verification—recommendations:

- Firms are encouraged to pursue independent verification. Verification applies to the entire firm's performance measurement practices and methods, not a selected composite.
- Verified firms should include the following disclosure language:

  "[Insert name of firm] has been verified for the periods [insert dates] by [name of verifier]. A copy of the verification report is available upon request."

GLOBAL INVESTMENT PERFORMANCE STANDARDS (GIPS®)

LOS 4.a: Describe the key features of the GIPS standards and the fundamentals of compliance.

CFA® Program Curriculum, Volume 1, page 170

GIPS Objectives

- To obtain global acceptance of calculation and presentation standards in a fair, comparable format with full disclosure.
- To ensure consistent, accurate investment performance data in areas of reporting, records, marketing, and presentations.
- To promote fair competition among investment management firms in all markets without unnecessary entry barriers for new firms.
- To promote global "self regulation."

Key Characteristics of GIPS

- To claim compliance, an investment management firm must define its "firm." This definition should reflect the "distinct business entity" that is held out to clients and prospects as the investment firm.
- GIPS are ethical standards for performance presentation which ensure fair representation of results and full disclosure.
- Include all actual fee-paying, discretionary portfolios in composites for a minimum of five years or since firm or composite inception. After presenting five years of compliant data, the firm must add annual performance each year going forward up to a minimum of ten years.
- Firms are required to use certain calculation and presentation standards and make specific disclosures.
- Input data must be accurate.
- GIPS contain both *required* and *recommended* provisions—firms are *encouraged* to adopt the *recommended* provisions.
- Firms are encouraged to present all pertinent additional and supplemental information.
- There will be no partial compliance and only full compliance can be claimed.
- Follow the local laws for cases in which a local or country-specific law or regulation conflicts with GIPS, but disclose the conflict.
- Certain recommendations may become requirements in the future.
- Supplemental private equity and real estate provisions contained in GIPS are to be applied to those asset classes.

Fundamentals of compliance contain both requirements and recommendations:

Definition of the firm—requirements:

- Apply GIPS on a firm-wide basis.
- Firm must be defined as a distinct business unit.
- Total firm assets include total market value of discretionary and non-discretionary assets, including fee-paying and non-fee-paying accounts.
- Include asset performance of sub-advisors, as long as the firm has discretion over sub-advisor selection.
- If a firm changes its organization, historical composite results cannot be changed.

Definition of the firm—recommendations:

- Include the broadest definition of the firm, including all geographical offices marketed under the same brand name.

Document policies and procedures—requirements:

- Document, in writing, policies and procedures the firm uses to comply with GIPS.

Claim of compliance—requirements:

- Once GIPS requirements have been met, the following compliance statement must be used:

  "[Insert name of firm] has prepared and presented this report in compliance with the Global Investment Performance Standards (GIPS®)."

- There is no such thing as partial compliance.
- There are to be no statements referring to calculation methodologies used in a composite presentation as being "in accordance with GIPS" or the like.
- Similarly, there should be no such statements referring to the performance of an individual, existing client as being "calculated in accordance with GIPS" or the like, unless a compliant firm is reporting results directly to the client.

Firm fundamental responsibilities—requirements:

- Firms must provide a compliant presentation to *all* prospects (prospect must have received a presentation within the previous 12 months).
- Provide a composite list and composite description to all prospects that make a request. List discontinued composites for at least five years.
- Provide, to clients requesting it, a compliant presentation and a composite description for any composite included on the firm's list.
- When jointly marketing with other firms, if one of the firms claims GIPS compliance, be sure it is clearly defined as separate from noncompliant firms.
- Firms are encouraged to comply with recommendations and must comply with all requirements. Be aware of updates, guidance statements, and the like.

LOS 4.b: Describe the scope of the GIPS standards with respect to an investment firm's definition and historical performance record.

CFA® Program Curriculum, Volume 1, page 170

The definition of the firm, for purposes of GIPS compliance, must be the corporation, subsidiary, or division that is held out to clients as a business entity. If a firm has different geographic locations (e.g., all doing business under the name of Bluestone Advisers), then the definition of the firm should include all the various geographic locations and their clients. Firms based in any country may present GIPS compliant performance histories.

A firm must initially present a minimum of five years of compliant performance presentation for the firm and each composite unless the firm or composite has been in existence less than five years. For firms or composites in existence less than five years, compliant performance since inception must be presented in order to claim compliance. After the initial compliant performance presentation, one year of compliant performance must be added each year to a required (minimum) performance history of ten years.

Firms may present periods of noncompliant performance immediately prior to the compliant performance history as long as no noncompliant performance is presented for any periods after January 1, 2000. Firms must specify which performance results are noncompliant and the ways in which such (noncompliant) performance does not comply with GIPS.

LOS 4.c: Explain how the GIPS standards are implemented in countries with existing standards for performance reporting and describe the appropriate response when the GIPS standards and local regulations conflict.

CFA® Program Curriculum, Volume 1, page 171

Firms that previously presented performance in compliance with a particular Country Version of GIPS (CVG) may claim GIPS compliance for any CVG-compliant results prior to January 1, 2006. Firms that report such CVG-compliant performance data must continue to include that performance data in subsequent GIPS-compliant presentations until a minimum of ten years of compliant performance is presented.

In any cases where country-specific regulations conflict with GIPS, firms must follow the applicable country-specific regulations but must also disclose the nature of the conflict with GIPS.

LOS 4.d: Describe the nine major sections of the GIPS standards.

CFA® Program Curriculum, Volume 1, page 174

0. *Fundamentals of compliance.* The fundamental issues involved in complying with GIPS are (a) definition of the firm, (b) documentation of firm policies and procedures with respect to GIPS compliance, (c) complying with GIPS updates, (d) claiming compliance

©2012 Kaplan, Inc.

in the appropriate manner, and (e) appropriate verification statement when a third-party verifier is employed.

1. *Input data.* Input data should be consistent in order to establish full, fair, and comparable investment performance presentations.

2. *Calculation methodology.* Certain methodologies are required for portfolio return calculations and certain other methodologies are required for composite return calculations. Uniformity in methods across firms is required so that their results are comparable.

3. *Composite construction.* Creation of meaningful, asset-weighted composites is important to achieve a fair presentation. Composite performance is based on the performance of one or more portfolios that have the same investment strategy or investment objective. Composite returns are the asset-weighted average (not a simple average) of the returns on the portfolios that are included in each composite.

4. *Disclosures.* The firm must disclose information about the presentation and the policies adopted by the firm so that the raw numbers presented in the report are understandable to the user. There are some disclosures that all firms must make, but some disclosures may not apply to all firms. If a disclosure is not applicable to a specific firm, the firm is not required to include any statement regarding it.

5. *Presentation and reporting.* Investment performance must be presented according to GIPS requirements. Other firm-specific information not specifically required by GIPS should be included when appropriate.

6. *Real estate.* Certain provisions apply to all real estate investments (land, buildings, etc.) regardless of the level of control the firm has over management of the investment. These provisions apply regardless of whether the asset is producing revenue or there is leverage involved in the investment.

7. *Private equity.* Private equity investments must be valued according to the GIPS Private Equity Valuation Principles, which are contained in Appendix D, unless the investment is an open-end or evergreen fund (which must follow regular GIPS). Private equity investments include all investment in companies that are not publicly traded, regardless of their stage of business development. This would include venture capital investments, ownership of a previously public company that has been purchased (taken private), and mezzanine financing, as well as limited partnership shares in such investments and fund-of-funds investments.

8. *Wrap fee/Separately Managed Account (SMA) portfolios.* For these portfolios, some of the requirements and recommendations in Sections 0 through 5 are supplemented or replaced by the requirements specified in this section.

CONCEPT CHECKERS

1. Which of the following statements *most accurately* describes the parties that GIPS are intended to apply to and serve? GIPS apply to:
   A. consultants who serve their existing and prospective clients.
   B. firms that issue securities and serve investment management firms.
   C. investment management firms and serve their existing and prospective clients.

2. For a composite to be constructed in compliance with GIPS, the portfolios included in the composite must:
   A. have been managed by the firm for the full performance reporting period.
   B. be selected immediately after the last business day of the period for which the composite's performance will be presented.
   C. include all fee-paying, discretionary portfolios that are managed according to the same strategy, mandate, or investment objective.

3. Verification of compliance with GIPS:
   A. may be performed on single composites.
   B. is required for a firm to claim GIPS compliance.
   C. requires the verification report to be issued for the entire firm.

4. Firms that claim to present investment performance in compliance with GIPS are required to:
   A. document the procedures and policies they use to ensure GIPS compliance.
   B. clearly disclose any calculations or other aspects of a presentation that are non-compliant with GIPS.
   C. calculate total firm assets as the fair value of all fee-paying discretionary portfolios managed by the firm.

5. Which of the following definitions of a firm would violate GIPS?
   A. Investment firm that has been in existence for less than five years.
   B. Regional branch of an investment management firm marketed under the name of its parent.
   C. Entity registered with the national regulator that oversees its investment management activities.

6. If a country has regulations in place that conflict with GIPS, firms that wish to claim GIPS compliance:
   A. may not do so because GIPS do not permit exceptions or partial compliance.
   B. must establish a subsidiary in a location where local law does not conflict with GIPS.
   C. must comply with local regulations and disclose the nature of the conflict in the presentation.

7.   Which of the following includes only sections of the Global Investment
        Performance Standards?
        A. Disclosure, Public Equity, Presentation and Reporting.
        B. Real Estate, Calculation Methodology, Fundamentals of Compliance.
        C. Input Data, Composite Construction, Wrap Fee/Speculative Margin
            Account (SMA) Portfolios.

ANSWERS – CONCEPT CHECKERS

1. **C** GIPS apply to investment management firms. They are intended to serve prospective and existing clients of investment firms and consultants who advise these clients.

2. **C** To comply with GIPS, a composite must include all fee-paying, discretionary portfolios managed according to the same investment objective, strategy, or mandate. The composite or composites in which a portfolio will be included must be determined on an ex-ante basis (i.e., before the period for which the composite's performance will be calculated). A GIPS-compliant composite must include terminated accounts.

3. **C** Verification of GIPS compliance is optional, but if a firm chooses to seek third-party verification, the report must be issued with respect to the whole firm. GIPS verification cannot be carried out for a single composite.

4. **A** GIPS Section 0, "Fundamentals of Compliance," states that firms must document their procedures for remaining in compliance with GIPS. Firms which state that they are in compliance with GIPS must comply fully and may not claim partial compliance. GIPS defines total firm assets as the fair value of all portfolios managed by the firm, including discretionary and non-discretionary, fee-paying and non-fee-paying portfolios.

5. **B** The definition of a firm for GIPS-compliant performance presentation should include all geographical offices marketed under the same name brand.

6. **C** Firms must always comply with the laws and regulations of the country in which they reside. In cases where local regulations conflict with GIPS, a firm can still claim GIPS compliance if they disclose the conflict fully in an otherwise compliant presentation.

7. **B** The nine major sections of GIPS are (0) Fundamentals of Compliance; (1) Input Data; (2) Calculation Methodology; (3) Composite Construction; (4) Disclosure; (5) Presentation and Reporting; (6) Real Estate; (7) Private Equity; and (8) Wrap Fee/Separately Managed Account (SMA) Portfolios.

SELF-TEST: ETHICS AND PROFESSIONAL STANDARDS

18 questions: 27 minutes

1. Karen Jones, CFA, is an outside director for Valley Manufacturing. At a director's meeting, Jones finds out that Valley Corp. has made several contributions to foreign politicians that she suspects were illegal. Jones checks with her firm's legal counsel and determines that the contributions were indeed illegal. At the next board meeting, Jones urges the board to disclose the contributions. The board, however, votes not to make a disclosure. Jones's *most appropriate* action would be to:
   A. protest the board's actions in writing to the executive officer of Valley.
   B. resign from the board and seek legal counsel as to her legal disclosure requirements.
   C. inform her supervisor of her discovery and cease attending meetings until the matter is resolved.

2. Over the past two days, Lorraine Quigley, CFA, manager of a hedge fund, has been purchasing large quantities of Craeger Industrial Products' common stock while at the same time shorting put options on the same stock. Quigley did not notify her clients of the trades although they are aware of the fund's general strategy to generate returns. Which of the following statements is *most likely* correct? Quigley:
   A. did not violate the Code and Standards.
   B. violated the Code and Standards by manipulating the prices of publicly traded securities.
   C. violated the Code and Standards by failing to disclose the transactions to clients before they occurred.

3. Melvin Byrne, CFA, manages a portfolio for James Martin, a wealthy client. Martin's portfolio is well diversified with a slight tilt toward capital appreciation. Martin requires very little income from the portfolio. Recently, Martin's brother, Cliff, has become a client of Byrne. Byrne proceeds to invest Cliff's portfolio in a similar manner to James's portfolio based on the fact that both brothers have a similar lifestyle and are only two years apart in age. Which of the following statements is *most likely* correct? Byrne:
   A. violated the Code and Standards by knowingly creating a conflict of interest between James's and Cliff's portfolios.
   B. violated the Code and Standards by failing to determine Cliff's objectives and constraints prior to investing his portfolio.
   C. did not violate the Code and Standards.

4. Robert Blair, CFA, Director of Research, has had an ongoing battle with his firm's management about the adequacy of its compliance system. Blair believes the firm's compliance procedures are inadequate in that they are not being monitored or carefully followed. Blair should *most appropriately*:
   A. resign from the firm unless the compliance system is strengthened and followed.
   B. send his superior a memo outlining the problem.
   C. decline in writing to continue to accept supervisory responsibility until reasonable compliance procedures are adopted.

5.   Beth Anderson, CFA, is a portfolio manager for several wealthy clients including Reuben Carlyle. Anderson manages Carlyle's personal portfolio of stock and bond investments. Carlyle recently told Anderson that he is under investigation by the IRS for tax evasion related to his business, Carlyle Concrete. After learning about the investigation, Anderson informs a friend at a local investment bank so that they may withdraw their proposal to take Carlyle Concrete public. Anderson has *most likely*:

   A. violated the Code and Standards by failing to maintain the confidentiality of her client's information.
   B. violated the Code and Standards by failing to detect and report the tax evasion to the proper authorities.
   C. not violated the Code and Standards since the information she conveyed pertained to illegal activities on the part of her client.

6.   A research report states: "Based on the fact that the South American utilities sector has seen rapid growth in new service orders, we expect that most companies in the sector will be able to convert the revenue increases into significant profits. We also believe the trend will continue for the next three to five years." The report goes on to describe the major risks of investing in this market. The author of this report:

   A. has not violated the Code and Standards.
   B. violated the Code and Standards by failing to properly distinguish factual information from opinions.
   C. violated the Code and Standards by failing to properly identify details related to the operations of South American utilities.

7.   Frist Investments, Inc. has just hired Michael Pulin to manage institutional portfolios, most of which are pension related. Pulin has just taken the Level III CFA exam and is awaiting his results. Pulin has more than 15 years of investment management experience with individual clients but has never managed an institutional portfolio. Pulin joined the CFA Institute as an affiliate member two years ago and is in good standing with the organization. Which of the following statements would be *most appropriate* for Frist to use in advertising Pulin as a new member of the firm? Pulin:

   A. has many years of investment experience which, along with his participation in the CFA program, will allow him to deliver superior investment performance relative to other managers.
   B. is a CFA Level III and passed the first two exams on the first attempt. He is an affiliate member of the CFA Institute. We expect him to become a regular member if he passes the Level III examination.
   C. is a Level III CFA candidate and has many years of excellent performance in the investment management industry. Pulin is an affiliate member of the CFA Institute and will be eligible to become a CFA charterholder and regular member if he passes the Level III CFA Exam.

8. Zanuatu, an island nation, does not have any regulations precluding the use of nonpublic information. Alfredo Romero has a friend and fellow CFA charterholder there, Donna Gordon, with whom he has shared nonpublic information regarding firms outside his industry. The information concerns several firms' internal earnings and cash flow projections. Gordon may:

   A. trade on the information under the laws of Zanuatu, which govern her behavior.

   B. not trade on the information under CFA Institute Standards, which govern her behavior.

   C. trade on the information under CFA Institute Standards since the firms concerned are outside Romero's industry.

9. Samantha Donovan, CFA, is an exam proctor for the Level II CFA exam. The day before the exam is to be administered, Donovan faxes a copy of one of the questions to two friends, James Smythe and Lynn Yeats, who are Level II candidates in the CFA program. Donovan, Smythe, and Yeats had planned the distribution of an exam question months in advance. Smythe used the fax to prepare for the exam. Yeats, however, had second thoughts and threw the fax away without looking at its contents. Which of the following statements is *most likely* correct?

   A. Smythe violated the Code and Standards, but Yeats did not.

   B. Donovan violated the Code and Standards, but Smythe did not.

   C. Donovan and Yeats both violated the Code and Standards.

10. Sally Albright, CFA, works full time for Frank & Company, an investment management firm, as a fixed income security analyst. Albright has been asked by a business contact at KDG Enterprises to accept some analytical work from KDG on a consulting basis. The work would entail investigating potential distressed debt securities in the small-cap market. Albright should *most appropriately*:

    A. accept the work as long as she obtains consent to all the terms of the engagement from Frank & Company.

    B. not accept the work as it violates the Code and Standards by creating a conflict of interest.

    C. accept the work as long as she obtains written consent from KDG and does it on her own time.

11. Josef Karloff, CFA, acts as liaison between Pinnacle Financial (an investment management firm) and Summit Inc. (an investment banking boutique specializing in penny stocks). When Summit underwrites an IPO, Karloff routinely has Pinnacle issue vague statements implying that the firm has cash flows, financial resources, and growth prospects that are better than is the case in reality. This action is *most likely* a violation of the section of the Standards concerning:

    A. fair dealing.

    B. nonpublic information.

    C. misconduct.

12. Steve Matthews, CFA, is a principal at Carlson Brothers, a leading regional investment bank specializing in initial public offerings of small to mid-sized biotech firms. Just before many of the IPOs are offered to the general public, Matthews arranges for 10% of the shares to be distributed to management of the firm going public. This action is a violation of the Standard concerning:
    A. additional compensation.
    B. disclosure of conflicts of interest.
    C. fair dealing.

13. Will Hunter, CFA, is a portfolio manager at NV Asset Managers. An investment banker asks Hunter to purchase shares in a new IPO to support the price long enough for insiders to liquidate their holdings. Hunter realizes that the price of the shares will almost certainly fall dramatically after his buying support ceases. NV management "strongly suggests" that Hunter honor the investment banker's request since NV has had a longstanding relationship with the investment bank. If Hunter agrees to make the purchases, he will:
    A. not violate the Code and Standards.
    B. violate the Standard concerning market manipulation.
    C. violate the Standard concerning priority of transactions.

14. Neiman Investment Co. receives brokerage business from Pick Asset Management in exchange for referring prospective clients to Pick. Pick advises clients—in writing, at the time the relationship is established—of the nature of its arrangement with Neiman. With regard to this practice, Pick has:
    A. complied with the Code and Standards.
    B. violated the Code and Standards by failing to preserve the confidentiality of the agreement with Neiman.
    C. violated the Code and Standards by participating in an agreement that creates a conflict of interest.

15. Ralph Salley, a Level I candidate in the CFA Program, is explaining Standard VI(B) Priority of Transactions, to his supervisor. Salley states, "The Standard recommends, but does not require, that members and candidates should not participate in initial public offerings. The Standard also recommends that trades for accounts of family members be made after those for other clients, but before those for the account of the members and candidates responsible for executing the transactions." Salley's explanation of the Standard is:
    A. correct.
    B. incorrect, because the Standard does not recommend that trades for family members be made after those for other clients.
    C. incorrect, because the Standard requires that members and candidates not participate in initial public offerings.

16. Which of the following policies is required to comply with GIPS?
    A. Compliance with GIPS must be verified by an independent third party.
    B. Restructuring of the firm's organization cannot be used as a basis to change the historical performance results of a composite.
    C. The definition of the firm must include the firm's offices in all countries and regions.

17. Mason Smith is trying to decide which of the following composite definitions, submitted by his junior analysts, would be considered an acceptable composite according to GIPS. An acceptable composite can include all:
     A. accounts that are managed directly from the firm's Hong Kong office.
     B. actively managed portfolios, but exclude passively managed portfolios.
     C. portfolios that are managed to provide a return approximately equal to that of the S&P 500 Index.

18. An investment management firm, Investco, Inc., was recently audited by the United States Securities and Exchange Commission (SEC). Investco included the following statement in its performance presentation report: "This report has been verified as GIPS compliant by Investco's Compliance Department and the United States Securities and Exchange Commission." Does this constitute acceptable verification under GIPS?
     A. No, only one party may perform GIPS verification.
     B. No, neither party involved in the audit constitutes an acceptable GIPS verification.
     C. Yes, because an audit was performed implicitly by the SEC and explicitly by the firm's audit team.

SELF-TEST ANSWERS: ETHICS AND PROFESSIONAL STANDARDS

1. **B** According to Standard I(A) Knowledge of the Law, since she has taken steps to stop the illegal activities and the board has ignored her, Jones must dissociate from the board and seek legal advice as to what other actions would be appropriate in this instance. She may need to inform legal or regulatory authorities of the illegal activities.

2. **A** Quigley's trades are most likely an attempt to take advantage of an arbitrage opportunity that exists between Craeger's common stock and its put options. She is not manipulating the prices of securities in an attempt to mislead market participants, which would violate Standard II(B) Market Manipulation. She is pursuing a legitimate investment strategy. Participants in her hedge fund are aware of the fund's investment strategy, and thus Quigley did not violate the Code and Standards by not disclosing this specific set of trades in advance of trading.

3. **B** Standard III(C) Suitability requires that before taking investment action, members and candidates must make a reasonable inquiry into a client's or prospect's investment objectives and constraints as well as their prior investment experience. Byrne cannot assume that because the brothers have similar lifestyles and are close in age that they should have similarly managed portfolios. Byrne should have interviewed Cliff directly before investing his portfolio.

4. **C** According to Standard IV(C) Responsibilities of Supervisors, because he is aware that the firm's compliance procedures are not being monitored and followed and because he has repeatedly tried to get company management to correct the situation, Blair should decline supervisory responsibility until adequate procedures to detect and prevent violations of laws, regulations, and the Code and Standards are adopted and followed. If he does not do so, he will be in violation of the Code and Standards.

5. **A** Anderson must maintain the confidentiality of client information according to Standard III(E) Preservation of Confidentiality. Confidentiality may be broken in instances involving illegal activities on the part of the client, but the client's information may only be relayed to proper authorities. Anderson did not have the right to inform the investment bank of her client's investigation.

6. **A** Historical growth can be cited as a fact. The report states that the firm *expects* further growth and profitability, which phrases the statement as an opinion. Under Standard V(B) Communication with Clients and Prospective Clients, it is not necessary to include every detail about a potential investment in a report. Members and candidates are expected to use their judgment and identify the most important factors to include.

7. **C** Standard VII(B) governs acceptable methods of referencing the CFA Institute, CFA designation, and CFA Program. Candidates may reference their candidacy if they are enrolled for, or waiting for the results of, a CFA exam. Pulin may also reference his membership status with the CFA Institute as well as his remaining eligibility requirements to become a CFA charterholder.

8. **B** Even though the laws of Zanuatu would not preclude trading on the information, as a CFA Charterholder, Gordon is bound by the CFA Institute Code and Standards. Standard II(A) prohibits the use of material nonpublic information, and Gordon may not trade the stocks about which she has such information under any circumstances.

9. **C**   In this situation, Donovan, Smythe, and Yeats all violated Standard VII(A) Conduct as Members and Candidates in the CFA Program. The Standard prohibits conduct that compromises the integrity, validity, or security of the CFA exams. Donovan clearly breached the exam security. Smythe and Yeats both compromised the integrity of the exams by planning to use the actual exam question to gain an advantage over other candidates. Even though Yeats did not ultimately use the information to study for the exam, she participated in a scheme to cheat on the CFA exam.

10. **A**   Albright may accept work for which she receives outside compensation and which may compete with her employer only if she obtains her employer's consent. Under Standard IV(A) Loyalty, such consent must be obtained from her employer prior to beginning the work.

11. **C**   Since the statements are vague, we have no direct evidence that a violation of securities law has occurred. However, under Standard I(D) Misconduct, members and candidates are prohibited from engaging in activities involving deceit. Karloff's action is a clear attempt to mislead the investing public regarding the value of Summit IPOs.

12. **C**   Standard III(B) Fair Dealing requires that members not use their position to disadvantage clients, specifically in the case of IPOs.

13. **B**   NV management is asking Hunter to violate Standard II(B) Market Manipulation, which prohibits actions that are designed to distort prices or artificially increase trading volume. The intent is to mislead market participants and allow corporate insiders to take advantage of artificially high prices.

14. **A**   Pick has not violated the Standards. The referral arrangement is fully disclosed to clients before they agree to do business with Pick. Therefore, clients can fully assess the effect of the agreement on the referral and how the agreement may affect their accounts before hiring Pick as their asset manager.

15. **B**   Standard VI(B) Priority of Transactions recommends that members and candidates avoid the appearance of conflict of interest by not participating in IPOs. If a family member is a fee-paying client, the member or candidate should treat them like any other client, not giving any advantage or disadvantage to their accounts.

16. **B**   Firms cannot alter historical performance records of composites simply because of a reorganization of the firm. This is required by GIPS Standard 0.A.15. Third-party verification of GIPS compliance and including all geographical offices in the definition of the firm are recommended, but not required.

17. **C**   Composites are groups of portfolios that represent a similar investment strategy, objective, or mandate. Clearly, grouping all portfolios managed to mirror the S&P 500 Index return constitutes a composite according to this definition. Organizing composites by office or by a generic active management category is not acceptable as these categories do not reflect any sort of strategy, objective, or mandate.

18. **B**   GIPS verification must be performed by an independent third party. The SEC audit does not constitute a GIPS verification.

The following is a review of the Quantitative Methods: Basic Concepts principles designed to address the learning outcome statements set forth by CFA Institute. This topic is also covered in:

THE TIME VALUE OF MONEY

EXAM FOCUS

This topic review covers time value of money concepts and applications. Procedures are presented for calculating the future value and present value of a single cash flow, an annuity, and a series of uneven cash flows. The impact of different compounding periods is examined, along with the procedures for solving for other variables in time value of money problems. Your main objective in this chapter is to master time value of money mechanics (i.e., learn how to crunch the numbers). Work all the questions and problems found at the end of this review. Make sure you know how to grind out all the time value of money problems on your calculator. The more rapidly you can do them (correctly), the more time you will have for the more conceptual parts of the exam.

TIME VALUE OF MONEY CONCEPTS AND APPLICATIONS

The concept of **compound interest** or **interest on interest** is deeply embedded in time value of money (TVM) procedures. When an investment is subjected to compound interest, the growth in the value of the investment from period to period reflects not only the interest earned on the original principal amount but also on the interest earned on the previous period's interest earnings—the interest on interest.

TVM applications frequently call for determining the **future value** (FV) of an investment's cash flows as a result of the effects of compound interest. Computing FV involves projecting the cash flows forward, on the basis of an appropriate compound interest rate, to the end of the investment's life. The computation of the **present value** (PV) works in the opposite direction—it brings the cash flows from an investment back to the beginning of the investment's life based on an appropriate compound rate of return.

Being able to measure the PV and/or FV of an investment's cash flows becomes useful when comparing investment alternatives because the value of the investment's cash flows must be measured at some common point in time, typically at the end of the investment horizon (FV) or at the beginning of the investment horizon (PV).

Using a Financial Calculator

It is very important that you be able to use a financial calculator when working TVM problems because the exam is constructed under the assumption that candidates have the ability to do so. There is simply no other way that you will have time to solve TVM problems. *CFA Institute allows only two types of calculators to be used for the exam—the TI BAII Plus® (including the BAII Plus Professional) and the HP 12C® (including the HP 12C Platinum). This topic review is written primarily with the TI BAII Plus in mind. If you don't already own a calculator, go out and buy a TI BAII Plus!* However, if you already own the HP 12C and are comfortable with it, by all means continue to use it.

The TI BAII Plus comes preloaded from the factory with the periods per year function (P/Y) set to 12. This automatically converts the annual interest rate (I/Y) into monthly rates. While appropriate for many loan-type problems, this feature is not suitable for the vast majority of the TVM applications we will be studying. So prior to using our SchweserNotes™, please set your P/Y key to "1" using the following sequence of keystrokes:

[2nd] [P/Y] "1" [ENTER] [2nd] [QUIT]

As long as you do not change the P/Y setting, it will remain set at one period per year until the battery from your calculator is removed (it does not change when you turn the calculator on and off). If you want to check this setting at any time, press [2nd] [P/Y]. The display should read P/Y = 1.0. If it does, press [2nd] [QUIT] to get out of the "programming" mode. If it doesn't, repeat the procedure previously described to set the P/Y key. With P/Y set to equal 1, it is now possible to think of I/Y as the interest rate per compounding period and N as the number of compounding periods under analysis. Thinking of these keys in this way should help you keep things straight as we work through TVM problems.

Before we begin working with financial calculators, you should familiarize yourself with your TI by locating the TVM keys noted below. These are the only keys you need to know to work virtually all TVM problems.

- N   Number of compounding periods.
- I/Y   = Interest rate per compounding period.
- PV   Present value.
- FV   = Future value.
- PMT = Annuity payments, or constant periodic cash flow.
- CPT   Compute.

 Professor's Note: We have provided an online video in the Schweser Library on how to use the TI calculator. You can view it by logging in at www.schweser.com.

Time Lines

It is often a good idea to draw a time line before you start to solve a TVM problem. A **time line** is simply a diagram of the cash flows associated with a TVM problem. A cash flow that occurs in the present (today) is put at time zero. Cash outflows (payments) are given a negative sign, and cash inflows (receipts) are given a positive sign. Once the cash flows are assigned to a time line, they may be moved to the beginning of the investment period to calculate the PV through a process called discounting or to the end of the period to calculate the FV using a process called compounding.

Figure 1 illustrates a time line for an investment that costs $1,000 today (outflow) and will return a stream of cash payments (inflows) of $300 per year at the end of each of the next five years.

Figure 1: Time Line

Please recognize that the cash flows occur at the end of the period depicted on the time line. Furthermore, note that the end of one period is the same as the beginning of the next period. For example, the end of the second year (t = 2) is the same as the beginning of the third year, so a cash flow at the beginning of Year 3 appears at time t = 2 on the time line. Keeping this convention in mind will help you keep things straight when you are setting up TVM problems.

 Professor's Note: Throughout the problems in this review, rounding differences may occur between the use of different calculators or techniques presented in this document. So don't panic if you are a few cents off in your calculations.

LOS 5.a: Interpret interest rates as required rates of return, discount rates, or opportunity costs.

CFA® Program Curriculum, Volume 1, page 244

Interest rates are our measure of the time value of money, although risk differences in financial securities lead to differences in their equilibrium interest rates. Equilibrium interest rates are the **required rate of return** for a particular investment, in the sense that the market rate of return is the return that investors and savers require to get them to willingly lend their funds. Interest rates are also referred to as **discount rates** and, in fact, the terms are often used interchangeably. If an individual can borrow funds at an interest rate of 10%, then that individual should *discount* payments to be made in the future at that rate in order to get their equivalent value in current dollars or other currency. Finally, we can also view interest rates as the **opportunity cost** of current consumption. If the market rate of interest on 1-year securities is 5%, earning an additional 5% is the opportunity forgone when current consumption is chosen rather than saving (postponing consumption).

LOS 5.b: Explain an interest rate as the sum of a real risk-free rate, and premiums that compensate investors for bearing distinct types of risk.

CFA® Program Curriculum, Volume 1, page 244

The **real risk-free rate** of interest is a theoretical rate on a single-period loan that has no expectation of inflation in it. When we speak of a real rate of return, we are referring to an investor's increase in purchasing power (after adjusting for inflation). Since expected inflation in future periods is not zero, the rates we observe on U.S. Treasury bills (T-bills), for example, are risk-free rates but not *real* rates of return. T-bill rates are *nominal risk-free rates* because they contain an *inflation premium*. The approximate relation here is:

nominal risk-free rate = real risk-free rate + expected inflation rate

Securities may have one or more **types of risk**, and each added risk increases the required rate of return on the security. These types of risk are:

- **Default risk.** The risk that a borrower will not make the promised payments in a timely manner.
- **Liquidity risk.** The risk of receiving less than fair value for an investment if it must be sold for cash quickly.
- **Maturity risk.** As we will cover in detail in the section on debt securities, the prices of longer-term bonds are more volatile than those of shorter-term bonds. Longer maturity bonds have more maturity risk than shorter-term bonds and require a maturity risk premium.

Each of these risk factors is associated with a risk premium that we add to the nominal risk-free rate to adjust for greater default risk, less liquidity, and longer maturity relative to a very liquid, short-term, default risk-free rate such as that on T-bills. We can write:

required interest rate on a security = nominal risk-free rate
+ default risk premium
+ liquidity premium
+ maturity risk premium

LOS 5.c: Calculate and interpret the effective annual rate, given the stated annual interest rate and the frequency of compounding.

CFA® Program Curriculum, Volume 1, page 253

Financial institutions usually quote rates as stated annual interest rates, along with a compounding frequency, as opposed to quoting rates as periodic rates—the rate of interest earned over a single compounding period. For example, a bank will quote a savings rate as 8%, compounded quarterly, rather than 2% per quarter. The rate of interest that investors actually realize as a result of compounding is known as the effective annual rate (EAR). EAR represents the annual rate of return actually being earned *after adjustments have been made for different compounding periods.*

EAR may be determined as follows:

$$EAR = (1 + periodic\ rate)^m - 1$$

where:
periodic rate = stated annual rate/m
m = the number of compounding periods per year

Obviously, the EAR for a stated rate of 8% *compounded annually* is not the same as the EAR for 8% *compounded semiannually*, or *quarterly*. Indeed, whenever compound interest is being used, the stated rate and the actual (effective) rate of interest are equal only when interest is compounded annually. Otherwise, the greater the compounding frequency, the greater the EAR will be in comparison to the stated rate.

The computation of EAR is necessary when comparing investments that have different compounding periods. It allows for an apples-to-apples rate comparison.

Example: Computing EAR

Compute EAR if the stated annual rate is 12%, compounded quarterly.

Answer:

Here m = 4, so the periodic rate is $\frac{12}{4} = 3\%$.

Thus, $EAR = (1 + 0.03)^4 - 1 = 1.1255 - 1 = 0.1255 = 12.55\%$.

This solution uses the [y^x] key on your financial calculator. The exact keystrokes on the TI for the above computation are 1.03 [y^x] 4 [=]. On the HP, the strokes are 1.03 [ENTER] 4 [y^x].

Example: Computing EARs for a range of compounding frequencies

Using a stated rate of 6%, compute EARs for semiannual, quarterly, monthly, and daily compounding.

Answer:

EAR with:

semiannual compounding = $(1 + 0.03)^2 - 1$	= 1.06090 - 1	= 0.06090 = 6.090%
quarterly compounding = $(1 + 0.015)^4 - 1$	= 1.06136 - 1	= 0.06136 = 6.136%
monthly compounding = $(1 + 0.005)^{12} - 1$	= 1.06168 - 1	= 0.06168 = 6.168%
daily compounding = $(1 + 0.00016438)^{365} - 1$	= 1.06183 - 1	= 0.06183 = 6.183%

Notice here that the EAR increases as the compounding frequency increases.

The limit of shorter and shorter compounding periods is called continuous compounding. To convert an annual stated rate to the EAR with continuous compounding, we use the formula $e^r - 1 = \text{EAR}$.

For 6%, we have $e^{0.06} - 1 = 6.1837\%$. The keystrokes are 0.06 [2nd] [e^x] [−] 1 [=] 0.061837.

LOS 5.d: Solve time value of money problems for different frequencies of compounding.

CFA® Program Curriculum, Volume 1, page 250

When compounding periods are other than annual, we must take account of that fact in our calculations. Consider the following two examples.

Example: Growth with quarterly compounding

John plans to invest $2,500 in an account that will earn 8% per year with quarterly compounding. How much will be in the account at the end of two years?

Answer:

There are eight quarterly compounding periods in two years, and the effective quarterly rate is 8 / 4 = 2%. The account will grow to $2,500(1.02)^8 = \$2,929.15$. Alternatively, since the EAR is $1.02^4 - 1 = 0.082432$, we can grow the $2,500 at 8.2432% for two years to get $2,500(1.082432)^2 = \$2,929.15$, which is the same result.

Example: Present value with monthly compounding

Alice would like to have $5,000 saved in an account at the end of three years. If the return on the account is 9% per year with monthly compounding, how much must Alice deposit today in order to reach her savings goal in three years?

Answer:

The effective monthly rate is 9 / 12 = 0.75%, and we can calculate the present value of $5,000 three years (36 months) from now as $5,000 / (1.0075)^{36} = \$3,820.74$. Alternatively, since the EAR is $1.0075^{12} - 1 = 0.093807$, we can calculate the present value by discounting $5,000 at the EAR for three years. $5,000 / 1.093807^3 = \$3,820.74$, which is the same result.

LOS 5.e: Calculate and interpret the future value (FV) and present value (PV) of a single sum of money, an ordinary annuity, an annuity due, a perpetuity (PV only), and a series of unequal cash flows.

CFA® Program Curriculum, Volume 1, page 245

Future Value of a Single Sum

Future value is the amount to which a current deposit will grow over time when it is placed in an account paying compound interest. The FV, also called the compound value, is simply an example of compound interest at work.

The formula for the FV of a *single* cash flow is:

$$FV = PV(1 + I/Y)^N$$

where:
PV = amount of money invested today (the present value)
I/Y = rate of return per compounding period
N = total number of compounding periods

In this expression, the investment involves a single cash outflow, PV, which occurs today, at t = 0 on the time line. The single sum FV formula will determine the value of an investment at the end of N compounding periods, given that it can earn a fully compounded rate of return, I/Y, over all of the periods.

The factor $(1 + I/Y)^N$ represents the compounding rate on an investment and is frequently referred to as the future value factor, or the **future value interest factor**, for a single cash flow at I/Y over N compounding periods. These are the values that appear in interest factor tables, which we will not be using.

Example: FV of a single sum

Calculate the FV of a $300 investment at the end of ten years if it earns an annually compounded rate of return of 8%.

Answer:

To solve this problem with your calculator, input the relevant data and compute FV.

N = 10; I/Y = 8; PV = –300; CPT → FV = $647.68

 Professor's Note: Note the negative sign on PV. This is not necessary, but it makes the FV come out as a positive number. If you enter PV as a positive number, ignore the negative sign that appears on the FV.

This relatively simple problem could also be solved using the following equation:

$$FV = 300(1 + 0.08)^{10} = \$647.68$$

On the TI calculator, enter 1.08 [y^x] 10 [×] 300 [=].

Present Value of a Single Sum

The PV of a single sum is today's value of a cash flow that is to be received at some point in the future. In other words, it is the amount of money that must be invested today, at a given rate of return over a given period of time, in order to end up with a specified FV. As previously mentioned, the process for finding the PV of a cash flow is known as *discounting* (i.e., future cash flows are "discounted" back to the present). The interest rate used in the discounting process is commonly referred to as the **discount rate** but may also be referred to as the **opportunity cost, required rate of return**, and the **cost of capital**. Whatever you want to call it, it represents the annual compound rate of return that can be earned on an investment.

The relationship between PV and FV can be seen by examining the FV expression stated earlier. Rewriting the FV equation in terms of PV, we get:

$$PV = FV \times \left[\frac{1}{(1 + I/Y)^N} \right] = \frac{FV}{(1 + I/Y)^N}$$

Note that for a single future cash flow, PV is always less than the FV whenever the discount rate is positive.

The quantity $1 / (1 + I/Y)^N$ in the PV equation is frequently referred to as the **present value factor, present value interest factor**, or **discount factor** for a single cash flow at I/Y over N compounding periods.

Example: PV of a single sum

Given a discount rate of 9%, calculate the PV of a $1,000 cash flow that will be received in five years.

Answer:

To solve this problem, input the relevant data and compute PV.

N = 5; I/Y = 9; FV = 1,000; CPT → PV = −$649.93 (ignore the sign)

Professor's Note: With single sum PV problems, you can either enter FV as a positive number and ignore the negative sign on PV or enter FV as a negative number.

This relatively simple problem could also be solved using the following PV equation:

$$PV = \frac{1,000}{(1+0.09)^5} = \$649.93$$

On the TI, enter 1.09 [y^x] 5 [=] [1/x] [×] 1,000 [=].

The PV computed here implies that at a rate of 9%, an investor will be indifferent between $1,000 in five years and $649.93 today. Put another way, $649.93 is the amount that must be invested today at a 9% rate of return in order to generate a cash flow of $1,000 at the end of five years.

Annuities

An **annuity** is a stream of *equal cash flows* that occurs at *equal intervals* over a given period. Receiving $1,000 per year at the end of each of the next eight years is an example of an annuity. There are two types of annuities: **ordinary annuities** and **annuities due**. The *ordinary annuity* is the most common type of annuity. It is characterized by cash flows that occur at the *end* of each compounding period. This is a typical cash flow pattern for many investment and business finance applications. The other type of annuity is called an *annuity due*, where payments or receipts occur at the beginning of each period (i.e., the first payment is today at t = 0).

Computing the FV or PV of an annuity with your calculator is no more difficult than it is for a single cash flow. You will know four of the five relevant variables and solve for the fifth (either PV or FV). The difference between single sum and annuity TVM problems is that instead of solving for the PV or FV of a single cash flow, we solve for the PV or FV of a stream of equal periodic cash flows, where the size of the periodic cash flow is defined by the payment (PMT) variable on your calculator.

Example: FV of an ordinary annuity

What is the future value of an ordinary annuity that pays $150 per year at the end of each of the next 15 years, given the investment is expected to earn a 7% rate of return?

Answer:

This problem can be solved by entering the relevant data and computing FV.

N = 15; I/Y = 7; PMT = −150; CPT → FV = $3,769.35

Implicit here is that PV = 0; clearing the TVM functions sets both PV and FV to zero.

The time line for the cash flows in this problem is depicted in the figure below.

FV of an Ordinary Annuity

As indicated here, the sum of the compounded values of the individual cash flows in this 15-year ordinary annuity is $3,769.35. Note that the annuity payments themselves amounted to $2,250 = 15 × $150, and the balance is the interest earned at the rate of 7% per year.

To find the PV of an ordinary annuity, we use the future cash flow stream, PMT, that we used with FV annuity problems, but we discount the cash flows back to the present (time = 0) rather than compounding them forward to the terminal date of the annuity.

Here again, the PMT variable is a *single* periodic payment, *not* the total of all the payments (or deposits) in the annuity. The PVA$_O$ measures the collective PV of a stream of equal cash flows received at the end of each compounding period over a stated number of periods, N, given a specified rate of return, I/Y. The following examples illustrate how to determine the PV of an ordinary annuity using a financial calculator.

Example: PV of an ordinary annuity

What is the PV of an annuity that pays $200 per year at the end of each of the next 13 years, given a 6% discount rate?

Answer:

The payments occur at the end of the year, so this annuity is an ordinary annuity. To solve this problem, enter the relevant information and compute PV.

N = 13; I/Y = 6; PMT = −200; FV = 0; CPT → PV = $1,770.54

The $1,770.54 computed here represents the amount of money that an investor would need to invest *today* at a 6% rate of return to generate 13 end-of-year cash flows of $200 each.

Example: PV of an ordinary annuity beginning later than t = 1

What is the present value of four $100 end-of-year payments if the first payment is to be received three years from today and the appropriate rate of return is 9%?

Answer:

The time line for this cash flow stream is shown in the following figure.

PV of an Annuity Beginning at t = 3

Step 1: Find the present value of the annuity as of the end of year 2 (PV_2).

Input the relevant data and solve for PV_2.

$$N = 4; I/Y = 9; PMT = -100; FV = 0; CPT \rightarrow PV = PV_2 = \$323.97$$

Step 2: Find the present value of PV_2.

Input the relevant data and solve for PV_0.

$$N = 2; I/Y = 9; PMT = 0; FV = -323.97; CPT \rightarrow PV = PV_0 = \$272.68$$

In this solution, the annuity was treated as an ordinary annuity. The PV was computed one period before the first payment, and we discounted $PV_2 = \$323.97$ over two years. We need to stress this important point. The PV annuity function on your calculator set in "END" mode gives you the value *one period before the annuity begins*. Although the annuity begins at t = 3, we discounted the result for only two periods to get the present (t = 0) value.

Example: PV of a bond's cash flows

A bond will make coupon interest payments of 70 euros (7% of its face value) at the end of each year and will also pay its face value of 1,000 euros at maturity in five years. If the appropriate discount rate is 8%, what is the present value of the bond's promised cash flows?

Answer:

The five annual coupon payments of 70 euros each can be viewed as an ordinary annuity. The maturity value of 1,000 euros is the future value of the bond at the time the last coupon payment is made. On a time line, the promised payment stream is as shown below.

Cash flows for a 5-year, 7%, 1,000 euro bond

The PV of the bond's cash flows can be broken down into the PV of a 5-payment ordinary annuity, plus the PV of a 1,000 euro lump sum to be received five years from now.

The calculator solution is:

N = 5; PMT = 70; I/Y = 8; FV = 1,000; CPT PV = –960

With a yield to maturity of 8%, the value of the bond is 960 euros.

Note that the PMT and FV must have the same sign, since both are cash flows paid to the investor (paid by the bond issuer). The calculated PV will have the opposite sign from PMT and FV.

Future Value of an Annuity Due

Sometimes it is necessary to find the *FV of an annuity due* (FVA_D), an annuity where the annuity payments (or deposits) occur at the beginning of each compounding period. Fortunately, our financial calculators can be used to do this, but with one slight modification—the calculator must be set to the beginning-of-period (BGN) mode. To switch between the BGN and END modes on the TI, press [2nd] [BGN] [2nd] [SET]. When this is done, "BGN" will appear in the upper right corner of the display window. If the display indicates the desired mode, press [2nd] [QUIT]. You will normally want your calculator to be in the ordinary annuity (END) mode, so remember to switch out of BGN mode after working annuity due problems. Note that nothing appears in the upper right corner of the display window when the TI is set to the END mode. It should be mentioned that while annuity due payments are made or received at the beginning of each period, the FV of an annuity due is calculated as of the end of the last period.

Another way to compute the FV of an annuity due is to calculate the FV of an ordinary annuity, and simply multiply the resulting FV by [1 + periodic compounding rate (I/Y)]. Symbolically, this can be expressed as:

$$FVA_D = FVA_O \times (1 + I/Y)$$

The following examples illustrate how to compute the FV of an annuity due.

Example: FV of an annuity due

What is the future value of an annuity that pays $100 per year at the beginning of each of the next three years, commencing today, if the cash flows can be invested at an annual rate of 10%? Note in the time line in the figure below that the FV is computed as of the end of the last year in the life of the annuity, Year 3, even though the final payment occurs at the beginning of Year 3 (end of Year 2).

Answer:

To solve this problem, put your calculator in the BGN mode ([2nd] [BGN] [2nd] [SET] [2nd] [QUIT] on the TI or [g] [BEG] on the HP), then input the relevant data and compute FV.

N = 3; I/Y = 10; PMT = –100; CPT → FV = $364.10

FV of an Annuity Due

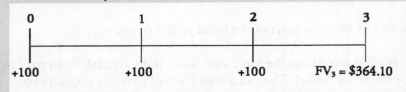

Alternatively, we could calculate the FV for an ordinary annuity and multiply it by (1 + I/Y). Leaving your calculator in the END mode, enter the following inputs:

N = 3; I/Y = 10; PMT = –100; CPT → FVA_O = $331.00

$$FVA_D = FVA_O \times (1 + I/Y) = 331.00 \times 1.10 = \$364.10$$

Example: FV of an annuity due

If you deposit $1,000 in the bank today and at the beginning of each of the next *three* years, how much will you have six years from today at 6% interest? The time line for this problem is shown in the following figure.

Answer:

FV of an Annuity Due

Step 1: Compute the FV of the annuity due at the end of Year 4 (FV_4).

Set your calculator to the annuity due (BGN) mode, enter the relevant data, and compute FV_4.

$N = 4$; $I/Y = 6$; $PMT = -1,000$; $CPT \rightarrow FV = \$4,637.09$

Step 2: Find the future value of FV_4 two years from Year 4.

Enter the relevant data and compute FV_6.

$N = 2$; $I/Y = 6$; $PV = -4,637.09$; $CPT \rightarrow FV = \$5,210.23$

or

$4,637.09(1.06)^2 = \$5,210.23$

Note that the FV function for an annuity when the calculator is set to BGN is the value one period after the last annuity deposit, at $t = 4$ in this example.

Present Value of an Annuity Due

While less common than those for ordinary annuities, some problems may require you to find the *PV of an annuity due* (PVA_D). Using a financial calculator, this really shouldn't be much of a problem. With an annuity due, *there is one less discounting period* since the first cash flow occurs at $t = 0$ and thus is already its PV. This implies that, all else equal, the PV of an annuity due will be greater than the PV of an ordinary annuity.

As you will see in the next example, there are two ways to compute the PV of an annuity due. The first is to put the calculator in the BGN mode and then input all the relevant variables (PMT, I/Y, and N) as you normally would. The second, and far easier way, is to treat the cash flow stream as an ordinary annuity over N compounding periods, and simply multiply the resulting PV by [1 + periodic compounding rate (I/Y)].

Symbolically, this can be stated as:

$$PVA_D = PVA_O \times (1 + I/Y)$$

The advantage of this second method is that you leave your calculator in the END mode and won't run the risk of forgetting to reset it. Regardless of the procedure used, the computed PV is given as of the beginning of the first period, t = 0.

Example: PV of an annuity due

Given a discount rate of 10%, what is the present value of a 3-year annuity that makes a series of $100 payments at the beginning of each of the next three years, starting today? The time line for this problem is shown in the following figure.

Answer:

First, let's solve this problem using the calculator's BGN mode. Set your calculator to the BGN mode ([2nd] [BGN] [2nd] [SET] [2nd] [QUIT] on the TI or [g] [BEG] on the HP), enter the relevant data, and compute PV.

N = 3; I/Y = 10; PMT = –100; CPT -→ PVA_D = $273.55

PV of an Annuity Due

PV = $273.55

Alternatively, this problem can be solved by leaving your calculator in the END mode. First, compute the PV of an ordinary 3-year annuity. Then multiply this PV by (1 + I/Y). To use this approach, enter the relevant inputs and compute PV.

N = 3; I/Y = 10; PMT = –100; CPT → PVA_O = $248.69

$$PVA_D = PVA_O \times (1 + I/Y) = \$248.69 \times 1.10 = \$273.55$$

Present Value of a Perpetuity

A **perpetuity** is a financial instrument that pays a fixed amount of money at set intervals over an *infinite* period of time. In essence, a perpetuity is a perpetual annuity. British consul bonds and most preferred stocks are examples of perpetuities since they promise fixed interest or dividend payments forever. Without going into all the excruciating mathematical details, the discount factor for a perpetuity is just one divided by the appropriate rate of return (i.e., $1/r$). Given this, we can compute the PV of a perpetuity.

$$PV_{perpetuity} = \frac{PMT}{I/Y}$$

The PV of a perpetuity is the fixed periodic cash flow divided by the appropriate periodic rate of return.

As with other TVM applications, it is possible to solve for unknown variables in the $PV_{perpetuity}$ equation. In fact, you can solve for any one of the three relevant variables, given the values for the other two.

Example: PV of a perpetuity

Kodon Corporation issues preferred stock that will pay $4.50 per year in annual dividends beginning next year and plans to follow this dividend policy forever. Given an 8% rate of return, what is the value of Kodon's preferred stock today?

Answer:

Given that the value of the stock is the PV of all future dividends, we have:

$$PV_{perpetuity} = \frac{4.50}{0.08} = \$56.25$$

Thus, if an investor requires an 8% rate of return, the investor should be willing to pay $56.25 for each share of Kodon's preferred stock. Note that the PV of a perpetuity is its value one period before its next payment.

Example: Rate of return for a perpetuity

Using the Kodon preferred stock described in the preceding example, determine the rate of return that an investor would realize if she paid $75 per share for the stock.

Answer:

Rearranging the equation for $PV_{perpetuity}$, we get:

$$I/Y = \frac{PMT}{PV_{perpetuity}} = \frac{4.50}{75.00} = 0.06 = 6.0\%$$

This implies that the return (yield) on a $75 preferred stock that pays a $4.50 annual dividend is 6.0%.

PV and FV of Uneven Cash Flow Series

It is not uncommon to have applications in investments and corporate finance where it is necessary to evaluate a cash flow stream that is not equal from period to period. The time line in Figure 2 depicts such a cash flow stream.

Figure 2: Time Line for Uneven Cash Flows

This 6-year cash flow series is not an annuity since the cash flows are different every year. In fact, there is one year with zero cash flow and two others with negative cash flows. In essence, this series of uneven cash flows is nothing more than a stream of annual single sum cash flows. Thus, to find the PV or FV of this cash flow stream, all we need to do is sum the PVs or FVs of the individual cash flows.

Example: Computing the FV of an uneven cash flow series

Using a rate of return of 10%, compute the future value of the 6-year uneven cash flow stream described above at the end of the sixth year.

Answer:

The FV for the cash flow stream is determined by first computing the FV of each individual cash flow, then summing the FVs of the individual cash flows. Note that we need to preserve the signs of the cash flows.

FV_1: PV = –1,000; I/Y = 10; N = 5; CPT → FV = FV_1 = –1,610.51

FV_2: PV = –500; I/Y = 10; N = 4; CPT → FV = FV_2 = –732.05

FV_3: PV = 0; I/Y = 10; N = 3; CPT → FV = FV_3 = 0.00

FV_4: PV = 4,000; I/Y = 10; N = 2; CPT → FV = FV_4 = 4,840.00

FV_5: PV = 3,500; I/Y = 10; N = 1; CPT → FV = FV_5 = 3,850.00

FV_6: PV = 2,000; I/Y = 10; N = 0; CPT → FV = FV_6 = **2,000.00**

FV of cash flow stream = $\sum FV_{individual}$ = 8,347.44

Example: Computing PV of an uneven cash flow series

Compute the present value of this 6-year uneven cash flow stream described above using a 10% rate of return.

Answer:

This problem is solved by first computing the PV of each individual cash flow, then summing the PVs of the individual cash flows, which yields the PV of the cash flow stream. Again the signs of the cash flows are preserved.

PV_1: FV = −1,000; I/Y = 10; N = 1; CPT → PV = PV_1 = −909.09

PV_2: FV = −500; I/Y = 10; N = 2; CPT → PV = PV_2 = −413.22

PV_3: FV = 0; I/Y = 10; N = 3; CPT → PV = PV_3 = 0

PV_4: FV = 4,000; I/Y = 10; N = 4; CPT → PV = PV_4 = 2,732.05

PV_5: FV = 3,500; I/Y = 10; N = 5; CPT → PV = PV_5 = 2,173.22

PV_6: FV = 2,000; I/Y = 10; N = 6; CPT → PV = PV_6 = **1,128.95**

PV of cash flow stream = $\sum PV_{individual}$ = $4,711.91

It is also possible to compute PV of an uneven cash flow stream by using the cash flow (CF) keys and the *net present value* (NPV) function on your calculator. This procedure is illustrated in the tables in Figures 3 and 4. In Figure 3, we have omitted the F01, F02, etc. values because they are all equal to 1. The Fn variable indicates how many times a particular cash flow amount is repeated.

Figure 3: NPV Calculator Keystrokes—TI BAII Plus®

Key Strokes	Explanation	Display
[CF] [2nd] [CLR WORK]	Clear CF Memory Registers	CF0 = 0.00000
0 [ENTER]	Initial Cash Outlay	CF0 = 0.00000
[↓] 1,000 [+/−] [ENTER]	Period 1 Cash Flow	C01 = −1,000.00000
[↓] [↓] 500 [+/−] [ENTER]	Period 2 Cash Flow	C02 = −500.00000
[↓] [↓] 0 [ENTER]	Period 3 Cash Flow	C03 = 0.00000
[↓] [↓] 4,000 [ENTER]	Period 4 Cash Flow	C04 = 4,000.00000
[↓] [↓] 3,500 [ENTER]	Period 5 Cash Flow	C05 = 3,500.00000
[↓] [↓] 2,000 [ENTER]	Period 6 Cash Flow	C06 = 2,000.00000
[NPV] 10 [ENTER]	10% Discount Rate	I = 10.00000
[↓] [CPT]	Calculate NPV	NPV = 4,711.91226

Note that the BAII Plus Professional will also give the NFV of 8,347.44 if you press the ↓ key.

Figure 4: NPV Calculator Keystrokes—HP12C®

Key Strokes	Explanation	Display
[f] [FIN] [f] [REG]	Clear Memory Registers	0.00000
0 [g] [CF$_0$]	Initial Cash Outlay	0.00000
1,000 [CHS] [g] [CF$_j$]	Period 1 Cash Flow	−1,000.00000
500 [CHS] [g] [CF$_j$]	Period 2 Cash Flow	−500.00000
0 [g] [CF$_j$]	Period 3 Cash Flow	0.00000
4,000 [g] [CF$_j$]	Period 4 Cash Flow	4,000.00000
3,500 [g] [CF$_j$]	Period 5 Cash Flow	3,500.00000
2,000 [g] [CF$_j$]	Period 6 Cash Flow	2,000.00000
10 [i]	10% Discount Rate	10.00000
[f] [NPV]	Calculate NPV	4,711.91226

Solving Time Value of Money Problems When Compounding Periods Are Other Than Annual

While the conceptual foundations of TVM calculations are not affected by the compounding period, more frequent compounding does have an impact on FV and PV computations. Specifically, since an increase in the frequency of compounding increases the effective rate of interest, it also *increases* the FV of a given cash flow and *decreases* the PV of a given cash flow.

Example: The effect of compounding frequency on FV and PV

Compute the FV one year from now of $1,000 today and the PV of $1,000 to be received one year from now using a stated annual interest rate of 6% with a range of compounding periods.

Answer:

Compounding Frequency Effect

Compounding Frequency	Interest Rate per Period	Effective Annual Rate	Future Value	Present Value
Annual (m = 1)	6.000%	6.00%	$1,060.00	$943.396
Semiannual (m = 2)	3.000	6.090	1,060.90	942.596
Quarterly (m = 4)	1.500	6.136	1,061.36	942.184
Monthly (m = 12)	0.500	6.168	1,061.68	941.905
Daily (m = 365)	0.016438	6.183	1,061.83	941.769

There are two ways to use your financial calculator to compute PVs and FVs under different compounding frequencies:

1. Adjust the number of periods per year (P/Y) mode on your calculator to correspond to the compounding frequency (e.g., for quarterly, P/Y = 4). WE DO NOT RECOMMEND THIS APPROACH!

2. Keep the calculator in the annual compounding mode (P/Y = 1) and enter I/Y as the interest rate per compounding period, and N as the number of compounding periods in the investment horizon. Letting *m* equal the number of compounding periods per year, the basic formulas for the calculator input data are determined as follows:

    I/Y = the annual interest rate / m

    N = the number of years × m

The computations for the FV and PV amounts in the previous example are:

PV_A: FV = –1,000; I/Y = 6 / 1 = 6; N = 1 × 1 = 1:
CPT → PV = PV_A = 943.396

PV_S: FV = –1,000; I/Y = 6 / 2 = 3; N = 1 × 2 = 2:
CPT → PV = PV_S = 942.596

PV_Q: FV = –1,000; I/Y = 6 / 4 = 1.5; N = 1 × 4 = 4:
CPT → PV = PV_Q = 942.184

PV_M: FV = –1,000; I/Y = 6 / 12 = 0.5; N = 1 × 12 = 12:
CPT → PV = PV_M = 941.905

PV_D: FV = –1,000; I/Y = 6 / 365 = 0.016438; N = 1 × 365 = 365:
CPT → PV = PV_D = 941.769

FV_A: **PV** = –1,000; I/Y = 6 / 1 = 6; N = 1 × 1 = 1:
CPT → FV = FV_A = 1,060.00

FV_S: PV = –1,000; I/Y = 6 / 2 = 3; N = 1 × 2 = 2:
CPT → FV = FV_S = 1,060.90

FV_Q: PV = –1,000; I/Y = 6 / 4 = 1.5; N = 1 × 4 = 4:
CPT → FV = FV_Q = 1,061.36

FV_M: PV = –1,000; I/Y = 6 / 12 = 0.5; N = 1 × 12 = 12:
CPT → FV = FV_M = 1,061.68

FV_D: PV = –1,000; I/Y = 6 / 365 = 0.016438; N = 1 × 365 = 365:
CPT → FV = FV_D = 1,061.83

Example: FV of a single sum using quarterly compounding

Compute the FV of $2,000 today, five years from today using an interest rate of 12%, compounded quarterly.

Answer:

To solve this problem, enter the relevant data and compute FV:

$$N = 5 \times 4 = 20; \; I/Y = 12 / 4 = 3; \; PV = -\$2,000; \; CPT \rightarrow FV = \$3,612.22$$

LOS 5.f: Demonstrate the use of a time line in modeling and solving time value of money problems.

CFA® Program Curriculum, Volume I, page 247

In most of the PV problems we have discussed, cash flows were discounted back to the current period. In this case, the PV is said to be indexed to t = 0, or the time index is t = 0. For example, the PV of a 3-year ordinary annuity that is indexed to t = 0 is computed at the beginning of Year 1 (t = 0). Contrast this situation with another 3-year ordinary annuity that doesn't start until Year 4 and extends to Year 6. It would not be uncommon to want to know the PV of this annuity at the beginning of Year 4, in which case the time index is t = 3. The time line for this annuity is presented in Figure 5.

Figure 5: Indexing Time Line to Other Than t = 0

Loan Payments and Amortization

Loan **amortization** is the process of paying off a loan with a series of periodic loan payments, whereby a portion of the outstanding loan amount is paid off, or amortized, with each payment. When a company or individual enters into a long-term loan, the debt is usually paid off over time with a series of equal, periodic loan payments, and each payment includes the repayment of principal and an interest charge. The payments may be made monthly, quarterly, or even annually. Regardless of the payment frequency, the size of the payment remains fixed over the life of the loan. The amount of the principal and interest component of the loan payment, however, does not remain fixed over the term of the loan. Let's look at some examples to more fully develop the concept of amortization.

Example: Loan payment calculation: Annual payments

A company plans to borrow $50,000 for five years. The company's bank will lend the money at a rate of 9% and requires that the loan be paid off in five equal end-of-year payments. Calculate the amount of the payment that the company must make in order to fully amortize this loan in five years.

Answer:

To determine the annual loan payment, input the relevant data and compute PMT.

$$N = 5;\ I/Y = 9;\ PV = -50,000;\ CPT \rightarrow PMT = \$12,854.62$$

Thus, the loan can be paid off in five equal annual payments of $12,854.62. Please note that FV = 0 in this computation; the loan will be fully paid off (amortized) after the five payments have been made.

Example: Loan payment calculation: Quarterly payments

Using the loan described in the preceding example, determine the payment amount if the bank requires the company to make quarterly payments.

Answer:

The quarterly loan payment can be determined by inputting the relevant data and computing the payment (PMT):

$$N = 5 \times 4 = 20;\ I/Y = 9\ /\ 4 = 2.25;\ PV = -50,000;\ CPT \rightarrow PMT = \$3,132.10$$

Example: Constructing an amortization schedule

Construct an amortization schedule to show the interest and principal components of the end-of-year payments for a 10%, 5-year, $10,000 loan.

Answer:

The first step in solving this problem is to compute the amount of the loan payments. This is done by entering the relevant data and computing PMT:

$$N = 5;\ I/Y = 10\%;\ PV = -\$10,000;\ CPT \rightarrow PMT = \$2,637.97$$

Thus, the loan will be repaid via five equal $2,637.97 end-of-year payments. Each payment is made up of an interest component (profit to the lender) plus the partial recovery of loan principal, with principal recovery being scheduled so that the full amount of the loan is paid off by the end of Year 5. The exact amount of the principal and interest components of each loan payment are presented and described in the amortization table shown in the following figure.

Amortization Table

Period	Beginning Balance	Payment	Interest Component (1)	Principal Component (2)	Ending Balance (3)
1	$10,000.00	$2,637.97	$1,000.00	$1,637.97	$8,362.03
2	8,362.03	2,637.97	836.20	1,801.77	6,560.26
3	6,560.26	2,637.97	656.03	1,981.94	4,578.32
4	4,578.32	2,637.97	457.83	2,180.14	2,398.18
5	2,398.18	2,638.00*	239.82	2,398.18	0.00

* There is usually a slight amount of rounding error that must be recognized in the final period. The extra $0.03 associated with payment five reflects an adjustment for the rounding error and forces the ending balance to zero.

1. Interest component = beginning balance × periodic interest rate. In period 3, the interest component of the payment is $6,560.26 × 0.10 = $656.03.

2. Principal component = payment – interest. For example, the period 4 principal component is $2,637.97 – $457.83 = 2,180.14.

3. The ending balance in a given period, t, is the period's beginning balance minus the principal component of the payment, where the beginning balance for period t is the ending balance from period t – 1. For example, the period 2 ending balance equals $8,362.03 – $1,801.77 = $6,560.26, which becomes the period 3 beginning balance.

 Professor's Note: Once you have solved for the payment, $2,637.97, the remaining principal on any payment date can be calculated by entering N = number of remaining payments and solving for the PV.

Example: Principal and interest component of a specific loan payment

Suppose you borrowed $10,000 at 10% interest to be paid semiannually over ten years. Calculate the amount of the outstanding balance for the loan after the second payment is made.

Answer:

First, the amount of the payment must be determined by entering the relevant information and computing the payment.

PV = –$10,000; I/Y = 10 / 2 = 5; N = 10 × 2 = 20; CPT → PMT = $802.43

The principal and interest component of the second payment can be determined using the following process:

Payment 1:   Interest = ($10,000)(0.05) = $500

                   Principal = $802.43 – $500 = $302.43

Payment 2:   Interest = ($10,000 – $302.43)(0.05) = $484.88

                   Principal = $802.43 – $484.88 = $317.55

Remaining balance = $10,000 – $302.43 – $317.55 = $9,380.02

The following examples will illustrate how to compute I/Y, N, or PMT in annuity problems.

Example: Computing an annuity payment needed to achieve a given FV

At an expected rate of return of 7%, how much must be deposited at the end of each year for the next 15 years to accumulate $3,000?

Answer:

To solve this problem, enter the three relevant known values and compute PMT.

     N = 15; I/Y = 7; FV = +$3,000; CPT → PMT = –$119.38 (ignore sign)

Example: Computing a loan payment

Suppose you are considering applying for a $2,000 loan that will be repaid with equal end-of-year payments over the next 13 years. If the annual interest rate for the loan is 6%, how much will your payments be?

Answer:

The size of the end-of-year loan payment can be determined by inputting values for the three known variables and computing PMT.

     N = 13; I/Y = 6; PV = –2,000; CPT → PMT = $225.92

Example: Computing the number of periods in an annuity

How many $100 end-of-year payments are required to accumulate $920 if the discount rate is 9%?

Answer:

The number of payments necessary can be determined by inputting the relevant data and computing N.

$$I/Y = 9\%; \ FV = \$920; \ PMT = -\$100; \ CPT \rightarrow N = 7 \ years$$

It will take seven annual $100 payments, compounded at 9% annually, to accrue an investment value of $920.

 Professor's Note: Remember the sign convention. PMT and FV must have opposite signs or your calculator will issue an error message.

Example: Computing the number of years in an ordinary annuity

Suppose you have a $1,000 ordinary annuity earning an 8% return. How many annual end-of-year $150 withdrawals can be made?

Answer:

The number of years in the annuity can be determined by entering the three relevant variables and computing N.

$$I/Y = 8; \ PMT = 150; \ PV = -1,000; \ CPT \rightarrow N = 9.9 \ years$$

Example: Computing the rate of return for an annuity

Suppose you have the opportunity to invest $100 at the end of each of the next five years in exchange for $600 at the end of the fifth year. What is the annual rate of return on this investment?

Answer:

The rate of return on this investment can be determined by entering the relevant data and solving for I/Y.

$$N = 5; \ FV = \$600; \ PMT = -100; \ CPT \rightarrow I/Y = 9.13\%$$

Example: Computing the discount rate for an annuity

What rate of return will you earn on an ordinary annuity that requires a $700 deposit today and promises to pay $100 per year at the end of each of the next ten years?

Answer:

The discount rate on this annuity is determined by entering the three known values and computing I/Y.

$N = 10$; $PV = -700$; $PMT = 100$; $CPT \rightarrow I/Y = 7.07\%$

Other Applications of TVM Functions

Example: Calculating the rate of compound growth

Sales at Acme, Inc., for the last five years (in millions) have been €4.5, €5.7, €5.3, €6.9, and €7.1.

What is the compound annual growth rate of sales over the period?

Answer:

The five years of sales represent four years of growth. Mathematically, the compound annual growth rate of sales is $(7.1 / 4.5)^{¼} -1 = 12.1\%$. The interim sales figures do not enter into the 4-year compound growth rate.

The calculator solution using the TVM keys is:

$FV = 7.1$; $PV = -4.5$; $N = 4$; $CPT \rightarrow I/Y = 12.08\%$

Note that if sales were 4.5 and grew for four years at an annual compound rate of 12.08%, they would grow to $4.5 (1.1208)^4 = 7.1$.

Example: Calculating the number of periods for specific growth

How many years will it take for an investment of $1,000 to grow to $2,000 at an annual compound rate of 14.87%?

Answer:

$FV = 2,000$; $PV = -1,000$; $I/Y = 14.87$; $CPT \rightarrow N = 4.9999$

It will take five years for money to double at an annual compound rate of 14.87%.

Funding a Future Obligation

There are many TVM applications where it is necessary to determine the size of the deposit(s) that must be made over a specified period in order to meet a future liability. Two common examples of this type of application are (1) setting up a funding program for future college tuition and (2) the funding of a retirement program. In most of these applications, the objective is to determine the size of the payment(s) or deposit(s) necessary to meet a particular monetary goal.

Example: Computing the required payment to fund an annuity due

Suppose you must make five annual $1,000 payments, the first one starting at the beginning of Year 4 (end of Year 3). To accumulate the money to make these payments, you want to make three equal payments into an investment account, the first to be made one year from today. Assuming a 10% rate of return, what is the amount of these three payments?

The time line for this annuity problem is shown in the following figure.

Funding an Annuity Due

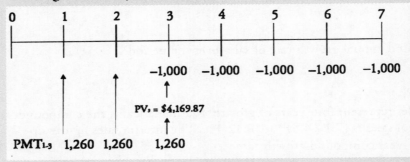

Answer:

The first step in this type of problem is to determine the amount of money that must be available at the beginning of Year 4 (t = 3) in order to satisfy the payment requirements. This amount is the PV of a 5-year annuity due at the beginning of Year 4 (end of Year 3). To determine this amount, set your calculator to the BGN mode, enter the relevant data, and compute PV.

$$N = 5; \; I/Y = 10; \; PMT = -1,000; \; CPT \rightarrow PV = PV_3 = \$4,169.87$$

Alternatively, you can leave your calculator in the END mode, compute the PV of a 5-year ordinary annuity, and multiply by 1.10.

$$N = 5; \; I/Y = 10; \; PMT = -1,000;$$
$$CPT \rightarrow PV = 3,790.79 \times 1.1 = PV_3 = \$4,169.87$$

A third alternative, with the calculator in END mode, is to calculate the t = 3 value of the last four annuity payments and then add $1,000.

$$N = 4; \; I/Y = 10; \; PMT = -1,000;$$
$$CPT \rightarrow PV = 3,169.87 + 1,000 = \$4,169.87 = PV_3$$

PV_3 becomes the FV that you need three years from today from your three equal end-of-year deposits. To determine the amount of the three payments necessary to meet this funding requirement, be sure that your calculator is in the END mode, input the relevant data, and compute PMT.

N = 3; I/Y = 10; FV = −4,169.87; CPT → PMT = $1,259.78

The second part of this problem is an ordinary annuity. If you changed your calculator to BGN mode and failed to put it back in the END mode, you will get a PMT of $1,145, which is incorrect.

Example: Funding a retirement plan

Assume a 35-year-old investor wants to retire in 25 years at the age of 60. She expects to earn 12.5% on her investments prior to her retirement and 10% thereafter. How much must she deposit at the end of each year for the next 25 years in order to be able to withdraw $25,000 per year at the beginning of each year for the 30 years from age 60 to 90?

Answer:

This is a 2-step problem. First, determine the amount that must be on deposit in the retirement account at the end of Year 25 in order to fund the 30-year, $25,000 annuity due. Second, compute the annuity payments that must be made to achieve the required amount.

Step 1: Compute the amount required to meet the desired withdrawals.

The required amount is the present value of the $25,000, 30-year annuity due at the beginning of Year 26 (end of Year 25). This can be determined by entering the relevant data, with the calculator in the END mode, and computing PV.

N = 29; I/Y = 10; PMT = −$25,000; CPT → PV = $234,240 (for 29 years)

Now, add the first annuity payment to get $234,240 + $25,000 = $259,240. The investor will need $259,240 at the end of Year 25.

Please note that we could have also performed this computation with our calculator in BGN mode as an annuity due. To do this, put your calculator in BGN mode [2nd] [BGN] [2nd] [SET] [2nd] [QUIT] on the TI or [g] [BEG] on the HP. Then enter:

N = 30; PMT = −25,000; I/Y = 10; CPT → PV = 259,240.14

If you do it this way, make certain you reset your calculator to the END mode.

Step 2: The annuity payment that must be made to accumulate the required amount over 25 years can be determined by entering the relevant data and computing PMT.

N = 25; I/Y = 12.5; FV = −259,240; CPT → PMT = $1,800.02

Thus, the investor must deposit $1,800 per year at the end of each of the next 25 years in order to accumulate $259,240. With this amount, she will be able to withdraw $25,000 per year for the following 30 years.

Note that all these calculations assume that the investor will earn 12.5% on the payments prior to retirement and 10% on the funds held in the retirement account thereafter.

The Connection Between Present Values, Future Values, and Series of Cash Flows

As we have explained in the discussion of annuities and series of uneven cash flows, the sum of the present values of the cash flows is the present value of the series. The sum of the future values (at some future time = n) of a series of cash flows is the future value of that series of cash flows.

One interpretation of the present value of a series of cash flows is how much would have to be put in the bank today in order to make these future withdrawals and exhaust the account with the final withdrawal. Let's illustrate this with cash flows of $100 in Year 1, $200 in Year 2, $300 in Year 3, and an assumed interest rate of 10%.

Calculate the present value of these three cash flows as:

$$\frac{100}{1.1} + \frac{200}{1.1^2} + \frac{300}{1.1^3} = \$481.59$$

If we put $481.59 in an account yielding 10%, at the end of the year we would have $481.59 \times 1.1 = \$529.75$. Withdrawing $100 would leave $429.75.

Over the second year, the $429.75 would grow to $429.75 \times 1.1 = \$472.73$. Withdrawing $200 would leave $272.73.

Over the third year, $272.73 would grow to $272.73 \times 1.1 = \$300$, so that the last withdrawal of $300 would empty the account.

The interpretation of the future value of a series of cash flows is straightforward as well. The FV answers the question, "How much would be in an account when the last of a series of deposits is made?" Using the same three cash flows—$100, $200, and $300—and the same interest rate of 10%, we can calculate the future value of the series as:

$$100(1.1)^2 + 200(1.1) + 300 = \$641$$

This is simply the sum of the t = 3 value of each of the cash flows. Note that the t = 3 value and the t = 0 (present) value of the series are related by the interest rate, $481.59(1.1)^3 = 641$.

The $100 cash flow (deposit) comes at t = 1, so it will earn interest of 10% compounded for two periods (until t = 3). The $200 cash flow (deposit) will earn 10% between t = 2 and t = 3, and the final cash flow (deposit) of $300 is made at t = 3, so $300 is the future (t = 3) value of that cash flow.

We can also look at the future value in terms of how the account grows over time. At t = 1 we deposit $100, so at t = 2 it has grown to $110 and the $200 deposit at t = 2 makes the account balance $310. Over the next period, the $310 grows to 310 × 1.1 = $341 at t = 3, and the addition of the final $300 deposit puts the account balance at $641. This is, of course, the future value we calculated initially.

Professor's Note: This last view of the future value of a series of cash flows suggests a quick way to calculate the future value of an uneven cash flow series. The process described previously for the future value of a series of end-of-period payments can be written mathematically as [(100 × 1.1) + 200] × 1.1 + 300 = 641, and this might be a quick way to do some future value problems.

Note that questions on the future value of an *annuity due* refer to the amount in the account one period after the last deposit is made. If the three deposits considered here were made at the beginning of each period (at t = 0, 1, 2) the amount in the account at the end of three years (t = 3) would be 10% higher (i.e., 641 × 1.1 = $705.10).

The **cash flow additivity principle** refers to the fact that present value of any stream of cash flows equals the sum of the present values of the cash flows. There are different applications of this principle in time value of money problems. If we have two series of cash flows, the sum of the present values of the two series is the same as the present values of the two series taken together, adding cash flows that will be paid at the same point in time. We can also divide up a series of cash flows any way we like, and the present value of the "pieces" will equal the present value of the original series.

Example: Additivity principle

A security will make the following payments at the end of the next four years: $100, $100, $400, and $100. Calculate the present value of these cash flows using the concept of the present value of an annuity when the appropriate discount rate is 10%.

Answer:

We can divide the cash flows so that we have:

t = 1	t = 2	t = 3	t = 4	
100	100	100	100	cash flow series #1
0	0	300	0	cash flow series #2
$100	$100	$400	$100	

The additivity principle tells us that to get the present value of the original series, we can just add the present values of series #1 (a 4-period annuity) and series #2 (a single payment three periods from now).

For the annuity: N = 4; PMT = 100; FV = 0, I/Y = 10; CPT → PV = –$316.99

For the single payment: N = 3; PMT = 0; FV = 300; I/Y = 10;
                     CPT → PV = –$225.39

The sum of these two values is 316.99 + 225.39 = $542.38.

The sum of these two (present) values is identical (except for rounding) to the sum of the present values of the payments of the original series:

$$\frac{100}{1.1} + \frac{100}{1.1^2} + \frac{400}{1.1^3} + \frac{100}{1.1^4} = \$542.38$$

KEY CONCEPTS

LOS 5.a

An interest rate can be interpreted as the rate of return required in equilibrium for a particular investment, the discount rate for calculating the present value of future cash flows, or as the opportunity cost of consuming now, rather than saving and investing.

LOS 5.b

The real risk-free rate is a theoretical rate on a single-period loan when there is no expectation of inflation. Nominal risk-free rate = real risk-free rate + expected inflation rate.

Securities may have several risks, and each increases the required rate of return. These include default risk, liquidity risk, and maturity risk.

The required rate of return on a security = real risk-free rate + expected inflation + default risk premium + liquidity premium + maturity risk premium.

LOS 5.c

The effective annual rate when there are m compounding periods =

$\left(1 + \dfrac{\text{stated annual rate}}{m}\right)^m - 1$. Each dollar invested will grow to

$\left(1 + \dfrac{\text{stated annual rate}}{m}\right)^m$ in one year.

LOS 5.d

For non-annual time value of money problems, divide the stated annual interest rate by the number of compounding periods per year, m, and multiply the number of years by the number of compounding periods per year.

LOS 5.e

Future value: $FV = PV(1 + I/Y)^N$

Present value: $PV = FV / (1 + I/Y)^N$

An annuity is a series of equal cash flows that occurs at evenly spaced intervals over time. Ordinary annuity cash flows occur at the end of each time period. Annuity due cash flows occur at the beginning of each time period.

Perpetuities are annuities with infinite lives (perpetual annuities):

$PV_{perpetuity} = \dfrac{PMT}{I/Y}$

The present (future) value of any series of cash flows is equal to the sum of the present (future) values of the individual cash flows.

LOS 5.f

Constructing a time line showing future cash flows will help in solving many types of TVM problems. Cash flows occur at the end of the period depicted on the time line. The end of one period is the same as the beginning of the next period. For example, a cash flow at the beginning of Year 3 appears at time t = 2 on the time line.

CONCEPT CHECKERS

1. The amount an investor will have in 15 years if $1,000 is invested today at an annual interest rate of 9% will be *closest* to:
    A. $1,350.
    B. $3,518.
    C. $3,642.

2. Fifty years ago, an investor bought a share of stock for $10. The stock has paid no dividends during this period, yet it has returned 20%, compounded annually, over the past 50 years. If this is true, the share price is now *closest* to:
    A. $4,550.
    B. $45,502.
    C. $91,004.

3. How much must be invested today at 0% to have $100 in three years?
    A. $77.75.
    B. $100.00.
    C. $126.30.

4. How much must be invested today, at 8% interest, to accumulate enough to retire a $10,000 debt due seven years from today? The amount that must be invested today is *closest* to:
    A. $5,835.
    B. $6,123.
    C. $8,794.

5. An analyst estimates that XYZ's earnings will grow from $3.00 a share to $4.50 per share over the next eight years. The rate of growth in XYZ's earnings is *closest* to:
    A. 4.9%.
    B. 5.2%.
    C. 6.7%.

6. If $5,000 is invested in a fund offering a rate of return of 12% per year, approximately how many years will it take for the investment to reach $10,000?
    A. 4 years.
    B. 5 years.
    C. 6 years.

7. An investment is expected to produce the cash flows of $500, $200, and $800 at the end of the next three years. If the required rate of return is 12%, the present value of this investment is *closest* to:
    A. $835.
    B. $1,175.
    C. $1,235.

8. Given an 8.5% discount rate, an asset that generates cash flows of $10 in Year 1, –$20 in Year 2, $10 in Year 3, and is then sold for $150 at the end of Year 4, has a present value of:
   A. $108.29.
   B. $135.58.
   C. $163.42.

9. An investor has just won the lottery and will receive $50,000 per year at the end of each of the next 20 years. At a 10% interest rate, the present value of the winnings is *closest* to:
   A. $425,678.
   B. $637,241.
   C. $2,863,750.

10. If $10,000 is invested today in an account that earns interest at a rate of 9.5%, what is the value of the equal withdrawals that can be taken out of the account at the end of each of the next five years if the investor plans to deplete the account at the end of the time period?
   A. $2,453.
   B. $2,604.
   C. $2,750.

11. An investor is to receive a 15-year, $8,000 annuity, with the first payment to be received today. At an 11% discount rate, this annuity's worth today is *closest* to:
   A. $55,855.
   B. $57,527.
   C. $63,855.

12. Given an 11% rate of return, the amount that must be put into an investment account at the end of each of the next ten years in order to accumulate $60,000 to pay for a child's education is *closest* to:
   A. $2,500.
   B. $3,588.
   C. $4,432.

13. An investor will receive an annuity of $4,000 a year for ten years. The first payment is to be received five years from today. At a 9% discount rate, this annuity's worth today is *closest* to:
   A. $16,684.
   B. $18,186.
   C. $25,671.

14. If $1,000 is invested today and $1,000 is invested at the beginning of each of the next three years at 12% interest (compounded annually), the amount an investor will have at the end of the fourth year will be *closest* to:
   A. $4,779.
   B. $5,353.
   C. $6,792.

15. An investor is looking at a $150,000 home. If 20% must be put down and the balance is financed at 9% over the next 30 years, what is the monthly mortgage payment?
    A. $799.33.
    B. $895.21.
    C. $965.55.

16. Given daily compounding, the growth of $5,000 invested for one year at 12% interest will be *closest* to:
    A. $5,600.
    B. $5,628.
    C. $5,637.

17. Terry Corporation preferred stocks are expected to pay a $9 annual dividend forever. If the required rate of return on equivalent investments is 11%, a share of Terry preferred should be worth:
    A. $81.82.
    B. $99.00.
    C. $122.22.

18. A share of George Co. preferred stock is selling for $65. It pays a dividend of $4.50 per year and has a perpetual life. The rate of return it is offering its investors is *closest* to:
    A. 4.5%.
    B. 6.9%.
    C. 14.4%.

19. If $10,000 is borrowed at 10% interest to be paid back over ten years, how much of the second year's payment is interest (assume annual loan payments)?
    A. $937.26.
    B. $954.25.
    C. $1,037.26.

20. What is the effective annual rate for a credit card that charges 18% compounded monthly?
    A. 15.38%.
    B. 18.81%.
    C. 19.56%.

CHALLENGE PROBLEMS

1. The Parks plan to take three cruises, one each year. They will take their first cruise 9 years from today, the second cruise one year after that, and the third cruise 11 years from today. The type of cruise they will take currently costs $5,000, but they expect inflation will increase this cost by 3.5% per year on average. They will contribute to an account to save for these cruises that will earn 8% per year. What equal contributions must they make today and every year until their first cruise (ten contributions) in order to have saved enough at that time for all three cruises? They pay for cruises when taken.

2. A company's dividend in 1995 was $0.88. Over the next eight years, the dividends were $0.91, $0.99, $1.12, $0.95, $1.09, $1.25, $1.42, and $1.26. Calculate the annually compounded growth rate of the dividend over the whole period.

3. An investment (a bond) will pay $1,500 at the end of each year for 25 years and on the date of the last payment will also make a separate payment of $40,000. If your required rate of return on this investment is 4%, how much would you be willing to pay for the bond today?

4. A bank quotes certificate of deposit (CD) yields both as annual percentage rates (APR) without compounding and as annual percentage yields (APY) that include the effects of monthly compounding. A $100,000 CD will pay $110,471.31 at the end of the year. Calculate the APR and APY the bank is quoting.

5. A client has $202,971.39 in an account that earns 8% per year, compounded monthly. The client's 35th birthday was yesterday and she will retire when the account value is $1 million.
    A. At what age can she retire if she puts no more money in the account?
    B. At what age can she retire if she puts $250 per month into the account every month, beginning one month from today?

ANSWERS – CONCEPT CHECKERS

1. **C**   N = 15; I/Y = 9; PV = –1,000; PMT = 0; CPT → FV = $3,642.48

2. **C**   N = 50; I/Y = 20; PV = –10; PMT = 0; CPT → FV = $91,004.38

3. **B**   Since no interest is earned, $100 is needed today to have $100 in three years.

4. **A**   N = 7; I/Y = 8; FV = –10,000; PMT = 0; CPT → PV = $5,834.90

5. **B**   N = 8; PV = –3; FV = 4.50; PMT = 0; CPT → I/Y = 5.1989

6. **C**   PV = –5,000; I/Y = 12; FV = 10,000; PMT = 0; CPT → N = 6.12.
   Rule of 72 → 72 / 12 = six years.

   Note to HP 12C users: One known problem with the HP 12C is that it does not have the capability to round. In this particular question, you will come up with 7, although the correct answer is 6.1163. CFA Institute is aware of this problem, and hopefully you will not be faced with a situation on exam day where the incorrect solution from the HP is one of the answer choices.

7. **B**   Using your cash flow keys, CF_0 = 0; CF_1 = 500; CF_2 = 200; CF_3 = 800; I/Y = 12; NPV = $1,175.29.

   Or you can add up the present values of each single cash flow.

   PV_1 = N = 1; FV = –500; I/Y = 12; CPT → PV = 446.43
   PV_2 = N = 2; FV = –200; I/Y = 12; CPT → PV = 159.44
   PV_3 = N = 3; FV = –800; I/Y = 12; CPT → PV = 569.42

   Hence, 446.43 + 159.44 + 569.42 = $1,175.29.

8. **A**   Using your cash flow keys, CF_0 = 0; CF_1 = 10; CF_2 = –20; CF_3 = 10; CF_4 = 150; I/Y = 8.5; NPV = $108.29.

9. **A**   N = 20; I/Y = 10; PMT = –50,000; FV = 0; CPT → PV = $425,678.19

10. **B**   PV = –10,000; I/Y = 9.5; N = 5; FV = 0; CPT → PMT = $2,604.36

11. **C**   This is an annuity due. Switch to BGN mode.

   N = 15; PMT = –8,000; I/Y = 11; FV = 0; CPT → PV = 63,854.92. Switch back to END mode.

12. **B**   N = 10; I/Y = 11; FV = –60,000; PV = 0; CPT → PMT = $3,588.08

13. **B**   Two steps: (1) Find the PV of the 10-year annuity: N = 10; I/Y = 9; PMT = –4,000; FV = 0; CPT → PV = 25,670.63. This is the present value as of the end of Year 4; (2) Discount PV of the annuity back four years: N = 4; PMT = 0; FV = –25,670.63; I/Y = 9; CPT → PV = 18,185.72.

14. **B**   The key to this problem is to recognize that it is a 4-year annuity due, so switch to BGN mode: N = 4; PMT = –1,000; PV = 0; I/Y = 12; CPT → FV = 5,352.84. Switch back to END mode.

15. **C** $N = 30 \times 12 = 360$; $I/Y = 9 / 12 = 0.75$; $PV = -150,000(1 - 0.2) = -120,000$; $FV = 0$;
CPT → PMT = \$965.55

16. **C** $N = 1 \times 365 = 365$; $I/Y = 12 / 365 = 0.0328767$; $PMT = 0$; $PV = -5,000$;
CPT → FV = \$5,637.37

17. **A** $9 / 0.11 = \$81.82$

18. **B** $4.5 / 65 = 0.0692$ or 6.92%

19. **A**   To get the annual payment, enter $PV = -10,000$; $FV = 0$; $I/Y = 10$; $N = 10$;
CPT → PMT = 1,627.45. The first year's interest is $\$1,000 = 10,000 \times 0.10$, so the
principal balance going into year 2 is $10,000 - 627.45 = \$9,372.55$. Year 2 interest
$= \$9,372.55 \times 0.10 = \$937.26$.

20. **C** $EAR = [(1 + (0.18 / 12))]^{12} - 1 = 19.56\%$

ANSWERS – CHALLENGE PROBLEMS

1.   Our suggested solution method is:

cost of first cruise $= 5,000 \times 1.035^9$
$= 6,814.49$

PV of first cruise cost $= \dfrac{6,814.49}{(1.08)^9} = \$3,408.94$

PV of second cruise cost $= \dfrac{(1.035)^{10}}{(1.08)^{10}} \times 5,000 = \$3,266.90$

PV of third cruise cost $= \left(\dfrac{1.035}{1.08}\right)^{11} \times 5,000 = \$3,130.78$

PV of all three = 3,408.94 + 3,266.90 + 3,130.78 = \$9,806.62. This is the amount
needed in the account today, so it's the PV of a 10-payment annuity due. Solve for
payment at 8% = \$1,353.22.

2. This problem is simpler than it may appear. The dividend grew from \$0.88 to \$1.26 in eight years. We know, then, that $0.88(1 + i)^8 = 1.26$, where i is the compound growth rate. Solving for i we get $\left(\dfrac{1.26}{0.88}\right)^{\frac{1}{8}} - 1 = 4.589\%$. could also just enter $\dfrac{1.26}{0.88}$, press

    $\left[\sqrt{}\right]$ three times, get 1.045890, and see that the answer is 4.589%.

    This technique for solving for a compound growth rate is a very useful one, and you will see it often.

    Calculator solution: PV = 0.88; N = 8; FV = –1.26; PMT = 0; CPT → I/Y = 4.589.

3. We can take the present value of the payments (a regular annuity) and the present value of the \$40,000 (lump sum) and add them together. N = 25; PMT = –1,500; i = 4;

    CPT → PV = 23,433.12 and $40,000 \times \left(\dfrac{1}{1.04}\right)^{25} = 15,004.67$, for a total value of

    \$38,437.79.

    Alternatively, N = 25; PMT = –1,500; i = 4; FV = –40,000; CPT → PV = 38,437.79.

4. For APR, PV = 100,000; FV = –110,471.31; PMT = 0; N = 12; CPT I/Y 0.8333, which is the monthly rate. The APR = 12 × 0.8333, or 10%.

    APY = 110,471.31 / 100,000 – 1 = 0.10471 = 10.471% (equivalent to a compound monthly rate of 0.8333%)

    Note that the APY, which includes the effects of compounding, must logically be larger than the APR, which does not.

5. A. PV = –202,971.39; I/Y = 8 / 12 = 0.6667; PMT = 0; FV = 1,000,000; CPT → N = 240. 240 months is 20 years; she will be 55 years old.
    B. Don't clear TVM functions. PMT = –250; CPT → N = 220, which is 18.335 years, so she will be 53. (N is actually 220.024, so the HP calculator displays 221.)

DISCOUNTED CASH FLOW APPLICATIONS

EXAM FOCUS

This review has a mix of topics, but all are important and useful. You must be able to use the cash flow functions on your calculator to calculate net present value and internal rate of return. We will use both of these in the Corporate Finance section and examine their strengths and weaknesses more closely there; but you must learn how to calculate them here. The time-weighted and money-weighted return calculations are standard tools for analysis. Calculating the various yield measures and the ability to calculate one from another are must-have skills. Don't hurry here; these concepts and techniques are foundation material that turns up repeatedly at all three levels of the CFA® curriculum.

LOS 6.a: Calculate and interpret the net present value (NPV) and the internal rate of return (IRR) of an investment.

CFA® Program Curriculum, Volume 1, page 294

The net present value (NPV) of an investment project is the present value of expected cash inflows associated with the project less the present value of the project's expected cash outflows, discounted at the appropriate cost of capital. The following procedure may be used to compute NPV:

- Identify all costs (outflows) and benefits (inflows) associated with an investment.
- Determine the appropriate discount rate or opportunity cost for the investment.
- Using the appropriate discount rate, find the PV of each cash flow. Inflows are positive and increase NPV. Outflows are negative and decrease NPV.
- Compute the NPV, the sum of the DCFs.

Mathematically, NPV is expressed as:

$$NPV = \sum_{t=0}^{N} \frac{CF_t}{(1+r)^t}$$

where:
CF_t = the expected net cash flow at time t
N = the estimated life of the investment
r = the discount rate (opportunity cost of capital)

NPV is the PV of the cash flows less the initial (time = 0) outlay.

Example: Computing NPV

Calculate the NPV of an investment project with an initial cost of $5 million and positive cash flows of $1.6 million at the end of Year 1, $2.4 million at the end of Year 2, and $2.8 million at the end of Year 3. Use 12% as the discount rate.

Answer:

The NPV for this project is the sum of the PVs of the project's individual cash flows and is determined as follows:

$$\text{NPV} = -\$5.0 + \frac{\$1.6}{1.12} + \frac{\$2.4}{(1.12)^2} + \frac{\$2.8}{(1.12)^3}$$

$$= -\$5.0 + \$1.42857 + \$1.91327 + \$1.99299$$

$$= \$0.3348 \text{ million, or } \$334,800$$

The procedures for calculating NPV with a TI BAII Plus® and an HP 12C® hand-held financial calculator are presented in Figures 1 and 2.

Figure 1: Calculating NPV with the TI Business Analyst II Plus®

Key Strokes	Explanation	Display
[CF] [2nd] [CLR WORK]	Clear CF Memory Registers	CF0 = 0.00000
5 [+/–] [ENTER]	Initial Cash Outlay	CF0 = –5.00000
[↓]1.6 ENTER]	Period 1 Cash Flow	C01 = 1.60000
[↓] [↓] 2.4 [ENTER]	Period 2 Cash Flow	C02 = 2.40000
[↓] [↓] 2.8 [ENTER]	Period 3 Cash Flow	C03 = 2.80000
[NPV] 12 [ENTER]	12% discount rate	I = 12.00000
[↓] [CPT]	Calculate NPV	NPV = 0.33482

Figure 2: Calculating NPV with the HP12C®

Key Strokes	Explanation	Display
[f] [FIN] [f] [REG]	Clear Memory Registers	0.00000
5 [CHS] [g] [CF$_0$]	Initial Cash Outlay	–5.00000
1.6 [g] [CF$_j$]	Period 1 Cash flow	1.60000
2.4 [g] [CF$_j$]	Period 2 Cash flow	2.40000
2.8 [g] [CF$_j$]	Period 3 Cash flow	2.80000
12 [i]	12% discount rate	12.00000
[f] [NPV]	Calculate NPV	0.33482

On the TI BAII Plus calculator, the sequence of [↓][↓] scrolls past the variables F01, F02, et cetera. The F here stands for frequency, and this is set to 1 by default. We did not enter anything because each cash flow amount occurred only once. If the period 2 cash flow, C02, were repeated three times (at t = 2, 3, and 4) we could input F02 = 3 to account for all three of these. The next input, C03, would then refer to the cash flow at t = 5.

On the HP 12C, you can also account for a repeated cash flow amount. Referring to the above example for the TI BAII Plus, the fact that the cash flow at period 2 is repeated for three periods is indicated by the sequence 3 [g] N_j immediately after the CF_j keystroke to input the amount of the period 2 cash flow.

Professor's Note: The NPV function can also be used to find the present value of any series of cash flows (positive or negative) over future periods. Just set $CF_0 = 0$ and input the cash flows CF_1 through CF_N as outlined above. The NPV is the present value of these cash flows since there is now no initial negative cash flow (initial cost).

The **internal rate of return** (IRR) is defined as the rate of return that equates the PV of an investment's expected benefits (inflows) with the PV of its costs (outflows). Equivalently, the IRR may be defined as the discount rate for which the NPV of an investment is zero.

Calculating IRR requires only that we identify the relevant cash flows for the investment opportunity being evaluated. Market-determined discount rates, or any other external (market-driven) data, are not necessary with the IRR procedure. The general formula for the IRR is:

$$0 = CF_0 + \frac{CF_1}{1+IRR} + \frac{CF_2}{(1+IRR)^2} + \cdots + \frac{CF_N}{(1+IRR)^N}$$

In the majority of IRR applications to capital budgeting, the initial cash flow, CF_0, represents the initial cost of the investment opportunity, and is therefore a negative value. As such, any discount rate less than the IRR will result in a positive NPV, and a discount rate greater than the IRR will result in a negative NPV. This implies that the NPV of an investment is zero when the discount rate used equals the IRR.

Example: Computing IRR

What is the IRR for the investment described in the preceding example?

Answer:

Substituting the investment's cash flows into the previous IRR equation results in the following equation:

$$0 = -5.0 + \frac{1.6}{1+IRR} + \frac{2.4}{(1+IRR)^2} + \frac{2.8}{(1+IRR)^3}$$

Solving this equation yields an IRR = 15.52%.

It is possible to solve IRR problems through a trial-and-error process. That is, keep guessing IRRs until you get the one that provides an NPV equal to zero. Practically speaking, a financial calculator or an electronic spreadsheet can and should be employed. The procedures for computing IRR with the TI BA II Plus and HP 12C financial calculators are illustrated in the following figures, respectively.

Calculating IRR with the TI Business Analyst II Plus®

Key Strokes	Explanation	Display
[CF] [2nd] [CLR WORK]	Clear Memory Registers	CF0 = 0.00000
5 [+/–] [ENTER]	Initial Cash Outlay	CF0 = –5.00000
[↓] 1.6 [ENTER]	Period 1 Cash Flow	C01 = 1.60000
[↓] [↓] 2.4 [ENTER]	Period 2 Cash Flow	C02 = 2.40000
[↓] [↓] 2.8 [ENTER]	Period 3 Cash Flow	C03 = 2.80000
[IRR] [CPT]	Calculate IRR	IRR = 15.51757

Calculating IRR with the HP12C®

Key Strokes	Explanation	Display
[f] [FIN] [f] [REG]	Clear Memory Registers	0.00000
5 [CHS] [g] [CF$_0$]	Initial Cash Outlay	–5.00000
1.6 [g] [CF$_j$]	Period 1 Cash flow	1.60000
2.4 [g] [CF$_j$]	Period 2 Cash flow	2.40000
2.8 [g] [CF$_j$]	Period 3 Cash flow	2.80000
[f] [IRR]	Calculate IRR	15.51757

LOS 6.b: Contrast the NPV rule to the IRR rule, and identify problems associated with the IRR rule.

CFA® Program Curriculum, Volume 1, page 298

NPV decision rule. The basic idea behind NPV analysis is that if a project has a positive NPV, this amount goes to the firm's shareholders. As such, if a firm undertakes a project with a positive NPV, shareholder wealth is increased.

The NPV decision rules are summarized:

- Accept projects with a positive NPV. Positive NPV projects will increase shareholder wealth.
- Reject projects with a negative NPV. Negative NPV projects will decrease shareholder wealth.
- When two projects are mutually exclusive (only one can be accepted), the project with the higher positive NPV should be accepted.

IRR decision rule. Analyzing an investment (project) using the IRR method provides the analyst with a result in terms of a rate of return.

The following are decision rules of IRR analysis:

- Accept projects with an IRR that is greater than the firm's (investor's) required rate of return.
- Reject projects with an IRR that is less than the firm's (investor's) required rate of return.

Note that for a single project, the IRR and NPV rules lead to exactly the same accept/reject decision. If the IRR is greater than the required rate of return, the NPV is positive, and if the IRR is less than the required rate of return, the NPV is negative.

Problems Associated With the IRR Method

When the acceptance or rejection of one project has no effect on the acceptance or rejection of another, the two projects are considered to be independent projects. When only one of two projects may be accepted, the projects are considered to be mutually exclusive. For mutually exclusive projects, the NPV and IRR methods can give conflicting project rankings. This can happen when the projects' initial costs are of different sizes or when the timing of the cash flows is different. Let's look at an example that illustrates how NPV and IRR can yield conflicting results.

Example: Conflicting decisions between NPV and IRR

Assume NPV and IRR analysis of two mutually exclusive projects produced the results shown in the following figure. As indicated, the IRR criteria recommends that Project A should be accepted. On the other hand, the NPV criteria indicates acceptance of Project B. Which project should be selected?

Ranking Reversals With NPV and IRR

Project	Investment at t = 0	Cash Flow at t = 1	IRR	NPV at 10%
A	−$5,000	$8,000	60%	$2,272.72
B	−$30,000	$40,000	33%	$6,363.64

Answer:

Investing in Project A increases shareholder wealth by $2,272.72, while investing in Project B increases shareholder wealth by $6,363.64. Since the overall goal of the firm is to maximize shareholder wealth, Project B should be selected because it adds the most value to the firm.

Mathematically speaking, the NPV method assumes the reinvestment of a project's cash flows at the opportunity cost of capital, while the IRR method assumes that the reinvestment rate is the IRR. The discount rate used with the NPV approach represents the market-based opportunity cost of capital and is the required rate of return for the shareholders of the firm.

Given that shareholder wealth maximization is the ultimate goal of the firm, always *select the project with the greatest NPV when the IRR and NPV rules provide conflicting decisions.*

LOS 6.c: Calculate and interpret a holding period return (total return).

CFA® Program Curriculum, Volume 1, page 301

A holding period can be any period of time. The holding period of an investment may be a matter of days or as long as several years. The **holding period return** is simply the percentage change in the value of an investment over the period it is held. If the asset has cash flows, such as dividend or interest payments, we refer to the return, including the value of these interim cash flows, as the **total return**.

As an example, consider a Treasury bill purchased for $980 and sold three months later for $992. The holding period return can be calculated as:

$$\text{HPR} = \frac{\text{ending value} - \text{beginning value}}{\text{beginning value}} = \frac{\text{ending value}}{\text{beginning value}} - 1$$

and we have $\frac{992}{980} - 1 = 0.0122$ or 1.22%

We would say that the investor's 3-month holding period return was 1.22%.

As an example of a security that has interim cash payments, consider a stock that is purchased for $30 and is sold for $33 six months later, during which time it paid $0.50 in dividends. The holding period return (total return in this case) can be calculated as:

$$\text{HPR} = \frac{\text{ending value} - \text{beginning value} + \text{cash flow received}}{\text{beginning value}}$$

$$= \frac{\text{ending value} + \text{cash flow received}}{\text{beginning value}} - 1$$

and we have $\frac{33 + 0.50}{30} - 1 = 0.1167$ or 11.67%,

which is the investor's total return over the holding period of six months.

LOS 6.d: Calculate and compare the money-weighted and time-weighted rates of return of a portfolio and evaluate the performance of portfolios based on these measures.

CFA® Program Curriculum, Volume 1, page 301

The **money-weighted return** applies the concept of IRR to investment portfolios. The money-weighted rate of return is defined as the internal rate of return on a portfolio, taking into account all cash inflows and outflows. The beginning value of the account is an inflow, as are all deposits into the account. All withdrawals from the account are outflows, as is the ending value.

Example: Money-weighted rate of return

Assume an investor buys a share of stock for $100 at t = 0 and at the end of the next year (t = 1), she buys an additional share for $120. At the end of Year 2, the investor sells both shares for $130 each. At the end of each year in the holding period, the stock paid a $2.00 per share dividend. What is the money-weighted rate of return?

Step 1: Determine the timing of each cash flow and whether the cash flow is an inflow (+), into the account, or an outflow (–), available from the account.

| t = 0: | purchase of first share | = +$100.00 inflow to account |

t = 1:	purchase of second share	= +$120.00
	dividend from first share	= −$2.00
	Subtotal, t = 1	+$118.00 inflow to account

t = 2:	dividend from two shares	= −$4.00
	proceeds from selling shares =	−$260.00
	Subtotal, t = 2	−$264.00 outflow from account

Step 2: Net the cash flows for each time period and set the PV of cash inflows equal to the present value of cash outflows.

$$PV_{inflows} = PV_{outflows}$$

$$\$100 + \frac{\$118}{(1+r)} = \frac{\$264}{(1+r)^2}$$

Step 3: Solve for *r* to find the money-weighted rate of return. This can be done using trial and error or by using the IRR function on a financial calculator or spreadsheet.

The intuition here is that we deposited $100 into the account at t = 0, then added $118 to the account at t = 1 (which, with the $2 dividend, funded the purchase of one more share at $120), and ended with a total value of $264.

To compute this value with a financial calculator, use these net cash flows and follow the procedure(s) described to calculate the IRR.

Net cash flows: CF_0 = +100; CF_1 = +120 − 2 = +118; CF_2 = −260 + −4 = −264

Calculating money-weighted return with the TI Business Analyst II Plus®

Note that the values for F01, F02, etc., are all equal to one.

Key Strokes	*Explanation*	*Display*
[CF] [2nd][CLR WORK]	Clear Cash Flow Registers	CF0 = 0.00000
100 [ENTER]	Initial Cash Outlay	CF0 = +100.00000
[↓] 118 [ENTER]	Period 1 Cash Flow	C01 = +118.00000
[↓] [↓] 264 [+/−] [ENTER]	Period 2 Cash Flow	C02 = −264.00000
[IRR] [CPT]	Calculate IRR	IRR = 13.86122

Calculating money-weighted return with the HP12C®

Key Strokes	Explanation	Display
[f] [FIN] [f] [REG]	Clear Memory Registers	0.00000
100 [g] [CF$_0$]	Initial Cash Outlay	+100.00000
118 [g] [CF$_j$]	Period 1 Cash Flow	+118.00000
264 [CHS] [g] [CF$_j$]	Period 2 Cash Flow	−264.00000
[f] [IRR]	Calculate IRR	13.86122

The money-weighted rate of return for this problem is 13.86%.

Professor's Note: In the preceding example, we entered the flows into the account as positive and the ending value as a negative (the investor could withdraw this amount from the account). Note that there is no difference in the solution if we enter the cash flows into the account as negative values (out of the investor's pocket) and the ending value as a positive value (into the investor's pocket). As long as payments into the account and payments out of the account (including the ending value) are entered with opposite signs, the computed IRR will be correct.

Time-weighted rate of return measures compound growth. It is the rate at which $1 compounds over a specified performance horizon. Time-weighting is the process of averaging a set of values over time. The *annual* time-weighted return for an investment may be computed by performing the following steps:

Step 1: Value the portfolio immediately preceding significant additions or withdrawals. Form subperiods over the evaluation period that correspond to the dates of deposits and withdrawals.

Step 2: Compute the holding period return (HPR) of the portfolio for each subperiod.

Step 3: Compute the product of (1 + HPR) for each subperiod to obtain a total return for the entire measurement period [i.e., (1 + HPR$_1$) × (1 + HPR$_2$) ... (1 + HPR$_n$)]. If the total investment period is greater than one year, you must take the geometric mean of the measurement period return to find the annual time-weighted rate of return.

Example: Time-weighted rate of return

An investor purchases a share of stock at t = 0 for $100. At the end of the year, t = 1, the investor buys another share of the same stock for $120. At the end of Year 2, the investor sells both shares for $130 each. At the end of both years 1 and 2, the stock paid a $2 per share dividend. What is the annual time-weighted rate of return for this investment? (This is the same investment as the preceding example.)

Answer:

Step 1: Break the evaluation period into two subperiods based on timing of cash flows.

Holding period 1:   Beginning value   = $100
                    Dividends paid   = $2
                    Ending value   = $120

Holding period 2:   Beginning value   = $240 (2 shares)
                    Dividends paid   = $4 ($2 per share)
                    Ending value   = $260 (2 shares)

Step 2: Calculate the HPR for each holding period.

$$HPR_1 = [(\$120 + 2) / \$100] - 1 = 22\%$$

$$HPR_2 = [(\$260 + 4) / \$240] - 1 = 10\%$$

Step 3: Find the compound annual rate that would have produced a total return equal to the return on the account over the 2-year period.

$$(1 + \text{time-weighted rate of return})^2 = (1.22)(1.10)$$

$$\text{time-weighted rate of return} = [(1.22)(1.10)]^{0.5} - 1 = 15.84\%$$

This is the *geometric mean* return, which we examine in more detail later. This allows us to express the time-weighted return as an annual compound rate, even though we have two years of data. In the investment management industry, *the time-weighted rate of return is the preferred method of performance measurement, because it is not affected by the timing of cash inflows and outflows.*

In the preceding examples, the time-weighted rate of return for the portfolio was 15.84%, while the money-weighted rate of return for the same portfolio was 13.86%. The results are different because the money-weighted rate of return gave a larger weight to the Year 2 HPR, which was 10%, versus the 22% HPR for Year 1. This is because there was more money in the account at the beginning of the second period.

If funds are contributed to an investment portfolio just before a period of relatively poor portfolio performance, the money-weighted rate of return will tend to be lower than the time-weighted rate of return. On the other hand, if funds are contributed to a portfolio at a favorable time (just prior to a period of relatively high returns), the money-weighted rate of return will be higher than the time-weighted rate of return. The use of the time-weighted return removes these distortions and thus provides a better measure of a manager's ability to select investments over the period. If the manager has complete control over money flows into and out of an account, the money-weighted rate of return would be the more appropriate performance measure.

LOS 6.e: Calculate and interpret the bank discount yield, holding period yield, effective annual yield, and money market yield for U.S. Treasury bills and other money market instruments.

CFA® Program Curriculum, Volume 1, page 307

Pure discount instruments such as U.S. T-bills are quoted differently from U.S. government bonds. T-bills are quoted on a *bank discount basis*, which is *based on the face value* of the instrument instead of the purchase price. The **bank discount** yield (BDY) is computed using the following formula:

$$r_{BD} = \frac{D}{F} \times \frac{360}{t}$$

where:

r_{BD} = the annualized yield on a bank discount basis

D = the dollar discount, which is equal to the difference between the face value of the bill and the purchase price

F = the face value (par value) of the bill

t = number of days remaining until maturity

360 = bank convention of number of days in a year

The *key distinction* of the bank discount yield is that it expresses the dollar discount from the face (par) value as a fraction of the face value, not the market price of the instrument. Another notable feature of the bank discount yield is that it is annualized by multiplying the discount-to-par by 360/t, where the market convention is to use a 360-day year versus a 365-day year. This type of annualizing method assumes no compounding (i.e., simple interest).

Example: Bank discount yield

Calculate the bank discount yield for a T-bill priced at $98,500, with a face value of $100,000 and 120 days until maturity.

Answer:

Substituting the relevant values into the bank discount yield equation in our example, we get:

$$r_{BD} = \frac{1,500}{100,000} \times \frac{360}{120} = 4.5\%$$

It is important for candidates to realize that a yield quoted on a bank discount basis is not representative of the return earned by an investor for the following reasons:

- Bank discount yield annualizes using simple interest and ignores the effects of compound interest.
- Bank discount yield is based on the face value of the bond, not its purchase price—investment returns should be evaluated relative to the amount invested.
- Bank discount yield is annualized based on a 360-day year rather than a 365-day year.

Holding period yield (HPY), or holding period return, is the total return an investor earns between the purchase date and the sale or maturity date. HPY is calculated using the following formula:

$$HPY = \frac{P_1 - P_0 + D_1}{P_0} = \frac{P_1 + D_1}{P_0} - 1$$

where:
P_0 = initial price of the instrument
P_1 = price received for instrument at maturity
D_1 = interest payment (distribution)

Example: HPY

What is the HPY for a T-bill priced at $98,500 with a face value of $100,000 and 120 days remaining until maturity?

Answer:

Using the HPY equation stated above, we have:

HPY = ($100,000 − $98,500) / $98,500
= $1,500 / $98,500
= 1.5228%

$D_1 = 0$ here because T-bills are a pure discount instrument (i.e., they make no interest payments).

The **effective annual** yield (EAY) is an annualized value, based on a 365-day year, that accounts for compound interest. It is calculated using the following equation:

$$EAY = (1 + HPY)^{365/t} - 1$$

Example: EAY

Compute the EAY using the 120-day HPY of 1.5228% from the previous example.

Answer:

The HPY is converted to an EAY as follows:

$$EAY = (1.015228)^{365/120} - 1 = 1.047042 - 1 = 4.7042\%$$

Note that we can convert from an EAY to HPY by using the reciprocal of the exponent and $(1.047042)^{120/365} - 1 = 1.5228\%$

The money market yield (or CD equivalent yield) is equal to the annualized holding period yield, *assuming a 360-day year*. Using the money market yield makes the quoted yield on a T-bill comparable to yield quotes for interest-bearing money market instruments that pay interest on a 360-day basis. The money market yield is $\frac{360}{\#\,days} \times HPY$.

$$r_{MM} = HPY \times (360/t)$$

Given the bank discount yield, r_{BD}, the money market yield, r_{MM}, may be calculated using the equation:

$$r_{MM} = \frac{360 \times r_{BD}}{360 - (t \times r_{BD})}$$

 Professor's Note: I couldn't remember this formula with a gun to my head, but I (and you) can easily convert a BDY to an HPY and the HPY to a money market yield using the previous formulas.

Example: Money market yield, r_{MM}

What is the money market yield for a 120-day T-bill that has a bank discount yield of 4.50%?

Answer:

Given the r_{BD} for the T-bill, the first equation for r_{MM} is applied as follows:

$$r_{MM} = \frac{360 \times 0.045}{360 - (120 \times 0.045)}$$

$$= 16.2 \ / \ 354.6$$

$$= 4.569\%$$

Alternatively, we could first calculate the HPY for the T-bill and then annualize that.

Actual discount is $0.045 \times \dfrac{120}{360} = 0.015$. Based on a $1,000 face value,

price = 1,000 (1 – 0.015) = 985, so that $HPY = \dfrac{1,000}{985} - 1$ and

$$r_{MM} = \left(\frac{1,000}{985} - 1 \right) \times \frac{360}{120} = 0.04569 = 4.569\%.$$

LOS 6.f: Convert among holding period yields, money market yields, effective annual yields, and bond equivalent yields.

CFA® Program Curriculum, Volume 1, page 307

Once we have established HPY, EAY, or r_{MM}, we can use one as a basis for calculating the other two. Remember:

- The HPY is the actual return an investor will receive if the money market instrument is held until maturity.
- The EAY is the annualized HPY on the basis of a 365-day year and incorporates the effects of compounding.
- The r_{MM} is the annualized yield that is based on price and a *360-day year* and does not account for the effects of compounding—it assumes simple interest.

Example: Converting among EAY, HPY, and r_{MM}

Assume you purchased a $100,000 T-bill that matures in 150 days for a price of $98,000. The broker who sold you the T-bill quoted the money market yield at 4.898%. Compute the HPY and the EAY.

Answer:

The T-bill HPY is simply $\dfrac{2,000}{98,000} = 2.041\%$, which we can also derive from the money market yield.

Money market to holding period yield—r_{MM} is an annualized yield based on a 360-day year. To change the r_{MM} in this example into its HPY, we need to convert it to a 150-day holding period by multiplying it by (150 / 360). Thus:

$$HPY = r_{MM} \times (150 / 360)$$

$$= 0.04898 \times (150 / 360)$$

$$= 0.02041 = 2.041\%$$

Holding period yield to effective annual yield—the EAY is equal to the annualized HPY based on a 365-day year. Now that we have computed the HPY, simply annualize using a 365-day year to calculate the EAY as follows:

$$EAY = (1 + 0.02041)^{365 / 150} - 1$$

$$= 1.05039 - 1 = 5.039\%$$

Note that to convert the EAY back into the HPY, apply the reciprocal of the exponent to the EAY. This is the same as taking one plus the EAY to the power (t/365). For example, we can convert the EAY we just calculated back to the HPY as follows:

$$HPY = (1.05039)^{150 / 365} - 1 = 2.041\%$$

> *Professor's Note: On the Level I CFA® exam, you may be asked to convert from any one of these three yields into one of the others. You should note that the EAY and r_{MM} are merely annualized versions of the HPY. If you concentrate on converting back and forth between the HPY and the other yield figures, you will be well-prepared to answer these types of questions on the Level I exam.*

Bond Equivalent Yield

The bond-equivalent yield refers to 2 × the semiannual discount rate. This convention stems from the fact that yields on U.S. bonds are quoted as twice the semiannual rate, because the coupon interest is paid in two semiannual payments.

Example: Bond-equivalent yield calculation (1)

A 3-month loan has a holding period yield of 2%. What is the yield on a bond-equivalent basis?

Answer:

The first step is to convert the 3-month yield to an effective semiannual (6-month) yield:

$$1.02^2 - 1 = 4.04\%$$

The second step it to double it ($2 \times 4.04 = 8.08\%$) to get the bond-equivalent yield.

Example: Bond-equivalent yield calculation (2)

The effective annual yield on an investment is 8%. What is the yield on a bond-equivalent basis?

Answer:

The first step is to convert the effective annual yield to an effective semiannual yield.

$$1.08^{0.5} - 1 = 3.923\%$$

The second step is to double it: $2 \times 3.923 = 7.846\%$.

Professor's Note: There is an alternative definition of the bond equivalent yield in the Corporate Finance topic review on Working Capital Management:

$$\left(HPR \times \frac{365}{\text{days to maturity}} \right)$$

KEY CONCEPTS

LOS 6.a
The NPV is the present value of a project's future cash flows, discounted at the firm's cost of capital, less the project's cost. IRR is the discount rate that makes the NPV = 0 (equates the PV of the expected future cash flows to the project's initial cost).

The NPV rule is to accept a project if NPV > 0; the IRR rule is to accept a project if IRR > required rate of return. For an independent (single) project, these rules produce the exact same decision.

LOS 6.b
For mutually exclusive projects, IRR rankings and NPV rankings may differ due to differences in project size or in the timing of the cash flows. Choose the project with the higher NPV as long as it is positive.

A project may have multiple IRRs or no IRR.

LOS 6.c
The holding period return (or yield) is the total return for holding an investment over a certain period of time and can be calculated as:

$$\text{HPY} = \frac{P_1 - P_0 + D_1}{P_0} = \frac{P_1 + D_1}{P_0} - 1$$

LOS 6.d
The money-weighted rate of return is the IRR calculated using periodic cash flows into and out of an account and is the discount rate that makes the PV of cash inflows equal to the PV of cash outflows.

The time-weighted rate of return measures compound growth. It is the rate at which $1 compounds over a specified performance horizon.

If funds are added to a portfolio just before a period of poor performance, the money-weighted return will be lower than the time-weighted return. If funds are added just prior to a period of high returns, the money-weighted return will be higher than the time-weighted return.

The time-weighted return is the preferred measure of a manager's ability to select investments. If the manager controls the money flows into and out of an account, the money-weighted return is the more appropriate performance measure.

LOS 6.e

Given a $1,000 T-bill with 100 days to maturity and a discount of $10 (price of $990):

- Bank discount yield = $\dfrac{10}{1,000} \times \dfrac{360}{100} = 3.60\%$

- Holding period yield = $\dfrac{1,000 - 990}{990} = 1.01\%$

- Effective annual yield = $1.0101^{365/100} - 1 = 3.74\%$

- Money market yield = $1.01\% \times \dfrac{360}{100} = 3.636\%$

LOS 6.f

Given a money market security with n days to maturity:

- Holding period yield = $\dfrac{\text{bank discount yield}\left(\dfrac{n}{360}\right)}{1 - \text{bank discount yield}\left(\dfrac{n}{360}\right)}$

- Money market yield = holding period yield $\times \dfrac{360}{n}$

- Effective annual yield = $(1 + \text{holding period yield})^{365/n} - 1$

- Holding period yield = $(1 + \text{effective annual yield})^{n/365} - 1$

- Bond equivalent yield = $[(1 + \text{effective annual yield})^{1/2} - 1] \times 2$

CONCEPT CHECKERS

1.   Which of the following statements *least accurately* describes the IRR and NPV methods?
   A. The discount rate that gives an investment an NPV of zero is the investment's IRR.
   B. If the NPV and IRR methods give conflicting decisions for mutually exclusive projects, the IRR decision should be used to select the project.
   C. The NPV method assumes that a project's cash flows will be reinvested at the cost of capital, while the IRR method assumes they will be reinvested at the IRR.

2.   Which of the following statements *least accurately* describes the IRR and NPV methods?
   A. A project's IRR can be positive even if the NPV is negative.
   B. A project with an IRR equal to the cost of capital will have an NPV of zero.
   C. A project's NPV may be positive even if the IRR is less than the cost of capital.

3.   Which of the following statements *least accurately* describes the IRR and NPV methods?
   A. The NPV tells how much the value of the firm has increased if you accept the project.
   B. When evaluating independent projects, the IRR and NPV methods always yield the same accept/reject decisions.
   C. When selecting between mutually exclusive projects, the project with the highest NPV should be accepted regardless of the sign of the NPV calculation.

4.   A company is considering entering into a joint venture that will require an investment of $10 million. The project is expected to generate cash flows of $4 million, $3 million, and $4 million in each of the next three years, respectively. Assuming a discount rate of 10%, what is the project's NPV?
   A. –$879,000.
   B. –$309,000.
   C. +$243,000.

5.   A company is considering entering into a joint venture that will require an investment of $10 million. The project is expected to generate cash flows of $4 million, $3 million, and $4 million in each of the next three years, respectively. Assuming a discount rate of 10%, what is the project's *approximate* IRR?
   A. 5%.
   B. 10%.
   C. 15%.

6. What should an analyst recommend based on the following information for two independent projects?

Project	Investment at t = 0	Cash Flow at t = 1	IRR	NPV at 12%
A	−$3,000	$5,000	66.67%	$1,464.29
B	−$10,000	$15,000	50.00%	$3,392.86

A. Accept A and reject B.
B. Reject A and accept B.
C. Accept A and accept B.

7. What should an analyst recommend based on the following information for two mutually exclusive projects?

Project	Investment at t = 0	Cash Flow at t = 1	IRR	NPV at 12%
A	−$3,000	$5,000	66.67%	$1,464.29
B	−$10,000	$15,000	50.00%	$3,392.86

A. Accept A and reject B.
B. Reject A and accept B.
C. Accept A and accept B.

8. Goodeal, Inc., is considering the purchase of a new material handling system for a cost of $15 million. This system is expected to generate a positive cash flow of $1.8 million per year in perpetuity. What is the NPV of the proposed investment if the appropriate discount rate is 10.5%?
A. $2,142,857.
B. $13,200,000.
C. $17,142,857.

9. Goodeal, Inc., is considering the purchase of a new material handling system for a cost of $15 million. This system is expected to generate a positive cash flow of $1.8 million per year in perpetuity. What is the IRR of the proposed investment if the appropriate hurdle rate is 10.5%?
A. 8.3%.
B. 10.5%.
C. 12.0%.

10. Should a company accept a project that has an IRR of 14% and an NPV of $2.8 million if the cost of capital is 12%?
A. Yes, based only on the NPV.
B. Yes, based on the NPV and the IRR.
C. No, based on both the NPV and IRR.

11. Which of the following statements *least likely* represents a characteristic of the time-weighted rate of return? It is:
    A. not affected by the timing of cash flows.
    B. used to measure the compound rate of growth of $1 over a stated measurement period.
    C. defined as the internal rate of return on an investment portfolio, taking into account all inflows and outflows.

Use the following data to answer Questions 12 and 13.

Assume an investor purchases a share of stock for $50 at time t = 0, and another share at $65 at time t = 1, and at the end of Year 1 and Year 2, the stock paid a $2 dividend. Also, at the end of Year 2, the investor sold both shares for $70 each.

12. The money-weighted rate of return on the investment is:
    A. 15.45%.
    B. 16.73%.
    C. 18.02%.

13. The time-weighted rate of return on the investment is:
    A. 18.27%.
    B. 20.13%.
    C. 21.83%.

14. What is the bank discount yield for a T-bill that is selling for $99,000, with a face value of $100,000 and 95 days remaining until maturity?
    A. 1.51%.
    B. 3.79%.
    C. 6.00%.

15. What is the holding period yield for a T-bill that is selling for $99,000 if it has a face value of $100,000 and 95 days remaining until maturity?
    A. 1.01%.
    B. 2.03%.
    C. 3.79%.

16. What is the effective annual yield for a T-bill that is selling for $99,000 if it has a face value of $100,000 and 95 days remaining until maturity?
    A. 3.79%.
    B. 3.94%.
    C. 4.50%.

17. What is the money market yield for a T-bill that is selling for $99,000 if it has a face value of $100,000 and 95 days remaining until maturity?
   A. 3.79%.
   B. 3.83%.
   C. 3.90%.

18. Which of the following is *least accurate* regarding a bank discount yield?
   A. It ignores the opportunity to earn compound interest.
   B. It is based on the face value of the bond, not its purchase price.
   C. It reflects the nonannualized return an investor will earn over a security's life.

19. A 175-day T-bill has an effective annual yield of 3.80%. Its money-market yield is *closest* to:
   A. 1.80%.
   B. 3.65%.
   C. 3.71%.

CHALLENGE PROBLEMS

1. Allison Rogers, CFA, makes the following statement: "The problems with bank discount yields quoted for T-bills is that they aren't yields, they ignore compounding, and they are based on a short year."
   A. Is she correct in all regards?

   B. Which of these problems is/are remedied by using the holding period yield?

   C. Which of these problems is/are remedied by using a money market yield?

   D. Which of these problems is/are remedied by using effective annual yields?

2.   L. Adams buys 1,000 shares of Morris Tool stock for $35 per share. One year later the stock is $38 per share and has paid a dividend of $1.50 per share. Adams reinvests the dividends in additional shares at the time. At the end of the second year, the shares are trading for $37 and have paid $2 dividends over the period.

    L. Burns buys 500 shares of Morris Tool stock for $35 per share. One year later the stock is $38 per share and has paid a dividend of $1.50 per share. Burns reinvests the dividends in additional shares at that time and also buys 500 additional shares. At the end of the second year, the shares are trading for $37 and have paid $2 in dividends over the period.

    A.   Compare the annual time-weighted returns for the accounts of the two investors (no calculation required).

    B.   Compare the annual money-weighted returns for the accounts of the two investors (no calculation required).

3.   At retirement nine years from now, a client will have the option of receiving a lump sum of £400,000 or 20 annual payments of £40,000, with the first payment made at retirement. What is the annual rate the client would need to earn on a retirement investment to be indifferent between the two choices?

ANSWERS – CONCEPT CHECKERS

1. **B** If the NPV and IRR methods give conflicting decisions when selecting among mutually exclusive projects, always select the project with the greatest positive NPV.

2. **C** A project will have a negative NPV if its IRR is less than the firm's cost of capital.

3. **C** When selecting between two mutually exclusive projects, neither project should be accepted if they both have a negative NPV.

4. **A** $NPV = 4 / 1.10 + 3 / (1.10)^2 + 4 / (1.10)^3 - \$10 = -\$0.879038$ million, or $-\$879,038$

   Calculator approach: CF0 = –10; CF1 = 4; CF2 = 3; CF3 = 4; I = 10 → NPV = –$0.879038 (million)

5. **A** Use your test-taking skills here. You know from the previous question that the NPV is negative at 10%. Thus, the IRR must be less than 10%. This leaves only choice **A** to be the answer. Calculator solution: IRR = 4.9%.

6. **C** Both projects should be accepted since both projects have positive NPVs and will thus increase shareholder wealth.

7. **B** When the NPV and IRR rankings conflict, always select the project with the highest positive NPV in order to maximize shareholder wealth.

8. **A** $NPV = PV(\text{cash inflows}) - CF_0 = (\$1.8 \text{ million} / 0.105) - \$15 \text{ million} = \$2,142,857$
   Accept the project.

9. **C** As a perpetuity, the following relationship applies: $1.8 million / IRR = $15 million. Thus, IRR = 1.8 / 15 = 12%. Since IRR > cost of capital (hurdle rate), accept the project.

10. **B** The project should be accepted on the basis of its positive NPV and its IRR, which exceeds the cost of capital.

11. **C** The money-weighted rate of return is the IRR of an investment's net cash flows.

12. **C** One way to do this problem is to set up the cash flows so that the PV of inflows = PV of outflows and plug in each of the multiple choices. $50 + 65 / (1 + r) = 2 / (1 + r) + 144 / (1 + r)^2 \rightarrow r = 18.02\%$. Or on your financial calculator, solve for IRR:

$$-50 - \frac{65-2}{1+\text{IRR}} + \frac{2(70+2)}{(1+\text{IRR})^2} = 0$$

Calculating Money-Weighted Return With the TI Business Analyst II Plus®

Key Strokes	Explanation	Display
[CF] [2ⁿᵈ] [CLR WORK]	Clear CF Memory Registers	CF0 = 0.00000
50 [+/–] [ENTER]	Initial cash inflow	CF0 = –50.00000
[↓] 63 [+/–][ENTER]	Period 1 cash inflow	C01 = –63.00000
[↓] [↓] 144 [ENTER]	Period 2 cash outflow	C02 = 144.00000
[IRR] [CPT]	Calculate IRR	IRR = 18.02210

13. **C** $HPR_1 = (65 + 2) / 50 - 1 = 34\%$, $HPR_2 = (140 + 4) / 130 - 1 = 10.77\%$

Time-weighted return $= [(1.34)(1.1077)]^{0.5} - 1 = 21.83\%$

14. **B** $(1,000 / 100,000) \times (360 / 95) = 3.79\%$

15. **A** $(100,000 - 99,000) / 99,000 = 1.01\%$

16. **B** $(1 + 0.0101)^{365/95} - 1 = 3.94\%$

17. **B** $(360 \times 0.0379) / [360 - (95 \times 0.0379)] = 3.83\%$, or $(1,000 / 99,000)(360 / 95) = 3.83\%$

18. **C** This is actually the definition of the holding period yield. The other answers are true statements regarding the bank discount yield.

19. **C** Since the effective yield is 3.8%, we know $\left[\dfrac{1,000}{price}\right]^{\frac{365}{175}} = 1.038$ and

$$price = \left[\dfrac{1,000}{1.038^{\frac{175}{365}}}\right] = \$982.28 \text{ per } \$1,000 \text{ face.}$$

The money market yield is

$$\left(\dfrac{360}{175}\right) \times HPY = \left(\dfrac{360}{175}\right)\left(\dfrac{1,000}{982.28} - 1\right) = \dfrac{360}{175}(0.01804) = 3.711\%.$$

Alternatively, we can get the HPY from the EAY of 3.8% as $(1.038)^{\frac{175}{365}} - 1 = 1.804\%$.

ANSWERS – CHALLENGE PROBLEMS

1. A. She is correct in all regards. Bank discount yields are not true yields because they are based on a percentage of face (maturity) value instead of on the original amount invested. They are annualized without compounding since the actual discount from face value is simply multiplied by the number of periods in a "year." The "year" used is 360 days, so that is a shortcoming as well.

   B. The holding period yield uses the increase in value divided by the amount invested (purchase price), so it solves the problem that the BDY is not a true yield.

   C. The money market yield is also a true yield (a percentage of the initial investment) but does not solve the other two problems since it does not involve compounding and is based on a 360-day year.

   D. The effective annual yield solves all three shortcomings. It is based on the holding period yield (so it is a true yield), is a compound annual rate, and is based on a 365-day year.

2. A. Both investors have held the same single stock for both periods, so the time-weighted returns must be identical for both accounts.

   B. The performance of the stock (annual total return) was better in the first year than in the second. Since Burns increased his holdings for the second period by more than Adams, the Burns account has a greater weight on the poorer returns in a money-weighted return calculation and will have a lower annual money-weighted rate of return over the two-year period than Adams.

3. Setting the retirement date to t = 0 we have the following choices:

t = 0	t = 1	t = 2	...	t = 20
400,000				
40,000	40,000	40,000	...	40,000

One method: PV = 400,000 – 40,000 = 360,000; PMT = –40,000; N = 19; FV = 0; CPT → I/Y = 8.9196%

Or in *BGN mode*: PV = 400,000; N = 20; FV = 0; PMT = –40,000; CPT → I/Y = 8.9196%

STATISTICAL CONCEPTS AND MARKET RETURNS

Study Session 2

EXAM FOCUS

This quantitative review is about the uses of descriptive statistics to summarize and portray important characteristics of large sets of data. The two key areas that you should concentrate on are (1) measures of central tendency and (2) measures of dispersion. Measures of central tendency include the arithmetic mean, geometric mean, weighted mean, median, and mode. Measures of dispersion include the range, mean absolute deviation, and the most important measure for us, variance. These measures quantify the variability of data around its "center." When describing investments, measures of central tendency provide an indication of an investment's expected return. Measures of dispersion indicate the riskiness of an investment. For the Level I exam, you should know the properties of a normal distribution and be able to recognize departures from normality, such as lack of symmetry (skewness) or the extent to which a distribution is peaked (kurtosis).

LOS 7.a: Distinguish between descriptive statistics and inferential statistics, between a population and a sample, and among the types of measurement scales.

CFA® Program Curriculum, Volume 1, page 325

The word **statistics** is used to refer to data (e.g., the average return on XYZ stock was 8% over the last ten years) and to the methods we use to analyze data. Statistical methods fall into one of two categories, **descriptive statistics** or **inferential statistics**.

Descriptive statistics are used to summarize the important characteristics of large data sets. The focus of this topic review is on the use of descriptive statistics to consolidate a mass of numerical data into useful information.

Inferential statistics, which will be discussed in subsequent topic reviews, pertain to the procedures used to make forecasts, estimates, or judgments about a large set of data on the basis of the statistical characteristics of a smaller set (a sample).

A **population** is defined as the set of all possible members of a stated group. A cross-section of the returns of all of the stocks traded on the New York Stock Exchange (NYSE) is an example of a population.

It is frequently too costly or time consuming to obtain measurements for every member of a population, if it is even possible. In this case, a sample may be used. A **sample** is defined as a subset of the population of interest. Once a population has been defined, a sample can be drawn from the population, and the sample's characteristics can be used to describe the population as a whole. For example, a sample of 30 stocks may be selected from among all of the stocks listed on the NYSE to represent the population of all NYSE-traded stocks.

Types of Measurement Scales

Different statistical methods use different levels of measurement, or measurement scales. Measurement scales may be classified into one of four major categories:

- **Nominal scales.** Nominal scales are the level of measurement that contains the least information. Observations are classified or counted with no particular order. An example would be assigning the number 1 to a municipal bond fund, the number 2 to a corporate bond fund, and so on for each fund style.
- **Ordinal scales.** Ordinal scales represent a higher level of measurement than nominal scales. When working with an ordinal scale, every observation is assigned to one of several categories. Then these categories are ordered with respect to a specified characteristic. For example, the ranking of 1,000 small cap growth stocks by performance may be done by assigning the number 1 to the 100 best performing stocks, the number 2 to the next 100 best performing stocks, and so on, assigning the number 10 to the 100 worst performing stocks. Based on this type of measurement, it can be concluded that a stock ranked 3 is better than a stock ranked 4, but the scale reveals nothing about performance differences or whether the difference between a 3 and a 4 is the same as the difference between a 4 and a 5.
- **Interval scale.** Interval scale measurements provide relative ranking, like ordinal scales, plus the assurance that differences between scale values are equal. Temperature measurement in degrees is a prime example. Certainly, 49°C is hotter than 32°C, and the temperature difference between 49°C and 32°C is the same as the difference between 67°C and 50°C. The weakness of the interval scale is that a measurement of zero does not necessarily indicate the total absence of what we are measuring. This means that interval-scale-based ratios are meaningless. For example, 30°F is not three times as hot as 10°F.
- **Ratio scales.** Ratio scales represent the most refined level of measurement. Ratio scales provide ranking and equal differences between scale values, and they also have a true zero point as the origin. Order, intervals, and ratios all make sense with a ratio scale. The measurement of money is a good example. If you have zero dollars, you have no purchasing power, but if you have $4.00, you have twice as much purchasing power as a person with $2.00.

 Professor's Note: Candidates sometimes use the French word for black, noir, to remember the types of scales in order of precision: Nominal, Ordinal, Interval, Ratio.

LOS 7.b: Define a parameter, a sample statistic, and a frequency distribution.

CFA® Program Curriculum, Volume 1, page 325

A measure used to describe a characteristic of a population is referred to as a parameter. While many population parameters exist, investment analysis usually utilizes just a few, particularly the mean return and the standard deviation of returns.

In the same manner that a parameter may be used to describe a characteristic of a population, a sample statistic is used to measure a characteristic of a sample.

A **frequency distribution** is a tabular presentation of statistical data that aids the analysis of large data sets. Frequency distributions summarize statistical data by assigning it to specified groups, or intervals. Also, the data employed with a frequency distribution may be measured using any type of measurement scale.

 Professor's Note: Intervals are also known as classes.

The following procedure describes how to construct a frequency distribution.

Step 1: Define the intervals. The first step in building a frequency distribution is to define the intervals to which data measurements (observations) will be assigned. An interval, also referred to as a class, is the set of values that an observation may take on. The range of values for each interval must have a lower and upper limit and be all-inclusive and nonoverlapping. Intervals must be *mutually exclusive* in a way that each observation can be placed in only one interval, and the total set of intervals should cover the total range of values for the entire population.

The number of intervals used is an important consideration. If too few intervals are used, the data may be too broadly summarized, and important characteristics may be lost. On the other hand, if too many intervals are used, the data may not be summarized enough.

Step 2: Tally the observations. After the intervals have been defined, the observations must be tallied, or assigned to their appropriate interval.

Step 3: Count the observations. Having tallied the data set, the number of observations that are assigned to each interval must be counted. The *absolute frequency,* or simply the frequency, is the actual number of observations that fall within a given interval.

Example: Constructing a frequency distribution

Use the data in Table A to construct a frequency distribution for the returns on Intelco's common stock.

Table A: Annual Returns for Intelco, Inc. Common Stock

10.4%	22.5%	11.1%	−12.4%
9.8%	17.0%	2.8%	8.4%
34.6%	−28.6%	0.6%	5.0%
−17.6%	5.6%	8.9%	40.4%
−1.0%	−4.2%	−5.2%	21.0%

Answer:

Step 1: *Defining the interval.* For Intelco's stock, the range of returns is 69.0% (−28.6% → 40.4%). Using a return interval of 1% would result in 69 separate intervals, which in this case is too many. So let's use eight nonoverlapping intervals with a width of 10%. The lowest return intervals will be −30% ≤ R_t < −20%, and the intervals will increase to 40% ≤ R_t ≤ 50%.

Step 2: *Tally the observations and count the observations within each interval.* The tallies and counts of the observations are presented in Table B.

Table B: Tally and Interval Count for Returns Data

Interval	Tallies	Absolute Frequency
−30% ≤ R < −20%	/	1
−20% ≤ R_t −10%	//	2
−10% ≤ R_t < 0%	///	3
0% ≤ R_t < 10%	///// //	7
10% ≤ R_t < 20%	///	3
20% ≤ R_t < 30%	//	2
30% ≤ R_t < 40%	/	1
40% ≤ R_t ≤ 50%	/	1
Total		20

Tallying and counting the observations generates a frequency distribution that summarizes the pattern of annual returns on Intelco common stock. Notice that the interval with the greatest (absolute) frequency is the (0% ≤ R_t < 10%) interval, which includes seven return observations. For any frequency distribution, the interval with the greatest frequency is referred to as the **modal interval**.

LOS 7.c: Calculate and interpret relative frequencies and cumulative relative frequencies, given a frequency distribution.

CFA® Program Curriculum, Volume 1, page 330

The **relative frequency** is another useful way to present data. The relative frequency is calculated by dividing the absolute frequency of each return interval by the total number of observations. Simply stated, relative frequency is the percentage of total observations falling within each interval. Continuing with our example, the relative frequencies are presented in Figure 1.

©2012 Kaplan, Inc.

Figure 1: Absolute and Relative Frequencies of Intelco Returns

Interval	Absolute Frequency	Relative Frequency
$-30\% \leq R_t < -20\%$	1	1/20 = 0.05, or 5%
$-20\% \leq R_t < -10\%$	2	2/20 = 0.10, or 10%
$-10\% \leq R_t < 0\%$	3	3/20 = 0.15, or 15%
$0\% \leq R_t < 10\%$	7	7/20 = 0.35, or 35%
$10\% \leq R_t < 20\%$	3	3/20 = 0.15, or 15%
$20\% \leq R_t < 30\%$	2	2/20 = 0.10, or 10%
$30\% \leq R_t < 40\%$	1	1/20 = 0.05, or 5%
$40\% \leq R_t \leq 50\%$	1	1/20 = 0.05, or 5%
Total	20	100%

It is also possible to compute the **cumulative absolute frequency** and **cumulative relative frequency** by summing the absolute or relative frequencies starting at the lowest interval and progressing through the highest. The cumulative absolute frequencies and cumulative relative frequencies for the Intelco stock returns example are presented in Figure 2.

Figure 2: Absolute, Relative, and Cumulative Frequencies of Intelco Returns

Interval	Absolute Frequency	Relative Frequency	Cumulative Absolute Frequency	Cumulative Relative Frequency
$-30\% \leq R_t < -20\%$	1	5%	1	5%
$-20\% \leq R_t < -10\%$	2	10%	3	15%
$-10\% \leq R_t < 0\%$	3	15%	6	30%
$0\% \leq R_t < 10\%$	7	35%	13	65%
$10\% \leq R_t < 20\%$	3	15%	16	80%
$20\% \leq R_t < 30\%$	2	10%	18	90%
$30\% \leq R_t < 40\%$	1	5%	19	95%
$40\% \leq R_t \leq 50\%$	1	5%	20	100%
Total	20	100%		

Notice that the cumulative absolute frequency or cumulative relative frequency for any given interval is the sum of the absolute or relative frequencies up to and including the given interval. For example, the cumulative absolute frequency for the $(0\% \leq R_t < 10\%)$ interval is 13 = 1 + 2 + 3 + 7 and the cumulative relative frequency for this interval is 5% + 10% + 15% + 35% = 65%.

LOS 7.d: Describe the properties of a data set presented as a histogram or a frequency polygon.

CFA® Program Curriculum, Volume 1, page 335

A **histogram** is the graphical presentation of the absolute frequency distribution. A histogram is simply a bar chart of continuous data that has been classified into a frequency distribution. The attractive feature of a histogram is that it allows us to quickly see where most of the observations are concentrated.

To construct a histogram, the intervals are scaled on the horizontal axis and the absolute frequencies are scaled on the vertical axis. The histogram for the Intelco returns data in Table B from the previous example is provided in Figure 3.

Figure 3: Histogram of Intelco Stock Return Data

To construct a **frequency polygon**, the midpoint of each interval is plotted on the horizontal axis, and the absolute frequency for that interval is plotted on the vertical axis. Each point is then connected with a straight line. The frequency polygon for the returns data used in our example is illustrated in Figure 4.

Figure 4: Frequency Polygon of Intelco Stock Return Data

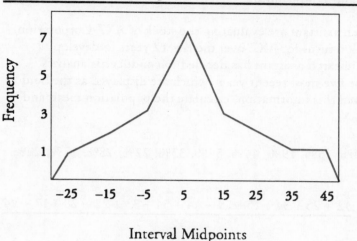

LOS 7.e: Calculate and interpret measures of central tendency, including the population mean, sample mean, arithmetic mean, weighted average or mean, geometric mean, harmonic mean, median, and mode.

CFA® Program Curriculum, Volume 1, page 339

Measures of central tendency identify the center, or average, of a data set. This central point can then be used to represent the typical, or expected, value in the data set.

To compute the **population** mean, all the observed values in the population are summed (ΣX) and divided by the number of observations in the population, N. Note that the population mean is unique in that a given population only has one mean. The population mean is expressed as:

$$\mu = \frac{\sum_{i=1}^{N} X_i}{N}$$

The **sample mean** is the sum of all the values in a sample of a population, ΣX, divided by the number of observations in the sample, n. It is used to make *inferences* about the population mean. The sample mean is expressed as:

$$\overline{X} = \frac{\sum_{i=1}^{n} X_i}{n}$$

Note the use of n, the sample size, versus N, the population size.

Example: Population mean and sample mean

Assume you and your research assistant are evaluating the stock of AXZ Corporation. You have calculated the stock returns for AXZ over the last 12 years to develop the following data set. Your research assistant has decided to conduct his analysis using only the returns for the five most recent years, which are displayed as the bold numbers in the data set. Given this information, calculate the population mean and the sample mean.

Data set: 12%, **25%**, **34%**, 15%, **19%**, 44%, **54%**, 33%, 22%, 28%, 17%, 24%

Answer:

$$\mu = \text{population mean} = \frac{12+25+34+15+19+44+54+33+22+28+17+24}{12}$$
$$= 27.25\%$$

$$\overline{X} = \text{sample mean} = \frac{25+34+19+54+17}{5} = 29.8\%$$

The population mean and sample mean are both examples of **arithmetic means**. The arithmetic mean is the sum of the observation values divided by the number of observations. It is the most widely used measure of central tendency and has the following properties:

- All interval and ratio data sets have an arithmetic mean.
- All data values are considered and included in the arithmetic mean computation.
- A data set has only one arithmetic mean (i.e., the arithmetic mean is unique).
- The sum of the deviations of each observation in the data set from the mean is always zero.

The arithmetic mean is the only measure of central tendency for which the sum of the deviations from the mean is zero. Mathematically, this property can be expressed as follows:

$$\text{sum of mean deviations} = \sum_{i=1}^{n}(X_i - \overline{X}) = 0$$

Example: Arithmetic mean and deviations from the mean

Compute the arithmetic mean for a data set described as:

Data set: [5, 9, 4, 10]

Answer:

The arithmetic mean of these numbers is:

$$\overline{X} = \frac{5+9+4+10}{4} = 7$$

The sum of the deviations from the mean (of 7) is:

$$\sum_{i=1}^{n}(X_i - \overline{X}) = (5-7)+(9-7)+(4-7)+(10-7) = -2+2-3+3 = 0$$

Unusually large or small values can have a disproportionate effect on the computed value for the arithmetic mean. The mean of 1, 2, 3, and 50 is 14 and is not a good indication of what the individual data values really are. On the positive side, the arithmetic mean uses all the information available about the observations. The arithmetic mean of a sample from a population is the best estimate of both the true mean of the sample and the value of the next observation.

The computation of a **weighted mean** recognizes that different observations may have a disproportionate influence on the mean. The weighted mean of a set of numbers is computed with the following equation:

$$\overline{X}w = \sum_{i=1}^{n} w_i X_i = (w_1 X_1 + w_2 X_2 + \ldots + w_n X_n)$$

where:

$X_1, X_2, \ldots X_n$ = observed values
$w_1, w_2, \ldots w_n$ = corresponding weights associated with each of the observations
such that $\Sigma w_i = 1$

Example: Weighted mean as a portfolio return

A portfolio consists of 50% common stocks, 40% bonds, and 10% cash. If the return on common stocks is 12%, the return on bonds is 7%, and the return on cash is 3%, what is the portfolio return?

Answer:

$$\overline{X}w = w_{stock}R_{stock} + w_{bonds}R_{bonds} + w_{cash}R_{cash}$$

$$\overline{X}w = (0.50 \times 0.12) + (0.40 \times 0.07) + (0.10 \times 0.03) = 0.091, \text{ or } 9.1\%$$

The example illustrates an extremely important investments concept: *the return for a portfolio is the weighted average of the returns of the individual assets in the portfolio.* Asset weights are market weights, the market value of each asset relative to the market value of the entire portfolio.

The **median** is the midpoint of a data set when the data is arranged in ascending or descending order. Half the observations lie above the median and half are below. To determine the median, arrange the data from the highest to the lowest value, or lowest to highest value, and find the middle observation.

The median is important because the arithmetic mean can be affected by extremely large or small values (outliers). When this occurs, the median is a better measure of central tendency than the mean because it is not affected by extreme values that may actually be the result of errors in the data.

Example: The median using an odd number of observations

What is the median return for five portfolio managers with 10-year annualized total returns record of: 30%, 15%, 25%, 21%, and 23%?

Answer:

First, arrange the returns in descending order.

30%, 25%, 23%, 21%, 15%

Then, select the observation that has an equal number of observations above and below it—the one in the middle. For the given data set, the third observation, 23%, is the median value.

Example: The median using an even number of observations

Suppose we add a sixth manager to the previous example with a return of 28%. What is the median return?

Answer:

Arranging the returns in descending order gives us:

30%, 28%, 25%, 23%, 21%, 15%

With an even number of observations, there is no single middle value. The median value in this case is the arithmetic mean of the two middle observations, 25% and 23%. Thus, the median return for the six managers is 24.0% = 0.5(25 + 23).

Consider that while we calculated the mean of 1, 2, 3, and 50 as 14, the median is 2.5. If the data were 1, 2, 3, and 4 instead, the arithmetic mean and median would both be 2.5.

The **mode** is the value that occurs most frequently in a data set. A data set may have more than one mode or even no mode. When a distribution has one value that appears most frequently, it is said to be **unimodal**. When a set of data has two or three values that occur most frequently, it is said to be **bimodal** or **trimodal**, respectively.

Example: The mode

What is the mode of the following data set?

Data set: [30%, 28%, 25%, 23%, 28%, 15%, 5%]

Answer:

The mode is 28% because it is the value appearing most frequently.

The geometric mean is often used when calculating investment returns over multiple periods or when measuring compound growth rates. The general formula for the geometric mean, G, is as follows:

$$G = \sqrt[n]{X_1 \times X_2 \times ... \times X_n} = (X_1 \times X_2 \times ... \times X_n)^{1/n}$$

Note that this equation has a solution only if the product under the radical sign is non-negative.

When calculating the geometric mean for a returns data set, it is necessary to add 1 to each value under the radical and then subtract 1 from the result. The geometric mean return (R_G) can be computed using the following equation:

$$1 + R_G = \sqrt[n]{(1 + R_1) \times (1 + R_2) \times ... \times (1 + R_n)}$$

where:
R_t = the return for period t

Example: Geometric mean return

For the last three years, the returns for Acme Corporation common stock have been −9.34%, 23.45%, and 8.92%. Compute the compound annual rate of return over the 3-year period.

Answer:

$$1 + R_G = \sqrt[3]{(-0.0934 + 1) \times (0.2345 + 1) \times (0.0892 + 1)}$$

$$1 + R_G = \sqrt[3]{0.9066 \times 1.2345 \times 1.0892} = \sqrt[3]{1.21903} = (1.21903)^{1/3} = 1.06825$$

$$R_G = 1.06825 - 1 = 6.825\%$$

Solve this type of problem with your calculator as follows:

- On the TI, enter 1.21903 [y^x] 0.33333 [=], or 1.21903 [y^x] 3 [1/x] [=]
- On the HP, enter 1.21903 [ENTER] 0.33333 [y^x], or 1.21903 [ENTER] 3 [1/x] [y^x]

Note that the 0.33333 represents the one-third power.

Professor's Note: The geometric mean is always less than or equal to the arithmetic mean, and the difference increases as the dispersion of the observations increases. The only time the arithmetic and geometric means are equal is when there is no variability in the observations (i.e., all observations are equal).

A harmonic mean is used for certain computations, such as the average cost of shares purchased over time. The harmonic mean is calculated as $\dfrac{N}{\displaystyle\sum_{i=1}^{N}\dfrac{1}{X_i}}$, where there are N values of X_i.

> **Example: Calculating average cost with the harmonic mean**
>
> An investor purchases $1,000 of stock each month, and over the last three months the prices paid per share were $8, $9, and $10. What is the average cost per share for the shares acquired?
>
> **Answer:**
>
> $$\bar{X}_H = \frac{3}{\frac{1}{8} + \frac{1}{9} + \frac{1}{10}} = \$8.926 \text{ per share}$$
>
> To check this result, calculate the total shares purchased as
> $$\frac{1,000}{8} + \frac{1,000}{9} + \frac{1,000}{10} = 336.11 \text{ shares.}$$
> The average price is $\dfrac{\$3,000}{336.11} = \$8.926$ per share.

The previous example illustrates the interpretation of the harmonic mean in its most common application. Note that the average price paid per share ($8.93) is less than the arithmetic average of the share prices, $\dfrac{8+9+10}{3} = 9$.

For values that are not all equal: harmonic mean < geometric mean < arithmetic mean. This mathematical fact is the basis for the claimed benefit of purchasing the same dollar amount of mutual fund shares each month or each week. Some refer to this practice as "dollar cost averaging."

LOS 7.f: Calculate and interpret quartiles, quintiles, deciles, and percentiles.

CFA® Program Curriculum, Volume 1, page 355

Quantile is the general term for a value at or below which a stated proportion of the data in a distribution lies. Examples of quantiles include:

- *Quartiles*—the distribution is divided into quarters.
- *Quintile*—the distribution is divided into fifths.
- *Decile*—the distribution is divided into tenths.
- *Percentile*—the distribution is divided into hundredths (percents).

Note that any quantile may be expressed as a percentile. For example, the third quartile partitions the distribution at a value such that three-fourths, or 75%, of the observations fall below that value. Thus, the third quartile is the 75th percentile.

The formula for the position of the observation at a given percentile, y, with n data points sorted in ascending order is:

$$L_y = (n+1)\frac{y}{100}$$

Quantiles and measures of central tendency are known collectively as **measures of location.**

Example: Quartiles

What is the third quartile for the following distribution of returns?

8%, 10%, 12%, 13%, 15%, 17%, 17%, 18%, 19%, 23%

Answer:

The third quartile is the point below which 75% of the observations lie. Recognizing that there are 10 observations in the data set, the third quartile can be identified as:

$$L_y = (10+1) \times \frac{75}{100} = 8.25$$

When the data is arranged in ascending order, the third quartile is one-fourth (0.25) of the way from the eighth data point (18%) to the ninth data point (19%), or 18.25%. This means that 75% of all observations lie below 18.25%.

LOS 7.g: Calculate and interpret 1) a range and a mean absolute deviation and 2) the variance and standard deviation of a population and of a sample.

CFA® Program Curriculum, Volume 1, page 361

Dispersion is defined as the *variability around the central tendency*. The common theme in finance and investments is the tradeoff between reward and variability, where the central tendency is the measure of the reward and dispersion is a measure of risk.

The **range** is a relatively simple measure of variability, but when used with other measures it provides extremely useful information. The range is the distance between the largest and the smallest value in the data set, or:

range = maximum value − minimum value

Example: The range

What is the range for the 5-year annualized total returns for five investment managers if the managers' individual returns were 30%, 12%, 25%, 20%, and 23%?

Answer:

range = 30 − 12 = 18%

The **mean absolute deviation (MAD)** is the average of the absolute values of the deviations of individual observations from the arithmetic mean.

$$MAD = \frac{\sum_{i=1}^{n} |X_i - \overline{X}|}{n}$$

The computation of the MAD uses the absolute values of each deviation from the mean because the sum of the actual deviations from the arithmetic mean is zero.

Example: MAD

What is the MAD of the investment returns for the five managers discussed in the preceding example? How is it interpreted?

Answer:

annualized returns: [30%, 12%, 25%, 20%, 23%]

$$\overline{X} = \frac{[30 + 12 + 25 + 20 + 23]}{5} = 22\%$$

$$MAD = \frac{[|30 - 22| + |12 - 22| + |25 - 22| + |20 - 22| + |23 - 22|]}{5}$$

$$MAD = \frac{[8 + 10 + 3 + 2 + 1]}{5} = 4.8\%$$

This result can be interpreted to mean that, on average, an individual return will deviate ±4.8% from the mean return of 22%.

The **population** variance is defined as the average of the squared deviations from the mean. The population variance (σ^2) uses the values for all members of a population and is calculated using the following formula:

$$\sigma^2 = \frac{\sum_{i=1}^{N}(X_i - \mu)^2}{N}$$

Example: Population variance, σ^2

Assume the 5-year annualized total returns for the five investment managers used in the earlier example represent *all* of the managers at a small investment firm. What is the population variance of returns?

Answer:

$$\mu = \frac{[30+12+25+20+23]}{5} = 22\%$$

$$\sigma^2 = \frac{\left[(30-22)^2 + (12-22)^2 + (25-22)^2 + (20-22)^2 + (23-22)^2\right]}{5} = 35.60\left(\%^2\right)$$

Interpreting this result, we can say that the average variation from the mean return is 35.60% squared. Had we done the calculation using decimals instead of whole percents, the variance would be 0.00356. What is a percent squared? Yes, this is nonsense, but let's see what we can do so that it makes more sense.

As you have just seen, a major problem with using the variance is the difficulty of interpreting it. The computed variance, unlike the mean, is in terms of squared units of measurement. How does one interpret squared percents, squared dollars, or squared yen? This problem is mitigated through the use of the *standard deviation*. The **population standard deviation**, σ, is the square root of the population variance and is calculated as follows:

$$\sigma = \sqrt{\frac{\sum_{i=1}^{N}(X-\mu)^2}{N}}$$

Example: Population standard deviation, σ

Using the data from the preceding examples, compute the population standard deviation.

Answer:

$$\sigma = \sqrt{\frac{(30-22)^2 + (12-22)^2 + (25-22)^2 + (20-22)^2 + (23-22)^2}{5}}$$

$$= \sqrt{35.60} = 5.97\%$$

Calculated with decimals instead of whole percents, we would get:

$$\sigma^2 = 0.00356 \text{ and } \sigma = \sqrt{0.00356} = 0.05966 = 5.97\%$$

Since the population standard deviation and population mean are both expressed in the same units (percent), these values are easy to relate. The outcome of this example indicates that the mean return is 22% and the standard deviation about the mean is 5.97%. Note that this is greater than the MAD of 4.8%, a result (σ > MAD) that holds in general.

The sample variance, s^2, is the measure of dispersion that applies when we are evaluating a sample of n observations from a population. The sample variance is calculated using the following formula:

$$s^2 = \frac{\sum_{i=1}^{n}(X_i - \overline{X})^2}{n-1}$$

The most noteworthy difference from the formula for population variance is that the denominator for s^2 is n − 1, one less than the sample size n, where σ^2 uses the entire population size N. Another difference is the use of the sample mean, $\overline{X}$, instead of the population mean, μ. Based on the mathematical theory behind statistical procedures, the use of the entire number of sample observations, n, instead of n − 1 as the divisor in the computation of s^2, will systematically *underestimate* the population parameter, σ^2, particularly for small sample sizes. This systematic underestimation causes the sample variance to be what is referred to as a biased estimator of the population variance. Using n − 1 instead of n in the denominator, however, improves the statistical properties of s^2 as an estimator of σ^2. Thus, s^2, as expressed in the equation above, is considered to be an unbiased estimator of σ^2.

Example: Sample variance

Assume that the 5-year annualized total returns for the five investment managers used in the preceding examples represent only a sample of the managers at a large investment firm. What is the sample variance of these returns?

Answer:

$$X = \frac{[30 + 12 + 25 + 20 + 23]}{5} = 22\%$$

$$s^2 = \frac{\left[(30-22)^2 + (12-22)^2 + (25-22)^2 + (20-22)^2 + (23-22)^2\right]}{5-1} = 44.5\left(\%^2\right)$$

Thus, the sample variance of 44.5($\%^2$) can be interpreted to be an unbiased estimator of the population variance. Note that 44.5 "percent squared" is 0.00445 and you will get this value if you put the percent returns in decimal form [e.g., $(0.30 - 0.22)^2$, etc.].

As with the population standard deviation, the **sample standard deviation** can be calculated by taking the square root of the sample variance. The sample standard **deviation**, *s,* is defined as:

$$s = \sqrt{\dfrac{\sum\limits_{i=1}^{n}(X_i - \overline{X})^2}{n-1}}$$

Example: Sample standard deviation

Compute the sample standard deviation based on the result of the preceding example.

Answer:

Since the sample variance for the preceding example was computed to be 44.5(%²), the sample standard deviation is:

$$s = [44.5(\%^2)]^{1/2} = 6.67\% \text{ or } \sqrt{0.00445} = 0.0667$$

The results shown here mean that the sample standard deviation, s = 6.67%, can be interpreted as an unbiased estimator of the population standard deviation, σ.

LOS 7.h: Calculate and interpret the proportion of observations falling within a specified number of standard deviations of the mean using Chebyshev's inequality.

CFA® Program Curriculum, Volume 1, page 371

Chebyshev's inequality states that for any set of observations, whether sample or population data and regardless of the shape of the distribution, the percentage of the observations that lie within *k* standard deviations of the mean is *at least* $1 - 1/k^2$ for all k > 1.

Example: Chebyshev's inequality

What is the minimum percentage of any distribution that will lie within ±2 standard deviations of the mean?

Answer:

Applying Chebyshev's inequality, we have:

$$1 - 1/k^2 = 1 - 1/2^2 = 1 - 1/4 = 0.75 \text{ or } 75\%$$

According to Chebyshev's inequality, the following relationships hold for any distribution. At least:

- 36% of observations lie within ±1.25 standard deviations of the mean.
- 56% of observations lie within ±1.50 standard deviations of the mean.
- 75% of observations lie within ±2 standard deviations of the mean.
- 89% of observations lie within ±3 standard deviations of the mean.
- 94% of observations lie within ±4 standard deviations of the mean.

The importance of Chebyshev's inequality is that it applies to any distribution. If we actually know the underlying distribution is normal, for example, we can be even more precise about the percentage of observations that will fall within 2 or 3 standard deviations of the mean.

LOS 7.i: Calculate and interpret the coefficient of variation and the Sharpe ratio.

CFA® Program Curriculum, Volume 1, page 372

A direct comparison between two or more measures of dispersion may be difficult. For instance, suppose you are comparing the annual returns distribution for retail stocks with a mean of 8% and an annual returns distribution for a real estate portfolio with a mean of 16%. A direct comparison between the dispersion of the two distributions is not meaningful because of the relatively large difference in their means. To make a meaningful comparison, a relative measure of dispersion must be used. **Relative dispersion** is the amount of variability in a distribution relative to a reference point or benchmark. Relative dispersion is commonly measured with the **coefficient of variation** (CV), which is computed as:

$$CV = \frac{s_x}{\overline{X}} = \frac{\text{standard deviation of x}}{\text{average value of x}}$$

CV measures the amount of dispersion in a distribution relative to the distribution's mean. It is useful because it enables us to make a direct comparison of dispersion across different sets of data. In an investments setting, the CV is used to measure the risk (variability) per unit of expected return (mean).

Example: Coefficient of variation

You have just been presented with a report that indicates that the mean monthly return on T-bills is 0.25% with a standard deviation of 0.36%, and the mean monthly return for the S&P 500 is 1.09% with a standard deviation of 7.30%. Your unit manager has asked you to compute the CV for these two investments and to interpret your results.

Answer:

$$CV_{T\text{-bills}} = \frac{0.36}{0.25} = 1.44$$

$$CV_{S\&P\,500} = \frac{7.30}{1.09} = 6.70$$

These results indicate that there is less dispersion (risk) per unit of monthly return for T-bills than there is for the S&P 500 (1.44 versus 6.70).

 Professor's Note: To remember the formula for CV, remember that the coefficient of variation is a measure of variation, so standard deviation goes in the numerator. CV is variation per unit of return.

The Sharpe Ratio

The Sharpe measure (a.k.a., the *Sharpe ratio* or *reward-to-variability ratio*) is widely used for investment performance measurement and measures *excess* return per unit of risk. The Sharpe measure appears over and over throughout the CFA® curriculum. It is defined according to the following formula:

$$\text{Sharpe ratio} = \frac{\bar{r}_p - r_f}{\sigma_p}$$

where:
$\bar{r}_p$ = portfolio return
r_f = risk-free return
σ_p = standard deviation of portfolio returns

Notice that the numerator of the Sharpe ratio uses a measure for a risk-free return. As such, the quantity $(\bar{r}_p - r_f)$, referred to as the **excess return** on Portfolio P, measures the extra reward that investors receive for exposing themselves to risk. Portfolios with large positive Sharpe ratios are preferred to portfolios with smaller ratios because it is assumed that rational investors prefer return and dislike risk.

Example: The Sharpe ratio

Assume that the mean monthly return on T-bills is 0.25% and that the mean monthly return and standard deviation for the S&P 500 are 1.30% and 7.30%, respectively. Using the T-bill return to represent the risk-free rate, as is common in practice, compute and interpret the Sharpe ratio.

Answer:

$$\text{Sharpe ratio} = \frac{1.30 - 0.25}{7.30} = 0.144$$

The Sharpe ratio of 0.144 indicates that the S&P 500 earned 0.144% of excess return per unit of risk, where risk is measured by standard deviation of portfolio returns.

Analysts should be aware of two limitations of the Sharpe ratio: (1) If two portfolios have negative Sharpe ratios, it is not necessarily true that the higher Sharpe ratio implies superior risk-adjusted performance. Increasing risk moves a negative Sharpe ratio closer to zero (i.e., higher). (2) The Sharpe ratio is useful when standard deviation is an appropriate measure of risk. However, investment strategies with option characteristics have asymmetric return distributions, reflecting a large probability of small gains coupled with a small probability of large losses. In such cases, standard deviation may underestimate risk and produce Sharpe ratios that are too high.

LOS 7.j: Explain skewness and the meaning of a positively or negatively skewed return distribution.

CFA® Program Curriculum, Volume 1, page 377

A distribution is symmetrical if it is shaped identically on both sides of its mean. Distributional symmetry implies that intervals of losses and gains will exhibit the same frequency. For example, a symmetrical distribution with a mean return of zero will have losses in the –6% to –4% interval as frequently as it will have gains in the +4% to +6% interval. The extent to which a returns distribution is symmetrical is important because the degree of symmetry tells analysts if deviations from the mean are more likely to be positive or negative.

Skewness, or skew, refers to the extent to which a distribution is not symmetrical. Nonsymmetrical distributions may be either positively or negatively skewed and result from the occurrence of outliers in the data set. Outliers are observations with extraordinarily large values, either positive or negative.

- A *positively skewed* distribution is characterized by many outliers in the upper region, or right tail. A positively skewed distribution is said to be skewed right because of its relatively long upper (right) tail.
- A *negatively skewed* distribution has a disproportionately large amount of outliers that fall within its lower (left) tail. A negatively skewed distribution is said to be skewed left because of its long lower tail.

LOS 7.k: Describe the relative locations of the mean, median, and mode for a unimodal, nonsymmetrical distribution.

CFA® Program Curriculum, Volume 1, page 380

Skewness affects the location of the mean, median, and mode of a distribution.

* For a symmetrical distribution, the mean, median, and mode are equal.
* For a positively skewed, unimodal distribution, the mode is less than the median, which is less than the mean. The mean is affected by outliers; in a positively skewed distribution, there are large, positive outliers which will tend to "pull" the mean upward, or more positive. An example of a positively skewed distribution is that of housing prices. Suppose that you live in a neighborhood with 100 homes; 99 of them sell for $100,000, and one sells for $1,000,000. The median and the mode will be $100,000, but the mean will be $109,000. Hence, the mean has been "pulled" upward (to the right) by the existence of one home (outlier) in the neighborhood.
* For a negatively skewed, unimodal distribution, the mean is less than the median, which is less than the mode. In this case, there are large, negative outliers that tend to "pull" the mean downward (to the left).

Professor's Note: The key to remembering how measures of central tendency are affected by skewed data is to recognize that skew affects the mean more than the median and mode, and the mean is "pulled" in the direction of the skew. The relative location of the mean, median, and mode for different distribution shapes is shown in Figure 5. Note the median is between the other two measures for positively or negatively skewed distributions.

Figure 5: Effect of Skewness on Mean, Median, and Mode

LOS 7.l: Explain measures of sample skewness and kurtosis.

CFA® Program Curriculum, Volume 1, page 380

Kurtosis is a measure of the degree to which a distribution is more or less "peaked" than a normal distribution. **Leptokurtic** describes a distribution that is more peaked than a normal distribution, whereas **platykurtic** refers to a distribution that is less peaked, or flatter than a normal distribution. A distribution is **mesokurtic** if it has the same kurtosis as a normal distribution.

As indicated in Figure 6, a leptokurtic return distribution will have more returns clustered around the mean and more returns with large deviations from the mean (fatter tails). Relative to a normal distribution, a leptokurtic distribution will have a greater percentage of small deviations from the mean and a greater percentage of extremely large deviations from the mean. This means that there is a relatively greater probability of an observed value being either close to the mean or far from the mean. With regard to an investment returns distribution, a greater likelihood of a large deviation from the mean return is often perceived as an increase in risk.

Figure 6: Kurtosis

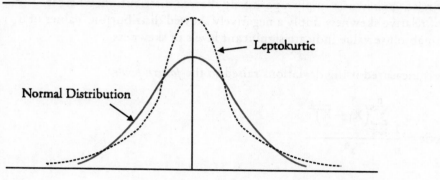

A distribution is said to exhibit **excess kurtosis** if it has either more or less kurtosis than the normal distribution. The computed kurtosis for all normal distributions is three. Statisticians, however, sometimes report excess kurtosis, which is defined as kurtosis minus three. Thus, a normal distribution has excess kurtosis equal to zero, a leptokurtic distribution has excess kurtosis greater than zero, and platykurtic distributions will have excess kurtosis less than zero.

Kurtosis is critical in a risk management setting. Most research about the distribution of securities returns has shown that returns are not normally distributed. Actual securities returns tend to exhibit both skewness and kurtosis. Skewness and kurtosis are critical concepts for risk management because when securities returns are modeled using an assumed normal distribution, the predictions from the models will not take into account the potential for extremely large, negative outcomes. In fact, most risk managers put very little emphasis on the mean and standard deviation of a distribution and focus more on the distribution of returns in the tails of the distribution—that is where the risk is. In general, greater positive kurtosis and more negative skew in returns distributions indicates increased risk.

Measures of Sample Skew and Kurtosis

Sample skewness is equal to the sum of the cubed deviations from the mean divided by the cubed standard deviation and by the number of observations. Sample skewness for large samples is computed as:

$$\text{sample skewness}(S_K) = \frac{1}{n} \frac{\sum_{i=1}^{n}(X_i - \overline{X})^3}{s^3}$$

where:
s = sample standard deviation

Note that the denominator is always positive, but that the numerator can be positive or negative, depending on whether observations above the mean or observations below the mean tend to be further from the mean on average. When a distribution is right skewed, sample skewness is positive because the deviations above the mean are larger on average. A left-skewed distribution has a negative sample skewness.

Dividing by standard deviation cubed standardizes the statistic and allows interpretation of the skewness measure. If relative skewness is equal to zero, the data is not skewed. Positive levels of relative skewness imply a positively skewed distribution, whereas negative values of relative skewness imply a negatively skewed distribution. Values of S_K in excess of 0.5 in absolute value indicate significant levels of skewness.

Sample kurtosis is measured using deviations raised to the *fourth power*.

$$\text{sample kurtosis} = \frac{1}{n} \frac{\sum_{i=1}^{n}(X_i - \bar{X})^4}{s^4}$$

where:
s = sample standard deviation

To **interpret kurtosis**, note that it is measured relative to the kurtosis of a normal distribution, which is 3. Positive values of excess kurtosis indicate a distribution that is leptokurtic (more peaked, fat tails), whereas negative values indicate a platykurtic distribution (less peaked, thin tails). Excess kurtosis values that exceed 1.0 in absolute value are considered large. We can calculate kurtosis relative to that of a normal distribution as:

excess kurtosis = sample kurtosis – 3

LOS 7.m: Explain the use of arithmetic and geometric means when analyzing investment returns.

CFA® Program Curriculum, Volume 1, page 386

Since past annual returns are compounded each period, the geometric mean of past annual returns is the appropriate measure of past performance. It gives us the average annual *compound* return. With annual returns of 5%, 12%, and 9% over three years, the geometric mean return of $[(1.05)(1.12)(1.09)]^{1/3} - 1 = 8.63\%$ tells us the single rate that, if compounded over the three periods, would lead to the same increase in wealth as the individual annual rates of return.

The arithmetic mean of (5% + 12% + 9%)/3 = 8.67% is, however, the statistically best estimator of the *next* year's returns given only the three years of return outcomes. To estimate *multi-year* returns (e.g. expected annual return over the next three years), the geometric mean of 8.63% is the appropriate measure.

Consider also a forward-looking model where returns will be either +100% or –50% each year for two years. Note that when returns are +100% in Year 1 and –50% in Year 2, the annual geometric mean return is $[(1 + 100\%)(1 - 50\%)]^{1/2} - 1 = 0\%$ and the arithmetic mean annual return is (100% – 50%)/2 = 25%.

Consider the following tree model for two years where the outcomes of +100% and −50% are equally likely and beginning wealth is $1,000:

Each of the four possible ending wealth values has a 25% probability, so the expected ending wealth is simply (4,000 + 1,000 + 1,000 + 250)/4 = $1,562.50, or 0.25(4,000) + 0.50(1,000) + 0.25(250) = $1,562.50. This is consistent with earning a compound annual rate of return equal to the arithmetic mean of 25%, $(1.25^2 − 1)\$1,000 =$ $1,562.50, but not with earning the geometric mean return of 0%. For each single year, the expected rate of return is simply the average of +100% and −50% since those outcomes are equally likely.

KEY CONCEPTS

LOS 7.a

Descriptive statistics summarize the characteristics of a data set; inferential statistics are used to make probabilistic statements about a population based on a sample.

A population includes all members of a specified group, while a sample is a subset of the population used to draw inferences about the population.

Data may be measured using different scales.
- Nominal scale—data is put into categories that have no particular order.
- Ordinal scale—data is put into categories that can be ordered with respect to some characteristic.
- Interval scale—differences in data values are meaningful, but ratios, such as twice as much or twice as large, are not meaningful.
- Ratio scale—ratios of values, such as twice as much or half as large, are meaningful, and zero represents the complete absence of the characteristic being measured.

LOS 7.b

Any measurable characteristic of a population is called a parameter.

A characteristic of a sample is given by a sample statistic.

A frequency distribution groups observations into classes, or intervals. An interval is a range of values.

LOS 7.c

Relative frequency is the percentage of total observations falling within an interval.

Cumulative relative frequency for an interval is the sum of the relative frequencies for all values less than or equal to that interval's maximum value.

LOS 7.d

A histogram is a bar chart of data that has been grouped into a frequency distribution. A frequency polygon plots the midpoint of each interval on the horizontal axis and the absolute frequency for that interval on the vertical axis, and connects the midpoints with straight lines. The advantage of histograms and frequency polygons is that we can quickly see where most of the observations lie.

LOS 7.e

The arithmetic mean is the average. $\bar{X} = \dfrac{\sum_{i=1}^{n} X_i}{n}$. Population mean and sample mean are examples of arithmetic means.

The geometric mean is used to find a compound growth rate. $G = \sqrt[n]{X_1 \times X_2 \times ... \times X_n}$.

The weighted mean weights each value according to its influence. $\bar{X}_W = \sum_{i=1}^{n} w_i X_i$.

The harmonic mean can be used to find an average purchase price, such as dollars per share for equal periodic investments.

$$\bar{X}_H = \frac{N}{\displaystyle\sum_{i=1}^{N} \frac{1}{x_i}}.$$

The median is the midpoint of a data set when the data is arranged from largest to smallest.

The mode of a data set is the value that occurs most frequently.

LOS 7.f

Quantile is the general term for a value at or below which a stated proportion of the data in a distribution lies. Examples of quantiles include:

- Quartiles—the distribution is divided into quarters.
- Quintile—the distribution is divided into fifths.
- Decile—the distribution is divided into tenths.
- Percentile—the distribution is divided into hundredths (percents).

LOS 7.g

The range is the difference between the largest and smallest values in a data set.

Mean absolute deviation (MAD) is the average of the absolute values of the deviations from the arithmetic mean:

$$MAD = \frac{\displaystyle\sum_{i=1}^{n} |X_i - \bar{X}|}{n}$$

Variance is defined as the mean of the squared deviations from the arithmetic mean or from the expected value of a distribution.

- Population variance = $\sigma^2 = \dfrac{\displaystyle\sum_{i=1}^{N}(X_i - \mu)^2}{N}$, where μ = population mean and

  N = size.

- Sample variance = $s^2 = \dfrac{\displaystyle\sum_{i=1}^{N}(X_i - \bar{X})^2}{n-1}$, where $\bar{X}$ = sample mean and

  n = sample size.

Standard deviation is the positive square root of the variance and is frequently used as a quantitative measure of risk.

LOS 7.h

Chebyshev's inequality states that the proportion of the observations within k standard deviations of the mean is at least $1 - 1/k^2$ for all k > 1. It states that for any distribution, at least:

36% of observations lie within +/– 1.25 standard deviations of the mean.

56% of observations lie within +/– 1.5 standard deviations of the mean.

75% of observations lie within +/– 2 standard deviations of the mean.

89% of observations lie within +/– 3 standard deviations of the mean.

94% of observations lie within +/– 4 standard deviations of the mean.

LOS 7.i

The coefficient of variation for sample data, $CV = \dfrac{s}{\overline{X}}$, is the ratio of the standard deviation of the sample to its mean (expected value of the underlying distribution).

The Sharpe ratio measures excess return per unit of risk:

$$\text{Sharpe ratio} \frac{\left(\overline{r}_p - r_f\right)}{\sigma_p}$$

LOS 7.j

Skewness describes the degree to which a distribution is not symmetric about its mean. A right-skewed distribution has positive skewness. A left-skewed distribution has negative skewness.

Sample skew with an absolute value greater than 0.5 is considered significantly different from zero.

LOS 7.k

For a positively skewed, unimodal distribution, the mean is greater than the median, which is greater than the mode.

For a negatively skewed, unimodal distribution, the mean is less than the median, which is less than the mode.

LOS 7.l

Kurtosis measures the peakedness of a distribution and the probability of extreme outcomes (thickness of tails).

- Excess kurtosis is measured relative to a normal distribution, which has a kurtosis of 3.
- Positive values of excess kurtosis indicate a distribution that is leptokurtic (fat tails, more peaked) so that the probability of extreme outcomes is greater than for a normal distribution.
- Negative values of excess kurtosis indicate a platykurtic distribution (thin tails, less peaked).
- Excess kurtosis with an absolute value greater than 1 is considered significant.

LOS 7.m

The arithmetic mean return is appropriate for forecasting single period returns in future periods, while the geometric mean is appropriate for forecasting future compound returns over multiple periods.

CONCEPT CHECKERS

1. The intervals in a frequency distribution should always have which of the following characteristics? The intervals should always:
    A. be truncated.
    B. be open ended.
    C. be nonoverlapping.

Use the following frequency distribution for Questions 2 through 4.

Return, R	Frequency
−10% up to 0%	3
0% up to 10%	7
10% up to 20%	3
20% up to 30%	2
30% up to 40%	1

2. The number of intervals in this frequency table is:
    A. 1.
    B. 5.
    C. 16.

3. The sample size is:
    A. 1.
    B. 5.
    C. 16.

4. The relative frequency of the second interval is:
    A. 10.0%.
    B. 16.0%.
    C. 43.8%.

Use the following data to answer Questions 5 through 13.

XYZ Corp. Annual Stock Prices

2003	2004	2005	2006	2007	2008
22%	5%	−7%	11%	2%	11%

5. What is the arithmetic mean return for XYZ stock?
    A. 7.3%.
    B. 8.0%.
    C. 11.0%.

6. What is the median return for XYZ stock?
   A. 7.3%.
   B. 8.0%.
   C. 11.0%.

7. What is the mode of the returns for XYZ stock?
   A. 7.3%.
   B. 8.0%.
   C. 11.0%.

8. What is the range for XYZ stock returns?
   A. 11.0%.
   B. 22.0%.
   C. 29.0%.

9. What is the mean absolute deviation for XYZ stock returns?
   A. 5.20%.
   B. 7.33%.
   C. 29.0%.

10. Assuming that the distribution of XYZ stock returns is a population, what is the population variance?
    A. $6.8\%^2$.
    B. $7.7\%^2$.
    C. $80.2\%^2$.

11. Assuming that the distribution of XYZ stock returns is a population, what is the population standard deviation?
    A. 5.02%.
    B. 8.96%.
    C. 46.22%.

12. Assuming that the distribution of XYZ stock returns is a sample, the sample variance is *closest* to:
    A. $5.0\%^2$.
    B. $72.4\%^2$.
    C. $96.3\%^2$.

13. Assuming that the distribution of XYZ stock returns is a sample, what is the sample standard deviation?
    A. 9.8%.
    B. 72.4%.
    C. 96.3%.

14. For a skewed distribution, what is the minimum percentage of the observations that will lie between ±2.5 standard deviations of the mean based on Chebyshev's Inequality?
    A. 56%.
    B. 75%.
    C. 84%.

Use the following data to answer Questions 15 and 16.

The annual returns for FJW's common stock over the years 2003, 2004, 2005, and 2006 were 15%, 19%, −8%, and 14%.

15.   What is the arithmetic mean return for FJW's common stock?
        A. 10.00%.
        B. 14.00%.
        C. 15.25%.

16.   What is the geometric mean return for FJW's common stock?
        A. 9.45%.
        B. 14.21%.
        C. It cannot be determined because the 2005 return is negative.

17.   A distribution of returns that has a greater percentage of small deviations from the mean and a greater percentage of extremely large deviations from the mean compared to a normal distribution:
        A. is positively skewed.
        B. has positive excess kurtosis.
        C. has negative excess kurtosis.

18.   Which of the following is *most accurate* regarding a distribution of returns that has a mean greater than its median?
        A. It is positively skewed.
        B. It is a symmetric distribution.
        C. It has positive excess kurtosis.

19.   The harmonic mean of 3, 4, and 5 is:
        A. 3.74.
        B. 3.83.
        C. 4.12.

CHALLENGE PROBLEMS

1. Year-end prices and dividends for Nopat Mutual Fund for each of six years are listed below along with the actual yield (return) on a money market fund called Emfund.

Year	Nopat Fund Year-End Price	Nopat Fund Year-End Dividend	Nopat Annual Holding Period Return	Emfund Return for the Year
2004	$28.50	$0.14		3.00%
2005	$26.80	$0.15	?	4.00%
2006	$29.60	$0.17	?	4.30%
2007	$31.40	$0.17	?	5.00%
2008	$34.50	$0.19	?	4.10%
2009	$37.25	$0.22	?	6.00%

Average risk-free rate over the five years 2005–2009 is 2.8%. Risk-free rate for 2004 is 2.8%.

A. Calculate the annual holding period returns for a beginning-of-year investment in Nopat fund for each of the five years over the period 2005–2009 (% with two decimal places).

B. What is the arithmetic mean annual total return on an investment in Nopat fund shares (dividends reinvested) over the period 2005–2009?

C. What is the average compound annual rate of return on an investment in Nopat fund made at year end 2004 if it were held (dividends reinvested) until the end of 2009?

D. What is the median annual return on an Emfund investment over the 6-year period 2004–2009?

E. What is the sample standard deviation of the annual returns on money market funds over the 6-year period, using the Emfund returns as a sample?

F. What is the holding period return on a 6-year investment in Emfund made at the beginning of 2004?

G. If an investor bought $10,000 of Nopat Fund shares at the end of the year in each of the three years 2007–2009, what is the average price paid per share? What is the arithmetic mean of the three year-end prices?

H. What would have been the 1-year holding period return on a portfolio that had $60,000 invested in Nopat Fund and $40,000 invested in Emfund as of the beginning of 2009?

I.   What is the coefficient of variation of the Nopat Fund annual total returns 2005–2009 and of the Emfund annual returns for the six years 2004–2009? Which is riskier?

J.   What is the Sharpe ratio for an investment in the Nopat Fund over the five years from 2005–2009? What is the Sharpe ratio for an investment in the Emfund over the six years 2004–2009? Which Sharpe ratio is more preferred?

K.   Calculate the range and mean absolute deviation of returns for an investment in the Emfund over the 6-year period 2004–2009.

L.   What is the annual growth rate of dividends on Nopat Fund over the period from 2004–2009?

2.   Identify the type of scale for each of the following:

A.   Cars ranked as heavy, medium, or light.

B.   Birds divided into categories of songbirds, birds of prey, scavengers, and game birds.

C.   The height of each player on a baseball team.

D.   The average temperature on 20 successive days in January in Chicago.

E.   Interest rates on T-bills each year for 60 years.

3.   Explain the difference between descriptive and inferential statistics.

4.   An analyst has estimated the following parameters for the annual returns distributions for four portfolios:

Portfolio	Mean Return E(R)	Variance of returns	Skewness	Kurtosis
Portfolio A	10%	625	1.8	0
Portfolio B	14%	900	0.0	3
Portfolio C	16%	1250	−0.85	5
Portfolio D	19%	2000	1.4	2

She has been asked to evaluate the portfolios' risk and return characteristics. Assume that a risk-free investment will earn 5%.

A.   Which portfolio would be preferred based on the Sharpe performance measure?

B.   Which portfolio would be the most preferred based on the coefficient of variation?

C.   Which portfolio(s) is/are symmetric?

D.   Which portfolio(s) has/have fatter tails than a normal distribution?

E.   Which portfolio is the riskiest based on its skewness?

F.   Which portfolio is the riskiest based on its kurtosis?

5.   Which measure of central tendency is most affected by including rare but very large positive values?

6.   A manager is responsible for managing part of an institutional portfolio to mimic the returns on the S&P 500 stock index. He is evaluated based on his ability to exactly match the returns on the index. His portfolio holds 200 stocks but has exactly the same dividend yield as the S&P 500 portfolio. Which of the statistical measures from this review would be an appropriate measure of his performance and how would you use it?

7.   Below are the returns on 20 industry groups of stocks over the past year:

12%, –3%, 18%, 9%, –5%, 21%, 2%, 13%, 28%, –14%,

31%, 32%, 5%, 22%,   28%, 7%, 9%, 12%,   17%, 6%

A.   What is the return on the industry group with the lowest rate of return in the top quartile?

B.   What is the 40th percentile of this array of data?

C.   What is the range of the data?

D.   Based on a frequency distribution with 12 intervals, what is the relative frequency and cumulative relative frequency of the 10th interval (ascending order)?

ANSWERS – CONCEPT CHECKERS

1. **C** Intervals within a frequency distribution should always be nonoverlapping and closed ended so that each data value can be placed into only one interval. Intervals have no set width and should be set at a width so that data is adequately summarized without losing valuable characteristics.

2. **B** An interval is the set of return values that an observation falls within. Simply count the return intervals on the table—there are five of them.

3. **C** The sample size is the sum of all of the frequencies in the distribution, or $3 + 7 + 3 + 2 + 1 = 16$.

4. **C** The relative frequency is found by dividing the frequency of the interval by the total number of frequencies.

   $$\frac{7}{16} = 43.8\%$$

5. **A** $[22\% + 5\% + -7\% + 11\% + 2\% + 11\%] / 6 = 7.3\%$

6. **B** To find the median, rank the returns in order and take the middle value: -7%, 2%, 5%, 11%, 11%, 22%. In this case, because there is an even number of observations, the median is the average of the two middle values, or $(5\% + 11\%) / 2 = 8.0\%$.

7. **C** The mode is the value that appears most often, or 11%.

8. **C** The range is calculated by taking the highest value minus the lowest value.

   $22\% - (-7\%) = 29.0\%$

9. **B** The mean absolute deviation is found by taking the mean of the absolute values of the deviations from the mean.

   $(|22 - 7.3| + |5 - 7.3| + |-7 - 7.3| + |11 - 7.3| + |2 - 7.3| + |11 - 7.3|) / 6 = 7.33\%$

10. **C** The population variance, σ^2, is found by taking the mean of all squared deviations from the mean.

    $\sigma^2 = [(22 - 7.3)^2 + (5 - 7.3)^2 + (-7 - 7.3)^2 + (11 - 7.3)^2 + (2 - 7.3)^2 + (11 - 7.3)^2] / 6$
    $= 80.2\%^2$

11. **B** The population standard deviation, σ, is found by taking the square root of the population variance.

    $\sigma = \{[(22 - 7.3)^2 + (5 - 7.3)^2 + (-7 - 7.3)^2 + (11 - 7.3)^2 + (2 - 7.3)^2 + (11 - 7.3)^2] / 6\}^{1/2}$
    $= (80.2\%^2)^{0.5}$
    $= 8.96\%$

12. **C** The sample variance, s^2, uses $n - 1$ in the denominator.

    $s^2 = [(22 - 7.3)^2 + (5 - 7.3)^2 + (-7 - 7.3)^2 + (11 - 7.3)^2 + (2 - 7.3)^2 + (11 - 7.3)^2] / (6 - 1) = 96.3\%^2$

13. **A**   The sample standard deviation, s, is the square root of the sample variance.

$s = \{[(22 - 7.3)^2 + (5 - 7.3)^2 + (-7 - 7.3)^2 + (11 - 7.3)^2 + (2 - 7.3)^2 + (11 - 7.3)^2] / (6 - 1)\}^{0.5} = (96.3)^{0.5} = 9.8\%$

14. **C**   Applying Chebyshev's inequality, $1 - [1 / (2.5)^2] = 0.84$, or 84%.

15. **A** $(15\% + 19\% + (-8\%) + 14\%) / 4 = 10\%$

16. **A** $(1.15 \times 1.19 \times 0.92 \times 1.14)^{0.25} - 1 = 9.45\%$

 Professor's Note: This question could have been answered very quickly since the geometric mean must be less than the arithmetic mean computed in the preceding problem.

17. **B**   A distribution that has a greater percentage of small deviations from the mean and a greater percentage of extremely large deviations from the mean will be leptokurtic and will exhibit excess kurtosis (positive). The distribution will be more peaked and have fatter tails than a normal distribution.

18. **A**   A distribution with a mean greater than its median is positively skewed, or skewed to the right. The skew "pulls" the mean. *Note: Kurtosis deals with the overall shape of a distribution and not its skewness.*

19. **B** $\bar{X}_H = \dfrac{3}{\frac{1}{3} + \frac{1}{4} + \frac{1}{5}} = 3.83$

ANSWERS – CHALLENGE PROBLEMS

1. **A.**   The annual holding period returns (total returns) are given in the table and are each calculated as (year-end price + year-end dividend)/previous year-end price – 1.

Year	Nopat Fund Year-End Price	Nopat Fund Year-End Dividend	Nopat Annual Holding Period Return	Emfund Return for the Year
2004	$28.50	$0.14		3.00%
2005	$26.80	$0.15	–5.44%	4.00%
2006	$29.60	$0.17	11.08%	4.30%
2007	**$31.40**	**$0.17**	6.66%	5.00%
2008	$34.50	$0.19	10.48%	4.10%
2009	$37.25	$0.22	8.61%	6.00%

  B.   The arithmetic mean of the holding period returns is 6.28%.

  C. $((1 - 0.0544)(1.1108)(1.0666)(1.1048)(1.0861))^{1/5} - 1 = 6.10\%$

  D.   Median = (4.3 + 4.1) / 2 = 4.2%.

E.   Sample standard deviation of Emfund returns over the six years is:

$$\{[(3 - 4.4)^2 + (4 - 4.4)^2 + (4.3 - 4.4)^2 + (5 - 4.4)^2 + (4.1 - 4.4)^2 + (6 - 4.4)^2] / 5\}^{1/2}$$

$$= \left(\frac{5.14}{5}\right)^{1/2} = 1.01\%$$

F. $(1.03)(1.04)(1.043)(1.05)(1.041)(1.06) - 1 = 29.45\%$.
The HPR is the percentage difference between the ending value and the beginning value. Starting with a value of $1, the ending value is $1(1.03)(1.04)(1.043)(1.05)(1.041) (1.06) = $1.2945, or 29.45% greater than the beginning value.

G.   The harmonic mean is $3/(1/31.4 + 1/34.5 + 1/37.25) = $34.22 average purchase price per share. Arithmetic mean price $= (31.4 + 34.5 + 37.25)/ 3 = $34.38.

H.   The portfolio return is a weighted average, $0.6 \times 8.61\% + 0.4 \times 6\% = 7.57\%$.

I.   CV for Nopat $= 6.77/6.28 = 1.08$. CV for Emfund $= 1.01/4.4 = 0.23$. Emfund is less risky by this measure.

J.   Sharpe ratio for Nopat is $(6.28 - 2.8)/ 6.77 = 0.51$. Sharpe measure for Emfund is $(4.4 - 2.8) / 1.01 = 1.58$. The Emfund is preferred using this criterion because it has higher excess returns per unit of risk.

K.   Range is $6\% - 3\% = 3\%$. MAD is $0.73\% = [(4.4\% - 3\%) - (4.4\% - 4\%) + (4.4\% - 4.3\%) + (5\% - 4.4\%) - (4.4\% - 4.1\%) + (6\% - 4.4\%)] / 6$. Remember to use absolute values; we show all differences as positive to reflect that.

L.   Average annual growth rate of dividends is the geometric mean rate of growth: $(0.22/0.14)^{1/5} - 1 = 9.46\%$.

2.   A.   An ordinal scale.

B.   A nominal scale.

C.   A ratio scale.

D.   An interval scale.

E.   A ratio scale.

3.   Descriptive statistics are used to summarize the important characteristics of large data sets to consolidate a mass of numerical data into useful information. Inferential statistics refers to using statistics to make forecasts, estimates, or judgments about a large set of data on the basis of the statistical characteristics of a smaller set (a sample).

4.   A.   Portfolio D has the highest Sharpe ratio, $\dfrac{19-5}{\sqrt{2000}} = 0.313$ and is therefore the most preferred.

B.   Portfolio B has the lowest coefficient of variation, $\dfrac{\sqrt{900}}{14} = 2.1429$ and is therefore the most preferred.

C.   Portfolio B has no skew and is therefore a symmetric distribution (about its mean of 14%).

D. The kurtosis of a normal distribution is 3, so only portfolio C has positive excess kurtosis, indicating fatter tails (and more peakedness) relative to a normal distribution.

E. Negative skew indicates that returns below the mean are more extreme, so we would consider Portfolio C to be the most risky based on skew alone.

F. Larger kurtosis indicates greater likelihood of extreme outcomes and from a risk-management standpoint this indicates greater risk. Portfolio C has the greatest kurtosis.

5. The mean is most affected by large outliers in a distribution, compared to the median and mode, which may be unaffected.

6. Since the goal is to match the index returns, we must focus on the differences between the returns on the manager's portfolio and those on the index he is attempting to mimic. These differences are referred to as "tracking error." The standard deviation or variance of the differences between his portfolio returns and the returns of the index over a number of periods would be a suitable measure of his performance. If you said mean absolute deviation, that is defensible as well as it is certainly one way to measure tracking error. It is, however, not the measure of tracking error we see used in practice.

7. A. With 20 datapoints, the top quartile ($\frac{1}{4}$) is the top 5. Count down from the greatest value to find the 5th from the top is 21%.

B. The location of the 40th percentile is $(20 + 1)(40/100) = 8.4$. The 8th and 9th lowest returns are 6% and 7%, so the 40th percentile is $6 + 0.4(7 - 6) = 6.4\%$.

C. The range of the data is $32 - (-28) = 60$.

D. Divide the range by 12 to get 5. The 10th interval from the bottom is the 3rd from the top. The top three intervals are $27 < x < 32$, $22 < x < 27$, and $17 < x < 22$. There are only two observations in the 10th interval, 18% and 21%. The relative frequency is $2/20 = 10\%$. Since there are four observations $\geq 22\%$, the cumulative relative frequency of the 10th interval is $(20 - 4)/20 = 80\%$.

The following is a review of the Quantitative Methods: Basic Concepts principles designed to address the learning outcome statements set forth by CFA Institute. This topic is also covered in:

PROBABILITY CONCEPTS

EXAM FOCUS

This topic review covers important terms and concepts associated with probability theory. Random variables, events, outcomes, conditional probability, and joint probability are described. Probability rules such as the addition rule and multiplication rule are introduced. These rules are frequently used by finance practitioners. Expected value, standard deviation, covariance, and correlation for individual asset and portfolio returns are discussed. A well-prepared candidate will be able to calculate and interpret these widely used measures. This review also discusses counting rules, which lay the foundation for the binomial probability distribution that is covered in the next topic review.

LOS 8.a: Define a random variable, an outcome, an event, mutually exclusive events, and exhaustive events.

CFA® Program Curriculum, Volume 1, page 412

- A **random variable** is an uncertain quantity/number.
- An **outcome** is an observed value of a random variable.
- An **event** is a single outcome or a set of outcomes.
- **Mutually exclusive events** are events that cannot both happen at the same time.
- **Exhaustive events** are those that include all possible outcomes.

Consider rolling a 6-sided die. The number that comes up is a *random variable*. If you roll a 4, that is an *outcome*. Rolling a 4 is an *event*, and rolling an even number is an *event*. Rolling a 4 and rolling a 6 are *mutually exclusive events*. Rolling an even number and rolling an odd number is a set of mutually exclusive and *exhaustive events*.

LOS 8.b: State the two defining properties of probability and distinguish among empirical, subjective, and a priori probabilities.

CFA® Program Curriculum, Volume 1, page 413

There are **two defining properties of probability.**

- The probability of occurrence of any event (E_i) is between 0 and 1 (i.e., $0 \leq P(E_i) \leq 1$).
- If a set of events, $E_1, E_2, \ldots E_n$, is mutually exclusive and exhaustive, the probabilities of those events sum to 1 (i.e., $\Sigma P(E_i) - 1$).

The first of the defining properties introduces the term $P(E_i)$, which is shorthand for the "probability of event *i*." If $P(E_i) - 0$, the event will never happen. If $P(E_i) - 1$, the event is certain to occur, and the outcome is not random.

The probability of rolling any one of the numbers 1–6 with a fair die is 1/6 = 0.1667 = 16.7%. The set of events—rolling a number equal to 1, 2, 3, 4, 5, or 6—is exhaustive, and the individual events are mutually exclusive, so the probability of this set of events is equal to 1. We are certain that one of the values in this set of events will occur.

An **empirical probability** is established by analyzing past data. An **a priori probability** is determined using a formal reasoning and inspection process. A **subjective probability** is the least formal method of developing probabilities and involves the use of personal judgment. An analyst may know many things about a firm's performance and have expectations about the overall market that are all used to arrive at a subjective probability, such as, "I believe there is a 70% probability that Acme Foods will outperform the market this year." Empirical and a priori probabilities, by contrast, are **objective probabilities**.

LOS 8.c: State the probability of an event in terms of odds for and against the event.

CFA® Program Curriculum, Volume 1, page 414

Stating the **odds** that an event will or will not occur is an alternative way of expressing probabilities. Consider an event that has a probability of occurrence of 0.125, which is one-eighth. The *odds* that the event will occur are $\frac{0.125}{(1-0.125)} = \frac{1/8}{7/8} = \frac{1}{7}$, which we state as, "the odds for the event occurring are one-to-seven." The *odds against* the event occurring are the reciprocal of 1/7, which is seven-to-one.

We can also get the probability of an event from the odds by reversing these calculations. If we know that the odds for an event are one-to-six, we can compute the probability of occurrence as $\frac{1}{1+6} = \frac{1}{7} = 0.1429 = 14.29\%$. Alternatively, the probability that the event will not occur is $\frac{6}{1+6} = \frac{6}{7} = 0.8571 = 85.71\%$.

> *Professor's Note: While I am quite familiar with the use of odds rather than probabilities at the horse track, I can't remember encountering odds for a stock or bond. The use of odds at the horse track lets you know how much you will win per $1 bet on a horse (less the track's percentage). If you bet on a 15-1 long shot and the horse wins, you will receive $15 and your $1 bet will be returned, so the profit is $15. Of course, if the horse loses, you would lose the $1 you bet and the "profit" is --$1.*
>
> *One last point is that the expected return on the bet is zero, based on the probability of winning expressed in the odds. The probability of the horse winning when the odds are 15-to-1 is $\frac{1}{15+1} = \frac{1}{16}$ and the probability of the horse losing is 15/16. The expected profit is $\frac{1}{16} \times \$15 + \frac{15}{16} \times (-\$1) = 0$.*

LOS 8.d: Distinguish between unconditional and conditional probabilities.

CFA® Program Curriculum, Volume 1, page 416

- Unconditional probability (a.k.a. *marginal probability*) refers to the probability of an event regardless of the past or future occurrence of other events. If we are concerned with the probability of an economic recession, regardless of the occurrence of changes in interest rates or inflation, we are concerned with the unconditional probability of a recession.
- A conditional probability is one where the occurrence of one event affects the probability of the occurrence of another event. For example, we might be concerned with the probability of a recession *given* that the monetary authority increases interest rates. This is a conditional probability. The key word to watch for here is "given." Using probability notation, "the probability of A *given* the occurrence of B" is expressed as $P(A \mid B)$, where the vertical bar (|) indicates "given," or "conditional upon." For our interest rate example above, the probability of a recession *given* an increase in interest rates is expressed as P(*recession | increase in interest rates*). A conditional **probability** of an occurrence is also called its **likelihood**.

LOS 8.e: Explain the multiplication, addition, and total probability rules.

CFA® Program Curriculum, Volume 1, page 417

The multiplication rule of probability is used to determine the joint probability of two events:

$$P(AB) = P(A \mid B) \times P(B)$$

The addition rule of probability is used to determine the probability that at least one of two events will occur:

$$P(A \text{ or } B) = P(A) + P(B) - P(AB)$$

The total probability rule is used to determine the unconditional probability of an event, given conditional probabilities:

$$P(A) = P(A \mid B_1)P(B_1) + P(A \mid B_2)P(B_2) + \ldots + P(A \mid B_N)P(B_N)$$

where $B_1, B_2, \ldots B_N$ is a mutually exclusive and exhaustive set of outcomes.

Professor's Note: Applications of all three probability rules are illustrated in subsequent LOS within this topic review.

LOS 8.f: Calculate and interpret 1) the joint probability of two events, 2) the probability that at least one of two events will occur, given the probability of each and the joint probability of the two events, and 3) a joint probability of any number of independent events.

CFA® Program Curriculum, Volume 1, page 417

The **joint probability** of two events is the probability that they will both occur. We can calculate this from the conditional probability that A will occur given B occurs (a conditional probability) and the probability that B will occur (the unconditional probability of B). This calculation is sometimes referred to as the *multiplication rule of probability*. Using the notation for conditional and unconditional probabilities we can express this rule as:

$$P(AB) = P(A \mid B) \times P(B)$$

This expression is read as follows: "The joint probability of A and B, $P(AB)$, is equal to the conditional probability of A *given* B, $P(A \mid B)$, times the unconditional probability of B, $P(B)$."

This relationship can be rearranged to define the conditional probability of A given B as follows:

$$P(A \mid B) = \frac{P(AB)}{P(B)}$$

Example: Multiplication rule of probability

Consider the following information:

- $P(I) = 0.4$, the probability of the monetary authority increasing interest rates (I) is 40%.
- $P(R \mid I) = 0.7$, the probability of a recession (R) given an increase in interest rates is 70%.

What is $P(RI)$, the joint probability of a recession *and* an increase in interest rates?

Answer:

Applying the multiplication rule, we get the following result:

$$P(RI) = P(R \mid I) \times P(I)$$

$$P(RI) = 0.7 \times 0.4$$

$$P(RI) = 0.28$$

Don't let the cumbersome notation obscure the simple logic of this result. If an interest rate increase will occur 40% of the time and lead to a recession 70% of the time when it occurs, the joint probability of an interest rate increase and a resulting recession is $(0.4)(0.7) = (0.28) = 28\%$.

Calculating the Probability That at Least One of Two Events Will Occur

The *addition rule* for probabilities is used to determine the probability that at least one of two events will occur. For example, given two events, A and B, the addition rule can be used to determine the probability that either A or B will occur. If the events are *not* mutually exclusive, double counting must be avoided by subtracting the joint probability that *both* A and B will occur from the sum of the unconditional probabilities. This is reflected in the following general expression for the addition rule:

$$P(A \text{ or } B) = P(A) + P(B) - P(AB)$$

For mutually exclusive events, where the joint probability, $P(AB)$, is zero, the probability that either A or B will occur is simply the sum of the unconditional probabilities for each event, $P(A \text{ or } B) = P(A) + P(B)$.

Figure 1 illustrates the addition rule with a Venn Diagram and highlights why the joint probability must be subtracted from the sum of the unconditional probabilities. Note that if the events are *mutually exclusive* the sets do not intersect, $P(AB) = 0$, and the probability that one of the two events will occur is simply $P(A) + P(B)$.

Figure 1: Venn Diagram for Events That Are Not Mutually Exclusive

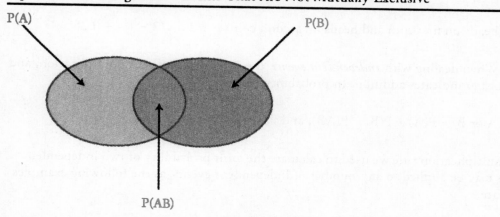

P(A)   P(B)

P(AB)

> **Example: Addition rule of probability**
>
> Using the information in our previous interest rate and recession example and the fact that the unconditional probability of a recession, $P(R)$, is 34%, determine the probability that either interest rates will increase *or* a recession will occur.

Answer:

Given that P(R) – 0.34, P(I) – 0.40, and P(RI) – 0.28, we can compute P(R or I) as follows:

P(R or I) = P(R) ɪ P(I)   P(RI)

P(R or I) = 0.34 ɪ 0.40 – 0.28

P(R or I) = 0.46

Calculating a Joint Probability of any Number of Independent Events

On the roll of two dice, the joint probability of getting two 4s is calculated as:

P(4 on first die and 4 on second die) = P(4 on first die) × P(4 on second die)
– 1/6 × 1/6 – 1/36 – 0.0278

On the flip of two coins, the probability of getting two heads is:

P(heads on first coin and heads on second coin) – 1/2 × 1/2 – 1/4 – 0.25

Hint: When dealing with *independent events*, the word *and* indicates multiplication, and the word *or* indicates addition. In probability notation:

P(A or B) = P(A) + P(B)   P(AB), and P(A **and** B) = P(A) × P(B)

The multiplication rule we used to calculate the joint probability of two independent events may be applied to any number of independent events, as the following examples illustrate.

Example: Joint probability for more than two independent events (1)

What is the probability of rolling three 4s in one simultaneous toss of three dice?

Answer:

Since the probability of rolling a 4 for each die is 1/6, the probability of rolling three 4s is:

P(three 4s on the roll of three dice) = 1/6 × 1/6 × 1/6 = 1/216 = 0.00463

Similarly:

P(four heads on the flip of four coins) =1/2 × 1/2 × 1/2 × 1/2 = 1/16 = 0.0625

Example: Joint probability for more than two independent events (2)

Using empirical probabilities, suppose we observe that the DJIA has closed higher on two-thirds of all days in the past few decades. Furthermore, it has been determined that up and down days are independent. Based on this information, compute the probability of the DJIA closing higher for five consecutive days.

Answer:

P(DJIA up five days in a row) - $2/3 \times 2/3 \times 2/3 \times 2/3 \times 2/3 - (2/3)^5 - 0.132$

Similarly:

P(DJIA down five days in a row) = $1/3 \times 1/3 \times 1/3 \times 1/3 \times 1/3 = (1/3)^5 = 0.004$

LOS 8.g: Distinguish between dependent and independent events.

CFA® Program Curriculum, Volume 1, page 420

Independent events refer to events for which the occurrence of one has no influence on the occurrence of the others. The definition of independent events can be expressed in terms of conditional probabilities. Events A and B are independent if and only if:

$P(A \mid B) - P(A)$, or equivalently, $P(B \mid A) - P(B)$

If this condition is not satisfied, the events are dependent events (i.e., the occurrence of one is dependent on the occurrence of the other).

In our interest rate and recession example, recall that events I and R are not independent; the occurrence of I affects the probability of the occurrence of R. In this example, the independence conditions for I and R are violated because:

$P(R) - 0.34$, but $P(R \mid I) - 0.7$; the probability of a recession is greater when there is an increase in interest rates.

The best examples of independent events are found with the a priori probabilities of dice tosses or coin flips. A die has "no memory." Therefore, the event of rolling a 4 on the second toss is independent of rolling a 4 on the first toss. This idea may be expressed as:

P(4 on second toss | 4 on first toss) = P(4 on second toss) = $1/6$ or 0.167

The idea of independent events also applies to flips of a coin:

P(heads on first coin   heads on second coin) - P(heads on first coin) - $1/2$ or 0.50

LOS 8.h: Calculate and interpret an unconditional probability using the total probability rule.

CFA® Program Curriculum, Volume 1, page 423

The *total probability rule* highlights the relationship between unconditional and conditional probabilities of mutually exclusive and exhaustive events. It is used to explain the unconditional probability of an event in terms of probabilities that are conditional upon other events.

In general, the unconditional probability of event R, $P(R) = P(R \mid S_1) \times P(S_1) + P(R \mid S_2) \times P(S_2) + \ldots + P(R \mid S_N) \times P(S_N)$, where the set of events $\{S_1, S_2, \ldots S_N\}$ is mutually exclusive and exhaustive.

Example: An investment application of unconditional probability

Building upon our ongoing example about interest rates and economic recession, we can assume that a recession can only occur with either of the two events   interest rates increase (I) or interest rates do not increase (I^C)—since these events are mutually exclusive and exhaustive. I^C is read "the complement of I," which means "not I." Therefore, the probability of I^C is $1 - P(I)$. It is logical, therefore, that the sum of the two joint probabilities must be the unconditional probability of a recession. This can be expressed as follows:

$$P(R) = P(RI) + P(RI^C)$$

Applying the multiplication rule, we may restate this expression as:

$$P(R) = P(R \mid I) \times P(I) + P(R \mid I^C) \times P(I^C)$$

Assume that $P(R \mid I) = 0.70$, $P(R \mid I^C)$, the probability of recession if interest rates do not rise, is 10% and that $P(I) = 0.40$ so that $P(I^C) = 0.60$. The unconditional probability of a recession can be calculated as follows:

$$
\begin{aligned}
P(R) &= P(R \mid I) \times P(I) + P(R \mid I^C) \times P(I^C) \\
&= (0.70)(0.40) + (0.10)(0.60) \\
&= 0.28 + 0.06 = 0.34
\end{aligned}
$$

In Figure 2 we illustrate the relation between conditional and unconditional probability.

Figure 2: Unconditional, Conditional, and Joint Probabilities

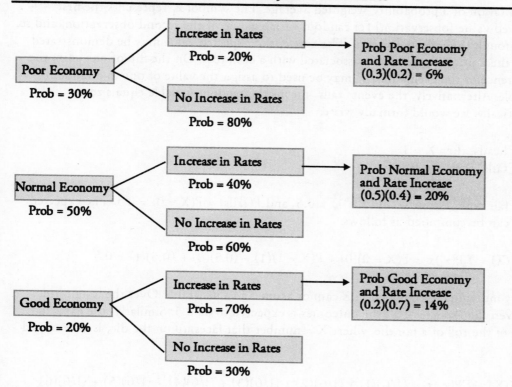

The probabilities for a poor, normal, and good economy are unconditional probabilities. The probabilities of rate increases are conditional probabilities [e.g., Prob (increase in rates | poor economy) = 20%]. The third column has joint probabilities [e.g., Prob (poor economy *and* increase in rates) – 6%]. The unconditional probability of a rate increase is the sum of the joint probabilities, 6% + 20% + 14% = 40% = Prob (increase in rates).

EXPECTED VALUE

Now that we have developed some probability concepts and tools for working with probabilities, we can apply this knowledge to determine the average value for a random variable that results from multiple experiments. This average is called an expected value.

In any given experiment, the observed value for a random variable may not equal its expected value, and even if it does, the outcome from one observation to the next will be different. The degree of dispersion of outcomes around the expected value of a random variable is measured using the variance and standard deviation. When pairs of random variables are being observed, the covariance and correlation are used to measure the extent of the relationship between the observed values for the two variables from one observation to the next.

The expected value is the weighted average of the possible outcomes of a random variable, where the weights are the probabilities that the outcomes will occur. The mathematical representation for the expected value of random variable X is:

$$E(X) = \Sigma P(x_i)x_i = P(x_1)x_1 + P(x_2)x_2 + \ldots + P(x_n)x_n$$

Here, E is referred to as the expectations operator and is used to indicate the computation of a probability-weighted average. The symbol x_1 represents the first observed value (observation) for random variable X, x_2 is the second observation, and so on, through the nth observation. The concept of expected value may be demonstrated using the a priori probabilities associated with a coin toss. On the flip of one coin, the occurrence of the event "heads" may be used to assign the value of one to a random variable. Alternatively, the event "tails" means the random variable equals zero. Statistically, we would formally write:

if heads, then $X = 1$
if tails, then $X = 0$

For a fair coin, $P(\text{heads}) = P(X = 1) = 0.5$, and $P(\text{tails}) = P(X = 0) = 0.5$. The expected value can be computed as follows:

$$E(X) = \Sigma P(x_i)x_i = P(X = 0)(0) + P(X = 1)(1) = (0.5)(0) + (0.5)(1) = 0.5$$

In any individual flip of a coin, X cannot assume a value of 0.5. Over the long term, however, the average of all the outcomes is expected to be 0.5. Similarly, the expected value of the roll of a fair die, where X = number that faces up on the die, is determined to be:

$$E(X) = \Sigma P(x_i)x_i = (1/6)(1) + (1/6)(2) + (1/6)(3) + (1/6)(4) + (1/6)(5) + (1/6)(6)$$
$$E(X) = 3.5$$

We can never roll a 3.5 on a die, but over the long term, 3.5 should be the average value of all outcomes.

The expected value is, statistically speaking, our "best guess" of the outcome of a random variable. While a 3.5 will never appear when a die is rolled, the average amount by which our guess differs from the actual outcomes is minimized when we use the expected value calculated this way.

Professor's Note: When we had historical data in an earlier topic review, we calculated the mean or simple arithmetic average and used deviations from the mean to calculate the variance and standard deviation. The calculations given here for the expected value (or weighted mean) are based on probability models, whereas our earlier calculations were based on samples or populations of outcomes. Note that when the probabilities are equal, the simple mean is the expected value. For the roll of a die, all six outcomes are equally likely, so

$$\frac{1+2+3+4+5+6}{6} = 3.5 \text{ gives us the same expected value as the probability}$$

model. However, with a probability model, the probabilities of the possible outcomes need not be equal, and the simple mean is not necessarily the expected outcome, as the following example illustrates.

Example: Expected earnings per share

The probability distribution of EPS for Ron's Stores is given in the figure below. Calculate the expected earnings per share.

EPS Probability Distribution

Probability	Earnings Per Share
10%	£1.80
20%	£1.60
40%	£1.20
30%	£1.00
100%	

Answer:

The expected EPS is simply a weighted average of each possible EPS, where the weights are the probabilities of each possible outcome.

$$E[EPS] = 0.10(1.80) + 0.20(1.60) + 0.40(1.20) + 0.30(1.00) = £1.28$$

Once we have expected EPS we can use that to calculate the variance of EPS from the probability model in the previous example. The variance is calculated as the probability-weighted sum of the squared differences between each possible outcome and expected EPS.

Example: Calculating variance from a probability model

Calculate the variance and standard deviation of EPS for Ron's Stores using the probability distribution of EPS from the table in the previous example.

Answer:

Variance of EPS for Ron's Stores is:

$$\sigma^2_{EPS} = 0.10\,(1.80 - 1.28)^2 + 0.20\,(1.60 - 1.28)^2 + 0.40\,(1.20 - 1.28)^2$$
$$+ 0.30\,(1.00 - 1.28)^2 = 0.0736$$

The standard deviation of EPS for Ron's Stores is:

$$\sigma_{EPS} = (0.0736)^{1/2} = 0.27$$

Note that the units of standard deviation are the same as that of EPS, so we would say that the standard deviation of EPS for Ron's Stores is £0.27.

LOS 8.i: Explain the use of conditional expectation in investment applications.

CFA® Program Curriculum, Volume 1, page 427

Expected values or returns can be calculated using conditional probabilities. As the name implies, *conditional expected values* are contingent upon the outcome of some other event. An analyst would use a conditional expected value to revise his expectations when new information arrives.

Consider the effect of a tariff on steel imports on the returns of a domestic steel stock. The stock's expected return, given that the government imposes the tariff, will be higher than the expected return if the tariff is not imposed.

Using the total probability rule. we can estimate the (unconditional) expected return on the stock as the sum of the expected return given no tariff times the probability a tariff will not be enacted plus the expected return given a tariff times the probability a tariff will be enacted.

LOS 8.j: Explain the use of a tree diagram to represent an investment problem.

CFA® Program Curriculum, Volume 1, page 428

You might well wonder where the returns and probabilities used in calculating expected values come from. A general framework called a **tree diagram** is used to show the probabilities of various outcomes. In Figure 3. we have shown estimates of EPS for four different outcomes: (1) a good economy and relatively good results at the company, (2) a good economy and relatively poor results at the company, (3) a poor economy and relatively good results at the company, and (4) a poor economy and relatively poor results at the company. Using the rules of probability. we can calculate the probabilities of each of the four EPS outcomes shown in the boxes on the right-hand side of the "tree."

Figure 3: A Tree Diagram

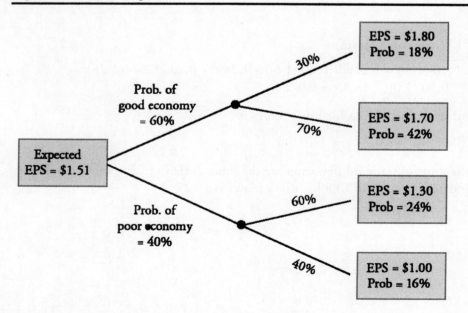

The expected EPS of $1.51 is simply calculated as:

$$0.18 \times 1.80 + 0.42 \times 1.70 + 0.24 \times 1.30 + 0.16 \times 1.00 = \$1.51$$

Note that the probabilities of the four possible outcomes sum to 1.

LOS 8.k: Calculate and interpret covariance and correlation.

CFA® Program Curriculum, Volume 1, page 434

The variance and standard deviation measure the dispersion, or volatility, of only one variable. In many finance situations, however, we are interested in how two random variables move in relation to each other. For investment applications, one of the most frequently analyzed pairs of random variables is the returns of two assets. Investors and managers frequently ask questions such as, "what is the relationship between the return for Stock A and Stock B?" or, "what is the relationship between the performance of the S&P 500 and that of the automotive industry?"

Covariance is a measure of how two assets move together. It is the expected value of the product of the deviations of the two random variables from their respective expected values. A common symbol for the covariance between random variables X and Y is $Cov(X,Y)$. Since we will be mostly concerned with the covariance of asset returns, the following formula has been written in terms of the covariance of the return of asset i, R_i, and the return of asset j, R_j:

$$Cov(R_i,R_j) = E\{[R_i - E(R_i)][R_j - E(R_j)]\}$$

The following are *properties of the covariance*:

- The covariance is a general representation of the same concept as the variance. That is, the variance measures how a random variable moves with itself, and the covariance measures how one random variable moves with another random variable.
- The covariance of R_A with itself is equal to the variance of R_A; that is, $Cov(R_A,R_A) = Var(R_A)$.
- The covariance may range from negative infinity to positive infinity.

To aid in the interpretation of covariance, consider the returns of a stock and of a put option on the stock. These two returns will have a negative covariance because they move in opposite directions. The returns of two automotive stocks would likely have a positive covariance, and the returns of a stock and a riskless asset would have a zero covariance because the riskless asset's returns never move, regardless of movements in the stock's return. While the formula for covariance given above is correct, the method of computing the covariance of returns from a joint probability model uses a probability-weighted average of the products of the random variable's deviations from their means for each possible outcome. The following example illustrates this calculation.

Example: Covariance

Assume that the economy can be in three possible states (S) next year: boom, normal, or slow economic growth. An expert source has calculated that P(boom) = 0.30, P(normal) – 0.50, and P(slow) – 0.20. The returns for Stock A, R_A, and Stock B, R_B, under each of the economic states are provided in the probability model below. What is the covariance of the returns for Stock A and Stock B?

Probability Distribution of Returns

Event	P(S)	R_A	R_B
Boom	0.3	0.20	0.30
Normal	0.5	0.12	0.10
Slow	0.2	0.05	0.00

Answer:

First, the expected returns for each of the stocks must be determined.

$$E(R_A) - (0.3)(0.20) + (0.5)(0.12) + (0.2)(0.05) - 0.13$$

$$E(R_B) = (0.3)(0.30) + (0.5)(0.10) + (0.2)(0.00) - 0.14$$

The covariance can now be computed using the procedure described in the following table.

Covariance Computation

Event	P(S)	R_A	R_B	$P(S) \times [R_A - E(R_A)] \times [R_B - E(R_B)]$
Boom	0.3	0.20	0.30	$(0.3)(0.2 - 0.13)(0.3 - 0.14) - 0.00336$
Normal	0.5	0.12	0.10	$(0.5)(0.12 - 0.13)(0.1 - 0.14) - 0.00020$
Slow	0.2	0.05	0.00	$(0.2)(0.05 - 0.13)(0 - 0.14) = 0.00224$

$$Cov(R_A, R_B) = \sum P(S) \times [R_A - E(R_A)] \times [R_B - E(R_B)] = 0.00580$$

The preceding example illustrates the use of a joint probability function. A *joint probability function* for two random variables gives the probability of the joint occurrence of specified outcomes. In this case, we only had three joint probabilities:

$$P(R_A = 0.2 \text{ and } R_B = 0.3) = 0.30$$

$$P(R_A = 0.12 \text{ and } R_B = 0.1) = 0.50$$

$$P(R_A = 0.05 \text{ and } R_B = 0.0) = 0.20$$

Joint probabilities are often presented in a table such as the one shown in the following table. According to the following table, $P(R_A = 0.12 \text{ and } R_B = 0.10) = 0.50$. This is the probability represented in the cell at the intersection of the column labeled $R_B = 0.10$ and the row labeled $R_A = 0.12$. Similarly, $P(R_A = 0.20 \text{ and } R_B = 0.10) = 0$.

Joint Probability Table

Joint Probabilities	$R_B = 0.30$	$R_B = 0.10$	$R_B = 0.00$
R_A 0.20	0.30	0	0
$R_A = 0.12$	0	0.50	0
$R_A = 0.05$	0	0	0.20

In more complex applications, there would likely be positive values where the zeros appear in the previous table. In any case, the sum of all the probabilities in the cells on the table must equal 1.

In practice, the covariance is difficult to interpret. This is mostly because it can take on **extremely** large values, ranging from negative to positive infinity, and, like the variance, **these** values are expressed in terms of square units.

To make the covariance of two random variables easier to interpret, it may be divided by the product of the random variables' standard deviations. The resulting value is called the **correlation** coefficient, or simply, correlation. The relationship between covariances, standard deviations, and correlations can be seen in the following expression for the correlation of the returns for asset i and j:

$$\text{Corr}\left(R_i, R_j\right) = \frac{\text{Cov}\left(R_i, R_j\right)}{\sigma\left(R_i\right)\sigma\left(R_j\right)}, \text{ which implies } \text{Cov}\left(R_i, R_j\right) = \text{Corr}\left(R_i, R_j\right)\sigma\left(R_i\right)\sigma\left(R_j\right)$$

The correlation between two random return variables may also be expressed as $\rho(R_i, R_j)$, or $\rho_{i,j}$.

Properties of correlation of two random variables R_i and R_j are summarized here:

- Correlation measures the strength of the linear relationship between two random variables.
- Correlation has no units.
- The correlation ranges from −1 to −1. That is, $-1 < \text{Corr}(R_i, R_j) < +1$.
- If $\text{Corr}(R_i, R_j) = 1.0$, the random variables have perfect positive correlation. This means **that** a movement in one random variable results in a proportional positive movement in the other relative to its mean.
- If **$\text{Corr}(R_i, R_j)$ =** −1.0, the random variables have perfect negative correlation. This means **that a** movement in one random variable results in an exact opposite proportional movement in the other relative to its mean.
- If $\text{Corr}(R_i, R_j) - 0$, there is no linear relationship between the variables, indicating that prediction of R_i cannot be made on the basis of R_j using linear methods.

Example: Correlation

Using our previous example, compute and interpret the correlation of the returns for stocks A and B, given that $\sigma^2(R_A) = 0.0028$ and $\sigma^2(R_B) = 0.0124$ and recalling that $\text{Cov}(R_A, R_B) = 0.0058$.

Answer:

First, it is necessary to convert the variances to standard deviations.

$$\sigma(R_A) - (0.0028)^{1/2} - 0.0529$$

$$\sigma(R_B) = (0.0124)^{1/2} = 0.1114$$

Now, the correlation between the returns of Stock A and Stock B can be computed as follows:

$$\text{Corr}(R_A, R_B) = \frac{0.0058}{(0.0529)(0.1114)} = 0.9842$$

The fact that this value is close to +1 indicates that the linear relationship is not only positive but very strong.

LOS 8.1: Calculate and interpret the expected value, variance, and standard deviation of a random variable and of returns on a portfolio.

CFA® Program Curriculum, Volume 1, page 425

The **expected value and variance for a portfolio of assets** can be determined using the properties of the individual assets in the portfolio. To do this, it is necessary to establish the portfolio weight for each asset. As indicated in the formula, the weight, *w*, of portfolio asset *i* is simply the market value currently invested in the asset divided by the current market value of the entire **portfolio**.

$$w_i = \frac{\text{market value of investment in asset i}}{\text{market value of the portfolio}}$$

Portfolio expected value. The expected value of a portfolio composed of *n* assets with weights, w_i, and expected values, R_i, can be determined using the following formula:

$$E\left(R_p\right) = \sum_{i=1}^{N} w_i E\left(R_i\right) = w_1 E(R_1) + w_2 E(R_2) + \ldots + w_n E(R_n)$$

More often, we have expected returns (rather than expected prices). When the R_i are returns, the expected return for a portfolio, $E(R_p)$, is calculated using the asset weights and the same formula as above.

Portfolio variance. The variance of the portfolio return uses the portfolio weights also, but in a more complicated way:

$$\text{Var}\left(R_p\right) = \sum_{i=1}^{N}\sum_{j=1}^{N} w_i w_j \text{Cov}\left(R_i, R_j\right)$$

The way this formula works, particularly in its use of the double summation operator, $\sum\sum$, is best explained using 2-asset and 3-asset portfolio examples.

Example: Variance of a 2-asset portfolio

Symbolically express the variance of a portfolio composed of risky asset A and risky asset B.

Answer:

Application of the variance formula provides the following:

$$\text{Var}(R_p) = w_A w_A \text{Cov}(R_A, R_A) + w_A w_B \text{Cov}(R_A, R_B) + w_B w_A \text{Cov}(R_B, R_A) + w_B w_B \text{Cov}(R_B, R_B)$$

Now, since $\text{Cov}(R_A, R_B) = \text{Cov}(R_B, R_A)$, and $\text{Cov}(R_A, R_A) = \sigma^2(R_A)$, this expression reduces to the following:

$$\text{Var}(R_p) = w_A^2 \sigma^2(R_A) + w_B^2 \sigma^2(R_B) + 2 w_A w_B \text{Cov}(R_A, R_B)$$

Since $\text{Cov}(R_A, R_B) = \sigma(R_B)\sigma(R_A)\rho(R_A, R_B)$, another way to present this formula is:

$$\mathbf{Var(R_p) = w_A^2 \sigma^2(R_A) + w_B^2 \sigma^2(R_B) + 2 w_A w_B \sigma(R_A)\sigma(R_B)\rho(R_A, R_B)}$$

Example: Variance of a 3-asset portfolio

A portfolio composed of risky assets A, B, and C will have a variance of return determined as:

$$Var(R_P) = w_A w_A Cov(R_A,R_A) + w_A w_B Cov(R_A,R_B) + w_A w_C Cov(R_A,R_C)$$
$$+ w_B w_A Cov(R_B,R_A) + w_B w_B Cov(R_B,R_B) + w_B w_C Cov(R_B,R_C)$$
$$+ w_C w_A Cov(R_C,R_A) + w_C w_B Cov(R_C,R_B) + w_C w_C Cov(R_C,R_C)$$

which can be reduced to the following expression:

$$Var(R_P) = w_A^2 \sigma^2(R_A) + w_B^2 \sigma^2(R_B) + w_C^2 \sigma^2(R_C)$$
$$+ 2w_A w_B Cov(R_A,R_B) + 2w_A w_C Cov(R_A,R_C) + 2w_B w_C Cov(R_B,R_C)$$

A portfolio composed of four assets will have four $w_i^2 \sigma^2(R_i)$ terms and six terms. A portfolio with five assets will have five $w_i^2 \sigma^2(R_i)$ terms and ten terms. In fact, the expression for the variance of an n-asset portfolio will have $n(n-1)/2$ unique $Cov(R_i,R_j)$ terms since $Cov(R_i,R_j) = Cov(R_j,R_i)$.

 Professor's Note: I would expect that if there is a problem on the exam that requires the calculation of the variance (standard deviation) of a portfolio of risky assets, it would involve only two risky assets.

The following formula is useful when we want to compute covariances, given correlations and variances:

LOS 8.m: Calculate and interpret covariance given a joint probability function.

CFA® Program Curriculum, Volume 1, page 436

Example: Expected value, variance, and covariance

What is the expected value, variance, and covariance(s) for a portfolio that consists of $400 in Asset A and $600 in Asset B? The joint probabilities of the returns of the two assets are in the following figure.

Probability Table

Joint Probabilities	$R_B = 0.40$	$R_B = 0.20$	$R_B = 0.00$
$R_A = 0.20$	0.15	0	0
$R_A = 0.15$	0	0.60	0
$R_A = 0.04$	0	0	0.25

Answer:

The asset weights are:

$$w_A = \$400 \,/\, (\$400 + \$600) = 0.40$$

$$w_B = \$600 \,/\, (\$400 + \$600) = 0.60$$

The expected returns for the individual assets are determined as:

$$E(R_A) = P(R_{A1}, R_{B1})R_{A1} + P(R_{A2}, R_{B2})R_{A2} + P(R_{A3}, R_{B3})R_{A3}$$

$$E(R_A) = (0.15)(0.20) + (0.60)(0.15) + (0.25)(0.04) = 0.13$$

$$E(R_B) = P(R_{B1}, R_{A1})R_{B1} + P(R_{B2}, R_{A2})R_{B2} + P(R_{B3}, R_{A3})R_{B3}$$

$$E(R_B) = (0.15)(0.40) + (0.60)(0.20) + (0.25)(0.00) = 0.18$$

The variances for the individual asset returns are determined as:

$$\textbf{Var(R}_A\textbf{)} = P(R_{A1}, R_{B1})[(R_{A1} - E(R_A)]^2 + P(R_{A2}, R_{B2})[(R_{A2} - E(R_A)]^2 + P(R_{A3}, R_{B3})[(R_{A3} - E(R_A)]^2$$

$$Var(R_A) = (0.15)(0.20 - 0.13)^2 + (0.6)(0.15 - 0.13)^2 + (0.25)(0.04 - 0.13)^2 = 0.0030$$

$$Var(R_B) = P(R_{B1}, R_{A1})[(R_{B1} - E(R_B)]^2 + P(R_{A2}, R_{B2})[(R_{B2} - E(R_B)]^2 + P(R_{B3}, R_{A3})[(R_{B3} - E(R_B)]^2$$

$$Var(R_B) = (0.15)(0.40 - 0.18)^2 + (0.6)(0.20 - 0.18)^2 + (0.25)(0.00 - 0.18)^2 = 0.0156$$

The covariance of the individual asset returns is determined as:

$$
\begin{aligned}
Cov(R_A, R_B) = \; & P(R_{A1}, R_{B1})[R_{A1} - E(R_A)][(R_{B1} - E(R_B)] \\
& + P(R_{A2}, R_{B2})[R_{A2} - E(R_A)][(R_{B2} - E(R_B)] \\
& + P(R_{A3}, R_{B3})[R_{A3} - E(R_A)][(R_{B3} - E(R_B)]
\end{aligned}
$$

$$
\begin{aligned}
Cov(R_A, R_B) = \; & 0.15(0.20 - 0.13)(0.40 - 0.18) \\
& + 0.60(0.15 - 0.13)(0.20 - 0.18) \\
& + 0.25(0.04 - 0.13)(0.00 - 0.18) \\
& = 0.0066
\end{aligned}
$$

Using the weights $w_A = 0.40$ and $w_B = 0.60$, the expected return and variance of the portfolio are computed as:

$$E(R_p) \quad\quad - w_A E(R_A) + w_B E(R_B) = (0.4)(0.13) + (0.6)(0.18) = 0.16$$

$$Var(R_p) \quad\quad = (0.40)^2(0.003) + (0.60)^2(0.0156) + 2(0.4)(0.60)(0.0066)$$
$$\quad\quad - 0.009264$$

Please note that as tedious as this example was, if more of the cells in the joint probability matrix were not zero, it could have been even more tedious.

Example: Correlation and covariance

Consider a portfolio of three assets, X, Y, and Z, where the individual market value of these assets is $600, $900, and $1,500, respectively. The market weight, expected return, and variance for the individual assets are presented below. The correlation matrix for the asset returns are shown in the following figure. Using this information, compute the variance of the portfolio return.

$$E(R_X) = 0.10 \quad\quad Var(R_X) - 0.0016 \quad\quad w_X - 0.2$$
$$E(R_Y) = 0.12 \quad\quad Var(R_Y) - 0.0036 \quad\quad w_Y = 0.3$$
$$E(R_Z) - 0.16 \quad\quad Var(R_Z) - 0.0100 \quad\quad w_Z - 0.5$$

Stock X, Y, and Z Returns Correlation

Returns	R_X	R_Y	R_Z
	Correlation Matrix		
R_X	1.00	0.46	0.22
R_Y	0.46	1.00	0.64
R_Z	0.22	0.64	1.00

Answer:

The expected return for the portfolio may be determined as:

$$E(R_p) = \sum w_i E(R_i) = w_1 E(R_1) + w_2 E(R_2) + w_3 E(R_3)$$

$$E(R_p) - (0.20)(0.10) + (0.30)(0.12) + (0.50)(0.16)$$

$$E(R_p) = 0.136$$

The variance of a 3-asset portfolio return is determined using the formula:

$$Var(R_p) = w_X^2\sigma^2(R_X) + w_Y^2\sigma^2(R_Y) + w_Z^2\sigma^2(R_Z) + 2w_Xw_YCov(R_X,R_Y) + 2w_Xw_ZCov(R_X,R_Z) + 2w_Yw_ZCov(R_Y,R_Z)$$

Here we must make use of the relationship $Cov(R_i,R_j) = \sigma(R_i)\sigma(R_j)\rho(R_i,R_j)$, since we are not provided with the covariances.

Let's solve for the covariances, then substitute the resulting values into the portfolio return variance equation.

$$Cov(R_X,R_Y) = (0.0016)^{1/2}(0.0036)^{1/2}(0.46) = 0.001104$$
$$Cov(R_X,R_Z) = (0.0016)^{1/2}(0.0100)^{1/2}(0.22) = 0.000880$$
$$Cov(R_Y,R_Z) = (0.0036)^{1/2}(0.0100)^{1/2}(0.64) = 0.003840$$

Now we can solve for the variance of the portfolio returns as:

$$Var(R_p) = (0.20)^2(0.0016) + (0.30)^2(0.0036) + (0.50)^2(0.01) +$$
$$(2)(0.2)(0.3)(0.001104) + (2)(0.2)(0.5)(0.00088) +$$
$$(2)(0.3)(0.5)(0.00384)$$

$$Var(R_p) = 0.004348$$

The standard deviation of portfolio returns = $(0.004348)^{1/2} = 0.0659 = 6.59\%$

Example: Covariance matrix

Assume you have a portfolio that consists of Stock S and a put option O on Stock S. The corresponding weights of these portfolio assets are $w_S = 0.90$ and $w_O = 0.10$. Using the covariance matrix provided in the following table, calculate the variance of the return for the portfolio.

Returns Covariance for Stock S and Put O

Returns	Covariance Matrix	
	R_S	R_O
R_S	0.0011	−0.0036
R_O	−0.0036	0.016

Answer:

This is the simplest type of example because the most tedious calculations have already been performed. Simply extract the appropriate values from the covariance matrix and insert them into the variance formula.

Recall that the covariance of an asset with itself is its variance. Thus, the terms along the diagonal in the covariance matrix are return variances.

The portfolio return variance can be computed as:

$$Var(R_p) = (0.90)^2(0.0011) + (0.10)^2(0.016) + 2(0.90)(0.10)(-0.0036)$$
$$= 0.000403$$

LOS 8.n: Calculate and interpret an updated probability using Bayes' formula.

CFA® Program Curriculum, Volume 1, page 441

Bayes' formula is used to update a given set of prior probabilities for a given event in response to the arrival of new information. The rule for updating prior probability of an event is:

updated probability =

$$\frac{\text{probability of new information for a given event}}{\text{unconditional probability of new information}} \times \text{prior probability of event}$$

Note in the following example of the application of Bayes' formula that we can essentially reverse a given set of conditional probabilities. This means that given P(B), P(A | B), and P(A | B^C), it is possible to use Bayes' formula to compute P(B | A).

Example: Bayes' formula (1)

Electcomp Corporation manufactures electronic components for computers and other devices. There is speculation that Electcomp is about to announce a major expansion into overseas markets. The expansion will occur, however, only if Electcomp's managers estimate overseas demand to be sufficient to support the necessary sales. Furthermore, if demand is sufficient and overseas expansion occurs, Electcomp is likely to raise its prices.

Using O to represent the event of overseas expansion, I to represent a price increase, and I^C to represent no price increase, an industry analyst has estimated the unconditional and conditional probabilities shown as follows:

P(I)	= 0.3
P(I^C)	= 0.7
P(O | I)	= 0.6
P(O | I^C)	= 0.4

The analyst's estimates for $P(I)$ and $P(I^C)$ are called the *priors* because they reflect what is already known. They do not reflect the current information about the possible overseas expansion.

Application of Bayes' formula allows us to compute $P(I \mid O)$, the probability that prices will increase given that Electcomp announces that it will expand overseas (the new information). Using the multiplication rule, we can express the joint probability of I and O:

$$P(O \mid I) = P(IO) \,/\, P(I), \text{ and } P(IO) = P(I \mid O) \times P(O)$$

Based on these relationships, Bayes' formula can be expressed using the information from this example, as indicated below {i.e., substitute the second equation into the first [for $P(IO)$] and solve for $P(I \mid O)$}:

$$P(I \mid O) = \frac{P(O \mid I)}{P(O)} \times P(I)$$

In order to solve this equation, $P(O)$ must be determined. This can be done using the total probability rule:

$$P(O) = P(O \mid I) \times P(I) + P(O \mid I^C) \times P(I^C)$$
$$P(O) = (0.6 \times 0.3) + (0.4 \times 0.7)$$
$$P(O) = 0.46$$

Now the updated probability of the increase in prices, given that Electcomp expands overseas, can be computed:

$$P(I \mid O) = \frac{0.60}{0.46} \times 0.30 = 0.3913$$

This means that if the new information of "expand overseas" is announced, the prior probability estimate of $P(I) = 0.30$ must be increased to 0.3913.

Example: Bayes' formula (2)

Another illustration of the use of Bayes' formula may make it easier to remember and apply. Consider the following possibilities. There is a 60% probability the economy will outperform, and if it does, there is a 70% chance a stock will go up and a 30% chance the stock will go down. There is a 40% chance the economy will underperform, and if it does, there is a 20% chance the stock in question will increase in value (have gains) and an 80% chance it will not. Let's diagram this situation.

A Probability Model

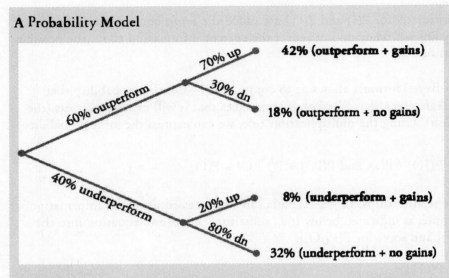

In the figure above, we have multiplied the probabilities to calculate the probabilities of each of the four outcome pairs. Note that these sum to 1. Given that the stock has gains, what is our updated probability of an outperforming economy? We sum the probability of stock gains in both states (outperform and underperform) to get 42% + 8% = 50%. Given that the stock has gains, the probability that the economy has outperformed is $\frac{42\%}{50\%} = 84\%$. In the previous notation the priors are as follows:

probability of economic outperformance = $P(O)$ = 60%, the probability of stock gains given economic outperformance is $P(G \mid O)$ = 70%, and the (unconditional) probability of a gain in stock price is 50%.

We are seeking $P(O \mid G)$, the probability of outperformance given gains. Bayes' formula says:

$$P(O|G) = \frac{P(G|O) \times P(O)}{P(G)}, \text{ which is our } \frac{42\%}{50\%} = 84\%$$

LOS 8.o: Identify the most appropriate method to solve a particular counting problem, and solve counting problems using the factorial, combination, and permutation notations.

CFA® Program Curriculum, Volume 1, page 444

Labeling refers to the situation where there are *n* items that can each receive one of *k* different labels. The number of items that receives label 1 is n_1 and the number that receive label 2 is n_2, and so on, such that $n_1 + n_2 + n_3 + ... + n_k = n$. The total number of ways that the labels can be assigned is:

$$\frac{n!}{(n_1!) \times (n_2!) \times ... \times (n_k!)}$$

where:
the symbol "!" stands for **factorial**. For example, 4! = 4 × 3 × 2 × 1 = 24, and 2! = 2 × 1 = 2.

The general expression for *n* factorial is:

$$n! = n \times (n - 1) \times (n - 2) \times (n - 3) \times \ldots \times 1, \text{ where by definition, } 0! = 1$$

Calculator help: On the TI, factorial is [2nd] [x!] (above the multiplication sign). On the HP, factorial is [g] [n!]. To compute 4! on the TI, enter [4][2nd][x!] = 24. On the HP, press [4][ENTER][g][n!].

Example: Labeling

Consider a portfolio consisting of eight stocks. Your goal is to designate four of the stocks as "long-term holds," three of the stocks as "short-term holds," and one stock as "sell." How many ways can these eight stocks be labeled?

Answer:

There are 8! = 40,320 total possible sequences that can be followed to assign the three labels to the eight stocks. However, the order that each stock is assigned a label does not matter. For example, it does not matter which of the first three stocks labeled "long-term" is the first to be labeled. Thus, there are 4! ways to assign the long-term label. Continuing this reasoning to the other categories, there are 4! × 3! × 1! equivalent sequences for assigning the labels. To eliminate the counting of these redundant sequences, the total number of possible sequences (8!) must be divided by the number of redundant sequences (4! × 3! × 1!).

Thus, the number of *different* ways to label the eight stocks is:

$$\frac{8!}{4! \times 3! \times 1!} = \frac{40,320}{24 \times 6 \times 1} = 280$$

If there are *n* labels (k = n), we have $\frac{n!}{1} = n!$. The number of ways to assign *n* different labels to *n* items is simply *n!*.

A special case of labeling arises when the number of labels equals 2 (k = 2). That is, the *n* items can only be in one of two groups, and $n_1 + n_2 = n$. In this case, we can let $r = n_1$ and $n_2 = n - r$. Since there are only two categories, we usually talk about choosing *r* items. Then (n − r) items are not chosen. The general formula for labeling when k = 2 is called the **combination formula** (or *binomial formula*) and is expressed as:

$$_nC_r = \frac{n!}{(n-r)!r!},$$

where $_nC_r$ is the number of possible ways (combinations) of selecting *r* items from a set of *n* items when the order of selection is not important. This is also written $\binom{n}{r}$ and read "n choose r."

Another useful formula is the permutation **formula**. A permutation is a specific ordering of a group of objects. The question of how many different groups of size r in specific order can be chosen from n objects is answered by the permutation formula. The number of permutations of r objects from n objects $= \dfrac{n!}{(n-r)!}$. We will give an example using this formula shortly.

> *Professor's Note: The combination formula $_nC_r$ and the permutation formula $_nP_r$ are both available on the TI calculator. To calculate the number of different groups of three stocks from a list of eight stocks (i.e., $_8C_3$), the sequence is 8 [2nd] [$_nC_r$] 3 [=], which yields 56. If we want to know the number of differently ordered groups of three that can be selected from a list of eight, we enter 8 [2nd] [$_nP_r$] 3 [=] to get 336, which is the number of permutations,*
>
> $$\frac{8!}{(8-3)!}.$$ *This function is not available on the HP calculator. Remember, current policy permits you to bring both calculators to the exam if you choose.*

Example: Number of choices in any order

How many ways can three stocks be sold from an 8-stock portfolio?

Answer:

This is similar to the preceding labeling example. Since order does not matter, we take the total number of possible ways to select three of the eight stocks and divide by the number of possible redundant selections. Thus, the answer is:

$$\frac{8!}{5! \times 3!} = 56$$

In the preceding two examples, ordering did not matter. The order of selection could, however, be important. For example, suppose we want to liquidate only one stock position per week over the next three weeks. Once we choose three particular stocks to sell, the order in which they are sold must be determined. In this case, the concept of permutation comes into play. The *permutation formula* is:

$$_nP_r = \frac{n!}{(n-r)!},$$

where $_nP_r$ is the number of possible ways (permutations) to select r items from a set of n items when the order of selection is important. The permutation formula implies that there are $r!$ *more* ways to choose r items if the order of selection *is important* than if order is not important.

Example: Permutation

How many ways are there to sell three stocks out of eight if the order of the sales is important?

Answer:

$$_nP_r = {}_8P_3 = \frac{8!}{(8-3)!} = \frac{8!}{5!} = 336$$

This is 3! times the 56 possible combinations computed in the preceding example for selecting the three stocks when the order was not important.

There are five guidelines that may be used to determine which counting method to employ when dealing with counting problems:

- The *multiplication rule of counting* is used when there are *two or more groups*. The key is that only *one* item may be selected from each group. If there are k steps required to complete a task and each step can be done in n ways, the number of different ways to complete the task is $n_1! \times n_2! \times \ldots \times n_k!$.
- *Factorial* is used by itself when there are *no groups*—we are only arranging a given set of n items. Given n items, there are n! ways of arranging them.
- The *labeling formula* applies to *three or more sub-groups* of predetermined size. Each element of the entire group must be assigned a place, or label, in one of the three or more sub-groups.
- The *combination formula* applies to *only two groups* of predetermined size. Look for the word "choose" or "combination."
- The *permutation formula* applies to *only two groups* of predetermined size. Look for a specific reference to "order" being important.

KEY CONCEPTS

LOS 8.a

A random variable is an uncertain value determined by chance.

An outcome is the realization of a random variable.

An event is a set of one or more outcomes. Two events that cannot both occur are termed "mutually exclusive" and a set of events that includes all possible outcomes is an "exhaustive" set of events.

LOS 8.b

The two properties of probability are:
* The sum of the probabilities of all possible mutually exclusive events is 1.
* The probability of any event cannot be greater than 1 or less than 0.

A priori probability measures predetermined probabilities based on well-defined inputs; empirical probability measures probability from observations or experiments; and subjective probability is an informed guess.

LOS 8.c

Probabilities can be stated as odds that an event will or will not occur. If the probability of an event is A out of B trials (A/B), the "odds for" are A to (B − A) and the "odds against" are (B − A) to A.

LOS 8.d

Unconditional probability (marginal probability) is the probability of an event occurring.

Conditional probability, P(A | B), is the probability of an event A occurring given that event B has occurred.

LOS 8.e

The multiplication rule of probability is used to determine the joint probability of two events:

$$P(AB) = P(A \mid B) \times P(B)$$

The addition rule of probability is used to determine the probability that at least one of two events will occur:

$$P(A \text{ or } B) = P(A) + P(B) - P(AB)$$

The total probability rule is used to determine the unconditional probability of an event, given conditional probabilities:

$$P(A) = P(A \mid B_1)P(B_1) + P(A \mid B_2)P(B_2) + \ldots + P(A \mid B_N)P(B_N)$$

where $B_1, B_2, \ldots B_N$ is a mutually exclusive and exhaustive set of outcomes.

LOS 8.f

The joint probability of two events, P(AB), is the probability that they will both occur. P(AB) = P(A | B) × P(B). For independent events, P(A | B) = P(A), so that P(AB) = P(A) × P(B).

The probability that at least one of two events will occur is P(A or B) = P(A) + P(B) – P(AB). For mutually exclusive events, P(A or B) = P(A) + P(B), since P(AB) = 0.

The joint probability of any number of independent events is the product of their individual probabilities.

LOS 8.g

The probability of an independent event is unaffected by the occurrence of other events, but the probability of a dependent event is changed by the occurrence of another event. Events A and B are independent if and only if:

P(A | B) = P(A), or equivalently, P(B | A) = P(B)

LOS 8.h

Using the total probability rule, the unconditional probability of A is the probability weighted sum of the conditional probabilities:

$$P(A) = \sum_{i=1}^{n}\left[P_i\left(B_i\right)\right] \times P\left(A \mid B_i\right),$$

where B_i is a set of mutually exclusive and exhaustive events.

LOS 8.i

Conditional expected values depend on the outcome of some other event.

Forecasts of expected values for a stock's return, earnings, and dividends can be refined, using conditional expected values, when new information arrives that affects the expected outcome.

LOS 8.j

A tree diagram shows the probabilities of two events and the conditional probabilities of two subsequent events.

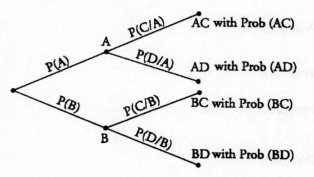

LOS 8.k

Covariance measures the extent to which two random variables tend to be above and below their respective means for each joint realization. It can be calculated as:

$$Cov(A,B) = \sum_{i=1}^{N} P_i\left(A_i - \bar{A}\right)\left(B_i - \bar{B}\right)$$

Correlation is a standardized measure of association between two random variables; it ranges in value from –1 to +1 and is equal to $\dfrac{Cov(A,B)}{\sigma_A \sigma_B}$.

LOS 8.l

The expected value of a random variable, $E(X)$, equals $\sum_{i=1}^{n} P_i(x_i)X_i$.

The variance of a random variable, $Var(X)$, equals $\sum_{i=1}^{n} P(x_i)[X_i - E(X)]^2 = \sigma_X^2$.

Standard deviation: $\sigma_X = \sqrt{\sigma_X^2}$.

The expected returns and variance of a 2-asset portfolio are given by:

$$
\begin{aligned}
E(R_P) &= w_1 E(R_1) + w_2 E(R_2) \\
Var(R_P) &= w_1^2 \sigma_1^2 + w_2^2 \sigma_2^2 + 2w_1 w_2 Cov_{1,2} \\
&= w_1^2 \sigma_1^2 + w_2^2 \sigma_2^2 + 2w_1 w_2 \sigma_1 \sigma_2 \rho_{1,2}
\end{aligned}
$$

LOS 8.m

Given the joint probabilities for X_i and Y_i, i.e., $P(X_i Y_i)$, the covariance is calculated as:

$$\sum_{i=1}^{n} P(X_i Y_i)[X_i - E(X)][Y_i - E(Y)]$$

LOS 8.n

Bayes' formula for updating probabilities based on the occurrence of an event O is:

$$P(I \mid O) = \frac{P(O \mid I)}{P(O)} \times P(I)$$

Equivalently, based on the tree diagram below, $P(A \mid C) = \dfrac{P(AC)}{P(AC) + P(BC)}$.

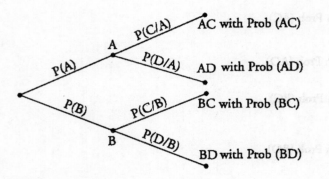

©2012 Kaplan, Inc.

LOS 8.o

The number of ways to order n objects is n factorial, $n! = n \times (n-1) \times (n-2) \times \ldots \times 1$.

There are $\dfrac{N!}{n_1! \times n_2! \times \ldots \times n_k!}$ ways to assign k different labels to n items, where n_i is the number of items with the label i.

The number of ways to choose a subset of size r from a set of size n when order doesn't matter is $\dfrac{n!}{(n-r)!r!}$ combinations; when order matters, there are $\dfrac{n!}{(n-r)!}$ permutations.

CONCEPT CHECKERS

1. Given the conditional probabilities in the table below and the unconditional probabilities $P(Y = 1) = 0.3$ and $P(Y = 2) = 0.7$, what is the expected value of X?

x_i	$P(x_i \mid Y = 1)$	$P(x_i \mid Y = 2)$
0	0.2	0.1
5	0.4	0.8
10	0.4	0.1

   A. 5.0.
   B. 5.3.
   C. 5.7.

Use the following data to answer Questions 2 through 6.

	Joint Probabilities		
Returns	$R_B = 0.5$	$R_B = 0.2$	$R_B = -0.3$
$R_A = -0.1$	0.4	0	0
$R_A = 0.1$	0	0.3	0
$R_A = 0.3$	0	0	0.3

2. Given the joint probability table, the expected return of Stock A is *closest* to:
   A. 0.08.
   B. 0.12.
   C. 0.15.

3. Given the joint probability table, the standard deviation of Stock B is *closest* to:
   A. 0.11.
   B. 0.22.
   C. 0.33.

4. Given the joint probability table, the variance of Stock A is *closest* to:
   A. 0.03.
   B. 0.12.
   C. 0.17.

5. Given the joint probability table, the covariance between A and B is *closest* to:
   A. −0.160.
   B. −0.055.
   C. 0.004.

6. Given the joint probability table, the correlation between R_A and R_B is *closest* to:
   A. −0.99.
   B. 0.02.
   C. 0.86.

©2012 Kaplan, Inc.

7.   The probability that the DJIA will increase tomorrow is 2/3. The probability of an increase in the DJIA stated as odds is:
     A. two-to-one.
     B. one-to-three.
     C. two-to-three.

8.   A discrete uniform distribution (each event has an equal probability of occurrence) has the following possible outcomes for **X**: [1, 2, 3, 4]. The variance of this distribution is *closest* to:
     A. 1.00.
     B. 1.25.
     C. 2.00.

9.   If events A and B are mutually exclusive, then:
     A. $P(A \mid B) = P(A)$.
     B. $P(AB) = P(A) \times P(B)$.
     C. $P(A \text{ or } B) = P(A) + P(B)$.

10. At a charity ball, 800 names are put into a hat. Four of the names are identical. On a random draw, what is the probability that one of these four names will be drawn?
     A. 0.004.
     B. 0.005.
     C. 0.010.

11. Among 900 taxpayers with incomes below $100,000, 35 were audited by the IRS. The probability that a randomly chosen individual with an income below $100,000 was audited is *closest* to:
     A. 0.039.
     B. 0.125.
     C. 0.350.

12. Which of the following values *cannot* be the probability of an event?
     A. 0.00.
     B. 1.00.
     C. 1.25.

13. Two mutually exclusive events:
     A. always occur together.
     B. cannot occur together.
     C. can sometimes occur together.

14. Two events are said to be independent if the occurrence of one event:
     A. means that the second event cannot occur.
     B. means that the second event is certain to occur.
     C. does not affect the probability of the occurrence of the other event.

Use the following conditional probabilities to answer Questions 15 through 18.

State of the Economy	Probability of the Economic State	Stock Performance	Conditional Probability of Stock Performance
Good	0.30	Good	0.60
		Neutral	0.30
		Poor	0.10
Neutral	0.50	Good	0.30
		Neutral	0.40
		Poor	0.30
Poor	0.20	Good	0.10
		Neutral	0.60
		Poor	0.30

15. What is the conditional probability of having good stock performance in a poor economic environment?
    A. 0.02.
    B. 0.10.
    C. 0.30.

16. What is the joint probability of having a good economy and a neutral stock performance?
    A. 0.09.
    B. 0.20.
    C. 0.30.

17. What is the total probability of having a good performance in the stock?
    A. 0.35.
    B. 0.65.
    C. 1.00.

18. Given that the stock had good performance, the probability the state of the economy was good is *closest* to:
    A. 0.35.
    B. 0.46.
    C. 0.51.

19. Consider a universe of ten bonds from which an investor will ultimately purchase six bonds for his portfolio. If the order in which he buys these bonds is not important, how many potential 6-bond combinations are there?
    A. 7.
    B. 210.
    C. 5,040.

20. The correlation of returns between Stocks A and B is 0.50. The covariance between these two securities is 0.0043, and the standard deviation of the return of Stock B is 26%. The variance of returns for Stock A is:
    A. 0.0011.
    B. 0.0331.
    C. 0.2656.

21. There are ten sprinters in the finals of a race. How many different ways can the gold, silver, and bronze medals be awarded?
    A. 120.
    B. 720.
    C. 1,440.

22. Which of the following is *least likely* a probability distribution?

    A. $X = [1,2,3,4]$; Prob $[X_i] = \dfrac{X_i^2}{30}$.

    B. $X = [5,10]$; Prob $[X_i] = \dfrac{8 - X_i}{5}$.

    C. $X = [5,10]$; Prob $[X_i] = \dfrac{X_i - 3}{9}$.

CHALLENGE PROBLEMS

1. Given the following probability data for the return on the market and the return on Best Oil, calculate the covariance of returns between Best Oil and the market.

   Joint Probability Table

	$R_{Best} = 20\%$	$R_{Best} = 10\%$	$R_{Best} = 5\%$
$R_{Mkt} = 15\%$	0.4	0	0
$R_{Mkt} = 10\%$	0	0.2	0
$R_{Mkt} = 0\%$	0	0	0.4

2. The correlation of returns between the returns on Cape Products and Dogger Industries is 0.6. The standard deviation of returns for Cape is 15%, and the standard deviation of returns for Dogger is 20%. The expected return for Dogger is 18%, and the expected return for Cape is 12%. Calculate the expected returns and standard deviation of returns on a portfolio that has $300,000 invested in Dogger and $200,000 invested in Cape.

3.   M. Atwood, an analyst, has developed a scoring system for bonds and found that if the score from a bond is less than 20, there is an 85% probability that it will default within five years. If a bond's score is greater than or equal to 20, there is only a 40% chance that it will default within five years. Given that a randomly chosen bond currently has a 25% probability of a score less than 20, what is the probability that a bond that defaults within the next five years had a score of 20 or higher?

4.   A bond that matures in one year is priced at $950 today. You estimate that it has a 10% probability of default. If the bond defaults, you expect to recover $600. If it does not default, it will pay $1,080 at maturity. The nominal 1-year risk-free rate is 7.5%.

A.   What are the odds against this bond defaulting?

B.   What is the expected payoff on the bond in one year?

C.   What is the expected return on the bond?

D.   What would be the price of the bond if its expected return were equal to the risk-free rate?

5.   You are considering a portfolio of three stocks:
   - Stock A (55% of the portfolio) has an expected return of 8%, with a standard deviation of 24%.
   - Stock B (25% of the portfolio) has an expected return of 4%, with a standard deviation of 18%.
   - Stock C (20% of the portfolio) has an expected return of 3%, with a standard deviation of 15%.

The correlations between these stocks' returns are:
   - Stock A with Stock B: 0.85.
   - Stock A with Stock C: 0.30.
   - Stock B with Stock C: −0.15.

A. Based on these data, construct a covariance matrix for the returns on the three stocks.

B. Calculate the expected return and standard deviation of the portfolio.

C. Provide a set of three mutually exclusive and exhaustive events with respect to the relation between this portfolio's realized return and its expected return.

D. If you add three more stocks to the portfolio, how many variances and how many unique covariances will you need to calculate the portfolio variance?

6.   You are forecasting the sales of a building materials supplier by assessing the expansion plans of its largest customer, a homebuilder. You estimate the probability that the customer will increase its orders for building materials to 25%. If the customer does increase its orders, you estimate the probability that the homebuilder will start a new development at 70%. If the customer does not increase its orders from this supplier, you estimate only a 20% chance that it will start the new development. Later, you find out that the homebuilder will start the new development. In light of this new information, what is your new (updated) probability that the builder will increase its orders from this supplier?

ANSWERS – CONCEPT CHECKERS

1. **B** $E(X \mid Y = 1) = (0.2)(0) + (0.4)(5) + (0.4)(10) = 6$ and $E(X \mid Y = 2) = (0.1)(0) + (0.8)(5) + (0.1)(10) = 5$

   $E(X) = (0.3)(6) + (0.7)(5) = 5.30$

2. **A** Expected return of Stock A $= (0.4)(-0.1) + (0.3)(0.1) + (0.3)(0.3) = 0.08$

3. **C** Expected return of Stock B $= (0.4)(0.5) + (0.3)(0.2) + (0.3)(-0.3) = 0.17$

   $Var(R_B) = 0.4(0.5 - 0.17)^2 + 0.3(0.2 - 0.17)^2 + 0.3(-0.3 - 0.17)^2 = 0.1101$

   Standard deviation $= \sqrt{0.1101} = 0.3318$

4. **A** $E(R_A) = 0.08$ (from #2 above)

   $Var(R_A) = 0.4(-0.1 - 0.08)^2 + 0.3(0.1 - 0.08)^2 + 0.3(0.3 - 0.08)^2 = 0.0276$

5. **B** $Cov(R_A, R_B) = 0.4(-0.1 - 0.08)(0.5 - 0.17) + 0.3(0.1 - 0.08)(0.2 - 0.17) + 0.3(0.3 - 0.08)(-0.3 - 0.17) = -0.0546$

6. **A** $Corr(R_A, R_B) = Cov(R_A, R_B) / \sigma(R_A)\sigma(R_B)$

   $Cov(R_A, R_B) = -0.0546$ (from #5 above)

   $Var(R_A) = 0.0276$ (from #4 above); $\sigma(R_A) = \sqrt{0.0276} = 0.1661$

   $\sigma(R_B) = 0.3318$ (from #3 above)

   $Corr(R_A, R_B) = -0.0546 / (0.1661)(0.3318) = -0.9907$

7. **A** Odds for $E = P(E) / [1 - P(E)] = \dfrac{2/3}{1/3} = 2/1 = $ two-to-one

8. **B** Expected value $= (1/4)(1 + 2 + 3 + 4) = 2.5$

   Variance $= (1/4)[(1 - 2.5)^2 + (2 - 2.5)^2 + (3 - 2.5)^2 + (4 - 2.5)^2] = 1.25$

   Note that since each observation is equally likely, each has 25% (1/4) chance of occurrence.

9. **C** There is no intersection of events when events are mutually exclusive. $P(A \mid B) = P(A) \times P(B)$ is only true for independent events. Note that since A and B are mutually exclusive (cannot both happen), $P(A \mid B)$ and $P(AB)$ must both be equal to zero.

10. **B** P(name 1 or name 2 or name 3 or name 4) $= 1/800 + 1/800 + 1/800 + 1/800 = 4/800 = 0.005$

11. **A** $35 / 900 = 0.0389$

12. **C** Probabilities may range from 0 (meaning no chance of occurrence) through 1 (which means a sure thing).

13. **B** One or the other may occur, but not both.

14. **C** Two events are said to be independent if the occurrence of one event does not affect the probability of the occurrence of the other event.

15. **B** Go to the poor economic state and read off the probability of good performance [i.e., P(good performance | poor economy) = 0.10].

16. **A** P(good economy and neutral performance) = P(good economy)P(neutral performance | good economy) = (0.3)(0.3) = 0.09.

17. **A** (0.3)(0.6) + (0.5)(0.3) + (0.2)(0.1) = 0.35. This is the sum of all the joint probabilities for good performance over all states [i.e., $\sum$P(economic state$_i$) P(good performance | economic state$_i$)].

18. **C** This is an application of Bayes' formula. P(good economy | good performance) = P(good stock performance | good economy) × P(good economy) / P(good stock performance).

$$= \frac{(0.6)(0.3)}{(0.3)(0.6) + (0.5)(0.3) + (0.2)(0.1)} = \frac{0.18}{0.35} = 0.5143$$

19. **B** $_nC_r = \frac{n!}{(n-r)!r!} = {}_{10}C_6 = \frac{10!}{(10-6)!6!} = \frac{10!}{4!6!} = 210$

20. **A** $Corr(R_A, R_B) = \frac{Cov(R_A, R_B)}{[\sigma(R_A)][\sigma(R_B)]}$

$$\sigma^2(R_A) = \left[\frac{Cov(R_A, R_B)}{\sigma(R_B)Corr(R_A, R_B)}\right]^2 = \left[\frac{0.0043}{(0.26)(0.5)}\right]^2 = 0.0331^2 = 0.0011$$

21. **B** Since the order of the top three finishers matters, we need to use the permutation formula.
$$_{10}P_3 = \frac{10!}{(10-3)!} = 720$$

22. **B** $\frac{8-5}{5} + \frac{8-10}{5} = \frac{1}{5}$, and $\frac{8-10}{5}$ is negative, so this satisfies neither of the requirements for a probability distribution. The others have P[X$_i$] between zero and one and $\sum$ P[X$_i$] = 1, and thus satisfy both requirements for a probability distribution.

ANSWERS – CHALLENGE PROBLEMS

1. E(R$_{Best}$) = 0.4(20%) + 0.2(10%) + 0.4(5%) = 12%

   E(R$_{Mkt}$) = 0.4(15%) + 0.2(10%) + 0.4(0%) = 8%

   Cov(R$_{Best}$, R$_{Mkt}$) = 0.4(20% − 12%)(15% − 8%)

   + 0.2(10% − 12%)(10% − 8%)

   + 0.4(5% − 12%)(0% − 8%)

   = 0.4(8)(7) + 0.2(−2)(2) + 0.4(−7)(−8) = 44

Remember the units of covariance (like variance) are percent squared here. We used whole number percents in the calculations and got 44; if we had used decimals, we would have gotten 0.0044.

2. The portfolio weight for Dogger (W_D) is $\frac{300}{500} = 60\%$ and for Cape, the portfolio weight is $\frac{200}{500} = 40\%$. The expected return on the portfolio is 0.6(18%) + 0.4(12%) = 15.6%.

    The variance is $(0.6)^2(0.2)^2 + (0.4)^2(0.15)^2 + 2(0.6)(0.4)(0.6)(0.2)(0.15) = 0.02664$.

    The standard deviation of portfolio returns is $\sqrt{0.02664} = 16.32\%$.

3. Construct the following tree:

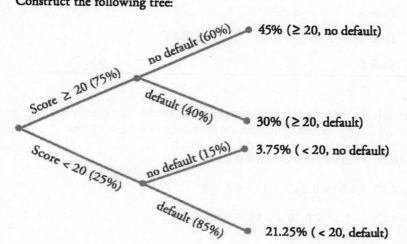

45% (≥ 20, no default)

no default (60%)

Score ≥ 20 (75%)

default (40%)

30% (≥ 20, default)

3.75% (< 20, no default)

Score < 20 (25%)

no default (15%)

default (85%)

21.25% (< 20, default)

    Total probability of default = 30% + 21.25% = 51.25%. Percent of defaulting bonds with score ≥ 20 = $\frac{30\%}{51.25\%} = 58.5\%$. A bond that defaults in the next five years has a 58.5% probability of having a current score greater than or equal to 20. Note that we have employed Bayes' theorem here to update the score expectation, based on the additional information that a bond has defaulted.

4. A. The odds for the bond defaulting are $\frac{0.10}{1-0.10} = \frac{1}{9}$, or 1-to-9. The odds against the bond defaulting are the reciprocal, or 9-to-1.

    B. The expected payoff on the bond at maturity is:

        P(default) × bond value if it defaults + P(no default) × bond value if it does not default = 0.1(600) + 0.9(1,080) = 60 + 972 = $1,032

    C. The expected return is 1,032 / 950 – 1 = 0.0863, or 8.63%.

    D. $\frac{1,032}{\text{price}} - 1 = 0.075$ so price would need to be $\frac{1,032}{1.075} = \$960$.

5.   A.   First, calculate the variances on each of the three stocks:

$Var(A) = (0.24)^2 = 0.0576$

$Var(B) = (0.18)^2 = 0.0324$

$Var(C) = (0.15)^2 = 0.0225$

These will be the diagonal entries in the covariance matrix:

Covariance Matrix of Returns for Stocks A, B, and C

	Stock A	Stock B	Stock C
Stock A	0.0576		
Stock B		0.0324	
Stock C			0.0225

Next, calculate the covariance for each pair of stocks. The correlation (ρ_{xy}) = $Cov(x,y) / \sigma_x\sigma_y$. Rearranging that, we get $Cov(x,y) = \rho_{xy} \sigma_x\sigma_y$. So:

$Cov(A,B) = 0.85 \times 0.24 \times 0.18 = 0.0367$

$Cov(A,C) = 0.30 \times 0.24 \times 0.15 = 0.0108$

$Cov(B,C) = -0.15 \times 0.18 \times 0.15 = -0.0041$

These results complete the covariance matrix:

Covariance Matrix of Returns for Stocks A, B, and C

	Stock A	Stock B	Stock C
Stock A	0.0576	0.0367	0.0108
Stock B	0.0367	0.0324	−0.0041
Stock C	0.0108	−0.0041	0.0225

B.   The expected return on the portfolio is a weighted average of the individual stock returns:

$E[R_p] = 0.55(0.08) + 0.25(0.04) + 0.20(0.03) = 0.06$, or 6%

For a 3-asset portfolio, the portfolio variance is calculated as:

$$Var(R_p) = W_A^2\sigma^2(R_A) + W_B^2\sigma^2(R_B) + W_C^2\sigma^2(R_C) + 2W_AW_BCov(R_A,R_B) + 2W_AW_CCov(R_A,R_C) + 2W_BW_CCov(R_B,R_C)$$

Substituting, we get:

$$Var(R_p) = 0.55^2\,(0.0576) + 0.25^2\,(0.0324) + 0.20^2\,(0.0225) + 2(0.55)(0.25)$$
$$(0.0367) + 2(0.55)(0.20)(0.0108) + 2(0.25)(0.20)(-0.0041)$$

$$= 0.0174 + 0.0020 + 0.0009 + 0.0101 + 0.0024 - 0.0004$$

$$= 0.0324$$

The portfolio standard deviation is $\sqrt{0.0324} = 0.1800$, or 18%.

C. You can answer this question any number of different ways, but here is the most obvious:

Event 1: The realized return is greater than the expected return.

Event 2: The realized return is equal to the expected return.

Event 3: The realized return is less than the expected return.

D. With six assets in the portfolio, there will be 6 variance terms and 15 unique covariance terms. The covariance matrix will have 6 × 6 = 36 cells. The covariance of a stock return with itself is its variance; those will be the six entries on the diagonal. The other 30 cells are the covariance pairs, but since each pair appears twice in the matrix—Cov(A,B) is the same as Cov(B,A)—the number of unique covariance pairs is half of that, or 15. For any portfolio of n assets, the portfolio variance calculation would involve n variance terms and $n(n-1)/2$ unique covariance terms.

6. The prior probability that the builder will increase its orders is 25%.

P(increase) = 0.25

P(no increase) = 0.75

There are four possible outcomes:
- Builder increases its orders and starts new development.
- Builder increases its orders and does not start new development.
- Builder does not increase its orders and starts new development.
- Builder does not increase its orders and does not start new development.

The probabilities of each outcome are as follows:
- P(increase and development) = (0.25)(0.70) = 0.175.
- P(increase and no development) = (0.25)(0.30) = 0.075.
- P(no increase and development) = (0.75)(0.20) = 0.15.
- P(no increase and no development) = (0.75)(0.80) = 0.60.

We want to update the probability of an increase in orders, given the new information that the builder is starting the development. We can apply Bayes' formula:

$$P(\text{increase} \mid \text{development}) = \frac{P(\text{development} \mid \text{increase}) \times P(\text{increase})}{P(\text{development})}$$

From our assumptions, P(development | increase) = 0.70, and P(increase) = 0.25, so the numerator is (0.70)(0.25) = 0.175.

P(development) is the sum of P(development and increase) and P(development and no increase).

P(development) = 0.175 + 0.15 = 0.325

Thus, P(increase | development) $= \dfrac{(0.7)\times(0.25)}{0.175+0.15} = \dfrac{0.175}{0.325} = 0.5385$, or 53.8

> *Professor's Note: I can never remember this formula, so I set these problems up like the probability model (tree) in the notes and focus on the probabilities of the new information—development in this case. Total probability of development is 17.5 + 15 = 32.5. Of that probability, 17.5 / 32.5, or 53.85% of the time, development is paired with an increase in sales!*

COMMON PROBABILITY DISTRIBUTIONS

EXAM FOCUS

This topic review contains a lot of key material. Learn the difference between discrete and continuous probability distributions. The binomial and normal distributions are the most important here. You must learn the properties of both distributions and memorize the formulas for the probability of a particular value when given a binomial probability distribution. Learn what shortfall risk is and how to calculate and use Roy's safety-first criterion. Know how to standardize a normally distributed random variable, use a z-table, and construct confidence intervals. These skills will be used repeatedly in the topic reviews that follow. Additionally, understand the basic features of the lognormal distribution, Monte Carlo simulation, and historical simulation. Finally, it would be a good idea to know how to get continuously compounded rates of return from holding period returns. Other than that, no problem.

LOS 9.a: Define a probability distribution and distinguish between discrete and continuous random variables and their probability functions.

LOS 9.b: Describe the set of possible outcomes of a specified discrete random variable.

CFA® Program Curriculum, Volume 1, page 464

A **probability distribution** describes the probabilities of all the possible outcomes for a random variable. The probabilities of all possible outcomes must sum to 1. A simple probability distribution is that for the roll of one fair die; there are six possible outcomes and each one has a probability of 1/6, so they sum to 1. The probability distribution of all the possible returns on the S&P 500 Index for the next year is a more complex version of the same idea.

A **discrete random** variable is one for which the number of possible outcomes can be counted, and for each possible outcome, there is a measurable and positive probability. An example of a discrete random variable is the number of days it rains in a given month, because there is a finite number of possible outcomes—the number of days it can rain in a month is defined by the number of days in the month.

A **probability function**, denoted p(x), specifies the probability that a random variable is equal to a specific value. More formally, p(x) is the probability that random variable X takes on the value x, or $p(x) = P(X = x)$.

The two key properties of a probability function are:

- $0 \leq p(x) \leq 1$.
- $\sum p(x) = 1$, the sum of the probabilities for *all* possible outcomes, x, for a random variable, X, equals 1.

Example: Evaluating a probability function

Consider the following function: $X = \{1, 2, 3, 4\}$, $p(x) = \dfrac{x}{10}$, else $p(x) = 0$

Determine whether this function satisfies the conditions for a probability function.

Answer:

Note that all of the probabilities are between 0 and 1, and the sum of all probabilities equals 1:

$$\sum p(x) = \frac{1}{10} + \frac{2}{10} + \frac{3}{10} + \frac{4}{10} = 0.1 + 0.2 + 0.3 + 0.4 = 1$$

Both conditions for a probability function are satisfied.

A **continuous random variable** is one for which the number of possible outcomes is infinite, even if lower and upper bounds exist. The actual amount of daily rainfall between zero and 100 inches is an example of a continuous random variable because the actual amount of rainfall can take on an infinite number of values. Daily rainfall can be measured in inches, half inches, quarter inches, thousandths of inches, or even smaller increments. Thus, the number of possible daily rainfall amounts between zero and 100 inches is essentially infinite.

The assignment of probabilities to the possible outcomes for discrete and continuous random variables provides us with discrete probability distributions and continuous probability distributions. The difference between these types of distributions is most apparent for the following properties:

- For a *discrete distribution*, $p(x) = 0$ when x cannot occur, or $p(x) > 0$ if it can. Recall that $p(x)$ is read: "the probability that random variable $X = x$." For example, the probability of it raining on 33 days in June is zero because this cannot occur, but the probability of it raining 25 days in June has some positive value.
- For a *continuous distribution*, $p(x) = 0$ even though x can occur. We can only consider $P(x_1 \leq X \leq x_2)$ where x_1 and x_2 are actual numbers. For example, the probability of receiving two inches of rain in June is zero because two inches is a single point in an infinite range of possible values. On the other hand, the probability of the amount of rain being between 1.99999999 and 2.00000001 inches has some positive value. In the case of continuous distributions, $P(x_1 \leq X \leq x_2) = P(x_1 < X < x_2)$ because $p(x_1) = p(x_2) = 0$.

In finance, some discrete distributions are treated as though they are continuous because the number of possible outcomes is very large. For example, the increase or decrease in the price of a stock traded on an American exchange is recorded in dollars and cents. Yet, the probability of a change of exactly $1.33 or $1.34 or any other specific change is almost zero. It is customary, therefore, to speak in terms of the probability of a range of possible price change, say between $1.00 and $2.00. In other words p(price change = 1.33) is essentially zero, but p($1 < price change < $2) is greater than zero.

LOS 9.c: Interpret a cumulative distribution function.

LOS 9.d: Calculate and interpret probabilities for a random variable, given its cumulative distribution function.

CFA® Program Curriculum, Volume 1, page 466

A **cumulative distribution function** (cdf), or simply *distribution function*, defines the probability that a random variable, *X*, takes on a value equal to or less than a specific value, *x*. It represents the sum, or *cumulative value*, of the probabilities for the outcomes up to and including a specified outcome. The cumulative distribution function for a random variable, *X*, may be expressed as $F(x) = P(X \leq x)$.

Consider the probability function defined earlier for X = {1, 2, 3, 4}, p(x) = x / 10. For this distribution, F(3) = 0.6 = 0.1 + 0.2 + 0.3, and F(4) = 1 = 0.1 + 0.2 + 0.3 + 0.4. This means that F(3) is the cumulative probability that outcomes 1, 2, or 3 occur, and F(4) is the cumulative probability that one of the possible outcomes occurs.

Figure 1 shows an example of a cumulative distribution function (for a standard normal distribution, described later in this topic). There is a 15.87% probability of a value less than –1. This is the total area to the left of –1 in the pdf in Panel (a), and the y-axis value of the cdf for a value of –1 in Panel (b).

Figure 1: Standard Normal Probability Density and Cumulative Distribution Functions

(a) Probability density function

(b) Cumulative distribution function

LOS 9.e: Define a discrete uniform random variable, a Bernoulli random variable, and a binomial random variable.

LOS 9.f: Calculate and interpret probabilities given the discrete uniform and the binomial distribution functions.

CFA® Program Curriculum, Volume 1, page 466

A **discrete uniform random variable** is one for which the probabilities for all possible outcomes for a discrete random variable are equal. For example, consider the *discrete uniform probability distribution* defined as X = {1, 2, 3, 4, 5}, p(x) = 0.2. Here, the probability for each outcome is equal to 0.2 [i.e., p(1) = p(2) = p(3) = p(4) = p(5) = 0.2]. Also, the cumulative distribution function for the *n*th outcome, $F(x_n) = np(x)$, and the probability for a range of outcomes is p(x)k, where *k* is the number of possible outcomes in the range.

Example: Discrete uniform distribution

Determine p(6), F(6), and $P(2 \leq X \leq 8)$ for the discrete uniform distribution function defined as:

X = {2, 4, 6, 8, 10}, p(x) = 0.2

Answer:

p(6) = 0.2, since p(x) = 0.2 for all *x*. $F(6) = P(X \leq 6) = np(x) = 3(0.2) = 0.6$. Note that n = 3 since 6 is the third outcome in the range of possible outcomes. $P(2 \leq X \leq 8) = 4(0.2) = 0.8$. Note that k = 4, since there are four outcomes in the range $2 \leq X \leq 8$. The following figures illustrate the concepts of a probability function and cumulative distribution function for this distribution.

Probability and Cumulative Distribution Functions

X = x	Probability of x Prob (X = x)	Cumulative Distribution Function Prob (X < x)
2	0.20	0.20
4	0.20	0.40
6	0.20	0.60
8	0.20	0.80

Cumulative Distribution Function for X ~ Uniform {2, 4, 6, 8, 10}

The Binomial Distribution

A binomial random variable may be defined as the number of "successes" in a given number of trials, whereby the outcome can be either "success" or "failure." The probability of success, p, is constant for each trial, and the trials are independent. A binomial random variable for which the number of trials is 1 is called a **Bernoulli random variable**. Think of a trial as a mini-experiment (or "Bernoulli trial"). The final outcome is the number of successes in a series of n trials. Under these conditions, the binomial probability function defines the probability of x successes in n trials. It can be expressed using the following formula:

$$p(x) = P(X = x) = \text{(number of ways to choose } x \text{ from } n)p^x(1-p)^{n-x}$$

where:

(number of ways to choose x from n) = $\dfrac{n!}{(n-x)!x!}$ which may also be denoted as

$$\binom{n}{x} \text{ or stated as "}n \text{ choose } x\text{"}$$

p = the probability of "success" on each trial [don't confuse it with $p(x)$]

So the probability of exactly x successes in n trials is:

$$p(x) = \frac{n!}{(n-x)!x!}p^x(1-p)^{n-x}$$

Example: Binomial probability

Assuming a binomial distribution, compute the probability of drawing three black beans from a bowl of black and white beans if the probability of selecting a black bean in any given attempt is 0.6. You will draw five beans from the bowl.

Answer:

$$P(X = 3) = p(3) = \frac{5!}{2!3!}(0.6)^3(0.4)^2 = (120 / 12)(0.216)(0.160) = 0.3456$$

Some intuition about these results may help you remember the calculations. Consider that a (very large) bowl of black and white beans has 60% black beans and that each time you select a bean, you replace it in the bowl before drawing again. We want to know the probability of selecting exactly three black beans in five draws, as in the previous example.

One way this might happen is BBBWW. Since the draws are independent, the probability of this is easy to calculate. The probability of drawing a black bean is 60%, and the probability of drawing a white bean is 1 − 60% = 40%. Therefore, the probability of selecting BBBWW, in order, is 0.6 × 0.6 × 0.6 × 0.4 × 0.4 = 3.456%. This is the $p^3(1-p)^2$ from the formula and p is 60%, the probability of selecting a black bean on any single draw from the bowl. BBBWW is not, however, the only way to choose exactly three black beans in five trials. Another possibility is BBWWB, and a third is BWWBB. Each of these will have exactly the same probability of occurring as our initial outcome, BBBWW. That's why we need to answer the question of how many ways (different orders) there are for us to choose three black beans in five draws. Using the formula, there are $\dfrac{5!}{3!(5-3)!} = 10$ ways; 10 × 3.456% = 34.56%, the answer we computed above.

Expected Value and Variance of a Binomial Random Variable

For a given series of n trials, the expected number of successes, or $E(X)$, is given by the following formula:

expected value of X = $E(X) = np$

The intuition is straightforward; if we perform n trials and the probability of success on each trial is p, we expect np successes.

The variance of a binomial random variable is given by:

variance of X = $np(1-p)$

Example: Expected value of a binomial random variable

Based on empirical data, the probability that the Dow Jones Industrial Average (DJIA) will increase on any given day has been determined to equal 0.67. Assuming that the only other outcome is that it decreases, we can state p(UP) = 0.67 and p(DOWN) = 0.33. Further, assume that movements in the DJIA are independent (i.e., an increase in one day is independent of what happened on another day).

Using the information provided, compute the expected value of the number of up days in a 5-day period.

Answer:

Using binomial terminology, we define success as UP, so p = 0.67. Note that the definition of success is critical to any binomial problem.

E(X | n = 5, p = 0.67) = (5)(0.67) = 3.35

Recall that the "|" symbol means *given*. Hence, the preceding statement is read as: the expected value of X given that n = 5, and the probability of success = 67% is 3.35.

We should note that since the binomial distribution is a discrete distribution, the result X = 3.35 is not possible. However, if we were to record the results of many 5-day periods, the average number of up days (successes) would converge to 3.35.

LOS 9.g: Construct a binomial tree to describe stock price movement.

CFA® Program Curriculum, Volume 1, page 476

A binomial model can be applied to stock price movements. We just need to define the two possible outcomes and the probability that each outcome will occur. Consider a stock with current price S that will, over the next period, either increase in value by 1% or decrease in value by 1% (the only two possible outcomes). The probability of an up-move (the **up transition** probability, *u*) is *p* and the probability of a down-move (the **down transition** probability, *d*) is (1 – p). For our example, the up-move factor (*U*) is 1.01 and the down-move factor (*D*) is 1 / 1.01. So there is a probability *p* that the stock price will move to S(1.01) over the next period and a probability (1 – p) that the stock price will move to S / 1.01.

A binomial tree is constructed by showing all the possible combinations of up-moves and down-moves over a number of successive periods. For two periods, these combinations are UU, UD, DU, and DD. Importantly, UD and DU result in the same stock price S after two periods since S (1.01)(1/1.01) = S and the order of the moves does not change the result. Each of the possible values along a binomial tree is a **node**. Figure 2 illustrates a binomial tree for three periods.

Figure 2: A Binomial Tree

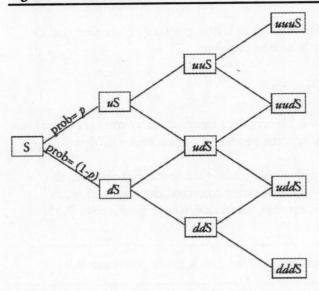

With an initial stock price S = 50, U = 1.01, D = $\frac{1}{1.01}$, and Prob(U) = 0.6, we can calculate the possible stock prices after two periods as:

$$uuS = 1.01^2 \times 50 = 51.01 \text{ with probability } (0.6)^2 = 0.36$$

$$udS = 1.01\left(\frac{1}{1.01}\right) \times 50 = 50 \text{ with probability } (0.6)(0.4) = 0.24$$

$$duS = \left(\frac{1}{1.01}\right)(1.01) \times 50 = 50 \text{ with probability } (0.4)(0.6) = 0.24$$

$$ddS = \left(\frac{1}{1.01}\right)^2 \times 50 = 49.01 \text{ with probability } (0.4)^2 = 0.16$$

Since a stock price of 50 can result from either UD or DU moves, the probability of a stock price of 50 after two periods (the middle value) is 2 × (0.6)(0.4) = 48%. A binomial tree with S = 50, U = 1.1, and Prob(U) = 0.7 is illustrated in Figure 3. Note that the middle value after two periods (50) is equal to the beginning value. The probability that the stock price is down (<50) after two periods is simply the probability of two down movements, $(1 - 0.7)^2 = 9\%$.

Figure 3: A Two-Period Binomial Tree   S = $50, U = 1.10, Prob(U) = 0.7

One of the important applications of a binomial stock price model is in pricing options. We can make a binomial tree for asset prices more realistic by shortening the length of the periods and increasing the number of periods and possible outcomes.

LOS 9.h: Calculate and interpret tracking error.

CFA® Program Curriculum, Volume 1, page 473

Tracking error is the difference between the total return on a portfolio and the total return on the benchmark against which its performance is measured. For example, if a portfolio of U.S. stocks has a return of 4% in a period when a comparable U.S. stock index increases by 7% (both on a total return basis), the portfolio's tracking error for that period is –3%.

> *Professor's Note: The expression "tracking error" is sometimes used interchangeably with "tracking risk," which refers to the standard deviation of the differences between a portfolio's return and its benchmark return.*

LOS 9.i: Define the continuous uniform distribution and calculate and interpret probabilities, given a continuous uniform distribution.

CFA® Program Curriculum, Volume 1, page 477

The continuous uniform distribution is defined over a range that spans between some lower limit, *a*, and some upper limit, *b*, which serve as the parameters of the distribution. Outcomes can only occur between *a* and *b*, and since we are dealing with a continuous distribution, even if a < x < b, P(X = x) = 0. Formally, the properties of a continuous uniform distribution may be described as follows:

- For all $a \leq x_1 < x_2 \leq b$ (i.e., for all x_1 and x_2 between the boundaries a and b).
- P(X < a or X > b) = 0 (i.e., the probability of X outside the boundaries is zero).
- $P(x_1 \leq X \leq x_2) = (x_2 - x_1)/(b - a)$. This defines the probability of outcomes between x_1 and x_2.

Don't miss how simple this is just because the notation is so mathematical. For a continuous uniform distribution, the probability of outcomes in a range that is one-half the whole range is 50%. The probability of outcomes in a range that is one-quarter as large as the whole possible range is 25%.

Example: Continuous uniform distribution

X is uniformly distributed between 2 and 12. Calculate the probability that X will be between 4 and 8.

Answer:

$$\frac{8-4}{12-2} = \frac{4}{10} = 40\%$$

The figure below illustrates this continuous uniform distribution. Note that the area bounded by 4 and 8 is 40% of the total probability between 2 and 12 (which is 100%).

Continuous Uniform Distribution

Since outcomes are equal over equal-size possible intervals, the cdf is linear over the variable's range. The cdf for the distribution in the above example, Prob (X < x), is shown in Figure 4.

Figure 4: CDF for a Continuous Uniform Variable

LOS 9.j: Explain the key properties of the normal distribution.

CFA® Program Curriculum, Volume 1, page 481

The normal distribution is important for many reasons. Many of the random variables that are relevant to finance and other professional disciplines follow a normal distribution. In the area of investment and portfolio management, the normal distribution plays a central role in portfolio theory.

The **normal distribution** has the following key properties:

- It is completely described by its mean, μ, and variance, σ^2, stated as $X \sim N(\mu, \sigma^2)$. In words, this says that "X is normally distributed with mean μ and variance σ^2."
- Skewness = 0, meaning that the normal distribution is symmetric about its mean, so that $P(X \leq \mu) = P(\mu \leq X) = 0.5$, and mean = median = mode.
- Kurtosis = 3; this is a measure of how flat the distribution is. Recall that excess kurtosis is measured relative to 3, the kurtosis of the normal distribution.
- A linear combination of normally distributed random variables is also normally distributed.
- The probabilities of outcomes further above and below the mean get smaller and smaller but do not go to zero (the tails get very thin but extend infinitely).

Many of these properties are evident from examining the graph of a normal distribution's probability density function as illustrated in Figure 5.

Figure 5: Normal Distribution Probability Density Function

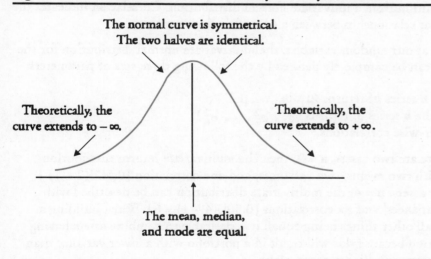

The normal curve is symmetrical.
The two halves are identical.

Theoretically, the curve extends to $-\infty$.

Theoretically, the curve extends to $+\infty$.

The mean, median, and mode are equal.

LOS 9.k: Distinguish between a univariate and a multivariate distribution, and explain the role of correlation in the multivariate normal distribution.

CFA® Program Curriculum, Volume 1, page 482

Up to this point, our discussion has been strictly focused on **univariate distributions** (i.e., the distribution of a single random variable). In practice, however, the relationships between two or more random variables are often relevant. For instance, investors and investment managers are frequently interested in the interrelationship among the returns of one or more assets. In fact, as you will see in your study of asset pricing models and modern portfolio theory, the return on a given stock and the return on the S&P 500 or some other market index will have special significance. Regardless of the specific variables, the simultaneous analysis of two or more random variables requires an understanding of multivariate distributions.

A multivariate distribution specifies the probabilities associated with a group of random variables and is meaningful only when the behavior of each random variable in the group is in some way dependent upon the behavior of the others. Both discrete and continuous random variables can have multivariate distributions. Multivariate distributions between two discrete random variables are described using joint probability tables. For continuous random variables, a multivariate *normal* distribution may be used to describe them if all of the individual variables follow a normal distribution. As previously mentioned, one of the characteristics of a normal distribution is that a linear combination of normally distributed random variables is normally distributed as well. For example, if the return of each stock in a portfolio is normally distributed, the return on the portfolio will also be normally distributed.

The Role of Correlation in the Multivariate Normal Distribution

Similar to a univariate normal distribution, a multivariate normal distribution can be described by the mean and variance of the individual random variables. Additionally, it is necessary to specify the correlation between the individual pairs of variables when describing a multivariate distribution. Correlation is the feature that distinguishes a multivariate distribution from a univariate normal distribution. Correlation indicates the strength of the linear relationship between a pair of random variables.

Using asset returns as our random variables, the multivariate normal distribution for the returns on n assets can be completely defined by the following three sets of parameters:

- n means of the n series of returns (μ_1, μ_2, ..., μ_n).
- n variances of the n series of returns (σ_1^2, σ_2^2, ..., σ_n^2).
- $0.5n(n - 1)$ pair-wise correlations.

For example, if there are two assets, n = 2, then the multivariate returns distribution can be described with two means, two variances, and one correlation [0.5(2)(2 – 1) = 1]. If there are four assets, n = 4, the multivariate distribution can be described with four means, four variances, and six correlations [0.5(4)(4 – 1) = 6]. When building a portfolio of assets, all other things being equal, it is desirable to combine assets having low returns correlation because this will result in a portfolio with a lower variance than one composed of assets with higher correlations.

LOS 9.1: Determine the probability that a normally distributed random variable lies inside a given interval.

CFA® Program Curriculum, Volume 1, page 483

A confidence interval is a range of values around the expected outcome within which we expect the actual outcome to be some specified percentage of the time. A 95% confidence interval is a range that we expect the random variable to be in 95% of the time. For a normal distribution, this interval is based on the expected value (sometimes called a point estimate) of the random variable and on its variability, which we measure with standard deviation.

Confidence intervals for a normal distribution are illustrated in Figure 6. For any normally distributed random variable, 68% of the outcomes are within one standard deviation of the expected value (mean), and approximately 95% of the outcomes are within two standard deviations of the expected value.

Figure 6: Confidence Intervals for a Normal Distribution

In practice, we will not know the actual values for the mean and standard deviation of the distribution, but will have estimated them as $\overline{X}$ and s. The three confidence intervals of most interest are given by:

- The 90% confidence interval for X is $\overline{X} - 1.65s$ to $\overline{X} + 1.65s$.
- The 95% confidence interval for X is $\overline{X} - 1.96s$ to $\overline{X} + 1.96s$.
- The 99% confidence interval for X is $\overline{X} - 2.58s$ to $\overline{X} + 2.58s$.

Example: Confidence intervals

The average return of a mutual fund is 10.5% per year and the standard deviation of annual returns is 18%. If returns are approximately normal, what is the 95% confidence interval for the mutual fund return next year?

Answer:

Here μ and σ are 10.5% and 18%, respectively. Thus, the 95% confidence interval for the return, R, is:

$$10.5 \pm 1.96(18) = -24.78\% \text{ to } 45.78\%$$

Symbolically, this result can be expressed as:

$$P(-24.78 < R < 45.78) = 0.95 \text{ or } 95\%$$

The interpretation is that the annual return is expected to be within this interval 95% of the time, or 95 out of 100 years.

LOS 9.m: Define the standard normal distribution, explain how to standardize a random variable, and calculate and interpret probabilities using the standard normal distribution.

CFA® Program Curriculum, Volume 1, page 484

The **standard normal distribution** is a normal distribution that has been standardized so that it has a mean of zero and a standard deviation of 1 [i.e., N~(0,1)]. To standardize an observation from a given normal distribution, the *z-value* of the observation must be calculated. The *z-value* represents the number of standard deviations a given observation is from the population mean. *Standardization* is the process of converting an observed value for a random variable to its *z*-value. The following formula is used to standardize a random variable:

$$z = \frac{\text{observation} - \text{population mean}}{\text{standard deviation}} = \frac{x - \mu}{\sigma}$$

Professor's Note: The term z-value *will be used for a standardized observation in this document. The terms* z-score *and* z-statistic *are also commonly used.*

Example: Standardizing a random variable (calculating *z*-values)

Assume that the annual earnings per share (EPS) for a population of firms are normally distributed with a mean of $6 and a standard deviation of $2.

What are the *z*-values for EPS of $2 and $8?

Answer:

If EPS = x = $8, then z = (x − μ) / σ = ($8 − $6) / $2 = +1

If EPS = x = $2, then z = (x − μ) / σ = ($2 − $6) / $2 = −2

Here, z = +1 indicates that an EPS of $8 is one standard deviation above the mean, and z = −2 means that an EPS of $2 is two standard deviations below the mean.

Calculating Probabilities Using *z*-Values

Now we will show how to use standardized values (*z*-values) and a table of probabilities for Z to determine probabilities. A portion of a table of the cumulative distribution function for a standard normal distribution is shown in Figure 7. We will refer to this table as the *z*-table, as it contains values generated using the cumulative density function for a standard normal distribution, denoted by F(Z). Thus, the values in the *z*-table are the probabilities of observing a *z*-value that is less than a given value, *z* [i.e., P(Z < z)]. The numbers in the first column are *z*-values that have only one decimal place. The columns to the right supply probabilities for *z*-values with two decimal places.

Note that the z-table in Figure 7 only provides probabilities for positive z-values. This is not a problem because we know from the symmetry of the standard normal distribution that $F(-Z) = 1 - F(Z)$. The tables in the back of many texts actually provide probabilities for negative z-values, but we will work with only the positive portion of the table because this may be all you get on the exam. In Figure 7, we can find the probability that a standard normal random variable will be less than 1.66, for example. The table value is 95.15%. The probability that the random variable will be less than −1.66 is simply $1 - 0.9515 = 0.0485 = 4.85\%$, which is also the probability that the variable will be greater than +1.66.

> *Professor's Note: When you use the standard normal probabilities, you have formulated the problem in terms of standard deviations from the mean. Consider a security with returns that are approximately normal, an expected return of 10%, and standard deviation of returns of 12%. The probability of returns greater than 30% is calculated based on the number of standard deviations that 30% is above the expected return of 10%. 30% is 20% above the expected return of 10%, which is 20 / 12 = 1.67 standard deviations above the mean. We look up the probability of returns less than 1.67 standard deviations above the mean (0.9525 or 95.25% from Figure 7) and calculate the probability of returns more than 1.67 standard deviations above the mean as $1 - 0.9525 = 4.75\%$.*

Figure 7: Cumulative Probabilities for a Standard Normal Distribution

				Cdf Values for the Standard Normal Distribution: The z-Table					
z	.00	.01	.02	.03	.04	.05	.06	.07	.08	.09
0.0	.5000	.5040	.5080	.5120	.5160	.5199	.5239	.5279	.5319	.5359
0.1	.5398	.5438	.5478	.5517	.5557	.5596	.5636	.5675	.5714	.5753
0.2	.5793	.5832	.5871	.5910	.5948	.5987	.6026	.6064	.6103	.6141
0.5	.6915	Please note that several of the rows have been deleted to save space.*								
1.2	.8849	.8869	.8888	.8907	.8925	.8944	.8962	.8980	.8997	.9015
1.6	.9452	.9463	.9474	.9484	.9495	.9505	.9515	.9525	.9535	.9545
1.8	.9641	.9649	.9656	.9664	.9671	.9678	.9686	.9693	.9699	.9706
1.9	.9713	.9719	.9726	.9732	.9738	.9744	.9750	.9756	.9761	.9767
2.0	.9772	.9778	.9783	.9788	.9793	.9798	.9803	.9808	.9812	.9817
2.5	.9938	.9940	.9941	.9943	.9945	.9946	.9948	.9949	.9951	.9952
3.0	.9987	.9987	.9987	.9988	.9988	.9989	.9989	.9989	.9990	.9990

* A complete cumulative standard normal table is included in Appendix A.

Example: Using the z-table (1)

Considering again EPS distributed with μ = $6 and σ = $2, what is the probability that EPS will be $9.70 or more?

Answer:

Here we want to know P(EPS > $9.70), which is the area under the curve to the right of the z-value corresponding to EPS = $9.70 (see the figure below).

The z-value for EPS = $9.70 is:

$$z = \frac{(x - \mu)}{\sigma} = \frac{(9.70 - 6)}{2} = 1.85$$

That is, $9.70 is 1.85 standard deviations above the mean EPS value of $6.

From the z-table we have F(1.85) = 0.9678, but this is P(EPS ≤ 9.70). We want P(EPS > 9.70), which is 1 − P(EPS ≤ 9.70).

P(EPS > 9.70) = 1 − 0.9678 = 0.0322, or 3.2%

P(EPS>$9.70)

Example: Using the z-table (2)

Using the distribution of EPS with μ = $6 and σ = $2 again, what percent of the observed EPS values are likely to be less than $4.10?

Answer:

As shown graphically in the figure below, we want to know P(EPS < $4.10). This requires a 2-step approach like the one taken in the preceding example.

First, the corresponding z-value must be determined as follows:

$$z = \frac{(\$4.10 - \$6)}{2} = -0.95,$$

So $4.10 is 0.95 standard deviations below the mean of $6.00.

Now, from the z-table for negative values in the back of this book, we find that F(−0.95) = 0.1711, or 17.11%.

Finding a Left-Tail Probability

The z-table gives us the probability that the outcome will be more than 0.95 standard deviations below the mean.

LOS 9.n: Define shortfall risk, calculate the safety-first ratio, and select an optimal portfolio using Roy's safety-first criterion.

CFA® Program Curriculum, Volume 1, page 487

Shortfall risk is the probability that a portfolio value or return will fall below a particular (target) value or return over a given time period.

Roy's safety-first criterion states that the optimal portfolio minimizes the probability that the return of the portfolio falls below some minimum acceptable level. This minimum acceptable level is called the **threshold level.** Symbolically, Roy's safety-first criterion can be stated as:

minimize $P(R_p < R_L)$

where:
R_p = portfolio return
R_L = threshold level return

If portfolio returns are normally distributed, then Roy's safety-first criterion can be stated as:

maximize the SFRatio where SFRatio = $\dfrac{\left[E\left(R_P \right) - R_L \right]}{\sigma_P}$

Professor's Note: Notice the similarity to the Sharpe ratio:

$$Sharpe = \frac{\left[E\left(R_p\right) - R_f\right]}{\sigma_p}$$ *. The only difference is that the SFRatio utilizes the*

excess return over the threshold return, R_L, where the Sharpe ratio uses the excess return over the risk-free rate, R_f. When the threshold level is the risk-free rate of return, the SFRatio is also the Sharpe ratio.

The reasoning behind the safety-first criterion is illustrated in Figure 8. Assume an investor is choosing between two portfolios: Portfolio A with expected return of 12% and standard deviation of returns of 18%, and Portfolio B with expected return of 10% and standard deviation of returns of 12%. The investor has stated that he wants to minimize the probability of losing money (negative returns). Assuming that returns are normally distributed, the portfolio with the larger SFR using 0% as the threshold return (R_L) will be the one with the lower probability of negative returns.

Figure 8: The Safety-First Criterion and Shortfall Risk

A. Normally Distributed Returns

Portfolio A: E(R)=12% σ_A=18%   Portfolio B: E(R)=10% σ_B=12%

Probability of returns < 0%
– i.e. short fall risk

0% 12%

$$SFR_A = \frac{12 - 0}{18} = 0.667$$

0%   10%

$$SFR_B = \frac{10 - 0}{12} = 0.833$$

B. Standard Normal

25.14%

−0.67   0

20.13%

−0.83   0

Panel B of Figure 8 relates the SFRatio to the standard normal distribution. Note that the SFR is the number of standard deviations *below* the mean. Thus, the portfolio with the larger SFR has the lower probability of returns below the threshold return, which is a return of 0% in our example. Using a *z*-table for negative values, we can find the probabilities in the left-hand tails as indicated. These probabilities (25% for Portfolio A and 20% for Portfolio B) are also the shortfall risk for a target return of 0%, that is, the probability of negative returns. Portfolio B has the higher SFR which means it has the lower probability of negative returns.

In summary, when choosing among portfolios with normally distributed returns using Roy's safety-first criterion, there are two steps:

Step 1: Calculate the SFRatio = $\dfrac{\left[E\left(R_P\right)-R_L\right]}{\sigma_p}$.

Step 2: Choose the portfolio that has the *largest* SFRatio.

> **Example: Roy's safety-first criterion**
>
> For the next year, the managers of a $120 million college endowment plan have set a minimum acceptable end-of-year portfolio value of $123.6 million. Three portfolios are being considered which have the expected returns and standard deviation shown in the first two rows of the table below. Determine which of these portfolios is the most desirable using Roy's safety-first criterion and the probability that the portfolio value will fall short of the target amount.
>
> **Answer:**
>
> The threshold return is R_L = (123.6 – 120) / 120 = 0.030 = 3%. The SFRs are shown in the table below. As indicated, the best choice is Portfolio A because it has the largest SFR.
>
> **Roy's Safety-First Ratios**
>
> | Portfolio | Portfolio A | Portfolio B | Portfolio C |
> |-----------|-------------|-------------|-------------|
> | $E(R_p)$ | 9% | 11% | 6.6% |
> | σ_p | 12% | 20% | 8.2% |
> | SFRatio | $0.5 = \dfrac{(9-3)}{12}$ | $0.4 = \dfrac{(11-3)}{20}$ | $0.44 = \dfrac{(6.6-3)}{8.2}$ |
>
> The probability of an ending value for Portfolio A less than $123.6 million (a return less than 3%) is simply F(–0.5) which we can find on the z-table for negative values. The probability is 0.3085 = 30.85%.

LOS 9.o: Explain the relationship between normal and lognormal distributions and why the lognormal distribution is used to model asset prices.

CFA® Program Curriculum, Volume 1, page 489

The **lognormal distribution** is generated by the function e^x, where x is normally distributed. Since the natural logarithm, ln, of e^x is x, the logarithms of lognormally distributed random variables are normally distributed, thus the name.

Figure 9 illustrates the differences between a normal distribution and a lognormal distribution.

Figure 9: Normal vs. Lognormal Distributions

In Figure 9, we can see that:

- The lognormal distribution is skewed to the right.
- The lognormal distribution is bounded from below by zero so that it is useful for modeling asset prices which never take negative values.

If we used a normal distribution of returns to model asset prices over time, we would admit the possibility of returns less than –100%, which would admit the possibility of asset prices less than zero. Using a lognormal distribution to model *price relatives* avoids this problem. A price relative is just the end-of-period price of the asset divided by the beginning price (S_1/S_0) and is equal to (1 + the holding period return). To get the end-of-period asset price, we can simply multiply the price relative times the beginning-of-period asset price. Since a lognormal distribution takes a minimum value of zero, end-of-period asset prices cannot be less than zero. A price relative of zero corresponds to a holding period return of –100% (i.e., the asset price has gone to zero). Recall that we used price relatives as the up-move and down-move (multiplier) terms in constructing a binomial tree for stock price changes over a number of periods.

LOS 9.p: Distinguish between discretely and continuously compounded rates of return, and calculate and interpret a continuously compounded rate of return, given a specific holding period return.

CFA® Program Curriculum, Volume 1, page 491

Discretely compounded returns are just the compound returns we are familiar with, given some discrete compounding period, such as semiannual or quarterly. Recall that the more frequent the compounding, the greater the effective annual return.

For a stated rate of 10%, semiannual compounding results in an effective yield of $\left(1+\dfrac{0.10}{2}\right)^2 -1 = 10.25\%$ and monthly compounding results in an effective yield of $\left(1+\dfrac{0.10}{12}\right)^{12} -1 = 10.47\%$. Daily or even hourly compounding will produce still larger effective yields. The limit of this exercise, as the compounding periods get shorter and shorter, is called **continuous compounding**. The effective annual rate, based on continuous compounding for a stated annual rate of R_{cc}, can be calculated from the formula:

$$\text{effective annual rate} = e^{R_{cc}} -1$$

Based on a stated rate of 10%, the effective rate with continuous compounding is $e^{0.10} -1 = 10.5171\%$. Please verify this by entering 0.1 in your calculator and finding the e^x function.

Since the natural log, ln, of e^x is x, we can get the continuously compounded rate from an effective annual rate by using the ln calculator function. Using our previous example, ln (1 + 10.517%) = ln 1.105171 = 10%. Verify this by entering 1.105171 in your calculator and then entering the ln key. (Using the HP calculator, the keystrokes are 1.105171 [g] [ln].)

We can use this method to find the continuously compounded rate that will generate a particular holding period return. If we are given a holding period return of 12.5% for the year, the equivalent continuously compounded rate is ln 1.125 = 11.778%. Since the calculation is based on 1 plus the holding period return, we can also do the calculation directly from the *price relative*. The price relative is just the end-of-period value divided by the beginning of period value. The continuously compounded rate of return is:

$$\ln\left(\frac{S_1}{S_0}\right) = \ln(1+\text{HPR}) = R_{cc}$$

Example: Calculating continuously compounded returns

A stock was purchased for $100 and sold one year later for $120. Calculate the investor's annual rate of return on a continuously compounded basis.

Answer:

$$\ln\left(\frac{120}{100}\right) = 18.232\%$$

If we had been given the return (20%) instead, the calculation is:

$$\ln(1 + 0.20) = 18.232\%$$

One property of continuously compounded rates of return is that they are additive for multiple periods. Note that the (effective) holding period return over two years is calculated by doubling the continuously compounded annual rate. If R_{cc} = 10%, the (effective) holding period return over two years is $e^{(0.10)2} - 1$ = 22.14%. In general, the holding period return after T years, when the annual continuously compounded rate is R_{cc}, is given by:

$$HPR_T = e^{Rcc \times T} - 1$$

Given investment results over a 2-year period, we can calculate the 2-year continuously compounded return and divide by two to get the annual rate. Consider an investment that appreciated from $1,000 to $1,221.40 over a 2-year period. The 2-year continuously compounded rate is ln(1,221.40 / 1,000) = 20%, and the annual continuously compounded rate (R_{cc}) is 20% / 2 = 10%.

LOS 9.q: Explain Monte Carlo simulation and describe its major applications and limitations.

CFA® Program Curriculum, Volume 1, page 494

Monte Carlo simulation is a technique based on the repeated generation of one or more risk factors that affect security values, in order to generate a distribution of security values. For each of the risk factors, the analyst must specify the parameters of the probability distribution that the risk factor is assumed to follow. A computer is then used to generate random values for each risk factor based on its assumed probability distributions. Each set of randomly generated risk factors is used with a pricing model to value the security. This procedure is repeated many times (100s, 1,000s, or 10,000s), and the distribution of simulated asset values is used to draw inferences about the expected (mean) value of the security and possibly the variance of security values about the mean as well.

As an example, consider the valuation of stock options that can only be exercised on a particular date. The main risk factor is the value of the stock itself, but interest rates could affect the valuation as well. The simulation procedure would be to:

1. Specify the probability distributions of stock prices and of the relevant interest rate, as well as the parameters (mean, variance, possibly skewness) of the distributions.

2. Randomly generate values for both stock prices and interest rates.

3. Value the options for each pair of risk factor values.

4. After many iterations, calculate the mean option value and use that as your estimate of the option's value.

Monte Carlo simulation is used to:

- Value complex securities.
- Simulate the profits/losses from a trading strategy.
- Calculate estimates of value at risk (VAR) to determine the riskiness of a portfolio of assets and liabilities.

- Simulate pension fund assets and liabilities over time to examine the variability of the difference between the two.
- Value portfolios of assets that have non-normal returns distributions.

The **limitations of Monte Carlo simulation** are that it is fairly complex and will provide answers that are no better than the assumptions about the distributions of the risk factors and the pricing/valuation model that is used. Also, simulation is not an analytic method, but a statistical one, and cannot provide the insights that analytic methods can.

LOS 9.r: Compare Monte Carlo simulation and historical simulation.

CFA® Program Curriculum, Volume 1, page 500

Historical simulation is based on actual changes in value or actual changes in risk factors over some prior period. Rather than model the distribution of risk factors, as in Monte Carlo simulation, the set of all changes in the relevant risk factors over some prior period is used. Each iteration of the simulation involves randomly selecting one of these past changes for each risk factor and calculating the value of the asset or portfolio in question, based on those changes in risk factors.

Historical simulation has the advantage of using the actual distribution of risk factors so that the distribution of changes in the risk factors does not have to be estimated. It suffers from the fact that past changes in risk factors may not be a good indication of future changes. Events that occur infrequently may not be reflected in historical simulation results unless the events occurred during the period from which the values for risk factors are drawn. An additional limitation of historical simulation is that it cannot address the sort of "what if" questions that Monte Carlo simulation can. With Monte Carlo simulation, we can investigate the effect on the distribution of security/portfolio values if we increase the variance of one of the risk factors by 20%; with historical simulation we cannot do this.

KEY CONCEPTS

LOS 9.a

A probability distribution lists all the possible outcomes of an experiment, along with their associated probabilities.

A discrete random variable has positive probabilities associated with a finite number of outcomes.

A continuous random variable has positive probabilities associated with a range of outcome values—the probability of any single value is zero.

LOS 9.b

The set of possible outcomes of a specific discrete random variable is a finite set of values. An example is the number of days last week on which the value of a particular portfolio increased. For a discrete distribution, $p(x) = 0$ when x cannot occur, or $p(x) > 0$ if it can.

LOS 9.c

A cumulative distribution function (cdf) gives the probability that a random variable will be less than or equal to specific values. The cumulative distribution function for a random variable X may be expressed as $F(x) = P(X \leq x)$.

LOS 9.d

Given the cumulative distribution function for a random variable, the probability that an outcome will be less than or equal to a specific value is represented by the area under the probability distribution to the left of that value.

LOS 9.e

A discrete uniform distribution is one where there are n discrete, equally likely outcomes.

The binomial distribution is a probability distribution for a binomial (discrete) random variable that has two possible outcomes.

LOS 9.f

For a discrete uniform distribution with n possible outcomes, the probability for each outcome equals $1/n$.

For a binomial distribution, if the probability of success is p, the probability of x successes in n trials is:

$$p(x) = P(X = x) = \frac{n!}{(n-x)!x!} p^x (1-p)^{n-x} = {}_nC_x \times p^x (1-p)^{n-x}$$

LOS 9.g

A binomial tree illustrates the probabilities of all the possible values that a variable (such as a stock price) can take on, given the probability of an up-move and the magnitude of an up-move (the up-move factor).

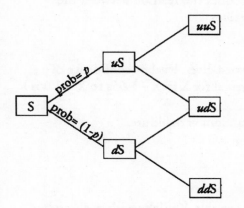

With an initial stock price S = 50, U = 1.01, D = $\frac{1}{1.01}$, and prob(U) = 0.6, the possible

stock prices after two periods are:

$uuS = 1.01^2 \times 50 = 51.01$ with probability $(0.6)^2 = 0.36$

$udS = 1.01\left(\frac{1}{1.01}\right) \times 50 = 50$ with probability $(0.6)(0.4) = 0.24$

$duS = \left(\frac{1}{1.01}\right)(1.01) \times 50 = 50$ with probability $(0.4)(0.6) = 0.24$

$ddS = \left(\frac{1}{1.01}\right)^2 \times 50 = 49.01$ with probability $(0.4)^2 = 0.16$

LOS 9.h

Tracking error is calculated as the total return on a portfolio minus the total return on a benchmark or index portfolio.

LOS 9.i

A continuous uniform distribution is one where the probability of X occurring in a possible range is the length of the range relative to the total of all possible values. Letting a and b be the lower and upper limit of the uniform distribution, respectively, then for:

$$a \leq x_1 \leq x_2 \leq b, \ P\left(x_1 \leq X \leq x_2\right) = \frac{(x_2 - x_1)}{(b - a)}$$

LOS 9.j

The normal probability distribution and normal curve have the following characteristics:
- The normal curve is symmetrical and bell-shaped with a single peak at the exact center of the distribution.
- Mean = median = mode, and all are in the exact center of the distribution.
- The normal distribution can be completely defined by its mean and standard deviation because the skew is always zero and kurtosis is always 3.

LOS 9.k

Multivariate distributions describe the probabilities for more than one random variable, whereas a univariate distribution is for a single random variable.

The correlation(s) of a multivariate distribution describes the relation between the outcomes of its variables relative to their expected values.

LOS 9.l

A confidence interval is a range within which we have a given level of confidence of finding a point estimate (e.g., the 90% confidence interval for X is $\bar{X} - 1.65s$ to $\bar{X} + 1.65s$).

Confidence intervals for any normally distributed random variable are:
- 90%: $\mu \pm 1.65$ standard deviations.
- 95%: $\mu \pm 1.96$ standard deviations.
- 99%: $\mu \pm 2.58$ standard deviations.

The probability that a normally distributed random variable X will be within A standard deviations of its mean, μ, [i.e., $P(\mu - A\sigma \leq X \leq \mu + A\sigma)$], is calculated as two times [1 – the cumulative left-hand tail probability, $F(-A)$], or two times {1 – the right-hand tail probability, $[1 - F(A)]$}, where $F(A)$ is the cumulative standard normal probability of A.

LOS 9.m

The standard normal probability distribution has a mean of 0 and a standard deviation of 1.

A normally distributed random variable X can be standardized as $Z = \dfrac{x - \mu}{\sigma}$ and Z will be normally distributed with mean = 0 and standard deviation 1.

The z-table is used to find the probability that X will be less than or equal to a given value.
- $P(X < x) = F(x) = F\left[\dfrac{x - \mu}{\sigma}\right] = F(z)$, which is found in the standard normal probability table.
- $P(X > x) = 1 - P(X < x) = 1 - F(z)$.

LOS 9.n

The safety-first ratio for portfolio P, based on a target return R_T, is:

$$SFRatio = \frac{E(R_P) - R_T}{\sigma_P}$$

Shortfall risk is the probability that a portfolio's value (or return) will fall below a specific value over a given period of time. Greater safety-first ratios are preferred and indicate a smaller shortfall probability. Roy's safety-first criterion states that the optimal portfolio minimizes shortfall risk.

LOS 9.o

If x is normally distributed, e^x follows a lognormal distribution. A lognormal distribution is often used to model asset prices, since a lognormal random variable cannot be negative and can take on any positive value.

LOS 9.p

As we decrease the length of discrete compounding periods (e.g., from quarterly to monthly) the effective annual rate increases. As the length of the compounding period in discrete compounding gets shorter and shorter, the compounding becomes continuous, where the effective annual rate = $e^i - 1$.

For a holding period return (HPR) over any period, the equivalent continuously compounded rate over the period is $\ln(1 + \text{HPR})$.

LOS 9.q

Monte Carlo simulation uses randomly generated values for risk factors, based on their assumed distributions, to produce a distribution of possible security values. Its limitations are that it is fairly complex and will provide answers that are no better than the assumptions used.

LOS 9.r

Historical simulation uses randomly selected past changes in risk factors to generate a distribution of possible security values, in contrast to Monte Carlo simulation, which uses randomly generated values. A limitation of historical simulation is that it cannot consider the effects of significant events that did not occur in the sample period.

CONCEPT CHECKERS

1. Which of the following is *least likely* an example of a discrete random variable?
   A. The number of stocks a person owns.
   B. The time spent by a portfolio manager with a client.
   C. The number of days it rains in a month in Iowa City.

2. For a continuous random variable X, the probability of any single value of X is:
   A. one.
   B. zero.
   C. determined by the cdf.

Use the following table to answer Questions 3 through 7.

Probability distribution of a discrete random variable X							
X	0	1	2	3	4	5	6	7
P(X)	0.04	0.11	0.18	0.24	0.14	0.17	0.09	0.03

3. The probability that X = 3 is:
   A. 0.18.
   B. 0.24.
   C. 0.43.

4. The cdf of 5, or F(5) is:
   A. 0.17.
   B. 0.71.
   C. 0.88.

5. The probability that X is *greater* than 3 is:
   A. 0.24.
   B. 0.43.
   C. 0.67.

6. What is $P(2 \leq X \leq 5)$?
   A. 0.17.
   B. 0.38.
   C. 0.73.

7. The expected value of the random variable X is:
   A. 3.35.
   B. 3.70.
   C. 5.47.

8. Which of the following is *least likely* a condition of a binomial experiment?
   A. There are only two trials.
   B. The trials are independent.
   C. If p is the probability of success, and q is the probability of failure, then
      $p + q = 1$.

9.   A recent study indicated that 60% of all businesses have a fax machine. From the binomial probability distribution table, the probability that exactly four businesses will have a fax machine in a random selection of six businesses is:
A. 0.138.
B. 0.276.
C. 0.311.

10.   Ten percent of all college graduates hired stay with the same company for more than five years. In a random sample of six recently hired college graduates, the probability that exactly two will stay with the same company for more than five years is *closest* to:
A. 0.098.
B. 0.114.
C. 0.185.

11.   Assume that 40% of candidates who sit for the CFA® examination pass it the first time. Of a random sample of 15 candidates who are sitting for the exam for the first time, what is the expected number of candidates that will pass?
A. 0.375.
B. 4.000.
C. 6.000.

12.   For the standard normal distribution, the z-value gives the distance between the mean and a point in terms of the:
A. variance.
B. standard deviation.
C. center of the curve.

13.   For a standard normal distribution, F(0) is:
A. 0.0.
B. 0.1.
C. 0.5.

14.   For the standard normal distribution, $P(0 \leq Z \leq 1.96)$ is:
A. 0.4713.
B. 0.4745.
C. 0.4750.

Use the following data to answer Questions 15 through 17.

A study of hedge fund investors found that their annual household incomes are normally distributed with a mean of $175,000 and a standard deviation of $25,000.

15.   The percent of hedge fund investors that have incomes less than $100,000 is *closest* to:
A. 0.05%.
B. 0.10%.
C. 0.13%.

16.   The percent of hedge fund investors that have incomes greater than $225,000 is *closest* to:
      A. 0.50%.
      B. 1.10%.
      C. 2.28%.

17.   The percent of hedge fund investors that have incomes greater than $150,000 is *closest* to:
      A. 34.13%.
      B. 68.26%.
      C. 84.13%.

Use the following table to answer Questions 18 and 19.

Portfolio	Portfolio A	Portfolio B	Portfolio C
$E(R_p)$	5%	11%	18%
σ_p	8%	21%	40%

18.   Given a threshold level of return of 4%, use Roy's safety-first criterion to choose the optimal portfolio. Portfolio:
      A. A.
      B. B.
      C. C.

19.   Given a threshold level of return of 0%, use Roy's safety-first criterion to choose the optimal portfolio. Portfolio:
      A. A.
      B. B.
      C. C.

20.   If a stock's initial price is $20 and its year-end price is $23, then its continuously compounded annual rate of return is:
      A. 13.64%.
      B. 13.98%.
      C. 15.00%.

21.   For a lognormal distribution, the:
      A. mean equals the median.
      B. probability of a negative outcome is zero.
      C. probability of a positive outcome is 50%.

22.   Using hypothesized parameter values and a random number generator to study the behavior of certain asset returns is part of:
      A. historical analysis.
      B. Monte Carlo simulation.
      C. standardizing a random variable.

23. A continuous uniform distribution has the parameters a = 4 and b = 10. The F(20) is:
   A. 0.25.
   B. 0.50.
   C. 1.00.

24. Which of the following statements *least accurately* describes the binomial distribution?
   A. It is a discrete distribution.
   B. The probability of an outcome of zero is zero.
   C. The combination formula is used in computing probabilities.

25. Approximately 95% of all observations for a normally distributed random variable fall in the interval:
   A. $\mu \pm \sigma$.
   B. $\mu \pm 2\sigma$.
   C. $\mu \pm 3\sigma$.

26. The probability that a normally distributed random variable will be more than two standard deviations above its mean is:
   A. 0.0228.
   B. 0.4772.
   C. 0.9772.

27. A stock doubled in value last year. Its continuously compounded return over the period was *closest* to:
   A. 18.2%.
   B. 69.3%.
   C. 100.0%.

28. Portfolio A has a safety-first ratio of 1.3 with a threshold return of 2%. What is the shortfall risk for a threshold return of 2%?
   A. 9.68%.
   B. 40.30%.
   C. 90.30%.

CHALLENGE PROBLEMS

1. A stock's price is $8.50 today. You decide to model the stock price over time using a binomial model (as a Bernoulli random variable) with a probability of an up-move of 60%. The up-move factor is 1.05.

   A. How many different prices are possible for the stock at the end of two periods?

   B. What are the possible prices after two periods?

   C. What is the probability that the stock price will be $8.50 after three periods?

   D. What is the probability that the stock price will be $8.925 after three periods?

   E. What is the probability that the stock price will be unchanged after six periods?

2. An analyst has developed a model of option prices as a function of a short-term interest rate and the price of the underlying stock. She decides to test the model with a Monte Carlo simulation.

    A. What steps does she need to perform to run the simulation?

    B. What limitations of Monte Carlo simulation does she need to keep in mind when she interprets the results?

    C. What would be the advantages of using historical simulation instead of Monte Carlo simulation? What would be the drawbacks?

3. The monthly returns on an index of investment-grade corporate bonds for the last ten years have averaged 0.7% with a standard deviation of 2.0%.

    A. Assuming the returns are approximately normally distributed, what are the 90%, 95%, and 99% confidence intervals for the monthly return on this index?

    B. You are considering whether to use a lognormal distribution to model the value of one of the bonds in the index. In what ways is the lognormal distribution different from the normal distribution? What property of the lognormal distribution makes it useful for modeling asset prices?

ANSWERS – CONCEPT CHECKERS

1. **B**   Time is usually a continuous random variable; the others are discrete.

2. **B**   For a continuous distribution p(x) = 0 for all X; only ranges of value of X have positive probabilities.

3. **B**   From the table.

4. **C**   (0.04 + 0.11 + 0.18 + 0.24 + 0.14 + 0.17) = 0.88

5. **B**   (0.14 + 0.17 + 0.09 + 0.03) = 0.43

6. **C**   (0.18 + 0.24 + 0.14 + 0.17) = 0.73

7. **A**   0 + 1(0.11) + 2(0.18) + 3(0.24) + 4(0.14) + 5(0.17) + 6(0.09) + 7(0.03) = 3.35

8. **A**   There may be any number of independent trials, each with only two possible outcomes.

9. **C**   Success = having a fax machine. $[6! / 4!(6 - 4)!](0.6)^4(0.4)^{6-4}$ = 15(0.1296)(0.16) = 0.311.

10. **A**   Success = staying for five years. $[6! / 2!(6 - 2)!](0.10)^2(0.90)^{6-2}$ = 15(0.01)(0.656) = 0.0984.

11. **C**   Success = passing the exam. Then, E(success) = np = 15 × 0.4 = 6.

12. **B**   This is true by the formula for z.

13. **C**   By the symmetry of the z-distribution and F(0) = 0.5. Half the distribution lies on each side of the mean.

14. **C**   From the table F(1.96) = 0.9750; thus, the answer is 0.9750 – 0.5 = 0.4750. Knowing that 95% lie between –1.96 and +1.96, and that 0 is the midpoint, we can say that $\frac{95\%}{2}$ = 47.5% lie between 0 and +1.96.

15. **C**   z = (100 – 175) / 25 = –3, F(–3) = 1 – 0.9987 = 0.0013

16. **C**   1 – F(2), where F(2) equals 0.9772. Hence, 1 – 0.9772 = 0.0228.

17. **C**   1 – F(–1) = F(1) = 0.8413

18. **C**   SFR = (18 – 4) / 40 is the largest value.

19. **A**   SFR = (5 – 0) / 8 is the largest value.

20. **B**   ln(23 / 20) = 0.1398

21. **B**   A lognormally distributed variable is never negative.

22. **B**   Monte Carlo simulation involves modeling asset prices or returns by generating random values for the risk factors that affect the price of a security.

23. **C** F(x) is the cumulative probability, P(x < 20) here. Because all the observations in this distribution are between 4 and 10, the probability of an outcome less than 20 is 100%.

24. **B** With only two possible outcomes, there must be some positive probability for each. If this were not the case, the variable in question would not be a random variable, and a probability distribution would be meaningless. It does not matter if one of the possible outcomes happens to be zero.

25. **B** $\mu \pm 2\sigma$. Approximately 95% of the outcomes for a normally distributed random variable are within two standard deviations of the mean.

26. **A** $1 - F(2) = 1 - 0.9772 = 0.0228$

27. **B** $\ln(2) = 0.6931$

28. **A** Using the tables, the cdf for −1.3 is 9.68%, which is the probability of returns less than 2%.

ANSWERS – CHALLENGE PROBLEMS

1. **A.** Using u for an up move and d for a down move, there are four possible outcomes (price paths) over two periods: uu, ud, du, and dd. Since ud and du result in the same price at the end of two periods ($8.50), there are three possible prices after two periods.

    B. An up-move factor of 1.05 means the down-move factor is 1 / 1.05. Therefore, the possible prices for each path are as follows:
    - uu: Price = $8.50(1.05)^2 = 9.37
    - ud: Price = $8.50(1.05)(1 / 1.05) = 8.50
    - du: Price = $8.50(1 / 1.05) (1.05) = 8.50
    - dd: Price = $8.50(1 / 1.05)^2 = 7.71

    C. For a 3-period model, there is no possible way that the up moves and down moves can exactly offset since the possibilities are: uuu, uud, udu, duu, ddu, dud, udd, ddd. The probability of a price of $8.50 is zero.

    D. $8.925 is the result of a single up move, 8.50(1.05) = 8.925. With three periods, this price could only result from two up moves and one down move (in any order). The probabilities of prices after n periods follow a binomial distribution. Define an up move as a success so that the probability of a success (p) is 0.60, the probability of an up move. The probability of two successes in three trials is $_3C_2 (0.6)^2 (1 - 0.6) = 43.2\%$. This calculation takes account of all three possible price paths that include two up moves and one down move: uud, udu, and duu.

    E. The price will be unchanged after six periods only if the price path includes three up moves and three down moves. The probability of three successes (up moves) in six trials is: $_6C_3 (0.6)^3 (1 - 0.6)^3 = 27.65\%$.

2. A. To construct a Monte Carlo simulation, the analyst would need to:

   1. Identify the distributions that the input variables follow and their means, variances, and any other relevant parameters, such as skewness.

   2. Generate random values from these distributions for both input variables.

   3. Price the option using the randomly generated inputs.

   4. Repeat steps 2 and 3 for many trials. Calculate the mean option price from all the trials. This value is the simulation's estimate of the option value.

   B. Whether the results from a Monte Carlo simulation are useful depends on how well the analyst has specified the distributions of the interest rate and the stock price (the old, garbage in—garbage out problem). Also, the simulation results contain no information about whether the valuation model itself is valid.

   C. The main advantages of historical simulation are that it uses actual historical values for the model inputs so that the analyst does not need to make assumptions about their probability distributions, and it is a less computer-intensive procedure. A disadvantage of historical simulation is that it assumes the past behavior of the variables is a reliable indicator of their future behavior, which might not be the case. Historical simulation also lacks the Monte Carlo approach's ability to model "what if" questions by changing the assumed probability distributions of the model inputs.

3. A. The 90% confidence interval is the mean ± 1.65 standard deviations.
      0.7 + 1.65(2.0) = 4.0%
      0.7 − 1.65(2.0) = −2.6%

      The 95% confidence interval is the mean ± 1.96 standard deviations.
      0.7 + 1.96(2.0) = 4.62%
      0.7 − 1.96(2.0) = −3.22%

      The 99% confidence interval is the mean ± 2.58 standard deviations.
      0.7 + 2.58(2.0) = 5.86%
      0.7 − 2.58(2.0) = −4.46%

   B. The lognormal distribution is skewed to the right, whereas the normal distribution is symmetrical. The lognormal distribution can only have positive values, whereas the normal distribution includes both positive and negative values. This property makes the lognormal distribution useful for modeling asset prices.

SAMPLING AND ESTIMATION

EXAM FOCUS

This topic review covers random samples and inferences about population means from sample data. It is essential that you know the central limit theorem, for it allows us to use sampling statistics to construct confidence intervals for point estimates of population means. Make sure you can calculate confidence intervals for population means given sample parameter estimates and a level of significance, and know when it is appropriate to use the z-statistic versus the t-statistic. You should also understand the basic procedures for creating random samples, and recognize the warning signs of various sampling biases from nonrandom samples.

APPLIED STATISTICS

In many real-world statistics applications, it is impractical (or impossible) to study an entire population. When this is the case, a subgroup of the population, called a sample, can be evaluated. Based upon this sample, the parameters of the underlying population can be estimated.

For example, rather than attempting to measure the performance of the U.S. stock market by observing the performance of all 10,000 or so stocks trading in the United States at any one time, the performance of the subgroup of 500 stocks in the S&P 500 can be measured. The results of the statistical analysis of this sample can then be used to draw conclusions about the entire population of U.S. stocks.

LOS 10.a: Define simple random sampling and a sampling distribution.

LOS 10.b: Explain sampling error.

CFA® Program Curriculum, Volume 1, page 514

Simple random sampling is a method of selecting a sample in such a way that each item or person in the population being studied has the same likelihood of being included in the sample. As an example of simple random sampling, assume that you want to draw a sample of five items out of a group of 50 items. This can be accomplished by numbering each of the 50 items, placing them in a hat, and shaking the hat. Next, one number can be drawn randomly from the hat. Repeating this process (experiment) four more times results in a set of five numbers. The five drawn numbers (items) comprise a simple random sample from the population. In applications like this one, a random-number table or a computer random-number generator is often used to create the sample. Another way to form an approximately random sample is systematic sampling, selecting every nth member from a population.

Sampling error is the difference between a sample statistic (the mean, variance, or standard deviation of the sample) and its corresponding population parameter (the true mean, variance, or standard deviation of the population). For example, the sampling error for the mean is as follows:

$$\text{sampling error of the mean} = \text{sample mean} - \text{population mean} = \bar{x} - \mu$$

A Sampling Distribution

It is important to recognize that the sample statistic itself is a random variable and, therefore, has a probability distribution. The **sampling distribution** of the sample statistic is a probability distribution of all possible sample statistics computed from a set of equal-size samples that were randomly drawn from the same population. Think of it as the probability distribution of a statistic from many samples.

For example, suppose a random sample of 100 bonds is selected from a population of a major municipal bond index consisting of 1,000 bonds, and then the mean return of the 100-bond sample is calculated. Repeating this process many times will result in many different estimates of the population mean return (i.e., one for each sample). The distribution of these estimates of the mean is the *sampling distribution of the mean*.

It is important to note that this sampling distribution is distinct from the distribution of the actual prices of the 1,000 bonds in the underlying population and will have different parameters.

LOS 10.c: Distinguish between simple random and stratified random sampling.

CFA® Program Curriculum, Volume 1, page 515

Stratified random sampling uses a classification system to separate the population into smaller groups based on one or more distinguishing characteristics. From each subgroup, or stratum, a random sample is taken and the results are pooled. The size of the samples from each stratum is based on the size of the stratum relative to the population.

Stratified sampling is often used in bond indexing because of the difficulty and cost of completely replicating the entire population of bonds. In this case, bonds in a population are categorized (stratified) according to major bond risk factors such as duration, maturity, coupon rate, and the like. Then, samples are drawn from each separate category and combined to form a final sample.

To see how this works, suppose you want to construct a bond portfolio that is indexed to the major municipal bond index using a stratified random sampling approach. First, the entire population of 1,000 municipal bonds in the index can be classified on the basis of maturity and coupon rate. Then, cells (stratum) can be created for different maturity/coupon combinations, and random samples can be drawn from each of the maturity/coupon cells. To sample from a cell containing 50 bonds with 2- to 4-year maturities and coupon rates less than 5%, we would select five bonds. The number of bonds drawn from a given cell corresponds to the cell's weight relative to the population (index), or $(50 / 1000) \times (100) = 5$ bonds. This process is repeated for all of the maturity/coupon cells, and the individual samples are combined to form the portfolio.

By using stratified sampling, we guarantee that we sample five bonds from this cell. If we had used simple random sampling, there would be no guarantee that we would sample any of the bonds in the cell. Or, we may have selected more than five bonds from this cell.

LOS 10.d: Distinguish between time-series and cross-sectional data.

CFA® Program Curriculum, Volume 1, page 517

Time-series data consist of observations taken *over a period of time* at specific and equally spaced time intervals. The set of monthly returns on Microsoft stock from January 1994 to January 2004 is an example of a time-series data sample.

Cross-sectional data are a sample of observations taken *at a single point in time*. The sample of reported earnings per share of all NASDAQ companies as of December 31, 2004, is an example of a cross-sectional data sample.

Time-series and cross-sectional data can be pooled in the same data set. **Longitudinal data** are observations over time of multiple characteristics of the same entity, such as unemployment, inflation, and GDP growth rates for a country over 10 years. **Panel data** contain observations over time of the same characteristic for multiple entities, such as debt/equity ratios for 20 companies over the most recent 24 quarters. Panel and longitudinal data are typically presented in table or spreadsheet form.

LOS 10.e: Explain the central limit theorem and its importance.

CFA® Program Curriculum, Volume 1, page 520

The **central limit theorem** states that for simple random samples of size n from a *population* with a mean μ and a finite variance σ^2, the sampling distribution of the sample mean $\bar{x}$ approaches a normal probability distribution with mean μ and a variance equal to $\dfrac{\sigma^2}{n}$ as the sample size becomes large.

The central limit theorem is extremely useful because the normal distribution is relatively easy to apply to hypothesis testing and to the construction of confidence intervals. Specific inferences about the population mean can be made from the sample mean, *regardless of the population's distribution*, as long as the sample size is "sufficiently large," which usually means $n \geq 30$.

Important properties of the central limit theorem include the following:

- If the sample size n is sufficiently large ($n \geq 30$), the sampling distribution of the sample means will be approximately normal. Remember what's going on here, random samples of size n are repeatedly being taken from an overall larger population. Each of these random samples has its own mean, which is itself a random variable, and this set of sample means has a distribution that is approximately normal.

- The mean of the population, μ, and the mean of the distribution of all possible sample means are equal.

- The variance of the distribution of sample means is $\dfrac{\sigma^2}{n}$, the population variance divided by the sample size.

LOS 10.f: Calculate and interpret the standard error of the sample mean.

CFA® Program Curriculum, Volume 1, page 520

The standard error of the sample mean is the standard deviation of the distribution of the sample means.

When the standard deviation of the population, σ, is *known*, the standard error of the sample mean is calculated as:

$$\sigma_{\bar{x}} = \frac{\sigma}{\sqrt{n}}$$

where:
$\sigma_{\bar{x}}$ = standard error of the sample mean
σ = standard deviation of the population
n = size of the sample

Example: Standard error of sample mean (known population variance)

The mean hourly wage for Iowa farm workers is $13.50 with a *population standard deviation* of $2.90. Calculate and interpret the standard error of the sample mean for a sample size of 30.

Answer:

Because the population standard deviation, σ, *is known*, the standard error of the sample mean is expressed as:

$$\sigma_{\bar{x}} = \frac{\sigma}{\sqrt{n}} = \frac{\$2.90}{\sqrt{30}} = \$0.53$$

 Professor's Note: On the TI BAII Plus, the use of the square root key is obvious. On the HP 12C, the square root of 30 is computed as: [30] [g] [$\sqrt{x}$].

This means that if we were to take all possible samples of size 30 from the Iowa farm worker population and prepare a sampling distribution of the sample means, we would get a distribution with a mean of $13.50 and standard error of $0.53.

Practically speaking, the *population's standard deviation is almost never known*. Instead, the standard error of the sample mean must be estimated by dividing the standard deviation of *the sample* mean by $\sqrt{n}$:

$$s_{\bar{x}} = \frac{s}{\sqrt{n}}$$

Example: Standard error of sample mean (unknown population variance)

Suppose a sample contains the past 30 monthly returns for McCreary, Inc. The mean return is 2% and the *sample* standard deviation is 20%. Calculate and interpret the standard error of the sample mean.

Answer:

Since σ is unknown, the standard error of the sample mean is:

$$s_{\overline{x}} = \frac{s}{\sqrt{n}} = \frac{20\%}{\sqrt{30}} = 3.6\%$$

This implies that if we took all possible samples of size 30 from McCreary's monthly returns and prepared a sampling distribution of the sample means, the mean would be 2% with a standard error of 3.6%.

Example: Standard error of sample mean (unknown population variance)

Continuing with our example, suppose that instead of a sample size of 30, we take a sample of the past 200 monthly returns for McCreary, Inc. In order to highlight the effect of sample size on the sample standard error, let's assume that the mean return and standard deviation of this larger sample remain at 2% and 20%, respectively. Now, calculate the standard error of the sample mean for the 200-return sample.

Answer:

The standard error of the sample mean is computed as:

$$s_{\overline{x}} = \frac{s}{\sqrt{n}} = \frac{20\%}{\sqrt{200}} = 1.4\%$$

The result of the preceding two examples illustrates an important property of sampling distributions. Notice that the value of the standard error of the sample mean decreased from 3.6% to 1.4% as the sample size increased from 30 to 200. This is because as the sample size increases, the sample mean gets closer, on average, to the true mean of the population. In other words, the distribution of the sample means about the population mean gets smaller and smaller, so the standard error of the sample mean decreases.

Professor's Note: I get a lot of questions about when to use σ and σ / √n . Just remember that the standard deviation of the mean of many observations is less than the standard deviation of a single observation. If the standard deviation of monthly stock returns is 2%, the standard error (deviation) of the average monthly return over the next six months is 2% / √6 = 0.82%. The average of several observations of a random variable will be less widely dispersed (have lower standard deviation) around the expected value than will a single observation of the random variable.

LOS 10.g: Identify and describe desirable properties of an estimator.

CFA® Program Curriculum, Volume 1, page 523

Regardless of whether we are concerned with point estimates or confidence intervals, there are certain statistical properties that make some estimates more desirable than others. These desirable **properties of an estimator** are **unbiasedness, efficiency,** and **consistency.**

- An *unbiased* estimator is one for which the expected value of the estimator is equal to the parameter you are trying to estimate. For example, because the expected value of the sample mean is equal to the population mean $[E(\bar{x}) = \mu]$, the sample mean is an unbiased estimator of the population mean.
- An unbiased estimator is also *efficient* if the variance of its sampling distribution is smaller than all the other unbiased estimators of the parameter you are trying to estimate. The sample mean, for example, is an unbiased and efficient estimator of the population mean.
- A *consistent* estimator is one for which the accuracy of the parameter estimate increases as the sample size increases. As the sample size increases, the standard error of the sample mean falls, and the sampling distribution bunches more closely around the population mean. In fact, as the sample size approaches infinity, the standard error approaches zero.

LOS 10.h: Distinguish between a point estimate and a confidence interval estimate of a population parameter.

CFA® Program Curriculum, Volume 1, page 523

Point estimates are single (sample) values used to estimate population parameters. The formula used to compute the point estimate is called the estimator. For example, the sample mean, $\bar{x}$, is an estimator of the population mean μ and is computed using the familiar formula:

$$\bar{x} = \frac{\sum x}{n}$$

The value generated with this calculation for a given sample is called the *point estimate* of the mean.

A *confidence interval* is a range of values in which the population parameter is expected to lie. The construction of confidence intervals is described later in this topic review.

LOS 10.i: Describe the properties of Student's *t*-distribution and calculate and interpret its degrees of freedom.

CFA® Program Curriculum, Volume 1, page 527

Student's *t*-distribution, or simply the *t*-distribution, is a bell-shaped probability distribution that is symmetrical about its mean. It is the appropriate distribution to use when constructing confidence intervals based on *small samples* (n < 30) from populations with *unknown variance* and a normal, or approximately normal, distribution. It may also be appropriate to use the *t*-distribution when the population variance is unknown and the sample size is large enough that the central limit theorem will assure that the sampling distribution is approximately normal.

Student's *t*-distribution has the following properties:

- It is symmetrical.
- It is defined by a single parameter, the **degrees of freedom (df)**, where the degrees of freedom are equal to the number of sample observations minus 1, n – 1, for sample means.
- It has more probability in the tails ("fatter tails") than the normal distribution.
- As the degrees of freedom (the sample size) gets larger, the shape of the *t*-distribution more closely approaches a standard normal distribution.

When *compared to the normal distribution*, the *t*-distribution is flatter with more area under the tails (i.e., it has fatter tails). As the degrees of freedom for the *t*-distribution increase, however, its shape approaches that of the normal distribution.

The degrees of freedom for tests based on sample means are n – 1 because, given the mean, only n – 1 observations can be unique.

The *t*-distribution is a symmetrical distribution that is centered about zero. The shape of the *t*-distribution is dependent on the number of degrees of freedom, and degrees of freedom are based on the number of sample observations. The *t*-distribution is flatter and has thicker tails than the standard normal distribution. As the number of observations increases (i.e., the degrees of freedom increase), the *t*-distribution becomes more spiked and its tails become thinner. As the number of degrees of freedom increases without bound, the *t*-distribution converges to the standard normal distribution (*z*-distribution). The thickness of the tails relative to those of the *z*-distribution is important in hypothesis testing because thicker tails mean more observations away from the center of the distribution (more outliers). Hence, hypothesis testing using the *t*-distribution makes it more difficult to reject the null relative to hypothesis testing using the *z*-distribution.

The table in Figure 1 contains one-tailed critical values for the *t*-distribution at the 0.05 and 0.025 levels of significance with various degrees of freedom (df). Note that, unlike the *z*-table, the *t*-values are contained within the table, and the probabilities are located at the column headings. Also note that the level of significance of a *t*-test corresponds to the *one-tailed probabilities, p,* that head the columns in the *t*-table.

Figure 2 illustrates the different shapes of the *t*-distribution associated with different degrees of freedom. The tendency is for the *t*-distribution to look more and more like the normal distribution as the degrees of freedom increase. Practically speaking, the greater the degrees of freedom, the greater the percentage of observations near the center of the distribution and the lower the percentage of observations in the tails, which are thinner as degrees of freedom increase. This means that confidence intervals for a random variable that follows a *t*-distribution must be wider (narrower) when the degrees of freedom are less (more) for a given significance level.

Figure 1: Table of Critical *t*-Values

df	One-Tailed Probabilities, p	
	p = 0.05	p = 0.025
5	2.015	2.571
10	1.812	2.228
15	1.753	2.131
20	1.725	2.086
25	1.708	2.060
30	1.697	2.042
40	1.684	2.021
50	1.676	2.009
60	1.671	2.000
70	1.667	1.994
80	1.664	1.990
90	1.662	1.987
100	1.660	1.984
120	1.658	1.980
∞	1.645	1.960

Figure 2: *t*-Distributions for Different Degrees of Freedom (df)

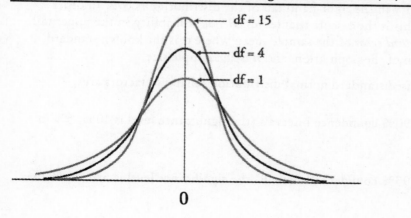

LOS 10.j: Calculate and interpret a confidence interval for a population mean, given a normal distribution with 1) a known population variance, 2) an unknown population variance, or 3) an unknown variance and a large sample size.

CFA® Program Curriculum, Volume 1, page 525

Confidence interval estimates result in a range of values within which the actual value of a parameter will lie, given the probability of 1 – α. Here, alpha, α, is called the *level of significance* for the confidence interval, and the probability 1 – α is referred to as the *degree of confidence*. For example, we might estimate that the population mean of random variables will range from 15 to 25 with a 95% degree of confidence, or at the 5% level of significance.

Confidence intervals are usually constructed by adding or subtracting an appropriate value from the point estimate. In general, confidence intervals take on the following form:

point estimate $\pm$ (reliability factor $\times$ standard error)

where:
point estimate = value of a sample statistic of the population parameter
reliability factor = number that depends on the sampling distribution of the point estimate and the probability that the point estimate falls in the confidence interval, $(1 - \alpha)$
standard error = standard error of the point estimate

If the population has a *normal distribution with a known variance*, a **confidence interval for the population mean** can be calculated as:

$$\bar{x} \pm z_{\alpha/2} \frac{\sigma}{\sqrt{n}}$$

where:
$\bar{x}$ = *point estimate* of the population mean (sample mean).
$z_{\alpha/2}$ = *reliability factor*, a standard normal random variable for which the probability in the right-hand tail of the distribution is $\alpha/2$. In other words, this is the z-score that leaves $\alpha/2$ of probability in the upper tail.
$\frac{\sigma}{\sqrt{n}}$ = the *standard error* of the sample mean where σ is the known standard deviation of the population, and n is the sample size.

The most commonly used standard normal distribution reliability factors are:

$z_{\alpha/2}$ = 1.645 for 90% confidence intervals (the significance level is 10%, 5% in each tail).

$z_{\alpha/2}$ = 1.960 for 95% confidence intervals (the significance level is 5%, 2.5% in each tail).

$z_{\alpha/2}$ = 2.575 for 99% confidence intervals (the significance level is 1%, 0.5% in each tail).

Do these numbers look familiar? They should! In our review of common probability distributions, we found the probability under the standard normal curve between $z = -1.96$ and $z = +1.96$ to be 0.95, or 95%. Owing to symmetry, this leaves a probability of 0.025 under each tail of the curve beyond $z = -1.96$ or $z = +1.96$, for a total of 0.05, or 5%—just what we need for a significance level of 0.05, or 5%.

Example: Confidence interval

Consider a practice exam that was administered to 36 Level I candidates. The mean score on this practice exam was 80. Assuming a population standard deviation equal to 15, construct and interpret a 99% confidence interval for the mean score on the practice exam for 36 candidates. *Note that in this example the population standard deviation is known, so we don't have to estimate it.*

Answer:

At a confidence level of 99%, $z_{\alpha/2} = z_{0.005} = 2.58$. So, the 99% confidence interval is calculated as follows:

$$\bar{x} \pm z_{\alpha/2} \frac{\sigma}{\sqrt{n}} = 80 \pm 2.58 \frac{15}{\sqrt{36}} = 80 \pm 6.45$$

Thus, the 99% confidence interval ranges from 73.55 to 86.45.

Confidence intervals can be interpreted from a probabilistic perspective or a practical perspective. With regard to the outcome of the CFA® practice exam example, these **two** perspectives can be described as follows:

- *Probabilistic interpretation.* After repeatedly taking samples of CFA candidates, administering the practice exam, and constructing confidence intervals for each sample's mean, 99% of the resulting confidence intervals will, in the long run, include the population mean.
- *Practical interpretation.* We are 99% confident that the population mean score is between 73.55 and 86.45 for candidates from this population.

Confidence Intervals for the Population Mean: Normal With Unknown Variance

If the distribution of the *population is normal with unknown variance*, we can use the *t*-distribution to construct a confidence interval:

$$\bar{x} \pm t_{\alpha/2} \frac{s}{\sqrt{n}}$$

where:

$\bar{x}$ = the point estimate of the population mean

$t_{\alpha/2}$ = the *t*-reliability factor (a.k.a. *t*-statistic or critical *t*-value) corresponding to a *t*-distributed random variable with n − 1 degrees of freedom, where *n* is the sample size. The area under the tail of the *t*-distribution to the right of $t_{\alpha/2}$ is $\alpha/2$

$\frac{s}{\sqrt{n}}$ = standard error of the sample mean

s = sample standard deviation

Unlike the standard normal distribution, the reliability factors for the *t*-distribution depend on the sample size, so we can't rely on a commonly used set of reliability factors.

Instead, reliability factors for the t-distribution have to be looked up in a table of Student's t-distribution, like the one at the back of this book.

Owing to the relatively fatter tails of the t-distribution, confidence intervals constructed using t-reliability factors ($t_{\alpha/2}$) will be more conservative (wider) than those constructed using z-reliability factors ($z_{\alpha/2}$).

Example: Confidence intervals

Let's return to the McCreary, Inc. example. Recall that we took a sample of the past 30 monthly stock returns for McCreary, Inc. and determined that the mean return was 2% and the sample standard deviation was 20%. Since the population variance is unknown, the standard error of the sample was estimated to be:

$$s_{\bar{x}} = \frac{s}{\sqrt{n}} = \frac{20\%}{\sqrt{30}} = 3.6\%$$

Now, let's construct a 95% confidence interval for the mean monthly return.

Answer:

Here, we will use the t-reliability factor because the population variance is unknown. Since there are 30 observations, the degrees of freedom are 29 = 30 − 1. Remember, because this is a two-tailed test at the 95% confidence level, the probability under each tail must be $\alpha/2 = 2.5\%$, for a total of 5%. So, referencing the one-tailed probabilities for Student's t-distribution at the back of this book, we find the critical t-value (reliability factor) for $\alpha/2 = 0.025$ and df = 29 to be $t_{29,\ 2.5} = 2.045$. Thus, the 95% confidence interval for the population mean is:

$$2\% \pm 2.045 \left(\frac{20\%}{\sqrt{30}} \right) = 2\% \pm 2.045(3.6\%) = 2\% \pm 7.4\%$$

Thus, the 95% confidence has a lower limit of −5.4% and an upper limit of +9.4%.

We can interpret this confidence interval by saying that we are 95% confident that the population mean monthly return for McCreary stock is between −5.4% and +9.4%.

Professor's Note: You should practice looking up reliability factors (a.k.a. critical t-values or t-statistics) in a t-table. The first step is always to compute the degrees of freedom, which is n − 1. The second step is to find the appropriate level of alpha or significance. This depends on whether the test you're concerned with is one-tailed (use α) or two-tailed (use $\alpha/2$). In this review, our tests will always be two-tailed because confidence intervals are designed to compute an upper and lower limit. Thus, we will use $\alpha/2$. To look up $t_{29,\ 2.5}$ find the 29 df row and match it with the 0.025 column; t = 2.045 is the result. We'll do more of this in our study of hypothesis testing.

Confidence Interval for a Population Mean When the Population Variance Is Unknown Given a Large Sample From Any Type of Distribution

We now know that the *z*-statistic should be used to construct confidence intervals when the population distribution is normal and the variance is known, and the *t*-statistic should be used when the distribution is normal but the variance is unknown. But what do we do when the distribution is *nonnormal?*

As it turns out, the size of the sample influences whether or not we can construct the appropriate confidence interval for the sample mean.

- If the *distribution is nonnormal* but the *population variance is known*, the *z*-statistic can be used as long as the sample size is large (n ≥ 30). We can do this because the central limit theorem assures us that the distribution of the sample mean is approximately normal when the sample is large.
- If the *distribution is nonnormal* and the *population variance is unknown*, the *t*-statistic can be used as long as the sample size is large (n ≥ 30). It is also acceptable to use the *z*-statistic, although use of the *t*-statistic is more conservative.

This means that if we are sampling from a nonnormal distribution (which is sometimes the case in finance), *we cannot create a confidence interval if the sample size is less than 30.* So, all else equal, make sure you have a sample of at least 30, and the larger, the better.

Figure 3 summarizes this discussion.

 Professor's Note: You should commit the criteria in this table to memory.

Figure 3: Criteria for Selecting the Appropriate Test Statistic

When sampling from a:	Test Statistic	
	Small Sample (n < 30)	Large Sample (n ≥ 30)
Normal distribution with *known* variance	*z*-statistic	*z*-statistic
Normal distribution with *unknown* variance	*t*-statistic	*t*-statistic*
Nonnormal distribution with *known* variance	not available	*z*-statistic
Nonnormal distribution with *unknown* variance	not available	*t*-statistic*

* The *z*-statistic is theoretically acceptable here, but use of the *t*-statistic is more conservative.

All of the preceding analysis depends on the sample we draw from the population being random. If the sample isn't random, the central limit theorem doesn't apply, our estimates won't have the desirable properties, and we can't form unbiased confidence intervals. Surprisingly, creating a *random sample* is not as easy as one might believe. There are a number of potential mistakes in sampling methods that can bias the results.

These biases are particularly problematic in financial research, where available historical data are plentiful, but the creation of new sample data by experimentation is restricted.

LOS 10.k: Describe the issues regarding selection of the appropriate sample size, data-mining bias, sample selection bias, survivorship bias, look-ahead bias, and time-period bias.

CFA® Program Curriculum, Volume 1, page 530

We have seen so far that a larger sample reduces the sampling error and the standard deviation of the sample statistic around its true (population) value. Confidence intervals are narrower when samples are larger and the standard errors of the point estimates of population parameters are less.

There are two limitations on this idea of "larger is better" when it comes to selecting an appropriate sample size. One is that larger samples may contain observations from a different population (distribution). If we include observations which come from a different population (one with a different population parameter), we will not necessarily improve, and may even reduce, the precision of our population parameter estimates. The other consideration is cost. The costs of using a larger sample must be weighed against the value of the increase in precision from the increase in sample size. Both of these factors suggest that the largest possible sample size is not always the most appropriate choice.

Data-Mining Bias, Sample Selection Bias, Survivorship Bias, Look-Ahead Bias, and Time-Period Bias

Data mining occurs when analysts repeatedly use the same database to search for patterns or trading rules until one that "works" is discovered. For example, empirical research has provided evidence that value stocks appear to outperform growth stocks. Some researchers argue that this anomaly is actually the product of data mining. Because the data set of historical stock returns is quite limited, it is difficult to know for sure whether the difference between value and growth stock returns is a true economic phenomenon, or simply a chance pattern that was stumbled upon after repeatedly looking for any identifiable pattern in the data.

Data-mining bias refers to results where the statistical significance of the pattern is overestimated because the results were found through data mining.

When reading research findings that suggest a profitable trading strategy, make sure you heed the following warning signs of data mining:

- Evidence that many different variables were tested, most of which are unreported, until significant ones were found.
- The lack of any economic theory that is consistent with the empirical results.

The best way to avoid data mining is to test a potentially profitable trading rule on a data set different from the one you used to develop the rule (i.e., use out-of-sample data).

Sample selection bias occurs when some data is systematically excluded from the analysis, usually because of the lack of availability. This practice renders the observed sample to be nonrandom, and any conclusions drawn from this sample can't be applied to the population because the observed sample and the portion of the population that was not observed are different.

Survivorship bias is the most common form of sample selection bias. A good example of the existence of survivorship bias in investments is the study of mutual fund performance. Most mutual fund databases, like Morningstar®'s, only include funds currently in existence—the "survivors." They do not include funds that have ceased to exist due to closure or merger.

This would not be a problem if the characteristics of the surviving funds and the missing funds were the same; then the sample of survivor funds would still be a random sample drawn from the population of mutual funds. As one would expect, however, and as evidence has shown, the funds that are dropped from the sample have lower returns relative to the surviving funds. Thus, the surviving sample is biased toward the better funds (i.e., it is not random). The analysis of a mutual fund sample with survivorship bias will yield results that overestimate the average mutual fund return because the database only includes the better-performing funds. The solution to survivorship bias is to use a sample of funds that all started at the same time and not drop funds that have been dropped from the sample.

Look-ahead bias occurs when a study tests a relationship using sample data that was not available on the test date. For example, consider the test of a trading rule that is based on the price-to-book ratio at the end of the fiscal year. Stock prices are available for all companies at the same point in time, while end-of-year book values may not be available until 30 to 60 days after the fiscal year ends. In order to account for this bias, a study that uses price-to-book value ratios to test trading strategies might estimate the book value as reported at fiscal year end and the market value two months later.

Time-period bias can result if the time period over which the data is gathered is either too short or too long. If the time period is too short, research results may reflect phenomena specific to that time period, or perhaps even data mining. If the time period is too long, the fundamental economic relationships that underlie the results may have changed.

For example, research findings may indicate that small stocks outperformed large stocks during 1980–1985. This may well be the result of time-period bias—in this case, using too short a time period. It's not clear whether this relationship will continue in the future or if it is just an isolated occurrence.

On the other hand, a study that quantifies the relationship between inflation and unemployment during the period from 1940–2000 will also result in time-period bias—because this period is too long, and it covers a fundamental change in the relationship between inflation and unemployment that occurred in the 1980s. In this case, the data should be divided into two subsamples that span the period before and after the change.

KEY CONCEPTS

LOS 10.a

Simple random sampling is a method of selecting a sample in such a way that each item or person in the population being studied has the same probability of being included in the sample.

A sampling distribution is the distribution of all values that a sample statistic can take on when computed from samples of identical size randomly drawn from the same population.

LOS 10.b

Sampling error is the difference between a sample statistic and its corresponding population parameter (e.g., the sample mean minus the population mean).

LOS 10.c

Stratified random sampling involves randomly selecting samples proportionally from subgroups that are formed based on one or more distinguishing characteristics, so that the sample will have the same distribution of these characteristics as the overall population.

LOS 10.d

Time-series data consists of observations taken at specific and equally spaced points in time.

Cross-sectional data consists of observations taken at a single point in time.

LOS 10.e

The central limit theorem states that for a population with a mean μ and a finite variance σ^2, the sampling distribution of the sample mean of all possible samples of size n (for n ≥ 30) will be approximately normally distributed with a mean equal to μ and a variance equal to σ^2 / n.

LOS 10.f

The standard error of the sample mean is the standard deviation of the distribution of the sample means and is calculated as $\sigma_{\bar{x}} = \dfrac{\sigma}{\sqrt{n}}$, where σ, the population standard

deviation, is known, and as $s_{\bar{x}} = \dfrac{s}{\sqrt{n}}$, where s, the sample standard deviation, is used

because the population standard deviation is unknown.

LOS 10.g

Desirable statistical properties of an estimator include unbiasedness (sign of estimation error is random), efficiency (lower sampling error than any other unbiased estimator), and consistency (variance of sampling error decreases with sample size).

LOS 10.h

Point estimates are single value estimates of population parameters. An estimator is a formula used to compute a point estimate.

Confidence intervals are ranges of values, within which the actual value of the parameter will lie with a given probability.

confidence interval = point estimate ± (reliability factor × standard error)

The reliability factor is a number that depends on the sampling distribution of the point estimate and the probability that the point estimate falls in the confidence interval.

LOS 10.i

The t-distribution is similar, but not identical, to the normal distribution in shape—it is defined by the degrees of freedom and has fatter tails compared to the normal distribution.

Degrees of freedom for the t-distribution are equal to n – 1. Student's t-distribution is closer to the normal distribution when df is greater, and confidence intervals are narrower when df is greater.

LOS 10.j

For a normally distributed population, a confidence interval for its mean can be constructed using a z-statistic when variance is known, and a t-statistic when the variance is unknown. The z-statistic is acceptable in the case of a normal population with an unknown variance if the sample size is large (30+).

In general, we have:

- $\bar{X} \pm Z_{\alpha/2} \dfrac{\sigma}{\sqrt{n}}$ when the variance is known, and

- $\bar{X} \pm t_{\alpha/2} \dfrac{s}{\sqrt{n}}$ when the variance is unknown and the sample standard deviation

must be used.

LOS 10.k

Increasing the sample size will generally improve parameter estimates and narrow confidence intervals. The cost of more data must be weighed against these benefits, and adding data that is not generated by the same distribution will not necessarily improve accuracy or narrow confidence intervals.

Potential mistakes in the sampling method can bias results. These biases include data mining (significant relationships that have occurred by chance), sample selection bias (selection is non-random), look-ahead bias (basing the test at a point in time on data not available at that time), survivorship bias (using only surviving mutual funds, hedge funds, etc.), and time-period bias (the relation does not hold over other time periods).

CONCEPT CHECKERS

1. A simple random sample is a sample drawn in such a way that each member of the population has:
   A. some chance of being selected in the sample.
   B. an equal chance of being included in the sample.
   C. a 1% chance of being included in the sample.

2. Sampling error is defined as:
   A. an error that occurs when a sample of less than 30 elements is drawn.
   B. an error that occurs during collection, recording, and tabulation of data.
   C. the difference between the value of a sample statistic and the value of the corresponding population parameter.

3. The mean age of all CFA candidates is 28 years. The mean age of a random sample of 100 candidates is found to be 26.5 years. The difference of 1.5 years is called the:
   A. random error.
   B. sampling error.
   C. population error.

4. If n is large and the population standard deviation is unknown, the standard error of the sampling distribution of the sample mean is *equal* to the:
   A. sample standard deviation divided by the sample size.
   B. population standard deviation multiplied by the sample size.
   C. sample standard deviation divided by the square root of the sample size.

5. The standard error of the sampling distribution of the sample mean for a sample size of n drawn from a population with a mean of μ and a standard deviation of σ is:
   A. sample standard deviation divided by the sample size.
   B. sample standard deviation divided by the square root of the sample size.
   C. population standard deviation divided by the square root of the sample size.

6. To apply the central limit theorem to the sampling distribution of the sample mean, the sample is usually considered to be large if n is *greater* than:
   A. 20.
   B. 25.
   C. 30.

7. Assume that a population has a mean of 14 with a standard deviation of 2. If a random sample of 49 observations is drawn f_____ population, the standard error of the sample mean is *closest* to:
   A. 0.04.
   B. 0.29.
   C. 2.00.

8.   The population's mean is 30 and the mean of a sample of size 100 is 28.5. The variance of the sample is 25. The standard error of the sample mean is *closest* to:
      A. 0.05.
      B. 0.25.
      C. 0.50.

9.   A random sample of 100 computer store customers spent an average of $75 at the store. Assuming the distribution is normal and the population standard deviation is $20, the 95% confidence interval for the population mean is *closest* to:
      A. $71.08 to $78.92.
      B. $73.89 to $80.11.
      C. $74.56 to $79.44.

10.   Best Computers, Inc., sells computers and computer parts by mail. A sample of 25 recent orders showed the mean time taken to ship out these orders was 70 hours with a sample standard deviation of 14 hours. Assuming the population is normally distributed, the 99% confidence interval for the population mean is:
      A. 70 ± 2.80 hours.
      B. 70 ± 6.98 hours.
      C. 70 ± 7.83 hours.

11.   The sampling distribution of a statistic is the probability distribution made up of all possible:
      A. observations from the underlying population.
      B. sample statistics computed from samples of varying sizes drawn from the same population.
      C. sample statistics computed from samples of the same size drawn from the same population.

12.   The sample of debt/equity ratios of 25 publicly traded U.S. banks as of fiscal year-end 2003 is an example of:
      A. a point estimate.
      B. cross-sectional data.
      C. a stratified random sample.

13.   Which of the following is *least likely* a desirable property of an estimate?
      A. Reliability.
      B. Efficiency.
      C. Consistency.

14.   If the variance of the sampling distribution of an estimator is smaller than all other unbiased estimators of the parameter of interest, the estimator is:
      A. efficient.
      B. unbiased.
      C. consistent.

15. Which of the following is *least likely* a property of Student's *t*-distribution?
    A. As the degrees of freedom get larger, the variance approaches zero.
    B. It is defined by a single parameter, the degrees of freedom, which is equal to n − 1.
    C. It has more probability in the tails and less at the peak than a standard normal distribution.

16. An analyst who uses historical data that was not publicly available at the time period being studied will have a sample with:
    A. look-ahead bias.
    B. time-period bias.
    C. sample selection bias.

17. The 95% confidence interval of the sample mean of employee age for a major corporation is 19 years to 44 years based on a *z*-statistic. The population of employees is more than 5,000 and the sample size of this test is 100. Assuming the population is normally distributed, the standard error of mean employee age is *closest* to:
    A. 1.96.
    B. 2.58.
    C. 6.38.

18. Which of the following is *most closely* associated with survivorship bias?
    A. Price-to-book studies.
    B. Stratified bond sampling studies.
    C. Mutual fund performance studies.

19. What is the *most appropriate* test statistic for constructing confidence intervals for the population mean when the population is normally distributed, but the variance is unknown?
    A. The *z*-statistic at α with *n* degrees of freedom.
    B. The *t*-statistic at α/2 with *n* degrees of freedom.
    C. The *t*-statistic at α/2 with n − 1 degrees of freedom.

20. When constructing a confidence interval for the population mean of a nonnormal distribution when the population variance is unknown and the sample size is large (n > 30), an analyst may acceptably use:
    A. either a *z*-statistic or a *t*-statistic.
    B. only a *z*-statistic at α with *n* degrees of freedom.
    C. only a *t*-statistic at α/2 with *n* degrees of freedom.

21. Jenny Fox evaluates managers who have a cross-sectional population standard deviation of returns of 8%. If returns are independent across managers, how large of a sample does Fox need so the standard error of sample means is 1.265%?
    A. 7.
    B. 30.
    C. 40.

22. Annual returns on small stocks have a population mean of 12% and a population standard deviation of 20%. If the returns are normally distributed, a 90% confidence interval on mean returns over a 5-year period is:
   A. 5.40% to 18.60%.
   B. −2.75% to 26.75%.
   C. −5.52% to 29.52%.

CHALLENGE PROBLEMS

1. Using random sampling, a manager wants to construct a portfolio of 50 stocks that will approximate the returns of a broad market index that contains 200 stocks. Explain how he could use simple random sampling and stratified random sampling to select stocks from the index and the possible advantages of stratified random sampling.

2. An analyst has taken a random sample of 50 observations from a population for which she wants to estimate the population mean. She believes this population's distribution is negatively skewed.

   A. Can she use the sample mean to estimate the population mean and construct a confidence interval? Explain.

   B. What are the desirable statistical properties of an estimator?

   C. Which of these properties does the sample mean possess as an estimator of the population mean?

3. A random sample of analyst earnings estimates has a mean of $2.84 and a standard deviation of $0.40. What can we say about the 90% confidence interval for earnings next period if:

   A. the sample size is 20?

   B. the sample size is 40?

   What probabilistic statement could we make at the 90% confidence level if:

   C. the sample size were 15?

   D. the sample size were 60?

ANSWERS – CONCEPT CHECKERS

1. **B** In a simple random sample, each element of the population has an equal probability of being selected. Choice C allows for an equal chance, but only if there are 100 elements in the population from which the random sample is drawn.

2. **C** An example might be the difference between a particular sample mean and the average value of the overall population.

3. **B** The sampling error is the difference between the population parameter and the sample statistic.

4. **C** The formula for the standard error when the population standard deviation is unknown is $s_{\bar{x}} = \dfrac{s}{\sqrt{n}}$.

5. **C** The formula for the standard error when the population standard deviation is known is $\sigma_{\bar{x}} = \dfrac{\sigma}{\sqrt{n}}$.

6. **C** By definition.

7. **B** $s_{\bar{X}} = \dfrac{s}{\sqrt{n}}$. Given $s = 2$, $s_{\bar{X}} = \dfrac{2}{\sqrt{49}} = \dfrac{2}{7} = 0.2857$.

8. **C** $s_{\bar{X}} = \dfrac{\sigma}{\sqrt{n}}$. Given $\sigma^2 = 25$, $s_{\bar{X}} = \dfrac{5}{\sqrt{100}} = \dfrac{5}{10} = 0.5$.

9. **A** Since the population variance is known and $n \geq 30$, the confidence interval is determined as $\bar{x} \pm z_{\alpha/2}\,(\sigma/\sqrt{n})$. $z_{\alpha/2} = z_{0.025} = 1.96$. So, the confidence interval is $75 \pm 1.96(20/10) = 75 \pm 3.92 = 71.08$ to 78.92.

10. **C** Since the population variance is unknown and $n < 30$, the confidence interval is determined as $\bar{x} \pm t_{\alpha/2}\,(s/\sqrt{n})$. Look up $t_{\alpha/2}$ and $df = n - 1$ to get critical t-value. $t_{0.01/2}$ and $df = 24$ is 2.797. So, the confidence interval is $70 \pm 2.797(14 / 5) = 70 \pm 7.83$.

11. **C** Suppose you have a population of 10,000 employees. If you take 100 samples of 50 employees each, the distribution of the 100 sample means is the sampling distribution.

12. **B** Cross-sectional data is a set of data that are all collected as of the same point in time.

13. **A** Efficiency, consistency, and unbiasedness are desirable properties of an estimator.

14. **A** An estimator is efficient if the variance of its sampling distribution is smaller than that of all other unbiased estimators of the parameter.

15. **A** As the degrees of freedom get larger, the t-distribution approaches the normal distribution. As the degrees of freedom fall, the peak of the t-distribution flattens and its tails get fatter (more probability in the tails—that's why, all else the same, the critical t increases as the df decreases).

16. **A**   The primary example of look-ahead bias is using year-end financial information in conjunction with market pricing data to compute ratios like the price/earnings (P/E). The E in the denominator is typically not available for 30–60 days after the end of the period. Hence, data that was available on the test date (P) is mixed with information that was not available (E). That is, the P is "ahead" of the E.

17. **C**   At the 95% level of significance, with sample size n = 100 and mean 31.5 years, the appropriate test statistic is $z_{\alpha/2} = 1.96$. *Note: The mean of 31.5 is calculated as the midpoint of the interval, or (19 + 44) / 2.* Thus, the confidence interval is $31.5 \pm 1.96 s_{\bar{X}}$, where $s_{\bar{X}}$ is the standard error of the sample mean. If we take the upper bound, we know that $31.5 + 1.96 s_{\bar{X}} = 44$, or $1.96 s_{\bar{X}} = 12.5$, or $s_{\bar{X}} = 6.38$ years.

18. **C**   Mutual fund performance studies are most closely associated with survivorship bias because only the better-performing funds remain in the sample over time.

19. **C**   Use the *t*-statistic at $\alpha/2$ and n – 1 degrees of freedom when the population variance is unknown. While the *z*-statistic is acceptable when the sample size is large, sample size is not given here, and the *t*-statistic is always appropriate under these conditions.

20. **A**   When the sample size is large, and the central limit theorem can be relied upon to assure a sampling distribution that is normal, either the *t*-statistic or the *z*-statistic is acceptable for constructing confidence intervals for the population mean. The *t*-statistic, however, will provide a more conservative range (wider) at a given level of significance.

21. **C** $1.265 = \dfrac{8}{\sqrt{N}}, N = \left(\dfrac{8}{1.265}\right)^2 \approx 40$

22. **B**   With a known population standard deviation of returns and a normally distributed population, we can use the *z*-distribution. The sample mean for a sample of five years will have a standard deviation of $\dfrac{20}{\sqrt{5}} = 8.94\%$. A 90% confidence interval around the mean return of 12% is $12\% \pm 1.65(8.94\%) = -2.75\%$ to 26.75%.

ANSWERS – CHALLENGE PROBLEMS

1.   In simple random sampling, the analyst would select any 50 stocks using a process that gives each stock in the index an equal chance of being chosen.

   Stratified sampling involves dividing a population into subgroups based on key characteristics, selecting random samples from each subgroup in accordance with the proportion of the population contained in each subgroup, and pooling the results. For example, the analyst could divide the index stocks by capitalization and industry to form the subgroups, and then select stocks randomly from each subgroup. In this context, stratified random sampling has the advantage that the sample will have the same proportion of exposure to each industry and firms of, for example, large, small, and medium size. If these subgroups successfully capture different risk characteristics, tracking error for the portfolio relative to the index can be reduced.

2. A. She can use the sample mean to estimate the population mean. The central limit theorem states that for a large enough sample size n (typically more than 30) from a population with a mean μ and variance σ^2, the probability distribution for the sample mean will be approximately normal with mean μ and variance σ^2/n. The theorem allows us to use the normal distribution to test hypotheses about the population mean, whether the population's distribution is normal or not.

    B. An estimator should be:
    - Unbiased—the expected value of the estimator should be equal to the population parameter.
    - Efficient—the variance of its sampling distribution is smaller than that of all the other unbiased estimators of the parameter.
    - Consistent—the standard error of the estimator should decrease as the sample size increases.

    C. The sample mean has all of these properties.

3. A,B. This is a bit tricky. We have no direct information about the distribution of possible earnings for the next period. We have information about the distribution of analysts' estimates of next period earnings. Based on the information given, we can make no statement about the 90% confidence interval for earnings next period.

    C. Since we cannot assume that the distribution of analyst estimates is normal, we cannot make any inferences about the mean of the population of analyst estimates with a sample size of only 15.

    D. With a sample size of 60, we can make a statement about a confidence interval for the mean of the population of analyst estimates. The t-statistic for a 90% confidence interval with 59 degrees of freedom is approximated by using the value for 60 degrees of freedom, which is 1.671.

    The confidence interval is $2.84 \pm 1.671\left(\dfrac{0.40}{\sqrt{60}}\right)$, or \$2.75 to \$2.93. We are 90% confident the true mean of the population of analyst estimates is within this range.

ANSWERS – CHALLENGE PROBLEMS

The following is a review of the Quantitative Methods: Application principles designed to address the learning outcome statements set forth by CFA Institute. This topic is also covered in:

HYPOTHESIS TESTING

Study Session 3

EXAM FOCUS

This review addresses common hypothesis testing procedures. These procedures are used to conduct tests of population means, population variances, differences in means, differences in variances, and mean differences. Specific tests reviewed include the z-test, t-test, chi-square test, and F-test. You should know when and how to apply each of these. A standard hypothesis testing procedure is utilized in this review. Know it! You should be able to perform a hypothesis test on the value of the mean without being given any formulas. Confidence intervals, levels of significance, the power of a test, and types of hypothesis testing errors are also discussed. Don't worry about memorizing the messy formulas on testing for the equalities and differences in means and variances at the end of this review, but be able to interpret these statistics.

HYPOTHESIS TESTING

Hypothesis testing is the statistical assessment of a statement or idea regarding a population. For instance, a statement could be as follows: "The mean return for the U.S. equity market is greater than zero." Given the relevant returns data, hypothesis testing procedures can be employed to test the validity of this statement at a given significance level.

LOS 11.a: Define a hypothesis, describe the steps of hypothesis testing, describe and interpret the choice of the null and alternative hypotheses, and distinguish between one-tailed and two-tailed tests of hypotheses.

CFA® Program Curriculum, Volume 1, page 552

A hypothesis is a statement about the value of a population parameter developed for the purpose of testing a theory or belief. Hypotheses are stated in terms of the population parameter to be tested, like the population mean, μ. For example, a researcher may be interested in the mean daily return on stock options. Hence, the hypothesis may be that the mean daily return on a portfolio of stock options is positive.

Hypothesis testing procedures, based on sample statistics and probability theory, are used to determine whether a hypothesis is a reasonable statement and should not be rejected or if it is an unreasonable statement and should be rejected. The process of hypothesis testing consists of a series of steps shown in Figure 1.

Figure 1: Hypothesis Testing Procedure*

State the hypothesis

↓

Select the appropriate test statistic

↓

Specify the level of significance

↓

State the decision rule regarding the hypothesis

↓

Collect the sample and calculate the sample statistics

↓

Make a decision regarding the hypothesis

↓

Make a decision based on the results of the test

* *(Source:* Wayne W. Daniel and James C. Terrell, *Business Statistics, Basic Concepts and Methodology,* Houghton Mifflin, Boston, 1997.)

 Professor's Note: You should know this process!

The Null Hypothesis and Alternative Hypothesis

The null hypothesis, designated H_0, is the hypothesis that the researcher wants to reject. It is the hypothesis that is actually tested and is the basis for the selection of the test statistics. The null is generally stated as a simple statement about a population parameter. Typical statements of the null hypothesis for the population mean include $H_0: \mu = \mu_0$, $H_0: \mu \leq \mu_0$, and $H_0: \mu \geq \mu_0$, where μ is the population mean and μ_0 is the hypothesized value of the population mean.

 Professor's Note: The null hypothesis always includes the "equal to" condition.

The alternative hypothesis, designated H_a, is what is concluded if there is sufficient evidence to reject the null hypothesis. It is usually the alternative hypothesis that you are really trying to assess. Why? Since you can never really prove anything with statistics, when the null hypothesis is discredited, the implication is that the alternative hypothesis is valid.

One-Tailed and Two-Tailed Tests of Hypotheses

The alternative hypothesis can be one-sided or two-sided. A one-sided test is referred to as a one-tailed test, and a two-sided test is referred to as a two-tailed test. Whether the test is one- or two-sided depends on the proposition being tested. If a researcher wants to test whether the return on stock options is greater than zero, a one-tailed test should be used. However, a two-tailed test should be used if the research question is whether the return on options is simply different from zero. Two-sided tests allow for deviation on both sides of the hypothesized value (zero). In practice, most hypothesis tests are constructed as two-tailed tests.

A **two-tailed** test for the population mean may be structured as:

$$H_0: \mu = \mu_0 \text{ versus } H_a: \mu \neq \mu_0$$

Since the alternative hypothesis allows for values above and below the hypothesized parameter, a two-tailed test uses two **critical values** (or **rejection points**).

The *general decision rule for a two-tailed test* is:

Reject H_0 if: test statistic > upper critical value or
                     test statistic < lower critical value

Let's look at the development of the decision rule for a two-tailed test using a z-distributed test statistic (a z-test) at a 5% level of significance, $\alpha = 0.05$.

- At $\alpha = 0.05$, the computed test statistic is compared with the critical z-values of ± 1.96. The values of ± 1.96 correspond to $\pm z_{\alpha/2} = \pm z_{0.025}$, which is the range of z-values within which 95% of the probability lies. These values are obtained from the cumulative probability table for the standard normal distribution (z-table), which is included at the back of this book.
- If the computed test statistic falls outside the range of critical z-values (i.e., test statistic > 1.96, or test statistic < -1.96), we reject the null and conclude that the sample statistic is sufficiently different from the hypothesized value.
- If the computed test statistic falls within the range ± 1.96, we conclude that the sample statistic is not sufficiently different from the hypothesized value ($\mu = \mu_0$ in this case), and we fail to reject the null hypothesis.

The *decision rule* (rejection rule) *for a two-tailed z-test* at $\alpha = 0.05$ can be stated as:

Reject H_0 if: test statistic < -1.96 or
              test statistic > 1.96

Figure 2 shows the standard normal distribution for a two-tailed hypothesis test using the z-distribution. Notice that the significance level of 0.05 means that there is 0.05 / 2 = 0.025 probability (area) under each tail of the distribution beyond ± 1.96.

Figure 2: Two-Tailed Hypothesis Test Using the Standard Normal (z) Distribution

Professor's Note: The next two examples are extremely important. Don't move on until you understand them!

Example: Two-tailed test

A researcher has gathered data on the daily returns on a portfolio of call options over a recent 250-day period. The mean daily return has been 0.1%, and the sample standard deviation of daily portfolio returns is 0.25%. The researcher believes that the mean daily portfolio return is not equal to zero. Construct a hypothesis test of the researcher's belief.

Answer:

First we need to specify the null and alternative hypotheses. The null hypothesis is the one the researcher expects to reject.

$$H_0: \mu_0 = 0 \text{ versus } H_a: \mu_0 \neq 0$$

Since the null hypothesis is an equality, this is a two-tailed test. At a 5% level of significance, the critical z-values for a two-tailed test are ±1.96, so the decision rule can be stated as:

Reject H_0 if test statistic < -1.96 or test statistic $> +1.96$

The *standard error* of the sample mean is the adjusted standard deviation of the sample. When the sample statistic is the sample mean, x, the standard error of the sample statistic for sample size n is calculated as:

$$s_{\overline{x}} = \frac{s}{\sqrt{n}}$$

Since our sample statistic here is a sample mean, the standard error of the sample mean for a sample size of 250 is $\dfrac{0.0025}{\sqrt{250}}$ and our test statistic is:

$$\frac{0.001}{\left(\dfrac{0.0025}{\sqrt{250}} \right)} = \frac{0.001}{0.000158} = 6.33$$

Since 6.33 > 1.96, we reject the null hypothesis that the mean daily option return is equal to zero. Note that when we reject the null, we conclude that the sample value is significantly different from the hypothesized value. We are saying that the two values are different from one another *after considering the variation in the sample*. That is, the mean daily return of 0.001 is statistically different from zero given the sample's standard deviation and size.

For a **one-tailed hypothesis** test of the population mean, the null and alternative hypotheses are either:

Upper tail: $H_0: \mu \leq \mu_0$ versus $H_a: \mu > \mu_0$, or
Lower tail: $H_0: \mu \geq \mu_0$ versus $H_a: \mu < \mu_0$

The appropriate set of hypotheses depends on whether we believe the population mean, μ, to be greater than (upper tail) or less than (lower tail) the hypothesized value, μ_0. Using a z-test at the 5% level of significance, the computed test statistic is compared with the critical values of 1.645 for the upper tail tests (i.e., $H_a: \mu > \mu_0$) or −1.645 for lower tail tests (i.e., $H_a: \mu < \mu_0$). These critical values are obtained from a z-table, where $-z_{0.05} = -1.645$ corresponds to a cumulative probability equal to 5%, and the $z_{0.05} = 1.645$ corresponds to a cumulative probability of 95% (1 − 0.05).

Let's use the upper tail test structure where $H_0: \mu \leq \mu_0$ and $H_a: \mu > \mu_0$.

- If the calculated test statistic is greater than 1.645, we conclude that the sample statistic is sufficiently greater than the hypothesized value. In other words, we reject the null hypothesis.
- If the calculated test statistic is less than 1.645, we conclude that the sample statistic is not sufficiently different from the hypothesized value, and we fail to reject the null hypothesis.

Figure 3 shows the standard normal distribution and the rejection region for a one-tailed test (upper tail) at the 5% level of significance.

Figure 3: One-Tailed Hypothesis Test Using the Standard Normal (z) Distribution

Example: One-tailed test

Perform a z-test using the option portfolio data from the previous example to test the belief that option returns are positive.

Answer:

In this case, we use a one-tailed test with the following structure:

$H_0: \mu \leq 0$ versus $H_a: \mu > 0$

The appropriate decision rule for this one-tailed z-test at a significance level of 5% is:

Reject H_0 if test statistic > 1.645

The test statistic is computed the same way, regardless of whether we are using a one-tailed or two-tailed test. From the previous example, we know that the test statistic for the option return sample is 6.33. Since 6.33 > 1.645, we reject the null hypothesis and conclude that mean returns are statistically greater than zero at a 5% level of significance.

The Choice of the Null and Alternative Hypotheses

The most common null hypothesis will be an "equal to" hypothesis. Combined with a "not equal to" alternative, this will require a two-tailed test. The alternative is often the hoped-for hypothesis. When the null is that a coefficient is equal to zero, we hope to reject it and show the significance of the relationship.

When the null is less than or equal to, the (mutually exclusive) alternative is framed as greater than, and a one-tail test is appropriate. If we are trying to demonstrate that a return is greater than the risk-free rate, this would be the correct formulation. We will have set up the null and alternative hypothesis so that rejection of the null will lead to acceptance of the alternative, our goal in performing the test.

LOS 11.b: Explain a test statistic, Type I and Type II errors, a significance level, and how significance levels are used in hypothesis testing.

CFA® Program Curriculum, Volume 1, page 555

Hypothesis testing involves two statistics: the test statistic calculated from the sample data and the *critical value* of the test statistic. The value of the computed test statistic relative to the critical value is a key step in assessing the validity of a hypothesis.

A test statistic is calculated by comparing the point estimate of the population parameter with the hypothesized value of the parameter (i.e., the value specified in the null hypothesis). With reference to our option return example, this means we are concerned with the difference between the mean return of the sample (i.e., $\overline{x} = 0.001$) and the hypothesized mean return (i.e., $\mu_0 = 0$). As indicated in the following expression, the test statistic is the difference between the sample statistic and the hypothesized value, scaled by the standard error of the sample statistic.

$$\text{test statistic} = \frac{\text{sample statistic} - \text{hypothesized value}}{\text{standard error of the sample statistic}}$$

The standard error of the sample statistic is the adjusted standard deviation of the sample. When the sample statistic is the sample mean, $\bar{x}$, the standard error of the sample statistic for sample size n, is calculated as:

$$\sigma_{\bar{x}} = \sigma / \sqrt{n}$$

when the population standard deviation, σ, *is known*, or

$$s_{\bar{x}} = s / \sqrt{n}$$

when the population standard deviation, σ, *is not known*. In this case, it is estimated using the standard deviation of the sample, s.

 Professor's Note: Don't be confused by the notation here. A lot of the literature you will encounter in your studies simply uses the term $\sigma_{\bar{x}}$ for the standard error of the test statistic, regardless of whether the population standard deviation or sample standard deviation was used in its computation.

As you will soon see, a test statistic is a random variable that may follow one of several distributions, depending on the characteristics of the sample and the population. We will look at four distributions for test statistics: the *t*-distribution, the *z*-distribution (standard normal distribution), the chi-square distribution, and the *F*-distribution. The critical value for the appropriate test statistic—the value against which the computed test statistic is compared—depends on its distribution.

Type I and Type II Errors

Keep in mind that hypothesis testing is used to make inferences about the parameters of a given population on the basis of statistics computed for a sample that is drawn from that population. We must be aware that there is some probability that the sample, in some way, does not represent the population, and any conclusion based on the sample about the population may be made in error.

When drawing inferences from a hypothesis test, there are two types of errors:

- **Type I error:** the rejection of the null hypothesis when it is actually true.
- **Type II error:** the failure to reject the null hypothesis when it is actually false.

The **significance** level is the probability of making a Type I error (rejecting the null when it is true) and is designated by the Greek letter alpha (α). For instance, a significance level of 5% ($\alpha = 0.05$) means there is a 5% chance of rejecting a true null hypothesis. When conducting hypothesis tests, a significance level must be specified in order to identify the critical values needed to evaluate the test statistic.

LOS 11.c: Explain a decision rule, the power of a test, and the relation between confidence intervals and hypothesis tests.

CFA® Program Curriculum, Volume 1, page 557

The decision for a hypothesis test is to either reject the null hypothesis or fail to reject the null hypothesis. Note that it is statistically incorrect to say "accept" the null hypothesis; it can only be supported or rejected. The **decision rule** for rejecting or failing to reject the null hypothesis is based on the distribution of the test statistic. For example, if the test statistic follows a normal distribution, the decision rule is based on critical values determined from the standard normal distribution (z-distribution). Regardless of the appropriate distribution, it must be determined if a one-tailed or two-tailed hypothesis test is appropriate before a decision rule (rejection rule) can be determined.

A decision rule is specific and quantitative. Once we have determined whether a one- or two-tailed test is appropriate, the significance level we require, and the distribution of the test statistic, we can calculate the exact critical value for the test statistic. Then we have a decision rule of the following form: if the test statistic is (greater, less than) the value X, reject the null.

The Power of a Test

While the significance level of a test is the probability of rejecting the null hypothesis when it is true, the **power of a test** is the probability of correctly rejecting the null hypothesis when it is false. The power of a test is actually one minus the probability of making a Type II error, or 1 – P(Type II error). In other words, the probability of rejecting the null when it is false (power of the test) equals one minus the probability of *not* rejecting the null when it is false (Type II error). When more than one test statistic may be used, the power of the test for the competing test statistics may be useful in deciding which test statistic to use. Ordinarily, we wish to use the test statistic that provides the most powerful test among all possible tests.

Figure 4 shows the relationship between the level of significance, the power of a test, and the two types of errors.

Figure 4: Type I and Type II Errors in Hypothesis Testing

Decision	True Condition	
	H_0 is true	H_0 is false
Do not reject H_0	Correct decision	Incorrect decision **Type II error**
Reject H_0	Incorrect decision **Type I error** Significance level, α, = P(Type I error)	Correct decision Power of the test = 1 – P(Type II error)

Sample size and the choice of significance level (Type I error probability) will together determine the probability of a Type II error. The relation is not simple, however, and calculating the probability of a Type II error in practice is quite difficult. Decreasing the significance level (probability of a Type I error) from 5% to 1%, for example, will increase the probability of failing to reject a false null (Type II error) and therefore reduce the power of the test. Conversely, for a given sample size, we can increase the power of a test only with the cost that the probability of rejecting a true null (Type I error) increases. For a given significance level, we can decrease the probability of a Type II error and increase the power of a test, only by increasing the sample size.

The Relation Between Confidence Intervals and Hypothesis Tests

A confidence interval is a range of values within which the researcher believes the true population parameter may lie.

A confidence interval is determined as:

$$\left\{ \left[\begin{array}{c} \text{sample} \\ \text{statistic} \end{array} - \left(\begin{array}{c} \text{critical} \\ \text{value} \end{array} \right) \left(\begin{array}{c} \text{standard} \\ \text{error} \end{array} \right) \right] \leq \begin{array}{c} \text{population} \\ \text{parameter} \end{array} \leq \left[\begin{array}{c} \text{sample} \\ \text{statistic} \end{array} + \left(\begin{array}{c} \text{critical} \\ \text{value} \end{array} \right) \left(\begin{array}{c} \text{standard} \\ \text{error} \end{array} \right) \right] \right\}$$

The interpretation of a confidence interval is that for a level of confidence of 95%, for example, there is a 95% probability that the true population parameter is contained in the interval.

From the previous expression, we see that a confidence interval and a hypothesis test are linked by the critical value. For example, a 95% confidence interval uses a critical value associated with a given distribution at the 5% level of significance. Similarly, a hypothesis test would compare a test statistic to a critical value at the 5% level of significance. To see this relationship more clearly, the expression for the confidence interval can be manipulated and restated as:

–critical value $\leq$ test statistic $\leq$ +critical value

This is the range within which we fail to reject the null for a two-tailed hypothesis test at a given level of significance.

Example: Confidence interval

Using option portfolio data from the previous examples, construct a 95% confidence interval for the population mean daily return over the 250-day sample period. Use a z-distribution. Decide if the hypothesis $\mu = 0$ should be rejected.

Answer:

Given a sample size of 250 with a standard deviation of 0.25%, the standard error can be computed as $s_{\bar{x}} = \dfrac{s}{\sqrt{n}} = 0.25/\sqrt{250} = 0.0158\%$.

At the 5% level of significance, the critical z-values for the confidence interval are $z_{0.025} = 1.96$ and $-z_{0.025} = -1.96$. Thus, given a sample mean equal to 0.1%, the 95% confidence interval for the population mean is:

$$0.1 - 1.96(0.0158) \leq \mu \leq 0.1 + 1.96(0.0158), \text{ or}$$

$$0.069\% \leq \mu \leq 0.1310\%$$

Since there is a 95% probability that the true mean is within this confidence interval, we can reject the hypothesis $\mu = 0$ because 0 is not within the confidence interval.

Notice the similarity of this analysis with our test of whether $\mu = 0$. We rejected the hypothesis $\mu = 0$ because the sample mean of 0.1% is more than 1.96 standard errors from zero. Based on the 95% confidence interval, we reject $\mu = 0$ because zero is more than 1.96 standard errors from the sample mean of 0.1%.

LOS 11.d: Distinguish between a statistical result and an economically meaningful result.

CFA® Program Curriculum, Volume 1, page 560

Statistical significance does not necessarily imply **economic significance**. For example, we may have tested a null hypothesis that a strategy of going long all the stocks that satisfy some criteria and shorting all the stocks that do not satisfy the criteria resulted in returns that were less than or equal to zero over a 20-year period. Assume we have rejected the null in favor of the alternative hypothesis that the returns to the strategy are greater than zero (positive). This does not necessarily mean that investing in that strategy will result in economically meaningful positive returns. Several factors must be considered.

One important consideration is transactions costs. Once we consider the costs of buying and selling the securities, we may find that the mean positive returns to the strategy are not enough to generate positive returns. Taxes are another factor that may make a seemingly attractive strategy a poor one in practice. A third reason that statistically significant results may not be economically significant is risk. In the above strategy, we have additional risk from short sales (they may have to be closed out earlier than in the test strategy). Since the statistically significant results were for a period of 20 years, it may be the case that there is significant variation from year to year in the returns from the strategy, even though the mean strategy return is greater than zero. This variation in returns from period to period is an additional risk to the strategy that is not accounted for in our test of statistical significance.

Any of these factors could make committing funds to a strategy unattractive, even though the statistical evidence of positive returns is highly significant. By the nature of statistical tests, a very large sample size can result in highly (statistically) significant results that are quite small in absolute terms.

LOS 11.e: Explain and interpret the *p*-value as it relates to hypothesis testing.

CFA® Program Curriculum, Volume 1, page 560

The *p*-value is the probability of obtaining a test statistic that would lead to a rejection of the null hypothesis, assuming the null hypothesis is true. It is the smallest level of significance for which the null hypothesis can be rejected. For one-tailed tests, the *p*-value is the probability that lies above the computed test statistic for upper tail tests or below the computed test statistic for lower tail tests. For two-tailed tests, the *p*-value is the probability that lies above the positive value of the computed test statistic *plus* the probability that lies below the negative value of the computed test statistic.

Consider a two-tailed hypothesis test about the mean value of a random variable at the 95% significance level where the test statistic is 2.3, greater than the upper critical value of 1.96. If we consult the *Z*-table, we find the probability of getting a value greater than 2.3 is $(1 - 0.9893) = 1.07\%$. Since it's a two-tailed test, our *p*-value is $2 \times 1.07 = 2.14\%$, as illustrated in Figure 5. At a 3%, 4%, or 5% significance level, we would reject the null hypothesis, but at a 2% or 1% significance level we would not. Many researchers report *p*-values without selecting a significance level and allow the reader to judge how strong the evidence for rejection is.

Figure 5: Two-Tailed Hypothesis Test with *p*-value = 2.14%

LOS 11.f: Identify the appropriate test statistic and interpret the results for a hypothesis test concerning the population mean of both large and small samples when the population is normally or approximately distributed and the variance is 1) known or 2) unknown.

CFA® Program Curriculum, Volume 1, page 561

When hypothesis testing, the choice between using a critical value based on the *t*-distribution or the *z*-distribution depends on sample size, the distribution of the population, and whether or not the variance of the population is known.

The *t*-Test

The *t*-test is a widely used hypothesis test that employs a test statistic that is distributed according to a *t*-distribution. Following are the rules for when it is appropriate to use the *t*-test for hypothesis tests of the population mean.

Use the t*-test if the population variance is **unknown*** and either of the following conditions exist:

- The sample is large (n ≥ 30).
- The sample is small (less than 30), but the distribution of the population is normal or approximately normal.

If the sample is small and the distribution is non-normal, we have no reliable statistical test.

The computed value for the test statistic based on the *t*-distribution is referred to as the *t*-statistic. For hypothesis tests of a population mean, a *t*-statistic with n − 1 degrees of freedom is computed as:

$$t_{n-1} = \frac{\overline{x} - \mu_0}{s / \sqrt{n}}$$

where:
$\overline{x}$ = sample mean
μ_0 = hypothesized population mean (i.e., the null)
s = standard deviation of the sample
n = sample size

 Professor's Note: This computation is not new. It is the same test statistic computation that we have been performing all along. Note the use of the sample standard deviation, s, in the standard error term in the denominator.

To conduct a *t*-test, the *t*-statistic is compared to a critical *t*-value at the desired level of significance with the appropriate degrees of freedom.

In the real world, the underlying variance of the population is rarely known, so the *t*-test enjoys widespread application.

The z-Test

The z-test is the appropriate hypothesis test of the population mean when the *population is normally distributed with known variance.* The computed test statistic used with the z-test is referred to as the z-statistic. The z-statistic for a hypothesis test for a population mean is computed as follows:

$$z\text{-statistic} = \frac{\overline{x} - \mu_0}{\sigma / \sqrt{n}}$$

where:
$\overline{x}$ = sample mean
μ_0 = hypothesized population mean
σ = standard deviation of the *population*
n = sample size

To test a hypothesis, the z-statistic is compared to the critical z-value corresponding to the significance of the test. Critical z-values for the most common levels of significance are displayed in Figure 6. You should have these memorized by now.

Figure 6: Critical z-Values

Level of Significance	Two-Tailed Test	One-Tailed Test
0.10 = 10%	±1.65	+1.28 or −1.28
0.05 = 5%	±1.96	+1.65 or −1.65
0.01 = 1%	±2.58	+2.33 or −2.33

When the *sample size is large* and the *population variance is unknown*, the z-statistic is:

$$z\text{-statistic} = \frac{\overline{x} - \mu_0}{s / \sqrt{n}}$$

where:
$\overline{x}$ = sample mean
μ_0 = hypothesized population mean
s = standard deviation of the *sample*
n = sample size

Note the use of the sample standard deviation, *s*, versus the population standard deviation, σ. Remember, this is acceptable if the sample size is large, although the *t*-statistic is the more conservative measure when the population variance is unknown.

Example: *z*-test or *t*-test?

Referring to our previous option portfolio mean return problem once more, determine which test statistic (*z* or *t*) should be used and the difference in the likelihood of rejecting a true null with each distribution.

Answer:

The population variance for our sample of returns is unknown. Hence, the *t*-distribution is appropriate. With 250 observations, however, the sample is considered to be large, so the *z*-distribution would also be acceptable. This is a trick question—either distribution, *t* or *z*, is appropriate. With regard to the difference in the likelihood of rejecting a true null, since our sample is so large, the critical values for the *t* and *z* are almost identical. Hence, there is almost no difference in the likelihood of rejecting a true null.

Example: The *z*-test

When your company's gizmo machine is working properly, the mean length of gizmos is 2.5 inches. However, from time to time the machine gets out of alignment and produces gizmos that are either too long or too short. When this happens, production is stopped and the machine is adjusted. To check the machine, the quality control department takes a gizmo sample each day. Today, a random sample of 49 gizmos showed a mean length of 2.49 inches. The population standard deviation is known to be 0.021 inches. Using a 5% significance level, determine if the machine should be shut down and adjusted.

Answer:

Let μ be the mean length of all gizmos made by this machine, and let $\bar{x}$ be the corresponding mean for the sample.

Let's follow the hypothesis testing procedure presented earlier in Figure 1. Again, you should know this process!

Statement of hypothesis. For the information provided, the null and alternative hypotheses are appropriately structured as:

H_0: μ = 2.5 (The machine does not need an adjustment.)

H_a: $\mu \neq$ 2.5 (The machine needs an adjustment.)

Note that since this is a two-tailed test, H_a allows for values above and below 2.5.

Select the appropriate test statistic. Since the population variance is known and the sample size is > 30, the z-statistic is the appropriate test statistic. The z-statistic is computed as:

$$z = \frac{\bar{x} - \mu_0}{\sigma / \sqrt{n}}$$

Specify the level of significance. The level of significance is given at 5%, implying that we are willing to accept a 5% probability of rejecting a true null hypothesis.

State the decision rule regarding the hypothesis. The $\neq$ sign in the alternative hypothesis indicates that the test is two-tailed with two rejection regions, one in each tail of the standard normal distribution curve. Because the total area of both rejection regions combined is 0.05 (the significance level), the area of the rejection region in each tail is 0.025. You should know that the critical z-values for $\pm z_{0.025}$ are ± 1.96. This means that the null hypothesis should not be rejected if the computed z-statistic lies between -1.96 and $+1.96$ and should be rejected if it lies outside of these critical values. The decision rule can be stated as:

Reject H_0 if $-z_{0.025} >$ z-statistic $> z_{0.025}$, or equivalently,

Reject H_0 if: $-1.96 >$ z-statistic $> +1.96$

Collect the sample and calculate the test statistic. The value of $\bar{x}$ from the sample is 2.49. Since σ is given as 0.021, we calculate the z-statistic using σ as follows:

$$z = \frac{\bar{x} - \mu_0}{\sigma / \sqrt{n}} = \frac{2.49 - 2.5}{0.021 / \sqrt{49}} = \frac{-0.01}{0.003} = -3.33$$

Make a decision regarding the hypothesis. The calculated value of the z-statistic is -3.33. Since this value is less than the critical value, $-z_{0.025} = -1.96$, it falls in the rejection region in the left tail of the z-distribution. Hence, there is sufficient evidence to reject H_0.

Make a decision based on the results of the test. Based on the sample information and the results of the test, it is concluded that the machine is out of adjustment and should be shut down for repair.

LOS 11.g: Identify the appropriate test statistic and interpret the results for a hypothesis test concerning the equality of the population means of two at least approximately normally distributed populations, based on independent random samples with 1) equal or 2) unequal assumed variances.

CFA® Program Curriculum, Volume 1, page 568

Up to this point, we have been concerned with tests of a single population mean. In practice, we frequently want to know if there is a difference between the means of two populations. There are two *t*-tests that are used to test differences between the means of two populations. Application of either of these tests requires that we are reasonably certain that our samples are independent and that they are taken from two populations that are normally distributed. Both of these t-tests can be used when the population variance is unknown. In one case, the population variances are assumed to be equal, and the sample observations are pooled. In the other case, however, no assumption is made regarding the equality between the two population variances, and the t-test uses an approximated value for the degrees of freedom.

Professor's Note: Please note the language of the LOS here. Candidates must "Identify the appropriate test statistic and interpret the results of a hypothesis test...." Certainly you should know that this is a t-test, and that we reject the hypothesis of equality when the test statistic is outside the critical t-values. Don't worry about memorizing the formulas given below. You should understand, however, that we can pool the data to get the standard deviation of the difference in means when we assume equal variances, while both sample variances are used to get the standard error of the difference in means when we assume the population variances are not equal.

A pooled variance is used with the t-test for testing the hypothesis that the means of two normally distributed populations are equal, when the variances of the populations are unknown but assumed to be equal.

Assuming independent samples, the t-statistic in this case is computed as:

$$t = \frac{\bar{x}_1 - \bar{x}_2}{\left(\dfrac{s_p^2}{n_1} + \dfrac{s_p^2}{n_2}\right)^{1/2}}$$

where:

$$s_p^2 = \frac{(n_1 - 1)s_1^2 + (n_2 - 1)s_2^2}{n_1 + n_2 - 2}$$

s_1^2 = variance of the first sample
s_2^2 = variance of the second sample
n_1 = number of observations in the first sample
n_2 = number of observations in the second sample

Note: The degrees of freedom, df, is $(n_1 + n_2 - 2)$.

Since we assume that the variances are equal, we just add the variances of the two sample means in order to calculate the standard error in the denominator.

The t-test for equality of population means when the populations are normally distributed and have **variances that are unknown and assumed to be unequal** uses the sample variances for both populations. Assuming independent samples, the t-statistic in this case is computed as follows:

$$t = \frac{\bar{x}_1 - \bar{x}_2}{\left(\frac{s_1^2}{n_1} + \frac{s_2^2}{n_2}\right)^{1/2}}$$

where:

$$\text{degrees of freedom} = \frac{\left(\frac{s_1^2}{n_1} + \frac{s_2^2}{n_2}\right)^2}{\frac{\left(s_1^2/n_1\right)^2}{n_1} + \frac{\left(s_2^2/n_2\right)^2}{n_2}}$$

and where:

s_1^2 = variance of the first sample
s_2^2 = variance of the second sample
n_1 = number of observations in the first sample
n_2 = number of observations in the second sample

With no assumption of equal variances, the denominator (standard error) is based on the individual sample variances for each sample.

You do not need to memorize these formulas, but should understand the numerator, the fact that these are t-statistics, and that the variance of the pooled sample is used when the sample variances are assumed to be equal. The intuition here is straightforward. If the sample means are very close together, the numerator of the t-statistic (and the t-statistic itself) are small, and we do not reject equality. If the sample means are far apart, the numerator of the t-statistic (and the t-statistic itself) are large, and we reject equality. Perhaps not as easy to remember is the fact that this test is only valid for two populations that are independent and normally distributed.

Example: Difference between means – equal variances

Sue Smith is investigating whether the abnormal returns for acquiring firms during merger announcement periods differ for horizontal and vertical mergers. She estimates the abnormal returns for a sample of acquiring firms associated with horizontal mergers and a sample of acquiring firms involved in vertical mergers. Her sample findings are reported in the following figure.

Abnormal Returns During Merger Announcement Periods

	Abnormal Returns Horizontal Mergers	Abnormal Returns Vertical Mergers
Mean	1.0%	2.5%
Standard deviation	1.0%	2.0%
Sample size (n)	64	81

Smith assumes that the samples are independent, the population means are normally distributed, and the population variances are equal.

Smith calculates the t-statistic as -5.474 and the degrees of freedom as 143. Should Smith reject or fail to reject the null hypothesis that the abnormal returns to acquiring firms during the announcement period are the same for horizontal and vertical mergers?

Answer:

State the hypothesis. Since this is a two-tailed test, the structure of the hypotheses takes the following form:

$$H_0: \mu_1 - \mu_2 = 0 \text{ versus } H_a: \mu_1 - \mu_2 \neq 0$$

where:
$\mu_1 =$ the mean of the abnormal returns for the horizontal mergers
$\mu_2 =$ the mean of the abnormal returns for the vertical mergers

Specify the level of significance. We will use the common significance level of 5% ($\alpha = 0.05$).

State the decision rule regarding the hypothesis. We must identify the critical t-value for a 5% level of significance and the *closest* degrees of freedom specified in a t-table. As you should verify with the partial t-table contained in the following figure, the closest entry for df = 143 is df = 120. At $\alpha / 2 = p = 0.025$ with df = 120, the critical t-value = 1.980.

Partial t-Table

df	One-Tailed Probabilities (p)		
	p = 0.10	p = 0.05	p = 0.025
110	1.289	1.659	1.982
120	1.289	1.658	1.980
200	1.286	1.653	1.972

Thus, the decision rule can be stated as:

Reject H_0 if t-statistic < -1.980 or t-statistic > 1.980

The rejection region for this test is illustrated in the following figure.

Decision Rule for Two-Tailed *t*-Test

(α = 0.05, df = 120)

2.5%   2.5%

−1.980   1.980

Reject H$_0$ Fail to Reject H$_0$ Reject H$_0$

Make a decision regarding the hypothesis. Since the test statistic, −5.474, falls to the left of the lower critical *t*-value, we reject the null hypothesis and conclude that the announcement period mean abnormal returns are different for horizontal and vertical mergers.

LOS 11.h: Identify the appropriate test statistic and interpret the results for a hypothesis test concerning the mean difference of two normally distributed populations.

CFA® Program Curriculum, Volume 1, page 572

While the tests considered in the previous section were of the difference between the means of two independent samples, sometimes our samples may be dependent. If the observations in the two samples both depend on some other factor, we can construct a "paired comparisons" test of whether the means of the differences between observations for the two samples are different. Dependence may result from an event that affects both sets of observations for a number of companies or because observations for two firms over time are both influenced by market returns or economic conditions.

For an example of a paired comparisons test, consider a test of whether the returns on two steel firms were equal over a 5-year period. We can't use the difference in means test because we have reason to believe that the samples are not independent. To some extent, both will depend on the returns on the overall market (market risk) and the conditions in the steel industry (industry specific risk). In this case, our pairs will be the returns on each firm over the same time periods, so we use the differences in monthly returns for the two companies. The paired comparisons test is just a test of whether the average difference between monthly returns is significantly different from zero, based on the standard error of the differences in monthly returns.

Remember, the paired comparisons test also requires that the sample data be normally distributed. Although we frequently just want to test the hypothesis that the mean of the differences in the pairs is zero ($\mu_{dz} = 0$), the general form of the test for any hypothesized mean difference, μ_{dz}, is as follows:

$$H_0: \mu_d = \mu_{dz} \text{ versus } H_a: \mu_d \neq \mu_{dz}$$

where:
μ_d = mean of the population of paired differences
μ_{dz} = hypothesized mean of paired differences, which is commonly zero

For one-tail tests, the hypotheses are structured as either:

$$H_0: \mu_d \leq \mu_{dz} \text{ versus } H_a: \mu_d > \mu_{dz}, \text{ or } H_0: \mu_d \geq \mu_{dz} \text{ versus } H_a: \mu_d < \mu_{dz}$$

For the paired comparisons test, the *t*-statistic with n − 1 degrees of freedom is computed as:

$$t = \frac{\bar{d} - \mu_{dz}}{s_{\bar{d}}}$$

where:

$$\bar{d} = \text{sample mean difference} = \frac{1}{n}\sum_{i=1}^{n} d_i$$

d_i = difference between the *i*th pair of observations

$$s_{\bar{d}} = \text{standard error of the mean difference} = \frac{s_d}{\sqrt{n}}$$

$$s_d = \text{sample standard deviation} = \left[\frac{\sum_{i=1}^{n}\left(d_i - \bar{d}\right)^2}{n-1}\right]^{1/2}$$

n = the number of paired observations

Example: Paired comparisons test

Joe Andrews is examining changes in estimated betas for the common stock of companies in the telecommunications industry before and after deregulation. Andrews believes that the betas may decline because of deregulation since companies are no longer subject to the uncertainties of rate regulation or that they may increase because there is more uncertainty regarding competition in the industry. The sample information he gathered is reported in the following figure. Determine whether there is a change in betas.

Beta Differences After Deregulation

Mean of differences in betas (before minus after)	0.23
Sample standard deviation of differences	0.14
Sample size	39

Answer:

State the hypothesis. There is reason to believe that the mean difference may be positive or negative, so a two-tailed test is in order here. Thus, the hypotheses are structured as:

$$H_0: \mu_d = 0 \text{ versus } H_a: \mu_d \neq 0$$

Select the appropriate test statistic. The test statistic for a paired comparisons test of whether the returns are equal is:

$$t = \frac{\overline{d}}{s_{\overline{d}}}$$

Specify the level of significance. Let's use a 5% level of significance.

State the decision rule regarding the hypothesis. There are 39 − 1 = 38 degrees of freedom. Using the *t*-distribution, the two-tailed critical *t*-values for a 5% level of significance with df = 38 is ±2.024. As indicated in the following table, the critical *t*-value of 2.024 is located at the intersection of the p = 0.025 column and the df = 38 row. The one-tailed probability of 0.025 is used because we need 2.5% in each tail for 5% significance with a two-tailed test.

Partial t-Table

df	One-Tailed Probabilities (p)		
	p = 0.10	P = 0.05	p = 0.025
38	1.304	1.686	2.024
39	1.304	1.685	2.023
40	1.303	1.684	2.021

Thus, the decision rule becomes:

Reject H_0 if t-statistic < -2.024, or t-statistic > 2.024

This decision rule is illustrated in the following figure.

Decision Rule for a Two-Tailed Paired Comparisons Test

($\alpha = 0.05$, df = 38)

2.5%   2.5%

-2.024 2.024

Reject H_0 Fail to Reject H_0 Reject H_0

Collect the sample and calculate the sample statistics. Using the sample data provided, the test statistic is computed as follows:

$$t = \frac{\overline{d}}{s_{\overline{d}}} = \frac{0.23}{0.14 / \sqrt{39}} = \frac{0.23}{0.022418} = 10.2596$$

Make a decision regarding the hypotheses. The computed test statistic, 10.2596, is greater than the critical *t*-value, 2.024—it falls in the rejection region to the right of 2.024 in the previous figure. Thus, we reject the null hypothesis of no difference, concluding that there *is* a statistically significant difference between mean firm betas before and after deregulation.

Make a decision based on the results of the test. We have support for the hypothesis that betas are lower as a result of deregulation, providing support for the proposition that deregulation resulted in decreased risk.

Keep in mind that we have been describing two distinct hypothesis tests, one about the significance of the difference between the means of two populations and one about the significance of the mean of the differences between pairs of observations. Here are rules for when these tests may be applied:

- The test of the differences in means is used when there are two *independent samples*.
- A test of the significance of the mean of the differences between paired observations is used when the samples are *not independent*.

 Professor's Note: The LOS here say "Identify the appropriate test statistic and interpret the results..." I can't believe candidates are expected to memorize these formulas (or that you would be a better analyst if you did). You should instead focus on the fact that both of these tests involve t-statistics and depend on the degrees of freedom. Also note that when samples are independent, you can use the difference in means test, and when they are dependent, the statistic is the average difference in (paired) observations divided by the standard error of the differences between observations.

LOS 11.i: Identify the appropriate test statistic and interpret the results for a hypothesis test concerning 1) the variance of a normally distributed population, and 2) the equality of the variances of two normally distributed populations based on two independent random samples.

CFA® Program Curriculum, Volume 1, page 576

The *chi-square test* is used for hypothesis tests concerning the variance of a normally distributed population. Letting σ^2 represent the true population variance and σ_0^2 represent the hypothesized variance, the hypotheses for a two-tailed test of a single population variance are structured as:

$$H_0: \sigma^2 = \sigma_0^2 \text{ versus } H_a: \sigma^2 \neq \sigma_0^2$$

The hypotheses for one-tailed tests are structured as:

$$H_0: \sigma^2 \leq \sigma_0^2 \text{ versus } H_a: \sigma^2 > \sigma_0^2, \text{ or}$$
$$H_0: \sigma^2 \geq \sigma_0^2 \text{ versus } H_a: \sigma^2 < \sigma_0^2$$

Hypothesis testing of the population variance requires the use of a chi-square distributed test statistic, denoted χ^2. The chi-square distribution is asymmetrical and approaches the normal distribution in shape as the degrees of freedom increase.

To illustrate the chi-square distribution, consider a two-tailed test with a 5% level of significance and 30 degrees of freedom. As displayed in Figure 7, the critical chi-square values are 16.791 and 46.979 for the lower and upper bounds, respectively. These values are obtained from a chi-square table, which is used in the same manner as a t-table. A portion of a chi-square table is presented in Figure 8.

Note that the chi-square values in Figure 8 correspond to the probabilities in the right tail of the distribution. As such, the 16.791 in Figure 7 is from the column headed *0.975* because 95% + 2.5% of the probability is to the right of it. The 46.979 is from the column headed *0.025* because only 2.5% probability is to the right of it. Similarly, at a 5% level of significance with 10 degrees of freedom, Figure 8 shows that the critical chi-square values for a two-tailed test are 3.247 and 20.483.

Figure 7: Decision Rule for a Two-Tailed Chi-Square Test

Figure 8: Chi-Square Table

Degrees of Freedom	Probability in Right Tail					
	0.975	0.95	0.90	0.1	0.05	0.025
9	2.700	3.325	4.168	14.684	16.919	19.023
10	3.247	3.940	4.865	15.987	18.307	20.483
11	3.816	4.575	5.578	17.275	19.675	21.920
30	16.791	18.493	20.599	40.256	43.773	46.979

The chi-square test statistic, χ^2, with $n - 1$ degrees of freedom, is computed as:

$$\chi_{n-1}^2 = \frac{(n-1)s^2}{\sigma_0^2}$$

where:

n	=	sample size
s^2	=	sample variance
σ_0^2	=	hypothesized value for the population variance.

Similar to other hypothesis tests, the chi-square test compares the test statistic, χ_{n-1}^2, to a critical chi-square value at a given level of significance and $n - 1$ degrees of freedom. Note that since the chi-square distribution is bounded below by zero, chi-square values cannot be negative.

Example: Chi-square test for a single population variance

Historically, High-Return Equity Fund has advertised that its monthly returns have a standard deviation equal to 4%. This was based on estimates from the 1990–1998 period. High-Return wants to verify whether this claim still adequately describes the standard deviation of the fund's returns. High-Return collected monthly returns for the 24-month period between 1998 and 2000 and measured a standard deviation of monthly returns of 3.8%. Determine if the more recent standard deviation is different from the advertised standard deviation.

Answer:

State the hypothesis. The null hypothesis is that the standard deviation is equal to 4% and, therefore, the variance of monthly returns for the population is $(0.04)^2 = 0.0016$. Since High-Return simply wants to test whether the standard deviation has changed, up or down, a two-sided test should be used. The hypothesis test structure takes the form:

$$H_0: \sigma_0^2 = 0.0016 \text{ versus } H_a: \sigma^2 \neq 0.0016$$

Select the appropriate test statistic. The appropriate test statistic for tests of variance using the chi-square distribution is computed as follows:

$$\chi^2 = \frac{(n-1)s^2}{\sigma_0^2}$$

Specify the level of significance. Let's use a 5% level of significance, meaning there will be 2.5% probability in each tail of the chi-square distribution.

State the decision rule regarding the hypothesis. With a 24-month sample, there are 23 degrees of freedom. Using the table of chi-square values at the back of this book, for 23 degrees of freedom and probabilities of 0.975 and 0.025, we find two critical values, 11.689 and 38.076. Thus, the decision rule is:

Reject H_0 if $\chi^2 < 11.689$, or $\chi^2 > 38.076$

This decision rule is illustrated in the following figure.

Decision Rule for a Two-Tailed Chi-Square Test of a Single Population Variance

$(\alpha = 0.05, df = 23)$

2.5%   2.5%

11.689   38.076

Reject H_0 | Fail to Reject H_0 | Reject H_0

Collect the sample and calculate the sample statistics. Using the information provided, the test statistic is computed as:

$$\chi^2 = \frac{(n-1)s^2}{\sigma_0^2} = \frac{(23)(0.001444)}{0.0016} = \frac{0.033212}{0.0016} = 20.7575$$

Make a decision regarding the hypothesis. Since the computed test statistic, χ^2, falls between the two critical values, we fail to reject the null hypothesis that the variance is equal to 0.0016.

Make a decision based on the results of the test. It can be concluded that the recently measured standard deviation is close enough to the advertised standard deviation that we cannot say that it is different from 4%, at a 5% level of significance.

Testing the Equality of the Variances of Two Normally Distributed Populations, Based on Two Independent Random Samples

The hypotheses concerned with the equality of the variances of two populations are tested with an *F*-distributed test statistic. Hypothesis testing using a test statistic that follows an *F*-distribution is referred to as the *F*-test. The *F*-test is used under the assumption that the populations from which samples are drawn are normally distributed and that the samples are independent.

If we let σ_1^2 and σ_2^2 represent the variances of normal Population 1 and Population 2, respectively, the hypotheses for the two-tailed F-test of differences in the variances can be structured as:

$$H_0: \sigma_1^2 = \sigma_2^2 \text{ versus } H_a: \sigma_1^2 \neq \sigma_2^2$$

and the one-sided test structures can be specified as:

$$H_0: \sigma_1^2 \leq \sigma_2^2 \text{ versus } H_a: \sigma_1^2 > \sigma_2^2, \text{ or } H_0: \sigma_1^2 \geq \sigma_2^2 \text{ versus } H_a: \sigma_1^2 < \sigma_2^2$$

The test statistic for the F-test is the ratio of the sample variances. The F-statistic is computed as:

$$F = \frac{s_1^2}{s_2^2}$$

where:

s_1^2 = variance of the sample of n_1 observations drawn from Population 1
s_2^2 = variance of the sample of n_2 observations drawn from Population 2

Note that $n_1 - 1$ and $n_2 - 1$ are the degrees of freedom used to identify the appropriate critical value from the F-table (provided in the Appendix).

Professor's Note: Always put the larger variance in the numerator (s_1^2). Following this convention means we only have to consider the critical value for the right-hand tail.

An F-distribution is presented in Figure 9. As indicated, the F-distribution is right-skewed and is truncated at zero on the left-hand side. The shape of the F-distribution is determined by *two separate degrees of freedom*, the numerator degrees of freedom, df_1, and the denominator degrees of freedom, df_2. Also shown in Figure 9 is that the *rejection region is in the right-side tail* of the distribution. This will always be the case as long as the F-statistic is computed with the largest sample variance in the numerator. The labeling of 1 and 2 is arbitrary anyway.

Figure 9: F-Distribution

numerator $df_1 = 10$, denominator $df_2 = 10$

0

5%

2.98

Fail to Reject H_0 Reject H_0

Example: F-test for equal variances

Annie Cower is examining the earnings for two different industries. Cower suspects that the earnings of the textile industry are more divergent than those of the paper industry. To confirm this suspicion, Cower has looked at a sample of 31 textile manufacturers and a sample of 41 paper companies. She measured the sample standard deviation of earnings across the textile industry to be $4.30 and that of the paper industry companies to be $3.80. Determine if the earnings of the textile industry have greater standard deviation than those of the paper industry.

Answer:

State the hypothesis. In this example, we are concerned with whether the variance of the earnings of the textile industry is greater (more divergent) than the variance of the earnings of the paper industry. As such, the test hypotheses can be appropriately structured as:

$$H_0: \sigma_1^2 \leq \sigma_2^2 \text{ versus } H_a: \sigma_1^2 > \sigma_2^2$$

where:
σ_1^2 = variance of earnings for the textile industry
σ_2^2 = variance of earnings for the paper industry
Note: $\sigma_1^2 > \sigma_2^2$

Select the appropriate test statistic. For tests of difference between variances, the appropriate test statistic is:

$$F = \frac{s_1^2}{s_2^2}$$

©2012 Kaplan, Inc.

Specify the level of significance. Let's conduct our hypothesis test at the 5% level of significance.

State the decision rule regarding the hypothesis. Using the sample sizes for the two industries, the critical *F*-value for our test is found to be 1.74. This value is obtained from the table of the *F*-distribution at the 5% level of significance with $df_1 = 30$ and $df_2 = 40$. Thus, if the computed *F*-statistic is greater than the critical value of 1.74, the null hypothesis is rejected. The decision rule, illustrated in the figure below, can be stated as:

Reject H_0 if F > 1.74

Decision Rule for *F*-Test

($\alpha = 0.05$, $df_1 = 30$, $df_2 = 40$)

5%

0   1.74

Fail to Reject H_0 Reject H_0

Collect the sample and calculate the sample statistics. Using the information provided, the *F*-statistic can be computed as:

$$F = \frac{s_1^2}{s_2^2} = \frac{\$4.30^2}{\$3.80^2} = \frac{\$18.49}{\$14.44} = 1.2805$$

 Professor's Note: Remember to square the standard deviations to get the variances.

Make a decision regarding the hypothesis. Since the calculated *F*-statistic of 1.2805 is less than the critical *F*-statistic of 1.74, we fail to reject the null hypothesis.

Make a decision based on the results of the test. Based on the results of the hypothesis test, Cower should conclude that the earnings variances of the industries are not statistically significantly different from one another at a 5% level of significance. More pointedly, the earnings of the textile industry are not more divergent than those of the paper industry.

LOS 11.j: Distinguish between parametric and nonparametric tests and describe the situations in which the use of nonparametric tests may be appropriate.

CFA® Program Curriculum, Volume 1, page 578

Parametric tests rely on assumptions regarding the distribution of the population and are specific to population parameters. For example, the z-test relies upon a mean and a standard deviation to define the normal distribution. The z-test also requires that either the sample is large, relying on the central limit theorem to assure a normal sampling distribution, or that the population is normally distributed.

Nonparametric tests either do not consider a particular population parameter or have few assumptions about the population that is sampled. Nonparametric tests are used when there is concern about quantities other than the parameters of a distribution or when the assumptions of parametric tests can't be supported. They are also used when the data are not suitable for parametric tests (e.g., ranked observations).

Situations where a nonparametric test is called for are the following:

1. The assumptions about the distribution of the random variable that support a parametric test are not met. An example would be a hypothesis test of the mean value for a variable that comes from a distribution that is not normal and is of small size so that neither the t-test nor the z-test are appropriate.

2. When data are ranks (an ordinal measurement scale) rather than values.

3. The hypothesis does not involve the parameters of the distribution, such as testing whether a variable is normally distributed. We can use a nonparametric test, called a runs test, to determine whether data are random. A runs test provides an estimate of the probability that a series of changes (e.g., +, +, −, −, +, −,….) are random.

The Spearman rank correlation test can be used when the data are not normally distributed. Consider the performance ranks of 20 mutual funds for two years. The ranks (1 through 20) are not normally distributed, so a standard t-test of the correlations is not appropriate. A large positive value of the Spearman rank correlations, such as 0.85, would indicate that a high (low) rank in one year is associated with a high (low) rank in the second year. Alternatively, a large negative rank correlation would indicate that a high rank in year 1 suggests a low rank in year 2, and vice versa.

KEY CONCEPTS

LOS 11.a

The hypothesis testing process requires a statement of a null and an alternative hypothesis, the selection of the appropriate test statistic, specification of the significance level, a decision rule, the calculation of a sample statistic, a decision regarding the hypotheses based on the test, and a decision based on the test results.

The null hypothesis is what the researcher wants to reject. The alternative hypothesis is what the researcher wants to prove, and it is accepted when the null hypothesis is rejected.

A two-tailed test results from a two-sided alternative hypothesis (e.g., H_a: $\mu \neq \mu_0$). A one-tailed test results from a one-sided alternative hypothesis (e.g., H_a: $\mu > \mu_0$, or H_a: $\mu < \mu_0$).

LOS 11.b

The test statistic is the value that a decision about a hypothesis will be based on. For a test about the value of the mean of a distribution:

$$\text{test statistic} = \frac{\text{sample mean} - \text{hypothesized mean}}{\text{standard error of sample mean}}$$

A Type I error is the rejection of the null hypothesis when it is actually true, while a Type II error is the failure to reject the null hypothesis when it is actually false.

The significance level can be interpreted as the probability that a test statistic will reject the null hypothesis by chance when it is actually true (i.e., the probability of a Type I error). A significance level must be specified to select the critical values for the test.

LOS 11.c

Hypothesis testing compares a computed test statistic to a critical value at a stated level of significance, which is the decision rule for the test.

The power of a test is the probability of rejecting the null when it is false. The power of a test = 1 – P(Type II error).

A hypothesis about a population parameter is rejected when the sample statistic lies outside a confidence interval around the hypothesized value for the chosen level of significance.

LOS 11.d

Statistical significance does not necessarily imply economic significance. Even though a test statistic is significant statistically, the size of the gains to a strategy to exploit a statistically significant result may be absolutely small or simply not great enough to outweigh transactions costs.

LOS 11.e

The p-value for a hypothesis test is the smallest significance level for which the hypothesis would be rejected. For example, a p-value of 7% means the hypothesis can be rejected at the 10% significance level but cannot be rejected at the 5% significance level.

LOS 11.f

With unknown population variance, the t-statistic is used for tests about the mean of a normally distributed population: $t_{n-1} = \dfrac{\bar{x} - \mu_0}{s / \sqrt{n}}$. If the population variance is known, the appropriate test statistic is $z = \dfrac{\bar{x} - \mu_0}{\sigma / \sqrt{n}}$ for tests about the mean of a population.

LOS 11.g

For two independent samples from two normally distributed populations, the difference in means can be tested with a t-statistic. When the two population variances are assumed to be equal, the denominator is based on the variance of the pooled samples, but when sample variances are assumed to be unequal, the denominator is based on a combination of the two samples' variances.

LOS 11.h

A paired comparisons test is concerned with the mean of the differences between the paired observations of two dependent, normally distributed samples. A t-statistic, $t = \dfrac{\bar{d}}{s_{\bar{d}}}$, where $s_{\bar{d}} = \dfrac{s_d}{\sqrt{n}}$, and $\bar{d}$ is the average difference of the n paired observations, is used to test whether the means of two dependent normal variables are equal. Values outside the critical t-values lead us to reject equality.

LOS 11.i

The test of a hypothesis about the population variance for a normally distributed population uses a chi-square test statistic: $\chi^2 = \dfrac{(n-1)s^2}{\sigma_0^2}$, where n is the sample size, s^2 is the sample variance, and σ_0^2 is the hypothesized value for the population variance. Degrees of freedom are $n - 1$.

The test comparing two variances based on independent samples from two normally distributed populations uses an F-distributed test statistic: $F = \dfrac{s_1^2}{s_2^2}$, where s_1^2 is the variance of the first sample and s_2^2 is the (smaller) variance of the second sample.

LOS 11.j

Parametric tests, like the t-test, F-test, and chi-square tests, make assumptions regarding the distribution of the population from which samples are drawn. Nonparametric tests either do not consider a particular population parameter or have few assumptions about the sampled population. Nonparametric tests are used when the assumptions of parametric tests can't be supported or when the data are not suitable for parametric tests.

CONCEPT CHECKERS

1. Which of the following statements about hypothesis testing is *most accurate*?
   A. A Type II error is rejecting the null when it is actually true.
   B. The significance level equals one minus the probability of a Type I error.
   C. A two-tailed test with a significance level of 5% has z-critical values of ±1.96.

2. Which of the following statements about hypothesis testing is *least accurate*?
   A. The power of test = 1 – P(Type II error).
   B. If the computed z-statistic = –2 and the critical z-value = –1.96, the null hypothesis is rejected.
   C. The calculated z-statistic for a test of a sample mean when the population variance is known is: $z = \dfrac{\bar{X} - \mu_0}{\dfrac{\sigma^2}{\sqrt{n}}}$.

Use the following data to answer Questions 3 through 7.

Austin Roberts believes that the mean price of houses in the area is greater than $145,000. A random sample of 36 houses in the area has a mean price of $149,750. The population standard deviation is $24,000, and Roberts wants to conduct a hypothesis test at a 1% level of significance.

3. The appropriate alternative hypothesis is:
   A. $H_a: \mu < \$145,000$.
   B. $H_a: \mu \geq \$145,000$.
   C. $H_a: \mu > \$145,000$.

4. The value of the calculated test statistic is *closest* to:
   A. 0.67.
   B. 1.19.
   C. 4.00.

5. Which of the following *most accurately* describes the appropriate test structure?
   A. Two-tailed test.
   B. One-tailed test.
   C. Chi-square test.

6. The critical value of the z-statistic is:
   A. ±1.96.
   B. +2.33.
   C. ±2.33.

7. At a 1% level of significance, Roberts should:
   A. reject the null hypothesis.
   B. fail to reject the null hypothesis.
   C. neither reject nor fail to reject the null hypothesis.

Use the following data to answer Questions 8 through 13.

An analyst is conducting a hypothesis test to determine if the mean time spent on investment research is different from three hours per day. The test is performed at the 5% level of significance and uses a random sample of 64 portfolio managers, where the mean time spent on research is found to be 2.5 hours. The population standard deviation is 1.5 hours.

8. The appropriate null hypothesis for the described test is:
   A. $H_0: \mu = 3$ hours.
   B. $H_0: \mu \leq 3$ hours.
   C. $H_0: \mu \geq 3$ hours.

9. This is a:
   A. one-tailed test.
   B. two-tailed test.
   C. paired comparisons test.

10. The calculated z-statistic is:
    A. −2.67.
    B. +0.33.
    C. +2.67.

11. The critical z-value(s) of the test statistic is (are):
    A. −1.96.
    B. +1.96.
    C. ±1.96.

12. The 95% confidence interval for the population mean is:
    A. $\{1.00 < \mu < 3.50\}$.
    B. $\{0.54 < \mu < 4.46\}$.
    C. $\{2.13 < \mu < 2.87\}$.

13. The analyst should *most appropriately*:
    A. reject the null hypothesis.
    B. fail to reject the null hypothesis.
    C. reach no conclusion because the sample standard deviation was not given.

14. A study was conducted to determine whether the standard deviation of monthly maintenance costs of a Pepper III aircraft is $300. A sample of 30 Pepper IIIs had a mean monthly maintenance cost of $3,025 and a standard deviation of $325. Using a 5% level of significance, which of the following is the *most appropriate* conclusion regarding the *difference* between the hypothesized value of the population variance and the sample variance?
    A. The population and sample variances are significantly different.
    B. The population and sample variances are not significantly different.
    C. There are no tests that may be used to test variance differences in small samples.

Use the following data to answer Questions 15 through 18.

Two samples were drawn from two normally distributed populations. For the first sample, the mean was $50 and the standard deviation was $5. For the second sample, the mean was $55 and the standard deviation was $6. The first sample consists of 25 observations and the second sample consists of 36 observations. (Note: In the questions below, the subscripts "1" and "2" indicate the first and second sample, respectively.)

15. Consider the hypotheses structured as $H_0: \mu_1 = \$48$ versus $H_a: \mu_1 \neq \$48$. At a 1% level of significance, the null hypothesis:
    A. cannot be rejected.
    B. should be rejected.
    C. cannot be tested using this sample information provided.

16. Using a 5% level of significance and a hypothesis test structure of $H_0: \sigma_1^2 \leq 24$ versus $H_a: \sigma_1^2 > 24$, the null hypothesis:
    A. cannot be rejected.
    B. should be rejected.
    C. cannot be tested using this sample information provided.

17. Consider the hypotheses structured as $H_0: \mu_1 \leq \$48$ versus $H_a: \mu_1 > \$48$. At a 5% level of significance, the null hypothesis:
    A. cannot be rejected.
    B. should be rejected.
    C. cannot be tested using the sample information provided.

18. Using a 5% level of significance for a test of the null of $H_0: \sigma_1^2 = \sigma_2^2$ versus the alternative of $H_a: \sigma_1^2 \neq \sigma_2^2$, the null hypothesis:
    A. cannot be rejected.
    B. should be rejected.
    C. cannot be tested using the sample information provided.

19. If the significance level of a test is 0.05 and the probability of a Type II error is 0.15, what is the power of the test?
    A. 0.850.
    B. 0.950.
    C. 0.975.

20. Which of the following statements about the *F*-distribution and chi-square distribution is *least accurate*? Both distributions:
    A. are asymmetrical.
    B. are bound by zero on the left.
    C. have means that are less than their standard deviations.

21. The appropriate test statistic for a test of the equality of variances for two normally distributed random variables, based on two independent random samples, is the:
    A. *t*-test.
    B. *F*-test.
    C. χ^2 test.

22. The appropriate test statistic to test the hypothesis that the variance of a normally distributed population is equal to 13 is the:
    A. t-test.
    B. F-test.
    C. χ^2 test.

23. William Adams wants to test whether the mean monthly returns over the last five years are the same for two stocks. If he assumes that the returns distributions are normal and have equal variances, the type of test and test statistic are *best* described as:
    A. paired comparisons test, t-statistic.
    B. paired comparisons test, F-statistic.
    C. difference in means test, t-statistic.

24. Which of the following assumptions is *least likely* required for the difference in means test based on two samples?
    A. The two samples are independent.
    B. The two populations are normally distributed.
    C. The two populations have equal variances.

25. For a hypothesis test with a probability of a Type II error of 60% and a probability of a Type I error of 5%, which of the following statements is *most accurate*?
    A. The power of the test is 40%, and there is a 5% probability that the test statistic will exceed the critical value(s).
    B. There is a 95% probability that the test statistic will be between the critical values if this is a two-tailed test.
    C. There is a 5% probability that the null hypothesis will be rejected when actually true, and the probability of rejecting the null when it is false is 40%.

CHALLENGE PROBLEMS

1. Ralph Rollins, a researcher, believes that the stocks of firms that have appeared in a certain financial newspaper with a positive headline and story return more on a risk-adjusted basis. He gathers data on the risk-adjusted returns for these stocks over the six months after they appear on the cover, and data on the risk-adjusted returns for an equal-sized sample of firms with characteristics similar to the cover-story firms matched by time period.

    A. State the likely null and alternative hypotheses for a test of his belief.

    B. Is this a one- or two-tailed test?

    C. Describe the steps in testing a hypothesis such as the null you stated in part A.

2. For each of the following hypotheses, describe the appropriate test, identify the appropriate test statistic, and explain under what conditions the null hypothesis should be rejected.

    A. A researcher has returns over 52 weeks for an index of natural gas stocks and for an index of oil stocks and wants to know if the weekly returns are equal. Assume that the returns are approximately normally distributed.

    B. A researcher has two independent samples that are approximately normally distributed. She wishes to test whether the mean values of the two random variables are equal and assumes that the variances of the populations from which the two samples are drawn are equal. As an additional question here, how should the degrees of freedom be calculated?

    C. A researcher wants to determine whether the population variances of two normally distributed random variables are equal based on two samples of sizes n_1 and n_2. As an additional question here, how should the degrees of freedom be calculated?

    D. A researcher wants to test whether the variance of a normally distributed population is equal to 0.00165. As an additional question here, how should the degrees of freedom be calculated?

ANSWERS – CONCEPT CHECKERS

1. **C** Rejecting the null when it is actually true is a Type I error. A Type II error is failing to reject the null hypothesis when it is false. The significance level equals the probability of a Type I error.

2. **C** $z = \dfrac{\overline{X} - \mu_0}{\dfrac{\sigma}{\sqrt{n}}}$ (σ^2 is the variance)

3. **C** $H_a: \mu > \$145,000$

4. **B** $z = \dfrac{149,750 - 145,000}{24,000 \ / \sqrt{36}} = 1.1875$

5. **B** The alternative hypothesis, $H_a: \mu > \$145,000$, only allows for values greater than the hypothesized value. Thus, this is a one-sided (one-tailed) test.

6. **B** For a one-tailed z-test at the 1% level of significance, the critical z-value is $z_{0.01} = 2.33$. Since the test is one-tailed on the upper end (i.e., $H_a: \mu > 145,000$), we use a positive z-critical value.

7. **B** The decision rule is to reject H_0 if z-computed > z-critical. Since $1.1875 < 2.33$, Roberts will fail to reject the null.

8. **A** $H_0: \mu = 3$ hours

9. **B** This is a two-sided (two-tailed) test. We want to test if the mean "differs from" 3 hours (i.e., $H_a: \mu \neq 3$ hours).

10. **A** The normally distributed test statistic $= z = \dfrac{(2.5 - 3.0)}{(1.5 \ / \sqrt{64})} = -2.67$.

11. **C** At $\alpha \ / 2 = 0.025$, the critical z-values are: $\pm z_{\alpha / 2} = \pm z_{0.025} = \pm 1.96$.

12. **C** The 95% confidence interval is $\{2.5 \pm (1.96)(0.1875)\} = \{2.5 \pm 0.3675\} \rightarrow \{2.1325 < \mu < 2.8675\}$.

13. **A** Decision rule: reject H_0 if $z_{computed} < -1.96$ or if $z_{computed} > +1.96$. Since $-2.67 < -1.96$, reject H_0.

14. **B** The wording of the proposition is a little tricky, but the test structure is $H_0: \sigma^2 = 300^2$ versus $H_a: \sigma^2 \neq 300^2$. The appropriate test is a two-tailed chi-square test. The decision rule is to reject H_0 if the test statistic is outside the range defined by the critical chi-square values at $\alpha \ / 2 = 0.025$ with df = 29. The test statistic is:

$$\chi^2 = \frac{(n-1)s^2}{\sigma_0^2} = \frac{(29)(105,625)}{90,000} = 34.035$$

The critical chi-square values are 16.047 on the left and 45.722 on the right. Since the χ^2 falls between these two values, we fail to reject the null hypothesis. This means the population standard deviation is not significantly different than $300.

©2012 Kaplan, Inc.

15. **A**   A two-tailed t-test is appropriate. The decision rule is to reject H_0 if the t-statistic is outside the range defined by $\pm t$ at $\alpha = 0.01$ with df = 24. The t-statistic = t_{24}
$$= \frac{\bar{x} - \mu_0}{s/\sqrt{n}} = \frac{50-48}{5/\sqrt{25}} = 2.0.\ \pm t_{24}\ \text{at}\ \alpha = 0.01 = \pm 2.797;$$ therefore, H_0 cannot be rejected.

16. **A**   The chi-square test is used to test hypotheses concerning a single population variance. Since this is a one-tailed test, the decision rule is to reject H_0 if $\chi^2 >$ the critical chi-square value at $\alpha = 0.05$ with df = 24.

$$\chi^2_{n-1} = \frac{(n-1)s^2}{\sigma_0^2} = \frac{(24)(25)}{24} = 25.0.$$ The right-tail critical chi-square value is 36.415.

Since $\chi^2 = 25 \leq 36.415$, H_0 cannot be rejected.

17. **B**   A one-tailed t-test is appropriate. The decision rule is to reject H_0 if the computed t-statistic > t-critical at $\alpha = 0.05$ with df = 24. The computed value of the t-statistic $= \frac{\bar{x} - \mu_0}{s/\sqrt{n}} = \frac{50-48}{5/\sqrt{25}} = 2.0$, and t-critical $= t_{24} = 1.711$. Since $t > t$-critical, H_0 should be rejected.

18. **A**   The F-test is appropriate to the equality of population variances. The decision rule is to reject H_0 if the computed test statistic, F, exceeds the critical F-value at $\alpha / 2$. For the information provided, $F = s_2^2 / s_1^2 = 36 / 25 = 1.44$. At a 0.025 level of significance with $d_1 = 24$ and $d_2 = 35$, F-critical $= 2.18$. Since $F < F$-critical $(1.44 < 2.18)$, we fail to reject the null hypothesis.

 Professor's Note: Many F-tables do not contain numerator df of 35. If the tables do not contain the exact df you need, interpolate the critical value based on the closest available df values.

19. **A**   The power of a test is $1 - P(\text{Type II error}) = 1 - 0.15 = 0.85$.

20. **C**   There is no consistent relationship between the mean and standard deviation of the chi-square distribution or F-distribution.

21. **B**   The F-test is the appropriate test.

22. **C**   A test of $\sigma^2 = \sigma_0^2$ is a χ^2 test.

23. **A**   Since the observations are likely dependent (both related to market returns), a paired comparisons (mean differences) test is appropriate and is based on a t-statistic.

24. **C**   When the variances are assumed to be unequal, we just calculate the denominator (standard error) differently and use both sample variances to calculate the t-statistic.

25. **C**   A Type I error is rejecting the null hypothesis when it's true. The probability of rejecting a false null is $[1 - \text{Prob Type II}] = [1 - 0.60] = 40\%$, which is called the power of the test. A and B are not necessarily true, since the null may be false and the probability of rejection unknown.

ANSWERS – CHALLENGE PROBLEMS

1. A. The null hypothesis is typically the one the researcher wants to disprove. In this case, that would be that the mean risk-adjusted return on the cover stocks is less than or equal to the mean risk-adjusted return on the control stocks. The alternative is that the mean risk-adjusted returns on the cover stocks is greater than the mean risk-adjusted return on the control stocks. Rejecting the null will offer statistical support for the proposition the researcher wants to "prove" (the alternative).

    B. This would be a one-tailed test since the alternative is "greater than."

    C. The steps in a hypothesis test are as follows:
    - State the hypothesis.
    - Select the appropriate test statistic.
    - Decide on the appropriate level of significance.
    - Determine the decision rule.
    - Collect the data.
    - Calculate the sample statistics.
    - Make a decision based on the decision rule for the test.
    - Make decisions or inferences based on the results.

2. A. Since these two returns likely exhibit significant correlation and are, therefore, not independent, a paired comparisons test is appropriate. Differences between the returns on the two indices each week will be used. The standard deviation of the differences is used to construct a t-test of the hypothesis that the mean weekly difference is significantly different from (not equal to) zero. Reject if the t-statistic is greater/less than the positive/negative critical value.

    B. This is a test of a difference in means and is a t-test. The test statistic is the difference in means over a standard deviation calculated from the pooled variances of the two samples. Reject if the t-statistic is greater/less than the positive/negative critical value. When the variances are assumed to be equal for a difference in means test, we can use the variance of the pooled samples, and the degrees of freedom are simply $n_1 + n_2 - 2$ (total number of observations in both samples minus two).

    C. The test statistic is the ratio of the larger sample variance to the smaller sample variance. This statistic follows an F-distribution with $n_1 - 1$ and $n_2 - 1$ degrees of freedom. Reject equality if the test statistic exceeds the upper critical value.

    D. The test of whether the population variance is equal to a particular value is done with a test statistic with $(n - 1)$ times the sample variance in the numerator and the

    hypothesized variance (0.00165 here) in the denominator $\dfrac{(n-1)s^2}{s_0^2}$.

    The test statistic follows a Chi-square distribution. Reject the null of a population variance equal to 0.00165 if the test statistic is greater than the upper critical value or less than the lower critical value. The degrees of freedom are simply $n - 1$.

TECHNICAL ANALYSIS

EXAM FOCUS

This topic review introduces the "story" that underlies technical analysis, and you should understand how this differs from fundamental analysis. You should learn what the technical indicator names mean and how they are used, but don't worry about being able to calculate them. The LOS for this topic ask you to "explain" and "describe." You are responsible for knowing about the assumptions and tools of technical analysis and understanding how technical analysts reach their conclusions. You are not required to believe technical analysis can create positive risk-adjusted returns on average over time.

LOS 12.a: Explain the principles of technical analysis, its applications, and its underlying assumptions.

CFA® Program Curriculum, Volume 1, page 602

Technical analysis is the study of collective market sentiment, as expressed in buying and selling of assets. It is based on the idea that prices are determined by the interaction of supply and demand. The market price equates supply and demand at any instant. Only participants who actually trade affect prices, and better-informed participants tend to trade in greater volume. Thus, price and volume reflect the collective behavior of buyers and sellers.

A key assumption of technical analysis is that market prices reflect both rational and irrational investor behavior. This assumption implies that the *efficient markets hypothesis* does not hold. (The efficient markets hypothesis is described in the Study Session on securities markets.) Technical analysts believe investor behavior is reflected in trends and patterns that tend to repeat and can be identified and used for forecasting prices.

Technical analysis can be contrasted with fundamental analysis, which attempts to determine the intrinsic value of an asset. While fundamental analysis of a firm uses the company's financial statements and other information to analyze its financial position and determine its value, technical analysis uses only the firm's share price and trading volume data to project a target price. Technical analysis is not concerned with identifying buyers' and sellers' reasons for trading, but only with the trades that have occurred.

An advantage of only using actual price and volume data is that they are observable. Much of the data used in fundamental analysis is subject to assumptions or restatements, and might not be available at all for assets such as currencies or commodities. (This does not, however, imply that technical analysis itself is objective; both kinds of analysis require subjective judgment.) Another advantage of technical analysis is that it can be applied to the prices of assets that do not produce future cash flows (dividends or interest), such as commodities. Technical analysis can also be useful when financial statement fraud occurs. Price and volume may reflect the true value of the company even before the fraud is widely known and before the financial statements are restated.

The usefulness of technical analysis is limited in markets where price and volume data might not truly reflect supply and demand. This may be the case in illiquid markets and in markets that are subject to outside manipulation (for example, currency market intervention by central banks). For stocks of bankrupt companies, short covering can create positive technical patterns even when it is known that the stock price will go to zero.

LOS 12.b: Describe the construction of and interpret different types of technical analysis charts.

CFA® Program Curriculum, Volume 1, page 606

Technical analysts primarily use charts of price and volume to analyze asset prices and overall market movement. Most of these charts have time on the horizontal axis. The time interval chosen (monthly, weekly, daily, or intraday periods) reflects the trading horizon of interest to the analyst. A technical analyst will typically start by observing longer-term trends on monthly and weekly charts, then look at recent activity on daily or intraday charts. If prices have changed exponentially (e.g., a stock index over several decades), an analyst may choose to draw charts on a logarithmic scale instead of the usual linear scale.

Line charts are the simplest technical analysis charts. They show closing prices for each period as a continuous line (see Figure 1).

Figure 1: Line Chart

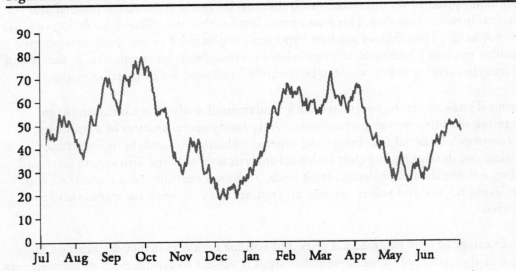

Bar charts add the high and low prices for each trading period and often include the opening price as well. Each period is displayed as a vertical line, with the closing price indicated as a point or dash on the right side of the line. If the chart includes opening prices, these are shown on the left side of each vertical line.

Candlestick charts use the same data as bar charts but display a box bounded by the opening and closing prices. The box is clear if the closing price is higher than the opening price, or filled if the close is lower than the opening price. Candlestick charts can make patterns easier to recognize (see Figure 2).

Figure 2: Bar and Candlestick Charts

Point and figure charts are helpful in identifying changes in the direction of price movements. These are drawn on graph paper, with price on the vertical axis. The price increment chosen is the "box size" for the chart. Unlike other technical charts, the horizontal axis does not represent discrete units of time. Instead, it represents the number of changes in direction. To determine when a change of direction has occurred, the analyst must choose a "reversal size" for the chart. A typical reversal size is three times the box size.

Starting from the opening price, the analyst will fill in a box in the first column if the closing price has changed by at least the box size. An X indicates an increase of one box size and an O indicates a decrease. If the price changes by more than one box size, the analyst will fill in multiple Xs or Os. If the price continues in the same direction in the next periods, the analyst will continue filling in the same column. When the price changes in the opposite direction by at least the reversal size, the analyst will begin the next column (see panel b of Figure 3).

Figure 3: Charts of Price Data

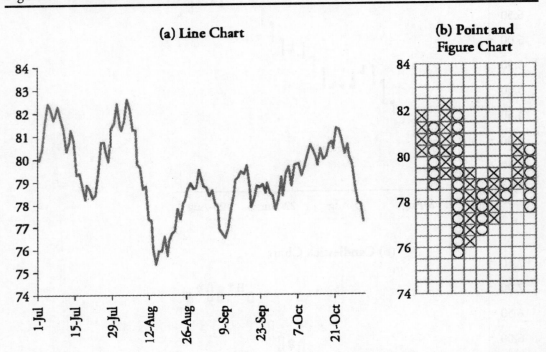

Technical analysts are concerned with volume as well as price. **Volume charts** are usually displayed below price charts with each period's volume shown as a vertical line (see Figure 4).

Figure 4: Volume Chart

To perform **relative strength analysis**, an analyst calculates the ratios of an asset's closing prices to benchmark values, such as a stock index or comparable asset, and draws a line chart of the ratios. An increasing trend indicates that the asset is outperforming the benchmark (positive relative strength) and a decrease shows that the asset is underperforming the benchmark (negative relative strength).

LOS 12.c: Explain the uses of trend, support, resistance lines, and change in polarity.

CFA® Program Curriculum, Volume 1, page 615

The most basic concept in technical analysis is the **trend** in prices. A market is said to be in an **uptrend** if prices are consistently reaching higher highs and retracing to higher lows. An uptrend means demand is increasing relative supply.

A market is in a **downtrend** if prices are consistently declining to lower lows and retracing to lower highs. A downtrend suggests supply (i.e., selling pressure) is increasing relative to demand.

Drawing a **trendline** on a chart can help to identify whether a trend is continuing or reversing. In an uptrend, a trendline connects the increasing lows in price. In a downtrend, the trendline connects the decreasing highs in price. When the price crosses the trendline by what the analyst considers a significant amount, a **breakout** from a downtrend or a **breakdown** from an uptrend is said to occur. Either a breakout or a breakdown may signal the end of the previous trend.

Breakouts and breakdowns are important because the trendline is thought to represent a level of support or resistance. At a **support** level, buying is expected to emerge that prevents further price decreases. At a **resistance** level, selling is expected to emerge that prevents further price increases. In addition to trendlines, support and resistance levels frequently appear at psychologically important prices such as round-number prices or historical highs and lows.

An important principle in technical analysis is the **change in polarity**. This refers to a belief that breached resistance levels become support levels and that breached support levels become resistance levels. In Figure 5, the area of 55 is viewed as as resistance level until the price breaks above that level, then 55 becomes a support level as prices decline from their new highs.

Figure 5: Change in Polarity

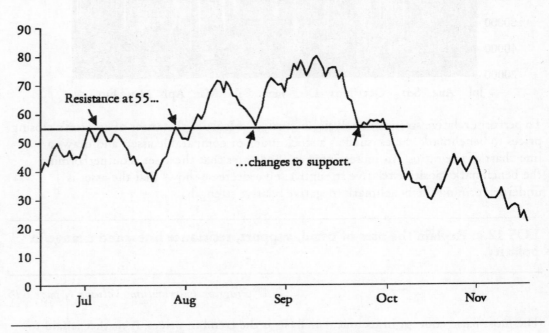

LOS 12.d: Identify and interpret common chart patterns.

CFA® Program Curriculum, Volume 1, page 618

Technical analysts look for recurring patterns in charts that suggest the future course of prices. Some patterns tend to appear at the end of trends, while other patterns indicate that a trend is likely to continue.

Reversal patterns occur when a trend approaches a range of prices but fails to continue beyond that range. A well-known example is the **head-and-shoulders** pattern, as shown in Figure 6. This pattern suggests the demand that has been driving the uptrend is fading, especially if each of the highs in the pattern occurs on declining volume.

Technical analysts commonly use the size of a head-and-shoulders pattern to project a price target for the ensuing downtrend. The size is the difference in price between the "head," the highest price reached, and the "neckline," the support level to which the price retraced after the left "shoulder" and the head have formed. If the price declines beyond the neckline after the right shoulder forms, the downtrend is projected to continue from that breakdown price by about the size of the head-and-shoulders pattern.

In Figure 6, the top of the head is at 80 and the neckline is at 55, so the size of the pattern is 80 – 55 = 25. The price target for the ensuing downtrend is 55 – 25 = 30.

Figure 6: Reversal Patterns

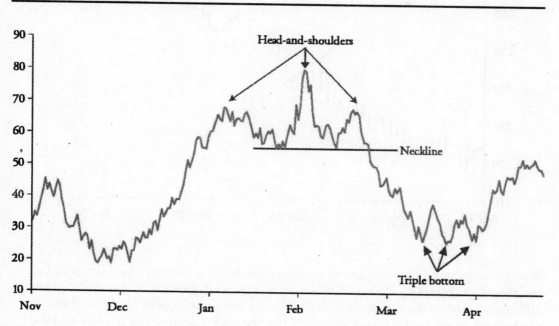

Double top and **triple top** patterns are similar to the head-and-shoulders pattern in that they indicate weakening in the buying pressure that has been driving an uptrend. In both cases, the price reaches a resistance level at which selling pressure appears repeatedly, preventing any further increase in the price. As with the head-and-shoulders, the size of a double or triple top pattern can be used to project a price target for the next downtrend.

Reversal patterns for downtrends are called **inverse head-and-shoulders, double bottom,** and **triple bottom** patterns and can be analyzed in the same way as the reversal patterns for uptrends.

Continuation patterns suggest a pause in a trend rather than a reversal. **Triangles** form when prices reach lower highs and higher lows over a period of time (see Figure 7). Trendlines on the highs and on the lows thus converge when they are projected forward. Triangles can be symmetrical (higher lows and lower highs), ascending (higher lows and a resistance level), or descending (lower highs and a support level).

Figure 7: Triangle Continuation Pattern

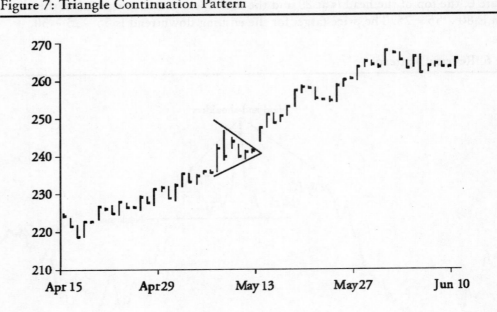

Triangles suggest buying and selling pressure have become roughly equal temporarily, but they do not imply a change in direction of the trend. The size of a triangle, or the difference between the two trendlines at the time when the pattern begins to form, can be used to set a price target, assuming the price breaks out of the triangle and the previous trend continues.

Rectangles form when trading temporarily forms a range between a support level and a resistance level. As with a triangle, a rectangle suggests the prevailing trend will resume and can be used to set a price target. Flags and pennants refer to rectangles and triangles that appear on short-term price charts.

LOS 12.e: Describe common technical analysis indicators: price-based, momentum oscillators, sentiment, and flow of funds.

CFA® Program Curriculum, Volume 1, page 629

Price-Based Indicators

Moving average lines are a frequently used to smooth the fluctuations in a price chart (or a chart of any time series). A moving average is simply the mean of the last *n* closing prices. The larger the chosen value of *n*, the smoother the moving average line. Analysts often use moving average periods that make intuitive sense, such as 20 days to represent the number of trading days in a month. In an uptrend, the price is higher than the moving average, and in a downtrend, the price is lower than the moving average. Moving average lines are often viewed as support or resistance levels.

Analysts use moving average lines to make changes in the trend easier to see. The longer the period used to calculate the moving average, the more short-term fluctuations are removed from the line. Overly long periods may, in fact, obscure changes in a price trend.

Moving averages for different periods can be used together, such as 20-day and 250-day averages. Points where the short-term average (more volatile) crosses the long-term average (smoother) can indicate changes in the price trend. When the short-term average crosses above long-term average (a "golden cross"), this is often viewed as an indicator of an emerging uptrend or a "buy" signal by technical analysts. The short-term average crossing below the long-term average (a "dead cross") is often viewed as an indicator of an emerging downtrend or a "sell" signal.

Bollinger bands are constructed based on the standard deviation of closing prices over the last n periods. An analyst can draw high and low bands a chosen number of standard deviations (typically two) above and below the n-period moving average. The bands move away from one another when price volatility increases and move closer together when prices are less volatile (see Figure 8).

Bollinger bands are viewed as useful for indicating when prices are extreme by recent standards on either the high or low side. Prices at or above the upper Bollinger band may be viewed as indicating an **overbought** market, one that is "too high" and likely to decrease in the near term. Likewise, prices at or below the lower Bollinger band may be viewed as indicating an **oversold** market, one that is "too low" and likely to increase in the near term. A possible trading strategy using Bollinger bands is to buy when the price is at the lower band or sell when the price is at the upper band. This is an example of a **contrarian strategy**—one that buys when most traders are selling and sells when most traders are buying. Contrarians believe markets get overbought or oversold because most investors tend to buy and sell at the wrong times, and thus it can be profitable to trade in the opposite direction.

Figure 8: Moving Average and Bollinger Bands

Oscillators

Oscillators are another group of tools technical analysts use to identify overbought or oversold markets. These indicators are based on market prices but scaled so that they "oscillate" around a given value, such as zero, or between two values such as zero and 100. Extreme high values of an oscillator are viewed as indicating that a market is overbought, while extreme low values are viewed as indicating an oversold market. Technical analysts use charts of oscillators over time to highlight periods when they are near their **high** or low extremes.

Oscillator charts can also be used to identify **convergence** or **divergence** of the oscillator and market prices. Convergence occurs when the oscillator shows the same pattern as prices (e.g., both reaching higher highs), and divergence occurs when the oscillator shows a different pattern than prices (e.g., failing to reach a higher high when the price does). Convergence suggests the price trend is likely to continue, while divergence may indicate a potential change in the price trend.

Examples of oscillators include the rate of change (ROC) oscillator, Relative Strength Index (RSI), moving average convergence/divergence (MACD) lines, and the stochastic oscillator.

- **Rate of change oscillator.** An ROC or *momentum oscillator* is calculated as 100 times the difference between the latest closing price and the closing price n periods earlier. Thus, it oscillates around zero. One way technical analysts use the ROC is to buy when the oscillator changes from negative to positive during an uptrend in prices, and sell when the ROC changes from positive to negative during a downtrend. Some analysts prefer to use the ratio of the current price to the past price in place of the difference. Calculated this way, the ROC oscillates around 100.
- **Relative Strength Index.** An RSI is based on the ratio of total price increases to total price decreases over a selected number of periods. This ratio is then scaled to oscillate between 0 and 100, with high values (typically those greater than 70) indicating an overbought market and low values (typically those less than 30) indicating an oversold market.
- **Moving average convergence/divergence.** MACD oscillators are drawn using exponentially smoothed moving averages, which place greater weight on more recent observations. The "MACD line" is the difference between two exponentially smoothed moving averages of the price, and the "signal line" is an exponentially smoothed moving average of the MACD line. The lines oscillate around zero but are not bounded. The MACD oscillator can be used to indicate overbought or oversold conditions or to identify convergence or divergence with the price trend. Points where the two lines cross can be used as trading signals, much like the use of two different moving averages discussed previously. The MACD line crossing above the smoother signal line is viewed as a buy signal and the MACD line crossing below the signal line is viewed as a sell signal.

- **Stochastic oscillator.** A stochastic oscillator is calculated from the latest closing price and highest and lowest prices reached in a recent period, such as 14 days. In a sustainable uptrend, prices tend to close nearer to the recent high, and in a sustainable downtrend, prices tend to close nearer to the recent low. Stochastic oscillators use two lines that are bounded by 0 and 100. The "%K" line is the difference between the latest price and the recent low as a percentage of the difference between the recent high and low. The "%D" line is a 3-period average of the %K line. Technical analysts typically use stochastic oscillators to identify overbought and oversold markets. Points where the %K line crosses the %D line can also be used as trading signals in the same way as the MACD lines.

 Professor's Note: Is this fun or what? Remember, no calculations are required. Just know the terms as best you can.

Non-Price-Based Indicators

While the technical indicators mentioned so far assume investor sentiment is reflected in price and volume data, technical analysts can also look at indicators of investor sentiment and capital flows to gain insight into potential emerging trends. **Sentiment indicators** can be used to discern the views of potential buyers and sellers. Market sentiment is said to be "bullish" when investors expect increasing prices and "bearish" when they expect decreasing prices.

Indicators can include **opinion polls** that try to measure investor sentiment directly, as well as several measures that are based on market data:

- **Put/call ratio.** Put options increase in value when the price of an underlying asset decreases, while call options increase in value if the price of the underlying asset increases. For financial assets that have actively traded options, the volume of put and call options reflects activity by investors with negative and positive outlooks, respectively, about the asset. The put/call ratio is put volume divided by call volume. Increases in the put/call ratio indicate a more negative outlook for the price of the asset. This ratio is generally viewed as a contrarian indicator. Extremely high ratios indicate strongly bearish investor sentiment and possibly an oversold market, while extremely low ratios indicate strongly bullish sentiment and perhaps an overbought market.
- **Volatility Index (VIX).** The Chicago Board Options Exchange calculates the VIX, which measures the volatility of options on the S&P 500 stock index. High levels of the VIX suggest investors fear declines in the stock market. Technical analysts most often interpret the VIX in a contrarian way, viewing a predominantly bearish investor outlook as a bullish sign.

- **Margin debt.** The amount of margin debt is a readily available indicator because brokers are required to report this data. Increases in total margin debt outstanding suggest aggressive buying by bullish margin investors. As margin investors reach their limits of margin credit, their ability to continue buying decreases, which can cause prices to begin declining. As prices decrease, investors may need to sell securities to meet margin calls, and these sales drive prices lower still. Increasing margin debt tends to coincide with increasing market prices and decreasing margin debt tends to coincide with decreasing prices.

- **Short interest ratio.** Just as an increase in margin debt suggests aggressive buying and strong positive sentiment, increases in shares sold short indicate strong negative sentiment. **Short interest** is the number of shares investors have borrowed and sold short. As with margin debt, short interest must be reported by brokerage firms. The short interest ratio is short interest divided by average daily trading volume. While a high short interest ratio means investors expect the stock price to decrease, it also implies future buying demand when short sellers must return their borrowed shares. Thus, technical analysts' opinions are divided as to how the short interest ratio should be interpreted.

Since technical analysis is based on changes in supply and demand conditions, indicators of the **flow of funds** in the financial markets can be useful for observing changes in the supply of securities and the demand for them.

- The **Arms index or short-term trading index (TRIN)** is a measure of funds flowing into advancing and declining stocks. The index is calculated as:

$$\text{TRIN} = \frac{\text{Number of advancing issues} \Big/ \text{Number of declining issues}}{\text{Volume of advancing issues} \Big/ \text{Volume of declining issues}}$$

An index value close to one suggests funds are flowing about evenly to advancing and declining stocks. Index values greater than one mean the majority of volume is in declining stocks, while an index less than one means more of the volume is in advancing stocks. On charts of the TRIN for U.S. stocks, spikes upward have coincided with large daily losses in the stock market, while spikes downward have coincided with large daily gains in the stock market.

- *Margin debt*, besides indicating investor sentiment as described above, is also a useful flow of funds indicator. Increasing margin debt may indicate that investors want to buy more stocks. Decreasing margin debt indicates increased selling.

- The **mutual fund cash position** is the ratio of mutual funds' cash to total assets. During uptrends, fund managers want to invest cash quickly because cash earns only the risk-free rate of return and thus decreases fund returns. During downtrends, fund cash balances increase overall fund returns. As a result, mutual fund cash positions tend to increase when the market is falling and decrease when the market is rising. Technical analysts typically view mutual fund cash as a contrarian indicator. When mutual funds accumulate cash, this represents future buying power in the market. A high mutual fund cash ratio therefore suggests market prices are likely to increase. On the other hand, when mutual funds' cash is low, they are already invested and market prices reflect their purchases.

- New equity issuance (i.e., initial public offerings) and secondary offerings (sales of additional shares by the issuer) add to the supply of stocks. Because issuers tend to sell new shares when stock prices are thought to be high, increases in issuance of new shares may often coincide with market peaks.

LOS 12.f: Explain the use of cycles by technical analysts.

LOS 12.g: Describe the key tenets of Elliott Wave Theory and the importance of Fibonacci numbers.

CFA® Program Curriculum, Volume 1, page 646

Cycle theory is the study of processes that occur in cycles, as many natural phenomena tend to do. Some technical analysts apply cycle theory to financial markets in an attempt to identify cycles in prices.

Some of the cycle periods favored by technical analysts are 4-year presidential cycles related to election years in the United States; decennial patterns or 10-year cycles; 18-year cycles; and 54-year cycles called the **Kondratieff** wave.

One of the more developed cycle theories is **Elliott wave theory.** Elliott wave theory is based on a belief that financial market prices can be described by an interconnected set of cycles. The cycle periods range from a few minutes (a "subminuette" cycle) to centuries (a "Grand Supercycle").

"Waves" refer to chart patterns associated with Elliott wave theory. In a prevailing uptrend, upward moves in prices consist of five waves and downward moves occur in three waves (see Figure 9). If the prevailing trend is down, downward moves have five waves and upward moves have three waves. Each of these waves, in turn, is composed of smaller waves of the same general form.

Figure 9: Elliott Wave Patterns

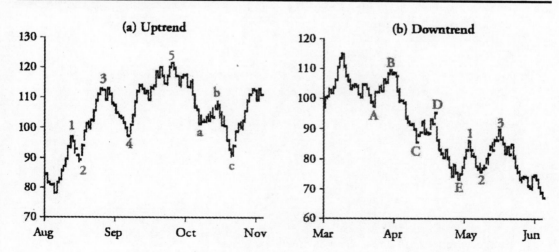

The sizes of these waves are thought to correspond with Fibonacci **ratios**. Fibonacci numbers are found by starting with 0 and 1, then adding each of the previous two numbers to produce the next (0, 1, 1, 2, 3, 5, 8, 13, 21, and so on). Elliott wave theorists believe that the ratios of Fibonacci numbers are useful for estimating price targets. For example, a down leg can be 1/2 or 2/3 the size of an up leg, or a price target can be 13/8 of the previous high. Ratios of consecutive Fibonacci numbers converge to 0.618 and 1.618 as the numbers in the sequence get larger. These two values are commonly used to project price targets.

LOS 12.h: Describe intermarket analysis as it relates to technical analysis and asset allocation.

CFA® Program Curriculum, Volume 1, page 649

Intermarket analysis refers to analysis of the interrelationships among the market values of major asset classes, such as stocks, bonds, commodities, and currencies. Relative strength ratios (described earlier in this topic review) are a useful tool for determining which asset classes are outperforming others. After identifying attractive asset classes, an analyst can apply relative strength analysis to identify which assets within these classes are outperforming others. This approach is also useful for comparing the relative performance of equity market sectors or industries, and of various international markets.

KEY CONCEPTS

LOS 12.a

Underlying all of technical analysis are the following assumptions:
- Prices are determined by investor supply and demand for assets.
- Supply and demand are driven by both rational and irrational behavior.
- While the causes of changes in supply and demand are difficult to determine, the actual shifts in supply and demand can be observed in market prices.
- Prices move in trends and exhibit patterns that can be identified and tend to repeat themselves over time.

LOS 12.b

Technical analysts use charts to identify trends and patterns in prices over time. A line chart is a continuous line that connects closing prices for each period. Bar charts and candlestick charts show the open, high, low, and close for each period. Volume charts often accompany price charts. Point-and-figure charts indicate significant changes in the direction of price trends.

LOS 12.c

In an uptrend, prices are reaching higher highs and higher lows. An uptrend line is drawn below the prices on a chart by connecting the increasing lows with a straight line.

In a downtrend, prices are reaching lower lows and lower highs. A downtrend line is drawn above the prices on a chart by connecting the decreasing highs with a straight line.

Support and resistance are price levels or ranges at which buying or selling pressure is expected to limit price movement. Commonly identified support and resistance levels include trendlines and previous high and low prices.

The change in polarity principle is the idea that breached resistance levels become support levels and breached support levels become resistance levels.

LOS 12.d

Technical analysts look for recurring patterns in price charts. Head-and-shoulders patterns, double tops, and triple tops are thought to be reversal patterns at the ends of uptrends. Inverse head-and-shoulders patterns, double bottoms, and triple bottoms are thought to be reversal patterns at the ends of downtrends.

Triangles, rectangles, flags, and pennants are thought to be continuation patterns, which indicate that the trend in which they appear is likely to go further in the same direction.

LOS 12.e

Price-based indicators include moving averages, Bollinger bands, and momentum oscillators such as the Relative Strength Index, moving average convergence/divergence lines, rate-of-change oscillators, and stochastic oscillators. These indicators are commonly used to identify changes in price trends, as well as "overbought" markets that are likely to decrease in the near term and "oversold" markets that are likely to increase in the near term.

Sentiment indicators include opinion polls, the put/call ratio, the volatility index, margin debt, and the short interest ratio. Margin debt, the Arms index, the mutual fund cash position, new equity issuance, and secondary offerings are flow-of-funds indicators. Technical analysts often interpret these indicators from a "contrarian" perspective, becoming bearish when investor sentiment is too positive and bullish when investor sentiment is too negative.

LOS 12.f

Some technical analysts believe market prices move in cycles. Examples include the Kondratieff wave, which is a 54-year cycle, and a 4-year cycle related to U.S. presidential elections.

LOS 12.g

Elliott wave theory suggests that prices exhibit a pattern of five waves in the direction of a trend and three waves counter to the trend. Technical analysts who employ Elliott wave theory frequently use ratios of the numbers in the Fibonacci sequence to estimate price targets and identify potential support and resistance levels.

LOS 12.h

Intermarket analysis examines the relationships among various asset markets such as stocks, bonds, commodities, and currencies. In the asset allocation process, relative strength analysis can be used to identify attractive asset classes and attractive sectors within these classes.

Study Session 3

CONCEPT CHECKERS

1. An assumption of technical analysis is that market prices:
    A. exhibit identifiable trends and patterns that persist and repeat.
    B. are the only information necessary to analyze a freely trading market.
    C. reflect supply and demand conditions because actual transactions reflect rational decisions by buyers and sellers.

2. From which of the following charts can an analyst read the opening price for a trading period?
    A. Line chart.
    B. Candlestick chart.
    C. Point-and-figure chart.

3. A stock has been in a downtrend for several days. When its price decreases to near $30, many investors enter orders to buy the stock and the price increases to $31. This is *most likely* an example of a:
    A. support level.
    B. resistance level.
    C. change in polarity.

4. An analyst who uses the standard deviation of recent prices to identify overbought or oversold conditions is *most likely* to employ:
    A. Bollinger bands.
    B. a Relative Strength Index.
    C. a rate of change oscillator.

5. A momentum indicator based on the ratio of price increases to price decreases over the last 14 days is *most likely* a:
    A. stochastic oscillator.
    B. Relative Strength Index.
    C. moving average convergence/divergence oscillator.

6. An increase in which of the following is *most likely* when stock market sentiment is becoming more bullish?
    A. Short interest ratio.
    B. Margin debt outstanding.
    C. Put/call ratio for a stock index.

7. The Kondratieff wave is a cycle of:
    A. 18 years.
    B. 36 years.
    C. 54 years.

8. For an asset with a current price of 100, which of the following price targets is *most likely* based on a Fibonacci ratio?
    A. 129.40.
    B. 145.60.
    C. 161.80.

9.   If a stock's relative strength ratio increases, the stock is:
A. increasing in price.
B. outperforming its benchmark.
C. increasing on high volume or decreasing on low volume.

Study Session 3

ANSWERS – CONCEPT CHECKERS

1. **A**   Technical analysis assumes persistent trends and repeating patterns in market prices can be used to forecast price behavior. Technical analysts believe prices reflect supply and demand, but that buying and selling can be motivated by both rational and irrational causes. Volume, along with price, is important information to a technical analyst.

2. **B**   Candlestick charts show the open, high, low, and close for each trading period. Line charts use only the closing price. Point-and-figure charts do not necessarily show distinct trading periods.

3. **A**   The downtrend reached a support level where buying demand sustained the price. A resistance level is a price at which selling pressure emerges that stops an uptrend. The change in polarity principle holds that breached support levels become resistance and breached resistance levels become support. With no information given on the stock's history, we cannot determine whether $30 had once been a resistance level.

4. **A**   Bollinger bands are based on the standard deviation of prices over some number of the most recent periods. An RSI is based on the sums of positive and negative price changes during a period. An ROC oscillator is based on the difference between the most recent closing price and the closing price a given number of periods earlier.

5. **B**   The RSI is calculated from the ratio of total price increases to total price decreases over a chosen number of days, then scaled to fluctuate between 0 and 100 using the formula RSI = 100 – [100 / (1 + ratio of increases to decreases)]. Stochastic oscillators are based on the highest and lowest prices over a chosen number of days. MACD oscillators are calculated based on exponentially smoothed moving averages.

6. **B**   "More bullish" means investors expect prices to increase in the near term. Increasing margin debt suggests investors are bullish and buying aggressively. Increases in put volume relative to call volume, or in the number of shares sold short, indicate bearish investor sentiment.

7. **C**   The Kondratieff wave is a 54-year cycle.

8. **C**   The value 1.618 is the ratio of large consecutive Fibonacci numbers. Technical analysts who employ Elliott wave theory frequently use Fibonacci ratios to set price targets.

9. **B**   If the relative strength ratio (stock price / benchmark value) increases, the stock is outperforming the benchmark stock or index against which it is being measured. This does not imply that the stock is increasing in price; if the stock price decreases but the benchmark decreases by a larger percentage, the ratio will increase. Volume is not an input into a relative strength ratio.

15 Questions: 22.5 Minutes

1. Allan Jabber invested $400 at the beginning of each of the last 12 months in the shares of a mutual fund that paid no dividends. Which method will he correctly choose in order to calculate his average price per share from the monthly share prices?
   A. Arithmetic mean.
   B. Harmonic mean.
   C. Geometric mean.

2. The central limit theorem and Chebyshev's inequality apply to which distributions?

	Central limit theorem	Chebyshev's inequality
A.	Normal only	Normal only
B.	Normal only	Any distribution
C.	Any distribution	Any distribution

3. Colonia has only two political parties, the Wigs and the Wags. If the Wags are elected, there is a 32% probability of a tax increase over the next four years. If the Wigs are elected, there is a 60% probability of a tax increase. Based on the current polls, there is a 20% probability that the Wags will be elected. The sum of the (unconditional) probability of a tax increase and the joint probability that the Wigs will be elected and there will be no tax increase are *closest* to:
   A. 55%.
   B. 70%.
   C. 85%.

4. Analysts at Wellborn Advisors are considering two well-diversified portfolios based on firm forecasts of their expected returns and variance of returns. James argues that Portfolio 1 will be preferred by the client because it has a lower coefficient of variation. Samantha argues that Portfolio 2 would be preferred by the client because it has a higher Sharpe ratio. The client states that he wishes to minimize the probability that his portfolio will produce returns less than the risk-free rate. Based on this information, the client would *most likely* prefer:
   A. 100% in Portfolio 1.
   B. 100% in Portfolio 2.
   C. some combination of Portfolios 1 and 2.

5. Ralph will retire 15 years from today and has saved $121,000 in his investment account for retirement. He believes he will need $37,000 at the beginning of each year for 25 years of retirement, with the first withdrawal on the day he retires. Ralph assumes that his investment account will return 8%. The amount he needs to deposit at the beginning of this year and each of the following 14 years (15 deposits in all) is *closest* to:
   A. $1,350.
   B. $1,450.
   C. $1,550.

6. The current price of Bosto shares is €50. Over the coming year, there is a 40% probability that share returns will be 10%, a 40% probability that share returns will be 12.5%, and a 20% probability that share returns will be 30%. Bosto's expected return and standard deviation of returns for the coming year are *closest* to:

	Expected return	Standard deviation
A.	15.0%	7.58%
B.	17.5%	5.75%
C.	17.5%	7.58%

7. Nikki Ali and Donald Ankard borrowed $15,000 to finance their wedding and reception. The fully-amortizing loan at 11% requires equal payments at the end of each of the next seven years. The principal portion of the first payment is *closest* to:
    A. $1,500.
    B. $1,530.
    C. $1,560.

8. Which of the following statements about probability distributions is *least accurate?*
    A. Continuous uniform distributions have cumulative distribution functions that are straight lines from zero to one.
    B. The probability that a continuously distributed random variable will take on a specific value is always zero.
    C. A normally distributed random variable divided by its standard deviation will follow a standard normal probability distribution.

9. Which of the following trading strategies is *most likely* using the change in polarity principle?
    A. Smith enters an order to buy a stock if the price decreases to 25, which had been the stock's historical high before it rallied to its current price of 30.
    B. Jones buys a stock when a momentum oscillator indicates an oversold condition and sells the stock when the oscillator indicates an overbought condition.
    C. Johnson buys a stock when its 5-day moving average crosses above its 20-day moving average and sells the stock when the 5-day average crosses below the 20-day average.

10. Given the following data:
    *   There is a 40% probability that the economy will be good next year and a 60% probability that it will be bad.
    *   If the economy is good, there is a 50% probability of a bull market, a 30% probability of an average market, and a 20% probability of a bear market.
    *   If the economy is bad, there is a 20% probability of a bull market, a 30% probability of an average market, and a 50% probability of a bear market.

    The unconditional probability of a bull market is *closest* to:
    A. 20%.
    B. 32%.
    C. 50%.

11. X, Y, and Z are independently distributed. The probability of X is 30%, the probability of Y is 40%, and the probability of Z is 20%. Which of the following is *closest* to the probability that either X or Y will occur?
    A. 70%.
    B. 58%.
    C. 12%.

12. Which will be *equal* for a 1-year T-bill with 360 days to maturity?
    A. Bank discount yield and money market yield.
    B. Money market yield and holding period yield.
    C. Effective annual yield and bond equivalent yield.

13. The percentage changes in annual earnings for a company are approximately normally distributed with a mean of 5% and a standard deviation of 12%. The probability that the average change in earnings over the next five years will be greater than 15.5% is *closest* to:
    A. 2.5%.
    B. 5.0%.
    C. 10.0%.

14. Which of the following is *least likely* correct concerning a random variable that is lognormally distributed?
    A. It has a symmetric distribution.
    B. The natural logarithms of the random variable are normally distributed.
    C. It is a univariate distribution.

15. A discrete random variable x can take on the values 1, 2, 3, 4, or 5. The probability function is Prob(x) = x/15, so the cumulative distribution function is $\sum_{n=1}^{x}\left(\frac{n}{15}\right)$. The cumulative probability, F(4), and P(2 < x ≤ 5) are:

	F(4)	P(2 < x ≤ 5)
A.	0.267	0.80
B.	0.267	0.93
C.	0.667	0.80

SELF-TEST ANSWERS: QUANTITATIVE METHODS

1. **B** The harmonic mean of the 12 purchase prices will be his average price paid per share.

2. **C** Both the central limit theorem and Chebyshev's inequality apply to any distribution.

3. **C** The unconditional probability of a tax increase is: $0.2(0.32) + 0.8(0.6) = 54.4\%$.

   The joint probability that the Wigs will be elected and there will be no tax increase is:

   $0.8(0.4) = 32\%$. The sum is: $54.4 + 32 = 86.4\%$.

4. **B** A portfolio that has a higher Sharpe ratio will have a lower probability of generating returns less than the risk-free rate. With a target return equal to the risk-free rate, the safety-first ratio for a portfolio is $(E[R_p] - R_f) / \sigma_p$, which is also the Sharpe ratio. Portfolio 2 will have a lower probability of returns less than the risk-free rate. Because both portfolios are well diversified and Portfolio 1 has a lower Sharpe ratio than Portfolio 2, any allocation to Portfolio 1 would decrease the overall portfolio's Sharpe and safety-first ratios, increasing the probability of returns less than the risk-free rate.

5. **B** Step 1: Calculate the amount needed at retirement at t = 15, with calculator in BGN mode.

   N = 25, FV = 0, I/Y = 8, PMT = 37,000, CPT PV = –426,564

   Step 2: Reduce this by the t = 15 value of current savings.

   $426,564 - 121,000(1.08)^{15} = 42,732$

   Step 3: Calculate the required deposits at t = 0,1,....,14 to result in a time 15 value of 42,732, with calculator still in BGN mode.

   PV = 0, N = 15, I/Y = 8, FV = 42,732, CPT PMT = –$1,457.22

   To check, in BGN mode, N = 15, I/Y = 8, PMT = 1,457.22, PV = 121,000,

   CPT FV = –426,564.39.

6. **A** $E[R] = (0.4)(10) + (0.4)(12.5) + (0.2)(30) = 15\%$

   Variance $= (0.4)(10 - 15)^2 + (0.4)(12.5 - 15)^2 + (0.2)(30 - 15)^2 = 57.5$

   Standard deviation $= \sqrt{57.5} = 7.58\%$

7. **B** The interest portion of the first payment is simply principal × interest rate = $(15,000 \times 0.11) = 1,650$.

   Using a financial calculator: PV = 15,000, FV = 0, I/Y = 11, N=7, CPT PMT= $3,183

   Principal = payment – interest = 3,183 – 1,650 = 1,533

8. **C** A standard normal probability distribution has a mean of zero, so subtracting the mean from a normal random variable before dividing by its standard deviation is necessary to produce a standard normal probability distribution.

9. **A** The change in polarity principle is the idea that a breached resistance level becomes a support level, and vice-versa. Here, Smith is projecting that the historical high of 25, having been breached, will act as a support level if the price decreases from 30.

10. **B** Using the total probability rule, the unconditional probability of a bull market is 0.50(0.40) + 0.20(0.60) = 32%.

11. **B** Probability of X or Y is P(X) + P(Y) − P(XY).

    0.3 + 0.4 − (0.3)(0.4) = 58%

12. **B** Because the money market yield is the holding period yield times #days / 360, HPY × 360 / 360 = HPY = **MMY**.

13. **A** The standard error of a 5-year average of earnings changes is $\dfrac{12\%}{\sqrt{5}}$ = 5.366%.

    15.5% is $\dfrac{15.5 - 5}{5.366}$ = 1.96 standard errors above the mean, and the probability of a

    5-year average more than 1.96 standard errors above the mean is 2.5% for a normal distribution.

14. **A** A lognormal distribution is skewed to the right (positively skewed).

15. **C** F(4) is the probability that x ≤ 4, which is (1 + 2 + 3 + 4) / 15 = 0.667, or 1 − 5 / 15 = 0.667.

    The probability that 2 < x ≤ 5, which is P(x = 3, 4, or 5), = (3 + 4 + 5) / 15 = 0.80. This is also F(5) − F(2) = (1 + 2 + 3 + 4 + 5) / 15 − (1 + 2) / 15 = 0.80.

FORMULAS

nominal risk-free rate = real risk-free rate + expected inflation rate

required interest rate on a security = nominal risk-free rate
+ default risk premium
+ liquidity premium
+ maturity risk premium

effective annual rate = $(1 + \text{periodic rate})^m - 1$

continuous compounding: $e^r - 1 = \text{EAR}$

$$PV_{perpetuity} = \frac{PMT}{I/Y}$$

$$FV = PV(1 + I/Y)^N$$

$$NPV = \sum_{t=0}^{N} \frac{CF_t}{(1+r)^t}$$

general formula for the IRR: $0 = CF_0 + \dfrac{CF_1}{1+IRR} + \dfrac{CF_2}{(1+IRR)^2} + \cdots + \dfrac{CF_N}{(1+IRR)^N}$

bank discount yield $= \dfrac{D}{F} \times \dfrac{360}{t}$

holding period yield $= \dfrac{P_1 - P_0 + D_1}{P_0} = \dfrac{P_1 + D_1}{P_0} - 1$

effective annual yield $= (1 + HPY)^{365/t} - 1$

money market yield $= HPY\left(\dfrac{360}{t}\right)$

population mean: $\mu = \dfrac{\displaystyle\sum_{i=1}^{N} X_i}{N}$

sample mean: $\overline{X} = \dfrac{\displaystyle\sum_{i=1}^{n} X_i}{n}$

geometric mean return (R_G): $1 + R_G = \sqrt[n]{(1+R_1) \times (1+R_2) \times \ldots \times (1+R_n)}$

harmonic mean: $\overline{X}_H = \dfrac{N}{\displaystyle\sum_{i=1}^{N} \dfrac{1}{x_i}}$

weighted mean: $\overline{X}_W = \sum_{i=1}^{n} w_i X_i$

position of the observation at a given percentile, y: $L_y = (n+1)\dfrac{y}{100}$

range = maximum value − minimum value

excess kurtosis = sample kurtosis − 3

$$MAD = \dfrac{\sum_{i=1}^{n} |X_i - \overline{X}|}{n}$$

population variance $= \sigma^2 = \dfrac{\sum_{i=1}^{N}(X_i - \mu)^2}{N}$,

where μ = population mean and N = number of possible outcomes

sample variance $= s^2 = \dfrac{\sum_{i=1}^{n}(X_i - \overline{X})^2}{n-1}$, where $\overline{X}$ = sample mean and n = sample size

coefficient of variation: $CV = \dfrac{s_x}{\overline{X}} = \dfrac{\text{standard deviation of } x}{\text{average value of } x}$

Sharpe ratio $= \dfrac{\overline{r}_p - r_f}{\sigma_p}$

joint probability: $P(AB) = P(A \mid B) \times P(B)$

addition rule: $P(A \text{ or } B) = P(A) + P(B) - P(AB)$

multiplication rule: $P(A \text{ and } B) = P(A) \times P(B)$

total probability rule:
$P(R) = P(R \mid S_1) \times P(S_1) + P(R \mid S_2) \times P(S_2) + \ldots + P(R \mid S_N) \times P(S_N)$

expected value: $E(X) = \Sigma P(x_i)x_i = P(x_1)x_1 + P(x_2)x_2 + \ldots + P(x_n)x_n$

$Cov(R_i, R_j) = E\{[R_i - E(R_i)][R_j - E(R_j)]\}$

$Corr(R_i, R_j) = \dfrac{Cov(R_i, R_j)}{\sigma(R_i)\sigma(R_j)}$

portfolio expected return: $E\left(R_p\right) = \sum_{i=1}^{N} w_i E(R_i) = w_1 E(R_1) + w_2 E(R_2) + \ldots + w_n E(R_n)$

portfolio variance: $Var\left(R_p\right) = \sum_{i=1}^{N}\sum_{j=1}^{N} w_i w_j Cov\left(R_i, R_j\right)$

where $w_i = \dfrac{\text{market value of investment in asset i}}{\text{market value of the portfolio}}$

Bayes' formula:

updated probability $= \dfrac{\text{probability of new information for a given event}}{\text{unconditional probability of new information}} \times \text{prior probability of event}$

combination (binomial) formula: $_nC_r = \dfrac{n!}{(n-r)!\,r!}$

permutation formula: $_nP_r = \dfrac{n!}{(n-r)!}$

binomial probability: $p(x) = \dfrac{n!}{(n-x)!\,x!} p^x \left(1-p\right)^{n-x}$

for a binomial random variable: $E(X) = np$; variance $= np(1-p)$

for a normal variable:

90% confidence interval for X is $\overline{X} - 1.65s$ to $\overline{X} + 1.65s$

95% confidence interval for X is $\overline{X} - 1.96s$ to $\overline{X} + 1.96s$

99% confidence interval for X is $\overline{X} - 2.58s$ to $\overline{X} + 2.58s$

$z = \dfrac{\text{observation} - \text{population mean}}{\text{standard deviation}} = \dfrac{x - \mu}{\sigma}$

$\text{SFRatio} = \dfrac{\left[E\left(R_p\right) - R_L\right]}{\sigma_p}$

continuously compounded rate of return: $r_{cc} = \ln\left(\dfrac{S_1}{S_0}\right) = \ln\left(1 + HPR\right)$

for a uniform distribution: $P\left(x_1 \le X \le x_2\right) = \dfrac{(x_2 - x_1)}{(b-a)}$

sampling error of the mean = sample mean − population mean = $\overline{x} - \mu$

standard error of the sample mean, known population variance: $\sigma_{\overline{x}} = \dfrac{\sigma}{\sqrt{n}}$

standard error of the sample mean, unknown population variance: $s_{\overline{x}} = \dfrac{s}{\sqrt{n}}$

confidence interval: point estimate ± (reliability **factor × standard error**)

confidence interval for the population mean: $\overline{x} \pm z_{\alpha/2} \dfrac{\sigma}{\sqrt{n}}$

tests for population mean = μ_0: z-statistic $= \dfrac{\overline{x} - \mu_0}{\sigma / \sqrt{n}}$, t-statistic $= \dfrac{\overline{x} - \mu_0}{s / \sqrt{n}}$

test for equality of variances: $F = \dfrac{s_1^2}{s_2^2}$, where $s_1^2 > s_2^2$

test of mean differences = 0: t-statistic $= \dfrac{\overline{d}}{s_d}$

test for equality of means:

t-statistic $= \dfrac{(\overline{x}_1 - \overline{x}_2)}{\left(\dfrac{s_1^2}{n_1} + \dfrac{s_2^2}{n_2}\right)^{1/2}}$ (sample variances assumed unequal)

t-statistic $= \dfrac{(\overline{x}_1 - \overline{x}_2)}{\left(\dfrac{s_P^2}{n_1} + \dfrac{s_P^2}{n_2}\right)^{1/2}}$ (sample variances assumed equal)

APPENDIX A:
AREAS UNDER THE NORMAL CURVE

Most of the examples in this book have used one version of the z-table to find the area under the normal curve. This table provides the cumulative probabilities (or the area under the entire curve to left of the z-value).

Probability Example

Assume that the annual earnings per share (EPS) for a large sample of firms is normally distributed with a mean of $5.00 and a standard deviation of $1.50. What is the approximate probability of an observed EPS value falling between $3.00 and $7.25?

If $EPS = x = \$7.25$, then $z = (x - \mu)/\sigma = (\$7.25 - \$5.00)/\$1.50 = +1.50$

If $EPS = x = \$3.00$, then $z = (x - \mu)/\sigma = (\$3.00 - \$5.00)/\$1.50 = -1.33$

Solving Using The Cumulative Z-Table

For z-value of 1.50: Use the row headed 1.5 and the column headed 0 to find the value 0.9332. This represents the area under the curve to the left of the critical value 1.50.

For z-value of −1.33: Use the row headed 1.3 and the column headed 3 to find the value 0.9082. This represents the area under the curve to the left of the critical value +1.33. The area to the left of −1.33 is $1 - 0.9082 = 0.0918$.

The area between these critical values is $0.9332 - 0.0918 = 0.8414$, or 84.14%.

Hypothesis Testing – One-Tailed Test Example

A sample of a stock's returns on 36 nonconsecutive days results in a mean return of 2.0 percent. Assume the population standard deviation is 20.0 percent. Can we say with 95 percent confidence that the mean return is greater than zero percent?

$H_0: \mu \leq 0.0\%$, $H_a: \mu > 0.0\%$. The test statistic = z-statistic = $\dfrac{\bar{x} - \mu_0}{\sigma/\sqrt{n}} = (2.0 - 0.0) / (20.0 / 6) = 0.60$.

The significance level = $1.0 - 0.95 = 0.05$, or 5%. Because we are interested in a return greater than 0.0 percent, this is a one-tailed test.

Using the Cumulative Z-Table

Because this is a one-tailed test with an alpha of 0.05, we need to find the value 0.95 in the cumulative z-table. The closest value is 0.9505, with a corresponding critical z-value of 1.65. Because the test statistic is less than the critical value, we fail to reject H_0.

Hypothesis Testing – Two-Tailed Test Example

Using the same assumptions as before, suppose that the analyst now wants to determine if he can say with 99% confidence that the stock's return is not equal to 0.0 percent.

$H_0: \mu = 0.0\%$, $H_a: \mu \neq 0.0\%$. The test statistic (z-value) = $(2.0 - 0.0) / (20.0 / 6) = 0.60$. The significance level = $1.0 - 0.99 = 0.01$, or 1%. Because we are interested in whether or not the stock return is nonzero, this is a two-tailed test.

Using the Cumulative Z-Table

Because this is a two-tailed test with an alpha of 0.01, there is a 0.005 rejection region in both tails. Thus, we need to find the value 0.995 (1.0 – 0.005) in the table. The closest value is 0.9951, which corresponds to a critical z-value of 2.58. Because the test statistic is less than the critical value, we fail to reject H_0 and conclude that the stock's return equals 0.0 percent.

CUMULATIVE Z-TABLE

STANDARD NORMAL DISTRIBUTION
$P(Z \leq z) = N(z)$ FOR $z \geq 0$

z	0.00	0.01	0.02	0.03	0.04	0.05	0.06	0.07	0.08	0.09
0.0	0.5000	0.5040	0.5080	0.5120	0.5160	0.5199	0.5239	0.5279	0.5319	0.5359
0.1	0.5398	0.5438	0.5478	0.5517	0.5557	0.5596	0.5636	0.5675	0.5714	0.5753
0.2	0.5793	0.5832	0.5871	0.5910	0.5948	0.5987	0.6026	0.6064	0.6103	0.6141
0.3	0.6179	0.6217	0.6255	0.6293	0.6331	0.6368	0.6406	0.6443	0.6480	0.6517
0.4	0.6554	0.6591	0.6628	0.6664	0.6700	0.6736	0.6772	0.6808	0.6844	0.6879
0.5	0.6915	0.6950	0.6985	0.7019	0.7054	0.7088	0.7123	0.7157	0.7190	0.7224
0.6	0.7257	0.7291	0.7324	0.7357	0.7389	0.7422	0.7454	0.7486	0.7517	0.7549
0.7	0.7580	0.7611	0.7642	0.7673	0.7704	0.7734	0.7764	0.7794	0.7823	0.7852
0.8	0.7881	0.7910	0.7939	0.7967	0.7995	0.8023	0.8051	0.8078	0.8106	0.8133
0.9	0.8159	0.8186	0.8212	0.8238	0.8264	0.8289	0.8315	0.8340	0.8365	0.8389
1.0	0.8413	0.8438	0.8461	0.8485	0.8508	0.8531	0.8554	0.8577	0.8599	0.8621
1.1	0.8643	0.8665	0.8686	0.8708	0.8729	0.8749	0.8770	0.8790	0.8810	0.8830
1.2	0.8849	0.8869	0.8888	0.8907	0.8925	0.8944	0.8962	0.8980	0.8997	0.9015
1.3	0.9032	0.9049	0.9066	0.9082	0.9099	0.9115	0.9131	0.9147	0.9162	0.9177
1.4	0.9192	0.9207	0.9222	0.9236	0.9251	0.9265	0.9279	0.9292	0.9306	0.9319
1.5	0.9332	0.9345	0.9357	0.9370	0.9382	0.9394	0.9406	0.9418	0.9429	0.9441
1.6	0.9452	0.9463	0.9474	0.9484	0.9495	0.9505	0.9515	0.9525	0.9535	0.9545
1.7	0.9554	0.9564	0.9573	0.9582	0.9591	0.9599	0.9608	0.9616	0.9625	0.9633
1.8	0.9641	0.9649	0.9656	0.9664	0.9671	0.9678	0.9686	0.9693	0.9699	0.9706
1.9	0.9713	0.9719	0.9726	0.9732	0.9738	0.9744	0.9750	0.9756	0.9761	0.9767
2.0	0.9772	0.9778	0.9783	0.9788	0.9793	0.9798	0.9803	0.9808	0.9812	0.9817
2.1	0.9821	0.9826	0.9830	0.9834	0.9838	0.9842	0.9846	0.9850	0.9854	0.9857
2.2	0.9861	0.9864	0.9868	0.9871	0.9875	0.9878	0.9881	0.9884	0.9887	0.9890
2.3	0.9893	0.9896	0.9898	0.9901	0.9904	0.9906	0.9909	0.9911	0.9913	0.9916
2.4	0.9918	0.9920	0.9922	0.9925	0.9927	0.9929	0.9931	0.9932	0.9934	0.9936
2.5	0.9938	0.9940	0.9941	0.9943	0.9945	0.9946	0.9948	0.9949	0.9951	0.9952
2.6	0.9953	0.9955	0.9956	0.9957	0.9959	0.9960	0.9961	0.9962	0.9963	0.9964
2.7	0.9965	0.9966	0.9967	0.9968	0.9969	0.9970	0.9971	0.9972	0.9973	0.9974
2.8	0.9974	0.9975	0.9976	0.9977	0.9977	0.9978	0.9979	0.9979	0.9980	0.9981
2.9	0.9981	0.9982	0.9982	0.9983	0.9984	0.9984	0.9985	0.9985	0.9986	0.9986
3.0	0.9987	0.9987	0.9987	0.9988	0.9988	0.9989	0.9989	0.9989	0.9990	0.9990

CUMULATIVE Z-TABLE (CONT.)

STANDARD NORMAL DISTRIBUTION

$P(Z \leq z) = N(z)$ FOR $z \leq 0$

z	0.00	0.01	0.02	0.03	0.04	0.05	0.06	0.07	0.08	0.09
0.0	0.5000	0.4960	0.4920	0.4880	0.4840	0.4801	0.4761	0.4721	0.4681	0.4641
-0.1	0.4602	0.4562	0.4522	0.4483	0.4443	0.4404	0.4364	0.4325	0.4286	0.4247
-0.2	0.4207	0.4168	0.4129	0.4090	0.4052	0.4013	0.3974	0.3936	0.3897	0.3859
-0.3	0.3821	0.3783	0.3745	0.3707	0.3669	0.3632	0.3594	0.3557	0.3520	0.3483
-0.4	0.3446	0.3409	0.3372	0.3336	0.3300	0.3264	0.3228	0.3192	0.3156	0.3121
-0.5	0.3085	0.3050	0.3015	0.2981	0.2946	0.2912	0.2877	0.2843	0.2810	0.2776
-0.6	0.2743	0.2709	0.2676	0.2643	0.2611	0.2578	0.2546	0.2514	0.2483	0.2451
-0.7	0.2420	0.2389	0.2358	0.2327	0.2297	0.2266	0.2236	0.2207	0.2177	0.2148
-0.8	0.2119	0.2090	0.2061	0.2033	0.2005	0.1977	0.1949	0.1922	0.1894	0.1867
-0.9	0.1841	0.1814	0.1788	0.1762	0.1736	0.1711	0.1685	0.1660	0.1635	0.1611
-1.0	0.1587	0.1562	0.1539	0.1515	0.1492	0.1469	0.1446	0.1423	0.1401	0.1379
-1.1	0.1357	0.1335	0.1314	0.1292	0.1271	0.1251	0.1230	0.1210	0.1190	0.1170
-1.2	0.1151	0.1131	0.1112	0.1093	0.1075	0.1057	0.1038	0.1020	0.1003	0.0985
-1.3	0.0968	0.0951	0.0934	0.0918	0.0901	0.0885	0.0869	0.0853	0.0838	0.0823
-1.4	0.0808	0.0793	0.0778	0.0764	0.0749	0.0735	0.0721	0.0708	0.0694	0.0681
-1.5	0.0668	0.0655	0.0643	0.0630	0.0618	0.0606	0.0594	0.0582	0.0571	0.0559
-1.6	0.0548	0.0537	0.0526	0.0516	0.0505	0.0495	0.0485	0.0475	0.0465	0.0455
-1.7	0.0446	0.0436	0.0427	0.0418	0.0409	0.0401	0.0392	0.0384	0.0375	0.0367
-1.8	0.0359	0.0351	0.0344	0.0336	0.0329	0.0322	0.0314	0.0307	0.0301	0.0294
-1.9	0.0287	0.0281	0.0274	0.0268	0.0262	0.0256	0.0250	0.0244	0.0239	0.0233
-2.0	0.0228	0.0222	0.0217	0.0212	0.0207	0.0202	0.0197	0.0192	0.0188	0.0183
-2.1	0.0179	0.0174	0.0170	0.0166	0.0162	0.0158	0.0154	0.0150	0.0146	0.0143
-2.2	0.0139	0.0136	0.0132	0.0129	0.0125	0.0122	0.0119	0.0116	0.0113	0.0110
-2.3	0.0107	0.0104	0.0102	0.0099	0.0096	0.0094	0.0091	0.0089	0.0087	0.0084
-2.4	0.0082	0.0080	0.0078	0.0076	0.0073	0.0071	0.0069	0.0068	0.0066	0.0064
-2.5	0.0062	0.0060	0.0059	0.0057	0.0055	0.0054	0.0052	0.0051	0.0049	0.0048
-2.6	0.0047	0.0045	0.0044	0.0043	0.0041	0.0040	0.0039	0.0038	0.0037	0.0036
-2.7	0.0035	0.0034	0.0033	0.0032	0.0031	0.0030	0.0029	0.0028	0.0027	0.0026
-2.8	0.0026	0.0025	0.0024	0.0023	0.0023	0.0022	0.0021	0.0021	0.0020	0.0019
-2.9	0.0019	0.0018	0.0018	0.0017	0.0016	0.0016	0.0015	0.0015	0.0014	0.0014
-3.0	0.0014	0.0013	0.0013	0.0012	0.0012	0.0011	0.0011	0.0011	0.0010	0.0010

APPENDIX B:
STUDENT'S *t*-DISTRIBUTION

df	Level of Significance for One-Tailed Test					
	0.100	0.050	0.025	0.01	0.005	0.0005

df	Level of Significance for Two-Tailed Test					
	0.20	0.10	0.05	0.02	0.01	0.001
1	3.078	6.314	12.706	31.821	63.657	636.619
2	1.886	2.920	4.303	6.965	9.925	31.599
3	1.638	2.353	3.182	4.541	5.841	12.294
4	1.533	2.132	2.776	3.747	4.604	8.610
5	1.476	2.015	2.571	3.365	4.032	6.869
6	1.440	1.943	2.447	3.143	3.707	5.959
7	1.415	1.895	2.365	2.998	3.499	5.408
8	1.397	1.860	2.306	2.896	3.355	5.041
9	1.383	1.833	2.262	2.821	3.250	4.781
10	1.372	1.812	2.228	2.764	3.169	4.587
11	1.363	1.796	2.201	2.718	3.106	4.437
12	1.356	1.782	2.179	2.681	3.055	4.318
13	1.350	1.771	2.160	2.650	3.012	4.221
14	1.345	1.761	2.145	2.624	2.977	4.140
15	1.341	1.753	2.131	2.602	2.947	4.073
16	1.337	1.746	2.120	2.583	2.921	4.015
17	1.333	1.740	2.110	2.567	2.898	3.965
18	1.330	1.734	2.101	2.552	2.878	3.922
19	1.328	1.729	2.093	2.539	2.861	3.883
20	1.325	1.725	2.086	2.528	2.845	3.850
21	1.323	1.721	2.080	2.518	2.831	3.819
22	1.321	1.717	2.074	2.508	2.819	3.792
23	1.319	1.714	2.069	2.500	2.807	3.768
24	1.318	1.711	2.064	2.492	2.797	3.745
25	1.316	1.708	2.060	2.485	2.787	3.725
26	1.315	1.706	2.056	2.479	2.779	3.707
27	1.314	1.703	2.052	2.473	2.771	3.690
28	1.313	1.701	2.048	2.467	2.763	3.674
29	1.311	1.699	2.045	2.462	2.756	3.659
30	1.310	1.697	2.042	2.457	2.750	3.646
40	1.303	1.684	2.021	2.423	2.704	3.551
60	1.296	1.671	2.000	2.390	2.660	3.460
120	1.289	1.658	1.980	2.358	2.617	3.373
∞	1.282	1.645	1.960	2.326	2.576	3.291

APPENDIX C:
F-TABLE AT 5 PERCENT (UPPER TAIL)

F-TABLE, CRITICAL VALUES, 5 PERCENT IN UPPER TAIL

Degrees of freedom for the numerator along top row
Degrees of freedom for the denominator along side row

	1	2	3	4	5	6	7	8	9	10	12	15	20	24	30	40
1	161	200	216	225	230	234	237	239	241	242	244	246	248	249	250	251
2	18.5	19.0	19.2	19.2	19.3	19.3	19.4	19.4	19.4	19.4	19.4	19.4	19.4	19.5	19.5	19.5
3	10.1	9.55	9.28	9.12	9.01	8.94	8.89	8.85	8.81	8.79	8.74	8.70	8.66	8.64	8.62	8.59
4	7.71	6.94	6.59	6.39	6.26	6.16	6.09	6.04	6.00	5.96	5.91	5.86	5.80	5.77	5.75	5.72
5	6.61	5.79	5.41	5.19	5.05	4.95	4.88	4.82	4.77	4.74	4.68	4.62	4.56	4.53	4.50	4.46
6	5.99	5.14	4.76	4.53	4.39	4.28	4.21	4.15	4.10	4.06	4.00	3.94	3.87	3.84	3.81	3.77
7	5.59	4.74	4.35	4.12	3.97	3.87	3.79	3.73	3.68	3.64	3.57	3.51	3.44	3.41	3.38	3.34
8	5.32	4.46	4.07	3.84	3.69	3.58	3.50	3.44	3.39	3.35	3.28	3.22	3.15	3.12	3.08	3.04
9	5.12	4.26	3.86	3.63	3.48	3.37	3.29	3.23	3.18	3.14	3.07	6.01	2.94	2.90	2.86	2.83
10	4.96	4.10	3.71	3.48	3.33	3.22	3.14	3.07	3.02	2.98	2.91	2.85	2.77	2.74	2.70	2.66
11	4.84	3.98	3.59	3.36	3.20	3.09	3.01	2.95	2.90	2.85	2.79	2.72	2.65	2.61	2.57	2.53
12	4.75	3.89	3.49	3.26	3.11	3.00	2.91	2.85	2.80	2.75	2.69	2.62	2.54	2.51	2.47	2.43
13	4.67	3.81	3.41	3.18	3.03	2.92	2.83	2.77	2.71	2.67	2.60	2.53	2.46	2.42	2.38	2.34
14	4.60	3.74	3.34	3.11	2.96	2.85	2.76	2.70	2.65	2.60	2.53	2.46	2.39	2.35	2.31	2.27
15	4.54	3.68	3.29	3.06	2.90	2.79	2.71	2.64	2.59	2.54	2.48	2.40	2.33	2.29	2.25	2.20
16	4.49	3.63	3.24	3.01	2.85	2.74	2.66	2.59	2.54	2.49	2.42	2.35	2.28	2.24	2.19	2.15
17	4.45	3.59	3.20	2.96	2.81	2.70	2.61	2.55	2.49	2.45	2.38	2.31	2.23	2.19	2.15	2.10
18	4.41	3.55	3.16	2.93	2.77	2.66	2.58	2.51	2.46	2.41	2.34	2.27	2.19	2.15	2.11	2.06
19	4.38	3.52	3.13	2.90	2.74	2.63	2.54	2.48	2.42	2.38	2.31	2.23	2.16	2.11	2.07	2.03
20	4.35	3.49	3.10	2.87	2.71	2.60	2.51	2.45	2.39	2.35	2.28	2.20	2.12	2.08	2.04	1.99
21	4.32	3.47	3.07	2.84	2.68	2.57	2.49	2.42	2.37	2.32	2.25	2.18	2.10	2.05	2.01	1.96
22	4.30	3.44	3.05	2.82	2.66	2.55	2.46	2.40	2.34	2.30	2.23	2.15	2.07	2.03	1.98	1.94
23	4.28	3.42	3.03	2.80	2.64	2.53	2.44	2.37	2.32	2.27	2.20	2.13	2.05	2.01	1.96	1.91
24	4.26	3.40	3.01	2.78	2.62	2.51	2.42	2.36	2.30	2.25	2.18	2.11	2.03	1.98	1.94	1.89
25	4.24	3.39	2.99	2.76	2.60	2.49	2.40	2.34	2.28	2.24	2.16	2.09	2.01	1.96	1.92	1.87
30	4.17	3.32	2.92	2.69	2.53	2.42	2.33	2.27	2.21	2.16	2.09	2.01	1.93	1.89	1.84	1.79
40	4.08	3.23	2.84	2.61	2.45	2.34	2.25	2.18	2.12	2.08	2.00	1.92	1.84	1.79	1.74	1.69
60	4.00	3.15	2.76	2.53	2.37	2.25	2.17	2.10	2.04	1.99	1.92	1.84	1.75	1.70	1.65	1.59
120	3.92	3.07	2.68	2.45	2.29	2.18	2.09	2.02	1.96	1.91	1.83	1.75	1.66	1.61	1.55	1.50
∞	3.84	3.00	2.60	2.37	2.21	2.10	2.01	1.94	1.88	1.83	1.75	1.67	1.57	1.52	1.46	1.39

APPENDIX D:
F-TABLE AT 2.5 PERCENT (UPPER TAIL)

F-TABLE, CRITICAL VALUES, 2.5 PERCENT IN UPPER TAILS

Degrees of freedom for the numerator along top row
Degrees of freedom for the denominator along side row

	1	2	3	4	5	6	7	8	9	10	12	15	20	24	30	40
1	648	799	864	900	922	937	948	957	963	969	977	985	993	997	1001	1006
2	38.51	39.00	39.17	39.25	39.30	39.33	39.36	39.37	39.39	39.40	39.41	39.43	39.45	39.46	39.46	39.47
3	17.44	16.04	15.44	15.10	14.88	14.73	14.62	14.54	14.47	14.42	14.34	14.25	14.17	14.12	14.08	14.04
4	12.22	10.65	9.98	9.60	9.36	9.20	9.07	8.98	8.90	8.84	8.75	8.66	8.56	8.51	8.46	8.41
5	10.01	8.43	7.76	7.39	7.15	6.98	6.85	6.76	6.68	6.62	6.52	6.43	6.33	6.28	6.23	6.18
6	8.81	7.26	6.60	6.23	5.99	5.82	5.70	5.60	5.52	5.46	5.37	5.27	5.17	5.12	5.07	5.01
7	8.07	6.54	5.89	5.52	5.29	5.12	4.99	4.90	4.82	4.76	4.67	4.57	4.47	4.41	4.36	4.31
8	7.57	6.06	5.42	5.05	4.82	4.65	4.53	4.43	4.36	4.30	4.20	4.10	4.00	3.95	3.89	3.84
9	7.21	5.71	5.08	4.72	4.48	4.32	4.20	4.10	4.03	3.96	3.87	3.77	3.67	3.61	3.56	3.51
10	6.94	5.46	4.83	4.47	4.24	4.07	3.95	3.85	3.78	3.72	3.62	3.52	3.42	3.37	3.31	3.26
11	6.72	5.26	4.63	4.28	4.04	3.88	3.76	3.66	3.59	3.53	3.43	3.33	3.23	3.17	3.12	3.06
12	6.55	5.10	4.47	4.12	3.89	3.73	3.61	3.51	3.44	3.37	3.28	3.18	3.07	3.02	2.96	2.91
13	6.41	4.97	4.35	4.00	3.77	3.60	3.48	3.39	3.31	3.25	3.15	3.05	2.95	2.89	2.84	2.78
14	6.30	4.86	4.24	3.89	3.66	3.50	3.38	3.29	3.21	3.15	3.05	2.95	2.84	2.79	2.73	2.67
15	6.20	4.77	4.15	3.80	3.58	3.41	3.29	3.20	3.12	3.06	2.96	2.86	2.76	2.70	2.64	2.59
16	6.12	4.69	4.08	3.73	3.50	3.34	3.22	3.12	3.05	2.99	2.89	2.79	2.68	2.63	2.57	2.51
17	6.04	4.62	4.01	3.66	3.44	3.28	3.16	3.06	2.98	2.92	2.82	2.72	2.62	2.56	2.50	2.44
18	5.98	4.56	3.95	3.61	3.38	3.22	3.10	3.01	2.93	2.87	2.77	2.67	2.56	2.50	2.44	2.38
19	5.92	4.51	3.90	3.56	3.33	3.17	3.05	2.96	2.88	2.82	2.72	2.62	2.51	2.45	2.39	2.33
20	5.87	4.46	3.86	3.51	3.29	3.13	3.01	2.91	2.84	2.77	2.68	2.57	2.46	2.41	2.35	2.29
21	5.83	4.42	3.82	3.48	3.25	3.09	2.97	2.87	2.80	2.73	2.64	2.53	2.42	2.37	2.31	2.25
22	5.79	4.38	3.78	3.44	3.22	3.05	2.93	2.84	2.76	2.70	2.60	2.50	2.39	2.33	2.27	2.21
23	5.75	4.35	3.75	3.41	3.18	3.02	2.90	2.81	2.73	2.67	2.57	2.47	2.36	2.30	2.24	2.18
24	5.72	4.32	3.72	3.38	3.15	2.99	2.87	2.78	2.70	2.64	2.54	2.44	2.33	2.27	2.21	2.15
25	5.69	4.29	3.69	3.35	3.13	2.97	2.85	2.75	2.68	2.61	2.51	2.41	2.30	2.24	2.18	2.12
30	5.57	4.18	3.59	3.25	3.03	2.87	2.75	2.65	2.57	2.51	2.41	2.31	2.20	2.14	2.07	2.01
40	5.42	4.05	3.46	3.13	2.90	2.74	2.62	2.53	2.45	2.39	2.29	2.18	2.07	2.01	1.94	1.88
60	5.29	3.93	3.34	3.01	2.79	2.63	2.51	2.41	2.33	2.27	2.17	2.06	1.94	1.88	1.82	1.74
120	5.15	3.80	3.23	2.89	2.67	2.52	2.39	2.30	2.22	2.16	2.05	1.94	1.82	1.76	1.69	1.61
∞	5.02	3.69	3.12	2.79	2.57	2.41	2.29	2.19	2.11	2.05	1.94	1.83	1.71	1.64	1.57	1.48

APPENDIX E:
CHI-SQUARED TABLE

Values of χ^2 (Degrees of Freedom, Level of Significance)
Probability in Right Tail

Degrees of Freedom	0.99	0.975	0.95	0.9	0.1	0.05	0.025	0.01	0.005
1	0.000157	0.000982	0.003932	0.0158	2.706	3.841	5.024	6.635	7.879
2	0.020100	0.050636	0.102586	0.2107	4.605	5.991	7.378	9.210	10.597
3	0.1148	0.2158	0.3518	0.5844	6.251	7.815	9.348	11.345	12.838
4	0.297	0.484	0.711	1.064	7.779	9.488	11.143	13.277	14.860
5	0.554	0.831	1.145	1.610	9.236	11.070	12.832	15.086	16.750
6	0.872	1.237	1.635	2.204	10.645	12.592	14.449	16.812	18.548
7	1.239	1.690	2.167	2.833	12.017	14.067	16.013	18.475	20.278
8	1.647	2.180	2.733	3.490	13.362	15.507	17.535	20.090	21.955
9	2.088	2.700	3.325	4.168	14.684	16.919	19.023	21.666	23.589
10	2.558	3.247	3.940	4.865	15.987	18.307	20.483	23.209	25.188
11	3.053	3.816	4.575	5.578	17.275	19.675	21.920	24.725	26.757
12	3.571	4.404	5.226	6.304	18.549	21.026	23.337	26.217	28.300
13	4.107	5.009	5.892	7.041	19.812	22.362	24.736	27.688	29.819
14	4.660	5.629	6.571	7.790	21.064	23.685	26.119	29.141	31.319
15	5.229	6.262	7.261	8.547	22.307	24.996	27.488	30.578	32.801
16	5.812	6.908	7.962	9.312	23.542	26.296	28.845	32.000	34.267
17	6.408	7.564	8.672	10.085	24.769	27.587	30.191	33.409	35.718
18	7.015	8.231	9.390	10.865	25.989	28.869	31.526	34.805	37.156
19	7.633	8.907	10.117	11.651	27.204	30.144	32.852	36.191	38.582
20	8.260	9.591	10.851	12.443	28.412	31.410	34.170	37.566	39.997
21	8.897	10.283	11.591	13.240	29.615	32.671	35.479	38.932	41.401
22	9.542	10.982	12.338	14.041	30.813	33.924	36.781	40.289	42.796
23	10.196	11.689	13.091	14.848	32.007	35.172	38.076	41.638	44.181
24	10.856	12.401	13.848	15.659	33.196	36.415	39.364	42.980	45.558
25	11.524	13.120	14.611	16.473	34.382	37.652	40.646	44.314	46.928
26	12.198	13.844	15.379	17.292	35.563	38.885	41.923	45.642	48.290
27	12.878	14.573	16.151	18.114	36.741	40.113	43.195	46.963	49.645
28	13.565	15.308	16.928	18.939	37.916	41.337	44.461	48.278	50.994
29	14.256	16.047	17.708	19.768	39.087	42.557	45.722	49.588	52.335
30	14.953	16.791	18.493	20.599	40.256	43.773	46.979	50.892	53.672
50	29.707	32.357	34.764	37.689	63.167	67.505	71.420	76.154	79.490
60	37.485	40.482	43.188	46.459	74.397	79.082	83.298	88.379	91.952
80	53.540	57.153	60.391	64.278	96.578	101.879	106.629	112.329	116.321
100	70.065	74.222	77.929	82.358	118.498	124.342	129.561	135.807	140.170

INDEX

A

absolute frequency 165
additional compensation arrangements 50
addition rule of probability 203, 205
additivity principle 127
alternative hypothesis 304
amortization 118
annuities 106
annuities due 106
a priori probability 202
arithmetic means 170
Arms index 354

B

bank discount yield (BDY) 147
bar charts 344
Bayes' formula 222
Bernoulli random variable 249
biased estimator 178
bimodal data set 172
binomial distribution 249
binomial formula 225
binomial random variable 249, 250
binomial tree 251
Bollinger bands 351
bond-equivalent yield (BEY) 151
breakdown 347
breakout 347

C

candlestick charts 345
cash flow additivity principle 127
CD equivalent yield 149
central limit theorem 282
change in polarity 348
Chebyshev's inequality 179
chi-square distribution 326
Code of Ethics 14
coefficient of variation 180
combination formula 225
communication with clients 57
composites 87
compounding frequency 116
compound interest 98, 99
conditional probability 203
conduct as members and candidates 69
confidence interval 256, 287
confidence interval for the population mean 288

consistent estimator 285
continuation patterns 349
continuous compounding 265
continuous distribution 246
continuous random variable 246
continuous uniform distribution 253
contrarian strategy 351
convergence 352
correlation 215, 256
cost of capital 105
Country Version of GIPS (CVG) 86
covariance 213
cross-sectional data 282
cumulative absolute frequency 167
cumulative distribution function 247
cumulative relative frequency 167

D

data mining 292
decennial patterns 355
decile 174
decision rule 305, 310
default risk premium 101
degrees of freedom 286
descriptive statistics 163
desirable properties of an estimator 285
diligence and reasonable basis 53
disclosure of conflicts 61
discount factor 105
discounting 99, 105
discount rate 100, 105, 123
discrete distribution 246
discretely compounded returns 264
discrete random variable 245
discrete uniform random variable 248
dispersion 175
distribution function 247
divergence 352
double bottom pattern 349
double top pattern 349
down transition probability 251
downtrend 347

E

effective annual rate (EAR) 101
effective annual yield (EAY) 148
efficient estimator 285
empirical probability 202
equality of variances 328

THE BUSN SOLUTION

Every 4LTR Press solution includes:

 + + (Tear-out Review Cards) + (Interactive eBook with magnified "1-1b")

Heading Numbers Connect Print & eBook

Visually Engaging Textbook | **Online Study Tools** | **Tear-out Review Cards** | **Interactive eBook**

STUDENT RESOURCES:

- Interactive eBook
- Auto-Graded Quizzes
- Flashcards
- Games: Crossword Puzzles, Beat the Clock, & Quiz Bowl
- PowerPoint® Slides
- Videos
- Review Cards

- Interactive Exhibits
- Cases & Exercises
- Career Transitions
- KnowNOW! Blog
- Interactive Business Decision-Making Scenarios

Students sign in at
www.cengagebrain.com

INSTRUCTOR RESOURCES:

- All Student Resources
- Engagement Tracker
- First Day of Class Instructions
- Instructor's Manual
- Test Bank
- PowerPoint® Slides
- Instructor Prep Cards

Instructors sign in at
www.cengage.com/login

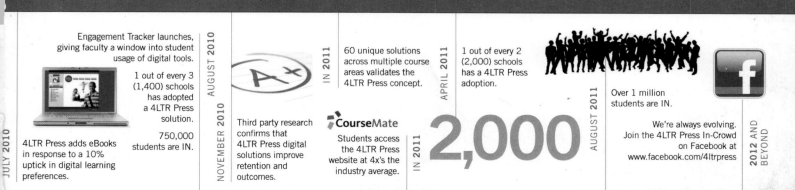

JULY 2010

4LTR Press adds eBooks in response to a 10% uptick in digital learning preferences.

AUGUST 2010

Engagement Tracker launches, giving faculty a window into student usage of digital tools.

1 out of every 3 (1,400) schools has adopted a 4LTR Press solution.

NOVEMBER 2010

750,000 students are IN.

Third party research confirms that 4LTR Press digital solutions improve retention and outcomes.

IN 2011

60 unique solutions across multiple course areas validates the 4LTR Press concept.

CourseMate

Students access the 4LTR Press website at 4x's the industry average.

APRIL 2011

1 out of every 2 (2,000) schools has a 4LTR Press adoption.

IN 2011

2,000

AUGUST 2011

Over 1 million students are IN.

We're always evolving. Join the 4LTR Press In-Crowd on Facebook at www.facebook.com/4ltrpress

2012 AND BEYOND

BUSN6
Marce Kelly, Jim McGowen, Chuck Williams

Senior Vice President, LRS/Acquisitions & Solutions
Planning: Jack W. Calhoun

Editorial Director, Business & Economics: Erin Joyner

Vice President 4LTR & Learning Solutions Strategy,
Institutional: Neil Marquardt

Acquisitions Editor: Jason Fremder

Developmental Editor: Julie Klooster

Editorial Assistant: Megan Fischer

Project Manager, 4LTR Press: Pierce Denny

Sr. Brand Manager: Kristen Hurd

Marketing Coordinator: Ilyssa Harbatkin

Sr. Content Project Manager: Martha Conway

Sr. Media Editor: Kristen Meere

Manufacturing Planner: Ron Montgomery

Production Service: MPS Limited

Sr. Art Director: Stacy Jenkins Shirley

Sr. Rights Acquisition Specialist, Images: Deanna Ettinger

Image Researcher: Charlotte Goldman

Rights Acquisition Specialist, Text: Amber Hosea

Text Permissions Researcher: Vinodh Ramachandran,
PreMedia Global

Cover and Internal Designer: KeDesign, Mason, OH

Cover Image: © Fancy Photography/Veer

Inside Front Cover Images: © iStockphoto.com/sdominick,
© iStockphoto.com/alexsl, © iStockphoto.com/A-Digit

Title Page Images: © iStockphoto.com/CostinT,
© iStockphoto.com/photovideostock,
© iStockphoto.com/Leontura

Back cover Image: © iStockphoto.com/René Mansi

Special Feature Images:
Spilled coffee: © iStockphoto.com/Aleksander Krol
Man with feet on desk: © iStockphoto.com/Lise Gagne
Green recycling: © iStockphoto.com/Radovan Marček
Thumbs up: © iStockphoto.com/Lasse Kristensen
Puzzle/iPad: © iStockphoto.com/Alex Slobodkin
Woman with business card: © iStockphoto.com/
Amanda Rohde

Library of Congress Control Number: 2012943273

Student Edition ISBN 13: 978-1-133-18893-3
Student Edition ISBN 10: 1-133-18893-1

Student Edition with CourseMate ISBN 13: 978-1-133-18892-6
Student Edition with CourseMate ISBN 10: 1-133-18892-3

South-Western
5191 Natorp Boulevard
Mason, OH 45040
USA

Cengage Learning is a leading provider of customized learning solutions
with office locations around the globe, including Singapore, the United
Kingdom, Australia, Mexico, Brazil, and Japan. Locate your local office at:
www.cengage.com/global

Cengage Learning products are represented in Canada by
Nelson Education, Ltd.

To learn more about 4LTR Press, visit **4ltr.cengage.com/busn**
Purchase any of our products at your local college store or at our
preferred online store **www.cengagebrain.com**

Printed in the United States of America
1 2 3 4 5 6 7 17 16 15 14 13

BUSN6

CONTENTS

PART 1 — The Business Environment

© iStockphoto.com/studiovision

© Brian A Jackson/Shutterstock.com

Chapter 4

Business Ethics and Social Responsibility:
Doing Well by Doing Good

Chapter 5

Business Communication:
Creating and Delivering Messages that Matter

PART 2 Creating a Business

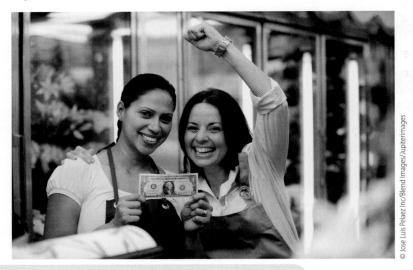

© Jose Luis Pelaez Inc/Blend Images/Jupiterimages

PART 3 — Financing a Business

Chapter 10
Financial Markets: Allocating Financial Resources

© Olga Danylenko/Shutterstock.com

© iStockphoto.com/Alex Slobodkin

Chapter 17

Operations Management: Putting It All Together

© iStockphoto.com/Jonathan Heger

Personal Finance Appendix 290

Endnotes 301

Glossary 317

Index 331

Tear-Out Cards

Visit www.cengagebrain.com to see the online appendices.

Online Appendix 1: Labor Unions and Collective Bargaining

Online Appendix 2: Business Law

To my family—
Scot, Justin, Lauren,
Allison, Cathy, and Shel.
You are my greatest blessing.

—Marce Kelly

To my grandsons,
Kyle and Xander.
Grandy loves you!

—Jim McGowen

To Jenny,
the book is done, let's play!

—Chuck Williams

The idea for this book—a whole new way of learning—began with students like you across the country. We paid attention to students who wanted to learn about business without slogging through endless pages of dry text. We listened to students who wanted to sit through class without craving a triple espresso. We responded to students who wanted to use their favorite gadgets to prepare for tests.

So we are confident that BUSN will meet your needs. The short, lively text covers all the key concepts without the fluff. The examples are relevant and engaging, and the visual style makes the book fun to read. But the text is only part of the package. You can access a rich variety of study tools via computer or iPod—the choice is yours.

We did one other thing we hope you'll like. We paid a lot of attention to students' concerns about the high price of college textbooks. We made it our mission to ensure that our package not only meets your needs but does so without busting your budget!

This innovative, student-focused package was developed by the authors—Marce Kelly, Jim McGowen, and Chuck Williams—and the experienced Cengage Learning publishers. The Cengage team contributed a deep understanding of students and professors across the nation, and the authors brought years of teaching and business experience.

Marce Kelly, who earned her MBA from UCLA's Anderson School of Management, spent the first 14 years of her career in marketing, building brands for Neutrogena and The Walt Disney Corporation. But her true love is teaching, so in 2000 she accepted a full-time teaching position at Santa Monica College. Professor Kelly has received seven Outstanding Instructor awards from the International Education Center and has been named four times to *Who's Who Among American Teachers*.

Jim McGowen is professor emeritus in the Business Division at Southwestern Illinois College. He has taught Introduction to Business for over a quarter of a century, and continues to teach several sections of the course each year. Professor McGowen chaired the Business Transfer Department at Southwestern Illinois College for 12 years, giving him the opportunity to work with faculty teaching a wide range of business courses. This experience gave him a deep appreciation for the role the Introduction to Business course plays in a business curriculum. Professor McGowen has a bachelor's degree in business administration and a master's degree in economics, both from Auburn University. He has received the Emerson Prize for Teaching Excellence and been recognized for teaching excellence by the Illinois Community College Trustees Association. He was named Faculty Member of the Year at Southwestern Illinois College in 2007.

Chuck Williams is the Dean of Butler's College of Business. His research interests include employee recruitment and turnover, performance appraisal, and employee training and goal-setting. He has taught in executive development programs at Oklahoma State University, the University of Oklahoma, Texas Christian University, and the University of the Pacific. Dr. Williams was honored by TCU's M.J. Neeley School of Business with the undergraduate Outstanding Faculty Teaching Award, was a recipient of TCU's Dean's Teaching Award, and was TCU's nominee for the U.S. Professor of the Year competition sponsored by the Carnegie Foundation for the Advancement of Teaching. He has written three other textbooks: *Management, Effective Management: A Multimedia Approach*, and *MGMT*.

We would appreciate any comments or suggestions you want to offer about this package. You can reach Jim McGowen at jmcgowen4@gmail.com, Chuck Williams at crwillia@butler.edu, and Marce Kelly at marcella.kelly@gmail.com. We wish you a fun, positive, productive term, and look forward to your feedback!

Marce Kelly   Jim McGowen   Chuck Williams

© Cengage Learning 2013   © Cengage Learning 2013   © Brent Smith, Butler University

1
Business Now:
Change Is the Only Constant

© Robert Daly/OJO Images/Jupiterimages

> # "BUSINESS IS IN ITSELF A POWER."
>
> —GARET GARRETT,
> AUTHOR AND FINANCIAL JOURNALIST

1-1 # Business Now: Moving at Breakneck Speed

Day by day, the business world simply spins faster. Industries rise—and sometimes fall—in the course of a few short months. Technologies forge instant connections across the globe. Powerful new trends surface and submerge, sometimes within less than a year. In this fast-paced, fluid environment, change is the only constant.

Successful firms lean forward and embrace the change. They seek the opportunities and avoid the pitfalls. They carefully evaluate risks. They completely understand their market, and they adhere to ethical practices. Their core goal: to generate long-term profits by delivering unsurpassed **value** to their customers.

Over the past few years, the explosive growth in Facebook and Twitter has played a pivotal part in forging a new role for both businesses and consumers in today's dynamic business environment. In a nod to Twitter, *AdvertisingAge* magazine dug through the most recent Census data and identified a host of trends in a "Twitter-Ready" 140-character format. Among the highlights:

- ➲ The median household income in the U.S. is roughly $50,000.
- ➲ The top 40% of Americans earn 75% of the money.
- ➲ Four in ten kids are born to single moms.
- ➲ By 2010, birthrates had dropped to an all-time record low.
- ➲ 60% of Americans now live in the South and West regions.
- ➲ 26% of men make six or more cell phone calls a day.[1]

1-1a Business Basics: Some Key Definitions

While you can certainly recognize a business when you see one, more formal definitions may help as you read through this book. A **business** is any organization that provides goods and services in an effort to earn a profit. **Profit** is the financial reward that comes from starting and running a business. More specifically, profit is the money that a business earns in sales (or revenue), minus expenses such as the cost of goods and the cost of salaries. But clearly, not every business earns a profit all the time. When a business brings in less money than it needs to cover expenses, it incurs a **loss**. If you launch a music label, for instance, you'll need to pay your artists, buy or lease a studio, and purchase equipment, among other expenses. If your label generates hits, you'll earn more than enough to cover all your expenses and make yourself rich. But a series of duds could leave you holding the bag. Just the possibility of earning a profit provides a powerful incentive for people of all backgrounds to launch their own enterprises. Despite the economic meltdown of 2008, American new business creation hit a 15-year high in 2009 and 2010.[2] You've probably noticed the entrepreneurial ambition among your peers as college students are flocking to entrepreneurship in the face of an uncertain economy.[3] People who risk their time, money, and other resources to start and manage a business are called **entrepreneurs.**

The *Forbes* list of the richest Americans highlights the astounding ability of the entrepreneurial spirit to build wealth. The top ten—featured in Exhibit 1.1—include multiple members of the Walton family who were not themselves entrepreneurs: their money comes from retail powerhouse Walmart, founded by brilliant, eccentric entrepreneur Sam Walton.

Interestingly, as entrepreneurs create wealth for themselves, they produce a ripple effect that enriches everyone around them. For instance, if your new website becomes

value The relationship between the price of a good or a service and the benefits that it offers its customers.

business Any organization that provides goods and services in an effort to earn a profit.

profit The money that a business earns in sales (or revenue), minus expenses, such as the cost of goods, and the cost of salaries. Revenue − Expenses = Profit (or Loss).

loss When a business incurs expenses that are greater than its revenue.

entrepreneurs People who risk their time, money, and other resources to start and manage a business.

the next Facebook, who will benefit? Clearly, *you* will. And you'll probably spend at least some of that money enriching your local clubs, clothing stores, and car dealerships. But others will benefit, too, including your members, advertisers on your site and the staff who support them, contractors who build your facilities, and the government that collects your taxes. The impact of one successful entrepreneur can extend to the far reaches of the economy. In fact, fast-growing new firms generate about 10% of all new jobs in any given year.[4] Multiply the impact by thousands of entrepreneurs—each working in his or her own self-interest—and you can see how the profit motive benefits virtually everyone.

From a bigger-picture perspective, business drives up the **standard of living** for people worldwide, contributing to a higher **quality of life**. Businesses not only provide the products and services that people enjoy but also provide the jobs that people need. Beyond the obvious, business contributes to society through innovation—think cars, TVs, and tablet computers. Business also helps raise the standard of living through taxes, which the government spends on projects that range from streetlights to environmental cleanup. Socially responsible firms contribute even more by actively advocating for the well-being of the society that feeds their success.

1-2 The History of Business: Putting It All in Context

You may be surprised to learn that—unlike today—business hasn't always been focused on what the customer wants. In fact, business in the United States has changed rather dramatically over the past 200–300 years. Most business historians divide the history of American business into five distinct eras, which overlap during the periods of transition:

➲ **The Industrial Revolution:** Technological advances fueled a period of rapid industrialization in America from the mid-1700s to the mid-1800s. As mass production took hold, huge factories replaced skilled artisan workshops. The factories hired large numbers of semiskilled workers who specialized in a limited number of tasks. The result was unprecedented production efficiency but also a loss of individual ownership and personal pride in the production process.

Exhibit 1.1
The Richest Americans 2011

NAME	NET WORTH	SOURCE OF WEALTH
BILL GATES	$59,000,000,000	Microsoft
WARREN BUFFETT	$39,000,000,000	Berkshire Hathaway
LARRY ELLISON	$33,000,000,000	Oracle
SHELDON ADELSON	$25,500,000,000	casinos
CHARLES KOCH	$25,000,000,000	diversified
DAVID KOCH	$25,000,000,000	diversified
CHRISTY WALTON	$24,500,000,000	Walmart
GEORGE SOROS	$22,000,000,000	hedge funds
JIM WALTON	$21,100,000,000	Walmart
ALICE WALTON	$20,900,000,000	Walmart
S. ROBSON WALTON	$20,500,000,000	Walmart
MICHAEL BLOOMBERG	$19,500,000,000	Bloomberg LP

Source: The Richest People in America, November 2011, Forbes magazine website, "http://www.forbes.com/forbes-400/list/, accessed January 10, 2012.

Ooops! What were they thinking?

Not Every Dumb Move Is an Utter Disaster...

In the wake of disastrous mistakes and outrageous misman-agement across our economy, it might be tough to remember that some mistakes are actually pretty amusing. But the *CBS MoneyWatch* website (formerly *BNET*) collected a number of examples that might help remind you.[5] A sampling:

- *"We care—NOT!!"* After shipping nearly 12 million poten-tially defective computers, a lawsuit against Dell alleges that the firm offered its sales force training that included tips such as: "Don't bring this to customer's attention pro-actively" and "Emphasize uncertainty."

- *The wrong kind of stimulus:* According to the Social Secu-rity Administration's Inspector General, more than 17,000 prison inmates and almost 72,000 dead people received economic stimulus checks from the federal government, totalling $22.3 million.

- *Do those chips come with ear plugs?* In 2010, PepsiCo, noisily introduced biodegradable packaging for its

Sun Chips brand but soon switched back to its non-recyclable bags after Facebook groups popped up with names such as: "Sorry but I can't hear you over this Sun Chips bag" and "I wanted Sun Chips but my roommate was sleeping." Testing indicated that the complainers had a legitimate point. Opening the biodegradable bags cre-ated more than 100 decibels of noise (similar to the noise level of a jet taking off at a distance of 300 meters).

- *Accidental cyber-snooping:* As Google sent its "Street View" cars all over the world collecting panoramic im-ages for uploading into GoogleMaps, the firm "uninten-tionally" collected and retained, among other things, passwords and complete email messages picked up from unsecured Wi-Fi networks.

- *Wasted time or well worthwhile?* To celebrate the 30th anniversary of Pac-Man in 2010, engineers at Google turned the site's home page into a fully functional ver-sion of the game, wasting an estimated 4.8 million hours of the world's time and more than $120 million in lost productivity.

- **The Entrepreneurship Era:** Building on the foun-dation of the industrial revolution, large-scale entre-preneurs emerged in the second half of the 1800s, building business empires. These industrial titans created enormous wealth, raising the overall standard of living across the country. But many also dominated their markets, forcing out competitors, manipu-lating prices, exploiting workers, and decimating the environment. Toward the end of the 1800s, the government stepped into the busi-ness realm, passing laws to regulate business and protect consumers and workers, creating more balance in the economy.

- **The Production Era:** In the early part of the 1900s, major businesses focused on further refining the pro-duction process and creating greater efficiencies. Jobs became even more specialized, increasing productivity and lowering costs and prices. In 1913, Henry Ford introduced

© Fotosearch/Archive Photos/Getty Images

When in doubt, we usually don't!

Most of us can probably think of a time when we should have taken some action, but instead we did nothing because doing nothing was easier. . . . Enter the choice architects, behavioral scientists who claim that businesses, governments, and other institutions can engineer our options to "nudge" us into making choices that are (ideally) more socially desirable or (from a business standpoint) more profitable than the choices that we'd make on our own. A couple of examples:

○ **Better Aim:** As most women who share toilets with men can attest, even the best-intentioned men don't seem to, uh, aim well when it comes to toilet hygiene. In busy restrooms, this is more than just a gross annoyance; dirty bathrooms increase cleaning costs and undermine brand image. Aad Kiedboom, an economist who worked for the Schiphol International Airport in Amsterdam, tackled this issue by etching the image of a black housefly onto the bowls of the airport's urinals, just to the left of the drain. As a result, "spillage" decreased 80%.

© iStockphoto.com/Dan Van Oss

○ **Musical Stairs:** In response to rising obesity rates, the city of Stockholm has retrofitted a staircase in its Odenplan subway station to resemble giant piano keys, which produce real sound, to encourage commuters to climb the stairs rather than ride the escalator. Hidden video footage suggests that so far it's been a resounding success—well used and fun for everyone.

Advocates argue that choice architects work for the good of society, encouraging—but never coercing—people to make positive choices. Critics argue that choice architects are manipulative—shoving rather than nudging, which interferes with peoples' freedom of choice. In the wrong hands, that can be dangerous. What is your perspective? In the hands of business, will choice architecture ultimately be positive or negative?[6]

---

the assembly line, which quickly became standard across major manufacturing industries. With managers focused on efficiency, the customer was an afterthought. But when customers tightened their belts during the Great Depression and World War II, businesses took notice. The "hard sell" emerged: aggressive persuasion designed to separate consumers from their cash.

○ **The Marketing Era:** After WWII, the balance of power shifted away from producers and toward consumers, flooding the market with enticing choices. To differentiate themselves from their competitors, businesses began to develop brands, or distinctive identities, to help consumers understand the differences among various products. The *marketing concept* emerged: a consumer focus that permeates

successful companies in every department, at every level. This approach continues to influence business decisions today as global competition heats up to unprecedented levels.

○ **The Relationship Era:** Building on the marketing concept, today, leading-edge firms look beyond each immediate transaction with a customer and aim to build long-term relationships. Satisfied customers can become advocates for a business, spreading the word with more speed and credibility than even the best promotional campaign. And cultivating current customers is more profitable than constantly seeking new ones. One key tool is technology. Using the Web and other digital resources, businesses gather detailed information about their customers and use these data to serve them better.

1-3 Nonprofits and the Economy: The Business of Doing Good

Nonprofit organizations play a critical role in the economy, often working hand-in-hand with businesses to improve the quality of life in our society. Focusing on areas such as health, human services, education, art, religion, and culture, **nonprofits** are business-*like* establishments, but their primary goals do not include profits. Chuck Bean, Executive Director of the Nonprofit Roundtable, explains: "By definition, nonprofits are not in the business of financial gain. We're in the business of doing good.

However, nonprofits are still businesses in every other sense—they employ people, they take in revenue, they produce goods and services and contribute in significant ways to our region's economic stability and growth." Nationwide, nonprofits employ about one in ten workers, accounting for more paid workers than the entire construction industry and more than the finance, insurance, and real-estate sectors combined. And nonprofit museums, schools, theaters, and orchestras have become economic magnets for many communities, drawing additional investment.[7]

Many businesses work with nonprofits to boost their impact in the community.

American Red Cross
Disaster Relief
ℹ REGISTRATION

AP Images/Tyler Morning Telegraph, Tom Worner

nonprofits Business-*like* establishments that employ people and produce goods and services with the fundamental goal of contributing to the community rather than generating financial gain.

factors of production Four fundamental elements—natural resources, capital, human resources, and entrepreneurship—that businesses need to achieve their objectives.

1-4 Factors of Production: The Basic Building Blocks

Both businesses and nonprofits rely on **factors of production**—four fundamental resources—to achieve their objectives. Some combination of these factors is crucial for an economic system to work and create wealth. As you read through the factors, keep in mind that they don't come free of charge. Human resources, for instance, require wages, while entrepreneurs need a profit incentive.

⊙ **Natural Resources:** This factor includes all inputs that offer value in their natural state, such as land, fresh water, wind, and mineral deposits. Most natural resources must be extracted, purified, or harnessed; people cannot actually create them. (Note that agricultural products, which people do create through planting and tending, are not a natural resource.) The value of all natural resources tends to rise with high demand, low supply, or both.

⊙ **Capital:** This factor includes machines, tools, buildings, information, and technology—the synthetic resources that a business needs to produce goods or services. Computers and telecommunications capability have become pivotal elements of capital across a surprising range of industries, from financial services to professional sports. You may be surprised to learn that in this context, capital does not include money, but, clearly, businesses use money to acquire, maintain, and upgrade their capital.

○ **Human Resources:** This factor encompasses the physical, intellectual, and creative contributions of everyone who works within an economy. As technology replaces a growing number of manual labor jobs, education and motivation have become increasingly important to human resource development. Given the importance of knowledge to workforce effectiveness, some business experts, such as management guru Peter Drucker, break out knowledge as its own category, separate from human resources.

○ **Entrepreneurship:** Entrepreneurs are people who take the risk of launching and operating their own businesses, largely in response to the profit incentive. They tend to see opportunities where others don't, and they use their own resources to capitalize on that potential. Entrepreneurial enterprises can kick-start an economy, creating a tidal wave of opportunity by harnessing the other factors of production. But entrepreneurs don't thrive in an environment that doesn't support them. The key ingredient is economic freedom: freedom of choice (whom to hire, for instance, or what to produce), freedom from excess regulation, and freedom from too much taxation. Protection from corruption and unfair competition is another entrepreneurial "must."

Clearly, all of these factors must be in place for an economy to thrive. But which factor is *most* important? One way to answer that question is to examine current economies around the world. Russia and China are both rich in natural resources and human resources, and both countries have a solid level of capital (growing in China, and deteriorating in Russia). Yet, neither country is wealthy; both rank relatively low in terms of gross national income per person. The missing ingredient seems to be entrepreneurship, limited in Russia largely through corruption and in China through government interference and taxes. Contrast those examples with, say, Hong Kong. The population is small, and the natural resources are severely limited, yet Hong Kong has consistently ranked among the richest regions in Asia. The

reason: operating for many years under the British legal and economic system, the government actively encouraged entrepreneurship, which fueled the creation of wealth. Recognizing the potential of entrepreneurship, China has recently done more to relax regulations and support free enterprise. The result has been tremendous growth, which may yet bring China into the ranks of the wealthier nations.[8]

1-5 The Business Environment: The Context for Success

No business operates in a vacuum. Outside factors play a vital role in determining whether each individual business succeeds or fails. Likewise, the broader **business environment** can make the critical difference in whether an overall economy thrives or disintegrates. The five key dimensions of the business environment are the economic environment, the competitive environment, the technological environment, the social environment, and the global environment, as shown in Exhibit 1.2.

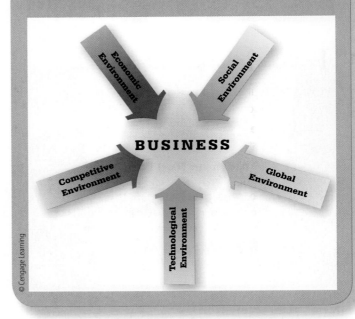

EXHIBIT 1.2
The Business Environment

Each dimension of the business environment affects both individual businesses and the economy in general.

Economic Environment

Social Environment

BUSINESS

Competitive Environment

Global Environment

Technological Environment

© Cengage Learning

1-5a The Economic Environment

In September 2008, the U.S. economy plunged into the worst fiscal crisis since the Great Depression. Huge, venerable financial institutions faced collapse, spurring unprecedented bailouts by the federal government and the Federal Reserve. By the end of the year, the stock market had lost more than a third of its value, and 11.1 million Americans were out of work. Housing prices fell precipitously, and foreclosure rates reached record levels. As fear swept through the banking industry, neither businesses nor individuals could borrow money to meet their needs. Economic turmoil in the United States spread quickly around the world, fueling a global economic crisis.

The U.S. economy continued to stagger through 2010 and 2011, with unemployment remaining stubbornly high, although signs of recovery began to emerge in late 2011 and early 2012. The Federal Reserve—the U.S. central banking system—took unprecedented, proactive steps to encourage an economic turnaround. And President Barack Obama spearheaded passage of a massive economic stimulus package, designed not only to create jobs but also to build infrastructure—with a focus on renewable energy—to position the U.S. economy for stability and growth in the decades to come. (The price, of course, was more national debt, which will ultimately counterbalance some of the benefits.)

The government also takes active steps on an ongoing basis to reduce the risks of starting and running a business. The result: free enterprise and fair competition flourish. Despite the economic crisis, research suggests that most budding entrepreneurs still plan to launch their

> "**A banker** is a fellow who lends you his umbrella when the sun is shining, but wants it back the minute it begins to rain."
>
> —MARK TWAIN, AUTHOR

firms in the next three years. One government policy that supports business is the relatively low federal tax rate, both for individuals and businesses. And President Obama has proposed lowering the tax rate even further for a large swath of individual taxpayers and businesses. A number of states—from Alabama to Nevada—make their local economies even more appealing by providing special tax deals to attract new firms. The federal government also runs entire agencies that support business, such as the Small Business Administration. Other branches of the government, such as the Federal Trade Commission, actively promote fair competitive practices, which help give every enterprise a chance to succeed.

Another key element of the U.S. economic environment is legislation that supports enforceable contracts. For instance, if you contract a company to supply your silk screening business with 1,000 blank tee shirts at $4.00 per piece, that firm must comply or face legal consequences. The firm can't wait until a day before delivery and jack up the price to $8.00 per piece because you would almost certainly respond with a successful lawsuit. Many U.S. businesspeople take enforceable contracts for granted,

Flex Your Creativity: Build Your Brainpower

In today's turbulent times, creativity matters more than ever. Here are some ideas to boost your brainpower:

○ **Exercise your mind:** Like any other skill, creativity must be trained to perform at full strength. So read about a wide range of topics. Do puzzles, turn off mindless TV, and nap when you need to.

○ **Listen to music:** Recent research from the National Science Foundation has affirmed that music is entwined in the neurological roots of the creative process in our brains.

○ **Take notes:** In school? Duh! But whenever inspiration strikes, jot down your ideas before you forget them. Reading your notes later, you may find that 99% of them are garbage, but 1% might well be brilliant.

○ **Embrace boredom:** Studies have shown that boredom can actually be "central to learning and creativity." So, next time you're bored, don't be too quick to whip out your smartphone—you may be cheating yourself (and the world) of your next big creative breakthrough.[9]

speed-to-market The rate at which a new product moves from conception to commercialization.

but in a number of developing countries—which offer some of today's largest business opportunities—contracts are often not enforceable (at least not in day-to-day practice).

Corruption also affects the economic environment. A low level of corruption and bribery dramatically reduces the risks of running a business by ensuring that everyone plays by the same set of rules—rules that are clearly visible to every player. Fortunately, U.S. laws keep domestic corruption mostly—but not completely—at bay. Other ethical lapses, such as shady accounting, can also increase the cost of doing business for everyone involved. But in the wake of ethical meltdowns at major corporations such as Enron and WorldCom, the federal government has passed tough-minded new regulations to increase corporate accountability. If the new legislation effectively curbs illegal and unethical practices, every business will have a fair chance at success.

Upcoming chapters on economics and ethics will address these economic challenges and their significance in more depth. But bottom line, we have reason for cautious (some would say *very* cautious) optimism. The American economy has a proven track record of flexibility and resilience, which will surely help us navigate this crisis and uncover new opportunities.

1-5b The Competitive Environment

As global competition intensifies yet further, leading-edge companies have focused on customer satisfaction like never before. The goal: to develop long-term, mutually beneficial relationships with customers. Getting current customers to buy more of your product is a lot less expensive than convincing potential customers to try your product for the first time. And if you transform your current customers into loyal advocates—vocal promoters of your product or service—they'll get those new customers for you more effectively than any advertising or discount program. Companies such as Amazon, Coca-Cola, and Nothwestern Mutual life insurance lead their industries in customer satisfaction, which translates into higher profits even when the competition is tough.[10]

Customer satisfaction comes in large part from delivering unsurpassed value. The best measure of value is the size of the gap between product benefits and price. A product has value when its benefits to the customer are equal to or greater than the price that the customer pays. Keep in mind that the cheapest product doesn't necessarily represent the best value. If a 99-cent toy from Big Lots breaks in

a day, customers may be willing to pay several dollars more for a similar toy from somewhere else. But if that 99-cent toy lasts all year, customers will be delighted by the value and will likely encourage their friends and family to shop at Big Lots. The key to value is quality, and virtually all successful firms offer top-quality products relative to their direct competitors.

A recent ranking study by consulting firm Interbrand highlights brands that use imagination and innovation to deliver value to their customers. Exhibit 1.3 shows the winners and the up-and-comers in the race to capture the hearts, minds, and dollars of consumers around the world.

Leading Edge versus Bleeding Edge Speed-to-market—the rate at which a firm transforms concepts into actual products—can be another key source of competitive advantage. And the pace of change just keeps getting faster. In this tumultuous setting, companies that stay ahead of the pack often enjoy a distinct advantage. But keep in mind that there's a difference between leading edge and bleeding edge. Bleeding-edge firms launch products that fail because

EXHIBIT 1.3:
2011 Global Brand Champions and the Ones to Watch, Interbrand

MOST VALUABLE BRANDS	BIGGEST GAINERS/ BRANDS	PERCENTAGE GAIN
COCA COLA	Apple	+58%
IBM	Google	+27%
MICROSOFT	Amazon	+32%
GOOGLE	Samsung	+20%
GE	Burberry	+20%
MCDONALD'S	Hyundai	+19%
INTEL	Caterpiller	+19%
APPLE	Cartier	+18%
DISNEY	eBay	+16%
HP	Adobe	+15%

Source: BestGlobal Brands 2011, Interbrand Website, http://www.interbrand.com/EN/best-global-brands/best-global-brands-2008/best-global-brands-2011.aspx, accessed August 16, 2012.

they're too far ahead of the market. During the late 1990s, for example, in the heart of the dot.com boom, WebVan, a grocery delivery service, launched to huge fanfare. But the firm went bankrupt just a few years later in 2001, partly because customers weren't yet ready to dump traditional grocery stores in favor of cyber-shopping. Leading-edge firms, on the other hand, offer products just as the market becomes ready to embrace them.[11]

Apple provides an excellent example of leading edge. You may be surprised to learn that Apple—which controls about 70%[12] of the digital music player market—did not offer the first MP3 player. Instead, it surveyed the existing market to help develop a new product, the iPod, which was far superior in terms of design and ease-of-use. But Apple didn't stop with one successful MP3 player. Racing to stay ahead, they soon introduced the colorful, more affordable iPod mini. And before sales reached their peak, they launched the iPod Nano, which essentially pulled the rug from under the blockbuster iPod mini just a few short months before the holiday selling season. Why? If they hadn't done it, someone else may well have done it instead. And Apple is almost maniacally focused on maintaining its competitive lead.[13]

1-5c **The Workforce Advantage**

Employees can contribute another key dimension to a firm's competitive edge. Recent research suggests that investing in worker satisfaction yields tangible, bottom-line results. The researchers evaluated the stock price of *Fortune* magazine's annual list of the "100 Best Companies to Work for in America" to the S&P 500, which reflects the overall market. In 2009, the heart of the Great Recession, the firms with the highest employee satisfaction provided a 10.3% annual return, compared to a 2.95% return for the firms in the S&P 500. While the critical difference in performance most likely stemmed from employee satisfaction, other factors—such as excellent product and superb top management—likely *also* played a role in both employee satisfaction and strong stock performance.[14]

Finding and holding the best talent will likely become a crucial competitive issue in the next decade, as the baby boom generation begins to retire. The 500 largest U.S. companies anticipate losing about half of their senior managers over the next five to six years. Since January 1, 2011, approximately 10,000 baby boomers began to turn 65 (the traditional retirement age) every day, and the Pew Research Center anticipates that this trend will continue for 19 years. Replacing the skills and experience these workers bring to their jobs may be tough: baby boomers include about 77 million people, while the generation that follows includes only 46 million. Firms that cultivate human resources now will find themselves better able to compete as the market for top talent tightens.[15]

1-5d **The Technological Environment**

The broad definition of **business technology** includes any tools that businesses can use to become more efficient and effective. But more specifically, in today's world, business technology usually refers to computers, telecommunications, and other digital tools. Over the past few decades, the impact of digital technology on business has been utterly transformative. New industries have emerged, while others have disappeared. And some fields—such as travel, banking, and music—have changed dramatically. Even in

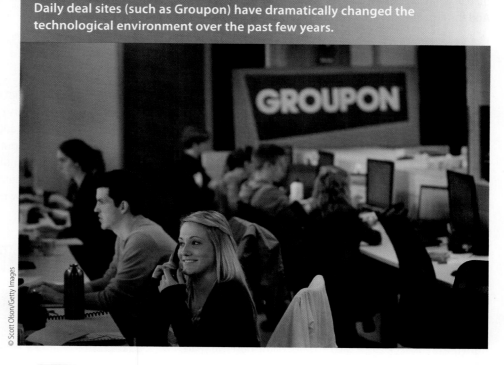

Daily deal sites (such as Groupon) have dramatically changed the technological environment over the past few years.

© Scott Olson/Getty Images

Innovation: For Better or for Worse

Creativity matters, not just for individual businesses, but also for the overall economy. And with global competition, the stakes are high. The editors of *Encyclopedia Britannica* recently explored creativity over time and across countries, compiling a list of the 100 greatest inventions of all time. The editors chose the winners—which they did not rank—based on how profoundly the innovations have affected human life—for better or for worse. Before you read further, consider which inventions you would place on the list. How have they affected human life? What inventions would you expect to find on the list in the future?

Many of the citations are not surprising, such as the computer, eyeglasses, gunpowder, candles, vaccinations, and the atomic bomb. Others are somewhat amusing, including disposable diapers (which *have* improved the quality of life for millions of parents worldwide!), cat litter, Astroturf (artificial grass), and Post-it notes. A few citations, such as Muzak (generic "elevator music") and bikinis, are somewhat puzzling, although they have clearly permeated contemporary culture.

While most of the inventions on this top 100 list are fairly recent, some are older than you might think. Flush toilets, for instance, have been around since the 1500s, although toilet tissue wasn't invented until 1857. Vending machines were invented in Egypt sometime between 200 and 100 BC. And the construction nail was invented by the Sumerians in about 3300 BC.

Interestingly, over the past century, corporations, rather than individuals, have been responsible for a growing number of key innovations. Examples include the Camcorder (Sony), the laptop computer (Radio Shack), and Viagra (Pfizer). This trend is only likely to build momentum as global competition intensifies.

The United States, despite our relatively short history, dominates the list of greatest inventions with 162 of 325 mentions, or just under 50%. One reason may be that our nation celebrates individuality, creativity, and, of course, the profit incentive. If we continue to flex our creative muscles, we could find ourselves with a competitive edge far into the twenty-first century.

Sometimes, accessing creativity is simply a matter of asking the right questions. Nottingham-Spirk, a successful industrial design firm responsible for a string of blockbuster new product hits, constantly asks questions of its own inventors, from the mild (e.g., "What can we do to make this 'NICE' product a 'WOW'?") to the wild (e.g., "What if the candy bar could levitate?"). And the firm uses the answers to all of these questions to drive innovation.[16]

categories with relatively unchanged products, companies have leveraged technology to streamline production and create new efficiencies. Examples include new processes such as computerized billing, digital animation, and robotic manufacturing. For fast-moving firms, the technological environment represents a rich source of competitive advantage, but it clearly can be a major threat for companies that are slow to adopt or to integrate new approaches.

The creation of the **World Wide Web** has transformed not only business, but also people's lives. Anyone, anywhere, anytime can use the Web to send and receive images and data (as long as access is available). One result is the rise of **e-commerce** or online sales, which allow businesses to tap into a worldwide community of potential customers. In the wake of the global economic crisis, e-commerce has slowed from the breakneck 20%+ growth rates of the past five years, but even so, analysts predict that solid growth will continue. Business-to-business selling comprises the vast majority of total e-commerce sales (and an even larger share of the profits). A growing number of businesses have also connected their digital networks with suppliers and distributors to create a more seamless flow of goods and services.[17]

"By 2014, there will probably be more **mobile** Web users than desktop users."

— UniversalMind

©iStockphoto.com/hohos

Alternative selling strategies thrive on the Internet, giving rise to a more individualized buying experience. If you've browsed seller reviews on eBay or received shopping recommendations from Amazon, you'll have a sense of how personal web marketing can feel. Online technology also allows leading-edge firms to offer customized products at prices that are comparable to standardized products. On the NikeID website, for instance, customers can "custom build" Nike shoes, clothing, and gear, all while sitting at home in their pajamas.

As technology continues to evolve at breakneck speed, the scope of change—both in everyday life and business operations—is almost unimaginable. In this environment, companies that welcome change and manage it well will clearly be the winners.

1-5e **The Social Environment**

The social environment embodies the values, attitudes, customs, and beliefs shared by groups of people. It also covers **demographics**, or the measurable characteristics of a population. Demographic factors include population size and density and specific traits such as age, gender, race, education, and income. Clearly, given all these influences, the social environment changes dramatically from country to country. And a nation as diverse as the United States features a number of different social environments. Rather than cover the full spectrum, this section will focus on the broad social trends that have the strongest impact on American business. Understanding the various dimensions

of the social environment is crucial since successful businesses must offer goods and services that respond to it.

Diversity While the American population has always included an array of different cultures, the United States has become more ethnically diverse in recent years. Caucasians continue to represent the largest chunk of the population at 66%, but the Hispanic and Asian populations are growing faster than any other ethnic groups. If current trends continue, according to the Pew Research Center, the overwhelming bulk of growth in the U.S. population in the coming decades will be due to immigration. In fact, by 2050, about 19% of Americans will be immigrants, compared with 12% in 2005. The Latino population will triple in size, and the Caucasian population will drop to less than half the U.S. population.[18] Exhibit 1.4 demonstrates the shifting population breakdown.

But the national statistics are somewhat misleading, since ethnic groups tend to cluster together. African Americans, for example, currently comprise about 37% of the Mississippi population, Asians comprise about 57% of the Hawaii population, and Hispanics comprise about 46% of the New Mexico population.[19]

So what does this mean for business? Growing ethnic populations offer robust profit potential for firms that pursue them. For instance, a number of major corporations such as AutoZone, Kellogg, Anheuser-Busch, PepsiCo, and

World Wide Web The service that allows computer users to easily access and share information on the Internet in the form of text, graphics, video, apps, and animation.

e-commerce Business transactions conducted online, typically via the Internet.

demographics The measurable characteristics of a population. Demographic factors include population size and density, as well as specific traits such as age, gender, and race.

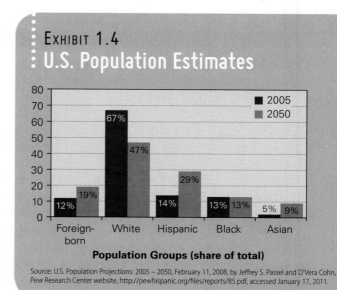

Exhibit 1.4
U.S. Population Estimates

Legend: ■ 2005 ■ 2050

Population Groups (share of total)	2005	2050
Foreign-born	12%	19%
White	67%	47%
Hispanic	14%	29%
Black	13%	13%
Asian	5%	9%

Source: U.S. Population Projections: 2005 – 2050, February 11, 2008, by Jeffrey S. Passel and D'Vera Cohn, Pew Research Center website, http://pewhispanic.org/files/reports/85.pdf, accessed January 17, 2011.

Say H₂No to "Mystery Chemicals"

Extreme sports athletes and their fans have become accustomed to both their venues and their top performers being flooded with sponsorship money. The flow is especially strong for snowboarders, given the relatively recent high profile of the sport (greater ESPN coverage, and inclusion in the Winter Olympics). Many athletes are thrilled, but two professional snowboarders, Bryan Fox and Austin Smith, rankled at being "a choice target-consumer for companies that sell 'energy drinks,'" such as Rockstar, Monster, and Red Bull. They feel "uncomfortable about how effective these companies have become at encouraging young people to consume their product: beverages of caffeine, sodium, sugar, high fructose corn syrup, and even some mystery chemicals about which little is known." In response, Fox and Austin launched a Drink Water movement, writing Drink Water on their snowboard decks alongside their sponsorship logos. Soon after, the duo started selling stickers, jackets, tee shirts, and sweatshirts with the Drink Water logo, and then launched a website. But Fox and Smith didn't stop there. Recognizing the very real danger of future global fresh water shortages, and the appalling fact that nearly one billion people today live without safe drinking water, Fox and Smith opted to donate 10% of Drink Water profits—driven from its apparel sales—to Water.org, a nonprofit that provides clean water and sanitation in Africa, southern Asia, and Central America. Fox and Smith clearly have entrepreneurial spirit that will make the world a better place in direct proportion to their success.[20]

Procter & Gamble have invested heavily in the Hispanic market over the past five years. In 2011, Kraft Foods tripled its spending on Hispanic marketing, spending more than half of its budget for Kool-Aid, in a first for any Kraft brand, on reaching Hispanics. Targeting an ethnic market can also yield remarkable results for products that cross over into mainstream culture. Music mogul and entrepreneur Russell Simmons, for example, initially targeted his music and clothing to the African American market, but his success quickly spilled over to mainstream culture, helping him build a hip-hop empire.[21]

Growing diversity also affects the workforce. A diverse staff—one that reflects an increasingly diverse marketplace—can yield a powerful competitive advantage in terms of both innovation and ability to reach a broad customer base. From global behemoths such as Coca-Cola and Verizon, to local corner stores, companies have taken proactive steps to hire and nurture people from a broad range of backgrounds. And that doesn't just reflect racial or ethnic roots. True diversity also includes differences in gender, age, religion, and nationality, among other areas. Leading-edge firms have also taken proactive steps to train their entire workforce to manage diversity for top performance.[22]

Effectively managing diversity should only become easier as time goes by. Multiple studies demonstrate that young American adults are the most tolerant age group, and they are moving in a more tolerant direction than earlier generations regarding racial differences, immigrants, and homosexuality. As this generation gathers influence and experience in the workforce, they are likely to leverage diversity in their organizations to hone their edge in a fiercely competitive marketplace.[23]

Aging Population As life spans increase and birthrates decrease, the American population is rapidly aging. As of the 2010 Census, its median age was 37.2, and it's increasing month by month. If current trends continue, the nation's elderly population will more than double between 2005 and 2050, and the number of working-age Americans will shrink from 63% to 58% of the population, dramatically increasing the number of people who are depending on each working American. And the United States isn't alone in this trend. The population is aging across the developed world, from Western Europe to Japan. China faces the same issue, magnified by its huge population. Demographers estimate that by the middle of the twenty-first century, China will be home to more than 330 million people age 65 or older, who will comprise a whopping 24% of its total population.[24]

The rapidly aging population brings opportunities and threats for business. Companies in fields that cater to the elderly—such as healthcare, pharmaceuticals, travel, recreation, and financial management—will clearly boom. But creative companies in other fields will capitalize on the trend as well by reimagining their current products to serve older clients. Possibilities include books, movies—maybe even video games—with mature characters; low-impact fitness programs such as water aerobics; and cell phones and PDAs with more readable screens. Again, the potential payoff of age diversity is clear: companies with older employees are more likely to find innovative ways to reach the aging consumer market.

But the larger numbers of retired people also pose significant threats to overall business success. With a smaller labor pool, companies will need to compete even harder for top talent, driving up recruitment and payroll costs. As state and federal governments stretch to serve the aging population, taxes may increase, putting an additional burden on business. And as mid-career workers spend more on elder care, they may find themselves with less to spend on other goods and services, shrinking the size of the consumer market.

Rising Worker Expectations Workers of all ages continue to seek flexibility from their employers. Moreover, following massive corporate layoffs in the early 2000s, employees are much less apt to be loyal to their firms. A 2011 MetLife survey showed that employee loyalty had hit a four-year low, although many employers were dangerously unaware of the morale meltdown. As young people today enter the workforce, they bring higher expectations for their employers in terms of salary, job responsibility, and flexibility—and less willingness to pay dues by working extra-long hours or doing a high volume of "grunt work." Smart firms are responding to the change in worker expectations by forging a new partnership with their employees. The goal is a greater level of mutual respect through open communication, information sharing, and training. And the not-so-hidden agenda, of course, is stronger, long-term performance.[25]

Ethics and Social Responsibility With high-profile ethical meltdowns dominating the headlines in the past few years, workers, consumers, and government alike have begun to hold businesses—and the people who run them—to a higher standard. Federal legislation, passed in the wake of the Enron fiasco, demands transparent financial management and more accountability from senior executives. And recognizing their key role in business success, a growing number of consumers and workers have begun to insist that companies play a proactive role in making their communities—and often the world community—better places. Sustainability—doing business today without harming

There need not be any conflict between the environment and the economy.

—AL GORE, NOBEL PEACE PRIZE WINNER

the ability of future generations to meet their needs—has become a core issue in the marketplace, driving business policies, investment decisions, and consumer purchases on an unprecedented scale.[26]

1-5f The Global Environment

The U.S. economy operates within the context of the global environment, interacting continually with other economies. In fact, over the past two decades, technology and free trade have blurred the lines between individual economies around the world. Technology has forged unprecedented

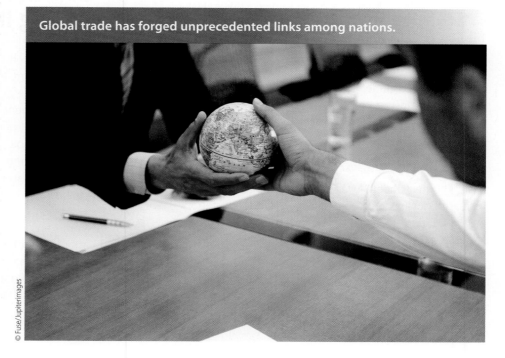

Global trade has forged unprecedented links among nations.

© Fuse/Jupiterimages

free trade An international economic and political movement designed to help goods and services flow more freely across international boundaries.

General Agreement on Tariffs and Trade (GATT) An international trade agreement that has taken bold steps to lower tariffs and promote free trade worldwide.

links among countries, making it cost effective—even efficient—to establish computer help centers in Bombay to service customers in Boston, or to hire programmers in Buenos Aires to make websites for companies in Stockholm. Not surprisingly, jobs have migrated to the lowest bidder with the highest quality—regardless of where that bidder is based.

Often, the lowest bidder is based in China or India. Both economies are growing at breakneck speed, largely because they attract enormous foreign investment. China has been a magnet for manufacturing jobs because of the high population and low wages—an average of $3.10 per hour versus $22.30 in the United States—although the gap is rapidly closing due to double digit annual wage inflation in China. And India has been especially adept at attracting high-tech jobs, in part because of their world-class, English-speaking university graduates who are willing to work for less than their counterparts around the globe.[27]

The migration of jobs relates closely to the global movement toward **free trade**. In 1995, a renegotiation of the **General Agreement on Tariffs and Trade (GATT)**—signed by 125 countries—took bold steps to lower tariffs (taxes on imports) and to reduce trade restrictions worldwide. The result: goods move more freely than ever across international boundaries. Individual groups of countries have gone even further, creating blocs of nations with virtually unrestricted trade. Mexico, Canada, and the United States have laid the groundwork for a free-trade mega-market through the North American Free Trade Agreement (NAFTA), and 25 European countries have created a powerful free-trading bloc through the European Union which has been weakened by a severe, ongoing financial crisis. The free-trade movement has lowered prices and increased quality across virtually every product category, as competition becomes truly global. We'll discuss these issues and their implications in more depth in Chapter 3.

A Multi-Pronged Threat In the past decade alone, war, terrorism, disease, and natural disasters have taken a horrific toll in human lives across the globe. The economic toll has been devastating as well, affecting businesses

"In Asia, the average person's living standards are currently set to rise by 10,000% in one lifetime!"

—Newsweek

© iStockphoto.com/Lasse Kristensen

around the world. The 9/11 terrorist attacks in New York and Washington, D.C., decimated the travel industry and led to multibillion-dollar government outlays for Homeland Security. In 2002, a terrorist bombing at an Indonesian nightclub killed nearly 200 people, destroying tourism on the holiday island of Bali. The 2003 deadly epidemic of the SARS flu dealt a powerful blow to the economies of Hong Kong, Beijing, and Toronto. Less than two years later, the Indian Ocean tsunami wiped out the fishing industry on long swaths of the Indian and Sri Lankan coastlines and crippled the booming Thai tourism industry. That same year, in 2005, Hurricane Katrina destroyed homes and businesses alike and brought the Gulf Coast oil industry to a virtual standstill. And the war in Iraq—while a boon to the defense industry—has dampened the economic potential of the Middle East. With nationalism on the rise, and growing religious and ethnic tensions around the world, the global economy may continue to suffer collateral damage.[28]

1-6 Business and You: Making It Personal

Whatever your career choice—from video game developer, to real estate agent, to web designer—business will affect your life. Both the broader economy and your own business skills will influence the level of your personal financial success. In light of these factors, making the right career choice can be a bit scary. But the good news is that experts advise graduating students to "Do what you love." This is a hardheaded strategy, not softhearted puffery. Following your passion makes dollars and sense in today's environment, which values less routine abilities such as creativity, communication, and caring. These abilities tend to be more rewarding for most people than routine, programmable skills that computers can easily emulate. Following your passion doesn't guarantee a fat paycheck, but it does boost your chances of both financial and personal success.[29]

THE BiG PICTURE

Business today is complex, global, and faster-moving than ever before. Looking forward, the rate of change seems likely to accelerate yet further. Although the full impact of the global economic crisis is still unclear, China and India seem poised to gain economic clout, raising worldwide competition to a whole new level. Technology will continue to change the business landscape. And a new focus on ethics and social responsibility will likely transform the role of business in society. This book will focus on the impact of change in every facet of business, from management to marketing to money, with an emphasis on how the elements of business relate to each other, and how business as a whole relates to you.

CAREERS

Business offers a growing range of exciting career opportunities. The possibilities include accounting, consulting, customer service, entrepreneurship, finance, human resources, marketing, real estate, retail, and sales. The specifics of each job are different depending on the industry and the company, although the core skills in each area usually transfer among industries. Entry-level pay is typically fairly low, but top jobs in business command top dollar. Most positions require at least a college degree, although some demand an advanced degree such as an MBA (Master of Business Administration) or a CPA (Certified Public Accountant). As customers, technology, and the business environment continue to change, your job will likely change considerably over the course of your career, regardless of your specific field. To succeed, you must be a fierce competitor, willing and able to actively embrace change.

What *else?*
RIP & REVIEW CARDS IN THE BACK
and visit www.cengagebrain.com!

2
Economics:
The Framework for Business

> ## "IN ECONOMICS IT IS A FAR, FAR WISER THING TO BE RIGHT THAN TO BE CONSISTENT."
>
> —John Kenneth Galbraith, Canadian American economist

2-1 Economics: Navigating a Crisis

In September 2008, the United States plunged into a deep economic crisis. The banking system hovered on the edge of collapse. Property values plummeted, and home foreclosure rates soared. Massive layoffs put more than a million Americans out of work. By the end of the year, the stock market had lost more than a third of its value, and financial turmoil in the United States had sparked sequential economic shocks from Europe, to South America, to Asia, and beyond. The outlook was grim.

How did this happen? Why? How could the economy get back on track?

Understanding these issues—and how the government responded to them—requires understanding some basic definitions: The **economy** is essentially a financial and social system. It represents the flow of resources through society, from production, to distribution, to consumption. **Economics** is the study of the choices that people, companies, and governments make in allocating those resources. The field of economics falls into two core categories: macroeconomics and microeconomics. **Macroeconomics** is the study of a country's overall economic dynamics, such as the employment rate, the gross domestic product, and taxation policies. While macroeconomic issues may seem abstract, they directly affect your day-to-day life, influencing key variables such as what jobs will be available for you, how much cash you'll actually take home after taxes,

or how much you can buy with that cash in any given month. **Microeconomics** focuses on smaller economic units such as individual consumers, families, and individual businesses. Both macroeconomics and microeconomics have played an integral role in the global economic crisis.

2-1a Global Economic Crisis: How Did This Happen?

The seeds of the crisis were planted more than a decade ago, during a time of prosperity. Through the last half of the 1990s, America enjoyed unprecedented growth. Unemployment was low, productivity was high, inflation was low, and the real standard of living for the average American rose significantly. The American economy grew by more than $2.4 trillion, a jump of nearly 33% in just five years. But the scene changed for the worse when the dot-com bubble burst in 2000, followed by the 9/11 terrorist attacks in 2001. As the stock market dropped and unemployment rose, economic experts feared that the country was hovering on the brink of a full-blown recession.[1]

In an effort to avert recession by increasing the money supply and encouraging investment, the Federal Reserve—the nation's central bank—decreased interest rates from 6.5% in mid-2000 to 1.25% by the end of 2002. As a result, the economy was awash with money, but opportunities to invest yielded paltry returns. This is when *subprime mortgage loans* came into play. Most experts define subprime mortgages as loans to borrowers with low credit scores, high debt-to-income ratios, or other signs of a reduced ability to repay the money they borrow.

These subprime mortgage loans were attractive to borrowers and lenders alike. For the borrowers, getting a loan suddenly became a cinch, and for the first time ever, hundreds of thousands of people could afford homes. The lenders were all too willing to give them mortgage loans, sometimes with little or no documentation (such as proof of income), and sometimes with little or no money down. As demand for homes skyrocketed, prices continued to rise year after year. Borrowers took on adjustable-rate loans assuming that when their loans adjusted up—usually sharply up—they could simply refinance their now-more-valuable homes for a new low starter rate and maybe even pull out some cash.

economy A financial and social system of how resources flow through society, from production, to distribution, to consumption.

economics The study of the choices that people, companies, and governments make in allocating society's resources.

macroeconomics The study of a country's overall economic dynamics, such as the employment rate, the gross domestic product, and taxation policies.

microeconomics The study of smaller economic units such as individual consumers, families, and individual businesses.

A *trillion* dollars? Say *what*??

Between stimulating the economy and bailing out the banking system, "a trillion dollars" is a figure you may have heard a lot lately. But getting your mind around what that actually means may be a little tricky, since it's just so much money. To understand the true magnitude of a trillion dollars, consider this:

- ❍ **If you had started spending a million dollars a day—every day, without fail—at the start of the Roman Empire, you still wouldn't have spent a trillion dollars by 2012; in fact, you'd have more than $250 billion left over.**

- ❍ **One trillion dollars, laid end-to-end, would stretch farther than the distance from the earth to the sun. You could also wrap your chain of bills more than 12,000 times around the earth's equator.**

- ❍ **If you were to fly a jet at the speed of sound, spooling out a roll of dollar bills behind you, it would take you more than 14 years to release a trillion dollars. But your plane probably couldn't carry the roll, since it would weigh more than one million tons.**

Turning the economy around may take even more than a trillion dollars, but make no mistake when you hear those numbers thrown around on the news—a trillion dollars is an awful lot of money!

Subprime loans were attractive to lenders because they provided a higher return than many other investments, and—given the growth in housing prices—they seemed relatively low risk. Banks and investment houses invented a range of stunningly complex financial instruments to slice up and resell the mortgages as specialized securities. Hedge funds swapped the new securities, convinced that they were virtually risk-free. With a lack of regulation—or any other government oversight—financial institutions did *not* maintain sufficient reserves in case those mortgage-backed funds lost value.

And they did indeed lose value. In 2006, housing prices peaked, and in the months that followed, prices began falling precipitously (see Exhibit 2.1), dropping nearly 35% from the market peak in 2006 through the market trough in 2009. Increasing numbers of subprime borrowers found themselves "upside down"—they owed their lenders more than the value of their homes. Once this happened, they couldn't refinance to lower their payments. Foreclosure rates climbed at an increasing pace. RealtyTrac, a leading online marketplace for foreclosure properties, reported that foreclosure rates were 33% higher in 2010 than they were in all of 2009. In 2011, the foreclosure rate dropped to the lowest level since 2007, when the recession began. Looking forward,

EXHIBIT 2.1 House Price Index

Source: Housing's Rise and Fall in 20 Cities, Dec. 27, 2011, *New York Times* website, http://www.nytimes.com/interactive/2011/05/31/business/economy/case-shiller-index.html#city/IND20, accessed January 25, 2012.

> "A billion here and a billion there, and pretty soon you're talking real **money.**"
>
> — U.S. Senator Everett Dirksen

RealtyTrac expects the 2012 foreclosure rate will be higher than 2011 but lower than the 2010 peak. The reasons are both continued high unemployment and a backlog of delinquencies working their way through the system.[2]

As mortgage values dropped, financial institutions began to feel the pressure—especially firms such as Bear Stearns that specialized in trading mortgage-backed securities, and firms such as Washington Mutual that focused on selling subprime mortgages. When financial institutions actually began to face collapse, a wave of fear washed over the entire banking industry. Banks became unwilling to lend money to each other or to clients, which meant that funds were not available for businesses to finance either day-to-day operations or longer-term growth. Company after company—from General Motors, to Yahoo!, to American Express, to countless small employers—began to announce layoffs. The December 2008 unemployment rate hit 7.2%. About 2.6 million Americans lost their jobs in 2008, making 2008 the worst year for jobs since 1945. And the unemployment rate continued to rise, hitting 9.3% in 2009, and 9.6% in 2010, leading to total Great Recession job losses of nearly 8 million, many of which will never come back as the economy continues to change, and old skills become obsolete.[3] The national average unemployment rate began to drop in late 2011–a hopeful sign–although it still remained much higher than ideal.

2-1b Moving in a Better Direction

Although the benefits were not immediately obvious in the face of a downward trend, the Federal Government and the Federal Reserve—known as "the Fed"—intervened in the economy at an unprecedented level to prevent total financial disaster. In March 2008, the Fed staved off bankruptcy at Bear Stearns. In early September 2008, the U.S. Department of the Treasury seized Fannie Mae and Freddie Mac, which owned about half of the U.S. mortgage market. A week later, the Fed bailed out tottering global insurance giant AIG with an $85 billion loan. But the bleeding continued.

The negative spiral spurred Congress to pass a $700 billion economic bailout plan in early October 2008, called TARP (the Troubled Assets Relief Program). By the end of the year, the Treasury had spent the first half of that money investing in banks, although early results were

"The President believes strongly that education is the economic defense budget of the 21st century."

— David Axelrod, President Obama's top political strategist

imperceptible for the economy. Just as the Treasury began to release funds to the banks, GM and Chrysler, two of the Big Three U.S. automakers, announced they also desperately needed a bailout. Both firms suggested that bankruptcy was imminent without government assistance. (Ford, the other member of the Big Three, also admitted to financial problems but claimed that it was not in the dire straits faced by its domestic competitors.) Facing the loss of more than 2.5 million jobs related to the auto industry, the Treasury agreed to spend a portion of what remained of the $700 billion in a partial auto industry bailout.[4] Although much of the public railed against the expensive government bailout program, by 2010 it appeared likely that TARP could end up costing taxpayers far less than anticipated, or even nothing, as insurance companies and banks began to break even, or in many cases earn profits, and pay back their government loans.[5]

As the new administration began, President Obama proposed, and Congress passed, an $825 billion economic stimulus package called the American Recovery and Reinvestment Act, designed to turn the economy around over the next two years. The plan included cutting taxes, building infrastructure, and investing $150 billion in green energy. By late 2011, the economy had begun to turn around at a very slow pace, although unemployment remained high, and economists predicted that the jobless rate would remain painfully high through the middle of the decade.[6]

All of these moves by the federal government and the Federal Reserve are part of fiscal and monetary policy.

2-2	# Managing the Economy Through Fiscal and Monetary Policy

While the free market drives performance in the American economy, the federal government and the Federal Reserve can help *shape* performance. During the recent crisis, both the government and the Fed have taken proactive roles to mitigate this economic contraction. The overarching goal is controlled, sustained growth, and both fiscal and monetary policy can help achieve this objective.

fiscal policy Government efforts to influence the economy through taxation and spending.

budget surplus Overage that occurs when revenue is higher than expenses over a given period of time.

budget deficit Shortfall that occurs when expenses are higher than revenue over a given period of time.

federal debt The sum of all the money that the federal government has borrowed over the years and not yet repaid.

2-2a Fiscal Policy

Fiscal policy refers to government efforts to influence the economy through taxation and spending decisions that are designed to encourage growth, boost employment, and curb inflation. Clearly, fiscal strategies are closely tied to political philosophy. But regardless of politics, most economists agree that lower taxes can boost the economy by leaving more money in people's pockets for them to spend or invest. Most also agree that government spending can boost the economy in the short term by providing jobs, such as mail carrier, bridge repairer, or park ranger; and in the long term by investing in critical public assets, such as a national renewable energy grid. Done well, both taxation and spending can offer economic benefits. The tricky part is finding the right balance between the two approaches.

Every year, the government must create a budget, or a financial plan, that outlines expected revenue from taxes and fees, and expected spending. If revenue is higher than spending, the government incurs a **budget surplus** (rare in recent years, but usually quite welcome!). If spending is higher than revenue, the government incurs a **budget deficit** and must borrow money to cover the shortfall. The sum of all the money borrowed over the years and not yet repaid is the total **federal debt**. Exhibit 2.2 shows key sources of revenue and key expenses for the federal government in 2011. Note that spending significantly outstrips receipts, creating a one-year budget deficit of more than a trillion dollars. Clearly, any additional spending without corresponding tax increases could dramatically increase the shortfall.

© Jose Luis Pelaez Inc./Blend Images/Jupiterimages

As of September 2012, the total U.S. federal debt stood at more than $16 trillion, a staggering $51,148.90 for every U.S.

EXHIBIT 2.2 Federal Government Revenue and Expenses

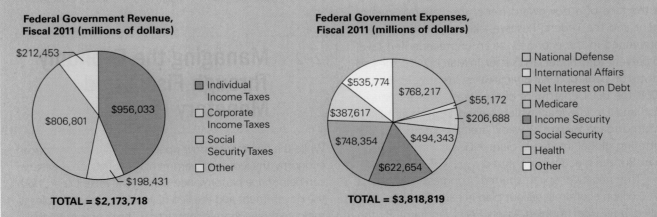

Federal Government Revenue, Fiscal 2011 (millions of dollars)

$212,453
$956,033
$806,801
$198,431

- Individual Income Taxes
- Corporate Income Taxes
- Social Security Taxes
- Other

TOTAL = $2,173,718

Federal Government Expenses, Fiscal 2011 (millions of dollars)

$535,774
$768,217
$55,172
$387,617
$206,688
$748,354
$494,343
$622,654

- National Defense
- International Affairs
- Net Interest on Debt
- Medicare
- Income Security
- Social Security
- Health
- Other

TOTAL = $3,818,819

Source: Economic Report of the President 2011, TABLE B–81. Federal receipts, outlays, surplus or deficit, and debt, fiscal years 2007–2012, http://www.gpoaccess.gov/eop/tables11.html, accessed January 25, 2012.

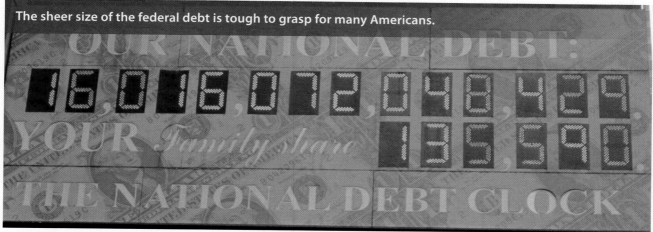

The sheer size of the federal debt is tough to grasp for many Americans.

OUR NATIONAL DEBT:

16,016,072,048,429.

YOUR *Family Share* 135,590.

THE NATIONAL DEBT CLOCK

© C. SCHNALL/Landov

citizen (see an online national debt clock at http://brillig.com/debt_clock/ for the latest figures).

The debt has only grown bigger every year since 1957, and the pace of growth will likely increase further in the wake of the economic crisis. This matters to each taxpayer because as the government repays the debt—not to mention paying the skyrocketing interest to finance this debt—less and less money will be available for other uses; services may be eliminated (e.g., student loans, veterans' benefits, housing subsidies), or taxes will soar, or perhaps even both.

PreOccupied with the 99%!

Fed up with big profits on Wall Street and bad news on Main Street, hordes of discouraged and disillusioned Americans took to the streets, public parks, and public lawns of the nation's cities in a loosely organized protest movement designed to demonstrate "that we are the 99% that will no longer tolerate the greed and corruption of the 1%." Central issues included:

- ◗ **The chronically high unemployment rate**
- ◗ **Income and wealth inequality**
- ◗ **The role of money in politics**
- ◗ **The high foreclosure rate**
- ◗ **The banking industry's perceived lack of accountability for the Great Recession**
- ◗ **Escalating college tuition and student loan burdens**

The Occupy Movement's "We are the 99%!" resonated with many Americans, especially in light of a report from the Congressional Budget Office stating that the top 1% of U.S. earners more than doubled their share of the nation's income over the past three decades.

Although inequality is clearly undesirable for those at the bottom, some may ask why it really matters, given that the American system gives everyone a chance to move into the top 1%. It matters most because inequality can actually *cause* economic crisis. When wealth concentrates at the top of the system, the wealthy encourage government to tax less and spend less on social programs such as unemployment benefits, worker retraining, public education, and the like. One result is that the quality of education suffers, and many college graduates are saddled with crushing student loan burdens—both of which effectively block the path to the top 1%. Another result is that the 99% have little or no cash on hand, which depresses broad-based consumption, which in turn depresses growth and employment. How we manage inequality may play a pivotal role in the long-term health of our economy.[7]

© MIKE GREENLAR/The Post-Standard/Landov

2-2b Monetary Policy

Monetary policy refers to actions that shape the economy by influencing interest rates and the supply of money. The Federal Reserve—essentially the central bank of the United States—manages U.S. monetary policy. For the first time in its history, the Fed has also taken an activist role in bailing out and propping up shaky financial firms during the economic crisis. Other Fed functions include banking services for member banks and the federal government.

The Fed is headed by a seven-member Board of Governors. The president appoints each member of the Board to serve a single 14-year term—though a member can also complete a former member's unexpired term and still be appointed to a full term of his or her own. These terms are staggered, with one expiring every two years, so that no single president can appoint all of the members. This structure helps ensure that the Fed can act independently of political pressure.

In addition to setting monetary policy, the Board of Governors oversees the operation of the 12 Federal Reserve Banks that carry out Fed policies and perform banking services for **commercial banks** in their districts. Interestingly, the federal government does not own these Federal Reserve Banks. Instead, they're owned by the member commercial banks in their individual districts.

The president appoints one of the seven members of the Board of Governors to serve as its Chairman—a position so powerful that many consider him the second most powerful person on Earth. For nearly 19 years, the chairman was Alan Greenspan. When Greenspan retired in early 2006, President Bush appointed economist Ben Bernanke to the chairman role. Bernanke has led the Fed's proactive efforts to turn the ailing economy around.

The core purpose of the Fed is to influence the size of the **money supply**—or the total amount of money within the overall economy. Clearly, you know what money is. But the formal definition of **money** is anything generally accepted as a medium of exchange, a measure of value, or a means of payment. The two most commonly used definitions of the money supply are M1 and M2:

- **M1**: All currency—paper bills and metal coins—plus checking accounts and traveler's checks.
- **M2**: All of M1 plus most savings accounts, money market accounts, and certificates of deposit (low-risk savings vehicles with a fixed term, typically less than one year).

As of July 2012, the M1 money supply totaled about $2.3 trillion, and the M2 version of the money supply totaled about $10.0 trillion. In practice, the term "money supply" most often refers to M2. (Note that credit cards are not part of the money supply, although they do have an unmistakable impact on the flow of money through the economy.)[8]

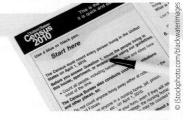

© iStockphoto.com/blackwaterimages

From Disruptive Demographics
Trends to Economic Aftershocks

The 2010 Census uncovered several major demographic shifts in the United States that will trigger significant economic change as they reverberate through our society.

- **South-shifting population:** More than half of the nation's population growth during the past decade occurred in Southern states.

- **Growing diversity:** Nonwhites accounted for about 85% of U.S. net population growth during the past decade.

- **More intermarriage:** Marriage across racial and ethnic lines has doubled since 1980.

- **Aging population:** About 8,000 Americans will turn 65 every day over the next five years, and they will live longer than previous generations.

- **Gender shift:** Women now hold nearly half of all paid U.S. jobs (49.8%), own 40% of all businesses, and hold 43% of executive, administrative, and managerial positions in the U.S. economy.

Researchers from the University of North Carolina point out that the trends bring both economic opportunities and challenges for businesses. For instance, the South now offers the largest and most diverse consumer markets for goods and services. Educated, high-income, older Americans will drive demand for new consumer electronics and other high-tech products related to "elder care." Meanwhile, a more diverse, multicultural population will require companies to develop new strategies for attracting customers and managing their workforces.[9]

When the economy contracts, the Fed typically increases the money supply. If more money is available, interest rates usually drop, encouraging businesses to expand and consumers to spend. But when prices begin to rise, the Fed attempts to reduce the money supply. Ideally, if less money is available, interest rates will rise. This will reduce spending, which should bring inflation under control. Specifically, the Fed uses three key tools to expand and contract the money supply: open market operations, discount rate changes, and reserve requirement changes.

Open Market Operations This is the Fed's most frequently used tool. **Open market operations** involve buying and selling government securities, which include treasury bonds, notes, and bills. These securities are the IOUs the government issues to finance its deficit spending.

How do open market operations work? When the economy is weak, the Fed *buys* government securities on the open market. When the Fed pays the sellers of these securities, money previously held by the Fed is put into circulation. This directly stimulates spending. In addition, any of the additional funds supplied by the Fed that are deposited in banks will allow banks to make more loans, making credit more readily available. This encourages even more spending and further stimulates the economy.

When inflation is a concern, the Fed *sells* securities. Buyers of the securities write checks to the Fed to pay for securities they bought, and the Fed withdraws these funds from banks. With fewer funds, banks must cut back on the loans they make, credit becomes tighter, and the money supply shrinks. This reduces spending and cools off the inflationary pressures in the economy.

Open market operations are set by the aptly named Federal Open Market Committee, which consists of the seven members of the Board of Governors and five of the twelve presidents of the Federal Reserve district banks. Each year, the Federal Open Market Committee holds eight regularly scheduled meetings to make decisions about open market operations, although they do hold additional meetings when the need arises. Both businesses and markets closely watch Open Market Committee rate setting and outlook statements in order to guide decision making.

© Keith Brofsky/Photodisc/Getty Images

Looking to Multiply Your Money? Look No Further Than Your Local Bank!

Everyone knows that banks help people save money, but most people don't realize that banks actually create money. While the process is complex, a simplified example illustrates the point. Say you deposit $5,000 in the bank. How much money do you have? Obviously, $5,000. Now imagine that your neighbor Anne goes to the bank for a loan. In line with Federal Reserve requirements, the bank must hold onto about 10% of its funds, so it loans Anne $4,500. She uses the money to buy a used car from your neighbor Jake, who deposits the $4,500 in the bank. How much money does Jake have? Clearly, $4,500. How much money do you have? Still, $5,000. Thanks to the banking system, our "money supply" has increased from $5,000 to $9,500. Multiply this phenomenon times millions of banking transactions, and you can see why cold, hard cash accounts for only about 10% of the total U.S. M2 money supply.[10]

But what happens if everyone goes to the bank at once to withdraw their money? The banking system would clearly collapse. And in fact, in 1930 and 1931, a run on the banks caused wave after wave of devastating bank failures. Panicked customers lost all their savings, ushering in the worst years of the Great Depression. To restore public confidence in the banking system, in 1933 Congress established the **Federal Deposit Insurance Corporation (FDIC)**. The FDIC insures deposits in banks and thrift institutions for up to $100,000 per customer, per bank. In the wake of the banking crisis, the FDIC temporarily increased its coverage to $250,000 per depositor at the end of 2008. Since the FDIC began operations on January 1, 1934, no depositor has lost a single cent of insured funds as a result of a bank failure.[11]

Discount Rate Changes Just as you can borrow money from your bank, your bank can borrow funds from the Fed. And, just as you must pay interest on your loan, your bank must pay interest on loans from the Fed. The **discount rate** is the interest rate the Fed charges on its loans to commercial banks. When the Fed reduces the discount rate, banks can obtain funds at a lower cost and use these funds to make more loans to their own customers. With the cost of acquiring funds from the Fed lower, interest rates on bank loans also tend to fall. The result: businesses and individuals are more likely to borrow money and spend it, which stimulates the economy. Clearly, the Fed is most likely to reduce the discount rate during recessions. In fact, during the early months of the financial crisis, the Fed cut the rate to less than 1%. But in response to inflation—usually a sign of a rapidly expanding economy—the Fed usually increases the discount rate. In response, banks raise the interest rates they charge their customers. Fewer businesses and individuals are willing to take loans, which ultimately slows down the economy and reduces inflation.[12]

Reserve Requirement Changes The Fed requires that all of its member banks hold funds called "reserves," equal to a stated percentage of the deposits held by their customers. This percentage is called the **reserve requirement** (or required reserve ratio). The reserve requirement helps protect depositors who may want to withdraw their money without notice. Currently, the reserve requirement stands at about 10%, depending on the size and type of a bank's deposits. If the Fed increases the reserve requirement, banks must hold more funds, meaning they will have fewer funds available to make loans. This makes credit tighter and causes interest rates to rise. If the Fed decreases the reserve requirement, some of the funds that banks were required to hold become available for loans. This increases the availability of credit and causes interest rates to drop. Since changes in the reserve requirement can have a dramatic impact on both the economy and the financial health of individual banks, the Fed uses this tool quite infrequently.

Other Fed Functions In addition to monetary policy, the Fed has several other core functions, including regulating financial institutions and providing banking services both for the government and for banks. In its role as a regulator, the Fed sets and enforces rules of conduct for

"About 20% of American households do not use standard **banking** services."

—TIME MAGAZINE

banks and oversees mergers and acquisitions to ensure fairness and compliance with government policy. The Fed will likely become even more proactive regarding regulation in the wake of the financial crisis. In its role as a banker for banks, the Fed coordinates the check-clearing process for checks on behalf of any banks that are willing to pay its fees. And as the government's bank, the Fed maintains the federal government's checking account and keeps the U.S. currency supply in good condition.

2-3 Capitalism: The Free Market System

It's a simple fact—more clear now than ever before—no one can get everything they want all of the time. We live in a world of finite resources, which means that societies must determine how to distribute resources among their members. An **economic system** is a structure for allocating limited resources. Over time and around the globe, nations have instituted different economic systems. But a careful analysis suggests that no system is perfect, which may explain why there isn't one standard approach. The next sections of this chapter examine each basic type of economic system and explore the trend toward mixed economies.

The economic system of the United States is called **capitalism**, also known as a "private enterprise system" or a "free market system." Brought to prominence by Adam

Smith in the 1700s, capitalism is based on private ownership, economic freedom, and fair competition. One core capitalist principle is the paramount importance of individuals, innovation, and hard work. In a capitalist economy, individuals, businesses, or nonprofit organizations privately own the vast majority of enterprises (with only a small fraction owned by the government). These private-sector businesses are free to make their own choices regarding everything from what they will produce, to how much they will charge, to whom they will hire and fire. Correspondingly, individuals are free to choose what they will buy, how much they are willing to pay, and where they will work.

To thrive in a free enterprise system, companies must offer value to their customers—otherwise, their customers will choose to go elsewhere. Businesses must also offer value to their employees and suppliers in order to attract top-quality talent and supplies. As companies compete to attract the best resources and offer the best values, quality goes up, prices remain reasonable, and choices proliferate, raising the standard of living in the economy as a whole.

2–3a The Fundamental Rights of Capitalism

For capitalism to succeed, the system must ensure some fundamental rights—or freedoms—to all of the people who live within the economy.

- ⊙ *The right to own a business and keep after-tax profits:* Remember that capitalism doesn't guarantee that anyone will actually *earn* profits. Nor does it promise that there won't be taxes. But if you do earn profits, you get to keep your after-tax income and spend it however you see fit (within the limits of the law, of course). This right acts as a powerful motivator for business owners in a capitalist economy; the lower the tax rate, the higher the motivation. The U.S. government strives to maintain low tax rates to preserve the after-tax profit incentive that plays such a pivotal role in the free enterprise system.

- ⊙ *The right to private property:* This means that individuals and private businesses can buy, sell, and use property—which includes land, machines, and buildings—in any way that makes sense to them. This right also includes the right to will property to family members. The only exceptions to private property rights are minimal government restrictions designed to protect the greater good. You can't, for instance, use your home or business to produce cocaine, abuse children, or spew toxic smoke into the air.

- ⊙ *The right to free choice:* Capitalism relies on economic freedom. People and businesses must be free to buy (or not buy) according to their wishes. They must be free to choose where to work (or not work) and where to live (or not live). Freedom of choice directly feeds competition, creating a compelling incentive for business owners to offer the best goods and services at the lowest prices. U.S. government trade policies boost freedom of choice by encouraging a wide array of both domestic and foreign producers to compete freely for our dollars.

- ⊙ *The right to fair competition:* A capitalist system depends on fair competition among businesses to drive higher quality, lower prices, and more choices. Capitalism can't achieve its potential if unfair practices—such as deceptive advertising, predatory pricing, and broken contracts—mar the free competitive environment. The government's role is to create a level playing field by establishing regulations and monitoring the competition to ensure compliance.

2–3b Four Degrees of Competition

Although competition is essential for the free market system to function, not all competition works the same. Different industries experience different degrees of competition, ranging from pure competition to monopolies.

- ⊙ **Pure competition** is a market structure with many competitors selling virtually identical products. Since customers can't (or won't) distinguish one product from another, no single producer has any control over the price. And new producers can easily enter and leave purely competitive markets. In today's U.S. economy, examples of pure competition have virtually disappeared. Agriculture probably comes closest—corn is basically corn, for example—but with the dramatic growth of huge corporate farms and the success of major cooperatives such as Sun-Maid, the number of competitors in agriculture has dwindled, and new farmers have trouble entering the market. Not only that, segments of the agriculture market—such as organic farms and hormone-free dairies—have emerged with hit products that command much higher prices than the competition.

- ⊙ **Monopolistic competition** is a market structure with many competitors selling differentiated products. (Caution! Monopolistic competition is quite different from

pure competition A market structure with many competitors selling virtually identical products. Barriers to entry are quite low.

monopolistic competition A market structure with many competitors selling differentiated products. Barriers to entry are low.

oligopoly A market structure with only a handful of competitors selling products that can be similar or different. Barriers to entry are typically high.

monopoly A market structure with one producer completely dominating the industry, leaving no room for any significant competitors. Barriers to entry tend to be virtually insurmountable.

a *monopoly,* which we will cover shortly.) Producers have some control over the price of their wares, depending on the value that they offer their customers. And new producers can fairly easily enter categories marked by monopolistic competition. In fact, in monopolistic competition, a successful product usually attracts new suppliers quite quickly. Examples of monopolistic competition include the clothing industry and the restaurant business.

Think about the clothing business, for a moment, in local terms. How many firms do you know that sell tee shirts? You could probably think of at least 50 without too much trouble. And the quality and price are all over the board: designer tee shirts can sell for well over $100, but plenty of options go for less than $10. How hard would it be to start your own tee shirt business? Probably not hard at all. In fact, chances are strong that you know at least one person who sells tee shirts on the side. In terms of product and price variation, number of firms, and ease of entry, the tee shirt business clearly demonstrates the characteristics of monopolistic competition.

⊙ **Oligopoly** is a market structure with only a handful of competitors selling products that can be similar or different. The retail gasoline business and the car manufacturing industry, for instance, are both oligopolies, even though gas stations offer very similar products, and car companies offer quite different models and features. Other examples of oligopoly include the soft drink industry, the computer business, and network television. Breaking into a market characterized by oligopoly can be tough because it typically requires a huge upfront investment.

Pay as You Throw

Admit it! Every so often, you've thrown away a can or a bottle that you really should have recycled, right? Would you have made the same choice if you had to pay your city for every piece of trash you threw away? A growing number of communities across the country are implementing "pay as you throw" (PAYT) programs that charge residents for waste collection based on the amount of waste they throw away—in the same way that they are charged for electricity, gas, and other utilities. As a result, residents are motivated not only to recycle more but also to think about ways to generate less waste in the first place. In fact, communities with PAYT programs report average reductions in waste amounts ranging from 25 to 35%. Recycling tends to increase significantly as well, further cutting down on the amount of waste requiring disposal. This can mean lower disposal costs, savings in waste transportation expenses, potentially greater revenues from the sale of recovered materials, and other cost savings. Obviously, PAYT programs work for the environment, but more recycling also works for the economy. According to the EPA, the American recycling industry is larger than our auto industry. In addition, for every 10,000 tons of solid waste going to landfills, 1 job is created. That same amount of waste—kept out of landfills—can create 10 recycling jobs or 75 materials reuse jobs. In fact, a recent study showed that a stronger recycling economy would create 1.5 million new jobs in manufacturing, collection, and other careers with family-supporting wages. So next time you're tempted to chuck an empty bottle or a finished newspaper, take an extra moment, and find a recycling bin.[13]

© Apollofoto/Shutterstock.com

You could start making tee shirts in your kitchen, for instance, but you'd need a pretty expensive facility to start manufacturing cars. Oligopolies typically avoid intense price competition, since they have nothing to gain—every competitor simply makes less money. When price wars do flare up, the results can be devastating for entire industries.

⊙ **Monopoly** is a market structure with just a single producer completely dominating the industry, leaving no room for any significant competitors. Monopolies usually aren't good for anyone but the company that has control since without competition there isn't any incentive to hold down prices or increase quality and choices. Because monopolies can harm the economy, most are illegal according to federal legislation, such as the Sherman Antitrust Act of 1890 and the Clayton Antitrust Act of 1914. Microsoft is the latest example of an industry giant that ran afoul of antimonopoly laws due to its position and policies in the software business. Even though Microsoft is not an actual monopoly, it was convicted of "monopolistic practices" that undermined fair competition.

However, in a few instances, the government not only allows monopolies but actually encourages them. This usually occurs when it would be too inefficient for each competitor to build its own infrastructure to serve the public. A **natural monopoly** arises. Cable television offers a clear example. Would it really make sense for even a handful of competitors to wire neighborhoods separately for cable? Clearly, that's not practical. Just imagine the chaos! Instead, the government has granted cable franchises—or monopolies—to individual companies and then regulated them (with mixed results) to ensure that they don't abuse the privilege. In addition to natural monopolies, the government grants patents and copyrights, which create artificial monopoly situations (at least temporarily) to encourage innovation.

2-3c Supply and Demand: Fundamental Principles of a Free Market System

In a free market system, the continual interplay between buyers and sellers determines the selection of products and prices available in the economy. If a business makes something that few people actually want, sales will be low, and the firm will typically yank the product from the market. Similarly, if the price of a product is too high, low sales will dictate a price cut. But if a new good or service becomes a hit, you can bet that similar offerings from other firms will pop up almost immediately (unless barriers—such as government-granted patents—prevent new entrants). The concepts of supply and demand explain how the dynamic interaction between buyers and sellers directly affects the range of products and prices in the free market.

Supply Supply refers to the quantity of products that producers are willing to offer for sale at different market prices. Since businesses seek to make as much profit as possible, they are likely to produce more of a product

that commands a higher market price and less of a product that commands a lower price. Think about it in terms of pizza. Assume it costs a local restaurant about $5 to make a pizza. If the market price for pizza hits, say, $20, you can bet that restaurant will start cranking out pizza. But if the price drops to $6, the restaurant has much less incentive to focus on pizza and will probably invest its limited resources in cooking other, more pricy, dishes.

The relationship between price and quantity from a supplier standpoint can be shown on a graph called the **supply curve.** The supply curve maps quantity on the x-axis (or horizontal axis) and price on the y-axis (or vertical axis). In most categories, as the price rises, the quantity produced rises correspondingly, yielding a graph that curves up as it moves to the right. Exhibit 2.3 shows a possible supply curve for pizza.

Demand Demand refers to the quantity of products that consumers are willing to buy at different market prices.

EXHIBIT 2.3 Supply Curve

Price per Pizza ($) vs. Quantity of Pizza Supplied per Day (in Thousands)

© Cengage Learning 2013

demand curve The graphed relationship between price and quantity from a customer demand standpoint.

equilibrium price The price associated with the point at which the quantity demanded of a product equals the quantity supplied.

socialism An economic system based on the principle that the government should own and operate key enterprises that directly affect public welfare.

Since consumers generally seek to get the products they need (or want) at the lowest possible prices, they tend to buy more products with lower prices and fewer products with higher prices. Pizza and tacos, for instance, are both popular meals. But if pizza costs a lot less than tacos, most people will get pizza more often than tacos. Likewise, if the price of pizza were out of hand, people would probably order tacos (or some other option) more often, reserving their pizza-eating for special occasions.

The relationship between price and quantity from a demand standpoint can be shown on a graph called the **demand curve.** Like the supply curve, the demand curve maps quantity on the x-axis and price on the y-axis. But different from the supply curve, the demand curve for most goods and services slopes downward as it moves to the right, since the quantity demanded tends to drop as prices rise. Exhibit 2.4 shows how a demand curve for pizza could look.

Equilibrium Price It's important to remember that supply and demand don't operate in a vacuum. The constant interaction between the two forces helps determine the market price in any given category. In theory, market prices adjust toward the point where the supply

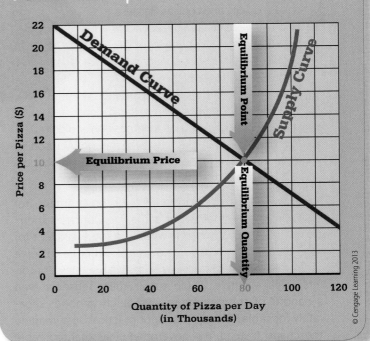

EXHIBIT 2.5 Equilibrium

© Cengage Learning 2013

curve and the demand curve intersect (see Exhibit 2.5). The price associated with this point of intersection—the point where the quantity demanded equals the quantity supplied—is called the **equilibrium price**, and the quantity associated with this point is called the "equilibrium quantity."

EXHIBIT 2.4 Demand Curve

© Cengage Learning 2013

2-4 Planned Economies: Socialism and Communism

In capitalist economies, private ownership is paramount. Individuals own businesses, and their personal fortunes depend on their success in the free market. But in planned economies, the government plays a more heavy-handed role in controlling the economy. The two key categories of planned economies are socialism and communism.

2-4a Socialism

Socialism is an economic system based on the principle that the government should own and operate key enterprises that directly affect public welfare, such as utilities, telecommunications, and healthcare. Although the official government goal is to run these enterprises in the best interest of the overall public, inefficiencies and corruption often interfere with effectiveness. Socialist economies also tend to have higher taxes, which are designed to distribute wealth more evenly through society. Tax revenues typically fund services that citizens in free enterprise systems would have to pay for themselves in countries with lower tax rates. Examples range from free childcare to free university education to free public healthcare systems. Critics of the recent government intervention in the U.S. economy believe that the new moves have pushed us too far in a socialist direction.

Most Western European countries—from Sweden, to Germany, to the United Kingdom—developed powerful socialist economies in the decades after World War II. But more recently, growth in these countries has languished. Although many factors have contributed to the slowdown, the impact of high taxes on the profit incentive and lavish social programs on the work incentive has clearly played a role. Potential entrepreneurs may migrate to countries that let them keep more of their profits, and workers with abundant benefits may find themselves losing motivation. In late 2010, many of these economies imposed stiff austerity measures to control government spending, eliminating some public benefits many took for granted.

2-4b Communism

Communism is an economic and political system that calls for public ownership of virtually all enterprises, under the direction of a strong central government. The communist concept was the brainchild of political philosopher Karl Marx, who outlined its core principles in his 1848 *Communist Manifesto*. The communism that Marx envisioned was supposed to dramatically improve the lot of the worker at the expense of the super-rich.

But countries that adopted communism in the 1900s—most notably the former Soviet Union, China, Cuba, North Korea, and Vietnam—did not thrive. Most imposed authoritarian governments that suspended individual rights and choices. People were unable to make even basic choices such as where to work or what to buy. Without the free market to establish what to produce, crippling shortages and surpluses developed. Corruption infected every level of government. Under enormous pressure from their own people and the rest of the world, communism began to collapse across the Soviet Union

and its satellite nations. At the end of the 1980s, it was replaced with democracy and the free market. Over the past two decades, China has also introduced significant free market reforms across much of the country, fueling its torrid growth rate. And in the 1990s, Vietnam launched free market reforms, stimulating rapid, sustained growth. The remaining communist economic systems— North Korea and Cuba—continue to falter, their people facing drastic shortages and even starvation.

communism An economic and political system that calls for public ownership of virtually all enterprises, under the direction of a strong central government.

mixed economies Economies that embody elements of both planned and market-based economic systems.

privatization The process of converting government-owned businesses to private ownership.

Mixed Economies: The Story of the Future

In today's world, pure economies—market or planned— are practically nonexistent, since each would fall far short of meeting the needs of its citizens. A pure market economy would make insufficient provision for the old, the young, the sick, and the environment. A pure planned economy would not create enough value to support its people over the long term. Instead, most of today's nations have **mixed economies**, falling somewhere along a spectrum that ranges from pure planned at one extreme to pure market at the other.

Even the United States—one of the most market-oriented economies in the world—does not have a *pure* market economy. The various departments of the government own a number of major enterprises, including the postal service, schools, parks, libraries, entire systems of universities, and the military. In fact, the federal government is the nation's largest employer, providing jobs for more than 4 million Americans. And—although the government does not directly *operate* firms in the financial sector—the federal government has become part owner in a number of financial institutions as part of the recent bailouts. The government also intervenes extensively in the free market by creating regulations that stimulate competition and protect both consumers and workers. Regulations are likely to become stronger in the wake of the economic crisis.[14]

Over the past 30 years, most economies of the world have begun moving toward the market end of the spectrum. Government-owned businesses have converted to private ownership via a process called **privatization**. Socialist governments have reduced red tape, cracked down on corruption, and created new laws to protect economic rights. Extravagant human services—from free healthcare to education subsidies—have shrunk. And far-reaching tax reform has created new incentives for both domestic and foreign investment in once-stagnant planned economies.[15]

Unfortunately, the price of economic restructuring has been a fair amount of social turmoil in many nations undergoing market reforms. Countries from France to China have experienced sometimes violent demonstrations in response to social and employment program cutbacks. Change is challenging, especially when it redefines economic winners and losers. But countries that have taken strides toward the market end of the spectrum—from small players such as the Czech Republic, to large players such as China—have seen the payoff in rejuvenated growth rates that have raised the standard of living for millions of people.

2-6 Evaluating Economic Performance: What's Working?

Clearly, economic systems are complex—very complex. So you probably won't be surprised to learn that no single measure captures all the dimensions of economic performance. To get the full picture, you need to understand a range of terms and measures, including gross domestic product, employment level, the business cycle, inflation rate, and productivity.

2-6a Gross Domestic Product

Real **gross domestic product**, or GDP, measures the total value of all final goods and services produced within a nation's physical boundaries over a given period of time, adjusted for inflation. (Nominal GDP does not include an inflation adjustment.) All domestic production is included in the GDP, even when the producer is foreign-owned. The U.S. GDP, for instance, includes the value of Hyundai cars built in Alabama, even though Hyundai is a South Korean firm. Likewise, the Indonesian GDP includes the value of Nike shoes manufactured in Indonesian factories, even though Nike is an American firm.

GDP is a vital measure of economic health. Business people, economists, and political leaders use GDP to measure the economic performance of individual nations and

"Raising a child from birth to age 17 costs about $235,000 (not including college!)."

— U.S. Department of Agriculture

to compare the growth among nations. Interestingly, GDP levels tend to be somewhat understated, since they don't include any illegal activities—such as paying undocumented nannies and gardeners, or selling illegal drugs—which can represent a significant portion of some countries' production. The GDP also ignores legal goods that are not reported to avoid taxation, plus output produced within households. In 2011, the GDP of the United States was just over $15.29 trillion, reflecting sluggish 1.7% growth rate versus 2010.[16] Check out Chapter 3 for a survey of the world's key economies according to total GDP and GDP growth rate.

2-6b Employment Level

The overall level of employment is another key element of economic health. When people have jobs, they have money, which allows them to spend and invest, fueling economic growth. Most nations track employment levels largely through the **unemployment rate**, which includes everyone age 16 and older who doesn't have a job and is actively seeking one. The U.S. unemployment rate climbed precipitously through the Great Recession, rising from 5.8% in 2008 to 9.3% in 2009, to 9.4% by December 2010. As the economy began its glacially slow turnaround, unemployment dropped to 8.1% in April 2012, but competition for new job openings remains fierce, since the recession wiped out a staggering 8 million jobs, leaving a record 70 applicants to contend for each open position.[17]

GDP is a vital measure of economic health.

© James Shearman/Atomic Imagery/Digital Vision/Jupiterimages

Interestingly, some unemployment is actually good—it reflects your freedom to change jobs. If you have an awful boss, for instance, you may just quit. If you quit, are you unemployed? Of course you are. Are you glad? You probably are, and in normal times, the chances are good that you'll find another position that's a better fit for you. This type of job loss is called *frictional unemployment*, and it tends to be ultimately positive. *Structural unemployment*, on the other hand, is usually longer term. This category encompasses people who don't have jobs because the economy no longer needs their skills. In the United States, growing numbers of workers in the past decade have found themselves victims of structural unemployment as manufacturing jobs have moved overseas. Often their only option is expensive retraining. Two other categories of unemployment are *cyclical*, which involves layoffs during recessions, and *seasonal*, which involves job loss related to the time of year. In some areas of the country, construction and agricultural workers are seasonally unemployed, but the best example may be the department store Santa who has a job only during the holiday season!

2-6c The Business Cycle

The **business cycle** is the periodic contraction and expansion that occurs over time in virtually every economy. But the word "cycle" may be a little misleading, since it implies that the economy contracts and expands in a predictable pattern. In reality, the phases of the cycle are different each time they happen, and—despite the efforts of countless experts—no one can accurately predict when changes will occur or how long they will last. Those who make the best guesses stand to make fortunes, but bad bets can be financially devastating. The two key phases of the business cycle are contraction and expansion, shown in Exhibit 2.6.

❍ **Contraction** is a period of economic downturn, marked by rising unemployment. Businesses cut back on production, and consumers shift their buying patterns to more basic products and fewer luxuries. The economic "feel-good factor" simply disappears. Economists declare an official **recession** when GDP decreases for two consecutive quarters. A **depression** is an especially deep and long-lasting recession. Fortunately, economies seldom spiral into severe depressions, thanks in large part to proactive intervention from the government. The last depression in the United States was the Great Depression of the 1930s. Whether a downturn is mild or severe, the very bottom of the contraction is called the "trough," as shown in Exhibit 2.6.

business cycle The periodic contraction and expansion that occur over time in virtually every economy.

contraction A period of economic downturn, marked by rising unemployment and falling business production.

recession An economic downturn marked by a decrease in the GDP for two consecutive quarters.

depression An especially deep and long-lasting recession.

> It's a recession when your neighbor loses his job; it's a depression when you lose yours.
>
> — HARRY TRUMAN

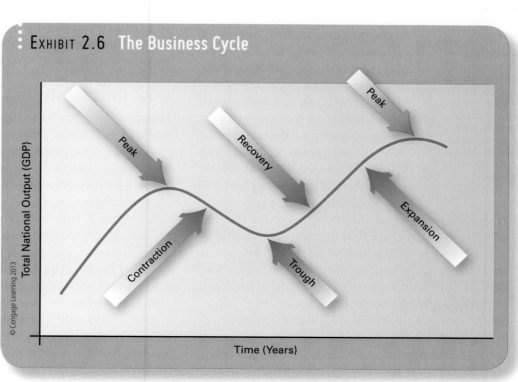

EXHIBIT 2.6 The Business Cycle

© Cengage Learning 2013

Total National Output (GDP)

Time (Years)

Peak · Contraction · Trough · Recovery · Expansion · Peak

recovery A period of rising economic growth and employment.

expansion A period of robust economic growth and high employment.

inflation A period of rising average prices across the economy.

hyperinflation An average monthly inflation rate of more than 50 percent.

disinflation A period of slowing average price increases across the economy.

deflation A period of falling average prices across the economy.

consumer price index (CPI) A measure of inflation that evaluates the change in the weighted-average price of goods and services that the average consumer buys each month.

producer price index (PPI) A measure of inflation that evaluates the change over time in the weighted-average wholesale prices.

productivity The basic relationship between the production of goods and services (output) and the resources needed to produce them (input) calculated via the following equation: output/input = productivity.

⊙ **Recovery** is a period of rising economic growth and increasing employment, following a contraction. Businesses begin to expand. Consumers start to regain confidence, and spending begins to rise. The recovery is essentially the transition period between contraction and expansion.

⊙ **Expansion** is a period of robust economic growth and high employment. Businesses expand to capitalize on emerging opportunities. Consumers are optimistic and confident, which fuels purchasing, which fuels production, which fuels further hiring. As Exhibit 2.6 demonstrates, the height of economic growth is called the peak of the expansion. The U.S. economy had the longest growth spurt on record during the ten-year period from 1991 to 2001. After a relatively mild slowdown in 2001–2002, the U.S. economy again expanded for several years before it plunged into a full-blown recession in 2008.[18]

2-6d Price Levels

The rate of price changes across the economy is another basic measure of economic well-being. **Inflation** means that prices, on average, are rising. Similar to unemployment, a low level of inflation is not so bad. It reflects a healthy economy—people have money, and they are willing to spend it. But when the Federal Reserve—the nation's central bank—manages the economy poorly, inflation can spiral out of control, which can lead to **hyperinflation**, when average prices increase more than 50% per month. In Hungary, for example, inflation in its unstable, post–World War II economy climbed so quickly that prices doubled every 15 hours from 1945 to 1946. More recently, prices in the war-torn former Yugoslavia doubled every 16 hours between October 1993 and January 1994.

When the rate of price increases slows down, the economy is experiencing **disinflation**, which was the situation in the United States in the mid-1990s and more recently in the second half of 2008. But when prices actually decrease, the economy is experiencing **deflation**, typically a sign of economic trouble that

goes hand-in-hand with very high unemployment. People don't have money and simply won't spend unless prices drop. During the Great Depression in the 1930s, the U.S. economy experienced deflation, with prices dropping 9% in 1931 and nearly 10% in 1932. Despite some economic turmoil, inflation in the United States was relatively low from 2000 to 2007, hovering at around 3%. But inflation picked up in the first half of 2008, only to fall during the first months of the economic crisis, remaining low throughout 2009 and 2010, and picking back up to an annual average of 3.2% for 2011.

The government uses two major price indexes to evaluate inflation: the **consumer price index (CPI)** and the **producer price index (PPI)**. The CPI measures the change in weighted-average price over time in a consumer "market basket" of goods and services that the average person buys each month. The U.S. Bureau of Labor Statistics creates the basket—which includes hundreds of items such as housing, transportation, haircuts, wine, and pet care—using data from more than 30,000 consumers. Although the market basket is meant to represent the average consumer, keep in mind that the "average" includes a lot of variation, so the CPI may not reflect your personal experience. For example, as a college student, you may be painfully sensitive to increases in tuition and the price of textbooks—a fact the authors of this particular textbook fully realize! But tuition and textbook prices aren't a big part of the "average" consumer's budget, so increases in these prices have a relatively small impact on the CPI.

The PPI measures the change over time in weighted-average wholesale prices, or the prices that businesses pay each other for goods and services. Changes in the PPI can sometimes predict changes in the CPI because producers tend to pass on price increases (and sometimes also price decreases) to consumers within a month or two of the changes.

2-6e Productivity

Productivity refers to the relationship between the goods and services that an economy produces and the resources needed to produce them. The amount of output—goods and services—divided by the amount of input (e.g., hours worked) equals productivity. The goal, of course, is to produce more goods and services, using fewer hours and other inputs. A high level of productivity typically correlates with healthy GDP growth, while low productivity tends to correlate with a more stagnant economy.

Over the past couple of decades, the United States has experienced strong productivity growth, due largely to infusions of technology that help workers produce more output, more quickly. But keep in mind that that productivity doesn't measure quality. That's why it's so important to examine multiple measures of economic health rather than relying on simply one or two dimensions.

THE BIG PICTURE

From a business standpoint, one key goal of economics is to guide your decision-making by offering a deeper understanding of the broad forces that affect both your business and your personal life. Knowing even basic economic principles can help you make better business decisions in virtually every area—from production, to marketing, to accounting, to name just a few—regardless of your specific function or level within an organization.

But you won't find an economics department within many (if any) businesses—rather, you'll find people across the organization applying economic theories and trends to their work, even in the face of continual economic flux. As you read through the other chapters in this book, take a moment to consider both the macroeconomic and microeconomic forces that affect each area you study. You're likely to find a surprising number of examples.

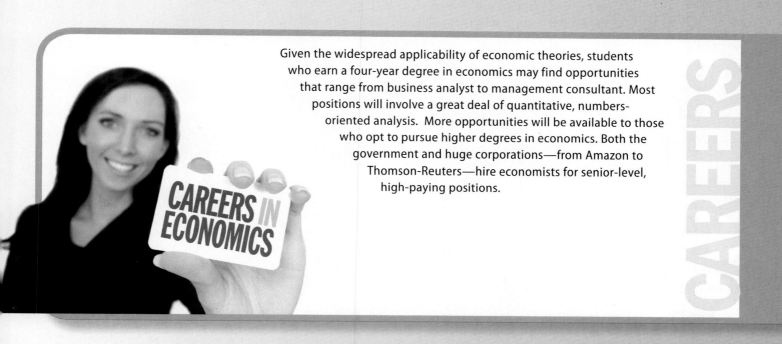

Given the widespread applicability of economic theories, students who earn a four-year degree in economics may find opportunities that range from business analyst to management consultant. Most positions will involve a great deal of quantitative, numbers-oriented analysis. More opportunities will be available to those who opt to pursue higher degrees in economics. Both the government and huge corporations—from Amazon to Thomson-Reuters—hire economists for senior-level, high-paying positions.

CAREERS IN ECONOMICS

CAREERS

What *else?*
RIP & REVIEW CARDS **IN THE BACK**
and visit www.cengagebrain.com!

3

The World Marketplace:
Business Without Borders

LEARNING OBJECTIVES

After studying this chapter, you will be able to:

3-1 Discuss business opportunities in the world economy

3-2 Explain the key reasons for international trade

3-3 Describe the tools for measuring international trade

3-4 Analyze strategies for reaching global markets

3-5 Discuss barriers to international trade and strategies to surmount them

3-6 Describe the free-trade movement and discuss key benefits and criticisms

> "A COMPANY THAT KEEPS ITS EYE ON TOM, DICK, AND HARRY IS GOING TO MISS PIERRE, HANS, AND YOSHIO."
>
> — AL RIES, MARKETING STRATEGIST AND AUTHOR

3-1 An Unprecedented Opportunity

As access to technology skyrockets and barriers to trade continue to fall, individual economies around the world have become more interdependent than ever before. The result is a tightly woven global economy marked by intense competition and huge, shifting opportunities. The long-term potential for U.S. business is enormous. Although the global economic crisis caused the world GDP to contract in 2009 for the first time since World War II, compared with average increases of about 3.5% per year since 1946, world GDP growth turned positive again in 2010 and 2011, led by growth in emerging markets that more than tripled growth in advanced economies.[1] See Exhibit 3.1 for a sampling of some specific higher- and lower-growth countries.

A quick look at population trends validates the global business opportunity, especially in developing nations. In late 2011, the world's population surpassed 7 billion people. With 313 million people, the United States accounts for less than 4.5% of the world's total population. More than 6.6 billion people live beyond our borders, representing more than 95% of potential customers for U.S. firms. But even though the growth rates in many high-population countries are strong, most of these nations remain behind the United States in terms of development and prosperity, posing considerable challenges for foreign firms. (In other words, most of their populations may not have the resources to buy even basic goods and services.) The issue is likely to become even more severe in the wake of the global economic crisis. Exhibit 3.1, a comparison of population, GDP growth rate, and per capita GDP for the world's six largest nations, highlights some of the discrepancies. Note that even though U.S. consumers clearly have money, China and India represent a much bigger opportunity in terms of both sheer size and economic growth.

The growing number of people with cell phones offers an interesting indicator of economic growth. Several

EXHIBIT 3.1 Selected Population and GDP Figures

NATION	POPULATION*	PER CAPITA GDP (U.S. DOLLARS)**	GDP GROWTH RATE***
CHINA	1,333,671,015	$8,400	+9.4%
INDIA	1,189,172,906	$3,700	+7.8%
EUROPEAN UNION	492,387,344	$34,000	+1.6%
UNITED STATES	313,232,044	$48,100	+1.5%
INDONESIA	245,613,043	$4,700	+6.4%
BRAZIL	203,429,773	$11,600	+2.8%

* *CIA World FactBook* Population Estimates, updated February 2012

** *CIA World FactBook* GDP Estimates, updated February 2012

*** *CIA World FactBook* GDP Growth Estimates, updated February 2012

Source: Rank Order Estimates, CIA—The World Factbook website: https://www.cia.gov/library/publications/the-world-factbook/rankorder/2004rank.html, accessed February 7, 2012; https://www.cia.gov/library/publications/the-world-factbook/rankorder/2003rank.html, accessed February 7, 2012; https://www.cia.gov/library/publications/the-world-factbook/rankorder/2119rank.html, accessed February 7, 2012.

recent studies have found that if a country increases cell phone penetration by 10 percentage points, GDP will likely increase by anywhere from +.5% to +1.2%. That may seem small, but it equates to somewhere between $49 and $118 billion for an economy the size of China. In other words, when the percentage of the population with cell phones goes up, the entire economy benefits.

Not surprisingly, cell phone penetration in India and China is skyrocketing. China currently boasts the world's largest base of cell phone users—more than 900 million—and the growth will likely continue. India's current subscriber base is nearly 900 million; it has grown explosively over the past five years and seems likely to follow suit in the next decade. The growth may well continue until China and India hit the 100%+ cell phone penetration rates that characterize a number of developed nations such as Taiwan, Hong Kong, Germany, and Argentina, which have more than one phone per person. In the United States, Europe, and Japan, cell phones followed landlines, but large swaths of developing nations aren't bothering to build conventional phone service. Rather, they're moving directly to cell phone networks. This trend is particularly marked across Africa, where cell phone penetration rates

"49.9% of households in India have a toilet, while more than 53% own a mobile phone."

— CNN

in 2009 were approximately 21% versus 9% for landlines. In Zimbabwe, for instance, cell phone penetration grew from 4% in 2008 to about 30% in 2009. David Knapp, general director of Motorola Vietnam, points out that many developing nations "can leapfrog technology." And Vietnamese micro-entrepreneur Nguyen Huu Truc says, "It's no longer something that only the rich can afford. Now, it's a basic means of communication." As more people get the chance to get connected, better communication will likely feed economic growth. The upshot is that millions of people worldwide will have a higher standard of living.[2]

Facing Facts: Facebook around the World

Despite how it seems in the United States, Facebook is not the only player in the social media market. In China, home-grown copycat sites such as Renren and Kaixin001 own the social networking landscape, especially since Facebook is officially blocked by Chinese censors. In Russia, as well, local copycats rule. But overall, Facebook dominates. Facebook's membership, which hit 800 million in 2011, will reach 1 billion in 2012, with the biggest growth occurring in Asia and the developing world. More than half of Facebook's users log in at least once per day. As of early 2011, almost 72% of all U.S. Internet users were on Facebook, while 70% of the entire user base was located outside of the United States. In just 20 minutes on Facebook, more than 1 million links are shared, 2 million friend requests are accepted, and almost 3 million messages are sent. With its recent $100 million public offering, Facebook is only likely to gain momentum in the months to come, spreading its social networking culture around the world. Facebook's long-term dominance, however, is far from guaranteed. Privacy advocates—particularly in Europe—are furious with certain Facebook business practices. And Facebook debuted on the American Customer Satisfaction Index with a score of 64 of 100, a ranking lower than that of the IRS and in the bottom 5% of all the private companies the report measured, which included airlines and cable companies. Low customer satisfaction could be the vulnerability that eventually topples Facebook, if its competitors can find a way to do better.[3]

© Cienpies Design/Shutterstock.com

3–2 Key Reasons for International Trade

Companies engage in global trade for a range of reasons beyond the obvious opportunity to tap into huge and growing new markets. The benefits include better access to factors of production, reduced risk, and an inflow of new ideas.

- ⊙ *Access to factors of production:* International trade offers a valuable opportunity for individual firms to capitalize on factors of production that simply aren't present in the right amount for the right price in each individual country. India, China, and the Philippines, for example, attract multibillion-dollar investments because of their large cohort of technically skilled university graduates who work for about one-fifth the pay of comparable American workers. Russia and the OPEC nations offer a rich supply of oil, and Canada, like other forested nations, boasts an abundant supply of timber. The United States offers plentiful capital, which is less available in other parts of the world. International trade helps even out some of the resource imbalances among nations.

- ⊙ *Reduced risk:* Global trade reduces dependence on one economy, lowering the economic risk for multinational firms. When the Japanese economy entered a deep, sustained slump in the 1990s, for instance, Sony and Toyota thrived through their focus on other, healthier markets around the world. But a word of caution is key: as national economies continue to integrate, an economic meltdown in one part of the world can have far-reaching impact. Major foreign banks, for example, were badly burned by the U.S. subprime market mess, due to heavy investments in U.S. mortgage markets.

- ⊙ *Inflow of innovation:* International trade can also offer companies an invaluable source of new ideas. Japan, for instance, is far ahead of the curve regarding cell phone service. Japanese cell phone "extras," including games, ringtones, videos, and stylish new accessories, set the standard for cell service around the world. In Europe, meanwhile, consumers are showing a growing interest

"More than 60% of the world's gross domestic product comes from global trade."

— New York Times

© Dmitry Melnikov/Shutterstock.com

in traditional and regional foods, which allow them to picture where their ingredients come from. Companies with a presence in foreign markets experience budding trends like these firsthand, giving them a jump in other markets around the world.[4]

3-2a Competitive Advantage

Beyond individual companies, industries tend to succeed on a worldwide basis in countries that enjoy a competitive advantage. But to understand competitive advantage, you need to first understand how **opportunity cost** relates to international trade. When a country produces more of one good, it must produce less of another good (assuming that resources are finite). The value of the second-best choice—the value of the production that a country gives up in order to produce the first product—represents the opportunity cost of producing the first product.

A country has an **absolute advantage** when it can produce more of a good than other nations, using the same amount of resources. China, for example, has an absolute advantage in terms of clothing production, relative to the United States. But having an absolute advantage isn't always enough. Unless they face major trade barriers, the industries in any country tend to produce products for which they have a **comparative advantage**—meaning that they tend to turn out those goods that have the lowest opportunity cost compared to other countries. The United States, for instance, boasts a comparative advantage versus most countries in movie and television program production; Germany has a comparative advantage in the production of high-performance cars; and South Korea enjoys a comparative advantage in electronics.

But keep in mind that comparative advantage seldom remains static. As technology changes and the workforce evolves (through factors such as education and experience), nations may gain or lose comparative advantage in various industries. China and India, for example, are both seeking to build a comparative advantage versus other nations in technology production by investing in their infrastructure and their institutions of higher education.

3-3 Global Trade: Taking Measure

After a decade of robust growth, global trade began slowing in 2007, due largely to turbulence in the worldwide financial markets. In 2008, the rate of growth in world trade slid below 5%, as the global recession tightened its grip. In 2009, global trade plummeted nearly 25% in U.S. dollar terms, and 12% in terms of overall volume from the 2008 level, the largest single-year drop since World War II. Global gross fixed investment fell about 4% year over year, or by roughly $800 billion. The global trade volume surged a record +14.5%, but economists anticipate a more modest +6.5% expansion in 2011. Global gross fixed investment grew one percentage point in 2011 to hit 24% of global world product. Measuring the impact of international trade on individual nations requires a clear understanding of balance of trade, balance of payments, and exchange rates.[5]

3-3a Balance of Trade

The **balance of trade** is a basic measure of the difference between a nation's exports and imports. If the total value of exports is higher than the total value of imports, the country has a **trade surplus**. If the total value of imports is higher than the total value of exports, the country has a **trade deficit**. Balance of trade includes the value of both goods and services, and it incorporates trade with all foreign nations. Although a trade deficit signals the wealth of an economy that can afford to buy huge amounts of foreign products, a large deficit can be destabilizing. It indicates, after all, that as goods and services flow into a nation, money flows out—a challenge with regard to long-term economic health. The United States has had an overall trade deficit since 1976, and as the American appetite for foreign goods has grown, the trade deficit has ballooned. But that growth may slow over the next few years if demand remains sluggish in response to the global economic crisis.

3-3b Balance of Payments

Balance of payments is a measure of the total flow of money into or out of a country. Clearly, the balance of trade plays a central role in determining the balance of payments. But the balance of payments also includes other financial flows such as foreign borrowing and lending, foreign aid payments and receipts, and foreign investments. A **balance of payments surplus** means that more money flows in than out, while a **balance of payments deficit** means that more money flows out than in. Keep in mind that the balance of payments typically corresponds to the balance of trade because trade is, in general, the largest component.

3-3c Exchange Rates

Exchange rates measure the value of one nation's currency relative to the currency of other nations. While the exchange rate does not directly measure global commerce, it certainly has a powerful influence on how global trade affects individual nations and their trading partners. The exchange rate of a given currency must be expressed in terms of another currency. Here are some examples of how the exchange rate can influence the economy, using the dollar and the euro.

STRONG DOLLAR VERSUS EURO: WHO BENEFITS? (EXAMPLE: $1.00 · 1.20 EUROS)	WEAK DOLLAR VERSUS EURO: WHO BENEFITS? (EXAMPLE: $1.00 · .60 EUROS)
U.S. travelers to Europe: Their dollars can buy more European goods and services.	*European travelers to the United States:* Their dollars buy more American goods and services.
American firms with European operations: Operating costs—from buying products to paying workers—are lower.	*European firms with American operations:* Operating costs—from buying products to paying workers—are lower.
European exporters: Their products are less expensive in the United States, so Europe exports more, and we import more.	*American exporters:* Their products are less expensive in Europe, so we export more, and Europe imports more.

© Cengage Learning 2013

3-3d Countertrade

A complete evaluation of global trade must also consider exchanges that don't actually involve money. A surprisingly large chunk of international commerce—possibly as much as 25%—involves the barter of products for products rather than for currency. Companies typically engage in **countertrade** to meet the needs of customers that don't have access to hard currency or credit, usually in developing countries. Individual countertrade agreements range from simple barter

to a complex web of exchanges that end up meeting the needs of multiple parties. Done poorly, countertrading can be a confusing nightmare for everyone involved. But done well, countertrading is a powerful tool for gaining customers and products that would not otherwise be available.[6]

3-4 Seizing the Opportunity: Strategies for Reaching Global Markets

There is no one "right way" to seize the opportunity in global markets. In fact, the opportunity may not even make sense for every firm. While international trade can offer new profit streams and lower costs, it also introduces a higher level of risk and complexity to running a business. Being ready to take on the challenge can mean the difference between success and failure.

Firms ready to tap the opportunity have a number of options for how to move forward. One way is to seek foreign suppliers through outsourcing and importing. Another possibility is to seek foreign customers through exporting, licensing, franchising, and direct investment. These market development options fall in a spectrum from low cost–low control to high cost–high control, as shown in Exhibit 3.2. In other words, companies that choose to export products to a foreign country spend less to enter that market than companies that choose to build their own factories. But companies that build their own factories have a lot more

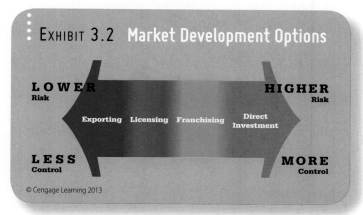

EXHIBIT 3.2 Market Development Options

LOWER Risk — HIGHER Risk

Exporting Licensing Franchising Direct Investment

LESS Control — MORE Control

© Cengage Learning 2013

control than exporters over how their business unfolds. Keep in mind that profit opportunity and risk—which vary along with cost and control—also play a critical role in how firms approach international markets.

Smaller firms tend to begin with exporting and move along the spectrum as the business develops. But larger firms may jump straight to the strategies that give them more control over their operations. Large firms are also likely to use a number of different approaches in different countries, depending on the goals of the firm and the structure of the foreign market. Regardless of the specific strategy, most large companies—such as General Electric, Nike, and Disney—both outsource with foreign suppliers and sell their products to foreign markets.

3-4a Foreign Outsourcing and Importing

Foreign outsourcing means contracting with foreign suppliers to produce products, usually at a fraction of the cost of domestic production. Gap, for instance, relies on a network of manufacturers in 50 different countries, mostly in less-developed parts of the world, from Asia, to Africa, to Central America. Apple depends on firms in China and Taiwan to produce the iPhone. And countless small companies contract with foreign manufacturers as well. The key benefit, of course, is dramatically lower wages, which drive down the cost of production.

But while foreign outsourcing lowers costs, it also involves significant risk. Quality control typically requires very detailed specifications to ensure that a company

Most of the clothing you're wearing right now was probably produced in another country.

© LUCIOPIX/ALAMY

gets what it actually needs. Another key risk of foreign outsourcing involves social responsibility. A firm that contracts with foreign producers has an obligation to ensure that those factories adhere to ethical standards. Deciding what those standards should be is often quite tricky, given different cultures, expectations, and laws in different countries. And policing the factories on an ongoing basis can be even harder than determining the standards. But companies that don't get it right face the threat of significant consumer backlash in the United States and Europe. This has been a particular issue with products produced in China. In the recent past, for instance, product defects forced U.S. firms to recall a host of Chinese-produced toys, including Thomas the Tank Engine trains that were coated with toxic lead paint, ghoulish fake eyeballs that were filled with kerosene, and Polly Pocket dolls that posed a swallowing hazard.[7]

Many Americans have become personally familiar with the quality/cost tradeoff as a growing number of companies have outsourced customer service to foreign call centers. Research suggests that the approximate cost of offering a live, American-based, customer service agent averages about $7.50 per call, while outsourcing those calls to live agents in another country drops the average cost down to about $3.25 per call. But customers end up paying the difference in terms of satisfaction, reporting high levels of misunderstanding, frustration, and inefficiency. A number of firms—such as jetBlue and Amazon.com—have enjoyed the best of both worlds by outsourcing customer service calls to U.S. agents who work from their own homes.[8]

Importing means buying products from overseas that have already been produced, rather than contracting with overseas manufacturers to produce special orders. Imported products, of course, don't carry the brand name of the importer, but they also don't carry as much risk. Pier 1 Imports, a large retail chain, has built a powerful brand around the importing concept, creating stores that give the customer the sense of a global shopping trip without the cost or hassle of actually leaving the country.

3-4b Exporting

Exporting is the most basic level of international market development. It simply means producing products domestically and selling them abroad. Exporting represents an especially strong opportunity for small and mid-sized companies. Ernest Joshua, for instance, developed a thriving Arkansas-based hair care company that specializes in products for African Americans. Recognizing opportunity abroad, his firm now exports products to Africa and the Caribbean.[9]

3-4c Foreign Licensing and Foreign Franchising

Foreign licensing and foreign franchising, the next level of commitment to international markets, are quite similar. **Foreign licensing** involves a domestic firm granting a foreign firm the rights to produce and market its product or to use its trademark/patent rights in a defined geographical area. The company that offers the rights, or the *licensor*, receives a fee from the company that buys the rights, or the *licensee*. This approach allows firms to expand into foreign markets with little or no investment, and it also helps circumvent government restrictions on importing in closed markets. But maintaining control of licensees can be a significant challenge. Licensors also run the risk that unethical licensees may become their competitors, using information that they gained from the licensing agreement. Foreign licensing is especially common in the food and beverage industry. The most high-profile examples include Coke and Pepsi, which grant licenses to foreign bottlers all over the world.

© Mystic Arabia/Alamy

Foreign franchising is a specialized type of licensing. A firm that expands through foreign franchising, called a *franchisor*, offers other businesses, or *franchisees*, the right to produce and market its products if the franchisee agrees to specific operating requirements—a complete package of how to do business. Franchisors also often offer their franchisees management guidance, marketing support, and even financing. In return, franchisees pay both a start-up fee and an ongoing percentage of sales to the franchisor. One key difference between franchising and licensing is that franchisees assume the identity of the franchisor. A McDonald's franchise in Paris, for instance, is clearly a McDonald's, not, say, a Pierre's Baguette outlet that also carries McDonald's products.

3-4d Foreign Direct Investment

Direct investment in foreign production and marketing facilities represents the deepest level of global involvement. The cost is high, but companies with direct investments have more control over how their business operates in a given country. The high-dollar commitment also represents significant risk if the business doesn't go well. Most direct investment takes the form of either acquiring foreign firms or developing new facilities from the ground up. Another increasingly popular approach is strategic alliances or partnerships that allow multiple firms to share risks and resources for mutual benefit.

Foreign acquisitions enable companies to gain a foothold quickly in new markets. In 2009, for example, Italian carmaker Fiat took over struggling U.S. auto giant Chrysler, with plans to more fully exploit the American market in the wake of the Great Recession. A number of other global giants, such as Microsoft, General Electric, and Nestlé, tend to follow a foreign acquisition strategy.[10]

Developing new facilities from scratch—or "offshoring"—is the most costly form of direct investment. It also involves significant risk. But the benefits include complete control over how the facility develops and the potential for high profits, which makes the approach attractive for corporations that can afford it. Intel, for instance, plans to build a $2.5 billion specialized computer chip manufacturing plant in northeastern China. And foreign car companies, from German Daimler-Benz, to Korean Hyundai, to Japanese Toyota, have built factories in the southern United States.[11]

Joint ventures involve two or more companies joining forces—sharing resources, risks, and profits, but not merging companies—to pursue specific opportunities. A formal, long-term agreement is usually called a **partnership**, while a less formal, less encompassing agreement is usually called a **strategic alliance**. Joint ventures are a popular, though controversial, means of entering foreign markets. Often a foreign company connects with a local firm to ease its way into the market. In fact, some countries, such as Malaysia, require that foreign investors have local partners. But research from Harvard finance professor Mihir Desai finds that joint ventures between multinational firms and

foreign licensing Authority granted by a domestic firm to a foreign firm for the rights to produce and market its product or to use its trademark/patent rights in a defined geographical area.

foreign franchising A specialized type of foreign licensing in which a firm expands by offering businesses in other countries the right to produce and market its products according to specific operating requirements.

direct investment (or foreign direct investment) When firms either acquire foreign firms or develop new facilities from the ground up in foreign countries.

joint ventures When two or more companies join forces—sharing resources, risks, and profits, but not actually merging companies—to pursue specific opportunities.

partnership A voluntary agreement under which two or more people act as co-owners of a business for profit.

strategic alliance An agreement between two or more firms to jointly pursue a specific opportunity without actually merging their businesses. Strategic alliances typically involve less formal, less encompassing agreements than partnerships.

"Obstacles are those frightful things you see when you take your eyes off your goal."

— HENRY FORD, FOUNDER OF FORD MOTOR COMPANY

domestic partners can be more costly and less rewarding than they initially appear. He and his team suggest that they make sense only in countries that require local political and cultural knowledge as a core element of doing business.[12]

3-5 Barriers to International Trade

Every business faces challenges, but international firms face more hurdles than domestic firms. Understanding and surmounting those hurdles is the key to success in global markets. Most barriers to trade fall into the following categories: sociocultural differences, economic differences, and legal/political differences. As you think about these barriers, keep in mind that each country has a different mix of barriers. Often countries with the highest barriers have the least competition, which can be a real opportunity for the first international firms to break through.

3-5a Sociocultural Differences

Sociocultural differences include differences among countries in language, attitudes, and values. Some specific, and perhaps surprising, elements that affect business include nonverbal communication, forms of address, attitudes toward punctuality, religious celebrations and customs, business

practices, and expectations regarding meals and gifts. Understanding and responding to sociocultural factors are vital for firms that operate in multiple countries. But since the differences often operate at a subtle level, they can undermine relationships before anyone is aware that it's happening. The best way to jump over sociocultural barriers is to conduct thorough consumer research, cultivate firsthand knowledge, and practice extreme sensitivity. The payoff can be a sharp competitive edge. Hyundai, for instance, enjoys a whopping 18% share of the passenger car market in India. It beat the competition with custom features that reflect Indian culture, such as elevated rooflines to provide more headroom for turban-wearing motorists.[13]

3-5b Economic Differences

Before entering a foreign market, it's critical to understand and evaluate the local economic conditions. Key factors to consider include population, per capita income, economic growth rate, currency exchange rate, and stage of economic development. But keep in mind that low scores for any of these measures don't necessarily equal a lack of opportunity. In fact, some of today's biggest opportunities are in countries with low per capita income. For example, the Indian division of global giant Unilever gets 50% of its sales from rural India by selling products to individual consumers in tiny quantities, such as two-cent sachets of shampoo. The rural Indian market has been growing so dramatically that in 2010,

Working Hard versus Hardly Working...

Americans have a reputation around the world for being relentless workaholics; and a 2011 survey from Expedia suggests that may not be far from the truth. Americans earn on average 14 days of paid vacation per year, compared to 30 days for their peers in Germany, France, and Brazil, and 25 days for their peers in India. Not only that, many Americans don't even end up taking the vacation they earn. Altogether, Americans forfeited 226 million unused vacation days in 2011, which equates to $34.3 billion worth of time (with the average full-time worker earning $39,416 a year, according to the Bureau of Labor Statistics). One in three American adults doesn't take his or her vacation at all in any given year. Most Europeans earn far more paid vacation days than Americans—30 days is common—and they typically use every single day. Only the Asian countries place less emphasis on vacation. The Japanese, for instance, earn an average of 11 paid vacation days and typically only use 5. And Americans really are getting more done during that extra time at work. The American workforce is among the most productive in the world, largely due to effective use of technology, rather than the extra hours in the office.[14]

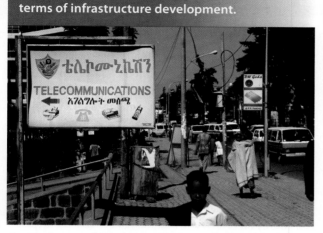
Foreign markets can differ dramatically in terms of infrastructure development.

the Chairman of Hindustan Unilever declared, "What we have done in the last 25 years we want to do it in the next two years," scaling up the reach of its consumer products from about 250,000 rural retail outlets to about 750,000. And Hewlett-Packard has recently joined forces with Unilever to give microdistributors in rural India the ability to check prices and place orders online from "what are now distinctively offline villages and regions." Also capitalizing on the rapid growth and increased demand, Samsung has introduced Guru, a mobile phone that can be charged with solar power, to rural India.[15]

Effectively serving less-developed markets requires innovation and efficiency. Emerging consumers often need different product features, and they almost always need lower costs. C. K. Prahalad, an influential business scholar, believed that forward-thinking companies can make a profit in developing countries if they make advanced technology affordable. Many markets are simply so large that high-volume sales can make up for low-profit margins.

Overall, the profit potential is clear and growing. And as consumers in developing countries continue to gain income—although at a much slower pace in the wake of the economic crisis—companies that established their brands early will have a critical edge over firms that enter the market after them.

Infrastructure should be another key economic consideration when entering a foreign market. Infrastructure refers to a country's physical facilities that support economic activity. It includes basic systems in each of the following areas:

- Transportation (e.g., roads, airports, railroads, and ports)
- Communication (e.g., TV, radio, Internet, and cell phone coverage)
- Energy (e.g., utilities and power plants)
- Finance (e.g., banking, checking, and credit)

The level of infrastructure can vary dramatically among countries. In Africa, for instance, only 11% of the population has Internet access, compared to 78% in North America. In

infrastructure A country's physical facilities that support economic activity.

Veggie Surprise, Anyone?

Travel around the world, and you're likely to see American fast-food franchisees in virtually every city. Although you'll surely recognize the names of these fast-food behemoths, you may not be as familiar with the food that they serve, since many of the dishes have been completely changed in response to local culture.

Some favorites from the Domino's international menus:

- **Japan: squid pizza**
- **England: tuna and sweet corn pizza**
- **Guatemala: black beans**
- **Netherlands: grilled lamb pizza**

Pizza Hut:

- **Japan: crust stuffed with shrimp nuggets and injected with mayonnaise**
- **South Korea: crust filled with sweet potato mousse**
- **China: lemon-flavored salmon pastry roll and scallop croquettes with crushed seaweed**

KFC:

- **China: spicy tofu chicken rice**
- **India: Chana Snacker (a chickpea burger topped with Thousand Island sauce)**

McDonald's:

- **India: Paneer Salsa Wrap (cottage cheese with Mexican-Cajun coating)**
- **Australia: Bacon and Egg Roll ("rashers of quality bacon and fried egg")**
- **Kuwait: Veggie Surprise Burger (no detailed description…yikes!)[16]**

Vietnam and Thailand, many consumers buy products directly from vendors in small boats, compared to firmly grounded stores in Europe. Although credit card purchases are still relatively low in much of the world, particularly in Asia, recent growth has been explosive and will probably continue for the next few years.[17]

3-5c Political and Legal Differences

Political regimes obviously differ around the world, and their policies have a dramatic impact on business. The specific laws and regulations that governments create around business are often less obvious, yet they can still represent a significant barrier to international trade. To compete effectively—and to reduce risk—managers must carefully evaluate these factors and make plans to respond to them both now and as they change.

Laws and Regulations International businesses must comply with international legal standards, the laws of their own countries, and the laws of their host countries. This can be a real challenge, since many developing countries change business regulations with little notice and less publicity. The justice system can pose another key challenge, particularly with regard to legal enforcement of ownership and contract rights. Since 2003, The World Bank has published a "Doing Business" report that ranks the ease of doing business for small and medium-sized companies in 183 different countries. The 2012 "Doing Business" report presented the encouraging news that there was a 13% increase in worldwide regulatory reforms versus the prior year. For the sixth year running, Singapore leads in the ease of doing business, followed by Hong Kong SAR China, New Zealand, the United States and Denmark. China, India, and the Russian Federation are among the top 30 most-improved economies. The "Doing Business" project examines the ease of doing business from nine different angles, including the ease of dealing with construction permits to paying taxes to enforcing contracts.[18] The key benefit of an effective legal system is that it reduces risk for both domestic and foreign businesses.

Bribery, the payment of money for favorable treatment, and corruption, the solicitation of money for favorable treatment, are also major issues throughout the world. While bribery and corruption are technically illegal in virtually every major country, they are often accepted as a standard way of doing business. Regardless, U.S. corporations and American citizens are subject to prosecution by U.S. authorities for offering bribes in any nation. See Chapter 4 for more details.

Desert Snow?

Dubai is a jewel of a city, built largely with oil money, at the edge of the Arabian Peninsula and the Persian Gulf. Inhabited mostly by foreigners, Dubai is characterized by conspicuous consumption. Upscale malls feature designer boutiques, and fine dining establishments offer a range of international cuisine.

Given its desert location, the weather in Dubai is often scorching. Summer days can hit 130°F, cooling to the 80s and 90s at night. Both tourists and residents can take a break from the heat by spending the day at Ski Dubai, one of the world's largest indoor ski resorts, covered with real snow year round, and maintained at −29°–30° F (just below freezing). Ski Dubai is a fun experience. But Ski Dubai's very existence only exacerbates Dubai's biggest environmental challenge—providing adequate fresh water to support rapid development in the desert climate.

Recognizing the looming issues, Dubai's leadership has begun to impose tougher sustainability standards on new construction, but environmentalists have begun to attack the irony of year-round recreational skiing on artificial snow at the edge of a desert in a bustling metropolis with a near-dire fresh water shortage. Maybe virtual skiing will be the next big business opportunity in Dubai.[19]

Political Climate The political climate of any country deeply influences whether that nation is attractive to foreign business. Stability is crucial. A country subject to strife from civil war, riots, or other violence creates huge additional risk for foreign business. Yet, figuring out how to operate in an unstable environment such as Russia, Bolivia, or the Middle East, can give early movers a real advantage. Grant Winterton, Coca-Cola's regional manager for Russia, commented to *Time* magazine that "the politics do concern us." But having snagged 50% of the $1.9 billion carbonated-soft-drink market, he concludes that "the opportunity far outweighs the risk." Poor enforcement of intellectual property rights across international borders is another tough issue for business. Fortunately, there has been some progress. The Business Software Alliance piracy-tracking study found that worldwide piracy rates dropped by one percentage point to 42% in 2010 (vs. 2009), but the total value of software theft hit a record $59 billion. The highest-piracy countries are Georgia, Zimbabwe, Bangladesh, Moldava, and Yemin, all 90% or higher.[20]

International Trade Restrictions National governments also have the power to erect barriers to international business through a variety of international trade restrictions. The arguments for and against trade restrictions—also called **protectionism**—are summarized below. As you read, note that most economists find the reasons to eliminate trade restrictions much more compelling than the reasons to create them.

Just as trade restrictions have a range of motivations, they can take a number of different forms. The most common trade restrictions are tariffs, quotas, voluntary export restraints, and embargoes.

- **Tariffs** are taxes levied against imports. Governments tend to use protective tariffs either to shelter fledgling industries that couldn't compete without help, or to shelter industries that are crucial to the domestic economy. In 2002, for instance, the United States imposed tariffs of 8% to 30% on a variety of imported steel products for a period of three years, in order to give some relief to the large, but ailing, U.S. steel industry.

- **Quotas** are limitations on the amount of specific products that may be imported from certain countries during a given time period. Russia, for instance, has specific quotas for U.S. meat imports.

- **Voluntary export restraints (VERs)** are limitations on the amount of specific products that one nation will export to another nation. Although the government of the exporting country typically imposes VERs, they usually do so out of fear that the importing country would impose even more onerous restrictions. As a result, VERs often aren't as "voluntary" as the name suggests. The United States, for instance, insisted on VERs with Japanese auto exports in the early 1980s (which many economists believe ultimately precipitated the decline of the U.S. auto industry).

- An **embargo** is a total ban on the international trade of a certain item, or a total halt in trade with a particular nation. The intention of most embargoes is to pressure the targeted country to change political policies or to protect national security. The U.S. embargo against trade with Cuba offers a high-profile example.

Quotas, VERs, and embargoes are relatively rare compared to tariffs, and tariffs are falling to new lows. But as tariffs decrease, some nations are seeking to control imports through nontariff barriers such as:

- Requiring red-tape-intensive import licenses for certain categories
- Establishing nonstandard packaging requirements for certain products
- Offering less-favorable exchange rates to certain importers
- Establishing standards on how certain products are produced or grown
- Promoting a "buy national" consumer attitude among local people

Nontariff barriers tend to be fairly effective because complaints about them can be hard to prove and easy to counter.[21]

protectionism National policies designed to restrict international trade, usually with the goal of protecting domestic businesses.

tariffs Taxes levied against imports.

quotas Limitations on the amount of specific products that may be imported from certain countries during a given time period.

voluntary export restraints (VERs) Limitations on the amount of specific products that one nation will export to another nation.

embargo A complete ban on international trade of a certain item, or a total halt in trade with a particular nation.

free trade The unrestricted movement of goods and services across international borders.

General Agreement on Tariffs and Trade (GATT) An international trade treaty designed to encourage worldwide trade among its members.

3-6 Free Trade: The Movement Gains Momentum

Perhaps the most dramatic change in the world economy has been the global move toward **free trade**—the unrestricted movement of goods and services across international borders. Even though *complete* free trade is not a reality, the emergence of regional trading blocks, common markets, and international trade agreements has moved the world economy much closer to that goal.

3-6a GATT and the World Trade Organization

The **General Agreement on Tariffs and Trade (GATT)** is an international trade accord designed to encourage worldwide trade among its members. Established in 1948 by 23 nations, GATT has undergone a number of revisions. The most significant changes stemmed from the 1986–1994 Uruguay Round of negotiations, which took bold steps to slash average tariffs by about 30%

and to reduce other trade barriers among the 125 nations that signed.

The Uruguay Round also created the **World Trade Organization (WTO)**, a permanent global institution to promote international trade and to settle international trade disputes. The WTO monitors provisions of the GATT agreements, promotes further reduction of trade barriers, and mediates disputes among members. The decisions of the WTO are binding, which means that all parties involved in disputes must comply to maintain good standing in the organization.

Ministers of the WTO meet every two years to address current world trade issues. As the world economy has shifted toward services rather than goods, the emphasis of WTO meetings has followed suit. Controlling rampant piracy of intellectual property is a key concern for developed countries. For less-developed countries, one central issue is U.S. and European agricultural subsidies, which may unfairly distort agricultural prices worldwide.

In fact, both the broader agenda and the individual decisions of the WTO have become increasingly controversial over the past ten years. Advocates for less-developed nations are deeply concerned that free trade clears the path for major multinational corporations to push local businesses into economic failure. A local food stand, for instance, probably won't have the resources to compete with a global giant such as McDonald's. If the food stand closes, the community has gained inexpensive hamburgers, but the entrepreneur has lost his livelihood, and the community has lost the local flavor that contributes to its unique culture. Other opponents of the WTO worry that the acceleration of global trade encourages developing countries to fight laws that protect the environment and workers' rights, for fear of losing their low-cost advantage on the world market. The concerns have sparked significant protests during the past few meetings of the WTO ministers, and the outcry may well grow louder as developing nations gain economic clout.

3-6b The World Bank

Established in the aftermath of World War II, the **World Bank** is an international cooperative of 187 member countries, working together to reduce poverty in the developing world. The World Bank influences the global economy by providing financial and technical advice to the governments of developing countries for projects in a range of areas, including infrastructure, communications, health, and education. The financial assistance usually comes in the form of low-interest loans. But to secure a loan, the borrowing nation must often agree to conditions that can involve rather arduous economic reform.

3-6c The International Monetary Fund

Like the World Bank, the **International Monetary Fund (IMF)** is an international organization accountable to the governments of its 187 member nations. The basic mission of the IMF is to promote international economic cooperation and

> ## "We must create a kind of globalization that works for everyone... and not just for a few."
>
> — NESTOR KIRCHNER, ARGENTINE STATESMAN

REASONS TO *CREATE* TRADE RESTRICTIONS	REASONS TO *ELIMINATE* TRADE RESTRICTIONS
Protect domestic industry (e.g., the U.S. steel industry)	Reduce prices and increase choices for consumers by encouraging competition from around the world
Protect domestic jobs in key industries (but perhaps at the cost of domestic jobs in other industries)	Increase domestic jobs in industries with a comparative advantage versus other countries
Protect national security interests	Increase jobs—both at home and abroad—from foreign companies
Retaliate against countries who have engaged in unfair trade practices	Build exporting opportunities through better relationships with other countries
Pressure other countries to change their policies and practices	Use resources more efficiently on a worldwide basis

stable growth. Funding comes from the member nations, with the United States contributing more than twice as much as any other country. To achieve these goals, the IMF:

- ● Supports stable exchange rates
- ● Facilitates a smooth system of international payments
- ● Encourages member nations to adopt sound economic policies
- ● Promotes international trade
- ● Lends money to member nations to address economic problems

Although all of its functions are important, the IMF is best known as a lender of last resort to nations in financial trouble. This policy has come under fire in the past few years. Critics accuse the IMF of encouraging poor countries to borrow more money than they can ever hope to repay, which actually cripples their economies over the long term, creating even deeper poverty.

At the end of 2005, the IMF responded to its critics by implementing a historic debt relief program for poor countries. Under this program, which has since been expanded to include other agencies, the IMF and its partners have extended 100% debt forgiveness to 40 poor countries, erasing about $75 billion in debt. The managing director of the IMF pointed out that the canceled debt will allow these countries to increase spending in priority areas to reduce poverty and promote growth (although some experts worry that debt cancellation sets a troubling precedent for future lending). The result should be a higher standard of living for some of the poorest people in the world.[22]

International cooperation leads to global economic development.

AP Images/J. Scott Applewhite

> **"Almost**
> half the world—over three billion people—live on less than $2.50 a day."
>
> —GlobalIssues.org

3-6d Trading Blocs and Common Markets

Another major development in the past decade is the emergence of regional **trading blocs**, or groups of countries that have reduced or even eliminated all tariffs, allowing the free flow of goods among the member nations. A **common market** goes even further than a trading bloc by attempting to harmonize all trading rules. The United States, Mexico, and Canada have formed the largest trading bloc in the world, and the 27 countries of the European Union have formed the largest common market.

NAFTA The **North American Free Trade Agreement (NAFTA)** is the treaty that created the free-trading zone among the United States, Mexico, and Canada. The agreement took effect in 1994, gradually eliminating trade barriers and investment restrictions over a 15-year period. Despite dire predictions of American jobs flowing to Mexico, the U.S. economy has grown significantly since the implementation of NAFTA. The Canadian and Mexican economies have thrived as well (although all three economies have slowed significantly during the global economic crisis).

But NAFTA critics point out that the U.S. trade deficit with both Mexico and Canada has skyrocketed. While exports to both nations have increased, imports have grown far faster; both countries are among the top ten contributors to the total U.S. trade deficit, threatening the long-term health of the American economy. Other criticisms of NAFTA include increased pollution and worker abuse. Companies that move their factories to Mexico to capitalize on lower costs also take advantage of looser environmental and worker-protection laws, creating major ethical concerns. But the full impact of NAFTA—for better or for worse—is tough to evaluate because so many other variables affect all three economies.[23]

European Union Composed of 27 nations and nearly half a billion people, and boasting a combined GDP of nearly $15 trillion, the **European Union (EU)** is the world's

trading bloc A group of countries that have reduced or even eliminated tariffs, allowing for the free flow of goods among the member nations.

common market A group of countries that have eliminated tariffs and harmonized trading rules to facilitate the free flow of goods among the member nations.

North American Free Trade Agreement (NAFTA) The treaty among the United States, Mexico, and Canada that eliminated trade barriers and investment restrictions over a fifteen-year period starting in 1994.

European Union (EU) The world's largest common market, composed of twenty-seven European nations.

largest common market. Exhibit 3.3 shows a map of the 2011 EU countries plus the three countries that have applied to join.[24]

The overarching goal of the EU is to bolster Europe's trade position and to increase its international political and economic power. To help make this happen, the EU has removed all trade restrictions among member nations and unified internal trade rules, allowing goods and people to move freely among EU countries. The EU has also created standardized policies for import and export between EU countries and the rest of the world, giving the member nations more clout as a bloc than each would have had on its own. Perhaps the EU's most economically significant move was the introduction of a single currency, the euro, in 2002. Of the 15 EU members at the time, 12 adopted the euro (exceptions were the United Kingdom, Sweden, and Denmark). The EU also affects the global economy with its leading-edge approach to environmental protection, quality production, and human rights.

In 2010 and 2011, hobbled by overwhelming debt and slow growth, several of the weaker EU countries—most notably Greece—spiraled into economic crisis. Fearing a financial domino effect, due to the close ties among the nations, the economically stronger EU countries cobbled together several bailout packages. But many economists still fear that its weaker members could drag the EU overall into a deep, damaging recession, and that one or more

EXHIBIT 3.3 European Union 2011

© Cengage Learning 2013

countries could default on its debt, withdraw from using the euro as currency, or both, with devastating financial consequences for both the EU and the world economy.

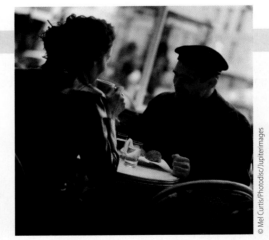

© Mel Curtis/Photodisc/Jupiterimages

A Pricey Post-Euro
Wake-up Call

Europe is famous for its café culture, but if key members of the euro-zone do indeed ditch the euro, *Time* magazine has estimated that the price of a cup of coffee (among many other staples) may rocket out of reach for many locals. In Athens, for instance, two cups of coffee a day, post-euro, could cost the average Greek nearly a quarter of his or her salary. Specific estimated price increases in post-Euro coffee include:

Brussels	+24%	Paris	+6%
Athens	+91%	Dublin	+25%
Madrid	+38%	Amsterdam	+2%
Rome	+28%	Berlin	no change[25]

THE BIG PICTURE

The past decade has been marked by extraordinary changes in the world economy. The boundaries between individual countries have fallen lower than ever before, creating a new level of economic connectedness. The growing integration has created huge opportunities for visionary companies of every size. But integration also means risk. The dangers became clear in 2008, when the economic crisis in the United States rapidly reverberated around the globe, fueling a deep, worldwide recession.

To succeed abroad—especially in tough economic times—individual firms must make the right choices about how to structure their operations, surmount barriers to trade, meet diverse customer needs, manage a global workforce, and handle complex logistics. Human rights and environmental protection continue to be especially critical for international businesses. Both are vital components of social responsibility and will only gain importance as advocates raise awareness around the world. In the face of economic, political, and social flux, effective global business leaders must master both strategy and implementation at a deeper level than ever before.

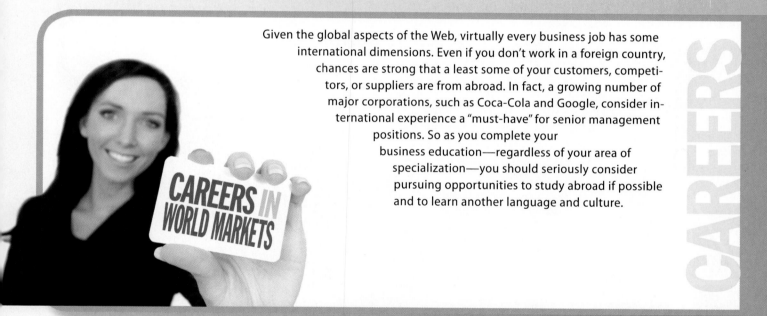

CAREERS

Given the global aspects of the Web, virtually every business job has some international dimensions. Even if you don't work in a foreign country, chances are strong that a least some of your customers, competitors, or suppliers are from abroad. In fact, a growing number of major corporations, such as Coca-Cola and Google, consider international experience a "must-have" for senior management positions. So as you complete your business education—regardless of your area of specialization—you should seriously consider pursuing opportunities to study abroad if possible and to learn another language and culture.

What *else?*
RIP & REVIEW CARDS IN THE BACK
and visit www.cengagebrain.com!

4

Business Ethics and Social Responsibility:
Doing Well by Doing Good

LEARNING OBJECTIVES

After studying this chapter, you will be able to:

4-1 Define ethics and explain the concept of universal ethical standards

4-2 Describe business ethics and ethical dilemmas

4-3 Discuss how ethics relates to both the individual and the organization

4-4 Define social responsibility and examine the impact on stakeholder groups

4-5 Explain the role of social responsibility in the global arena

4-6 Describe how companies evaluate their efforts to be socially responsible

> "THE SUCCESS OF OUR ECONOMY HAS ALWAYS DEPENDED... ON THE ABILITY TO EXTEND OPPORTUNITY TO EVERY WILLING HEART—NOT OUT OF CHARITY, BUT BECAUSE IT IS THE SUREST ROUTE TO OUR COMMON GOOD."
>
> — President Barack Obama

4-1a Defining Ethics: Murkier Than You'd Think

ethics A set of beliefs about right and wrong, good and bad.

In the most general sense, **ethics** refer to sets of beliefs about right and wrong, good and bad. While your individual ethics stem from who you are as a human being, your family, your social group, and your culture also play a significant role in shaping your ethics. And therein lies the challenge: in the United States, people come from such diverse backgrounds that establishing broad agreement on specific ethical standards can be daunting. The global arena only amplifies the challenge.

A given country's legal system provides a solid starting point for examining ethical standards. The function of laws in the United States (and elsewhere) is to establish and enforce ethical norms that apply to everyone within our society. Laws provide basic standards of behavior. But truly ethical behavior goes beyond the basics. In other words, your actions can be completely legal, yet still unethical. But since the legal system is far from perfect, in rare instances your actions can be illegal, yet still ethical. Exhibit 4.1 shows some examples

4-1 Ethics and Social Responsibility: A Close Relationship

Ethics and social responsibility—often discussed in the same breath—are closely related, but they are definitely not the same. Ethics refers to sets of beliefs about right and wrong, good and bad; business ethics involve the application of these issues in the workplace. Clearly, ethics relate to individuals and their day-to-day decision making. Just as clearly, the decisions of each individual can affect the entire organization.

Social responsibility is the obligation of a business to contribute to society. The most socially responsible firms feature proactive policies that focus on meeting the needs of all their stakeholders—not just investors but also employees, customers, the broader community, and the environment. The stance of a company regarding social responsibility sets the tone for the organization and clearly influences the decisions of individual employees.

Although this chapter discusses ethics and social responsibility separately, keep in mind that the two areas have a dynamic, interactive relationship that plays a vital role in building both profitable businesses and a vibrant community.

Exhibit 4.1 Legal–Ethical Matrix

LEGAL AND UNETHICAL	LEGAL AND ETHICAL
Promoting high-calorie/low-nutrient foods with inadequate information about the risks	Producing high-quality products
Producing products that you know will break before their time	Rewarding integrity Leading by example
Paying non living wages to workers in developing countries	Treating employees fairly Contributing to the community Respecting the environment

ILLEGAL AND UNETHICAL	ILLEGAL AND ETHICAL
Embezzling money	Providing rock-bottom prices *only* to distributors in underserved areas
Engaging in sexual harassment	Collaborating with other medical clinics to guarantee low prices in low-income countries (collusion)
Practicing collusion with competitors	
Encouraging fraudulent accounting	

© Cengage Learning 2013

of how business conduct can fall within legal and ethical dimensions. Clearly, legal and ethical actions should be your goal. Legality should be the floor—not the ceiling—for how to behave in business and elsewhere.

Do all actions have ethical implications? Clearly not. Some decisions fall within the realm of free choice with no direct link to right and wrong, good and bad. Examples might include where you watch your morning news, what features your company includes on its new tablet computers, or what cell phone you decide to purchase.

universal ethical standards Ethical norms that apply to all people across a broad spectrum of situations.

business ethics The application of right and wrong, good and bad, in a business setting.

ethical dilemma A decision that involves a conflict of values; every potential course of action has some significant negative consequences.

4-1b Universal Ethical Standards: A Reasonable Goal or Wishful Thinking?

Too many people view ethics as relative. In other words, their ethical standards shift depending on the situation and how it relates to them. Here are a few examples:

- ❍ "It's not okay to steal paper clips from the stationery store…*but* it's perfectly fine to 'borrow' supplies from the storage closet at work. Why? The company owes me a bigger salary."

- ❍ "It's wrong to lie…*but* it's okay to call in sick when I have personal business to take care of. Why? I don't want to burn through my limited vacation days."

- ❍ "Everyone should have a level playing field…*but* it's fine to give my brother the first shot at my company's contract. Why? I know he really needs the work."

This kind of two-faced thinking is dangerous because it can help people rationalize bigger and bigger ethical deviations. But the problem can be fixed by identifying **universal ethical standards** that apply to everyone across a broad spectrum of situations. Some people argue that we could never find universal standards for a country as diverse as the United States. But the nonprofit, nonpartisan Character Counts organization has worked

© STOCKBYTE/GETTY IMAGES

Exhibit 4.2 Universal Ethical Standards

TRUSTWORTHINESS	Be honest.
	Don't deceive, cheat, or steal.
	Do what you say you'll do.
RESPECT	Treat others how you'd like to be treated.
	Be considerate.
	Be tolerant of differences.
RESPONSIBILITY	Persevere.
	Be self-controlled and self-disciplined.
	Be accountable for your choices.
FAIRNESS	Provide equal opportunity.
	Be open-minded.
	Don't take advantage of others.
CARING	Be kind.
	Be compassionate.
	Express gratitude.
CITIZENSHIP	Contribute to the community.
	Protect the environment.
	Cooperate whenever feasible.

Source: © 2009 Josephson Institute. Reprinted from the Josephson Institute's Report Card on the Ethics of American Youth Summary with permission.

with a diverse group of educators, community leaders, and ethicists to identify six core values, listed in Exhibit 4.2, that transcend political, religious, class, and ethnic divisions.

4-2 Business Ethics: Not an Oxymoron

Quite simply, **business ethics** is the application of right and wrong, good and bad in a business setting. But this isn't as straightforward as it may initially seem. The most challenging business decisions seem to arise when values are in conflict…when whatever you do will have negative consequences, forcing you to choose among bad options. These are true **ethical dilemmas**. (Keep in mind that ethical *dilemmas* differ from ethical *lapses*, which

Bad News Today— Worse News Tomorrow!

In 2010, the Josephson Institute Center for Youth Ethics produced a Report Card on the Ethics of American Youth, based on a survey of 43,000 students in high schools across the United States. The results suggest that students are disturbingly willing to lie, cheat, steal, or intimidate others, despite a sky-high opinion of their own personal character. Some highlights (or perhaps we should call them lowlights):

- **59% admitted that they cheated on a test at school within the past 12 months (34% admitted doing so two or more times).**
- **39% believe that a person has to lie or cheat sometime in order to succeed, even though 84% agree that it's not worth it to lie or cheat because it hurts your character.**
- **18% admitted that they stole something from a friend within the past 12 months.**
- **21% admitted that they stole something from their parents within the past 12 months.**
- **72% agree that it's sometimes OK to hit or threaten a person who makes me very angry.**
- **28% admitted that they stole something from a store within the past 12 months.**

Sadly, the actual rates of bad behavior are probably understated, since more than 25% admitted that they lied on one or two questions, and experts agree that dishonesty on surveys usually reflects an attempt to conceal misconduct.

Despite rampant lying, cheating, and stealing, 98% of respondents agreed that it's important to be a person of good character, and 79% would rate their own character higher than that of their peers. Furthermore, 92% said they were satisfied with their personal character.

A number of analysts find it easy to dismiss the long-term implications of these findings, claiming that as teenagers mature, their judgment and morals will mature as well and their conduct will reflect stronger values. A recent large-scale study by the Josephson Institute of Ethics found unequivocally that high-school attitudes and behaviors and actions are a clear predictor of adult behavior across a range of situations. Cheaters in high school are far more likely as adults to lie to their spouses, customers, bosses, and employers and to cheat on expense reports, taxes, and insurance claims.

Clearly, now is the time for smart companies to clarify their standards and establish safeguards to head off costly ethical meltdowns in their future workforce.[1]

---

involve clear misconduct.) Here are a couple of hypothetical examples of ethical dilemmas:

- You've just done a great job on a recent project at your company. Your boss has been very vocal about acknowledging your work and the increased revenue that resulted from it. Privately, she said that you clearly earned a bonus of at least 10%, but due to company politics, she was unable to secure the bonus for you. She also implied that if you were to submit inflated expense reports for the next few months, she would look the other way, and you could pocket the extra cash as well-deserved compensation for your contributions.

- One of the engineers on your staff has an excellent job offer from another company and asks your advice on whether or not to accept the position. You need him to complete a project that is crucial to your company (and to your own career). You also have been told—in strictest confidence by senior management—that when this project is complete, the company will lay off all internal engineers. If you advise him to stay, he would lose the opportunity (and end up without a job), but if you advise him to go, you would violate the company's trust (and jeopardize your own career).

4-3 Ethics: Multiple Touchpoints

Although each person must make his or her own ethical choices, the organization can have a significant influence on the quality of those decisions. The next two sections discuss the impact of both the individual and the organization on ethical decision making, but as you read them, keep in mind that the interaction between the two is dynamic: sometimes it's hard to tell where one stops and the other starts.

4-3a Ethics and the Individual: The Power of One

Ethical choices begin with ethical individuals. Your personal needs, your family, your culture, and your religion all influence your value system. Your personality traits—self-esteem, self-confidence, independence, and sense of humor—play a significant role as well. These factors all come into play as you face ethical dilemmas. The challenge can be overwhelming, which has led a range of experts to develop frameworks for reaching ethical decisions. While the specifics vary, the key principles of most decision guides are very similar:

- ❂ Do you fully understand each dimension of the problem?
- ❂ Who would benefit? Who would suffer?
- ❂ Are the alternative solutions legal? Are they fair?
- ❂ Does your decision make you comfortable at a "gut feel" level?
- ❂ Could you defend your decision on the nightly TV news?
- ❂ Have you considered and reconsidered your responses to each question?

The approach seems simple, but in practice it really isn't. Workers—and managers, too—often face enormous pressure to do what's right for the company or right for their career, rather than simply what's right. And keep in mind that it's completely possible for two people to follow the framework and arrive at completely different decisions, each feeling confident that he or she has made the right choice.

4-3b Ethics and the Organization: It Takes a Village

Although each person is clearly responsible for his or her own actions, the organization can influence those actions to a startling degree. Not surprisingly, that influence starts at the top, and actions matter far more than words. The president of the Ethics Resource Center states, "CEOs in particular must communicate their personal commitment to high ethical standards and consistently drive the message down to employees through their actions." Any other approach—even just the *appearance* of shaky ethics—can be deeply damaging to a company's ethical climate. Here are a couple of examples from the news:

- ❂ High Flyers: When the CEOs of the Big Three automakers—two of them hovering on the edge of bankruptcy—went to Washington to request a $25 billion bailout package, they flew in three separate corporate jets at an estimated cost of $20,000 per round-trip flight. All three were operating in line with official corporate travel policies, but it just didn't look right. One lawmaker pointedly asked, "Couldn't you all have downgraded to first class or jet-pooled or something to get here? It would have at least sent a message that you do get it." Not surprisingly, the execs left empty-handed.[2]

> ❝ You have to do your own growing no matter how tall your grandfather was.
>
> — ABRAHAM LINCOLN

- ❂ Beach Junket: A few days after the Fed committed $85 billion to keep AIG out of bankruptcy, the insurer spent more than $440,000 on a sales "retreat" at a luxury resort in California. Expenditures included $150,000 for food, $23,000 in spa charges, and $7,000 for golf. Rather than apologizing, CEO Edward Liddy only committed that the company would examine its expenses.[3]

- ❂ Retirement Perks: When Jack Welch retired from his post as CEO of General Electric, the Board awarded him a generous financial package and an eye-popping collection of perks. His perks ranged from use of an $80,000 per month apartment, to country club fees, to corporate jet privileges. These perks did not represent an ethical breach—Welch negotiated them in good faith—but when the list surfaced in the press a year after his retirement, he voluntarily gave up his perks to mitigate a public relations problem that could have tarnished his reputation as a tough, ethical, and highly successful CEO.[4]

- ❂ Gross Excess: In the mid-1990s, Disney CEO Michael Eisner hired his friend Michael Ovitz as Disney's president. Fourteen months later, Disney fired Ovitz for incompetence, and he walked away with a $140 million settlement. Disgruntled stockholders sued the Disney Board for mismanagement, which led to the release of Ovitz's Disney expense account documents. In 14 months, he spent $4.8 million (that's about $80,000 per week!). Specifics included $54,330 for basketball tickets, a $946 gun for movie director Robert Zemeckis, and $319 for breakfast. Was he stealing? *No.* Was he unethical? You decide.[5] How do you feel about the business decisions described in Exhibit 4.3?

4-3c Creating and Maintaining an Ethical Organization

Research from the Ethics Resource Center (ERC) suggests that organizational culture has more influence than any other variable on the ethical conduct of individual employees. According to the ERC, key elements of a strong culture include displays of ethics-related actions at all levels of an organization and accountability for actions. The impact of these elements can be dramatic. Consider, for example, the following research results:

- A 61 percentage-point favorable difference in the level of observed misconduct when employees say they work in a strong ethical culture.

- When employees felt that the great recession negatively impacted the ethical culture of their company, misconduct rose by 16 percentage points.

- ERC research showed that companies behave differently during economic difficulties. The decisions and behaviors of their leaders are perceived by employees as a heightened commitment to ethics. As a result, employees adopt a higher standard of conduct for themselves.[6]

Robert Lane, former CEO of Deere, a highly performing, highly ethical corporation, believes in the importance of senior management commitment to ethics, but he points out that the "tone at the top" must be reinforced by the actual behavior observed by suppliers, dealers, customers, and employees. At Deere, this is summed up in highly visible, frequently referenced shorthand known as "the how." Lane declares that to establish an ethical culture, ethical words must be "backed up with documented practices, processes, and procedures, all understood around the globe."[7]

A strong organizational culture works in tandem with formal ethics programs to create and maintain ethical work environments. A written **code of ethics** is the cornerstone of any formal ethics program. The purpose of a written code is to give employees the information they need to make ethical decisions across a range of situations. Clearly, an ethics code becomes even more important for multinational companies, since it lays out unifying values and priorities for divisions that are rooted in different cultures. But a written code is worthless if it doesn't reflect living principles. An effective code of ethics flows directly from ethical corporate values and leads directly to ongoing communication, training, and action.

> **code of ethics** A formal, written document that defines the ethical standards of an organization and gives employees the information they need to make ethical decisions across a range of situations.

© Brian A. Jackson/Shutterstock.com

EXHIBIT 4.3 Ethics at Work: How Would You Judge the Actions of These Business Leaders?

Pierre Omidyar eBay creator Omidyar has contributed $100 million to the Tufts University Micro Finance Fund. His goal is to give economic power to poor people around the world through small business loans. Ultimately, he hopes to create entrepreneurial self-sufficiency as eBay has done for so many avid users.

Sherron Watkins Despite intense pressure and high personal stakes, Watkins, a former vice president of Enron, reported the accounting irregularities that led to the discovery of staggering corporate fraud.

Stanley O'Neal As investment house Merrill Lynch began racking up losses that led to its collapse, CEO O'Neal announced his "retirement" and walked away with a compensation package worth more than $160 million.

John A. Thain The ousted Merrill Lynch executive, under pressure from President Obama, agreed to reimburse federal bailout recipient Bank of America for an expensive renovation of his office that included an $87,000 area rug and a $35,000 commode.

Bill Gates As Microsoft CEO, Bill Gates made some ethically shaky moves, but he and his wife also established the Bill and Melinda Gates Foundation, by far the largest U.S. charity. Working for the foundation, Gates applies his famous problem-solving skills to global health, global development, and American education.

John Mackey From 1999 until 2006, Whole Foods CEO John Mackey posted thousands of anonymous comments on Yahoo! Finance, hyping his company and occasionally attacking rival Wild Oats, which he hoped to purchase for an advantageous price.

whistle-blowers
Employees who report their employer's illegal or unethical behavior to either the authorities or the media.

social responsibility
The obligation of a business to contribute to society.

stakeholders Any groups that have a stake—or a personal interest—in the performance and actions of an organization.

Specific codes of ethics vary greatly among organizations. Perhaps the best-known code is the Johnson & Johnson Credo, which has guided the company profitably—with a soaring reputation—through a number of crises that would have sunk lesser organizations. One of the striking elements of the Credo is the firm focus on fairness. It carefully refrains from overpromising financial rewards, committing instead to a "fair return" for stockholders.

To bring a code of ethics to life, experts advocate a forceful, integrated approach to ethics that virtually always includes the following steps:

1. Get executive buy-in and commitment to follow-through. Top managers need to communicate—even overcommunicate—about the importance of ethics. But talking works only when it's backed up by action: senior management must give priority to keeping promises and leading by example.

2. Establish expectations for ethical behavior at all levels of the organization, from the CEO to the night-time cleaning crew. Be sure that outside parties such as suppliers, distributors, and customers understand the standards.

3. Integrate ethics into mandatory staff training. From new-employee orientation to ongoing training, ethics must play a role. Additional, more specialized training helps employees who face more temptation (e.g., purchasing agents, overseas sales reps).

4. Ensure that your ethics code is both global and local in scope. Employees in every country should understand both the general principles and the specific applications. Be sure to translate it into as many languages as necessary.

5. Build and maintain a clear, trusted reporting structure for ethical concerns and violations. The structure should allow employees to seek anonymous guidance for ethical concerns and to report ethics violations anonymously.

6. Establish protection for **whistle-blowers**, people who report illegal or unethical behavior. Be sure that no retaliation occurs, in compliance with both ethics and the Sarbanes-Oxley Act (see discussion later in the chapter). Some have even suggested that whistle-blowers

should receive a portion of the penalties levied against firms that violate the law.

7. Enforce the code of ethics. When people violate ethical norms, companies must respond immediately and—whenever appropriate—publicly to retain employee trust. Without enforcement, the code of ethics becomes meaningless.

4-4 Defining Social Responsibility: Making the World a Better Place

Social responsibility is the obligation of a business to contribute to society. Similar to ethics, the broad definition is clear, but specific implementation can be complex. Obviously, the number-one goal of any business is long-term profits; without profits, other contributions are impossible. But once a firm achieves a reasonable return, the balancing act begins: how can a company balance the need to contribute against the need to boost profits, especially when the two conflict? The answer depends on the business's values, mission, resources, and management philosophy, which lead in turn to its position on social responsibility. Business approaches fall across the spectrum, from no contribution to proactive contribution, as shown in Exhibit 4.4.

4-4a The Stakeholder Approach: Responsibility to Whom?

Stakeholders are any groups that have a stake—or a personal interest—in the performance and actions of an organization. Different stakeholders have different needs, expectations, and levels of interest. The federal government, for instance, is a key stakeholder in pharmaceutical companies but a very minor stakeholder in local art studios. The community at large is a key stakeholder for a coffee shop chain but a minor stakeholder for a web design firm. Enlightened organizations identify key stakeholders for their business and consider stakeholder priorities in their decision making. The goal is to balance their needs and priorities as effectively as possible, with an eye toward building their business over the long term. Core stakeholder groups for most businesses are employees, customers, investors, and the broader community.

Responsibility to Employees: Creating Jobs That Work Jobs alone aren't enough. The starting point for socially responsible employers is to meet legal standards, and the

© Feng Yu/Shutterstock.com

Exhibit 4.4 The Spectrum of Social Responsibility

LESS Responsible

No Contribution
Some businesses do not recognize an obligation to society and do only what's legally required.

Responsive Contributions
Some businesses choose to respond on a case-by-case basis to market requests for contributions.

Proactive Contributions
Some businesses choose to integrate social responsibility into their strategic plans, contributing as part of their business goals.

MORE Responsible

---

requirements are significant. How would you judge the social responsibility of the firms listed in Exhibit 4.5? Employers must comply with laws that include equal opportunity, workplace safety, minimum-wage and overtime requirements, protection from sexual harassment, and family and medical unpaid leaves. We will discuss these legal requirements (and others) in Chapter 15 on Human Resource Management.

But socially responsible employers go far beyond the law. They create a workplace environment that respects the dignity and value of each employee. They ensure that hard work, commitment, and talent pay off. They move beyond minimal safety requirements to establish proactive protections, such as ergonomically correct chairs and computer screens that reduce eyestrain. And the best employers respond to the ongoing employee search for a balance between work and personal life. With an increasing number of workers facing challenges such as raising kids and caring for elderly parents, responsible companies are stepping in with programs such as on-site day care, company-sponsored day camp, and referral services for elder care.

Responsibility to Customers: Value, Honesty, and Communication One core responsibility of business is to deliver consumer value by providing quality products at fair prices. Honesty and communication are critical components of this equation. **Consumerism**—a widely accepted social movement—suggests that consumer rights should be the starting point. In the early 1960s, President Kennedy defined these rights, which most businesses respect in response to both consumer expectations and legal requirements:

- The Right to Be Safe: Businesses are legally responsible for injuries and damages caused by their

products—even if they have no reason to suspect that their products might cause harm. This makes it easy for consumers to file suits. In some cases, the drive to avert lawsuits has led to absurdities such as the warning on some coffee cups: "Caution! Hot coffee is hot!" (No kidding…)

- The Right to Be Informed: The law requires firms in a range of industries—from mutual funds, to groceries, to pharmaceuticals—to provide the public with extensive information. The Food and Drug Administration, for instance, mandates that most grocery foods feature a very specific "Nutrition Facts" label. Beyond legal requirements, many firms use the Web to provide a wealth of extra information about their products. KFC, for example, offers an interactive Nutrition Calculator that works with all of its menu items (and it's fun to use, too).

- The Right to Choose: Freedom of choice is a fundamental element of the capitalist U.S. economy. Our economic system works largely because consumers freely choose to purchase the products that best meet their needs. As businesses compete, consumer value increases. Socially responsible firms support consumer choice by following the laws that prevent anticompetitive behavior such as predatory pricing, collusion, and monopolies.

- The Right to Be Heard: Socially responsible companies make it easy for consumers to express legitimate complaints. They also develop highly

> **consumerism** A social movement that focuses on four key consumer rights: (1) the right to be safe, (2) the right to be informed, (3) the right to choose, and (4) the right to be heard.

trained customer service people to respond to complaints. In fact, smart businesses view customer complaints as an opportunity to create better products and stronger relationships. Statistics suggest that 1 in 50 dissatisfied customers takes the time to complain. The other 49 quietly switch brands. By soliciting feedback, you're not only being responsible, but also building your business.[8]

Delivering quality products is another key component of social responsibility to consumers. **Planned obsolescence**—deliberately designing products to fail in order to shorten the time between consumer repurchases—represents a clear violation of social responsibility. In the long term, the market itself weeds out offenders. After all, who would repurchase a product that meets a premature end? But in the short term, planned obsolescence thins consumer wallets and abuses consumer trust.

When businesses do make mistakes, apologizing to consumers won't guarantee renewed sales. But a sincere apology can definitely restore a company's reputation, which can ultimately lead to greater profits. Three recent examples make this point clear:

❍ *Going with the Flow*: In late 2010, Johnson & Johnson discontinued the popular o.b. Ultra tampons. Loyal users stripped the shelves of remaining stock (bidding the price of a box of Ultras up to more than $100 on eBay) and bombarded the manufacturer

"More than 75% of consumers say that social responsibility is an important factor in their purchase decisions, and 70% say they are willing to pay a premium for products from a socially responsible company."

— Knowledge@Wharton

© iStockphoto.com/Lasse Kristensen

Social Responsibility at Work

How would you judge the actions of these firms?

The Clorox Company   In early 2008, Clorox introduced a line of "99% natural" cleaning products called Green Works. This is the first such effort from a major consumer products company, and also the first time that the Sierra Club has endorsed a product line by allowing the use of its logo on the labels. In return, Clorox makes an annual contribution to the Sierra Club, the amount based on total Green Works sales.

Tyson Foods   Tyson has been accused of unfair business practices, unsavory labor and environmental practices, and controversial chicken-raising protocols, but in 2009, the factory farmer gave nearly 11% of its profits to charity.

Kraft   As obesity among kids spirals out of control, Kraft has taken a brave stand: a pledge to stop advertising unhealthy—yet highly profitable—foods to young children. Kraft also plans to eliminate in-school marketing and drop some unhealthy snacks from school vending machines. As the king of the food business, Kraft has chosen what's right for kids over what's right for its own short-term profits.

Enron/Arthur Andersen (now defunct)   Enron, once hailed as a shining example of corporate excellence, collapsed in late 2001 due to massive accounting fraud, which bilked employees and other small investors out of millions of dollars. Arthur Andersen, hired to audit Enron's accountings, participated in the scandal by masking the issues and shredding documents containing potential evidence.

Bank of America   After receiving $45 billion in taxpayer bailout funds, Bank of America sponsored a five-day carnival-like event outside the 2009 Super Bowl stadium called the NFL Experience. The high-profile attraction included 850,000 square feet of sports games, plus marketing solicitations for football-themed B of A banking products. The bank defended the event as an effective growth strategy, while critics blasted it as an abuse of taxpayer dollars.

Toyota   In 2009, Toyota stonewalled for months before admitting to a defect in some of its most popular cars that appeared to cause fatal accidents due to unintended acceleration. Even after announcing a large-scale recall, Toyota waited five days before halting new sales on models affected by the recall. Some analysts believe that Toyota knew about the defects long before the problems began and opted to do nothing.

© Cengage Learning 2013

Investors count on companies to spend money wisely and fully disclose all key facts.

© Jose Luis Pelaez/JLP Studios/Jupiterimages

with complaints. In late 2011, Johnson & Johnson announced that Ultras would be back on shelf by late 2012, and offered an apology video rife with every cliché imaginable, including a handsome, male singer. The music video was customizable; viewer names appeared throughout in the video, and the video closed with a coupon offer. The video represented a masterful attempt to regain loyalty for a product that had yet to reappear on the shelf.[9]

- *Deleted without Warning*: In mid-2009, Amazon remotely and abruptly deleted some digital editions of books from the Kindle devices of customers who had already purchased them (because Amazon hadn't obtained proper rights to make those sales in the first place). Indignant customers were furious at this violation of their privacy, which many felt was akin to theft, despite an automatic refund of the purchase price from Amazon. Amazon founder and CEO Jeff Bezos issued a characteristically blunt apology, stating that the company's actions were "stupid, thoughtless, and painfully out of line with its principles." But fortunately for Amazon, not too much harm was done; by the end of 2009, Kindle remained Amazon's bestselling product, and sales of Kindle digital books hit 48% of the sales of physical books.[10]

- *Apple Angst*: Apple introduced the iPhone on June 29, 2007, to rave reviews and stellar sales, despite the $599 price tag. But two months later, Apple dropped the price of the phone by $200, in order to expand the user base yet further. Not surprisingly, early adopters were livid—why, they demanded, did

© David Robertson/Alamy

Apple repay their trust and support by ripping them off? CEO Steve Jobs quickly apologized and offered every $599 iPhone customer a $100 Apple store credit. The response seemed to work. In 2008, Apple's ranking in the American Customer Satisfaction Index climbed 8%, a full ten percentage points ahead of its nearest competitor, maintaining a dramatic lead through 2011.[11]

Responsibility to Investors: Fair Stewardship and Full Disclosure

The primary responsibility of business to investors is clearly to make money—to create an ongoing stream of profits. But companies achieve and maintain long-term earnings in the context of responsibility to *all* stakeholders, which may mean trading short-term profits for long-term success. Responsibility to investors starts by meeting legal requirements, and in the wake of recent corporate scandals, the bar is higher than ever. The 2002 **Sarbanes-Oxley Act** limits conflict-of-interest issues by restricting the consulting services that accounting firms can provide for the companies they audit. Sarbanes-Oxley also requires that financial officers and CEOs personally certify the validity of their financial statements. (See Chapter 8 for more detail on the Sarbanes-Oxley Act.)

But beyond legal requirements, companies have a number of additional responsibilities to investors. Spending money wisely would be near the top of the list. For instance, are executive retreats to the South Pacific on the company tab legal? They probably are. Do they represent a responsible use of corporate dollars? Now that seems unlikely. Honesty is another key responsibility that relates directly to financial predictions. No one can anticipate exactly how a company will perform, and an overly optimistic or pessimistic assessment is perfectly legal. But is it socially responsible? It probably isn't, especially if it departs too far from the objective facts—which is, of course, a subjective call.

Responsibility to the Community: Business and the Greater Good

Beyond increasing everyone's standard of living, businesses can contribute to society in two main ways: philanthropy and responsibility. **Corporate philanthropy** includes

Sarbanes–Oxley Act
Federal legislation passed in 2002 that sets higher ethical standards for public corporations and accounting firms. Key provisions limit conflict–of–interest issues and require financial officers and CEOs to certify the validity of their financial statements.

corporate philanthropy
All business donations to nonprofit groups, including money, products, and employee time.

all business donations to nonprofit groups, including both money and products. The Giving USA Foundation reported that total corporate donations grew an estimated 10.6% in 2010, and the total change from 2008 to 2010 was a whopping +23.6%, which was surprisingly high in light of the Great Recession. Not only that, 65% of the surveyed corporations increased their contributions from 2009 to 2010. Much of the growth may have been fueled by pharmaceutical companies, which substantially boosted giving of both cash and products.[12]

Corporate philanthropy also includes donations of employee time; in other words, some companies pay their employees to spend time volunteering at nonprofits. In 2011, Eli Lilly & Co. launched an international volunteer program, which pays for 200 employees to travel to developing nations to work with and for the local populations.[13]

Some companies contribute to nonprofits through **cause-related marketing**. This involves a partnership between a business and a nonprofit, designed to spike sales for the company and raise money for the nonprofit. Unlike outright gifts, these dollars are not tax deductible for the company, but they can certainly build the company's brands.

Corporate responsibility relates closely to philanthropy but focuses on the actions of the business itself rather than donations of money and time. GE actively recruits and nurtures members of the U.S. military, currently employing more than 10,000 U.S. veterans. The firm provides special recognition and support for military employees and

iHurt—Working Conditions for Employees at Apple Contractors in China May Be Painfully Bad

As demand for iPads and iPhones has skyrocketed throughout the West, pressure to produce has intensified for the factory workers in China who pump out the products in increasingly high numbers. Conditions may be especially tough for workers at Foxconn, one of Apple's key suppliers in China. After a spate of worker suicides in 2010, managers at the factories ordered new staff to sign pledges that they would not attempt to commit suicide. At the advice of psychologists, Foxconn also erected anti-suicide nets around worker dormitory buildings. An independent investigation uncovered some appalling conditions that may have contributed to the suicides:

- **Excessive overtime was rife, despite a legal limit of 36 hours a month. One worker's pay slip showed 98 hours of overtime in one month.**

- **During peak periods of demand for the iPad, workers were allowed only one day off in 13.**

- **Badly performing workers were humiliated in front of colleagues.**

- **Workers were banned from talking and forced to stand up for their 12-hour shifts.**

Apple's supplier code of conduct demands that employees are treated with respect and dignity, but its own audit reports suggest suppliers in China may not meet up to these standards. The situation is especially deplorable given that in early 2011, Apple reported one of the most lucrative quarters of any corporation in history, with $13.06 billion in profits on $46.3 billion in sales. Its sales would have been even higher, executives said, if overseas factories had been able to produce more.

Responding to the controversy, Apple entered a partnership with the Fair Labor Association (FLA). In doing so, the company agreed to uphold the FLA's workplace code of conduct throughout their entire supply chain. But the FLA may not have been the best choice, since some experts have pointed out that the FLA is in part funded by the companies it investigates. In fact, recent research suggests that labor rights violations remain the norm in some key Foxconn factories, and in June, 2012, yet another worker killed himself.[14]

Should Your Tap Water Go to the Dogs?

Practically everyone has watched a thirsty dog eagerly slurp water from an open toilet. Leaving the yuck factor aside, can all those dogs really be wrong? Both research and experience suggest that "toilet to tap" (or repurposing wastewater) may be the long-term solution to the looming worldwide fresh water shortage. In fact, recycled water has long been used for agriculture and industry. But the city-state of Singapore and swaths of Orange County, California, have gone even further, purifying sewage water on a large scale to meet much of their populations' general water needs, claiming that the recycled wastewater is nearly as pure as distilled water. Still, before the reclaimed water reaches the tap, both Singapore and Orange County mix it with other water sources to increase public acceptance. Orange County officials believe that in another ten years, they may be able to pump the recycled wastewater directly to taps. The business opportunities have already begun to emerge. Currently, companies such as GE Water and Siemens Water Technologies are doing advanced water research and helping to design and build filtration facilities.[15]

of future generations to meet their needs. This means weaving environmentalism throughout the business decision-making process. Since sustainable development can mean significant long-term cost savings, the economic crisis may even push forward environmentally friendly programs.

The results of sustainability programs have been impressive across a range of industries. McDonald's, for instance, produces mountains of garbage each year, as do virtually all major fast-food chains. But the Golden Arches stands above the others in its attempts to reduce the problem. Following are some encouraging statistics:

- By the end of 2008, McDonald's UK was recycling 100% of its used cooking oil for biodiesel to fuel delivery trucks. This equates to 1,500 family cars being removed from the road each year.

- "Soft drinks were shipped as syrup in cardboard containers. The local restaurants added the water and the fizz. Now the syrup is delivered by trucks that pump it directly into receiving tanks at the restaurants. No packaging is needed at all. Savings: 68 million pounds of cardboard per year."[16]

Reducing the *amount* of trash is better than recycling, but recycling trash clearly beats dumping it in a landfill. McDonald's participates in this arena as well, through their extensive recycling programs, but more importantly as a big buyer of recycled products.

Taking an even broader perspective, some firms have started to measure their carbon footprint, with an eye toward reducing it. **Carbon footprint** refers to the amount

sustainable development Doing business to meet the needs of the current generation, without harming the ability of future generations to meet their needs.

carbon footprint Refers to the amount of harmful greenhouse gases that a firm emits throughout its operations, both directly and indirectly.

families before, during, and after deployments. Taking a different approach to corporate responsibility, Starbucks pays its suppliers a premium for "ethically sourced" coffee. A fair portion of the price must get to the farmers, and measures are in place to ensure safe and humane working conditions. These policies of both corporations ultimately benefit society as a whole.

Responsibility to the Environment Protecting the environment is perhaps the most crucial element of responsibility to the community. Business is a huge consumer of the world's limited resources, from oil, to timber, to fresh water, to minerals. In some cases, the production process decimates the environment and spews pollution into the air, land, and water, sometimes causing irreversible damage. And the products created by business can cause pollution as well, such as the smog generated by cars, and the sometimes-toxic waste caused by junked electronic parts.

The government sets minimum standards for environmental protection at the federal, state, and local levels. But a growing number of companies are going further, developing innovative strategies to build their businesses while protecting the environment. Many have embraced the idea of **sustainable development**: doing business to meet the needs of this generation without harming the ability

McDonald's has been a worldwide leader in sustainable development.

© CHUCK BERMAN/MCT/Landov

of harmful greenhouse gases that a firm emits throughout its operations, both directly and indirectly. The ultimate goal is to become carbon neutral—either to emit zero harmful gasses or to counteract the impact of emissions by removing a comparable amount from the atmosphere through projects such as planting trees. Dell Inc. became fully carbon neutral in mid-2008, fulfilling its quest to become "the greenest technology on the planet." More recently, PepsiCo calculated the carbon footprint for its Tropicana orange juice brand and was surprised to learn that about a third of its emissions came from applying fertilizer to the orange groves. According to the Conference Board, business leaders have begun to see their carbon footprint—both measurement and reduction—as a burgeoning opportunity.[17] Many large corporations track three different types of emissions. The first, called Scope 1, refers to direct emissions produced by corporate operations. The second, called Scope 2, refers to emissions that result from purchased electricity, heat, and steam. Scope 3 emissions, which are more complex to track, are emissions that occur outside a company's boundary, but over which it has some control. This category includes areas such as employee commutes, supplier emissions, and product-use emissions. Examining Scope 3 emissions has motivated Sony Electronics to make energy efficiency a priority in new product development, and spurred the Coca Cola Corporation to focus on developing more environmentally friendly "cold drink equipment" (e.g., vending machines and fountain drink dispensers). Coke was surprised and dismayed to learn that emissions from their combined cold drink equipment accounted for three times the level of emissions of their total manufacturing.[18]

A growing number of companies use **green marketing** to promote their businesses. This means marketing environmental products and practices to gain a competitive edge. Patagonia, for example, markets outdoor clothing using 100% organic cotton and natural fibers such as hemp. But green marketing represents a tough challenge: while most people support the idea of green products, the vast majority won't sacrifice price, performance, or convenience to actually buy those products. Sometimes, however, green marketing can be quite consistent with profitability. The Toyota Prius hybrid car offers an interesting example. The Prius costs several thousand dollars more than a standard car, but as gas prices skyrocketed through the summer of 2008, consumers flooded the dealerships, snapping up Prius hybrids faster than Toyota could ship them. Yet, when the economy dropped in late 2008, Toyota sales plummeted along with the rest of the industry, suggesting that the environment may be a fair-weather priority for consumers.[19]

> **"Surprisingly**, workplace ethics actually improved during the Great Recession."
>
> — Ethics Resource Center

4-5 Ethics and Social Responsibility in the Global Arena: A House of Mirrors?

Globalization has made ethics and social responsibility even more complicated for workers at every level. Bribery and corruption are among the most challenging issues faced by companies and individuals that are involved in international business. Transparency International, a leading anticorruption organization, publishes a yearly index of "perceived corruption" across 146 countries. No country scores a completely clean 10 out of 10, and the United States scores a troubling 7.1, which was quite a bit higher than China at 3.5 and India at 3.3, but lower than most of the European countries that dominate the top of the list. Not surprisingly, the world's poorest countries fall largely in the bottom half of the index, suggesting that rampant corruption is part of their business culture.[20]

Corruption wouldn't be possible if companies didn't offer bribes, so Transparency International also researched the likelihood of firms from industrialized countries to pay bribes abroad. The 2011 results indicated that firms from export powers Russia, China, and Mexico rank among the worst, with India following close behind. U.S. corporations, forbidden to offer bribes since 1977 under the Foreign Corrupt Practices Act, show a disturbing inclination to flout the law. The United States scored 8.1 out of a possible 10, falling below many Western European countries.[21]

These statistics raise some thought-provoking questions:

- When does a gift become a bribe? The law is unclear, and perceptions differ from country to country.
- How can corporations monitor corruption and enforce corporate policies in their foreign branches?
- What are other ways to gain a competitive edge in countries where bribes are both accepted and expected?

Other challenging issues revolve around business responsibility to workers abroad. At minimum, businesses should pay a living wage for reasonable hours in a safe

Going Green—It's Not Just Governments

While governments and grassroots groups around the world have led the global push to "go green," make no mistake, multinational businesses have played a leadership role as well, making major contributions to the greening of the planet, some using strikingly innovative methods (e.g., on-site worm farms to hasten recycling). Here are some examples from *Newsweek*'s 2011 Green Rankings:

- For every new employee hired at Indian technology services giant, Infosys, the company plants a sapling to help replenish natural resources. In addition, the company's environmental programs have combined to reduce its energy consumption, water consumption, and carbon footprint by 5%.

- In 2010, Tata Consultancy Services, another Indian technology giant, reduced its carbon footprint by 14.07%, reduced paper consumption by 34%, and increased waste conversion to manure by 60%. In addition, between 2009 and 2010, 100,000 employees participated in sustainability training.

- Technology services firm CA, Inc., launched an innovative print-management program, which eliminates the need for cover pages when printing, and saved an estimated 16.3 million sheets of paper between April 2009 and October 2010. The company's new $30 million building in India includes an on-site worm farm to recycle all nonplastic waste.

- Computer giant Dell uses biodegradable mushroom and bamboo packaging to wrap the products it ships. Dell also provides an easy way for customers to recycle old computers and products, by returning them to a Goodwill store for refurbishment, reuse, or recycling. The company says that this program has kept more than 190 million pounds of e-waste from landfills and created 250 green jobs.

- Walmart de Mexico introduced reusable bags in 2008, and by 2010, the company had sold more than 4.2 million of the bags, which helped it reach a 58% reduction in plastic bags use, three years ahead of schedule.[22]

working environment. But exactly what this means is less clear-cut. Does a living wage mean enough to support an individual or a family? Does "support" mean enough to subsist day to day or enough to live in modest comfort? Should American businesses ban child labor in countries where families depend on their children's wages to survive? Companies must address these questions individually,

bringing together their own values with the laws of both the United States and their host countries.

The most socially responsible companies establish codes of conduct for their vendors, setting clear policies for human rights, wages, safety, and environmental impact. In 1991, Levi Strauss became the first global company to establish a comprehensive code of conduct for its contractors. Over the years, creative thinking has helped it maintain its high standards, even in the face of cultural clashes. An example from Bangladesh, outlined in the *Harvard Business Review*, illustrates its preference for win-win solutions. In the early 1990s, Levi Strauss "discovered that two of its suppliers in Bangladesh were employing children under the age of 14—a practice that violated the company's principles but was tolerated in Bangladesh. Forcing the suppliers to fire the children would not have ensured that the children received an education, and it would have caused serious hardship for the families depending on the children's wages. In a creative arrangement, the suppliers agreed to pay the children's regular wages while they attended school and to offer each child a job at age 14. Levi Strauss, in turn, agreed to pay the children's tuition and provide books and uniforms." This creative solution allowed the suppliers to maintain their valuable contracts from Levi Strauss, while Levi Strauss upheld its values and improved the quality of life for its most vulnerable workers.[23]

Clearly, codes of conduct work best with monitoring, enforcement, and a commitment to finding solutions that work for all parties involved. Gap Inc. offers an encouraging example. In 1996, Gap published a rigorous Code of Vendor Conduct and required compliance from all of its vendors. Its vendor-compliance officers strive

"In 2010, the environmental impact of recycling and composting equaled to removing 36 million cars from the road."

—Environmental Protection Agency

social audit A systematic evaluation of how well a firm is meeting its ethics and social responsibility goals.

to visit each of its 3,000 factories at least once a year. The company has uncovered a troubling number of violations, proactively pulling contracts from serious violators and rejecting bids from suppliers who don't meet its standards.

Gap and Levi Strauss seem to be doing their part, but the world clearly needs universal standards and universal enforcement to ensure that the benefits of globalization don't come at the expense of the world's most vulnerable people.[24]

4–6 Monitoring Ethics and Social Responsibility: Who Is Minding the Store?

Actually, many firms are monitoring themselves. The process is called a **social audit**, which is a systematic evaluation of how well a firm is meeting its ethics and social responsibility objectives. Establishing goals is the starting point for a social audit, but the next step is to determine how to measure the achievement of those goals, and measurement can be a bit tricky. As You Sow, an organization dedicated to promoting corporate social responsibility, recommends that companies measure their success by evaluating a "double bottom line," one that accounts for traditional financial indicators, such as earnings, and one that accounts for social-responsibility indicators, such as community involvement.

Other groups are watching as well, which helps keep businesses on a positive track. Activist customers, investors, unions, environmentalists, and community groups all play a role. In addition, the threat of government legislation keeps some industries motivated to self-regulate. One example is the entertainment industry, which uses a self-imposed rating system for both movies and TV, largely to fend off regulation. Many people argue that the emergence of salads at fast-food restaurants represents an effort to avoid regulation as well.

Choosing Between a Loaf of Bread and a Packet of Shampoo

© imagebroker/Alamy

Three-quarters of the world's population—nearly 4 billion people—earn less than $2 per day. But C. K. Prahalad, a well-respected consultant and economist, claims that if the "aspirational poor" had a chance to consume, they could add about $13 trillion in annual sales to the global economy. Unilever, a global marketing company headquartered in Europe, has aggressively pursued this market with consumer products. Their customers might not have electricity, running water, or even enough for dinner, but many of them do have packets of Sunsilk shampoo and Omo detergent. Electronics companies have experienced marketing success as well. In Dharavi, for instance—one of the largest urban slums in India—more than 85% of households own a television.

Critics suggest that the corporate push to reach impoverished consumers will enrich multinationals at the expense of their customers, representing exploitation of the world's poorest people. Ashvin Dayal, East Asia director for the antipoverty group Oxfam UK, expressed concern to *Time* magazine that corporate marketing might unseat locally produced products or encourage overspending by those who truly can't afford it. Citing heavily marketed candy and soda, he points out that "companies have the power to create needs rather than respond to needs."

But Prahalad counters that many people at the bottom of the economic pyramid accept that some of the basics—running water, for instance—are not likely to ever come their way. Instead, they opt to improve their quality of life through affordable "luxuries," such as single-use sachets of fragrant shampoo. He argues that "It's absolutely possible to do very well while doing good." Furthermore, he suggests that corporate marketing may kick-start the poorest economies, triggering entrepreneurial activity and economic growth. Since globalization shows no signs of slowing, let's hope that he's right.[25]

What do you think? Is targeting the poor with consumer goods exploitation or simply smart marketing?

THE BIG PICTURE

Clearly, the primary goal of any business is to earn long-term profits for its investors. But profits alone are not enough. As active participants in society, firms must also promote ethical actions and social responsibility throughout their organizations and their corresponding customer and supplier networks. Although every area matters, a few warrant special mention:

- In tough economic times, effective business leaders focus more than ever on integrity, transparency, and a humane approach to managing the workforce—especially during cutbacks.
- Building or maintaining a presence in foreign markets requires particularly careful attention to human rights and local issues.
- Sustainable development and other environmentally sound practices are not only fiscally prudent and customer-friendly but also crucial for the health of our planet.

Virtually all organizations seek to hire individuals with a proven track record of ethical behavior and a strong commitment to integrity in both their personal decision making and actions. But over the past two decades, a number of large corporations—such as BellSouth, Dell, Dow, and Xerox—have established separate offices of ethics and compliance, offering a new career track for professionals eager to work specifically in the field of ethics. Offices of ethics and compliance can focus on a number different areas, but key areas of interest typically include mitigating employee-filed lawsuits, monitoring employee use of the Internet, overseeing corporate compliance with legislation, and taking steps to ensure that the corporate code of ethics moves "off the walls and into the halls." Qualifications for these positions often include education and experience in human resource management, accounting, or law. Many large corporations, such as Disney, Target, and Hasbro, also hire social responsibility professionals, often focused on sustainability and environmental initiatives, or auditing factories— typically foreign factories—to ensure compliance with company standards and local laws. These positions almost always require at least a four-year degree and exceptional communication skills.

CAREERS IN BUSINESS ETHICS AND SOCIAL RESPONSIBILITY

What *else?*
RIP & REVIEW CARDS IN THE BACK
and visit www.cengagebrain.com!

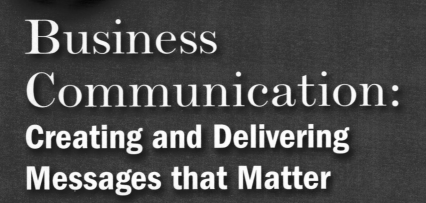

5

Business Communication:
Creating and Delivering Messages that Matter

LEARNING OBJECTIVES

After studying this chapter, you will be able to:

5-1 Explain the importance of excellent business communication

5-2 Describe the key elements of nonverbal communication

5-3 Compare, contrast, and choose effective communication channels

5-4 Choose the right words for effective communication

5-5 Write more effective business memos, letters, and emails

5-6 Create and deliver successful verbal presentations

> ## "WHAT YOU *DO* SPEAKS SO LOUD THAT I CANNOT HEAR WHAT YOU *SAY*."
>
> — RALPH WALDO EMERSON

5-1 | Excellent Communication Skills: Your Invisible Advantage

Much of your success in business will depend on your ability to influence the people around you. Can you land the right job? Close the deal that makes the difference? Convince the boss to adopt your idea? Motivate people to buy your products? Excellent communicators are not only influential but also well liked, efficient, and effective. Great communication skills can dramatically boost your chance for success, while poor communication skills can bury even the most talented people.

So what exactly are "excellent communication skills"? Many students believe that great business communication equates to a knack for speaking or a flair for writing. But if that's where you stop, you're likely to hit a brick wall again and again as you attempt to achieve your goals. Effective **communication** happens only when you transmit meaning—*relevant* meaning—to your audience.

Communication must be dynamic, fluid, and two-way, which includes listening. Seeking and understanding feedback from your audience—and responding appropriately—form the core of successful business communication. And it isn't as easy as you may think. American novelist Russell Hoban neatly summarized the issue: "When you come right down to it, how many people speak the same language even when they speak the same language?"

5-1a Communication Barriers: "That's Not What I Meant!"

Why is effective communication so challenging? The key issue is **noise**, which is any interference that causes the message

you send to be different from the message your audience understands. Some experts define noise in terms of **communication barriers**, which arise in a number of different forms. As you read the definitions, keep in mind that with a bit of extra effort, most are surmountable, and we'll discuss strategies and tips as we move through the chapter.

- ⊘ **Physical Barriers:** These can range from a document that looks like a wall of type, to a room that's freezing cold, to chairs in your office that force your visitors to sit at a lower level than you.

- ⊘ **Language Barriers:** Clearly, if you don't speak the language, you'll have trouble communicating. But even among people who do share the same language, slang, jargon, and regional accents can interfere with meaning.

- ⊘ **Body Language Barriers:** Even if your words are inviting, the wrong body language can alienate and distract your audience so completely that they simply won't absorb the content of your message.

- ⊘ **Perceptual Barriers:** How your audience perceives you and your agenda can create a significant obstacle to effective communication. If possible, explore their perceptions—both positive and negative—in advance!

- ⊘ **Organizational Barriers:** Some companies have built-in barriers to effective communication, such as an unspoken rule that the people at the top of the organization don't talk to the people at the bottom. These barriers are important to understand but hard to change.

- ⊘ **Cultural Barriers:** These can include everything from how you greet colleagues and establish eye contact to how you handle disagreement, eat business meals, and make small talk at meetings. As globalization gains speed, **intercultural communication** will become increasingly pivotal to long-term business success.

Identifying and understanding communication barriers is a vital first step toward dismantling them in order to communicate more effectively with any audience.

communication The transmission of information between a sender and a recipient.

noise Any interference that causes the message you send to be different from the message your audience understands.

communication barriers Obstacles to effective communication, typically defined in terms of physical, language, body language, cultural, perceptual, and organizational barriers.

intercultural communication Communication among people with differing cultural backgrounds.

5-2 Nonverbal Communication: Beyond the Words

Most of us focus on what we want to say, but *how* we say it matters even more. In fact, studies cited in *The Wall Street Journal's Career Journal* suggest that during face-to-face communication, only 7% of meaning comes from the verbal content of the message—38% comes from tone of voice, and 55% comes from body language such as facial expressions, gestures, and posture.[1]

The goal of **nonverbal communication** should be to reinforce the meaning of your message. Random facial expressions and disconnected body language—arbitrary arm thrusts, for example—are at best distracting, and at worst clownish. But strong, deliberate nonverbal communication can dramatically magnify the impact of your messages. Here are a few examples of how this can work (but keep in mind that these examples do not necessarily translate from culture to culture):

- **Eye Contact:** Within American culture, sustained eye contact (different from a constant cold stare) indicates integrity, trust, and respectful attention, whether you're communicating with a subordinate, a superior, or a peer.

- **Tone of Voice:** Variation is the key to effectiveness, since paying attention to a monotone takes more concentration than most people are willing to muster. Also, even when you're angry or frustrated, try to keep your voice in a lower pitch to encourage listeners to stay with your message.

- **Facial Expressions:** People vary widely in terms of how much emotion they show on their faces, but virtually everyone communicates, whether or not they know it, through a wide range of expressions that include shy smiles, focused frowns, clenched jaws, squinted eyes, and furrowed brows.

- **Gestures and Posture:** How you handle your body speaks for you. For example, leaning forward can indicate interest, shrugging can suggest a lack of authority, and fidgeting can imply either impatience or nervousness. To increase the power of your message, both your gestures and your posture should be confident, open, and coherent.

As silly as it sounds, one of the easiest, most effective ways to improve your body language is to practice nonverbal communication in front of the mirror. Check out your gestures, notice your facial expressions, and focus on eye contact. If you have the time and ability, it's also helpful (though humbling!) to videotape yourself delivering both a formal and informal message, and ask a trusted friend to dissect the results with you.

Accurately discerning the body language of others is another powerful business communication tool. But keep in mind that you must evaluate others in the context of common sense. When your boss keeps yawning, she may be bored, *or* she may just be tired. When your colleague crosses his arms, he may be indicating defensiveness, *or* he might just normally stand that way.

Dress for Success—Redefined!

The way you look and dress in the office makes a statement about what people can expect from you and how you feel about yourself. Your appearance is among the most powerful forms of business communication. Some experts believe that more than 50% of another person's perception of you is driven by how you look. By the time you get to college, you've probably heard again and again that a mainstream, conservative look is the best approach for business. But no one seems to have told that to several of today's best-known technology entrepreneurs who nailed top spots on *GQ* magazine's Worst Dressed Men of Silicon Valley list. *GQ* snipes that Craig Newmark, who launched Craig's List, dresses (unsurprisingly) like a guy who stalks Craigslist—wrinkled shirts, oversized blazers, and a beret fetish. *GQ* also criticizes several of the "winners" for sporting "dad jeans" and college logo-emblazoned hoodies. Mark Zuckerberg, founder of Facebook, scored the number one spot on the worst-dressed list, with style so poor that it even inspired a mock fashion-free men's clothing line, Mark By Mark Zuckerberg (http://www.markbymarkzuckerberg.com/). What lessons can you learn from this? In addition to being fashion DON'Ts, every man on the *GQ* list has already proven his worth through his measurable contributions to the tech business. So until you prove your worth, your best strategy may be to cultivate a mainstream appearance, and table your edgy look until *after* you've made it big.[2]

Social Media Kaleidoscope

If you take a stroll across any American college campus, you are likely to see hordes of students with cell phones virtually glued to their ears or dancing under their fingertips from the moment one class ends until the moment the next class begins, and sometimes well into the next class. Social media absorb much of this time and energy. The social media scene has taken hold in China as well. About a quarter of all social media users in the world are Chinese—almost 500 million people—and about half of them have more than one social media profile. But in China, social media has a whole different look and feel. Facebook, Twitter, and YouTube are officially blocked, but a raft of homegrown alternatives is thriving in their absence. The average Chinese Internet user is online for a hefty 2.7 hours per day. Interestingly, young people in China tend to have even more friends online than offline. The most popular alternative to Twitter in China is Sina Weibo, which—because each character in Chinese represents an entire word—allows for much longer messages within the 140-character limited micro-blogging format. Businesses in China have jumped on the opportunity to use Sina Weibo to deliver relatively long promotional messages, including web links, directly to their target consumers. In today's global environment, businesses must learn to communicate effectively via social media across a dazzling array of platforms and countries.[3]

5-2a Active Listening: The Great Divider

How we listen (or don't listen) also sends a high-impact, nonverbal message. In fact, an old Chinese proverb asserts that to listen well is as powerful a means of influence as to talk well. Those who do both are unstoppable.

Strong listening skills—**active listening**—play an obvious role in business success. The higher you go in an organization, the more you find that people are listening. Hourly employees may spend 30% of their time listening, while managers often spend 60%, and executives might spend 75% or more. Interestingly, top salespeople also tend to spend about 75% of their communication time listening.[4]

According to the International Listening Association website, 85% of our learning is derived from listening, yet listeners are distracted, forgetful, and preoccupied 75% of the time. If listening is so crucial, why do most of us have such a hard time engaging completely? One reason may be that people *listen* at about 125 to 250 words per minute, but *think* at about 1,000 to 3,000 words per minute—that's a significant gap. Common ways to fill the void include daydreaming, thinking about the past (e.g., last night), and planning for the future (e.g., later in the day).[5]

When you listen, try to use the extra thinking time to make yourself pay closer attention to the speaker. You'll find that people tend to tell more to those who listen better, so if you polish your listening skills, you're also likely to buff up the quality of what you know and when you know it. Exhibit 5.1 highlights some listening do's and don'ts (specific to American culture).[6]

5-3 Choose the Right Channel: A Rich Array of Options

Figuring out the right way to send a message can be a daunting challenge, especially in light of the growing number of choices. The various options are called **communication channels**. Understanding the impact of each channel will help you make the best decision regarding which to use.

active listening Attentive listening that occurs when the listener focuses his or her complete attention on the speaker.

communication channels The various ways in which a message can be sent, ranging from one-on-one in-person meetings to Internet message boards.

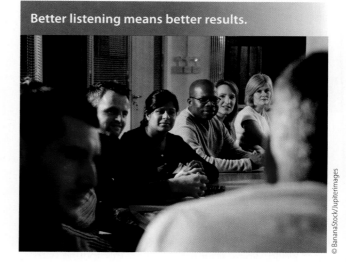

Better listening means better results.

Exhibit 5.1 Tips for Better Listening

LISTENING DO'S	LISTENING DON'TS
Use your extra mental capacity to summarize (to yourself!) what the speaker is saying. Ask yourself: Why does this matter? What's the key point?	Don't even glance at your emails or text messages. You won't fool anyone with those surreptitious peeks.
Take a few notes. It will not only help you concentrate but also communicate to the speaker that his or her thoughts really matter.	Don't begin speaking the moment the person stops talking. Take a brief pause to indicate that you're absorbing the message.
Listen with both your ears and your eyes. Notice any inconsistency between the speaker's words and body language.	Don't get overly comfortable. If your body is too relaxed, your mind may wander more easily.
Use nonverbal communication—nods, smiles, leaning forward—to indicate interest in the speaker.	Don't pick up your phone—or even look at your phone—when you're listening. And whenever it's practical, set your cell phone to vibrate when others are speaking.
Use verbal feedback and questions to indicate understanding and empathy: "So you're saying that…," or "Why do you think that?"	Don't interrupt or finish other people's sentences. There are few better ways to cut off future communication.

© Cengage Learning 2013

Communication channels differ from one another in terms of how much information—or richness—they communicate to the recipient. Exhibit 5.2 provides a brief overview of key channels. Other channels might include intranet postings, WebEx, Facebook, and text messaging Where would these additional channels fall on the spectrum? Why?

5-3a Consider the Audience: It's Not about You!

Clearly, the needs and expectations of your audience play a crucial role in your choice of communication channel. Even if the recipient's preferences seem absurd—for example, we probably all know someone who refuses to check email or voice mail—remember that your first priority is to communicate your message. If you send it through a channel that the audience doesn't expect, understand, or like, you've crippled your chance for successful communication.

Analysis and consideration of your audience should also be a top priority after you choose your communication channel. Meeting the needs of your audience will give you a crucial edge in developing a message that works.

5-4 Pick the Right Words: Is That Car Pre-Loved or Just Plain Used?!

Mark Twain once said, "The difference between the right word and almost the right word is the difference between lightning and the lightning bug." Perhaps that's a little extreme, but it may not be too far from the truth. In the business world, where your messages are competing with so

many others for the all-too-limited attention of the recipient, the right words can encourage your audience to stay with you long enough to absorb your message.

5-4a Analyze Your Audience

To find the right words, begin with the needs of your audience. Consider:

- **Expectations:** What kind of language do most people use in the organization? Is it formal or informal? Is it direct or roundabout? Should you differ from the norm? Why or why not?
- **Education:** The education level of the audience should drive the level of vocabulary and the complexity of the message.
- **Profession:** Some professions (e.g., website development) are rife with jargon and acronyms. How should this influence your message?

5-4b Be Concise

Comedian Jerry Seinfeld once said "I will spend an hour editing an eight-word sentence into five." While Jerry might be going a bit too far, it pays to be clear and concise in business communication. But don't be concise at the expense of completeness; include all information that your audience may need. (It'll save you time down the road.)

5-4c Avoid Slang

Unless you're absolutely certain that your audience will understand and appreciate it, do not use slang in either written or verbal communication. The risk of unintentionally alienating yourself from your audience is simply too high.

5-4d Avoid Bias

Intentionally or unintentionally, words can communicate biases that can interfere with your message, alienate your audience, and call your own character into question. As a result, you will be less effective in achieving the immediate goals of your communication (and possibly any future communication as well). Three kinds of **bias** are common.

Gender Bias Gender bias consists of words that suggest stereotypical attitudes toward a specific gender. Avoiding bias becomes tricky when you simply don't know the gender of your audience, which often happens when you apply for a job in writing. The best solution, of course, is to find out the recipient's name, but if you can't do that, do not address your message to "Dear Sir" or "Dear Madam"; rather, use the title of the position (e.g., "Dear Hiring Manager").

> "Improvement in a firm's communication effectiveness is associated with a nearly 16% increase in its market value."
>
> —Watson Wyatt, Consulting firm

Another common challenge is to establish agreement in your sentences without creating gender bias. Consider the following example:

The guitarist who loses his instrument must buy a new one.

Technically, this sentence is correct, but it implies that all guitarists are men. A simple solution would be to convert to plural:

Guitarists who lose their instruments must buy new ones.

This approach almost always works to help you sidestep the gender bias issue. In the rare case that it doesn't, you can simply use the "his or her" option.

Age Bias Age bias refers to words that suggest stereotypical attitudes toward people of specific ages. In American culture, older people tend to experience negative age bias much

bias A preconception about members of a particular group. Common forms of bias include gender bias; age bias; and race, ethnicity, or nationality bias.

EXHIBIT 5.2 Communication Channels

COMMUNICATION CHANNEL	CHANNEL RICHNESS	WHEN SHOULD YOU USE THIS CHANNEL?
MEMOS/REPORTS	Very low: Your audience won't gain any information from your tone or your body language.	When your content is uncontroversial When you must reach a number of people with the same message When you must communicate lengthy or detailed information
EMAIL	Very low: Here, too, your audience learns nothing beyond your words themselves.	When your content is uncontroversial When you must reach a number of people with the same message
INSTANT MESSAGE/ TEXTING	Very low: Because so many of us IM or text with as few words as possible, your audience will pick up only the basics.	When your content is uncontroversial When you want a quick response regarding relatively simple issues When you know that your audience won't be annoyed by it
VOICE MAIL	Low: Your audience has the benefit of hearing your tone but not seeing your body language.	When your content is uncontroversial When you don't need a record of your message (but don't forget that the recipient can easily save or forward your voice mail)
TELEPHONE CONVERSATION	Moderate: Your audience benefits from hearing your tone and how it changes through the call.	When you need to either deliver your message or get a response quickly When your content is more personal or controversial When you need or want a spontaneous, dynamic dialogue with the recipient
VIDEOCONFERENCING	High: Especially with state-of-the-art equipment, the channel conveys much of the richness of actually being there.	When you need to reach multiple people with complex or high-priority content When you need or want a spontaneous, dynamic dialogue with an audience that you cannot reach in person
IN-PERSON PRESENTATION	High: Your audience directly experiences every element of your communication, from verbal content, to tone, to body language.	When you need to reach a large audience with an important message When you need or want to experience the immediate response of your audience
FACE-TO-FACE MEETING	Very high: Your audience experiences your full message even more directly.	When your message is personal, emotional, complex, or high-priority (but if the recipient might be volatile, consider using a less-immediate channel) When you need or want instant feedback from your audience

© Cengage Learning 2013

Say What??!!

Between the Beijing Olympics in 2008 and the Shanghai World Expo in 2010, China has gained an increasingly high profile on the world stage, and so has Chinglish, a sometimes-bizarre blend of Chinese and mangled English language that seems to pop up on signs, menus, and labels throughout the tourist-heavy cities of China. For example:

- Plus-sized shoppers at the Scat clothing chain might find themselves needing to buy "fatso" or "lard-bucket" sizes.

- Before the Beijing Olympics, tourists could visit Racist Park, later rechristened Minorities Park to avoid sending a misleadingly negative message to visitors about Chinese culture.

- A sign at the Terracotta Warriors Museum in Xi'an reads "Cherishing Flowers and Trees" rather than "Keep Off the Grass."

- The sign pointing to the information desk in a major train station reads "Question Authority," which has somewhat startling overtones in this Communist country.

- In the past, the sick may have sought treatment at the Dongda Anus Hospital, now called the Dongda Proctology Hospital.

Although many of these language goofs are highly amusing, a number of Chinese find the snickers humiliating rather than funny. In fact, as the World Expo approached in 2010, the Chinese government established the Shanghai Commission for the Management of Language Use to eradicate by fiat the worst examples of mangled English. Many Chinese agree with translator Jeffrey Yao, who underscores that the purpose of signs is communication, not entertainment. "I want to see people nodding that they understand the message on these signs. I don't want to see them laughing."[7]

此段200米,当心
落石,请靠岩壁行走,
快速通过请勿逗留.
Within 200 meters,notice
the rockslide,please is run
about by cliff.

© John Henshall/Alamy

> **active voice** Sentence construction in which the subject performs the action expressed by the verb (e.g., *My sister wrote the paper*). The active voice works better for the vast majority of business communication.

more often than younger people. This happens despite specific federal legislation outlawing employment discrimination against people over 40 years old. The reason may be that American culture associates youth with highly valued qualities such as creativity, speed, independence, and individualism. This bias will become increasingly detrimental as the workforce ages. Here is an example of age bias:

We need someone young and dynamic in this position!

You could easily eliminate the negative bias by simply deleting the word "young" or by replacing it with the word "energetic." One clear benefit of eliminating bias in this case would be a broader applicant pool that might include an older person who is more dynamic than any of the younger applicants.

Race, Ethnicity, and Nationality Bias Words can also suggest stereotypical attitudes toward specific races, ethnicities, and nationalities. Leaving aside prejudice—which is clearly wrong—the problems in this area are usually unintentional and stem from unarticulated assumptions about a person's attitudes, opinions, and experiences. Your best plan for avoiding bias is to forgo any references to race, ethnicity, or nationality unless they are directly relevant and clearly necessary. And, of course, never simply assume

> **If you have nothing to say, say nothing.**
> — MARK TWAIN

© iStockphoto.com/Newbird

that one person embodies the attitudes, opinions, and experiences of a larger group. If you communicate with each person as an individual, you will not only avoid bias but also develop deeper, more effective channels of communication.

5-4e Use the Active Voice Whenever Possible

Active voice facilitates direct, powerful, concise communication. You have used the **active voice** when the subject of

Minding your Manners in the Digital World >:-P

Good manners today involve so much more than the please and thank you basics. Most likely, you are very comfortable with polite digital communication in your social world, but the story can change dramatically in the business world, with the potential for embarrassment around every corner. Here are some sticky situations and some thoughts on how to handle them:

- *Should you friend your boss or coworkers?* Before doing so, you should definitely get a feel for how involved your workplace is in digital networking. Needless to say, if you *do* connect with people from work, you must be careful not to publicly post either comments or pictures that relate to work. You should also consider using privacy controls and different friend

lists to control how and with whom you share information. And you'll need to vet postings from your other friends as well to make sure that no inappropriate information is shared.

- *Will your Facebook profile interfere with your job search, even if it's on a privacy lockdown?* Keep in mind that Facebook can change its privacy features at any time without notification, so it's always prudent to post conservatively on your profile, assuming anything you post online can become public at any time.

- *What's the best way to decline a request to connect with someone?* It's perfectly OK to simply ignore the request, without explaining your reasons, especially if the person is a relative stranger.[8]

---

your sentence *is* doing the action described by the verb. You have used the **passive voice** when the subject of your sentence *is not* doing the action described by the verb.

Here's an example of a sentence that uses the active voice:

Our team made a mistake in the sales forecast.

Our team, the subject of the sentence, did the action described by the verb (making a mistake). The same sentence in the passive voice would read as follows:

A mistake was made in the sales forecast.

In this version, the subject of the sentence is the mistake, which clearly did not do the action. As you can see from these examples, another benefit of active voice is accountability, which can create deeper trust between you and your audience.

5-5 Write High-Impact Messages: Breaking through the Clutter

For many businesspeople, checking email—or even regular mail—is like approaching a fire hose for a sip of water. Goal number one is to crank down the pressure to get what you need without being knocked over by all the rest. To attain this goal, many people simply press the delete button.

Your challenge as a writer is to make your message a must-read, and the starting point should be the needs of your audience. Consider how the audience will respond to your message—think about how they will feel, not what they will

do—and use that information to guide your writing. But keep in mind that it's hard to know for sure how the recipient will respond. For instance, each of the responses in Exhibit 5.3 could be reasonable for different people.

How do you know how your audience will respond? In most cases, you must simply guess based on as much evidence as you can find. The value of making a thoughtful guess is that the chances of achieving your goal will soar if you happen to be correct.

The anticipated audience response should directly affect how you structure your writing.

○ If the recipient will feel positive or neutral about your message, the memo or email should begin with your bottom line. What is your request or recommendation or conclusion? Why should the audience care? After

passive voice Sentence construction in which the subject does not do the action expressed by the verb; rather the subject is acted upon (e.g., *The paper was written by my sister*). The passive voice tends to be less effective for business communication.

Exhibit 5.3 Messages and Responses

MESSAGE	POSSIBLE RESPONSES
Please note the new computer password procedures.	Positive: *Great! We've really needed this.* Neutral: *OK, no big deal.* Negative: *Not another change…*
The company plans to restructure your work team when the project is complete.	Positive: *I can hardly wait to work with new people!* Neutral: *It's all part of the job…* Negative: *Not another change!*

you've clarified those points, follow up with your rationale and explanations (keeping in mind that less is usually more for time-starved businesspeople).

- If the recipient will feel negative about your message, start the memo or email with a couple of lines that present the rationale before you give the bottom line. Follow up with alternatives if there are any, and be sure to end on a positive note (rather than an apology). This structure is less straightforward, but it's a more effective way to communicate your message.

See Exhibit 5.4 for sample emails based on different anticipated responses to messages in an Internet game development firm.

5-5a Strike the Right Tone

Good business writing sounds natural—it flows like spoken language and reads like a conversation on paper. To strike the right tone for any given message, remember that you can choose from a wide variety of conversational styles, from formal to chatty. Imagine yourself speaking to the recipient of your message, and you'll find that the right tone emerges naturally. A few guidelines will also help:

- Use common words in most situations (e.g., *use* versus *utilize*).

- Use the active voice (e.g., *We made a mistake* versus *A mistake was made*).

- Use personal pronouns (*I, you*) whenever appropriate.

- Use contractions (*I'll, don't, here's*) as often as you would when speaking.

5-5b Don't Make Grammar Goofs

Grammatical errors will distract your reader from your writing and undermine your credibility. Most businesspeople are aware of the more common grammatical errors, so they tend to jump off the page before the content of the message. But if you're uncertain about a particular point, look at how professionally edited publications handle similar issues. Finally, don't be afraid to do a commonsense check on any grammatical question.

Edward P. Bailey, noted professor and business communication author, points out that many writers make grammar mistakes based on phantom knowledge—"mythical" grammar rules that aren't even in grammar handbooks. His research firmly reassures us that:

- It is OK to end a sentence with a preposition when doing so sounds natural and does not involve excess words (e.g., *Where is this book from?* is much better than *From where is this book?*).

- It is OK to begin sentences with "And" or "But" (e.g., *Most teens enjoy videogames with a moderate level of violence. But a small, vocal minority strongly advocates a more clean-cut approach.*).

- It is OK to split infinitives (e.g., *Try to effectively film the next scene* is a perfectly acceptable sentence, even though "effectively" is inserted between "to" and "film.").

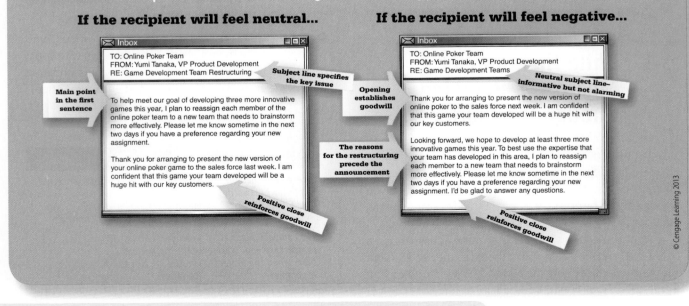

EXHIBIT 5.4 Sample Emails: Same Message, Different Approach

If the recipient will feel neutral...

TO: Online Poker Team
FROM: Yumi Tanaka, VP Product Development
RE: Game Development Team Restructuring

To help meet our goal of developing three more innovative games this year, I plan to reassign each member of the online poker team to a new team that needs to brainstorm more effectively. Please let me know sometime in the next two days if you have a preference regarding your new assignment.

Thank you for arranging to present the new version of your online poker game to the sales force last week. I am confident that this game your team developed will be a huge hit with our key customers.

Main point in the first sentence

Subject line specifies the key issue

Positive close reinforces goodwill

If the recipient will feel negative...

TO: Online Poker Team
FROM: Yumi Tanaka, VP Product Development
RE: Game Development Teams

Thank you for arranging to present the new version of online poker to the sales force next week. I am confident that this game your team developed will be a huge hit with our key customers.

Looking forward, we hope to develop at least three more innovative games this year. To best use the expertise that your team has developed in this area, I plan to reassign each member to a new team that needs to brainstorm more effectively. Please let me know sometime in the next two days if you have a preference regarding your new assignment. I'd be glad to answer any questions.

Neutral subject line—informative but not alarming

Opening establishes goodwill

The reasons for the restructuring precede the announcement

Positive close reinforces goodwill

© Cengage Learning 2013

If you follow these principles, your writing not only will sound more natural but also will flow more easily. Winston Churchill, a renowned writer and speaker, was on-board with this commonsense approach decades ago, as we can see from his joking comment that poked fun at tortured writing: "From now on, ending a sentence with a preposition is something up with which I will not put."[9]

5-5c Use Block Paragraphs

There are three elements to block paragraphs (1) use single spacing, (2) double space between paragraphs, and (3) do not indent the first sentence of your paragraphs. This approach has become standard for business writing over the past decade, as writers have begun to include an increasing number of additional elements such as headings and illustrations. The block paragraphs create a more organized look for your page, guiding the reader's eye through the key elements of your structure.

5-5d Use Headings and Bulleted Lists Wherever Appropriate

Both headings and bulleted lists will guide your reader more easily through your writing. And the easier it is for your reader, the more likely that he or she will absorb your message, which is, of course, your ultimate goal.

- **Headings:** A heading is not a title; rather, it is a label for one of several parts. If you have only one part, skip the heading and use a title or a subject line. Consider using informative headings (e.g., "Recruitment has stalled," rather than simply "Recruitment"), or question headings (e.g., "Have we met our recruitment goals for this campaign?"). And remember, headings are just as effective for letters and emails as they are for memos, and they are perfectly OK in one-page documents.

- **Bulleted Lists:** A bulleted list is invaluable tool that you can use to engage your reader's attention whenever you have more than one of anything in your writing (e.g., next steps, similar sections, questions). By formatting your lists with bullets, you are directing your reader's eye through your writing.

EXHIBIT 5.5 Ten Tips for Excellent Email

1. Consider both your primary and secondary readers. In other words, never forget that your reader may forward your email without considering the potential impact on you.

2. Keep it short! Many readers won't scroll down past whatever shows on their screen, so be sure to get your bottom line close to the top of your message.

3. Don't forget to proofread. This is especially important if you're asking someone to do something for you. And remember that your spell checker won't catch every mistake.

4. Use standard writing. Smiley faces, abbreviations, and five exclamation points are all fine if you're emailing your buddies, but in more formal messages they can make you look silly (or like you just don't care).

5. Avoid attachments if possible. They take time and space to open, and they don't always translate well to cell phones and PDAs. Instead, cut and paste relevant sections of the attachment into your email.

6. Don't assume privacy. Think of your emails as postcards that anyone (especially computer system administrators and managers) can read along the way. In that light, try not to use email to communicate negative or critical messages.

7. Respond promptly to emails. If you don't have time to respond to the email itself, consider sending a message such as "Sorry, but I'm swamped right now—will get back to you early next week."

8. Assume the best. Because emails are often brief, they can cause unintentional offense. If you receive an off-key message, don't be afraid to inquire: "I'm not sure what you mean . . . could you please explain?"

9. Create a compelling subject line. Make your reader want to open your message. Briefly communicate the topic of your message and why your reader should care.

10. Think before you write, and think again before you send! Too many people send messages in an emotional moment that they later regret. Take time to think and think again.

© Cengage Learning 2013

> # "We have two ears and one mouth so that we can listen twice as much as we speak."
>
> — Epictetus, Stoic philosopher

© Ilya Andriyanov/Shutterstock.com

5-6 Create and Deliver Successful Verbal Presentations: Hook 'Em and Reel 'Em In!

What do people fear most? The *Book of Lists* asserts that public speaking ranks number one for the majority of people, high above the fear of death at number four. So, when people say they would rather die than give a speech, they may really mean it! This section is designed to mitigate any fear you might have about public speaking by giving you guidance on how to create and deliver a high-impact verbal presentation.

As with most communication, the needs of the audience are the best place to begin. How does your audience feel about you and your topic? Are they interested? Hostile? Positive? What were they doing before your presentation? Dragging themselves out of bed after a late night at a sales meeting? Eating lunch? Use this information to guide how you develop your presentation. For instance, an eager, educated audience might not need as much background as a more lethargic, less-interested audience.

Giving great presentations may be easier than you think.

© Jon Feingersh/Iconica/Getty Images

5-6a Opening

The opening of your presentation gives you a chance to grab the attention of the audience. If your opening hooks them, you've boosted the likelihood that you will hold their attention throughout the presentation. But developing that hook can be a challenge. The following are some suggestions for effective hooks:

- **An Interesting or Startling Statistic:** In a presentation regarding a risk management program, you could open by sharing that "Your odds of being killed in a plane crash are about one in twenty-five million, while your odds of being killed falling out of bed are about one in two million. What does this mean for us?"

- **Audience Involvement:** Pulling the audience into your opening can be very effective. For instance, in a presentation for a clothing company: "Imagine yourself with me at 11 P.M. on a Friday night, standing in line for admission to the hottest club in New York. As we inch forward, we suddenly realize that three other women in line are wearing the exact same dress as you…."

- **A Compelling Story or Anecdote:** This approach works best when it's completely genuine, using specific details that are directly relevant to the audience. For instance, in a presentation about employee benefits, you might want to share the story of a colleague who beat cancer using the company's innovative healthcare program.

- **A Relevant Simile or Metaphor:** Patricia Fripp, an award-winning keynote speaker, shares a simile that worked well to open a presentation for a colleague: "Being a scientist is like doing a jigsaw puzzle in a snowstorm at night… you don't have all the pieces… and you don't have the picture to work from."

- **Engaging Questions:** In a presentation about customer service, you could open by asking: "How many of you have spent far too long waiting on hold for customer service that was finally delivered by a surly agent who clearly knew nothing about your question?"

5-6b Body

The most common presentation mistake is to include too many key ideas in the body of your presentation. Audiences simply cannot absorb more than two to four main points, and three are ideal. Specific examples and vivid comparisons will illustrate your points and bring them to life, while trusted sources, specific data, and expert quotations will increase your credibility and persuasiveness. Regardless of the length of your presentation, be sure to use clear transitions as you move from point to point.

Just before launching into the body of your presentation, you should tell the audience your key points, ideally with visual reinforcement. Then as you move to each new point, you can refer to the blueprint that you established upfront. A clear, explicit structure will help the audience track with you as you move through your material.

5-6c Close

Ideally, the close of your presentation will summarize your key points. Then circle back to your introduction, so that the beginning and the end serve as "bookends" for the body of your presentation. For instance, if you began by asking questions, end by answering them. If you began with an anecdote, end by referring to the same story. As an alternative (or maybe an addition), consider sharing a quotation or a bit of humor relevant to your content.

Also, keep in mind that you should verbally signal to your audience that you are about to conclude. After you do so—by saying, "In summary," for instance—be sure that you actually do conclude. Nothing alienates an audience more quickly than launching into another point after you've told them you're finished! Your body language will support your conclusion if you turn off your projector and move toward the audience to answer questions. And even if you aren't so eager to field questions, try to paste a receptive look on your face—it'll increase your credibility and set a positive tone for the Q&A session.

5-6d Questions

At the start of your presentation, decide whether you want to handle questions throughout your talk or save them for the end. Tell your audience your preference upfront; most of the time they will respect it. But if you do receive unwanted questions in the middle of your presentation, don't ignore them. Simply remind the questioner that you'll leave plenty of time for questions at the end.

Not surprisingly, the best tip for handling questions is to be prepared. Since it's tough to anticipate questions for your own presentation, you may want to enlist the help of a trusted colleague to brainstorm the possibilities. And don't just come up with the questions—prepare the answers, too!

5-6e Visual Aids

Studies suggest that three days after a presentation, people retain 10% of what they heard from an oral presentation, 35% from a visual presentation, and 65% from a combined visual and oral presentation. The numbers are compelling: visual aids matter. Depending on your audience, effective, high-impact visual aids could range from props to charts to mounted boards. But in business communication, PowerPoint slides are the most common option. If you use PowerPoint, consider these suggestions:

- ○ **Showing Works Better Than Simply Telling:** Use pictures and other graphics whenever possible.

- ○ **Less Is More:** Keep this helpful guideline in mind: no more than seven words per line, no more than seven lines per slide.
- ○ **Don't Just Read Your Slides Aloud:** Instead, paraphrase, add examples, and offer analysis and interpretation.
- ○ **Go Easy on the Special Effects:** Too many sounds and too much animation can be painfully distracting.
- ○ **Don't Let Your Slides Upstage You:** Look at your audience, not at the slides. And dim the screen when you're not specifically using it.[10]

5-6f Google Presentations

Although Microsoft PowerPoint remains the software option of choice for business presentations, Google Presentations software is swiftly gaining ground. Google Presentations is one of a growing number of applications based in "the cloud." This means that when you buy a new computer, you don't need to spend hundreds of dollars buying PowerPoint. You simply log into your Google account, use the Google Presentations software, and save your finished product on Google's servers. Since your work is stored on the Internet, you can access it from any device with a web connection—you don't need to email it to yourself, or store it on a temperamental local drive, or worry about saving your changes as you move from work to home to school.

But Google Presentations is far from perfect. If you temporarily lose your Internet connection—while on a plane or a bus, for instance—you cannot access your work. Security might be a worry, since web-based data may be vulnerable to hackers. If Google disables your account for any reason, your work is lost. And Google Presentations does not yet include all the features available in PowerPoint, such as chart-making tools and advanced slide animations. The price, though, is pretty attractive: free! And that includes new versions and updates.

From a long-term perspective, another key benefit of Google Presentations—and all other cloud computing applications—is environmental. *Newsweek* writer Brian Braiker points out that "conducting affairs in the cloud is not only convenient, it's also greener: less capital and fewer printouts means less waste." All of which suggests that the forecast for Google Presentations is far from cloudy.[11]

5-6g Handling Nerves

Believe it or not, most experts agree that nervousness can be useful before a presentation. A little adrenalin can help you perform better, think faster, and focus more completely. But we all know that out-of-control nerves can interfere with effectiveness. Here are some ideas to mitigate speech anxiety:

❍ Send yourself positive messages; visualize success. Examples: "I will be dynamic and engaging." "They will completely support my new product idea."

❍ Take ten slow, deep breaths—use the yoga approach of breathing in through your nose and out through your mouth.

❍ Take a sip of water to loosen your throat muscles and mitigate a shaking voice. (Water also gives you a way to fill pauses.)

❍ Pick a friendly face or two in the audience, and imagine yourself speaking only to those people (but don't stare at them!).

❍ Remind yourself that the audience wants you to succeed. Focus on their needs rather than your own nerves.

If possible, have a handful of one-on-one conversations with audience members before your presentation. This will almost certainly reinforce that they want you to succeed, which will likely take the edge off your nerves.

5-6h Handling Hostility

We've all seen hostile questioners who seem determined to undermine presenters. It can be awful to watch, but it's surprisingly easy to handle. Here are a few tips:

❍ Stay calm and professional. Rightly or wrongly, the hostile questioner has won the day if you get defensive or nervous.

❍ Don't be afraid to pause before you answer to gather your thoughts and allow the hostility to diffuse. (A sip of water can provide good cover for a thought-gathering moment.)

❍ Once you've answered the question, don't reestablish eye contact with the questioner. Doing so would suggest that you are seeking approval for your response, which only invites further hostile follow-up.

❍ If the questioner insists on follow-up, you may need to agree to disagree. If so, be decisive: "Sounds like we have two different points of view on this complex issue."

❍ Use body language to reinforce that you are done interacting with the questioner. Take a couple of steps away, and ask another part of the group whether they have any questions.

5-6i Incorporating Humor

Everyone likes to be funny, but incorporating humor in a business presentation can be risky. Only do it if you're very, very sure that it's funny. Even so, double-check that your jokes are appropriate and relevant. You should never, ever laugh at the expense of any member of your audience. Even laughing at yourself is chancy, since you risk diminishing your credibility. (But a joke at your own expense is always effective if you make a mistake; there's no better way to recover the goodwill of your audience.)

5-6j A Spot on the Back Wall?

Many people have heard the old myth that no one will know the difference if you calm your nerves by looking at a spot on the back wall rather than at the audience. Don't do it! While *you* may be more comfortable, your audience will be mystified . . . more often than not, they'll keep turning around to find out what's so interesting back there!

5-6k Delivery

Some people are naturals, but for the rest of us, **dynamic delivery** is a learned skill. It begins and ends with preparation, but keep in mind that practice doesn't always make perfect—in fact, practice more often just makes permanent. So be sure that you practice with an eye toward improvement. If possible, you should set up a practice situation that's close to the real thing. If you'll be standing to present, stand while you practice, since standing makes many people feel more vulnerable. Consider practicing in front of a mirror to work on eye contact and gestures. Also, try recording your voice to work on a lively tone.

Finally, practice in front of a trusted friend or two who can give you valuable feedback. See Exhibit 5.6 for Ten Tips for Dynamic Delivery.

EXHIBIT 5.6 Ten Tips for Dynamic Delivery

1. PRACTICE!
2. Know your material, but never memorize it word for word.
3. Look directly at members of your audience at least 50% of the time.
4. Vary your voice, your facial expressions, and your body language.
5. Use selective notes (but keep them inconspicuous).
6. Stick to your allotted time.
7. Slow down and listen to yourself.
8. Don't apologize (unless you really did something wrong!).
9. Remember to use natural gestures.
10. PRACTICE!

© Cengage Learning 2013

THE BIG PICTURE

Effective communication saves time and money—boosting performance and morale—across every area of business. But one vital principle holds true regardless of the more specific nature of your communication: the best way to achieve your goals is to focus on your audience, not on yourself. If you understand the goals, expectations, and needs of your audience, you can tailor your communication to boost your chances (sometimes dramatically) of accomplishing your objectives.

As globalization and technological change continue to accelerate, new communication challenges will likely develop across the spectrum of business. To ensure that your communication continues to be effective, keep an open mind. Pay attention to differences among cultures, to language usage in professional publications, and to new communication technology. And don't be afraid to consult an up-to-date communication website or handbook every so often. When other resources aren't available, rely on courtesy, consideration, and common sense—valuable tools to guide your communication in any situation.

CAREERS IN BUSINESS COMMUNICATION

Clearly, superb communication skills are essential for any career in business, and they become even more important as you climb the ranks of an organization. In fact, even in fields that traditionally have emphasized more analytical skills (such as accounting and finance), recruiters are now seeking candidates with strong writing and speaking skills. These skills have become even more important in the face of increased globalization. But business careers that center almost exclusively on communication are typically in the marketing realm, such as advertising, public relations, sales, and related fields, which we will discuss in more detail later in the text.

What else?
RIP & REVIEW CARDS IN THE BACK
and visit www.cengagebrain.com!

6
Business Formation:
Choosing the Form that Fits

LEARNING OBJECTIVES

After studying this chapter, you will be able to:

6-1 Describe the characteristics of the four basic forms of business ownership

6-2 Discuss the advantages and disadvantages of a sole proprietorship

6-3 Evaluate the pros and cons of the partnership as a form of business ownership

6-4 Explain why corporations have become the dominant form of business ownership

6-5 Explain why limited liability companies are becoming an increasingly popular form of business ownership

6-6 Evaluate the advantages and disadvantages of franchising

> "THE LIMITED LIABILITY CORPORATION IS THE *GREATEST* SINGLE DISCOVERY OF MODERN TIMES."
>
> — NICHOLAS MURRAY BUTLER
> PRESIDENT OF COLUMBIA UNIVERSITY, 1902–1945

6-1 Business Ownership Options: The Big Four

One of the most important decisions entrepreneurs make when they start a new business is the form of ownership they'll use. The form they choose affects virtually every aspect of establishing and operating their firm, including the initial cost of setting up the business, the way the profits are distributed, the types of taxes (if any) the business must pay, and the types of regulations it must follow. Choice of ownership also determines the degree to which each owner is personally liable for the firm's debts and the sources of funds available to the firm to finance future expansion.

The vast majority of businesses in the United States are owned and organized under one of four forms:

1. A **sole proprietorship** is a business that is owned, and usually managed, by a single individual. As far as the law is concerned, a sole proprietorship is simply an extension of the owner. Company earnings are treated just like the owner's income; likewise, any debts the company incurs are considered to be the owner's personal debts.

2. A **partnership** is a voluntary agreement under which two or more people act as co-owners of a business for profit. As we'll see later in the chapter, there are several types of partnerships. In its most basic form, known as a **general partnership**, each partner has the right to participate in the company's management and share in profits—but also has unlimited liability for any debts the company incurs.

3. A **corporation** is a business entity created by filing a form (known in most states as the **articles of incorporation**) with the appropriate state agency, paying the state's incorporation fees, and meeting other requirements. (The specifics vary among states.) Unlike a sole proprietorship or a partnership, a corporation is considered to be a legal entity that is separate and distinct from its owners. In many ways, a corporation is like an artificial person. It can legally engage in virtually any business activity a natural person can pursue. For example, a corporation can enter into binding contracts, borrow money, own property, pay taxes, and initiate legal actions (such as lawsuits) in its own name. It can even be a partner in a partnership or an owner of another corporation. Because of a corporation's status as a separate legal entity, the owners of a corporation have **limited liability**—meaning they aren't personally responsible for the debts and obligations of their company.

4. A **limited liability company (LLC)** is a hybrid form of business ownership that is similar in some respects to a corporation while having other characteristics that are similar to a partnership. Like a corporation, a limited liability company is considered a legal entity separate from its owners. Also like a corporation—and as its name implies—an LLC offers its owners limited liability for the debts of their business. But it offers more flexibility than a corporation in terms of tax treatment; in fact, one of the most interesting characteristics of an LLC is that its owners can elect to have their business taxed either as a corporation *or* a partnership. Many states even allow individuals to form single-person LLCs that are taxed as if they were sole proprietorships.

Sole proprietorships, partnerships, and corporations have been around in some form since the beginning of our nation's history, but limited liability companies are a relatively new form of ownership in the United States. In 1977, Wyoming passed the first

---

sole proprietorship A form of business ownership with a single owner who usually actively manages the company.

partnership A voluntary agreement under which two or more people act as co-owners of a business for profit.

general partnership A partnership in which all partners can take an active role in managing the business and have unlimited liability for any claims against the firm.

corporation A form of business ownership in which the business is considered a legal entity that is separate and distinct from its owners.

articles of incorporation The document filed with a state government to establish the existence of a new corporation.

limited liability When owners are not personally liable for claims against their firm. Owners with limited liability may lose their investment in the company, but their other personal assets are protected.

limited liability company (LLC) A form of business ownership that offers both limited liability to its owners and flexible tax treatment.

state statute allowing LLCs, and Florida became the second state to do so in 1982. But it wasn't until a ruling by the Internal Revenue Service (IRS) in 1988 clarifying the tax treatment of LLCs that most other states followed suit. Today every state has enacted LLC legislation, and the LLC has become a very popular ownership option. In many states, filings to form LLCs now outnumber filings to form corporations.[1]

Exhibits 6.1 and 6.2 provide some interesting insights about the relative importance of each form of ownership. As shown in Exhibit 6.1, the sole proprietorship is by far the most common type of business organization in the United States. In 2008, 22.6 million individuals reported operating nonfarm sole proprietorships. This represented more than 71% of the total number of business enterprises. As a group, these sole proprietorships reported $1.37 trillion in revenue and $265 billion in net income (profit). But while these figures are impressive in the aggregate, most individual sole proprietorships are quite small. According to the U.S. Census Bureau's *2012 Statistical Abstract*, more than two-thirds of all sole proprietorships reported annual revenue of less than $25,000, while less than 1% reported receipts in excess of $1 million.[2]

As Exhibit 6.2 shows, when it comes to economic impact, the corporate form of ownership rules. Though corporations comprised only 18.5% of all business entities, in 2008 they reported about 58% of all business profits. Corporations such as Walmart, ExxonMobil, General Electric, Apple, and Boeing have annual sales revenues measured in the billions (sometimes hundreds of billions) of dollars. But not all corporations are multibillion-dollar enterprises. In 2008, about 25% of all corporations reported total revenues of less than $25,000.[3]

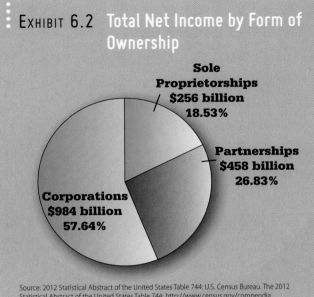

Exhibit 6.2 Total Net Income by Form of Ownership

Sole Proprietorships $256 billion 18.53%

Partnerships $458 billion 26.83%

Corporations $984 billion 57.64%

Source: 2012 Statistical Abstract of the United States Table 744: U.S. Census Bureau. The 2012 Statistical Abstract of the United States Table 744: http://www.census.gov/compendia /statab/2012/tables/12s0744.pdf, accessed May 29, 2012.

As you can see from Exhibit 6.1, partnerships are less common than sole proprietorships or corporations. Still, in 2008, more than 3.1 million businesses were classified as partnerships in the United States. And partnerships tend to be both larger and more profitable than sole proprietorships. As Exhibit 6.2 shows, in the aggregate, partnerships earned 1.7 times more total net income than sole proprietorships, despite the fact that sole proprietorships outnumbered partnerships by a ratio of almost four to one![4]

You've probably noticed that Exhibits 6.1 and 6.2 don't include specific information about limited liability companies. That's because these exhibits are based on information taken from annual tax returns submitted to the Internal Revenue Service (IRS). The IRS doesn't track LLC information separately. Instead, it classifies each LLC based on the tax treatment the company selects. LLCs that choose to be taxed as partnerships are classified as partnerships, while those choosing to be taxed as corporations are classified as corporations. (The vast majority of LLCs elect to be taxed as partnerships, so most LLC earnings are reported in the partnership category.)

We'll see that each form of ownership has distinct advantages and disadvantages. As a company grows

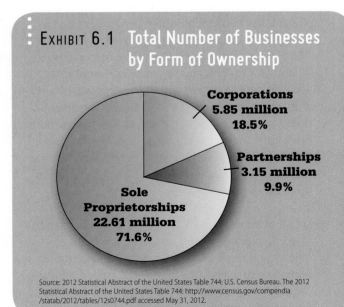

Exhibit 6.1 Total Number of Businesses by Form of Ownership

Corporations 5.85 million 18.5%

Partnerships 3.15 million 9.9%

Sole Proprietorships 22.61 million 71.6%

Source: 2012 Statistical Abstract of the United States Table 744: U.S. Census Bureau. The 2012 Statistical Abstract of the United States Table 744: http://www.census.gov/compendia /statab/2012/tables/12s0744.pdf accessed May 31, 2012.

"Corporation: an ingenious device for obtaining profit without individual responsibility."

— AMBROSE BIERCE, 19TH-CENTURY COMPILER OF *THE DEVIL'S DICTIONARY* and matures, the form of ownership that's best suited to its needs may change. Fortunately, the form of ownership for a business isn't set in stone. For example, it is possible—and in fact quite common—for business owners to convert from a sole proprietorship to a corporation, or from a corporation to a limited liability company.

6-2 Advantages and Disadvantages of Sole Proprietorships

Our look at Exhibits 6.1 and 6.2 raises two questions about sole proprietorships. First, why is this form of ownership so popular? Second, why do sole proprietorships usually remain relatively small? A look at the advantages and disadvantages of sole proprietorships can help answer these questions.

6-2a Advantages

Sole proprietorships offer some very attractive advantages to people starting a business:

- **Ease of Formation:** Compared to the other forms of ownership we'll discuss, the paperwork and costs involved in forming a sole proprietorship are minimal. No special forms must be filed, and no special fees must be paid. Entrepreneurs who are eager to get a business up and running quickly can find this a compelling advantage.

- **Retention of Control:** As the only owner of a sole proprietorship, you're in control. You have the ability to manage your business the way you want. If you want to "be your own boss," a sole proprietorship might look very attractive.

- **Pride of Ownership:** One of the main reasons many people prefer a sole proprietorship is the feeling of pride and the personal satisfaction they gain from owning and running their own business.

- **Retention of Profits:** If your business is successful, *all* the profits go to you—minus your personal taxes, of course.

- **Possible Tax Advantage:** No taxes are levied directly on the earnings of sole proprietorships as a business. Instead, the earnings are taxed only as income of the proprietor. As we'll see when we discuss corporations, this avoids the undesirable possibility of double taxation of earnings.

© David Gilder/Shutterstock.com

6-2b Disadvantages

Entrepreneurs thinking about forming sole proprietorships should also be aware of some serious drawbacks:

- **Limited Financial Resources:** Raising money to finance growth can be tough for sole proprietors. With only one owner responsible for a sole proprietorship's debts, banks and other financial institutions are often reluctant to lend it money. Likewise, suppliers may be unwilling to provide supplies on credit. This leaves sole proprietors dependent on their own wealth plus the money that their firms generate.

- **Unlimited Liability:** Because the law views a sole proprietorship as an extension of its owner, the debts of the firm become the owner's personal debts. If someone sues your business and wins, the court can seize your personal possessions—even those that have nothing to do with your business—and sell them to pay the damages. This unlimited personal liability means that operating as a sole proprietorship is a risky endeavor.

- **Limited Ability to Attract and Maintain Talented Employees:** Most sole proprietors are unable to pay the high salaries and substantial perks that highly qualified, experienced employees get when they work for big, well-established companies.

- **Heavy Workload and Responsibilities:** Being your own boss can be very rewarding, but it can also mean very long hours and a lot of stress. Sole proprietors—as the ultimate authority in their business—often must perform tasks or make decisions in areas where they lack expertise.

- **Lack of Permanence:** Because sole proprietorships are just extensions of their owners, they lack permanence. If the owner dies, retires, or withdraws from the business for some other reason, the company legally ceases to exist. Even if the company continues to operate under new ownership, in the eyes of the law, it becomes a different firm.

6-3 Partnerships: Two Heads (and Bankrolls) Can Be Better Than One

There are several types of partnerships, each with its own specific characteristics. We'll focus our discussion mainly on the most basic type, known as a general partnership.

However, we'll also take a quick look at limited partnerships and limited liability partnerships.

6-3a Formation of General Partnerships

There is no limit on the number of partners who can participate in a general partnership, but most partnerships consist of only a few partners—often just two. The partnership is formed when the partners enter into a voluntary partnership agreement. It is legally possible to start a partnership on the basis of a verbal agreement, but doing so is often a recipe for disaster. It's much safer to get everything in writing and to seek expert legal assistance when drawing up the agreement. A typical partnership agreement spells out details, such as the initial financial contributions each partner will make, the specific duties and responsibilities each will assume, how they will share profits (and losses), how they will settle disagreements, and how they will deal with the death or withdrawal of one of the partners. Well-written agreements can prevent common misunderstandings.

6-3b Advantages of General Partnerships

Partnerships offer some key advantages relative to both sole proprietorships and corporations:

- **Ability to Pool Financial Resources:** With more owners investing in the company, a partnership is likely to have a stronger financial base than a sole proprietorship.

- **Ability to Share Responsibilities and Capitalize on Complementary Skills:** Partners can share the burden of running the business, which can ease the workload. Tasks and jobs can also be divided based on complementary skills, using each partner's talents to best advantage.

- **Ease of Formation:** In theory, forming a partnership is easy. As we've already noted, it's possible (but not advisable) to establish a partnership based on a simple verbal agreement. But we shouldn't overemphasize this advantage. Working out all of the details of a partnership agreement can sometimes be a complex and time-consuming process.

- **Possible Tax Advantages:** Similar to a sole proprietorship, the earnings of a partnership "pass through" the business—untouched by the Internal Revenue Service (IRS)—and are taxed only as the partners' personal income. Again, this avoids the potential for double taxation endemic to corporations.

6-3c Disadvantages of General Partnerships

General partnerships also have some serious disadvantages. Well-written partnership agreements, however, can mitigate some of these major drawbacks:

© Jose Luis Pelaez Inc/Blend Images/Jupiterimages

- **Unlimited Liability:** As a general partner, you're not only liable for your own mistakes but also for those of your partners. In fact, all general partners have unlimited liability for the debts and obligations of their business. So, if the assets they've invested in the business aren't sufficient to meet these claims, the personal assets of the partners are at risk. When someone sues a general partnership, the lawsuit can target *any* individual partner or group of partners. In fact, lawsuits often go after the partners with the deepest pockets, even if they did not personally participate in the act that caused the legal action. In other words, if you have more personal wealth than the other partners, you could lose more than they do even if they were the ones at fault!

- **Potential for Disagreements:** If general partners can't agree on how to run the business, the conflict can complicate and delay decision making. A well-drafted partnership agreement usually specifies how disputes will be resolved, but disagreements among partners can create friction and hard feelings that harm morale and undermine the cooperation needed to keep the business on track.

- **Lack of Continuity:** If a current partner withdraws from the partnership, the relationships among the

A friendship founded on business is a good deal better than a business founded on friendship.

<small>JOHN D. ROCKEFELLER, ON BUSINESS PARTNERSHIPS</small>

participants will clearly change, potentially ending the partnership. This creates uncertainty about how long a partnership will remain in business.

- ⊃ **Difficulty in Withdrawing from a Partnership:** A partner who withdraws from a partnership remains personally liable for any debts or obligations the firm had *at the time of withdrawal*—even if those obligations were incurred by the actions of other partners.

6-3d Limited Partnerships

The risks associated with unlimited liability make general partnerships unattractive to many individuals who would otherwise be interested in joining a business partnership. Fortunately, two other types of partnerships allow some partners to limit their personal liability to some extent, although each comes with particular requirements.

The first of these, known as a **limited partnership**, is a partnership arrangement that includes at least one general partner *and* at least one limited partner. Both types of partners contribute financially to the company and share in its profits. But in other respects they play different roles:

- ⊃ General partners have the right to participate fully in managing their partnership, but they also assume unlimited personal liability for any of its debts—just like the partners in a general partnership.

- ⊃ Limited partners *cannot* actively participate in its management, but they have the protection of limited liability. This means that, as long as they do not actively participate in managing the company, their personal wealth is not at risk.

6-3e Limited Liability Partnerships

The **limited liability partnership (LLP)** is another partnership arrangement that is attractive to partners who want to limit their personal risk. It is similar to a limited partnership in some ways, but it has the advantage of allowing *all* partners to take an active role in management, while also offering *all* partners some form of limited liability. In other words, there's no need to distinguish between limited and general partners in an LLP.

limited partnership A partnership that includes at least one general partner who actively manages the company and accepts unlimited liability and one limited partner who gives up the right to actively manage the company in exchange for limited liability.

limited liability partnership (LLP) A form of partnership in which all partners have the right to participate in management and have limited liability for company debts.

The Name Game

One of the first tasks facing entrepreneurs starting a new business is the selection of the company's name. It turns out that the process involved in naming a company depends on the form of ownership the entrepreneur chooses. The specific requirements differ somewhat from state to state. (You can check out the details for any specific state at http://www. business.gov/register/business-name/ dba.html.)

Most sole proprietorships and general partnerships operate under the names of their owners. But others use a "fictitious" name to create a more memorable impression. Owners that use a fictitious name must do a name search to make sure that no other company in the area is already using the same name—or one so similar that the two names could be easily confused. Failure to take this precaution could result in being on the losing end of a trademark infringement lawsuit! In many states, companies using fictitious names also must file a document known as a DBA ("Doing Business As")

© Oliver Suckling/Shutterstock.com

certificate with the county clerk where the business is located. This informs the government and the general public that the company is doing business under a fictitious name and identifies the actual owners.

The process for naming corporations and limited liability companies has different requirements. In most states, the name of a corporation or LLC must be registered with the secretary of state where the business is formed. The name also must include specific wording to indicate that the owners are not personally liable for the debts of their company. For example, corporate names typically *must* include one of the following words: "corporation," "incorporated," "company," or "limited" (or a corresponding abbreviation such as "Corp.," "Inc.," "Co.," or "Ltd."). Similarly, the name of a limited liability company typically *must* include either the words "limited liability company" or the abbreviation "LLC." Certain other words, such as "bank" or "cooperative," *cannot* be used in the name of a corporation or limited liability company without approval by an appropriate regulatory agency.[5]

The amount of liability protection offered by LLPs varies among states. In some states, LLPs offer "full-shield" protection, meaning that partners have limited liability for all claims against their company, except those resulting from *their own* negligence or malpractice. In other states, partners in LLPs have a lesser "partial-shield" protection. In these states, each partner has limited liability for the negligence or malpractice of other partners but still has unlimited liability for any other debts. Another drawback is that some states only allow specific types of professional businesses to form limited liability partnerships. For example, California law allows only accountants, lawyers, and architects to form LLPs.

6-4 Corporations: The Advantages and Disadvantages of Being an Artificial Person

There are several types of corporations. The most common is called a **C corporation**; when people use the term "corporation" without specifying which type, they are generally referring to a C corporation. Because it's the most common, we'll devote most of our discussion to C corporations. However, we'll also describe three other types of corporations: S corporations, statutory close (or closed) corporations, and nonprofit corporations.

6-4a Forming a C Corporation

As mentioned earlier, the formation of a corporation requires filing articles of incorporation and paying filing fees. It also requires the adoption of **corporate bylaws**, which are detailed rules that govern the way the corporation is organized and managed. Because of these requirements, forming a corporation tends to be more expensive and complex than forming a sole proprietorship or partnership. The requirements, however, vary among the states. Some states are known for their simple forms, inexpensive fees, low corporate tax rates, and "corporation-friendly" laws and court systems. In those states, forming a corporation is not much harder or more expensive than setting up a sole proprietorship and sometimes can be simpler than forming a partnership. Not surprisingly, many large companies choose to incorporate in states with such favorable environments—even if they intend to do the majority of their business in other states. Delaware, in particular, has been very successful at attracting corporations. You may not think of Delaware as the home of corporate power, but more than half of all publicly traded corporations—and 63% of the firms listed in the Fortune 500—are incorporated in Delaware.[6]

6-4b Ownership of C Corporations

Ownership of C corporations is represented by shares of stock, so owners are called "**stockholders**" (or "shareholders"). Common stock represents the basic ownership interest in a corporation, but some firms also issue preferred stock. One key difference between the two types of stock involves voting rights; common stockholders normally have the right to vote in stockholders' meetings, while preferred stockholders do not. As shown in Exhibit 6.3, many large corporations issue billions of shares of stock and have hundreds of thousands—or even millions—of stockholders.

Stock in large corporations is usually publicly traded, meaning that anyone with the money and inclination to do so can buy shares—and that anyone who owns shares is free to sell them. But many smaller corporations are owned by just a handful of stockholders who don't actively trade their stock. It's even possible for individuals to incorporate their business and be the sole shareholder in their corporation.[7]

Stockholders don't have to be individuals. **Institutional investors**, such as mutual funds, insurance companies, pension funds, and endowment funds, pool money from a large number of individuals and use these funds to buy stocks and other securities. As Exhibit 6.3 illustrates, such institutional investors own the majority of stock in many large corporations.

6-4c The Role of the Board of Directors

It's not practical for all of the stockholders of a large corporation to actively participate in the management of their company. Besides, most stockholders don't have the time, management skills, or desire to effectively manage such a complex business enterprise. Thus, in accordance with corporate bylaws, the stockholders elect a **board of directors** and rely on this board to oversee the operation of their company and protect their interests.

The board of directors establishes the corporation's mission and sets its broad objectives. But board members seldom take an active role in the day-to-day management of their company. Instead, again in accordance with corporate bylaws, the board appoints a chief executive officer (CEO) and other corporate officers to manage the company on a daily basis. The board also sets the level of compensation for these officers and monitors their performance to ensure that they act in a manner consistent with stockholder interests. It also provides advice to these officers on broad policy

Exhibit 6.3 Stock Ownership in Selected Major U.S. Corporations

CORPORATION	SHARES OF COMMON STOCK OUTSTANDING (BILLIONS)	TOTAL NUMBER OF STOCKHOLDERS	PERCENTAGE OF SHARES OWNED BY INSTITUTIONAL INVESTORS
AT&T	5.86	1,291,207	92.10
COCA-COLA	2.26	250,275	64.00
FORD	8.10	158,445	30.00
GE	10.59	598,000	54.20
MCDONALD'S	1.02	1,583,000	67.20
MICROSOFT	8.40	134,854	67.10
WALMART	3.41	275,525	31.10
WALT DISNEY	1.79	994,425	67.10

Source: Shares outstanding and percentage of institutional ownership is from the Key Statistics for each corporation reported in Yahoo! Finance (http://finance. yahoo.com/); Information about the number of shareholders is found in Item 5 (Market for the Company's Common Equity) of each firm's 2011 10-K annual report filed with the SEC accessed through the Edgar database (http://www.sec.gov/edgar.shtml) accessed May 31, 2012.

issues, approves their major proposals, and ensures that the company adheres to major regulatory requirements.

6-4d Advantages of C Corporations

Corporations have become the dominant form of business ownership for several reasons:

- **Limited Liability:** As already explained, stockholders are not personally liable for the debts of their company. If a corporation goes bankrupt, the stockholders might find that their stock is worthless, but their other personal assets are protected.

- **Permanence:** Unless the articles of incorporation specify a limited duration, corporations can continue operating as long as they remain financially viable and the majority of stockholders want the business to continue. Unlike a sole proprietorship or partnership, a general corporation is unaffected by the death or withdrawal of an owner.

- **Ease of Transfer of Ownership:** It's easy for stockholders of publicly traded C corporations to withdraw from ownership—they simply sell their shares of stock.

- **Ability to Raise Large Amounts of Financial Capital:** Corporations can raise large amounts of financial capital by issuing shares of

A New Form of Business Aims for Social Responsibility

In April of 2010, Maryland became the first state to pass a law allowing the formation of an entirely new business entity called a benefit corporation. Formation of a benefit corporation is similar to that of a C corporation, but with the additional requirement that the company's bylaws must include provisions identifying specific social or environmental goals, which the law then holds the board of directors accountable for achieving.

Despite their social orientation, benefit corporations aren't nonprofit organizations. They are allowed—indeed, expected—to earn a satisfactory financial return for their owners. But Maryland's law explicitly allows directors of benefit corporations to give equal or greater priority to other stakeholders such as employees, customers, or environmentalists. This gives a benefit corporation's board legal cover to pursue social and environmental goals without fear of stockholder lawsuits. As Maryland state senator Jamie Raskin, one of the sponsors of the Maryland law, put it, "We are giving companies a way to do good and do well at the same time. The benefit corporations will tie public and private purposes together."

It is too early to tell whether benefit corporations will become a popular type of business entity. But some early developments suggest that it has attracted considerable attention. Many privately held corporations have already expressed interest in converting to this new business entity. And benefit corporation legislation has already been introduced in several other states, with Vermont becoming the second state to allow the formation of benefit corporations in May 2010.[8]

stock or by selling formal IOUs called *corporate bonds*. The ability to raise money by issuing these securities gives corporations a major financial advantage over most other forms of ownership.

○ **Ability to Make Use of Specialized Management:** Large corporations often find it easier to hire highly qualified professional managers than proprietorships and partnerships. Major corporations can typically offer attractive salaries and benefits, and their permanence and potential for growth offer managers opportunities for career advancement.

6-4e Disadvantages of C Corporations

In addition to their significant benefits, C corporations have a number of drawbacks:

○ **Expense and Complexity of Formation and Operation:** As we've already seen, establishing a corporation can be more complex and expensive than forming a sole proprietorship or partnership. Corporations are also subject to more formal operating requirements. For example, they are required to hold regular board meetings and keep accurate minutes.

○ **Complications When Operating in More Than One State:** When a business that's incorporated in one state does business in other states, it's called a "*domestic* corporation" in the state where it's incorporated, and a "*foreign* corporation" in the other states. A corporation must register (or "qualify") as a foreign corporation in order to do business in any state other than the one in which it incorporated. This typically requires additional paperwork, fees, and taxes. But registration as a foreign corporation is only necessary if the company is involved in substantial business

> "General Electric, one of the largest corporations in America, filed a whopping 57,000-page federal tax return... [which] would have been 19 feet high if printed out and **stacked.**"
>
> — WEEKLY STANDARD

activities within the state. Businesses that only engage in minor business activities typically are exempt from the registration requirement. For example, a firm operating a production facility or maintaining a district office in a state other than its corporate home would need to register as a foreign corporation, but a firm that simply held a bank account or solicited sales to customers in that state through the mail would not be required to do so.

○ **Double Taxation of Earnings and Additional Taxes:** The IRS considers a C corporation to be a separate legal entity and taxes its earnings accordingly. Then any dividends (earnings the corporation distributes to stockholders) are taxed *again* as the personal income of the stockholders. This double taxation can take a big bite out of the company's earnings that are distributed to shareholders. But note that corporations often reinvest some or all of their profits back into the business. Shareholders don't pay income taxes on these *retained earnings*. Many states also impose separate income taxes on corporations.

EXHIBIT 6.4 How Double Taxation Reduces Earnings for Stockholders

Pre-Tax Corporate Earnings — Corporate Taxes — After Tax Corporate Earnings — Stockholders — Personal Income Taxes — Stockholder's After-Tax Income

© Cengage Learning 2013

In addition, most states also impose an annual franchise tax on both domestic and foreign corporations that operate within their borders.

- **More Paperwork, More Regulation, and Less Secrecy:** Corporations are more closely regulated and are required to file more government paperwork than other forms of business. Large, publicly traded corporations are required to send annual statements to all shareholders and to file detailed quarterly and annual reports with the Securities and Exchange Commission (SEC). The annual report filed with the SEC (called a Form 10-K) is often hundreds of pages long and includes a wealth of information about the company's operations and financial condition. Anyone can look at these forms, making it difficult to keep key corporate information secret from competitors.

- **Possible Conflicts of Interest:** The corporate officers appointed by the board are supposed to further the interests of stockholders. But some top executives pursue policies that further their *own* interests (such as prestige, power, job security, high pay, and attractive perks) at the expense of the stockholders. The board of directors has an obligation to protect the interests of stockholders, but in recent years the boards of several major corporations have come under criticism for continuing to approve high compensation packages for top executives even when their companies performed poorly.

6-4f Other Types of Corporations: Same but Different

Now that we've described C corporations, let's take a quick look at three other types of corporations: **S corporations**, **statutory close corporations**, and **nonprofit corporations**. Like C corporations, each is created by filing the appropriate paperwork with a government agency. Also like general corporations, these corporations are considered legal entities that stand apart from their owners and can enter into contracts, own property, and take legal action in their own names. But in other key respects they are quite different from C corporations—and from each other. Exhibit 6.5 summarizes the basic features of these corporations.

6-4g Corporate Restructuring

Large corporations constantly look for ways to grow and achieve competitive advantages. Some corporations work to achieve these goals, at least in part, through mergers, acquisitions, and divestitures. We'll close our discussion of corporations by taking a quick look at these forms of corporate restructuring.

Mergers and Acquisitions In the news and casual conversation, the terms "merger" and "acquisition" are often used

S corporation A form of corporation that avoids double taxation by having its income taxed as if it were a partnership.

statutory close (or closed) corporation A corporation with a limited number of owners that operates under simpler, less formal rules than a C corporation.

nonprofit corporation A corporation that does not seek to earn a profit and differs in several fundamental respects from C corporations.

EXHIBIT 6.5 Characteristics of S, Statutory Close, and Nonprofit Corporations

TYPE	KEY ADVANTAGES	LIMITATIONS
S CORPORATION	- The IRS does not tax earnings of S corporations separately. Earnings pass through the company and are taxed only as income to stockholders, thus avoiding the problem of double taxation associated with C corporations. - Stockholders have limited liability.	- It can have no more than 100 stockholders. - With only rare exceptions, each stockholder must be a U.S. citizen or permanent resident of the United States. (No ownership by foreigners or other corporations.)
STATUTORY CLOSE (OR CLOSED) CORPORATION	- It can operate under simpler arrangements than conventional corporations. For example, it doesn't have to elect a board of directors or hold an annual stockholders' meeting. - All owners can actively participate in management while still having limited liability.	- The number of stockholders is limited. (The number varies among states but is usually no more than 50.) - Stockholders normally can't sell their shares to the public without first offering the shares to existing owners. - Not all states allow formation of this type of corporation.
NONPROFIT (OR NOT-FOR-PROFIT) CORPORATION	- Earnings are exempt from federal and state income taxes. - Members and directors have limited liability. - Individuals who contribute money or property to the nonprofit can take a tax deduction, making it easier for these organizations to raise funds from donations.	- It has members (who may pay dues) but cannot have stockholders. - It cannot distribute dividends to members. - It cannot contribute funds to a political campaign. - It must keep accurate records and file paperwork to document tax-exempt status.

© Cengage Learning 2013

acquisition A corporate restructuring in which one firm buys another.

merger A corporate restructuring that occurs when two formerly independent business entities combine to form a new organization.

divestiture The transfer of total or partial ownership of some of a firm's operations to investors or to another company.

interchangeably. However, there's a difference between the two. An **acquisition** occurs when one firm buys another firm. The firm making the purchase is called the "acquiring firm," and the firm being purchased is called the "target firm." After the acquisition, the target firm ceases to exist as an independent entity while the purchasing firm continues in operation, and its stock is still traded. But not all acquisitions are on friendly terms. When the acquiring firm buys the target firm despite the opposition of the target's board and top management, the result is called a "hostile takeover."

In a **merger**, instead of one firm buying the other, the two companies agree to a combination of equals, joining together to form a new company out of the two previously independent firms. Exhibit 6.6 describes the three most common types of corporate combinations.

Divestitures: When Less Is More Sometimes corporations restructure by subtraction rather than by addition. A **divestiture** occurs when a firm transfers total or partial ownership of some of its operations to investors or to another company. Firms often use divestitures to rid themselves of a part of their company that no longer fits well with their strategic plans. This allows them to streamline their operations and focus on their core businesses. In many (but not all) cases, divestitures involve the sale of assets to outsiders, which raises financial capital for the firm.

One common type of divestiture, called a "spin-off," occurs when a company issues stock in one of its own divisions or operating units and sets it up as a separate company—complete with its own board of directors and corporate officers. It then distributes the stock in the new company to its existing stockholders. After the spin-off, the stockholders end up owning two separate companies rather than one. They can then buy, sell, or hold either (or both) stocks as they see fit. While a spin-off allows a corporation to eliminate a division that no longer fits in its plans, it doesn't actually generate any additional funds for the firm.

A "carve-out" is like a spin-off in that the firm converts a particular unit or division into a separate company and issues stock in the newly created corporation. However, instead of distributing the new stock to its current stockholders, it sells

Stockholders "Say on Pay"

A corporation's board of directors is ethically bound to put the financial interests of stockholders who own the company above all else. Critics charge, however, that boards have too often increased executive pay regardless of company performance. Beginning in 2011, however, the Wall Street Reform and Consumer Protection Act of 2010 (or Dodd-Frank Act) gave stockholders of publicly traded corporations the right to cast advisory votes on executive compensation. Although nonbinding, these votes give stockholders the chance to publicly review board-recommended compensation policies. Are these so-called say on pay votes making a difference?

Early results across 5,300 companies are that 98% of executive compensation plans are approved by a majority of stockholders, typically with 90% of stockholders in favor. But when not approved, the average vote is just 42% in favor. However, most companies and outside groups, such as independent advisory firm Institutional Shareholder Services, treat anything less than 70% approval as problematic. When only 58% of Allstate's shareholders approved executive compensation plans, CEO Tom Wilson communicated with 30% of shareholders to learn why people were concerned: "My job is to make our shareholders happy."

So, what typically leads to rejection or low levels of approval? In short, paying managers much more than comparable managers at similar companies, not linking executive pay to company performance, excessive severance pay (more than three times annual salary plus bonus), exorbitant benefits, or giving executives additional compensation to pay personal taxes (i.e., tax gross-ups).

Solutions are straightforward. Like Allstate's Wilson, communicating with shareholders is key. Then make sure pay is comparable, transparent, easily understood by shareholders, and that it increases or decreases along with goals related to long-term company financial performance. For instance, even though Family Dollar Stores saw earnings increase 19%, revenue rise by 9%, and its stock price rise by 27%, it missed its goal for pretax earnings. So, the board cut the CEO's bonus by 37% and his total compensation by 11%. A company spokesman said, "We had some aggressive goals last year, and we didn't reach those goals."[9]

Corporate mergers involve a combination of equals.

the stock to outside investors, thus raising additional financial capital. In many cases, the firm sells only a minority of the total shares, so that it maintains majority ownership.

6-5 The Limited Liability Company: The New Kid on the Block

As the newest form of business ownership, state laws concerning the legal status and formation of LLCs are still evolving. Several states have recently revised their statutes to make forming LLCs simpler and to make transfer of ownership easier. Other states have kept more restrictive requirements intact. This diversity of state requirements, and the continuing evolution of LLC statutes, makes it difficult to provide meaningful generalizations about this form of ownership.[10]

6-5a Forming and Managing an LLC

In many respects, forming an LLC is similar to forming a corporation. As with corporations, LLCs are created by filing a document (which goes by a variety of names, such as *certificate of organization* or *articles of organization*) and paying filing fees in the state where the business is organized. Organizers of most LLCs also draft an operating agreement, which is similar to the bylaws of a corporation. Some states also require LLCs to publish a notice of intent to operate as a limited liability company.

Because LLCs are neither corporations nor partnerships, their owners are called *members* rather than stockholders or partners. Members of LLCs often manage their own company

horizontal merger
A combination of two firms that are in the same industry.

vertical merger A combination of firms at different stages in the production of a good or service.

conglomerate merger A combination of two firms that are in unrelated industries.

EXHIBIT 6.6 Types of Mergers and Acquisitions

TYPE OF MERGER	DEFINITION	COMMON OBJECTIVE	EXAMPLE
HORIZONTAL MERGER	A combination of firms in the same industry.	Increase size and market power within the industry. Improve efficiency by eliminating duplication of facilities and personnel.	United Airlines' acquisition of Continental Airlines in 2010.
VERTICAL MERGER	A combination of firms that are at different stages in the production of a good or service, creating a "buyer-seller" relationship.	Provide tighter integration of production and increased control over the supply of crucial inputs.	Google's announcement in 2011 of its acquisition of Motorola Mobility, a company that manufactures cell phones using Google's Android operating system.
CONGLOMERATE MERGER	A combination of firms in unrelated industries.	Reduce risk by making the firm less vulnerable to adverse conditions in any single market.	The 2006 acquisition by Berkshire Hathaway (a highly diversified company that holds stock in a wide variety of companies) of Iscar, a privately held company that makes cutting tools.

© Cengage Learning 2013

under an arrangement similar to the relationship among general partners in a partnership. However, some LLCs hire professional managers who have responsibilities much like those of the CEO and other top officers of corporations.

6–5b Advantages of LLCs

Why are LLCs becoming so popular? This form of ownership offers significant advantages:

- ○ **Limited Liability:** Similar to a corporation, *all* owners of an LLC have limited liability.

- ○ **Tax Pass-Through:** As mentioned at the beginning of this chapter, for tax purposes the owners of LLCs may elect to have their companies treated as either a corporation or a partnership—or even as a sole proprietorship if owned by a single person. The default tax classification for LLCs with more than one owner—and the one most LLCs choose—is the partnership option. Under this arrangement, there is no separate tax on the earnings of the company. Instead, earnings "pass through" the company and are taxed only as income of the owners. This eliminates the double taxation of profits that is endemic to general corporations. However, there are some cases where it makes sense for LLCs to elect to be taxed as a corporation. For example, the owner of a single-person LLC can avoid paying self-employment taxes by electing to have

the LLC treated as a corporation rather than as a sole proprietorship.

- ○ **Simplicity and Flexibility in Management and Operation:** Unlike corporations, LLCs aren't required to hold regular board meetings. Also, LLCs are subject to less paperwork and fewer reporting requirements than corporations.

- ○ **Flexible Ownership:** Unlike S corporations, LLCs can have any number of owners. Also unlike S corporations, the owners of LLCs can include foreign investors and other corporations. However, some states do make it difficult to transfer ownership to outsiders.

6–5c Limitations and Disadvantages of LLCs

Despite their increasing popularity, LLCs have some limitations and drawbacks:

- ○ **Complexity of Formation:** Because of the need to file articles of organization and pay filing fees, LLCs can take more time and effort to form than sole proprietorships. In general, forming an LLC is also more difficult than creating a partnership. But as we mentioned earlier, the formation of a partnership requires a "meeting of the minds" of the partners, which isn't always easy to achieve. So in some

Lowering Apple's Tax Bite

Although double taxation is a major drawback to corporate ownership, tax laws provide corporations ways to reduce their tax liabilities, such as incorporating or doing business in low-tax locations. When Apple sells an iPad or iPhone in the United States, the profits are invested by Braeburn Capital, an Apple subsidiary in Reno, Nevada, where the capital gains tax rate is zero, thus avoiding California's 10.33% capital gains tax. With nearly $35 billion to manage, that saves Apple billions in California taxes!

Apple's most creative tax strategy is the "Double Irish with a Dutch Sandwich." No, that's not a double Irish whiskey with an Uitsmitjer, a Dutch sandwich with meat, cheese, and fried eggs. Facebook, Google, and Microsoft also do this, but here's how it works at Apple specifically. Apple Sales International (ASI), located in Ireland, is registered to Baldwin Holdings, an Apple subsidiary in the British Virgin Islands that has no corporate taxes. Apple Sales International owns the rights to the international sale of Apple's technology patents, which are worth billions per year. Yet, rather than selling them, it licenses them to Ireland-based Apple Operations International (AOI), which then sells Apple's technology globally. AOI's profits are then transferred to Apple's Dutch subsidiary (i.e., the Dutch sandwich). This avoids an Irish withholding tax because the European Union views this as an internal company transfer. Finally, the Dutch subsidiary transfers the profits back to Bermuda and Baldwin Holdings.

Confused? Just know that like you, companies go to great lengths to legally reduce their taxes. You do so to increase your tax refund, but companies do so to increase dividends that can be paid to shareholders and to retain earnings that can be reinvested in the company.[11]

cases, the formation of a partnership can prove to be every bit as challenging as the formation of an LLC.

- ⊙ **Annual Franchise Tax:** Even though they may be exempt from corporate income taxes, many states require LLCs to pay an annual franchise tax.

- ⊙ **Foreign Status in Other States:** Like corporations, LLCs must register or qualify to operate as "foreign" companies when they do business in states other than the state in which they were organized. This results in additional paperwork, fees, and taxes.

- ⊙ **Limits on Types of Firms That Can Form LLCs:** Most states do not permit banks, insurance companies, and nonprofit organizations to operate as LLCs.

- ⊙ **Differences in State Laws:** As we've already mentioned, LLC laws are still evolving—and their specific requirements vary considerably among the states. In 2006, the National Conference of Commissioners on Uniform State Laws created a Revised Uniform Limited Liability Company Act that could be used as a model by all states. To date, only a few states have adopted this law. Until there is more uniformity in state laws, operating LLCs in more than one state is likely to remain a complex endeavor.[12]

6-6 | Franchising: Proven Methods for a Price

A **franchise** is a licensing arrangement under which one party (the **franchisor**) allows another party (the **franchisee**) to use its name, trademark, patents, copyrights, business methods, and other property in exchange for monetary payments and other considerations. Franchising has become a very popular way to operate a business and an important source of employment and income. A 2012 study conducted by Global Insight for the International Franchising Association's Education Foundation reported that almost 740,000 franchise establishments operated in the United States, employing over 7.9 million workers. And according to another franchising study published by the Bureau of the Census in 2010, franchise establishments dominate several major markets such as fast food, auto dealerships, convenience stores, and private mail distribution centers.[13]

The two most popular types of franchise arrangements are **distributorships** and **business format franchises**. In a distributorship, the franchisor makes a product and grants distributors a license to sell it. The most common example of this type of franchise is the arrangement between automakers and the dealerships that sell their cars. In a business format franchise, the franchisor grants the franchisee the right to both make *and* sell its good or service. Under this arrangement, the franchisor usually provides a wide range of services to the franchisee, such as help with site selection, training, and help in obtaining financing, but also requires the franchisee to follow very specific guidelines while operating the business. You're no doubt very familiar with business format franchises; examples include Wendy's, Supercuts, Jiffy Lube, and Massage Envy.

6-6a Franchising in Today's Economy

Franchising is now a well-established method of operating a business—but that doesn't mean it's static. Let's look at some ways the world of franchising is changing.

One of the biggest trends in franchising for the past several years has been an expansion into foreign markets. Franchisors in a variety of industries have found that opportunities for franchise growth are greater in foreign countries because competition is less intense, and markets are less saturated than in the United States. At the end of 2011, McDonald's had 13,407 franchise outlets in foreign countries (slightly more than it had in the United States), Subway had 8,704, and Curves had 3,087.[14] Of course, operating in foreign countries can pose special challenges. Differences in culture, language, laws, demographics, and economic development mean that franchisors, like other types of business owners, must adjust their business methods—and the specific products they offer—to meet the needs of foreign consumers.

Another notable trend has been the growth in the number of women franchisees. Reliable statistics on women in franchising are difficult to find, but the International Franchising Association (IFA) estimates that women now own about 30% of all franchises, and anecdotal evidence suggests that the trend toward more

franchise A licensing arrangement under which a franchisor allows franchisees to use its name, trademark, products, business methods, and other property in exchange for monetary payments and other considerations.

franchisor The business entity in a franchise relationship that allows others to operate its business using resources it supplies in exchange for money and other considerations.

franchisee The party in a franchise relationship that pays for the right to use resources supplied by the franchisor.

distributorship A type of franchising arrangement in which the franchisor makes a product and licenses the franchisee to sell it.

business format franchise A broad franchise agreement in which the franchisee pays for the right to use the name, trademark, and business and production methods of the franchisor.

women-owned franchises is continuing. A number of women, such as JoAnne Shaw (founder of the Coffee Beanery), Maxine Clark (founder of Build-A-Bear), and Linda Burzynski (owner and CEO of Liberty Fitness), also have become very successful franchisors. But, despite these highly visible success stories, the number of women franchisors hasn't grown nearly as fast as the number of women franchisees.[15]

Minority participation in franchises, both as franchisees and franchisors, has been relatively low. African Americans, Hispanics, Asian Americans, and Native Americans make up about a third of the population, and that share is expected to steadily grow over the next several decades. Yet, according to C. Everett Wallace, a past chair of the IFA's Minorities in Franchising Committee, fewer than 10% of all franchisees are minorities. One of the main reasons for such low minority involvement in franchising is a lack of awareness of franchising opportunities within minority communities. But many franchisors are now making a strong effort to actively recruit minority franchisees.[16]

Two major initiatives have given the efforts to reach minority franchising a boost in recent years. The first, known as the National Minority Franchising Initiative (NMFI), was founded in 2000. The NMFI's website currently maintains a directory of more than 500 franchisors who actively promote minority franchise ownership. The second initiative, called MinorityFran, was established in early 2006 by the IFA. This initiative has the cooperation of a variety of organizations interested in promoting minority business ownership, including the National Urban League, the Association of Small Business Development Centers, the U.S. Pan Asian American Chamber of Commerce, and the Minority Business Development Agency. Franchisors participating in the program receive information and marketing materials designed to help them reach potential minority franchisees more effectively. As of late 2010, MinorityFran had more than 100 participating franchisors, including such major players as ExxonMobil, McDonald's, and YUM! Brands (which owns KFC, Taco Bell, and Pizza Hut), all pledging to actively recruit minority franchisees.[17]

6-6b Advantages of Franchising

Both the franchisee and the franchisor must believe they'll benefit from the franchise arrangement; otherwise, they wouldn't participate. The advantages of franchising for the franchisor are fairly obvious. It allows the franchisor to expand the business and bring in additional revenue (in the form of franchising fees and royalties) without investing its own capital. Also, franchisees—business owners who are motivated to earn a profit—may have a greater incentive than salaried managers to do whatever it takes to maximize the success of their outlets.

From the franchisee's perspective, franchising offers several advantages:

- **Less Risk:** Franchises offer access to a proven business system and product. The systems and methods offered by franchisors have an established track record. People who are interested in buying a franchise can do research to see how stores in the franchise have performed and can talk to existing franchisees before investing.

- **Training and Support:** The franchisor normally provides the franchisee with extensive training and support. For example, Subway offers two weeks of training at its headquarters and additional training at meetings. The franchisor also sends out newsletters, provides Internet support, maintains a toll-free number for phone support, and provides on-site evaluations.[18]

- **Brand Recognition:** Operating a franchise gives the franchisee instant brand-name recognition, which can be a big help in attracting customers.

- **Easier Access to Funding:** Bankers and other lenders may be more willing to lend money if the business is part of an established franchise than if it is a new, unproven business.

6-6c Disadvantages of Franchising

Franchising also has some drawbacks. From the franchisor's perspective, operating a business with perhaps thousands of semi-independent owner–operators can be complex and challenging. With such a large number of owners, it can be difficult to keep all of the franchisees satisfied, and disappointed franchisees sometimes go public with their complaints, damaging the reputation of the franchisor. In fact, it isn't unusual for disgruntled franchisees to sue their franchisors.

Franchisees are also likely to find some disadvantages:

- **Costs:** The typical franchise agreement requires franchisees to pay an initial franchise fee when they enter into the franchise agreement and an ongoing royalty (usually a percentage of monthly sales revenues) to the franchisor. In addition, the franchisor may assess other fees to support national advertising campaigns or for other purposes. These costs vary considerably, but for high-profile franchises, they can be substantial. Exhibit 6.7 compares the franchise fees, royalties, and minimum total investment for several well-established franchises. (Total investment reflects the fact that the cost of starting a franchise generally requires the franchisee to invest in property, equipment, and inventory in addition to paying the franchise fee. The actual total investment that franchisees make is often substantially higher than the estimated minimum investment cited in Exhibit 6.7.)

- **Lack of Control:** The franchise agreement usually requires the franchisee to follow the franchisor's procedures to the letter. People who want the freedom and flexibility to be their own boss can find these restrictions frustrating.

- **Negative Halo Effect:** The irresponsible or incompetent behavior of a few franchisees can create a negative perception that adversely affects not only the franchise as a whole but also the success of other franchisees.

- **Growth Challenges:** While growth and expansion are definitely possible in franchising (many franchisees own multiple outlets), strings are attached. Franchise agreements usually limit the franchisee's territory and require franchisor approval before expanding into other areas.

- **Restrictions on Sale:** Franchise agreements normally prevent franchisees from selling their franchises to other investors without prior approval from the franchisor.

- **Poor Execution:** Not all franchisors live up to their promises. Sometimes the training and support are of poor quality, and sometimes the company does a poor job of screening franchisees, leading to the negative halo effect we mentioned previously.

These considerations suggest that before buying a franchise, potential owners should carefully research the franchise opportunity.

franchise agreement
The contractual arrangement between a franchisor and franchisee that spells out the duties and responsibilities of both parties.

6-6d Entering into a Franchise Agreement

To obtain a franchise, the franchisee must sign a **franchise agreement**. This agreement is a legally binding contract that specifies the relationship between the franchisor and the franchisee in great detail. There's no standard form for the contract, but some of the key items normally covered include the following:

- **Terms and Conditions:** The franchisee's rights to use the franchisor's trademarks, patents, and signage, and any restrictions on those rights. It also covers how long the agreement will last and under what terms (and at what cost) it can be renewed.

- **Fees and Other Payments:** The fees the franchisee must pay for the right to use the franchisor's products and methods, and when these payments are due.

- **Training and Support:** The types of training and support the franchisor will provide to the franchisee.

EXHIBIT 6.7 Franchisee Costs for Selected Franchises

FRANCHISE	TYPE OF BUSINESS	FRANCHISE FEE	ROYALTY*	ESTIMATED MINIMUM TOTAL INVESTMENT
COFFEE NEWS	Local newsletters	$8,500	$80/wk.	$9,425
MERLE NORMAN	Cosmetics and skin care	$0	0%	$33,300
ANYTIME FITNESS	Health club	$18,999	$499/mo.	$46,299
SUBWAY	Fast food	$15,000	8%	$84,800
PAPA JOHN'S	Pizza delivery	$25,000	5%	$115,823
SUPERCUTS	Hair styling	$27,500	6%	$103,560
JENNY CRAIG	Weight loss	$25,000	7%	$169,600
JIFFY LUBE	Automobile maintenance	$35,000	4%	$196,500

*Royalty is expressed as a percentage of gross revenues unless otherwise specified.

Source: Individual franchise opportunity pages for each listed franchise on the Entrepreneur.com website, http://www.entrepreneur.com/franchiseopportunities/index.html, accessed June 1, 2012.

○ **Specific Operational Requirements:** The methods and standards established by the franchisor that the franchisee is required to follow.

○ **Conflict Resolution:** How the franchisor and franchisee will handle disputes.

○ **Assigned Territory:** The geographic area in which the franchisee will operate and whether the franchisee has exclusive rights in that area.

It's vital for anyone thinking about entering into a franchise agreement to know all the facts before signing on the dotted line. Fortunately, the Federal Trade Commission (FTC) requires franchisors to provide potential franchisees with a document known as a **Franchise Disclosure Document (FDD)**. This long, complex document (covering 23 separate major topics and sometimes running well over 100 pages) can be an invaluable source of information about virtually every aspect of the franchise arrangement. For example, the FDD must provide

> **"If you** told me 30 years ago that one day I'd be sitting in a Subway store in Russia, I'd have said you were crazy."
>
> —Fred DeLuca, Founder, Subway Restaurants

contact information for at least 100 current franchisees. (If the franchisor has fewer than 100 current franchisees, it must list all of them.) This gives a potential franchisee the ability to contact other franchisees and ask them about their experiences with the franchisor. As an added bonus, the FTC requires the FDD to be written in "plain English" rather than in the complex legal jargon that often characterizes such documents. This rule means you actually have a chance to understand what you're reading![19]

Under FTC rules, the franchisor must give the franchisee at least 14 calendar days to review the FDD before the franchise agreement can be signed. A careful study of the FDD can go a long way toward ensuring that the franchisee makes an informed decision. Even though the FDD is written in "plain English," it's a good idea to have a lawyer who is knowledgeable about franchise law review it. You'll have to pay for any legal advice, but entering into a bad franchise agreement can be a lot more expensive (and stressful) than a lawyer's fees.

© iStockphoto.com/Johnny Greig

Franchise Consultants: Would You Like Fries with That Franchise?

You've saved your money and decided that franchising is how you will become a business owner. But which franchisor is right for you? After two decades of trading at the Chicago Stock Exchange, Mike Grace wanted his own company, but he was having trouble evaluating franchise options. So he began working with Mike Waller of Entrepreneurs Source, Inc. Waller, a franchise consultant, gets paid 20% to 40% of the franchise fee when someone signs up with a franchisor. He's a franchise matchmaker, helping franchisors and franchisees select the right business opportunity. Dan Martin, chief executive of IFX International Inc., a franchise-consulting firm in San Diego, says, "A franchise consultant will have a portfolio of brands but is searching for the best lead for those brands. In representing a client, they're going to gauge the appropriateness of that client for a specific brand."

To pick the right franchise broker, start with these questions:

○ **How long have you been a franchise broker?**

○ **What is your franchise experience?**

○ **Do you offer in-person meetings and coaching?**

○ **Can you provide a list of people who are in franchising thanks to you?**

According to Mike Grace, having franchise consultant Mike Waller around was, "The difference between jumping into something with your fingers crossed or feeling confident that you're doing the right thing." Grace bought a ServPro cleanup and restoration franchise.

What franchise business is attractive to you? Would you like fries with that franchise?[20]

THE BIG PICTURE

This chapter discusses the four major forms of business ownership. Each form of ownership has both advantages and limitations, so no single form of ownership is the best in all situations.

Sole proprietorships are appealing to entrepreneurs who want to start a business quickly, with few formalities or fees, and who want to be their own boss. But sole proprietorships aren't well suited for raising financing from external sources, so growth opportunities are limited. And sole proprietors have unlimited liability for their company's debts and obligations.

General partnerships allow two or more owners to pool financial resources and take advantage of complementary skills. But each owner must assume the risk of unlimited liability, and disagreements among partners can complicate and delay important decisions.

Corporations are more complex and expensive to create than other forms of business. Another potentially serious drawback is the double taxation of earnings. But corporations have the greatest potential for raising financial capital and provide owners with the protection of limited liability.

The limited liability company (LLC) is a relatively new form of business ownership that offers many of the advantages of corporations without as many regulations. One major advantage of LLCs compared to corporations is that its earnings can be taxed as if the company is a partnership, thus avoiding double taxation. But the laws governing limited liability companies vary considerably among states, making it a challenge to operate an LLC in multiple states.

Many Americans view business ownership as a means of achieving both personal satisfaction and financial success. In fact, millions of Americans each year choose to pursue those goals by starting (or buying) and operating their own small business. Between 1990 and 2008, the number of nonfarm sole proprietorships in the United States grew from 14.8 million to more than 22.6 million, the number of partnerships increased from 1.6 million to 3.1 million, and the number of corporations from 3.7 million to 5.8 million. Even during the depths of the recent recession, business formation boomed, in part because many unemployed workers who were unable to find jobs with existing firms viewed starting their own business as the key to economic survival. In 2008, in the face of the deepening recession, American adults started new businesses at the rate of 530,000 per month.[21]

Individuals who want to own and operate a business but don't want to build their organization from the ground up, often find franchising to be an attractive alternative. Today, there are almost 800,000 franchise establishments in the United States, and current projections suggest that franchise opportunities will continue to grow.[22] One notable trend is that many franchisors are seeking to grow by reaching out to minorities and women.

Starting and running a business requires an entrepreneurial mindset that not everyone possesses. Another way to participate in business ownership and pursue financial goals is to buy stock in publicly traded corporations. Corporate stock has proven a popular investment for many people. And historically, stock ownership has yielded attractive financial returns over the long run. But as the ups and downs in stock prices over the past few years indicate, investing in the stock market isn't for the faint of heart!

CAREERS IN BUSINESS

CAREERS

What else?

RIP & REVIEW CARDS IN THE BACK
and visit www.cengagebrain.com!

7

Small Business and Entrepreneurship:
Economic Rocket Fuel

> "DO WHAT YOU *LOVE*. THIS WAY, WHETHER YOU MAKE MONEY AT IT OR NOT, AT LEAST YOU'RE *ENJOYING* YOURSELF."
>
> — GUY KAWASAKI, VENTURE CAPITALIST

entrepreneurs, such as Bill Gates and Paul Allen (founders of Microsoft), Phil Knight (founder of Nike), Michael Dell (founder of Dell Inc.), and Sergey Brin and Larry Page (founders of Google). And many people feel that their chances of even moderate financial success are higher if they're working for themselves rather than someone else. The opportunity to make more money is a primary motivator for many entrepreneurs, although other factors clearly play a role as well.[4]

> **entrepreneurs** People who risk their time, money, and other resources to start and manage a business.

7-1 Launching a New Venture: What's in It for Me?

Over time, the entrepreneurship rate has played a powerful, positive role in the U.S. economy. Despite the raging recession, new business creation increased steadily from 2007 to 2009. In 2010, overall U.S. entrepreneurship rates reached their highest level in 15 years, driven in part by unemployed workers looking to stay afloat as they sought new jobs. This represented a hopeful sign for the future of our economy—job seekers becoming potential job creators. Unfortunately, in 2011, the entrepreneurship rate declined slightly.[1] But 54% of Generation Y (born 1984–1995) either want to start a business or already have started one, a critically important element to long-term economic recovery.[2]

Starting a new business can be tough—very tough. Yet for the right person, the advantages of business ownership far outweigh the risk and hard work. Although people start their own ventures for a variety of reasons, most are seeking some combination of greater financial success, independence, flexibility, and challenge. Others are simply seeking survival.

7-1a Greater Financial Success

Although you can make a pretty good living working for someone else, your chances of getting really rich may be higher if you start your own business. The *Forbes* magazine annual list of the 400 richest Americans is dominated by

7-1b Independence

Being your own boss is a huge benefit of starting your own business. You answer to no one other than yourself and any investors whom you invite to participate in your business. Bottom line: you are the only one who is ultimately responsible for your success or failure. This setup is especially compelling for people who have trouble being subordinates because of their personalities (and we probably all know someone who fits that description!). But while independence is nice, it's important to keep in mind that every business depends on meeting the needs of its customers, who can be even more demanding than the toughest boss.

7-1c Flexibility

The ability to set your own hours and control your own schedule is a hugely appealing benefit for many business owners, especially parents seeking more time with their kids or retirees looking for extra income. Given current technological tools—from email to eBay—it's easy for small business owners to manage their firms on the go or after hours. Of course, there's often a correlation between hours worked and dollars earned. (It's rare to work less and earn more.) But when more money isn't the primary goal, the need for flexibility can be enough to motivate many entrepreneurs to launch their own enterprise.

7-1d Challenge

Running your own business provides a level of challenge unmatched by many other endeavors. Most business owners—especially new business owners—never find themselves bored! Starting a business also offers endless opportunities for learning that can provide more profound satisfaction for many people than grinding out the hours as an employee.

7-1e Survival

Although most entrepreneurs launch their business in response to an opportunity with hopes of improving their lives, some entrepreneurs—called "necessity entrepreneurs"—launch their business because they believe it is their *only* economic option. Necessity entrepreneurs range from middle-aged workers laid off from corporate jobs, to new immigrants with limited English and heavy accents, to those who experience discrimination in the standard workplace. For each of these types of people, small business ownership can be the right choice in the face of few other alternatives.

> "Anything that's really awesome takes a lot of work."
>
> —Mark Zuckerberg, founder, Facebook

of Amazon—aims to change the world through blockbuster goods or services. That isn't the case for all small-business owners. Most people who launch new firms expect to better themselves, but they don't expect huge, transformative growth. In fact, nearly 70% of small business owners say they don't want to grow any larger.[5]

However, classic entrepreneurs who deliver on the promise of their best ideas can dramatically change the economic and social landscape worldwide. Examples of business owners who thought and delivered big include Henry Ford, founder of the Ford Motor Company and originator of assembly line production; Walt Disney, founder of The Walt Disney Company and creator of Mickey Mouse; Mary Kay Ash, founder of a cosmetics powerhouse; Martha Stewart, lifestyle innovator for the masses; J.K. Rowling, creator of the *Harry Potter* franchise; and Mark Zuckerberg, founder of Facebook.

7-2 The Entrepreneur: A Distinctive Profile

Successful entrepreneurs tend to stand out from the crowd in terms of both their mindset and their personal characteristics. As you read this section, consider whether you fit the entrepreneurial profile.

7-2a The Entrepreneurial Mindset: A Matter of Attitude

Almost every entrepreneur starts as a small businessperson—either launching a firm or buying a firm—but not every small businessperson starts as an entrepreneur. The difference is a matter of attitude. From day one, a true entrepreneur—such as Sam Walton of Walmart, Steve Jobs of Apple, or Jeff Bezos

7-2b Entrepreneurial Characteristics

While experts sometimes disagree about the specific characteristics of successful entrepreneurs, virtually all include vision, self-reliance, energy, confidence, tolerance of uncertainty, and tolerance of failure. (See Exhibit 7.1.) Most successful entrepreneurs have all of these qualities and more, but they come in a huge variety of combinations that highlight the complexity of personality: there is no one successful entrepreneurial profile.

App - surd? Or not so much?

Facebook's purchase of Instagram for a cool billion dollars added fuel to the already overheated market for mobile apps. In fact, in the race to create the next killer app, *The Wall Street Journal* reports "it is getting tough to tell the difference between a joke and the next big thing." For instance, iPoo, a social-networking app that connects people sitting on toilets, sounds like a joke, but it really exists. More than 200,000 people have paid $1 apiece to download iPoo since it launched two years ago, say the app's creators, enough to help put one of them through Harvard Business School. And they claim that tens of thousands actually use it every day. Another spoof app that made it big is Jotly, a rate-anything app that lets users rate anything they can photograph, from "personal hiding places," to good meals, to whatever… While Jotly started as a digital designer's joke, within a couple of months, it had thousands of users and two legitimate venture-backed competitors. The idea certainly sounds app-surd, but perhaps Instagram didn't sound so great either before it took the iPhone world by storm.[5a]

> # "Never be the smartest person in the room. If you are, I suggest you invite smarter people ... or find a different room."
>
> — MICHAEL DELL

Vision Most entrepreneurs are wildly excited about their own new ideas, which many seem to draw from a bottomless well. Entrepreneurs find new solutions to old problems, and they develop new products that we didn't even know we needed until we had them. And entrepreneurs stay excited about their ideas, even when friends and relatives threaten to call the loony bin. For instance, Fred Smith, founder of the FedEx empire, traces the concept for his business to a term paper he wrote at Yale, which supposedly received a C from a skeptical professor. But that didn't stop him from creating a business logistics system that transformed the industry, and along with UPS, enabled e-commerce to flourish.

Self-Reliance As an entrepreneur, the buck stops with you. New business owners typically need to do everything themselves, from getting permits, to motivating employees, to keeping the books—all in addition to producing the product or service that made them start the business in the first place. Self-reliance seems to come with an **internal locus of control**, or a deep-seated sense

that the individual is personally responsible for what happens in his or her life. When things go well, people with an internal locus of control feel that their efforts have been validated, and when things go poorly, those same people feel that they need to do better next time. This sense of responsibility encourages positive action. In contrast, people with an **external locus of control** rely less on their own efforts, feeling buffeted by forces such as random luck and the actions of others, which they believe will ultimately control their fate.

Energy Entrepreneurs simply can't succeed without an enormous amount of energy. Six or seven 12-hour workdays are not atypical in the start-up phase of running a business. In fact, 61% of small business owners report working six or more days per week, compared to only 22% of workers in the general population. And for small business owners, even a day off isn't *really* off. Only 27% of small business owners define a day off as not working at all, while 57% of small business owners say they always or most of the time work on holidays. But Discover Financial Services also learned that many small business owners seem to find the grind worthwhile: 47% of small business owners said that if they won $10 million in the lottery, they would still work in their current job. Only 9% would stop working, and 8% would combine work, volunteering, and other areas of interest.[6]

Confidence Successful entrepreneurs typically have confidence in their own ability to achieve, and their confidence encourages them to act boldly. But too much confidence has a downside. Entrepreneurs must take care not to confuse likelihood with reality. In fact, many could benefit from the old adage "Hope for the best and plan for the worst." A study for the Small Business Administration Office of Advocacy confirmed that entrepreneurs are typically overconfident regarding their own abilities. As a result they're sometimes willing to plunge into a new business, but they don't always have the skills to succeed.[7]

> **internal locus of control** A deep-seated sense that the individual is personally responsible for what happens in his or her life.
>
> **external locus of control** A deep-seated sense that forces other than the individual are responsible for what happens in his or her life.

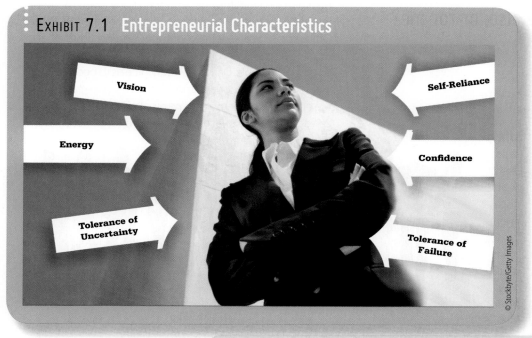

EXHIBIT **7.1** **Entrepreneurial Characteristics**

Vision

Energy

Tolerance of Uncertainty

Self-Reliance

Confidence

Tolerance of Failure

© Stockbyte/Getty Images

Entrepreneurship: Do you have what it takes?

How about YOU? Are YOU ready to start your own business? Successful entrepreneurs clearly have a wide range of personalities and characteristics. But these four questions, posed by Andy Swan on the Small Biz Survival website, may help separate those who *want* to launch a business from those who actually *can*.[8]

1. "Do you enjoy working? No... not thinking... not ideating... working. Executing. You have to execute. A mediocre idea well-executed is worth 100 times as much as a great idea that isn't carried out. Yes, having your own business is WORK, that dirty four-letter word that some have the misguided impression does not apply when you are the boss."

2. "Do you gamble? I really think that there is something deep inside of some people that makes them CRAVE risk, thrive on it. This one is hard—if not impossible—to fake, since entrepreneurs face risk every day of the week. The ones who are good at it typically flourish, the ones who are not, usually fail in business."

3. "Can you fake it? A lot of entrepreneurship is promotion. You can't wear your emotions on your sleeve, or you're DEAD. Why? Because 90–95% of the time, your company is in trouble, and you have major doubts. But guess what... investors, customers, partners... everyone... they DO NOT want to hear it, see it, or sense it. They want confidence. Yes.... later you HAVE to deliver quality.... but today, you have to deliver confidence."

   How true is that statement? The ability to roll with the punches and come up smiling can get a new business owner a long way. How's your duck 'n' dodge?

4. "Are you good on your feet? Things change. ALL the time... Poof... the business plan you spent 6 months perfecting is gone. A lot of people can't stand it when plans change at the last minute. Others expect it and stay up late."

I'm going to put 150% of myself into whatever I do. Would I rather do that for someone else, or for me?

—Chantel Waterbury, founder, Chloe and Isabel

Tolerance of Uncertainty

More often than others, entrepreneurs see the world in shades of gray, rather than simply black and white. They tend to embrace uncertainty in the business environment, turning it to their advantage rather than shying away. Uncertainty also relates to risk, and successful entrepreneurs tend to more willingly accept risk—financial risk, for instance, such as mortgaging their home for the business, and professional risk, such as staking their reputation on the success of an unproven product.

Tolerance of Failure Even when they fail, entrepreneurs seldom label themselves losers. They tend to view failure as a chance to learn, rather than as a sign that they just can't do it (whatever "it" may be for them at any given moment). Interestingly, Isaac Fleischmann, director of the U.S. Patent Office for 36 years, pointed out that "During times of economic decline when unemployment increases, so does the number of patents. Dark days often force us to become more ingenious, to monitor and modify the ways we reached failure and reshape them into a new pattern of success." Failure can actually be an effective springboard for achievement.[9]

Entrepreneurs are a diverse group of people who tend to share some similar personal characteristics.

Elevating Hoodies

What would you do if you won the lottery? Buy a baseball team? Bail out Greece? Many of today's technology entrepreneurs have rather suddenly earned millions (sometimes billions) of dollars, beyond many people's wildest lottery dreams. In mid-2012, 28-year old Mark Zuckerberg, founder of Facebook, suddenly became one of the richest people in the world and faced the enviable challenge of figuring out how to spend his money. For starters, Zuckerberg joined Bill Gates and Warren Buffet in signing the "Giving Pledge," promising to donate half his wealth to charity. He also donated $100 million to the Newark, NJ, public school system, and invested in a high-tech open source social networking firm. Personal finance guru, Suze Orman, gives Zuckerberg—famous for wearing hoodies to even the most formal events—this investing advice: "Mark, you're now a multi-multibillionaire: maybe invest in a hoodie factory or something. Put a logo on it. Just something to take the look one step up."[10]

A surprising number of twentieth-century entrepreneurial stars experienced significant failure in their careers yet bounced back to create wildly successful ventures. Early in his career, for instance, Walt Disney was fired from an ad agency (in hindsight, a rather foolish ad agency) for a "singular lack of drawing ability." Ray Kroc, the man who made McDonald's into a fast-food empire, couldn't make a go of real estate, so he sold milkshake machines for much of his life. He was 52 years old, and in failing health, when he discovered the McDonald brothers' hamburger stand and transformed it into a fast food empire. And Steve Jobs, founder of Apple computer, found himself unceremoniously dumped by his board of directors less than ten years after introducing the world's first personal computer. After another decade, he returned in triumph, restoring Apple's polish with blockbuster new products such as the iPod and the iPhone. So next time you fail, keep your eyes open for opportunity—your failure may be the first step of the next big thing.[11]

7-3 Finding the Money: Funding Options for Small Businesses

For many entrepreneurs, finding the money to fund their business is the top challenge of their start-up year. The vast majority of new firms are funded with the personal resources of their founder. In fact, about 95% of entrepreneurs raise start-up funds from personal accounts, family, and friends. Other key funding sources include bank loans, angel investors, and venture capital firms.[12]

7-3a Personal Resources

While the idea of using just your own money to open a business sounds great, the financial requirements of most new firms typically force entrepreneurs to also tap personal resources such as family, friends, and credit cards. According to *Consumer Reports*, 68% of total start-up financing comes from personal resources.[13] If you do borrow from family or friends, virtually every small business expert recommends that you keep the relationship as professional as possible. If the business fails, a professional agreement can preserve personal ties. And if the business succeeds, you'll need top-quality documentation of financing from family and friends to get larger-scale backing from outside sources.

Personal credit cards can be an especially handy—though highly risky—financing resource. In fact, a recent survey found that nearly half of all start-ups are funded with plastic. (It's no wonder, given that those solicitations just keep on coming.) Credit cards do provide fast, flexible money, but watch out—if you don't pay back your card company fast, you'll find yourself socked with financing fees that can take years to pay off.[14]

7-3b Loans

Getting commercial loans for a new venture can be tough. Banks and other lenders are understandably hesitant to fund a business that doesn't have a track record. And when they do, they require a lot of paperwork and often a fairly long waiting period. Given these hurdles, only 20% of new business owners launch with commercial loans. In 2011, small business loans unfortunately fell to a 12-year low.[14a] And virtually no conventional lending source—private or government—will lend 100% of the start-up dollars for a new business. Most require that the entrepreneur provide a minimum of

25 to 30% of total start-up costs from personal resources.[15]

Another source for loans may be the U.S. Small Business Administration (SBA). The SBA doesn't give free money to start-up businesses—neither grants nor interest-free loans—but it does partially guarantee loans from local commercial lenders. This reduces risk for the lenders, who are, in turn, more likely to lend money to a new business owner. The SBA also has a microloan program that lends small amounts of money—$13,000 on average—to start-up businesses through community nonprofit organizations.[16]

Peer-to-peer lending offers yet another potential funding source for new business start-ups. Websites such as Prosper.com and LendingClub.com bring together borrowers and investors so that both can benefit financially. Many entrepreneurs have found this is an easier way to get money, at more favorable terms, than through more-established sources.

7-3c Angel Investors

Angel investors aren't as saintly—or as flighty—as they sound. They are wealthy individuals who invest in promising start-up companies for one basic reason: to make money for themselves. According to Jeffrey Sohl, director of the Center for Venture Research, angels look for companies that seem likely to grow at 30 to 40% per year and will then either be bought or go public. He estimates that 10 to 15% of private companies fit that description, but points out that finding those firms isn't easy. It doesn't help, he says, that "80% of entrepreneurs think they're in that 10 to 15%." In the first half of 2010, the number of firms that received angel funding increased 3% versus 2009, despite the

Angel investors and venture capitalists actively seek to invest in high growth potential start-up firms.

© Colin Anderson/Blend Images/Jupiterimages

economic crisis. In 2011, the size of median angel funding rounds grew 40%, and angels began to focus on early stage start-ups, an encouraging sign for long-term economic health.[17]

7-3d Venture Capital

Venture capital firms fund high-potential new companies in exchange for a share of ownership, which can sometimes be as high as 60%. These deals tend to be quite visible, but keep in mind that only a tiny fraction of new businesses receive any venture capital money. The advice and guidance that come with the dollars can also be quite significant. David Barger, chief executive officer of jetBlue Airways, remembers that he and jetBlue's founder, David Neeleman, originally planned to call the airline Taxi and to fly bright yellow planes. But an influential venture capitalist changed their minds. He called them into his office and said, "If you call this airline Taxi, we're not going to invest." The name changed, and the venture capitalist stayed.[18]

Although the economic crisis drastically reduced venture capital spending, 2011 saw a 22% increase in venture capital dollars and a 4% increase in the number of deals, making 2011 one of the top three years of the past decade for venture funding. **The environment continued to be a bright spot: Investments in clean technology firms in 2011 grew 12% in terms of both dollars and number of deals versus 2010, hitting the highest total level ever recorded for a single year. For the full year 2011, three of the top ten deals were in the Clean Tech category. The flow of money suggests that the clean tech sector continues to be a ripe segment for new business start-ups.[19]**

7-4 Opportunities and Threats for Small Business: A Two-Sided Coin

Most small businesses enjoy a number of advantages as they compete for customers. But they also must defuse a range of daunting potential threats in order to succeed over the long term.

Small Business Opportunities Small businesses enjoy a real competitive edge across a range of different areas. Because of their size, many small firms can exploit narrow but profitable market niches, offer personal customer service, and maintain lower overhead costs. And due to advances in technology, small firms can compete more effectively than ever in both global and domestic markets.

Market Niches Many small firms are uniquely positioned to exploit small, but profitable, **market niches**. These sparsely

"Nearly 80% of Americans trust small business owners to create jobs versus about 40% who trust leaders of Congress."

— Gallup

Nutty Market Niches

Small businesses can do especially well in market niches, even niches that initially seem somewhat wacky. Here are a handful of wacky businesses that have really worked:

- *Neuticles*: Did you worry about your dog's self-esteem after he got neutered? Entrepreneur Greg Miller did, which was why he invented Neuticles, artificial testicular implants for dogs. Despite the giggle factor, Neuticles have become a huge commercial success, recently featured in *BusinessWeek* magazine, where he points out that at first, many people thought the idea was nuts.

- *The Smashing Place*: Ever been so mad you just wanted to smash something? If you live in Tokyo, you're in luck! You can just visit The Smashing Place, buy a plate or a cup of your choice, and smash it against a concrete wall—the staff will even cheer you on, and recycle the scraps afterwards.

- *Rent-a-Chicken*: Your first question may be why? As interest in local food and urban farming has grown, more families have shown interest in keeping chickens, which can be a bit of a commitment—especially baby chicks. That's where Rent-a-Chicken can help, by providing two full-grown hens, and everything needed to keep them for the summer. Founder Leslie Suitor claims, "Chickens are about as easy as goldfish. Really. Families can expect to gather about a dozen eggs a week." Eggcellent![21]

So the next time inspiration strikes, you may want to write down your idea and get to work, no matter how wacky it may initially seem.

---

occupied spaces in the market tend to have fewer competitors because they simply aren't big enough—or high-profile enough—for large firms. They nonetheless offer more than enough potential for small, specialized companies. For example, Kazoo & Company, a relatively small toy store, competes effectively with Walmart, Target, and Kmart by stocking different—and complementary—products, deliberately zigging when the big players zag.[20]

Personal Customer Service With a smaller customer base, small firms can develop much more personal relationships with individual customers. Shel Weinstein, for instance, former owner of a Los Angeles corner pharmacy, knew his customers so well that they would call him at home in the middle of the night for help with medical emergencies. The personal touch can be especially beneficial in some foreign markets, where clients prize the chance to deal directly with top management.

Lower Overhead Costs With entrepreneurs wearing so many hats, from CEO to customer service rep, many small firms have lower overhead costs. They can hire fewer managers and fewer specialized employees. Perhaps more importantly, smaller firms—due to a lack of resources—tend to work around costs with tactics such as establishing headquarters in the owner's garage or offering employees flexible schedules instead of costly healthcare benefits.

Technology The Internet has played a powerful role in opening new opportunities for small businesses. Using a wealth of online tools, from eBay to eMachineshop, companies-of-one can create, sell, publish, and even manufacture goods and services more easily than ever before. The Internet has also created international opportunities, transforming small businesses into global marketers. The London-based Anything Left-Handed retail store, for instance, evolved into an award-winning global wholesaler of left-handed items within a year of launching its website. Founder Keith Milsom comments that "our website has allowed us to communicate with potential customers and market our business worldwide at very little cost, making international development possible."[22]

Small Business Threats While small businesses do enjoy some advantages, they also face intimidating obstacles, from a high risk of failure to too much regulation.

High Risk of Failure Starting a new business involves risk—a lot of risk—but the odds improve significantly if you make it past the crucial four-year mark. Check out the seven-year survival rate in Exhibit 7.2. Notice that it declines much more slowly after Year 4.

Even though these numbers may look daunting, it's important to remember that owners shut down their businesses for many reasons other than the failure of the firm itself. The possibilities include poor health, divorce, better opportunities elsewhere, and interestingly, an unwillingness to make the enormous time commitment of running a business. Small business expert David Birch jokingly calls this last reason—which is remarkably common—the "I had no idea!" syndrome. It highlights the importance of anticipating what you're in for *before* you open your doors.[23]

Lack of Knowledge and Experience People typically launch businesses because they either have expertise in a particular area—like designing websites or cooking Vietnamese food—or because they have a breakthrough idea—like a new way to develop computer chips or run an airline. But in-depth knowledge in a specific area doesn't necessarily mean expertise in running a business. Successful business owners must know everything from finance to human resources to marketing.

Too Little Money The media is filled with stories of business owners who made it on a shoestring, but lack of start-up money is a major issue for most new firms. Ongoing profits don't usually begin for a while, which means that entrepreneurs must plan on some lean months—or even years—as the business develops momentum. That means a real need to manage money wisely and to resist the temptation to invest in fixed assets, such as fancy offices and advanced electronics, before sufficient regular income warrants it. It also requires the nerve to stay the course despite initial losses.[24]

Bigger Regulatory Burden Complying with federal regulations can be challenging for any business, but it can be downright overwhelming for small firms. A study sponsored by the federal government shows that firms with fewer than 20 employees spend an average of $10,585 per employee abiding by federal regulations, compared with $7,755 spent by firms with more than 500 employees. The overall burden is new number: +36% greater for small business than for its larger business counterparts. But relief may be on the way: Congress continues to examine ways to reduce the growing regulatory burden on small businesses—an urgent need in the face of the struggling economy.[25]

Higher Health Insurance Costs Administrative costs for small health plans are much higher than for large businesses, making it even tougher for small firms to offer coverage to their employees. Given skyrocketing healthcare costs in general, the best employees are likely to demand a great insurance plan, putting small business at a real disadvantage in terms of building a competitive workforce.[26] But this may change as healthcare reform goes into effect over the next decade.

7-5 Launch Options: Reviewing the Pros and Cons

When you imagine starting a new business, the first thought that comes to mind would probably be the process of developing your own big idea from an abstract concept to a thriving enterprise. But that's not the only option. In fact, it may make more sense to purchase an established business, or even buy a franchise such as a Pizza Hut or Subway restaurant. Each choice, of course, involves pros and cons. The trick is finding the best fit for you: the combination that offers you the least harmful downsides and the most meaningful upsides. Broadly speaking, it's less risky to buy an established business or franchise, but it can be more satisfying to start from scratch. Exhibit 7.3 offers a more detailed overview of the pros and cons.

7-5a Making It Happen: Tools for Business Success

Whatever way you choose to become a small business owner, several strategies can help you succeed over the long term: gain experience in your field, learn from others, educate yourself, access **Small Business Administration (SBA)** resources, and develop a business plan.

EXHIBIT 7.2 New Business Survival Rates

YEAR IN BUSINESS	SURVIVAL RATE	CHANGE VS. PRIOR YEAR (PERCENTAGE POINTS)
YEAR 1	81%	−19
YEAR 2	66%	−15
YEAR 3	54%	−12
YEAR 4	44%	−10
YEAR 5	38%	−6
YEAR 6	34%	−4
YEAR 7	31%	−3

Source: Business Employment Dynamics data: survival and longevity, II, by Amy E. Knaup and Merissa C. Piazza, September 2007, Monthly Labor Review, Bureau of Labor Statistics website, http://www.bls.gov/opub/mlr/2007/09/art1full.pdf, accessed February 15, 2009.

Gain Experience Getting roughly three years of experience working for someone else in the field that interests you is a good rule of thumb. That way, you can learn what does and doesn't fly in your industry with relatively low personal risk (and you'd be making any mistakes on someone else's dime). You can also start developing a vibrant, relevant network before you need to ask for favors. But if you stay much longer than three years, you may get too comfortable to take the plunge and launch your own venture.

Learn from Others You should actively seek opportunities to learn from people who've succeeded in your field. If you don't know anyone personally, use your network to get introductions. And don't forget industry associations, local events, and other opportunities to build relationships. Also, remember that people who failed in your field may be able to give you valuable insights (why make the same mistakes they did?). As a bonus, they may be more willing to share their ideas and their gaffes if they're no longer struggling to develop a business of their own.

Educate Yourself The opportunities for entrepreneurial learning have exploded in the past decade. Many colleges and universities now offer full-blown entrepreneurship programs that help students both develop their plans and secure their initial funding. But education shouldn't stop there. Seek out relevant press articles, workshops, websites, and blogs so that your ongoing education will continue to boost your career.

Access SBA Resources The SBA offers a number of resources beyond money (which we'll discuss in the next section). The SBA website, www.sba.gov, provides a wealth of information from industry-specific statistics, to general trends, to updates on small business regulations. The SBA also works hand in hand with individual states to fund local **Small Business Development Centers (SBDCs)**. SBDCs provide a range of free services for small businesses from developing your concept,

Small Business Development Centers (SBDCs) Local offices—affiliated with the Small Business Administration—that provide comprehensive management assistance to current and prospective small business owners.

EXHIBIT 7.3 Pros and Cons of Starting a Business from Scratch versus Buying an Established Business

STARTING YOUR BUSINESS FROM SCRATCH

Key Pros	Key Cons
It's all *you:* Your concept, your decisions, your structure, and so on.	It's all *you.* That's a lot of pressure.
You don't have to deal with the prior owner's bad decisions.	It takes time, money, and sheer sweat equity to build a customer base.
	Without a track record, it's harder to get credit from both lenders and suppliers.
	From securing permits to hiring employees, the logistics of starting a business can be challenging.

BUYING AN ESTABLISHED BUSINESS

Key Pros	Key Cons
The concept, organizational structure, and operating practices are already in place.	Working with someone else's idea can be a lot less fun for some entrepreneurs.
Relationships with customers, suppliers, and other stakeholders are established.	You may inherit old mistakes that can range from poor employee relations to pending lawsuits.
Getting financing and credit is less challenging.	

BUYING A FRANCHISE

Key Pros	Key Cons
In most cases, you're buying your own piece of a well-known brand and proven way of doing business.	You have less opportunity for creativity since most agreements tie you to franchise requirements.
Typically, management expertise and consulting come with the franchise package.	If something goes wrong with the national brand (e.g., *E. coli* at a burger joint), your business will suffer, too.
Franchisers occasionally offer not just advice but also the financing that can make the purchase possible.	The initial purchase price can be steep, and that doesn't include the ongoing percent-of-sales royalty fee.
These advantages add up to a very low 5% first-year failure rate.	

Source: Five Reasons Why Franchises Flop, by Steve Strauss, February 28, 2005, *USA Today* Money website, http://www.usatoday.com/money/smallbusiness/columnist/strauss/2005-02-28-franchise_x.htm.

to consulting on your business plan, to helping with your loan applications. And the SBA supports **SCORE**, the Service Corps of Retired Executives at www.score.org. They provide free, comprehensive counseling for small businesses from qualified volunteers.

Develop a Business Plan Can a business succeed without a plan? Of course. Many do just fine by simply seizing opportunity as it arises, and changing direction as needed. Some achieve significant growth without a plan. But a **business plan** does provide an invaluable way to keep you and your team focused on success. And it's absolutely crucial for obtaining outside funding, which is why many entrepreneurs write a business plan after they've used personal funding sources (such as savings, credit cards, and money from family and friends) to get themselves up and running. Even then, the plan may be continually in flux if the industry is rapidly changing.

An effective business plan, which is usually 25 to 50 pages long, takes about six months to write. While the specifics may change by industry, the basic elements of any business plan answer these core questions:

- ➲ What service or product does your business provide, and what needs does it fill?
- ➲ Who are the potential customers for your product or service, and why will they purchase it from you?
- ➲ How will you reach your potential customers?
- ➲ Where will you get the financial resources to start your business?
- ➲ When can you expect to achieve profitability?

The final document should include all of the following information:

- ➲ Executive summary (two to three pages)
- ➲ Description of business (include both risks and opportunities)

"More than 30% of the richest people in the world do not have a college degree, but 57% of those who start a business in high-income countries do have a college degree."
— GLOBAL ENTREPRENEURSHIP MONITOR AND *FORBES*

© razihusin/Shutterstock.com

- ➲ Marketing
- ➲ Competition (don't underestimate the challenge)
- ➲ Operating procedures
- ➲ Personnel
- ➲ Complete financial data and plan, including sources of start-up money (be realistic!)
- ➲ Appendix (be sure to include all your research on your industry)[27]

Check out the SBA business-planning site for more information on how to write your own business plan and for samples of actual business plans (http://www.sba.gov/smallbusinessplanner/index .html). Other excellent resources (among many) on the Internet include the sample business plan resource center (www.bplans.com/) and the business plan pages of AllBusiness.com (www .allbusiness.com/).

| 7-6 | **Small Business and the Economy: An Outsized Impact** |

The most successful entrepreneurs create goods and services that change the way people live. Many build blockbuster corporations that power the stock market and dominate pop culture through ubiquitous promotion. But small businesses—despite their lower profile—also play a vital role in the U.S. economy. Here are a few statistics from the U.S. Small Business Administration:

- ➲ In 2009, 99.9% of the 27,500,000 businesses in the United States had fewer than 500 employees.
- ➲ More than three-quarters of those business owners—21,400,000 people, totaling about 7% of the population—ran their businesses without any employees.

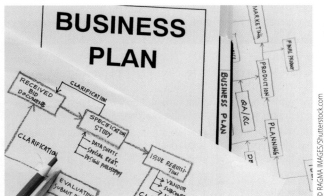

BUSINESS PLAN

© RAGMA IMAGES/Shutterstock.com

Accidental Inventions

Every new business begins with a great idea, but not all great ideas begin with careful planning—a number of successful businesses have been built on inventions that happened by accident. But that doesn't mean that you shouldn't be prepared; first-century philosopher Seneca said, "Luck is what happens when preparation meets opportunity." A sampling of "accidental inventions":[28]

© haveseen/Shutterstock.com

○ *Microwave Ovens*: When World War II scientist, Percy Spencer, was inspecting a magnetron tube at a Raytheon lab, he noticed that a candy bar in his pocket had melted, which sparked the idea of using microwaves for cooking. Today, more than 90% of households have microwave ovens.

○ *Coca-Cola*: Atlanta pharmacist John Pemberton was mixing ingredients to create a new headache remedy when he discovered, instead, a tasty beverage, Coca-Cola,

which was sold from his pharmacy for eight years before it was popular enough to be sold in bottles.

○ *Post-it Notes*: 3M scientist Spencer Silver developed the repositionable adhesive for Post-it Notes. But they didn't become a product until his co-worker, Art Fry, was looking for a sticky, reusable bookmark to replace the paper bookmarks that kept slipping out of his church hymnal. Fry proposed the product, which quickly became a worldwide hit for 3M.

○ Yet, these small businesses generate about half of the U.S. gross domestic product.

○ Over the past 17 years, small businesses created 65% of the net new jobs in the United States.

○ In total, small business provides jobs for about half of the nation's private workforce.[29]

The statistics, of course, depend on the definition of small business. For research purposes, the SBA defines small business as companies with up to 500 employees, including the self-employed. But the SBA also points out that the meaning of small business differs across industries. To officially count as "small," the number of employees can range from fewer than 100 to 1,500, and the average revenue can range from $0.75 million to $28.5 million, depending on the type of business. But regardless of the specific definition, the fact is clear: small business is a big player in the U.S. economy.

Beyond the sheer value of the goods and services they generate, small businesses make a powerful contribution to the U.S. economy in terms of creating new jobs, fueling innovation, and vitalizing inner cities.

○ Creating New Jobs: Small businesses with employees start up at a rate of about 600,000 per year. Five years after they launch, about half of those businesses—and many of the jobs they create—remain viable. But while small businesses are quick to add new jobs, they're often the first to contract when times are tough; instability comes with the territory.[30]

○ Fueling Innovation: Small businesses are much more likely to develop revolutionary new ideas. Small patenting firms produce about 13% more patents per employee than their large-firm counterparts, and those patents are twice as likely to be found among the top 1% of highest-impact patents. Small firms tend to be effective innovators for a number of reasons. Perhaps most importantly, their very reason for being often ties to a brand new idea. In the early years, they need innovation in order to simply survive. And they often display a refreshing lack of bureaucracy that allows new thinking to take hold.[31]

○ Vitalizing Inner Cities: New research shows that small businesses are the backbone of urban economies, finding opportunity in niches that may not be worthwhile for larger firms. Small business comprises more than 99% of inner-city business establishments. In addition to creating new jobs, these small businesses generate 80% of total employment in American inner cities, providing a springboard for economic development.[32]

7-6a Entrepreneurship Around the World

Research suggests that entrepreneurship has an economic impact in countries around the world. Societies need entrepreneurs to ensure that new ideas actualize and to ensure that people are able to self-employ when their economy

© BSH Stock/Image Source

does not provide for their basic needs. For the past 12 years, the Global Entrepreneurship Monitor (GEM) has measured the annual rate of new business start-ups across a range of countries across the globe. The thirteenth annual GEM study included 54 countries. According to lead author, Donna Kelley, the overall findings were very positive: "Thanks to an uptick in entrepreneurship worldwide, we now have nearly 400 million entrepreneurs starting and running businesses in the 54 economies surveyed. Even better news is that more than 140 million of these entrepreneurs expect to add at least five new jobs over the next five years. These figures and growth projections affirm that entrepreneurial activity is flourishing across the globe and that entrepreneurship, as an economic engine, is the best hope for reviving a weakened world economy."

According to GEM, the most effective way to evaluate entrepreneurship levels is by phase. A country's total early-phase entrepreneurship rate includes the percentage of adults who have been running their own business from 3 months to 3.5 years. The current entrepreneurship rate varies dramatically from country to country, ranging from a high of 24.6% in China to a low of 5.8% in Spain and Sweden. (See Exhibit 7.4 for the ten nations with the highest and lowest entrepreneurship rates.) The differences among countries seem to depend largely on several key factors: What is the national per capita income? What will the entrepreneur need to give up (i.e., the opportunity costs)? How high is the risk of failure? How strongly do the national culture and political environment support business start-ups?

Per Capita Income In lower-income countries, such as China and Chile, a high percentage of entrepreneurs start their own businesses because they simply have no other options. This contributes heavily to the startlingly high overall level of entrepreneurship. The rate of such "necessity entrepreneurship" declines in higher-income countries, such as the United States and Japan, where entrepreneurs are more likely to strike out on their own in response to an opportunity that they spot in the marketplace.

> "In 2011, about 24% of the Chilean population was actively involved in early stage entrepreneurial activity."
>
> —GLOBAL ENTREPRENEURSHIP MONITOR

Opportunity Costs Entrepreneurship rates are significantly lower in countries that provide a high level of employment protection (it's hard to get fired) and strong unemployment insurance (financial support if you do get fired). With these benefits in place, the sense of urgency regarding entrepreneurship tends to fall, in part because fear of failure is much lower. The European Union provides a number of clear examples.

Cultural/Political Environment Extensive, complex regulations can hinder entrepreneurship by raising daunting barriers. And a lack of cultural support only compounds the problem. These factors certainly contribute to the relatively low entrepreneurship rates in much of the European Union and Japan. Entrepreneurs in more supportive nations such as the United States and New Zealand get a boost from limited regulation and strong governmental support. A thriving "cowboy culture" helps, too—standout individuals who break free of old ways attract attention and admiration in many of the countries with higher entrepreneurship rates.[33]

EXHIBIT 7.4 Early Phase Entrepreneurship Rates 2011

TOP TEN ENTREPRENEURSHIP RATES		BOTTOM TEN ENTREPRENEURSHIP RATES	
COUNTRY	RATE	COUNTRY	RATE
CHINA	24.6%	Slovenia	3.7%
TRINIDAD	19.5%	Denmark	4.6%
CHILE	23.7%	Russia	4.6%
PERU	22.9%	Malaysia	4.9%
COLUMBIA	21.4%	Japan	5.2%
ARGENTINA	20.8%	Germany	5.6%
PANAMA	20.8%	Belgium	5.7%
THAILAND	19.5%	France	5.7%
GUATEMALA	19.3%	Spain	5.8%
VENEZUELA	15.4%	Sweden	5.8%

Source: Global Entrepreneurship Monitor Report 2011 by Donna J. Kelley, Slavica Singer, and Mike Herrington, May 10, 2012, GEM Consortium website, http://gemconsortium.org/docs/download/2012, accessed June 13, 2012.

Successful entrepreneurs need more than simply a great idea. Bringing that idea to market—and earning a profit in the process—requires deep knowledge of every area of business. Finding money, attracting customers, and absorbing risk are only some of the challenges. But for the right person, the payoff can be huge in terms of everything from financial success to scheduling flexibility. The key is finding something you love to do that offers value to others. While that doesn't guarantee success, building on a passion suggests that you'll at least enjoy the journey. Looking forward from the global economic crisis, entrepreneurship seems likely to become a way of life, either part-time or full-time, for a growing swath of the population. The ideal result would be a higher standard of living—and a higher quality of life—for business owners and their customers worldwide.

CAREERS

If your personality fits the entrepreneurial profile, you may want to consider launching your own business as a means of achieving your financial and your lifestyle goals in an uncertain and rapidly changing economic environment. And no need to wait until you've earned your degree to realize your dreams. A recent large-scale survey by the Young Entrepreneurs Council found that 36% of college students are sidepreneurs–they have started their own businesses in addition to getting their degrees.[34] If you do decide to pursue entrepreneurship, be sure to seek as much information and support as possible from your local Small Business Development Center.

CAREERS IN ENTERPRENEURSHIP

What *else?*
RIP & REVIEW CARDS IN THE BACK
and visit www.cengagebrain.com!

8

Accounting:

Decision Making by the Numbers

LEARNING OBJECTIVES

After studying this chapter, you will be able to:

8-1 Define accounting and describe how accounting information is used by a variety of stakeholders

8-2 Identify the purposes and goals of generally accepted accounting principles

8-3 Describe the key elements of the major financial statements

8-4 Describe several methods stakeholders can use to obtain useful insights from a company's financial statements

8-5 Explain the role of managerial accounting and describe the various cost concepts identified by managerial accountants

8-6 Explain how the budget process can help managers plan, motivate, and evaluate their organization's performance

> ## "THE *PEN* IS MIGHTIER THAN THE SWORD, BUT NO MATCH FOR THE *ACCOUNTANT.*"
> —Jonathan Glancey, British journalist

multiple times—layoffs might be in the offing, so many employees might decide to polish their résumés!

○ Creditors: The late, great comedian Bob Hope once defined a bank as a place that would only lend you money if you could prove you didn't really need it. That's a bit of an exaggeration, but it is true that before granting a loan, responsible bankers and other lenders will want to assess a firm's creditworthiness by looking at its financial statements.

○ Suppliers: Like bankers, companies that provide supplies want to know that the company can pay for the orders it places.

○ Government agencies: Accurate accounting information is critical for meeting the reporting requirements of the Internal Revenue Service (IRS), the Securities and Exchange Commission (SEC), and other federal and state agencies.

A number of other groups—including the news media, competitors, and unions—might also have a real interest in a firm's accounting information—whether the firm wants them to have it or not! If you have any interest in managing, investing in, or working for a business, the ability to understand accounting information is extremely valuable.

8-1 Accounting: Who Needs It—and Who Does It?

Accounting is a system for recognizing, organizing, analyzing, and reporting information about the financial transactions that affect an organization. The goal of this system is to provide its users with relevant, timely information that helps them make better economic decisions.

Who uses the information that accounting provides? It's a long list; after all, everyone wants to make good decisions! In fact, a variety of business stakeholders rely so heavily on accounting information that it's sometimes called the "language of business."

8-1a Accounting: Who Uses It?

Key users of accounting information include:

○ Managers: Marketing managers, for instance, need information about sales in various regions and for various product lines. Financial managers need up-to-date facts about debt, cash, inventory, and capital.

○ Stockholders: As owners of the company, most stockholders have a keen interest in its financial performance, especially as indicated by the firm's financial statements. Has management generated a strong enough return on their investment?

○ Employees: Strong financial performance would help employees make their case for nice pay raises and hefty bonuses. But if earnings drop—especially

8-1b Accounting: Who Does It?

Accountants work in a variety of positions to provide all of this information. Let's take a quick look at some of the roles accountants play:

○ **Public accountants** provide services such as tax preparation, external auditing (a process we'll describe later in this chapter), or management consulting to clients on a fee basis.

○ **Management accountants** work within a company and provide analysis, prepare reports and financial

financial accounting
The branch of accounting that prepares financial statements for use by owners, creditors, suppliers, and other external stakeholders.

generally accepted accounting principles (GAAP) A set of accounting standards that is used in the preparation of financial statements.

Financial Accounting Standards Board (FASB) The private board that establishes the generally accepted accounting principles used in the practice of financial accounting.

statements, and assist managers in their own organization. *Internal auditors* also work within their organizations to detect internal problems such as waste, mismanagement, embezzlement, and employee theft.

> "**If my** father had hugged me even once, I'd be an accountant right now."
>
> —Ray Romano, comedian

🡢 **Government accountants** perform a variety of accounting functions for local, state, or federal government agencies. Some ensure that the government's own tax revenues and expenditures are recorded and reported in accordance with regulations and requirements. Others work for the IRS to audit tax returns or for other government agencies, such as the SEC or FDIC, to help ensure that our nation's banks and other financial institutions comply with the rules and regulations governing their behavior.

Many jobs performed by accountants require expertise in complex subject areas. For this reason, accountants who want to move up in their profession often seek certification in a particular field. But achieving such recognition isn't easy. For example, in order to be recognized as a *certified public accountant* in most states, a candidate must complete the equivalent of 150 semester hours (five years) of college education with a heavy emphasis in accounting and other business-related courses, must pass a rigorous two-day, four-part exam (very few candidates pass all four parts on their first try), and must complete at least one year of direct work experience in the field of accounting. Individuals seeking to become *certified management accountants* or *certified fraud examiners* must satisfy similarly challenging requirements.

8–2 Financial Accounting: Intended for Those on the Outside Looking In

Financial accounting is the branch of accounting that addresses the needs of external stakeholders, including stockholders, creditors, and government regulators. These stakeholders are seldom interested in poring over detailed accounting information about the individual departments or divisions within

a company. Instead, they're interested in the financial performance of the firm as a whole. They often want to know how a firm's financial condition has changed over a period of several years, or to compare its results to those of other firms in the same industry. The major output of financial accounting is a set of financial statements designed to provide this broad type of information. We'll describe these statements in the next section.

8–2a Role of the Financial Standards Accounting Board

Imagine how confused and frustrated investors, creditors, and regulators would become if every firm could make its own financial accounting rules as it went along and change them whenever it wanted! To reduce confusion and provide external stakeholders with consistent and accurate financial statements, the accounting profession has adopted a set of **generally accepted accounting principles (GAAP)** that guide the practice of financial accounting. In the United States, the Securities and Exchange Commission (SEC) has the ultimate legal authority to set and enforce accounting standards. In practice, however, the SEC has delegated the responsibility for developing these rules to a private organization known as the **Financial Accounting Standards Board (FASB)**. This board consists of seven members appointed by the Financial Accounting Foundation. Each member serves a five-year term and can be reappointed to serve one additional term. In order to preserve independence and impartiality, the members are required to sever all ties with any firms or institutions they served prior to joining the Board.

Through GAAP, the FASB aims to ensure that financial statements are:

🡢 Relevant: They must contain information that helps the user understand the firm's financial performance and condition.

🡢 Reliable: They must provide information that is objective, accurate, and verifiable.

🡢 Consistent: They must provide financial statements based on the same core assumptions and procedures over time; if a firm introduces any significant changes in how it prepares its financial statements, GAAP requires it to clearly identify and describe these changes.

🡢 Comparable: They must present accounting statements in a reasonably standardized way, allowing users to track the firm's financial performance over a period of years and compare its results with those for other firms.

Accounting Fraud, the Not-So-Usual Suspects: Friends, Neighbors, Co-Workers, Bosses, and Relatives

Stealing cash, faking bills or expense reports, or falsifying revenues or expenses to misstate profits, that is, accounting fraud, "Can happen to people who are otherwise good-intentioned; maybe they are trying to make a mortgage payment or put food on the table. These aren't hardened or overly sophisticated criminals," says Dave Recker at Willis Executive Risks. Barry Pollack, a partner in the Washington D.C. law firm of Miller & Chevalier, says, "People don't just set out and say, 'I'm going to commit a fraud.' Most of the time they're good people who have complied with the rules. Then pressure sets in, and they go closer and closer to the line." Many cases have involved family members, people who have known each other since childhood, or even the best man at your wedding. "There are no boundaries as far as who commits fraud," says CPA and Certified Fraud Examiner (CFE) Frank Suponcic.

According to the Association for Certified Fraud Examiners (AFCE), 85% of those committing fraud are doing so for the first time. And because you wouldn't normally suspect them, fraud typically lasts 18 months before being detected, costs a company 5% of annual revenues, and averages $140,000 per incident where there's only a 50% chance of recovering what's been stolen.

So if 85% of people who commit fraud have never done so before, how can you detect who is committing fraud? AFCE's John Warren says, "There are three factors usually associated with fraud—opportunity, the ability to rationalize it, and financial need." Opportunity means "no one is watching." So hire a CFE to conduct a fraud audit to identify weaknesses and recommend strong accounting controls and procedures, such as dual signoffs for all transactions. Suponcic says, "You can't let your guard down." Rationalization and financial need are evident in 81% of fraud cases, where people were living above their means, experiencing financial difficulties, or had unusually close associations with vendors or customers, which gave them opportunity. Finally, since most fraud is initially detected by tips from employees, customers, or vendors, establish and publicize an independent hotline that people can call to report suspicions.[1]

The FASB is constantly modifying, clarifying, and expanding GAAP as business practices evolve and new issues arise. Perhaps the most important focus in recent years has been a move by the FASB and its international counterpart, the International Accounting Standards Board (IASB), to find ways to make U.S. accounting practices more consistent with those in other nations. This effort is likely to have far-reaching consequences.

8-2b Ethics in Accounting

Even clear and well-established accounting principles won't result in accurate and reliable information if managers and accountants flaunt them. A series of accounting scandals rocked the American business world during the late 1990s and the first few years of the twenty-first century. Between October 2001 and July 2002, several large corporations—Enron, Tyco, WorldCom, and Adelphia, to name only a few—were implicated in major accounting scandals. In many cases, these firms overstated earnings by billions of dollars or hid billions of dollars in debts. Once their accounting improprieties became known, most of these firms suffered severe financial difficulties. Some of the companies went bankrupt, leaving stockholders with worthless stock, and employees without jobs or pension plans. Many of the CEOs and top financial officers for these companies ended up in prison.[2]

These scandals served as a wake-up call to the accounting profession that their ethical training and standards need major improvement. In the wake of the scandals, many state accounting boards passed new ethics-related requirements.

8-3 Financial Statements: Read All About Us

One of the major responsibilities of financial accounting is the preparation of three basic financial statements: the balance sheet, income statement, and statement of cash flows. Taken together, these financial statements provide external stakeholders with a broad picture of an organization's financial condition and its recent financial performance. Large corporations with publicly traded stock must provide an annual report containing all three statements to all stockholders. They also must file quarterly and annual reports, including financial statements, with the SEC. Let's take a look at the information each statement provides.

8-3a The Balance Sheet: What We Own and How We Got It

The **balance sheet** summarizes a firm's financial position at a specific point in time. Though the balance sheets of different firms vary in specifics, all of them are organized to reflect the most famous equation in all of accounting—so famous that it is usually referred to simply as the **accounting equation**:

Assets = Liabilities + Owners' Equity

Exhibit 8.1 shows a simplified balance sheet for Bigbux, a hypothetical company we'll use to illustrate the information provided by financial statements. As you look over this exhibit, keep in mind that real-world balance sheets may include additional accounts and that different firms sometimes use different names for the same type of account. Despite these differences, Exhibit 8.1 should help you understand the basic structure common to all balance sheets. Notice that the three major sectors of this statement reflect the key terms in the accounting equation. Once we've defined each of these terms, we'll explain the logic behind the accounting equation and how the balance sheet illustrates this logic.

⊙ **Assets** are things of value that the firm owns. Balance sheets usually classify assets into at least two major categories. The first category, called *current assets,* consists of cash and other assets that the firm expects to use up or convert into cash within a year. For example, in Bigbux's balance sheet, the value for *accounts receivable* refers to money owed to Bigbux by customers who bought its goods on credit. (These receivables are converted into cash when customers pay their bills.) *Inventory* is the other current asset listed on Bigbux's balance sheet. For a wholesale or retail company, inventory consists of the stock of goods it has available for sale. For a manufacturing firm, inventory includes not only

Is There an Easier Way to Do Accounting?

Assets = Liabilities + Owner's Equity. What? If you're confused about accounting, you're in good company. Most businesspeople struggle, too. One of them was entrepreneur, Jessica Mah, who has been starting businesses since she was a teenager. She said, "I started my first business when I was 13—an eBay store—and later I had a web hosting company. To this day, I don't know how profitable the eBay store was. And I thought the web hosting business was doing well, but we were barely breaking even." She found popular accounting programs such as Intuit's QuickBooks frustrating and time consuming. Says Mah, "It seemed like a simple problem to solve, but accounting software isn't the answer. It isn't only complex, but it's built with accountants in mind."

So she started inDinero.com, a website that gives businesspeople meaningful accounting information without requiring them to learn accounting. inDinero eliminates data entry by electronically pulling information from company bank, credit card, and PayPal accounts, as well as websites like FreshBooks, which automate expenses and invoices. It

sets up budgets, automatically categorizes revenues and expenditures, and generates reports providing a real-time financial dashboard of company performance. Says Mah, "In less than 5 minutes, you'll know precisely how much you're earning, spending, what your cash situation looks like, and more. Since inDinero understands your spending, we can also remind you of upcoming bills to pay, and warn you about low balances and unusual account activity."

In short, says Mah, "Entrepreneurs don't want to spend hours reconciling transactions and learning about double-entry bookkeeping. We got rid of the complexity, so business owners can quickly see how they're doing." So, if you want to know the financial performance of your company without having to learn accounting, try inDinero.[3]

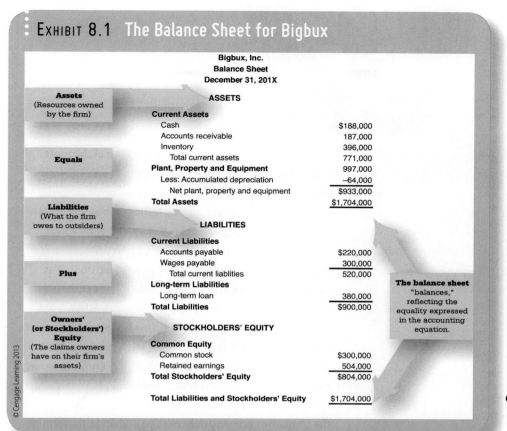

EXHIBIT 8.1 The Balance Sheet for Bigbux

Assets
(Resources owned by the firm)

Equals

Liabilities
(What the firm owes to outsiders)

Plus

Owners'
(or Stockholders')
Equity
(The claims owners have on their firm's assets)

© Cengage Learning 2013

Bigbux, Inc.
Balance Sheet
December 31, 201X

ASSETS

Current Assets	
Cash	$188,000
Accounts receivable	187,000
Inventory	396,000
Total current assets	771,000
Plant, Property and Equipment	997,000
Less: Accumulated depreciation	−64,000
Net plant, property and equipment	$933,000
Total Assets	$1,704,000

LIABILITIES

Current Liabilities	
Accounts payable	$220,000
Wages payable	300,000
Total current liablties	520,000
Long-term Liabilities	
Long-term loan	380,000
Total Liabilities	$900,000

STOCKHOLDERS' EQUITY

Common Equity	
Common stock	$300,000
Retained earnings	504,000
Total Stockholders' Equity	$804,000
Total Liabilities and Stockholders' Equity	$1,704,000

The balance sheet "balances," reflecting the equality expressed in the accounting equation.

finished goods but also materials and parts used in the production process as well as any unfinished goods.

The other major category of assets on Bigbux's balance sheets is *Property, plant, and equipment.* It lists the value of the company's land, buildings, machinery, equipment, and other long-term assets. With the exception of land, these assets have a limited useful life, so accountants subtract *accumulated depreciation* from the original value of these assets to reflect the fact that these assets are being used up over time.

Though Bigbux doesn't do so, some companies list a third category of assets, called *intangible assets.* These are assets that have no physical existence—you can't see or touch them—but they still have value. Examples include patents, copyrights, trademarks, and even the goodwill a company develops with its stakeholders.

○ **Liabilities** indicate what the firm owes to non-owners— in other words, the claims non-owners have against the firm's assets. Balance sheets usually organize liabilities into two broad categories: current liabilities and long-term liabilities. *Current liabilities* are debts that come due within a year of the date on the balance sheet. Accounts payable—what the firm owes suppliers when it buys supplies on credit—is a common example of a current liability. Wages payable, which indicate what the firm

owes to workers for work they have already performed, is another example. *Long-term liabilities* are debts that don't come due until more than a year after the date on the balance sheet. The only long-term liability that Bigbux lists is a long-term loan, which is a formal written IOU with a due date more than a year after the date on the balance sheet.

○ **Owners' (or Stockholders') equity** refers to the claims the owners have against their firm's assets. The specific accounts listed in the owners' equity section of a balance sheet depend on the form of business ownership. As Exhibit 8.1 shows, common stock is a key owners' equity account for corporations. So, for corporations such as Bigbux, the owners' equity section is usually titled *stockholders' equity.* Also notice that retained earnings, which are the accumulated earnings reinvested in the company (rather than paid to owners), is another major component of the owners' equity section.

The logic behind the accounting equation is based on the fact that firms must finance the purchase of their assets, and owners and non-owners are the only two sources of funding. The accounting equation tells us that the value of a firm's assets must equal the amount of financing provided by owners (as measured by owners' equity) plus the amount

"It sounds extraordinary, but it's a fact that balance sheets can make fascinating reading."

— BARONESS MARY ARCHER, CAMBRIDGE UNIVERSITY LECTURER AND CHAIRWOMAN OF THE NATIONAL ENERGY FOUNDATION

JUST BECAUSE THEY CAN...

...DOESN'T MEAN THEY SHOULD.

Firms often create special purpose entities (SPEs) to help them achieve their financial objectives. An SPE is a trust, partnership, or subsidiary corporation set up for a limited and well-defined purpose, such as obtaining money for a special project on more favorable terms. The use of SPEs can be a legitimate part of a firm's financial strategy, but in recent years, some firms have used them to hide financial problems from stakeholders.

In the late 1990s, Enron appeared to be one of the most successful (and fastest growing) corporations in the U.S. Unfortunately, most of the company's reported success was due to "creative" accounting rather than actual performance. In reality, during the late 1990s and early 2000s, Enron was saddled with extremely high debt and suffered from a string of questionable investment decisions that were gradually pushing it toward bankruptcy.

Enron financed most of its apparent growth through the creation of hundreds of SPEs. One important feature of these SPEs was that they qualified as off-balance sheet financing, meaning that GAAP didn't require Enron to report their assets and liabilities on its own balance sheet. Enron's top management took advantage of this loophole to hide the company's growing debt burden and underperforming assets from regulators, investors, and employees. Thus, stakeholders were unaware that Enron was in trouble until its collapse was imminent—a collapse that cost thousands of workers their jobs (and pensions) and wiped out the investments of Enron's stockholders.

The FASB responded to the Enron scandal by revising GAAP to require disclosure of the assets and debts of SPEs on their parent company's consolidated balance sheet under certain circumstances. But new types of SPEs and other forms of off-balance sheet financing designed to circumvent these requirements surfaced during the financial meltdown in 2008–09, suggesting that the temptation to hide debt remains a problem.[4]

What do YOU think?

- What steps could the FASB take to minimize the adverse effects of off-balance sheet financing?
- What responsibility did Enron's board of directors have to oversee—and rein in—their company's aggressive use of SPEs?
- Suppose you owned stock in a major corporation. What steps would you take to find out whether the company used off-balance sheet financing?

provided by creditors (as indicated by the firm's liabilities) to purchase those assets. Because a balance sheet is based on this logic, it must *always* be in balance. In other words, the dollar value of the assets *must* equal the dollar value of the liabilities plus owners' equity. This is true for *all* firms, from the smallest sole proprietorship to the largest multinational corporation. Notice in Exhibit 8.1 that the $1,704,000 in total assets listed on Bigbux's balance sheet matches the $1,704,000 in liabilities plus owners' equity.

8-3b The Income Statement: So, How Did We Do?

The **income statement** summarizes the financial results of a firm's operations over a given period of time. The figure that attracts the most attention on the income statement is net income, which measures the company's profit or loss. In fact, another name for the income statement is the *profit and loss statement* (or, informally, the *P&L*). Just as with the balance sheet, we can use a simple equation to illustrate the logic behind the organization of the income statement:

$$\text{Revenue} - \text{Expenses} = \text{Net Income}$$

In this equation:

- **Revenue** represents the increase in the amount of cash and other assets (such as accounts receivable) the firm earns in a given time period as the result of its business activities. A firm normally earns revenue by selling goods or by charging fees for providing services (or both). Accountants use **accrual-basis accounting** when recognizing revenues. Under the accrual approach, revenues are recorded when they are earned, and payment is reasonably assured. It's important to realize that this is not always when the firm receives cash from its sales. For example, if a firm sells goods on credit, it reports revenue before it receives cash. (The revenue would show up initially as an increase in accounts receivable rather than as an increase in cash.)

- **Expenses** indicate the cash a firm spends, or other assets it uses up, to carry out the business activities necessary to generate its revenue. Under accrual-basis accounting, expenses aren't necessarily recorded when cash is paid. Instead, expenses are matched to the revenue they help generate. The specific titles given to the costs and expenses listed on an income statement vary among firms—as do the details provided. But the general approach remains the same: costs are deducted from revenue in several stages to show how net income is determined. The first step in this process is to deduct *costs of goods sold*, which are costs directly related to buying, manufacturing, or providing the goods and services the company sells. (Manufacturing companies often use the term *cost of goods manufactured* for these costs.) The difference between the firm's revenue and its cost of goods sold is its *gross profit*. The next step is to deduct *operating expenses* from gross profit. Operating expenses are costs the firm incurs in the regular operation of its business. Most income statements divide operating expenses into *selling expenses* (such as salaries and commissions to salespeople and advertising

expenses) and *general (or administrative) expenses* (such as rent, insurance, utilities, and office supplies). The difference between gross profit and operating expenses is *net operating income*. Finally, interest expense and taxes are deducted from net operating income to determine the firm's net income.

- **Net income** is the profit or loss the firm earns in the time period covered by the income statement. If net income is positive, the firm has earned a profit. If it's negative, the firm has suffered a loss. Net income is called the "bottom line" of the income statement because it is such an important measure of the firm's operating success. But income statements usually include additional information below the net income, so it isn't literally the bottom line. For example, the income statement for Bigbux indicates how much of the net income was retained and how much was distributed to stockholders in the form of dividends.

Take a look at Exhibit 8.2 to see how the income statement for Bigbux is organized. See if you can identify the

income statement The financial statement that reports the revenues, expenses, and net income that resulted from a firm's operations over an accounting period.

revenue Increases in a firm's assets that result from the sale of goods, provision of services, or other activities intended to earn income.

accrual-basis accounting The method of accounting that recognizes revenue when it is earned and matches expenses to the revenues they helped produce.

expenses Resources that are used up as the result of business operations.

net income The difference between the revenue a firm earns and the expenses it incurs in a given time period.

Exhibit 8.2 Income Statement for Bigbux

	Bigbux, Inc. Income Statement For Year Ending December 31, 201X	
Revenue: (What the firm earns)		
	Sales Revenue	890,000.00
	Cost of goods sold	550,000.00
Minus	**Gross Profit**	340,000.00
	Operating Expenses	
	Selling expenses	79,000.00
	Administrative expenses	86,000.00
Costs and Expenses (Cash spent and other resources used up)	**Total Operating Expenses**	165,000.00
	Net Operating Income	175,000.00
	Interest expense	12,000.00
	Taxable Income	163,000.00
Equals	Taxes	62,000.00
	Net Income	101,000.00
Net Income (Profit if positive or loss if negative)	Dividends	55,000.00
	Transfer to Retained Earnings	46,000.00

© Cengage Learning 2013

statement of cash flows The financial statement that identifies a firm's sources and uses of cash in a given accounting period.

accounts that represent the revenue, expense, and income concepts we've just described.

8-3c The Statement of Cash Flows: Show Me the Money

The last major financial statement is the **statement of cash flows**. Cash is the lifeblood of any business organization. A firm must have enough cash to pay what it owes to workers, creditors, suppliers, and taxing authorities—hopefully, with enough left to pay a dividend to its owners! So it's not surprising that a firm's stakeholders are very interested in how and why a company's cash balance changed over the past year. The statement of cash flows provides this information by identifying the amount of cash that flowed into and out of the firm from three types of activities:

1. Cash flows from *operating activities* show the amount of cash that flowed into the company from the sale of goods or services, as well as cash from dividends and interest received from ownership of the financial securities of other firms. It also shows the amount of cash used to cover expenses resulting from operations and any cash payments to purchase securities held for short-term trading purposes. Remember that under the accrual method, not all revenues and expenses on the income statement represent cash flows, so operating cash flows may differ substantially

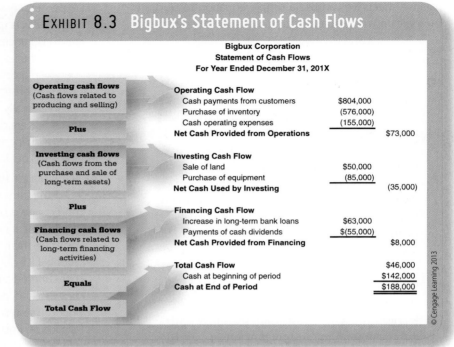

EXHIBIT 8.3 Bigbux's Statement of Cash Flows

Operating cash flows (Cash flows related to producing and selling)

Plus

Investing cash flows (Cash flows from the purchase and sale of long-term assets)

Plus

Financing cash flows (Cash flows related to long-term financing activities)

Equals

Total Cash Flow

Bigbux Corporation
Statement of Cash Flows
For Year Ended December 31, 201X

Operating Cash Flow		
Cash payments from customers	$804,000	
Purchase of inventory	(576,000)	
Cash operating expenses	(155,000)	
Net Cash Provided from Operations		$73,000
Investing Cash Flow		
Sale of land	$50,000	
Purchase of equipment	(85,000)	
Net Cash Used by Investing		(35,000)
Financing Cash Flow		
Increase in long-term bank loans	$63,000	
Payments of cash dividends	$(55,000)	
Net Cash Provided from Financing		$8,000
Total Cash Flow		$46,000
Cash at beginning of period		$142,000
Cash at End of Period		$188,000

© Cengage Learning 2013

from the revenues and expenses shown on the income statement.

2. Cash flows from *investing activities* show the amount of cash received from the sale of fixed assets (such as land and buildings) and financial assets bought as long-term investments. It also shows any cash used to buy fixed assets and long-term financial investments.

3. Cash flows from *financing activities* show the cash the firm received from issuing additional shares of its own stock or from taking out long-term loans. It also shows cash outflows from payment of dividends to shareholders and to repay principal on loans.

Exhibit 8.3 shows the Statement of Cash Flows for Bigbux. You can see that Bigbux experienced a substantial increase in its total cash balance. You can also see that this increase in cash was primarily due to two factors. First, a look at operating cash flows shows that the cash Bigbux collected from customer payments exceeded its cash payments for inventory and operating expenses by a significant margin. Second, the section on financing activities shows that Bigbux took out a large long-term loan. The net increases in cash from these sources more than offset the net cash outflow from investing due to the purchase of new equipment. Note that the cash balance at the end of the period matches the amount of cash reported in the current balance sheet (see Exhibit 8.1 again)—as it always should.

Luxury goods are the only area in which it is possible to make luxury margins.

— Bernard Arnault, business magnate and art collector

8-3d Other Statements: What Happened to the Owners' Stake?

In addition to the three major statements we've just described, firms usually prepare either a statement of retained earnings or a stockholders' equity statement. Let's take a quick look at each of these statements.

The *statement of retained earnings* is a simple statement that shows how retained earnings have changed from one accounting period to the next. The change in retained earnings is found by subtracting dividends paid to shareholders from net income.

Firms that have more complex changes in the owners' equity section sometimes report these changes in notes to the financial statements in the annual report. But they often disclose these changes by providing a *stockholders' equity statement*. Like the statement of retained earnings, this statement shows how net income and dividends affect retained earnings. But it also shows other changes in stockholders' equity, such as those that arise from the issuance of additional shares of stock.

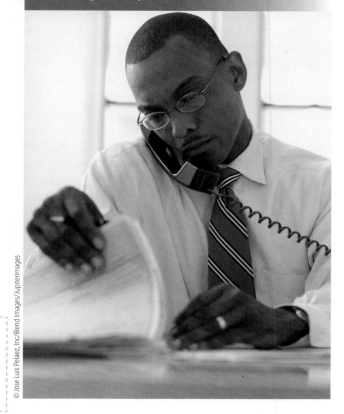

External auditors carefully examine a company's financial records before rendering their opinion.

© Jose Luis Pelaez, Inc/Blend Images/Jupiterimages

8-4 Interpreting Financial Statements: Digging Beneath the Surface

The financial statements we've just described contain a lot of important information. But they don't necessarily tell the whole story. In fact, the numbers they report can be misleading if they aren't put into proper context. Thus, in addition to looking at the statements, it's also important to check out the independent auditor's report and read the management discussion and footnotes that accompany these statements. It's also a good idea to compare the figures reported in current statements with those from earlier statements to see how key account values have changed.

8-4a The Independent Auditor's Report: Getting a Stamp of Approval

U.S. securities laws require publicly traded corporations in the United States to have an independent CPA firm (an accounting firm that specializes in providing public accounting services) perform an annual *external audit* of their financial statements. And many companies that aren't publicly traded also obtain external audits even though they aren't legally required to do so.

The purpose of an audit is to verify that the company's financial statements were properly prepared in accordance with generally accepted accounting principles and fairly present the financial condition of the firm. So external auditors don't just check the figures, they also examine the accounting *methods* the company used to *obtain* those figures. For example, auditors interview the company's accounting and bookkeeping staff to verify that they understand and properly implement procedures that are consistent with GAAP. They also examine a sample of specific source documents (such as sales receipts or invoices) and verify that the transactions they represent were properly posted to the correct accounts. Auditors also look for signs of fraud or falsified records. They often conduct an actual physical count of goods or supplies in inventory to determine the accuracy of the figures reported in the company's inventory records and contact the company's banker to verify its account balances. The audit process is rigorous, but it's important to realize that in large, public companies, it would be impossible for auditors to check the accuracy of every transaction.

The results of the audit are presented in an *independent auditor's report*, which is included in the annual report the firm sends to its stockholders. If the auditor doesn't find any problems with the way a firm's financial statements were prepared and presented, the report will offer an *unqualified* (or *"clean"*) *opinion*—which is by far the most common outcome. If the auditor identifies some minor concerns but believes that on balance the firm's statements remain a fair and accurate representation of the company's financial position, the report will offer a *qualified opinion*. But when auditors discover more serious and widespread problems with a firm's statements, they offer an *adverse opinion*. An adverse opinion indicates that the auditor believes the financial statements are seriously flawed and that they may be misleading and unreliable. (An adverse opinion must include an explanation of the specific reasons for the opinion.) Adverse opinions are very rare, so when an auditor renders one it should set off alarm bells, warning stakeholders to view the information in the firm's financial statements with real skepticism. Exhibit 8.4 shows the auditor's opinion for Groupon's 2012 financial statements. This is clearly an unqualified (clean) opinion since the auditor concludes in the third paragraph that the statements fairly present Groupon's financial condition.

In order for CPA firms to perform audits with integrity, they must be independent of the firms they audit. During the 1990s, many of the major CPA firms entered into very lucrative consulting contracts with some of the businesses they were auditing. It became increasingly difficult for these CPA firms to risk losing these high-paying contracts by raising issues about accounting practices when they audited the books of their clients. In other words, the auditors ceased to be truly independent and objective. The lack of rigorous oversight by external auditors contributed to the accounting scandals we mentioned earlier in this chapter.

In the aftermath of the scandals, Congress passed the Sarbanes-Oxley Act of 2002 (commonly referred to as "SOX" or "Sarbox"). This law banned business relationships that might create conflicts of interest between CPA firms and the companies they audit. It also established a private-sector nonprofit corporation known as the Public Company Accounting Oversight Board (PCAOB). The PCAOB defines its mission as "to protect the interests of investors and further the public interest in the preparation of informative, fair, and independent audit reports."[5]

8-4b Checking Out the Notes to Financial Statements: What's in the Fine Print?

Some types of information can't be adequately conveyed by numbers alone. Annual reports include notes (often *many* pages of notes) that disclose additional information about the firm's operations, accounting practices, and special circumstances that clarify and supplement

---

Exhibit 8.4 An External Auditor's Opinion

THE BOARD OF DIRECTORS AND STOCKHOLDERS OF GROUPON INC.

We have audited the accompanying consolidated balance sheets of Groupon, Inc. as of December 31, 2010 and 2011, and the related consolidated statements of operations, comprehensive loss, stockholders' equity, and cash flows for each of the three years in the period ended December 31, 2011. Our audits also included the financial statement schedule listed in the index at Item 15(b). These financial statements and schedule are the responsibility of the Company's management. Our responsibility is to express an opinion on these financial statements and schedule based on our audits.

We conducted our audits in accordance with the standards of the Public Company Accounting Oversight Board (United States). Those standards require that we plan and perform the audit to obtain reasonable assurance about whether the financial statements are free of material misstatement. We were not engaged to perform an audit of the Company's internal control over financial reporting. Our audits included consideration of internal control over financial reporting as a basis for designing audit procedures that are appropriate in the circumstances, but not for the purpose of expressing an opinion on the effectiveness of the Company's internal control over financial reporting. Accordingly, we express no such opinion. An audit also includes examining, on a test basis, evidence supporting the amounts and disclosures in the financial statements, assessing the accounting principles used and significant estimates made by management, and evaluating the overall financial statement presentation. We believe that our audits provide a reasonable basis for our opinion.

In our opinion, the financial statements referred to above present fairly, in all material respects, the consolidated financial position of Groupon, Inc. at December 31, 2010 and 2011, and the consolidated results of its operations, its comprehensive loss, and its cash flows for each of the three years in the period ended December 31, 2011, in conformity with U.S. generally accepted accounting principles. Also, in our opinion, the related financial statement schedule when considered in relation to the basic consolidated financial statements taken as a whole, presents fairly in all material respects the information set forth therein.

/s/   ERNST & YOUNG LLP

Chicago, Illinois
March 30, 2012

Lions and Tigers and Bears, Oh My! Management's Discussion and Analysis

A company's annual report (10-k) provides detailed financial reporting. In "Item 7: Management's Discussion and Analysis," the 10-k also contains management's explanation of the trends, events, or risks likely to affect the company's financial condition. "Item 7," in many ways, provides the stories and worries behind the 10-k's numbers.

For example, "Item 7" in Groupon's 10-k states, "A substantial number of group buying sites that attempt to replicate our business model have emerged around the world." Indeed, Groupon's business has been copied in 50 countries! China alone has 1,000 Groupon-type businesses, including one that copied Groupon's website down to a www.groupon.cn URL. In the U.S., Groupon's record growth has attracted numerous competitors such as Living Social, Tippr, Bloomspot, Scoutmob, and BuyWithMe, along with Google Offers and Facebook Check-in Deals. How worried is Groupon about director competitors? Worried enough to admit that intense competition could hurt its future financial performance.

By contrast, the management discussion and analysis section of Apple's 10-k discussed Japan's massive earthquake and tsunami, saying, "These geological events have caused significant damage in the region ... to nuclear power plants, and have impacted Japan's power and other infrastructure as well as its economy." Apple explained, though, that it had minimized disruptions to its parts supplies, saying, "To the extent that component production has been affected, the Company has generally obtained alternative sources of supply or implemented other measures."

Finally, Ford's 10-k discussed how weak economic conditions in Europe may slow its business. "The current economic performance in many European countries, particularly Greece, Ireland, Italy, Portugal, and Spain, is being hampered by excessive government debt levels and the resulting budget austerity measures that are contributing to weak economic growth... During 2012, economic growth is likely to remain weak in these markets."[6]

the numbers reported on the financial statements. These notes can be *very* revealing. For example, GAAP often allows firms to choose among several options when it comes to certain accounting procedures—and the choices the firm makes can affect the value of assets, liabilities, and owners' equity on the balance sheet and the revenues, costs, and net income on the income statement. The notes to financial statements explain the specific accounting methods used to recognize revenue, value inventory, and depreciate fixed assets. They might also provide details about the way the firm funds its pension plan or health insurance for its employees. They must also disclose *changes* in accounting methods that could affect the comparability of the current financial statements to those of previous years. Even more interesting, the notes might disclose important facts about the status of a lawsuit against the firm or other risks the firm faces. Stakeholders who ignore these notes are likely to miss out on important information.

Another important source of information is the section of the annual report usually titled "Management's Discussion and Analysis." As its name implies, this is where the top management team provides its take on the financial condition of the company. SEC guidelines require top management to disclose any trends, events, or risks likely to have a significant impact on the firm's financial condition in this section of the report.

8-4c Looking for Trends in Comparative Statements

The SEC requires publicly traded corporations to provide *comparative financial statements*. This simply means that

In 2004 a horse named "Read The Footnotes" ran in the Kentucky Derby.

— Securities and Exchange Commission

the balance sheet, income statement, and statement of cash flows must list two or more years of figures side by side, making it possible to see how account values have changed over a period of time. Many firms that aren't publicly traded also present comparative statements, even though they are not required to do so by GAAP.

Comparative balance sheets allow users to trace what has happened to key assets and liabilities over the past two or three years, and whether its owners' equity had increased. Comparative income statements show whether the firm's net income increased or decreased and what has happened to revenues and expenses over recent years. Using comparative statements to identify changes in key account values over time is called **horizontal analysis**.

8-5 Inside Intelligence: The Role of Managerial Accounting

Now that we've looked at financial accounting, let's turn our attention to the other major branch of accounting, **managerial (or management) accounting**. As its name implies, this branch of accounting is designed to meet the needs of a company's managers, though in recent years many firms have empowered other employees and given them access to some of this information as well. Exhibit 8.5 identifies several ways that managerial accounting differs from financial accounting.

Managers throughout an organization rely on information created by managerial accountants to make important decisions. The accuracy and reliability of this information can make a huge difference in the performance of a firm. In fact, many firms view their management accounting systems as a source of competitive advantage and regard the specifics of these systems as highly valuable company secrets.[7]

It's impossible to describe all the functions performed by managerial accountants in a single chapter. So we'll be selective and focus on only two of them—but the two we'll discuss often play a crucial role in managerial decision making: measuring and assigning costs, and developing budgets.

8-5a Cost Concepts: A Cost for All Reasons

Without good information on costs, managers would be operating in the dark as they try to set prices, determine the most desirable mix of products, and locate areas where efficiency is lagging. A firm's management accounting system helps managers throughout an organization measure costs and assign them to products, activities, and even whole divisions.

Accountants define **cost** as the value of what is given up in exchange for something else. Depending on the type of problem they are analyzing, managerial

Exhibit 8.5 Comparison of Financial and Managerial Accounting

	FINANCIAL ACCOUNTING	MANAGERIAL ACCOUNTING
PURPOSE	Primarily intended to provide information to external stakeholders, such as stockholders, creditors, and government regulators. Information provided by financial accounting is available to the general public.	Primarily intended to provide information to internal stakeholders, such as the managers of specific divisions or departments. This information is proprietary—meaning that it isn't available to the general public.
TYPE OF INFORMATION PRESENTED	Focuses almost exclusively on financial information.	Provides both financial and nonfinancial information.
NATURE OF REPORTS	Prepares a standard set of financial statements.	Prepares customized reports to deal with specific problems or issues.
TIMING OF REPORTS	Presents financial statements on a predetermined schedule (usually quarterly and annually).	Creates reports upon request by management rather than according to a predetermined schedule.
ADHERENCE TO ACCOUNTING STANDARDS?	Governed by a set of generally accepted accounting principles (GAAP).	Uses procedures developed internally that are not required to follow GAAP.
TIME PERIOD FOCUS	Summarizes past performance and its impact on the firm's present condition.	Provides reports dealing with past performance but also involves making projections about the future when dealing with planning issues.

© Cengage Learning 2013

A payment for materials to a supplier is an out-of-pocket cost.

accountants actually measure and evaluate several different types of costs. We'll begin our discussion by describing some of the cost concepts commonly used by managerial accountants.

At the most basic level, accountants distinguish between out-of-pocket costs and opportunity costs. **Out-of-pocket costs** (also called *explicit costs*) are usually easy to measure because they involve actual expenditures of money or other resources. The wages a company pays to its workers, the payments it makes to suppliers for raw materials, and the rent it pays for office space are examples.

But accountants realize that not all costs involve a monetary payment; sometimes what is given up is the *opportunity* to use an asset in some alternative way. Such costs are often referred to as **implicit costs**. For example, suppose a couple of lawyers form a partnership and set up their office in a building one of the partners already owns. They feel good about their decision because they don't have to make any out-of-pocket payments for rent. But a good managerial accountant would point out to the partners that they still incur an implicit cost, because by using the building themselves they forgo the opportunity to earn income by renting the office space to someone else.

Managerial accountants also distinguish between fixed costs and variable costs. As the name implies, **fixed costs** don't change when the firm changes its level of production. Examples of fixed costs include interest on a bank loan, property insurance premiums, rent on office space, and other payments that are set by a contract or by legal requirements. Many fixed costs are really only fixed for some "relevant range" of output. For example, if a company sees a dramatic rise in sales, it might have to move into bigger facilities, thus incurring a higher rent.

Variable costs are costs that rise (vary) when the firm produces more of its goods and services. As a company ramps up its production it is likely to need more labor and materials and to use more electrical power. Thus payments for many types of labor, supplies, and utilities are variable costs.

8-5b Assigning Costs to Products: As (Not So) Simple as ABC?

Finally, accountants often want to assign costs to specific *cost objects*, such as one of the goods or services their firm produces. When they assign costs to specific cost objects, accountants distinguish between *direct costs* and *indirect costs*. **Direct costs** are those that can be directly traced to the production of the product. For example, the wage payments made to workers directly involved in producing a good or service would be a direct cost for that product. On the other hand, the costs a firm incurs for plant maintenance, quality control, or depreciation on office equipment are usually classified as **indirect costs** since they tend to be the result of the firm's general operation rather than the production of any specific product.

Direct costs for labor and materials are usually easy to measure and assign, since they have an easily identifiable link to the object. Unfortunately, indirect costs aren't tied in such a simple and direct way to the production of a specific product. In the past, managerial accountants usually relied on simple rules to assign indirect costs to different products—and in some cases they still do. One such approach is to allocate indirect costs in proportion to the number of direct labor hours involved in the production of each product. Under this method, products that require the most labor to produce are assigned the most indirect costs. But, while this approach is simple, it can provide very misleading information. There is simply no logical reason for many types of indirect costs to be related to the amount of direct labor used to produce a product.

In recent years, managerial accountants have developed more sophisticated ways to allocate costs. One relatively new method is called **activity-based costing (ABC)**.

out-of-pocket cost A cost that involves the payment of money or other resources.

implicit cost The opportunity cost that arises when a firm uses owner-supplied resources.

fixed costs Costs that remain the same when the level of production changes within some relevant range.

variable costs Costs that vary directly with the level of production.

direct cost Costs that are incurred directly as the result of some specific cost object.

indirect costs Costs that are the result of a firm's general operations and are not directly tied to any specific cost object.

activity-based costing (ABC) A technique to assign product costs based on links between activities that drive costs and the production of specific products.

This approach is more complex and difficult to implement than the direct labor method. Basically, it involves a two-stage process. The first stage is to identify specific activities that create indirect costs and determine the factors that "drive" the costs of these activities. The second stage is to tie these cost drivers to the production of specific goods (or other cost objects). Once the relationships between cost drivers and specific products are identified, they can be used to determine how much of each indirect cost is assigned to each product.

Clearly, ABC is much more complex to implement than a system that assigns costs based on a simple "one size fits all" rule, such as the direct labor method. However, it's likely to provide more meaningful results because it is based on a systematic examination of how indirect costs are related to individual goods.

8-6 Budgeting: Planning for Accountability

Management accountants also play an important role in the development of budgets. **Budgeting** is a management tool that explicitly shows how a firm will acquire and allocate the resources it needs to achieve its goals over a specific time period. The budgetary process facilitates planning by requiring managers to translate goals into measurable quantities and identify the specific resources needed to achieve these goals. But budgeting offers other advantages as well. If done well, budgeting:

- Helps managers clearly specify how they intend to achieve the goals they set during the planning process. This should lead to a better understanding of how the organization's limited resources will be allocated.

- Encourages communication and coordination among managers and employees in various departments within the organization. For example, the budget process can give middle and first-line managers and employees an opportunity to provide top managers with important insights about the challenges facing their specialized areas—and the resources they need to meet those challenges. But, as we will explain in the next section, the extent to which this advantage is realized depends on the specific approach used in the budgeting process.

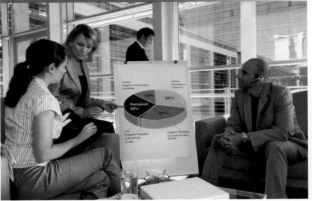

Budgeting encourages communication and coordination among managers and employees.

© unique pic/Cultura/Jupiterimages

- Serves as a motivational tool. Good budgets clearly identify goals *and* demonstrate a plan of action for acquiring the resources needed to achieve them. Employees tend to be more highly motivated when they understand the goals their managers expect them to accomplish and when they view these goals as ambitious but achievable.

- Helps managers evaluate progress and performance. Managers can compare actual performance to budgeted figures to determine whether various departments and functional areas are making adequate progress toward achieving their organization's goals. If actual performance falls short of budgetary goals, managers can look for reasons and, if necessary, take corrective action.

8-6a Preparing the Budget: Top-Down or Bottom-Up?

There are two broad approaches to budget preparation. In some organizations, top management prepares the budget with little or no input from middle and supervisory managers—a process known as *top-down budgeting*. Supporters of this approach point out that top management knows the long-term strategic needs of the company and is in a better position to see the big picture when making budget decisions.

The other approach to budgeting is called *bottom-up (or participatory) budgeting*. Organizations that use a participatory process allow middle and supervisory managers to participate actively in the creation of the budget. Proponents of this approach maintain that it has two major advantages. First, middle and supervisory managers are likely to know more about the

New Accounting Trend: Cloud-Based Accounting

For years, all-in-one products such as QuickBooks, Sage Peachtree, and Microsoft Dynamics have dominated accounting software sales, providing standardized accounting tools, such as general ledgers, accounts receivable and payable, payroll, and inventory. Companies bought this software, installed it on computer servers, paid for annual updates, and then used it throughout the organization.

Today, the trend is away from "installed" software programs and toward cloud-based accounting. Cloud computing means using Internet-based storage capacity, applications, and processing power. If you have a Dropbox account, use Google Docs, or sync your iPhone with Apple's iCloud, you have personal experience with cloud computing.

So why is cloud-based accounting software becoming popular? It cuts startup costs up to 50% because there's no need to buy, replace, or upgrade in-house servers. Instead, accounting software and data are hosted in huge data centers maintained by companies selling cloud-based accounting. Ongoing costs are cheaper because you only buy the services, processing time, and data storage that you need. Small companies don't have to buy the same products and services needed by large companies. Because cloud-based accounting runs within web browsers, programs and data can be accessed with a computer, smartphone, or tablet anywhere and anytime you've got Internet access. Finally, unlike with installed accounting packages where each server and computer must be manually updated with new versions of the software, upgrades are automatic. CPA David Cieslak says, "So when I log on, I'll always be using the latest apps. I'll have access to my data [that has] ... been backed up and secure... There's no product installation... I'm straight away working with my key applications and that data."

So, don't pull your head out of the clouds. Keep your head—and your accounting software and data—in the clouds where it's cheaper, accessible, and fully upgraded.[8]

issues and challenges facing their departments—and the resources it will take to address them—than top management. Second, middle and first-line managers are likely to be more highly motivated to achieve budgetary goals when they have a say in how those goals are developed. On the negative side, the bottom-up approach is more time consuming and resource intensive to carry out than the top-down approach. Also, some middle managers may be tempted to overstate their needs or set low budget goals in order to make their jobs easier—an outcome known as *budgetary slack*.[9] Despite these drawbacks, the participatory approach currently is more common than the top-down process.

8-6b Developing the Key Budget Components: One Step at a Time

The budgeting process actually requires the preparation of several different types of budgets. But all of these individual budgets can be classified into two broad categories: operating budgets and financial budgets.

Operating budgets are budgets that identify projected sales and production goals and the various costs the firm will incur to meet these goals. These budgets are developed in a specific order, with the information from earlier budgets used in the preparation of later budgets.

The preparation of operating budgets begins with the development of a *sales budget* that provides quarterly estimates of the number of units of each product the firm expects to sell, the selling price, and the total dollar value of expected sales. The sales budget *must* be created first because many of the production and cost figures that go into other operating budgets depend on the level of sales. Once the sales budget is complete, the budgeted sales level can be used to develop the production budget, the administrative expenses, and the selling expenses budgets. And once the production budget is completed, the information it contains is used to prepare budgets for direct labor costs, direct materials costs, and manufacturing overhead. The final stage in the preparation of operating budgets is the creation of a *budgeted income statement*. This budget looks much like the income statement we described earlier, but instead of describing the actual results of the firm's past operations, it combines the revenue projections from the sales budget and the cost projections from the other operating budgets to present a forecast of *expected* net income.

operating budgets
Budgets that communicate an organization's sales and production goals and the resources needed to achieve these goals.

Financial budgets focus on the firm's financial goals and identify the resources needed to achieve these goals. The two main financial budget documents are the *cash budget* and the *capital expenditure budget*. The cash budget identifies short-term fluctuations in cash flows, helping managers identify times when the firm might face cash flow problems—or when it might have a temporary surplus of cash that it could invest. The capital expenditure budget identifies the firm's planned investments in major fixed assets and long-term projects. The information from these two financial budgets and the budgeted income statement are combined to construct the *budgeted balance sheet*. This is the last financial budget; it shows how the firm's operations, investing, and financing activities are expected to affect all of the asset, liability, and owners' equity accounts.

The firm's **master budget** organizes the operating and financial budgets into a unified whole, representing the firm's overall plan of action for a specified time period. In other words, the master budget shows how all of the pieces fit together to form a complete picture. Exhibit 8.6 shows all of the budget documents that are included in a typical master budget. The arrows indicate the order in which the budgets are developed, starting with the sales budget and ending with the budgeted balance sheet.

8-6c Being Flexible: Clearing Up Problems with Static

The budget process, as we've described it so far, results in a *static* budget, meaning that it is based on a single assumed level of sales. Static budgets are excellent tools for planning, but they have weaknesses when they are used to measure progress, evaluate performance, and identify problem areas that need correcting.

The problem with a static budget is that real-world sales can (and often do) vary considerably from their forecasted value—often for reasons that aren't under the control of the firm's management. For example, the collapse of the U.S. economy into a deep recession, beginning in late 2007, caused sales to drop sharply and unexpectedly even at many well-managed companies.

As we mentioned earlier, many cost figures in budgets are based on the level of sales specified in the sales budget. When actual sales differ significantly from the sales volume assumed in a static budget all of these related budget figures will be erroneous. Using these inaccurate figures to evaluate real-world performance is likely to result in very poor assessments!

One common way managerial accountants avoid this problem is to develop a *flexible budget* for control purposes. A flexible budget is one that isn't based on a single assumed level of sales. Instead, it is developed over a *range* of possible sales levels, and is designed to show the appropriate budgeted level of costs for each different level of sales. This flexibility enables managers to make more meaningful comparisons between actual costs and budgeted costs.

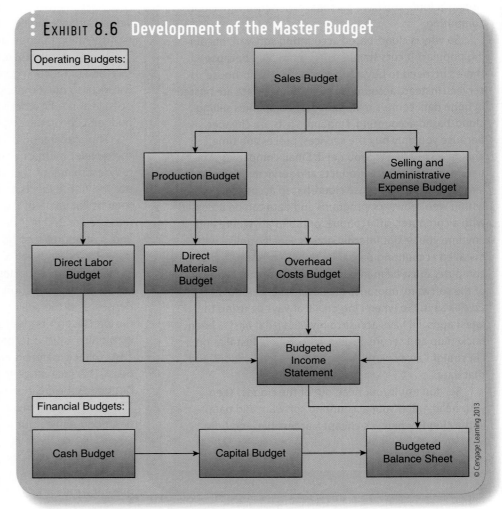

EXHIBIT 8.6 Development of the Master Budget

© Cengage Learning 2013

THE BIG PICTURE

Accounting provides vital information to both the internal and external stakeholders of a firm. The balance sheet, income statement, and statement of cash flows that are the main output of financial accounting help external stakeholders, such as owners and creditors, evaluate the financial performance of a firm. And managerial accounting helps managers throughout an organization make better decisions by providing them with relevant and timely information about the costs and benefits of the choices they have to make. Clearly, a basic knowledge of accounting concepts will help you succeed in just about any career path you choose.

CAREERS

CAREERS IN ACCOUNTING

Over 1.2 million jobs in the United States are in the accounting profession. And the most recent forecast by the Bureau of Labor Statistics predicts that employment in accounting will grow by 191,000 jobs in the next ten years.[10] One reason for this growth: the new regulations enacted in the aftermath of the recent financial meltdown will require many firms to keep more records and file more financial reports—and this extra workload will require more accountants. Another reason is that several recent high-profile cases of accounting and investment fraud have increased the demand for skilled internal auditors and forensic accountants to detect illegal behavior and trace the resulting money trails. On a more positive note, the desire of businesses to meet their environmental responsibilities has led to the development of new accounting techniques to measure the costs and benefits of "green" business practices—and a demand for accountants who know how to use and interpret them. Finally, the SEC's push to overhaul GAAP and make U.S. accounting practices more consistent with those in other nations may open up opportunities for a new breed of accountants who are well-versed in the application of these new principles.

What *else?*
RIP & REVIEW CARDS IN THE BACK
and visit www.cengagebrain.com!

9

Finance:
Acquiring and Using Funds to Maximize Value

LEARNING OBJECTIVES
After studying this chapter, you will be able to:

9-1 Identify the goal of financial management and explain the issues financial managers confront as they seek to achieve this goal

9-2 Describe the tools financial managers use to evaluate their company's current financial condition and develop financial plans

9-3 Evaluate the major sources of funds available to meet a firm's short-term and long-term financial needs

9-4 Identify the key issues involved in determining a firm's capital structure

9-5 Describe how financial managers acquire and manage current assets

9-6 Explain how financial managers evaluate capital budgeting proposals to identify the best long-term investment options for their company

> ## "MONEY IS LIKE A SIXTH SENSE — AND YOU CAN'T MAKE USE OF THE OTHER FIVE WITHOUT IT."
>
> — WILLIAM SOMERSET MAUGHAM, ENGLISH PLAYWRIGHT, NOVELIST, AND SHORT STORY WRITER

9-1 What Motivates Financial Decisions?

Financial capital refers to the funds a firm uses to acquire its assets and finance its operations. Firms use some of their capital to meet short-term obligations, such as paying bills from suppliers, meeting payroll, repaying loans from banks, and paying taxes owed to the government. Other funds are used to finance major long-term investments, such as the purchase of a plant and equipment or the launch of a new product line. And, of course, firms need some funds to pay a return to the owners for their investment in the company.

Companies also have a variety of ways to acquire the financial capital they need: direct contributions by owners, reinvestment of earnings, loans from banks, credit provided by suppliers, and (for corporations) newly issued stocks or bonds. This isn't a complete list by any means—in fact, we'll discuss additional sources later in the chapter—but you get the idea: firms often have several ways to raise money.

In a nutshell, **finance** is the functional area of business that is responsible for finding, among all these alternatives, the best sources of funds and the best way to use them. But which sources and uses are "best" depends on the goals of the financial managers. Historically, the most widely accepted goal of financial management has been to *maximize the value of the firm to its owners*. For corporations with publicly traded stock, this translates into finding the sources and uses of financial capital that will maximize the market price of the company's common stock.

Financial managers emphasize the goal of maximizing the market price of stock because they have a legal and ethical obligation (called a *fiduciary duty*) to make decisions consistent with the financial interests of their firm's owners. After all, the stockholders are the ones with their money at risk. The managers who work for the company have a fiduciary responsibility to act in the best interests of the stockholders, and that means increasing the value of their investment in the company.

Another reason for emphasizing shareholder wealth is more pragmatic. Firms that fail to create shareholder wealth are unlikely to be viewed as attractive investments. Thus, in order to continue attracting the financial capital needed to achieve its other goals, a firm must provide value to its existing stockholders.

But finding the mix of sources and uses of funds that maximize shareholder value isn't a simple process. Let's look at two major issues that confront financial managers as they seek to achieve their primary goal.

9-1a Shareholder Value and Social Responsibility: Does Good Behavior Pay Off?

The emphasis that financial managers place on maximizing shareholder value may seem to conflict with the modern view that a socially responsible firm has an obligation to respect the needs of *all* stakeholders—not just its owners but also its employees, customers, creditors, suppliers, and even society as a whole. The good news is that being socially responsible *can* be (and often is) a good strategy for also achieving the goal of shareholder wealth maximization—especially if managers take a *long-term* perspective.

When a company respects the needs of customers by providing high-quality goods and services at competitive prices, and when it listens and responds fairly to their concerns, those customers are more likely to keep coming back—and to recommend the company to friends and relatives. Similarly, when a firm provides its employees with a good work environment, those employees are likely to have better morale and greater loyalty, resulting in higher productivity and lower employee turnover. And when a company supports its local community through corporate philanthropy or cause-related marketing, the resulting goodwill may boost sales and create a more favorable business climate. All of these outcomes suggest that a commitment to meeting social responsibilities can contribute to a more profitable company and an increase in shareholder value.[1]

> **financial capital** The funds a firm uses to acquire its assets and finance its operations.
>
> **finance** The functional area of business that is concerned with finding the best sources and uses of financial capital.

But things aren't always that simple. Being socially responsible requires a long-term commitment to the needs of many different stakeholders. Unfortunately, the incentives of top executives (in the form of raises, bonuses, and other perks) are often tied to their firm's *short-term* performance. In such cases, some managers focus on policies that make their firm's stock price rise in the short run, but which are unsustainable over the long haul. And when managers fix their attention on raising the market price of the company's stock in the next year (or next quarter), concerns about social responsibility sometimes get lost in the shuffle.

It is also worth noting that responding to the needs of all stakeholders isn't always a simple and straightforward task. Diverse stakeholder groups can have very different goals, and finding the right balance among the competing interests of these groups can be difficult. For example, a firm's managers might believe they can increase profits (and the value of its stock) by shutting down a plant in the United States and outsourcing the work to China. While this might benefit shareholders, it would clearly be detrimental to its U.S. workforce and the community in which that current plant is located. When conflicts arise between the long-term interests of owners and those of other stakeholders, financial managers generally adopt the policies they believe are most consistent with the interests of ownership.

9-1b Risk and Return: A Fundamental Tradeoff in Financial Management

One of the most important lessons in financial management is that there is a tradeoff between risk and return. In financial management, **risk** refers to the degree of uncertainty about the actual outcome of a decision. The **risk-return tradeoff** suggests that sources and uses of funds that offer the potential for high rates of return tend to be more risky than sources and uses of funds that offer lower returns.

Financial managers want to earn an attractive rate of return for shareholders. But they also must realize that the higher the expected return they seek, the more they expose their company to risk. Our nation's recent economic history illustrates this point. In the years just prior to the Great Recession,

> **In a 2010** survey of 2,000 executives and investors, over 75% agreed that socially responsible policies create corporate value over the long run.
>
> —Harvard Business Review

many firms in the financial sector invested heavily in the housing market—a strategy that offered the potential for high returns but was very risky. Many of these same firms chose to finance most of their investments by increasing their own debt, which made the risk even greater.

When the housing market faltered, and prices dropped, these firms found themselves in serious trouble as their debts came due at the same time the value of their investments was falling.

Many of the companies who engaged in these risky strategies went belly-up during the early stages of the financial meltdown. The list of failures included some major banks and Wall Street firms that had been considered icons of free-market capitalism. In fact, firms with almost $1.2 trillion in assets filed for bankruptcy in 2008. To put that in perspective, the total asset value of all of the firms that went bankrupt in the post-9/11 recession of 2001–2002 (a downturn that included the bankruptcies of Enron, WorldCom, and several other huge corporations) was less than $500 billion. And it could have been worse; without massive assistance (what some critics call a "bailout") by the federal government, many other major corporations might have suffered the same fate.[2]

9-2 Identifying Financial Needs: Evaluation and Planning

Before financial managers can determine the best financial strategies for their firm, they must identify existing strengths and weaknesses. Then they must devise financial plans that provide a roadmap the firm can use to improve financial performance and acquire the resources needed to achieve its short-term and long-term objectives.

9-2a Using Ratio Analysis to Identify Current Strengths and Weaknesses

One way financial managers evaluate the firm's current strengths and weaknesses is by computing ratios that compare values of key accounts listed on their firm's financial statements—mainly its balance sheet and income statement. This technique is called **financial ratio analysis**. Over the years, financial managers have developed an impressive array of specific ratios. Most of the key ratios fall into one of four basic categories:

1. **Liquidity ratios**: In finance, a **liquid asset** is one that can be quickly converted into cash with little risk of loss. **Liquidity ratios** measure the ability of an organization to convert assets into the cash it needs to pay off liabilities that come due in the next year. Liquidity concerns became a major issue for many companies in 2008, when declining sales cut into operating cash flows and credit markets dried up with the onset of the recession.

   One of the simplest and most commonly used liquidity ratios is the *current ratio*, which is computed by dividing a firm's current assets by its current liabilities. Current assets include cash and other assets expected to be converted

JUST BECAUSE THEY CAN... ...DOESN'T MEAN THEY SHOULD.

The housing boom between 2003 and 2007 seemed like a win-win situation for everyone. The surge in housing construction created jobs and stimulated economic growth. Millions of Americans who had never owned a home found themselves moving into their dream house. Even Americans who already owned homes saw the value of their houses soar. And lenders in the mortgage market made huge profits.

But in reality, these gains were the result of an unsustainable bubble, due in part to the shortsighted—and sometimes unethical—behavior of mortgage brokers who arranged housing loans and the lenders who provided the funds. These brokers and lenders increasingly tapped the subprime mortgage market, consisting of borrowers who lacked the financial capacity to qualify for conventional loans. To make these loans *appear* affordable, brokers pushed variable rate mortgages with very low initial rates. They knew that subprime borrowers would be unable to make the higher payments if interest rates rose, but they often neglected to explain this fact to the borrowers. They also pushed many unsophisticated borrowers into mortgage agreements that generated high fees, which they folded into the mortgage. The result: more income for the brokers and lenders and higher payments for the borrower.

While such policies increased the profits of brokers and lenders at first, they were unsustainable in the long run. When interest rates on variable rate mortgages increased, a huge number of subprime borrowers defaulted on their loans. In many areas, the surge in foreclosures contributed to a steep decline in housing prices. Mortgage lending collapsed, and many of the most aggressive firms in the subprime market were wiped out.

Many observers believe more ethical mortgage lending practices could have resulted in a better outcome. As Nobel Prize winning economist Joseph Stiglitz put it, "Had the designers of these mortgages focused on the ends—what we actually wanted from our mortgage market—rather than how to maximize *their* revenues, then they might have devised products that *permanently* increased homeownership. They could have 'done well by doing good.'"[3]

What do YOU think?

- What ethical responsibilities do mortgage brokers and lenders have to their borrowers?
- What responsibility did subprime borrowers have to "read the fine print" in their loan agreements?
- How do the lessons of the mortgage crisis illustrate the need to focus on the long-term consequences of financial decisions?

into cash in the next year, while current liabilities are the debts that must be repaid in the next year. The larger the current ratio, the easier it should be for a firm to obtain the cash needed to pay its short-term debts. But, as we'll explain when we discuss how a firm manages its cash and other liquid assets, it is also possible to have too much liquidity.

2. **Asset management ratios: Asset management ratios** (also sometimes called *activity ratios*) provide measures of how effectively an organization is using its assets to generate net income. For example, the *inventory turnover ratio*—computed by dividing the firm's cost of goods sold by average inventory—measures how many times a firm's inventory is sold and replaced each year. Up to a point, a high turnover ratio is good because it indicates that the firm's products are moving quickly. On the other hand, a low inventory turnover indicates that goods may be sitting on the firm's shelves or stored in its warehouses for long periods of time—usually not a positive sign. However, it is possible for an inventory turnover ratio to be *too* high. For instance, a high ratio could mean that the company isn't keeping enough goods in stock, causing frequent stockouts. This can frustrate customers and result in lost sales if they take their business elsewhere.

For firms that sell a lot of goods on credit, the *average collection period* is another important asset management ratio. This ratio is computed by dividing accounts receivable by average daily credit sales. A value of 45 for this ratio means that customers take 45 days (on average) to pay for their credit purchases. In general, the smaller the ratio the better, since a lower value indicates that the firm's customers are paying for their purchases more quickly. But we'll see in our discussion of working capital management that low collection periods can also have drawbacks.

3. **Leverage ratios: Financial leverage** is the use of debt to meet a firm's financing needs; a *highly leveraged* firm is one that relies heavily on debt. While the use of leverage can benefit a firm when times are good, a high degree of leverage is very risky. As we mentioned earlier, the extensive use of debt financing by big banks and major Wall Street

firms played a major role in the financial meltdown that began during the latter part of the past decade.

Leverage ratios measure the extent to which a firm uses financial leverage. One common measure of leverage is the *debt-to-asset ratio* (sometimes just called the *debt ratio*), which is computed by dividing a firm's total liabilities by its total assets. If a firm financed half its assets with debt and half with owners' equity, its debt ratio would be .5 (or 50%). The higher the debt-to-asset ratio, the more heavily leveraged the firm is.

4. **Profitability ratios:** Firms are in business to earn a profit, and **profitability ratios** provide measures of how successful they are at achieving this goal. There are many different profitability ratios, but we'll look at just a couple of examples. *Return-on-equity* (ROE), calculated by dividing net income (profit) by owners' equity, measures the income earned per dollar invested by the stockholders. If a firm issues both common and preferred stock, the computation of this ratio typically measures only the return to the common stockholders, since they are considered to be the true owners of the company. Thus, dividends paid to preferred stockholders are subtracted from net income in the numerator when computing ROE because these dividends aren't available to common stockholders. Similarly, the denominator of this ratio includes only equity provided by common stockholders and retained earnings.

Another profitability ratio, called *earnings per share* (EPS), indicates how much net income a firm earned per share of common stock outstanding. It is calculated by dividing net income minus preferred dividends by the average number of shares of common stock outstanding.

Exhibit 9.1 defines each of the ratios we've just described and shows how it is computed. As you look at the exhibit, keep in mind that it represents only a sample of the financial ratios used by financial managers.

9-2b Planning Tools: Creating a Road Map to the Future

Ratio analysis helps managers identify their firm's current financial strengths and weaknesses. The next step is to develop plans that build on the firm's strengths and correct its weaknesses. Financial planning is an important part of the firm's overall planning process. Assuming that the overall planning process has established appropriate goals and objectives for the firm, financial planning must answer the following questions:

⊙ What specific assets must the firm obtain in order to achieve its goals?

- How much additional financing will the firm need to acquire these assets?
- How much financing will the firm be able to generate internally (through additional earnings), and how much must it obtain from external sources?
- When will the firm need to acquire external financing?
- What is the best way to raise these funds?

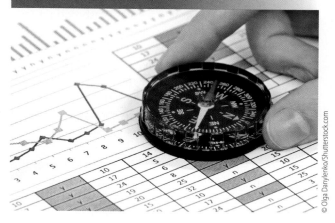

Financial planning points managers in the right direction.

© Olga Danylenko/Shutterstock.com

The planning process involves input from a variety of areas. In addition to seeking input from managers in various functional areas of their business, financial managers usually work closely with the firm's accountants during the planning process.

9-2c Basic Planning Tools: Budgeted Financial Statements and the Cash Budget

The budgeting process provides financial managers with much of the information they need for financial planning. In fact, the **budgeted income statement** and **budgeted balance sheet** are two key financial planning tools. Also called *pro forma financial statements*, they provide a framework for analyzing the impact of the firm's plans on the financing needs of the company.

- The budgeted income statement uses information from the sales budget and various cost budgets (as well as other assumptions) to develop a forecast of

---

EXHIBIT 9.1 Key Financial Ratios

RATIO NAME	TYPE	WHAT IT MEASURES	HOW IT IS COMPUTED
CURRENT	Liquidity: measures ability to pay short-term liabilities as they come due.	Compares current assets (assets that will provide cash in the next year) to current liabilities (debts that will come due in the next year).	$\dfrac{Current\ Assets}{Current\ Liabilities}$
INVENTORY TURNOVER	Asset management: measures how effectively a firm is using its assets to generate revenue.	How quickly a firm sells its inventory to generate revenue.	$\dfrac{Cost\ of\ Goods\ Sold}{Average\ Inventory}$
AVERAGE COLLECTION PERIOD	Asset management: measures how effectively a firm is using its assets to generate revenue.	How long it takes for a firm to collect from customers who buy on credit.	$\dfrac{Accounts\ Receivable}{\left(\dfrac{Annual\ Credit\ Sales}{365}\right)}$
DEBT-TO-ASSETS	Leverage: measures the extent to which a firm relies on debt to meet its financing needs.	Similar to debt-to-equity, but compares debt to assets rather than equity. This is another way of measuring the degree of financial leverage, or debt, the firm is using.	$\dfrac{Total\ Debt}{Total\ Assets}$
RETURN ON EQUITY	Profitability: compares the amount of profit to some measure of resources invested.	Indicates earnings per dollar invested by the owners of the company. Since common stockholders are the true owners, preferred stockholders' dividends are deducted from net income before computing this ratio.	$\dfrac{Net\ Income - Preferred\ Dividend}{Average\ Common\ Stockholders\ Equity}$
EARNINGS PER SHARE	Profitability: compares the amount of profit to some measure of resources invested.	Measures the net income per share of common stock outstanding.	$\dfrac{Net\ Income - Preferred\ Dividend}{Average\ Number\ of\ Common\ Share\ Outstanding}$

© Cengage Learning 2013

net income for the planning period. This can help the firm evaluate how much internal financing (funds generated by earnings) will be available.

➲ The budgeted balance sheet forecasts the types and amounts of assets a firm will need to implement its future plans. It also helps financial managers determine the amount of additional financing (liabilities and owners' equity) the firm must arrange in order to acquire those assets.

The **cash budget** is another important financial planning tool. Cash budgets normally cover a one-year period and show projected cash inflows and outflows for each month. Financial managers use cash budgets to get a better understanding of the *timing* of cash flows within the planning period. This is important because most firms experience uneven inflows and outflows of cash over the course of a year, which can lead to cash shortages and cash surpluses. Projecting cash flows helps financial managers determine when the firm is likely to need additional

funds to meet short-term cash shortages, and when surpluses of cash will be available to pay off loans or to invest in other assets.

Even firms with growing sales can experience cash flow problems, especially if many of their customers buy on credit. To meet increasing sales levels, a growing firm must hire more labor and buy more supplies. These workers and suppliers may expect to be paid well before the company's customers pay their bills, leading to a temporary cash crunch.

Exhibit 9.2 illustrates this type of situation by presenting a partial cash budget for a hypothetical firm called Oze-Moore. The cash budget shows that, despite its increasing sales, Oze-Moore will have cash shortages in March and April. Knowing this in advance gives financial managers time to find the best sources of short-term financing to cover these shortages. The cash budget also shows that Oze-Moore will experience a big cash surplus in May as the customers start paying for the purchases they made in March and April. Knowing this ahead of time helps managers forecast when they will be able to repay the loans they took out to cover their previous cash shortages. It also gives them time to evaluate short-term interest-earning investments they could make to temporarily "park" their surplus cash.

©iStockphoto.com/Henrik Jonsson

EXHIBIT 9.2 Cash Budget for Oze-Moore

Cash Budget for Oze-Moore

	February	March	April	May	
Sales	$75,000	$110,000	$125,000	$90,000	
Cash balance at beginning of month		$10,000	$10,000	$10,000	Sales increase in both March and April. But since most of Oze-Moore's customers buy on credit, its receipt of cash lags behind these sales increases.
Receipts of Cash					
Cash sales		$16,500	$18,750	$13,500	
Collection of accounts receivable from last month's sales		$63,750	$93,500	$106,250	
Total Cash Available		$90,250	$122,250	$129,750	
Disbursements of Cash					While receipts of cash lag behind sales, Oze-Moore's payments of wages and accounts payable are due in the same month as sales.
Payment of accounts payable		$60,500	$68,750	$49,500	
Wages and salaries		$27,500	$31,250	$22,500	
Fixed costs (rent, interest on debt, etc.)		$8,000	$8,000	$8,000	
Purchase of new computers			$6,500		
Total Cash Payments		$96,000	$114,500	$80,000	
Excess or Deficit of Cash for Month		-$5,750	$7,750	$49,750	
Loans needed to maintain cash balance of $10,000		$15,750	$2,250	$0	
Amount of cash available to repay short-term loans		$0	$0	$39,750	
Cash balance at end of month		$10,000	$10,000	$31,750	
Cumulative loans		$15,750	$18,000	$0	

Despite big increases in sales in March and April, Oze-Moore suffers a shortfall of cash because of the difference in *timing* between cash receipts and cash payments.

Financial managers want to have at least $10,000 in the cash balance at the beginning of each month. When cash falls below this amount they take out a short-term loan.

In May, Oze-Moore has a surplus in cash. This gives it enough cash to pay off the loans from earlier months.

© Cengage Learning 2013

9-3 Finding Funds: What Are the Options?

Once financial managers have identified the amount of financial capital needed to carry out their firm's plans, the next step is to determine which sources of funds to tap. The most appropriate sources of funds for a business depend on several factors. One of the most important considerations is the firm's stage of development. Start-up firms face different challenges and have different needs than more established firms. Another factor is the reason the funds are needed. Funds used to meet short-term needs, such as meeting payroll, paying suppliers, or paying taxes, typically come from different sources than funds used to finance major investments in plants, property, and equipment.

The financing options available to new firms are generally much more limited than those available to more mature firms with an established track record. In fact, for start-up firms the main source of funds is likely to be the personal wealth of the owner (or owners), supplemented by loans from relatives and friends. Given how risky new business ventures are, banks and other established lenders often hesitate to make loans to new, unproven companies. (In some cases, the Small Business Administration overcomes this reluctance by guaranteeing loans for start-ups and other small businesses that satisfy its criteria.) As the firms grow and become more established, they typically are able to obtain financing from other sources.

Some start-ups with the potential for generating rapid growth may be able to attract funds from wealthy individuals, called *angel investors*, or from venture capital firms. Both angel investors and venture capitalists typically invest in risky opportunities that offer the possibility of high rates of return. Both also typically provide funds in exchange for a share of ownership.

9-3a Sources of Short-Term Financing: Meeting Needs for Cash

Firms that have survived the start-up phase of the business life cycle often have several sources of short-term financing. Let's take a look at some of the most common options.

Trade Credit One of the most important sources of short term financing for many firms is **trade credit**, which arises when suppliers ship materials, parts, or goods to a firm without requiring payment at the time of delivery. By allowing the firms to "buy now, pay later," they help the firm conserve its existing cash, thus avoiding the need to acquire funds from other sources.

Strong Profits = Private Equity + EcoValueScreen

Private equity (PE), another form of long-term financing, occurs when investors buy private companies (as opposed to publicly held companies). PE firms invest in underperforming businesses and then fix and sell them, usually for substantial returns. PE investing is risky, and investors only make money if their companies improve enough to command higher prices.

David M. Rubenstein, managing director of the Carlyle Group, one of the world's largest PE firms, says, "In the old days when we would buy a company, we would say, 'What are the risks we're going to take in the environment? What are the risks we're going to take in the energy area?' Now we say, 'How can we improve these areas and how can we actually make money doing this?'"

To do that, Carlyle partnered with the Environmental Defense Fund (EDF), a nonprofit advocacy group that uses scientists, lawyers, and economists to solve environmental problems. Together, they developed the EcoValuScreen tool to identify ways to improve energy efficiencies, lower costs, and reduce environmental impact on forest products, greenhouse emissions, chemicals, waste, and water use. For instance, when Carlyle bought NBTY, a maker of nutritional supplements, the EcoValueScreen identified decreasing energy usage, reducing packaging, and minimizing solid waste as ways to save substantial money while sustaining the environment.

EDF's Kirk Hourdajian said that, "EDF shows businesses that they can save money, mitigate risk, and drive business value and performance improvements through environmental initiatives." Carlyle's Rubenstein agrees, saying that, "Sustainability equals more cash flow. And if you are willing to put in the time to improve the sustainability principles of a company, you can in fact make more money."

Carlyle spokesperson Bryan Corbett says, "Private equity is always looking for ways to create value. EDF wanted to provide concrete case studies to prove that environmental strategy is a robust long-term value creation lever." In the end, "Being a good corporate citizen represents good business practice and creates long-term value for our investors."[4]

In most cases, the terms of trade credit are presented on the invoice the supplier includes with the shipment. For example, the invoice might list the terms as 2/10 net 30. The "net 30" indicates that the supplier allows the buyer 30 days before payment is due. But the "2/10" tells the buyer that the supplier is offering a 2% discount off the invoice price if the buyer pays within 10 days.

At first glance, the 2% discount in our example may not seem like a big deal. But failing to take the discount can be very costly. Consider the terms we mentioned above: 2/10, net 30. If the firm fails to pay within 10 days, it loses the discount and must pay the full amount 20 days later. Paying 2% more for the use of funds for only 20 days is equivalent to an *annual* finance charge of over 37%![5]

Suppliers will grant trade credit only after they've evaluated the creditworthiness of the firm. But once they've granted this credit to a company, they generally continue offering it as long as the firm satisfies the terms of the credit arrangements. Trade credit is sometimes called **spontaneous financing** because it is granted when the company places its orders without requiring any additional paperwork or special arrangements. The level of trade credit automatically adjusts as business conditions change and the company places larger or smaller orders with its suppliers.

Although firms of all sizes use this type of financing, trade credit is a particularly important source of financing for small businesses. The Federal Reserve Board's *Survey of Small Business Finances* indicates that about 60% of small firms rely on trade credit as a major source of short-term financial capital.[6]

Factoring The money that customers owe a firm when they buy on credit shows up in accounts receivable on the company's balance sheet. A **factor** buys the accounts receivables of other firms. The factor makes a profit by purchasing the receivables at a discount and collecting the full amount from the firm's customers.

Although firms that use factors don't receive the full amount their customers owe, factoring offers some definite advantages. Instead of having to wait for customers to pay, the firm gets its money almost immediately. Also, since the factor is responsible for collection efforts, the firm using the factor may be able to save money by eliminating its own collection department. Finally, the factor typically assumes the risk for bad debts on any receivables it buys. (However, factors typically perform a careful evaluation of the quality of accounts receivable before they buy them and may refuse to buy receivables that are high risk.) According to the Commercial Finance Association, factoring has typically provided more than $130 billion dollars in short-term funds to American businesses in recent years.[7]

Short-Term Bank Loans Banks are another common source of short-term business financing. Short-term bank loans are usually due in 30 to 90 days, though they can be up to a year in length. When a firm negotiates a loan with a bank, it signs a *promissory note*, which specifies the length of the loan, the rate of interest the firm must pay, and other terms and conditions of the loan. Banks sometimes require firms to pledge collateral, such as inventories or accounts receivable, to back the loan. That way, if the borrower fails to make the required payments, the bank has a claim on specific assets that can be used to pay off the amount due.

Rather than going through the hassle of negotiating a separate loan each time they need more funds, many firms work out arrangements with their bankers to obtain pre-approval so that they can draw on funds as needed. One way they do this is by establishing a **line of credit**. Under this arrangement, a bank agrees to provide the firm with funds up to some specified limit, as long as the borrower's credit situation doesn't deteriorate, and the bank has sufficient funds—conditions that aren't always met, as the recent financial meltdown clearly illustrated.

A **revolving credit agreement** is similar to a line of credit, except that the bank makes a formal, legally binding commitment to provide the agreed-upon funds. In essence, a revolving credit agreement is a *guaranteed* line of credit. In exchange for the binding commitment to provide the funds, the bank requires the borrowing firm to pay a commitment fee based on the *unused* amount of funds. Thus, under the terms of a revolving credit agreement, the firm will pay interest on any funds it borrows, and a commitment fee on any funds it does not borrow. The commitment fee is lower than the interest on the borrowed funds, but it can amount to a fairly hefty charge if the firm has a large unused balance.

Commercial Paper Well-established corporations have some additional sources of short-term financial capital. For instance, many large corporations with strong credit ratings issue **commercial paper**, which consists of short-term promissory notes (IOUs). Historically, commercial paper issued by corporations has been unsecured—meaning it isn't backed by a pledge of collateral. Because it is normally unsecured, commercial paper is only offered by firms with excellent credit ratings; firms with less-than-stellar financial reputations that try to issue unsecured commercial paper are unlikely to find buyers. In recent years, a new class of commercial paper has emerged, called *asset-backed commercial paper,* which, as its name implies, is backed by some form of collateral.

Commercial paper can be issued for up to 270 days, but most firms typically issue it for much shorter periods—sometimes for as little as two days. One key reason commercial paper is popular with companies is that it typically carries a lower interest rate than commercial banks charge on short-term loans. By far the biggest issuers of commercial paper are financial institutions, but other large corporations also use this form of financing.

The market for commercial paper normally is huge—often close to $2 trillion—but it can fluctuate dramatically as economic conditions change. Because most commercial paper is unsecured, investors tend to view it as risky when business conditions deteriorate. In fact, when the economy spiraled into the Great Recession of 2008–2009, the market for commercial paper essentially dried up. This put a tremendous strain on many struggling financial institutions that relied on commercial paper to meet their short-term cash needs. The situation became so grim that in October of 2008 the Fed established the Commercial Paper Funding Facility, a limited liability company funded by the Federal Reserve Bank of New York. This facility, which the Fed operated until February 1, 2010, ultimately purchased several hundred billion dollars of commercial paper, providing a crucial infusion of cash into this stressed market.[8]

9-3b Sources of Long-Term Funds: Providing a Strong Financial Base

The sources of financial capital we've looked at so far have been appropriate for dealing with cash needs that arise from short-term fluctuations in cash flows. But financial managers typically seek more permanent funding to finance major investments and provide a secure financial base for their company. Let's take a look at some of the more common sources of long-term funds.

Direct Investments from Owners One key source of long-term funds for a firm is the money the owners themselves invest in their company. For corporations, this occurs when it sells *newly issued* stock—and it's important to realize that the *only* time the corporation receives financial capital from the sale of its stock is when it is initially issued. If Google issued new shares of stock which you bought, the funds would go to Google. But once you own Google's stock, if you decide to sell your shares to another investor, Google gets nothing. The money from the sale is all yours—minus, of course, the commission you pay to your broker and the taxes on any gains you make on the sale.

Another way firms can meet long-term financial needs is by reinvesting their earnings. The profits that a firm reinvests are called **retained earnings**. This source isn't a pool of cash; it simply reflects the share of the firm's earnings that has been used to finance the purchase of assets and pay off liabilities. If you want to know how much cash a firm has, check the figure in the cash account at the top of its balance sheet. You'll typically find that the value in the firm's cash account is quite different from the amount listed as the retained earnings!

retained earnings The part of a firm's net income it reinvests.

Retained earnings are a major source of long-term capital for many corporations, but the extent to which they are used depends on the state of the economy. When the economy is booming and profits are high, retained earnings tend to soar. But when the economy slides into a recession, most corporations find they have few earnings to reinvest. For instance, in 2006 (the last real "boom" year prior to the Great Recession), corporate retained earnings exceeded $430 billion, while in the recession year of 2008, the figure fell to $157 billion—a drop of well over 60%.[9]

The decision to retain earnings involves a tradeoff because firms have another way to use their earnings: they can pay out some or all of their profits to their owners by declaring a dividend. You might think that stockholders would be unhappy with a firm that retained most of its earnings, since that would mean they would receive a smaller dividend. But many stockholders actually prefer their companies to reinvest earnings—at least if management invests them wisely—because doing so can help finance their firm's growth. And a growing, more profitable firm usually translates into an increase in the market price of the firm's stock.

Billionaire Warren Buffet's company, Berkshire Hathaway, has never paid dividends, choosing to reinvest all of its substantial profits. This strategy paid off handsomely for stockholders. During the ten-year period between March 1, 2001, and February 18, 2011, Berkshire's stock soared from $72,000 to $120,750 per share.[10] Despite the fact that it paid them no dividend, you can bet that most of Berkshire's shareholders were pleased with the capital gains that resulted from this strategy!

Long-Term Debt In addition to contributions from owners, firms can also raise long-term funds by borrowing from banks and other lenders or by issuing bonds.

Term Loans There are many different types of long-term loans, but the most typical arrangement—sometimes simply called a *term loan*—calls for a regular schedule of fixed payments sufficient to ensure that the principal (the amount initially borrowed) and interest are repaid by the end of the loan's term.

Lenders often impose requirements on long-term loans to ensure repayment. Most lenders require that the loans be backed by a pledge of some type of collateral. Banks and other lenders also often include *covenants* in their loan agreements. A **covenant** is a requirement a lender imposes on the borrower as a condition of the loan. One common covenant requires the borrower to carry a specified amount of liability insurance. Another requires the borrower to agree not to borrow any *additional* funds until the current loan is paid off. Covenants sometimes even restrict the size of bonuses or pay raises the firm can grant to employees. The purpose of covenants is to protect creditors by preventing the borrower from pursuing policies that might undermine its ability to repay the loan. While covenants are great for lenders, borrowers often view them as highly restrictive.[11]

Corporate Bonds Rather than borrow from banks or other lenders, corporations sometimes issue their own formal IOUs, called *corporate bonds*, which they sell to investors. Bonds often have due dates (maturities) of ten or more years after issuance. Like corporate stock, bonds are marketable, meaning that bondholders can sell them to other investors before they mature. But it is important to realize that unlike shares of stock, which represent ownership in a corporation, bonds are certificates of debt.

9-4 Leverage and Capital Structure: How Much Debt Is Too Much Debt?

Most firms use a combination of **equity** and **debt financing** to acquire needed assets and to finance their operations. Owners provide equity financing, while creditors (lenders) provide debt

Decisions about capital structure require managers to weigh the risks and rewards of financial leverage.

© Christopher T Stein/Chaos/Digital Vision/Jupiterimages

financing. Thus, when a company issues and sells new stock or uses retained earnings to meet its financial needs, it is using equity financing. But when it takes out a bank loan, or issues and sells corporate bonds, it is relying on debt financing.

Both equity and debt financing have advantages and drawbacks. The extent to which a firm relies on various forms of debt and equity to satisfy its financing needs is called that firm's **capital structure**. To simplify our discussion, we'll focus mainly on the capital structure of corporations, but many of the basic principles apply to other forms of ownership.

9-4a Pros and Cons of Debt Financing

When a firm borrows funds, it enters into a contractual agreement with the lenders. This arrangement creates a *legally binding* requirement to repay the money borrowed (called the principal) *plus interest*. These payments take precedence over any payments to owners. In fact, lenders often require the firm to pledge collateral, such as real estate, financial securities, or equipment, to back the loan. Should the firm be unable to make the required payments, the lenders can use this collateral to recover what they are owed.

Debt financing offers some advantages to firms. For instance, the interest payments a firm makes on debt are a tax-deductible expense. So Uncle Sam (in the form of the IRS) subsidizes the interest payments. For example, if the corporation's tax rate is 30%, then each dollar of interest expense reduces the firm's taxes by $.30—meaning the true cost to the firm of each dollar of interest is only $.70.

Another advantage of debt is that it enables the firm to acquire additional funds without requiring existing stockholders to invest more of their own money or the sale of stock to new investors (which would dilute the ownership of existing owners). Moreover, if the firm invests the borrowed funds profitably, the use of debt can substantially improve the return on equity to the shareholders. We'll illustrate this result in our discussion of financial leverage.

One obvious disadvantage of debt is the requirement to make fixed payments. This can create real problems when the firm finds itself in an unexpectedly tight financial situation. In bad times, required interest payments can eat up most (or all) of the earnings, leaving little or no return to the firm's owners. And if the firm is unable to meet these payments, its creditors can force it into bankruptcy.

As we mentioned earlier, another disadvantage of debt financing is that creditors often impose covenants on the borrower. These covenants can hamper the firm's flexibility and might result in unintended problems. For example, a covenant that restricts bonuses and pay raises to employees might undermine the morale of key workers and tempt them to seek employment elsewhere. Similarly, restrictions on dividends or on the ability of the firm to borrow additional funds may make it difficult for the firm to raise more money.

9-4b Pros and Cons of Equity Financing

For corporations, equity financing comes from two major sources: retained earnings and money directly invested by stockholders who purchase newly issued stock. Equity financing is more flexible and less risky than debt financing. Unlike debt, equity imposes no required payments. A firm can skip dividend payments to stockholders without having to worry that it will be pushed into bankruptcy. And a firm doesn't have to agree to burdensome covenants to acquire equity funds.

On the other hand, equity financing doesn't yield the same tax benefits as debt financing. In addition, existing owners might not want a firm to issue more stock, since doing so might dilute their share of ownership. Finally, a company that relies mainly on equity financing forgoes the opportunity to use financial leverage. But as we've already noted, leverage can be a two-edged sword. We'll illustrate the risks and rewards of leverage in our next section.

9-4c Financial Leverage: Using Debt to Magnify Gains (and Losses)

As mentioned in our discussion of ratios, firms that rely on a lot of debt in their capital structure are said to be *highly leveraged*. The main advantage of financial leverage is that it magnifies the return on the stockholders' investment when times are good. Its main disadvantage is that it also reduces the financial return to stockholders when times are bad.

Let's illustrate both the advantages and disadvantages of financial leverage with a simple example. Exhibit 9.3 shows the revenues, expenses, and earnings that two firms—Eck-Witty Corporation and Oze-Moore International—would experience for two different levels of sales, one representing a strong year and the other a weak year. To make the impact of leverage easy to see, we'll assume that Eck-Witty and Oze-Moore are *identical* in all respects *except* their capital structure. In particular, our example assumes that the two companies have the same amount of assets and experienced exactly the same *earnings before interest and taxes* (abbreviated as EBIT). Thus, any differences in the net income of these firms results from differences in their use of debt and equity financing. We'll use return on equity (ROE) to measure the financial return each firm offers its stockholders. (See Exhibit 9.1 if you need a reminder about how to interpret or compute this ratio.)

Note that *both* firms have a total of $1 million in assets, but they've financed the purchase of their assets in very different ways. Eck-Witty used only common stock and retained earnings in its capital structure, so it has $1 million in equity financing and no debt. Oze-Moore's capital structure consists of $200,000 in owners' equity and $800,000 in debt, so it is highly leveraged. The interest rate on its debt is 10%, so Oze-Moore has to make required interest payments of $80,000 per year to its lenders. Both companies must pay taxes equal to 25% of their earnings, but Oze-Moore's total tax bill will be lower than Eck-Witty's because its interest payments are tax deductible.

As Exhibit 9.3 shows, when sales are strong, Oze-Moore's use of leverage really pays off. Eck-Witty's ROE of 12% under

© ZEF NIKOLLA/HO/HO/EPA/Landov

Liking Facebook's IPO: Too Early for Thumbs Down?

An initial public offering (IPO) is the first time that a company sells stock to the public, usually to finance growth. There are three parties in an IPO: the company selling its stock, the investment bank underwriting the stock sale that advises the company, and the public who buy the initial shares via a stock exchange. As the underwriter, the investment bank buys the company's stock, reselling it to the public at the issue price, which it determines with the company. If the issue price is too high, investors won't buy as much, and the investment bank ends up with less money than it paid the company. If it's too low, investors will buy more because they perceive a bargain, but the company and investment bank "leave money on the table." When that happens, the stock generally rises in value, and the public, which paid a low price, resells the stock to others for a profit. With so much at risk, intense analysis goes into determining the issue price.

Facebook's $38 issue price quickly rose to $44, finished at $38.23 by day's end, and fell to $27 a month later, reducing Facebook's market cap from $105 billion to $74 billion. What happened?

Just three days before, Facebook decided to sell 25% more shares to the public, most likely exceeding demand. Furthermore, a decline in recent sales and profits led large institutional buyers to reduce how much they planned to buy.

David Sze, at Greylock Partners, an early Facebook investor said, "Two moments from now, this moment won't matter." Google's stock dropped below issue price, from $108 to $85, as did Amazon's, from $18 to $14. Today, Google stock exceeds $500, and Amazon's exceeds $200. The IPO raised billions for Facebook. What matters in the long run is successfully using that capital to improve Facebook's long-term performance.[12]

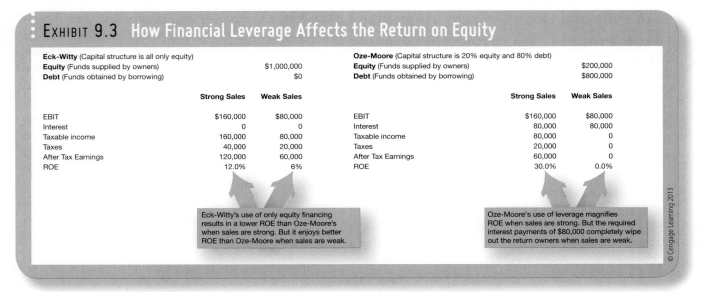

EXHIBIT 9.3 How Financial Leverage Affects the Return on Equity

Eck-Witty (Capital structure is all only equity)			Oze-Moore (Capital structure is 20% equity and 80% debt)		
Equity (Funds supplied by owners)	$1,000,000		**Equity** (Funds supplied by owners)	$200,000	
Debt (Funds obtained by borrowing)	$0		**Debt** (Funds obtained by borrowing)	$800,000	
	Strong Sales	**Weak Sales**		**Strong Sales**	**Weak Sales**
EBIT	$160,000	$80,000	EBIT	$160,000	$80,000
Interest	0	0	Interest	80,000	80,000
Taxable income	160,000	80,000	Taxable income	80,000	0
Taxes	40,000	20,000	Taxes	20,000	0
After Tax Earnings	120,000	60,000	After Tax Earnings	60,000	0
ROE	12.0%	6%	ROE	30.0%	0.0%

Eck-Witty's use of only equity financing results in a lower ROE than Oze-Moore's when sales are strong. But it enjoys better ROE than Oze-Moore when sales are weak.

Oze-Moore's use of leverage magnifies ROE when sales are strong. But the required interest payments of $80,000 completely wipe out the return owners when sales are weak.

© Cengage Learning 2013

the strong sales scenario isn't bad, but it pales in comparison to the 30% return Oze-Moore generates for its owners under the same scenario. Oze-Moore's higher ROE occurs because its interest payments are *fixed*. It pays its creditors $80,000—no more, no less—whether EBIT is high or low. When Oze-Moore can borrow funds at an interest rate of 10% and invest them in assets that earn *more* than 10% (as it does in the strong sales scenario), the extra return goes to the *owners* even though creditors provided the funds. This clearly adds a significant boost to the returns enjoyed by the stockholders!

But in the weak sales scenario, the results are quite different. In this case, the $80,000 of *required* interest payments eats up all of Oze-Moore's earnings, leaving it with no net income for its owners, so its ROE is zero. If EBIT had been anything less than $80,000, Oze-Moore wouldn't have had enough earnings to cover the interest—and if it failed to come up with the money to pay its creditors they could force it into bankruptcy. This illustrates the risk associated with financial leverage. In comparison, notice that Eck-Witty still earns a positive ROE for its owners in the weak sales scenario; granted an ROE of 6% isn't spectacular, but it sure beats the 0% return Oze-Moore experienced!

Our leverage example contains important lessons for the real world—lessons that recent financial history clearly illustrates. During the economic boom between 2003 and early 2007, many companies found that the use of leverage magnified their ROEs. When the economy slowed, the required interest and principal payments on their debt became a heavy burden on highly leveraged firms. As we mentioned at the beginning of this chapter, many of these firms ended up in bankruptcy.

By late 2008, many of the highly leveraged firms that survived the initial carnage were frantically looking for ways to replace much of the debt in their capital structure with more equity—a strategy known as *deleveraging*.

> **"Always live within your income, even if you have to borrow money to do so. Never run into debt, not if you can find anything else to run into."**
>
> — JOSH BILLINGS, 19TH CENTURY AMERICAN HUMORIST

Unfortunately, most companies found deleveraging to be a slow and painful process. Their poor financial performance during the financial meltdown meant their earnings were low (or even negative), so they couldn't use retained earnings to build their equity capital. And the plummeting stock market and lack of investor confidence made it difficult to sell new stock. The moral of the story: if the financial returns of leverage seem too good to be true, over the long run they probably are. Sound financial management requires keeping a level head and considering the riskiness of financial decisions as well as their return.[13]

In the wake of the financial crisis, the federal government enacted new legislation designed to reduce the likelihood of similar meltdowns in the future. The **Dodd–Frank Act** included requirements for large firms in the financial sector to hold more equity and less debt in their capital structures and established a Financial Stability Oversight Council to monitor financial markets and to identify and respond to emerging risks. If also created a Consumer Financial Protection Bureau to protect consumers from predatory lending practices by financial institutions.[14]

9-5 Acquiring and Managing Current Assets

Let's turn our attention to how a firm determines the amount and type of current assets to hold. As we'll see, holding current assets involves tradeoff; either too much or too little of these assets can spell trouble.

9-5a Managing Cash: Is It Possible to Have *Too Much Money*?

A company must have cash to pay its workers, suppliers, creditors, and taxes. Many firms also need cash to pay dividends. And most firms also want to hold enough cash to meet unexpected contingencies. But cash has one serious shortcoming compared to other assets: it earns little or no return. If a firm holds much more cash than needed to meet its required payments, stockholders are likely to ask why the excess cash isn't being invested in more profitable assets. And if the firm can't find a profitable way to invest the money, the stockholders are likely to ask management why it doesn't use the excess cash to pay them a higher dividend—most shareholders can think of plenty of ways *they'd* like to use the cash!

In the narrowest sense, a firm's cash refers to its holdings of currency (paper money and coins issued by the government) plus demand deposits (the balance in its checking account). However, when most firms report their cash holdings on their balance sheet, they take a broader view, including **cash equivalents** along with their actual cash. Cash equivalents are very safe and highly liquid assets that can be converted into cash quickly and easily. Commercial paper, U.S. Treasury Bills (T-bills), and money market mutual funds are among the most popular cash equivalents. The advantage of these cash equivalents is that they offer a better financial return (in the form of interest) than currency or demand deposits.

> "The Dodd-Frank Act was 2,319 pages in length. Apparently there was a lot about our financial system in 2010 that Congress wanted to change!"
> — David Skeel, The New Financial Deal

© Picsfive/Shutterstock.com

As we explained in our discussion of short-term sources of funds, major corporations with strong credit ratings often *sell* commercial paper to raise needed short-term funds. On the other side of such transactions are firms that *buy* commercial paper as part of their portfolio of cash equivalents because—at least under normal economic conditions—it is a safe and liquid way to earn some interest. But during economic downturns the appeal of commercial paper as a cash equivalent plummets due to increased risk.

U.S. Treasury bills, or "T-bills," are short-term IOUs issued by the U.S. government. Most T-bills mature (come due) in 4, 13, or 26 weeks. There is a very active secondary market for T-bills, meaning that their owners can sell them to other investors before they mature. Thus, T-bills are highly liquid. And, unlike commercial paper, T-bills are backed by the U.S. government, so they are essentially risk-free. The safety and liquidity of T-bills make them very attractive cash equivalents even in times of economic distress.

Money market mutual funds raise money by selling shares to large numbers of investors. They then pool these funds to purchase a portfolio of short-term, liquid securities. (In fact, money market mutual funds often include large holdings of commercial paper and T-bills.) Money market mutual funds are an affordable way for small investors to get into the market for securities, which would otherwise be beyond their means. This affordability also makes these funds a particularly attractive cash equivalent for smaller firms.

9-5b Managing Accounts Receivable: Pay Me Now or Pay Me Later

Accounts receivable represents what customers who buy on credit owe the firm. Allowing customers to buy on credit can significantly increase sales. However, as our discussion of the cash budget showed, credit sales can create cash flow problems because they delay the receipt of cash the firm needs to meet its financial obligations. Customers who pay late or don't pay at all only exacerbate the problem. So it's important for firms to have a well-thought-out policy that balances the advantages of offering credit with the costs. The key elements of this policy should include:

➔ Setting credit terms: For how long should the firm extend credit? What type of cash discount should the firm offer to encourage early payments?

➔ Establishing credit standards: How should the firm decide which customers qualify for credit? What type of

Dodd–Frank Act A law enacted in the aftermath of the financial crisis of 2008–2009 that strengthened government oversight of financial markets and placed limitations on risky financial strategies such as heavy reliance on leverage.

cash equivalents Safe and highly liquid assets that many firms list with their cash holdings on their balance sheet.

U.S. Treasury bills (T-bills) Short-term marketable IOUs issued by the U.S. federal government.

money market mutual funds A mutual fund that pools funds from many investors and uses these funds to purchase very safe, highly liquid securities.

credit information should it require? How strict should its standards be?

- Deciding on an appropriate collection policy: How aggressive should the firm be at collecting past-due accounts? At what point does it make sense to take (or at least threaten to take) legal action against late-paying customers, or to turn over the accounts to collection agencies? When does it make sense to work out compromises?

In each area, financial managers face tradeoffs. For example, a firm that extends credit for only 30 days will receive its payments sooner than a firm that allows customers 90 days. But setting short credit periods may also result in lost sales. Similarly, setting high credit standards reduces the likelihood a firm will have problems with customers who pay late (or not at all). However, strict standards may prevent many good customers from getting credit, resulting in lower sales. Finally, an aggressive collection policy may help the firm collect payments that it would otherwise lose. But an aggressive policy is costly, and it might alienate customers who make honest mistakes, causing them to take future business to competitors.

Some small businesses have found that being flexible and creative about the form of payment can help them get at least some of what they are owed. Barter arrangements sometimes work better than demanding cash—especially in troubled times such as the recent recession. For example, a health spa took payments from one of its customers in the form of hundreds of granola bars. Similarly, the owner of a bookkeeping firm agreed to accept payment from a veterinarian in the form of emergency surgery on her pet cat![16]

9-5c Managing Inventories: Taking Stock of the Situation

Inventories are stocks of finished goods, work-in-process, parts, and materials that firms hold as a part of doing business. Clearly, businesses must hold inventories to operate. For example, you'd probably be disappointed if you visited a Best Buy store and were confronted with empty shelves rather than with a wide array of electronic gadgets to compare and try out. Similarly, a manufacturing firm wouldn't be able to assemble its products without an inventory of parts and materials.

But for many firms, the costs of storing, handling, and insuring inventory items are significant expenses. In recent years, many manufacturing firms have become very aggressive about keeping inventories as low as possible in an attempt to reduce costs and improve efficiency. Such "lean" inventory policies can be very effective, but they leave the firm vulnerable to supply disruptions. Honda had to shut down some of its Ohio assembly lines for eight days in late 2011 after 15 feet of floodwater swamped the Taiwanese factories of key suppliers, delaying shipments of four-wheel drive systems for its cars. If Honda held larger inventories, it might have been able to continue operating its assembly lines until its Taiwanese suppliers could resume shipments.[17]

Robin Hood? Big Customers Help Themselves by Paying Accounts Receivable Later

In weak economies, businesses stretch payments to manage cash flows. When Anatta Design, a website developer, billed an online retailer $6,600 for redesigning the shopping cart section of its website, the retailer paid 404 days after the bill was due!

How common is late payment? In the U.S., the average company pays 29.2 days late. Likewise, in the United Kingdom, it's 25.6 days late, with large companies paying 34 days late. And, large companies are taking longer than they used to. Walmart pays in 29.5 days, up from 27 three years ago, while Apple pays in 52 days, up from 43 days. A study by Experian, a global consumer and business credit reporting company, confirms late payments are up by 14% in 2012, except for large companies whose late payments are up 28%!

While good accounts receivables policies determine how long credit is extended, who qualifies for credit, and how aggressively past-due accounts should be pursued, those policies don't help much when your largest customers pay late. Chris Shult, president of Bevco Engineering, says, "The choice they give you is take it or leave it." The problem, says Shult, is, "You're collecting a lot slower than you're paying out, so it stunts your growth."

Solutions include expanding your line of bank credit. Or, using a lender such as PrimeRevenue, which provides loans to small suppliers at the much cheaper interest rate of their larger customers. Another option is ReceivablesExchange.com, where lenders bid for the chance to lend against your accounts receivable. The average starting cost is 4% of receivables, and the cash is received in 24 to 48 hours. If paid on time, costs can quickly drop to just 1% of receivables.[15]

PAST DUE

© Stephen VanHorn/Shutterstock.com

Capital Budgeting: In It for the Long Haul

We'll conclude the chapter with a look at how firms evaluate proposals to invest in long-term assets or undertake major new projects. **Capital budgeting** refers to the procedure a firm uses to plan for investments in assets or projects that it expects will yield benefits for more than a year. The capital budgeting process evaluates proposals such as:

- ❏ Replacing old machinery and equipment with new models to reduce cost and improve the efficiency of current operations

- ❏ Buying additional plant, machinery, and equipment to expand production capacity in *existing* markets

- ❏ Investing in plant, property, and equipment needed to expand into *new* markets

- ❏ Installing new, or modifying existing, plant and equipment to achieve goals not directly related to expanding production, such as reducing pollution or improving worker safety

The number of capital budgeting proposals a firm considers each year can be quite large. But it's unlikely that all proposals will be worth pursuing. How do financial managers decide whether or not to accept a proposal?

9-6a Evaluating Capital Budgeting Proposals

Financial managers measure the benefits and costs of long-term investment proposals in terms of the cash flows they generate. These cash flows are likely to be negative at the start of a project because money must be spent to get a long-term investment project up and running before it begins generating positive cash flows. But a project must eventually generate enough positive cash flows to more than offset these negative initial cash outflows if it is to benefit the company.

9-6b Accounting for the Time Value of Money

One of the most challenging aspects of the evaluation of a long-term project's cash flows is that they are spread out over a number of years. When financial managers compare cash flows that occur at different times, they must take the **time value of money** into account. The time value of money reflects the fact that, from a financial manager's perspective, a dollar received today is worth *more* than a dollar received in the future because the sooner you receive a sum of money, the sooner you can put that money to work to earn even *more* money.

Suppose, for example, that you were given the choice of receiving $1,000 either today or the same amount one year from today. If you think like a financial manager, this choice is a no-brainer! Let's be conservative and say that if you receive the money today you can deposit it in an insured one-year **certificate of deposit (CD)** at your local bank that pays 4% interest. (A CD is similar to a savings account, except that it requires the funds to remain on deposit for a fixed term; in our example, the term is one year. You would incur a penalty if you withdrew your funds early.) Investing in your 4% CD means that a year from today you would have $1,040 (the $1,000 you deposited plus $40 in interest). But if you wait until next year to receive the $1,000, you'll lose the opportunity to earn that $40 in interest. Clearly, receiving the cash today is the better option.

© iStockphoto.com/VikZa

Because money has a time value, a cash flow's value depends not only on the *amount* of cash received but also on *when* it is received. Financial managers compare cash flows occurring at different times by converting them to their present values. The **present value** of a cash flow received in a future time period is the amount of money that, if invested *today* at an assumed rate of interest (called the *discount rate*), would grow to become that future amount of money. Exhibit 9.4 shows that $10,000 invested today at 3% grows to a future value of $11,254.88 in four years. Thus, $10,000 is the present value of $11,254.88 received in four years.

9-6c The Risk-Return Tradeoff Revisited

Unfortunately, financial managers don't have crystal balls, so they don't know the *actual* cash flows a proposed project will generate. Instead, they base their analysis on the cash flows the proposal is *expected* to generate. Once a company actually invests in a project, it may find that the *actual* cash flows are quite different from these estimated flows. This uncertainty means that capital budgeting decisions must consider risk.

In general, projects with the potential for high returns are also the projects with a high degree of uncertainty and risk. This is another example of the risk-return tradeoff we introduced at the beginning of this chapter. Clearly, financial managers must take this tradeoff into account when they compare different capital budgeting proposals; they must determine whether riskier proposals generate a high enough expected return to justify their greater risk.

capital budgeting The process a firm uses to evaluate long-term investment proposals.

time value of money The principle that a dollar received today is worth more than a dollar received in the future.

certificate of deposit (CD) An interest-earning deposit that requires the funds to remain deposited for a fixed term. Withdrawal of the funds before the term expires results in a financial penalty.

present value The amount of money that, if invested today at a given rate of interest (called the discount rate), would grow to become some future amount in a specified number of time periods.

net present value (NPV) The sum of the present values of expected future cash flows from an investment, minus the cost of that investment.

One common way financial managers try to do this is to use a higher discount rate when they compute the present values of cash flows for risky projects than when they compute present values for less risky projects. This reflects the idea that a higher return is required to compensate for the greater risk.

9-6d Net Present Value: A Decision Rule for Capital Budgeting

The most common method financial managers use to evaluate capital budgeting proposals is to compute their **net present value (NPV)**. The NPV of an investment proposal is found by adding the present values of *all* of its estimated future cash flows and subtracting the initial cost of the investment from the sum. A positive NPV means that the present value of the expected cash flows from the project is greater than the cost of the project. In other words, the benefits from the project exceed its cost even after accounting for the time value of money. Financial managers approve projects with positive NPVs. A negative NPV means that the present value of the expected future cash flows from the project is less than the cost of the investment. This would indicate that the cost of the project outweighs its cash flow benefits. Financial managers would reject proposals with negative NPVs. (See Exhibit 9.5.)

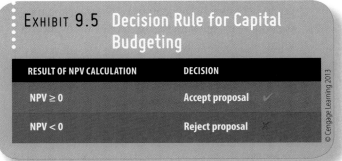

EXHIBIT 9.4 How a Present Value of $10,000 Grows to a Future Value of $11,254.88 in Four Years

Now
- Deposit $10,000.00 (Present value)
- Earn 3% per year

After 1 year you have
- $10,000 + $300 interest earned over first year (3% of 10,000) =
- $10,300.00

After 2 years you have
- $10,300.00 + $309 interest earned over second year (3% of $10,300) =
- $10,609

After 3 years you have
- $10,609.00 + $318.27 interest earned over third year (3% of $10,609) =
- $10,927.07

After 4 years you have
- $10,927.07 + $327.82 interest earned over fourth year (3% of $10,927.07) =
- $11,254.88 (Future Value)

© Cengage Learning 2013

EXHIBIT 9.5 Decision Rule for Capital Budgeting

RESULT OF NPV CALCULATION	DECISION
NPV ≥ 0	Accept proposal ✓
NPV < 0	Reject proposal ✗

© Cengage Learning 2013

Apple's "Walking Around Money": What Do You Do with $100 Billion in Cash?

© Don Farrall/Photodisc/Getty Images

Companies need cash to pay workers, bills, taxes, and dividends. In June 2011, Apple had $76.2 billion in cash, more than the gross domestic product of 126 countries! Financial analyst Toni Sacconaghi of Sanford C. Bernstein & Co. said, "We're talking about a level of cash that's preposterous by any metric." By February 2012, Apple had nearly $100 billion in cash, $64 billion overseas and $33.6 billion in the U.S. "If they can't find ways to use it to grow, they should be returning it to shareholders," stated Tim Ghriskey of Solaris Asset Management. CEO Tim Cook admitted, "It's more than we need to run the company."

Unfortunately, cash earns little or no return, and Apple has poorly managed its mountains of cash, earning a minuscule 0.75% return compared to Google's 2.8% and Microsoft's 3.7%.

Managing its cash like Microsoft would have given Apple an extra $2.95 billion!

With record cash and profits, Apple declared its first ever dividend in 2012, paying $2.65 per shareholder, or $5 billion per year. It will also spend $10 billion annually for stock buybacks to neutralize "dilution from future employee equity grants and employee stock purchase programs." CEO Tim Cook said, "Even with these [$15 billion in] investments, we can maintain a war chest for strategic opportunities and have plenty of cash to run our business." Yes, even with $15 billion a year toward dividends and stock buybacks, Apple's cash will double to $200 billion by September 2014! If so, stockholders will pressure Cook to better manage Apple's cash.[18]

THE BIG PICTURE

In this chapter, we described the tasks financial managers perform as they attempt to find the "best" sources and uses of financial resources—meaning those that will maximize the value of the firm to its owners. We saw that in their attempts to achieve this goal, financial managers face two challenges. The first is to balance the needs of owners against those of the other stakeholders; the second is to balance the potential rewards of their decisions against the risks.

Recent history illustrates how important sound financial management is to the success of a firm—and how devastating poor financial decisions can be. Indeed, the recent decline and fall of some of the biggest and best-known U.S. corporations can be traced in large measure to poor financial decisions—especially decisions that failed to adequately take risk into account, resulting in the use of too much leverage.

These lessons from the recent past will probably result in a different approach to financial management over the next several years. While memories of the Great Recession are still relatively fresh, firms may be more conservative in their view of what constitutes the best sources and uses of funds. In particular, they are likely to shy away from excessive debt and put more emphasis on equity financing. They also are less likely to use their funds to invest in highly risky or speculative assets. These more conservative tendencies are likely to be reinforced by the major regulatory reforms designed to curb aggressive (and risky) behavior introduced by the Dodd-Frank Act.

Financial managers are employed by firms in every sector of the economy, but the greatest numbers are in the insurance, banking, and financial services sectors. About 527,000 financial managers were employed in the United States in 2012. Financial managers need strong computer and analytical skills. The work often involves long hours, can be mentally challenging, and is sometimes stressful. But salaries and other compensation tend to be attractive. The median salary in 2010 was $103,910—a figure that doesn't include bonuses or stock options, which, for many financial managers, have been a significant source of additional income.[19] However, bonuses may be less generous in the wake of the financial crisis.

The Bureau of Labor Statistics (BLS) projects that job growth in financial management will grow by 9% between 2010 and 2020, which is slower than the average rate of growth for all occupations. However, the BLS also projects that the competition for these jobs is likely to be intense because the number of applicants may increase even faster than the number of jobs. Thus, even though the minimum requirements for most financial management positions is a bachelor's degree in finance, economics, or business administration, an advanced degree in one of these fields, such as a master's in business administration (MBA), may be necessary to be considered for the more desirable jobs.[20]

CAREERS IN FINANCIAL MANAGEMENT

CAREERS

What *else?*

RIP & REVIEW CARDS IN THE BACK
and visit www.cengagebrain.com!

10

Financial Markets:
Allocating Financial Resources

LEARNING OBJECTIVES

After studying this chapter, you will be able to:

10-1 Explain the role of financial markets in the U.S. economy and identify the key players in these markets

10-2 Identify the key laws that govern the way financial markets operate and explain the impact of each law

10-3 Describe and compare the major types of securities that are traded in securities markets

10-4 Explain how securities are issued in the primary market and traded on secondary markets

10-5 Compare several strategies that investors use to invest in securities

10-6 Interpret the information provided in the stock quotes available on financial websites

> "SOMETIMES YOUR BEST INVESTMENTS ARE THE ONES YOU DON'T MAKE."
>
> — DONALD TRUMP

10-1 The Role of Financial Markets and Their Key Players

Financial markets perform a vital function: they transfer funds from savers (individuals and organizations willing to defer the use of some of their income in order to earn a financial return and build their wealth) to borrowers (individuals and organizations that need additional funds to achieve their financial goals in the current time period). Without these markets, companies would find it difficult to obtain the financial resources they need to meet their payrolls, invest in new facilities, develop new products, and compete effectively in global markets.

But it's not just businesses that benefit from these markets. You'll almost certainly participate on both sides of financial markets. In fact, you already participate in these markets as a borrower when you use a credit card to finance daily purchases or when you take out a loan to pay college tuition. And you'll participate as a saver when you put money into a savings account to accumulate the money you'll need for a down payment on your first house, or when you invest in financial securities to build up a nest egg for your retirement years.

In the U.S. and other well-developed market economies, the vast majority of financing occurs indirectly, with *financial intermediaries* coming between the ultimate savers and borrowers. We'll see that they perform a variety of functions, but what they all have in common is that they help channel funds from savers to borrowers.

10-1a Depository Institutions

Depository institutions are financial intermediaries that obtain funds by accepting checking or savings deposits (or both) from individuals, businesses, and other institutions, and then lend these funds to borrowers.

- Commercial banks are the most common depository institutions. When you make a deposit into a checking or savings account at your bank, you are providing funds that the bank can use for making loans to businesses, governments, or other individuals.

  At the start of 2012, over half (54%) of total bank assets were in the form of loans, including over $4.4 trillion in real estate and mortgage loans, more than $1.4 trillion in consumer loans, and over $2 trillion in commercial and other loans. And compared to historical trends, this was relatively high. In the immediate aftermath of the Great Recession, banks were still quite conservative in their loan-making decisions. For comparison, in 2007 loans comprised 57% of all bank assets.[1]

- **Credit unions** are cooperatives, meaning that they are not-for-profit organizations that are owned by their depositors. As not-for-profit organizations, they strive to pay higher interest rates on member deposits and charge lower interest rates on loans.

  Credit unions are open to individuals who belong to a specific "field of membership." For example, membership in some credit unions is limited to the employees who work for a specific employer and their family members; other credit unions base membership on church or union affiliation or are open to people living in a certain geographic area.[2]

  Credit unions are a much smaller player in financial markets than commercial banks, but in early 2012 they held more than $321 billion in mortgage financing and $223 billion in consumer credit on their books.[3]

- **Savings and loan associations** (also called "S&Ls" or "thrifts") traditionally accepted only savings account deposits and used them to make mortgage loans. During the early 1980s, regulations on S&Ls were relaxed, allowing them to accept checking account deposits and make a broader range of loans. Still, the major focus of the savings and loan industry remains mortgage loans.

---

financial markets
Markets that transfer funds from savers to borrowers.

depository institution
A financial intermediary that obtains funds by accepting checking or savings deposits (or both) and uses these funds to make loans to borrowers.

credit union A depository institution that is organized as a cooperative, meaning that it is owned by its depositors.

savings and loan association A depository institution that has traditionally obtained most of its funds by accepting savings deposits, which have been used primarily to make mortgage loans.

Marginal glossary terms:

securities broker A financial intermediary that acts as an agent for investors who want to buy and sell financial securities. Brokers earn commissions and fees for the services they provide.

securities dealer A financial intermediary that participates directly in securities markets, buying and selling stocks and other securities for its own account.

investment bank A financial intermediary that specializes in helping firms raise financial capital by issuing securities in primary markets.

At the end of 2011, S&Ls held about $586 billion in mortgage financing on their books—not a trivial sum by any means, but a big drop from 2006 when the figure was almost $1.1 trillion.[4] In large part, this reflected the collapse of the housing market at the end of the past decade. But S&Ls began declining in importance well before the Great Recession.[5]

10-1b Nondepository Financial Institutions

In addition to banks and other depository institutions, a number of other financial intermediaries play important roles in financial markets.

⊃ **Institutional Investors** don't accept deposits but amass huge pools of financial capital from other sources and use these funds to acquire a portfolio of many different assets. Mutual funds obtain money by selling shares to investors; insurance companies obtain money by collecting premiums from policyholders; and pension funds obtain money by collecting funds employers and their employees contribute for the employees' retirement. These institutions invest heavily in corporate stock; the majority of shares in most major U.S. corporations are held by institutional investors. They are also major holders of corporate bonds and government securities.

⊃ **Securities brokers** act as agents for investors who want to buy or sell financial securities, such as corporate stocks or bonds. In addition to handling the trades, many brokers provide their clients with additional services such as financial planning and market research. Brokers are compensated by charging fees and commissions for the services they provide.

⊃ **Securities dealers** participate directly in securities markets, buying and selling stocks and bonds for their own account. They earn a profit by selling securities for higher prices than they paid to purchase them. (The difference between the prices at which they buy and sell a security is called the *spread*.)

⊃ **Investment banks** are financial intermediaries that help firms issue new securities to raise financial capital. Sometimes investment banks actually buy the newly issued securities themselves; in other cases, they simply help arrange for their sale. Today's investment

© Erik Lam/Shutterstock.com

Woof! Dividends and Dogs of the Dow

Stock returns come in two forms. If a stock grows in value after being purchased, the price appreciation is called a capital gain. Historically, most investors prefer such growth stocks. If a corporation distributes part of its earnings to shareholders, a stock dividend is paid for each share of stock. Unfortunately, most investors don't include dividend-paying stocks in their portfolios. That's a mistake. Since 1927, non-dividend paying stocks have earned an average annual return of 8.4%, while stocks with the small dividend payouts averaged 10.2%, stocks with moderate dividends averaged 10.2%, and stocks with large dividends averaged 11.1%.

While there aren't any guarantees, companies that start paying dividends often go to great lengths to continue doing so. Procter & Gamble has paid dividends each year since 1890, General Mills since 1899, and ExxonMobil since 1984. Likewise, Procter & Gamble and ExxonMobil have been increasing their dividends annually since 1957 and 1984, respectively.

How can you take advantage of dividend-paying stocks in your investment portfolio? One simple strategy is the "Dogs of the Dow," in which you buy the ten highest yielding dividend stocks listed on the Dow Jones Industrial Average. Such stocks have high dividends relative to their stock prices, which are lower than they should be. This approach gives you a strong dividend and a likelihood that the stock price will appreciate off of its lows. Invest equally in each "dog." Hold them for a year. Then replace those that are no longer dogs with that year's new dogs. Sometimes this strategy underperforms the market, but over 20 years, it matched the returns of the Dow Jones Industrial Average but slightly exceeded Standard & Poor's. On the day this was written, the "dogs" were all Fortune 500 companies, such as AT&T and Verizon.

Most stock advisors, though, recommend a mix of growth stocks and dividend-paying stocks. Furthermore, they caution that dividend-paying stocks are not a substitute for bonds, which typically pay higher yields against much lower risk.[6]

banks aren't actually independent companies. Instead, they are typically divisions of huge bank holding companies that also own commercial banks.

10-2 Regulating Financial Markets to Protect Investors and Improve Stability

Financial markets only work well when savers and borrowers have confidence in the soundness of key financial institutions and in the fairness of the market outcomes. When depositors lose confidence in their banks, or when investors discover that financial markets are rigged by practices such as insider trading or unethical and deceptive accounting, the financial system breaks down.

The financial crisis of 2008 is only the latest example of the disruptions that result when financial markets malfunction. From the early twentieth century to the present day, the U.S. economy has experienced several other major financial crises. The economy experienced massive bank failures in 1907 and in the early 1930s. It also weathered a savings and loan crisis in the late 1980s that brought the failure of over 1,000 S&Ls and required a federal bailout that cost over $120 billion.[7] And a variety of scandals involving ethical lapses (and in many cases outright fraud) roiled financial markets at the turn of the century.

10-2a Financial Regulation: Early Efforts

During most of the twentieth century, the federal government responded to financial upheavals by introducing new laws and regulations. This trend first emerged in the wake of the banking panic of 1907, which created pressure for Congress to find a way to stabilize the nation's banking system. The result was the **Federal Reserve Act of 1913**. As its name implies, this act created the Federal Reserve System (the Fed) to serve as the central bank in the United States. The law gave the Fed the primary responsibility for overseeing our nation's banking system.

Unfortunately, the creation of the Fed didn't solve all of the nation's banking problems. Another wave of bank failures occurred in the early 1930s as the economy sank into the Great Depression. Congress responded by passing the **Banking Act of 1933**, also known as the *Glass-Steagall Act*. This law established the Federal Deposit Insurance Corporation, which insured depositors against financial losses when a bank failed. The insurance initially covered only $2,500 of deposits—but $2,500 bought a lot more in the 1930s than it does today! Over the years, coverage has been increased several times. Today, the FDIC insures up to $250,000 in deposits.

Another major provision of the Glass-Steagall Act banned commercial banks from dealing in securities markets, selling insurance, or otherwise competing with nondepository institutions such as insurance companies and investment banks. The rationale for these restrictions was that involvement in such activities exposed banks and their depositors to higher levels of risk.

Congress responded to the stock market crash that occurred in 1929 with two laws that are still the foundation of U.S. securities markets regulation. The first of these was the **Securities Act of 1933**, which dealt mainly with the process of issuing new securities. It prohibited misrepresentation or other forms of fraud in the sale of newly issued stocks and bonds. It also required firms issuing new stock in a public offering to file a registration statement with the SEC. The next year, Congress passed the **Securities Exchange Act of 1934**, which regulated the trading of previously issued securities. This law created the **Securities and Exchange Commission** (SEC) and gave it broad powers to oversee the securities industry. The law required that all publicly traded firms with at least 500 shareholders and $10 million in assets file quarterly and annual financial reports with the SEC, and that brokers and dealers register with the SEC.

The Securities Exchange Act also gave the SEC the power to prosecute individuals and companies that engaged in fraudulent securities market activities. For example, the SEC has the authority to go after individuals who engage in illegal *insider trading*, which is the practice of using inside information (important information about a company that isn't available to the general investing public) to profit unfairly from trading in a company's securities.

10-2b Deregulation During the 1980s and 1990s: Temporarily Reversing Course

The passage of these laws ushered in a period of more stable financial markets. But critics argued that the laws—especially the Glass-Steagall Act—represented an onerous government intrusion into the financial sector that stifled competition and impeded financial innovation. During the 1980s and 1990s Congress responded to these criticisms by easing restrictions

Federal Reserve Act of 1913 The law that established the Federal Reserve System as the central bank of the United States.

Banking Act of 1933 The law that established the Federal Deposit Insurance Corporation (FDIC) to insure bank deposits. It also prohibited commercial banks from selling insurance or acting as investment banks.

Securities Act of 1933 The first major federal law regulating the securities industry. It requires firms issuing new stock in a public offering to file a registration statement with the SEC.

Securities and Exchange Act of 1934 A federal law dealing with securities regulation that established the Securities and Exchange Commission to regulate and oversee the securities industry.

Securities and Exchange Commission The federal agency with primary responsibility for regulating the securities industry.

Financial Services Modernization Act of 1999 An act that overturned the section of the Banking Act of 1933 that prohibited commercial banks from selling insurance or performing the functions of investment banks.

common stock The basic form of ownership in a corporation

on banks and other depository institutions. For instance, the **Financial Services Modernization Act of 1999**, also known as the *Gramm-Bliley-Leach Act*, reversed the Glass-Steagall Act's prohibition of banks selling insurance or acting as investment banks.

The financial sector initially seemed to prosper under its less regulated environment. It responded to its increased freedom with a variety of new services. And new technologies such as ATMs and online banking made financial transactions easier and more convenient.

10-2c Recent Developments: Re-regulation in the Aftermath of Financial Turmoil

But the wave of deregulation didn't last. A series of accounting scandals at the beginning of the twenty-first century, followed by a near collapse of the financial system in 2008, created pressure for new laws.

Congress reacted to the accounting scandals in the first years of the new century by passing the Sarbanes-Oxley Act in 2002. This law included provisions to ensure that external auditors offered fair, unbiased opinions when they examined a company's financial statements. It also increased the SEC's authority to regulate financial markets and investigate charges of fraud and unethical behavior.[8]

In the wake of the financial crisis of 2008–2009 Congress passed the Dodd-Frank Act of 2010. This far-reaching law expanded the Fed's regulatory authority over nondepository financial institutions, such as hedge funds and mortgage brokers, that had previously operated with little regulatory oversight or accountability. It also created the Financial Stability Oversight Council to identify emerging risks in the financial sector so that action could be taken to rein in risky practices *before* they led to a crisis. The council was given the authority to recommend new rules to the Federal Reserve that would limit risky practices of the nation's largest, most complex financial institutions.[9]

10-3 Investing in Financial Securities: What Are the Options?

Financial securities markets are critical to corporations that rely on them to obtain much of their long-term financial capital. They also provide one of the most important venues

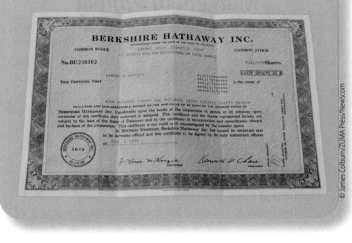

EXHIBIT 10.1 Stock Certificates Represent Shares of Ownership in a Corporation.

Common stock is the basic form of ownership in a corporation.

© James Colburn/ZUMA Press/Newscom

that individuals can use to build their long-term wealth and earn significant financial returns.

10-3a Common Stock: Back to Basics

Common stock is the basic form of ownership in a corporation. Exhibit 10.1 shows a stock certificate for Berkshire Hathaway, Inc. As owners of corporations, common stockholders have certain basic rights:

⊃ **Voting Rights:** Owners of common stock have the right to vote on important issues in the annual stockholders' meeting. Under the most common arrangement, stockholders can cast one vote for each share of stock they own. One of the key issues that stockholders vote on is the selection of members to the corporation's board of directors, but they also may vote on other major issues, such as the approval of a merger with another firm or a change in the corporation's by-laws. As you learned in Chapter 6, the Dodd-Frank Act of 2010 gives stockholders the right to vote on their company's executive compensation policies. While non-binding, a "say on pay" vote gives shareholders a way to make their feelings known about executive compensation.[10]

⊃ **Right to Dividends:** Dividends are a distribution of earnings to the corporation's stockholders. All common stockholders have the right to receive a dividend *if* their corporation's board of directors declares one. The "catch" is that the board has no legal obligation to declare a dividend. In fact, many rapidly growing

> **"I never attempt** to make money on the Stock Market. I buy on the assumption that they could close the market the next day and not reopen it for five years."

— Warren Buffett, American business magnate, investor, and philanthropist

companies routinely choose to skip dividends and reinvest most or all of their earnings to finance growth.

🡢 **Capital Gains:** Stockholders receive another type of return on their investment, called a **capital gain**, *if* the price of the stock rises above the amount they paid for it. Capital gains can create very attractive financial returns for stockholders. Of course, there is no guarantee the stock's price will rise. If it falls, stockholders would experience a capital loss rather than a capital gain.

🡢 **Preemptive Right:** If a corporation issues new stock, existing stockholders sometimes have a preemptive right to purchase new shares in proportion to their existing holdings before the stock is offered to the other investors. For example, if you own 5% of the existing shares of stock, then the preemptive right gives you the right to purchase 5% of the new shares. This could be important for large stockholders who want to maintain their share of ownership. However, the conditions under which existing stockholders have preemptive rights vary among the states. In several states, a preemptive right is only available if it is specifically identified in the corporation's charter.

🡢 **Right to a Residual Claim on Assets:** The final stockholder right is a residual claim on assets. If the corporation goes out of business and liquidates its assets, stockholders have a right to share in the proceeds in proportion to their ownership. But note that this is a *residual* claim—it comes *after all other claims* have been satisfied. In other words, the firm must pay any back taxes, legal expenses, wages owed to workers, and debts owed to creditors before the owners get anything. By the time all of these other claims have been paid, nothing may be left for the owners.

10-3b Preferred Stock: Getting Preferential Treatment

Common stock is the basic form of corporate ownership, but some companies also issue **preferred stock**, so named because it offers its holders preferential treatment in two respects:

🡢 **Claim on Assets:** Holders of preferred stock have a claim on assets that comes before common stockholders if the company goes out of business. This gives preferred stockholders a better chance than common stockholders of recovering their investment if the company goes bankrupt.

🡢 **Payment of Dividends:** Unlike dividends on common stock, dividends on preferred stock are usually a stated amount. And a corporation can't pay *any* dividend to its common stockholders unless it pays the full stated dividend on its preferred stock. Still, it is important to note that a corporation has no *legal* obligation to pay a dividend to *any* stockholders, not even those who hold preferred stock.

Preferred stock sometimes includes a *cumulative feature*. This means that if the firm skips a preferred dividend in one period, the amount it must pay the next period is equal to the dividend for that period *plus* the amount of the dividend it skipped in the previous period. Additional skipped dividends continue to accumulate, and the firm can't pay *any* dividends to common stockholders until *all* accumulated dividends are paid to preferred stockholders.

Preferred stock isn't necessarily "preferred" to common stock in all respects. For instance, preferred stockholders normally don't have voting rights, so they can't vote on issues that come up during stockholders meetings. And even though preferred stockholders are more likely to receive a dividend, they aren't guaranteed a *better* dividend; the board can declare a dividend to common stockholders that offers a higher return.[11] Finally, when a company experiences strong earnings, the market price of its common stock can—and often does—appreciate more in value than the price of its preferred shares, thus offering common shareholders a greater capital gain.

10-3c Bonds: Earning Your Interest

A **bond** is a formal IOU issued by a corporation or government entity. Bonds come in many different varieties. Our discussion will focus on the basic characteristics of long-term bonds issued by corporations.

capital gain The return on an asset that results when its market price rises above the price the investor paid for it.

preferred stock A type of stock that gives its holder preference over common stockholders in terms of dividends and claims on assets.

bond A formal debt instrument issued by a corporation or government entity.

maturity date The date when a bond will come due.

par value (of a bond) The value of a bond at its maturity; what the issuer promises to pay the bondholder when the bond matures.

coupon rate The interest paid on a bond, expressed as a percentage of the bond's par value.

current yield The amount of interest earned on a bond, expressed as a percentage of the bond's current market price.

The date a bond comes due is called its **maturity date**, and the amount the issuer owes the bondholder at maturity is called the bond's **par value** (or face value). Long-term bonds issued by corporations usually mature ten to thirty years after issuance, but longer maturities are possible. In 2012, several major corporations, including IBM and Coca-Cola, issued *century bonds* that matured 100 years after they were issued.[12]

Bondholders can sell their bonds to other investors before they mature, but the price they receive might not correspond to the bond's par value because bond prices fluctuate with conditions in the bond market. When a bond's market price is above its par value, it is selling at a *premium*; when its price is below par value, it is selling at a *discount*.

Most bonds require their issuers to pay a stated amount of interest to bondholders each year until the bond matures. The **coupon rate** on the bond expresses the annual interest payment as a percentage of the bond's par value. For example, investors who own a bond with a par value of $1,000 and a coupon rate of 7.5% receive $75 in interest (7.5% of $1,000) each year until the bond reaches

maturity—or until they sell their bonds to someone else. But since bonds can sell at a premium or a discount, the coupon rate doesn't necessarily represent the rate of return that investors earn on the amount they actually *paid* for the bond. The **current yield** expresses a bond's interest payment as a percentage of the bond's *current market price* rather than its par value. If the market price of the bond in our example was $833.33, then the current yield would be 9% (found by dividing the $75 interest payment by $833.33).

Unlike dividends on stock, a firm has a *legal obligation* to pay interest on bonds—and to pay the bondholder the par value of the bond when it matures. Thus, bondholders are more likely to receive a financial return than stockholders. But that doesn't mean that bonds are without risk. Corporations that get into serious financial difficulties sometimes *default* on their bonds, meaning that they are unable to make required payments. When that happens, bankruptcy proceedings usually allow bondholders to recover some (but not all) of what they are owed; historically, the average amount recovered has been about 72 cents on the dollar. While that is better than what stockholders can expect, it is far short of being risk free![13]

QE? Queen Elizabeth? Quod Est? Quantitative Easing?

© fstockfoto/Shutterstock.com

In the U.S. banking system, the Federal Reserve Bank, or central bank (CB), influences the economy by changing the interest rates it charges banks for borrowing. If the economy slows, for example, the CB lowers interest rates. Banks then lower their rates, which encourages companies and consumers to borrow and spend, stimulating growth and eventually increasing profits and stock prices.

But if interest rates are already low or close to zero, like we've seen over the past four years, cutting bank interest rates doesn't help. In such instances, the CB uses quantitative easing to put more cash into the economy by buying assets such as long-term bonds. When you buy bonds, you want a high coupon rate because it increases your returns. The company issuing the bonds, though, wants a low coupon rate to reduce the costs of borrowing money from bondholders. Since the CB only cares about stimulating the economy, it is willing to spend trillions to buy bonds at low rates. Each time the CB buys bonds, the money it spends goes to bondholders who then have more cash to spend.

Does QE work? Yes! Studies show that QE cuts bond rates by a significant 1.5% to 3%. That, in turn, puts more cash into the economy. Between December 2008 and March 2010 when the CB spent $1.7 trillion on QE, stocks rose by 80%! When the CB spent $600 billion for QE between November 2010 and June 2011, stocks rose another 30%. Why learn about quantitative easing? Because it can significantly affect your investments![14]

10-3d Convertible Securities: The Big Switch

Corporations sometimes issue **convertible securities**, which are bonds or shares of preferred stock that investors can exchange for a given number of shares of the issuing corporation's common stock. A *conversion ratio* indicates the number of shares of common stock exchanged for each convertible security. For example, if the conversion ratio is 20, then each convertible security can be exchanged for 20 shares of common stock. The ratio is set at the time the convertible securities are issued so that it is only financially desirable to convert the securities if the price of the common stock increases.

Owning a convertible security allows investors to gain from an increase in the price of common stock, while limiting their risk if the price of the stock falls. If the price of the common stock increases, the holders of convertible securities can convert them into the now more valuable stock. But if the price of the company's common stock falls, investors can continue to hold their convertible securities and collect their interest or preferred dividends.

The firm also can benefit from issuing convertible bonds because the popularity of this feature with investors allows it to offer a lower coupon rate on convertible bonds (or a lower dividend on preferred stock), thus reducing its fixed payments. And if investors convert to common stock, the firm no longer has to make these fixed payments at all. But there is one important group that may be unhappy with this arrangement; the corporation's existing stockholders may be displeased if the new stock issued to holders of convertible securities dilutes their share of ownership—and their share of any profits!

Mutual Funds and ETFs: Diversification Made Easy **Financial diversification**—the practice of holding many different securities in many different sectors—is generally considered a desirable strategy because it helps reduce (but not completely eliminate) risk. If you hold many different securities in different sectors of the economy, then losses on some securities may be offset by gains on others.

Many investors who want to hold diversified portfolios find that investing in large numbers of individual stocks and bonds is prohibitively expensive. And even if they could afford to do so, investors often lack the time and expertise to select a large number of individual securities. Faced with these limitations, many investors find that **mutual funds** and exchange traded funds are attractive options.

Mutual Funds: Portfolios Made Easy There are two ways mutual funds can be structured. A *closed-end fund* issues a fixed number of shares and invests the money received from selling these shares in a portfolio of assets. Shares of closed-end funds can be traded among investors

much like stocks. An *open-end mutual fund* doesn't have a fixed number of shares, nor are its shares traded like stocks. Instead, the fund issues additional shares when demand increases and redeems (buys back) old shares when investors want to cash in.

The price at which shares of an open-end mutual fund are issued and redeemed is based on the fund's **net asset value per share** (NAVPS), which is computed by dividing the total value of the fund's cash, securities, and other assets (less any liabilities) by the number of fund shares outstanding. Though the NAVPS is the basis for the price of a fund's shares, investors often also pay commissions and purchase fees.

Several features make mutual funds a popular choice for investors:

○ **Diversification at Relatively Low Cost:** By pooling the funds of thousands of investors, mutual funds have the financial resources to invest in a broader portfolio of securities than individual investors could afford. This high level of diversification can help reduce risk.

○ **Professional Management:** Most mutual funds are managed by a professional fund manager who selects the assets in the fund's portfolio. This can be appealing to investors who lack the time and expertise to make complex investment decisions.

With today's technology, investors can track the assets in their portfolios at any time and from just about any place.

© iStockphoto.com/Skip Odonnell

Does Green Investing Earn Green Returns?

Is it possible to meet your personal financial goals while also satisfying your desire to invest in companies that pursue environment-friendly policies? Several so-called "green" mutual funds claim to help you do just that. The New Alternatives Fund, established in 1982, was the first fund that selected stocks based primarily on environmental considerations. In recent years the fund's portfolio has emphasized firms that develop alternative energy sources, recycle waste, and produce pollution abatement equipment.

Green funds vary in terms of the criteria they use for selecting their stocks. For instance, the Winslow Green Growth Fund invests aggressively in small-growth firms that meet their environmental responsibilities. The more conservative Portfolio 21 selects large, well-established companies that emphasize environmental sustainability. Its portfolio of over 100 stocks typically includes such well-known corporations as Nike, Staples, Google, and Johnson & Johnson.

An obvious question is whether these *environmentally* green funds provide investors with the other type of "green" investors seek—namely, an attractive *financial* return. Over the long haul, the answer appears to be yes. The Winslow Green Growth Fund had an average annual return of 12.27% from its inception in 1994 through March 2011. That significantly outperformed the average return on stock indices such as the S&P 500 over the same time period. Likewise, the Portfolio 21 Fund also performed much better than the S&P 500 over the five-year period ending on March 31, 2011. The New Alternative Fund hasn't performed quite as well, but its returns over the same five-year period have come close to matching the S&P performance.

These average returns concealed big fluctuations over shorter time periods. The Winslow fund earned an eye-popping total return of 92% in 2003, but saw returns drop by 60% in 2008—and then rise again by 43.7% in 2009. The returns reported by New Alternatives and Portfolio 21 fluctuated by similar amounts over the same time period.[15]

○ **Variety:** Whatever your investment goals and philosophy, you can probably find a fund that's a good match. There are many different types of funds; some invest only in certain types of securities (such as municipal bonds or stocks of large corporations), others invest in specific sectors of the economy (such as energy, technology or healthcare), and yet others seek more balanced and broad-based portfolios. Some funds simply invest in a portfolio of stocks that matches those in a specific stock index, such as the Standard & Poor 500 or the Wilshire 5000. These *index funds* have become very popular in recent years.

○ **Liquidity:** It's easy to withdraw funds from a mutual fund. For a closed-end fund, you simply sell your shares. For an open-end fund, you redeem your shares from the fund itself. However, regardless of when you initiate your withdrawal, redemptions of an open-end fund are not carried out until its NAVPS is determined after the *next* trading session is completed.

Mutual funds do have some drawbacks. Perhaps the most serious is that the professional management touted by many funds doesn't come cheap. Investors in mutual funds pay a variety of fees that typically range from 1% to 3% of the amount invested. The fees charged by mutual funds can make a serious dent in the overall return received by the fund's investors. And funds assess these fees even when they perform poorly. One reason for the popularity of index funds is that they don't require professional management, so their fees are lower.

Another drawback of actively managed funds is that when their professional managers engage in a lot of trading, any financial gains can have significant tax consequences. It is also important to realize that some of the specialized mutual funds that invest in only one sector of the economy or only one type of security may not provide enough diversification to reduce risk significantly.

10-3e Exchange Traded Funds: Real Basket Cases (and We Mean That in a Good Way)

An **exchange traded fund (ETF)** is similar to a mutual fund in some respects but differs in how it is created and how its shares are initially distributed. ETFs allow investors to buy ownership in what is called a *market basket* of many different securities. In fact, the market basket for most ETFs reflects the composition of a broad-based stock index, much like an index mutual fund. But in recent years more specialized ETFs that focus on narrower market baskets of assets have appeared on the market. Like closed-end mutual funds—but unlike the more common open-end funds—ETFs are traded just like stocks. Thus, you can buy and sell ETFs any time of the day.

Compared to most actively managed mutual funds, ETFs usually have lower costs and fees. However, since ETFs are bought and sold like stocks, you do have to pay brokerage commissions every time you buy or sell shares.

> " There are approximately 8,000 mutual funds now in the United States—far more than the total number of actively traded individual stocks in the United States. "
>
> —Investment Company Institute

10-4

Issuing and Trading Securities: The Primary and Secondary Markets

There are two distinct types of securities markets: the primary securities market and the secondary securities market. The **primary securities market** is where corporations raise additional financial capital by selling *newly issued* securities. The **secondary securities market** is where *previously issued* securities are traded.

10-4a The Primary Securities Market: Where Securities Are Issued

There are two methods of issuing securities in the primary market:

⊃ In a **public offering**, securities are sold (in concept, at least) to anyone in the investing public who is willing and financially able to buy them.

⊃ In a **private placement**, securities are sold to one or more private investors (who may be individuals or institutions) under terms negotiated between the issuing firm and the private investors.

Public Offerings Many corporations are initially owned by a small number of people who don't sell the stock to outsiders. But growing corporations often need to obtain more financial capital than such a small group can provide. Such firms may *go public* by issuing additional stock and offering it to investors outside their group. The first time a corporation sells its stock in a public offering, the sale is called an **initial public offering (IPO)**.

Going public is a complicated and high-stakes process; obtaining sufficient funds in an IPO is often critical to the firm's success. So, almost all firms that go public enlist the help and advice of an investment bank that specializes in helping firms issue new securities. The investment bank assists the firm at every step of the IPO, from the planning and market assessment phase until the actual securities are distributed to investors after the offering is conducted.

One of the key responsibilities of the investment bank is to arrange for the actual sale of the securities. The investment bank uses either a *best efforts* or a *firm commitment* approach. Under the best efforts approach the bank provides advice about pricing and marketing the securities and assists in finding potential buyers. But it doesn't guarantee that the firm will sell all of its securities at a high enough price to meet its financial goals. The investment bank earns a commission on all of the shares sold under a best efforts approach.

Under a *firm-commitment* arrangement, the investment bank **underwrites** the issue. This means that the investment bank itself purchases *all* of the shares at a specified price, thus guaranteeing that the firm issuing the stock will receive a known amount of new funds. The investment bank that underwrites the offer seeks to earn a profit by reselling the stock to investors at a higher price. For large public offerings a group of investment banks, called an *underwriting syndicate*, may temporarily work together to underwrite the securities.

Before going public, a firm must file a **registration statement** with the Securities and Exchange Commission (SEC). This long, complex document must include the firm's key financial statements plus additional information about the company's management, its properties, its competition, and the intended uses for the funds it plans to obtain from the offering. The corporation cannot legally offer its new securities for sale until the SEC has examined this statement and declared it effective.

Private Placements In a private placement, the issuing firm negotiates the terms of the offer directly with a

exchange traded fund (ETF) Shares traded on securities markets that represent the legal right of ownership over part of a basket of individual stock certificates or other securities.

primary securities market The market where newly issued securities are traded. The primary market is where the firms that issue securities raise additional financial capital.

secondary securities market The market where previously issued securities are traded.

public offering A primary market issue in which new securities are offered to any investors who are willing and able to purchase them.

private placement A primary market issue that is negotiated between the issuing corporation and a small group of accredited investors.

initial public offering (IPO) The first time a company issues stock that may be bought by the general public.

underwriting An arrangement under which an investment banker agrees to purchase all shares of a public offering at an agreed-upon price.

registration statement A long, complex document that firms must file with the SEC when they sell securities through a public offering.

market order An order telling a broker to buy or sell a specific security at the best currently available price.

limit order An order to a broker to buy a specific stock only if its price is below a certain level, or to sell a specific stock only if its price is above a certain level.

Investing in securities requires you to think carefully about your specific situation, your personal goals, and your attitudes:

- ❍ What are your short-term and long-term goals?
- ❍ Given your budget, how much are you able to invest?
- ❍ How long can you leave your money invested?
- ❍ How concerned are you about the tax implications of your investments?
- ❍ How much tolerance do you have for risk?

Notice that the last question deals with your attitudes toward risk. Most people are not comfortable with high levels of risk. But no investment strategy completely avoids risk. And in general, the riskier the approach, the greater the *potential* rewards. To achieve your goals, you'll need to find the balance between risk and return that works for you.

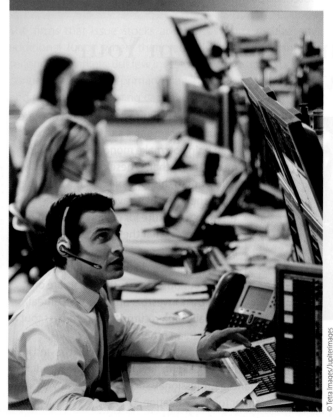

Stockbrokers place orders to buy and sell stocks and other securities for their clients.

© Tetra Images/Jupiterimages

10–5a Choosing a Broker: Gaining Access to the Markets

Members of the general public cannot directly trade stocks and other securities on the exchanges, the over-the-counter market, or ECNs we described earlier in the chapter. Thus, most investors enlist the services of a brokerage firm to carry out their trades. Choosing the right broker is the first step in implementing your investment plans.

A *full service broker* provides a wide range of services—such as market research, investment advice, and tax planning—in addition to carrying out your trades. *Discount brokers* provide the basic services needed to buy and sell securities but offer fewer additional services. They may also restrict your ability to trade certain types of securities. For example, some discount brokers don't offer the ability to buy and sell foreign securities. Discount brokers tend to charge significantly lower commissions than full service brokers. In fact, many discount brokers charge flat fees of only a few dollars per trade for basic transactions. But brokerage firms also charge a variety of fees—sometimes including "inactivity fees" if you don't place enough orders! Once these fees are considered, brokerage, firms that offer low commissions may not be as inexpensive as they first appear!

In recent years, competition among brokerage firms has blurred the distinction between full service and discount brokers. To stop clients from defecting to discount brokers, many full-service firms have lowered their commissions. At the same time, many discount brokers have begun to offer a broader range of services to attract more clients. Now many brokerage firms offer investors the choice of discount or full-service accounts.

Once you've decided on a broker, you need to open an account. This is a fairly simple process; it requires filling out some forms (usually available online) and making an initial investment. The minimum initial investment varies, but $1,000 to $3,000 is fairly typical.

10–5b Buying Securities: Let's Make a Deal

Once you've set up your account, you can trade securities by contacting your broker and indicating the security you want to trade and the quantity you want to buy or sell. You can also specify the type of order you want to place. The most common types of orders are market orders and limit orders:

- ❍ **Market orders** instruct the broker to buy or sell a security at the current market price. Placing a market

JUST BECAUSE THEY CAN...

...DOESN'T MEAN THEY SHOULD.

Normally, the way to make money in the stock market is to "buy low, sell high." This is a logical strategy, but it only works if the price of the stock increases. Investors who believe the price of a company's stock will fall sometimes turn to a different strategy called "short selling." This approach simply reverses the standard procedure: the investor sells high *then* buys low. Short sellers do this by borrowing shares of stock and selling them. (They usually borrow the shares from their broker.) Then they wait for the price to fall, buy the stock at the lower price, and replace the shares they borrowed. They profit from the difference between the high price at which they sold the borrowed shares and the lower price they paid for the replacement shares.

Short selling is legal—and even desirable. As certified financial analyst Alex Dumortier puts it, "Short selling is an integral part of a well-functioning market, since it allows market participants to voice their view that a stock is overpriced. Without short sellers, the market would be inherently positively biased, and stocks would be priced less efficiently."

But short selling sometimes tempts investors to behave in unethical ways. One questionable tactic is called "naked short selling." This occurs when a short seller sells shares without first borrowing them—meaning that the seller actually has no stock to sell. The sale isn't actually completed until the seller furnishes the shares, but it is still recorded. This can put downward pressure on the price of the stock. The short seller benefits from the lower price, but other investors find the value of their stock declining because of transactions that haven't occurred.

An even more appalling tactic is called "short and distort." This involves selling borrowed stock and then spreading negative (and unfounded) rumors about the company to put downward pressure on its stock. As with naked short selling, the lower stock prices that result from these distortions benefit the short seller but can cause significant harm to the company and losses to investors who aren't part of the scam.

What do YOU think?

- What are the risks involved in short selling?
- Why are short-and-distort tactics likely to be more successful in recessions?
- How can abusive naked short selling be controlled?[17]

OCTOBER

"October. This is one of the peculiarly dangerous months to speculate in stocks. The others are July, January, September, April, November, May, March, June, December, August and February."

— MARK TWAIN IN PUDD'NHEAD WILSON

order virtually guarantees that your order will be executed. The downside is that you may end up buying at a higher price than you expected to pay (or selling your stock for less than you expected to receive).

- **Limit orders** place limits on the prices at which orders are executed. A buy limit order tells a broker to buy a stock *only* if its price is at or below a specified value. You'd use this approach if you wanted to make sure you didn't pay more for the stock than you thought it was worth. A sell limit order tells your broker to sell the shares only if the price is at or above a specified value. This prevents your broker from selling your stock at a price you believe is too low.

10-5c Strategies for Investing in Securities

There are several strategies you can use to guide your investment decisions. We'll provide an overview of the more common approaches, but none of these approaches is foolproof—alas, there is no known strategy that is guaranteed to earn you millions.

Investing for Income Some investors focus on buying bonds and preferred stocks in order to generate a steady, predictable flow of income. This approach is popular with retirees who want to supplement their retirement income. But the return on such low-risk securities is relatively low, and their market value seldom increases much over time. Thus, it probably isn't the best strategy for younger investors who are trying to grow their wealth.

Market Timing Investors who rely on *market timing* use a variety of analytical techniques to try to predict when prices of specific stocks are likely to rise and fall. Market timers try to make quick gains by buying low and selling high over a relatively short time horizon.

The problem with market timing is that so many factors can influence stock prices—some of them random in nature—that it's tough to consistently identify the timing and direction of changes in stock prices. Market timing also requires investors to make frequent trades. Given the commissions paid on trades and the taxes incurred on short-term capital gains, this approach may do a better job of enriching the broker than enriching the trader!

Value Investing Investors who favor *value investing* try to find stocks that are undervalued in the market. They believe that the market price will rise over time to reflect its true value, thus generating a capital gain. This approach requires a lot of research to identify discrepancies between a company's true (or intrinsic) value and its current market price.

The drawback with value investing is that you are one of thousands of investors all trying to do the same thing, so the competition to locate undervalued stocks is intense. Unless you're among the first to discover a good value, the investors who beat you to it will rush to buy up the stock, increasing demand and driving up the stock's price so that it is no longer undervalued.

Investing for Growth Investors who focus on growth look for companies that have the potential to grow much faster than average for a sustained period of time, which they believe will lead to a steady (and sometimes spectacular) rise in the stock's price. Investors using this strategy often invest in stocks of relatively new companies with innovative products in a hot sector of the economy.

Investing for growth entails a lot of risk. Small new companies don't have an established track record. And rapidly expanding industries tend to attract a lot of start-up companies, so competition can be intense. Finally, given the rapid pace of technological change, today's hot prospects may soon be dethroned by the next big thing. It's hard to predict which firms will be winners; even experts often make the wrong choice.

Buying and Holding If you're a patient person with steady nerves, a buy-and-hold approach might appeal to you. This strategy involves purchasing a diversified set of securities and holding them for a long period of time. Buy-and-hold investors put their faith in the ability of the *overall market* to continue the long-run upward trend it has exhibited throughout its history. One way that many buy-and-hold investors do this is by investing in index mutual funds and ETFs. The buy-and-hold strategy seldom allows investors to "get rich quick," but it usually results in a solid financial return over the long haul.

Obviously, the buy-and-hold strategy will work only if you can afford to leave your money invested for a long time. When the stock market takes a dive, it can sometimes take years for stocks to recover and start to show solid returns. Some people who think they're comfortable with a buy-and-hold strategy end up getting "happy feet" after a few weeks of declining stock prices. They panic and sell off their stocks at exactly the wrong time, locking in big losses. For the buy-and-hold strategy to work, you've got to have the patience—and mental toughness—to ride out short-term downturns in the market.

10-6 Keeping Tabs on the Market

Once you've begun to invest in securities, you'll want to keep track of how your investments are doing. Using the Internet, you can easily find information about both general market trends and the performance of specific securities.

10-6a Stock Indices: Tracking the Trends

One of the most common ways to track general market conditions and trends is to follow what's happening to various stock indices. A **stock index** tracks the prices of a large group of stocks that meet certain defined criteria. Many investors like to compare how the stocks in their own portfolio compare to the performance of these broad indices. Two of the best-known indices are the Dow Jones Industrial Average and the S&P 500.

- The **Dow Jones Industrial Average (DJIA)**: Often called just "the Dow," this is the most widely followed stock index. The Dow is based on the adjusted average price of 30 stocks picked by the editors of *The Wall Street Journal*. All of the Dow firms are large, well-established corporations, such as American Express, General Electric, Coca-Cola, Hewlett-Packard, and Disney.

- The **Standard & Poor's 500**: With 500 stocks instead of just 30, the S&P 500 is a much broader index than the DJIA. Still, like the Dow, all of the companies included in the S&P 500 are large, well-established American corporations.

Exhibit 10.2 identifies several other well-known indices, including some that track prices of stocks in foreign securities markets.

10-6b Tracking the Performance of Specific Securities

Many financial websites offer detailed stock quotes that provide the current price of a company's stock and a wealth of related information. To check out a specific stock, you simply type its *stock symbol*—a short combination of letters that uniquely identifies a corporate security—into a "Get Quote" box. (Most sites have a lookup feature that finds the symbol if you type in the company's name.)

Exhibit 10.3 illustrates the information a popular financial website, Yahoo! Finance (http://finance.yahoo.com/), provides about Procter & Gamble's common stock. Some of the key figures reported for Procter & Gamble include:

- *Last trade*: The price of Procter & Gamble's common stock for the most recent trade was $62.76.

- *Change*: The last trade of Procter & Gamble's stock was $0.05 higher than the closing price for the stock on the previous day.

- *Bid and Ask*: The highest price currently offered (bid) to buy Procter & Gamble stock is $62.80 for 100 shares. The lowest price currently offered (asked) to sell the stock is $62.97 for 100 shares.

- *Day's range*: The highest price for the stock during the day was $62.77, and the lowest price was $62.21.

- *52-Week range*: The highest price for Procter & Gamble stock over the previous 52 weeks was $67.95, while its lowest price was $57.56.

- *Volume*: 7,814,492 shares of the stock have been traded up to this point in the current trading session.

- *Market Cap*: The total market value of all shares of Procter & Gamble common stock outstanding was $171.97 billion. This is found by multiplying the price per share times the number of shares of common stock outstanding.

stock index A statistic that tracks how the prices of a specific set of stocks have changed.

Dow Jones Industrial Average An index that tracks stock prices of thirty large, well-known U.S. corporations.

Standard & Poor's 500 A stock index based on prices of 500 major U.S. corporations in a variety of industries and market sectors.

Exhibit 10.2 Major Stock Price Indices

INDEX	WHAT IT TRACKS
NASDAQ COMPOSITE	All of the domestic and foreign common stocks traded on the NASDAQ exchange.
WILSHIRE 5000	Stock prices of all U.S. corporations with actively traded stock. Despite the 5000 in its name, this index actually includes well over 6000 stocks. (The exact number changes frequently.)
RUSSELL 2000	Stock prices of 2000 relatively small but actively traded U.S. corporations.
FTSE 100	Stock prices of 100 of the largest and most actively traded companies listed on the London Stock Exchange.
NIKKEI 225	Stock prices of 225 of the largest and most actively traded companies listed on the Tokyo Stock Exchange.
SSE COMPOSITE	Stock prices of all stocks listed on the Shanghai Stock Exchange.

© Cengage Learning 2013

Exhibit 10.3 Yahoo! Finance Quote for a Stock

Procter & Gamble Co. Common St (NYSE: PG)
Real-time 62.60 ↓ .10 (−0.2%) 3:00 PM EDT

Last Trade:	62.59	Day's Range:	62.21 − 62.77
Trade Time:	2:59 PM EDT	52wk Range:	57.56 − 67.95
Change:	↑0.22 (0.35%)	Volume:	7,814,492
Prev Close:	62.54	Avg Vol (3m):	10,581,800
Open:	62.50	Market Cap:	171.97B
Bid:	62.80 x 100	P/E (ttm):	19.24
Ask:	62.97 x 100	EPS (ttm):	3.26
1y Target Est:	71.12	Div & Yield:	2.25 (3.60%)

Source: Yahoo! Finance stock quote accessed June 12, 2012. Reproduced with permission of Yahoo! Inc. YAHOO! and the YAHOO! logo are registered trademarks of Yahoo! Inc.

○ *P/E*: The price-to-earnings ratio is found by dividing the stock's price per share by its earnings per share. In general, a higher P/E ratio means investors expect a greater growth in earnings over time.

○ *EPS (earnings per share)*: Procter & Gamble earned $3.26 per share of common stock outstanding. EPS is computed by dividing the net income available to common stockholders by the number of shares of common stock outstanding.

○ *Div & Yield*: The sum of dividends paid by Procter & Gamble over the past 12 months was $2.25 per share. Yield is found by dividing the dividend per share by the previous day's price per share. It tells us that at that price the dividend paid by Procter & Gamble represented a 3.60% return to the investor. (But since the total return to stockholders may also include a capital gain or loss, this yield doesn't tell us the whole story.)

Financial websites also provide information about other types of securities such as mutual funds, ETFs, and bonds.

THE BIG PICTURE

Many different organizations participate in financial markets, including banks, finance companies, securities brokers and dealers, investment banks and institutional investors such as mutual funds, insurance companies, and pension funds. Although they differ in their functions, each of these participants helps financial markets achieve their primary purpose of channeling funds from savers to borrowers.

In this chapter, we focused on one particular type of financial market, namely the market for financial securities. The financial capital that corporations raise when they issue stocks and bonds in these markets is critical to every functional area of their operations. Without these funds, the marketing department would lack the resources needed to develop new products, information technology professionals would be unable to update hardware and software, and operations managers would be unable to acquire the machinery and equipment needed to produce the goods and services the company sells to earn its profits.

On the other side of these markets, investors who buy corporate securities do so to acquire assets that they believe will help them achieve their own financial goals. But investing in securities involves risk. Over any short-run time period, there is simply no guarantee that stocks and bonds will provide investors with the returns they expect. The good news—at least if you plan to invest—is that history shows that, over the long run, the return on these securities is positive. Given enough time and patience, investing in stocks and other securities is likely to result in a substantial increase in wealth.

Financial markets offer employment opportunities in a wide range of occupations.

Securities brokers advise clients on appropriate investments based on their needs and financial ability. When a client makes an investment decision, the broker electronically sends the order to the floor of the securities exchange to complete the transaction.

Brokerage firms normally require brokers to have a minimum of a bachelor's degree in business, finance, accounting, or economics. In addition, brokers must register with the Financial Industry Regulatory Authority (FINRA). Before they can register, they must be an employee of a registered brokerage firm for at least four months and pass a rigorous exam administered by FINRA.

Brokers earn most of their income in the form of commissions based on the amount of stocks, bonds, and other securities they trade for their clients. The average annual income of brokers in 2010 was $70,190. The BLS projects that over the next several years, job opportunities for brokers will grow about as fast as the average for all occupations.[17a]

Financial analysts assess the performance of stocks, bonds, commodities, and other types of investments and make recommendations about investments. They normally work for banks, pension funds, insurance companies, mutual funds, and securities firms.

Most firms require financial analysts to have a bachelor's degree in finance, economics, or statistics; large firms strongly prefer a master's degree in one of these fields. Licensure is sometimes required, but the type of license (if any) depends on the specific job.

Financial analysts are well paid; their average income in 2010 was $74,350 (a figure that doesn't include bonuses). The BLS projects that job growth for this profession will be faster than average for the next several years. However, the BLS also projects that competition for these jobs will be intense.[18]

CAREERS IN FINANCIAL MARKETS

What *else?*
RIP & REVIEW CARDS IN THE BACK
and visit www.cengagebrain.com!

11
Marketing:
Building Profitable Customer Connections

LEARNING OBJECTIVES
After studying this chapter, you will be able to:

11-1 Discuss the objectives, the process, and the scope of marketing

11-2 Identify the role of the customer in marketing

11-3 Explain each element of marketing strategy

11-4 Describe the consumer and business decision-making process

11-5 Discuss the key elements of marketing research

11-6 Explain the roles of social responsibility and technology in marketing

> "MAKE THE
> *CUSTOMER*
> THE HERO
> OF YOUR STORY."
>
> — Ann Hadley, Chief Content Officer,
> MarketingProfs

11-1 Marketing: Getting Value by Giving Value

What comes to mind when you hear the term **marketing**? Most people think of the radio ad they heard this morning, or the billboard they saw while driving to school. But advertising is only a small part of marketing; the whole story is much bigger. The American Marketing Association defines marketing as *the activity, set of institutions, and processes for creating, communicating, delivering, and exchanging offerings that have value for customers, clients, partners, and society at large.*

The ultimate benefit that most businesses seek from marketing is long-term profitability. But attaining this benefit is impossible without first delivering value to customers and other stakeholders. A successful marketer delivers value by filling customer needs in ways that exceed their expectations. As a result, you get sales today and sales tomorrow and sales the next day, which—across the days and months and years—can translate into long-term profitability. Alice Foote MacDougall, a successful entrepreneur in the 1920s, understood this thinking early on: "In business you get what you want by giving other people what they want." **Utility** is the ability of goods and services to satisfy these wants. And since there is a wide range of wants, products can provide utility in a number of different ways:

➲ *Form utility* satisfies wants by converting inputs into a finished form. Clearly, the vast majority of products provide some kind of form utility. For example, Subway slaps together bread, meat, veggies, and condiments into delicious sandwiches, and UGG Australia stretches, treats, and sews sheepskins into comfortable, stylish boots.

➲ *Time utility* satisfies wants by providing goods and services at a convenient time for customers. For example, UPS offers next day delivery, LensCrafters makes eyeglasses within about an hour, 7-Eleven opens early and closes late, and most fast-food restaurants offer 24-hour drive through windows.

➲ *Place utility* satisfies wants by providing goods and services at a convenient place for customers. For example, ATMs offer banking services in many large supermarkets, Starbucks serves coffee in many office buildings, and vending machines refuel tired students on virtually every college campus.

➲ *Ownership utility* satisfies wants by smoothly transferring ownership of goods and services from seller to buyer. Virtually every product provides some degree of ownership utility, but some offer more than others. Apple, for example, has created a hassle-free purchase process that customers can follow by phone, by computer, and in person.

Satisfying customer wants—in a way that exceeds expectations—is a job that never ends. Jay Levinson, a recognized expert in breakthrough marketing, comments, "Marketing is … a process. You improve it, perfect it, change it, even pause it. But you never stop it completely."

11-1a The Scope of Marketing: It's Everywhere!

For many years, businesspeople have actively applied the principles of marketing to goods and services that range from cars, to fast food, to liquor, to computers, to movies. But within the past decade or two, other organizations have successfully adopted marketing strategies and tactics to further their goals.

Nonprofit organizations—in both the private and public sectors—play a significant role in our economy, employing more people than the federal government and all 50 state governments combined (not to mention an army of volunteers!). These organizations use marketing, sometimes quite assertively, to achieve their

marketing An organizational function and a set of processes for creating, communicating, and delivering value to customers and for managing customer relationships in ways that benefit the organization and its stakeholders.

utility The ability of goods and services to satisfy consumer "wants."

objectives. The U.S. Army's marketing communications budget, for example, sometimes approaches as much as $200 million per year. Your own college probably markets itself to both prospective students and potential alumni donors. Private-sector nonprofit organizations also use marketing strategies for everything from marshalling Girl Scout leaders for kids, to boosting attendance at the local zoo, to planning cultural events.[1]

Nonprofit organizations play a pivotal role in the expansion of marketing across our economy to include people, places, events, and ideas. But for-profit enterprises have also begun to apply marketing strategies and tactics beyond simply goods and services.

The city of Las Vegas and many of its individual hotels do an excellent job with place marketing.

© Rolf_52/Shutterstock.com

- **People Marketing:** Sports, politics, and art dominate this category, but even some businesspeople merit mentioning. Top banking executives, for instance, took a beating from a marketing standpoint during the financial meltdown at the end of 2008. Also in 2008, President Barack Obama was named Ad Age Marketer of the Year, edging out powerhouse consumer brands that were also on the short list, such as Apple, Nike, and Coors. He became a living symbol of change in the minds of his supporters. Countless entertainers and athletes have used people marketing to their advantage as well. Consider, for example, Kim Kardashian, who appeared to build her career on promotion alone. In fact, as you pursue your personal goals—whether you seek a new job or a Friday night date—people marketing principles can help you achieve your objective. Start by figuring out what your "customer" needs, and then ensure that your "product" (you!) delivers above and beyond expectations.[2]

- **Place Marketing:** This category involves drawing people to a particular place. Cities and states use place marketing to attract businesses. Delaware, for instance, the second-smallest state in the Union, is home to more than half of the Fortune 500 firms because it deliberately developed a range of advantages for corporations. But more visibly, cities, states, and nations use place marketing to attract tourists. Thanks to powerful place marketing, most people have probably heard that "What happens in Vegas stays in Vegas." In late 2008, Las Vegas shelved the high-rolling campaign in favor of a more "recession-proof," but less successful strategy: the "Take a Break USA" campaign. By late 2009, Vegas had reverted to the "What Happens…" campaign that fueled visitors since its launch in 2003.[3]

- **Event Marketing:** This category includes marketing—or sponsoring—athletic, cultural, or charitable events. Partnerships between the public and private sectors are increasingly common. Examples include the Olympics, the Super Bowl, and Rapper Jay-Z's 2012 concert to benefit the Shawn Carter Scholarship Foundation, which helps low-income students cover college costs.

- **Idea Marketing:** A whole range of public and private organizations market ideas that are meant to change how people think or act. Recycle, don't drink and drive, buckle your seatbelt, support our political party, donate blood, and don't smoke are all examples of popular causes. Often, idea marketing and event marketing are combined, as we see in the annual Avon

Walk for Breast Cancer. The planners actively market the idea of annual mammograms, as they solicit contributions for breast cancer research and participation in the event itself.

11-1b The Evolution of Marketing: From the Product to the Customer

The current approach to marketing evolved through a number of overlapping stages, as you'll see in Exhibit 11.1. But as you read about these eras, keep in mind that some businesses have remained lodged—with varying degrees of success—in the thinking of a past era.

Production Era Marketing didn't always begin with the customer. In fact, in the early 1900s, the customer was practically a joke. Henry Ford summed up the prevailing mindset when he reportedly said "You can have your Model T in any color you want as long as it's black." This attitude made sense from a historical perspective, since consumers didn't have the overwhelming number of choices that are currently available; most products were purchased as soon as they were produced and distributed to consumers. In this context, the top business priority was to produce large quantities of goods as efficiently as possible.

Selling Era By the 1920s, production capacity had increased dramatically. For the first time, supply in many categories exceeded demand, which caused the emergence of the hard sell. The selling focus gained momentum in the 1930s and 1940s, when the Depression and World War II made consumers even more reluctant to part with their limited money.

Marketing Era The landscape changed dramatically in the 1950s. Many factories that had churned out military supplies converted to consumer production, flooding the market with choices in virtually every product category. An era of relative peace and prosperity emerged, and—as soldiers returned from World War II—marriage and birthrates soared. To compete for the consumer's dollar, marketers attempted to provide goods and services that met customer needs better than anything else on the market. As a result, the marketing concept materialized in the 1950s. The **marketing concept** is a philosophy that makes customer satisfaction—now and in the future—the central focus of the entire organization. Companies that embrace this philosophy strive to delight customers, integrating this goal into all business activities. The marketing concept holds that delivering unmatched value to customers is the only effective way to achieve long-term profitability.

Relationship Era The marketing concept has gathered momentum across the economy, leading to the current era, unfolding over the last decade, which zeros in on long-term customer relationships. Acquiring a new customer can cost five times more than keeping an existing customer. Retaining your current customers—and getting them to spend additional dollars—is clearly cost-effective. Moreover, satisfied customers can develop into advocates for your business, becoming powerful generators of positive "word-of-mouth."

marketing concept A business philosophy that makes customer satisfaction—now and in the future—the central focus of the entire organization.

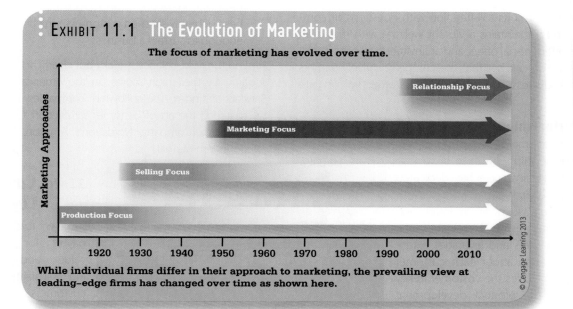

EXHIBIT 11.1   The Evolution of Marketing

The focus of marketing has evolved over time.

Marketing Approaches

Relationship Focus

Marketing Focus

Selling Focus

Production Focus

1920   1930   1940   1950   1960   1970   1980   1990   2000   2010

© Cengage Learning 2013

While individual firms differ in their approach to marketing, the prevailing view at leading-edge firms has changed over time as shown here.

11-2 The Customer: Front and Center

11-2a Customer Relationship Management (CRM)

Customer relationship management (CRM) is the centerpiece of successful, twenty-first century marketing. Broadly defined, CRM is the ongoing process of acquiring, maintaining, and growing profitable customer relationships by delivering unmatched value. CRM works best when marketers combine marketing communication with one-on-one personalization. Amazon is a champion player at CRM, greeting customers by name, recommending specific products, and providing streamlined checkout. Clearly, information is an integral part of this process—you simply can't do CRM without collecting, managing, and applying the right data at the right time for the right person (and every repeat customer is the "right person"!).

Limited Relationships The scope of your relationships will depend not just on the data you gather but also on your industry. Colgate-Palmolive, for example, can't forge a close personal bond with every person who buys a bar of Irish Spring soap. However, the company does invite customers to call its toll-free line with questions or comments, and it maintains a vibrant website with music, an e-newsletter, special offers, and an invitation to contact the company. You can bet that the company actively gathers data and pursues a connection with customers who initiate contact.

Full Partnerships If you have a high-ticket product and a smaller customer base, you're much more likely to pursue a full partnership with each of your key clients. Colgate-Palmolive, for instance, has dedicated customer service teams working with key accounts such as Walmart and Costco. With a full partnership, the marketer gathers and leverages extensive information about each customer and often includes the customer in key aspects of the product development process.

Value You know you've delivered **value** when your customers believe that your product has a better relationship between the cost and the benefits than any competitor. By this definition, low cost does not always mean high value. In fact, a recent survey suggests that loyal customers are often willing to pay *more* for their products rather than switch to lower-cost competitors. Apple provides a clear example. We probably all know at least a handful of Apple fanatics who gladly pay far more for their PowerBooks (or iPhones or iPads) than they would pay for a competing product.

11-2b Perceived Value Versus Actual Value

The operative idea here is *perceived*. Simply creating value isn't enough; you also must help customers believe that your product is uniquely qualified to meet their needs. This becomes a particular challenge when you're a new business competing against a market leader with disproportionately strong perceived value.

11-2c Customer Satisfaction

You know you've satisfied your customers when you deliver perceived value above and beyond their expectations. But achieving **customer satisfaction** can be tricky. Less savvy marketers frequently fall into one of two traps:

- The first trap is overpromising. Even if you deliver more value than anyone else, your customers will be disappointed if your product falls short of overly high expectations. The messages that you send regarding your product influence expectations—keep them real!

- The second trap is underpromising. If you don't set expectations high enough, too few customers will be willing to try your product. The result will be a tiny base of highly satisfied customers, which usually isn't enough to sustain a business.

Finding the right balance is tricky but clearly not impossible. Judging by their high scores on the American Customer Satisfaction Index, the following companies come close to mastering the art of customer satisfaction: Costco, State Farm, Clorox Company, Nordstrom, Amazon, Lexus, and Northwestern Mutual.[4]

11-2d Customer Loyalty

Customer loyalty is the payoff for delivering value and generating satisfaction. Loyal customers purchase from you again and again—and they sometimes even pay more for your product. They forgive your mistakes. They provide valuable feedback. They may require less service. They refer their friends (and sometimes even strangers). Moreover, studying your loyal customers can give you a competitive edge for acquiring new ones, since people with a similar profile would likely be a great fit for your products.[5]

11-3 Marketing Strategy: Where Are You Going, and How Will You Get There?

In marketing terms, the questions become: Who is your target audience, and how will you reach them? Many successful firms answer this question by developing a formal **marketing plan**, updated on a yearly basis; other firms handle their planning on a more informal basis. But regardless of the specific approach, the first step in planning your marketing strategy should be to determine where to target your efforts. Who are those people who are most likely to buy your products? The first step is **market segmentation**—dividing your marketing into groups of people, or segments, that are similar to one another and different from everyone else. One or more of these segments will be your target market. Once you've identified your target market, your next step is to determine how you can best use marketing tools to reach them. And finally, you need to anticipate and respond to changes in the external environment. This section will define target market, explain market segmentation, introduce the marketing mix, and review the key factors in the marketing environment. Taken together, these elements will shape an effective marketing strategy, as shown in Exhibit 11.2.

The marketer creates the marketing mix but responds to the marketing environment with a single-minded focus on the target market.

11-3a Target Market

Your **target market** is the group of people who are most likely to buy your product. This is where you should concentrate your marketing efforts. But why not target your efforts toward everyone? After all, even if most middle-aged moms wouldn't buy purple polka-dotted miniskirts, an adventurous few just might do it. Well, you can always hope for the adventurous few, but virtually every business has limited resources, and marketing toward the people who are most likely to buy your flamboyant minis—say,

teenage girls—will maximize the impact of each dollar you spend. A well-chosen target market embodies the following characteristics:

- ➲ Size: There must be enough people in your target group to support a business.

- ➲ Profitability: The people must be willing and able to spend more than the cost of producing and marketing your product.

- ➲ Accessibility: Your target must be reachable through channels that your business can afford.

- ➲ Limited competition: Look for markets with limited competition; a crowded market is much tougher to crack.

11-3b Consumer Markets Versus Business Markets

Consumer marketers (B2C) direct their efforts to people who are buying products for personal consumption (e.g., candy bars, shampoo, and clothing), whereas **business marketers (B2B)** direct their efforts to customers who are

marketing plan A formal document that defines marketing objectives and the specific strategies for achieving those objectives.

market segmentation Dividing potential customers into groups of similar people, or segments.

target market The group of people who are most likely to buy a particular product.

consumer marketers (also known as business-to-consumer or B2C) Marketers who direct their efforts toward people who are buying products for personal consumption.

business marketers (also known as business-to-business or B2B) Marketers who direct their efforts toward people who are buying products to use either directly or indirectly to produce other products.

EXHIBIT **11.2** Marketing Strategy

Competitive

Social/Cultural

Product Strategy

Pricing Strategy

Economic

Promotion Strategy

TARGET MARKET

Distribution Strategy

Technological

Political/Legal

© Cengage Learning 2013

buying products to use either directly or indirectly to produce other products (e.g., lumber, insulation, and robots). But keep in mind that the distinction between the market categories is not in the products themselves; rather, it lies in how the buyer will use the product. For instance, shoes that you buy for yourself are clearly a consumer product, but shoes that a bowling alley buys for its customers are a business product. Similarly, a computer that you buy for yourself is a consumer product, but a computer that your school buys for the computer lab is a business product. Both B2C and B2B marketers need to choose the best target, but they tend to follow slightly different approaches.

11-3c Consumer Market Segmentation

Choosing the best target market (or markets) for your product begins with dividing your market into segments, or groups of people who have similar characteristics. But people can be similar in a number of different ways, so, not surprisingly, marketers have several options for segmenting potential consumers.

Demographic B2C **demographic segmentation** refers to dividing the market based on measurable characteristics about people such as age, income, ethnicity, and gender. Demographics are a vital starting point for most marketers. Chapstick, for instance, targets young women with the Shimmer version of its lip balm, and Chevy Camaro targets young men with money. Sometimes the demographic makeup of a given market is tough to discern; African American artists, for instance, create the bulk of rap music, yet Caucasian suburban males form the bulk of the rap music market.

Geographic B2C **geographic segmentation** refers to dividing the market based on where consumers live. This process can incorporate countries, or cities, or population density as key factors. For instance, Ford Expedition does not concentrate on European markets, where tiny, winding streets and nonexistent parking are common in many cities. Cosmetic surgeons tend to market their services more heavily in urban rather than rural areas. And finding the perfect surfboard is easy in Hawaii but more challenging in South Dakota.

Tony Hsieh, CEO of Zappos.com, has tapped into the stylish, fun-loving mind-set of his target customers.

© 2012 Zappos.com, Inc. or its affiliates.

Psychographic B2C **psychographic segmentation** refers to dividing the market based on consumer attitudes, interests, values, and lifestyles. Toyota Prius, for instance, targets consumers who care about protecting the environment. A number of companies have found a highly profitable niche providing upscale wilderness experiences for people who seek all the pleasure with none of the pain (you enjoy the great outdoors, while someone else lugs your gear, pours your wine, slices your goat cheese, and inflates your extra-comfy air mattress). Both magazine racks and the Internet are filled with products geared toward psychographic segments, including adventure travel sites, Adventure Center .com, shoe-selling mega site Zappos.com, and business and financial powerhouse WallStreetJournal.com. NOTE: Marketers typically use psychographics to complement other segmentation approaches rather than to provide the core definition.

Behavioral B2C **behavioral segmentation** refers to dividing the market based on how people behave toward various products. This category includes both the benefits that consumers seek from products and how consumers use the product. The Neutrogena Corporation, for example, built a multimillion-dollar hair care business by targeting consumers who wanted an occasional break from their favorite shampoo. Countless products such as Miller Lite actively target the low-carbohydrate consumer. But perhaps the most common type of behavioral segmentation is based on usage patterns. Fast-food restaurants, for instance, actively target heavy users (who, ironically, tend to be slender): young men in their 20s and 30s. This group consumes about 17% of their total calories from fast food, compared to 12% for adults in general. Understanding the usage patterns of your customer base gives you the option of either focusing on your core users or trying to pull light users into your core market.

11-3d Business Market Segmentation

B2B marketers typically follow a similar process in segmenting their markets, but they use slightly different categories:

Geographic B2B geographic segmentation refers to dividing the market based on the concentration of customers. Many industries tend to be highly clustered in certain areas, such as technology in California, and auto suppliers in the "auto corridor" that stretches south from Michigan to Tennessee. Geographic segmentation, of course, is especially common on an international basis, where variables such as language, culture, income, and regulatory differences can play crucial roles.

Customer-Based B2B customer-based segmentation refers to dividing the market based on the characteristics of customers. This approach includes a range of possibilities. Some B2B marketers segment based on customer size. Others segment based on customer type. Johnson & Johnson, for example, has a group of salespeople dedicated exclusively to retail accounts such as Target and Publix, while other salespeople focus solely on motivating doctors to recommend their products. Other potential B2B markets include institutions—schools and hospitals, for instance, are key segments for Heinz Ketchup—and the government.

Product-Use–Based B2B product-use–based segmentation refers to dividing the market based on how customers will use the product. Small and midsized companies find this strategy especially helpful in narrowing their target markets. Possibilities include the ability to support certain software packages or production systems or the desire to serve certain customer groups, such as long-distance

© David P. Smith/Shutterstock.com

Color me... hungry?!

Have you ever noticed that fast-food restaurants typically feature vivid shades of red, yellow, and orange in both their logos and their décor? Think McDonald's, KFC, Burger King, and Pizza Hut. The color choice is no coincidence.

Marketing researchers have learned that consumers in the United States associate red with energy, passion, and speed. Yellow suggests happiness and warmth, while orange suggests playfulness, affordability, and fun. A simulated cocktail party study found that partygoers in red rooms reported feeling hungrier and thirstier than others, and guests in yellow rooms ate twice as much as others. The implication? Surrounding customers with red, yellow, and orange encourages them to eat a lot quickly and leave, which aligns nicely with the goals of most fast-food chains.

Color psychology is a powerful—though often overlooked—marketing tool. Colors evoke emotions and trigger specific behaviors, which can dramatically influence how people buy your product. Here is a list of common colors and some of their associations in U.S. mainstream culture.

Keep in mind that while some color associations are universal, others can differ significantly among cultures. White, for instance, signifies death and mourning in Chinese culture, while purple represents death in Brazil.

As a marketer, your goal should be to align your color choice with the perceptions of your target market and the features of your product. The result should be more green for your bottom line![6]

RED — Love, passion, warmth, food, excitement, action, danger, need to stop

BLUE — Power, trustworthiness, calm, success, seriousness, boredom

GREEN — Money, nature, health, healing, decay, illness

ORANGE — Playfulness, affordability, youth, fun, low quality, cheap

PURPLE — Royalty, luxury, dignity, spirituality, nightmares, craziness

WHITE — Purity, innocence, simplicity, mildness

BLACK — Sophistication, elegance, seriousness, sexuality, mystery, evil truckers or restaurants that deliver food.

11-3e The Marketing Mix

Once you've clearly defined your target market, your next challenge is to develop compelling strategies for product, price, distribution, and promotion. The blending of these elements becomes your **marketing mix**, as shown below in Exhibit 11.3.

⊙ **Product Strategy:** Your product involves far more than simply a tangible good or a specific service. Product strategy decisions range from brand name, to product image, to package design, to customer service, to guarantees, to new product development, and more. Designing the best product clearly begins with understanding the needs of your target market.

⊙ **Pricing Strategy:** Pricing is a challenging area of the marketing mix. To deliver customer value, your prices must be fair, relative to the benefits of your product. Other factors include competition, regulation, and public opinion. Your product category plays a critical role as well. A low-cost desk, for instance, might be appealing, but who would want discount-priced knee surgery?

⊙ **Distribution Strategy:** The goal is to deliver your product to the right people, in the right quantities, at the right time, in the right place. The key decisions include shipping, warehousing, and selling outlets (e.g., the

"Give them quality — That's the best kind of advertising."

—Milton Hershey, Founder, The Hershey Chocolate Company

Web versus network marketing versus brick-and-mortar stores). The implications of these decisions for product image and customer satisfaction can be significant.

⊙ **Promotion Strategy:** Promotion includes all of the ways that marketers communicate about their products. The list of possibilities is long and growing, especially as the Internet continues to evolve at breakneck speed. Key elements today include advertising, personal selling, sales promotion, public relations, word-of-mouth, and product placement. Successful promotional strategies typically evolve in response to both customer needs and competition. A number of innovative companies are even inviting their customers to participate in creating their advertising through venues such as YouTube. Check out Exhibit 11.4 to see how easily you can analyze promotional strategies.

11-3f The Global Marketing Mix

As you decide to enter foreign markets, you'll need to reevaluate your marketing mix for each new country. Should it change? If so, how should it change? Many business goods simply don't require much change in the marketing mix, since their success isn't dependent on culture. Examples include heavy machinery, cement, and farming equipment. Consumer products, however, often require completely new marketing mixes to effectively reach their consumers.

Nike's approach to marketing in China offers an interesting example of how one firm managed the complex process of building a successful business in a foreign market. When Nike first entered China in the 1990s, the

EXHIBIT 11.3 Marketing Mix

Product Strategy

Pricing Strategy

Promotion Strategy

Distribution Strategy

© Cengage Learning 2013

company seemed to face an insurmountable challenge: not only did a pair of Nike sneakers cost twice the Chinese average monthly salary, but most Chinese just didn't play sports, according to Terry Rhoads, then director of Nike sports marketing. So he boldly set out to change that. Rhoads created a Nike high-school basketball league, which has since spread to 17 cities. To loosen up fans, he blasted canned cheering during games and arranged for national TV coverage of the finals. He even leveraged connections with the NBA to bring Michael Jordan for visits.

The gamble quickly paid off, as the Chinese middle class emerged—along with more individualistic values, which are a strong fit with the Nike ethos. By 2001, Nike had dubbed its marketing approach "hip hoop," which they described as an effort to "connect Nike with a creative lifestyle." Sales in 2011 exceeded $2 billion, driven largely by basketball shoes. Nike currently strives to build current Chinese sales on its existing basketball fans by further developing an individual and team-sports culture. Nike executive Don Blair comments that, "China has one of the biggest populations who are tuned in to sports, but they aren't yet participants."[7]

11-3g The Marketing Environment

While marketers actively influence the elements of the marketing mix, they must anticipate and respond to the elements of the external environment, which they typically cannot control. **Environmental scanning** is a key tool; the goal is simply to continually collect information from sources that range from informal networks, to industry newsletters, to the general press, to customers, to suppliers, to the competition, among others. The key elements of the external environment include the following components:

Competitive The dynamic competitive environment probably affects marketers on a day-to-day basis more than any other element. Understanding the competitive environment often begins with analysis of **market share**, or the percentage of the marketplace that each firm controls. To avoid ambushes—and to uncover new opportunities—you must continually monitor how both dominant and emerging competitors handle each element of their marketing mix. And don't forget indirect competitors, who meet the same consumer needs as you but with a completely different product (e.g., Red Bull vs. 5-Hour Energy).

Economic The only certainty in the economic environment is change, but the timing of expansions and contractions is virtually impossible to predict. Your goal as a marketer is to identify and respond to changes as soon as possible, keeping in mind that a sharp eye sees opportunity even in economic downturns. For instance, affordable luxuries and do-it-yourself enterprises can thrive during recessions.

Social/Cultural The social/cultural element covers a vast array of factors, including lifestyle, customs, language, attitudes, interests, and population shifts. Trends can change rapidly, with a dramatic impact on marketing

environmental scanning The process of continually collecting information from the external marketing environment.

market share The percentage of a market controlled by a given marketer.

EXHIBIT 11.4 Analyzing Promotional Strategies

Who is the target audience for each of these ads? How does each ad position the product relative to the competition? Which strategy is most effective? Why?

FAMILY MISTAKES MINI'S TLC PACKAGE FOR ACTUAL TLC. FEELS A BIT SILLY. THE END.

IT'S A MINI ADVENTURE

the car in front is a TOYOTA

Fancy a breath of fresh air?

Image courtesy of The Advertising Archives

JUST BECAUSE THEY CAN... ...DOESN'T MEAN THEY SHOULD.

With every visit to the hospital, patients leave reams of personal information, sometimes multiple times. Most of us assume that information will remain private. But faced with an increasingly competitive healthcare market, a growing number of hospitals are giving patient records to marketing firms, which slice and dice the data, and even combine it with other data, to develop highly targeted marketing pieces, designed to "inform" potential patients—especially those who are likely to have high-paying health insurance—about specific services that may be relevant for them. Many of these pieces are quite successful. While hospitals may profit from offering cholesterol tests and mammograms, the big payoff comes later—in additional tests and procedures, including surgery. For instance, in 2010 and 2011, St. Anthony's Medical in St. Louis spent $25,000 on a targeted mailing to 40,000 women for mammogram screenings. The letters led 1,000 women to get the test, which generated $530,000 in revenue from screenings, biopsies, and other related services, she says.

Although somewhat unsettling, this kind of marketing is legal. According to Deven McGraw, director of the health privacy project at the Center for Democracy and Technology in Washington, federal law allows hospitals to use confidential medical records to keep patients informed about services that may help them. "You want health providers to communicate to patients about health options that may be beneficial," McGraw says. "But sometimes this is about generating business for a new piece of equipment that the hospital just bought." Doug Heller, executive director of Consumer Watchdog, furthers the criticism, saying, "When marketing is picking and choosing based on people's financial status, it is inherently discriminating against patients who have every right and need for medical information." Advocates argue that hospitals are only using completely legal strategies that sophisticated consumer product firms have used successfully for years.

What do YOU think?

- How do you feel about this kind of marketing? Does it seem fair? Ethical?
- Should hospitals market to everyone, regardless of their ability to pay? Why or why not?[8]

decisions. Anticipating and responding to trends can be especially important in industries such as entertainment, fashion, and technology. In late 2009, for instance, Facebook removed some key privacy controls from its News Feed. The social media giant did not anticipate the black eye it received from outraged consumers who believed that Facebook had violated their privacy. Facebook was also surprised that the privacy controls it implemented in May 2010, which required consumers to opt out of sharing, would not be enough to appease privacy advocates.[9]

Technological Changes in technology can be very visible to consumers (e.g., the introduction of the iPhone). However, technology often affects marketers in ways that are less directly visible. For example, technology allows mass customization of Levi's blue jeans at a reasonable price and facilitates just-in-time inventory management for countless companies that see the results in their bottom lines.

Political/Legal The political/legal area includes laws, regulations, and political climate. Most U.S. laws and regulations are clear (e.g., those declaring dry counties in certain states), but others are complex and evolving (e.g., qualifications for certain tax breaks). Political climate includes changing levels of governmental support for various business categories. Clearly, the political/legal issues affect heavily regulated sectors (e.g., telecommunications and pharmaceuticals) more than others.

11-3h The Global Marketing Environment

As the Internet has grown, the world market has become accessible to virtually every business. This boosts the importance of understanding each element of the marketing

© Yuri Arcurs/Shutterstock.com

environment—competitive, economic, social/cultural, technological, and political/legal—in each of your key markets. Among the biggest global challenges are researching opportunities in other countries and delivering your product to customers in other countries.

11-4 Customer Behavior: Decisions, Decisions, Decisions!

If successful marketing begins with the customer, then understanding the customer is critical. Why do people buy one product but not another? How do they use the products they buy? When do they get rid of them? Knowing the answers to these questions will clearly help you better meet customer needs.

11-4a Consumer Behavior

Consumer behavior refers specifically to how people act when they are buying products for their own personal consumption. The decisions they make often seem spontaneous (after all, how much thought do you give to buying a pack of gum?), but they often result from a complex set of influences, as shown in Exhibit 11.5.

Marketers, of course, add their own influence through the marketing mix. For instance, after smelling pretzels in the mall and tasting pretzel morsels from the sample tray, many of us would at least be tempted to cough up the cash for a hot, buttery pretzel of our own . . .

Exhibit 11.5 Elements That Influence the Consumer Decision-Making Process

INFLUENCE	DESCRIPTION
CULTURAL	*Culture:* The values, attitudes, and customs shared by members of a society *Subculture:* A smaller division of the broader culture *Social Class:* Societal position driven largely by income and occupation
SOCIAL	*Family:* A powerful force in consumption choices *Friends:* Another powerful force, especially for high-profile purchases *Reference Groups:* Groups that give consumers a point of comparison
PERSONAL	*Demographics:* Measurable characteristics such as age, gender, or income *Personality:* The mix of traits that determines who you are
PSYCHOLOGICAL	*Motivation:* Pressing needs that tend to generate action *Attitudes:* Lasting evaluations of (or feelings about) objects or ideas *Perceptions:* How people select, organize, and interpret information *Learning:* Changes in behavior based on experience

© Cengage Learning 2013

regardless of any other factors! Similarly, changes in the external environment—for example, a series of hurricanes in Florida—dramatically affect consumer decisions about items such as flashlights, batteries, and plywood.

All these forces shape consumer behavior in each step of the process regarding purchase decisions. Exhibit 11.6 shows how the consumer decision process works.

Clearly, marketing can influence the purchase decision every step of the way, from helping consumers identify needs (or problems), to resolving that awful feeling of **cognitive dissonance** (or kicking oneself) after a major purchase. Some marketers attempt to avoid cognitive dissonance altogether by developing specific programs to help customers validate their purchase choices. One example might be postpurchase mailings that highlight the accolades received by an expensive product.

But does every consumer go through every step of the process all the time? That's clearly not the case! People make low-involvement decisions (such as buying that pack of gum) according to habit ... or even just on a whim. But when the stakes are high—either financially or socially—most people move through the five steps of the classic decision-making process. For example, most of us wouldn't think of buying a car, a computer, or the "right" pair of blue jeans without stepping through the decision-making process.

11-4b Business Buyer Behavior

Business buyer behavior refers to how people act when they're buying products to use either directly or indirectly to produce other products (e.g., chemicals, copy paper, computer servers). Business buyers typically have purchasing training and apply rational criteria to their decision-making process. They usually buy according to purchase specifications and objective standards, with a minimum of personal judgment or whim. Often, business buyers are integrating input from a number of internal sources, based on a relatively formal process. And finally, business buyers tend to seek (and often secure) highly customized goods, services, and prices.

11-5 Marketing Research: So What Do They REALLY Think?

If marketing begins with the customer, marketing research is the foundation of success. **Marketing research** involves gathering, interpreting, and applying information to uncover opportunities and challenges. The goal, of course, is better marketing decisions: more value for consumers and more profits for businesses that deliver. Companies use marketing research to:

- Identify external opportunities and threats (from social trends to competition).
- Monitor and predict customer behavior.
- Evaluate and improve each area of the marketing mix.

11-5a Types of Data

There are two main categories of marketing research data—**secondary data** and **primary data**—each with its own set of benefits and drawbacks, as shown in Exhibit 11.7.

EXHIBIT 11.6 Consumer Decision Process

Need Recognition
Your best friend suddenly notices that she is the only person she knows who still wears high-rise blue jeans to class...problem alert!

Information Search
Horrified, your friend not only checks out your style but also notices what the cool girls on campus are wearing. AND she snitches your copy of *Cosmo* to leaf through the ads.

Evaluation of Alternatives
Your friend compares the prices and styles of the various brands of blue jeans that she identifies.

Purchase Decision
After a number of conversations, your friend finally decides to buy True Religion jeans for $215.

Postpurchase Behavior
Three days later, she begins to kick herself for spending so much money on jeans because she can no longer afford her daily Starbucks habit.

© Cengage Learning 2013

Ooops! What were they thinking?

"If you can't be a good example, then you'll just have to serve as a horrible warning."

Even the heavy hitters make marketing gaffes. Their biggest mistakes are often entertaining, but they also serve as a powerful warning to consult with the customer *before* taking action. A few amusing examples:

- ⊃ In 2011, Nivea ran a campaign called "Look Like You Give A Damn" for a men's line that featured sharply turned out guys chucking the remains of their former scruffy selves, with the tagline "Re-civilize yourself". One of the ads featured an image of a well-groomed Black man holding what is supposed to be his own severed head with an Afro and a beard, his "uncivilized" self. After outrage in the Black community, Nivea apologized and vowed never to run the ad again.

- ⊃ In 2007, Hershey's introduced Ice Breakers Pacs, nickel-sized dissolvable pouches with a powdered sweetener inside. But they discontinued production in early 2008, in response to concerns from police narcotics officers and other community leaders that the mints too closely resembled tiny heat-sealed bags used to sell powdered street drugs. Announcing that the candy would be discontinued, Hershey's CEO commented that the company was "sensitive to these concerns." Apparently they weren't sensitive soon enough.

- ⊃ In 2009, Tropicana introduced a new package for its premium orange juice. The redesign supplanted the longtime Tropicana brand symbol—an orange from which a straw protrudes—with a picture of a glass of orange juice. Consumers were outraged. They described the package as "ugly," "stupid," and "generic." One even asked, "Do any of these package design people actually shop for orange juice?" Deluged with negative feedback, the company scrapped the new packaging less than two months after they introduced it.

- ⊃ In 2011, Groupon ran a Super Bowl ad that featured Timothy Hutton talking about Tibet's human rights crisis and then pivoting blithely to chatter about a Groupon discount at a Tibetan restaurant. Following social media-driven backlash about the ad, Groupon's CEO apologized and took a pass on Super Bowl advertising in 2012.

These fiascos only highlight the importance of *marketing research*. But sometimes, of course, even research isn't enough to identify marketing issues before they hit. At that point, the priority should shift to dealing with the mistake openly, honestly, and quickly, which can help a company win the game, despite the gaffe.[10]

Clearly, it makes sense to gather secondary data before you invest in primary research. Look at your company's internal information. What does previous research say? What does the press say? What can you find on the Web? Once you've looked at the secondary research, you may find that primary research is unnecessary. But if not, your secondary research will guide your primary research and make it more focused and relevant, which ends up saving time and money.

Exhibit 11.7 Research Data Comparison

SECONDARY DATA:	PRIMARY DATA:
Existing data that marketers gather or purchase	New data that marketers compile for the first time
Tends to be lower cost	Tends to be more expensive
May not meet your specific needs	Customized to meet your needs
Frequently outdated	Fresh, new data
Available to your competitors	Proprietary—no one else has it
Examples: U.S. census, *The Wall Street Journal*, *Time* magazine, your product sales history	Examples: Your own surveys, focus groups, customer comments, mall interviews

© Cengage Learning 2013

observation
research Marketing
research that *does not*
require the researcher to
interact with the research
subject.

survey
research Marketing
research that requires the
researcher to interact with
the research subject.

11-5b Primary Research Tools

There are two basic categories of primary research: observation and survey. **Observation research** happens when the researcher *does not* directly interact with the research subject. The key advantage of watching versus asking is that what people actually *do* often differs from what they *say*—sometimes quite innocently. For instance, if an amusement park employee stands outside an attraction and records which way people turn when they exit, he may be conducting observation research to determine where to place a new lemonade stand. Watching would be better than asking because many people could not honestly say which way they'd likely turn. Examples of observation research include:

- Scanner data from retail sales
- Traffic counters to determine where to place billboards
- Garbage analysis to measure recycling compliance

Observation research can be both cheap and amazingly effective. A car dealership, for instance, can survey the preset radio stations on every car that comes in for service. That information helps them choose which stations to use for advertising. But the biggest downside of observation research is that it doesn't yield any information on consumer motivation—the reasons behind consumer decisions. The preset radio stations wouldn't matter, for example, if the bulk of drivers listen only to their iPods in the car.

Survey research happens when the researcher *does* interact with research subjects. The key advantage is that you can secure information about what people are thinking and feeling, beyond what you can observe. For example, a carmaker might observe that the majority of its purchasers are men. They could use this information to tailor their advertising to men, or they could do survey research and possibly learn that even though men do the actual purchasing, women often make the purchase decision ... a very different scenario! But the key downside of survey research is that many people aren't honest or accurate about their experiences, opinions, and motivations, which can make survey research quite misleading. Examples of survey research include:

- Telephone and online questionnaires
- Door-to-door interviews
- Mall-intercept interviews
- Focus groups
- Mail-in questionnaires

11-5c An International Perspective

Doing marketing research across multiple countries can be an overwhelming challenge. In parts of Latin America, for instance, many homes don't have telephone

"It ain't easy being green"

Consumer appetite for green products has increased significantly in the past year, according to findings from the annual ImagePower® Global Green Brands Study. Now more savvy about how green choices in personal care, food, and household products directly affect them and their families, global consumers are expanding their green purchase interest to higher-ticket items such as cars and technology. More than 60% of consumers globally want to buy from environmentally responsible companies.

1. Seventh Generation
2. Whole Foods
3. Tom's of Maine
4. Burt's Bees
5. Trader Joe's
6. The Walt Disney Company
7. S.C. Johnson
8. Dove
9. Apple
10. Starbucks, Microsoft (tied)

Packaging was of particular concern to U.S. consumers; 71% believe companies use too much material in product packaging—though only 34% say they consciously purchase products that use less packaging. In 2011, U.S. consumers ranked the above brands "greenest."

For the first time since the inception of the survey, the four brands perceived to be the greenest are "born green" companies, rather than mainstream companies with green add-on benefits. Delivering green benefits *and* performance—without a wallet-busting price—is a tough challenge that more and more marketers are racing to meet.[11]

connections, so the results from telephone surveys could be very misleading. Door-to-door tends to be a better approach. But in parts of the Middle East, researchers could be arrested for knocking on a stranger's door, especially if they aren't dressed according to local standards. Because of these kinds of issues, many companies hire research firms with a strong local presence (often based in-country) to handle their international marketing research projects.

"On average, consumer spending on goods and services accounts for around 70% of U.S. GDP."

—Robert Reich, economist

11-6 Social Responsibility and Technology: A Major Marketing Shift

Two key factors have had a dramatic impact on marketing in the past couple of decades: a surge in the social responsibility movement, and the dramatic emergence of the Internet and digital technology. This section will cover how each factor has influenced marketing.

11-6a Marketing and Society: It's Not Just About You!

Over the past couple of decades, the social responsibility movement has accelerated in the United States, demanding that marketers actively contribute to the needs of the broader community. Leading-edge marketers have responded by setting a higher standard in key areas such as environmentalism, abolishment of sweatshops, and involvement in the local community. Starbucks, Target, and General Electric, for instance, all publish corporate responsibility reports that evaluate the social impact of how the companies run their businesses, and all highlight their programs on their corporate websites.

Innovation: Unleashed!

In today's hyper-competitive marketplace, businesses must differentiate their products from an astonishing array of alternatives. While life-changing innovation is rare, many successful products simply provide a new twist on an existing product. Examples include Wish-Bone's salad dressing spritzers, Nike's air cushioning for athletic shoes, and Nabisco's 100 Calorie cookie packs.

To help you make those kinds of jumps, the game in this box uses rebus puzzles to stretch your creativity. Rebus puzzles present common words and phrases in novel orientation to each other. The goal is to determine the meaning. The puzzles are below, and the answers are at the bottom of the box.

ARREST YOU'RE	HISTORY HISTORY HISTORY	SK8 iiiiiiiiiiiiiiiiiii	print	BAN ANA	Shut Sit
funny funny words words words words	ST4ANCE	herring	MEREPEAT	Jack	Symphon

Answers: You're under arrest, too funny for words, history repeats itself, for instance, small print, repeat after me, red herring, skate on thin ice, banana split, Jack-in-the-Box, sit down and shut up, unfinished symphony

green marketing The development and promotion of products with ecological benefits.

mass customization The creation of products tailored for individual consumers on a mass basis.

Green Marketing Companies employ **green marketing** when they actively promote the ecological benefits of their products. Toyota has been especially successful promoting the green benefits of its Prius (although like all carmakers, Toyota has struggled during the global financial crisis and more recently, during the Japanese earthquake and tsunami). Its strategy highlights fuel economy and performance, implying that consumers can "go green" without making any real sacrifices. Environmentally friendly fashion offers another emerging example of green marketing. Over the past few years, a number of designers have rolled out their versions of upscale ecofashion. In addition to clothing made of organic cotton, recent entries include vegan stilettos with four-inch heels, bamboo dresses, biodegradable umbrellas, and solar-powered jackets. (These jackets feature solar cells, integrated into the collar, that collect solar energy and route it to charge devices.) Green marketing items are aimed at a growing number of consumers who make purchase decisions based (at least in part) on their convictions. But reaching these consumers may be an increasing challenge in tough economic times, when low prices trump all other considerations for a growing swath of the population.[12]

11-6b Technology and Marketing: Power to the People!

The emergence of the digital age has revolutionized every element of marketing. Perhaps the most dramatic change has been a shift in power from producers to customers. The Internet gives customers 24/7 access to information and product choices from all over the world. In response, competition has intensified as marketers strive to meet an increasingly high standard of value.

Just over 20% of people say they think most creatively in their cars, while 5% say they think most creatively in the shower, and—surprisingly—only 1% say they think most creatively while listening to music.

— M.I.T. Invention Index

But technology has also created opportunities for marketers. The Internet has opened the door for **mass customization**: creating products tailored for individual consumers on a mass basis. Using sophisticated data collection and management systems, marketers can now collect detailed information about each customer, which allows them to develop one-on-one relationships and to identify high-potential new customers. Through the Web, marketers can tap into (or even create) communities of users that yield valuable information about their goods and services. Technology also helps marketers lower costs, so they can deliver greater value to their customers.

The digital boom has also created an abundance of promotional opportunities as marketers reach out to consumers via new tools, such as interactive advertising, virtual reality displays, text messaging, and video kiosks. We'll discuss these tools in more detail in Chapter 12.

THE BIG PICTURE

Since the ultimate goal of most marketing is long-term profitability, a core marketing principle must infuse every facet of a successful organization: the need to deliver products that exceed customer expectations. The customer must come first for *every* department—including finance, accounting, engineering, manufacturing, and human resources—although the specifics of how that plays out will clearly differ for each organizational function. Competition in the future will only intensify. Customer choices will continue to multiply as globalization and technology march forward. While these forces will weed out the weaker players, firms with a deeply engrained marketing orientation and a strong customer focus will continue to flourish—delivering value to their stakeholders, and dollars to their bottom line.

CAREERS

Since the marketing concept permeates every aspect of successful organizations, you won't be surprised to learn that virtually every position in business requires an understanding of basic marketing principles. Furthermore, the spectrum of marketing positions is very wide, ranging from sales, to advertising, to public relations, to brand management, to marketing research, and increasingly, social media marketing. Entry-level positions will have titles such as assistant, analyst, and coordinator, moving up to manager and director slots, and top-level positions are typically at the vice-presidential or corporate officer level. Most positions require a college degree, and many also demand an MBA. In 2011 and 2012, the starting median salary for undergraduate marketing majors was $38,200 and the median mid-career salary was $73,500. According to the Bureau of Labor Statistics, marketing management jobs are likely to increase about 13% by 2018.[13]

What *else?*

RIP & REVIEW CARDS IN THE BACK
and visit www.cengagebrain.com!

12

Product and Promotion:

Creating and Communicating

Value

"DON'T BE AFRAID TO GET CREATIVE AND *EXPERIMENT* WITH YOUR MARKETING."

— Mike Volpe, CMO, Hubspot

Product and promotional strategy are the two most visible elements of the promotional mix: What benefits are you offering consumers, and how are you communicating those benefits? This chapter covers product and promotional strategies separately, but as you read, keep in mind that effective marketers carefully interweave all the elements of the marketing mix—including distribution and pricing strategies—to create a coherent whole that's even stronger than the sum of the parts.

12-1 Product: It's Probably More Than You Thought

When most people hear the term "product," they immediately think of the material things that we buy, use, and consume every day: for example, an Android cell phone or a pair of 7 jeans. But from a marketing standpoint, product means much more. A **product** can be anything that a company offers to satisfy consumer needs and wants; the possibilities include not only physical goods but also services and ideas. A car wash, laser eye surgery, and a cooking lesson all qualify as products.

When you buy a product, you also "buy" all of the attributes associated with the product. These encompass a broad range of qualities, such as the brand name, the image, the packaging, the reputation, and the guarantee. From a consumer standpoint, these attributes (or the lack of these attributes) are part of the product purchase, even if they don't add to its value. As a marketer, it's worth your while to carefully consider each element of your product

to ensure that you're maximizing value without sacrificing profitability. With the introduction of the translucent, multicolored iMac computers in 1998, Apple established its reputation for creating value through product design—an attribute that other PC manufacturers completely overlooked as they churned out their inventories of boring, beige boxes. Over the years, Apple has continued to polish its reputation by introducing sleek, elegantly designed products such as its iPad tablet computers and its iPhones.

> **product** Anything that an organization offers to satisfy consumer needs and wants, including both goods and services.

12-1a Services: A Product by Any Other Name...

If a "product" includes anything that satisfies consumer needs, services clearly fit the bill. But services have some obvious differences from tangible goods. You often cannot see, hear, smell, taste, or touch a service, and you can virtually never "own" it. After math tutoring, for example, you might possess sharper calculus skills, but you don't own the tutoring experience (at least not literally). Most services embody these qualities:

- **Intangibility:** You typically cannot see, smell, taste, or touch a service before you buy it. Clearly, this creates a lot of uncertainty. Will the purchase really be worthwhile? Smart marketers mitigate the uncertainty by giving clues that suggest value. For example, the Formosa Café, a funky, old-time Hollywood bar and restaurant, plasters the walls with signed pictures of movie stars, providing "evidence" of its movie biz credentials.

- **Inseparability:** Try as you might, you simply can't separate the buyer of a service from the person who renders it. Delivery requires interaction between the buyer and the provider, and the customer directly contributes to the quality of the service. Consider a trip to the doctor. If you accurately describe your symptoms, you're likely to get a correct diagnosis. But if you simply say, "I just don't feel normal," the outcome will likely be different.

- **Variability:** This one ties closely to inseparability. A talented masseuse would probably help you relax, whereas a mediocre one might actually create tension. And even the talented masseuse might give better service at the end of the day than at the beginning, or worse service on the day she breaks up with her boyfriend. Variability also applies to the difference among providers. A massage at a top-notch spa is likely to be better than a massage at your local gym.

◐ **Perishability:** Marketers cannot store services for delivery at peak periods. A restaurant, for instance, only has so many seats; they can't (reasonably) tell their 8 p.m. dinner customers to come back the next day at 5 p.m. Similarly, major tourist destinations, such as Las Vegas, can't store an inventory of room service deliveries or performances of Cirque du Soleil. This creates obvious cost issues; is it worthwhile to prepare for a peak crowd but lose money when it's slow? The answer depends on the economics of your business.

12-1b Goods Versus Services: A Mixed Bag

Identifying whether a product is a good or a service can pose a considerable challenge, since many products contain elements of both. A meal at your local Italian restaurant obviously includes tangible goods: you definitely own that calzone. But someone else took your order, brought it to the table, and (perhaps most importantly) did the dishes! Service was clearly a crucial part of the package.

A goods and services spectrum can provide a valuable tool for analyzing the relationship between the two. (See Exhibit 12.1.) At one extreme, **pure goods** don't include any services. Examples include a bottle of ketchup or a package of socks. At the other extreme, **pure services** don't include any goods. Examples include financial consulting or a piano lesson. Other products—such as a meal at Pizza Hut—fall somewhere between the poles.

12-1c Product Layers: Peeling the Onion

When customers buy products, they actually purchase more than just the good or service itself. They buy a complete product package that includes a core benefit, the actual product, and product augmentations. Understanding

these layers is valuable, since the most successful products delight consumers at each one of them.

Core Benefit   At the most fundamental level, consumers buy a core benefit that satisfies their needs. When you go to a movie, the core benefit is entertainment. When you buy a smartphone, the core benefit is communication. And when you go to the doctor, the core benefit is better health. Most products also provide secondary benefits that help distinguish them from other goods and services that meet the same customer needs. A secondary benefit of a smartphone might include entertainment, since it probably plays your music, too.

12-1d Actual Product

The *actual product* layer, of course, is the product itself: the physical good or the delivered service that provides the core benefit. The *Avengers* movie was an actual "service" that provided entertainment to millions of people in 2012. A Motorola Droid is an actual smartphone that provides communication and entertainment services. Identifying the actual product is sometimes tough when the product is a service. For example, the core benefit of visiting a doctor might be better health, but the actual product may be someone in a white coat poking and prodding you. Keep in mind that the actual product includes all of the attributes that make it unique, such as the brand name, the features, and the packaging.

Augmented Product   Most marketers wrap their actual products in additional goods and services, called the *augmented product*, that sharpen their competitive edge. Augmentations come in a range of different forms. Many upscale movie theaters in L.A. display props from movies that have played in that theater. Most smartphones come with warranties or insurance and offer at least some customer service. And some doctors might give you sample pills until you can get your prescription filled.

12-1e Product Classification: It's a Bird, It's a Plane...

Products fall into two broad categories—consumer products and business products—depending on the reason for the purchase. **Consumer products** are purchased for personal use or consumption,

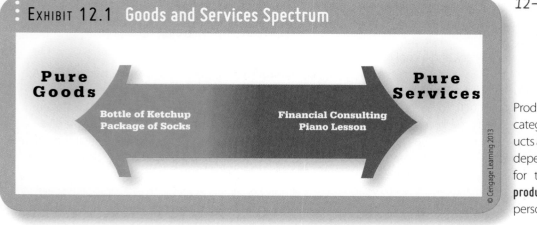

Exhibit 12.1   Goods and Services Spectrum

Pure Goods

Bottle of Ketchup
Package of Socks

Pure Services

Financial Consulting
Piano Lesson

© Cengage Learning 2013

while **business products** are purchased to use either directly or indirectly in the production of another product. The computer you have at home is a consumer product, while the computer in your college's computer lab is a business product.

Consumer Product Categories Marketers further divide consumer products into several different subcategories, as shown below. Understanding the characteristics of the subcategories can help marketers develop better strategies.

- ⊃ *Convenience products* are the inexpensive goods and services that consumers buy frequently with limited consideration and analysis. Distribution tends to be widespread, with promotion by the producers. Examples include staples such as eggs and toilet paper, impulse items such as gum and soda, and emergency products such as cough drops and towing services.

- ⊃ *Shopping products* are the more expensive products that consumers buy less frequently. Typically, as consumers shop, they search for the best value and learn more about features and benefits through the shopping process. Distribution is widespread but more selective than for convenience products. Both producers and retailers tend to promote shopping products. Examples include electronics, insurance services, and appliances.

- ⊃ *Specialty products* are those much more expensive products that consumers seldom purchase. Most people perceive specialty products as being so important that they are unwilling to accept substitutes. Because of this, distribution tends to be highly selective. (Consumers are willing to go far out of their way for the "right" brand.) Both producers and retailers are apt to promote specialty products but to a highly targeted audience. Some specialty product examples are Lamborghini sports cars, Tiffany jewelry, and cosmetic surgery.

- ⊃ *Unsought products* are the goods and services that hold little interest (or even negative interest) for consumers. Price and distribution vary wildly, but promotion tends to be aggressive to drum up consumer interest. Disability insurance, prepaid burial plots, and blood donations are some examples.

Business Product Categories Marketers also divide business products into subcategories. Here, too, understanding the subcategories can lead to better marketing strategies.

- ⊃ *Installations* are large capital purchases designed for a long productive life. The marketing of installations emphasizes personal selling and customization. Examples include industrial robots, new buildings, airplanes, and railroad cars.

- ⊃ *Accessory equipment* includes smaller, movable capital purchases, designed for a shorter productive life than installations. Marketing focuses on personal selling but includes less customization than installations. Examples include personal computers, power tools, and furniture.

- ⊃ The *maintenance, repair, and operating products* category consists of small-ticket items that businesses consume on an ongoing basis but don't become part of the final product. Marketing tactics emphasize efficiency. Examples include brooms, lightbulbs, and copy paper.

- ⊃ *Raw materials* include the farm and natural products used in producing other products. Marketing emphasizes price and service rather than product differentiation. Examples include cotton, timber, and wheat.

- ⊃ *Component parts and processed materials* include finished (or partially finished) products used in producing other products. Marketing emphasizes product quality as well as price and service. Examples include batteries and spark plugs for cars and aluminum ingots for soda cans.

- ⊃ *Business services* are those services that businesses purchase to facilitate operations. Marketing focuses on quality and relationships; the role of price can vary. Examples include payroll services, janitorial services, marketing research, and legal services.

> **business products**
> Products purchased to use either directly or indirectly in the production of other products.
>
> **product differentiation**
> The attributes that make a good or service different from other products that compete to meet the same or similar customer needs.

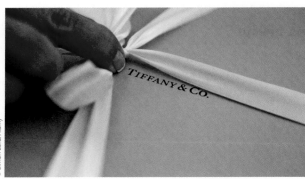
© Simon Lord/Alamy

Product Differentiation and Planning: A Meaningful Difference

While some products have succeeded with little or no forethought, you'll dramatically boost your chance of a hit with careful planning. **Product differentiation** should be a key

quality level How well a product performs its core functions.

product consistency How reliably a product delivers its promised level of quality.

product features The specific characteristics of a product.

customer benefit The advantage that a customer gains from specific product features.

consideration. Winning products must embody a real or perceived difference versus the glut of goods and services that compete in virtually every corner of the market. But different alone isn't enough; different from, and better than, the competition are both critical in order to create the shortest path to success. A quick look at some high-profile product failures illustrates the point.

○ **Clear Beer:** In the 1990s, several companies introduced clear beers, reflecting an ill-fated obsession with clear products, including shampoo, soap, and the short-lived, clear Crystal Pepsi.

○ **iSmell:** In 2001, DigiScents attempted to create a computer-peripheral device to emit smells to go with sites visited or emails opened. It held a cartridge carrying different primary odors to be emitted in combinations to create "appropriate" scents. PC World Magazine deemed it one of the world's worst tech products.

○ **Funky French Fries:** In 2002, Ore-Ida introduced Funky Fries. The flavors included cinnamon-sugar, chocolate, and "radical blue." Not surprisingly, they were off the market in less than a year.

12-2a **Product Quality**

Product quality relates directly to product value, which comes from understanding your customer. Peter Drucker, a noted business thinker, writer, and educator, declared:

Quality in a product or service is not what the supplier puts in. It's what the customer gets out and is willing to pay for. A product is not quality because it is hard to make and costs a lot of money ... this is incompetence. Customers pay only for what is of use to them and gives them value. Nothing else constitutes quality.

EXHIBIT 12.2 Product Quality Indicators

PRODUCT CATEGORY	SOME QUALITY INDICATORS
INTERNET SEARCH ENGINES	Fast, relevant, and far-reaching results
PURSES	High-profile designer, high price, and celebrity customers
COPY MACHINES	Reliability, flexibility, and customer service
ROLLER COASTERS	Thrill factor, design, and setting
CUPCAKES	Taste, design of frosting, high price, and natural ingredients

© Cengage Learning 2013

In other words, a high-quality product does a great job meeting customer needs. Seimans, a huge electronics conglomerate, embodies this thinking in its approach to quality: "Quality is when our customers come back and our products don't."

But the specific definition of quality—and the attributes that indicate quality—changes across product categories. See Exhibit 12.2 for a few examples.

Regardless of product category, the two key aspects of quality are level and consistency. **Quality level** refers to how well a product performs its core functions. You might think that smart companies deliver the highest possible level of performance, but this is seldom profitable, or even desirable. For instance, only a tiny group of consumers would pay for a speed boat to go 200 mph, when 80 mph offers a sufficient thrill (at least for most of us!). The right level of product performance is the level that meets the needs of your consumers, and those needs include price. Decisions about quality level must also consider the competition. The goal is to outperform the other players in your category while maintaining profitability.

The second dimension of quality is **product consistency**. How consistently does your product actually deliver the promised level of quality? With a positive relationship between price and performance, consistent delivery can offer a competitive edge at almost any quality level.

Honda offers an excellent example. When most people consider the Accord, the Civic, and the CRV, all Honda-owned models, quality quickly comes to mind. And all three dominate their markets. But clearly, the quality *levels* (and price) are different for each. The Accord serves the upper, more conservative end of the market; the Civic tends to appeal to younger, hipper, more budget-minded consumers; the CRV tends to appeal to middle-of-the-road shoppers seeking a reliable, small SUV. In short, Honda succeeds at delivering product consistency at several markedly different quality levels.

12-2b **Features and Benefits**

Product features are the characteristics of the product you offer. If a product is well designed, each feature corresponds to a meaningful **customer benefit**. The marketer's challenge is to design a package of features that offers the highest level of value for an acceptable price. And the equation must also account for profitability goals.

One winning formula may be to offer at least some low-cost features that correspond to high-value benefits. Creating an "open kitchen" restaurant, for instance, has limited impact on costs but gives patrons an exciting, up-close view of the drama and hustle of professional food preparation. Exhibit 12.3 lists some other examples of product features and their corresponding customer benefits.

> **"Quality** *means doing it right when no one is looking."*
>
> — Henry Ford

12-2c Product Lines and the Product Mix

Some companies focus all of their efforts on one product, but most offer a number of different products to enhance their revenue and profits. A **product line** is a group of products that are closely related to each other, in terms of either how they work or the customers they serve. Amazon's first product line was books. To meet the needs of as many book lovers as possible, Amazon carries well over a million different titles in its product line. A **product mix** is the total number of product lines and individual items sold by a single firm. Amazon's product mix includes a wide range of product lines, from books, to electronics, to toys (to name just a few).

Decisions regarding how many items to include in each product line and in the overall product mix can have a huge impact on a firm's profits. With too few items in each line, the company may be leaving money on the table. With too many items, the company may be spending unnecessarily to support its weakest links.

One reason that firms add new product lines is to reach completely new customers. Gap, for instance, added Old Navy to reach younger, lower-income customers, and Banana Republic to reach older, higher-income customers. Each line includes a range of different products designed to meet the needs of their specific customers. But one risk of adding new lines—especially lower-priced lines—is **cannibalization**, which happens when a new entry "eats" the sales of an existing line.

This is especially dangerous when the new products are lower-priced than the current ones. You could see the problem, for instance, if a $20 blue jean purchase from Old Navy replaces a $50 blue jean purchase from Gap; the company has lost more than half its revenue on the sale. Like other companies with multiple lines, Gap carefully monitors the cannibalization issue and works to differentiate its lines as fully as possible.

12-2d Branding

At the most basic level, a **brand** is a product's identity that sets it apart from other players in the same category. Typically, brands represent the combination of elements such as product name, symbol, design, reputation, and image. But today's most powerful emerging brands go far beyond the sum of their attributes. They project a compelling group identity that creates brand fanatics: loyal customers who advocate for the brand better than any advertising a marketer could buy. The overall value of a brand to an organization—the extra money that consumers will spend to buy that brand—is called **brand equity**.

Since 2001, *BusinessWeek* and Interbrand, a leading brand consultancy, have teamed up to publish a ranking of the 100 Best Global Brands by dollar value. The top ten brands are listed in Exhibit 12.4, but you can find the complete list at Interbrand's website.

product line A group of products that are closely related to each other, either in terms of how they work, or the customers they serve.

product mix The total number of product lines and individual items sold by a single firm.

cannibalization When a producer offers a new product that takes sales away from its existing products.

brand A product's identity—including product name, symbol, design, reputation, and image—that sets it apart from other players in the same category.

brand equity The overall value of a brand to an organization.

Exhibit 12.3 Product Features and Customer Benefits

PRODUCT	PRODUCT FEATURE	CUSTOMER BENEFIT
SUBWAY SANDWICHES	Lower fat	Looser pants
GROUPON	Great deals on valuable products and services	More cash for other needs
WHOLE FOODS MARKET	Organic produce	A healthier planet
STELLA McCARTNEY CLUTCH	Highly fashionable	You feel chic
TRIPLE LATTE	Caffeine, caffeine, caffeine	More time to, uh, study

© Cengage Learning 2013

Exhibit 12.4 *BusinessWeek*/Interbrand Top Ten Global Brands

BRAND	COUNTRY OF OWNERSHIP
COCA-COLA	United States
IBM	United States
MICROSOFT	United States
GOOGLE	United States
GE	United States
MCDONALD'S	United States
INTEL	United States
APPLE	United States
DISNEY	United States
HP	United States

Source: 2011 Ranking of the Top 100 Brands, Interbrand Website, http://www.interbrand.com/en/best-global-brands/best-global-brands-2008/best-global-brands-2011.aspx, accessed June 20, 2012.

Brand Name A catchy, memorable name is among the most powerful elements of your brand. While the right name will never save a bad business, it can launch a good business to new heights. But finding the right name can be tough. According to the respected Brighter Naming consulting group, the following characteristics can help:

1. Short, sweet, and easy to pronounce and spell: Examples include Sprite, H&M, GE, Nike, and Visa.

2. Unique within the industry: Think Caterpillar, Yahoo!, Starbucks, Zara, and Google.

3. Good alliteration, especially for long names: The words should roll off your tongue. Some examples are Coca-Cola, BlackBerry, Dunkin Donuts, and Minute Maid.[1]

Brand names typically fall into four categories, as described in Exhibit 12.5.

Line Extensions versus Brand Extensions As companies grow, marketers look for opportunities to grow their businesses. **Line extensions** are similar products offered under the same brand name. Possibilities include new flavors, sizes, colors, ingredients, and forms. One example is Lays potato chips, which offers more than 45 versions, including BBQ, Baked, Flamin Hot, Chili Limon, mustard flavored, and lightly salted. The marketing challenge is to ensure that line extensions steal market share from competitors rather than from the core brand.

Brand extensions, on the other hand, involve launching a product in a new category under an existing brand name. The Bic brand, for instance, is quite elastic, stretching nicely to include diverse products such as pens, glue, cigarette lighters, and disposable razors. The Virgin brand demonstrates similar elasticity, covering more than 350 companies that range from airlines, to cell phones, to soft drinks, to cars. But the concept of brand extension becomes most clear (and most entertaining) through examining brand extension failures. Examples include Bic perfume, Budweiser Dry, Colgate (yes, the toothpaste brand!) frozen dinners, and Harley-Davidson Cologne.[2]

Licensing Some companies opt to license their brands from other businesses. **Licensing** means purchasing—often for a substantial fee—the right to use another company's brand name or symbol. The benefits, of course, are instant name recognition, an established reputation, and a proven track record. On a worldwide basis, the best-known licensing arrangements are probably character names, which range from Bart Simpson to Sponge Bob and appear on everything from cereal, to toys, to underwear. Many movie producers also do high-profile licensing, turning out truckloads of merchandise that features movie properties such as Batman and *Twilight*.

Another fast-growing area is the licensing of corporate or college names. Coca-Cola, for instance, claims to have more than 300 licensees who sell over a billion dollars of licensed merchandise each year. The potential benefits for Coca-Cola are clear: more promotion, increased exposure, and enhanced image. But the risk is significant. If licensed products are of poor quality or overpriced, the consumer backlash hits the core brand rather than the producer of the licensed product.

Cobranding Cobranding is when established brands from different companies join forces to market the same product. This cooperative approach has a long history but is currently enjoying a new popularity. Examples include:

- T.G.I. Friday's markets a broad (and very popular) range of Jack Daniel's flavored foods.

- Tim Horton's Cafe and Bake Shops opened Cold Stone Creamery venues at selected locations.

- As the official airline of SeaWorld, Southwest Airlines (LUV) has three Shamu planes in its fleet. Passengers are occasionally visited by penguins before take-off.

Cobranding can offer huge advantages to both partners, by leveraging their strengths to enter new markets and gain more exposure. But cobranding can be risky. If one partner makes a major goof, the fallout can damage the reputation of the other partner as well.

National Brands Versus Store Brands National brands, also called *manufacturers' brands*, are brands that the

Exhibit 12.5 Brand Name Categories

CATEGORY	DESCRIPTION	EXAMPLES
LOCATION-BASED	Refers to either the area served or the place of origin	Southwest Airlines, Bank of America, Best Western Hotels
FOUNDER'S NAME	Can include first name, last name, or both	McDonald's, Suzy's Sub Sandwiches, Ford, Disney, Hewlett-Packard
DESCRIPTIVE OR FUNCTIONAL	Describes what the product is or how it works	eBay, U.S. News and World Report, Weight Watchers, Krispy Kreme
EVOCATIVE	Communicates an engaging image that resonates with consumers	Yahoo!, Craftsman, Virgin, Intel, Lunchables, Cosmopolitan, Starbucks

© Cengage Learning 2013

producer owns and markets. Many are well-known and widely available, such as Oreo cookies, Dial soaps, and Nutella. Although most retailers carry lots of national brands, an increasing number have opted to also carry their own versions of the same products, called **store brands**, or *private label*. Deep discounters, such as Walmart and Costco, have had particular success with their private-label brands (e.g., Sam's Choice and Kirkland). *Private labels* play a growing role in grocery stores as well. In the United States, about one out of four grocery purchases is private label, and the numbers are even higher in Europe, hitting half of all grocery sales in a number of markets. As the global recession deepened in 2008 and 2009, private-label sales increased by more than 7%. But by 2011, as the economic recovery gained traction, fewer consumers traded down to private-label options. The growing influence and increasing quality of low-end private-label brands increase the pressure on national brands to continually innovate while holding down prices.[3]

© s70/ZUMA Press/Newscom

At the upper end of the market—especially in the clothing business—key retailers specialize in private brands to create and protect a consistent, upscale image. Examples include Neiman Marcus, Coldwater Creek, and Saks Fifth Avenue. Private-label clothing accounts for more than 40% of all U.S. apparel sales.[4]

> **store brands** Brands that the retailer both produces and distributes (also called private-label brands).

12-2e Packaging

Great packaging does more than just hold the product. It can protect the product, provide information, facilitate storage, suggest product uses, promote the product brand, and attract buyer attention. Great packaging is especially important in the crowded world of grocery stores and mass merchandisers. In the average supermarket, the typical shopper passes about 300 items per minute and makes anywhere from 20% to 70% of purchases on sheer impulse. In this environment, your package must call out to your target customers and differentiate your product from all

Ooops! What were they thinking?

Oops! Bank of America Busted!

Most months, most of us can scrape up an additional five dollars, which might be part of why Bank of America decided to levy a $5 monthly fee on debit card users in late 2011. This tone deaf move prompted instant outrage from consumers, who still blame big banks for busting the economy, bankrupting "Main Street," and sucking up bailout dollars. Many vocal consumer critics believed it wasn't fair for banks to suddenly charge them to access their own money—a service they had enjoyed free of charge for years. When the consumer outcry reached epic proportions, and after other banks refused to come on board with the idea, Bank of America finally ditched the plan. Apparently this was a wise move, since a recent poll

that showed 62% of consumers would leave their bank if it began charging a debit card fee, and the Progressive Change Campaign Committee said 21,500 consumers would remove their money from Bank of America in response to the fee. But despite dropping the fee, Bank of America still hasn't completely regained consumer confidence. Unfortunately, the debit card debacle was not Bank of America's only recent disaster. In June 2012, Moody's Investors Service downgraded Bank of America's credit rating, so that it was only two notches above junk. Banks are particularly sensitive to downgrades because they rely on the confidence of creditors and big customers. And consumer advocates still stand ready to "prove" that "by moving our money, we will make these irresponsible banks less 'too big to fail.'"[5]

the others lined up beside it. Yet, in attracting consumer attention, a good package cannot sacrifice the basics such as protecting the product.[6]

Bottom line: great packaging stems from consumer needs, but it usually includes at least a smidge of creative brilliance. Examples include yogurt in a pouch that doesn't need a spoon, soup-to-go that can be microwaved in the can, "anti-theft" clear sandwich bags printed with mold-like green splotches (seriously!), and single-serving baby carrot packets that moms can toss into kids' lunches.

12-3 Innovation and the Product Life Cycle: Nuts, Bolts, and a Spark of Brilliance

For a business to thrive long term, effective new product development is vital. And the process works only if it happens quickly. As technological advances hit the market at breakneck speed, current products are becoming obsolete faster than ever before. The need for speed compounds as hungry competitors crowd every niche of the market. But the rush is risky, since new product development costs can be in the millions, and the success rate is less than a third. Marketers who succeed in this challenging arena devote painstaking effort to understanding their customers, but they also nurture the creativity they need to generate new ideas. An example of how this can work: The 3M Corporation—makers of Post-It Notes and Scotch Tape—introduces about 500 new products per year by pushing its employees to "relentlessly ask, 'What if?'" 3M also encourages workers to spend 15% of their work time (paid work time!) on projects of personal interest.[7]

12-3a Types of Innovation

Clearly, the first personal computer represented a higher degree of newness than the first personal computer with a color screen. And the computer with a color screen represented a higher degree of newness than the first low-cost knockoff. Levels of innovation fall along a spectrum, as shown in Exhibit 12.6.

Discontinuous Innovation *Discontinuous innovations* are brand-new ideas that radically change how people live. Examples include the first car, the first television, and the first computer. These dramatic innovations require extensive customer learning, which should guide the marketing process.

Exhibit 12.6 Levels of Innovation

Discontinuous Innovation

Dynamically Continuous Innovation

Continuous Innovation

© Cengage Learning 2013

Dynamically Continuous Innovation *Dynamically continuous innovations* are characterized by marked changes to existing products. Examples include cell phones, MP3 players, and digital cameras. These types of innovations require a moderate level of consumer learning in exchange for significant benefits.

Continuous Innovation A slight modification of an existing product is called a *continuous innovation*. Examples include new sizes, flavors, shapes, packaging, and design. The goal of continuous innovation is to distinguish a product from the competition. The goal of a knockoff is simply to copy a competitor and offer a lower price.

12-3b The New Product Development Process

An efficient, focused development process will boost your chances of new product success. The standard model includes six stages:

Idea Generation

Idea Screening

Analysis

Development

Testing

Commercialization

© Cengage Learning 2013

Each stage requires management to "green light" ideas before moving forward, to ensure that the company doesn't waste resources on marginal concepts.

- **Idea Generation:** Some experts estimate that it takes 50 ideas for each new product that makes it to market, so you should definitely cast a wide net. Ideas can come from almost anywhere, including customer research, customer complaints, salespeople, engineers, suppliers, and competitors.

- **Idea Screening:** The purpose of this stage is to weed out ideas that don't fit with the company's objectives and ideas that would clearly be too expensive to develop. The Walt Disney Company, for instance, would

Innovation is creativity with a job to do.

—John Emmerling, Innovation Consultant

certainly eliminate the idea of a XXX cable channel because it just doesn't fit their mission.

◐ **Analysis:** The purpose of the analysis stage is to estimate costs and forecast sales for each idea to get a sense of the potential profit and of how the product might fit within the company's resources. Each idea must meet rigorous standards to remain a contender.

◐ **Development:** The development process leads to detailed descriptions of each concept with specific product features. New product teams sometimes also make prototypes, or samples, that consumers can actually test. The results help fully refine the concept.

◐ **Testing:** This stage involves the formal process of soliciting feedback from consumers by testing the product concept. Do they like the features? Are the benefits meaningful? What price makes sense? Some companies also test-market their products or sell them in a limited area to evaluate the consumer response.

◐ **Commercialization:** This stage entails introducing the product to the general market. Two key success factors are gaining distribution and launching promotions. But a product that tested well doesn't always mean instant success. The VW Beetle, for example, sold only 330 cars during its first year in the United States, but it later became a hit.

12-3c New Product Adoption and Diffusion

In order to become a commercial success, new products must spread throughout a market after they are introduced. That process is called *diffusion*. But diffusion clearly happens at different speeds, depending on the individual consumer and on the product itself.

Product Adoption Categories Some consumers like to try new things; others seem terrified of change. These attitudes clearly affect the rate at which individual people are willing to adopt (or begin buying and using) new products. The first adopters, about 2.5% of the total, are adventurous risk takers. The laggards, about 16% of the total, sometimes adopt products so late that earlier adopters have already moved to the next new thing. The rest of the population falls somewhere in between. Keep in mind that individuals tend to adopt new products at different rates. For instance, we probably all know someone who is an innovator in technology but a laggard in fashion, or vice versa.

Product Diffusion Rates Some new products diffuse into the population much more quickly than others. For example, Apple iPods and Segway Human Transporters appeared on the market around the same time; iPods have become a pop culture icon, while Segways remain on the fringe. What accounts for the difference? Researchers have identified five product characteristics that affect the rate of adoption and diffusion. The

Wacky Warnings

As product lawsuits take on a life of their own, manufacturers are responding with warning labels that seem increasingly wacky. To call attention to this trend, a Michigan anti-lawsuit group called M-LAW sponsors the annual Wacky Warning Label Contest. Top finishers over the past few years have included the following gems:

◐ A toilet brush tag that says: "Do not use for personal hygiene."

◐ An electric razor for men warns: "Never use while sleeping."

◐ An electric skillet warns: "Caution: griddle surface may be hot during and after cooking."

◐ A label on a scooter for children cautions: "This product moves when used."

◐ A label on a collapsible baby stroller warns: "Remove child before folding."[8]

©Login/Shutterstock.com

more characteristics a product has, the faster it will diffuse into the population.

○ **Observability:** How visible is the product to other potential consumers? Some product categories are easier to observe than others. If you adopt a new kind of car, the whole neighborhood will know, plus anyone else who sees you on the streets and highways.

○ **Trialability:** How easily can potential consumers sample the new product? Trial can be a powerful way to create new consumers, which is why many markets fill their aisles with sample tables during popular shopping hours. Other examples of trial-boosting strategies include test-driving cars, sampling music, and testing new fragrances.

○ **Complexity:** Can potential consumers easily understand what your product is and how it works? If your product confuses people—or if they find it hard to explain to others—adoption rates will slow. For example, many people who test-ride Segway Human Transporters love the experience, but they have trouble explaining to others how it works or why it beats other transportation options.

○ **Compatibility:** How consistent is your product with the existing way of doing things? Cordless phones,

for example, caught on almost instantly, since they were completely consistent with people's prior experiences—only better!

○ **Relative Advantage:** How much better are the benefits of your new product compared to existing products? When gas prices climb, for example, the benefits of a hybrid car take on a much higher value relative to standard cars. As a result, demand skyrockets.

12-3d The Product Life Cycle: Maximizing Results over Time

When marketers introduce a new product, they hope it will last forever, generating sales and profits for years to come. But they also realize that all products go through a **product life cycle**: a pattern of sales and profits that typically changes over time. The life cycle can be dramatically different across individual products and product categories, and predicting the exact shape and length of the life cycle is virtually impossible. But most product categories do move through the four distinct stages shown in Exhibit 12.7.

○ **Introduction:** This is a time of low sales and nonexistent profits as companies invest in raising awareness about the product and the product category. Some categories, such as the microwave, languish in this phase for years, while other categories, such as computer memory sticks, zoom through this phase. And some categories never get beyond introduction. (Think clear beers.)

○ **Growth:** During the growth period, sales continue to rise, although profits usually peak. Typically, competitors begin to notice emerging categories in the growth phase. They enter the market—often with new variations of existing products—which further fuels the growth. Hybrid cars are currently

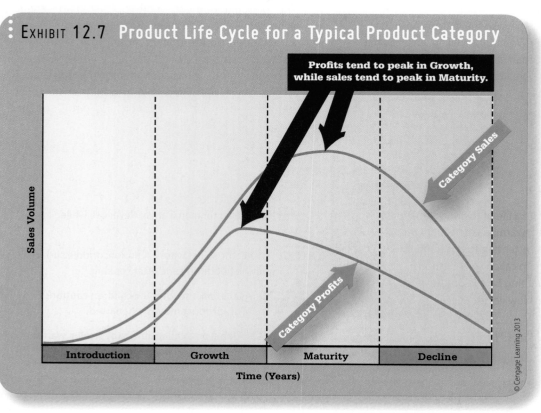

EXHIBIT 12.7 Product Life Cycle for a Typical Product Category

Profits tend to peak in Growth, while sales tend to peak in Maturity.

Category Sales

Category Profits

Sales Volume

Introduction | Growth | Maturity | Decline

Time (Years)

© Cengage Learning 2013

in the growth phase, and a number of competitors have recently entered the market.

- ⊙ **Maturity:** During maturity, sales usually peak. Profits continue to decline as competition intensifies. Once a market is mature, the only way to gain more users is to steal them from competitors, rather than to bring new users into the category. Weaker players begin to drop out of the category. Gasoline-powered cars, sugared soda, and network TV are in maturity in the United States.

- ⊙ **Decline:** During this period, sales and profits begin to decline, sometimes quite rapidly. The reasons usually relate to either technological change or change in consumer needs. For instance, the introduction of word processing pushed typewriters into decline, and a change in consumer taste and habits pushed hot cereal into decline. Competitors continue to drop out of the category.

Familiarity with the product life cycle helps marketers plan effective strategies for existing products and identify profitable categories for new products. Exhibit 12.8 summarizes typical marketing strategies and offers examples for each phase.

Individual products also have life cycles that usually follow the category growth pattern but sometimes vary dramatically. Clearly, it's in the marketer's best interest to extend the profitable run of an individual brand as long as possible. There are several ways to make this happen: finding new uses for the product, changing the product, and changing the marketing mix. For example, *American Idol* renewed interested in their franchise by introducing new celebrity judges.

promotion Marketing communication designed to influence consumer purchase decisions through information, persuasion, and reminders.

12-4 Promotion: Influencing Consumer Decisions

Promotion is the power to influence consumers—to remind them, to inform them, to persuade them. The best promotion goes one step further, building powerful consumer bonds that draw your customers back to your product again and again. But don't forget that great promotion only works with a great product. Bill Bernbach, an ad industry legend, captures this concept by noting that "A great ad campaign will make a bad product fail faster. It will get more people to know it's bad."

Marketers can directly control most promotional tools. From TV advertising to telephone sales, the marketer creates the message and communicates it directly to the target audience. But, ironically, marketers *cannot* directly control the most powerful promotional tools: publicity, such as a comment on *The View*, or a review in *Consumer Reports*, and word-of-mouth such as a recommendation from a close friend or even a casual acquaintance. Marketers can only influence these areas through creative promotional strategies.

12-4a Promotion in Chaos: Danger or Opportunity?

Not coincidentally, the Chinese symbol for crisis resembles the symbols for danger and opportunity—a perfect description of promotion in today's market. The pace of change is staggering. Technology has empowered consumers to choose how and when they interact with media, and they are grabbing control with dizzying speed. Cable-based on-demand video continues to soar, and digital movie downloads are poised for explosive growth. In 2012 Internet users spent nearly four hours per week surfing the Web, compared to nearly 33 per week watching TV. Meanwhile, more passive forms of entertainment, such as network television, are slowly losing their audience. And those people who do still watch TV are gleefully changing the schedules and zapping the ads with TiVo or similar devices. As media splinters across an array of entertainment options, usage patterns have changed as well: tech-savvy viewers are more prone to consume media in on-the-fly snacks rather than sit-down meals. Rising

EXHIBIT 12.8 The Product Life Cycle and Marketing Strategies

PHASE	EXAMPLES	SALES/PROFITS	KEY MARKETING STRATEGIES
Introduction	Virtual reality games, fuel cell technology	Low sales, low profits	Build awareness, trial, and distribution
Growth	Hybrid cars, flat-screen TVs, electronic book readers	Rapidly increasing sales and profits	Reinforce brand positioning, often through heavy advertising
Maturity	Airlines, DVD players, personal computers, online stock trading, energy drinks	Flat sales and declining profits	Target competitors, while defending franchise with new product features, competitive advertising, promotion, and price cuts
Decline	Pagers, videocassettes	Declining sales and profits	Reduce spending and consider terminating the product

© Cengage Learning 2013

consumer power and the breakneck pace of technology have created a growing need—and a stunning opportunity—for marketers to zero in on the right customers, at the right time, with the right message.[9]

12-4b Integrated Marketing Communication: Consistency and Focus

How many marketing messages have you gotten in the past 24 hours? Did you flip on the TV or radio? Surf the Web? Notice a billboard? Glance at the logo on a T-shirt or cap? Chat with a friend about some product he likes? Marketing exposure quickly snowballs: the typical consumer receives about 3,000 advertising messages each day. Some of those messages are hard to avoid as marketers find new, increasingly creative ways to promote their products to a captive audience. The venues include elevators, taxicabs, golf carts, and other surprising settings.[10]

Given the confounding level of clutter, smart companies use **integrated marketing communication** to coordinate their messages through every promotional vehicle—including their advertising, website, and salespeople—creating a coherent impression in the minds of their customers. Why bother coordinating all of these elements? The answer is clear. Consumers don't think about the specific source of the communication; instead, they combine—or integrate—the messages from *all* the sources to form a unified impression about your product. If the messages are out of sync or confusing, busy consumers won't bother to crack the code. They'll simply move on to the next best option.

Can you really control every message that every consumer sees or hears about your product? It's not likely. But if you accurately identify the key points of contact between your product and your target market, you can focus on those areas with remarkable effectiveness. For instance, the most common points of contact for McDonald's are probably advertising and the in-store experience. From upbeat commercials, to smiling employees, to brightly striped uniforms, McDonald's spends millions of dollars to support its core message of fast, tasty food in a clean, friendly environment—heavily concentrated in the areas that are key to its brand.

Other companies are likely to encounter the bulk of their customers through different channels. You'd probably learn about Dell computers, for example, through either its website or word-of-mouth. Dell has invested heavily in both areas. The company maintains an innovative, user-friendly website that allows even novice users to create customized systems. And Dell delivers award-winning customer service and technical support, which gets its customers to recommend its products to family and friends.

12-4c Coordinating the Communication

Even after you've identified the key points of contact, coordinating the messages remains a challenge. In many companies, completely different teams develop the different promotional areas. Salespeople and brand managers often have separate agendas, even when the same executive manages both departments. Frequently, disconnected outside agencies handle advertising, web development, and sales promotion programs. Coordinating the messages will happen only with solid teamwork, which must begin at the top of the organization.

Information also plays a crucial role. To coordinate marketing messages, everyone who creates and manages them must have free access to knowledge about the customer, the product, the competition, the market, and the strategy of the organization. Some of this information, such as strategic goals, will come from the top down, but a fair amount, such as information about the customer, should come from the bottom up. Information must also flow laterally, across departments and agencies. The marketing research department, for instance, might have critical information about product performance, which might help the web management agency create a feature page that might respond to competitive threats identified by the sales force. When all parties have access to the same data, they are much more likely to remain on the same page.

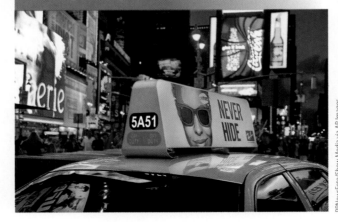

With so much clutter in the marketplace, coordinating messages can be a real challenge.

PRNewsFoto/Show Media via AP Images

12-5 A Meaningful Message: Finding the Big Idea

Your promotional message begins with understanding how your product is different from and better than the competition. But your **positioning statement**—a brief statement that articulates how you want your target market to envision your product relative to the competition—seldom translates directly into the promotional message. Instead, it marks the beginning of the creative development process, often spearheaded by ad agency creative professionals. When it works, the creative development process yields a *big idea*—a meaningful, believable, and distinctive concept that cuts through the clutter. Big ideas are typically based on either a rational or an emotional premise. Here are a few examples from the last decade:

RATIONAL:	Price:	Home Depot: "More saving. More doing."
	Engineering:	BMW: "The ultimate driving machine."
	Ingredients:	Snapple: "Made from the best stuff on earth."
EMOTIONAL:	Empowerment:	Burger King: "Have it your way."
	Humor:	Virgin Atlantic: "More experience than our name suggests"
	Fun:	Nintendo: "Born to play"

© Cengage Learning 2013

Not surprisingly, funny ads are a consumer favorite, although humor can be risky. For a record ten years in a row, from 1998 through 2008, Budweiser—known for using humor effectively—nabbed the top spot in *USA Today's* annual Ad Meter consumer ranking of Super Bowl ads. But in 2009, a very funny "Free Doritos" ad—created by talented amateurs in an online contest sponsored by Frito-Lay—knocked Budweiser off its pedestal. Budweiser regained the top spot in 2011, sharing the honor with Doritos, which, once again, took the top prize with a hilarious customer-created ad. Doritos used the same strategy to score a third win in 2012.[11]

The best big ideas have entrenched themselves in popular culture, spawning both imitators and parodies. A small sampling includes:

- The Energizer Bunny
- "Got Milk?"
- Budweiser: "Whassssuuup?!?!"
- GE: "We bring good things to life."
- Motel 6: "We'll leave the light on for you."

12-5a An International Perspective

Some big ideas translate well across cultures. The Marlboro Man now promotes rugged individualism across the globe. But other big ideas don't travel as smoothly. DeBeers tried running ads in Japan using their proven strategy in the West: fabulously dressed women smiling and kissing their husbands who have just given them glittering diamonds. The ads failed in Japan because a Japanese woman would be more likely to shed a few tears and feign anger

that her husband would spend so much money. The revised DeBeers campaign featured a hardworking husband and wife in their tiny apartment. Receiving a diamond, the wife chides her extravagant husband: "Oh, you stupid!" The campaign was a wild success. Taking a big idea to a foreign market can mean big money and a powerful brand, but careful research should still be your first step.[12]

promotional channels
Specific marketing communication vehicles, including traditional tools, such as advertising, sales promotion, direct marketing, and personal selling, and newer tools such as product placement, advergaming, and Internet minimovies.

12-6 The Promotional Mix: Communicating the BIG IDEA

Once you've nailed your message, you need to communicate the big idea to your target market. The traditional communication tools—or **promotional channels**—include advertising, sales promotion, direct marketing, and personal selling. But more recently, a number of new tools have emerged, ranging from advergaming to Internet minimovies. The combination of communication tools that you choose to promote your product is called your "promotional mix."

12-6a Emerging Promotional Tools: The Leading Edge

In the past decade, the promotional landscape has changed dramatically. Consumer expectations and empowerment have skyrocketed. Consumer tolerance for impersonal corporate communication has fallen. And digital technology has surged forward at breakneck speed. As a result, new promotional tools have emerged, and previously minor tools have burst into the mainstream. This section covers several leading-edge promotional tactics, but keep in mind that other tools—such as mobile phone promotion, social media marketing (e.g., Facebook) and widget-based marketing—are growing explosively, too.

Internet Advertising Internet advertising has been highly visible for more than a decade. But the industry has moved far beyond simple banner ads and annoying pop-up ads. The highest growth areas include paid search advertising, search engine optimization, and online video advertising.

Paid search advertising includes both sponsored links on Google that relate to the topic you've searched and targeted Google text ads on a number of different websites—both of which are at the heart of Google's outsized financial success. Industry expert *eMarketer* estimates that paid search advertising, including both Google and other similar services, will surpass $17 billion in 2012, and may surpass $20 billion by 2015. Paid search seems to be an especially attractive tactic during tough economic times, since it offers high accountability—marketers can tell exactly how well their limited advertising dollars are working.[13]

Search engine optimization (SEO) also demonstrated strong growth as the economy weakened. SEO involves taking specific steps to ensure that your website appears high on the list when customers look for your product or service via an Internet search engine such as Google or Yahoo!. Typically, the higher a firm appears, the more traffic that site will receive from potential customers. Predictions from *eMarketer* suggest that U.S. spending on search-engine marketing will nearly double from $12.2 billion in 2008 to $23.4 billion by 2013.[14]

Online video advertising represents another high-growth area. This includes the increasingly popular "pre-roll" ads, the 15- to 30-second spots that viewers often sit through before watching an online video on YouTube, Hulu, or many other sites. Online video advertising more than tripled in the first half of 2008 (although the base was miniscule compared to search advertising). According to *eMarketer* estimates, the growth will increase—more than triple again from $2.16 billion in 2011 to $7.13 billion in 2015, representing continued spectacular growth.[15]

Social Media Clearly, social media—including Facebook, Twitter, Blogger, Tumblr, Foursquare, and many others—is not a fad, but rather, a paradigm shift in how successful businesses market themselves. According to advertising heavyweight Alex Bogusky, "You can't buy attention anymore. Having a huge budget doesn't mean anything in social media…The old media paradigm was PAY to play. Now you get back what you authentically put in." And the evidence is building that social media offers a truly impressive return on investment, especially compared to traditional media. A few examples compiled by social media expert Erik Qualman underscore the potential return on investment:

- Wetpaint/Altimeter Study found companies that are both deeply and widely engaged in social media

significantly surpass their peers in both revenues and profits. The study also found the company sales with the highest levels of social media activity grew on average by +18%, while those companies with the least amount of social activity saw their sales decline by −6%.

- BlendTec increased its sales 5x by running the often humorous "Will It Blend" videos on YouTube, blending everything from an iPhone to a sneaker.

- Dell sold $3,000,000 worth of computers on Twitter.

- Ford Motor Company gave away 100 Fiestas to influential bloggers, resulting in 37% of Generation Y learning of the Ford Fiesta before it was launched in the United States.

- Debt relief firm CareOne found that customers gained through social media completed their first payment through the company, at a higher rate of +732%.

- Web host provider Moonfruit more than recouped its $15,000 social media investment as its website traffic soared +300% while sales increased +20%.

Looking ahead, smart marketers of both large and small businesses are investing their limited resources in social marketing and reaping an unprecedented return, forging the future of marketing promotion.[16]

Product Placement Product placement—the paid integration of branded products into movies and TV—exploded into big-screen prominence in 1982, when Reese's Pieces played a highly visible role in Steven Spielberg's blockbuster film *E.T.* Reese's Pieces sales shot up 65% (a major embarrassment for the marketers of M&Ms, who had passed on the opportunity). Over the years, product placement in movies has moved rapidly into the limelight. A few notable examples are:

- *Risky Business* (1983): This movie launched Tom Cruise and fueled a run on Ray-Ban sunglasses. The shades got another boost in 1997 with *Men in Black*.

- *You've Got Mail* (1998): AOL scored big in this Tom Hanks–Meg Ryan romance that etched the AOL signature mail call onto the national consciousness.

- James Bond: This longstanding movie icon hawked so many products in recent movies (e.g., Omega watches, Heineken beer, and British Airways) that it triggered a backlash from annoyed moviegoers and critics.[17]

Overall, Apple takes top honors in the movie product placement sweepstakes. In 2010, Apple products appeared in 30% of all films that were number one in the U.S. box office. That performance actually represents a decline from 2008, when Apple products appeared in 50% of all number one films. The decline happened because other electronics firms stepped up their product placement efforts in response to

"Marketing is experiencing a profound paradigm shift."

— Dr. Eli Cox, Marketing Professor

Apple. In fact, Sony Studios, pursuing corporate synergy, actually banned Apple products from all their films, replacing them with Sony VAIO products wherever possible.[18]

In an interesting combination of promotional tactics, product placement and online video have begun to merge. In 2010, Lady Gaga's, YouTube smash hit video *Telephone* featured no fewer than ten product placements. Some of the placements, for instance, Miracle Whip, were paid, while others, such as Virgin Mobile and Polaroid, were extensions of existing partnerships with Gaga. Given its efficacy in reaching younger consumers, this approach seems sure to grow in the future. According to Jonathan Feldman, a top executive at Atlantic Records, "Before, video was definitely to showcase creativity and content…today we look at video as another piece of pie and a way to generate revenue."

Product placement on TV has catapulted into the mainstream in response to the growing prominence of digital video recorders (DVRs) such as TiVo. Nielsen estimates that nearly 40% of U.S. households had at least one DVR in 2011, 43% in 2012, up from fewer than 10% in 2005. DVRs allow consumers not only to watch on their own schedule but also to zap ads. Worried marketers see product placement as a chance to "TiVo-proof" their messages by integrating them into the programming. Media experts anticipate that product placement will become a $6.1 billion market by 2014.[19]

Product placement works best for marketers if the product seamlessly integrates into the show as a player rather than simply a prop. For instance, it's hard to miss Coke in *American Idol*. The judges are seldom without their Coca-Cola–emblazoned cups, and the contestants sit on a Coca-Cola couch in a Coca-Cola room as they wait to hear their fate. The price tag for this exposure—including commercial time and online content—is about $35 million. Media buyers often negotiate product placement deals as part of a package that includes

Raising your F-Factor

For years, the implications of getting an F have been anything but positive. But in today's social media world, smart brands are doing everything they can to raise their F-Factor. F is for friends, fans, followers, who influence purchasing decisions in more sophisticated ways.

According to Trendingwatching, there are several different ways that the F-Factor can work:

1. **F-Discovery: Consumers rely on their social networks to *discover* new products and services. An increasing number of sites allow consumers to compile sets of merchandise that they "like" and share them with their friends.**

2. **F-Rated: A growing number social network sites automatically serve up *ratings, recommendations, and reviews* from friends next to products that they are researching.**

3. **F-Feedback: Consumers ask their friends and followers to *improve and validate* their buying decisions. Product recommendations from family (63%) and friends (31%) are the most trusted. However, 81% of U.S. consumers now go online to do additional research, with 55% looking for user reviews, and 10% soliciting advice from their social networks. Among people aged 25-34, however, this figure rises to 23%. And, 90% of people trust the recommendations of their Facebook friends.**

4. **F-Together: Shopping is becoming increasingly *social*, even when consumers and their peers are not physically together. In fact, 83% of consumers say they tell friends if they get a good deal. In April 2011, Facebook announced that every time a user posts about buying a ticket from Ticketmaster, the company estimates they receive an extra $5.30.**

5. **F-Me: Consumers' social networks are literally turned into products and services. A couple of examples: 1)*Twournal* enables users of Twitter to transform their tweets and pictures into a real-life published journal. In addition to creating their own "books," users can also buy and sell publications from other users, and 2) *CrowdedInk* offers an app that allows users, to generate mugs filled with pictures of their Facebook friends or Twitter followers.**

As the F-Factor gains momentum, customer satisfaction becomes more important than ever. Only brands that consistently deliver on their promises will fully capitalize on the benefits that the F-factor can offer.[20]

regular ads, which reinforce the product that appeared in the program (unless, of course, the ads are zapped).[21]

Whether in TV or movies, product placement offers marketers huge sales potential in a credible environment, which may account for its huge growth rate. But product placement is risky—if your show is a dud, your placement is worthless. And the cost is high and growing, which only increases the financial risk. The benefits of product placement are tough to measure as well, especially for existing brands. But in the end, the only measure that really counts is consumer acceptance, which may disappear if product placement intrudes too much on the entertainment value of movies and TV.

Advergaming Interactive games have exploded into pop culture, with about 72% of U.S. consumers playing some kind of video game. Not surprisingly, marketers have followed closely behind, developing a new promotional channel: **advergaming**. Market analysts expect that spending on all video game advertising will hit nearly $2 billion by 2012.[22]

According to Massive, an advertising network that specializes in video games, advergaming works for marketers. Gamers exposed to embedded ads show a 64% increase in brand familiarity, a 37% increase in brand rating, and a 41% increase in purchase consideration; furthermore, rather than despising the ads, 55% of gamers said they "look cool." But Massive isn't the only game in town. In early 2007, Google purchased AdScape, a nimble video game advertising company, and independent agency Double Fusion also provides fierce competition. Despite the strong research results, analysts anticipate that advergaming will move in a new direction over the next few years, with deals that link brands with tangible rewards for players. Dr. Pepper, for instance, seeded 500 million bottles and fountain drink cups in 2010

© MARIO ANZUONI/Reuters/Landov

with special codes that allowed gamers to download content such as virtual weapons for EA game. This approach still leaves room for purely promotional in-game ads to support the out-of-game campaigns. Given the effectiveness of advergaming and the explosive growth, gamers may soon see a cyberworld filled with as much promotion as the real world.[23]

Buzz Marketing A recent study defined "buzz" as the transfer of information from someone who is in the know to someone who isn't. Buzz is essentially word-of-mouth, which now influences two-thirds of all consumer product purchases. And it makes sense. In a world that's increasingly complex, people turn to people they know and trust to help sort the garbage from the good stuff. Other popular terms for **buzz marketing** are "guerrilla marketing" and "viral marketing."

Not surprisingly, marketers have actively pursued buzz for their brands, especially with the rising cost and diminishing effectiveness of more traditional media channels. Innovative buzz campaigns are typically custom-designed to meet their objectives, and they often cost significantly less than more traditional approaches. Here are some notable examples:

- ◉ **Whopper Sacrifice:** Burger King has been among the most successful buzz marketers, using the Internet to develop quirky and creative campaigns that have quickly gone viral. In late 2009, Burger King invited customers to download their Whopper Sacrifice Facebook application and use it to drop ten Facebook friends in exchange for a free Angry Whopper coupon worth $3.69. The application then bluntly notified each friend that he or she had been dumped in exchange for about $.37 worth of burger. Consumers responded in droves, apparently thankful for the excuse to purge their friend lists. Burger King terminated the campaign when Facebook requested that they terminate the "de-friending" notification. But Burger King could still loudly proclaim "Your love for the Whopper sandwich proved to be stronger than 233,906 friendships."

- ◉ **Tremor:** Procter & Gamble, known for its traditional marketing, has mobilized buzz marketing on an unprecedented scale. Its Tremor marketing group, launched in 2001, recruited about 200,000 sociable kids, ages 13 to 19, to talk up products to their peers. These teens talk for free—or if not for free, for the chance to influence companies and get the early inside scoop on new products. In addition to P&G brands, Tremorites have worked on heavy-hitters such as Sony Electronics, DreamWorks SKG, and Coca-Cola. The results have been impressive. A dairy foods firm, for instance, introduced a new chocolate malt milk in Phoenix and Tucson with the same marketing mix and the same spending level. One exception: they used Tremor teens in Phoenix. After six months, sales in Phoenix were 18% higher than in Tucson. That kind of success tells its own story.[24]

Sponsorships Sponsorships certainly aren't new, but they are among the fastest-growing categories of promotional spending, projected to hit nearly $19 billion in 2012, and forecast to grow faster than other advertising and promotional spending over the next decade. Sponsorships provide a deep association between a marketer and a partner (usually a cultural or sporting event). Even though sponsors can't usually provide more than simply their logo or slogan, consumers tend to view them in a positive light, since they are clearly connected to events that matter to the target audience. The best sponsorship investments, of course, occur when the target audience for the marketer completely overlaps the target audience for the event. The high level of integration between the sponsors and events can provide millions of dollars in valuable media coverage, justifying the hefty price.[25]

12-6b Traditional Promotional Tools: A Marketing Mainstay

Although new tools are gaining prominence, traditional promotional tools—advertising, sales promotion, public relations, and personal selling—remain powerful. In fact, many marketers use the new tools in conjunction with the traditional to create a balanced, far-reaching promotional mix.

Advertising The formal definition of **advertising** is paid, nonpersonal communication, designed to influence a

It no longer makes economic sense to send an advertising message to the many in hopes of persuading the few.

— Lawrence Light, former CMO, McDonald's

"By mid-2012, U.S. smartphone penetration reached 44%, and nearly half of owners search the Web in response to offline ads."

—Rochester Institute of Technology

target audience with regard to a product, service, organization, or idea. Most major brands use advertising not only to drive sales, but also to build their reputation, especially with a broad target market. Television (network broadcasts and cable combined) remains the number-one advertising media, with magazines and newspapers following. As mass media prices increase and audiences fragment, fringe media is roaring toward the mainstream. But measurement is tough, since alternative media tactics are buried in other categories, including magazines, outdoor, and Internet. The overall media spending patterns for 2010 are shown in Exhibit 12.9. As you review the table, note that Internet spending does not include search advertising or online video advertising, which are typically tracked separately. Also note that overall media spending has dropped significantly in response to the recession.

Each type of media offers advantages and drawbacks, as summarized in Exhibit 12.10. Your goal as a marketer should be to determine which media options reach your target

sponsorship A deep association between a marketer and a partner (usually a cultural or sporting event), which involves promotion of the sponsor in exchange for either payment or the provision of goods.

advertising Paid, nonpersonal communication, designed to influence a target audience with regard to a product, service, organization, or idea.

EXHIBIT 12.9	2010 Measured Media Spending (billions)	
MEASURED MEDIA	**2010 SPENDING**	**PERCENTAGE OF TOTAL**
BROADCAST TV	$25,000	19.1%
CABLE TV	$21,200	16.2%
SPOT TV	$16,300	12.4%
SYNDICATED TV	$4,100	3.1%
NEWSPAPERS	$20,000	15.2%
RADIO	$8,200	6.3%
MAGAZINES	$24,300	18.5%
OUTDOOR	$3,800	2.9%
INTERNET*	$8,200	6.3%
TOTAL	$131,100	100%

Source: 100 Leading National Advertisers 2011 Edition Index, June 21, 2011, *Advertising Age.* * Internet figures are based on display advertising. They do not include paid search or broadband video advertising.

EXHIBIT 12.10 Major Media Categories

MAJOR MEDIA	ADVANTAGES	DISADVANTAGES
BROADCAST TV	*Mass audience:* Top-rated shows garnered more than 20 million viewers in 2011. *High impact:* TV lends itself to vivid, complex messages that use sight, sound, and motion.	*Disappearing viewers:* The 20 million viewers for top-rated shows in 2011 are dwarfed by the 1983 record of 105 million viewers for the finale of M*A*S*H. *Jaded viewers:* Consumers who aren't zapping ads with TiVo are prone to simply tuning them out. *High cost:* A 30-second ad during Super Bowl 2012 cost a record $4 million, and a typical primetime ad cost $200,000 to $400,000, depending on the show.
CABLE TV	*Targeted programming:* Cable helps advertisers target highly specialized markets (Zhong Tian Channel, anyone?). *Efficient:* The cost per contact is relatively low, especially for local buys. *High impact:* Cable offers the same sight, sound, and motion benefits as broadcast.	*DVRs:* As with broadcast TV, many viewers simply aren't watching ads. *Uneven quality:* Many cable ads are worse than mediocre, providing a seedy setting for quality products.
NEWSPAPERS	*Localized:* Advertisers can tailor their messages to meet local needs. *Flexible:* Turnaround time for placing and pulling ads is very short. *Consumer acceptance:* Readers expect, and even seek, newspaper ads.	*Short life span:* Readers quickly discard their papers. *Clutter:* It takes two or three hours to read the average metro paper from cover to cover. Almost no one does it. *Quality:* Even top-notch color newsprint leaves a lot to be desired.
DIRECT MAIL	*Highly targeted:* Direct mail can reach very specific markets. *International opportunity:* Less jaded foreign customers respond well to direct mail. *Email option:* Opt-in email can lower direct mail costs.	*Wastes resources:* Direct mail uses a staggering amount of paper. And most recipients don't even read it before they toss it. *High cost:* Cost per contact can be high, although advertisers can limit the size of the campaign. *Spam:* Unsolicited email ads have undermined consumer tolerance for all email ads.
RADIO	*Highly targeted:* In L.A., for example, the dial ranges from Vietnamese talk radio, to urban dance music, each station with dramatically different listeners. *Low cost:* Advertisers can control the cost by limiting the size of the buy. *Very flexible:* Changing the message is quick and easy.	*Low impact:* Radio relies only on listening. *Jaded listeners:* Many of us flip stations when the ads begin.
MAGAZINES	*Highly targeted:* From Cosmo to Computerworld, magazines reach very specialized markets. *Quality:* Glossy print sends a high-quality message. *Long life:* Magazines tend to stick around homes and offices.	*High cost:* A full-page, four-color ad in *People* can cost more than $300,000. *Inflexible:* Advertisers must submit artwork months before publication.
OUTDOOR	*High visibility:* Billboards and building sides are hard to miss. *Repeat exposure:* Popular locations garner daily viewers. *Breakthrough ideas:* Innovative approaches include cars and buses "wrapped" in ads, video billboards, and blimps.	*Simplistic messages:* More than an image and a few words will get lost. *Visual pollution:* Many consumers object to outdoor ads. *Limited targeting:* It's hard to ensure that the right people see your ad.
INTERNET	*24/7 global coverage:* Offers a remarkable level of exposure. *Highly targeted:* Search engines are especially strong at delivering the right ad to the right person at the right time. *Interactive:* Internet ads can empower consumers.	*Intrusive:* The annoyance factor from tough-to-close pop-ups alienates consumers, infuriating many. *Limited readership:* Web surfers simply ignore the vast majority of ads.

© Cengage Learning 2013

market efficiently and effectively, within the limits of your budget.

Sales Promotion Sales promotion stimulates immediate sales activity through specific short-term programs aimed at either consumers or distributors. Traditionally, sales promotion has been subordinate to other promotional tools, but spending has accelerated in the past decade. Sales promotion falls into two categories: consumer and trade.

Consumer promotion is designed to generate immediate sales. Consumer promotion tools include premiums, promotional products, samples, coupons, rebates, and displays.

- **Premiums** are items that consumers receive free of charge—or for a lower than normal cost—in return for making a purchase. Upscale cosmetics companies use the gift-with-purchase approach on a regular basis. Successful premiums create a sense of urgency—"Buy me now!"—while building the value of the brand.

- **Promotional** products are also essentially gifts to consumers of merchandise that advertise a brand name. Or pizza delivery places give away refrigerator magnets with their logo and phone number. Promotional products work best when the merchandise relates to the brand, and it's so useful or fun that consumers will opt to keep it around.

- **Samples** reduce the risk of purchasing something new by allowing consumers to try a product before committing their cash. From 2009 to 2011, Muscle Milk hired hundreds of personal trainers to conduct promotions and distribute samples. Sampling also drives immediate purchases. At one time or another, most of us have probably bought food we didn't need after tasting a delicious morsel in the supermarket aisle. Costco and Trader Joe's do especially well with this angle on sampling.

- **Coupons** offer immediate price reductions to consumers. Instant coupons require even less effort, since they are attached to the package right there in the store. The goal is to entice consumers to try new products. But the downside is huge. Marketers who depend on coupons encourage consumers to focus on price rather than value, which makes it harder to differentiate brands and build loyalty. In categories with frequent coupons (such as soap and cereal), too many consumers wait for the coupon in order to buy. They end up getting great deals, but marketers pay the price in reduced profits.

- **Rebates,** common in the car industry and the electronics business, entice consumers with cash-back offers. This is a powerful tactic for higher-priced items, since rebates offer an appealing purchase motivator. And rebates provide an incentive for marketers as well: breakage. Most people who buy a product because of the rebate don't actually follow through and do the paperwork to get the money (some estimates suggest that breakage rates are as high as 90 to 95%). This means that marketers can offer hefty discounts without actually coughing up the cash, so it isn't surprising that rebates are a popular promotional tool!

- **Displays** generate purchases in-store. Most experts agree that consumers make a hefty chunk of their purchase decisions as they shop, which means that displays can play a crucial role in sales success. Marketers of consumer products often give prefabricated display materials to grocery stores and mass merchandisers to encourage promotion.

Trade Promotion is designed to stimulate wholesalers and retailers to push specific products more aggressively. Special deals and allowances are the most common form of trade promotion, especially for consumer products. The idea is that if you give your distributors a temporary price cut, they will pass the savings on to consumers via a short-term "special."

Trade shows are another popular form of trade promotion. Usually organized by industry trade associations, trade shows give exhibitors a chance to display and promote

sales promotion
Marketing activities designed to stimulate immediate sales activity through specific short-term programs aimed at either consumers or distributors.

consumer promotion
Marketing activities designed to generate immediate consumer sales, using tools such as premiums, promotional products, samples, coupons, rebates, and displays.

trade promotion
Marketing activities designed to stimulate wholesalers and retailers to push specific products more aggressively over the short term.

© Scott Olson/Getty Images

their products to their distributors. They typically attract hundreds of exhibitors and thousands of attendees. Trade shows are especially common in rapidly changing industries such as toys and consumer electronics. Every year the Consumer Electronics Association hosts "The world's largest annual trade show for consumer electronics!" in Las Vegas.

Other forms of trade promotion include contests, sweepstakes, and special events for distributors. A soda company might sponsor a contest to see which grocery store can build the most creative summer display for its soda brands. Or a cable TV programmer might take a group of system managers to Key West to "learn more about their programming" (really an excuse for a great party that makes the system managers more open to the programmer's pitch).

Public Relations In the broadest sense, **public relations (or PR)** involves the ongoing effort to create positive relationships with all of a firm's different "publics," including customers, employees, suppliers, the community, the general public, and the government. But in a more focused sense, PR aims to generate positive **publicity**, or unpaid stories in the media that create a favorable impression about a company or its products. The endgame, of course, is to boost demand.

For the most part, the media covers companies or products that they perceive as newsworthy. To get coverage, smart firms continually scan their own companies for potential news—a hot product or a major corporate achievement—and present that news to the media. But finding news on a regular basis can be tough. To fill the gaps, innovative PR people sometimes simply create "news." PR guru Bill Stoller offers some interesting ideas for how to invent stories that will grab media attention:

➲ **Launch a Hall of Fame:** Induct some luminaries from your industry, create a simple website, and send your press release to the media. Repeat each year, building your reputation along the way.

➲ **Make a List:** The best, the worst, the top ten, the bottom ten—the media loves lists, and the possible topics are endless! Just make sure that your list is relevant to your business.

➲ **Create a Petition:** The Web makes this tactic easy. Harness a growing trend or identify a need in your industry, and launch your petition. The more signatures you get, the better your chances for publicity.[26]

The biggest advantage of publicity is that it is usually credible. Think about it: Are you more likely to buy a product featured on the news or a product featured in a 30-second ad?

Are you more likely to read a book reviewed by *The New York Times* or featured on a billboard? Publicity is credible because most people believe that information presented by the media is based on legitimate opinions and facts rather than on the drive to make money. And it also helps that publicity is close to free (excluding any fees for a PR firm).

But publicity has a major downside: the marketer has no control over how the media presents the company or its products. For example, in an effort to protect customers from a growing tide of solicitors in front of its stores, Target banned Salvation Army bell ringers in front of all its stores in 2004. The press cried foul, focusing not on the service to consumers, but rather on the disrespect to a venerable charity. Target's archrival Walmart, spotting an opportunity for itself at Target's expense, announced that it would match customer donations to the Salvation Army at all of its locations.

Personal Selling Personal selling—the world's oldest form of promotion—is person-to-person presentation of products to potential buyers. But successful selling typically begins long before the actual presentation and ends long afterward. In today's competitive environment, selling means building relationships on a long-term basis.

Creating and maintaining a quality sales force are expensive. Experts estimate that each business-to-business sales call costs nearly $400. So why are so many people

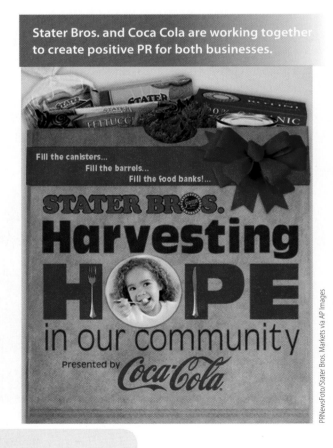

Stater Bros. and Coca Cola are working together to create positive PR for both businesses.

employed in sales?[27] Because nothing works better than personal selling for high-ticket items, complex products, and high-volume customers. In some companies, the sales team works directly with customers; in other firms, the sales force works with distributors who buy large volumes of products for resale.

Salespeople fall along a spectrum that ranges from order takers who simply process sales to order seekers who use creative selling to persuade customers. Most department stores hire order takers who stand behind the counter and ring up sales. But Nordstrom hires creative order seekers who actively garner sales by offering extra services such as tasteful accessory recommendations for a clothing shopper.

A separate category of salespeople focuses on *missionary selling*, which means promoting goodwill for a company by providing information and assistance to customers. The pharmaceutical industry hires a small army of missionary salespeople who call on doctors to explain and promote its products, even though the actual sales move through pharmacies.

The sales process typically follows six key stages. Keep in mind that well before the process begins, effective salespeople seek a complete understanding of their products, their industry, and their competition. A high level of knowledge permeates the entire selling process.

1. **Prospect and Qualify:** Prospecting means identifying potential customers. Qualifying means choosing those who are most likely to buy your product. Choosing the right prospects makes salespeople more efficient, since it helps them focus their limited time in areas that will yield results. Companies find prospects in a number of different ways, from trade shows, to direct mail, to cold calling. In a retail environment, everyone who walks in the door is a prospect, so salespeople either ask questions or look for visual cues to qualify customers.

2. **Prepare:** Before making a sales call, research is critical, especially in a business-to-business environment. What are your prospect's wants and needs? What are his or her current product lines? Who are the key competitors? What are the biggest internal and external challenges? How much time is your prospect willing to give you? The answers to these questions will help you customize your presentation for maximum effectiveness.

3. **Present:** You've probably heard that you don't get a second chance to make a good first impression, and that's especially true in sales. With so many options and so little time, buyers often look for reasons to eliminate choices; a weak first impression provides an easy reason to eliminate you. Your presentation itself should match the features of your product to the benefits that your customer seeks (a chance to use all that preparation). Testimonials, letters of praise from satisfied current customers, can push forward the sale by reducing risk for your prospect. A demonstration can be the clincher. When test-driving cars, a demonstration is a no-brainer. But in other categories, technology can help demonstrate products that are too big to move.

4. **Handle Objections:** The key to success here is to view objections as opportunities rather than criticism. Objections give you a chance to learn more about the needs of your prospects and to elaborate on the benefits of your product. You should definitely anticipate as many objections as possible and prepare responses. One response may be connecting prospects with others in your company who can better handle their concerns. This approach offers the additional benefit of deepening ties between your prospect and your company.

Don't look now… Somebody might be watching!

In fact, if you're on the Internet, somebody is almost certainly watching. *The Wall Street Journal* recently reported that the average visit to the world's 50 most popular websites in December 2011 triggered 56 instances of data collection, up from just 10 instances in November 2010. That staggering increase comes thanks to the online-advertising business, which increasingly relies on data about users' web surfing behavior to target ads. Advertisers buy data about users' web browsing. As soon as a user visits a web page, the visit is sold to the highest bidder, in real-time bidding, based on attributes such as the type of page visited or previous web browsing by the user. To make the auctions work, advertising companies are racing to place tracking technology on as many websites as possible. But don't blame your favorite site. Due to electronic "piggybacking," websites often don't know how much data are being collected about their users. So if the hair on the back of your neck stands up the next time you visit your favorite site, now you know why… you really are being watched![28]

© Andresr/Shutterstock.com

5. **Close Sale:** Closing the sale—or asking the prospect to buy—is at the heart of the selling process. The close should flow naturally from the prior steps, but often it doesn't—sealing the deal can be surprisingly tough. One approach may be a trial close: "Would you like the 15-inch screen or the 17-inch screen?" If your prospect is still reluctant to buy, you may want to offer another alternative, or a special financial incentive. Even if the prospect doesn't actually make the purchase, remember that he or she may be willing in the future, so keep the door open.

6. **Follow-up:** The sales process doesn't end when the customer pays. The quality of service and support plays a crucial role in future sales from the same customer, and getting those sales is much easier than finding brand-new prospects. Great relationships with current customers also lead to testimonials and referrals that build momentum for long-term sales success.

Two personal selling trends are gathering momentum in a number of organizations: consultative selling and team selling. *Consultative selling* involves shifting the focus from the products to the customers. On a day-to-day basis, the practice involves a deep understanding of customer needs. Through lots and lots of active listening, consultative salespeople offer practical solutions to customer problems—solutions that use their products. While consultative selling generates powerful customer loyalty, it involves a significant—and expensive—time investment from the sales force.

Team selling tends to be especially effective for large, complex accounts. The approach includes a group of specialists from key functional areas of the company—not just sales but also engineering, finance, customer service, and others. The goal is to uncover opportunities and respond to needs that would be beyond the capacity of a single salesperson. In these situations, a key part of the salesperson's role is to connect and coordinate the right network of contacts.

12-6c Choosing the Right Promotional Mix: Not Just a Science

There are no fail-safe rules for choosing the right combination of promotional tools. The mix varies dramatically among various industries but also within specific industry segments. The best approach may simply be to consider the following questions in developing the mix that works best for your products.

○ **Product Characteristics:** How can you best communicate the features of your product? Is it simple or complex? Is it high-priced or inexpensive? A specialized, high-priced item, for example, might require an investment in personal selling, whereas a simple, low-cost product might lend itself to billboard advertising.

○ **Product Life Cycle:** Where does your product stand in its life cycle? Are you developing awareness? Are you generating desire? What about driving purchases? And building loyalty? The answers will clearly affect your promotional focus. For instance, if you're developing awareness, you might focus more on advertising, but if you're aiming to drive immediate sales, you'll probably emphasize sales promotion.

○ **Target Audience:** How big is your target audience? Where do they live and work? A small target audience—especially if it's geographically dispersed—would lend itself to personal selling or direct mail. A sizable target audience might suggest advertising as an effective way to reach large numbers. Audience expectations should also play a role in your promotional mix decisions.

○ **Push Versus Pull:** Does your industry emphasize push or pull strategies? A **push strategy** involves motivating distributors to "push" your product to the final consumers, usually through heavy trade promotion and personal selling. A **pull strategy** involves creating demand from your final consumers so that they "pull" your products through the distribution channels. Many successful brands use a combination of push and pull strategies to achieve their goals. P&G recently launched a consumer marketing campaign for Crest toothpaste featuring an "Irresistibility IQ" quiz for club-goers, but it also promotes heavily to dentists, hoping that those dentists will recommend Crest to their patients.

○ **Competitive Environment:** How are your key competitors handling their promotional strategies? Would it make more sense for you to follow their lead or to forge your own promotional path? If all your competitors offer coupons, for instance, your customers may expect you to offer them as well. Or if the environment is cluttered, you might want to focus on emerging promotional approaches such as advergaming.

○ **Budget:** What are your promotional goals? How much money will it take to achieve them? (Answering this question is tough, but it's clearly important.) How much are your competitors spending in each area of the mix? And how much money do you have for promotion? Even though available budget shouldn't drive the promotional mix, it plays a crucial role, especially for smaller businesses.

THE BIG PICTURE

The possibilities in both product development and promotional strategy have rapidly multiplied in the past few years alone. But companies can't deliver on the potential without well-oiled teamwork throughout the organization. For instance, the operations group must focus on quality, the accounting group must focus on cost, and the finance group must focus on funding—but from a big picture standpoint, all groups must work toward the same overarching goal: maximizing customer value. Promotion also requires coordination within the organization and among the outside suppliers who provide promotional services. Finally, the best ideas for both product and promotion can come from any department. Marketers who stay ahead of the curve will only sharpen their competitive edge in the decade to come.

CAREERS

Product development decisions are often the bailiwick of the most senior managers who may work quite closely with engineering departments to bring their product development visions to life. The senior management team at Apple is famous for meticulously (some say relentlessly) guiding Apple's blockbuster product development process. In this scenario, a key role of marketers, whose titles may be product manager or brand manager is typically to provide input and feedback from consumers and distributers. Jobs in promotion are highly varied. Most medium and large firms use a sales force, but in small organizations, everyone typically participates in sales to varying degrees, helping to land clients and keep them happy. Marketing promotion is handled both within companies and within agencies that specialize in everything from website development to advertising. Given the growing role of the Internet in marketing promotion, creativity and technological savvy are critical success factors.

CAREERS IN PRODUCT AND PROMOTION

What else?
RIP & REVIEW CARDS IN THE BACK
and visit www.cengagebrain.com!

13

Distribution and Pricing:

Right Product, Right Person, Right Place, Right Price

LEARNING OBJECTIVES

After studying this chapter, you will be able to:

13-1 Define distribution and differentiate between channels of distribution and physical distribution

13-2 Describe the various types of wholesale distributors

13-3 Discuss strategies and trends in store and nonstore retailing

13-4 Explain the key factors in physical distribution

13-5 Outline core pricing objectives and strategies

13-6 Discuss pricing in practice, including the role of consumer perceptions

> "WE NOW LIVE IN AN AGE OF SURREAL ABUNDANCE."
>
> — JONAH LEHRER, AUTHOR

Distribution and pricing are not the most glamorous elements of the marketing mix, but managed effectively, they can provide a powerful competitive advantage. While this chapter will cover distribution and pricing strategies separately, keep in mind that the two are linked both with each other, and with the product and promotional strategies of any successful brand.

13-1 Distribution: Getting Your Product to Your Customer

Next time you go to the grocery store, look around—the average U.S. supermarket carries about 50,000 different products.[1] Is your favorite brand of soda part of the mix? Why? How did it get from the factory to your neighborhood store? Where else could you find that soda? How far would you be willing to go to get it? These are marketing distribution questions that contribute directly to the **distribution strategy**: getting the right product to the right person at the right place at the right time.

The distribution strategy has two elements: channels of distribution and physical distribution. A **channel of distribution** is the path that a product takes from the producer to the consumer, while **physical distribution** is the actual movement of products along that path. Some producers choose to sell their products directly to their customers through a **direct channel**. No one stands between the producer and the customer. Examples range from Dell computers, to local farmers markets, to factory outlet stores. But most producers use **channel intermediaries** to help their products move more efficiently and effectively from their factories to their consumers. Hershey's, for example, sells chocolate bars to Sam's Club—a channel intermediary—which may, in turn, sell them to you.

13-1a The Role of Distributors: Adding Value

You might be asking yourself why we need distributors. Wouldn't it be a lot less expensive to buy directly from the producers? The answer, surprisingly, is no. Distributors add value—additional benefits—to products. They charge for adding that value, but typically they charge less than it would cost for consumers or producers to add that value on their own. When distributors add to the cost of a product without providing comparable benefits, the middlemen don't stay in business. Fifteen years ago, for instance, most people bought plane tickets from travel agents. But when the Internet reduced the cost and inconvenience of buying tickets directly from airlines, thousands of travel agencies lost their customers.

One core role of distributors is to reduce the number of transactions—and the associated costs—for goods to flow from producers to consumers. As you'll see in Exhibit 13.1, even one marketing intermediary in the distribution channel can funnel goods from producers to consumers with far fewer costly transactions.

Distributors add value, or utility, in a number of different ways: form, time, place, ownership, information, and service. Sometimes the distributors deliver the value (rather than adding it themselves), but often they add new utility that wouldn't otherwise be present. As you read through the various types of utility, keep in mind that they are often interrelated, building on each other to maximize value.

Form utility provides customer satisfaction by converting inputs into finished products. Clearly, form utility is primarily a part of manufacturing. Nabisco provides form utility by transforming flour and sugar into cookies. But retailers

distribution strategy A plan for delivering the right product to the right person at the right place at the right time.

channel of distribution The network of organizations and processes that links producers to consumers.

physical distribution The actual, physical movement of products along the distribution pathway.

direct channel A distribution process that links the producer and the customer with no intermediaries.

channel intermediaries Distribution organizations—informally called "middlemen"—that facilitate the movement of products from the producer to the consumer.

can add form utility as well. Yogurtland, for instance, converts milky liquid into a soft-serve treat.

Time utility adds value by making products available at a convenient time for consumers. In our 24/7 society, consumers feel entitled to instant gratification, a benefit that distributors can provide more easily than most producers. Consider one-hour dry cleaning, or soda machines at your school. These distributors provide options for filling your needs at a time that works for you.

Place utility satisfies customer needs by providing the right products in the right place. Gas stations and fast food, for instance, often cluster conveniently at the bottom of freeway ramps. ATMs—essentially electronic distributors—are readily available in locations that range from grocery stores to college cafeterias.

Ownership utility adds value by making it easier for customers to actually possess the goods and services that they purchase. Providing credit, cashing checks, delivering goods,

Zappos has built its brand around superb customer service.

© Ethan Miller/Getty Images

and installing products are all examples of how distributors make it easier for customers to own their products.

Information utility boosts customer satisfaction by providing helpful information. Zappos.com, for instance, hires customer service experts to guide its customers through its website to the perfect pair of shoes. Similarly, most skateboard stores hire skater salespeople who gladly help customers find the best board for them.

Service utility adds value by providing fast, friendly, personalized service. Examples include placing a special order for that part you need to customize your computer, or picking out outfits that work for your body type in your local clothing boutique. Distributors that provide service utility typically create a loyal base of customers.

The Members of the Channel: Retailers versus Wholesalers Many producers sell their goods through multiple channels of distribution. Some channels have many members, while others have only a few. The main distinction among channel members is whether they are retailers or wholesalers. **Retailers** are the distributors that most of us know and use on a daily basis. They sell products directly to final consumers. Examples include 7-Eleven markets, Starbucks, and Urban Outfitters. **Wholesalers**, on the other hand, buy products from the producer and sell them to businesses (or other nonfinal users, such as hospitals, nonprofits, and the government). The businesses that buy from wholesalers can be retailers, other wholesalers, or business users. To complicate this fairly simple concept, some distributors act as both wholesalers and retailers. Costco, for example, sells directly to businesses *and* to consumers.

EXHIBIT 13.1 Reducing Transactions through Marketing Intermediaries

Manufacturer — Manufacturer — Manufacturer — Manufacturer

Customer — Customer — Customer — Customer

Manufacturer — Manufacturer — Manufacturer — Manufacturer

Marketing Intermediary

Customer — Customer — Customer — Customer

© Cengage Learning 2013

Wholesalers: Sorting Out the Options

Some wholesalers are owned by producers, while others are owned by retailers, but the vast majority—accounting for about two-thirds of all the wholesale trade—are **independent wholesaling businesses**. These companies represent a number of different producers, distributing their goods to a range of customers. Independent wholesalers fall into two categories: (1) **merchant wholesalers**, who take legal possession, or title, of the goods they distribute, and (2) **agents/brokers**, who don't take title of the goods.

13–2a Merchant Wholesalers

Merchant wholesalers comprise about 80% of all wholesalers. By taking legal title to the goods they distribute, merchant wholesalers reduce the risk of producers' products being damaged or stolen—or even that they just won't sell. Taking title also allows merchant wholesalers to develop their own marketing strategies, including pricing.

- ○ Full-service merchant wholesalers provide a complete array of services to the retailers or business users who typically purchase their goods. This includes warehousing, shipping, promotional assistance, product repairs, and credit.

- ○ Limited-service merchant wholesalers provide fewer services to their customers. For example, some might warehouse products but not deliver them. Others might warehouse and deliver but not provide credit or marketing assistance. The specific categories of limited-service merchant wholesalers include the following:

  - ○ *Drop Shippers:* Drop shippers take legal title of the merchandise, but they never physically process it. They simply organize and facilitate product shipments directly from the producer to their customers. Drop shippers are common in industries with bulky products, such as coal or timber. Amazon, however, successfully

AP Images/Ross D. Franklin

Who's the real hog in the food distribution system?

Today, if you crave a fresh peach in the middle of winter, you can probably buy it at the supermarket, thanks to modern agribusiness, technology, and transportation. Some might say this makes you an energy hog because that peach was likely shipped from the southern hemisphere, and you could just as easily have chosen locally-grown produce from your neighborhood farmer's market. They may support their argument by pointing out that the food at the supermarket has traveled an average of 1,500 miles to get there.

But locally grown does not mean environmentally friendly—harmful pesticides can be used in any location. The biggest part of fossil fuel use in industrial farming is not transportation or machinery, it's chemicals. As much as 40% of the energy used in the food system goes to produce fertilizers and pesticides.

But you're still not off the hook—no matter where you buy your produce, you're probably still an energy hog, simply by virtue of the American food storage and preparation systems. A single 10-mile round trip by car to the farmers' market will easily burn about 14,000 calories of fossil fuel energy. Refrigerator and freezer storage plus cooking also add energy hits. In total, household usage accounts for 22% of all the energy expenditures in the United States.

So what's the best approach? One expert advocates that "the best way to make the most of these truly precious resources of land, favorable climates, and human labor is to grow…all produce…in the places where they grow best and with the most efficient technologies—and then pay the relatively tiny energy cost to get them to market, as we do with every other commodity in the economy. Sometimes that means growing vegetables in your backyard. Sometimes that means buying vegetables grown in California or Costa Rica."[2]

pioneered the use of drop shipping in e-commerce, where it has become a standard shipping method for a number of major websites.

- ○ *Cash and Carry Wholesalers:* These distributors service customers who are too small to merit in-person sales calls from wholesaler reps. Customers must make the trip to the wholesaler themselves and cart their own products back to their stores. Costco and Staples are both examples.

multichannel retailing
Providing multiple distribution channels for consumers to buy a product.

○ *Truck Jobbers:* Typically working with perishable goods such as bread, truck jobbers drive their products to their customers, who are usually smaller grocery stores. Their responsibilities often include checking the stock, suggesting reorder quantities, and removing out-of-date goods.

13-2b Agents and Brokers

Agents and brokers connect buyers and sellers and facilitate transactions in exchange for commissions. But they do not take legal ownership of the goods they distribute. Many insurance companies, for instance, distribute via agents, while brokers often handle real estate and seasonal products such as fruits and vegetables.

13-3 Retailers: The Consumer Connection

Retailers represent the last stop on the distribution path, since they sell goods and services directly to final consumers. Given their tight consumer connection, retailers must keep in especially close touch with rapidly changing consumer needs and wants.

Smart retailers gain a competitive edge by providing more utility, or added value, than their counterparts. Low prices are only part of the equation. Other elements clearly include customer service, product selection, advertising, and location. The look and feel of the retailer—whether online or on-ground—is another critical element.

Retailing falls into two main categories: store and nonstore. But as we discuss each type, keep in mind that the lines between them are not always clear. In fact, **multichannel retailing**—or encouraging consumers to buy through different venues—is an emerging phenomenon. Some marketers have sold their products through multiple channels for many years. For example, on any given day, you could purchase a Coke from a grocery store, a restaurant, or a vending machine. But the emergence of the Internet has provided a host of new opportunities for firms that hadn't previously considered a multichannel approach. An active relationship between on-ground and online outlets has become pivotal for many retailers.

13-3a Store Retailers

While other retail channels are growing, traditional stores remain the 800-pound gorilla of the retail industry, accounting for well over 90% of total retail. Stores range in size from tiny mom-and-pop groceries to multi-acre superstores dwarfed only by their parking lots. Exhibit 13.2 highlights examples of different store types.

Both retailers and the producers who distribute through them must carefully consider their distribution strategy. The three key strategic options are intensive, selective, and exclusive.

Exhibit 13.2 Retail Store Categories

STORE TYPE	STORE DESCRIPTION	EXAMPLES
CATEGORY KILLER	Dominates its category by offering a huge variety of one type of product.	OfficeMax, Best Buy, Staples
CONVENIENCE STORE	Sells a small range of everyday and impulse products at easy-to-access locations with long hours and quick checkout.	7-Eleven, AM/PM markets, Famima, and a wide range of local stores
DEPARTMENT STORE	Offers a wide variety of merchandise (e.g., clothes, furniture, cosmetics), plus (usually) a high level of service.	Nordstrom, Macy's, JCPenney
DISCOUNT STORE	Offers a wide array of merchandise at significantly lower prices and with less service than most department stores.	Target, Walmart, Kmart
OUTLET STORE	Producer-owned store sells directly to the public at a huge discount. May include discontinued, flawed, or overrun items.	Nike, Versace, Quicksilver, Calvin Klein, Converse, GUESS
SPECIALTY STORE	Sells a wide selection of merchandise within a narrow category, such as auto parts.	Barnes & Noble, Victoria's Secret, Claire's, AutoZone
SUPERMARKET	Offers a wide range of food products, plus limited nonfood items (e.g., toilet paper).	Kroger, Safeway, Albertson's, Whole Foods, Trader Joe's
SUPERCENTER	Sells a complete selection of food and general merchandise at a steep discount in a single enormous location.	Walmart Supercenters, Super Target
WAREHOUSE CLUB	Sells discounted food and general merchandise to club members in a large warehouse format.	Costco, Sam's Club

© Cengage Learning 2013

"The size of supermarkets has increased more than 20% since 1994."

— JONAH LEHRER, AUTHOR

© italianestro/Shutterstock.com

Intensive Distribution Intensive distribution involves placing your products in as many stores as possible (or placing your stores themselves in as many locations as possible). This strategy makes the most sense for low-cost convenience goods that consumers won't travel too far to find. Marketers have chosen this strategy for McDonald's, Crest toothpaste, and *People* magazine, among thousands of other items.

Selective Distribution Selective distribution means placing your products only with preferred retailers (or establishing your stores only in limited locations). This approach tends to work best for medium- and higher-priced products or stores that consumers don't expect to find on every street corner. Marketers have chosen this strategy for Nordstrom, In & Out Burger, and most brands of paintball equipment, for instance.

Exclusive Distribution Exclusive distribution means establishing only one retail outlet in a given area. Typically, that one retailer has exclusive distribution rights and provides exceptional service and selection. This strategy tends to work for luxury-good providers with a customer base that actively seeks their products. Examples include top-end cars such as Lamborghini, and fashion trendsetters such as Versace.

The **wheel of retailing** offers another key strategic consideration. The wheel is a classic theory that suggests retail firms—sometimes even entire retail categories—become more upscale as they go through their life cycles. For instance, it's easiest to enter a business on a shoestring, gaining customers by offering low prices. But eventually businesses trade up their selection, service, and facilities to maintain and build their customer base. Higher prices then follow, creating vulnerability to new, lower-priced competitors. And thus the wheel keeps rolling.

Although the wheel of retailing theory does describe many basic retail patterns, it doesn't account for stores that launch at the high end of the market (e.g., Whole Foods) and those that retain their niche as deep discounters (e.g., Dollar General or Taco Bell). But the wheel theory does underscore the core principle that retailers must meet changing consumer needs in a relentlessly competitive environment.

> **wheel of retailing** A classic distribution theory that suggests that retail firms and retail categories become more upscale as they go through their life cycles.

13-3b Nonstore Retailers

While most retail dollars flow through brick-and-mortar stores, a growing number of sales go through other channels, or nonstore retailers. The key players represent online retailing, direct-response retailing, direct selling, and vending.

Online Retailing Also known as "e-tailing," online retailing grew at the astonishing rate of nearly 25% per year for most of the early 2000s. But the torrid pace began to slow in 2008 with the onset of the recession. Online retailing grew only 1.6% in 2009, but growth bounced back to over 12% in 2011. Looking forward, experts predict that annual growth will remain robust. Much of the growth will likely come at the expense of on-ground retail, as consumers continue to shift to online channels. The bigger name brands—including online-only brands, such as Amazon, and on-ground brands with a strong web presence, such as Best Buy—seem poised to benefit most, since cautious consumers are most familiar with them.[3]

Online retailers, like their on-ground counterparts, have learned that great customer service can be a powerful differentiator. Simply "getting eyeballs" isn't enough, since—depending on the industry—fewer than 5% of the people visiting a typical website convert into paying customers. Overstock.com, for instance, has been a pioneer in online customer service, hiring and training 60 specialists who engage customers in live chats, available 24/7. When a customer has a live chat with one of its specialists, the average purchase amount doubles. In fact, according to the National Retail Federation (NRF), shoppers have increasingly identified Internet-only retailers among those who offered the best customer service. In 2012, Amazon.com took top honors in the annual NRF/American Express Customers' Choice survey, and two other online retailers—Overstock.com and Zappos.com—placed in its top five positions for the fourth year in a row for retailers that offer the best customer service in any retail format.[4]

Despite the advantages, online retailers face two major hurdles. The first is that products must be delivered, and even the fastest deliery services typically take at least a couple of days. But the truly daunting hurdle is the lack of security on the Web. As online retailers and software developers create increasingly secure systems, hackers develop more sophisticated tools to crack their new codes.

Direct Response Retailing This category includes catalogs, telemarketing, and advertising (such as infomercials) meant to elicit direct consumer sales. While many traditional catalog retailers have also established successful websites, the catalog side of the business continues to thrive. Victoria's Secret, for instance, sends a mind-boggling 400 million catalogs each year—that's more than four catalogs for every American woman between the ages of 15 and 64. Telemarketing, both inbound and outbound, also remains a potent distribution channel, despite the popular National Do Not Call list established in 2003.

Direct Selling This channel includes all methods of selling directly to customers in their homes or workplaces. Door-to-door sales has enjoyed a resurgence in the wake of the National Do Not Call list, but the real strength of direct selling lies in **multilevel marketing**, or **MLM**. Multilevel marketing involves hiring independent contractors to sell products to their personal network of friends and colleagues and to recruit new salespeople in return for a percentage of their commissions. Mary Kay Cosmetics and The Pampered Chef have both enjoyed enormous success in this arena, along with pioneering companies such as Tupperware.

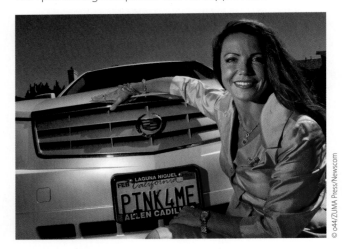

© 044/ZUMA Press/Newscom

Vending Until about a decade ago, vending machines in the United States sold mostly soft drinks and snacks. But more recently, the selection has expanded (and the machines have gone more upscale) as marketers recognize the value of providing their products as conveniently as possible to their target consumers. The Maine Lobster Game, for example, allows

customers to catch their own fresh lobster dinner with a metal claw in restaurants and bars. But other countries are far ahead of the United States in the vending arena. In Japan, for instance, people buy everything from blue jeans to beef from vending machines. As technology continues to roll forward, U.S. consumers are likely to see a growing number of vending machines for products as diverse as "fresh-baked" pizza, digital cameras, and specialty coffee drinks.

> # "Far eastern trade accounts for 90% of the shipments through the Port of Los Angeles."
> — CNBC

13-4 Physical Distribution: Planes, Trains, and Much, Much More

Determining the best distribution channels for your product is only the first half of your distribution strategy. The second half is the physical distribution strategy: determining how your product will flow through the channel from the producer to the consumer.

The **supply chain** for a product includes not only its distribution channels but also the string of suppliers who deliver products to the producers. (See Exhibit 13.3.) Planning and coordinating the movement of products along the supply chain—from the raw materials to the final consumers—is called **supply chain management** or **SCM**. **Logistics** is a subset of SCM that focuses more on tactics (the actual movement of products) than on strategy.

At one time, relationships among the members of the supply chain were contentious. But these days, companies that foster collaboration, rather than competition, have typically experienced more success. Vendor-managed inventory is an emerging strategy—pioneered by Walmart—that allows suppliers to determine buyer needs and automatically ship product. This strategy saves time and money but also requires an extraordinary level of trust and information-sharing among members of the supply chain.

In our turbocharged 24/7 society, supply chain management has become increasingly complex. Gap, for instance, contracts with more than 3,000 factories in more than 50 different countries, and distributes its products to

Exhibit 13.3 Elements of the Supply Chain

The supply chain highlights the links among the various organizations in the production and distribution process.

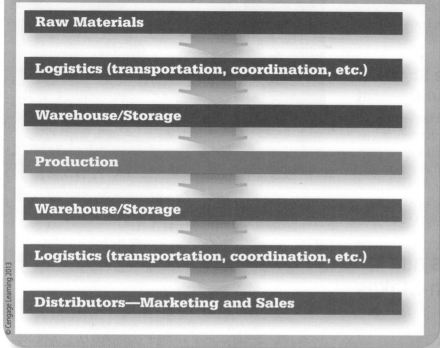

- Raw Materials
- Logistics (transportation, coordination, etc.)
- Warehouse/Storage
- Production
- Warehouse/Storage
- Logistics (transportation, coordination, etc.)
- Distributors—Marketing and Sales

© Cengage Learning 2013

○ **Order Processing:** How should we manage incoming and outgoing orders? What would be most efficient for our customers and suppliers?

○ **Customer Service:** How can we serve our customers most effectively? How can we reduce waiting times and facilitate interactions?

○ **Transportation:** How can we move products most efficiently through the supply chain? What are the key tradeoffs?

○ **Security:** How can we keep products safe from vandals, theft, and accidents every step of the way?

And fragile or perishable products, of course, require even more considerations.

modes of transportation The various transportation options—such as planes, trains, and railroads—for moving products through the supply chain.

about 3,000 stores in eight different countries. The coordination requirements are mind-boggling. Key management decisions include the following considerations:

○ **Warehousing:** How many warehouses do we need? Where should we locate our warehouses?

○ **Materials Handling:** How should we move products within our facilities? How can we best balance efficiency with effectiveness?

○ **Inventory Control:** How much inventory should we keep on hand? How should we store and distribute it? What about costs such as taxes and insurance?

13-4a Transportation Decisions

Moving products through the supply chain is so important that it deserves its own section. The various options—trains, planes, and railroads, for instance—are called **modes of transportation**. To make smart decisions, marketers must consider what each mode offers in terms of cost, speed, dependability, flexibility, availability, and frequency of shipments. The right choice, of course, depends on the needs of the business and on the product itself. See Exhibit 13.4 for a description of the transportation options.

Depending on factors such as warehousing, docking facilities, and accessibility, some distributors use several different

Exhibit 13.4 Modes of Transportation

MODE	PERCENTAGE OF U.S. VOLUME BASED ON 2007 TON-MILES	COST	SPEED	ON-TIME DEPENDABILITY	FLEXIBILITY IN HANDLING	FREQUENCY OF SHIPMENTS	AVAILABILITY
RAIL	39.5%	Medium	Slow	Medium	Medium	Low	Extensive
TRUCK	28.6%	High	Fast	High	Medium	High	Most extensive
SHIP	12.0%	Lowest	Slowest	Lowest	Highest	Lowest	Limited
PLANE	0.3%	Highest	Fastest	Medium	Low	Medium	Medium
PIPELINE	19.6%	Low	Slow	Highest	Lowest	Highest	Most limited

Source: Table 1-46b: U.S. Ton-Miles of Freight (BTS Special Tabulation), 2007 data, Bureau of Transportation website, http://www.bts.gov/publications/national_transportation_statistics/html/table_01_46b.html (accessed June 30, 2010).

modes of transportation. If you owned a clothing boutique in Las Vegas, for example, chances are that much of your merchandise would travel by boat from China to Long Beach, California, and then by truck from Long Beach to Las Vegas.

13-4b Proactive Supply Chain Management

A growing number of marketers have turned to supply chain management to build a competitive edge through greater efficiency. But given the complexity of the field, many firms choose to outsource this challenge to experts rather than handling it internally. Companies that specialize in helping other companies manage the supply chain—such as UPS—have done particularly well in today's market.

13-5 Pricing Objectives and Strategies: A High-Stakes Game

Pricing strategy clearly has a significant impact on the success of any organization. Price plays a key role in determining demand for your products, which directly influences a company's profitability. Most people, after all, have a limited amount of money and a practically infinite number of ways they could spend it. Price affects their spending choices at a more fundamental level than most other variables.

But ironically, price is perhaps the toughest variable for marketers to control. Both legal constraints and marketing intermediaries (distributors) play roles in determining the final price of most products. Marketers must also consider costs, competitors, investors, taxes, and product strategies.

In today's frenetic environment, stable pricing is no longer the norm. Smart marketers continually evaluate and refine their pricing strategies to ensure that they meet their goals. Even the goals themselves may shift in response to the changing market. Common objectives and strategies include building profitability, boosting volume, matching the competition, and creating prestige.

13-5a Building Profitability

Since long-term profitability is a fundamental goal of most businesses, profitability targets are often the starting point for pricing strategies. Many firms express these goals in terms of either return on investment (ROI) or return on sales (ROS). Keep in mind that profitability is the positive difference between revenue (or total sales) and costs. Firms can

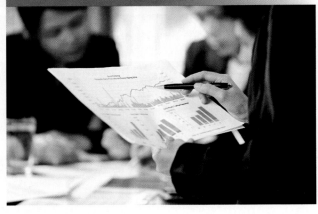

Many firms express long-term profitability goals in terms of either return on investment or return on sales.

© OtnaYdur/Shutterstock.com

boost profits by increasing prices or decreasing costs, since either strategy will lead to a greater spread between the two. Doing both, of course, is tricky, but companies that succeed—such as Apple—typically dominate their markets.

13-5b Boosting Volume

Companies usually express volume goals in terms of market share—the percentage of a market controlled by a company or a product. Amazon.com, for example, launched with volume objectives. Its goal was to capture as many "eyeballs" as possible, in hopes of later achieving profitability through programs that depend on volume, such as advertising on its site. A volume objective usually leads to one of the following strategies.

Penetration Pricing Penetration pricing, a strategy for pricing new products, aims to capture as much of the market as possible through rock-bottom prices. Each individual sale typically yields a tiny profit; the real money comes from the sheer volume of sales. One key benefit of this strategy is that it tends to discourage competitors, who may be scared off by the slim margins. But penetration pricing makes sense only in categories that don't have a significant group of consumers who would be willing to pay a premium (otherwise, the marketer would be leaving money on the table). For obvious reasons, companies that use penetration pricing are usually focused on controlling costs. JetBlue is a key example. Its prices are often unbeatable, but it strictly controls costs by using a single kind of jet, optimizing turnaround times at the gate, and using many non-major airports.

Everyday-Low Pricing Also known as "sustained discount pricing," everyday-low pricing (EDLP) aims to achieve long-term profitability through volume. Walmart is clearly the king of EDLP with "Always low prices. *Always!*" But Costco uses the same strategy to attract a much more upscale audience. The difference between the two customer groups quickly becomes apparent by glancing at the cars, while strolling through the two parking lots. Costco customers are typically seeking everyday discounts because they want to, not because they need to. The product mix—eclectic and upscale—reflects the customer base. (Costco sells discounted fine wine, low-priced rotisserie chickens, fresh king crab legs, and high-end electronics.) While Costco posted years of healthy, sustained growth, the firm ran into trouble at the end of 2008. As the recession tightened its grip, sales began to soften, especially in non-food categories, suggesting that EDLP may be most effective for less-upscale products.[5] By 2010, Costco had recovered and returned to its historical growth trajectory.

High/Low Pricing The high/low pricing strategy tries to increase traffic in retail stores by special sales on a limited number of products, and higher everyday prices on others. Often used—and overused—in grocery stores, drug stores, and department stores, this strategy can alienate customers who feel cheated when a product they bought for full price goes on sale soon afterward. High/low pricing can also train consumers to buy only when products are on sale.

Loss-Leader Pricing Closely related to high/low pricing, loss-leader pricing means pricing a handful of items—or loss leaders—temporarily below cost to drive traffic. The retailer loses money on the loss leaders but aims to make up the difference (and then some) on other purchases. To encourage other purchases, retailers typically place loss leaders at the back of the store, forcing customers to navigate past a tempting array of more profitable items. The loss-leader strategy has been used effectively by producers, as well. Gillette, for instance, gives away some shavers practically for free but reaps handsome profits as consumers buy replacement blades. Similarly, Microsoft has sold its Xbox systems at a loss in order to increase potential profits from high-margin video games. But the loss-leader strategy can't be used everywhere, since a number of states have made loss leaders illegal for anticompetitive reasons.[6]

> **"If automobiles** had followed the same development cycle as the computer, a Rolls-Royce would today cost $100, get a million miles per gallon, and explode once a year, killing everyone inside."
>
> — Robert Cringely, technology journalist

high/low pricing A pricing strategy designed to drive traffic to retail stores by special sales on a limited number of products, and higher everyday prices on others.

loss-leader pricing Closely related to high/low pricing, loss-leader pricing means pricing a handful of items—or loss leaders—temporarily below cost to drive traffic.

13-5c Matching the Competition

The key goal is to set prices based on what everyone else is doing. Usually, the idea is to wipe out price as a point of comparison, forcing customers to choose their product based on other factors. Examples include Coke and Pepsi, Honda and Toyota, Chevron and Mobil, and Delta and United. But sometimes one or two competitors emerge that drive pricing for entire industries. Marlboro, for instance, leads the pack in terms of cigarette pricing, with other brands falling into place behind.

Hide and Seek Pricing

Have you ever ordered the special at a restaurant and then been *shocked* at the size of the bill? Or maybe you've purchased a cheap printer and found yourself unhappily surprised at the outrageous monthly cost of ink cartridges to keep it in operation? This increasingly common practice—of marketers highlighting information that they want you to have (e.g., the low price of the printer) and deemphasizing the information that they would rather you don't have (e.g., the high cost of print cartridges)—is called price "shrouding." It isn't exactly fraud, but many consumers believe that it isn't quite ethical, either. The only practical solution is to become a smarter consumer. Always read the fine print. Ask questions when you aren't sure about pricing, even if asking feels a bit uncomfortable. Remember that we put ourselves in a vulnerable position every time we hesitate to ask. And be sure to keep in mind that if an offer seems too good to be true, it probably is—you just need to examine the details more carefully.[7]

Ooops! What were they thinking?

"Slippery Finger" Pricing Goofs

If a price seems too good to be true, it probably is. But seeking an incredible bargain can still make sense—dollars and cents. Due to "slippery finger" typos, frequent price changes, and programming glitches, online retailers are especially vulnerable to pricing mistakes. Without human cashier confirmation, it's tough to catch the goofs. And to magnify the problem, quick communication on the Web almost ensures a flood of customers placing orders as soon as the wrong price goes live.

A sampling of recent online "deals":

- ⟳ **Free flights from Los Angeles to Fiji**
- ⟳ **Round-trip tickets from San Jose, CA, to Paris for $27.98**
- ⟳ **$1,049 televisions wrongly listed for $99.99 on Amazon**
- ⟳ **$588 Hitachi monitors mistakenly marked down to $164**
- ⟳ **$379 Axim X3i PDAs wrongly priced at $79 on Dell's site**
- ⟳ **Five watches, worth $11,332, briefly sale-priced at $0.0 (with free shipping) on Ashford.com**

After the first few high-profile pricing disasters, online retailers have taken steps to protect themselves through specific disclaimers in their terms of use. And the courts have generally ruled that a company need not honor an offer if a reasonable person would recognize that it was a mistake.

But disclaimers and legal protections won't protect a retailer from customers who feel cheated. So companies that post pricing mistakes must choose between losing money by honoring offers or losing customer goodwill by canceling them—there simply isn't a winning option. But Travelocity—home of those unintended free tickets from Los Angeles to Fiji—has at least found a way to handle snafus with grace. Its Travelocity Guarantee program notes "If, say, we inadvertently advertise a fare that's just 'too good to be true,' like a free trip to Fiji, we'll work with you and our travel partners to make it up to you and find a solution that puts a smile on your face." So—happy shopping!

13-5d Creating Prestige

The core goal is to use price to send consumers a message about the high quality and exclusivity of a product—the higher the price, the better the product. Of course, this strategy works only if the product actually delivers top quality; otherwise, nobody would buy more than once (and those who do so would clearly spread the word). Rolex watches, Mont Blanc pens, and Bentley cars all use prestige pricing to reinforce their image.

Skimming Pricing This new product pricing strategy is a subset of prestige pricing. **Skimming pricing** involves offering new products at a premium price. The idea is to entice price-insensitive consumers—music fanatics, for example—to buy high when a product first enters the market. Once these customers have made their purchases, marketers will often introduce lower-priced versions of the same product to capture the bottom of the market. Apple used this strategy with its iPod, introducing its premium version for a hefty price tag. Once it had secured the big spenders, Apple introduced the lower-priced iPod Nanos and Shuffles with a powerful market response. But keep in mind that skimming works only when a product is tough to copy in terms of design, brand image, technology, or some other attribute. Otherwise, the fat margins will attract a host of competitors.

13-6 Pricing in Practice: A Real-World Approach

At this point, you may be wondering about economic theory. How do concepts such as supply and demand and price elasticity affect pricing decisions?

Even though most marketers are familiar with economics, they often don't have the information they need to apply the theories to their specific pricing strategies. Collecting data for supply and demand curves is expensive and time consuming, which may be unrealistic for rapidly changing markets. From a real-world standpoint, most marketers consider market-based factors—especially customer expectations and competitive prices—but they rely on cost-based pricing. The key question is: What price levels will allow me to cover my costs and achieve my objectives?

13-6a Breakeven Analysis

Breakeven analysis is a relatively simple process that determines the number of units a firm must sell to cover all costs. Sales above the breakeven point will generate a profit; sales below the breakeven point will lead to a loss. The actual equation looks like this:

$$\text{Breakeven Point (BP)} = \frac{\text{Total fixed costs (FC)}}{\text{Price/unit (P)} - \text{Variable cost/unit (VC)}}$$

If you were selling pizza, for example, your fixed costs might be $300,000 per year. Fixed costs stay the same regardless of how many pizzas you sell. Specific fixed costs might include the mortgage, equipment payments, advertising, insurance, and taxes. Suppose your variable cost per pizza—the cost of the ingredients and the cost of wages for the baker—were $4 per pizza. If your customers would pay $10 per pizza, you could use the breakeven equation to determine how many pizzas you'd need to sell in a year so that your total sales were equal to your total expenses. Remember: a company that is breaking even is not making a profit.

Here's how the break-even analysis would work for our pizza business:

$$BP = \frac{FC}{P - VC} = \frac{\$300,000}{\$10 - \$4} = \frac{\$300,000}{\$6} = 50,000 \text{ pizzas}$$

Over a one-year horizon, 50,000 pizzas would translate to about 303 pizzas per day. Is that reasonable? Could you do better? If so, fire up those ovens! If not, you have several choices, each with its own set of considerations:

⊃ **Raise Prices:** How much do other pizzas in your neighborhood cost? Are your pizzas better in some way? Would potential customers be willing to pay more?

⊃ **Decrease Variable Costs:** Could you use less expensive ingredients? Is it possible to hire less expensive help? How would these changes affect quality and sales?

⊃ **Decrease Fixed Costs:** Should you choose a different location? Can you lease cheaper equipment? Would

it make sense to advertise less often? How would these changes affect your business?

Clearly, there isn't one best strategy, but a break-even analysis helps marketers get a sense of where they stand and the hurdles they need to clear before actually introducing a product.

13-6b Fixed Margin Pricing

Many firms determine upfront how much money they need to make for each item they sell. The **profit margin**—which is the gap between the cost and the price on a per product basis—can be expressed as a dollar amount but more often is expressed as a percent. There are two key ways to determine margins.

1. **Cost-Based Pricing:** The most popular method of establishing a fixed margin starts with determining the actual cost of each product. The process is more complex than it may initially seem, since fixed costs must be allocated on a per-product basis, and some variable costs fluctuate dramatically on a daily or weekly basis. But once the per-product cost is set, the next step is to layer the margin on the cost to determine the price. Costco, for instance, has a strict policy that no branded item can be marked up by more than 14%, and no private-label item by more than 15%. Supermarkets, on the other hand, often mark up merchandise by 25%, and department stores by 50% or more. Margins in other industries can be much thinner.[8]

© pixelbully / Alamy

Putting iTunes on the Spot

The Apple iTunes store has enjoyed fantastic success since its introduction in 2001. The iTunes pay-99-cents-per-track pricing format revitalized a music industry badly battered by the wild popularity of music pirating sites such as Napster. Over the years, iTunes has had little or no meaningful competition, garnering 200 million accounts by 2011. But music fans in Europe may be just as likely to get their music from Swedish music subscription service, Spotify.com, which has a free, ad-supported option available to customers, as well as a premium service for unlimited access to the tracks on mobile phones and offline for about $16.50 per month. In mid-2011, Spotify announced a partnership with Facebook that allowed easy swapping of playlists and suddenly made downloaded music much more social—and a much better fit with today's social media-driven digital world. The result has been a significant competitive advantage for Spotify versus Apple iTunes.[9]

2. **Demand-Based Pricing:** This approach begins by determining what price consumers would be willing to pay. With that as a starting point, marketers subtract their desired margin, which yields their target costs. This method is more market-focused than cost-based pricing, but it's also more risky, since profits depend on achieving those target costs. A number of Japanese companies, such as Sony, have been very successful with this approach, achieving extraordinarily efficient production.

13-6c Consumer Pricing Perceptions: The Strategic Wild Card

You just don't know if you've found the right price until you figure out how consumers perceive it. And those perceptions can sometimes defy the straightforward logic of dollars and cents. Two key considerations are price–quality relationships and odd pricing.

The link between price and perceived quality can be powerful. Picture yourself walking into a local sporting goods store, looking for a new snowboard. They have several models of your favorite brand, most priced at around $450. But then you notice another option—same brand, same style—marked down to $79. Would you buy it? If you were like most consumers, you'd probably assume that something were wrong with a board that cheap. Would you be right? It's hard to know. Sometimes the relationship between price and quality is clear and direct, but that is not always the case. Regardless, consumers will use price as an indicator of quality unless they have additional information to guide their decision. Savvy marketers factor this tendency into their pricing strategies.

Marketers also must weigh the pros and cons of **odd pricing**, or ending prices in numbers below even dollars and

There are two kinds of fools in any market. One doesn't charge enough. The other charges too much.

— Russian Proverb

cents. A micro stereo system at Target, for instance, costs $99.99. Gasoline, of course, uses odd pricing to 99/100ths of a cent. But wouldn't round numbers be easier? Does that extra penny really make a difference? While the research is inconclusive, many marketers believe that jumping up to the "next" round number sends a message that prices have hit a whole new level. In other words, they believe that the *perceived* gap between $99.99 and $100.00 is much greater than the *actual* gap of 1%. And it certainly makes sense from an intuitive standpoint.

Odd prices have also come to signal a bargain, which is often—but not always—a benefit for the marketer. For instance, a big-screen TV for $999.99 might seem like a great deal, while knee surgery for $4,999.99 sounds kind of scary—you'd probably rather that your doctor charge $5,000. Likewise, a fast-food joint might charge $3.99 for its value meal, while fine restaurants almost always end their prices in zeros. Marketers can determine whether odd pricing would work for them by evaluating the strategy in light of the messages it sends to the target market.

© Fotogroove/Shutterstock.com

Go Figure!!

Classic economics—plus common sense—says that as consumers, we will research and weigh our options and make the best choice. But in the real world, consumers are not so rational. Our emotions can trump our minds. In fact, recent research shows that money can act like a drug on our brains. Even just counting your money can literally raise your pain threshold. Pricing hot buttons, such as "FREE!," "99 cents!," and "limited time!" can play games with our minds, too, luring us to purchase and consume products that we don't really even want! But the good news for marketers is that consumers are irrational in somewhat predictable ways—go figure!

Mere exposure to a high price makes a lower price seem reasonable, even if it isn't. So smart marketers often keep overpriced items in their line simply to promote sales of other items. For instance, if the most expensive necklace in a jewelry store is $100, and no one wants to buy it, the owner might add a $200 necklace to boost sales of the $100 necklace. Economists call this effect anchoring. And research shows that anchors are tough to shake. One key takeaway that goes beyond consumer goods: "be first to name a price in a negotiation—especially a salary negotiation—and don't worry about being overly reasonable."[10]

THE BIG PICTURE

Distribution and pricing are two fundamental elements of the marketing mix. In today's frenzied global economy, marketers are seeking a competitive edge through distribution management. Creating a profitable presence in multiple retail venues requires constant focus throughout the organization. And managing the supply chain—how products move along the path from raw materials to the final consumer—plays a crucial role in controlling costs and providing great customer service. Integrating effective technology during the entire process can separate the winners from the losers.

Pricing objectives and strategies are also pivotal since they directly impact both profitability and product image. As the market changes, successful companies continually reevaluate and modify their approach, working hand in hand with their accountants.

Looking ahead, a growing number of companies will probably move toward collaboration, rather than competition, as they manage their supply chains. And pricing will likely become even more dynamic in response to the changing market.

CAREERS

As the economy globalized, the process of distributing countless numbers of goods and services around the world as efficiently as possible led to the rise of the field of logistics, which encompasses transportation, warehousing, inventory management, and inspection. Specific jobs include truck driver, freight agent, warehouse manager, inspector, purchase agent, and scheduler. Some positions do not require higher education, but virtually all demand superior organizational skills and an entrenched detail orientation, plus a deep understanding of the complex web of rules, regulations, and laws that govern many aspects of logistics in our increasingly globalized world economy. In 2012, the median salary for logistics professionals was $91,000, with job growth anticipated in the south and southeast regions of the United States, plus significant opportunities abroad.[11]

In most companies, pricing is an integral part of the marketing manager's job—rather than a separate position—typically handled with support from cost accountants. Determining effective, profitable pricing strategies requires strong analytical skills and a broad strategic perspective with a focus on the long term.

CAREERS IN DISTRIBUTION AND PRICING

What *else?*

RIP & REVIEW CARDS **IN THE BACK**
and visit **www.cengagebrain.com!**

© Ben Bloom/Stone/Getty Images

14

Management, Motivation, and Leadership:
Bringing Business to Life

LEARNING OBJECTIVES
After studying this chapter, you will be able to:

14-1 Discuss the role of management and its importance to organizational success

14-2 Explain key theories and current practices of motivation

14-3 Outline the categories of business planning and explain strategic planning

14-4 Discuss the organizing function of management

14-5 Explain the role of managerial leadership and the key leadership styles

14-6 Describe the management control process

> # "MOVE FAST AND BREAK THINGS."
>
> — Mark Zuckerberg, Founder and CEO, Facebook

14-1 Bringing Resources to Life

To grow and thrive, every business needs resources—money, technology, materials—and an economic system that helps enterprise flourish. But those resources, or factors of production, are nothing without **management** to bring them to life. Managers provide vision and direction for their organizations, they decide how to use resources to achieve goals, and they inspire others—both inside and outside their companies—to follow their lead. By formal definition, managers achieve the goals of an organization through planning, organizing, leading, and controlling organizational resources, including people, money, and time.

In simple terms, **planning** means figuring out where to go and how to get there. **Organizing** means determining a structure for both individual jobs and the overall organization. **Leading** means directing and motivating people to achieve organizational goals. And **controlling** means checking performance and making adjustments as needed. In today's chaotic, hyper-competitive business environment, managers face daunting challenges. But for the right people, management positions can provide an exhilarating—though sometimes exhausting—career.

As the business pace accelerates and the environment continues to morph—especially in the wake of economic turmoil—the role of management is also radically transforming. The successful manager has changed from boss to coach, from disciplinarian to motivator, from dictator to team builder. But the bottom-line goal remains the same: to create value for the organization.

14-1a Management Hierarchy: Levels of Responsibility

Most medium-sized and large companies have three basic levels of management: **top management**, **middle management**, and **first-line (or supervisory) management**. The levels typically fall into a pyramid of sorts, with a small number of top managers and a larger number of supervisory managers. Responsibilities shift as managers move up the hierarchy, and the skills that they use must shift accordingly. Here are the differences between three key levels:

- **Top management** sets the overall direction of the firm. Top managers must articulate a vision, establish priorities, and allocate time, money, and other resources. Typical titles include chief executive officer (CEO), president, and vice president.

- **Middle management** manages the managers. (Say that three times!) Middle managers must communicate up and down the pyramid, and their primary contribution often involves coordinating teams and special projects with their peers from other departments. Typical titles include director, division head, and branch manager.

- **First-line management** manages the people who do the work. First-line managers must train, motivate, and evaluate nonmanagement employees, so they are heavily involved in day-to-day production issues. Typical titles include supervisor, foreman, and section leader.

Smaller companies usually don't have a hierarchy of management. Often the owner must act as the top-, middle-, and first-line manager, all rolled into one. This clearly requires enormous flexibility and well-developed management skills.

14-1b Management Skills: Having What It Takes to Get the Job Done

Given the turbulence of today's business world, managers must draw on a staggering range of skills to do their jobs efficiently and effectively. Most of these abilities cluster into three broad categories: technical skills, human skills, and conceptual skills.

- **Technical Skills:** Technical skills refer to expertise in a specific functional area or department. Keep in mind

---

management Achieving the goals of an organization through planning, organizing, leading, and controlling organizational resources including people, money, and time.

planning Determining organizational goals and action plans for how to achieve those goals.

organizing Determining a structure for both individual jobs and the overall organization.

leading Directing and motivating people to achieve organizational goals.

controlling Checking performance and making adjustments as needed.

top management Managers who set the overall direction of the firm, articulating a vision, establishing priorities, and allocating time, money, and other resources.

middle management Managers who supervise lower-level managers and report to a higher-level manager.

first-line management Managers who directly supervise nonmanagement employees.

technical skills Expertise in a specific functional area or department.

that technical skills don't necessarily relate to technology. People can have technical skills—or specific expertise—in virtually any field, from sales, to copywriting, to accounting, to airplane repair, to computer programming.

○ **Human Skills:** Human skills refer to the ability to work with and through other people in a range of different relationships. Human skills include communication, leadership, coaching, empathy, and team building. A manager with strong human skills can typically mobilize support for initiatives and find win–win solutions for conflicts.

○ **Conceptual Skills:** Conceptual skills refer to the ability to grasp a big-picture view of the overall organization and the relationship between its various parts. Conceptual skills also help managers understand how their company fits into the broader competitive environment. Managers with strong conceptual skills typically excel at strategic planning.

All three categories of skill are essential for management success. But their importance varies according to the level of the manager. Front-line managers must have a high degree of technical skills, which help them hire, train, and evaluate employees; avoid mistakes; and ensure high-quality production. Middle-level managers need an especially high level of human skills. They typically act as the bridge between departments, coordinating people and projects that sometimes have mismatched priorities. Top-level managers must demonstrate excellent conceptual skills in order to formulate a vision, interpret marketplace trends, and plan for the future. To move up in an organization, managers must constantly learn and grow, nurturing skills that reflect their new tasks.

Across all three skill sets, critical thinking and decision-making abilities have become increasingly important. Critical thinking helps managers find value even in an overload of information, while decision-making skills help them respond wisely and rapidly, with an unwavering focus on customer satisfaction.

Managers who expect to grow in the company hierarchy must expect to foster new skills. Too often, workers get promotions because of great technical skills—e.g., the top salesperson lands the sales manager slot—but they struggle to move further because they don't fully develop their human and conceptual skills.

The Power of One

Some people seem compelled to succeed no matter what . . . and those are the folks who tend to drive the economy. A quick survey of some well-known super-achievers suggests that a high level of motivation was part of their personalities from the very beginning:

○ *Mark Zuckerberg, Facebook founder:* **Before he went to college, Mark was recruited to work for Microsoft and AOL. As a toddler, he found a screwdriver and dismantled his crib when he thought he was too old for a "baby bed."**

○ *Martha Stewart, lifestyle mogul:* **Still in elementary school, Martha catered local birthday parties for other kids because the going rate for babysitting "wasn't quite enough money."**

○ *Jeff Bezos, Amazon founder:* **As a teenager, Jeff built amateur robots and an assortment of other electronic inventions.**

○ *Richard Branson, Virgin Group CEO:* **Branson attributes at least some of his motivation to his mom: when he was six, she would shove him out of the car and tell him to find his own way home.**

○ *Ronald Reagan, former U.S. President:* **In Reagan's first job as a lifeguard, he apparently saved 77 lives.**

But keep in mind that some high achievers don't gear up until well after childhood. True motivation requires clear goals, which people can develop at any point in their lives. When meaningful goals merge with energy and determination, anything becomes possible.[1]

© Yuri Arcurs/Shutterstock.com

Ooops! What were they thinking?

Bad Decisions, Big Impacts

Every day, managers around the globe make high-stakes decisions, from expanding overseas, to introducing new products, to closing factories. The great decisions have become the stuff of legends, shaping the business world as we know it today. Bad choices also abound. Consider these five business decisions that made history for their silliness:

- Faced with the opportunity to buy rights to the telephone in 1876, Western Union, the telegraph behemoth, rejected the newfangled device: "This 'telephone' has too many shortcomings to be seriously considered as a means of communication. The device is inherently of no value to us."

- In 1899, two young attorneys approached Asa Chandler—owner of the briskly selling new fountain drink Coca-Cola—with an innovative proposal to bottle the beverage. Chandler sold them exclusive rights to bottle Coke across most of the United States for the grand sum of $1. Oops.

- In 1981, Universal Studios offered Mars, Inc., the opportunity to feature M&M's in a family-friendly movie (*E.T.*) in return for exposure. Mars said no, so Universal took the offer to Hershey's, which offered Reese's Pieces. When *E.T.* became a top-grossing film, sales exploded. Hershey executives said the exposure the product received as "*E.T.'s* favorite candy" was worth millions of dollars.

- In 1999, fledgling search engine, Excite, rejected an offer to buy Google because it considered the $1 million asking price to be too high. Google is now worth nearly $300 billion, and Excite is defunct.

- Mike Smith, one of the executives in charge of evaluating new talent for the London office of Decca Records, rejected the Beatles in 1962 with the now infamous line: "Groups are out; four-piece groups with guitars particularly are finished." Not so much. . . .

With the help of hindsight, momentous decisions may seem almost inevitable. But these bloopers clearly show that in the fog of the moment, the right choice can be anything but clear.[1a]

14-2 Motivation: Lighting the Fire

Standout managers motivate others to reach for their best selves—to accomplish more than they ever thought possible. Motivated workers tend to feel great about their jobs, and workers who feel great tend to produce more. But the thinking about *how* to motivate workers has changed dramatically over time. In the early 1900s, key management thinkers focused on efficiency and productivity, dictating precisely how workers should do each element of their jobs. But more recent research suggests that people's thoughts and feelings play a vital role in motivation, which leads to a range of new theories.

14-2a Theories of Motivation

Maslow's Hierarchy of Needs Theory Noted psychologist Abraham Maslow theorized that people are motivated to satisfy only unmet needs. He proposed a hierarchy of human needs—from basic to abstract—suggesting that as each need is met, people become motivated to meet the next highest need in the pyramid. Maslow's five specific needs are shown in Exhibit 14.1. While his theory was not based on the workplace, Maslow's ideas can illuminate the needs behind motivation at work.

EXHIBIT 14.1 Maslow's Hierarchy of Needs and the Workplace

MASLOW'S NEED	DESCRIPTION	WORKPLACE EXAMPLES
PHYSIOLOGICAL	Need for basic survival—food, water, clothing, and shelter	A job with enough pay to buy the basics
SAFETY	Need to feel secure—free of harm and free of fear	Safety equipment, healthcare plans, life insurance, retirement plans, job security
SOCIAL (BELONGING)	Need to feel connected to others—accepted by family and friends	Teamwork, positive corporate culture, company lunchroom, department outings
ESTEEM	Need for self-respect and respect from others—recognition and status	Acknowledgment, feedback, promotions, perks
SELF-ACTUALIZATION	Need for fulfillment—the need to realize one's fullest potential	Challenging, creative jobs; meaningful work that ties to a greater good

© Cengage Learning 2013

From a workplace perspective, the idea that people are motivated only by unmet needs clearly holds true for the first two levels of the hierarchy. Finding a job that pays the bills, for instance, is the primary motivator for most people who don't have any job at all. People who have a job but no healthcare would find health insurance much more motivating than, say, a company picnic geared toward meeting social needs.

But after physiological and safety needs are met, the other needs are motivating to different degrees in different people. An employee with strong social connections outside work might be more motivated by a promotion that meets esteem needs than by a company outing that meets social needs. A number of firms actually use self-actualization needs as a starting point for motivating employees, by creating a mission statement that communicates the importance of the work. The House of Blues inspires employees through its lofty purpose: to promote racial and spiritual harmony through love, peace, truth, righteousness, and nonviolence.

14-2b Theory X and Theory Y

Psychologist Douglas McGregor, one of Maslow's students, studied workplace motivation from a different angle. He proposed that management attitudes toward workers would directly affect worker motivation. His research suggested that management attitudes fall into two opposing categories, which he called **Theory X and Theory Y**, described in Exhibit 14.2.

McGregor proposed that managers should employ Theory Y assumptions in order to capitalize on the imagination and intelligence of every worker. In American business today, some organizations use a Theory X approach, but a growing number have begun to at least experiment with Theory Y, tapping into a rich pool of employee input.

Leaders don't create followers, they create more leaders.

— Tom Peters, Management Consultant, author

Job Enrichment A number of researchers have focused on creating jobs with more meaningful content, under the assumption that challenging, creative work will motivate employees to give their best effort. **Job enrichment** typically includes the following factors:

1. **Skill Variety:** Workers can use a range of different skills.

2. **Task Identity:** Workers complete tasks with clear beginnings and endings.

3. **Task Significance:** Workers understand the impact of the task on others.

4. **Autonomy:** Workers have freedom and authority regarding their jobs.

5. **Feedback:** Workers receive clear, frequent information about their performance.

Richard Branson, maverick founder of the Virgin Group, relies on job enrichment, especially autonomy and feedback, to keep people motivated at his 350-company empire (which includes a startling range of firms, such as Virgin Atlantic Airlines, Virgin Music, Virgin mobile phones, and Virgin Galactic space travel). Branson gives his managers a stake in their companies and then tells them "to run it as if it's their own." He says, "I intervene as little as possible. Give them that, and they will give everything back." According to Virgin's website,

Exhibit 14.2 Theory X and Theory Y

THEORY X ASSUMPTIONS ABOUT WORKERS	THEORY Y ASSUMPTIONS ABOUT WORKERS
• Workers dislike work and will do everything they can to avoid it.	• Work is as natural as play or rest—workers do not inherently dislike it.
• Fear is motivating—coercion and threats are vital to get people to work toward company goals.	• Different rewards can be motivating—people can exercise self-direction and self-control to meet company goals.
• People prefer to be directed, avoiding responsibility and seeking security.	• People can accept and even seek responsibility. • The capacity for imagination, creativity, and ingenuity is widely distributed in the population. • The intellectual capacity of the average worker is underutilized in the workplace.

© Cengage Learning 2013

"we pretty much practice a collaborative and supportive style of custodianship." Due in large part to Branson's motivational approach, the Virgin workforce is fully engaged with the company, contributing to its remarkable long-term success.[2]

Expectancy Theory Usually attributed to researcher Victor Vroom, **expectancy theory** deals with the relationship among individual effort, individual performance, and individual reward. The key concept is that a worker will be motivated if he or she believes that effort will lead to performance, and performance will lead to a meaningful reward.

$$Effort \rightarrow Performance \rightarrow Reward$$

The theory suggests that if any link in the chain is broken, the employee will not be motivated.

Imagine if your professor announced on the first day of class that he or she had never given any student an A, as a matter of principle. Would you be motivated to perform in class? Not likely—the link between performance and reward would be broken. Retailer Hot Topic has done a particularly strong job implementing the link between effort and performance. A Hot Topic employee describes the connection, saying, "I've worked for HT for five years, and the best thing I've learned is that if you work hard enough and dedicate enough of yourself to something, you can achieve your goals!" Hot Topic has also established strong links between performance and rewards. Perhaps it's no coincidence that Hot Topic was one of the few retail chains that continued to perform well, even as the recession tightened its grip in late 2008 and early 2009.[3]

Equity Theory Pioneered by J. Stacy Adams, **equity theory** proposes that perceptions of fairness directly affect worker motivation. The key idea is that people won't be motivated if they believe that the relationship between what they contribute and what they earn is different from the relationship between what others contribute and what others earn. For example, if you worked ten-hour days, and earned less than the guy in the next cube who works seven-hour days, you'd

probably think it was pretty unfair. To restore a sense of balance, you might:

- ⊃ Demand a raise
- ⊃ Start coming in late, leaving early, and taking extra long lunch hours
- ⊃ Convince yourself that the other guy is about to be fired (or try to get him fired)
- ⊃ Look for another job

The response to perceived inequity almost always involves trying to change the system, changing your own work habits, distorting your perceptions, or leaving the company.

But keep in mind that equity theory is based on perceptions, which are not always on the mark. People are all too prone to overestimate their own contributions, which throws perceived equity out of balance. The best way to combat equity issues is through clear, open communication from management.[4]

14-2c **Motivation Today**

Companies today use a range of approaches to motivation, although several key themes have emerged. Most firms no longer seek to make their employees happy; instead, they want their workers to be productive and engaged. Yet, for employees, work is about more than just productivity. University of Michigan business school professor David Ulrich points out that even in today's hyper-competitive environment, "people still want to find meaning in their work and in the institutions that employ them."[5]

A growing emphasis on corporate culture has captured the best of both worlds for companies that do it right. A look at *Fortune* magazine's 100 Best Companies to Work for in 2012 demonstrates that a distinctive, positive culture tends to create productive employees who are deeply attached to their work and their companies. The winners tend to emphasize the health and well-being of their employees and to offer strong commitments to make the world a better place. Google, which earned the number one slot, offers employees a famous set of perks at their Silicon Valley headquarters, including on-site haircutting, massage services, game facilities, and 25 cafés company-wide, all free. As one happy Googler writes, "Employees are never more than 150 feet away from a well-stocked pantry." Despite—or perhaps in part *because* of the pricey perks—everything at Google is up: revenue, profits, share price, paid search clicks, and hiring. Wegmans' Food Markets has made employee health a religion. More than 2,000 workers have enrolled in a free smoking-cessation program since 2009; in 2012, it opened a 24/7 health hotline.

Many "Googlers" especially appreciate the top quality free food that's always available for employees.

© ERIN SIEGAL/Reuters /Landov

expectancy theory
A motivation theory that concerns the relationship among individual effort, individual performance, and individual reward.

equity theory A motivation theory that proposes that perceptions of fairness directly affect worker motivation.

strategic planning High-level, long-term planning that establishes a vision for the company, defines long-term objectives and priorities, determines broad action steps, and allocates resources.

tactical planning More specific, shorter-term planning that applies strategic plans to specific functional areas.

operational planning Very specific, short-term planning that applies tactical plans to daily, weekly, and monthly operations.

Computer storage firm NetApp is so serious about its pay for performance that employees have received pay-outs of up to 31% of their salary. After five years, Men's Wearhouse gives employees three-week paid sabbaticals and three weeks of paid vacation a year. Mattel, Inc. closes its offices at 1 p.m. every Friday and everyone gets paid time off to volunteer in schools. Starbucks' massive part-time work-force gets full health insurance ben-efits, stock awards, and free coffee. Employees at Umpqua Bank get 40 hours of paid time off every year to do volunteer work.[6]

Finally, a growing number of businesses have expanded their range of employee incentives beyond just cash. While money certainly matters, *Fortune* magazine points out that "telling employees they're doing a great job costs nothing but counts big." Employee training is a noncash motivational tactic gaining momentum across the economy in response to the growing array of complex skills needed by the workforce. The emphasis on training and education is especially motivating given that more and more employees identify themselves based on their field of expertise rather than their organization.[7]

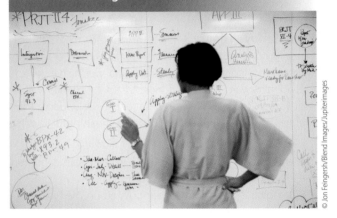

Effective planning can be complex and time-consuming.

© Jon Feingersh/Blend Images/Jupiterimages

14–3	**Planning: Figuring Out Where to Go and How to Get There**

The planning function—figuring out where to go and how to get there—is the core of effective management. A survey in *The Wall Street Journal* found that 80% of executives identify planning as their most valuable management tool. But even though planning is critical, it's also highly risky in light of cut-throat competition, rapid change, and economic uncertainty. The best plans keep the organization on track without sacri-ficing flexibility and responsiveness; they incorporate ways to respond to change both inside and outside the organization.[8]

Although all managers engage in planning, the scope of the process changes according to the manager's posi-tion as shown in Exhibit 14.3. Top-level managers focus on **strategic planning**. They establish a vision for the com-pany, define long-term objectives and priorities, determine broad action steps, and allocate resources. Middle manag-ers focus on **tactical planning**, or applying the strategic plan to their specific areas of responsibility. And first-line man-agers focus on **operational planning**, or applying the tactical plans to daily, weekly, and monthly operations. Successful firms often encourage a flow of feedback up and down the organization to ensure that all key plans are sound and that all key players "buy in." Some typical planning decisions and time frames are shown in Exhibit 14.3.

EXHIBIT 14.3 Managerial Planning

TYPE OF PLANNING	MANAGEMENT LEVEL	SCOPE OF PLANNING	EXAMPLES OF PLANNING QUESTIONS AND CONCERNS
STRATEGIC PLANNING	Senior management	Typically five-year time frame	Should we acquire a new company? Should we begin manufacturing in China? Should we expand to overseas markets? Should we take our company public?
TACTICAL PLANNING	Middle management	Typically one-year time frame	Should we spend more time servicing each customer? Should we hire a public relations agency to handle PR? Should we spend fewer ad dollars on TV and more on the Web?
OPERATIONAL PLANNING	First-line management	Daily, weekly, and monthly time frame	How should we schedule employees this week? When should we schedule delivery for each batch of product? How should customer service people answer the phones?

© Cengage Learning 2013

A fourth category of planning has gained new prominence in the past decade: **contingency planning**, or planning for unexpected events. Senior management usually spearheads contingency planning but with input from the other levels of management. Contingency plans consider what might go wrong—both inside the business and with the outside environment—and develop responses. Potential issues include:

- How should we respond if our competitors knock off our best-selling product?
- What should we do if the government regulates our industry?
- How should we respond if our data management/computer system fails?
- How can we restart our business if a natural disaster destroys our plant or supply channels?
- How will we evacuate employees if terrorists strike our headquarters?

Clearly, anticipating every potential problem is impossible (and impractical). Instead, effective contingency plans tend to focus only on the issues that are most probable, most potentially harmful, or both (see Exhibit 14.4). For example, a southern California amusement park (e.g., Disneyland) might concentrate its contingency plans on earthquake response, while an online retailing firm might focus its plans on responding to a computer hacker attack.

14-3a Strategic Planning: Setting the Agenda

Strategic planning is the most fundamental part of the planning process, since all other plans—and most major management decisions—stem from the strategic plan. The strategic planning process typically includes these steps:

1. Define the mission of the organization.
2. Evaluate the organization's competitive position.
3. Set goals for the organization.
4. Create strategies for competitive differentiation.
5. Implement strategies.
6. Evaluate results, and incorporate lessons learned.

Defining Your Mission The mission of an organization articulates its essential reason for being. The **mission** defines the organization's purpose, values, and core goals, providing the framework for all other plans (see Exhibit 14.5). Most large companies present their mission as a simple, vivid, compelling statement that everyone involved with the company—from the janitor to the CEO, from customers to investors—can easily understand. Mission statements tend to vary in their length, their language, and even their names, but they share a common goal: to provide a clear, long-term focus for the organization.

Evaluating Your Competitive Position Strategy means nothing in a vacuum—every firm must plan in the context of the marketplace. Many companies use a **SWOT analysis** (strengths, weaknesses, opportunities, and threats) to evaluate where they stand relative to the competition. Strengths and weaknesses are internal to the organization, and they include factors that would either build up or drag down the firm's performance. Opportunities and threats are external,

contingency planning Planning for unexpected events, usually involving a range of scenarios and assumptions that differ from the assumptions behind the core plans.

mission The definition of an organization's purpose, values, and core goals, which provides the framework for all other plans.

SWOT analysis A strategic planning tool that helps management evaluate an organization in terms of internal strengths and weakness, and external opportunities and threats.

Exhibit 14.4 Contingency Planning Paradigm

Businesses tend to focus their contingency plans on issues that are most probable *and* most potentially harmful.

Most Probable Issues

Most Harmful Issues

Focus Area for Contingency Plans

© Cengage Learning 2013

Exhibit 14.5 Examples of Mission Statements

COMPANY	MISSION STATEMENT
LEVI STRAUSS & CO	We will market the most appealing and widely worn casual clothing in the world. We will clothe the world.
BRISTOL-MYERS SQUIBB COMPANY	To discover, develop and deliver innovative medicines that help patients prevail over serious diseases.
GOOGLE	To organize the world's information and make it universally accessible and useful.
HARLEY-DAVIDSON, INC	We fulfill dreams through the experience of motorcycling.

© Cengage Learning 2013

and they include factors that would affect the company's performance but are typically out of the company's control. Exhibit 14.6 offers some examples.

Initial information about internal strengths and weaknesses usually comes from careful analysis of internal reports on topics such as budget and profitability. But to better understand strengths and weaknesses, executives should actively seek firsthand information—on a personal basis—from key people throughout the company, from front-line workers to the board of directors.

Gathering information about external opportunities and threats can be more complex, since these areas include both current and potential issues (which can be tough to predict). Information about external factors can come from many different sources, including the news, government reports, customers, and competitors.

EXHIBIT 14.6 SWOT Analysis

POTENTIAL INTERNAL STRENGTHS:	POTENTIAL EXTERNAL OPPORTUNITIES:
• Premium brand name • Proven management team • Lower costs/higher margins	• Higher consumer demand • Complacent competitors • Growth in foreign markets

POTENTIAL INTERNAL WEAKNESSES:	POTENTIAL EXTERNAL THREATS:
• Low employee satisfaction • Inadequate financial resources • Poor location	• A powerful new competitor • A deep recession • New government regulations

© Cengage Learning 2013

Slackers? Not so much...

© Yuri Arcurs/Shutterstock.com

Generation Y—which includes the 76 million kids born between 1978 and 1998—is changing the face of the workforce. These self-confident, outspoken young people have posed a new set of challenges for managers across the economy. A quick profile of Generation Y—also known as "millennials," "echo-boomers," and "Gen F" (for Facebook)—highlights their key characteristics. Keep in mind that no general overview can clearly describe each member of Generation Y. Yet, chances are strong that you recognize at least parts of yourself in this profile. Companies that understand you and your peers—and figure out how to harness your talents—will find themselves with a sharp competitive edge in the years to come.

Unfortunately, not all employers "get" Gen Y. According to a 2009 Pew Research Center study, three out of four Americans believe that today's youth are less virtuous and industrious than their elders. But the facts suggest otherwise. Volunteerism among young people has exploded. Between 1989 and 2006, the share of teenagers doing volunteer work doubled. Furthermore, millennials are more willing to accept that their work will bleed into evenings and weekends. Some experts also believe that millennials are better at switching quickly from one activity to another, a real plus in today's fast-paced work environment.[9] More Gen Y characteristics:

- **Goal Driven:** Gen Yers expect to perform for their rewards. But they tend to find smaller, short-term goals much more motivating than long-term goals. The reason: a week in their fast-paced world is more like a year was for their parents.

- **Facebook-Focused:** On average, Gen Yers have 696 Facebook friends, and 16 of them are work friends.

- **Change Oriented:** Gen Yers actively embrace change and excitement. Many anticipate—even hope—to change jobs frequently. They don't share the expectation of long-term employment that disillusioned so many of their parents.

- **Tech Savvy:** Gen Yers are masters of the Internet and the iPhone. They often expect top technology in the workplace, and they use virtually all of it (often at the same time!) to boost their performance.

- **Diverse:** Gen Y is among the most diverse demographic groups in America—one in three is a minority—and most don't believe that their ethnicity defines their character. Many were born in other countries and speak multiple languages fluently.

- **Entrepreneurial:** Only 7% of Gen Y works for a Fortune 500 company because start-ups are dominating the workforce. Even though most of their companies won't succeed, they are demonstrating an unprecedented entrepreneurial spirit. Companies can allow Gen Yers to operate entrepreneurially within the corporation by giving them control over their time, activities, and budgets as much as possible.

- **Fulfillment Focused:** Gen Yers tend to value their families and their personal lives deeply. They fully expect to achieve their lofty career goals without sacrificing time for themselves and the people they care about.[10]

Setting Your Goals Strategic goals represent concrete benchmarks that managers can use to measure performance in each key area of the organization. They must fit the firm's mission and tie directly to its competitive position. The three most effective goals are:

1. **Specific and Measurable:** Whenever possible, managers should define goals in clear numerical terms that everyone understands.

2. **Tied to a Time Frame:** To create meaning and urgency, goals should be linked to a specific deadline.

3. **Realistic but Challenging:** Goals that make people stretch can motivate exceptional performance.

Exhibit 14.7 offers examples of how weak goals can transform into powerful goals.

Creating Your Strategies Strategies are action plans that help the organization achieve its goals by forging the best fit between the firm and the environment. The underlying aim, of course, is to create a significant advantage versus the competition. Sources of competitive advantage vary, ranging from better product quality, to better technology, to more motivated employees. The most successful companies build their advantage across several fronts. Southwest Airlines, for example, has a more motivated workforce and a lower cost structure. H&M has lower prices and more fashionable clothing choices. And Procter & Gamble has more innovative new products and strong core brands.

The specifics of strategy differ by industry and by company, but all strategies represent a roadmap. The SWOT analysis determines the starting point, and the objectives signify the immediate destination. Since speed matters, you must begin mapping the next leg of the journey even before you arrive. For added complexity, you never know—given the turbulent environment—when you might hit roadblocks. This means that strategies must be dynamic and flexible. Top managers have responded to this challenge by encouraging front-line managers to participate in the process more than ever before.

Implementing Your Strategies Implementation should happen largely through tactical planning. Middle managers in each key area of the company must develop plans to carry out core strategies in their area. If the strategic plan, for example, calls for more new products, marketing would need to generate ideas, finance would need to find funding, and sales would need to prepare key accounts. And all of these steps would require tactical planning.

Evaluating Your Results and Incorporating Lessons Learned Evaluation of results should be a continual process, handled by managers at every level as part of their controlling function, covered further in this chapter. But for evaluation to be meaningful, the lessons learned must be analyzed objectively and factored back into the next planning cycle.

strategic goals Concrete benchmarks that managers can use to measure performance in each key area of the organization.

strategies Action plans that help the organization achieve its goals by forging the best fit between the firm and the environment.

14-4 Organizing: Fitting Together the Puzzle Pieces

The organizing function of management means creating a logical structure for people, their jobs, and their patterns of interaction. And clearly, the pieces can fit together in a number of different ways. In choosing the right structure for a specific company, management typically considers many factors, including the goals and strategies of the firm, its products, its use of technology, its size, and the structure of its competitors. Given the potential for rapid change in each of these factors, smart companies continually re-examine their structure and make changes whenever necessary. Microsoft, for instance, restructures its organization every couple of years as new challenges emerge.

But to be effective, reorganizations—and their purpose—must be clear to employees throughout the company. Xerox CEO Anne Mulcahy learned the hard way. Her comments: "During the 1990s, we had lots of consultants on organizational effectiveness. We sliced and diced the business into industries, product lines, and geographies . . . you name it. It looked good on paper, but fell apart in implementation. I found myself in a job where I couldn't look anybody in the eye and feel clear accountability for anything . . . I'll trade off organizational design for clarity and accountability any day of the week!"[11]

In order to help employees understand how they and their jobs fit within the broader organization, most

Exhibit 14.7 Goal Setting: Getting It Right

WEAK GOAL	POWERFUL GOAL
BECOME MORE INNOVATIVE.	Introduce one new product each quarter for the next three years.
REDUCE DELINQUENT ACCOUNTS.	Reduce delinquent accounts to no more than 1% of the total by the next quarter.
INCREASE MARKET SHARE.	Become the #1 or #2 brand in each market where we compete by the end of 2012.

© Cengage Learning 2013

organization chart A visual representation of the company's formal structure.

degree of centralization The extent to which decision-making power is held by a small number of people at the top of the organization.

firms issue an **organization chart**, or a visual representation of the company's formal structure, as shown in Exhibit 14.8.

Looking at the company represented by Exhibit 14.8, you would probably assume that the vice president of production has more power than a regular employee in the marketing department. And in terms of formal power, you'd be absolutely right. But if the marketing employee babysits on the weekend for the president's granddaughter, the balance of power may actually be a bit different than it seems. Make no mistake: the formal structure matters. But knowing how power flows on an informal basis could dramatically increase your effectiveness as well, by helping you target your ideas to the right managers and marshal the support of the most influential employees.

14-4a Key Organizing Considerations

In developing the organizational structure, management must make decisions about the degree of centralization, the span of management control, and the type of departmentalization that makes the most sense at any given time.

Centralization The **degree of centralization** relates directly to the source of power and control. In centralized companies, a small number of people at the top of the organization have the power to make decisions. This approach is simple and efficient, and the result tends to be a strong corporate image and a uniform customer approach across the

EXHIBIT 14.8 Sample Organization Chart

President

Vice President, Marketing

Vice President, Production

Employee

Employee

Employee

Employee

Employee

Employee

© Cengage Learning 2013

Should you work fewer hours?

You probably should work less but make sure you're working *better*. Many managers consider their employees who spend more time in the office to be more dedicated and more hardworking. But the truth is often more complicated. Those employees may simply be inefficient. According to Harvard Business School Professor Robert Pozen, many professionals are inefficient because their firm's hour-oriented culture hasn't forced them to think rigorously about what's really important. Sometimes, this leads professionals to spend too much time perfecting one particular task—say, the formatting of an internal presentation—instead of spending time where it might be more useful. Unfortunately for the sake of the rest of their lives, 62% of high-earning individuals in America work 50 hours or more per week; 35% work 60 hours or more per week. Pozen suggests the following strategies for stepping off the treadmill:

- Decline meetings whenever you can.
- Don't be afraid to use the "delete" button when reviewing your inbox.
- If you can't say "no" to a certain request, recognize that it may only require a B+ effort.[12]

front lines. But the downside is that centralized companies typically respond more slowly to customer needs and have lower employee morale. The trade-off may be worthwhile in steady, stable markets, but those are rare.

Faced with today's turbulent environment, most firms are moving toward greater decentralization, pushing power to the lower levels of the organization. Employees with the power to make decisions can respond to customer needs more quickly and effectively. They can also capitalize on opportunities that would likely vaporize in the time it would take to get permission to act. But for decentralization to work, every employee must fully understand the firm's mission, goals, and strategy; otherwise, the company could develop a fragmented image, which would undermine its long-term strength. Also, active communication across departments is

© David Stuart, Photographer/Shutterstock.com

essential so that all employees can benefit from innovations in other parts of the organization.

Span of Control The **span of control**, or span of management, refers to the number of people a manager supervises. There is no ideal number for every manager. The "right" span of control varies based on the abilities of both the manager and the subordinates, the nature of the work being done, the location of the employees, and the need for planning and coordination. Across industries, the general trend has moved toward wider spans of control as a growing number of companies have pruned layers of middle management to the bare minimum.

© iStockphoto.com/studiovision

Departmentalization **Departmentalization** means breaking workers into logical groups. A number of different options make sense, depending on the organization.

- ⊙ **Functional:** Dividing employees into groups based on area of expertise, such as marketing, finance, and engineering, tends to be efficient and easy to coordinate. For those reasons, it works especially well for small- to medium-sized firms.

- ⊙ **Product:** Dividing employees into groups based on the products that a company offers helps workers develop expertise about products that often results in especially strong customer relations.

- ⊙ **Customer:** Dividing employees into groups based on the customers that a company serves helps companies focus on the needs of specific customer groups. Many companies have separate departments for meeting the needs of business and consumer users. This approach is related to product departmentalization.

- ⊙ **Geographical:** Dividing employees into groups based on where customers are located can help different departments better serve specific regions within one country. Similarly, many international firms create a separate department for each different country they serve.

> **span of control** Span of management; refers to the number of people a manager supervises.
>
> **departmentalization** The division of workers into logical groups.

- ⊙ **Process:** Dividing into groups based on what type of work employees do is common in manufacturing, where management may divide departments by processes such as cutting, dyeing, and sewing.

As companies get larger, they usually adopt several different types of departmentalization at different levels of the organization. This approach, shown in Exhibit 14.9, is called "hybrid departmentalization."

EXHIBIT 14.9   An Example of Hybrid Departmentalization

© Cengage Learning 2013

line organizations
Organizations with a clear, simple chain of command from top to bottom.

line-and-staff organizations
Organizations with line managers forming the primary chain of authority in the company, and staff departments working alongside line departments.

line managers Managers who supervise the functions that contribute directly to profitability: production and marketing.

staff managers Managers who supervise the functions that provide advice and assistance to the line departments.

matrix organizations Organizations with a flexible structure that brings together specialists from different areas of the company to work on individual projects on a temporary basis.

14-4b Organization Models

Company structures tend to follow one of three different patterns: line organizations, line-and-staff organizations, and matrix organizations. But these organizational models are not mutually exclusive. In fact, many management teams build their structure using elements of each model at different levels of the organization.

Line Organizations A line organization typically has a clear, simple chain of command from top to bottom. Each person is directly accountable to the person immediately above, which means quick decision making and no fuzziness about who is responsible for what. The downside is a lack of specialists to provide advice or support for line managers. This approach tends to work well for small businesses, but for medium-sized and large companies, the result can be inflexibility, too much paperwork, and even incompetence, since experts aren't available to give their input on key decisions.

Line-and-Staff Organizations A line-and-staff organization incorporates the benefits of a line organization without all the drawbacks. **Line managers** supervise the functions that contribute directly to profitability: production and marketing. **Staff managers**, on the other hand, supervise the functions that provide advice and assistance to the line departments. Examples include legal, accounting, and human resources. In a line-and-staff organization, the line managers form the primary chain of authority in the company. Staff departments work alongside line departments, but there is no direct reporting relationship (except at the top of the company). Since staff people don't report to line people, their authority comes from their know-how. This approach, which overlays fast decision making with additional expertise, tends to work well for

"**Management** is doing things right; leadership is doing the right things."

— Peter Drucker, Management researcher, writer, and speaker

medium-sized and large companies. But in some firms, the staff departments gain so much power that they become dictatorial, imposing unreasonable limitations on the rest of the company.

Matrix Organizations Matrix organizations build on the line-and-staff approach by adding a lot more flexibility. A matrix structure brings together specialists from different areas of the company to work on individual projects on a temporary basis. A new-product-development team, for instance, might include representatives from sales, engineering, finance, purchasing, and advertising. For the course of the project, each specialist reports to the project manager and to the head of his or her own department (e.g., the vice president of marketing). The matrix approach has been particularly popular in the high-tech and aerospace industries.

The matrix structure offers several key advantages. It encourages teamwork and communication across the organization. It offers flexibility in deploying key people. It lends itself to innovative solutions. And not surprisingly—when managed well—the matrix structure creates a higher level of motivation and satisfaction for employees. But these advantages have a clear flip side. The need for constant communication can bog down a company in too many meetings. The steady state of flux can be overwhelming for both managers and employees. And having two bosses can cause conflict and stress for everyone.

<table>
<tr><td>14-5</td><td>

Leadership: Directing and Inspiring

</td></tr>
</table>

While most people easily recognize a great leader, defining the qualities of leaders can be more complex since successful leaders have a staggering range of personalities, characteristics, and backgrounds. Most researchers agree that true leaders are trustworthy, visionary, and inspiring. After all, we don't follow people who don't know where they're going, and we definitely don't follow people we don't trust. Other key leadership

© iStockphoto.com/Lasse Kristensen

traits include empathy, courage, creativity, intelligence, and fairness.

14-5a Leadership Style

How a leader uses power defines his or her leadership style. While the range of specific styles is huge, most seem to cluster into three broad categories: autocratic, democratic, and free-rein. The categories fall along a continuum of power, with the manager at one end and the employees at the other, as shown in Exhibit 14.10.

EXHIBIT 14.10 The Continuum of Leadership and Power

© Cengage Learning 2013

Autocratic leaders hoard decision-making power for themselves, and they typically issue orders without consulting their followers. **Democratic leaders** share power with their followers. Even though they still make final decisions, they typically solicit and incorporate input from their followers. **Free-rein leaders** set objectives for their followers but give them freedom to choose how they accomplish those goals.

Interestingly, the most effective leaders don't use just one approach. They tend to shift their leadership style, depending on the followers and the situation. When a quick decision is paramount, autocratic leadership may make the most sense. An army officer, for example, probably shouldn't take a vote on whether to storm a hill in the middle of a firefight. But when creativity is the top priority—during new product brainstorming, for instance—free-rein management would probably work best. Likewise, a brand-new worker might benefit from autocratic (but friendly)

management, while a talented, experienced employee would probably work best under free-rein leadership.

Another vital consideration is the customer. When the customer seeks consistency in the delivery of the product—in fast food, for instance—the autocratic leadership style may be appropriate. But when the customer needs flexibility and problem-solving assistance—a consulting client, for example—the free-rein leadership style may be most effective. The democratic leadership style typically provides customers with a balance of consistency and flexibility, which works across a wide range of industries.

autocratic leaders Leaders who hoard decision-making power for themselves and typically issue orders without consulting their followers.

democratic leaders Leaders who share power with their followers. While they still make final decisions, they typically solicit and incorporate input from their followers.

free-rein leaders Leaders who set objectives for their followers but give them freedom to choose how they will accomplish those goals.

14-6 Controlling: Making Sure It All Works

Controlling may be the least glamorous of the management functions, but don't be fooled: it's critically important. Controlling means monitoring performance of the firm—or individuals within the firm—and making improvements when necessary. As the environment changes, plans change. And as plans change, the control process must change as well, to ensure that the company achieves its goals. The control process includes three key steps:

1. Establish clear performance standards.
2. Measure actual performance against standards.
3. Take corrective action if necessary.

Establishing clear standards—or performance goals—begins with planning. At every level of planning, objectives should emerge that are consistent

"American employees admit that 68% of the mistakes they personally make never come to their manager's attention."

— FUTURE FOUNDATION

Successful Psychopaths
and Productive Narcissists

Watch out! That good-looking guy on the corporate fast track may be a psychopath…

Check out the profile: Psychopaths demonstrate hypnotic charm, coupled with a fundamental lack of empathy and conscience. They can perceive your feelings—often with spooky accuracy—but they just don't care. Canadian researcher Robert Hare describes them as "callous, cold-blooded individuals… They have no sense of guilt or remorse." And they take real pleasure from leveraging their power.

While not every psychopath is a budding Charles Manson, Hare has found that the psychopaths in the workplace share a basic personality profile with their more violent counterparts. Corporate psychopaths, however, score higher in the "selfish, callous, remorseless use of others" category, and much lower in the "unstable, antisocial, and socially deviant lifestyle" category that lands people in jail for more brutal crimes.

The headlines are filled with stories of corporate psychopaths gone way wrong for crimes that range from creative accounting to stock manipulation. CEOs such as Enron's Bernie Ebbers and Bernie Madoff have plundered their companies at the expense of thousands of people losing their jobs or their savings or both. But countless corporate psychopaths have stayed on the right side of the law, delivering bottom-line results at a staggering personal cost to the colleagues they betray and demoralize on a daily basis.

Another unpleasant personality in the corner office is the productive narcissist. These characters don't have much empathy either, but they often have a powerful vision, a flair for innovation, and a knack for attracting committed followers. While their goal may be helping humanity in the abstract, they're often insensitive to the real people around them. Bill Gates—widely respected for his razor-sharp mind, his visionary strategic management, and his world-changing philanthropic generosity—has been known to deflate eager subordinates with comments such as "That's the stupidest thing I've ever heard." And when engineers asked Steve Jobs why they were creating the iMac, he replied, "Because I'm the CEO, and I think it can be done." But despite their abrasive approach, productive narcissists are much less scary than psychopaths, since they're committed to their vision for the company rather than simply to themselves.

Today's chaotic, results-driven business environment may be a magnet for corporate psychopaths and productive narcissists, since both personalities thrive on constant, chaotic change. And the broader culture doesn't help. Americans idealize the idea of the corporate cowboy—the charismatic maverick who delivers against all odds, regardless of the cost. You can protect yourself by learning to recognize and steer clear of unhealthy personalities, no matter how charming they may initially seem.[13]

with the company's mission and strategic plan. The objectives must be (1) specific and measurable, (2) realistic but challenging, and (3) tied to a time frame. Individual managers may need to break these goals into smaller parts for specific employees, but the subgoals should retain the same three qualities as the original objective.

Measuring performance against standards should happen well before the end of the time frame attached to the goal. A strong information tracking system is probably management's best tool in this phase of the control process.

If the company or individual is not on track to meet the goals, management's first response should be communication. Employees with full information are far more likely to improve their performance than employees who never learn that they're falling behind. But sometimes workers need more than information—they may need additional resources or coaching in order to meet their goals. Apple's Steve Jobs was often accused of being a tyrannical boss—especially in the employee-evaluation process—but he defended himself by saying, "My job is not to be easy on people. My job is to make them better." If they still don't succeed, perhaps the goals themselves need re-examination as part of a dynamic planning process. Given the expense in both human and financial terms, disciplining employees for poor performance should come only after exploring the reasons for not meeting goals and making changes if necessary.

THE BIG PICTURE

In the past decade, management has become more complex and demanding than ever before. Managers in every area of the business must carry out their roles—planning, organizing, leading, and controlling—in a relentlessly fast-paced world, seething with constant change. While management isn't for everyone, it's often a fit for people with vision, courage, integrity, energy, and a passionate commitment to their companies.

Looking forward, the role of management will continue to evolve in response to the environment. Regardless of how the changes unfold, several key factors will be absolutely vital for successful managers in the twenty-first century: a constant focus on the customer, a commitment to globalization, excellent judgment, and the right mix of talented, motivated employees.

Every business field, from information technology to accounting, includes management jobs, and virtually all of those positions require experience in the field before promotion to management. If you are interested in pursuing a management track, your best strategy from a career development perspective would be to deliberately cultivate the skills required at the level above you, without neglecting the skills you need to excel at your current level. Managers typically have more accountability than employees—which often requires more work hours—and therefore have higher salary structures.

CAREERS

CAREERS IN MANAGEMENT

What *else?*
RIP & REVIEW CARDS **IN THE BACK**
and visit www.cengagebrain.com!

15
Human Resource Management:
Building a Top-Quality
Workforce

LEARNING OBJECTIVES
After studying this chapter, you will be able to:

15-1   Explain the importance of human resources to business success

15-2   Discuss key human resource issues in today's economy

15-3   Outline challenges and opportunities that the human resources function faces

15-4   Discuss human resource planning and core human resources responsibilities

15-5   Explain the key federal legislation that affects human resources

> # "IF SOMETHING GOES WRONG, IT'S MY PROBLEM; IF SOMETHING GOES *RIGHT*, IT'S THEIR SUCCESS."
>
> — PAMELA FIELDS, CEO, STETSON

Companies that get the most from their people often consider their human resources their biggest investment. They view the core goal of **human resource (HR) management** in a similar light: to nurture their human investment so that it yields the highest possible return. HR can achieve that goal by recruiting world-class talent, promoting career development, and boosting organizational effectiveness. But clearly, this can happen only in partnership with key managers throughout the company, especially senior executives. (In smaller companies, of course, the owners usually handle HR management in addition to their other responsibilities.)

> **human resource management** The management function focused on maximizing the effectiveness of the workforce by recruiting world-class talent, promoting career development, and determining workforce strategies to boost organizational effectiveness.

15-1 Human Resource Management: Bringing Business to Life

As competition accelerates across the globe, leading firms in every business category have recognized that a quality workforce can vault them over the competition. Southwest Airlines was early to recognize the untapped potential of its people. Executive Chairman Herb Kelleher declared, "We value our employees first. They're the most important, and if you treat them right, then they treat the customers right, and if you treat the customers right, then they keep coming back and shareholders are happy." His attitude has more than paid off. Southwest Airlines has posted profits for 39 consecutive years, even as other airlines have spiraled into decline.

As the Great Recession constricted the economy in 2009, managing human resources remained a top priority for Southwest CEO Gary Kelly. "We've never had a layoff. We've never had a pay cut. And we're going to strive mightily, especially this year, to avoid them once again . . ." Instead, he says, "We're being more creative about encouraging employees to move about the company. We are not threatening people with their jobs." He points out, "We're known for being the greatest company to work for and at the top of the customer service rankings." He maintains, "There is a devotion to the people and a commitment to our people, once we hire them, that we have lived up to. We have proven many times that we're going to be there for our employees in the bad times."[1]

15-2 Human Resource Management Challenges: Major Hurdles

Building a top-quality workforce can be tougher than it may initially seem. Human resource managers—and their counterparts throughout the company—face huge challenges. The best strategies still aren't clear, but forward-thinking firms tend to experiment with new approaches.

15-2a Layoffs and Outsourcing

As high-tech, high-end jobs follow low-tech, low-end jobs out of the country—or even just to local contractors—human resources find themselves in turmoil. Many jobs have disappeared altogether as companies have contracted in response to the Great Recession. In 2011 and 2012, many economists were concerned about a "jobless recovery," as labor markets faltered, and unemployment rates began to rise again. How can businesses boost the morale and the motivation level of the employees who are left behind? Does less job security translate to less worker loyalty? How can human resources continue to add value as the ground shifts beneath them—and as they wonder how long their own jobs will last?[2]

15-2b Wage Gap

Comparing CEO pay to worker pay demonstrates a startling wage gap, bigger in the United States than in any other developed country. In 2011, the average CEO earned 231 times the average worker. As a point of comparison,

Humble Beginnings

Everyone starts somewhere. Not even the rich and famous always had glamour jobs. In today's challenging economy, getting any job at all can be tough for young people, but whatever work you do get, consider that it might be the first step on the road to the next big thing. Some early job examples of the rich and famous:

© JustASC/Shutterstock.com

- ⊃ **Steve Jobs (Apple founder):** assembly line worker at HP. At age 13, Jobs put in screws on an HP assembly line. The young computer geek later described the first day of work as "bliss."

- ⊃ **Suze Orman (personal finance guru):** During her early years, Orman bused tables and washed dishes to make a buck.

- ⊃ **Donald Trump (real estate investor and former presidential candidate):** Got his start collecting soda bottles for the deposit money.

- ⊃ **Oprah Winfrey (media mogul):** Oprah began working at the corner grocery store next to her father's barber shop…and she hated every minute of it.

- ⊃ **Quentin Tarantino (writer and film director):** usher at an adult movie theatre. "I could care less about the movies and was totally bored by them."

- ⊃ **Barack Obama (President of the United States):** Obama's first job was scooping ice cream in a Honolulu Baskin Robbins.[2a]

30 years ago, chief executives averaged only 30 to 40 times the average American worker's paycheck. In 2009, median CEO salaries at 200 large, publicly held U.S. firms fell by 0.9%, while net income decreased by 5%. In 2010, the gap widened again, with the average CEO earning 343 times the average worker. Most observers don't object to the pay gap when top CEO pay is tied to top performance. But as the value of formerly high-flying corporations began to evaporate in 2008 and 2009, public rage over senior management salaries and bonuses hit new highs. But the tide turned in 2011, when data revealed CEO pay during 2011 was correlated to how well companies fared in the stock market, a change from 2010. Maintaining the link between pay and performance, clearly represents a strategic challenge for HR management.[3]

15-2c Older Workers

As the oversized Baby Boomer generation begins turning 60, their employers—which include virtually every major American company—face a potential crisis: the loss of key talent and experience through massive retirements. Beginning January 1, 2011 every single day more than 10,000 baby boomers reached the age of 65, and that will continue to happen every single day until 2030.[4] Enlightened companies have responded with programs to retain their best employees through flexible schedules, training opportunities, and creative pay schedules. But as companies aggressively trimmed their payrolls in 2008 and 2009, the priority of these kinds of programs plummeted, which may leave some firms with a critical dearth of highly experienced workers when the economy revs back up.

15-2d Younger Workers

As twenty-somethings enter the workforce, they often bring optimism, open minds, technological know-how, a team orientation, a proven ability to multitask, and a multicultural perspective. But a number of them also bring an unprecedented sense of entitlement. This can translate into startlingly high expectations for their pay, their responsibilities, and their job flexibility, but little willingness to "pay dues." Many have no expectation that their employers will be loyal to them, and they don't feel that they owe their

"Couples with similar jobs have more trouble finding work–life balance than those in different lines of work."

— USA Today

© Sashkin/Shutterstock.com

companies strong loyalty. Managing this group can sometimes be a challenge, but companies that do it well stand to deliver results for years to come.[5]

15-2e Women Workers

Over the past few decades, women have made enormous strides in terms of workplace equality. But several large-scale studies confirm that women continue to face daunting discrimination in terms of both pay and promotions. While unfair treatment has been an issue for many years, recent legal changes have made it easier for women to sue, costing companies millions of dollars in the past decade alone. And the flood of lawsuits shows no signs of slowing. Many women have responded to the unfriendly business environment by leaving the workforce; droves of highly qualified, professional women step out of the workforce early—usually to raise children, start their own companies, or pursue other interests. As a result, we are experiencing a harmful, ongoing brain drain. Human resource managers can help mitigate this issue by implementing specific retention plans for valued women workers and by taking proactive steps to reintegrate returning women back into the workforce.[6]

15-2f Work-Life Balance

Over the past decade, workers across all ages and both genders have actively pursued more flexibility and work–life balance in their jobs. But as the recession deepened in 2009, companies began to cut back on these initiatives, describing them as "nice to have" programs in a time when "need to have" goals—such as meeting payroll each month—are tough to attain. Middle-level managers are also apt to demonstrate bias against worker flexibility, even when top management actively supports work–life balance programs. In spite of these issues, insightful HR managers try hard to offer enough flexibility to keep their best workers without jeopardizing their company's business goals.[7]

15-2g Lawsuits

The United States has become a wildly litigious society, with employees, customers, and shareholders levying lawsuit after lawsuit against firms of all sizes. Even though many of the lawsuits are legitimate—some profoundly important—a good number are just plain silly. But even if a lawsuit is frivolous, and even if it's thrown out of court, it can still cost a company millions of dollars. Even more importantly, a frivolous lawsuit can cost a business its reputation. Avoiding employee lawsuits by knowing the law and encouraging legal practices is a growing human resources challenge.

15-3 Human Resources Managers: Corporate Black Sheep?

15-3a The Problem

The human resource management function is clearly critical, but human resources departments—and the people who work in them—face major challenges. Leading-edge firms expect every department to offer "big picture," strategic contributions that boost company value. But a report in *Fast Company* suggests that most HR professionals lack sufficient strategic skills. Among other data, the report quotes a respected executive at a top U.S. company: "Business acumen is the single biggest factor that HR professionals in the U.S. lack today."[8]

But even highly qualified, strategically focused HR managers face daunting perception problems. A management professor at a leading school comments that "The best and the brightest just don't go into HR." Once in the workforce, many employees see the human resources department as irrelevant—or even worse, as the enemy. This perception clearly undermines their effectiveness.

15-3b The Solution

To gain respect from both senior management and their peers, human resources executives must earn a seat at the table. The first step is to know the company. What are the strategic goals? Who is the core customer? Who is the competition? Respected HR departments typically figure out ways to quantify their impact on the company in dollars and cents. They determine how to raise the value of the firm's human capital, which in turn increases the value of the firm itself. Effective HR people also remain open to exceptions even as they enforce broad company policies.

"Frivolous lawsuits cost American businesses over $865 billion per year."

— Pacific Research Institute

But clearly, these solutions will work only if senior management recognizes the potential value of effective human resource management. One simple test of senior management commitment is the reporting relationship. If the HR department reports to the CFO, it may be on the fast track to outsourcing. But if the HR department reports to the CEO, the strategic possibilities are unlimited.

15-4 Human Resource Planning: Drawing the Map

Great human resource management begins with great planning: Where should you go? And how should you get there? Your objectives should flow from the company's master plan, and your strategies must reflect company priorities.

One of the first steps in the HR planning process should be to figure out where the company stands in terms of human resources. What skills does the workforce already have? What skills does it need? A company-wide **job analysis** often goes hand in hand with evaluating the current workforce. Job analysis examines what exactly needs to be done in each position to maximize the effectiveness of the organization—independent of who might be holding each job at any specific time. Smaller companies often handle job analysis on an informal basis, but larger companies typically specify a formal **job description** and **job specifications** (or "specs").

A job description defines the jobholder's responsibilities, and job specs define the qualifications for doing the job. Consider the job of band manager. The job description might include finding engagements for the band, and settling disputes among band members. The job specs might include the type of education and experience required. Taken together, the two might look something like Exhibit 15.1.

The next step is to forecast future human resource requirements. The forecasting function requires a deep understanding of the company's goals and strategies. HR managers must also assess the future supply of workers. Assessing supply can be a real challenge, since the size and quality of the workforce shift continually. But key considerations should include retirement rates, graduation rates in relevant fields, and the pros and cons of the international labor market.

A complete HR plan—which falls under the company's strategic planning umbrella—must cover each core area of human resource management (see Exhibit 15.2):

- ➲ Recruitment
- ➲ Selection
- ➲ Training
- ➲ Evaluation
- ➲ Compensation
- ➲ Benefits
- ➲ Separation

15-4a Recruitment: Finding the Right People

Finding people to hire is easy—especially as the unemployment rate hit new highs in 2009 and spiked up in 2010 and 2011—but finding *qualified* employees can still be a daunting challenge. The U.S. Census Bureau points out that a college degree typically doubles earning power, and the U.S. Bureau of Labor Statistics attests that most of the fastest-growing fields in the next five years will require college graduates. But only 30% of adults in America over the age of 25 have a college degree. And as highly trained, highly educated baby boomers hit retirement, HR recruiters may face a hiring crunch. In addition to finding qualified hires, recruiters also must find new employees who fit with the company culture in terms of both personality and style.[9]

Exhibit 15.1 Job Description and Job Specifications: Band Manager

JOB DESCRIPTION	JOB SPECIFICATIONS
Work with the music group to help make major decisions regarding the creative and business direction of the band	A bachelor's degree in music management
Negotiate recording contracts and engagement fees	A minimum of three years' experience managing a high-profile band
Help band members understand their rights and responsibilities	Excellent communication and networking skills

© Cengage Learning 2013

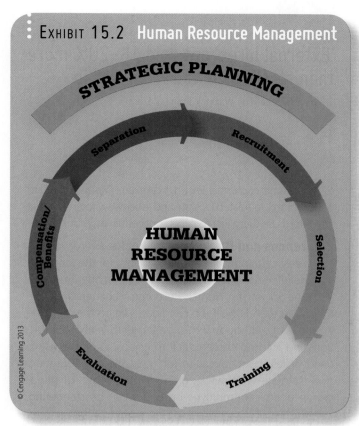

Exhibit 15.2 Human Resource Management

STRATEGIC PLANNING

HUMAN RESOURCE MANAGEMENT

Separation · Recruitment · Selection · Training · Evaluation · Compensation/Benefits

© Cengage Learning 2013

New employees come from two basic sources: internal and external. **Internal recruitment** involves transferring or promoting employees from other positions within the company. This approach offers several advantages:

➲ Boosts employee morale by reinforcing the value of experience within the firm

➲ Reduces risk for the firm, since current employees have a proven track record

➲ Lowers costs of both recruitment and training

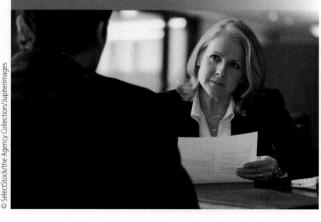

Selecting the best candidate for each job is much tougher than it may initially seem.

© SelectStock/the Agency Collection/Jupiterimages

But companies often find that they don't have the right person within their organization. The firm may be too small, or perhaps no one has the right set of skills to fill the immediate needs. Or maybe the firm needs the fresh thinking and energy that can come only from outside. When this is the case, companies turn to **external recruitment**.

External recruitment, or looking for employees outside the firm, usually means tapping into a range of different resources. The possibilities include employment websites, newspaper ads, trade associations, college and university employment centers, and employment agencies. But the most promising source of new hires may be referrals from current employees. A growing number of organizations offer their current employees a cash bonus—typically $1,000 to $2,000—for each person they refer to the company who makes it past a probationary period. As an added benefit, employees who come through referrals have an excellent chance at success, since the person who recommended them has a stake in their progress. Employee-referral programs also represent a real bargain for employers, compared to the average cost per new hire of more than $4,000. Not surprisingly, a higher level of employee referrals correlates to a higher level of shareholder returns, although lack of diversity may become a long-term problem with relying on employee referrals.[10]

> **internal recruitment**
> The process of seeking employees who are currently within the firm to fill open positions.
>
> **external recruitment**
> The process of seeking new employees from outside the firm.

15-4b Selection: Making the Right Choice

Once you have a pool of qualified candidates, your next step is to choose the best person for the job. This, too, is more easily said than done, yet making the right selection is crucial. The costs of a bad hire—both the direct costs such as placing ads, and the intangibles such as lost productivity and morale—can drain company resources. A typical selection process includes accepting applications, interviewing, testing, checking references and background, and making the job offer. Keep in mind that small businesses often follow a more streamlined process.

Applications Many companies use written applications simply as an initial screening mechanism. Questions about education and experience will determine whether a candidate gets any further consideration. In other words, the application is primarily a tool to reject unqualified candidates, rather than to actually choose qualified candidates.

Interviews Virtually every company uses interviews as a central part of the selection process. In larger companies, the HR department does initial interviews and then sends qualified candidates to the hiring manager for the actual selection. The hiring manager usually recruits co-workers to participate in the process.

Although employers frequently give interviews heavy weight in hiring decisions, interviews often say surprisingly little about whether a candidate will perform on the job. Too many managers use the interview as a get-to-know-you session rather than focusing on the needs of the position. To help ensure that interviews better predict performance, experts recommend a **structured interview** process: developing a list of questions beforehand and asking the same questions to each candidate. The most effective questions are typically behavioral: they ask the candidate to describe a situation that he or she faced at a previous job—or a hypothetical situation at the new job—and to explain the resolution. Interviewers should gear the specific questions toward behaviors and experiences that are key for the new position. Consider the following examples of how these questions could be worded:

- ● Describe a time when you had to think "outside the box" to find a solution to a pressing problem.

- ● Describe a situation that required you to do a number of things at the same time. How did you handle it? What was the outcome?

- ● If you realized that a co-worker was cheating on his expense report, how would you handle the situation?

- ● What would you do if your boss asked you to complete a key project within an unreasonable time frame?

Cultural differences also affect interview performance. As the U.S. labor pool becomes more diverse, even domestic companies must be aware of cultural differences. And it isn't simply a matter of legality or ethics. Firms that hire the best people regardless of cultural background will gain a critical edge in our increasingly competitive world.

Most colleges and universities offer comprehensive career services. Especially in today's competitive labor market, you would be wise to visit your career center early in your college career and use those services to prepare yourself for a smooth transition into the workforce.

Testing Either before or after the interview process (and sometimes at both points), a growing number of companies have instituted employment testing of various sorts. The main categories include skills testing, personality testing, drug testing, and physical exams. Skills testing and personality testing carry a fair amount of legal risk, since these tests must measure skills and aptitudes that relate directly to the job itself. Virtually 100% of Fortune 500 companies conduct pre-employment drug testing,

'External hires' get paid 18–20% more than staff promoted from within.

— Matthew Bidwell, Wharton Business School

as do most other companies. Physical exams are also standard but are highly regulated by state and federal law to ensure that firms don't use them just to screen out certain individuals.

References and Background Checks Even if you feel absolutely certain that a candidate is right for the job, don't skip the reference check before you make an offer. Research from the Society for Human Resource Managers suggests that more than 50% of job candidates lie on their résumé in some way. Although it may be tough to verify contributions and accomplishments at former jobs, it's pretty easy to uncover lies about education, job titles, and compensation. And it's quite worthwhile, given that the costs of bringing an unethical employee on board can be staggering. Furthermore, if you happen to hire a truly dangerous employee, you can open the door to negligent-hiring lawsuits for not taking "reasonable care." But surprisingly—despite the high risk—employment expert James Challenger estimates that only about 25% of candidates are thoroughly vetted by the companies that consider them.[11]

Job Offers After you find the right person, the next hurdle is to design the right job offer and get your candidate to accept it. To hook an especially hot contender, you may need to get creative. A phone call from top management, the royal treatment, and special perks go a long way, but most superb candidates also want to know in very specific terms how their contributions would affect the business. And no matter how excited you are about your candidate, be certain to establish a **probationary period** upfront. This means a specific time frame (typically three to six months) during which a new hire can prove his or her worth on the job. If everything works out, the employee will move from conditional to permanent status; if not, the company can fire the employee fairly easily.

Contingent Workers Companies that experience a fluctuating need for workers sometimes opt to hire **contingent workers**—or employees who don't expect regular, full-time jobs—rather than permanent, full-time workers. Specifically, contingent employees include temporary full-time workers, independent contractors, on-call workers, and temporary agency or contract agency workers. As a group, these contingent workers account for more than 30% of U.S. employment.[12]

Employers appreciate contingent workers because they offer flexibility, which can lead to much lower costs. But the hidden downside can be workers who are less committed and less experienced. Too much reliance on contingent workers could unwittingly sabotage company productivity and the customer experience.

15-4c Training and Development: Honing the Competitive Edge

For successful companies in virtually every field, training and development have become an ongoing process rather than a one-time activity. Even in a recession, training and development must gather speed for companies and individuals to maintain their competitive edge. Experts offer five key reasons that relate directly to a healthy bottom line:

1. Increased innovation in strategies and products
2. Increased ability to adopt new technologies
3. Increased efficiency and productivity
4. Increased employee motivation and lower employee turnover
5. Decreased liability (e.g., sexual harassment lawsuits)

Training programs take a number of different forms, from orientation to skills training, to management development, depending on the specific employee and the needs of the organization.

Orientation Once you hire new employees, **orientation** should be the first step in the training and development process. Effective orientation programs typically focus on introducing employees to the company culture (but without sacrificing need-to-know administrative information). Research consistently shows that strong orientation programs significantly reduce employee turnover, which lowers costs.

The Boeing aerospace company has mastered the art of employee orientation. Boeing Military Aircraft and Missile Systems revamped its orientation process to include mentoring, meetings with senior executives, and an after-work social program. One highlight of the orientation—meant to crystallize the "wow" factor of working at Boeing—is the chance to take the controls of an F/A-18 fighter plane flight simulator. Management rightfully sees the program as a chance to develop "future leaders…the ones who will

> **orientation** The first step in the training and development process, designed to introduce employees to the company culture and provide key administrative information.

Ooops! What were they thinking?

Interview Gaffes: The Top Ten Things NOT to Do

As you get ready to interview for your dream job, you'll almost certainly find yourself awash in a torrent of advice from family and friends, and flooded with tips found on the Web and elsewhere. "Don't be late, don't be early… Don't ask too many questions, don't ask too few… Don't look too casual, don't look too stuffy…. And whatever you do, never let anyone see that you're nervous!" But however you actually feel—and whatever you actually say—take heart from knowing that you probably won't top these "real-life" interview-question blunders:

1. Question: "What five or six adjectives best describe you?"
   Answer: "Really, really, really, really, really cool!"
2. Question: "Were you late because you got lost?"
   Answer: "No. It was such a nice day that I didn't mind driving slowly."
3. Question: "Why should I hire you?"
   Answer: "Because they say you should always hire people better than yourself."

4. Question: "What do you find interesting about this job?"
   Answer: "The money. I don't really care what your company does."
5. Question: "Is it important to you to get benefits right away?"
   Answer: "I don't believe in healthcare. If I broke my leg, I'd just live with it."
6. Question: "What is your greatest strength?"
   Answer: "I'm a quick learner if I'm in the mood to pay attention."
7. Question: "What can you tell me about your creative ability?"
   Answer: "My answers to most of your questions are pretty good indicators."
8. Question: "Would you be willing to take a drug test?"
   Answer: "Sure. What kind of drugs do I get to test?"
9. Question: "What would your boss say about you?"
   Answer: "That I'm insubordinate."
10. Question: "How would you define a 'problem person'?"
    Answer: "Anyone who disagrees with me."[13]

make sure that Boeing continues to be a great place to work."[14]

On-the-Job Training On-the-job training is popular because it's very low-cost. Employees simply begin their jobs—sometimes under the guidance of more experienced employees—and learn as they go. For simple jobs, this can make sense, but simple jobs are disappearing from the U.S. market due to the combined impact of offshoring and technology. On-the-job training can also compromise the customer experience. Have you ever waited much too long in a short line at the grocery store because the clerk couldn't figure out how to use the cash register? Multiplied across hundreds of customers, this kind of experience undermines the value of a company's brand.

Formal apprenticeship programs tend to be a more effective way of handling on-the-job training. **Apprenticeship** programs mandate that each beginner serve as an assistant to a fully trained worker for a specified period of time before gaining full credentials to work in the field. In the United States, apprenticeships are fairly common in trades such as plumbing and bricklaying. But in Europe, apprenticeships

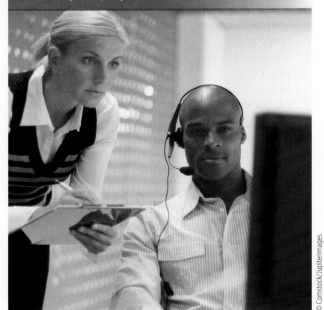

On-the-job training often works best for relatively simple jobs.

© Comstock/Jupiterimages

are much more common across a wide range of professionals, from bankers to opticians.

Off-the-Job Training Classroom training happens away from the job setting but typically during work hours. Employers use classroom training—either on-site or off-site—to teach a wide variety of topics from new computer programming languages, to negotiation skills, to stress management, and more. Going one step further than classroom training, some employers train workers off-site on "real" equipment (e.g., robots) similar to what they would actually use on the job. This approach is called "vestibule training." Police academies often use vestibule training for firearms. Job simulation goes even further than vestibule training, by attempting to duplicate the exact conditions that the trainee will face on the job. This approach makes sense for complex, high-risk positions such as astronaut or airline pilot.

Computer-Based Training Computer-based training—mostly delivered via the Web—now plays a crucial role in off-the-job training. Broadband technology has turbocharged audio and visual capabilities, which support engaging and interactive online training programs. Online training also standardizes the presentation of the material, since it doesn't depend on the quality of the individual instructor. And the Web helps employers train employees wherever they may be in the world, at their own pace and convenience. But there is a key drawback: it takes a lot of discipline to complete an online program, and some people simply learn better through direct human interaction.

Management Development As the bulk of top-level U.S. executives move toward retirement (or lose their jobs in the recession), developing new leaders has become a priority in many organizations. **Management development** programs help current and potential executives develop the skills they need to move into leadership positions. These programs typically cover specific issues that the business faces but also less-tangible—yet equally important—topics, such as communication, planning, business-analysis, change-management, coaching, and team-building skills.

15-4d Evaluation: Assessing Employee Performance

Straightforward, frequent feedback is a powerful tool to improve employee performance. The best managers provide informal feedback on a constant basis so that employees always know where they stand. But most companies also require that managers give formal feedback through periodic **performance appraisals**, usually every six months or once a year. Typically, managers conduct the appraisals by sitting down with each employee on a one-to-one basis and comparing actual results to expected results. The performance appraisal affects decisions regarding compensation, promotions, training, transfers, and terminations.

The HR role in performance appraisals begins with the strategic process of creating evaluation tools that tie directly into the company's big-picture objectives. Then, on a day-to-day basis, HR coordinates the actual appraisal process, which typically involves volumes of paperwork. HR must also ensure that managers are trained in providing relevant, honest, objective feedback, and that workers at every level know how to respond if they believe their appraisal is not fair.

Both giving and receiving evaluations tend to be awkward for everyone involved, and unfortunately, uncomfortable people tend to make mistakes. As you read the following list, you'll probably find that you've been on the receiving end of at least a couple of the most common appraisal goofs.

1. **Gotcha!** Too many managers use the performance appraisal as a chance to catch employees doing something wrong, rather than doing something right.

2. **The Once-a-Year Wonder** Many companies mandate annual reviews, but some managers use that as an excuse to give feedback only once a year.

3. **Straight from the Gut** Although "gut feel" can have real value, it's no substitute for honest, relevant documentation of both expectations and accomplishments.

4. **What Have You Done for Me Lately?** Many managers give far too much weight to recent accomplishments, discounting the early part of the review period.

5. **The "Me Filter"** While appraisals are a bit subjective by their very nature, some managers filter every comment through their personal biases. Here are some examples:

   - **Positive Leniency:** "I'm a nice guy, so I give everyone great scores."

   - **Negative Leniency:** "I have high expectations, so I give everyone low scores."

- **Halo Effect:** "I like this employee so I'll give her top scores across the board."

For a performance appraisal to be effective, the manager must focus on fairness, relevance, objectivity, and balance. Equally important, the manager should give feedback on a continual basis to eliminate surprises and maximize performance.

15-4e Compensation: Show Me the Money

The term **compensation** covers both pay and benefits, but when most people think about compensation, they think about cash. Yet your paycheck is only part of the picture. Many companies also offer noncash benefits such as healthcare, which can be worth up to 30% of each employee's pay. Researching, designing, and managing effective compensation systems are core HR functions.

From a company perspective, compensation—both cash and noncash—represents a big chunk of product costs, especially in labor-intensive businesses such as banks, restaurants, and airlines. Although many firms opt to cut labor costs as far as possible, others boost compensation above the norm to find and keep the best workers. In fact, research suggests that companies offering higher-than-average compensation generally outperform their competitors in terms of total return to shareholders—both stock price and dividend payouts.[15]

Regarding specific individuals and positions, companies typically base compensation on a balance of the following factors:

- **Competition:** How much do competing firms offer for similar positions?

- **Contribution:** How much does a specific person contribute to the bottom line?

- **Ability to Pay:** How much can the company afford?

- **Cost of Living:** What would be reasonable in light of the broader local economy?

- **Legislation:** What does the government mandate?

The most common compensation systems in the United States are wages and salaries. **Wages** refer to pay in exchange for the number of hours or days that an employee works. Variations can be huge, starting

performance appraisal A formal feedback process that requires managers to give their subordinates feedback on a one-to-one basis, typically by comparing actual results to expected results.

compensation The combination of pay and benefits that employees receive in exchange for their work.

wages The pay that employees receive in exchange for the number of hours or days that they work.

salaries The pay that employees receive over a fixed period, most often weekly or monthly.

benefits Noncash compensation, including programs such as health insurance, vacation, and childcare.

at the federal minimum wage of $7.25 per hour (as of mid-2012) and ranging up to more than $50 per hour. Jobs that require less education—such as flipping burgers—typically pay hourly wages. Federal law requires companies to pay nonexempt wage earners overtime, 50% more than their standard wage, for every hour worked over 40 hours per week.

Salaries, on the other hand, cover a fixed period, most often weekly or monthly. Most professional, administrative, and managerial jobs pay salaries. While salaries are usually higher than wages, salaried workers do not qualify for overtime, which means that sometimes a low-level manager's overall pay may be less than the pay of wage-based employees who work for that manager.

© Arkady/Shutterstock.com

Pay for Performance In addition to wages and salaries, many organizations link some amount of worker pay directly to performance. The idea, of course, is to motivate employees to excel. Exhibit 15.3 lists some common approaches.

As you look over the range of variable pay options, which would you find most motivating? Why? What type of business might use each form of variable pay? Why?

15-4f Benefits: From Birthday Cakes to Death Benefits

Benefits represent a significant chunk of money for employers, but for many years, workers took benefits for granted. No longer. As the unemployment rate skyrocketed in 2009, employees began to appreciate their benefits more than ever, recognizing that healthcare, dental care, paid sick days, retirement plans, and other perks add enormous value to their paychecks—and can be yanked at the discretion of their employer.[16]

Exhibit 15.3 Performance Pay Options

VARIABLE PAY SYSTEM	DESCRIPTION
COMMISSION	Commission involves payment as a percentage of sales. Usually, larger commissions go with smaller base pay.
BONUSES	Bonuses are lump-sum payments, typically to reward strong performance from individual employees.
PROFIT SHARING	Profit-sharing plans reward employees with a share of company profits above and beyond predetermined goals.
STOCK OPTIONS	Stock options are the right to buy shares of company stock at some future date for the price of the shares on the day that the company awarded the options.
PAY FOR KNOWLEDGE	This approach involves awarding bonuses and pay increases in exchange for increases in knowledge such as earning an MBA.

© Cengage Learning 2013

In fact, a number of budget-minded employers already stick to the legally mandated basics: Social Security and Medicare contributions, payments to state unemployment and workers' compensation programs, and job protection per the Federal Family and Medical Leave Act. However, socially responsible employers—and companies that seek a competitive advantage through a top-notch workforce—tend to offer far more. Optional benefits usually include some or all of the following:

- Paid vacation days and holidays
- Paid sick days
- Health insurance
- Retirement programs
- Product discounts

A smaller number of companies also offer less traditional benefits such as backup childcare options, free massage, pet health insurance, tuition reimbursement, and paid time off for volunteering. Since the recession of 2009, companies that offered "extras" have focused extra attention on perks that would boost morale without an outrageous price tag.[17]

In the past decade, a growing number of companies have begun to offer **cafeteria-style benefits**. This approach involves giving their employees a set dollar amount per person that they must spend on company benefits. The key to these plans is choice, which allows employees to tailor their benefits to their individual needs.

Over the past couple of decades, employees across the U.S. economy have demanded more flexibility from their employers, and companies have responded. Flexible scheduling options include flextime, telecommuting, and job-sharing plans, discussed in detail below. But unfortunately, as massive, widespread layoffs swept across the economy in 2009, workers began to give up flexible schedules—or to stop even asking about them in the first place—out of fear that they would appear less committed to their jobs.[18]

Flextime A **flextime** plan gives workers some degree of freedom in terms of when they start and finish their workday, as long as they complete the required number of hours. Typically, companies with flextime scheduling oblige their employees to start work between mandated hours in the morning—say, anytime between 7 A.M. and 10 A.M.—to take lunch between certain hours in the middle of the day, and to complete work at the end of eight hours. This approach ensures that everyone is present during core hours for communication and coordination, but it provides choice outside those parameters. Flextime tends to increase employee morale and retention, but it makes less sense in jobs that entail extensive teamwork and customer interaction. It also requires careful management to avoid abuse.

The **compressed workweek**, another version of flextime scheduling, allows employees to work a full-time number of hours in less than the standard workweek. The most popular option is to work four ten-hour days rather than five eight-hour days. Major companies, such as Intel, have developed successful compressed workweek programs at a number of their facilities.

Telecommuting Working remotely—most often from home—is a growing phenomenon on a global scale. Booming technological advances allow employees to "commute" to the office via phones, fax machines, and broadband networks. More than 60% of companies allow **telecommuting**, and about 30% of Americans telecommute at least occasionally. The bottom-line benefits for companies that embrace the approach can be significant. Over two-thirds of employers report increased productivity among their telecommuters. Telecommuting employees are 35%–40% more productive than their office-bound colleagues. And direct savings from decreased costs add up fast, as well. By establishing telecommuting programs, employers can realize annual cost savings of $5,000 per employee, which

Wacky Benefits

While most benefits are optional, you would not be unreasonable to expect your firm to offer standard perks, such as paid vacation days or sick time, but a handful of creative companies have developed a package of perks to create a unique, compelling corporate culture.[19] Some examples:

© Poulsons Photography/Shutterstock.com

- ◯ **Zappos.com:** Offers a full-time, on-site life coach who helps employees achieve work-life balance and "create fun and a little weirdness."

- ◯ **Goldman Sachs:** Its brand new Wall Street headquarters features a reading room, sky lobby, and 54,000-square-foot gym.

- ◯ **NetApp:** Actively supports employee volunteer work. Allowed one employee to take five straight weeks to get the required 200 hours of training to be a volunteer fire fighter. That employee says, "Now I'm a hero to my three children because I'm a fireman."

- ◯ **Quicken Loans:** Razor scooters move team members around the office, which is adorned with scratch-and-sniff wallpaper, custom graffiti by a local artist, and foosball tables.

Commuting at Zero Gallons per Mile

Countless studies confirm that telecommuting can offer real benefits for both employers and employees. But it can also make a world of difference for our planet.

According to the EPA, the U.S. economy could save $23 billion in transportation, environmental, and energy costs if the number of telecommuting workers increased by 10% to 20%. Telecommuting rates increased by 74% between 2005 and 2009, and with rates expected to continue growing by 15% each year, the savings in gas costs could be enormous. Telecommuting already saves 10 million barrels of oil per year by reducing traffic congestion and keeping cars off the roads.

With fewer workers in the office, employers can reduce their need for space, cut back on certain office supplies, and eliminate the need for duplicate equipment such as computers, printers, and phones. Teleworkers are also more likely to email documents instead of printing them, and may be more conservative with resources, such as water and paper products, at home than they are in the office.

Individual firms that encourage telemarketing also enjoy substantial benefits. At Sun Microsystems, nearly 60% of employees telecommute, and save an average of $1,500 per year on gas alone, plus three weeks of wasted time. Each employee also reduces energy consumption by 5,400 kW hours per year. Cisco estimates annual savings of more than $225 million in productivity due to telecommuting, plus a reduction in greenhouse gas emissions of 47,320 metric tons.

Telecommuting adds up to a winning strategy for all parties involved.[20]

adds up to hundreds of millions of dollars each year for big players, such as IBM, Sun Microsystems, and AT&T.[21]

While telecommuting sounds great at first glance, it offers benefits and drawbacks for organizations and employees alike, as you'll see in Exhibit 15.4.

Job Sharing Job sharing allows two or more employees to share a single full-time job. Typically, job-share participants split the salary equally, but they often need to allocate full benefits to just one of the partners. On a nationwide basis, fewer than 20% of employers (e.g., American Express and PricewaterhouseCoopers) offer job-sharing programs

and reap the benefits such as higher morale and better retention.[22]

15-4g Separation: Breaking Up Is Hard to Do

Employees leave jobs for a number of different reasons. Experiencing success, they may be promoted or lured to another firm. Experiencing failure, they may be fired. Or in response to changing business needs, their employer might transfer them or lay them off. And employees also leave jobs for completely personal reasons such as family needs, retirement, or a change in career aspirations.

When companies terminate employees, they must proceed very carefully to avoid wrongful-termination lawsuits. The best protection is honesty and documentation. Employers should always document sound business reasons for termination and share those reasons with the employee.

But employees can still lose their jobs for reasons that have little or nothing to do with their individual performance. In response to the recession, employers eliminated 5.1 million jobs between December 2007 and March 2009. And while the recession eased in 2011 and 2012, employment has not returned to pre-recession levels, and many experts anticipate that it will not fully rebound for many years. As companies have become leaner, the remaining workers have experienced enormous stress. Managers can mitigate the trauma most effectively by showing empathy and concern for employees who remain, and by treating the laid-off employees with visible compassion.[23]

15-5 Legal Issues: HR and the Long Arm of the Law

Even when the company is right—even when the company wins—employment lawsuits can cost millions of dollars and deeply damage the reputation of an organization, as we briefly discussed earlier in this chapter. To avoid employment lawsuits, most firms rely on HR to digest the complex, evolving web of employment legislation and court decisions, and to ensure that management understands the key issues.

The bottom-line goal of most employment legislation is to protect employees from unfair treatment by employers. Some would argue that the legislation goes so far that it hinders the ability of companies to grow. But regardless of your personal perspective, the obligation of an ethical employer is to understand and abide by the law as it stands—even if you're working within the system to change it.

The most influential piece of employment law may be the **Civil Rights Act of 1964**. **Title VII** of this act—which applies only to employers with 15 or more workers—outlaws discrimination in hiring, firing, compensation, apprenticeships, training, terms, conditions, or privileges of employment based on race, color, religion, sex, or national origin. Over time, Congress has supplemented Title VII with legislation that prohibits discrimination based on pregnancy, age (40+), and disability.

Title VII also created the **Equal Employment Opportunity Commission (EEOC)** to enforce its provisions. And in 1972, Congress beefed up the EEOC with additional powers to regulate and to enforce its mandates, making the EEOC a powerful force in the human resources realm.

Here are some additional key pieces of employment legislation:

⊃ **Fair Labor Standards Act of 1938:** Established a minimum wage and overtime pay for employees working more than 40 hours a week.

⊃ **Equal Pay Act of 1963:** Mandated that men and women doing equal jobs receive equal pay.

> **"75% of layoff survivors report that their productivity dropped after the layoff."**
>
> — *Psychology Today*

⊃ **Occupational Safety and Health Act of 1970:** Required safety equipment for employees and established maximum exposure limits for hazardous substances.

⊃ **Immigration Reform and Control Act of 1986:** Required employers to verify employment eligibility for all new hires.

⊃ **Americans with Disabilities Act of 1990:** Prohibited discrimination in hiring, promotion, and compensation against people with disabilities and required employers to make "reasonable" accommodations for them.

⊃ **Family and Medical Leave Act of 1993:** Required firms with 50 or more employees to provide up to 12 weeks of job-secure, unpaid leave on the birth or adoption of a child or the serious illness of a spouse, child, or parent.

Civil Rights Act of 1964 Federal legislation that prohibits discrimination in hiring, firing, compensation, apprenticeships, training, terms, conditions, or privileges of employment based on race, color, religion, sex, or national origin.

Title VII A portion of the Civil Rights Act of 1964 that prohibits discrimination in hiring, firing, compensation, apprenticeships, training, terms, conditions, or privileges of employment based on race, color, religion, sex, or national origin for employers with 15 or more workers.

Equal Employment Opportunity Commission (EEOC) A federal agency designed to regulate and enforce the provisions of Title VII.

Exhibit 15.4 An Analysis of Telecommuting

	BENEFITS	DRAWBACKS
ORGANIZATION	• Lower costs for office space, equipment, and upkeep • Higher employee productivity due to better morale, fewer sick days, and more focused performance • Access to a broader talent pool (not everyone needs to be local)	• Greater challenges maintaining a cohesive company culture • Greater challenges fostering teamwork • Greater challenges monitoring and managing far-flung employees
EMPLOYEE	• Much more flexibility • Zero commute time (less gas money) • Better work-family balance • Every day is casual Friday (or even pajama day!) • Fewer office politics and other distractions	• Less fast-track career potential • Less influence within the organization • Weaker connection to the company culture • Isolation from the social structure at work

Source: Flexible Hours and Telecommuting—Not the Ticket to the Top of Corporate America, Five Questions for Susan DePhillips, Workforce Management, September 2005, http://www.workforce.com/section/02/article/24/14/66.html

15-5a Affirmative Action: The Active Pursuit of Equal Opportunity

The term **affirmative action** refers to policies meant to increase employment and educational opportunities for minority groups—especially groups defined by race, ethnicity, or gender. Emerging during the American civil rights movement in the 1960s, affirmative action seeks to make up for the systematic discrimination of the past by creating more opportunities in the present.

Over the past couple of decades, affirmative action has become increasingly controversial. Opponents have raised concerns that giving preferential treatment to some groups amounts to "reverse discrimination" against groups who do not get the same benefits. They claim that affirmative action violates the principle that all individuals are equal under the law. But supporters counter that everyone who benefits from affirmative action must—by law—have relevant and valid qualifications. They argue that proactive measures are the only workable way to right past wrongs and to ensure truly equal opportunity.

Recent U.S. Supreme Court decisions have supported affirmative action, pointing out that government has a "compelling interest" in ensuring racial diversity. But the Court has rejected "mechanistic" affirmative action programs that amount to quota systems based on race, ethnicity, or gender.

The long-term fate of affirmative action remains unclear, but achieving the underlying goal—a diverse workplace with equal opportunity for all—stands to benefit both business and society as a whole.

15-5b Sexual Harassment: Eliminating Hostility

Sexual harassment—which violates Title VII of the Civil Rights Act of 1964—involves discrimination against a person based on his or her gender. According to the EEOC, sexual harassment can range from requests for sexual favors to the presence of a hostile work environment. The EEOC also points out that a sexual harasser may be either a woman or a man, and the harasser doesn't need to be the victim's supervisor. The victim could be anyone affected—either directly or indirectly—by the offensive conduct. And clearly, to qualify as sexual harassment, the conduct must be unwelcome. The total number of sexual harassment charges filed with the EEOC in the past decade dropped 27% from 2001 to 2011, but the number of charges filed by men rose from 13.7% to 16.3%.[24]

Not just the perpetrator is liable for sexual harassment; employers may share accountability if they did not take "reasonable care" to prevent and correct sexually harassing behavior, or if they did not provide a workable system for employee complaints. Simply adopting a written policy against sexual harassment is not enough. Taking "reasonable care" also means taking proactive steps—such as comprehensive training—to ensure that everyone in the organization understands 1) that the firm does not tolerate sexual harassment, and 2) that the firm has a system in place for complaints and will not tolerate retaliation against those who complain.[25]

Odd Jobs

As you contemplate your post-college career, chances are good that you are mostly considering the more typical fields, where people you know have built successful careers. Although there are many satisfying options, a number of folks have built rewarding careers in fields that initially appear somewhat odd. A few examples:[26]

- **Flavorists:** Also known as flavor chemists, flavorists synthesize and re-create natural flavors. Average pay for these specialists is up to $100,000 per year.

- **Dog Food Taster:** Just like any other meals, dog food needs to be inspected too. Since they can't use dogs to test the food, this delicious cuisine requires a professional taste tester.

- **Master Sommeliers:** Sommeliers help people dining decide which wines complement their meals. They also help restaurants craft their wine lists. Average pay is an impressive $80,000 to $160,000 per year.

- **Crash Designer:** One of Mattel's engineers has spent the past 27 years coming up with new, inventive ways to flip tiny cars around plastic tracks as a designer for Mattel's Hot Wheels brand. "If your toy is hurting, add loops and crashing. Crashing inside loops, even better," he says.

© Big Pants Production/Shutterstock.com

THE BIG PICTURE

Effective human resource management can create an unbeatable competitive edge—a fair, productive, empowering workplace pays off in bottom-line results. In good times, one core HRM goal is to find, hire, and develop the best talent. While that function remains crucial in tough economic times, the focus changes to managing HR costs while maintaining morale. Looking forward, a growing number of firms will most likely outsource traditional HR tasks such as payroll and benefits administration to companies that specialize in these areas. HR departments could then focus on their core mission: working with senior management to achieve business goals by cultivating the firm's investment in human resources.

The Bureau of Labor Statistics projects that jobs in human resources will experience much faster growth than average through 2018.[27] But attaining one of these positions will require much more than simply liking people. Human resources jobs include analysts, benefits administrators, negotiators, recruiters, trainers, managers, and more. Most positions require at least a four-year degree in business or human resources, several years of related experience, and excellent interpersonal skills.

CAREERS IN HUMAN RESOURCES

What *else?*
RIP & REVIEW CARDS IN THE BACK
and visit www.cengagebrain.com!

16

Managing Information and Technology:
Finding New Ways to Learn and Link

LEARNING OBJECTIVES

After studying this chapter, you will be able to:

16-1   Explain the basic elements of computer technology—including hardware, software, and networks—and describe key trends in each area

16-2   Discuss the reasons for the increasing popularity of cloud computing

16-3   Describe how data becomes information and how decision support systems can provide high-quality information that helps managers make better decisions

16-4   Explain how Internet-based technologies have changed business-to-consumer and business-to-business commerce

16-5   Describe the problems posed by the rapid changes in Internet-based technologies, and explain ways to address these problems

"THE INTERNET? IS THAT THING STILL *AROUND*?"

— HOMER SIMPSON

16-1 Information Technology: Explosive Change

Over the past few decades, computer and communications hardware and software have changed dramatically. The capabilities of hardware have increased by orders of magnitude. In the late 1950s, for example, you would have needed 50 24-inch disks—costing tens of thousands of dollars—to store 5 megabytes of data. Today you can buy a flash memory device, about the same size as a postage stamp, that stores 64 gigabytes of data—over 12,000 times more than that whole 1950s disk array—for under $60. And in terms of processing power, Apple's iPad tablet computer, introduced in 2012 with a base price under $500, can complete more than 3 *billion* mathematical operations *per second*—making it faster than many multimillion-dollar supercomputers from the early 1990s.[1] While more difficult to quantify with specific statistics, it's also clear that software has become more powerful, more flexible, and easier to use.

Perhaps an even more important development than the increased power of hardware and sophistication of software is the degree to which today's technology is linked by networks. These networks allow businesses to coordinate their internal functions, reach their customers, and collaborate with their suppliers and partners in ways that could not have been envisioned a quarter of a century ago. Networks have not only improved the efficiency and effectiveness of existing businesses, they've also opened up entirely new business opportunities. Of course, these new linkages pose challenges and threats as well as benefits and opportunities; a quarter of a century ago, people hadn't heard of computer viruses, spyware, phishing, or spam (except for the Hormel meat product variety). Over the course of this chapter, we'll take a look at both sides of this rapidly changing story.

16-1a Hardware and Software

Hardware refers to the physical components used to collect, input, store, and process data, and to display and distribute information. This hardware includes the various components of a computer system as well as communications and network equipment. Examples include barcode scanners, hard drives, printers, routers, and smartphones.

Software refers to the programs that provide instructions to a computer so that it can perform a desired task. There are two broad categories of software: system software and application software. Both types of software take advantage of the tremendous increase in hardware capabilities to become both more powerful and easier to use.

System software performs the critical functions necessary to operate a computer at the most basic level. The fundamental form of system software is the operating system, which controls the overall operation of the computer. It implements vital tasks, such as managing the file system, reading programs and data into main memory, and allocating system memory among various tasks to avoid conflicts.

Operating system software also provides the interface that enables users to interact with their computers. Early operating systems required users to type complex commands with very precise syntax in order to carry out tasks such as running programs or opening, saving, or deleting files. If you made an error while typing a command, your monitor would just sit there until you typed the correct command. Today's operating systems are much simpler and more intuitive. The *graphical user interface* (or GUI—pronounced "gooey") allows users to enter commands by clicking on icons on the computer screen or by tapping or swiping them on devices with a touch screen.

Utility programs supplement operating system software in ways that increase the security or abilities of the computer system. Examples include firewalls, antivirus software, and antispyware programs. Over the years, operating systems have incorporated many features that were originally provided by such utility programs.

Applications software is software that helps users perform a desired task. Horizontal applications software, such as word processing, spreadsheet, and personal information management

---

hardware The physical tools and equipment used to collect, input, store, organize, and process data and to distribute information.

software Programs that provide instructions to a computer so that it can perform a desired task.

system software Software that performs the critical functions necessary to operate the computer at the most basic level.

applications software Software that helps a user perform a desired task.

Internet The world's largest computer network; essentially a network of computer networks all operating under a common set of rules that allow them to communicate with each other.

broadband Internet connection An Internet connection that is capable of transmitting large amounts of information very quickly.

Internet2 (I2) A new high-tech Internet with access limited to a consortium of member organizations (and other organizations these members sponsor). I2 utilizes technologies that give it a speed and capacity far exceeding the current Internet.

software, is used by many different businesses and occupations. Vertical applications software is designed for a specific industry or profession. For example, brokerage firms have special software that allows them to transact business on the stock exchanges, and product designers have computer-aided design (CAD) software that enables them to produce technical drawings in three dimensions.

16-1b Networks

Today, most firms (and households) use networks that allow users to communicate with each other and share both files and hardware resources. A network links computer resources using either a wired or wireless connection. Firms usually want to prevent outsiders from obtaining access to their networks for privacy and security reasons, but they sometimes allow customers or suppliers partial access to their private networks to strengthen their relationships with these important stakeholders.

The Internet and the World Wide Web The development and growth of the **Internet** is one of the great networking stories of the past two decades. The Internet is often referred to as the world's largest computer network. It's actually a network of networks, consisting of hundreds of thousands of smaller networks operating under a common set of protocols (rules) so that they can communicate with each other.

One common way to experience the Internet is through the World Wide Web. But while the Internet supports the Web and provides access to it, only about a quarter of the traffic on the Internet involves the Web. (Other traffic includes, but isn't limited to, email, VoIP phone calls, Internet chat, online gaming, and machine-to-machine communications.)[2] Still, the Web is an incredibly rich environment; it consists of billions of documents—the number grows every day—written and linked together using Hypertext Markup Language (HTML).

The increased availability of broadband Internet connections has fueled the popularity of Internet applications. A **broadband Internet connection** has the capacity to transmit large amounts of data very quickly, allowing users to quickly download large files such as music, games, and movies. A survey by the Pew Internet and American Life Project, summarized in Exhibit 16.1, found that access to broadband Internet connections grew rapidly for much of the past decade. As Exhibit 16.1

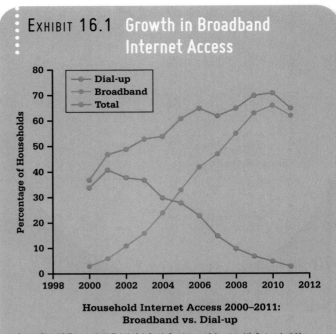

EXHIBIT 16.1 Growth in Broadband Internet Access

Household Internet Access 2000–2011: Broadband vs. Dial-up

Source: Digital Differences by K. Zickuhr & A. Smith, Pew Internet & American Life Project, April 13, 2012, http://www.pewinternet.org/~/media//Files/Reports/2012/PIP_Digital_differences_041312.pdf, accessed June 16, 2012.

shows, only 3% of American adults had access to high-speed Internet at home in 2000, but by 2012 that figure had climbed to 62%.[3] From a business perspective, the growth in broadband penetration allows companies to offer richer, more interactive experiences to customers who visit their websites or use their apps.

But even today's broadband connections are too slow and inefficient for many business and scientific applications. Such projects often require high-definition video and audio files to be shared among multiple sites at the same time. Beginning in 1996, several leading research universities, corporations, and other organizations formed a coalition to create a new generation of Internet technology in the United States based on fiber-optic cable. The resulting network became known as **Internet2** (or "I2").

Access to I2 was initially limited to dues-paying members of the Internet2 consortium, which today consists of over 200 major universities as well as 70 leading high-tech corporations, 45 government agencies, and about 50 international organizations.[4] But under an initiative begun in 2001, members of the I2 consortium can sponsor access to the network for other research and educational organizations that otherwise would be unable to qualify for membership. This initiative has given many elementary schools, high schools, community colleges, libraries, and museums access to I2 resources.[5]

Internet2 isn't simply a faster way to surf the Web or send email. In fact, such routine uses of the current Internet aren't even allowed. Instead, it is a noncommercial network that uses high-speed connectivity to improve education, research, and collaboration. Member organizations see Internet2 as a way to bring together their researchers, scientists, and engineers at various locations in a way that allows real-time collaboration on complex and important topics. It also allows corporations to collaborate with other companies, universities, and organizations located thousands of miles apart. One of the missions of the Internet2 consortium is to "facilitate the development, deployment and use of revolutionary Internet technologies."[6] So, the benefits of Internet2 will eventually become commonplace on the Internet that the rest of us use.

Intranets and Extranets An **intranet** is a private network that has the same look and feel as the Web and uses the same web browser software to display documents, but limits access to the employees of a single firm (or members of a single organization). When properly implemented, intranets enhance communication and collaboration among employees and provide an effective way to distribute information and applications throughout the organization. Employees can usually log onto their company's intranet from remote locations using password-protected Internet access, allowing them to use company resources when working on the road or from home.

> **"There are** only two industries that refer to their customers as 'users.'"
>
> — Edward Tufte, statistician

Firms sometimes also create **extranets** by giving key stakeholders, such as suppliers or customers, limited access to certain areas of their intranet. Extranets enable firms to provide additional services and information to their external stakeholders. For example, the firm might allow customers to check on the status of their order, or suppliers to check on the state of the firm's inventory to plan shipments of parts and materials.

intranet A private network that has the look and feel of the Internet and is navigated using a web browser, but which limits access to a single firm's employees (or a single organization's members).

extranet An intranet that allows limited access to a selected group of stakeholders, such as suppliers or customers.

16-1c The Role of the IT Department

Many business organizations have an information technology (IT) department to manage their information resources. But the role of this department varies significantly from one company to another. In some firms, the IT department plays a strategic role, making and implementing key decisions about the technologies the firm will use. In other organizations, the role of IT is largely operational; managers in functional departments make the key decisions about

Reply All: Instant Panic and Regret with the Rare Happy Ending

With a click, and a lack of attention, Reply All has produced many embarrassing workplace emails. Ben Baldanza, CEO of Spirit Airlines, responded to an email containing a customer complaint sent by his executives, "We owe him nothing as far as I'm concerned. Let him tell the world how bad we are. He's never flown us before anyway and will be back when we save him a penny." Of course, he mistakenly included the customer.

Reply All can sometimes end happily. When a spam email written in an Indian dialect was sent by gulfmalayaly.com, an online magazine, an automatic message at Business Wire, which distributes company press releases, resent the spam to the original recipients who responded angrily, with each complaint compounding the problem. One wrote, "Do people understand that, by replying to all, you're perpetuating this ridiculous spam cycle?" The negativity turned positive, however, after London writer Padraig Belton responded, "Personally, I feel that after this many emails from you lot, we should all knock off together to the pub." Then London businessperson Robert Peacok emailed, "Rather than getting steamed up about all this, maybe it is worth considering setting up a LinkedIn group in which we can exchange crazy banter or possibly even business opportunities if we can establish our common link." More than 75 people from around the world joined! Three days later, Belton and Peacok met for a drink. Belton said, "Whoever sent that spam may have done us an actual sort of favor."[7]

© blanche/Shutterstock.com

cloud computing The use of Internet-based storage capacity, processing power, and computer applications to supplement or replace internally owned information technology resources.

the computer and information resources their areas need, and the IT department simply maintains these resources and provides technical support to employees.

16-2 Cloud Computing: The Sky's the Limit!

In most companies, employees use applications and access data stored on their own computers or their companies' servers. But a relatively new trend called "cloud computing" is challenging that approach. **Cloud computing** means using Internet-based storage capacity, applications, and processing power to supplement or replace internally owned computer resources.

You're already familiar with consumer-focused cloud computing services if you share photos on Shutterfly, store your music on Apple's iCloud storage services, or use a service like Dropbox to access and share documents and files. These services clearly offer significant benefits, such as the ability to store large files without taking up valuable space on your computer's hard drive and the convenience of being able to access your documents, music, or photos from any computer (and many mobile devices) with an Internet connection.

Until recently, most businesses were reluctant to embrace cloud computing, citing concerns about security and reliability. But the rapid increase in the number of firms using cloud-based services suggests that more and more businesses are becoming convinced that the advantages of cloud computing outweigh its risks. John Engates, chief technology officer at Raskspace, a leading cloud data host, says, "We're definitely having more conversations about security with small- and medium-sized customers, and we're also selling more security services to those customers than ever before. It's on the rise."[8]

And for some organizations, moving to the cloud may actually increase data security. Jim Reavis, of Cloud Security Alliance, an industry group, says, "Small and medium businesses are insane not to leverage the advantages of cloud computing. It ends up being almost in all cases a security upgrade because they can't otherwise afford the practices." Eric Cooper, executive director of the San Antonio Food Bank, works with 150 employees, 5,000 volunteers, and a small technology budget. He said that basic data security practices were "well above our [in-house] technological

and intellectual capacity." So they put their critical data and supplier network in the cloud. He says, "It was a no-brainer. I can't be worried about whether there's someone hacking our system."[8a] Now his cloud provider does that for him. More specifically, the cloud offers to its users the ability to:

- ⊃ Access a vast array of computing resources without the need to invest heavily in expensive new hardware, software, and IT personnel.

- ⊃ Quickly adjust the amount of computer resources to meet their needs—and pay only for the resources that are actually used. This lowers costs and eliminates the problem of excess capacity. In fact, the cost reductions are often so great that even small firms can afford to take advantage of sophisticated and powerful cloud computing resources.

- ⊃ Encourage collaboration among employees and business partners. Cloud resources aren't confined to a specific platform or operating system, so it is easy for people using different computer systems to share files and programs. In addition, many cloud-based applications include tools specifically designed to facilitate collaboration.

Cloud computing may revolutionize the role of IT departments.

- ⊃ Take advantage of incredible gains in processing speed. Not only does cloud computing give users access to more resources, but it also enables them to use those resources more efficiently by taking advantage of a technique called *massively parallel computing*, which can combine the processing power of hundreds (or even thousands) of computers to work on different elements of a problem simultaneously. The result is that data processing projects that used to take weeks to complete on a firm's internal computer resources can be completed in less than a day using cloud resources.[9]

© iStockphoto.com/Luca di Filippo

16-3 Information Technology and Decision Making: A Crucial Aid

One of the vital functions of information technology—at least in relationship to business—is to transform data into useful information for decision makers. In order to make decisions, managers must have information about the current state of their business, their competitive environment, and the trends and market conditions that offer new opportunities. Where does this information come from? How can it be made more useful? How can managers process the information to make better decisions?

16-3a Data and Information

Let's start by distinguishing between data and information. **Data** are the facts and figures a firm collects. Data in their raw form have limited usefulness because they lack the context needed to give them meaning. Data become **information** when they are processed, organized, and presented in a way that makes them useful to a decision maker. Sometimes firms can obtain useful information from external sources, but sometimes they must create information by processing their own data. Given today's competitive environment, the speed with which managers obtain good-quality information can be a crucial competitive advantage.

Internally, every department of an organization generates facts and figures that the firm must store and track. Every time a financial transaction is completed, for example, the firm's accounting system must record the specific accounts affected. Similarly, a firm's human resources department must enter new data every time an employee is hired, fired, promoted, changes jobs, or retires. Firms must also keep track of the names, addresses, and credit information of each customer. This is hardly a complete list, but you get the picture; firms must store mountains of data and convert them into useful information.

Typically, today's businesses store their data in **databases**, which are files of related data organized according to a logical system and stored on hard drives or some other computer-accessible storage media. It isn't unusual for a company to have many different databases, each maintained by a different department or functional area to meet its specific needs. For example, the human resources department might have a database of employee pay rates, and the marketing department may have another database of customer history.

Once all these data are stored, the firm must convert them into information. One common method is to query a database. A query is a request for the database management software to search the database for data that match criteria specified by the user. Suppose, for instance, that a marketing manager plans to introduce a product

To err is human—and to blame it on a computer is even more so.

— ROBERT ORBEN, COMEDY WRITER AND SPEECHWRITER

upgrade. She can enter a query that asks for the email addresses of all customers who have purchased the product in the past year. She can use this information to send a targeted email message, promoting the upgrade to the customers who are most likely to buy it.

16-3b Characteristics of Good Information

We've seen that businesses have many sources of information. But not all information is of good quality. High-quality information is:

- ⊙ Accurate: It should be free of errors and biases.

- ⊙ Relevant: It should focus on issues that are important to decision makers.

- ⊙ Timely: It should be available in time to make a difference.

- ⊙ Understandable: It must help the user grasp its meaning.

- ⊙ Secure: Confidential information must be secure from hackers and competitors.

16-3c Using Information Technology to Improve Decision Making

A company's information technology (IT) department frequently works closely with managers throughout the organization to support decision making. In fact, many companies develop **decision support systems** (DSS) that give managers access to large amounts of data and the processing power to convert the data into high-quality information quickly and efficiently.

Over the past two decades, a new class of decision support system has evolved to take advantage of the dramatic increase in data storage and processing capabilities. Called **business intelligence systems**, these systems help businesses discover subtle and complex relationships hidden in their data. Such systems can be a source of competitive advantage for the businesses that develop them.

One of the most common approaches to implementing a business intelligence system is to create a data warehouse and use data mining to discover unknown relationships. A **data warehouse** is a very large, organization-wide database that provides a centralized location for storing

data Raw, unprocessed facts and figures.

information Data that have been processed in a way that make them meaningful to their user.

database A file consisting of related data organized according to a logical system and stored on a hard drive or some other computer-accessible media.

decision support system (DSS) A system that gives managers access to large amounts of data and the processing power to convert these data into high-quality information, thus improving the decision-making process.

business intelligence system A sophisticated form of decision support system that helps decision makers discover information that was previously hidden.

data warehouse A large, organization-wide database that stores data in a centralized location.

data from both the organization's own databases and external sources.

Data mining uses powerful statistical and mathematical techniques to analyze vast amounts of data to identify useful information that had been hidden. In recent years, data mining has had considerable success in areas as diverse as fraud and crime detection, quality control, scientific research, and even professional sports. When the San Francisco Giants used data mining to decide when to increase or decrease seat prices for single game tickets, ticket revenues jumped by 6%.[11]

16-3d Expert Systems

Managers who use decision-support systems usually already know quite a bit about the problem and how they want to solve it. They just need access to the right data and a system to "crunch the numbers" in a way that provides relevant, accurate, and timely information to help them make their decisions. But what happens when the problem is beyond the expertise of the manager? One way to deal with this problem is to set up an **expert system** (ES) to guide the manager through the decision-making process.

To develop expert systems, programmers ask experts in the relevant area to explain how they solve problems. They then devise a program to mimic the expert's approach, incorporating various rules or guidelines that the human

Data mining can help firms discover information previously hidden in vast amounts of data.

© Amy Walters/Shutterstock.com

expert uses. The finished program will ask a user a series of questions, basing each question on the response to the previous question. The program continues to ask questions until it has enough information to reach a decision and make a recommendation.

Expert systems routinely solve problems in areas as diverse as medical diagnoses, fraud detection, and consumer credit evaluation. The troubleshooting systems that many companies have on the customer-support pages of their websites are another type of expert system. If your product doesn't work, the troubleshooter will ask a series of questions designed to diagnose the problem and suggest solutions. Based on your responses to each question, the system selects the next question as it starts narrowing down the possible reasons for the problem until it identifies the cause and offers a solution. Often you can solve your problem without waiting on hold to talk to a human expert over the phone.[12]

Despite impressive results in many fields, expert systems have their limitations. Programming all of the decision rules into the system can be time-consuming, complicated, and expensive. In fact, it's sometimes impossible because the experts themselves can't clearly explain how they make their decisions—they just "know" the answer based on their years of experience. If the experts can't clearly explain how they reach their conclusions, then programmers can't include the appropriate decision rules in the system. Finally, an expert system has little flexibility and no common sense. It probably won't be able to find a solution to a problem that deviates in any significant way from the specific type of problem it was programmed to solve.[13]

16-4 Information Technology and the World of E-Commerce

Over the past 20 years, advances in information technology have had a dramatic and widespread effect on how companies conduct their business. But in this chapter, we'll just concentrate on one key area: the growth and development of e-commerce.

E-commerce refers to marketing, buying, selling, and servicing of products over a network (usually the Internet). You're probably most familiar with **business-to-consumer (B2C) e-commerce**. You participate in this form of e-commerce when you purchase songs from iTunes, use Expedia to make travel arrangements, or buy stocks through an online broker such as Charles Schwab. However, **business-to-business (B2B) e-commerce**, which consists of markets where businesses sell supplies, components, machinery, equipment, or services to other businesses, actually accounts for a much larger volume of business.

While both B2C and B2B involve exchanging goods over the Internet, they differ in some important ways, as shown in Exhibit 16.2. Given these structural differences, it isn't surprising that the two markets operate so differently.

While B2B and B2C are the most obvious forms of e-commerce, they aren't the *only* forms. For example, in C2C (consumer-to-consumer) e-commerce, consumers buy from and sell to other consumers—think eBay and Craigslist. And in B2G (business-to-government), e-commerce businesses sell information, goods, and services to government agencies.

16-4a Using Information Technology in the B2C Market

Firms in the B2C market use information technology in a variety of ways. In this section, we'll describe how firms use technology in general (and the Internet in particular) to attract new customers and strengthen the loyalty of existing customers.

Web 2.0 One major goal for most firms today is to develop stronger relationships with their customers. The Internet has proven to be an excellent tool for fostering such relationships—though it took a while for businesses to discover the best way to do so. In the early days of e-commerce, most companies tried to maintain tight control over all of the content presented on their websites. These websites presented information about products and allowed customers to place orders for goods and services but offered little opportunity for user participation or involvement. However, by the early years of the twenty-first century, innovative businesses were developing ways to make e-commerce more interactive and collaborative. In doing so, they not only forged stronger relationships with the customers who posted this content, they also created a richer, more interesting, and more useful experience for *others* who visited the site. This new approach became known as **Web 2.0**.

Many Web 2.0 sites rely on users (or members) to provide most of their content. For instance, the online encyclopedia Wikipedia uses wiki software to allow users to comment on and contribute to its articles. And social networking sites such as Facebook and Twitter wouldn't exist without user-created material. The more users who participate on these sites, the more useful (and entertaining) they become—and the easier it is for them to attract even more visitors and contributors.

Interestingly, many companies have found that techniques used to encourage collaboration among their customers can be used to accomplish the same result with their employees. Major corporations such as HP, Wells Fargo, and Procter & Gamble now use Web 2.0 techniques to help their own employees work more effectively together. The use of Web 2.0 technologies within organizations is called Enterprise 2.0.[14]

Advertising on the Internet Many B2C companies have large target markets, so advertising is an important part of their marketing strategy. Internet advertising revenue grew rapidly in the early twenty-first century, increasing almost fourfold from 2002 to 2008. It dropped slightly in early 2009 (as did most types of advertising expenditures during the onset of the recession) but began rising again later that year.

Web 2.0 Websites that incorporate interactive and collaborative features in order to create a richer, more interesting, and more useful experience for their users.

EXHIBIT 16.2 Key Differences between B2C and B2B e-Commerce

	B2C	B2B
TYPE OF CUSTOMERS	Individual final consumers	Other businesses
NUMBER OF CUSTOMERS IN TARGET MARKET	Very large	Often limited to a few major business customers
SIZE OF TYPICAL INDIVIDUAL TRANSACTION	Relatively small (usually a few dollars to a few hundred dollars)	Potentially very large (often several thousand dollars, sometimes several million dollars)
CUSTOMER BEHAVIOR	May do some research, but many purchases may be based on impulse.	Usually does careful multiple research and compares vendors. May take bids.
COMPLEXITY OF NEGOTIATIONS	Purchase typically involves little or no negotiation. Customer usually buys a standard product and pays the listed price.	Often involves extensive negotiation over specifications, delivery, installation, support, and other issues
NATURE OF RELATIONSHIP WITH CUSTOMERS	Firm wants to develop customer loyalty and repeat business but seldom develops a close working relationship with individual customers.	Buyers and sellers often eventually develop close and long-lasting relationships that allow them to coordinate their activities.

© Cengage Learning 2013

Want to Go Green? There Are Apps for That!

Looking for ways to be more environmentally responsible? If you own a smartphone or tablet computer, a good strategy is to check out the "green" apps available for your device. Literally hundreds of such apps are available. Some help you find places to recycle, others help you identify "green" businesses, and yet others provide tips to improve your fuel economy while driving. These apps not only allow you to be "green," they also allow you to save some "green" (as in money). Most green apps are priced under $5—in fact, several of them are free. Even the ones that cost a few bucks often quickly pay for themselves by helping you save on gasoline consumption or utility bills.

The greatest numbers of green apps are available for the iPhone and Android phones, but several are also available for other types of smartphones and for tablet computers. Here's an "apps sampler" to illustrate some of the possibilities:

iRecycle: Helps you find convenient locations for recycling over 240 categories of waste materials, including paper, plastics, electronics, and paint.

Good Guide: Provides ratings for thousands of products to help you pick the ones that are good for both you and the environment.

Green Genie: Provides lifestyle tips that help the environment while saving you money. This app also suggests green projects you can try and provides links to additional green resources.

Find Green: Uses your smartphone's GPS to determine your location and suggests nearby businesses that are environmentally friendly.

Green Gas Saver: Monitors your driving habits and offers tips and suggestions on ways to get better gas mileage—an outcome that both helps the environment and saves you money at the pump.

Avego: Dynamically matches drivers and riders who want to share rides. The app includes built-in safety and security measures. It uses GPS technology to measure the length of the shared ride, and electronically transfers micropayments from the rider to the driver.

Keep in mind that this is far from a complete list. There are hundreds of additional apps that can help you in your quest to be green—and more are being developed all the time. So be sure to check for new green apps on a regular basis.[15]

By the end of 2009, it surpassed magazine advertising revenue for the first time, and in 2011 it increased another 37% to over $31 billion. If current trends continue, it will soon surpass newspaper advertising—perhaps doing so by the time you read this. Ads placed on pages containing search results (such as those you see on Google or Bing) accounted for 46% of all Internet advertising revenues.[16]

Firms in B2C markets also use opt-in email as an advertising medium. Opt-in emails are messages that the receiver has explicitly chosen to receive. Customers often opt in when they register their products online and click to indicate that they would like to receive product information from the company. Since the customer has agreed to receive the message, opt-in emails tend to reach interested consumers. And, because email requires no envelopes, paper, or postage, it's much less expensive than direct mail.

Viral Marketing The Internet has also proven to be an effective medium for **viral marketing**, which attempts to get customers to communicate a firm's message to friends, family, and colleagues. Despite its name, legitimate viral marketing doesn't use computer viruses. Effective viral marketing campaigns can generate a substantial increase in consumer awareness of a product. As a strategy, viral marketing isn't unique to the Internet; even before the World Wide Web, marketers were adept at buzz marketing, the use of unconventional (and usually low-cost) tactics to stimulate word-of-mouth product promotion. But the Internet has made it possible to implement such strategies in clever ways and reach large numbers of people very quickly. Many viral marketing campaigns in recent years have used social media such as Facebook, Twitter, and YouTube.

Handling Payments Electronically B2C e-commerce normally requires customers to pay at the time the purchase is made. Clearly, the use of cash and paper checks isn't practical. In the United States, most payments in the B2C market are made by credit cards. To ensure that such transactions are secure, most sites transmit payment information using a secure socket layer (SSL) protocol. You can tell if a site on which you're doing business is using SSL in two fairly subtle ways. First, the URL will begin with

In 2011, users spent over 700 billion minutes each month on Facebook.

— USA TODAY

https:// instead of simply http://. (Note the "s" after http in the address.) Also, a small closed lock icon will appear near the bottom of your web browser (the exact location depends on the specific browser you are using). 🔒

Another common method of payment is to use a **cybermediary**—an Internet-based company that specializes in the secure electronic transfer of funds. By far the best-known cybermediary is PayPal. According to figures on its website, PayPal (which is owned by eBay) had 110 million active accounts worldwide as of mid-2012.[17]

A final way of making electronic payments is **electronic bill presentment and payment**. This is a relatively new method in which bills are sent to customers via email. The bill includes a simple mechanism (such as clicking on a button-shaped icon) that allows the customer to make a payment once the amount of the bill has been verified. Many banks now offer this payment method, as do services such as Quicken and Fiserv.

16-4b Using Information Technology in the B2B Market

B2B e-commerce generally requires a very different approach than B2C e-commerce. Not only do B2B transactions often involve much larger sums of money and require much more negotiation than B2C transactions, they also often result in long-term supply chain relationships that require close collaboration between buyer and seller. A *supply chain* is the network of organizations and activities needed to obtain materials and other resources, produce final products, and get those products to their final users. Forging tight and efficient supply chain relationships can be a key competitive advantage for firms.

An effective supply chain requires close coordination between a company and its suppliers. Information technology can provide the tools needed to foster this coordination. For example, the extranets we mentioned earlier can allow suppliers to keep tabs on their customers' inventories, thus anticipating when to make shipments of parts or materials.

Many firms involved in B2B business also make use of specialized Internet sites, called **e-marketplaces**, which provide a platform for businesses in specific B2B markets to interact. These platforms generally allow buyers in the market to solicit bids by posting requests for proposals (RFPs) on the site. Suppliers can then respond by bidding on RFPs that interest them.

E-marketplaces provide a number of advantages to their participants:

- ⊃ Compared to older methods, they reduce time, effort, and cost of doing business for both buyers and sellers.

- ⊃ Because they are Internet-based, they don't require expensive dedicated connections between firms, so even smaller firms can afford to participate.

- ⊃ They enable sellers and buyers to contact and negotiate with a large number of market participants on the other side of the market, thus maximizing the chances of finding good matches.

- ⊃ They often provide additional services—beyond simple trade—that allow firms to exchange information and collaborate, thus forging tighter supply chain relationships.

In recent years, many firms have begun using another information technology known as **radio frequency identification (RFID)** to improve the efficiency of their supply chains. This technology stores information on a microchip and transmits it to a reader when it's within range—up to several thousand feet. The chips can be extremely small—some are difficult to see with the naked eye—and can be embedded in most types of tangible products. The chips are usually powered by the energy in the radio signal sent by the reader so they don't need batteries.

RFID chips can store and transmit all sorts of information, but most commonly they transmit a serial number that uniquely identifies a product, vehicle, or piece of equipment. This type of information can be used to help track goods and

© Tatiana Popova/Shutterstock.com

"Getting information off the Internet is like taking a drink from a fire hydrant."

— MITCHELL KAPOR, ENTREPRENEUR, FOUNDER OF LOTUS DEVELOPMENT CORPORATION other resources as they move through a supply chain. Deliveries can be recorded automatically and electronically without the need to make manual records. The chips also can make taking inventory much quicker and simpler, since the items in stock identify themselves to readers. And the chips can be used to reduce the chances of pilferage. The results of these advantages are lower costs and a more efficient supply chain.

Australia-based Quantas Airlines uses RFID chips to eliminate paper itineraries, boarding passes, and luggage tags. To check in, frequent fliers "wave" a Quantas ID card with an embedded RFID chip while standing in front of a ticket kiosk. Likewise, frequent fliers receive permanent "Q Bag Tags" with RFID chips to attach to their luggage. So, when dropping bags off, they wave their Quantas ID card again to identify themselves, and put their luggage on the luggage belt. Automatically, the luggage is weighed and the Q Bag Tag is scanned, matching the bag to the ID card. At the gate, customers flash ID cards to receive seat assignments. Quantas customer Jake Coverdale says, "It's bloody good, actually. I go to America and Europe a lot and I think this is the best check-in in the world. It's incredibly efficient."[18]

<table>
<tr><td>16-5</td><td>

Challenges and Concerns Arising from New Technologies
</td></tr>
</table>

So far, we've concentrated on the benefits of advances in information technology—and it's clear that these benefits are enormous. But rapid technological advances also pose challenges and create opportunities for abuse. These problems affect businesses, their customers, and their employees, as well as the general public. In this section, we'll look at annoyances, security concerns, and legal and ethical issues.

16-5a Malware

The Internet—for all its advantages—creates the possibility that unwanted files and programs may land on your computer. In many cases, this happens without your knowledge, much less your permission. Some of these files and programs are relatively benign (even useful), but others can create major problems. Software that is created

© iStockphoto.com/Giorgio Magini

Use Two-Factor Authentication on Your Gmail Account So You're Not "Mugged in London"

If you've ever gotten an email from a friend claiming to be "mugged in Spain" or "mugged in London," then chances are his Gmail account has been hacked. This happens several thousand times daily, and the hacked accounts are then used to send spam and phishing attacks. In the mugged in Spain or London scams, hackers take over someone's Gmail account, and then, posing as the Gmail account holder, sends emails to the account holder's contacts claiming to have been mugged while traveling abroad. Their new bank card from the United States won't arrive for several days and they need you—dear friend or family member—to wire money via Western Union or MoneyGram. Someone often does. Google estimates that, on average, African- or Eastern European-based hackers make $500 a day from these scams.

How does this happen? Simple: people use the same password repeatedly for their online accounts. Michael Jones, Google's Chief Technology Advocate, says, "If you have ever used the same password in more than one place, you have reduced your overall safety record to whichever site had the lowest amount of protection. If you use your password in two places, it is not a valid password." Then, when hackers crack one password, they've got access to all of your accounts.

To prevent this from happening to you, sign up for Gmail's two-factor authentication. Authentication simply means making sure users are who they say they are. Two-factor means that it takes more than a password, the first factor, to gain access. Google will send a verification code, the second factor to your smartphone. Enter the code after your password. Since the hacker doesn't have your phone, your Gmail account is safe. And, Google requires you to reauthorize any device you use to read your Gmail every 30 days. What happens if you lose your phone? Nearly all smartphones can be remotely wiped and shut down. Also, set up your Gmail account with a "recovery email" to receive verification codes. But make sure it has a different password! Two-factor authentication is easy. Use it wherever available for your online accounts.[19]

and distributed with malicious intent is called **malware** (short for "malicious software"). Spyware, computer viruses, and worms are all examples of malware.

Spyware is software that installs itself on your computer without permission and then tracks your computer behavior in some way. It might track which Internet sites you visit to learn more about your interests and habits in order to send you targeted ads. Or, more alarmingly, it might log every keystroke (thus capturing passwords, account numbers, and user names to accounts as you enter them), allowing someone to steal your identity. Some spyware even goes beyond passive watching and takes control of your computer, perhaps sending you to websites you didn't want to visit.

Computer viruses are programs that install themselves on computers without the users' knowledge or permission and spread—sometimes very rapidly—by attaching themselves to other files that are transferred from computer to computer. Viruses are often attached to emails, instant messages, or files downloaded from the Internet. Some viruses are little more than pranks, but others can cause great harm. They can erase or modify data on your hard drive, prevent your computer from booting up, or find and send personal information you've stored on your computer to people who want to use it for identity theft. **Worms** are similar to viruses, except that they are independent programs that can spread across computer networks without being attached to other files.

How can you protect yourself from spyware, viruses, and worms? Take these common-sense steps:

- Perform regular backups. This can come in handy should a virus tamper with (or erase) the data on your hard drive. Store the backed-up data in a separate place.
- Install high-quality antivirus and antispyware software, and keep it updated. (Today's Internet security software usually has the ability to download and install updates automatically, but they may need to be configured to do so.)
- Update your operating system regularly so that any security holes it contains are patched as soon as possible.
- Don't open email messages or attachments if you don't know and trust the sender.
- Don't download files from websites unless you are sure they are legitimate. And be sure to read the licensing agreement of any programs you install—especially those of freeware you download from the Internet. The wording of these agreements will often indicate if other programs (such as spyware) will be installed along with your free program.

> **"Good** passwords are bad for people, and bad passwords are good for criminals."
>
> — Michael Jones, Chief Technology Advocate, Google

16–5b Spam, Phishing, and Pharming

Spam refers to unsolicited commercial emails, usually sent to huge numbers of people with little regard for whether they are interested in the product or not. It's hard to get exact measures of the amount of spam that is sent each year, but experts agree that it now comprises the vast majority of all email in the United States. It clogs email inboxes and makes it tough for people to find legitimate messages among all the junk. Spam filters exist that help detect and eliminate spam, but spammers are very good at eventually finding ways to fool these filters.[20]

The U.S. Congress enacted the Controlling the Assault of Non-Solicited Pornography and Marketing Act (usually called the CAN-SPAM Act) in 2003. This act requires senders of unsolicited commercial email to label their messages as ads and to tell the recipient how to decline further messages. It also prohibits the use of false or deceptive subject lines in email messages. But the rapid increase in the amount of spam in recent years suggests this law hasn't been an effective deterrent.

Phishing is another common use of spam. Phishers send email messages that appear to come from a legitimate business, such as a bank, credit card company, or retailer. The email attempts to get recipients to disclose personal information, such as their social security or credit card numbers, by claiming that there is a problem with their account—or sometimes simply that the account information needs to be verified or updated. The messages appear authentic; in addition to official-sounding language, they often include official-looking corporate logos. The email also usually provides a link to a website where the recipient is supposed to log in and enter the desired information. When the victims of the scam click on this link, they go to a website that can look amazingly like the site for the real company—but it's not. It's a clever spoof of the site where the phishers collect personal information and use it to steal identities.

malware A general term for malicious software, such as spyware, computer viruses, and worms.

spyware Software that is installed on a computer without the user's knowledge or permission for the purpose of tracking the user's behavior.

computer virus Computer software that can be spread from one computer to another without the knowledge or permission of the computer users by attaching itself to emails or other files.

worm Malicious computer software that, unlike viruses, can spread on its own without being attached to other files.

spam Unsolicited email advertisements usually sent to very large numbers of recipients, many of whom may have no interest in the message.

phishing A scam in which official-looking emails are sent to individuals in an attempt to get them to divulge private information such as passwords, usernames, and account numbers.

pharming A scam that seeks to steal identities by routing Internet traffic to fake websites.

hacker A skilled computer user who uses his or her expertise to gain unauthorized access to the computer (or computer system) of others, sometimes with malicious intent.

firewall Software and/ or hardware designed to prevent unwanted access to a computer or computer system.

One of the best ways to avoid such scams is to be skeptical of email requests for personal information; reputable businesses almost *never* ask you to divulge such information via email. Also, never click on a link in an email message to go to a website where you have financial accounts—if the message is from a phisher, that link is used to direct you to the fake site. Instead, use a link to the site that you've bookmarked, or type in the link to the real site yourself.

Not content with phishing expeditions, some scam artists have now taken to **pharming**. Like phishing, pharming uses fake websites to trick people into divulging personal information. But pharming is more sophisticated and difficult to detect than phishing because it doesn't require the intended victim to click on a bogus email link. Instead, it uses techniques to redirect Internet traffic to the fake sites. Thus, even if you type in the *correct* URL for a website you want to visit, you still might find yourself on a very realistic-looking pharming site. One way to check the validity of the site is to look for the indications that the site is secure, such as the https:// in the URL and the small closed lock icon mentioned earlier.[21]

Computers aren't the only devices plagued by these threats and annoyances. Cell phone users are facing increasing problems with spam delivered via text messaging. Even more alarming, some scammers have found ways to take their phishing expeditions to cell phones—a practice known as "smishing." One typical smishing ploy is to use text messaging to entice cell phone users to visit the scammer's fake website.[22]

16-5c Hackers: Break-Ins in Cyberspace

Hackers are skilled computer users who have the expertise to gain unauthorized access to other people's computers. Not all hackers intend to do harm, but some—called "black hat hackers" (or "crackers")—definitely have malicious intent. They may attempt to break into a computer system to steal identities or to disrupt a business.

Protecting against hackers requires individuals and businesses to be security conscious. Some of the precautions used against hackers, such as making frequent backups, are similar to those used to protect against viruses. Another key to protecting against hackers is to make sure that all data transmitted over a network are encrypted, or sent in encoded form that can only be read by those who have access to a key. Security experts also suggest that organizations restrict access to computer resources by requiring users to have strong passwords. According to Microsoft,

Hackers use their computer expertise to gain unauthorized access to other people's computers, often for malicious purposes.

© Photosani/Shutterstock.com

strong passwords are at least 14 characters in length; include a mix of letters, numbers and special characters; and don't contain any common words or personal information.[23]

Unfortunately, users struggle to remember strong passwords, so they reuse one or two passwords. "Having the same password for everything is like having the same key for your house, your car, your gym locker, your office," says PayPal's Michael Barrett. With password management software, such as LastPass, users memorize just one master password. LastPass works with any browser on any computer, tablet, or smart phone. It generates unique, strong passwords, synchronizes encrypted data across devices, and autofills forms so you don't have to manually enter personal information or passwords.[24]

Firewalls are another important tool to guard against hackers and other security threats. A firewall uses hardware or software (or sometimes both) to create a barrier that prevents unwanted messages or instructions from entering a computer system. As threats from spyware, hackers, and other sources have developed, the use of firewalls has become commonplace.

16-5d Ethical and Legal Issues

Information technology raises a number of legal and ethical challenges, such as the need to deal with privacy issues and to protect intellectual property rights. These issues are controversial and don't have simple solutions.

Personal Privacy Firms now have the ability to track customer behavior in ways that were never before possible. This has advantages for you because it allows firms to offer better, more personalized service. But all this extra information comes at the expense of your privacy. Does the fact that firms know so much about your preferences and behavior make you a bit nervous?

Does it bother you that your email messages lack confidentiality? When you send an email, it could be stored on several computers: your personal computer, the server of your email provider, the server of your recipient's provider, and your recipient's own computer. If you send the email from your company's system, it's also likely to be stored when the company backs up its information. If you thought that deleting an email message from your own computer erased it permanently and completely, you need to think again.

The list of other ways in which information technology can erode your personal privacy is long and getting longer. For example, RFID chips are now embedded in U.S. passports and in many states' driver's licenses. Some privacy experts are concerned that such chips will make it easy for government organizations to track individuals. One reason government officials gave for embedding RFID chips in passports and driver's licenses was to make it harder for criminals and terrorists to forge IDs. But in 2009, a hacker publicly demonstrated the ability to read the information in these chips from a distance of several yards, leading to fears that identity thieves could use similar techniques to obtain personal information and perhaps even create convincing copies of these important identification

documents. Encryption and protective sleeves, however, can prevent unauthorized scanning. Thieves are more likely to be successful by stealing your actual ID or passport the old fashioned way.[25]

The bottom line is that there's no simple way to solve privacy concerns. Privacy is an elusive concept, and there is no strong consensus about how much privacy is enough.

intellectual property
Property that is the result of creative or intellectual effort, such as books, musical works, inventions, and computer software.

Protecting Intellectual Property Rights Intellectual property refers to products that result from creative and intellectual efforts. There are many types of intellectual property, but we'll focus on forms of intellectual property that are protected by copyright law, such as books, musical works, computer programs, video games, and movies. Copyright law gives the creators of this property the exclusive right to produce, record, perform, and sell their work for a specified time period.

Piracy of intellectual property occurs when someone reproduces and distributes copyrighted work without obtaining permission from—or providing compensation to—the owner of the copyrighted material. When piracy becomes widespread, creators of intellectual property receive much less income for their efforts. This can substantially reduce their incentive to continue developing creative material.

The Business Software Alliance estimates that globally 42% of all business software installed on personal computers in 2011 was pirated, resulting in the loss of over $63 billion in revenue to software companies. In several smaller

Multitasking Makes You Stupid!

© iStockphoto.com/Troels Graugaard

New emails arrive with a "ding" and a two-second preview flashes on your screen. Smartphones buzz with every text and email. Phones play different ringtones for every caller. Add in discussions and interruptions from co-workers, plus constant switching between the various open programs and windows on your computer, and is it any wonder you can't get anything done? Multitasking isn't efficient. Multitasking prevents you from paying attention long enough to get anything done! Stanford University researcher Clifford Nass says, "It's unequivocally the case that workers who are doing multiple things at one time are doing them poorly. The human brain just really isn't built to switch rapidly from one task to another. Workers who constantly multitask are hurting their ability to get work done, even when they are not multitasking. People become much more distracted [and] can't manage their memory very well."

The solution according to Nass is, "When you start to do something, do it and nothing else for 20 minutes. This trains you to focus, to think deeply. It trains you not to think that distraction is a positive, and it teaches your brain to be able to focus." Also, prevent distractions by turning off email sounds and notifications. Set smartphones to buzz only for phone calls. Don't listen to music with lyrics, which will break your concentration. Instead, listen to classical music, opera, or foreign singers who don't speak your language. Most importantly, do one thing at a time![26]

JUST BECAUSE THEY CAN... ...DOESN'T MEAN THEY SHOULD.

In early May of 2011 Burson-Marsteller, a high-powered public relations firm, contacted several newspaper reporters and technology bloggers claiming that Google was using an initiative called Social Circle to collect, mine, and share the personal information of millions of people without their knowledge or consent. The firm implied that Google's tactics were unethical—perhaps even illegal— and urged the reporters and bloggers to write stories about Google's misdeeds. In fact, it even offered to help at least one of the bloggers actually write his anti-Google piece.

Some bloggers and newspapers looked into the claims made by the PR firm—but the results weren't what Burson-Marsteller was hoping for. The reporters all concluded that the allegations were either overblown or misrepresented how Social Circle worked. One of the reporters even characterized Burson-Marsteller's efforts as a "smear campaign" against Google.

It was clear that Burson-Marsteller wasn't making the allegations on its own but was rather working under the direction of a client. But the firm refused to identify who had hired it. The mystery was solved when Facebook issued a press release admitting that it was the client behind the efforts. It justified its actions by claiming that it had legitimate concerns about Google's tactics and was just trying to get its concerns investigated by the independent press.

Even if Facebook had legitimate concerns, launching an anonymous PR campaign that contained misleading information about a rival firm went against its core value of transparency. Facebook admitted that "The issues are serious, and we should have presented them in a serious and transparent way."

Burson-Marsteller also expressed embarrassment for its role in the incident. In a prepared statement, the PR firm concluded that "Whatever the rationale, this was not at all standard operating procedure and is against our policies, and the assignment on those terms should have been declined. When talking to the media, we need to adhere to strict standards of transparency about clients, and this incident underscores the absolute importance of that principle."[27]

What do YOU think?

- How concerned are you that your personal information on social networking sites might be used without your permission?
- What should Burson-Marsteller have done when Facebook approached them for this assignment?
- How does this incident affect your perception of Google, Facebook, and Burson-Marsteller?

---

countries, including Georgia, Bangladesh, and Libya, the rate of piracy was over 90%. Among larger nations, the piracy rate in China exceeded 77%, while in India it was 63%. The good news is that the piracy rate was much lower in the United States at 19%. But given the huge size of the U.S. software market, even this relatively low rate of piracy still resulted in losses of over $9.7 billion in revenue for software companies. Faced with such a widespread problem, many software publishers have become very aggressive at prosecuting firms and individuals engaged in software piracy.[28]

Music studios, video game developers, and motion picture producers also face significant problems with piracy. For instance, Japan's Computer Entertainment Suppliers Association estimated that video game piracy cost game developers for the Nintendo DS and PlayStation Portable $41.5 billion in sales between 2004 and 2009.[29]

Given how lucrative piracy can be, it's unlikely that this problem will go away anytime soon. You can expect the companies hurt by these practices to continue aggressively prosecuting pirates and to work on new technologies that make pirating digital media more difficult.

Information technology plays a vital role in virtually every aspect of business operations. For instance, marketing managers use information technology to learn more about customers, reach them in novel ways, and forge stronger relationships with them—as we showed in our discussion of Web 2.0. Operations managers use RFID technologies to coordinate the movement of goods within supply chains and to keep more accurate inventory records. And financial managers use IT to track financial conditions and identify investment opportunities. Managers in all areas of a business can use decision-support systems to improve their decision making. They also can apply techniques such as data mining to obtain interesting new insights hidden in the vast streams of data that flow into their companies.

Cloud computing represents the newest and one of the most exciting new approaches to how companies acquire and utilize IT resources. The use of cloud-based resources has the potential to not only lower costs and increase flexibility but also significantly magnify computation power. If cloud computing can overcome concerns about security and stability, it is likely to continue growing in popularity, which could result in significant changes to the role IT departments play within their organizations.

The rapid changes in IT in recent years—especially those related to the rise of Internet as a business venue—have opened up exciting new commercial opportunities. But these changes have also created a host of legal and ethical challenges and security. One thing is certain: business organizations that find ways to leverage the advantages of new IT developments while minimizing the accompanying risks are most likely to enjoy competitive success.

The rapidly changing nature of information technology and the increasing importance this technology plays in the success of modern businesses suggest that careers in this field are likely to see significant growth over the next several years. Let's take a look at two common occupations in information technology.

Computer support specialists provide technical assistance and advice to the users of their organization's information technology resources—which in today's business world is just about everyone in the organization! They diagnose and resolve computer- and network-related problems. They also may write training manuals and participate in sessions to train other workers in the proper use of new hardware and software. Finally, these workers often oversee the daily performance of their company's computer systems.

Requirements for employment as a computer support specialist vary. Some employers strongly prefer candidates with a bachelor's degree in computer science, computer engineering, or information technology. Other employers accept individuals with an associate's degree in a computer-related field. Still other firms will hire applicants with college degrees in any field as long as they possess strong technical and communications skills. The Bureau of Labor Statistics projects that employment opportunities for computer support specialists will be quite good for the next several years, with employment expected to grow about as fast as average. In 2010, the average salary for this occupation was $46,260.[29a]

Computer systems analysts design, maintain, and upgrade computer systems and select, install, and configure the hardware and software needed to implement their designs. They also devise ways to apply existing resources to meet new challenges. This work generally requires a high degree of technical competence, so most employers require systems analysts to have at least a bachelor's degree in a technical field such as computer science, information technology, or computer or software engineering. Many prefer candidates with advanced degrees in these fields. The Bureau of Labor Statistics forecasts that employment opportunities for computer system analysts will grow faster than average for the next several years. In 2010, the average salary for systems analysts was $77,740.[30]

CAREERS IN INFORMATION TECHNOLOGY

CAREERS

What *else?*
RIP & REVIEW CARDS **IN THE BACK**
and visit www.cengagebrain.com!

17

Operations Management:
Putting It All Together

© Ivan Kruk/Shutterstock.com

LEARNING OBJECTIVES

After studying this chapter, you will be able to:

17-1 Define operations management and describe how the role of operations management has changed over the past 50 years

17-2 Discuss the key responsibilities of operations managers

17-3 Describe how operations managers face the special challenges posed by the provision of services

17-4 Explain how changes in technology have revolutionized operations management

17-5 Describe the strategies operations managers have used to improve the quality of goods and services

17-6 Explain how lean and green practices can help both the organization and the environment

17-1 Operations Management: Producing Value in a Changing Environment

Operations management is concerned with managing all of the activities involved in creating value by producing goods and services and distributing them to customers. When operations managers do their job well, their firms produce the *right* goods and services in the *right* quantities and distribute these to the *right* customers at the *right* time—all the while keeping quality high and costs low. Obviously, the decisions of operations managers can have a major impact on a firm's revenues and its costs, and thus on its overall profitability.

17-1a Responding to a Changing Environment

The practice of operations management has changed dramatically over the past half century. New technologies, shifts in the structure of the economy, challenges posed by global competition and concerns about the impact of production on the environment have fueled this revolution. Let's begin by identifying the key changes that have characterized the practice of operations management over the past 50 years.

From a Focus on Efficiency to a Focus on Effectiveness
To operations managers, **efficiency** means producing a product at the *lowest cost*. **Effectiveness** means producing products that *create value* by providing customers with goods and services that offer a better relationship between price and perceived benefits. In other words, effectiveness means finding ways to give customers more for their money—while still making a profit.

In the 1960s, the focus of operations management was mainly on efficiency. The goal was to keep costs low so the firm could make a profit while keeping its prices competitive. In today's highly competitive global markets, efficiency remains important. But operations managers now realize that keeping costs (and prices) low are only part of the equation. Customers usually buy goods that offer the best value—and these aren't always the same as the goods that sell for the lowest price. A product that offers better features, more attractive styling and higher quality may provide more value—and attract more customers—than a product with a lower price. Thus, today's operations managers have broadened their focus to look at benefits as well as costs.

From Goods to Services Goods are tangible products that you can see and touch. *Durable goods* are expected to last three years or longer; examples include furniture, cars, and appliances. *Nondurable goods*, such as toothpaste, apples, and paper towels, are used up more quickly and are often perishable. **Services** are activities that yield benefits but don't directly result in a physical product. Examples include legal advice, entertainment, and medical care. Goods are consumed, while services are experienced.

In the 1960s, the U.S. economy was a manufacturing powerhouse, with more than a third of its labor force employed in the goods-producing sector. But over the past 50 years, the American economy has experienced a fundamental shift away from the production of goods and toward the provision of services. By 2011, less than 14% of the nonfarm labor force worked in the goods-producing sector. By contrast, employment in the service sector had risen to well over 86% of the labor force.[1]

From Mass Production to Mass Customization
Fifty years ago, one common production strategy was to keep costs low by producing large quantities of standardized products. The goal of this *mass production* strategy was to achieve reductions in average cost by taking advantage of specialization and the efficient use of capital. But today's technologies allow many firms to pursue *mass customization*—the production of small quantities of customized goods and services that more precisely meet

operations management Managing all of the activities involved in creating value by producing goods and services and distributing them to customers.

efficiency Producing output or achieving a goal at the lowest cost.

effectiveness Using resources to create value by providing customers with goods and services that offer a better relationship between price and perceived benefits.

goods Tangible products.

services Intangible products.

the needs of specific customers—with very little increase in costs.

From Local Competition to Global Competition For the first 25 years after World War II, American firms dominated key markets. This strength was based partly on the fact that the United States possessed a rich base of natural resources, a growing and increasingly well-educated labor force, an excellent infrastructure, and the strong incentive system inherent in a market economy. But it also reflected the fact that the production facilities and infrastructure in many European and Asian nations had been severely damaged during the war.

By the early 1970s, the economies of Japan, Germany, and other war-ravaged nations had been rebuilt, with many of their major companies boasting efficient new production facilities with state-of-the-art technology. In addition, many Japanese firms had adopted new techniques that greatly improved the quality of their products. With lower labor costs, impressive technology and world-class quality, these foreign producers quickly began to take market share from American firms. In more recent years, firms in Korea, India, and China have also become formidable competitors.

From Simple Supply Chains to Complex Value Chains Over the past 50 years, the increasingly competitive and global nature of markets has brought about major changes in how firms produce and distribute their goods and services. Many supply chains today span multiple organizations located in many different countries. The shift from a cost perspective to a value perspective has led operations managers to extend their view beyond the traditional supply chain to encompass a broader range of processes and organizations known as a *value chain*.

From Exploiting the Environment to Protecting the Environment In the 1960s, many operations managers viewed the natural environment as something to exploit. The emphasis on keeping costs low made it tempting to dispose of wastes as cheaply as possible—often by dumping them into rivers, lakes, or the atmosphere. But the serious consequences of environmental pollution have become increasingly apparent. Operations managers at socially responsible companies have responded by adopting a variety of green practices to produce goods and services in more environmentally responsible ways.

Exhibit 17.1 summarizes the discussion of the key ways in which operations management has changed over the past 50 years. We'll look at these changes in greater detail as we move through this chapter. But first let's take a look at the some of the key tasks operations managers perform.

> **"Nothing**
> is less productive than to make more efficient what should not be done at all."
>
> —Peter F. Drucker

EXHIBIT 17.1 Operations Management: Fifty Years of Change

Characteristics of Operations Management in 1962

- Focus on Minimizing Costs
- Production of Goods
- Mass Production
- Simple Supply Chains
- Exploit the Environment

Factors Promoting Change

- Improvements in Production and Information Technologies
- Rise of Global Competition and Global Opportunities
- Recognition of Quality as a Source of Competitive Advantage
- Adoption of Marketing Perspective and Customer Focus
- Recognition of Serious Environmental Problems

Characteristics of Operations Management in 2012

- Focus on Creating Value
- Provision of Services
- Mass Customization
- Complex Value Chains
- Sustain the Environment

What Do Operations Managers Do?

Understanding the marketing definition of *product* plays a pivotal role in understanding what operations managers do. A product consists of all of the tangible and intangible features (sometimes called the *customer benefit package*) that create value for consumers by satisfying their needs and wants. For example, when you purchase a car made by General Motors, you not only get the physical automobile, you also get (among other things) a warranty and (for many models) a year of OnStar services.

Marketing research typically determines which features a product should include to appeal to its target customers. Although operations managers don't normally have the primary responsibility for designing these goods and services, they provide essential information and advice during the product-design process, especially regarding the challenges and constraints involved in creating actual products on time and within budget.

Once the actual goods and services are designed, operations managers must determine the processes needed to produce them and get them to the customer. A **process** is a set of related activities that transform inputs into outputs, thus adding value. Once these processes are designed, operations managers also play a key role in determining where they will be performed, what organizations will perform them, and how the processes will be organized and coordinated.

The most obvious processes are those directly involved in the production of goods and services. But there are many other processes that play necessary "supporting roles." For example, purchasing and inventory management processes ensure that the firm has an adequate supply of high-quality materials, parts, and components needed to produce the goods without delays or disruptions.

Let's take a closer look at some of the functions that operations managers perform to move goods and services from the drawing board to the final user.

17–2a Process Selection and Facility Layout

Once a product is designed, operations managers must determine the best way to produce it. This involves determining the most efficient processes, deciding the best sequence in which to arrange those processes, and designing the appropriate layout of production and distribution facilities. Well-designed processes and facility layouts enable a firm to produce high-quality products effectively and efficiently, giving it a competitive advantage. Poorly designed processes can result in production delays, quality problems, and high costs.

process A set of related activities that transform inputs into outputs, thus adding value.

There are several ways to organize processes. The best approach depends on considerations such as the volume of production and the degree of standardization of the product.

- Firms often use a *product layout* when they produce goods that are relatively standardized and produced in large volumes. This type of layout organizes machinery, equipment, and other resources according to the specific sequence of operations that must performed. The machinery used in this type of layout is often highly specialized, designed to perform one specific task *very* efficiently. One classic example of a product layout is an assembly line, where the product being produced moves from one station to another in a fixed sequence, with the machinery and workers at each station performing specialized tasks. Services that provide a high volume of relatively standardized products also use flow-shop processes. For example, fast-food restaurants often use a simple product layout to prepare sandwiches, pizzas, or tacos in a standard sequence of steps.

- A *process layout* is used by many firms that need to produce small batches of goods that require a degree of customization. This approach arranges equipment according to the type of task performed. For example, in a machine shop, all of the drills may be located in one area, all of the lathes in another area, and all

© LYSTSEVA MARINA/ITAR-TASS/Landov

of the grinders in yet another. Unlike assembly lines and other product layouts, a process layout doesn't require work to be performed in a specific sequence; instead, the product can be moved from one type of machinery to another in whatever sequence is necessary. Thus, process layouts can be used to produce a variety of products without the need for expensive retooling. But this flexibility sometimes comes at the cost of longer processing times and more complex planning and control systems. Also, because the machinery and equipment used in a process layout is usually more general-purpose in nature and may be used to produce a greater variety of goods, the process layout requires workers to be more versatile than those employed in a product layout.

○ A *cellular layout* falls between the product layout and the process layout. It groups different types of machinery and equipment into self-contained cells. A production facility might have several cells, each designed to efficiently produce a family of parts (or entire products) that have similar processing requirements. Like an assembly line, the product moves from one station in the cell to the next in a specific sequence. However, unlike most assembly lines, cells are relatively small and are designed to be operated by a few workers who perform a wider array of tasks than assembly line workers.

○ A *fixed position layout* is used for goods that must be produced at a specific site (such as a building or a dam) or that are so large and bulky that it isn't feasible to move them from station to station (such as a ship or commercial airplane). Even some services, such as concerts or sporting events that are performed at a specific location, use this approach. In a

fixed position layout, the good or service stays in one place, and the employees, machinery, and equipment are brought to the fixed site when needed during various stages of the production process.

17–2b Facility Location

There is an old saying in real estate that the three most important factors determining the value of a property are "location, location, and location." There is no doubt that the location is also important to operations managers. The location of facilities can have an important influence on the efficiency and effectiveness of an organization's processes.

For some types of facilities, the location decision is dominated by one key consideration. A coal mine, for instance, must be located where there's coal. But for many other types of facilities, the decision is more complex. Exhibit 17.2 identifies some key factors that operations managers evaluate when they decide where to locate a facility, but the importance of each factor varies depending on the specific industry. For instance, many service firms place primary interest on locating close to their markets, while manufacturing firms are often more concerned about the cost and availability of land and labor and access to highways, railways, and port facilities.

Exhibit 17.2 Factors That Affect Location Decisions

GENERAL LOCATION FACTORS	EXAMPLES OF SPECIFIC CONSIDERATIONS
ADEQUACY OF UTILITIES	Is the supply of electricity reliable? Is clean water available?
LAND	Is adequate land available for a facility? How much does the land cost?
LABOR MARKET CONDITIONS	Are workers with the right skills available? How expensive is labor?
TRANSPORTATION FACTORS	Is the location near customers and suppliers? Is appropriate transportation nearby?
QUALITY OF LIFE FACTORS	What is the climate like? Are adequate healthcare facilities available?
LEGAL AND POLITICAL ENVIRONMENT	Does the local government support new businesses? What are the local taxes, fees, and regulations?

© Cengage Learning 2013

17-2c Inventory Control: Knowing When to Hold 'Em

Inventories are stocks of goods or other items held by an organization. Manufacturing firms usually hold inventories of raw materials, components and parts, work in process, and finished goods. Retail firms don't normally hold work in process or raw materials, but they do hold inventories of the finished goods they sell as well as basic supplies that they need.

Deciding how much inventory to hold can be a real challenge for operations managers because increasing (or decreasing) the amount of inventory involves both benefits and costs. For example, benefits of holding larger inventories include:

- ⊙ **Smoother Production Schedules:** A candy maker might produce more candy than it needs in August and September and hold the excess in inventory so that it can meet the surge in demand for Halloween treats without investing in more production capacity.

- ⊙ **Protection Against Stock-Outs and Lost Sales:** Holding larger inventories reduces the chance of stock-outs and lost sales due to supply disruptions or unexpected surges in demand.

- ⊙ **Reduced Ordering Costs:** Every time a company orders supplies, it incurs paperwork and handling costs. Holding a larger average inventory reduces the number of orders the firm must make and thus reduces ordering costs.

But holding larger inventories involves costs as well as benefits:

- ⊙ **Tied-Up Funds:** Items in inventory don't generate revenue until they're sold, so holding large inventories can tie up funds that could be better used elsewhere within the organization.

- ⊙ **Additional Holding Costs:** Bigger inventories require more storage space, which can mean extra costs for heating, cooling, taxes, insurance, and more.

- ⊙ **Increased Risk:** Holding large inventories exposes the firm to the risk of losses due to spoilage, depreciation, and obsolescence.

Operations managers determine the optimal amount of inventory by comparing the costs and benefits associated with different levels of inventory. In our discussion of lean manufacturing, we'll see that one recent trend has been toward finding ways to reduce inventory levels at every stage of the supply chain.

17-2d Project Scheduling

Projects such as constructing a new production facility, developing a new commercial airliner, or filming a movie are complex and expensive endeavors. It's vital to monitor them carefully to avoid major delays or cost overruns. The **critical path method (CPM)** is one of the most important tools that operations managers use to manage such projects. We can illustrate the basic idea behind this tool by looking at a simple example in which a theater company wants to stage a play. Exhibit 17.3 presents the steps involved in this project.

Notice that Exhibit 17.3 identifies **immediate predecessors** for all of the activities except activity A. *Immediate predecessors* are activities that must be completed before another activity can begin. For example, it is clear that the cast for the play cannot be determined until the play has been selected, so activity A (selecting the play) is an immediate predecessor to activity B (selecting the cast). Similarly, since sets can't be built without lumber, paint, and other materials, activity E (buying materials for the sets) is an immediate predecessor for activity G (building the sets).

Using the Critical Path Method to Focus Efforts Now look at Exhibit 17.4, which is a CPM network for the theater project. This network shows how all of the activities in the theater project are related to each other. The direction of the arrows shows the immediate predecessors for each activity. Notice that arrows go from activities B (selecting the cast) *and* F (purchasing material for the costumes) to activity H (making the costumes). This indicates that *both* of these activities are immediate predecessors for activity H—the costumes can't be made without material, and they must be made in the correct sizes to fit the actors. But also notice that no arrow links activities B and C. This shows that these are independent activities; in other words, the theater company doesn't have to select the cast before it designs the sets (or vice versa).

We can use Exhibit 17.4 to illustrate some basic concepts used in CPM analysis. A *path* is a sequence of activities that *must be completed in the order specified by the arrows* for the overall project to be completed. You can trace several paths in our example by following a series of arrows from start to finish. For example, one path is A → B → I → J → K, and another path is A → C → E → G → J → K.

The **critical path** consists of the sequence of activities that takes the longest to complete. A *delay in any activity on a critical path is likely to delay the completion of the entire project.* Thus, operations managers watch activities on the

EXHIBIT 17.3 Activities Involved in Presenting a Play

ACTIVITY	DESCRIPTION	IMMEDIATE PREDECESSOR(S)	ESTIMATED COMPLETION TIME (WEEKS)
A	Select Play	None	2
B	Select Cast	A (must know play to know what roles are available)	4
C	Design Sets	A (must know play before sets can be designed)	4
D	Design Costumes	A (must know play to determine what costumes are needed)	5
E	Buy Materials for Sets	C (set must be designed to determine types and quantities of materials needed to build it)	2
F	Buy Materials for Costumes	D (costumes must be designed before materials for costumes are determined)	2
G	Build Sets	E (must have materials in order to build the sets)	4
H	Make Costumes	B, F (must have materials in order to make the costumes, and must know actors' sizes to ensure that costumes fit)	6
I	Initial Rehearsals	B (actors must be selected for each role before they can rehearse their parts)	2
J	Final (Dress) Rehearsal	G, H, I (costumes and sets must be completed, and initial rehearsals performed, before the final rehearsal can occur)	1
K	Perform Play (end of project)	J	N/A

© Cengage Learning 2013

critical path very carefully and take actions to help ensure that they remain on schedule. We've shown the critical path for the theater project (A → D → F → H → J → K) with red arrows on our diagram.

Distinguishing between the critical path and other paths can help operations managers allocate resources more efficiently. Activities that aren't on the critical path can be delayed without causing a delay in the overall completion of the project—as long as the delay isn't too great. In CPM terminology, these activities have *slack*. When operations managers

see delays in critical path activities, they may be able to keep the project on track by diverting manpower and other resources from activities with slack to activities on the critical path.

17-2e Designing and Managing Value Chains

Perhaps the most important function of operations management is the design and management of value chains. A **value chain** is the network of relationships that channels the flow of inputs, information, and financial resources through all of the processes directly or indirectly involved in producing goods and services and distributing them to customers.

An organization's value chain clearly includes its supply chain, which consists of the organizations, activities, and processes involved in the physical flow of goods, from the raw materials stage

EXHIBIT 17.4 A CPM Network for Staging a Play

© Cengage Learning 2013

to the final consumer. In fact, some organizations use the terms *value chain* and *supply chain* interchangeably. But a value chain is a broader concept; in addition to the supply chain, it includes activities and processes involved in *acquiring customers*—such as contract negotiations and customer financing—as well as activities and processes involved in *keeping customers* by providing services after the sale, such as performing warranty repairs, offering call center assistance, and helping customers recycle used goods. In a value chain, the main focus is on the customer; in contrast, the supply chain is more oriented toward traditional production relationships.[2]

One of the most important issues that operations managers examine when they design value chains is the trade-off between vertical integration and outsourcing. **Vertical integration** occurs when a firm attempts to gain more control over its value chain by either developing the ability to perform processes previously performed by other organizations in the chain or by acquiring those organizations. **Outsourcing** is essentially the opposite of vertical integration; it involves arranging for other organizations to perform value chain functions that were previously performed internally.

In recent years, the trend in value chain design has been to rely more on outsourcing and less on vertical integration. Outsourcing allows a firm to shed functions it doesn't perform well in order to focus on its areas of strength. It also frees people, money, and other resources that had been tied up in the outsourced activities, allowing these resources to be employed in more profitable ways.

Even when a firm decides to perform processes itself, it still faces a choice: should it perform these functions domestically, or should it offshore these activities? **Offshoring** means moving processes previously performed domestically to a foreign location. It is important to realize that offshoring is *not* the same thing as outsourcing processes to other organizations. Offshoring doesn't require outsourcing; a firm often offshores processes by directly investing in its *own* foreign facilities. Similarly, outsourcing doesn't require a firm to go offshore; activities can be outsourced to other *domestic* firms. Despite this distinction, many firms have combined these approaches by hiring organizations in other countries to perform some of the processes that they previously performed at their own domestic facilities.

It is also worth noting that offshoring can go in both directions. Just as American firms offshore processes to other countries, some foreign companies offshore some of their processes to the U.S. For example, several Japanese, European, and Korean automakers now have extensive design and production facilities in the U.S.

One common reason for offshoring by U.S. firms is to take advantage of less expensive labor. But other factors can also play a role. Land and other resources also may be less expensive in developing nations than in the United States. And some foreign governments, eager to attract American investments, may offer financial incentives or other inducements. In addition, many foreign markets are growing much more rapidly than the relatively mature U.S. market. Firms often find it advantageous to locate production facilities close to these rapidly growing markets.

While foreign outsourcing can often reduce costs, it also can complicate value chains and create coordination problems. And it can expose the firm to certain types of risks. When a firm outsources important functions, it may have to entrust others in its value chain with confidential information and intellectual property, such as copyrighted material or patented designs. These strategic assets have less legal protection in some countries than in the United States, so providing access to foreign firms may increase the risk that the firm's intellectual property will be pirated or counterfeited. This issue has been of greatest concern when firms have outsourced some of their supply chain functions to organizations in China.[3]

Given the trend toward offshoring and outsourcing, value chains (and the supply chains at their core) have become increasingly complex, often involving many

> **value chain** The network of relationships that channels the flow of inputs, information, and financial resources through all of the processes directly or indirectly involved in producing goods and services and distributing them to customers.
>
> **vertical integration** Performance of processes internally that were previously performed by other organizations in a supply chain.
>
> **outsourcing** Arranging for other organizations to perform supply chain functions that were previously performed internally.
>
> **offshoring** Moving production or support processes to foreign countries.

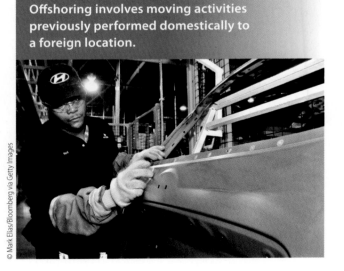

Offshoring involves moving activities previously performed domestically to a foreign location.

© Mark Elias/Bloomberg via Getty Images

different organizations and processes located in many different countries. Modern operations managers rely on sophisticated *supply chain management software* to streamline the communications among supply chain participants and to help them plan and coordinate their efforts.

The newest versions of **enterprise resource planning (ERP)** software take supply chain management to its highest level. ERP initially focused on integrating the flow of information among *all* aspects of a single organization's operations—accounting, finance, sales and marketing, production, and human resources. But the newest versions go beyond a single organization to help manage activities along an entire supply chain or value chain. The common information system makes it easier for organizations throughout the chain to communicate and coordinate their activities.

ERP systems do have some drawbacks. They are complex, expensive, and difficult to implement, and they require users to learn new ways to enter and access data. Productivity can actually fall until users become accustomed to these new methods. But despite these challenges, ERP systems have become very popular. And they continue to evolve and take advantage of new technologies. One of the newest developments is the arrival of web-based ERP systems that can be "rented" from online providers—a strategy that reduces the need to invest in new hardware and software. The use of web-based ERP services is an example of a relatively new trend in information technology known as *cloud computing*.[4]

17-3 Implications of a Service-Based Economy: Responding to Different Challenges

Exhibit 17.5 illustrates how services differ from tangible goods. These differences present a number of challenges to service providers. One key challenge arises because customers often participate in the provision of services, which means that service providers have less control over how the process is carried out, how long it takes to complete, and whether the result is satisfactory. For instance, the accuracy of a doctor's diagnosis depends on how honestly

EXHIBIT 17.5 Differences between Goods and Services

GOODS	SERVICES
Are tangible: They have a physical form and can be seen, touched, handled, etc.	Are intangible: They can be "experienced," but they don't have a physical form.
Can be stored in an inventory.	Must be consumed *when* they are produced.
Can be shipped.	Must be consumed *where* they are provided.
Are produced independently of the consumer.	Often require the customer to be actively involved in their production.
Can have at least *some* aspects of their quality determined objectively by measuring defects or deviations from desired values.	Intangible nature means quality is based mainly on customer perceptions.

© Cengage Learning 2013

and completely the patient answers the doctor's questions. And the amount of time the doctor spends with each patient will depend on the seriousness of the problem and the complexity of the diagnosis and treatment.

17-3a Designing the Servicescape

Because of the interaction between customers and service providers, the design of service facilities often must take the experiences of the participants into account. A **servicescape** is the environment in which the customer and service provider interact. A well-designed servicescape can have a positive influence on the attitudes and perceptions of both the customer and those who provide the service. A poor servicescape can have the opposite effect.[5]

The design of servicescapes centers on three types of factors: ambience; functionality; and signs, symbols, and artifacts.

- ⊃ *Ambience* refers to factors such as decor, background music, lighting, noise levels, and even scents. For example, massage therapists often use low light, soothing background music, and pleasant scents to create a relaxing atmosphere for a massage.

- ⊃ *Functionality* involves how easy is it for the customer to move through the facility and find what they are looking for.

- ⊃ *Signs, symbols,* and *artifacts* convey information to customers and create impressions. Obviously, signs like

"Place Your Order Here" and "Pick Up Your Order Here" provide useful information that helps consumers maneuver through the service encounter. But other signs and symbols can be used to create favorable impressions. For instance, lawyers and accountants often prominently display their diplomas, professional certifications, and awards in their offices to communicate their qualifications and accomplishments to their clients.

17-3b How Big Is Big Enough?

Because services are intangible and often must be experienced at the time they are created, service providers can't produce the service in advance and store it to meet temporary surges in demand. This can create challenges for operations managers because the demand for many types of services varies significantly, depending on the season, the day of the week, or the time of day. During peak lunch and dinner hours, popular restaurants tend to be very busy—often with crowds waiting to get a table. The same restaurants may be nearly empty during the mid-afternoon or late at night. Given such fluctuations in demand, the selection of *capacity*—the number of customers the service facility can accommodate per time period—becomes a crucial consideration.

If the capacity of a service facility is too small, customers facing long waits during periods of peak demand may well take their business elsewhere. But a facility large enough to handle peak capacity is more expensive to build; costs more to heat, cool, and insure; and may have substantial excess capacity during off-peak periods. Operations managers must weigh these drawbacks against the ability to handle a larger number of customers during peak hours.

Many service firms try to minimize this tradeoff by finding ways to spread out demand so that big surges don't occur. One way to do this is to give customers an incentive to use the service at off-peak times. Many bars and restaurants have "happy hours" or "early-bird specials." Similarly, movie theaters have lower prices for matinée showings, and resort hotels offer reduced rates during their off seasons.

17-4 The Technology of Operations

Now let's take a close look at how technology has revolutionized operations management. Some of the new technologies involve the increasing sophistication of machinery and equipment. Others involve advances in software and information technology. The impact of these technological advances is greatest when the automated machinery is directly linked to the new software running on powerful new computers.

17-4a Automation: The Rise of the Machine

For the past half century, one of the biggest trends in operations management has been increased **automation** of many processes. Automation means replacing human operation and control of machinery and equipment with some form of programmed control. The use of automated systems has become increasingly common—and increasingly sophisticated.

Automation began in the early 1950s with primitive programmed machines. But in recent decades, **robots** have taken automation to a whole new level. Robots are reprogrammable machines that can manipulate materials, tools, parts, and specialized devices in order to perform a variety of tasks. Some robots have special sensors that allow them to "see," "hear," or "feel" their environment. Many robots are mobile and can even be guided over rugged terrain.

Robots offer many advantages to firms:

- ➲ They often perform jobs that most human workers find tedious, dirty, dangerous, or physically demanding.

- ➲ They don't get tired, so they can work very long hours while maintaining a consistently high level of performance.

- ➲ They are flexible; unlike old dogs, robots *can* be taught new tricks because they are reprogrammable.

automation Replacing human operation and control of machinery and equipment with some form of programmed control.

robot A reprogrammable machine that is capable of manipulating materials, tools, parts, and specialized devices in order to perform a variety of tasks.

Automation involves programming machines and equipment to carry out tasks previously performed by humans.

© iStockphoto.com/Jonathan Heger

Robots are most commonly used for tasks such as welding, spray painting, and assembling products, but they can do many other things ranging from packaging frozen pizza to disposing of hazardous waste.

17-4b Software Technologies

Several types of software have become common in operations management, and as the processing power of computers has improved, the capabilities of these applications have become increasingly sophisticated. Some of the most common examples include:

- ➲ **Computer-aided design (CAD)** software provides powerful drawing and drafting tools that enable users to create and edit blueprints and design drawings quickly and easily. Current CAD programs allow users to create 3-D drawings.

> # "Customers don't expect you to be perfect. They do expect you to fix things when they go wrong."
>
> — Donald Porter, V.P. British Airways

- ➲ **Computer-aided engineering (CAE)** software enables users to test, analyze, and optimize their designs through computer simulations. CAE software can help engineers find and correct design flaws *before* production.
- ➲ **Computer-aided manufacturing (CAM)** software takes the electronic design for a product and creates the programmed instructions that robots and other automated equipment must follow to produce that product as efficiently as possible.

AP Images/Daily Progress, Bill Clark

Wall-E and R2D2:
Robots Lower Hospital Costs

Robots do boring, dangerous, and physically demanding work, and, though it takes time, they can be reprogrammed to perform new tasks. This is why robots are often used to find and retrieve parts, paint and weld things, and assemble big, heavy components in heavy manufacturing settings such as auto assembly plants.

Robots, however, are beginning to play a basic, but increasingly important, role in healthcare settings, especially when it comes to lowering costs. For example, guided by sensors and built-in GPS navigation, robots, which look like "a cabinet attached to a giant vacuum cleaner," deliver and collect food trays, medications, trash, and linens. A robot will roll up to a nurses' station and "tell" the nurse in a pre-recorded voice that it is delivering supplies. After the items have been removed, pressing a green button sends the robot on its way.

Ken King, chief of administrative services at El Camino Hospital in California's Silicon Valley said, "We were looking at having to hire 12 new staff at least, just to carry everything around." But leasing 20 robots costs just $350,000 per year, compared to $1 million a year for staff to do the same job. Furthermore, says King, "The staff is completely used to them. Visitors and patients, though, still see the robots as a novelty, and sometimes want to mess around with them. They will jump right in front of the robot, to see what happens. But these things stop on a dime." Donald Jones, an investor in Aethon, a robotics company, says, "My guess is that in five years, there will be 10 times the number of robots deployed in hospitals that there are today."[6]

Today, **computer-aided design and computer-aided manufacturing** software are often combined into a single system, called **CAD/CAM**. This enables CAD designs to flow directly to CAM programs, which then send instructions directly to the automated equipment on the factory floor to guide the production process.

When a CAD/CAM software system is integrated with robots and other high-tech equipment, the result is **computer-integrated manufacturing (CIM)**, in which the whole design and production process is highly automated. The speed of computers, the ability to reprogram computers rapidly, and the integration of all these functions make it possible to switch from the design and production of one good to another quickly and efficiently. CIM allows firms to produce custom-designed products for individual customers quickly and at costs almost as low as those associated with mass-production techniques, thus allowing firms to pursue the strategy of mass customization mentioned at the beginning of this chapter.

17-5 Focus on Quality

Almost everyone agrees that quality is important. But the concept of quality is tough to define—even expert opinions differ. For our purposes, we'll adopt the view that quality is defined in terms of how well a good or service satisfies customer preferences.

Why is quality so important? First, better quality clearly improves effectiveness (creates value) since consumers perceive high-quality goods as having greater value than low-quality goods. But finding ways to increase quality can also can lead to greater efficiency because the cost of poor quality can be very high. When a firm detects defective products, it must scrap, rework, or repair them. And the costs of poor quality can be even higher when a firm *doesn't* catch defects before shipping products to consumers. These costs include handling customer complaints, warranty repair work, loss of goodwill, and the possibility of bad publicity or lawsuits. In the long run, firms often find that improving quality reduces these costs by more than enough to make up for their investment.

These ideas aren't especially new. W. Edwards Deming, viewed by many as the father of the quality movement, first proposed the relationship between quality and business success in the early 1950s. His ideas, which came to be known as the *Deming Chain Reaction*, are summarized in Exhibit 17.6.

17-5a Waking Up to the Need for Quality

In the years immediately after World War II, most Japanese goods had a reputation for being cheap and shoddy. But during the 1950s, many Japanese firms sought advice from Deming and other U.S. quality gurus. They learned to view quality improvement as a *continuous* process that was the responsibility of all employees in the organization. During the 1950s and 1960s, the quality of Japanese goods slowly but steadily improved.

By the early 1970s, many Japanese firms had achieved a remarkable turnaround, with quality levels that exceeded those of companies in most other countries (including the U.S.) by a wide margin. This improved quality was a major reason why Japanese firms rapidly gained global market share, often at the expense of American firms that had faced little competition in years immediately following World War II.

computer-integrated manufacturing (CIM) A combination of CAD/CAM software with flexible manufacturing systems to automate almost all steps involved in designing, testing, and producing a product.

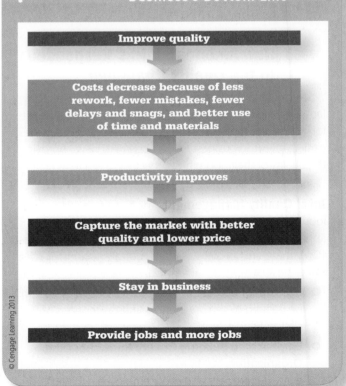

EXHIBIT 17.6 The Deming Chain Reaction: Improved Quality Helps the Business's Bottom Line

Improve quality

Costs decrease because of less rework, fewer mistakes, fewer delays and snags, and better use of time and materials

Productivity improves

Capture the market with better quality and lower price

Stay in business

Provide jobs and more jobs

© Cengage Learning 2013

Apple Stores: Predicted to Fail, Have Highest Sales in Retail

When launched a decade ago, Apple's retail stores were widely predicted to fail. This year, more than a quarter billion people will visit Apple's 326 stores, or four times the number of visitors to Walt Disney's four largest theme parks. Why? Quality built on problem solving, highly trained staff, and a customer focus built around empathy.

At Apple stores, high-quality services rests on a sales philosophy of not selling but helping customers solve problems. The Apple training manual reads, "Your job is to understand all of your customers' needs—some of which they may not even realize they have." David Ambrose, a former Apple store employee says, "You were never trying to close a sale. It was about finding solutions for a customer and finding their pain points."

Apple "geniuses," who staff the "Genius Bars" in each store are trained at Apple headquarters and, "can take care of everything from troubleshooting your problems to actual repairs." Geniuses are regularly tested on their knowledge and problem-solving skills to maintain their certification. Other Apple store employees are highly trained and are not allowed to help customers until they've spent two to four weeks shadowing experienced store employees.

The acronym, APPLE, instructs employees how to empathetically engage with customers: "Approach customers with a personalized warm welcome," "Probe politely to understand all the customer's needs," "Present a solution for the customer to take home today," "Listen for and resolve any issues or concerns," and "End with a fond farewell and an invitation to return." And when customers are frustrated and become emotional, the advice is to, "Listen and limit your responses to simple reassurances that you are doing so. 'Uh-huh,' 'I understand,' etc."

The results from Apple's retail approach speak for themselves, as Apple retail sales average $4,406 per square foot, higher than Tiffany jewelry stores ($3,070), Coach luxury retail ($1,776), or Best Buy ($880), a full-service computer and electronics store.[7]

17-5b How American Firms Responded to the Quality Challenge

When operations managers at American firms realized how far they trailed the Japanese in quality, they made a real effort to change their ways. Like the Japanese a few decades earlier, American business leaders began to view improving the quality of their goods and services as a key to regaining international competitiveness.

Total Quality Management The first result of this new-found emphasis on quality was the development of an approach called **total quality management**, better known as TQM. There are several variations, but all versions of TQM share the following characteristics:

- **Customer Focus:** TQM recognizes that quality should be defined by the preferences and perceptions of customers.

- **Emphasis on Building Quality throughout the Organization:** TQM views quality as the concern of every department and every employee.

- **Empowerment of Employees:** Most TQM programs give teams of workers the responsibility and authority to make and implement decisions to improve quality.

- **Focus on Prevention Rather Than Correction:** The TQM philosophy agrees with the old adage that an "ounce of prevention is worth a pound of cure." Thus, TQM pursues a strategy of preventing mistakes that create defects.

- **Long-Run Commitment to Continuous Improvement:** TQM requires firms to adopt a focus on making improvements in quality a way of life.

In many cases, American firms using TQM attempt to reduce defects by using **poka-yokes**—the Japanese term for "mistake proofing." Poka-yokes are simple procedures built into the production process that either prevent workers from making mistakes or help workers quickly catch and correct mistakes if they do occur. One simple example of a poka-yoke would be providing assembly workers with "kits" that contain exactly enough parts to complete one unit of work at a time. If the worker

> Quality is more important than quantity. One home run is much better than two doubles.
>
> — Steve Jobs, co-founder of Apple

completes an assembly and sees a part left over, it's clear that a mistake has been made, and he or she can correct it on the spot.[8]

The Move to Six Sigma During the 1990s, another approach to quality improvement, known as **Six Sigma**, became increasingly popular. Six Sigma shares some characteristics with TQM, such as an organization-wide focus on quality, emphasis on finding and eliminating causes of errors or defects (prevention rather than correction), and a long-term focus on continuous quality improvement. Also like TQM, it relies on teams of workers to carry out specific projects to improve quality. At any given time, a firm may have several Six Sigma projects under way, and the goal of each is to achieve the Six Sigma level of quality.

But Six Sigma differs from TQM in other respects. Unlike TQM, it has a single unifying measure: to reduce defects of any operation or process to a level of no more than 3.4 per million opportunities. Attaining this level of quality represents a rigorous and challenging goal. Six Sigma also differs from TQM in its reliance on extensive (and expensive) employee training and reliance on expert guidance. The techniques used in the Six Sigma approach are quite advanced, and their application requires a high level of expertise.

17-5c Quality Standards and Initiatives

Another way firms try to improve quality is to launch programs designed to achieve certification or recognition from outside authorities. Two common approaches are participation in the Baldrige National Quality Program and seeking certification under the International Organization for Standardization's ISO 9000 standards.

The Baldrige National Quality Program Congress passed the Malcolm Baldrige National Quality Improvement Act of 1987 in an effort to encourage American firms to become more competitive in the global economy by vigorously pursuing improvements in quality and productivity. Winners of the Baldrige Award must demonstrate excellence in seven areas: leadership; strategic planning; customer and market focus; measurement, analysis, and knowledge management; human resource focus; process management; and business results.

Firms that participate in the **Baldrige National Quality Program** receive benefits even if they don't win the award. Every participating firm receives a detailed report prepared by expert evaluators identifying areas of strength and areas where improvement is needed. Considering the normal fees that high-powered consulting firms charge for similar reports, the information and advice a firm gets for the fee charged to participate in the Baldrige program (which for manufacturing, service, and small businesses is $4,500 to $7,500) are a tremendous bargain![9]

ISO 9000 Certification Founded in 1947, ISO is a network of national standards institutes from more than 160 nations that have worked together to develop over 18,500 international standards for a wide array of industries. ISO standards ensure that goods produced in one country will meet the requirements of buyers in another country. This benefits buyers by giving them the ability to purchase from foreign sellers with confidence, thus giving them a wider array of choices. It also benefits sellers by allowing them to compete more successfully in global markets.[10]

Most of the standards established by the ISO are industry-specific. But in 1987, the ISO developed and published the **ISO 9000** family of standards. The goal of this effort was to articulate an international consensus on good quality-management practices that could be applied to virtually any company. Similar to the other quality initiatives we've

total quality management (TQM) An approach to quality improvement that calls for everyone within an organization to take responsibility for improving quality and emphasizes the need for a long-term commitment to continuous improvement.

poka-yokes Simple methods incorporated into a production process designed to eliminate or greatly reduce errors.

Six Sigma An approach to quality improvement characterized by very ambitious quality goals, extensive training of employees, and a long-term commitment to working on quality-related issues.

Baldrige National Quality Program A national program to encourage American firms to focus on quality improvement.

ISO 9000 A family of generic standards for quality management systems established by the International Organization for Standardization.

lean production An approach to production that emphasizes the elimination of waste in all aspects of production processes.

just-in-time (JIT) production A production system that emphasizes the production of goods to meet actual current demand, thus minimizing the need to hold inventories of finished goods and work in process at each stage of the supply chain.

discussed, ISO 9000 standards define quality in terms of the ability to satisfy customer preferences and require the firm to implement procedures for continuous quality improvement.

There are several standards in the ISO 9000 family, but the most basic—and the only one for which organizations can be certified—is ISO 9001, which specifies the requirements for a quality-management system. (Other ISO 9000 standards are concerned with the documentation, training, and the economic and financial aspects of quality management.) As of 2010, over one million organizations worldwide had earned ISO 9001 certificates, but the number of U.S. firms with ISO 9001 certification lags that of several other nations. Only about 25,000 U.S. organizations had been certified in 2010, compared to over 297,000 in China and 139,000 in Italy.[11]

17-6 The Move to Be Lean and Green: Cutting Cost and Cutting Waste

Lean production refers to a set of strategies and practices to eliminate waste, which is defined as any function or activity that uses resources but doesn't create value. Eliminating

waste can lead to dramatic improvements in efficiency. For example, Louis Vuitton produces some of the most expensive handmade bags and purses in the world. To increase productivity, it switched to teams of 6 to 12 workers who learned to complete multiple production steps. So instead of having 3 workers separately gluing, stitching, and finishing the edges of a flap over and over, 1 worker would do all three steps. Because of that, says CEO Ives Carcelle, "We were able to hire 300 new people without adding a factory."[12]

17-6a Reducing Investment in Inventory: Just-in-Time to the Rescue

One of the hallmarks of lean systems is a tight control on inventories. In part, this reflects recognition of the costs of holding large inventories that we discussed earlier. But the lean approach also offers another reason for minimizing inventories. Large inventories serve as a buffer that enables a firm to continue operations when problems arise due to poor quality, faulty equipment, or unreliable suppliers—making it easier for firms to live with these problems rather than correct them. Advocates of lean production argue that, in the long run, it is more efficient to improve quality, keep equipment in good working order, and develop reliable supply relationships than to continue compensating for these problems by holding large inventories.

Lean manufacturing avoids overproduction and holding large inventories of finished goods by using **just-in-time (JIT) production** methods. JIT produces

Just-in-Time: Not Too Small. Not Too Big. Just Right.

Only one factory worldwide makes Xirallic, a shiny pigment with coated glass flakes mixed into automotive paint. When the Xirallic factory in Onahama, Japan, was damaged and without power following Japan's earthquake and tsunami in 2011, auto manufacturers began rationing the inventory they had in stock. Ford stopped taking orders for red cars and for "Tuxedo Black" F-150 trucks, all of which used Xirallic. Likewise, Chrysler immediately reduced the number of orders it would take for ten different colors of cars made with Xirallic.

Ron DeFeo, CEO of Terex, a heavy-equipment manufacturer says, "Just-in-time (JIT) makes sense, but it's vulnerable to disruptions." Supply-chain consultant Paul Martyn says that for some companies running JIT systems, inventory is so low

that, "we aren't just lean, we've become anorexic."

© Dmitry Kalinovsky/Shutterstock.com

Consequently, some companies are increasing inventory levels to avoid potential disruptions. Alex Niemeyer, a supply-chain consultant at McKinsey & Co., says, "What we're seeing is a general move toward building safety back into the system." For instance, Al-jon, which makes equipment that trash companies use to process scrap metal and solid waste, has increased inventory and added another supplier in Germany. Al-jon's president, Kendig Kneen, says, "We've tried everything, but in essence it ends up that we have to lay more inventory in. But that's a challenge, because cash flow is tight." The key is a balance between JIT's low cost and the risk of production disruption.[13]

only enough goods to satisfy current demand. This approach is called a *pull system* because actual orders "pull" the goods through the production process. The workers at the end of the production process produce just enough of the final product to satisfy actual orders and use just enough parts and materials from preceding stages of production to satisfy their needs. Workers at each earlier stage are expected to produce just enough output at their workstations to replace the amount used by the processes further along in the process—and in so doing they withdraw just the needed amount of parts and other supplies from even earlier processes.

JIT techniques obviously result in very small inventories of finished goods and work in process. But lean firms also hold only small inventories of materials and parts, counting on suppliers to provide them with these items as they need them to meet current demand. In a lean system, *all* organizations in the supply chain use the JIT approach, so that inventories are minimized at each stage. Clearly, this type of system requires incredible coordination among all parts of the supply chain; in fact, the movement toward JIT is a key reason why supply chain management has become so crucial.

JIT does have some potential drawbacks. The most serious problem is that it can leave producers vulnerable to supply disruptions. If a key supplier is unable to make deliveries due to a natural disaster, labor strike, or other problem, the firms further along the supply chain may quickly run out of parts or materials and have to shut down production.

17-6b Lean Thinking in the Service Sector

Employing lean principles in the service sector can be quite a challenge because customers often participate in providing the service. This means a service firm usually has less control over how processes are conducted. But many service firms have benefited from creatively applying lean techniques. Southwest Airlines is well known for its efforts to reduce waste. It uses only one type of aircraft (the Boeing 737) to standardize maintenance and minimize training costs. It also has an extremely simple ticketing system (no assigned seating) and, when possible, flies into smaller or older airports where there is less congestion. This means that less time and less fuel are spent circling airports waiting to

LED Lightbulbs: Don't Change, Go Green!

Light-emitting diode (LED) lightbulbs are much more expensive than traditional, filament-based lightbulbs. But because they last so long, they're cheaper to use. Why? Because of the labor costs of changing lightbulbs. For example, at San Francisco's Intercontinental hotel, it costs $50 to change one lightbulb! Switching to longer-lasting LED bulbs that are changed every decade significantly reduces those costs. Eric Dominguez, director of energy services for Caesars Entertainment, which runs casinos with millions of lights, says, "Instead of replacing a bulb seven times a year, now you're talking about not touching a bulb for four or five years."

Changing lightbulbs is a labor-intensive task involving ladders, mechanical lifts, and, for large companies, the tracking and purchasing of thousands of lightbulbs. All of that takes time. And because traditional bulbs burn out quickly, bulb replacements are frequent. Charles Zimmerman, Walmart's vice president for international design and construction, says, "If you think about a 20- to 40-foot tall parking lot light pole, you need a bucket truck and electrician to replace those lamps every two years." Yet because LED bulbs last so long, the big savings is in labor and maintenance costs. A study by the U.S. Department of Energy estimated the savings for a Walmart parking lot in Kansas over the course of 10 years. The total cost of using standard bulbs was $248,134, compared to $220,396 for LED bulbs. While the LED bulbs cost more initially—$146,800 versus $103,490 for standard bulbs—they were substantially cheaper in terms of energy costs, $55,196 versus $89,884, and maintenance costs, $18,400 for LED bulbs versus $54,760 for standard bulbs.

Savings will increase even more as LED prices, which have already dropped by half, drop by another third within three years according to predictions by the U.S. Department of Energy. Walmart now uses LED lights in the parking lots of its new stores. As standard bulbs burn out, they will be replaced by LED lights in existing stores and their parking lots. Walmart's first all-LED store opened in Wichita, Kansas, this year.[14]

land or sitting on runways waiting to take off. Despite a no-frills approach, Southwest almost always ranks near the top of the list in terms of airline customer satisfaction.[15]

17-6c Green Practices: Helping the Firm by Helping the Environment

Many of today's leading firms have also tried to become "greener" by finding environmentally friendly ways to carry out the processes needed to produce and distribute their goods and services. Green practices include designing facilities to be more energy efficient; using renewable energy sources such as wind, solar, or geothermal power when possible;

One way some firms have tried to make their operations greener is by making use of renewable energy sources.

© Brian A Jackson/Shutterstock.com

making use of recyclable materials; switching to paints, lubricants, cleaning fluids, and solvents that are less harmful to the environment; and even providing labeling to help consumers find out which products are the most environmentally friendly.

The long-term goal of many green practices is to achieve *sustainability*, which means finding ways to meet the organization's current objectives while protecting and preserving the environment for future generations. One impediment to even greater acceptance of sustainability initiatives is that some sustainability efforts—such as switching to renewable sources of energy—add to costs.[16] But many firms have found that other sustainability efforts can actually benefit the bottom line. A recent study by Aberdeen Group, a well-known technology research firm, found that firms employing best-in-class sustainability practices not only saw an 8% drop in sustainability-related costs but also experienced a 16% increase in customer retention.[17]

In the late 1990s, the International Organization for Standardization developed a set of standards called **ISO 14000**. This new set of standards focuses on environmental management. As with ISO 9000, the term ISO 14000 actually refers to a family of standards. The broadest of these is ISO 14001. In order to receive ISO 14001 certification, a firm must:

- ⊃ demonstrate the ability to identify and control the environmental impact of their activities
- ⊃ make a commitment to continually improve their environmental performance
- ⊃ implement a systematic approach to setting environmental targets and to achieving those targets.

It is important to note that ISO 14000 standards do not establish specific goals for environmental performance; doing so would be very difficult, since ISO is intended to be a generic set of standards that apply to all industries, and each specific industry faces different environmental challenges.[18]

Operations managers are responsible for "putting it all together" by developing and implementing the processes needed to produce goods and services and distribute them to the target market. Their decisions affect both revenues and costs, going a long way toward determining whether a firm makes a profit or suffers a loss.

The responsibilities of operations managers require them to work closely with other managers throughout their organizations. For example, they must work with marketers and designers to ensure that the desired goods and services move from the drawing board to the final customer on time and within budget. They must work closely with financial managers to ensure that the company invests in the capital goods needed to produce goods and services in the most efficient manner. And they must work effectively with human resource managers to attract and develop workers who possess the knowledge and skills needed to become world-class competitors. Operations managers must even go beyond their own organization and work effectively with the suppliers and distributors who comprise the firm's value chain.

Operations managers must continuously adapt to changes in technology and in competitive conditions. Key challenges in recent years have centered on the need to continuously improve product quality while finding ways to reduce costs and protect the environment. You can expect the goals of becoming ever leaner—and ever greener—to remain a major focus of operations managers in years to come.

Operations management encompasses a number of different specific occupations, including quality management and control, product development, facilities management, and supply chain (or value chain) management. Operations research, which applies mathematical and statistical techniques to solving complex business problems, is a related field that might appeal to you if you have strong quantitative and problem-solving skills.

Operations managers typically need very strong technical skills and must be good problem solvers. Given the increasing use of value chain management software and computerized production methods, they also must be comfortable with information technology. Many companies require bachelor's degrees in operations management or a related field even for entry-level positions.

Job growth in operations management varies according to sector. Positions in the service sector should continue to increase more rapidly than those in the goods-producing sector.

Because operations management encompasses such a wide array of specific occupations, salaries vary widely. For many positions, the entry-level salary is in the $50,000 to $60,000 range. Experienced operations managers often earn base salaries in excess of $100,000 and may also receive substantial performance bonuses.[19]

What *else?*
RIP & REVIEW CARDS **IN THE BACK**
and visit **www.cengagebrain.com!**

Personal Finance Appendix

LEARNING OBJECTIVES

After studying this appendix, you will be able to...

A-1   Apply the principles of budgeting to your personal finances

A-2   Identify strategies to help build a sufficient savings

A-3   Explain the importance of using credit wisely

A-4   Discuss key wealth-building principles and the financial instruments that may be part of a wealth-building strategy

> "THE SAFE WAY TO DOUBLE YOUR *MONEY* IS TO FOLD IT ONCE OVER AND PUT IT IN YOUR POCKET."
>
> — FRANK "KIN" HUBBARD, CARTOONIST, HUMORIST, AND JOURNALIST

A-1a How Do I Get Started?

You can get a good handle on what should be included in your budget by carefully tracking and analyzing all of your financial transactions for several weeks. This takes discipline and careful record keeping, but once you know where your money comes from and where it goes, you'll have what you need to prepare your budget.

There are many approaches to setting up your budget. If you don't want to build your budget from scratch, you can check out several free online personal finance sites that can help you get started. Two of the most popular are Mint.com (http://www.mint.com) and Yodlee.com (http://www.yodlee.com). If you want more bells and whistles—and more support—than the free sites provide, you can purchase a commercial program such as Quicken, Moneydance, or AceMoney. Basic versions of these programs typically cost less than $50 and provide a wide range of features, such as online banking services, financial calculators, and stock quotes. Most also give you the ability to export data into tax preparation software, making tax filing much simpler.

If you are comfortable with Excel (or other spreadsheet software), another option is to build your own budget. Excel includes budget templates to help you get started, and even more are available online. These templates are generic, so you may want to tweak them to suit your own circumstances. You won't get all of the features provided by the commercial packages, but that isn't necessarily a bad thing. Some people actually find all of the bells and whistles in the commercial applications overwhelming and prefer the straightforward simplicity of a spreadsheet template. Also, the process of "building" the budget yourself may give you a sense of personal satisfaction and a greater appreciation for the budget relationships than you'd get using online sites or commercial software packages.

Assessing Revenues: Where Does My Money Come From? A budget starts with a forecast of your income—the money you bring in. This can come from many different sources. For many people, the paycheck from their job is their primary source of income. But the major source of income for entrepreneurs may be the profits they earn from their businesses. Some people also derive a substantial amount of income from financial investments, such as stocks and bonds, while others earn rental income. Retirees often depend on pensions, Social Security, and private investments for much of their income.

> **budget** (personal) A detailed forecast of financial inflows (income) and outflows (expenses) in order to determine your net inflow or outflow for a given period of time.

Personal financial management issues affect all of us, young and old alike. How successfully we manage our financial resources affects where we live, how well we can provide for our families, and when (or perhaps even if) we'll be able to retire comfortably. The financial decisions you make and habits you develop now will affect your personal and financial future.

New laws and regulations have changed the way many financial markets operate in recent years. The Dodd-Frank Wall Street Reform and Consumer Protection Act of 2010, passed in the wake of the financial crisis of 2008 and 2009, includes several provisions intended to protect the financial rights of consumers. But many of the law's requirements did not go into effect until mid-2011, so it is too soon to evaluate its long-term impact on consumer rights.

One key provision of the Dodd-Frank Act was the establishment of the Consumer Financial Protection Bureau (CFPB). One early goal of the CFPB was to eliminate confusing and deceptive banking practices related to mortgages, credit cards, and other loan agreements.[1]

A-1 Your Budget

One of the first steps in getting control over your financial situation is to develop a **budget**, which is a detailed forecast of your expected cash inflows (income) and cash outflows (expenditures). You can use your budget to develop your financial plan and to monitor your progress toward achieving your financial goals.

Assessing Expenses: Where Does It All Go? Once you have identified the amount of income you expect to receive from various sources, you can turn your focus to the spending side of your budget. In order to set up your budget, you'll need to be very specific about where your money goes. As we've already mentioned, carefully tracking your expenditures over a period of several weeks can help you identify your spending patterns. Many people who do this are surprised by the habits they uncover. You may find that you're spending a lot more than you thought on video games, music downloads, or clothes. Once you discover your spending patterns, you'll be in a better position to determine the categories of spending to include in your budget and to estimate the amount you'll spend in each category.

Understanding Your Spending Habits Your expenditures can be classified into discretionary and nondiscretionary categories. The payments you have the most control over are called your **discretionary payments**. Perhaps you like dining out, nightclubbing, or shopping. Perhaps you just have expensive taste in coffee. David Bach, author of *The Automatic Millionaire,* challenges us to

Rather go to bed without dinner than to rise in debt.

— BENJAMIN FRANKLIN

look at our "latté factors," meaning the little vices we each find hard to resist. You'll find that something as seemingly minor as a $4 cup of coffee each workday costs you $1,040 each year ($4 x 5 days per week x 52 weeks). Once you realize the true cost of these "latté factors," you'll have a greater incentive to bring them under control.[2] Your budget can be helpful in imposing the discipline you need to accomplish this goal.

Nondiscretionary payments are those you have little control over, such as your monthly rent or car payment, which are set by contract. Your lifestyle may also lock you into other costs that are at least partly nondiscretionary. Given your need to get to school and work, you may have to spend a significant amount of money on gas and car maintenance every month. But with a little flexibility and creativity, you may find that such costs aren't *completely* nondiscretionary. For instance, you might be able to significantly reduce your expenses for gas and car maintenance by carpooling or using mass transit.

You may also want to consider your attitude toward spending. Are you most likely to spend too much money when you are depressed or stressed out? Look at this aspect carefully, and try to be as honest as possible with yourself. The final thing you should consider is whom you are with

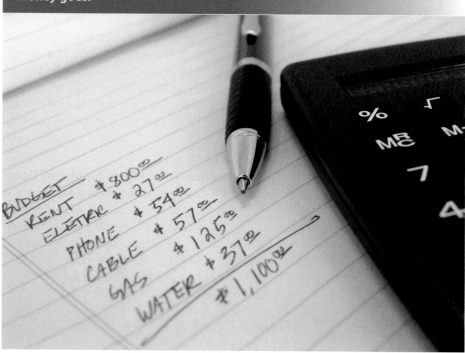

Setting up a budget requires you to be very specific about where your money goes.

BUDGET
RENT $800⁰⁰
ELETRIC $27⁰⁰
PHONE $54⁰⁰
CABLE $57⁰⁰
GAS $125⁰⁰
WATER $37⁰⁰
$1,100⁰⁰

© R. MACKAY PHOTOGRAPHY, LLC/Shutterstock.com

when you spend money. You may find that you tend to spend much more money while hanging out with certain friends.

After you have prepared your budget, you'll need to keep track of your actual expenses and compare them to your budget. And you'll need to adjust your budget periodically to reflect significant changes in your lifestyle, employment status, and financial goals.

A-2 Your Savings: Building a Safety Net

A **savings account** is an interest-earning account that is intended to satisfy obligations that your checking account cannot handle. Think of your savings account as a "safety net" for unexpected financial challenges, such as a major plumbing repair, the need to replace your car's transmission, or even the loss of your job. Many financial experts suggest that you have enough money in your savings to cover six months of your expenses. The good news is that if you're lucky enough to avoid major problems, your savings account will earn you a bit of interest income.

One technique for establishing a sizable savings balance is to "pay yourself first." This concept, popularized by David Bach, suggests that you have a predetermined amount from each paycheck automatically deposited into your savings account. Once you've accumulated enough in your savings account to provide an adequate safety net, you can use the "pay yourself first" approach to achieve other financial goals.[3]

Interest rates on savings accounts vary from bank to bank, so you should shop around to find the best rate. In recent years, online savings banks have often provided higher interest rates than traditional banks. Just be sure to look for reputable banks that are insured by the **Federal Deposit Insurance Corporation (FDIC)**. The FDIC is an independent agency created by Congress to maintain stability and public confidence in the nation's financial system, primarily by insuring bank deposits. The FDIC insures individual

deposits up to $250,000 per account in FDIC insured banks.[4]

A-3 Your Credit: Handle With Care!

Credit refers to your ability to obtain goods or resources without having to make immediate payment. One of the most important determinants of the amount of credit you can obtain is your **credit score**, which is a numerical indicator of your creditworthiness. Currently, the most commonly used credit scoring system is the Fair, Isaac and Company (FICO) scale. The FICO scale runs from 300 to 850.

Your individual FICO score is based on several factors, including your payment history, the amount you owe, the type of credit used, and the length of time you've held various credit accounts.[5] As Exhibit A.1 shows, about 72% of all Americans have scores between 600 and 800; only 2% have scores below 500, and 13% have scores above 800. A high score makes it easier to get credit on favorable terms.[5a] On a $250,000, 30-year fixed mortgage, a borrower with a below-average credit score of 620 will pay $89,000 more interest because of higher interest rates than a borrower with a fair to good credit score of 780.[6]

savings account An interest-bearing account holding funds not needed to meet regular expenditures.

Federal Deposit Insurance Corporation (FDIC) An independent agency created by Congress to maintain stability and public confidence in the nation's financial system, primarily by insuring bank deposits.

credit Allows a borrower to buy a good or acquire an asset without making immediate payment, and to repay the balance at a later time.

credit score A numerical measure of a consumer's creditworthiness.

© Ljupco Smokovski/Shutterstock.com

EXHIBIT A.1 What FICO Credit Scores Mean

WHAT FICO CREDIT SCORES MEAN		
SCORE	CREDITWORTHINESS	PERCENTAGE OF CONSUMERS
BELOW 500	Very poor	2%
500–599	Poor to below average	13%
600–699	Below average to fair	27%
700–799	Fair to good	45%
800 OR BETTER	Excellent	13%

© Cengage Learning 2013

credit card A card issued by a bank or finance company that allows the cardholder to make a purchase now and pay the credit card issuer later.

grace period The period of time that the credit card holder has to pay outstanding balances before interest or fees are assessed.

annual percentage rate (APR) The interest expense charged on a credit card, expressed as an annual percentage.

A-3a Credit Cards: Boon or Bane?

Now let's look at a specific source of credit that is near and dear to many college students' hearts: the **credit card**. A credit card allows its holder to make a purchase now and pay the credit card issuer later.

> "The average college student owes $4,100 in credit card debt. Just 9.4% pay off their debt in full each month."
>
> — Creditcards.com

There are several benefits to having and using credit cards. The most obvious is that credit cards are more convenient and safer than carrying a lot of cash. Credit cards also make it easy to track your expenditures, since you have access to a monthly summary of charges. And many cards offer perks, such as discounts on certain products, extended warranties on purchases, or frequent-flier miles. Another benefit of the *responsible* use of credit cards is that it can improve your credit score by allowing you to establish a history of prompt payments. This can make it easier for you to borrow money when you really need it—such as when you want to buy a car or your first home.

One downside of having a credit card is that the "buy now, pay later" aspect of credit card use makes it hard for some people to maintain financial discipline. Another problem is that interest rates on unpaid card balances tend to be very high. Many card issuers also impose a variety of fees that can make a noticeable dent in your wallet. And making late payments or failing to pay what you owe can damage your credit history, hurting your chances of getting additional credit when you need it.

A-3b The Devil in the Details — Understanding Your Credit Card Agreement!

Before you accept a credit card, make sure you read the credit card agreement and understand the main conditions for using that card. Some things to look for include:

⊃ **Grace period:** The period of time that you have to pay your balance before interest or fees are assessed. Some credit card companies expect to receive their payment within 21 days of the credit

card statement date. So, it becomes very important to get these bills paid as soon as possible to avoid the interest and other fees.

⊃ **APR (annual percentage rate):** The percentage financing cost charged on unpaid balances. The higher the APR, the greater your interest expense on unpaid balances. Your credit card company may charge different APRs for different types of transactions.

⊃ **Late fees:** May also be assessed if a payment is not received within the grace period. Federal law now caps late fees at $25 for a first offense and $35 for additional late payments.[7]

⊃ **Other fees:** Include *annual fees* (a charge just for the privilege of having a card, whether you use it or not), *over-the-credit-limit fees* if your charges exceed your credit limit, and *balance-transfer fees* if you transfer a balance from one card to another. This isn't a complete list, but it does reflect many of the most common types of fees you might incur. Not all cards are subject to all of these charges; the specific types and amounts of fees can vary considerably from one issuer to another—which is why reading the fine print is important!

A-3c Protection for Consumers: New Laws and Regulations

Two recent laws have had a significant impact on credit card practices. The Credit Card Accountability, Responsibility and Disclosure Act of 2009 (often called the CARD Act) requires issuers to give a 45-day notice before making significant changes to credit agreements and prohibits them from raising interest rates on existing balances unless the borrower is more than 60 days late in making required payments. It also requires anyone under the age of 21 who applies for a credit card to either verify proof of income or have an older adult cosign the application. And it places caps on certain types of fees that credit card issuers can charge.

As mentioned at the beginning of this appendix, the Dodd-Frank Act created the Consumer Financial Protection Bureau. One focus of the CFPB's early efforts has been to make it easier for consumers to compare the features and costs of various credit cards so that they can select the ones that best meet their needs. The Dodd-Frank Act also requires lenders, insurance companies, and others who reject your application to provide you with a free copy of your credit score.[8]

A-3d Using Credit Cards Wisely: The Need for Discipline

Although many young adults manage their credit cards without major problems, others are stunned when the credit card bill arrives. Many never read their credit card agreements, so they are taken by surprise by higher-than-expected interest charges and fees. Others simply lack discipline. They succumb to the temptations of a "buy now, pay later" mentality and run up big bills that they can't afford to pay.

The first rule when you have credit card difficulties is to "PUT THE CARD DOWN!" When you find yourself in trouble, stop using the card so you don't compound your difficulties. Make sure you don't use the card again until you've gotten your spending habits under control.

Once you've eliminated the temptation to dig a deeper hole, the next step is to make sure you consistently pay a substantial amount each month toward retiring the debt on that card. Given how high APRs are on the unpaid balances for most credit cards, it is usually a good idea to place a *very* high priority on eliminating these balances as quickly as possible.

If you just can't seem to shake the habit of overspending, consider using cash or a **debit card** instead of a credit card. While a debit card looks like a credit card, there is a big difference. When you use a debit card, money is immediately withdrawn from your bank account, so you "feel the pain" just as if you'd paid in cash. Many people spend less when they use cash or debit cards than when they use credit cards.

© iStockphoto.com/Burak Can OZTAS

A-4 Your Investments: Building for the Future

Investing involves reducing consumption today in order to acquire assets that build future wealth. In a very real way, investing is like the concept of sowing and reaping. A farmer plants a seed (makes an investment) in anticipation of a harvest (return) that will be much larger than the seed that was planted. When it comes to investing, early is better than late—but late is better than never.

A-4a Building Wealth: The Key Is Consistency—and an Early Start!

Don't talk yourself out of investing just because you don't have much to invest. Even if you start with a small amount, your wealth will eventually grow to a significant amount as long as you stick with it. And the earlier you start the better off you'll be. To see this, take a look at Exhibit A.2, which compares how big your retirement nest egg will be at age 65 for different monthly investment amounts beginning at different ages (and assuming you earn an annual return of 8%). A 30-year-old who invests $60 per month will end up with $137,633 at age 65. Compare this to someone who begins investing $60 per month at age 20, and the results are startling. The investor who starts at age 20 only directly invests $7,200 more ($60 per month for 120 more months) than the investor who starts at age 30. But the earlier investor ends up with a nest egg

> **debit card** A card issued by the bank that allows the customer to make purchases as if the transaction involved cash. In a debit card purchase, the customer's bank account is immediately reduced when the purchase is made.
>
> **investing** Reducing consumption in the current time period in order to build future wealth.

EXHIBIT A.2 Growing Your Investment: Starting Early Makes a Difference

MONTHLY SAVINGS	STARTING AGE			
	20	30	40	50
$30	$158,236	$ 68,816	$ 28,531	$10,381
$60	$316,472	$137,633	$ 57,062	$20,762
$90	$474,709	$206,449	$ 85,592	$31,143
$120	$632,945	$275,266	$114,123	$41,525
$150	$791,181	$344,082	$142,654	$51,906

Note: Figures in the table show the amount accumulated at age 65. Results are based on an assumed annual rate of return of 8% compounded monthly.

© Cengage Learning 2013

of $316,472—almost $179,000 more than that of the investor who started at age 30.

The reason for this result is that, over time, you earn interest not only on the money you directly invest but also on the *interest* you've earned in *previous* years—a process known as *compounding*. The earlier you begin investing, the more powerful the compounding effect becomes. By the time an investor reaches age 65, any dollars invested at age 20 have been compounded for a *very long* time, resulting in a big increase in the nest egg. The message of Exhibit A.2 is clear: an early start to investing can lead to dramatically more money when it comes time to retire.

Financial Securities: What Are My Investment Options?

Now that we've demonstrated the importance of investing, let's look at some specific types of financial instruments you might want to include in your investment portfolio. Our brief discussion can't hope to cover all of the possibilities, so we'll focus only on some of the most common choices. Keep in mind that, in addition to the financial instruments we describe in this section, many people also hold much of their wealth in other assets. The largest single asset for many households is the equity they have in their home.

Let's begin by looking at *common stock*, which represents ownership in a corporation. Common stock offers the possibility of two types of financial returns. The first, called a *dividend,* is a distribution of profits paid out to the stockholders. Dividends are paid only if the corporation's board of directors declares them—and there is no legal requirement for them to do so. If a corporation is in poor financial shape, its board of directors may decide that it is unable to pay a dividend. But even if a company is highly profitable, its board may decide to reinvest (retain) its profits rather than pay dividends to stockholders.

Investors can earn a second type of return, called a capital gain, if the market price of their stock rises relative to the price they paid for it. But stock prices can go down as well as up—as many investors have painfully discovered in recent years! Thus, it is possible for investors to experience *capital losses* as well as capital gains. Clearly, investing in common stock entails a significant degree of risk. But historically the average rate of return on stocks has been better than the return on many other types of investments.

In addition to common stock, some corporations also offer another type of stock, called *preferred stock.* The two types of stock have some important differences. From the perspective of many investors, the most important distinction is that owners of preferred stock are more likely to receive a dividend than owners of common stock. Preferred stock is normally issued with a stated dividend, and common stockholders can't be paid *any* dividend until the preferred dividend is paid in full. Still, even preferred stockholders have no guaranteed legal right to receive a dividend.

A *corporate bond* is another type of corporate security, but it is quite different from stock. A bond is a formal IOU issued by a corporation. While stockholders are the owners of a corporation, bondholders are its creditors. Most bonds are long-term debts that mature (come due) 10 to 30 years after they are issued, though bonds with shorter and longer maturities are sometimes issued.

As creditors, bondholders are legally entitled to receive interest payments from the issuing corporation every year until the bond matures, and to receive an amount known as the *principal* (or "face value") when the bond matures.

But bondholders don't have to hold their bonds until they mature. Like stocks, bonds can be bought and sold on securities markets, and their price can rise and fall. So, like stockholders, bondholders can experience capital gains or losses.

Because the issuing corporation is legally required to pay interest and principal on a fixed schedule, the returns on bonds are more predictable than returns on stocks. However, even bonds pose some risk. During the recent economic downturn, many firms defaulted on (failed to make) their legally required bond payments.

Government securities are IOUs issued by government entities when they borrow money. As with corporate bonds, government securities normally pay their holders a stated rate of interest until they mature. State and local governments often issue bonds. In fact, many investors like to invest in municipal bonds

© iStockphoto.com/DNY59

because interest income earned on these bonds is usually exempt from federal income taxes. But the biggest single issuer of government securities is the federal government. The U.S. Treasury markets a variety of securities, from long-term bonds that mature in 30 years, to short-term treasury bills (popularly called "T-bills") that can mature in as little as four weeks. Historically, securities issued by the federal government have been viewed as very safe investments. But in recent years, the rapid growth in federal debt has led some securities rating services to question this view.[9]

Certificates of deposit are offered by banks and other depository institutions like credit unions. They are similar to savings accounts but are issued for a fixed term—which could be as short as three months or as long as five years. The rate of interest paid on CDs is often higher than the rate on a regular savings account but usually lower than the interest rate on corporate bonds and most government securities. CDs with longer maturities typically earn a higher interest rate than CDs that have shorter terms. You can cash in a CD before it matures, but you'll incur a substantial penalty if you do.

One advantage of CDs is that they are insured by the FDIC. Because of this insurance and their predictable rate of return, CDs are considered to be among the safest investment options. The tradeoff is that they offer lower returns than most other types of investments.

Mutual funds sell shares to investors and pool the resulting funds to invest in financial instruments such as corporate stocks, corporate bonds, government securities, or other assets. Some mutual funds invest mainly in bonds, others invest mainly in stocks, and others in government securities. Some invest in specific sectors of the economy, such as technology, energy, or healthcare, while others invest in broader portfolios.

Most mutual funds are professionally managed, with the fund's manager selecting the specific securities that the fund will hold. This professional management appeals to many investors who don't have the time or expertise to evaluate investment alternatives. But it is also expensive—mutual funds charge fees to cover the cost of managing the fund and to meet other expenses. Investors must pay these fees even if the funds perform poorly.

Exchange Traded Funds (ETFs) are similar to mutual funds in that they represent ownership in a broad portfolio of securities. However, unlike most mutual funds, they are bought and sold just like shares of corporate stock. ETFs are a relatively new investment vehicle (first marketed in 1993), but they have become quite popular in recent years.

A-4b Acquiring Financial Assets: The Role of a Broker

Investors normally acquire many of their financial assets, including shares of common and preferred stocks, corporate bonds, and certain other financial assets (such as ETFs), by purchasing them in securities markets. However, individual investors can't directly participate in these markets. Instead, they normally rely on the services of a brokerage firm to buy and sell securities.

When choosing a broker, it's important to consider both the costs and the level of service. In addition to carrying out your trades, a *full-service broker* provides a wide range of services—such as research to identify good investment opportunities, financial planning, and tax advice. Most full-service brokerage firms charge commissions based on the dollar value of the orders their clients place. They also charge fees for the services they provide. In contrast, *discount brokers* buy and sell securities for their clients but offer few additional services. The commissions and fees charged by discount brokers are usually significantly lower than those of full-service brokers. Many discount brokerage firms charge flat fees of a few dollars per trade for simple transactions.

In recent years, competition among brokerage firms has blurred the distinction between full-service and discount brokers. Many full-service firms have lowered their commissions, while many discount brokers have begun offering investment advice and other services. Most major brokerage firms now offer their clients both discount and full-service options.

Before entrusting a brokerage firm with your financial transactions, you should check out its background. The Financial Industry Regulatory Authority's (FINRA's) BrokerCheck website (http://www.finra.org/Investors/ToolsCalculators/BrokerCheck/) is a good place to start. This site offers very detailed background information on over 1.3 million current and former FINRA-registered brokers and over 17,400 FINRA-registered brokerage firms.

A-4c Building a Portfolio: A Few Words about Diversification, Risk, and Return

The financial securities we've described are not mutually exclusive. It is possible—and usually desirable—to invest in a diversified financial portfolio consisting of a variety of stocks, bonds, CDs, government securities, and other assets.

The main advantage offered by diversification is that it reduces your risk. If you put a large part of your wealth into one specific investment, you could be wiped out if that investment goes sour. If you invest in several different assets, then losses in some are likely to be offset by gains in others. But diversification also has a downside—it not only reduces risk but also reduces the possibility of earning exceptionally high returns.

One widely accepted financial principle is that a tradeoff exists between risk and return; in other words, investments with the potential for generating high returns tend to be riskier than investments that offer lower returns. For example, stock prices sometimes decline sharply, so investing in stocks is considered quite risky. But historically, the long-run average return on stocks has been significantly higher than the average return on bonds, which offer safer, more predictable returns.

In general, younger investors are less concerned about risk than older investors. When you are young, you have more time to recover from adverse results, so you may be willing to take more risks and be more aggressive in pursuit of higher returns. If you invest mostly in stocks when you are young, and the stock market crashes, you still have time to recoup your losses and take advantage of future increases in stock prices. But older investors who hold a lot of stock might find that the same crash wiped out much of the wealth just when they were counting on it to supplement their retirement income. Older investors often become more conservative, adjusting their portfolio to include a greater percentage of relatively safe assets such as government securities, bonds of corporations with strong credit ratings, and CDs.

A-4d But What Is My Best Investment? (Hint: Look in the Mirror!)

So far, we have focused on investing in financial assets. But in many ways, the most important investment you can make is in yourself, by devoting your time, effort, and money to your education, training, health, and fitness. The Bureau of Labor Statistics reports that the median weekly earnings of high-school graduates in the first quarter of 2012 was $653, while for workers with bachelor's degrees, the figure was $1,158—a difference of $505 or 77%.[10] Over a typical worker's 40-year career, this amounts to a difference in earnings of over $1.25 million! And higher education not only increases your income, it also gives you more job security. In 2012, the unemployment rate for workers with a high-school education was 8.1% while the unemployment rate for workers with at least a bachelor's degree was 3.9%.[11]

Strategies to Become More Marketable One way to increase your marketability and your starting salary is to secure an internship during your college years. Such internships usually offer little or no monetary compensation, but they pay off in other ways. They give students a chance to gain first-hand experience

What Are the Best Personal Finance Apps for Smartphones?

Since your smartphone goes everywhere you do, why not use personal finance apps that pull together real-time data from your bank, credit cards, and financial service providers? As for security, data isn't stored on your phone or on providers' servers, accounts can be deactivated via web browsers, and 128-bit bank-level encryption is always used. Here are several highly recommended apps at the time this book went to press.

- **Mint:** The app version of acclaimed Mint.com aggregates financial information from all of your accounts. It categorizes spending, indicates when you're over budget and shows total cash, credit card debt, and monthly cash flow each time you use it. Free.

- **Hello Wallet:** Compares saving and spending patterns to people of similar incomes and ages, flags regrettable purchases, sends daily messages encouraging saving, and uses GPS to send feedback when it "knows" you're shopping. $8.95 a month.

- **Pageonce:** Similar to Mint, but this app generates numerous useful charts and graphics. The opening screen shows cash, bills, investments, credit card debt, credit score, and savings offers for shopping. Free, or upgrade to Gold for $4.99 a month for bill payment and other services.[12]

that supplements what they learn in the classroom and helps them determine whether a specific career is right for them. And the internship experience looks great on a résumé. But in 2010, the U.S. Department of Labor issued a ruling that makes it more difficult for profit-seeking firms to offer unpaid or low-wage internships. Many educators, business leaders, and politicians have called on the Department of Labor to modify its stance to make internships easier to establish. But unless and until such modifications are adopted, internships may remain difficult to find.[13]

Other Work Opportunities Don't despair if you are unable to secure an internship. There are other ways to gain experience in your field of interest. Consider taking a (gulp) pay cut from your temporary *job* to get experience in your *career* field. Or perhaps consider doing volunteer work in that field—not only will you be doing a good deed, you'll also be learning the ropes in your chosen field. Taking a temporary pay cut to gain relevant work experience often pays for itself many times over when you leave college and pursue a full-time position.

A–4e **Investing for the Long Term: Planning for Your Retirement**

One of the most important reasons people invest is to build up a nest egg for retirement. While your retirement might seem like it is a long way off, investing for your golden years now can really pay off, since it allows you to take advantage of the compounding effects we talked about earlier.

A key to a comfortable retirement is to start saving early.

© Blend Images/Shutterstock.com

One of the most popular ways to build wealth for retirement is to set up an individual retirement account, or **IRA**. There are several types of IRAs; the two most popular are the *traditional IRA* and the *Roth IRA*. Both types of IRAs are individual investments—you make the decisions about how much to invest (subject to maximum allowable contributions) and what specific investments to make. You can put your IRA money into stocks, government securities, CDs, mutual funds, or other types of financial securities.

> **IRA** An individual retirement account that provides tax benefits to individuals who are investing for their retirement.
>
> **401(k), 403(b), and 457 plans** Employee payroll deduction retirement plans that offer tax benefits.

Both traditional and Roth IRAs offer tax advantages intended to provide an incentive for people to invest for their retirement. But the nature and timing of the tax advantages are different. With a traditional IRA, the contributions you make reduce your taxable income in the same tax year, and the earnings on your contributions are tax deferred, allowing them to grow more rapidly.[14] But you must pay taxes on the money received from a traditional IRA when you begin making withdrawals. On the other hand, the contributions you make to a Roth IRA are *not* tax deductible at the time you make them, but earnings on these contributions are tax-free, and you pay no taxes on the distributions you receive from a Roth IRA after you retire.

One drawback to both traditional and Roth IRAs is that the amount that individuals can contribute each year is relatively small. In 2012, the maximum contribution for both types of plans was $5,000. (Individuals over the age of 50 could contribute up to $6,000.)

401(k), 403(b), and 457 plans are employee-contribution retirement plans that are named for the sections of the IRS tax code where they are described. These plans are similar in many respects; the main differences are in who qualifies for each type of plan. 401(k) plans are offered to employees of private-sector businesses, while 403(b) plans are for employees of certain types of nonprofit organizations such as schools, religious organizations, and charities. The 457 plans are primarily for state and local government employees and nonprofit organizations. Some employees in the nonprofit sector qualify for both 403(b) and 457 plans.

Unlike IRAs, all of these plans are implemented through a payroll-deduction process. Also, these plans have much higher contribution limits than traditional and Roth IRAs. In 2012, for example, employees could contribute up to $17,000 in a 401(k) plan, with individuals over 50 allowed to contribute up to an additional $5,500 *if* their

company matching An amount contributed by the employer to an employee's retirement account, matching the employee's retirement contributions either dollar-for-dollar or based on a percentage of each dollar contributed by the employee.

vesting period A specified period of time for which an employee must work for an employer in order to receive the full advantage of certain retirement benefits.

employer's plan contained a "catch-up" provision. Other potential advantages of these plans include:

⊙ **Tax advantages:** Any income employees invest in traditional 401(k), 403(b), and 457 plans are tax deductible, and the earnings on these investments are tax deferred. This reduces current taxes and allows the funds to grow more rapidly. However, retirees must pay taxes on funds distributed from their fund when they make withdrawals. As with IRAs, there are Roth versions of these plans. Employees who choose the Roth version pay taxes on the income they contribute, but earnings on these contributions and distributions after retirement are tax exempt.

⊙ **Company matching:** Some employers match employee contribution either dollar for dollar or with a percentage of each dollar you contribute up to a limit. This can be a big advantage of these plans over IRAs. If your company matches your 401(k) or 403(b) or 457 contributions, you should consider contributing as much as you can up to the maximum your company will match—it's like getting free money for your retirement.

There are also some important restrictions on these plans. First, not all employers offer these plans. Second, if your employer does offer a plan that offers matching contributions, you won't be entitled to all of the matching funds unless you've remained employed with the company for a stated period of time called the **vesting period**. The length of time for full vesting varies depending on the employer, but it is usually several years. Finally, keep in mind that these are *retirement* plans. There are restrictions on withdrawing the money in these plans prior to retirement, and you may pay significant penalties if you do.

Making sound personal financial decisions requires careful thought and discipline. You should start by establishing a budget; doing so will help you understand your current financial situation, plan for the future, and monitor your progress toward achieving your goals. One of your first goals should be to set aside enough savings to provide adequate protection against unforeseen financial challenges. One good strategy to build your savings is to "pay yourself first." Another key to financial success is to make careful decisions with respect to your use of credit cards and other forms of credit. Next, you should turn your attention to investing to build your wealth over time. You'll discover many different investment opportunities, each with their own pros and cons. No single investment strategy is foolproof, but two principles that have stood the test of time are: (1) start investing early to take full advantage of compounding, and (2) diversify your investments to protect against risk.

What *else?*
RIP & REVIEW CARDS IN THE BACK and visit www.cengagebrain.com!

1

1. 27 Twitter-Ready Consumer Trends you need to know by Matt Carmichael, *AdvertisingAge* magazine, October 20, 2010, accessed January 13, 2010.

2. Entrepreneurial activity rose to highest rate in 14 years, Kauffman Foundation press release, May 20, 2010, Kauffman Foundation website, http://www.techjournalsouth.com/2010/05/entrepreneurial-activity-rose-to-highest-rate-in-14-years/, accessed January 13, 2011; Startup rate at 15-year high by Catherine Clifford, March 7, 2011, CNN Money website, http://money.cnn.com/2011/03/07/smallbusiness/new_business_starts/index.htm, accessed January 10, 1012.

3. College Freshmen Show Increasing Interest in Entrepreneurship, Kauffman Foundation press release, November 18, 2009, Kauffman Foundation website, http://www.kauffman.org/newsroom/first-time-college-students-show-increasing-interest-in-entrepreneurship.aspx accessed January 13, 2011; From Books to Business: Student Entrepreneurs by Julia Aubuchon, November 14, 2009, ABC News website, http://abcnews.go.com/Business/SmallBiz/successful-student-entrepreneurs/story?id=9075154, accessed January 13, 2011; Student entrepreneurship in college is on the rise in poor economy by Amy Reinink, November 3, 2011, Washington Post website, http://www.washingtonpost.com/lifestyle/magazine/student-entrepreneurship-in-college-is-on-the-rise-in-poor-economy/2011/10/17/gIQAxEMuiM_print.html, accessed January 10, 2012

4. State of Entrepreneurship Address, January 19, 2010, Kauffman Foundation website, http://www.kauffman.org/newsroom/entrepreneurs-expect-to-limit-hiring-in-2010-according-to-new-kauffman-foundation-poll.aspx, accessed January 13, 2011.

5. *Business Blunders of the Year 2010* by Adam Horowitz, Martin Douglass, and Mike Grudowski, CBS moneywatch website, http://www.cbsnews.com/8334-505125_162-51493483/business-blunders-of-the-year/?tag=bnetdomain, accessed January 13, 2011.

6. Thaler, Richard H. and Sunstein, Cass R, *Nudge: Improving Decisions about Health, Wealth, and Happiness.* (New York: Penguin Group, 2009); Easy Does It: How to make lazy people do the right thing, by Thaler and Sunstein, *The New Republic*, April 9, 2008, New Republic website; Stephen J. Dubner, Who will climb the piano stairs? Freakonomics: The Hidden Side of Everything *New York Times*, October 13, 2009, http://freakonomics.blogs.nytimes.com/2009/10/13/who-will-climb-the-piano-stairs/?pagemode=print, retrieved March 22, 2010; http://articles.latimes.com/2008/apr/02/opinion/oe-thalerandsunstein2; http://www.marcgunther.com/2009/11/16/whats-for-lunch-behaviorial-economics-meets-climate-change/.

7. On the Nonprofit Sector and Community Solutions Act of 2010 by Leonard Jacobs, June 18, 2010, The Clyde Fitch Report, The Clyde Fitch Report Website, http://www.clydefitchreport.com/2010/06/introducing-hr-5533-the-nonprofit-sector-and-community-solutions-act-of-2010/, accessed January 16, 2011; 7.2% of Americans work for nonprofit groups, study finds, by Suzanne Perry, December 19, 2006, The Chronicle of Philanthropy website, http://philanthropy.com/free/update/2006/12/2006121901.htm, accessed January 19, 2009; Wages in the nonprofit sector: management, professional, and administrative support occupations by Amy Butler, October 28, 2008, Bureau of Labor Statistics website, http://www.bls.gov/opub/cwc/cm20081022ar01p1.htm, accessed January 19, 2008; Occupational Employment and Wages, 2007, May 9, 2008, Bureau of Labor Statistics website, http://www.bls.gov/news.release/pdf/ocwage .pdf, accessed January 19, 2009; Nonprofit sector needs to be better understood by Todd Cohen, February 22, 2010, Inside Philanthropy Blog, Philanthropy Journal website, http://philanthropyjournal.blogspot.com/2010/02/nonprofit-sector-needs-to-be-better.html, retrieved March 23, 2010.

8. GNI Per Capita 2007 World Bank Data, revised October 17, 2008, http://siteresources.worldbank.org/DATASTATISTICS/ Resources/GNIPC.pdf, accessed January 19, 2009; CIA World Factbook China, updated December 18, 2008, https://www.cia.gov/library/publications/the-world-factbook/geos/ch.html, accessed January 19, 2009; CIA World Factbook Russia, updated December 18, 2008, https://www.cia.gov/library/publications/the-world-factbook/geos/rs.html, accessed January 19, 2009; CIA World Factbook Hong Kong, updated December 18, 2008, https://www.cia .gov/library/publications/the-world-factbook/geos/hk.html, accessed January 19, 2009.

9. You're checked out but your brain is checked in by Benedict Carey, August 8, 2008, The *New York Times* website, http://www.nytimes.com/2008/08/05/health/research/05mind.html, accessed January 15, 2011; The Hidden Secrets of the Creative Mind, interview with R. Keith Sawyer, January 8, 2006, *Time* magazine website, July 24, 2008, http://www.time.com/time/magazine/article/0,9171,1147152-1,00.html; 10 Steps for Boosting Creativity by Jeffrey Baumgartner, Jeffrey Paul Baumgartner website, http://www.jpb.com/creative/creative.php, accessed January 15, 2012; Music and Creativity by Miles O'Brien, Science Nation website, http://www.nsf.gov/news/special_reports/science_nation/musiccreativity.jsp, accessed January 15, 2012.

10. American Customer Satisfaction Index, 2011 Results, ACSI website, http://www.theacsi.org/index.php?option=com_content&view=article&id=12&Itemid=110, accessed January 14, 2012.

11. Why Webvan drove off a cliff by Joanna Glasner, Wired News, July 10, 2001, http://www.wired.com/news/business/ 0,1367,45098,00.html.

12. Honey, I shrunk the iPod. A lot. by Steven Levy, September 19, 2005, *Newsweek* magazine; Behind Apple's strategy: be second to market by John Boddie, August 29, 2005, Harvard Business School Working Knowledge, http://hbswk.hbs.edu/item.jhtml?id=4970&t=technology. What's to become of Microsoft's answer to the iPod? by John Letzing July 29, 2009, Marketwatch website, http://www .marketwatch.com/story/microsofts-zune-continues-to-struggle-2009-07-29, accessed April 1, 2010.

13. See note 12 above.

14. Employee Satisfaction & Stock Performance by Jeffrey Henning on Fri, Aug 06, 2010, Voice of Vovici Blog, http://blog.vovici.com/blog/?Tag=Employee%20Satisfaction%20Surveys, accessed January 17, 2011; Giving employees what they want: the returns are huge, May 4, 2005, Knowledge@Wharton, Human Resources, http://knowledge.wharton.upenn.edu/article/1188.cfm, accessed January 19, 2009; How Investing in Intangibles—Like Employee Satisfaction—Translates into Financial Returns, January 9, 2008, Knowledge@ Wharton website, http://knowledge.wharton.upenn.edu/article.cfm?articleid=1873, accessed January 19, 2009.

15. 10,000—Baby Boomers Retire, Pew Research Center, January 17, 2011, Pew Research website, http://pewresearch.org/databank/dailynumber/?NumberID=1150, accessed January 11, 2011.

16. Ideas made here by Anne Fisher, Fortune magazine, June 11, 2007, page 35, CNNMoney website, http://money.cnn.com/magazines/fortune/fortune_archive/2007/06/11/100061499/index.htm, accessed January 17, 2011; Editors name the greatest inventions of all time, Encyclopedia Britannica News Release, January 30, 2003, http://corporate .britannica.com/press/releases/invention.html; Encyclopedia Britannica's Great Inventions, accessed October 11, 2005, http://corporate.britannica.com/press/inventions.html.

17. Retail E-Commerce Update by Jeffrey Grau, December 2008, eMarketer website, http://www.emarketer.com/Reports/All/Emarketer_2000545.aspx, accessed January 19, 2009; eMarketer: E-Commerce Expected to Grow Double Digits through 2012, by David Kaplan, PaidContent website, March 17, 2011, http://paidcontent.org/article/419-emarketer-e-commerce-expected-to-grow-double-digits-through-2012/, accessed January 15, 2012.

18. U.S. Population Projections: 2005–2050, February 11, 2008, by Jeffrey S. Passel and D'Vera Cohn, Pew Research Center website, http://pewhispanic.org/files/reports/85.pdf, accessed January 17, 2011.

19. State and County Quick Facts, Mississippi, U.S. Census, Bureau website, http://quickfacts.census.gov/qfd/states/28000.html Last Revised, February 23, 2010, retrieved March 30, 2010; Hawaii's Asian population at 55% is highest proportion in nation, May 1, 2009, Hawaii 24/7 website, http://www.hawaii247.org/2009/05/01/hawaiis-asian-population-at-55-is-highest-proportion-in-nation/, retrieved March 30, 2010; State and County Quick Facts, New Mexico, U.S. Census Bureau website, http://quickfacts.census.gov/qfd/states/35000.html, Last Revised, February, 23, 2010, retrieved March 30, 2010.

20. Wary of Energy Drinks in an Adrenaline Sport by Jeff Dinunzio, January 7, 2012, New York Times website, http://www.nytimes.com/2012/01/08/sports/pro-water-in-snowboarding-culture-heavy-on-energy-drinks.html, accessed January 16, 2012; Drink Water Launches website, December 5, 2011, Snowboarder Magazine website, http://www.snowboardermag.com/industry-news/drink-water-launches-website/, accessed January 16, 2012; Drink Water website, http://www.wedrinkwater.com/about, accessed January 16, 2012; Billions Daily Affected by Water Crisis, Water.Org website, http://water.org/water-crisis/one-billion-affected/, accessed January 16, 2012.

21. Translating Hispanic Marketing into Shareholder Value, Hispanic PR Wire/Business Wire, December 4, 2006, http://www.hispanicprwire.com/print.php?l=in&id=7660; Kraft Aims Kool-Aid Ads at a Growing Hispanic Market by Andrew Adam Newman, May 26, 2011, New York Times website, http://www.nytimes.com/2011/05/27/business/media/27adco.html, accessed January 16, 2012.

22. Diversity Awareness, Hershey Foods Corporation website, accessed October 4, 2005, https://www.hersheysjobs.com/Career/ControlPanel.aspx?ModuleCategoryID=1999999.

23. Attitudes of young people toward diversity, CIRCLE fact sheet, February 2005, http://www.civicyouth.org/PopUps/FactSheets/Attitudes%202.25.pdf.

24. U.S. Population Projections: 2005 – 2050, February 11, 2008, by Jeffrey S. Passel and D'Vera Cohn, Pew Research Center website, http://pewhispanic.org/files/reports/85.pdf, accessed January 17, 2011; China's concern over population aging and health by Toshiko Kaneda, Population Reference Bureau website, http://www.prb.org/Articles/2006/ChinasConcernOverPopulationAgingandHealth.aspx, accessed January 17, 2011.

25. Pending job flexibility act received mixed reviews by Sue Shellenbarger, WSJ Career Journal, http://www.careerjournal.com/columnists/workfamily/20010426-workfamily.html, accessed October 4, 2005; Bad attitudes in the workplace by Les Christie, Sept 6, 2005, CNNMoney, http://money.cnn.com/2005/08/24/pf/workplace_morale/?section=money_pf; Inspiring worker loyalty one tough job by John Ellis, July 1, 2005, East Bay Business Times website, http://www.bizjournals.com/eastbay/stories/2005/07/04/focus1.html; Employee loyalty is at a three-year low by Laura Petrecca, March 28, 2011, USA Today website, http://www.usatoday.com/money/workplace/2011-03-26-employees-less-loyal.htm, accessed January 16, 2012.

26. Sustainability: Balancing Opportunity and Risk in the Consumer Products Industry, 2007 Report, Deloitte website, http://www.deloitte.com/dtt/cda/doc/content/us_cb _sustainability-study_june2007opt.pdf, accessed January 20, 2009; While Everything Else Stops, Green Still Means Go by Sarah Fister Gale, January 19, 2009, GreenBiz website, http://www.planetthoughts.org/?pg=pt/Whole&qid=2675, accessed June 1, 2011.

27. How Rising Wages Are Changing the Game in China by Dexter Roberts, March 27, 2006, BusinessWeek website, http://www.businessweek.com/magazine/content/06_13/b3977049.htm, accessed January 20, 2009; Good Luck Competing Against Chinese Labor Costs, Mfg. Job Growth in China Is Headed Up, Not Down; 109 Million Mfg. Workers in China Dwarfs Number in U.S., by Richard McCormack, May 2, 2006, Manufacturing and Technology News website, http://www.manufacturingnews.com/news/06/0502/art1.html, accessed January 20, 2009; Cost of Chinese labor is on the rise by Scott Tong, July 6, 2007, Marketplace website, http://marketplace.publicradio.org/display/web/2007/07/06/cost_of_chinese_labor_is_on_the_rise/, accessed January 20, 2009; Manufacturing in China Today: Employment and Labor Compensation by Judith Banister, September 2007, The Conference Board website, http://www.conference-board.org/economics/workingpapers.cfm, accessed January 20, 2009; The End of Cheap Labor in China by Bill Powell, June 26, 2011, Time magazine website, http://www.time.com/time/magazine/article/0,9171,2078121,00.html, accessed January 16, 2012.

28. Asian tsunami devastates Sri Lankan fishing industry by Jason Beaubien, January 10, 2005, NPR Morning Edition, http://www.npr.org/templates/story/story.php?storyId=4276161; Phuket tourism industry crippled by mass cancellations by Sally Pook, January 8, 2005, Cyber Diver News Network, http://www.cdnn.info/news/travel/t050111.html; Homeland security scuffle by Veronique de Rugy, October 15, 2004, National Review website, http://www.nationalreview.com/comment/rugy200410150840.asp; Bush brushes aside rebuilding cost concerns, September 19, 2005, Reuters News Service, MSNBC website, http://www.msnbc.msn.com/id/9374106/.

29. Pomp and Circumspect by Daniel Pink, June 4, 2005, The New York Times website, http://select.nytimes.com/gst/abstract.html?res=F60C1FFD3F5C0C778CDDAF0894DD404482.

Pg. 13 Fact: http://www.universalmind.com/mindshare/entry/mobile-users-will-exceed-desktop-users-by-2014, accessed November 2012.

Pg. 16 Fact: http://www.thedailybeast.com/newsweek/2007/12/22/the-rise-of-a-fierce-yet-fragile-superpower.html , accessed November 2012.

2

1. TABLE B–1.—Gross domestic product, 1959–2008, Economic Report of the President: 2009 Spreadsheet Tables, updated January 14, 2009, Government Printing Office website, http://www.gpoaccess.gov/eop/tables09.html, accessed January 20, 2009.

2. More Foreclosures Expected in 2011 by Amy Hoak, December 12, 2010, The Wall Street Journal website, http://online.wsj.com/article/SB10001424052748703518604576014011451160994.html?mod=googlenews_wsj, accessed January 24, 2011; RealtyTrac's James J. Saccacio to Discuss Foreclosure Crisis Fallout at AFSA State Government Affairs Forum by RealtyTrac staff, RealityTrac website, October 1, 2008, http://www.realtytrac.com/ContentManagement/pressrelease.aspx? ChannelID=9&ItemID=5284&accnt=64847, accessed January 22, 2009; REALTYTRAC® Year-end Report Shows Record 2.8 Million U.S. Properties With Foreclosure Filings in 2009, RealtyTrac Staff, January 14, 2010, RealtyTrac website, http://www.realtytrac.com/contentmanagement/pressrelease.aspx?itemid=8333, accessed April 21, 2010; RealtyTrac: 2011 National Foreclosure Rate Lowest Since 2007, January 12, 2012, Commercial Record website, http://www.commercialrecord.com/news148166.html, accessed January 18, 2012.

3. 7.9 million jobs lost — many forever by Chris Isidore, July 2, 2010, CNNMoney website, http://money.cnn.com/2010/07/02/news/economy/jobs_gone_forever/index.htm, accessed, January 24, 2011.

4. Credit Crisis–The Essentials, Updated January 20, 2009, The New York Times website, Automakers say if they go, millions of jobs will vanish by Sharon Silke Carty and Barbara Hagenbaugh, Updated November 21, 2008, USA Today website, Auto Industry Bailout Overview, Updated January 20, 2009, The New York Times website, http://topics.nytimes.com/topics/reference/timestopics/subjects/c/credit_crisis/index.html, accessed January 21, 2009; http://www.usatoday.com/money/autos/2008-11-17-automakers-bailout-impact_N.htm, accessed January 21, 2009; http://topics.nytimes.com/top/reference/timestopics/subjects/c/credit_crisis/auto_industry/index.html, accessed January 21, 2009.

5. TARP Bailout to Cost Less Than Once Anticipated by Jackie Calmes, The New York Times website, October 1, 2010, http://dealbook.nytimes.com/2010/10/01/tarp-bailout-to-cost-less-than-once-anticipated/.

6. One Trillion Dollars by Micheal Grunwald, January 26, 2009, Time, pp. 27–31, http://www.time.com/time/politics/article/0,8599,1871769,00.html, accessed February 5, 2011; Economy adds jobs at fastest pace in three years by Jeannine Aversa and Christopher S. Rugaber, April 2, 2010, Associated Press, http://www.google.com/hostednews/ap/article/ALeqM5gNiyJ905Ho0Ur96V2TQhsBX19lGwD9ER6P402, accessed April 20, 2010; Bernanke declares 'recession is very likely over' by Greg Robb, September 15, 2009, MarketWatch website, http://www.marketwatch.com/story/bernanke-declares-the-recession-over-2009-09-15, accessed, April 20, 2010.

7. Sources: Struck in the Middle by Rana Foroohar, August 15, 2011, Time magazine website, http://www.time.com/time/magazine/article/0,9171,2086853,00.html, accessed January 24, 2012.

8. Money Stock Measures, Federal Reserve Statistical Release, February 5, 2009, Federal Reserve website, http://www.federalreserve.gov/releases/h6/hist/h6hist1.txt, accessed February 11, 2009.

9. UNC Researchers Spot Six Demographic Trends That Will Transform U.S., January 18, 2011, UNC website, http://uncnews.unc.edu/content/view/4227/67/, accessed January 24, 2012.

10. Money Stock Measures, Federal Reserve Statistical Release, January 22, 2009, http://www.federalreserve.gov/releases/h6/current/, accessed January 23, 2009.

11. Who is the FDIC?, FDIC website, October 27, 2008, http://www.fdic.gov/about/learn/symbol/index.html, accessed January 22, 2009.

12. Historical Changes of the Target Federal Funds and Discount Rates, Federal Reserve Bank of New York website, http://www.newyorkfed.org/markets/statistics/dlyrates/fedrate.html, accessed January 22, 2009.

13. Creating Green Jobs Through Recycling, EPA Region 9 Newsletter, February, 2011, EPA website, http://www.epa.gov/region9/newsletter/feb2011/greenjobs.html, accessed January 23, 2012; Pay as You Throw Fact Sheet for State Officials, updated July 26, 2011, EPA website, http://www.epa.gov/osw/conserve/tools/payt/tools/state.htm, accessed January 23 2012; More Recycling Will Create 1.5 Million New U.S. Jobs, November 14, 2011, Recycling Works Campaign website, http://www.recyclingworkscampaign.org/2011/11/more-jobs-less-pollution/, accessed January 31, 2012.

14. Federal Government, excluding Postal Services, U.S. Department of Labor Bureau of Labor Statistics website, March 12, 2008, http://stats.bls.gov/oco/cg/cgs041.htm, accessed August 16, 2008; Postal Service Workers, U.S. Department of Labor Bureau of Labor Statistics website, December 18, 2007, http://stats.bls.gov/oco/ocos141.htm, accessed August 16, 2008; Job Opportunities in the Armed Forces, U.S. Department of Labor Bureau of Labor Statistics website, December 18, 2007, http://stats.bls.gov/oco/ocos249.htm, accessed August 16, 2008.

15. Russia's flat tax miracle by Daniel J. Mitchell, PhD, The Heritage Foundation, March 24, 2003, http://www.heritage.org/Press/Commentary/ed032403.cfm; Russians do taxes right by Deroy Murdock, National Review Online, March 1, 2002, http://www.nationalreview.com/murdock/murdock030102.shtml; Russia: income taxes and tax laws, July 2005, Worldwide-Tax website, http://www.worldwide-tax.com/russia/russia_tax.asp; History of the U.S. taxsystem, U.S. Treasury website, http://www.ustreas.gov/education/fact-sheets/taxes/ustax.html,accessed March 9, 2006.

16. Central Intelligence Agency. The World Factbook, North America; The United States: Economy: Overview Updated February, 2011, https://www.cia.gov/library/publications/the-world-factbook/geos/us.html, accessed February 5, 2011.

17. Graduates warned of record 70 applicants for every job by Jeevan Vasagar, July 6, 2010, The Guardian website, http://www.guardian.co.uk/education/2010/jul/06/graduates-face-tougher-jobs-fight, accessed January 26, 2011.

18. Labor Force Statistics from the Current Population Survey: Unemployment Rate Table, U.S. Department of Labor Bureau of Labor Statistics website, http://data.bls.gov/PDQ/servlet/SurveyOutputServlet?data_tool=latest_numbers&series_id=LNS14000000, accessed January 22, 2009.

Pg. 26 Fact: http://business.time.com/2012/09/13/america-to-banks-were-just-not-that-into-you/, accessed November 18, 2012.

Pg. 32 Fact: http://money.cnn.com/2012/06/14/news/economy/cost-raising-child/index.htm, accessed November 2012.

3

1. CIA – The World Economy Overview, The World Factbook website, updated February, 2011, https://www.cia.gov/library/publications/the-world-factbook/geos/xx.html, accessed February 5, 2011; Global Economic Outlook 2012, The Conference Board, January 2012, Conference Board website, http://www.conference-board.org/data/globaloutlook.cfm, accessed February 2, 2012.

2. Zimbabwe: Mobile phone penetration linked to GDP growth, October 28, 2010, AllAfrica Global Media website, http://allafrica.com/stories/201011011088.html, accessed February 7, 2010; Mobile Phone Adoption in Developing Countries, WikiInvest website, http://www.wikinvest.com/concept/Mobile_Phone_Adoption_in_Developing_Countries, accessed February 8, 2011; Cell phones vital in developing world by Malcolm Foster, January 27, 2007, Washington Post website, http://www .washingtonpost.com/wp-dyn/content/article/2007/01/27/AR2007012700662.html, accessed January 28, 2009; China's mobile users top 600 million: govt, July 24, 2008, Kioskea website, http://en.kioskea.net/actualites/china-s-mobile-users-top-600-million-govt-10563-actualite.php3, accessed January 28, 2009; Telecom sector regaining momentum by Anand Kumar, August 25, 2008, Dawn website, http://www.dawn.com/2008/08/25/ebr15.htm, accessed January 28, 2009; Adam Hwang, China market: Mobile phone users increase to nearly 766 million in February, says MIIT, DigiTimes, April 2, 2010, http://www.digitimes.com/news/a20100402vl200.html, accessed May 4, 2010; Telecom Regulatory Authority of India, Press Release No. 20 /2010, New Delhi, April 26, 2010, Telecom Subscription Data as of March 31, 2010, http://www.trai.gov.in/writereaddata/trai/upload/pressreleases/732/pr26apr10no20.pdf, accessed May 4, 2010.

3. Social Climbers by Lev Grossman and Allie Townsend, January 9, 2012, Time magazine website, http://www.time.com/time/magazine/article/0,9171,2103284,00.html, accessed February 6, 2012; Facebook Statistics, Stats and Facts for 2011, January 18, 2011, Digital Buzz Blog, http://www.digitalbuzzblog.com/facebook-statistics-stats-facts-2011/, accessed February 6, 2012; Commentary on Internet News & Information, Internet Portals & Search Engines, and Internet Social Media, July 19, 2011, American Customer Satisfaction Index website, http://www.theacsi.org/index.php?option=com_content&view=article&id=258:acsi-commentary-july-2011&catid=14:acsi-results&Itemid=336, accessed February 19, 2012; Facebook Tops 500 Million Users Worldwide by Jessica Guynn, July 22, 2010, Los Angeles Times website, http://articles.latimes.com/2010/jul/22/business/la-fi-facebook-20100722, accessed February 19, 2012.

4. Insperiences, Trendwatching newsletter, http://www.trendwatching.com/trends/insperience.htm, accessed January 12, 2006; Ten Key Trends for Chocolate Products, January 23, 2012, Food and Drink Europe website, http://www.foodanddrinkeurope.com/Consumer-Trends/10-key-trends-for-chocolate-products?utm_source=copyright&utm_medium=OnSite&utm_campaign=copyright, accessed February 3, 2012.

5. Trade to expand by 9.5% in 2010 after a dismal 2009, WTO reports, WTO 2010 Press Release, March 26, 2010, WTO website, http://www.wto.org/english/news_e/pres10_e/pr598_e.htm, accessed

February 9, 2010; CIA, The World FactBook, The World Economy: Overview, CIA Website, https://www.cia.gov/library/publications/the-world-factbook/geos/xx.html, updated February 2010, accessed February 9, 2010; The CIA World FactBook, Economy, updated January 26, 2012, CIA FactBook website, https://www.cia.gov/library/publications/the-world-factbook/geos/xx.html, accessed February 3, 2012.

6. What is countertrade? by Neha Gupta, Barter News Weekly website, March 11, 2010, http://www.barternewsweekly.com/2010/03/11/what-is-counter-trade-1851/, accessed February 10, 2010; Countertrade—an innovative approach to marketing by Dan West, Chairman American Countertrade Association, BarterNews issue #36, 1996, http://barternews.com/approach_marketing.htm; Global Offset and Countertrade Association website, http://www.globaloffset.org/index.htm, accessed January 27, 2006.

7. Mattel Issues New Massive China Toy Recall, Associated Press, MSNBC website, August 14, 2007, http://www.msnbc.msn.com/id/20254745/ns/business-consumer_news/, accessed February 10, 2010; As More Toys Are Recalled, Trail Ends in China by Eric S. Lipton and David Barboza, June 19, 2007, The New York Times website, http://www.nytimes.com/2007/06/19/business/worldbusiness/19toys.html, accessed January 29, 2009.

8. Yellin, E. (2009). Your call is (not that) important to us. New York: Simon Schuster, Inc.; Outsourced call centers return, to U.S. homes by Carolyn Beeler, NPR Website, August 25, 2010, http://www.npr.org/templates/story/story.php?storyId=129406588, accessed February 10, 2010.

9. Thinking outside the border by Curtis, Minority Business Entrepreneur, September/October 2005, http://www.export .gov/comm_svc/pdf/MBE_article.pdf.

10. Fiat Nears Stake in Chrysler That Could Lead to takeover by Stacy Meichtry and John Stoll, The Wall Street Journal website, January 20, 2009, http://online.wsj.com/article/SB123238519459294991.html, accessed February 10, 2010; eBay to acquire Skype, Press Release, September 12, 2005, Skype website, http://www.skype.com/company/news/2005/skype_ebay.html, accessed February 10, 2010.

11. Intel to Build Advanced Chip-Making Plant in China by David Barboza, March 27, 2007, The New York Times website, http://www.nytimes.com/2007/03/27/technology/27chip.html, accessed January 30, 2009.

12. Rethink the value of joint ventures by Cynthia Churchwell, Harvard Business School Working Knowledge, May 10, 2004, http://hbswk.hbs.edu/item.jhtml?id=4113&t=globalization.

13. Hyundai grows up by Michael Schuman, Time Global Business, July 2005, http://www.time.com/time/globalbusiness/article/0,9171,1074141,00.html; At 5 feet 10 inches, I was too tall for Tokyo by Cathie Gandel, My Turn, Newsweek, December 12, 2005. Hyundai Bets Big On India and China by Moon Ihlwan, January 30, 2008, BusinessWeek website, http://www.businessweek.com/globalbiz/content/jan2008/gb20080130_061205.htm, accessed January 30, 2009; Maruti, Hyundai, Tata Motors Lose Market Share to Smaller Firms in 2010-11, April 10, 2011, India Times website, http://articles.economictimes.indiatimes.com/2011-04-10

/news/29403269_1_market-share-car-segment-passenger-car, accessed February 6, 2012.

14. U.N.: U.S. Workers Are World's Most Productive, September 3, 2007, MSNBC website, http://www.msnbc.msn.com/id/20572828/ns/business-world_business/t/un-us-workers-are-worlds-most-productive/#.Tyzz3IF-Euc, accessed February 3, 2012; Expedia.Com 2011 Vacation Deprivation Study, October 2011, Expedia website, http://media.expedia.com/media/content/expus/graphics/other/pdf/vacation-deprivation-fact-sheetnov2011.pdf, accessed February 3, 2012; Americans to forfeit $34.3 billion in vacation days by Jessica Dickler, November 30, 2011, CNNMoney, CNN website, http://money.cnn.com/2011/30/pf/unused_vacation/index.htm, accessed February 3, 2012.

15. Rural Market India Brand Equity Foundation, Updated December 10, 2010, IBEF website, http://www.ibef.org/artdispview.aspx?art_id=27581&cat_id=938&in=78, accessed February 10, 2010; Selling to rural India, Springwise Newsletter, June 2003, http://www.springwise.com/newbusinessideas/2003/06/shakti.html; Red herring: selling to the poor, April 11, 2004, The Next Practice website, http://www.thenextpractice.com/news/red_herring_selling_to_the_poor.php; Are you ready for globalization 2.0? by Tim Weber, January 28, 2005, BBC News website, http://news.bbc.co.uk/1/hi/business/4214687.stm.

16. McDonald's country/market sites, http://www.mcdonalds .com./countries.html, accessed February 10, 2011; http://www.dominos.com/Public-EN/Site+Content/Secondary/Inside+Dominos/Pizza+Particulars/International+Speciality+Toppings/; http://slice.seriouseats.com/archives/2008/02/crazy-weird-asian-pizza-crusts-japanese-korean-hong.html; http://recipes.howstuffworks.com/fresh-ideas/dinner-food-facts/favorite-pizza-toppings-in-10-countries.htm; http://slice.seriouseats.com/archives/2008/02/crazy weird-asian-pizza-crusts-japanese-korean-hong-kong.htm; McDonald's No Match for KFC in China as Colonel Rules Fast Food by William Mellor, January 26, 2011, Bloomberg website, http://www.bloomberg.com/news/2011-01-26/mcdonald-s-no-match-for-kfc-in-china-where-colonel-sanders-rules-fast-food.html, accessed February 6, 2012; Morocco Loving the McArabia by Erik German, May 30, 2010, Global Post website, http://www.globalpost.com/dispatch/morocco/090825/morocco-loving-the-mcarabia, accessed February 6, 2012.

17. Internet Usage Statistics, World Internet Users and Population Stats, June 2010, Internet World Stats Website, http://www.internetworldstats.com/stats.htm, accessed February 16, 2011; Asia-Pacific Region Embraces Use of Credit and Debit Cards by Kathy Chu, June 30, 2010, USAToday website, http://www.usatoday.com/money/world/2010-06-30-chinadebt30_CV_N.htm, accessed February 6, 2012; World Internet Statistics, World Internet Users and Population Stats, updated March 31, 2011, World InternetStats website, http://www.internetworldstats.com/stats.htm, accessed February 6, 2012.

18. Doing Business Economy Rankings 2011 Report, World Bank website, http://www.doingbusiness.org/rankings, accessed February 11, 2011.

19. Ski Dubai website, http://www.skidxb.com/, accessed February 3, 2012; Dubai Faces Environmental Problems After Growth by Liz Alderman, October 27, 2010, New York Times website, http://www.nytimes.com/2010/10/28/business/energy-environment/28dubai.html, accessed February 3, 2010; Eco-consciousness amidst Conspicuous Consumption by Nicole Wong, May 3, 2011, Technorati website, http://technorati.com/lifestyle/green/article/eco-consciousness-amidst-conspicuous-consumption/, accessed February 3, 2012.

20. Eighth Annual BSA Global Software Piracy Study, May 2011, Business Software Alliance website, http://Portal.Bsa.Org/Globalpiracy2010/Downloads/Study_Pdf/2010_BSA_Piracy_Study-Standard.Pdf, accessed February 6, 2012.

21. USTR releases 2002 inventory of trade barriers, Press Release, April 2, 2002, http://www.useu.be/Categories/Trade/Apr0202USTRReport-ForeignTradeBarriers.html; U.S. targets non-tariff barriers to global trade, News Release, April 3, 2002, http://www.usconsulate.org.hk/pas/pr/2002/040301.htm.

22. Debt Relief Under the Heavily Indebted Poor Countries (HIPC) Initiative, Factsheet–December 16, 2010, International Monetary Fund website, http://www.imf.org/external/np/exr/facts/hipc.htm, accessed February 11, 2010.

23. Top 10 Exporting Countries Causing the US Trade Deficit by Daniel Workman, April 27, 2010, Suite101 Website, http://www.suite101.com/content/top-10-exporting-countries-causing-the-us-trade-deficit-a226747, accessed February 11, 2011.

24. CIA The World FactBook European Union: The Economy-Overview: CIA website, https://www.cia.gov/library/publications/the-world-factbook/geos/ee.html, updated February, 2011, accessed February 11, 2011.

25. Euro-Free Zone: How Many Drachmas (or Lire or Francs) Will a Post-Euro Cup of Coffee Cost? By Stephen Gandel, January 9, 2012, Time magazine website, http://www.time.com/time/magazine/article/0,9171,2103292,00.html, accessed February 6, 2012.

Pg. 38 Fact: http://www.cnn.com/2012/09/17/world/asia/india-open-toilets-udas/index.html, accessed November, 2012.

Pg. 39 Fact: Workers of the World, Employed by David Bornstein, The New York Times, November 3, 2011, http://opinionator.blogs.nytimes.com/2011/11/03/workers-of-the-world-employed/, accessed November, 2012.

Pg. 49 Fact: http://www.globalissues.org/issue/2/causes-of-poverty, accessed November, 2012.

4

1. The Ethics of American Youth – 2008 summary, Josephson Institute Center for Youth Ethics website, http://charactercounts.org/programs/reportcard/index.html, accessed February 10, 2009; Josephson Institute, Character Study Reveals Predictors of Lying and Cheating, October 29, 2009, http://josephsoninstitute.org/surveys/index.html, accessed May 13, 2010; The Ethics of American Youth. What would Honest Abe say? Josephson Institute Press Release, February 10, 2011, Character Counts website, http://charactercounts.org/programs/reportcard/2010/installment02_report-card_honesty-integrity.html, accessed February 20, 2011.

2. Big Three auto CEOs flew private jets to ask for taxpayer money by Josh Levs, November 19, 2008, CNN website, http://www.cnn.com/2008/US/11/19/autos.ceo.jets/, accessed February 2, 2009.

3. Lawmakers, Questioning Fed Bailout, Seek AIG 'Junket' Refund by Ryan J. Donmoyer – October 9, 2008 Bloomberg website, http://www.bloomberg.com/apps/news?pid=newsarchive&sid=aPlPYw6JXIBU&refer=us, accessed February 21, 2011.

4. Divorce duel reveals Welch's perks, September 6, 2002, CNN Money website, http://money.cnn.com/2002/09/06/news/companies/welch_ge/, accessed February 2, 2009.

5. Why We'll Miss the Disney Trial by Barney Gimbel, Fortune, December 27, 2004, retrieved from CNNMoney website, http://money.cnn.com/magazines/fortune/fortune_archive/2004/12/27/8217949/index.htm; Disney's Basket Cases by Peter Bart, Variety, March 7, 2004, http://www.variety.com/article/VR1117901299.html?categoryid=1&cs=1.

6. National Business Ethics Survey: How Employees View Ethics in Their Organizations, 1994–2005, Ethics Resource Center, October 12, 2005, http://www.ethics.org/research/2005-press-release.asp; Ethics Resource Center, 2009 National Business Ethics Survey, http://www.ethics.org/nbes/files/nbes-final.pdf, (accessed May 14, 2010); 2011 NBES Key Findings, Ethics website, http://www.ethics.org/nbes/findings.html, accessed February 26, 2012.

7. The role of tone from the top by Bob Lane, December 28, 2009, Ethisphere website, http://ethisphere.com/the-role-of-tone-from-the-top/, accessed, February 21, 2011.

8. Complaining Customers Are Good for Business by Bob Leduc, Virtual Marketing Newsletter, May 11, 2004, http://www.marketingsource.com/newsletter/05-11-2004.html.

9. O.B. Ultra Tampons Are Coming Back, and the Company Apologizes with a Song by Jeannine Stein, December 8, 2011, Los Angeles Times website, http://articles.latimes.com/2011/dec/08/news/la-heb-ob-tampons-return-20111208, accessed February 29, 2012; o.b. video apology message, http://articles.latimes.com/2011/dec/08/news/la-heb-ob-tampons-return-20111208, accessed February 29, 2012.

10. The year in technology industry apologies by Bob Brown, Network World, 12/01/2009, Network World website, http://www.networkworld.com/slideshows/2009/120109-apologies.html#slide2, accessed February 22, 2011; Amazon Erases Orwell Books From Kindle by Brad Stone July 17, 2009, New York Times website, http://www.nytimes.com/2009/07/18/technology/companies/18amazon.html, accessed February 22, 2011; The Customer Is Always Right by Daniel Lyons, December 21, 2009, Newseeek website, http://www.newsweek.com/2009/12/20/the-customer-is-always-right.html, accessed February 22, 2011.

11. Open letter to iPhone customers, Apple website, http://www.apple.com/hotnews/openiphoneletter/, accessed February 3, 2009; Apple's customer satisfaction up despite struggling industry by Jeff Smykil, August 19, 2008, Ars Technica website, http://arstechnica.com/apple/news/2008/08/apples-customer-satisfaction-up-despite-struggling-industry.ars, accessed February 3, 2009; The American Customer Satisfaction Index Scores by Company, Personal Computers through 2011, the ACSI website, http://www.theacsi.org/index.php?option=com_content&view=article&id=149&catid=&Itemid=214&c=Apple+, accessed March 20, 2012.

12. Giving USA 2010, The Center on Philanthropy at Indiana University, Giving USA Website,

http://www.givingusareports.org/products/GivingUSA_2010_ExecSummary_Print.pdf, accessed February 24, 2011; Giving USA 2011 Executive Summary, The Annual Report on Philanthropy for 2010, Giving USA website, http://www.givingusareports.org/products/GivingUSA_2011_ExecSummary_Print.pdf, accessed March 22, 2012.

13. Charitable giving estimated to be $306.39 billion in 2007, June 23, 2008, Planned Giving Center website, http://www.pgdc.com/pgdc/us-charitable-giving-estimated-be-30639-billion-2007, accessed February 4, 2009; Corporate donors adjust to economic slump by Ret Boney, September 15, 2008, Philanthropy Journal website, http://www.philanthropyjournal.org/resources/special-reports/corporate-giving/corporate-donors-adjust-economic-slump, accessed February 4, 2009; Should Your Company Pay for You to Volunteer Abroad? By Kasia Moreno, March 21, 2012, Forbes website, http://www.forbes.com/sites/kasiamoreno/2012/03/21/should-your-company-pay-for-you-to-volunteer-abroad/, accessed March 23, 2012.

14. The Dirty Little Secrets of Search by David Segal, February 12, 2011, New York Times website, http://www.nytimes.com/2011/02/13/business/13search.html, accessed February 28, 2011.

15. Has Green Stopped Giving? by Jack Neff, November 9, 2010, AdvertisingAge website, http://adage.com/article/news/consumer-revolt-sprouting-green-friendly-products/146944/, accessed February 25, 2011; Buzzword: Green fatigue by Kimberly Janeway, Home and Garden Blog, Consumer Reports website, http://blogs.consumerreports.org/home/2010/11/buzzword-green-fatigue-.html, accessed February 25, 2011.

16. Bad and Good Environmental Marks for McDonald's by Donalla Meadows, Sustainability Institute website, http://www.sustainer.org/dhm_archive/search.php?display_article=vn304mcdonaldsed, accessed May 15, 2005.

17. 'Carbon Footprint' Gaining Business Attention, October 18, 2006, Press Release, Conference Board website, http://www.conference-board.org/UTILITIES/pressDetail.cfm?press_ID=2985, accessed February 4, 2009; Green goal of 'carbon neutrality' hits limit by Jeffery Ball, December 30, 2008, Wall Street Journal website, http://online.wsj.com/article/SB123059880241541259.html, accessed February 4, 2009; How green is my orange? by Andrew Martin, January 22, 2009, New York Times website, http://www.nytimes.com/2009/01/22/business/22pepsi.html?_r=1&scp=1&sq=How%20green%20is%20my%20orange&st=cse, accessed February 4, 2009.

18. U.S. Corporations Size Up Their Carbon Footprints by Rachel King, June 1, 2009, Bloomberg BusinessWeek, BusinessWeek website, http://www.businessweek.com/technology/content/jun2009/tc2009061_692661.htm, accessed February 24, 2011.

19. Marketing, Business and Sustainable Development: A Global Guide, Business and Sustainable Development website, http://www.bsdglobal.com/markets/green_marketing.asp, accessed February 4, 2009.

20. Transparency International Corruptions Perceptions Index 2020, Transparency International website, http://www.transparency.org/policy_research/surveys_indices/cpi/2010/results, accessed March 24, 2012.

21. Bribe Payers Index 2011, Transparency International website, http://bpi.transparency.org/results/, accessed March 24, 2012.

22. Newsweek 2011 Green Rankings, The Daily Beast website, October 16, 2011, http://www.thedailybeast.com/topics/green-rankings.html, accessed March 24, 2012.

23. Selling to the Poor by Kay Johnson, Time Bonus Section, May 2005; The Payoff for Investing in Poor Countries by C.K. Prahalad and Allen Hammond, Harvard Business School Working Knowledge website, http://hbswk.hbs.edu/item.jhtml?id=3180&t=nonprofit&noseek=one.

24. Gap, Inc. Social Reporting Award, December 20, 2004, Business Ethics website, http://www.business-ethics.com/annual.htm#Gap%20Inc.

25. Values in Tension: Ethics Away from Home by Thomas Donaldson, Harvard Business Review, September/October 1996.

Pg. 60 Fact: http://knowledge.wharton.upenn.edu/article.cfm?articleid=2966, accessed November 2012.

Pg. 64 Fact: http://www.ethicsworld.org/ethicsandemployees/nbes.php, accessed November 2012.

Pg. 65 Fact: http://www.epa.gov/epawaste/nonhaz/municipal/index.htm, accessed November 2012.

5

1. Body Language Tactics That Sway Interviewers by Eugene Raudsepp, The Wall Street Journal CareerJournal, December 5, 2002, http://www.careerjournal.com/jobhunting/interviewing/20021205-raudsepp.html.

2. How to dress for an interview by Alison Doyle, About website, http://jobsearch.about.com/od/interviewsnetworking/a/dressforsuccess.htm, accessed March 5, 2011; CTRL+ALT+DEL: The 15 Worst-Dressed Men Of Silicon Valley by Clover Hope, August 3, 2011, GQ website, http://www.gq.com/style/profiles/201108/worst-dressed-men-silicon-valley-mark-zuckerberg#slide=1, accessed May 20, 2012.

3. Social media in China: The same, but different by Thomas Crampton, February 25, 2011, Memeburn Website, http://memeburn.com/2011/02/social-media-in-china-the-same-but-different/, accessed March 4, 2011; INFOGRAPHIC: How Chinese Citizens Use Social Media by George Stroumboulopoulos, December 1, 2011, CBC/Radio Canada website, http://www.cbc.ca/strombo/world/infographic-how-chinese-citizens-use-social-media.html, accessed May 20, 2012.

4. The Listener Wins by Michael Purdy, Monster contributing writer, Monster.com, http://featuredreports.monster.com/listen/overview/, accessed August 22, 2006; The Human Side of Business by Stephen D. Boyd, Agency Sales Magazine, February 2004, page 35, accessed via Infotrac College Edition.

5. We Learn More by Listening Than Talking by Harvey Mackay, The Daily Herald, January 16, 2005, page E6[SB14], http://old.heraldextra.com/modules.php?op=modload&name=News&file=article&sid=45313; Listening Factoids, International Listening Association, http://www.listen.org/pages/factoids.html, accessed August 22, 2006.

6. The Human Side of Business by Stephen D. Boyd, Agency Sales Magazine, February 2004, page 35, accessed via Infotrac College Edition;

Learn to Listen: Closing the Mouth and Opening the Ears Facilitates Effective Communication by Marjorie Brody, Incentive, May 2004, page 57, accessed via Business and Company Resource Center.

7. Shanghai Is Trying to Untangle the Mangled English of Chinglish, by Andrew Jacobs The New York Times, May 2, 2010, New York Times website, http://www.nytimes.com/2010/05/03/world/asia/03chinglish.html?pagewanted=1, accessed May 20, 2010; China Clamping Down on Bad English Translations by Peter Leo, March 17, 2012, Pittsburgh Post-Gazette website, http://www.post-gazette.com/stories/local/morning-file/china-clamping-down-on-bad-english-translations-455101/, accessed May 20, 2012.

8. Sticky Business Etiquette Questions & Answers, 2012, Robert Half website, http://www.roberthalf.us/BusinessEtiquetteQuestions, accessed May 20, 2012.

9. Edward P. Bailey, Writing and Speaking at Work, (Prentice Hall, 2005), pages 82–89.

10. Presenting Effective Presentations with Visual Aids, U.S. Department of Labor, Occupational Safety and Health Administration, http://www.osha.gov/doc/outreachtraining/htmlfiles/traintec.html, accessed August 22, 2006.

11. Bringing the cloud with you by Philip Tucker, March 31, 2008, Google Docs Blog, http://googledocs.blogspot.com/2008/03/bringing-cloud-with-you.html, accessed February 13, 2009; Living in the Clouds by Brian Braiker, June 10, 2008, Newsweek website, http://www.newsweek.com/id/140864, accessed February 13, 2009; Comparing Google Docs with competing cloud computing applications by Michael Miller, February 9, 2009, InformIT website, http://www.informit.com/articles/article.aspx?p=1323244&seqNum=3, accessed February 13, 2009.

Pg. 73 Fact: http://robertoigarza.files.wordpress.com/2008/11/rep-effective-employee-communication-ww-2008.pdf, accessed November 2012.

Pg. 77 Fact: http://www.huffingtonpost.com/2012/02/10/teens-email-use-study_n_1268470.html, accessed November 2012.

6

1. Why States Should Adopt the Revised Uniform Limited Liability Company Act (2006), National Conference of Commissioners on Uniform State Laws website, http://www.nccusl.org/Update/uniformact_why/uniformacts-why-ullca.asp, accessed January 28, 2011.

2. U.S. Census Bureau. The 2011 Statistical Abstract of the United States Tables 743 and 744: http://www.census.gov/compendia/statab/2011/tables/11s0744.pdf, accessed January 23, 2011.

3. U.S. Census Bureau. The 2011 Statistical Abstract of the United States Tables 743 and 744: http://www.census.gov/compendia/statab/2011/tables/11s0744.pdf, accessed January 23, 2011.

4. U.S. Census Bureau. The 2011 Statistical Abstract of the United States Table 743: http://www.census.gov/compendia/statab/2011/tables/11s0744.pdf, accessed January 23, 2011.

5. Naming Your Business, Business Owner's Toolkit website, http://www.toolkit.com/small_business_guide/sbg.aspx?nid=P01_4800; Choosing the Right Name for My Corporation or Limited Liability Company, SCORE website, http://

www.score.org/leg_choosing_name.html; Business Name Registration (Doing Business As), Business.gov website, http://www.business.gov/register/business-name/dba.html.

6. Delaware Division of Corporations: http://www.corp.delaware.gov/, accessed January 26, 2011.

7. Setting Up a One Person Corporation by Karen Klein, November 7, 2007, *Business Week* website, http://www.businessweek.com/smallbiz/content/nov2007/sb2007117_803605.htm.

8. The Ben & Jerry's Law: Principles Before Profit, by John Tozzi, *Bloomberg Business Week*, April 26, 2010, pp. 65-66; Maryland Signs Benefit Corporation Law, by Tasha Petty, Little Green Submarine website, http://www.littlegreensubmarine.com/maryland-signs-benefit-corporation-law/; Maryland First State in Union to Pass Benefit Corporation Legislation, CSR Newswire website, http://www.csrwire.com/press/press_release/29332-Maryland-First-State-in-Union-to-Pass-Benefit-Corporation-Legislation.

9. Say-on-Pay Votes Show Results, by J. Lublin, *Wall Street Journal*, March 1, 2012, http://online.wsj.com/article/SB100014240529702045714045772556415315165 10.html; Dismay on Pay, by S. Johnson, *CFO*, March 2012, pages 25–26; Lessons Learned: The Inaugural Year of Say-on-Pay, by A. Sheehan & A. Mastagni, *The Corporate Governance Advisor*, May/June 2012; For CEOs, Pay Lags Behind Results; Missed Targets, Rise in Scrutiny Offset Profit, Revenue Increases, Survey Finds, by S. Thurm, *The Wall Street Journal*, March 26, 2012, *The Wall Street Journal* website, http://online.wsj.com/article/SB1000142405270230472440457729948348236 0926.html, accessed June 3, 2012; Say on Pay Best Practices for 2012, by J. Wilson & J. Agen, *The Corporate Board*, March/April 2012, pages 6–10.

10. Why States Should Adopt the Revised Uniform Limited Liability Company Act (2006), National Conference of Commissioners on Uniform State Laws website, http://www.nccusl.org/Update/uniformact_why/uniformacts-why-ullca.asp, accessed January 22, 2011.

11. How Apple Sidesteps Billions in Taxes, by C. Huhigg & D. Kocieniewski, *The New York Times*, April 28, 2012, page A1; Inside Google's $1 Billion-a-Year Tax Cutting Strategy, by J. Drucker & H. Zschiegner, Bloomberg Business-Week website, October 21, 2010, http://www.businessweek.com/technology/google-tax-cut/google-terminal.html, accessed June 2, 2012; Apple's Tax Avoidance: Evil Scheming, Good Business, or Both? by S. Gustin, *Time*, May 1, 2012, http://business.time.com/2012/05/01/apples-tax-avoidance-evil-scheming-good-business-or-both/, accessed June 2, 2012; The Double Irish and the Dutch Sandwich: The Explainer's Field Guide to Exotic Tax Dodges, by J. Lowder, Slate, http://www.slate.com/articles/news_and_politics/explainer/2011/04/the_double_irish_and_the_dutch_sandwich.html, accessed April 14, 2011; Apple to Pay Dividend, Plans $10 Billion Buyback; Company to Maintain a 'War Chest' for Strategic Opportunities, by I. Sherr & S. Tibken, *The Wall Street Journal*, March 19, 2012, http://online.wsj.com/article/SB1000142405270230472440457729107128985780 2.html, accessed June 2, 2012.

12. Why States Should Adopt the Revised Uniform Limited Liability Company Act (2006), National Conference of Commissioners on Uniform State Laws website, http://www.nccusl.org/Update/

uniformact_why/uniformacts-why-ullca.asp, accessed January 22, 2011.

13. Franchise Business Outlook: 2011, prepared by PwC for the International Franchise Association Educational Foundation, IFA website, http://emarket.franchise.org/News_Release/Outlook%20report%202011.pdf; Census Bureau's First Release of Comprehensive Franchise Data Shows Franchises Make Up More Than 10% of Employer Businesses, U.S. Census Bureau website, http://www.census.gov/newsroom/releases/archives/economic_census/cb10-141.html, accessed January 30, 2011; Franchise Business Economic Outlook: March 2012, by IHS Global Insight, International Franchise Association, March 22, 2011, http://emarket.franchise.org/FranchiseBusinessReport2012.pdf.

14. Entrepreneur.com website pages for individual franchisors, http://www.entrepreneur.com/franchises/mcdonalds/282570-0.html; http://www.entrepreneur.com/franchises/subway/282839-0.html; http://www.entrepreneur.com/franchises/curves/282265-0.html, accessed June 1, 2012.

15. Fit for Franchising by Taylor Mallory, *Pink* Magazine June/July 2007, pinkmagazine.com website, http://www.pinkmagazine.com/franchise/women/2007/burzynski.html; Franchising Attracts More Women, Minorities by Julie Bennett, Startup Journal, accessed through Entrepreneur.com website, http://www.entrepreneur.com/franchises/franchisezone/startupjournal/article61324.html; Female Franchisors Few and Far Between by Julie M. Young, e-magnify.com website, https://www.e-magnify.com/resources_articlearchiveresults.asp?categoryID=18; Fit to Be a Franchisee: Many Businesswomen Choose Franchises that Connect With Personal Interests by Nancy Lacewell, June 7, 2006 Business First of Louisville website, http://www.bizjournals.com/louisville/stories/2006/05/22/story2.html.

16. Boosting Diversity in Franchising by Joan Szabo, December 5, 2006, *Franchise Update* website, http://www.franchise-update.com/article/188/.

17. Bridging the Gap Between the Minority Community and the Franchising Industry, Minority Franchising website, http://www.minorityfranchising.com/, accessed January 20, 2011; MinorityFran, International Franchise Association website, http://www.franchise.org/files/MinorityFran%20Broch%20by%20page.pdf, accessed January 20, 2011.

18. Subway, Entrepreneur.com website, http://www.entrepreneur.com/franchises/subway/282839-2.html.

19. Franchise Rule Compliance Guide, Federal Trade Commission website, http://www.ftc.gov/bcp/edu/pubs/business/franchise/bus70.pdf, pages 20, 102-103, and 121.

20. 10 Questions to Ask a Franchise Broker/Consultant Before You Work with Them, The Franchise King website, November 14, 2007, http://thefranchiseking.com/10-questions-to-ask-franchise-brokers, accessed June 3, 2012; Franchising—Chain Links: Franchise Consultants can Help Prospective Buyers Find the Right Match, by L. Angus, *The Wall Street Journal*, June 13, 2011, R7.

21. U.S. Census Bureau. The 2011 Statistical Abstract of the United States Table 743, http://www.census.gov/compendia/statab/2011/tables/11s0744.pdf, accessed January 23, 2011; Recession, Layoffs Fuel Many to Start Small Businesses, by Laura Petrecca, *USA Today* website,

http://www.usatoday.com/money/smallbusiness/startup/week1-exploring-small-business-options.htm.

22. Franchise Business Outlook: 2011, prepared by PwC for the International Franchise Association Educational Foundation, IFA website, http://emarket.franchise.org/News_Release/Outlook%20report%202011.pdf.
Pg. 90 Fact: *The Weekly Standard*, April, 2012, http://www.weeklystandard.com/blogs/ge-filed-57000-page-tax-return-paid-no-taxes-14-billion-profits_609137.html.

7

1. New Business Startups Declined in 2011, Annual Kauffman Study Shows, March 19, 2012, Kauffman website, http://www.kauffman.org/research-and-policy/kiea-2012-infographic.aspx, accessed June 12, 2012.

2. Millennial Women Are Burning Out at Work By 30... And It's Great For Business by Meghan Casserly, January 12, 2012, Forbes website, http://www.forbes.com/sites/meghancasserly/2012/01/12/millennial-women-burning-out-great-for-business-entrepreneurs/, accessed June 12, 2012.

4. The *Forbes* 400 edited by Matthew Miller and Duncan Greenberg, September 17, 2008, *Forbes* website, http://www.forbes.com/2008/09/16/forbes-400-billionaires-lists-400list08_cx_mn_0917richamericans_land.html, accessed February 15, 2009.

5. Discover Polls Reveal True Character of the American *Entrepreneur*, October 22, 2007, Press Release, Discover Financial Services website, http://investorrelations.discoverfinancial.com/phoenix.zhtml?c=204177&p=irol-newsArticle&ID=1065373&highlight=, accessed February 15, 2009.

5a. Appsurd: In Silicon Valley, It's Hard to Make a Joke by Geoffrey A. Fowler, June 5, 2012, *The Wall Street Journal* website, http://online.wsj.com/article/SB1000142405270230350550457740428411 7534706.html, accessed June 13, 2012.

6. More than Half of Small Business Owners Work at Least Six-Day Weeks, Still Find Time for Personal Life, Wells Fargo News Release, August 9, 2005, https://www.wellsfargo.com/press/20050809_GallupPersonalLife. Discover Polls Reveal True Character of the American Entrepreneur, October 22, 2007, Press Release, Discover Financial Services website, http://investorrelations.discoverfinancial.com/phoenix.zhtml?c=204177&p=irol-newsArticle&ID=1065373&highlight=, accessed February 15, 2009; Small Business Owners Working Longer Hours, May 26, 2009, Rent to Own website, http://rtoonline.com/Content/Article/may09/smal-business-owners-work-hours-survey-052609.asp, accessed June 12, 2012.

7. Entrepreneurial Risk and Market Entry, by Brian Wu and Anne Marie Knott, SBA Office of Advocacy, January 2005, http://www.sba.gov/advo/research/wkpbw249.pdf.

8. Personality Test for Entrepreneurship Success, by Andy Swan, Small Biz Survival website, http://www.smallbizsurvival.com/2008/08/personality-test-for-entrepreneurship.html, posted August 4, 2008, accessed April 3, 2011.

9. Failure: Use It as a Springboard to Success, U.S. SBA Online Library, no attribution, http://www.sba.gov/library/successXIII/19-Failure-Use-it.doc, accessed December 28, 2005.

10. How to Spend It by Rebecca Dana, May 28, 2012, The Daily Beast website, http://www.thedailybeast.com/newsweek/2012/05/20/how-will-zuckerberg-spend-his-millions.html, accessed June 13, 2012.

11. Failure: Use It as a Springboard to Success, U.S. SBA Online Library, no attribution, http://www.sba.gov/library/successXIII/19-Failure-Use-it.doc, accessed December 28, 2005.

12. What Makes Them Tick, by Keith McFarland, Inc 500, 2005, Inc website, http://www.inc.com/resources/inc500/2005/articles/20051001/tick.html; Bootstrapping Your Startup? Make Money Before You Spend It, by Kwame Kuadey, June 12, 2012, Young Entrepreneurs Council website, http://theyec.org/bootstrapping-your-startup-make-money-before-you-spend-it/, accessed June 12, 2012.

13. How to finance a new business, April 2008, Consumer Reports website, http://www.consumerreports.org/cro/money/credit-loan/how-to-finance-a-new-business/overview/how-to-finance-a-new-business-ov.htm, accessed March 18, 2011.

14. Credit Cards Replace Small Business Loans, by John Tozzi, August 20, 2008, *Business Week* website, http://www.businessweek.com/small-biz/content/aug2008/sb20080820_288348.htm?chan=smallbiz_smallbiz+index+page_top+small+business+stories, accessed February 15, 2009.

14a. Bank Loans to Small Business Fall to 12-Year Low by Jacob Fenton, December 16, 2011, MSNBC website, http://bottomline.msnbc.msn.com/_news/2011/12/16/9470807-bank-loans-to-small-business-fall-to-12-year-low?lite, accessed June 12, 2012.

15. Start-up Information, updated April 28, 2008, Delaware Small Business Development Center website, http://www.delawaresbdc.org/DocumentMaster.aspx?doc=1003#6, accessed February 15, 2009.

16. Financial Assistance, Small Business Administration website, http://www.sba.gov/services/financialassistance/index.html, accessed February 15, 2009.

17. The Angel Investor Market in Q1Q2 2011: A Return to the Seed Stage by Jeffrey Sohl, Center for Venture Research, October 11, 2011, University of New Hampshire website, http://wsbe.unh.edu/sites/default/files/q1q2_2011_analysis_report.pdf, accessed June 12, 2012; Angel Investments Up 40% by Abby Tracy, March 13, 2012, Inc. website, http://wire.inc.com/2012/03/13/angel-investments-up-40/, accessed June 12, 2012.

18. The Steady, Strategic Assent of jetBlue Airways, Strategic Management Knowledge at Wharton, December 14, 2005–January 10, 2006, http://knowledge.wharton.upenn.edu/article/1342.cfm; Charging Ahead, by Bobbie Gossage, January 2004, Inc. Magazine, http://www.inc.com/magazine/20040101/gettingstarted.html.

19. Annual Venture Investment Dollars Increase 22% Over Prior Year, According to the Moneytree Report, January 20, 2012, PriceWaterhouseCoopers website, https://www.pwcmoneytree.com/MTPublic/ns/moneytree/filesource/exhibits/11Q4MTPressrelease.pdf, accessed June 12, 2012.

20. Amplestuff website, http://www.amplestuff.com/; Kazoo v. Walmart, Reveries Magazine, November 29, 2005, http://www.reveries.com/?p=232.

21. Odd Jobs: Prosthetic Dog-Testicle Maker by Eric Spitznagel, April 25, 2012, Bloomberg Businessweek website, http://www.businessweek.com/articles/2012-04-25/odd-jobs-prosthetic-dog-testicle-maker#disqus_thread, accessed June 14, 2012; 6 Weird But Successful Small Business Ideas by Heather Levin, September 11, 2011, MoneyCrashers website, http://www.moneycrashers.com/weird-successful-small-business-ideas/, accessed June 13, 2012; Kids Up North: Rent-a-Chicken in Traverse City Makes Urban Farming Child's Play by Kate Bassett, May 24, 2010, MY-North website, http://www.mynorth.com/My-North/May-2010/Kids-Up-North-Rent-a-Chicken-in-Traverse-City-Makes-Urban-Farming-Child-rsquos-Play/, accessed June 15, 2012.

22. E-Commerce Award—June 2002, Anything Left-Handed website, http://www.anythingleft-handed.co.uk/pressreleases.html.

23. Focus on Success, Not Failure by Rhonda Abrams, May 7, 2004, USA Today website money section, http://www.usatoday.com/money/smallbusiness/columnist/abrams/2004-05-06-success_x.htm.

24. Is Entrepreneurship for You? U.S. Small Business Administration, http://www.sba.gov/starting_business/startup/areyouready.html, accessed December 15, 2005.

25. Committee Examines Ways to Ease Growing Regulatory Burden on Small Businesses, July 30, 2008, U.S. House of Representatives Press Release, House of Representatives website, http://www.house.gov/smbiz/PressReleases/2008/pr-7-30-08-regulatory.html, accessed February 15, 2009.

26. Entrepreneurship in the 21st Century, Conference Proceedings, March 26, 2004, SBA Office of Advocacy and the Kauffman Foundation, http://www.sba.gov/advo/stats/proceedings_a.pdf; Health Care Costs Surface in Economic Stimulus Debate by Sharon McLoone, February 10, 2009, *Washington Post* website, http://voices.washingtonpost.com/small-business/2009/02/health_care_costs_surface_in_e.html, accessed February 15, 2009.

27. Business Plan Basics, U.S. SBA, http://www.sba.gov/starting_business/planning/basic.html, accessed February 15, 2009.

28. Top 10 Accidental Inventions, Science Channel website, http://science.discovery.com/brink/top-ten/accidental-inventions/inventions-01.html, accessed March 22, 2011.

29. Frequently Asked Questions, SBA Office of Advocacy, updated September 2009, SBA website, http://www.sba.gov/advo/stats/sbfaq.pde, accessed June 3, 2010.

30. Frequently Asked Questions, SBA Office of Advocacy, Updated September 2008, SBA website, http://www.sba.gov/advo/stats/sbfaq.pdf, accessed February 17, 2009.

31. Frequently Asked Questions, SBA Office of Advocacy, Updated September 2008, SBA website, http://www.sba.gov/advo/stats/sbfaq.pdf, accessed February 17, 2009.

32. Small Business Drives Inner City Growth and Jobs, NewsRelease, October 11, 2005, U.S. SBA Office of Advocacy, http://www.sba.gov/advo/press/05-32.html.

33. Global Entrepreneurship Monitor, 2008 Executive Report by Niels Bosma, Zoltan J. Acs, Erkko Autio, Alicia Coduras, and Jonathan Levie, Babson College and London School of Economics, http://www.gemconsortium.org/article.aspx?id=76, published January 15, 2009, accessed February 17, 2009.

34. Exclusive Survey Results: Tons of College Students Are Starting Businesses—And A Lot Are Doing It Because They Can't Find Jobs by Alyson Shontell, February 17, 2011, Business Insider website, http://www.businessinsider.com/youth-entrepreneurship-council-2011-2?op=1, accessed March 21, 2011.

Pg. 107 Fact: Americans Trust Small-Business Owners Most on Job Creation, November 3, 2011, Gallup website, http://www.gallup.com/poll/150545/americans-trust-small-business-owners-job-creation.aspx, accessed November, 2012.

Pg. 110 Fact: http://www.forbes.com/sites/johngreathouse/2012/06/05/business-tips-from-college-dropouts-zuckerberg-jobs-gates-dell-ellison-branson-and-disney/, and http://www.gemconsortium.org/docs/download/260, accessed November 2012.

Pg. 112 Fact: http://www.gemconsortium.org/docs/download/2313, accessed November 2012.

8

1. 2012 Global Fraud Study: Report to the Nations on Occupational Fraud and Abuse, Association of Certified Fraud Examiners, http://www.acfe.com/uploadedFiles/ACFE_Website/Content/rttn/2012-report-to-nations.pdf, accessed June 5, 2012; The Not-So-Usual Suspects, by B. Carlino, *Accounting Today*, December 2011, p. 9; Fraud Prevention: How to Implement Internal Controls to Prevent Employee Theft, by S. Ostrowski, *Smart Business Cleveland*, February 2012, p. 90; Employee Theft, Fraud Pose Growing Challenge, by J. Wojcik, *Business Insurance*, October 17, 2011, p. 6.

2. Scandal Sheet, CBS Marketwatch website, http://www.marketwatch.com/news/features/scandal_sheet.asp; Corporate Scandal Sheet, Citizen Works website, http://www.citizenworks.org/enron/corp-scandal.php; The Corporate Scandal Sheet, by Penelope Patsuris, *Forbes*, August 26, 2002, http://www.forbes.com/2002/07/25/accountingtracker.html.

3. Change Generation: Jessica Mah and inDinero.com Make Business Finance Simple, FastCompany, January 11, 2011, http://www.fastcompany.com/article/change-generation-jessica-mah-indinerocom, accessed June 6, 2012; Can a 20-Year-Old Help You Track Your Finances? by A. Gardella, *The New York Times*, September 29, 2010, http://boss.blogs.nytimes.com/2010/09/29/can-a-20-year-old-help-you-track-your-finances/, accessed June 6, 2012; How a 20 Year Old Female Entrepreneur Raises a Million Dollars and Gets Sh*t Done, by F. Gruber, Techcocktail.com, September 2, 2010, http://techcocktail.com/how-a-20-year-old-female-entrepreneur-raises-a-million-dollars-and-gets-sht-done-2010-09, accessed June 6, 2012; Indinero Makes Small Business Finances a Snap, J. Pepitone, CNNMoney, September 10, 2010, http://money.cnn.com/2010/09/10/smallbusiness/indinero/index.htm?section=money_smbusiness, accessed June 6, 2010.

4. Off-Balance Sheet Financing, riskglossary.com website, http://www.riskglossary.com/link/off_balance_sheet_finance.htm; Enron and the Use and Abuse of Special Purpose Entities in Corporate Structures, by Steven L. Schwarcz,

AEI-Brookings Joint Center for Regulatory Studies, reg-markets.org website, http://reg-markets.org/admin/authorpdfs/redirect-safely.php?fname=../pdffiles/phpUH.pdf; The Fall of Enron, Special Report, the Houston Chronicle website, http://www.chron.com/news/specials/enron/timeline.html; Accounting Issues at Enron, by Alan Reinstein and Thomas R. Weirich, *The CPA Journal* website, http://www.nysscpa.org/cpajournal/2002/1202/features/f122002.htm; Causes of the Financial Crisis, by Viral Acharya, the Commission on Growth and Development website, http://www.growthcommissionblog.org/content/causes-of-the-financial-crisis.

5. Mission statement on PCAOB website, http://www.pcaobus.org/index.aspx.

6. Form 10-K, Apple, United States Securities and Exchange Commission, January 25, 2012; Form 10-K, Groupon, United States Securities and Exchange Commission, March 30, 2012; Form 10-K, Ford Motor Company, United States Securities and Exchange Commission, February 21, 2012; Taobao to Launch Local Deals on Group-Buying Website, by L. Chao, *The Wall Street Journal*, February 23, 2011, http://online.wsj.com/article/SB10001424052748703775704576161340839989996.html, accessed June 7, 2012; U.S. Coupon Site Clicks on Europe–Groupon Buys Germany's CityDeal to Expand Base of Subscribers Who Get Daily Emails for Discounts at Local Businesses, by G. Fowler, *The Wall Street Journal*, May 17, 2010, B4; Groupon versus the World, by R. Underwood, *Inc.*, October 2010, 116 -118.

7. Albrecht, Stice, Stice, and Swain, *Accounting Concepts and Applications*, 9th ed. (Cengage Learning), p. 758.

8. Technology 2012 Preview: Part 1, by J. Drew, *Journal of Accountancy*, November 2011, p. 46-52; Top Cloud Computing Trends for 2012, by G. Hinchcliffe, Shoebooks Online Accounting Blog, April 11, 2012, http://onlineaccountingblog.shoebooks.com.au/2012/04/11/top-cloud-computing-trends-for-2012/, accessed June 8, 2012; Risks versus Value in Outsourced Cloud Computing, by R. Tisnovsky, *Financial Executive*, November 2010, p. 64-65.

9. *The Essentials of Finance and Budgeting*, Harvard Business School Press, Boston, MA, 2005, pp. 177–181.

10. Accountants and Auditors, Occupational Outlook Handbook, Bureau of Labor Statistics, U.S. Department of Labor, http://www.bls.gov/ooh/Business-and-Financial/Accountants-and-auditors.htm, accessed June 11, 2012.

Pg. 125 Fact: A Beginner's Guide to Financial Statements, SEC website, http://www.sec.gov/investor/pubs/begfinstmtguide.htm accessed March 29, 2009. ("Read The Footnotes" finished seventh in the 2004 Kentucky Derby.)

9

1. See, for example, Moyer, McGuigan, and Rao, *Fundamentals of Contemporary Financial Management, 2nd ed.* (South-Western, Cengage Learning), p. 3; Brigham and Houston, *Fundamentals of Financial Management, 11th ed.*, p. 2.

2. Numbers, *BusinessWeek*, February 9, 2009, p. 13.

3. Joseph E. Stiglitz, *Freefall* (W. W. Norton, 2010), pp. 31–32; Financial Crisis Inquiry Commission, *Financial Crisis Inquiry Report*, (Official Government Edition, January, 2011) pp. 109–114.

4. A Closer Look, by S. Gale, PM Network, July 2011, p. 30–33; A Short (Sometimes Profitable) History of Private Equity, by J. Gordon, *The Wall Street Journal*, January 18, 2012, p. A15; How Private Equity Works, by J. Macey, *The Wall Street Journal*, January 13, 2012, p. A13; The Private Equity/Sustainability Link; David M. Rubenstein of Carlyle Group on Why the Two Can Go Together, by J. Forsyth, *The Wall Street Journal*, March 26, 2012, http://online.wsj.com/article/SB1000142405270230463640457729965255321 9204.html, accessed June 9, 2012.

5. The approximate "finance charge" of not taking the discount on credit can be computed using the following formula:

$$\text{Cost of Not Taking discount} = \frac{\%\ \text{discount}}{(100 - \%\ \text{discount})} \times \frac{365}{(\text{Credit\_Period} - \text{Discount\_Period})}$$

where % discount is the discount the buyer receives for paying on or before the last day the discount is available, the Credit Discount Period is the number of days before payment of full invoice amount is due.

6. Financial Services Used by Small Businesses: Evidence from the 2003 Survey of Small Business Finances, by Traci Mack and John D. Wolken, *Federal Reserve Bulletin*, October 2006, p. A181.

7. Annual Asset-Based Lending and Factoring Surveys, 2009, Commercial Finance Association website, https://www.cfa.com/eweb/docs/2009_survey_nonmember.pdf accessed March 5, 2011.

8. Commercial Paper Funding Facility, New York Federal Reserve Bank website, http://www.federalreserve.gov/monetarypolicy/cpff.htm; New York Fed CPFF FAQs, New York Federal Reserve Bank website, http://www.newyorkfed.org/markets/cpff_faq.html , accessed March 15, 2010.

9. Table B-90: Corporate Profits with Inventory Valuation and Capital Consumption Adjustments, 1962-2010, Economic Report of the President, 2011, GPOaccess website, http://www.gpoaccess.gov/eop/tables11.html.

10. Berkshire Hathaway Inc., Historical Prices, Google Prices, http://www.google.com/finance/historical?cid=4376&startdate=Jun+13%2C+2011&enddate=Jun+11%2C+2012&num=30, accessed June 11, 2012.

11. Why do companies issue debt and bonds? Can't they just borrow from the bank?, Investopedia website, http://www.investopedia.com/ask/answers/05/reasonforcorporatebonds.asp.

12. Facebook Workers Shrug Off IPO, by G. Fowler & P. Tam, *The Wall Street Journal*, May 23, 2012, p. B4; Facebook's Early Buyers Burned, Too, by J. Light, *The Wall Street Journal*, June 7, 2002, http://online.wsj.com/article/SB1000142405270230350640457744865187720 4794.html, accessed June 10, 2012; Inside Fumbled Facebook Offering, by S. Raice, A. Das, & G. Chon, *The Wall Street Journal*, May 23, 2012, p. A1; Facebook's Launch Sputters—Underwriters Forced to Prop Up IPO of Social Network; Only a 23-cent Rise, by S. Raice, R. Dezember, & J. Bunge, *The Wall Street Journal*, May 19, 2012, p. A1.

13. Financial Sectors' New Buzzword Is Deleverage, by Chris Arnold, NPR website, http://www.npr.org/templates/story/story.php?storyId=94795760, accessed August 9, 2009; Deleveraging, Now Only in Early Stages, Will Transform the Banking Industry by James Saft, *New York Times* website, http://www.nytimes.com/2008/06/26/business/worldbusiness/26iht-col27.1.14006619.html?_r=1, accessed August,

9, 2009; Deleveraging: A Fate Worse than Debt, *Economist* website, http://www.economist.com/businessfinance/displaystory.cfm?story_id=12306060, accessed August 9, 2009.

14. Brief Summary of the Dodd-Frank Wall Street Reform and Consumer Protection Act. United States Senate Committee on Banking, Housing and Urban Affairs website, http://banking.senate.gov/public/_files/070110_Dodd_Frank_Wall_Street_Reform_comprehensive_summary_Final.pdf.

15. The Money Game—Getting Your Due: Entrepreneurs Are Trying to Take the Stigma out of Borrowing against Receivables, by S. Covel, *The Wall Street Journal*, May 11, 2009, p. R8; Big Customers Are Taking Longer to Pay, by A. Lotus, *The Wall Street Journal*, June 7, 2012, p. B7; Suppliers Suffer from 'Endemic' Late Payment, by R. Tyler, *The Telegraph*, January 27, 2012, http://www.telegraph.co.uk/finance/yourbusiness/9042484/Supplierssufferfromendemiclatepayment.html, accessed June 10, 2012.

16. Getting Tough with Customers by Matthew Boyle and Olga Kharif, *Business Week* March 9, 2009 p. 30.

17. Honda Profit Tumbles: Thai Floods Hit U.S. Output, by Y. Takahashi & M. Ramsey, *Dow Jones NewsPlus*, October 31, 2011, http://www.djnewsplus.com/rssarticle/SB132004240725505903.html, accessed June 11, 2012.

18. Apple Yields to Investor Cash Call, by L. Denning, *The Wall Street Journal*, March 20, 2012, p. C12; Corporate News: For Apple, a $76 Billion Dilemma As Cash Stockpile Swells, Investors Again Ask about Its Plans for Dividends, Share Repurchases, by Y. Kane, *The Wall Street Journal*, July 21, 2011, p. B9; Apple Announces Dividend, Share Buyback, by D. Moren, MacWorld, March 19, 2012, http://www.macworld.com/article/1165959/apple_announces_dividend_share_buyback.html, accessed June 10, 2012; Cash Returns: Where Apple Lags Google and Microsoft, by M. Peers, *The Wall Street Journal*, May 23, 2011, http://online.wsj.com/article/SB10001424052702304520804576339392545579346.html, accessed June 10, 2012; Corporate News: Cash Question Lingers over Apple Shareholders Show Support at First Annual Meeting without Steve Jobs, by J. Vascellaro & I. Sherr, *The Wall Street Journal*, February 24, 2012, p. B3.

19. Financial Managers, Occupational Outlook Handbook, Bureau of Labor Statistics, U.S. Department of Labor, http://www.bls.gov/ooh/management/financial-managers.htm, accessed June 11, 2012.

20. Financial Managers, Occupational Outlook Handbook, Bureau of Labor Statistics, U.S. Department of Labor, http://www.bls.gov/ooh/management/financial-managers.htm, accessed June 11, 2012.

Pg. 134 Fact: Capitalism for the Long Term, by Dominick Barton, *Harvard Business Review*, March, 2011, p. 89.

Pg. 145 Fact: David Skeel, *The New Financial Deal* (John Wiley & Sons, 2010), p. 4.

10

1. Flow of Funds Accounts of the United States, Table L.109, Federal Reserve Statistical Release, First Quarter 2012, June 7, 2012, http://www.federalreserve.gov/releases/z1/Current/z1.pdf, accessed June 12, 2012.

2. National Credit Union Administration website, http://www.ncua.gov/Resources/ConsumerInformation/aboutJoiningCUs.aspx.

3. Flow of Funds Accounts of the United States, Table L.113, Federal Reserve Statistical Release, First Quarter 2012, June 7, 2012, http://www.federalreserve.gov/releases/z1/Current/z1.pdf, accessed June 12, 2012.

4. Mortgage Debt Outstanding, Board of Governors of the Federal Reserve System, March 2012, http://www.federalreserve.gov/econresdata/releases/mortoutstand/current.htm, accessed June 13, 2012.

5. See, for example, Chart 1.1: Numbers and Assets, Office of Thrift Supervision 2009 Fact Book, accessed via Office of Thrift Supervision website, http://www.ots.treas.gov/_files/481165.pdf.

6. 2012 Dogs of the Dow, Dogsofthedow.com, http://www.dogsofthedow.com/dogs2012.htm, accessed June 15, 2012; In Dividends We Trust, by J. Buckingham, Forbes, November 21, 2011, p. 80; Dividends for 100 Years, by S. Marnjian, October 2, 2009, http://www.fool.com/investing/dividends-income/2009/10/02/dividends-for-100-years.aspx, accessed June 15, 2012; 'Dogs' Strategy Paid Dividends for Second Year in a Row, by S. Russolillo & B. Conway, The Wall Street Journal, January 3, 2012, http://online.wsj.com/article/SB1000142405297020 44644045777115084130393306.html, accessed June 15, 2012.

7. The Cost of the Savings and Loan Crisis, by Timothy Curry and Lynn Shibut, FDIC Review December, 2000, accessed on FDIC website, http://www.fdic.gov/bank/analytical/banking/2000dec/brv13n2_2.pdf.

8. Public Company Accounting Oversight Board website, http://pcaobus.org/Pages/default.aspx.

9. Brief Summary of the Dodd-Frank Wall Street Reform and Consumer Protection Act, United States Senate Committee on Banking, Housing and Urban Affairs website, http://banking.senate.gov/public/_files/070110_Dodd_Frank_Wall_Street_Reform_comprehensive_summary_Final.pdf.

10. Brief Summary of the Dodd-Frank Wall Street Reform and Consumer Protection Act, United States Senate Committee on Banking, Housing and Urban Affairs website, http://banking.senate.gov/public/_files/070110_Dodd_Frank_Wall_Street_Reform_comprehensive_summary_Final.pdf.

11. Some preferred stock contains a "participating" feature on its dividend. This means that if the dividend paid to common stockholders exceeds some specified amount, the board must also raise the dividend to preferred stockholders. See "Participating Preferred Stock," Investopedia website, http://www.investopedia.com/terms/p/participatingpreferredstock.asp.

12. Are Bond Buyers This Crazy? by Dan Caplinger, Motley Fool website, http://www.fool.com/investing/dividends-income/2010/08/26/are-bond-buyers-this-crazy.aspx; Investors, Issuers Plan for 2112 with 'Century Bonds, by A. Gara, Forbes, April 12, 2012, http://www.forbes.com/sites/thestreet/2012/04/12/investors-issuers-plan-for-2112-with-century-bonds/, accessed June 15, 2012.

13. The Coming Bond Default Wave, by Richard Lehmann, Forbes Magazine website, http://www.forbes.com/forbes/2008/1013/130.html.

14. Q&A: Quantitative Easing, Financial Times Lexicon, Financial Times, http://www.ft.com/intl/cms/s/0/edca4b66-cc67-11dd-9c43-000077b07658.html, accessed June 15, 2012; Quantitative Easing, Financial Times Lexicon, Financial Times, http://lexicon.ft.com/Term?term=quantitative-easing, accessed June 15, 2012; Let's Be Realistic about What the Fed Can Do about the Economy, by J. Cassidy, Fortune, September 5, 2011, p. 49; Have the Fed's Efforts Helped? by D. Wessel, The Wall Street Journal, June 6, 2012, http://online.wsj.com/article/SB100 01424052702303296604577450360972881958.html, accessed June 15, 2012.

15. Finding the Right Green Fund by Eugenia Levenson, Fortune magazine website, November 6, 2008, http://money.cnn.com/2008/11/05/magazines/fortune/levenson_greenfunds.fortune/index.htm; Green Investments for Launderers by Will Ashworth, Investopedia website, April 7, 2008, http://community.investopedia.com/news/IA/2008/Green_Investments_For_Launderers.aspx?partner=YahooSA; Winslow Green Growth Fund Performance, Winslow Management Company website, http://www.winslowgreen.com/fund/performance.aspx, accessed April 25, 2011; Portfolio 21 Performance, Portfolio 21 Investments website, http://www.portfolio21.com/in_depth_perf.php, accessed April 25, 2011; New Alternatives Fund Annual Report, December 31, 2010, http://www.newalternativesfund.com/returns/NAF-AR-2009.pdf, accessed April 25, 2011.

15a. Quick Facts, NYSE EURONEXT, http://www.nyx.com/en/who-we-are/quick-facts, accessed June 13, 2012; Markets, NASDAQ OMX, http://www.nasdaqomx.com/aboutus/ourmarkets/, accessed June 13, 2012.

16. Commission Warns Investors to Avoid Affinity Fraud: Beware of Swindlers Who Claim Loyalty to Your Group, Arizona Corporation Commission, April 1, 2009, https://docs.google.com/viewer?url=http://www.azinvestor.gov/News/2009/Apr%201-2009.pdf, accessed June 14, 2009; Fleecing the Flock, Economist, January 28, 2012, p. 63–64; A Bull Market for Investment Scams, by B. Burnsed, BusinessWeek Online, July 9, 2009, http://www.businessweek.com/bwdaily/dnflash/content/jul2009/db2009078_476479.htm, accessed June 14, 2012; Stanford Sentenced to 110 Years for Ponzi Scheme, by D. Gilbert, The Wall Street Journal, June 14, 2012, http://online.wsj.com/article/SB1000142405270230373420457746663406841746..html?mod=WSJ_hp_LEFTWhatsNewsCollection, accessed June 14, 2012; Birds of the Same Feather: The Dangers of Affinity Fraud, by F. Perri & R. Brody, Journal of Forensic Studies in Accounting and Business, Fall 2011, p. 3346.

17. Short and Distort Stock Scams, Fraud Guides website, http://www.fraudguides.com/investment-short-and-distort-scams.asp; What Is Naked Short Selling? by Annalyn Censky, CNNMoney.com website, http://money.cnn.com/2010/05/19/news/economy/naked_short_selling_wtf/; The Truth About Naked Shorts by Alex Dumortier, Motley Fool website, http://www.fool.com/investing/dividends-income/2008/09/22/the-truth-about-naked-shorts.aspx; The Short and Distort: Stock Manipulation in a Bear Market, by Rick Wayman, Investopedia website, http://www.investopedia.com/articles/analyst/030102.asp.

17a. Securities, Commodities, and Financial Services Sales Agents, Occupational Outlook Handbook, Bureau of Labor Statistics, U.S. Department of Labor, http://www.bls.gov/ooh/Sales/Securities-commodities-and-financial-services-sales-agents.htm, accessed June 12, 2012.

18. Financial Analysts, Occupational Outlook Handbook, Bureau of Labor Statistics, U.S. Department of Labor, http://www.bls.gov/ooh/business-and-financial/financial-analysts.htm, accessed June 12, 2012.

Pg. 159 Fact: Investment Company Institute Factbook, the Investment Company Institute website, http://www.icifactbook.org/fb_ch1.html, accessed April 25, 2011.

11

1. Army to Use Webcasts From Iraq for Recruiting, by Stuart Elliott, November 10, 2008, New York Times website, http://www.nytimes.com/2008/11/11/business/media/11adco.html, accessed February 22, 2009; Army Strong! Army Smash! October 11, 2006, Armchair Generalist website, http://armchairgeneralist.typepad.com/my_weblog/2006/10/army_strong_arm.html, accessed April 19, 2011; U.S. Army Searches New Agency, Defines Hispanic Market as Key Target, August 12, 2010, Portada website, http://www.portada-online.com/article.aspx?aid=6604, accessed April 19, 2010; U.S. Army Puts Marketing in Play by Andrew McMains, August 11, 2010, AdWeek website, http://www.adweek.com/news/advertising-branding/us-army-puts-marketing-in-play-103040, accessed June 16, 2012.

2. What marketers can learn from Obama's campaign, by Al Ries, November 5, 2008, Advertising Age website, http://adage.com/moy2008/article?article_id=131810, accessed February 22, 2009.

3. Vegas turns to reality show amid recession by Natalie Zmuda, January 2009, Advertising Age website, http://adage.com/abstract.php?article_id=134193, accessed February 22, 2009.

4. American Customer Satisfaction Index Quarterly Scores, Q1—Q4 2008, ASCI website, http://www.theacsi.org/index.php?option=com_content&task=view&id=13&Itemid=31, accessed February 24, 2009.

5. Eight reasons to keep your customers loyal by Rama Ramaswami, January 12, 2005, Mulitchannel Merchant website, http://multichannelmerchant.com/opsandfulfillment/advisor/Brandi-custloyal, accessed February 24, 2009.

6. The psychology of color in marketing by June Campbell, accessed March 19, 2005, UCSI website, http://www.ucsi.cc/webdesign/color-marketing.html; Color psychology in marketing by Al Martinovic, June 21, 2004, ImHosted website, http://developers.evrsoft.com/article/web-design/graphics-multimedia-design/color-psychology-in-marketing.shtml; Colors that sell by Suzanne Roman, November 29, 2004, ImHosted website, http://developers.evrsoft.com/article/web-design/graphics-multimedia-design/colors-that-sell.shtml; Reinvent Wheel? Blue Room. Defusing a Bomb? Red Room by Pam Belluck, February 6, 2009, New York Times website, http://www.nytimes.com/2009/02/06/science/06color.html, accessed February 26, 2009.

7. Shoe makers gunning for Olympian feat by Andria Cheng, May 9, 2008, Market Watch website, http://www.marketwatch.com/news/story/story.aspx?guid={781CC2E2-2B3F-4FF5-A0C5-0FB962D7E204}, accessed February 24, 2009;

Nike Climbs to Record as Orders Surge, Profit Rises by Matt Townsend and Robert Fenne, September 24, 2010, Bloomberg website, http://www.businessweek.com/news/2010-09-24/nike-climbs-to-record-as-orders-surge-profit-rises.html, accessed April 12, 2011; In China, Nike Sets Out to Alter Sports Mindset by Laurie Burkitt, *The Wall Street Journal* website, http://online.wsj.com/article/SB10001424052970204450804576624900309968790.html, accessed June 17, 2012.

8. Hospitals Mine Patient Records in Search of Customers by Phil Galewitz, February 5, 2012, *USA Today* website, http://www.usatoday.com/money/industries/health/story/2012-01-18/hospital-marketing/52974858/1, accessed June 17, 2012.

9. Facebook: Friend, Foe, or Frenemy? May 27, 2010, *Newsweek* website, http://www.newsweek.com/blogs/techtonic-shifts/2010/05/26/facebook-friend-foe-or-frenemy-.html, accessed April 11, 2010.

10. Groupon Passing on Super Bowl Ads This Year, by Tribune Staff, January 6, 2012, Chicago Tribune website, http://articles.chicagotribune.com/2012-01-06/news/chi-groupon-passing-on-super-bowl-ads-this-year-20120106_1_celebrity-narrated-public-service-announcements-himalayan-restaurant-super-bowl-ads, accessed June 17, 2012; Why This Nivea For Men Ad Is 'Uncivilized' by Jerry Barrow, August 17, 2011, The Urban Daily website, http://theurbandaily.com/1485855/why-this-nivea-for-men-ad-is-uncivilized-opinion/, accessed June 17, 2012; Marketing Muck-Ups: The Biggest Follies of 2011, December 12, 2011, AdvertisingAge website, http://adage.com/article/special-report-book-of-tens-2011/marketing-muck-ups-biggest-follies-2011/231468/, accessed June 17, 2012.

11. Consumer Interest in Green Products Expands across Categories, June 8, 2011, PRNewWire website, http://www.prnewswire.com/news-releases/consumer-interest-in-green-products-expands-across-categories-123473189.html, accessed June 18, 2012.

12. Environment a fair-weather priority for consumers, June 3, 2008, Penn, Schoen & Bergland Press Release, Penn, Schoen & Bergland website, http://www.psbresearch.com/press_release_Jun3-2008.htm, accessed February 24, 2009; Green Fashion: Is It More Than Marketing Hype? by Gloria Sin, May 28, 2008, *Fast Company* website, http://www.fastcompany.com/articles/2008/05/green-fashion-hype.html, accessed February 24, 2009; 'Green Fashion,' Formerly Hippie, Now Hip! February 21, 2008, CBS News website, http://www.cbsnews.com/stories/2008/02/21/earlyshow/living/beauty/main3855868.shtml, accessed February 24, 2009.

13. Smart job picks for 2010 by Michelle Goodman, February 17, 2010, PayScale website, http://blogs.payscale.com/content/2010/02/projected-job-growth-2010.html, accessed April 14, 2011; Best Undergrad College Degrees by Salary, 2010 – 10 College Salary Report, PayScale Website, http://www.payscale.com/best-colleges/degrees.asp, accessed April 14, 2011; 2011 – 2012 PayScale College Salary Report, PayScale website, http://www.payscale.com/best-colleges, accessed June 18, 2012.

Pg. 183 Fact: Sustainable Consumption Facts and Trends from a Business Perspective, World Business Council for Sustainable Development Website, December 2008, http://www.wbcsd.org/DocRoot/I9Xwhv7X5V8cDIHbHC3G/WBCSD_Sustainable_Consumption_web.pdf, accessed April 22, 2011.

Pg. 184 Fact: Lemulson-MIT Invention Index, http://mit.edu/invent/n-pressreleases/n-press-05index.html, accessed August 29, 2008.

12

1. Characteristics of a Great Name, The Brand Name Awards by Brighter Naming, http://www.brandnameawards.com/top10factors.html, accessed April 10, 2005.

2. Brand Extensions: Marketing in Inner Space, by Adam Bass, Brand Channel website, http://www.brandchannel.com/papers_review.asp?sp_id=296 accessed March 25, 2007; Brand Extensions We Could Do Without, by Reena Jana, August 7, 2006, *BusinessWeek* website, http://www.businessweek.com/magazine/content/06_32/b3996420.htm; The 20 Worst Product Failures, Sales HQ website, http://saleshq.monster.com/news/articles/2655-the-20-worst-product-failures, accessed June 20, 2012.

3. Private Label Growing Rapidly by Alex Palmer, September 22, 2009, *BrandWeek* website, http://www.brandweek.com/bw/content_display/news-and-features/packaged-goods/e3i7c69fb437bbee15e35345c87bdf679fe, accessed June 14, 2010; Ten Private Label Trends that Shook North America, PlanetRetail website, http://www1.planetretail.net/_data/assets/pdf_file/0016/43063/10-PL-Trends-That-Shook-North-America-Final.pdf, accessed May 2, 2011; IRI: Fewer Shoppers Buying Private Label Versus Last Year, Store Brands Decisions website, http://www.storebrandsdecisions.com/news/2011/04/05/iri-fewer-shoppers-buying-private-label-versus-last-year, posted April 5, 2011, accessed May 2, 2011.

4. The USA Apparel Market Research Report, June 2010, *Fashion*, http://www.infomat.com/fido/getpublication.fcn?&type=research&SearchString=apparel&id=737870ST0000927&start=1&tr=17 Infomat, accessed June 14, 2010.

5. Bank of America Axes $5 Debit Card Fee by Jason Kessler and Blake Ellis, November 1, 2011, CNNMoney website, http://money.cnn.com/2011/11/01/pf/bank_of_america_debit_fee/index.htm, accessed June 20, 2012; Bank of America Corporation, June 21, 2012, *The New York Times* website, http://topics.nytimes.com/top/news/business/companies/bank_of_america_corporation/index.html, accessed June 25, 2012.

6. Not on the List? The Truth about Impulse Purchases, January 7, 2009, Knowledge@Wharton website, http://knowledge.wharton.upenn.edu/article.cfm?articleid=2132, accessed February 28, 2009.

7. 3M: Commitment to Sustainability, GreenBiz Leaders website, 1999.

8. Wacky Warning Labels 2009 Winners Announced, August 16, 2009, Foundation for Fair Civil Justice website, http://www.foundationforfairciviljustice.org/news/in_depth/wacky_warning_labels_2009_winners_announced/, accessed June 14, 2010 ; Wacky Warning Labels Show Toll of Frivolous Lawsuits by Bob Dorigo Jones, June 8, 2012, Bob Dorigo Jones website, http://www.bobdorigojones.com/, accessed June 20, 2012; Deadline for Entering 15th Annual Wacky Warning Labels™ Contest Is May 15 by Bob Dorigo Jones, May 7, 2012, Bob Dorigo Jones website, http://www.bobdorigojones.com/, accessed June 20, 2012.

9. U.S. Consumer Online Behavior Survey Results 2007_Part One: Wireline Usage, International Data Corporation website, February 19, 2008, http://www.idc.com/getdoc.jsp?containerId=prUS21096308, accessed March 3, 2009; Why Video On Demand Is Still Cable's Game to Lose by Dan Frommer, September 5, 2008, The Business Insider website, http://www.businessinsider.com/2008/9/why-video-on-demand-is-still-cable-s-game-to-lose, accessed March 3, 2009; Streaming vids boost Netflix profits, by Glenn Abel, January 29, 2009, Download Movies 101 website, http://downloadmovies101.com/wordpress-1/2009/01/29/streaming-vids-boost-netflix-profits/, accessed March 3, 2009; Casting the Big Movie Download Roles, September 7, 2007, eMarketer website, http://www.emarketer.com/Article.aspx?id=1005346, accessed March 3, 2009 Time Watching TV Still Tops Internet posted by Clark Fredricksen, December 15, 2010, eMarketer Blog, http://www.emarketer.com/blog/index.php/time-spent-watching-tv-tops-internet/, accessed May 4, 2011; Average time spent online per U.S. visitor in 2010, posted January 11, 2011, ComScore Data Mine website, http://www.comscoredatamine.com/2011/01/average-time-spent-online-per-u-s-visitor-in-2010/, accessed May 4, 2011; How People Watch TV Online and Off by Erick Schonfeld, January 8, 2012, TechCrunch website, http://techcrunch.com/2012/01/08/how-people-watch-tv-online/, accessed June 20, 2012.

10. Permission Marketing by William C. Taylor, December 18, 2007, *Fast Company* website, http://www.fastcompany.com/magazine/14/permission.html, accessed March 3, 2009.

11. 'Two nobodies from nowhere' craft winning Super Bowl ad by Bruce Horovitz, February 4, 2009, *USA Today* website, http://www.usatoday.com/money/advertising/admeter/2009admeter.htm, accessed March 4, 2009.

12. Professor Paul Herbig, Tristate University, International Marketing Lecture Series, Session 6, International Advertising, www.tristate.edu/faculty/herbig/pahimadvstg.htm, accessed June 1, 2005; Taking Global Brands to Japan by Karl Moore and Mark Smith, The Conference Board website, http://www.conference-board.org/worldwide/worldwide_article.cfm?id=243&pg=1, accessed June 1, 2005.

13. Search Marketing Trends: Back to Basics, eMarketer website, February 2009, http://www.emarketer.com/Report.aspx?code=emarketer_2000559, accessed June 18, 2010; eMarketer: Display ad growth catching up with search, posted by Leah McBride Mensching on December 16, 2010, sfnblog, http://www.sfnblog.com/advertising/2010/12/emarketer_display_ad_growth_catching_up.php, accessed May 11, 2011; US Online Ad Spend Poised to Grow 20% in 2011, June 8, 2011, eMarketer website, http://www.emarketer.com/Article.aspx?R=1008431, accessed June 20, 2012.

14. eMarketer: Search Is Vital in a Recession by *Adweek* staff, February 25, 2009, *Brandweek* website, http://www.brandweek.com/bw/content_display/news-and-features/digital/e3i195c363ab252f976a2dabde4d8ef2549, accessed March 3, 2009.

15. U.S. Online Advertising Video Spending 2007–2013, August 2008, eMarketer website,

http://www.marketingcharts.com/television/
emarketer-revises-online-video-ad-spend-
projections-downward-5679/emarketer-online-
video-ad-spend-us-2007-2013jpg/, accessed June
18, 2010; Promises, promises: Will online video
ads deliver this year? posted by David Hallerman,
December 9, 2010, The eMarketer Blog, http://
www.emarketer.com/blog/index.php/promises-
promises-online-video-ads-deliver-year/, accessed
May 11, 2011; US Online Ad Spend Poised to
Grow 20% in 2011, June 8, 2011, eMarketer
website, http://www.emarketer.com/Article.
aspx?R=1008431, accessed June 20, 2012.
16. Social media claims more of our attention.
But email's not dead yet, posted August 2, 2010
by Meghan Keane, eConsultancy website, http://
econsultancy.com/us/blog/6366-social-media-
might-claim-a-lot-of-our-attention-but-email-
s-not-dead-yet, accessed May 11, 2011; Social
Media ROI Examples & Video, by Erik Qualman,
posted November 12, 2009, Socialnomics, Social
Media Blog, http://socialnomics.net/2009/11/12/
social-media-roi-examples-video/, accessed June
28, 2010; The ROI of Social Media: 10 Case
Studies by Lauren Fisher, July 16, 2011, The Next
Web website, http://thenextweb.com/socialme-
dia/2011/07/16/the-roi-of-social-media-10-case-
studies/, accessed June 21, 2012.
17. Brandchannel's 2004 Product Placement
Awards by Abram Sauer, February 21, 2005,
http://www.brandchannel.com/start1.asp?
fa_id=251; A Product Placement Hall of Fame
by Dale Buss, *Business Week* Online, June 22,
1998, http://www.businessweek.com/1998/25/
b3583062.htm.
18. Apple tops 2010 film product placement
awards, by Eric Slivka, February 22, 2011,
MacRumors website, http://www.macrumors
.com/2011/02/22/apple-tops-2010-film-product-
placement-awards/, accessed May 11, 2011.
19. PQ Media Market Analysis Finds Global
Product Placement Spending Grew 37% in 2006;
Forecast to Grow 30% in 2007, Driven by Relaxed European Rules, Emerging Asian Markets;
Double-Digit Growth in U.S. Decelerates, PQ
Media website, March 14, 2007, http://www
.pqmedia.com/about-press-20070314-gppf.html,
accessed September 4, 2008; DVR Households
Swelling Ranks by Jose Fermoso, December 16,
2008, Portfolio website, http://www.portfolio
.com/views/blogs/the-tech-observer/2008/12/16/
dvr-households-swelling-ranks, accessed March 4,
2009; FCC opens inquiry into stealthy TV product
placement, June 26, 2008, *USA Today* website,
http://www.usatoday.com/life/television/2008-
06-26-fcc-advertising_N.htm, accessed March
4, 2009; DVRs now in 30.6% of U.S. Households, by Bill Gorman, April 30, 2009, TV by
the Numbers website, http://tvbythenumbers.
com/2009/04/30/dvrs-now-in-306-of-us-
households/17779, accessed June 16, 2010;
Product Placement Dipped Last Year for the
First Time by Andrew Hampp, June 29, 2010,
AdAge website, http://adage.com/article/
madisonvine-news/product-placement-dipped-
year-time/144720/, accessed May 11, 2011;
DVR Penetration grows to 39.7% of households,
42.2% of viewers by Robert Seidman,
March 23, 2011, TV by the numbers website,
http://tvbythenumbers.zap2it.com/2011/03/23/
dvr-penetration-grows-to-39-7-of-households-
42-2-of-viewers/86819/, accessed May 11,
2011; Product Placement Grows in Music

Videos by Joseph Plambeck, July 5, 2010, *The
New York Times* website, http://www.nytimes.
com/2010/07/06/business/media/06adco.html?_
r=1, accessed June 21, 2012; DVRs and Streaming
Prompt a Shift in the Top-Rated TV Shows by
Bill Carter and Brian Stelter, March 4, 2012, *The
New York Times* website, http://www.nytimes.
com/2012/03/05/business/media/dvrs-and-stream-
ing-prompt-a-shift-in-the-top-rated-tv-shows.
html?pagewanted=all, accessed June 21, 2012.
20. The F-Factor Trendwatching May 2011,
http://trendwatching.com/briefing/, accessed
May 16, 2011.
21. Ford, Coke & AT&T Pay More to Sponsor
American Idol by Susan Gunelius, January 18,
2008, Bizzia website, http://www.bizzia.com/
brandcurve/ford-coke-att-pay-more-to-sponsor-
american-idol/, accessed March 4, 2009; Global
Paid Product Placement to Reach $7.6 billion by
2010: Report, by Amy Johannes, August 17, 2006,
PromoMagazine website, http://promomagazine.
com/research/paidplacementreport/, accessed June
16, 2010.
22. All Time High: 72% of U.S. Population Plays
Video Games, by Matt Peckham, April 3, 2008,
PC World website, http://blogs.pcworld.com/
gameon/archives/006748.html, accessed
March 5, 2009; Video Game Advertising report,
eMarketer website, http://www.emarketer.com/
Report.aspx?code=emarketer_2000485, accessed
March 5, 2009.
23. Massive Summary Research—Significant
Findings, Massive website, http://www.massiv-
eincorporated.com/casestudiesa.html, accessed
March 4, 2009; Google to Buy Adscape by
Nick Gonzalez, TechCrunch website, February 16, 2007, http://www.techcrunch.
com/2007/02/16/google-to-buy-adscape-for-
23-million/, accessed March 5, 2009; IN-game
advertising is a massive market, May 15, 2011,
The Telegraph website, http://www.telegraph.
co.uk/technology/news/5312188/In-game-
advertising-is-a-massive-market.html, accessed
May 16, 2011; Report: Video Game Ads to
Reach $1 Bil. by 2012 by Mike Shields, March
4, 2008, AdWeek website, http://www.adweek.
com/news/television/report-video-game-ads-
reach-1-bil-2012-95119, accessed June 21, 2012;
Let the Games Begin Advertising! April 6, 2007,
eMarketer website, http://www.emarketer.com/
Article.aspx?1004739&R=1004739, accessed
June 21, 2012.
24. Kid Nabbing, by Melanie Wells, February 2,
2004, *Forbes* website, http://www.forbes.com/
free_forbes/2004/0202/084.html; Tremor
website, http://tremor.com/index.html, accessed
March 5, 2009; General Mills, Kraft Launch
Word of Mouth Networks by Elaine Wong,
October 5, 2008, *BrandWeek* website, http://
www.brandweek.com/bw/content_display/
news-and-features/packaged-goods/e3i2db03fb-
29d573ec52722456845f5c274, accessed March 5,
2009.
25. Sponsorship Spending To Rise 2.2 Percent
in 2009, IEG Press Release, February 11, 2009,
Sponsorship.Com website, http://www.sponsor-
ship.com/About-IEG/Press-Room/Sponsorship-
Spending-To-Rise-2.2-Percent-in-2009.aspx,
accessed March 5, 2009; Sponsorship Spending To
Rise 2.2 Percent in 2009, August 28, 2009, Som-
merville Baddley Marketing website, http://www.
sbmktg.net/2009/08/sponsorship-spending-to-
rise-22-percent-in-2009/ (accessed June 16, 2010);

Sponsorship Spending: 2010 Proves Better Than
Expected; Bigger Gains Set For 2011, IEG Press
Release, January 12, 2011, http://www
.prweb.com/releases/2011/01/prweb4958744.htm,
accessed May 15, 2011; Economic Uncertainty to
Slow Sponsorship Growth in 2012, January 11,
2012, IEG website, http://www.sponsorship.com/
About-IEG.aspx, accessed June 22, 2012.
26. Publicity from Thin Air (Don't Just Wait for
News to Happen), by Bill Stoller, Article Point
website, http://www.articlepoint.com/articles/
public-relations/publicity-from-thin-air.php,
accessed June 15, 2005.
27. The Employment Situation – April 2011,
Bureau of Labor Statistics News Release, May 6,
2011, Bureau of Labor Statistics website, http://
www.bls.gov/news.release/pdf/empsit.pdf, accessed
May 16, 2011.
28. Online Tracking Ramps Up by Julia Angwin,
June 17, 2012, *The Wall Street Journal* website,
http://online.wsj.com/article/SB10001424052702
303836404577472491637833420.html, accessed
June 23, 2012.
Pg. 203 Fact: Offline Ads Drive Mobile Response,
May 30, 2012, Print in the Mix, Rochester In-
stitute of Technology, http://printinthemix.com/
Fastfacts/Show/570, accessed June, 2012.

13

1. Supermarket Facts, Industry Overview 2008,
Food Marketing Institute website, http://www.fmi.
org/facts_figs/?fuseaction=superfact, accessed June
30, 2010.
2. Math Lessons for Locavores by Stephen Bu-
diansky, August 19, 2010, *The New York Times*
website, http://www.nytimes.com/2010/08/20/
opinion/20budiansky.html, accessed June 23,
2012.
3. Report: Online retail could reach $156B
in 2009 by Rachel Metz, January 29, 2009,
The Industry Standard website, http://
www.thestandard.com/news/2009/01/29/
report-online-retail-could-reach-156b-2009,
accessed March 13, 2009; eMarketer revises
e-commerce forecast by Jeffrey Grau, March
5, 2009, eMarketer website, http://www.emar-
keter.com/Article.aspx?id=1006948, http://
www.emarketer.com/Article.aspx?id=1006948;
Inside the Secret World of Trader Joes by Beth
Kowitt, August 23, 2010, *Fortune* website,
http://money.cnn.com/2010/08/20/news/com-
panies/inside_trader_joes_full_version.fortune/
index.htm, accessed May 30, 2011; Healthy
Growth for Ecommerce as Retail Continues
Shift to Web, eMarketer Blog, March 17,
2011, http://www.emarketer.com/Article.
aspx?R=1008284, accessed May 30, 2011;
http://mashable.com/2011/02/28/forrester-e-
commerce/.
4. Fireclick Index, Top Line Growth, Fireclick
website, http://index.fireclick.com/fireindex.
php?segment=0, accessed March 13, 2009; L.L.
Bean Once Again Number One in Customer
Service, According to NRF Foundation/American
Express Survey, January 13, 2009, National Retail
Federation website, http://www.nrf.com/modules
.php?name=News&op=viewlive&sp_id=653,
accessed May 30, 2011; Amazon.com Tops
in Customer Service, According to NRF
Foundation/American Express Survey,
January 17, 2012, National Retail Federation

Website: http://www.nrf.com/modules.php?name=News&op=viewlive&sp_id=1293, accessed June 23, 2012.

5. Sales soften at Costco, March 4, 2009, Retail Analysis IGD website, http://www.igd.com/analysis/channel/news_hub.asp?channelid=1&channelitemid=9&nidp=&nid=5616, accessed March 13, 2009.

6. Loss Leader Strategy, Investopedia website (a *Forbes* Digital Company), http://www.investopedia.com/terms/l/lossleader.asp, accessed March 14, 2009; Walmart not crying over spilt milk by Al Norman, August 22, 2008, *The Huffington Post* website, http://www.huffingtonpost.com/al-norman/wal-mart-not-crying-over_b_120684.html, accessed March 14, 2009.

7. Goodbye, Bait-and-Switch. Hello, 'Shrouding' by Jean Chatzky, May 26, 2005, MSNBC website, http://today.msnbc.msn.com/id/7966877/ns/today-money/t/goodbye-bait-and-switch-hello-shrouding/, accessed June 23, 2012.

8. How Costco Became the Anti Walmart by Steven Greenhouse, July 17, 2005, *New York Times* website, http://www.nytimes.com/2005/07/17/business/yourmoney/17costco.html?adxnnl=1&pagewanted=1&adxnnlx=1122004143-8Vfn2DFl1MJfernM1navLA; Why Costco is so addictive by Matthew Boyle, October 25, 2006, CNNMoney website, http://money.cnn.com/magazines/fortune/fortune_archive/2006/10/30/8391725/index.htm, accessed March 14, 2009.

9. Spotify cozies up to iPod, takes aim at iTunes by Don Reisinger, May 4, 2011, cNet News Website, http://news.cnet.com/8301-13506_3-20059630-17.html, accessed June 1, 2011.

10. Why we fall for this by David Kestenbaum, AARP Magazine, May/June 2011 issue, http://www.aarp.org/money/scams-fraud/info-04-2011/marketing-mind-tricks.html, accessed May 29, 2011; Why the Price Is Rarely Right, by Peter Coy, January 10, 2010, *BusinessWeek* website, http://www.businessweek.com/magazine/content/10_05/b4165077443953.htm, accessed July 1, 2010.

11. Logistics Management 27th Annual Salary Survey: Ready to Move Up, by Patrick Burnson, Executive Editor of Logistics Management, April 07, 2011, Logistics Management, website, http://www.logisticsmgmt.com/article/27th_annual_salary_survey_ready_to_move_up, accessed June 2, 2011; Logistics Management 2012 Salary Survey, Supply Chain Management Review website, http://www.logisticsmgmt.com/article/2012_salary_survey/, accessed June 23, 2012.

Pg. 216 Fact: http://www.cnbc.com/id/46385183/Busiest_U_S_Trade_Hubs?slide=16, accessed November 2012.

14

1. The Importance of Being Richard Branson, Leadership and Change, Knowledge@Wharton, January 12, 2005, http://knowledge.wharton.upenn.edu/article/1109.cfm; Ambition: Why Some People are Most Likely to Succeed, by Jeffrey Kluger, *Time* magazine, November 14, 2005, p. 48–59, http://www.time.com/time/archive/preview/0,10987,1126746,00.html. Jeff Bezos, Reference for Business website, 2nd Edition, http://www.referenceforbusiness.com/businesses/A-F/Bezos-Jeff.html, accessed June 24, 2012; The Roller Coaster Ride of Mark Zuckerberg by Matt Melvin, 2011, Teen Ink website, http://www.teenink.com/nonfiction/academic/article/292887/The.., accessed June 24, 2012; Reagan Trail Days, The Ronald Reagan Trail website, http://www.ronaldreagantrail.net/Pages/ReaganTrail.php?city=2&page=Dixon, accessed June 24, 2012.

1a. Top Ten Bad Business Decisions, October 10, 2010, Business Excellence website, http://www.bus-ex.com/article/top-ten-bad-business-decisions, accessed June 24, 2012.

2. The Importance of Being Richard Branson, Leadership and Change, Knowledge@Wharton, January 12, 2005, http://knowledge.wharton.upenn.edu/article/1109.cfm.

3. Hot Topic, Inc. Reports Fourth Quarter EPS Increases 19% to $0.32 Per Diluted Share; Provides Guidance for the 1st Quarter of 2009, March 11, 2009, News Blaze website, http://newsblaze.com/story/2009031112554500001.pz/topstory.html, accessed March 25, 2009.

4. Motivate Your Staff, by Larry Page, How to Succeed in 2005, Business 2.0 magazine, December 1, 2004, http://money.cnn.com/magazines/business2/business2_archive/2004/12/01/8192529/index.htm.

5. A New Game at the Office: Many Young Workers Accept Fewer Guarantees by Steve Lohr, *The New York Times*, December 5, 2005, http://select.nytimes.com/gst/abstract.html?res=F00F12FE38550C768CDDAB0994DD404482.

6. 100 Best Companies to Work For 2012, Fortune website, http://money.cnn.com/magazines/fortune/best-companies/, accessed June 24, 2012.

7. The 100 Best Companies to Work For 2006, *Fortune* magazine, January 23, 2006, pp. 71–74; Why the Economy Is a Lot Stronger Than You Think by Michael Mandel, *BusinessWeek* Online, February 13, 2006, http://www.businessweek.com/magazine/content/06_07/b3971001.htm.

8. Don't Get Hammered by Management Fads by Darrell Rigby, *The Wall Street Journal*, May 21, 2001.

9. A Generation of Slackers? Not So Much by Catherine Rampell, May 28, 2811, *New York Times* website, http://www.nytimes.com/2011/05/29/weekinreview/29graduates.html, accessed June 29, 2011.

10. Managing Generation Y—Part 1, Book Excerpt by Bruce Tulgan and Carolyn A. Martin, *BusinessWeek* online, September 28, 2001, http://www.businessweek.com/smallbiz/content/sep2001/sb20010928_113.htm; Managing Generation Y—Part 2, Book Excerpt by Bruce Tulgan and Carolyn A. Martin, *BusinessWeek* online, October 4, 2001, http://www.businessweek.com/smallbiz/content/oct2001/sb2001105_229.htm; Generation Y: They've Arrived at Work with a New Attitude by Stephanie Armour, *USA Today*, November 6, 2005, http://www.usatoday.com/money/workplace/2005-11-06-gen-y_x.htm; The Facebook Generation vs. the Fortune 500 by Gary Hamel, March 24, 2009, The *Wall Street Journal* Blogs website, http://blogs.wsj.com/management/2009/03/24/the-facebook-generation-vs-the-fortune-500/, accessed March 30, 2009; What Gen Y Really Wants by Penelope Trunk, July 5, 2007, *Time* magazine website, http://www.time.com/time/magazine/article/0,9171,1640395,00.html, accessed March 30, 2009; Managing Generation Y as they change the workforce by Molly Smith, January 8, 2008, Reuters website, http://www.reuters.com/article/pressRelease/idUS129795+08-Jan-2008+BW20080108, accessed March 30, 2009; Millennial Branding Survey Reveals that Gen-Y Is Connected to an Average of 16 Co-Workers on Facebook, by Dan Schawbel, January 9, 2012, Millennial Branding website, http://millennialbranding.com/2012/01/millennial-branding-gen-y-facebook-study/, accessed June 23, 2012.

11. The cow in the ditch: how Anne Mulcahy Rescued Xerox, Special Section: Knowledge at Wharton, November 16–29, 2005, http://knowledge.wharton.upenn.edu/index.cfm?fa=viewArticle&id=1318&specialId=41.

12. Stop Working All Those Hours by Robert C. Pozen, June 15, 2012, Harvard Business Review website, http://blogs.hbr.org/hbsfaculty/2012/06/stop-working-all-those-hours.html, accessed June 24, 2012.

13. Is your boss a psychopath? by Alan Deutschman, July 2005, Fast Company, http://www.fastcompany.com/magazine/96/open_boss.html; Corporate psychopaths at large by Lisa Desai, September 3, 2004, CNN.com International, http://edition.cnn.com/2004/BUSINESS/08/26/corporate.psychopaths/; How Apple does it, by Lev Grossman, October 24, 2005, Time Inside Innovation.

Pg. 237 Fact: Future Foundation survey referenced in The Hidden Costs of Poor People Management by Laurence Karsh, December 1, 2004, Inc Website, http://www.inc.com/articles/2004/12/karsh.html, accessed July 2012.

15

1. Gary Kelly Southwest Airlines CEO on the Business of Building Trust by Kate McCann, October 11, 2005, McCombs School of Business website, http://www.mccombs.utexas.edu/news/pressreleases/lyceum05_kelly_wrap05.asp, accessed July 2, 2010; Southwest Airlines Reports Fourth Quarter Profit and 37th Consecutive Year of Profitability, January 21, 2010, PRNewsWire website, http://www.prnewswire.com/news-releases/southwest-airlines-reports-fourth-quarter-profit-and-37th-consecutive-year-of-profitability-82241197.html, accessed July 2, 2010; 1106 HR Magazine: Views from the Top, November 1, 2006, SHRM website, http://www.shrm.org/Publications/hrmagazine/EditorialContent/Pages/1106ceoex.aspx, accessed July 5, 2011.

2. America's jobless recovery. Not again. June 3, 2011, *Economist* website, http://www.economist.com/blogs/freeexchange/2011/06/americas-jobless-recovery, accessed July 5, 2011; A New Game at the Office: Many Young Workers Accept Fewer Guarantees, by Steve Lohr, *New York Times*, December 5, 2005, http://select.nytimes.com/gst/abstract.html?res=F00F12FE38550C768CDDAB0994DD404482.

2a. The Humbling First Jobs of 25 Very Successful Celebrities and Business Leaders by HR World Editors, September 24, 2010, Focus website, http://www.focus.com/fyi/humbling-first-jobs-25-very-successful-celebrities-and-busin/, accessed June 27, 2012; Celebrities' First Jobs, Oprah's website, November 3, 2009, http://www.oprah.com/entertainment/Oprahs-Live-Newscast-and-Celebrities-First-Jobs/1, accessed June 27, 2012.

3. CEO pay vs. performance – Still a roll of the dice, (WSJ) by Dionysus on April 1, 2010, posted on Economatrix website, http://www.economatix.com/ceo-pay-vs-performance-still-a-roll-of-the-dice-wsj, accessed September 6, 2011; Figure 3AE from Lawrence Mishel, Jared Bernstein, and Heidi Shierholz, *The State of Working America 2009/2009. An Economic Policy Institute Book*. Ithaca, N.Y.: ILR Press, An Imprint of Cornell University Press, 2009, http://www.stateofworkingamerica.org/tabfig/2008/03/SWA08_Chapter3_Wages_r2_Fig-3AE.jpg. accessed July 1, 2010; We Knew They Got Raises. But This?, by Pradnya Joshi, July 2, 2011, *New York Times* website, http://www.nytimes.com/2011/07/03/business/03pay.html, accessed July 5, 2011; U.S. CEO's Pay 231 Times Higher Than That of Average Workers by Marla Dickerson, May 2, 2012, Los Angeles Times website, http://articles.latimes.com/2012/may/02/business/la-fi-mo-us-ceo-pay-231-times-more-than-average-workers-20120502, accessed June 30, 2012; CEO Pay Moves with Corporate Results by Scott Thurm, May 23, 2012, The Wall Street Journal website, http://online.wsj.com/article/SB10001424052702304019404577416210712022298.html, accessed July 2, 2012.

4. In 2011 The Baby Boomers Start To Turn 65: 16 Statistics About The Coming Retirement Crisis That Will Drop Your Jaw, December 30, 2010, The American Dream website, http://endoftheamericandream.com/archives/in-2011-the-baby-boomers-start-to-turn-65-16-statistics-about-the-coming-retirement-crisis-that-will-drop-your-jaw, accessed July 5, 2011.

5. Facing Young Workers' High Job Expectations, from Associated Press, *Los Angeles Times*, June 27, 2005; *Not Everyone by Bruce Tulgan Gets a Trophy*, San Francisco: Jossey-Bass (Wiley Imprint), 2009.

6. How Corporate America Is Betraying Women, by Betsy Morris, *Fortune*, January 10, 2005; Jane Drain – women leaving your workforce, Smart Manager website, http://www.smartmanager.com.au/web/au/smartmanager/en/pages/89_jane_drain—women_leaving_workforce.html, accessed July 5, 2011; Educated Women Quit Work as Spouses Earn More by Tiziana Barghini, March 8, 2012, Reuters website, http://www.reuters.com/article/2012/03/08/us-economy-women-idUSBRE8270AC20120308, accessed June 25, 2012; Highly Achieved Women Leaving the Traditional Workforce Final Report March 2008, U.S. Department of Labor, http://www.choose2lead.org/Publications/Are%20We%20Losing%20the%20Best%20and%20the%20Brightest.pdf, accessed June 25, 2012.

7. Featured Employee Rap Sheet, Hot Topic website, http://www.hottopic.com/community/rapsheets/emp_jodi.asp?LS=0&, accessed April 11, 2006; A New Game at the Office: Many Young Workers Accept Fewer Guarantees by Steve Lohr, *New York Times*, December 5, 2005, http://select.nytimes.com/gst/abstract.html?res=F00F12FE38550C768CDDAB0994DD404482; Work-life benefits fall victim to slow economy, by Andrea Shim, April 4, 2009, *Los Angeles Times* website, http://www.latimes.com/business/la-fi-flexible4-2009apr04,0,4344887.story, accessed April 4, 2009; Pending Job Flexibility Act Received Mixed Reviews by Sue Shellenbarger, *WSJ Career Journal*, http://www.careerjournal.com/columnists/workfamily/20010426-workfamily.html, accessed

August 9, 2005; Work-life benefits fall victim to slow economy by Andrea Shim, April 4, 2009, *Los Angeles Times* website, http://www.latimes.com/business/la-fi-flexible4-2009apr04,0,4344887.story, accessed April 4, 2009.

8. Why We Hate HR by Keith W. Hammonds, December 19, 2007, *Fast Company* website, http://www.fastcompany.com/magazine/97/open_hr.html?page=0%2C1, accessed April 4, 2009.

9. Table 1. The 30 fastest growing occupations covered in the 2008–2009 *Occupational Outlook Handbook*, Economic News Release, December 18, 2007, Bureau of Labor Statistics website, http://www.bls.gov/news.release/ooh.t01.htm, accessed April 7, 2009; Census Bureau Data Underscore Value of College Degree, U.S. Census Bureau News, October 26, 2006, Census Bureau website, http://www.census.gov/Press-Release/www/releases/archives/education/007660.html, accessed April 7, 2009; Increasing Share of Adults Have College Degrees, Census Bureau Finds by Derek Quizon, April 26, 2011, *The Chronicle of Higher Education* website, http://chronicle.com/article/Increasing-Share-of-Adults/127264/, accessed July 5, 2011.

10. SHRM Human Capital Benchmarking Study, 2008 Executive Summary, page 14, SHRM website, http://www.shrm.org/Research/Documents/2008%20Executive%20Summary_FINAL.pdf, accessed April 7, 2009; Effective Recruiting Tied to Stronger Financial Performance, Watson Wyatt Worldwide news release, August 16, 2005, Watson Wyatt Worldwide website, http://www.watsonwyatt.com/news/press.asp?ID=14959, accessed April 7, 2009.

11. Top Five Resume Lies by Jeanne Sahadi, December 9, 2004, CNN Money website, http://money.cnn.com/2004/11/22/pf/resume_lies/.

12. You're Hired. At Least for Now by Anne Kates Smith, March 2010, Kiplinger website, http://www.kiplinger.com/magazine/archives/employers-choose-temps-contract-workers.html accessed July 13, 2010); Special Report on Contingent Staffing—The Future of Contingent Staffing Could Be Like Something Out of a Movie, by Irwin Speizer, October 19, 2009, Workforce Management website, http://www.workforce.com/section/recruiting-staffing/feature/special-report-contingent-staffingthe-future-contingent/, accessed July 5, 2011; The Rise of the Independent Work Force by Alexandra Levit, April 14, 2012, *The New York Times* website, http://www.nytimes.com/2012/04/15/jobs/independent-workers-are-here-to-stay.html, accessed June 25, 2012.

13. The Questions: How Not to Answer compiled by Barry Shamis of Selecting Winners, Inc., FacilitatorGuy Resume Resource Center, http://resume.bgolden.com/res/interview-bloopers.php, accessed September 1, 2005; Interview Bloopers: What Not to Do! by Maureen Bauer, Channel 3000 website, http://html.channel3000.com/sh/employment/stories/ employment—20001002-144946.html, accessed September 1, 2005; More Interview Bloopers by Maureen Bauer, Channel 3000 website, http://html.channel3000.com/sh/employment/stories/employment—20001002-152818.html.

14. Orientation: Not Just a Once-over-Lightly Anymore, by Matt DeLuca HRO Today, April/May 2005, http://www.hrotoday.com/Magazine.asp?artID=928; New Emphasis on First Impressions by Leslie Gross Klaff, March 2008, Workforce Management website, http://www.workforce.com/archive/feature/25/41/58/index.

php?ht=, accessed April 7, 2009; Show and Tell—Disney Institute's Four-Day Seminar on HR Management by Leon Rubis, *HR* magazine, April 1998; New Employee Experience Aims for Excitement Beyond the First Day by Daryl Stephenson, Boeing Frontiers Online, May 2002, http://www.boeing.com/news/frontiers/archive/2002/may/i_mams.html.

15. Labor-Intensive, by Sean McFadden, *Boston Business Journal*, November 19, 2004, http://www.bizjournals.com/boston/stories/2004/11/22/smallb1.html; The Costco Way; Higher Wages Mean Higher Profits. But Try Telling Wall Street by Stanley Holmes and Wendy Zelner, *Business-Week*, April 12, 2004; Study: Moderation in Hiring Practices Boosts Business Performance by Todd Raphael, Workforce Management, August 19, 2005, http://www.workforce.com/section/00/article/24/14/03.html.

16. Appreciating Benefits as Times Gets Tough, by Carroll Lachnit, March 24, 2009, Blog: The Business of Management, Workforce Management website, http://workforce.com/wpmu/bizmgmt/2009/03/24/benefits_in_tough_times/, accessed April 9, 2009.

17. Perking Up: Some Companies Offer Surprising New Benefits by Sue Shellenbarger, March 18, 2009, *Wall Street Journal* website, http://online.wsj.com/article/SB123733195850463165.html, accessed April 9, 2009.

18. Questions and Answers about Flexible Work Schedules: A Sloan Work and Family Research Network Fact Sheet, updated September 2008, Sloan Work and Family Research Network website, http://wfnetwork.bc.edu/pdfs/flexworksched.pdf, accessed April 9, 2009; Work-life benefits fall victim to slow economy by Andrea Shim, April 4, 2009, *Los Angeles Times* website, http://www.latimes.com/business/la-fi-flexible4-2009apr04,0,4344887.story, accessed April 4, 2009.

19. 100 Best Companies to Work for 2011, Best benefits: Unusual Perks, *Fortune* website, http://money.cnn.com/magazines/fortune/best-companies/2011/benefits/unusual.html, accessed July 5, 2011; 100 Best Companies to Work for 2011, *Fortune* website, 2012, http://Money.Cnn.Com/Magazines/Fortune/Bestcompanies/2011/Full_List/, accessed June 27, 2012.

20. Home Sweet Office: Telecommute Good for Business, Employees, and Planet by Brendan I. Koerner, September 22, 2008, *Wired* website, http://www.wired.com/culture/culturereviews/magazine/16-10/st_essay, accessed April 11, 2009; Give telecommuting the green light by Ted Samson, June 2, 2007, InfoWorld website, http://www.infoworld.com/d/green-it/give-telecommuting-green-light-628, accessed April 11, 2009; Sun, employees find big savings from Open Work telecommuting program by Ted Samson, June 19, 2008, InfoWorld website, http://www.infoworld.com/d/green-it/sun-employees-find-big-savings-open-work-telecommuting-program-821, accessed April 11, 2009; National Study Finds Electronics Significantly Reduce Energy, Press Release, September 19, 2007, Telecommute Connecticut! website, http://www.telecommutect.com/employers/pr_9_27_07.php, accessed July 2, 2010; Telecommuting Creates Happier and More Productive Employees by Diann Daniel, May 3, 2012, HP website, http://h30565.www3.hp.com/t5/Feature-Articles/Telecommuting-Creates-Happier-and-More-Productive-Employees/ba-p/1834,

accessed June 28, 2012; Benefits of Telework (aka Telecommuting), March 23, 2011, EcoCoach website, http://www.eco-coach.com/blog/2011/03/23/benefits-of-telework-aka-telecommuting/, accessed June 28, 2012.

21. Give telecommuting the green light by Ted Samson, June 7, 2007, InfoWorld website, http://www.infoworld.com/d/green-it/give-telecommuting-green-light-628, accessed April 10, 2009; Home Sweet Office: Telecommute Good for Business, Employees, and Planet by Brendan I. Koerner, September 22, 2008, *Wired* website, http://www.wired.com/culture/culturereviews/magazine/16-10/st_essay, accessed April 10, 2009; Skype: More companies allow telecommuting by Ginger Christ, April 5, 2011, Dayton Business Journal Website, http://www.bizjournals.com/dayton/news/2011/04/05/more-companies-allow-telecommuting.html, accessed July 5, 2011; Costs and Benefits, Advantages of Telecommuting for Companies, Telework Research Network website, http://www.teleworkresearchnetwork.com/costs-benefits, accessed July 5, 2011.

22. The New Job Sharers by Michelle V. Rafter, May 2008, Workforce Management website, http://www.workforce.com/archive/feature/25/53/28/index.php, accessed April 10, 2009; Study Attempts To Dispel Five Myths of Job Sharing by Stephen Miller, May 9, 2007, Society for Human Resource Management website, http://moss07.shrm.org/Publications/HRNews/Pages/XMS_021497.aspx, accessed April 10, 2009.

23. 5.1 million jobs lost in this recession so far by Rex Nutting, April 3, 2009, MarketWatch website, http://www.marketwatch.com/news/story/51-million-jobs-lost-recession/story.aspx?guid={CF54164C-6F7B-4501-B6FB-D7D1C8D710B9}&dist=msr_8, accessed April 10, 2009; Boost Employee Morale After Layoffs, Workforce Management website, http://www.workforce.com/archive/article/22/14/10.php, accessed April 10, 2009.

24. Sexual Harassment Charges, EEOC & FEPAs Combined: FY 1997–FY 2008, EEOC website, updated March 11, 2009, http://www.eeoc.gov/stats/harass.html, accessed April 10, 2009.

25. Sexual Harassment, updated March 11, 2009, http://www.eeoc.gov/types/sexual_harassment.html, accessed April 10, 2009.

26. 8 Wacky Jobs at Best Companies, 100 Best Companies to Work for 2011, Fortune website, http://money.cnn.com/galleries/2011/pf/jobs/1101/gallery.best_companies_craziest_jobs.fortune/index.html, accessed July 5, 2011; 8 Wacky Jobs, Fortune website, http://money.cnn.com/galleries/2011/fortune/1105/gallery.fortune500_fun_jobs.fortune/index.html, accessed July 5; Strangest jobs in the world; Odd travel industry jobs include bath sommelier, dog surf instructor by Katrina Brown Hunt and Darrin Tobias, June 13, 2011, *New York Daily News* website, http://www.nydailynews.com/lifestyle/2011/06/13/2011-06-13_strangest_jobs_in_the_world_odd_travel_industry_jobs_include_bath_sommelier_dog_.html, accessed July 12, 2011; Unusual Jobs and Their Paydays by Jason Daniels, May 17th, 2012, PayDayOne website, http://news.paydayone.com/general-finance/jobs-and-their-paydays/, accessed June 27, 2012; Unusual Jobs That Pay Surprisingly Well by Jaquelyn Smith, May 25, 2012, Forbes website, http://www.forbes.com/sites/jacquelynsmith/2012/05/25/unusual-jobs-that-pay-surprisingly-well/.

27. Human Resources, Training, and Labor Relations Managers and Specialists, Occupational Outlook Handbook, 2011, Bureau Labor Statistics website, http://www.bls.gov/oco/ocos021.htm, accessed July 5, 2011.
Pg. 242 Fact: http://usatoday30.usatoday.com/news/health/wellness/story/2012-01-15/Work-life-balance-tougher-for-couples-with-similar-jobs/52537324/1, accessed November 2012.
Pg. 243 Fact: Frivolous Lawsuits, America's Best website, April 2008, http://www.americasbestcompanies.com/magazine/articles/frivolous-lawsuits.aspx, accessed November 27, 2012.
Pg. 253 Fact: http://www.psychologytoday.com/blog/wired-success/201006/the-impact-layoffs-surviving-employees, accessed November 2012.

16

1. The iPad in Your Hand: As Fast as a Supercomputer of Yore by John Markoff, *New York Times* website, http://bits.blogs.nytimes.com/2011/05/09/the-ipad-in-your-hand-as-fast-as-a-supercomputer-of-yore/; What Makes the New iPad Tick: A Peek Inside, IT News Post, March 11, 2012, http://www.itnewspost.com/apple/what-makes-the-new-ipad-tick-a-peek-inside/, accessed June 16, 2012.
2. The Web Is Dead. Long Live the Internet, by Chris Anderson, Wired website, http://www.wired.com/magazine/2010/08/ff_webrip/all/1.
3. Home Broadband 2010: Trends in Broadband Adoption by Aaron Smith, Pew Internet and American Life Project, http://www.pewinternet.org/Reports/2010/Home-Broadband-2010/Part-1/Little-change-in-home-broadband-in-2010.aspx, accessed May 16, 2011.
4. Internet2 Member and Partner List, Internet2 website, http://www.internet2.edu/resources/list-forweb.pdf.
5. Muse website, http://k20.internet2.edu/about/goals.
6. About Us, Internet2 website, http://www.internet2.edu/about/, accessed May 16, 2011.
7. 9 'Reply All' Email Disasters, The Week, November 1, 2009, http://theweek.com/article/index/102900/9-reply-all-email-disasters, accessed June 17, 2012; 'Reply-All' Emails Overwhelm German Parliament, NPR, January 30, 2012, http://www.npr.org/2012/01/30/146075544/the-last-word-in-business, accessed June 17, 2012; Reply All: The Button Everyone Loves to Hate by E. Bernstein, *The Wall Street Journal*, March 8, 2011, http://online.wsj.com/article/SB10001424052748703386704576186520353326558.html, accessed June 17, 2012; Changing the Subject: Spam Makes Friends Across Continents 'Reply All' Spread the Distress, But Outrage Gave Way to Camaraderie by L. Meckler, *The Wall Street Journal*, March 12, 2012, p. A1.
8. Seeking Safety in Clouds by J. Bussey, *The Wall Street Journal*, September 15, 2011, http://online.wsj.com/article/SB10001424053111904060604576572930344327162.html, accessed June 16, 2012.
8a. Seeking Safety in Clouds by J. Bussey, *The Wall Street Journal*, September 15, 2011, http://online.wsj.com/article/SB10001424053111904060604576572930344327162.html, accessed June 16, 2012.
9. Self-service, Prorated Super Computing Fun by Derek Gottfrid, The *New York Times*, November 1, 2007, http://open.blogs.nytimes.com/2007/11/01/self-service-prorated-super-computing-fun/; NY Times AWS Cloud Computing

Mistake Costs $240, Green Data Center Blog, November 5, 2008, http://www.greenm3.com/2008/11/nytimes-cloud-c.html; Early Experiments in Cloud Computing by Galen Gruman, InfoWorld website April 7, 2008: http://www.infoworld.com/d/virtualization/early-experiments-in-cloud-computing-020.
11. The Price Is Right, *The Economist*, January 9, 2012, http://www.economist.com/blogs/gametheory/2012/01/sports-ticketing, accessed June 16, 2012.
12. *Management Information Systems*, 5th ed. by Effy Oz, *Course Technology*, Cengage Learning, 2006, pp. 332–338; Expert Systems, AlanTuring.Net, http://www.cs.usfca.edu/www.AlanTuring.net/turing_archive/pages/Reference%20Articles/what_is_AI/What%20is%20AI07.html.
13. *Experiencing MIS* by David M. Kroenke Pearson Prentice Hall, 2008, pp. 340–341; What Are Expert Systems? Thinkquest.org website, http://library.thinkquest.org/11534/expert.htm, accessed May 24, 2009.
14. Web 2.0 Definition Updated and Enterprise 2.0 Emerges by Dion Hinchcliffe, ZDnet website, http://blogs.zdnet.com/Hinchcliffe/?p=71; The Ethics of Web 2.0: YouTube vs. Flickr, Revver, Eyespot, Bliptv, and Even Google, Lessig.org website, http://www.lessig.org/blog/2006/10/the_ethics_of_web_20_youtube_v.html, accessed May 24, 2009; Twitter, Blogs and Other Web 2.0 Tools Revolutionize Government Business by Doug Beizer, *Federal Computer Week* website, March 6, 2009, http://www.fcw.com/Articles/2009/03/09/Web-2.0-in-action.aspx.
15. 7 Best Green Apps for Mobile Phones by Jaymi Heimbuch, PlanetGreen.com website, http://planetgreen.discovery.com/feature/green-phone/green-apps-mobile-phones.html; The Top Ten Apps to Make You More Green by Matylda Czarnecka, TechCrunch website, http://techcrunch.com/2010/08/10/top-ten-green-apps/; Green Apps that Can Save You Money by Deborah Zabarenko, Reuters website, http://blogs.reuters.com/environment/2011/02/18/green-apps-that-can-save-you-money/.
16. IAB Internet Advertising Revenue Report: 2010 Full Year Results by Pricewaterhouse Coopers, IAB website, http://www.iab.net/media/file/IAB_Full_year_2010_0413_Final.pdf, accessed May 17, 2011; A Milestone for Internet Ad Revenue by Teddy Wayne, *New York Times* website, April 25, 2010, http://www.nytimes.com/2010/04/26/business/media/26drill.html; Internet Ad Revenues Hit $31 Billion in 2011, Historic High Up 22% Over 2010 Record-Breaking Numbers, Internet Advertising Bureau, June 11, 2012, www.iab.net/about_the_iab/recent_press_releases/press_release_archive/press_release/pr-041812, accessed June 16, 2012.
17. Paypal website, https://www.paypal-media.com/aboutus.cfm, accessed May 17, 2011; About PayPal, Welcome to the Press Center: Get the Latest on PayPal, https://www.paypal-media.com/about, accessed June 21, 2012.
18. The Middle Seat: The Trump Card at CheckIn With HighTech IDs, Qantas Fliers Get A Fast, Practically Paperless Experience by S. McCartney, *The Wall Street Journal*, December 29, 2011, p. D1.
19. Advanced Sign-In Security for Your Google Account, Google Official Blog, http://googleblog.blogspot.com/2011/02/advanced-sign-in-security-for-your.html, accessed June 17, 2012; Getting

Started with 2-Step Verification, Google, https://support.google.com/accounts/bin/answer.py?hl=en&topic=1056283&answer=185839, accessed June 17, 2012; Recovery Email Address, Google, http://support.google.com/accounts/bin/answer.py?hl=en&p=oz&ctx=ch_b%2F0%2FUpdateAccountRecoveryOptions&answer=183726, accessed June 17, 2012.

20. Spammers Target Email Newsletters by David Utter, January 19, 2007, WebProWorld Security Forum, http://www.securitypronews.com/insider-reports/insider/spn-49-20070119Spammers TargetEmailNewsletters.html; Spammers Turn to Images to Fool Filters by Anick Jesdanun, *USA Today*, June 28, 2006, http://www.usatoday.com/tech/news/computersecurity/wormsviruses/2006-06-28-spam-images_x.htm.

21. Pharming: Is Your Trusted Website a Clever Fake? Microsoft website January 3, 2007, http://www.microsoft.com/protect/yourself/phishing/pharming.mspx; Online Fraud: Pharming, Symantic website, http://www.symantec.com/norton/cybercrime/pharming.jsp, accessed May 24, 2009; Advisory: Watch Out for Drive-by-Pharming Attacks, Pharming.org website, http://www.pharming.org/index.jsp, accessed May 24, 2009.

22. 'Smishing' Emerges as New Threat to Cell Phone Users by Mark Huffman, Consumer Affairs.com website, http://www.consumeraffairs.com/news04/2006/11/smishing.html accessed May 22, 2009; 'SMiShing' Fishes for Personal Data Over Cell Phone by Eleanor Mills, CNet News website, February 24, 2009, http://news.cnet.com/8301-1009_3-10171241-83.html.

23. Create Strong Passwords, Microsoft Safety & Security Center, Microsoft website, http://www.microsoft.com/security/online-privacy/passwords-create.aspx.

24. What Makes a Password Stronger with Concern about Hackers, Tools for Remembering So Many Codes by S. Woo, *The Wall Street Journal*, June 23, 2011, p. D2.

25. Passport RFIDs Cloned Wholesale by $250 eBay Shopping Spree by Dan Goodin, *The Register* website February 2, 2009, http://www.theregister.co.uk/2009/02/02/low_cost_rfid_cloner/; Life With Big Brother: Radio Chips Coming Soon to Your Driver's License? by Bob Unruh, World Net Daily website February 28, 2009, http://www.worldnetdaily.com/index.php?fa=PAGE.view&pageId=90008; RFID Driver's Licenses Debated by Mark Baard, *Wired* website October 6, 2004, http://www.wired.com/politics/security/news/2004/10/65243; A Threat Analysis of RFID Passports by A. Ramos, W. Scott, W. Scott, D. Lloyd, K. O'Leary & J. Waldo, Communications of the ACM, December 2009, p. 38-42.

26. Multitasking: More Is Less by R. Mantell, *The Wall Street Journal*, July 10, 2011, http://online.wsj.com/article/SB10001424052702303544604576436572369558128.html, accessed June 17, 2012; The Ethics of Multitasking, Business-Week Online by B. Weinstein, September 7, 2009, http://www.businessweek.com/managing/content/sep2009/ca2009094_935233.htm, accessed June 17, 2012.

27. Facebook, Burson discuss role in Google Circle dispute by byron Acohido, Scott Martin and Jon Swartz, *USA Today* website, http://www.usatoday.com/tech/news/2011-05-12-google-whisper-campaign_n.htm; Oops: Facebook Caught Planting Anti-Google Stories to Press by Devindra Hardawar, VentureBeat website, http://venturebeat.com/2011/05/12/

facebook-anti-google-smear/; Facebook Busted in Clumsy Smear of Google by Dan Lyons, The Daily Beast website, http://www.thedailybeast.com/blogs-and-stories/2011-05-12/facebook-busted-in-clumsy-smear-attempt-on-google/; Burson-Marsteller Statement, Burson-Marsteller website, http://www.burson-marsteller.com/Newsroom/Pages/Burson-MarstellerStatement.aspx; Burson-Marsteller Caught Deleting Facebook Criticism; Facebook Delivers Statement, by David Murphy, PC Magazine website, http://www.pcmag.com/article2/0,2817,2385394,00.asp.

28. Eighth Annual BSA Global Software 2010 Piracy Study: May 2011, Business Software Alliance website, http://portal.bsa.org/globalpiracy2010/downloads/study_pdf/2010_BSA_Piracy_Study-InBrief.pdf; Shadow Market: 2011 BSA Global Software Piracy Study, Business Software Alliance, May 2012, http://portal.bsa.org/globalpiracy2011/downloads/study_pdf/2011_BSA_Piracy_Study-Standard.pdf, accessed June 16, 2012.

29. CESA: Portable Piracy Cost Game Industry $41.5 Billion, Gamasutra website, http://www.gamasutra.com/view/news/28848/CESA_Portable_Piracy_Cost_Game_Industry_415_Billion.php.

29a. Computer Support Specialists, Occupational Outlook Handbook, Bureau of Labor Statistics, U.S. Department of Labor,http://www.bls.gov/ooh/Computer-and-Information-Technology/Computer-support-specialists.htm, accessed June 16, 2012.

30. Computer System Analysts, Occupational Outlook Handbook, Bureau of Labor Statistics, U.S. Department of Labor, http://www.bls.gov/ooh/computer-and-information-technology/computer-systems-analysts.htm, accessed June 16, 2012; All information about the nature of work, educational requirements, earnings and projected growth in employment in this section are based on the Occupational Outlook Handbook, 2010–2011 edition, accessed from the Bureau of Labor Statistics website, http://www.bls.gov/oco/ocos287.htm and http://www.bls.gov/oco/ocos306.htm.
Pg. 264 Fact: http://usatoday30.usatoday.com/NEWS/usaedition/2011-05-11-Marketers-turn-to-Facebook-to-se_ST_U.htm, accessed November 2012.

17

1. Establishment Data: Historical Employment, Bureau of Labor Statistics, ftp://ftp.bls.gov/pub/suppl/empsit.ceseeb1.txt, accessed June 18, 2012.

2. *OM*, *2nd ed.* by David A. Collier and James R. Evans, Mson, OH: South-Western, Cengage Learning, 2010, pages 27–28.

3. Outsourcing: Ripoff Nation, BW Smallbiz Front Line, Winter 2006, *Business Week* website, http://www.businessweek.com/magazine/content/06_52/b4015435.htm?chan=rss_topStories_ssi_5; Outsourcing in China: Five Basic Rules for Reducing Risk by Steve Dickinson, ezinearticles.com website, http://ezinearticles.com/?Outsourcing-in-China:-Five-Basics-for-Reducing-Risk&id=17214.

4. ERP and Cloud Computing: Delivering a Virtual Feast by David Stodder, Information-Week website, May 20, 2010, http://www.informationweek.com/news/software/bi/224701329, accessed Dec. 6, 2011.

5. Servicescapes: The Impact of Physical Surroundings on Customers and Employees by M. J. Bitner, *Journal of Marketing*, April 1992, pp. 57–71.

6. The Robots Are Coming to Hospitals: A New Breed of BlueCollar Robots is Handling the Dirty Work, Transporting Linens and Laundry by T. Hay, *The Wall Street Journal*, March 15, 2002, http://online.wsj.com/article/SB100014240527023044598045772813505258709 34.html, accessed June 20, 2012; Soon, That Nearby Worker Might Be a Robot by R. King, BusinessWeek, June 2, 2010, p. 3.

7. Penney Picks Boss From Apple — Secrets From Genius Bar: Full Loyalty, No Negativity by Y, Kane & I. Sherr, *The Wall Street Journal*, June 15, 2011, p. A1.

8. Poka Yoke Mistake Proofing by Kerri Simon, iSixSigma website, http://www.isixsigma.com/library/content/c020128a.asp; Make No Mistake by Mark Hendricks, *Entrepreneur* Magazine, October 1996, http://www.entrepreneur.com/magazine/entrepreneur/1996/october/13430.html, accessed July 30, 2007.

9. Baldrige FAQs: Applying for the Malcolm Baldrige National Quality Award, National Institutes of Standards and Technology, http://www.nist.gov/baldrige/about/faqs_applying.cfm, accessed June 18, 2012.

10. About ISO, ISO website, http://www.iso.org/iso/about.htm, accessed June 5, 2011; ISO Standards, ISO website, http://www.iso.org/iso/iso_catalogue.htm, accessed June 5, 2011.

11. ISO 9001 - Quality management systems - Requirements, International Organization for Standardization, http://www.iso.org/iso/iso-survey2010.pdf, accessed June 18, 2012.

12. At Vuitton, Growth in Small Batches—Luxury-Goods Maker's New French Factory Adds to Capacity but Sticks to Strategy of Tight Rein, *The Wall Street Journal*, June 27, 2011, p. B1.

13. Multitasking: More Is Less by R. Mantell, *The Wall Street Journal*, July 10, 2011, http://online.wsj.com/article/SB10001424052702303544604576436572369558128.html, accessed June 17, 2012.

14. The Math Changes on Bulbs by K. Linebaugh, *The Wall Street Journal*, November 30, 2011, http://online.wsj.com/article/SB10001424052970203537304577031912827196558.html, accessed June 18, 2012.

15. *OM*, *2nd ed.* by David A.Collier and James R. Evans, Mason, OH: South-Western, Cengage Learning, 2010, pages 328–330.

16. One reason renewable energy is more expensive than energy from carbon-based sources such as coal or oil is that the market prices of such carbon-based sources do not reflect their environmental costs.

17. Sustainability Initiatives Cut Costs 6-10%, Environmental Leader website, http://www.environmentalleader.com/2009/06/09/sustainability-initiatives-cut-costs-by-6-10/.

18. ISO 14000 Essentials, ISO website, http://www.iso.org/iso/iso_14000_essentials, accessed June 4, 2011.

19. Careers in Operations Management Salaries, Careers-in-Business, http://www.careers-in-business.com/omsal.htm, accessed June 18, 2012; Careers in Operations Management, Careers-in-Business, http://www.careers-in-business.com/om.htm, accessed June 18, 2012.

Personal Finance Appendix

1. Learn About the Bureau, Consumer Finance Protection Bureau website, http://www.consumerfinance.gov/the-bureau/.

2. Bach, David, *The Automatic Millionaire* New York, Broadway Books, 2004.

3. Bach, David, *The Automatic Millionaire* New York, Broadway Books, 2004.

4. FDIC Insurance Coverage Basics, FDIC website, http://www.fdic.gov/deposit/deposits/insured/basics.html; Note that, in accordance with provisions in the Dodd-Frank Act of 2010, the FDIC provided temporary, unlimited coverage to noninterest-bearing accounts. However, this would not affect coverage on savings accounts, since they do pay interest. Moreover, at the time this text went to print, the unlimited coverage was scheduled to expire on December 31, 2012. (See Temporary Unlimited Coverage for Noninterest-bearing Transactions Accounts, FDIC website, http://www.fdic.gov/deposit/deposits/insured/temporary.html); Your Insured Deposits, FDIC Insurance Basics, Federal Deposit Insurance Corporation, http://www.fdic.gov/deposit/deposits/insured/basics.html, accessed June 23, 2012.

5. What's In Your FICO Score?, myFICO website, http://www.myfico.com/CreditEducation/WhatsInYourScore.aspx; How Credit Scores Work, How a Score Is Calculated by Pat Curry, Bankrate.com website, http://www.bankrate.com/brm/news/credit-scoring/20031104a1.asp.

5a. About Credit Scores, Money-Zine.com, http://www.money-zine.com/Financial-Planning/Debt-Consolidation/About-Credit-Scores/, accessed June 23, 2012.

6. How Your Credit Score Affects Your Mortgage, U.S. News and World Report, March 2, 2011, http://money.usnews.com/money/blogs/my-money/2011/03/02/how-your-credit-score-affects-your-mortgage, accessed June 23, 2012.

7. Feds Cap Credit Card Late Fees at $25 by Susan Ladika, Creditcards.com website, http://www.creditcards.com/credit-card-news/feds-cap-credit-card-late-payment-fee-25.php; Does Law Cap Credit Card Rates?, BankRate.com, http://www.bankrate.com/finance/credit-cards/does-law-cap-credit-card-interest-rates.aspx, accessed June 23, 2012.

8. What the Dodd-Frank Law Means for You by Leslie McFadden, Bankrate.com website, http://www.bankrate.com/financing/credit-cards/what-the-dodd-frank-act-means-for-you/.

9. Fresh Downgrade Threat to U.S. Debt by Carol E. Lee and Janet Hook, *Wall Street Journal* website, http://online.wsj.com/article/SB1000142405270230477830457637399271172366.html.

10. Table 5. Quartiles and Selected Deciles of Usual Weekly Earnings of Full-Time Wage and Salary Workers by Selected Characteristics, First Quarter 2012 Averages, Not Seasonally Adjusted, Economic News Release, Bureau of Labor Statistics, April 17, 2012, http://www.bls.gov/news.release/wkyeng.t05.htm, accessed June 23, 2012.

11. Table A-4. Employment Status of the Civilian Population 25 Years and Over by Educational Attainment, Economic News Release, Bureau of Labor Statistics, June 1, 2012, http://www.bls.gov/news.release/empsit.t04.htm/, accessed June 23, 2012.

12. The Best New Personal Finance Apps by A. Tergesen & J. Light, SmartMoney, June 18, 2012, http://www.smartmoney.com/invest/mutual-funds/conflict-of-interest-at-blackrock-funds-1340036191929/, accessed June 23, 2012; Best Personal Finance Mobile Apps by S. Yin, PC Magazine, February 23, 2012, http://www.pcmag.com/article2/0,2817,2400562,00.asp, accessed June 23, 2012.

13. U.S. Department of Labor Advisory by Janet Oates (Assistant Secretary, Employment and Training Administration) and Nancy Leppink (Deputy Administrator, Wage and Hour Division), U.S. Department of Labor website, http://wdr.doleta.gov/directives/attach/TEGL/TEGL12-09acc.pdf; The Unpaid Intern, Legal or Not by Steven Greenhouse, *New York Times* website, http://www.nytimes.com/2010/04/03/business/03intern.html.

14. While earnings on traditional IRA contributions are always tax deferred, there are income-based limits on the deductibility of contributions. Thus, high-income taxpayers are unable to deduct any money they contribute to a traditional IRA. For more specifics, see the IRS guidelines at: http://www.irs.gov/retirement/participant/article/0,,id=202516,00.html.

Pg. 294 Fact: Study finds rising number of college students using credit cards for tuition, SallieMae, https://www1.salliemae.com/about/news_info/newsreleases/041309.htm, April 13, 2009.

401(k), 403(b), and 457 plans
Employee payroll deduction retirement plans that offer tax benefits.

absolute advantage
The benefit a country has in a given industry when it can produce more of a product than other nations using the same amount of resources.

accounting
A system for recognizing, organizing, analyzing, and reporting information about the financial transactions that affect an organization.

accounting equation
Assets = Liabilities + Owners' Equity

accredited investor
An organization or individual investor who meets certain criteria established by the SEC and so qualifies to invest in unregistered securities.

accrual-basis accounting
The method of accounting that recognizes revenue when it is earned and matches expenses to the revenues they helped produce.

acquisition
A corporate restructuring in which one firm buys another.

active listening
Attentive listening that occurs when the listener focuses his or her complete attention on the speaker.

active voice
Sentence construction in which the subject performs the action expressed by the verb (e.g., *My sister wrote the paper*). The active voice works better for the vast majority of business communication.

activity-based costing (ABC)
A technique to assign product costs based on links between activities that drive costs and the production of specific products.

administrative law
Laws that arise from regulations established by government agencies.

advergaming
A relatively new promotional channel that involves integrating branded products and advertising into interactive games.

advertising
Paid, nonpersonal communication, designed to influence a target audience with regard to a product, service, organization, or idea.

affirmative action
Policies meant to increase employment and educational opportunities for minority groups—especially groups defined by race, ethnicity, or gender.

agent
A party who agrees to represent another party, called the principal.

agents/brokers
Independent distributors who do not take title of the goods they distribute (even though they may take physical possession on a temporary basis before distribution).

angel investors
Individuals who invest in start-up companies with high growth potential in exchange for a share of ownership.

annual percentage rate (APR)
The interest expense charged on a credit card, expressed as an annual percentage.

applications software
Software that helps a user perform a desired task.

apprenticeships
Structured training programs that mandate that each beginner serve as an assistant to a fully trained worker before gaining full credentials to work in the field.

arbitration
A process in which a neutral third party has the authority to resolve a dispute by rendering a binding decision.

articles of incorporation
The document filed with a state government to establish the existence of a new corporation.

asset management ratios
Financial ratios that measure how effectively a firm is using its assets to generate revenues or cash.

assets
Resources owned by a firm.

autocratic leaders
Leaders who hoard decision-making power for themselves and typically issue orders without consulting their followers.

automation
Replacing human operation and control of machinery and equipment with some form of programmed control.

balance of payments
A measure of the total flow of money into or out of a country.

balance of payments deficit
Shortfall that occurs when more money flows out of a nation than into that nation.

balance of payments surplus
Overage that occurs when more money flows into a nation than out of that nation.

balance of trade
A basic measure of the difference in value between a nation's exports and imports, including both goods and services.

balance sheet
A financial statement that reports the financial position of a firm by identifying and reporting the value of the firm's assets, liabilities, and owners' equity.

Baldrige National Quality Program
A national program to encourage American firms to focus on quality improvement.

Banking Act of 1933
The law that established the Federal Deposit Insurance Corporation (FDIC) to insure bank deposits. It also prohibited commercial banks from selling insurance or acting as investment banks.

behavioral segmentation
Dividing the market based on how people behave toward various products. This category includes both the benefits that consumers seek from products and how consumers use the products.

benefits
Noncash compensation, including programs, such as health insurance, vacation, and childcare.

bias
A preconception about members of a particular group. Common forms of bias include gender bias, age bias, and race, ethnicity, or nationality bias.

board of directors
The individuals who are elected by stockholders of a corporation to represent their interests.

bond
A formal debt instrument issued by a corporation or government entity.

boycott
A tactic in which a union and its supporters and sympathizers refuse to do business with an employer with which they have a labor dispute.

brand
A product's identity—including product name, symbol, design, reputation, and image—that sets it apart from other players in the same category.

brand equity
The overall value of a brand to an organization.

brand extension
A new product, in a new category, introduced under an existing brand name.

breach of contract
The failure of one party to a contract to perform his or her contractual obligations.

breakeven analysis
The process of determining the number of units a firm must sell to cover all costs.

broadband Internet connection
An Internet connection that is capable of transmitting large amounts of information very quickly.

budget (personal)
A detailed forecast of financial inflows (income) and outflows (expenses) in order to determine your net inflow or outflow for a given period of time.

budget deficit
Shortfall that occurs when expenses are higher than revenue over a given period of time.

budget surplus
Overage that occurs when revenue is higher than expenses over a given period of time.

budgeted balance sheet
A projected financial statement that forecasts the types and amounts of assets a firm will need to implement its future plans and how the firm will finance those assets. (Also called a *pro forma* balance sheet.)

budgeted income statement
A projection showing how a firm's budgeted sales and costs will affect expected net income. (Also called a *pro forma* income statement.)

budgeting
A management tool that explicitly shows how firms will acquire and allocate the resources needed to achieve its goals over a specific time period.

business
Any organization that provides goods and services in an effort to earn a profit.

business buyer behavior
Describes how people act when they are buying products to use either directly or indirectly to produce other products.

business cycle
The periodic contraction and expansion that occur over time in virtually every economy.

business environment
The setting in which business operates. The five key components are: economic environment, competitive environment, technological environment, social environment, and global environment.

business ethics
The application of right and wrong, good and bad in a business setting.

business format franchise
A broad franchise agreement in which the franchisee pays for the right to use the name, trademark, and business and production methods of the franchisor.

business intelligence system
A sophisticated form of decision support system that helps decision makers discover information that was previously hidden.

business law
The application of laws and legal principles to business relationships and transactions.

business marketers (also known as business-to-business or B2B)
Marketers who direct their efforts toward people who are buying products to use either directly or indirectly to produce other products.

business plan
A formal document that describes a business concept, outlines core business objectives, and details strategies and timelines for achieving those objectives.

business products
Products purchased to use either directly or indirectly in the production of other products.

business technology
Any tools—especially computers, telecommunications, and other digital products—that businesses can use to become more efficient and effective.

business-to-business (B2B) e-commerce
E-commerce in markets where businesses buy from and sell to other businesses.

business-to-consumer (B2C) e-commerce
E-commerce in which businesses and final consumers interact.

buzz marketing
The active stimulation of word of mouth via unconventional, and often relatively low-cost, tactics. Other terms for buzz marketing are "guerrilla marketing" and "viral marketing."

C corporation
The most common type of corporation, which is a legal business entity that offers limited liability to all of its owners, who are called *stockholders*.

cafeteria-style benefits
An approach to employee benefits that gives all employees a set dollar amount that they must spend on company benefits, allocated however they wish within broad limitations.

cannibalization
When a producer offers a new product that takes sales away from its existing products.

capital budgeting
The process a firm uses to evaluate long-term investment proposals.

capital gain
The return on an asset that results when its market price rises above the price the investor paid for it.

capital structure
The mix of equity and debt financing a firm uses to meet its permanent financing needs.

capitalism
An economic system—also known as the private enterprise or free market system—based on private ownership, economic freedom, and fair competition.

carbon footprint
Refers to the amount of harmful greenhouse gases that a firm emits throughout its operations, both directly and indirectly.

case law (also called common law)
Laws that result from rulings, called precedents, made by judges who initially hear a particular type of case.

cash budget
A detailed forecast of future cash flows that helps financial managers identify when their firm is likely to experience temporary shortages or surpluses of cash.

cash equivalents
Safe and highly liquid assets that many firms list with their cash holdings on their balance sheet.

cause-related marketing
Marketing partnerships between businesses and nonprofit organizations, designed to spike sales for the company and raise money for the nonprofit.

certificate of deposit (CD)
An interest-earning deposit that requires the funds to remain deposited for a fixed term. Withdrawal of the funds before the term expires results in a financial penalty.

channel intermediaries
Distribution organizations—informally called "middlemen"—that facilitate the movement of products from the producer to the consumer.

channel of distribution
The network of organizations and processes that links producers to consumers.

Chapter 7 bankruptcy
A form of bankruptcy that discharges a debtor's debts by liquidating assets and using the proceeds to pay off creditors.

Chapter 11 bankruptcy
A form of bankruptcy used by corporations and individuals that allows the debtor to reorganize operations under a court-approved plan.

Chapter 13 bankruptcy
A form of bankruptcy that allows individual debtors to set up a repayment plan to adjust their debts.

Civil Rights Act of 1964
Federal legislation that prohibits discrimination in hiring, firing, compensation, apprenticeships, training, terms, conditions, or privileges of employment based on race, color, religion, sex, or national origin.

closed shop
An employment arrangement in which the employer agrees to hire only workers who already belong to the union.

cloud computing
The use of Internet-based storage capacity, processing power, and computer applications to supplement or replace internally owned information technology resources.

cobranding
When established brands from different companies join forces to market the same product.

code of ethics
A formal, written document that defines the ethical standards of an organization and gives employees the information they need to make ethical decisions across a range of situations.

cognitive dissonance
Consumer discomfort with a purchase decision, typically for a higher-priced item.

collective bargaining
The process by which representatives of union members and employers attempt to negotiate a mutually acceptable labor agreement.

commercial banks
Privately owned financial institutions that accept demand deposits and make loans and provide other services for the public.

commercial paper
Short-term (and usually unsecured) promissory notes issued by large corporations.

common market
A group of countries that has eliminated tariffs and harmonized trading rules to facilitate the free flow of goods among the member nations.

common stock
The basic form of ownership in a corporation.

communication
The transmission of information between a sender and a recipient.

communication barriers
Obstacles to effective communication, typically defined in terms of physical, language, body language, cultural, perceptual, and organizational barriers.

communication channels
The various ways in which a message can be sent, ranging from one-on-one, in-person meetings to Internet message boards.

communism
An economic and political system that calls for public ownership of virtually all enterprises, under the direction of a strong central government.

company matching
An amount contributed by the employer to an employee's retirement account, matching the employee's retirement contributions either dollar for dollar or based on a percentage of each dollar contributed by the employee.

comparative advantage
The benefit a country has in a given industry if it can make products at a lower opportunity cost than other countries.

compensation
The combination of pay and benefits that employees receive in exchange for their work.

compensatory damages
Monetary payments that a party who breaches a contract is ordered to pay in order to compensate the injured party for the actual harm suffered by the breach of contract.

compressed workweek
A version of flextime scheduling that allows employees to work a full-time number of hours in less than the standard workweek.

computer-aided design (CAD)
Drawing and drafting software that enables users to create and edit blueprints and design drawings quickly and easily.

computer-aided design/computer-aided manufacturing (CAD/CAM)
A combination of software that can be used to design output and send instructions to automated equipment to perform the steps needed to produce this output.

computer-aided engineering (CAE)
Software that enables users to test, analyze, and optimize their designs.

computer-aided manufacturing (CAM)
Software that takes the electronic design for a product and creates the programmed instructions that robots must follow to produce that product as efficiently as possible.

computer-integrated manufacturing (CIM)
A combination of CAD/CAM software with flexible manufacturing systems to automate almost all steps involved in designing, testing, and producing a product.

computer virus
Computer software that can be spread from one computer to another without the knowledge or permission of the computer users.

conceptual skills
The ability to grasp a big-picture view of the overall organization, the relationship between its various parts, and its fit in the broader competitive environment.

conglomerate merger
A combination of two firms that are in unrelated industries.

consideration
Something of value that one party gives another as part of a contractual agreement.

constitution
A code that establishes the fundamental rules and principles that govern a particular organization or entity.

consumer behavior
Description of how people act when they are buying, using, and discarding goods and services for their own personal consumption. Consumer behavior also explores the reasons behind people's actions.

consumer marketers (also known as business-to-consumer or B2C)
Marketers who direct their efforts toward people who are buying products for personal consumption.

consumer price index (CPI)
A measure of inflation that evaluates the change in the weighted-average price of goods and services that the average consumer buys each month.

consumer products
Products purchased for personal use or consumption.

consumer promotion
Marketing activities designed to generate immediate consumer sales, using tools such as premiums, promotional products, samples, coupons, rebates, and displays.

consumerism
A social movement that focuses on four key consumer rights: (1) the right to be safe, (2) the right to be informed, (3) the right to choose, and (4) the right to be heard.

contingency planning
Planning for unexpected events, usually involving a range of scenarios and assumptions that differ from the assumptions behind the core plans.

contingent workers
Employees who do not expect regular, full-time jobs, including temporary full-time workers, independent contractors, and temporary agency or contract agency workers.

contract
An agreement that is legally enforceable.

contraction
A period of economic downturn, marked by rising unemployment and falling business production.

controlling
Checking performance and making adjustments as needed.

convertible security
A bond or share of preferred stock that gives its holder the right to exchange it for a stated number of shares of common stock.

copyright
The exclusive legal right of an author, artist, or other creative individual to use, copy, display, perform, and sell their own creations and to license others to do so.

corporate bylaws
The basic rules governing how a corporation is organized and how it conducts its business.

corporate philanthropy
All business donations to nonprofit groups, including money, products, and employee time.

corporate responsibility
Business contributions to the community through the actions of the business itself rather than donations of money and time.

corporation
A form of business ownership in which the business is considered a legal entity that is separate and distinct from its owners.

cost
The value of what is given up in exchange for something.

countertrade
International trade that involves the barter of products for products rather than for currency.

coupon rate
The interest paid on a bond, expressed as a percentage of the bond's par value.

covenant
A restriction lenders impose on borrowers as a condition of providing long-term debt financing.

craft union
A union comprising workers who share the same skill or work in the same profession.

credit
Allows a borrower to buy a good or acquire an asset without making immediate payment, and to repay the balance at a later time.

credit card
A card issued by a bank or finance company that allows the cardholder to make a purchase now and to pay the credit card issuer later.

credit score
A numerical measure of a consumer's creditworthiness.

credit union
A depository institution that is organized as a cooperative, meaning that it is owned by its depositors.

crime
A wrongful act against society, defined by law and prosecuted by the state.

critical path
The sequence of activities in a project that is expected to take the longest to complete.

critical path method (CPM)
A project-management tool that illustrates the relationships among all the activities involved in completing a project and identifies the sequence of activities likely to take the longest to complete.

current yield
The amount of interest earned on a bond expressed as a percentage of the bond's current market price.

customer benefit
The advantage that a customer gains from specific product features.

customer loyalty
When customers buy a product from the same supplier again and again—sometimes paying even more for it than they would for a competitive product.

customer-relationship management (CRM)
The ongoing process of acquiring, maintaining, and growing profitable customer relationships by delivering unmatched value.

customer satisfaction
When customers perceive that a good or service delivers value above and beyond their expectations.

cybermediary
An Internet-based firm that specializes in the secure electronic transfer of funds.

data
Raw, unprocessed facts and figures.

data mining
The use of sophisticated statistical and mathematical techniques to analyze data and discover hidden patterns and relationships among data, thus creating valuable information.

data warehouse
A large, organization-wide database that stores data in a centralized location.

database
A file consisting of related data organized according to a logical system and stored on a hard drive or some other computer-accessible media.

debit card
A card issued by the bank that allows the customer to make purchases as if the transaction involved cash. In a debit card purchase, the customer's bank account is immediately reduced when the purchase is made.

debt financing
Funds provided by lenders (creditors).

decision support system (DSS)
A system that gives managers access to large amounts of data and the processing power to convert these data into high-quality information, thus improving the decision-making process.

deflation
A period of falling average prices across the economy.

degree of centralization
The extent to which decision-making power is held by a small number of people at the top of the organization.

demand
The quantity of products that consumers are willing to buy at different market prices.

demand curve
The graphed relationship between price and quantity from a customer demand standpoint.

democratic leaders
Leaders who share power with their followers. While they still make final decisions, they typically solicit and incorporate input from their followers.

demographic segmentation
Dividing the market into smaller groups based on measurable characteristics about people such as age, income, ethnicity, and gender.

demographics
The measurable characteristics of a population. Demographic factors include population size and density, as well as specific traits such as age, gender, and race.

departmentalization
The division of workers into logical groups.

depository institution
A financial intermediary that obtains funds by accepting checking or savings deposits (or both) and uses these funds to make loans to borrowers.

depression
An especially deep and long-lasting recession.

direct channel
A distribution process that links the producer and the customer with no intermediaries.

direct costs
Costs that are incurred directly as the result of some specific cost object.

direct investment
(or foreign direct investment) When firms either acquire foreign firms or develop new facilities from the ground up in foreign countries.

discount rate
The rate of interest that the Federal Reserve charges when it loans funds to banks.

discretionary payments
Expenditures for which the spender has significant control in terms of the amount and timing.

disinflation
A period of slowing average price increases across the economy.

distribution strategy
A plan for delivering the right product to the right person at the right place at the right time.

distributive bargaining
The traditional adversarial approach to collective bargaining.

distributorship
A type of franchising arrangement in which the franchisor makes a product and licenses the franchisee to sell it.

divestiture
The transfer of total or partial ownership of some of a firm's operations to investors or to another company.

Dodd-Frank Act
A law enacted in the aftermath of the financial crisis of 2008–2009 that strengthened government oversight of financial markets and placed limitations on risky financial strategies such as heavy reliance on leverage.

Dow Jones Industrial Average
An index that tracks stock prices of thirty large, well-known U.S. corporations.

dynamic delivery
Vibrant, compelling presentation delivery style that grabs and holds the attention of the audience.

e-commerce
Business transactions conducted online, typically via the Internet.

economic system
A structure for allocating limited resources.

economics
The study of the choices that people, companies, and governments make in allocating society's resources.

economy
A financial and social system of how resources flow through society, from production, to distribution, to consumption.

effectiveness
Using resources to create the value by providing customers with goods and services that offer a better relationship between price and perceived benefits.

efficiency
Producing output or achieving a goal at the lowest cost.

electronic bill presentment and payment
A method of bill payment that makes it easy for the customer to make a payment, often by simply clicking on a payment option contained in an email.

electronic communications network (ECN)
An automated, computerized securities trading system that automatically matches buyers and sellers, executing trades quickly and allowing trading when securities exchanges are closed.

e-marketplace
A specialized Internet site where buyers and sellers engaged in business-to-business e-commerce can communicate and conduct business.

embargo
A complete ban on international trade of a certain item, or a total halt in trade with a particular nation.

employment at will
A legal doctrine that views employment as an entirely voluntary relationship that both the employee and employer are free to terminate at any time and for any reason.

enterprise resource planning (ERP)
Software-based approach to integrate an organization's (and in the sophisticated versions, a value chain's) information flows.

entrepreneurs
People who risk their time, money, and other resources to start and manage a business.

environmental scanning
The process of continually collecting information from the external marketing environment.

Equal Employment Opportunity Commission (EEOC)
A federal agency designed to regulate and enforce the provisions of Title VII.

equilibrium price
The price associated with the point at which the quantity demanded of a product equals the quantity supplied.

equity financing
Funds provided by the owners of a company.

equity theory
A motivation theory that proposes that perceptions of fairness directly affect worker motivation.

ethical dilemma
A decision that involves a conflict of values; every potential course of action has some significant negative consequences.

ethics
A set of beliefs about right and wrong, good and bad.

European Union (EU)
The world's largest common market, composed of 27 European nations.

everyday-low-pricing (EDLP)
Long-term discount pricing, designed to achieve profitability through high sales volume.

exchange rates
A measurement of the value of one nation's currency relative to the currency of other nations.

exchange traded fund (ETF)
Shares traded on securities markets that represent the legal right of ownership over part of a basket of individual stock certificates or other securities.

expansion
A period of robust economic growth and high employment.

expectancy theory
A motivation theory that concerns the relationship among individual effort, individual performance, and individual reward.

expenses
Resources that are used up as the result of business operations.

expert system (ES)
A decision-support system that helps managers make better decisions in an area where they lack expertise.

exporting
Selling products in foreign nations that have been produced or grown domestically.

external locus of control
A deep-seated sense that forces other than the individual are responsible for what happens in his or her life.

external recruitment
The process of seeking new employees from outside the firm.

extranet
An intranet that allows limited access to a selected group of stakeholders, such as suppliers or customers.

factor
A company that provides short-term financing to firms by purchasing their accounts receivable at a discount.

factors of production
Four fundamental elements—natural resources, capital, human resources, and entrepreneurship—that businesses need to achieve their objectives.

federal debt
The sum of all the money that the federal government has borrowed over the years and not yet repaid.

Federal Deposit Insurance Corporation (FDIC)
A federal agency that insures deposits in banks and thrift institutions for up to $250,000 per customer, per bank.

Federal Reserve Act of 1913
The law that established the Federal Reserve System as the central bank of the United States.

Financial Services Modernization Act of 1999
An act that overturned the section of the Banking Act of 1933 that prohibited commercial banks from selling insurance or performing the functions of investment banks.

finance
The functional area of business that is concerned with finding the best sources and uses of financial capital.

financial accounting
The branch of accounting that prepares financial statements for use by owners, creditors, suppliers, and other external stakeholders.

Financial Accounting Standards Board (FASB)
The private board that establishes the generally accepted accounting principles used in the practice of financial accounting.

financial budgets
Budgets that focus on the firm's financial goals and identify the resources needed to achieve those goals.

financial capital
The funds a firm uses to acquire its assets and finance its operations.

financial diversification
A strategy of investing in a wide variety of securities in order to reduce risk.

financial leverage
The use of debt in a firm's capital structure.

financial markets
Markets that transfer funds from savers to borrowers.

financial ratio analysis
Computing ratios that compare values of key accounts listed on a firm's financial statements.

Financial Services Modernization Act of 1999
An act that overturned the section of the Banking Act of 1933 that prohibited commercial banks from selling insurance or performing the functions of investment banks.

firewall
Software and/or hardware designed to prevent unwanted access to a computer or computer system.

first-line management
Managers who directly supervise nonmanagement employees.

fiscal policy
Government efforts to influence the economy through taxation and spending.

fixed costs
Costs that remain the same when the level of production changes within some relevant range.

flextime
A scheduling option that allows workers to choose when they start and finish their workdays, as long as they complete the required number of hours.

foreign franchising
A specialized type of foreign licensing in which a firm expands by offering businesses in other countries the right to produce and market its products according to specific operating requirements.

foreign licensing
Authority granted by a domestic firm to a foreign firm for the rights to produce and market its product or to use its trademark/patent rights in a defined geographical area.

foreign outsourcing
(also contract manufacturing) Contracting with foreign suppliers to produce products, usually at a fraction of the cost of domestic production.

franchise
A licensing arrangement under which a franchisor allows franchisees to use its name, trademark, products, business methods, and other property in exchange for monetary payments and other considerations.

franchise agreement
The contractual arrangement between a franchisor and a franchisee that spells out the duties and responsibilities of both parties.

Franchise Disclosure Document (FDD)
A detailed description of all aspects of a franchise that the franchisor must provide to the franchisee at least fourteen calendar days before the franchise agreement is signed.

franchisee
The party in a franchise relationship that pays for the right to use resources supplied by the franchisor.

franchisor
The business entity in a franchise relationship that allows others to operate its business using resources it supplies in exchange for money and other considerations.

free-rein leaders
Leaders who set objectives for their followers but give them freedom to choose how they will accomplish those goals.

free trade
An international economic and political movement designed to help goods and services flow more freely across international boundaries.

General Agreement on Tariffs and Trade (GATT)
An international trade agreement that has taken bold steps to lower tariffs and promote free trade worldwide.

general partnership
A partnership in which all partners can take an active role in managing the business and have unlimited liability for any claims against the firm.

generally accepted accounting principles (GAAP)
A set of accounting standards that is used in the preparation of financial statements.

geographic segmentation
Dividing the market into smaller groups based on where consumers live. This process can incorporate countries, cities, or population density as key factors.

goods
Tangible products.

grace period
The period of time that the credit-card holder has to pay outstanding balances before interest or fees are assessed.

green marketing
Developing and promoting environmentally sound products and practices to gain a competitive edge.

grievance
A complaint by a worker that the employer has violated the terms of the collective bargaining agreement.

gross domestic product (GDP)
The total value of all final goods and services produced within a nation's physical boundaries over a given period of time.

hacker
A skilled computer user who uses his or her expertise to gain unauthorized access to the computer (or computer system) of others, sometimes with malicious intent.

hardware
The physical tools and equipment used to collect, input, store, organize, and process data and to distribute information.

high/low pricing
A pricing strategy designed to drive traffic to retail stores by special sales on a limited number of products, and higher everyday prices on others.

horizontal analysis
Analysis of financial statements that compares account values reported on these statements over two or more years to identify changes and trends.

horizontal merger
A combination of two firms that are in the same industry.

human resource management
The management function focused on maximizing the effectiveness of the workforce by recruiting world-class talent, promoting career development, and determining workforce strategies to boost organizational effectiveness.

human skills
The ability to work effectively with and through other people in a range of different relationships.

hyperinflation
An average monthly inflation rate of more than 50 percent.

implicit cost
The opportunity cost that arises when a firm uses owner-supplied resources.

immediate predecessors
Activities in a project that must be completed before some other specified activity can begin.

importing
Buying products domestically that have been produced or grown in foreign nations.

income statement
The financial statement that reports the revenues, expenses, and net income that resulted from a firm's operations over an accounting period.

independent wholesaling businesses
Independent distributors that buy products from a range of different businesses and sell those products to a range of different customers.

indirect costs
Costs that are the result of a firm's general operations and are not directly tied to any specific cost object.

industrial union
A union comprising workers employed in the same industry.

inflation
A period of rising average prices across the economy.

information
Data that have been processed in a way that makes them meaningful to their user.

infrastructure
A country's physical facilities that support economic activity.

initial public offering (IPO)
The first time a company issues stock that may be bought by the general public.

institutional investor
An organization that pools contributions from investors, clients, or depositors and uses these funds to buy stocks and other securities.

integrated marketing communication
The coordination of marketing messages through every promotional vehicle to communicate a unified impression about a product.

intellectual property
Property that is the result of creative or intellectual effort, such as books, musical works, inventions, and computer software.

intercultural communication
Communication among people with differing cultural backgrounds.

interest-based bargaining
A form of collective bargaining that emphasizes cooperation and problem solving in an attempt to find a "win–win" outcome.

internal locus of control
A deep-seated sense that the individual is personally responsible for what happens in his or her life.

internal recruitment
The process of seeking employees who are currently within the firm to fill open positions.

International Monetary Fund (IMF)
An international organization of 187 member nations that promotes international economic cooperation and stable growth.

Internet
The world's largest computer network; essentially a network of computer networks all operating under a common set of rules that allow them to communicate with each other.

Internet2 (I2)
A new high-tech Internet restricted to dues-paying members of a consortium. I2 utilizes technologies that give it a speed and capacity far exceeding the current Internet.

intranet
A private network that has the look and feel of the Internet and is navigated using a web browser, but which limits access to a single firm's employees (or a single organization's members).

inventory
Stocks of goods or other items held by organizations.

investment bank
A financial intermediary that specializes in helping firms raise financial capital by issuing securities in primary markets.

investing
Reducing consumption in the current time period in order to build future wealth.

IRA
An individual retirement account that provides tax benefits to individuals who are investing for their retirement.

ISO 9000
A family of generic standards for quality management systems established by the International Organization for Standardization.

ISO 14000
A family of generic standards for environmental management established by the International Organization for Standardization.

job analysis
The examination of specific tasks that are assigned to each position, independent of who might be holding the job at any specific time.

job description
An explanation of the responsibilities for a specific position.

job enrichment
The creation of jobs with more meaningful content, under the assumption that challenging, creative work will motivate employees.

job specifications
The specific qualifications necessary to hold a particular position.

joint ventures
When two or more companies join forces— sharing resources, risks, and profits, but not actually merging companies— to pursue specific opportunities.

just-in-time (JIT) production
A production system that emphasizes the production of goods to meet actual current demand, thus minimizing the need to hold inventories of finished goods and work in process at each stage of the supply chain.

Labor–Management Relations Act (Taft–Hartley Act)
Law passed in 1947 that placed limits on union activities, outlawed the closed shop, and allowed states to pass right-to-work laws that made union shops illegal.

labor union
A group of workers who have organized to work together to achieve common job-related goals, such as higher wages, better working conditions, and greater job security.

laws
Rules that govern the conduct and actions of people within a society that are enforced by the government.

leading
Directing and motivating people to achieve organizational goals.

lean production
An approach to production that emphasizes the elimination of waste in all aspects of production processes.

leverage ratios
Ratios that measure the extent to which a firm relies on debt financing in its capital structure.

liabilities
Claims that outsiders have against a firm's assets.

licensing
Purchasing the right to use another company's brand name or symbol.

limit order
An order to a broker to buy a specific stock only if its price is below a certain level, or to sell a specific stock only if its price is above a certain level.

limited liability
When owners are not personally liable for claims against their firm. Owners with limited liability may lose their investment in the company, but their personal assets are protected.

limited liability company (LLC)
A form of business ownership that offers both limited liability to its owners and flexible tax treatment.

limited liability partnership (LLP)
A form of partnership in which all partners have the right to participate in management and have limited liability for company debts.

limited partnership
A partnership that includes at least one general partner who actively manages the company and accepts unlimited liability and one limited partner who gives up the right to actively manage the company in exchange for limited liability.

line-and-staff organizations
Organizations with line managers forming the primary chain of authority in the company, and staff departments working alongside line departments.

line extensions
Similar products offered under the same brand name.

line managers
Managers who supervise the functions that contribute directly to profitability: production and marketing.

line of credit
A financial arrangement between a firm and a bank in which the bank pre-approves credit up to a specified limit, provided that the firm maintains an acceptable credit rating.

line organizations
Organizations with a clear, simple chain of command from top to bottom.

liquid asset
An asset that can quickly be converted into cash with little risk of loss.

liquidity ratios
Financial ratios that measure the ability of a firm to obtain the cash it needs to pay its short-term debt obligations as they come due.

lockout
An employer-initiated work stoppage.

logistics
A subset of supply chain management that focuses largely on the tactics involved in moving products along the supply chain.

loss
When a business incurs expenses that are greater than its revenue.

loss-leader pricing
Closely related to high/low pricing, loss-leader pricing means pricing a handful of items—or loss leaders—temporarily below cost to drive traffic.

M1 money supply
Includes all currency plus checking accounts and traveler's checks.

M2 money supply
Includes all of M1 money supply plus most savings accounts, money market accounts, and certificates of deposit.

macroeconomics
The study of a country's overall economic dynamics, such as the employment rate, the gross domestic product, and taxation policies.

malware
A general term for malicious software, such as spyware, computer viruses, and worms.

management
Achieving the goals of an organization through planning, organizing, leading, and controlling organizational resources including people, money, and time.

management development
Programs to help current and potential executives develop the skills they need to move into leadership positions.

managerial (or management) accounting
The branch of accounting that provides reports and analysis to managers to help them make informed business decisions.

market makers
Securities dealers that make a commitment to continuously offer to buy and sell the stock of a specific corporation listed on the NASDAQ exchange or traded in the OTC market.

market niche
A small segment of a market with fewer competitors than the market as a whole. Market niches tend to be quite attractive to small firms.

market order
An order telling a broker to buy or sell a specific security at the best currently available price.

market segmentation
Dividing potential customers into groups of similar people, or segments.

market share
The percentage of a market controlled by a given marketer.

marketing
An organizational function and a set of processes for creating, communicating, and delivering value to customers and for managing customer relationships in ways that benefit the organization and its stakeholders.

marketing concept
A business philosophy that makes customer satisfaction—now and in the future—the central focus of the entire organization.

marketing mix
The blend of marketing strategies for product, price, distribution, and promotion.

marketing plan
A formal document that defines marketing objectives and the specific strategies for achieving those objectives.

marketing research
The process of gathering, interpreting, and applying information to uncover marketing opportunities and challenges, and to make better marketing decisions.

Maslow's hierarchy of needs theory
A motivation theory that suggests that human needs fall into a hierarchy and that as each need is met, people become motivated to meet the next-highest need in the pyramid.

mass customization
The creation of products tailored for individual consumers on a mass basis.

master budget
A presentation of an organization's operational and financial budgets that represents the firm's overall plan of action for a specified time period.

matrix organizations
Organizations with a flexible structure that brings together specialists from different areas of the company to work on individual projects on a temporary basis.

maturity date
The date when a bond will come due.

mediation
A method of dealing with an impasse between labor and management by bringing in a neutral third party to help the two sides reach agreement by reducing tensions and making suggestions for possible compromises.

merchant wholesalers
Independent distributors who take legal possession, or title, of the goods they distribute.

merger
A corporate restructuring that occurs when two formerly independent business entities combine to form a new organization.

microeconomics
The study of smaller economic units, such as individual consumers, families, and individual businesses.

middle management
Managers who supervise lower-level managers and report to a higher-level manager.

mission
The definition of an organization's purpose, values, and core goals, which provides the framework for all other plans.

mixed economies
Economies that embody elements of both planned and market-based economic systems.

modes of transportation
The various transportation options—such as planes, trains, and railroads—for moving products through the supply chain.

monetary policy
Federal Reserve decisions that shape the economy by influencing interest rates and the supply of money.

money
Anything generally accepted as a medium of exchange, a measure of value or a means of payment.

money market mutual fund
A mutual fund that pools funds from many investors and uses these funds to purchase very safe, highly liquid securities.

money supply
The total amount of money within the overall economy.

monopolistic competition
A market structure with many competitors selling differentiated products. Barriers to entry are low.

monopoly
A market structure with one producer completely dominating the industry, leaving no room for any significant competitors. Barriers to entry tend to be virtually insurmountable.

multichannel retailing
Providing multiple distribution channels for consumers to buy a product.

mutual fund
An institutional investor that raises funds by selling shares to investors and uses the accumulated funds to buy a portfolio of many different securities.

national brands
Brands that the producer owns and markets.

National Labor Relations Act (Wagner Act)
Landmark pro-labor law enacted in 1935. This law made it illegal for firms to discriminate against union members and required employers to recognize certified unions and bargain with these unions in good faith.

natural monopoly
A market structure with one company as the supplier of a product because the nature of that product makes a single supplier more efficient than multiple competing ones. Most natural monopolies are government sanctioned and regulated.

negligence
An unintentional tort that arises due to carelessness or irresponsible behavior.

Net Asset Value Per Share (NAV)
The value of a mutual fund's securities and cash holdings, minus any liabilities, divided by the number of shares of the fund outstanding.

net income
The difference between the revenue a firm earns and the expenses it incurs in a given time period.

net present value (NPV)
The sum of the present values of expected future cash flows from an investment, minus the cost of that investment.

noise
Any interference that causes the message you send to be different from the message your audience understands.

nondiscretionary payments
Expenditures that the spender has little or no control over.

nonprofit corporation
A corporation that does not seek to earn a profit and differs in several fundamental respects from C corporations.

nonprofits
Business-*like* establishments that employ people and produce goods and services with the fundamental goal of contributing to the community rather than generating financial gain.

nonverbal communication
Communication that does not use words. Common forms of nonverbal communication include gestures, posture, facial expressions, tone of voice, and eye contact.

North American Free Trade Agreement (NAFTA)
The treaty among the United States, Mexico, and Canada that eliminated trade barriers and investment restrictions over a fifteen-year period starting in 1994.

observation research
Marketing research that *does not* require the researcher to interact with the research subject.

odd pricing
The practice of ending prices in numbers below even dollars and cents in order to create a perception of greater value.

offshoring
Moving production or support processes to foreign countries.

oligopoly
A market structure with only a handful of competitors selling products that can be similar or different. Barriers to entry are typically high.

on-the-job training
A training approach that requires employees to simply begin their jobs—sometimes guided by more experienced employees—and to learn as they go.

open market operations
The Federal Reserve function of buying and selling government securities, which include treasury bonds, notes, and bills.

open shop
An employment arrangement in which workers are not required to join a union or pay union dues.

operating budgets
Budgets that communicate an organization's sales and production goals and the resources needed to achieve those goals.

operational planning
Very specific, short-term planning that applies tactical plans to daily, weekly, and monthly operations.

operations management
Managing all of the activities involved in creating value by producing goods and services and distributing them to customers.

opportunity cost
The opportunity of giving up the second-best choice when making a decision.

organization chart
A visual representation of the company's formal structure.

organizing
Determining a structure for both individual jobs and the overall organization.

orientation
The first step in the training and development process, designed to introduce employees to the company culture and provide key administrative information.

outsourcing
Arranging for other organizations to perform supply chain functions that were previously performed internally.

out-of-pocket cost
A cost that involves the payment of money or other resources.

over-the-counter (OTC) market
The market where securities that are not listed on exchanges are traded.

owners' equity
The claims a firm's owners have against their company's assets (often called "stockholders' equity" on balance sheets of corporations).

par value (of a bond)
The value of a bond at its maturity; what the issuer promises to pay the bondholder when the bond matures.

partnership
A voluntary agreement under which two or more people act as co-owners of a business for profit.

passive voice
Sentence construction in which the subject does not do the action expressed by the verb; rather the subject is acted upon (e.g., *The paper was written by my sister*). The passive voice tends to be less effective for business communication.

patent
A legal monopoly that gives an inventor the exclusive right over an invention for a limited time period.

penetration pricing
A new product pricing strategy that aims to capture as much of the market as possible through rock-bottom prices.

performance appraisal
A formal feedback process that requires managers to give their subordinates feedback on a one-to-one basis, typically by comparing actual results to expected results.

personal selling
The person-to-person presentation of products to potential buyers.

pharming
A scam that seeks to steal identities by routing Internet traffic to fake websites.

phishing
A scam in which official-looking emails are sent to individuals in an attempt to get them to divulge private information such as passwords, user names, and account numbers.

physical distribution
The actual, physical movement of products along the distribution pathway.

picketing
A union tactic during labor disputes in which union members walk near the entrance of the employer's place of business, carrying signs to publicize their position and concerns.

planned obsolescence
The strategy of deliberately designing products to fail in order to shorten the time between purchases.

planning
Determining organizational goals and action plans for how to achieve those goals.

poka-yokes
Simple methods incorporated into a production process designed to eliminate or greatly reduce errors.

positioning statement
A brief statement that articulates how the marketer would like the target market to envision a product relative to the competition.

preferred stock
A type of stock that gives its holder preference over common stockholders in terms of dividends and claims on assets.

present value
The amount of money that, if invested today at a given rate of interest (called the "discount rate"), would grow to become some future amount in a specified number of time periods.

primary data
New data that marketers compile for a specific research project.

primary securities market
The market where newly issued securities are traded. The primary market is where the firms that issue securities raise additional financial capital.

principal
A party who agrees to have someone else (called an agent) act on his or her behalf.

principal–agent relationship
A relationship in which one party, called the principal, gives another party, called the agent, the authority to act in place of, and bind the principal when dealing with, third parties.

private placement
A primary market issue that is negotiated between the issuing corporation and a small group of accredited investors.

privatization
The process of converting government-owned businesses to private ownership.

probationary period
A specific timeframe (typically three to six months) during which a new hire can prove his or her worth on the job before he or she becomes permanent.

process
A set of related activities that transform inputs into outputs, thus adding value.

producer price index (PPI)
A measure of inflation that evaluates the change over time in the weighted-average wholesale prices.

product
Anything that an organization offers to satisfy consumer needs and wants, including both goods and services.

product consistency
How reliably a product delivers its promised level of quality.

product differentiation
The attributes that make a good or service different from other products that compete to meet the same or similar customer needs.

product features
The specific characteristics of a product.

product life cycle
A pattern of sales and profits that typically changes over time.

product line
A group of products that are closely related to each other, in terms of either how they work or the customers they serve.

product mix
The total number of product lines and individual items sold by a single firm.

product placement
The paid integration of branded products into movies, television, and other media.

productivity
The basic relationship between the production of goods and services (output) and the resources needed to produce them (input), calculated via the following equation: output/input = productivity.

profit
The money that a business earns in sales (or revenue), minus expenses, such as the cost of goods, and the cost of salaries. Revenue – Expenses = Profit (or Loss)

profit margin
The gap between the cost and the price of an item on a per-product basis.

profitability ratios
Ratios that measure the rate of return a firm is earning on various measures of investment.

promotion
Marketing communication designed to influence consumer purchase decisions through information, persuasion, and reminders.

promotional channels
Specific marketing communication vehicles, including traditional tools, such as advertising, sales promotion, direct marketing, and personal selling, and newer tools, such as product placement, advergaming, and Internet minimovies.

property
The legal right of an owner to exclude non-owners from having control over a particular resource.

protectionism
National policies designed to restrict international trade, usually with the goal of protecting domestic businesses.

psychographic segmentation
Dividing the market into smaller groups based on consumer attitudes, interests, values, and lifestyles.

public offering
A primary market issue in which new securities are offered to any investors who are willing and able to purchase them.

public relations (PR)
The ongoing effort to create positive relationships with all of a firm's different "publics," including customers, employees, suppliers, the community, the general public, and the government.

publicity
Unpaid stories in the media that influence perceptions about a company or its products.

pull strategy
A marketing approach that involves creating demand from the ultimate consumers so that they "pull" your products through the distribution channels by actively seeking them.

pure competition
A market structure with many competitors selling virtually identical products. Barriers to entry are quite low.

pure goods
Products that do not include any services.

pure services
Products that do not include any goods.

push strategy
A marketing approach that involves motivating distributors to heavily promote—or "push"—a product to the final consumers, usually through heavy trade promotion and personal selling.

quality level
How well a product performs its core functions.

quality of life
The overall sense of well-being experienced by either an individual or a group.

quotas
Limitations on the amount of specific products that may be imported from certain countries during a given time period.

radio frequency identification (RFID)
A technology that stores information on small microchips that can transmit the information when they are within range of a special reader.

recession
An economic downturn marked by a decrease in the GDP for two consecutive quarters.

recovery
A period of rising economic growth and employment.

registration statement
A long, complex document that firms must file with the SEC when they sell securities through a public offering.

reserve requirement
A rule set by the Fed, which specifies the minimum amount of reserves (or funds) a bank must hold, expressed as a percentage of the bank's deposits.

retailers
Distributors that sell products directly to the ultimate users, typically in small quantities, that are stored and merchandized on the premises.

retained earnings
The part of a firm's net income it reinvests.

revenue
Increases in a firm's assets that result from the sale of goods, provision of services, or other activities intended to earn income.

revolving credit agreement
A guaranteed line of credit in which a bank makes a binding commitment to provide a business with funds up to a specified credit limit at any time during the term of the agreement.

right-to-work law
A state law that makes union shops illegal within that state's borders.

risk
The degree of uncertainty regarding the outcome of a decision.

risk-return tradeoff
The observation that financial opportunities that offer high rates of return are generally riskier than opportunities that offer lower rates of return.

robot
A reprogrammable machine that is capable of manipulating materials, tools, parts, and specialized devices in order to perform a variety of tasks.

S corporation
A form of corporation that avoids double taxation by having its income taxed as if it were a partnership.

salaries
The pay that employees receive over a fixed period, most often weekly or monthly.

sale
A transaction in which the title (legal ownership) to a good passes from one party to another in exchange for a price.

sales promotion
Marketing activities designed to stimulate immediate sales activity through specific short-term programs aimed at either consumers or distributors.

Sarbanes-Oxley Act
Federal legislation passed in 2002 that sets higher ethical standards for public corporations and accounting firms. Key provisions limit conflict-of-interest issues and require financial officers and CEOs to certify the validity of their financial statements.

savings account
An interest-bearing account holding funds not needed to meet regular expenditures.

savings and loan association
A depository institution that has traditionally obtained most of its funds by accepting savings deposits, which have been used primarily to make mortgage loans.

scope of authority (for an agent)
The extent to which an agent has the authority to act for and represent the principal.

SCORE (Service Corps of Retired Executives)
An organization—affiliated with the Small Business Administration—that provides free, comprehensive business counseling for small business owners from qualified volunteers.

secondary data
Existing data that marketers gather or purchase for a research project.

secondary securities market
The market where previously issued securities are traded.

Securities Act of 1933
first major federal law regulating the securities industry. It requires firms issuing new stock in a public offering to file a registration statement with the SEC.

securities broker
A financial intermediary that acts as an agent for investors who want to buy and sell financial securities. Brokers earn commissions and fees for the services they provide.

securities dealer
A financial intermediary that participates directly in securities markets, buying and selling stocks and other securities for its own account.

Securities and Exchange Commission
The federal agency with primary responsibility for regulating the securities industry.

Securities Exchange Act of 1934
A federal law dealing with securities regulation that established the Securities and Exchange Commission to oversee the securities industry.

services
Intangible products.

servicescape
The environment in which a customer and service provider interact.

sexual harassment
Workplace discrimination against a person based on his or her gender.

Six Sigma
An approach to quality improvement characterized by very ambitious quality goals, extensive training of employees, and a long-term commitment to working on quality-related issues.

skimming pricing
A new product pricing strategy that aims to maximize profitability by offering new products at a premium price.

Small Business Administration (SBA)
An agency of the federal government designed to maintain and strengthen the nation's economy by aiding, counseling, assisting, and protecting the interests of small businesses.

Small Business Development Centers (SBDCs)
Local offices—affiliated with the Small Business Administration—that provide comprehensive management assistance to current and prospective small business owners.

social audit
A systematic evaluation of how well a firm is meeting its ethics and social responsibility goals.

social responsibility
The obligation of a business to contribute to society.

socialism
An economic system based on the principle that the government should own and operate key enterprises that directly affect public welfare.

sociocultural differences
Differences among cultures in language, attitudes, and values.

software
Programs that provide instructions to a computer so that it can perform a desired task.

sole proprietorship
A form of business ownership with a single owner who usually actively manages the company.

spam
Unsolicited email advertisements usually sent to very large numbers of recipients, many of whom may have no interest in the message.

span of control
Span of management; refers to the number of people that a manager supervises.

specific performance
A remedy for breach of contract in which the court orders the party committing the breach to do exactly what the contract specifies.

speed-to-market
The rate at which a new product moves from conception to commercialization.

sponsorship
A deep association between a marketer and a partner (usually a cultural or sporting event), which involves promotion of the sponsor in exchange for either payment or the provision of goods.

spontaneous financing
Financing that arises during the natural course of business without the need for special arrangements.

spyware
Software that is installed on a computer without the user's knowledge or permission for the purpose of tracking the user's behavior.

staff managers
Managers who supervise the functions that provide advice and assistance to the line departments.

stakeholders
Any groups that have a stake—or a personal interest—in the performance and actions of an organization.

Standard & Poor's 500
A stock index based on prices of 500 major U.S. corporations in a variety of industries and market sectors.

standard of living
The quality and quantity of goods and services available to a population.

statement of cash flows
The financial statement that identifies a firm's sources and uses of cash in a given accounting period.

statute of frauds
A requirement that certain types of contracts must be in writing in order to be enforceable.

statute of limitations
The time period within which a legal action must be initiated.

statutory close (or closed) corporation
A corporation with a limited number of owners that operates under simpler, less formal rules than a C corporation.

statutory law
Law that is the result of legislative action.

stock (or securities) exchange
An organized venue for trading stocks and other securities that meet its listing requirements.

stock index
A statistic that tracks how the prices of a specific set of stocks have changed.

stockholder
An owner of a corporation.

store brands
Brands that the retailer both produces and distributes (also called "private-label brands").

strategic alliance
An agreement between two or more firms to jointly pursue a specific opportunity without actually merging their businesses. Strategic alliances typically involve less formal, less encompassing agreements than partnerships.

strategic goals
Concrete benchmarks that managers can use to measure performance in each key area of the organization.

strategic planning
High-level, long-term planning that establishes a vision for the company, defines long-term objectives and priorities, determines broad action steps, and allocates resources.

strategies
Action plans that help the organization achieve its goals by forging the best fit between the firm and the environment.

strike
A work stoppage initiated by a union.

structured interviews
An interviewing approach that involves developing a list of questions beforehand and asking the same questions in the same order to each candidate.

supply
The quantity of products that producers are willing to offer for sale at different market prices.

supply chain
All organizations, processes, and activities involved in the flow of goods from their raw materials to the final consumer.

supply chain management (SCM)
Planning and coordinating the movement of products along the supply chain, from the raw materials to the final consumers.

supply curve
The graphed relationship between price and quantity from a supplier standpoint.

survey research
Marketing research that requires the researcher to interact with the research subject.

sustainable development
Doing business to meet the needs of the current generation, without harming the ability of future generations to meet their needs.

SWOT analysis
A strategic planning tool that helps management evaluate an organization in terms of internal strengths and weakness, and external opportunities and threats.

system software
Software that performs the critical functions necessary to operate the computer at the most basic level.

tactical planning
More specific, shorter-term planning that applies strategic plans to specific functional areas.

target market
The group of people who are most likely to buy a particular product.

tariffs
Taxes levied against imports.

technical skills
Expertise in a specific functional area or department.

telecommuting
Working remotely—most often from home—and connecting to the office via phone lines, fax machines, or broadband networks.

Theory X and Theory Y
A motivation theory that suggests that management attitudes toward workers fall into two opposing categories based on management assumptions about worker capabilities and values.

time value of money
The principle that a dollar received today is worth more than a dollar received in the future.

title
Legal evidence of ownership.

Title VII
A portion of the Civil Rights Act of 1964 that prohibits discrimination in hiring, firing, compensation, apprenticeships, training, terms, conditions, or privileges of employment based on race, color, religion, sex, or national origin for employers with 15 or more workers.

top management
Managers who set the overall direction of the firm, articulating a vision, establishing priorities, and allocating time, money, and other resources.

tort
A private wrong that results in physical or mental harm to an individual, or damage to that person's property.

total quality management (TQM)
An approach to quality improvement that calls for everyone within an organization to take responsibility for improving quality and emphasizes the need for a long-term commitment to continuous improvement.

trade credit
Spontaneous financing granted by sellers when they deliver goods and services to customers without requiring immediate payment.

trade deficit
Shortfall that occurs when the total value of a nation's imports is higher than the total value of its exports.

trade promotion
Marketing activities designed to stimulate wholesalers and retailers to push specific products more aggressively over the short term.

trade surplus
Overage that occurs when the total value of a nation's exports is higher than the total value of its imports.

trademark
A mark, symbol, word, phrase, or motto used to identify a company's goods.

trading bloc
A group of countries that has reduced or even eliminated tariffs, allowing for the free flow of goods among the member nations.

underwriting
An arrangement under which an investment banker agrees to purchase all shares of a public offering at an agreed-upon price.

unemployment rate
The percentage of people in the labor force over age 16 who do not have jobs and are actively seeking employment.

Uniform Commercial Code (UCC)
A uniform act governing the sale of goods, leases, warranties, transfer of funds, and a variety of other business-related activities.

union shop
An employment arrangement in which a firm can hire nonunion workers, but these workers must join the union within a specified time period to keep their jobs.

universal ethical standards
Ethical norms that apply to all people across a broad spectrum of situations.

U.S. Treasury bills (T-bills)
Short-term marketable IOUs issued by the U.S. government.

utility
The ability of goods and services to satisfy consumer "wants."

value
The relationship between the price of a good or a service and the benefits that it offers its customers.

value chain
The network of relationships that channels the flow of inputs, information, and financial resources through all of the processes directly or indirectly involved in producing goods and services and distributing them to customers.

variable costs
Costs that vary directly with the level of production.

venture capital firms
Companies that invest in start-up businesses with high growth potential in exchange for a share of ownership.

vertical integration
Performance of processes internally that were previously performed by other organizations in a supply chain.

vertical merger
A combination of firms at different stages in the production of a good or service.

vesting period
A specified period of time for which an employee must work for an employer in order to receive the full advantage of certain retirement benefits.

viral marketing
An Internet marketing strategy that tries to involve customers and others not employed by the seller in activities that help promote the product.

voluntary export restraints (VERs)
Limitations on the amount of specific products that one nation will export to another nation.

wages
The pay that employees receive in exchange for the number of hours or days that they work.

Web 2.0
Websites that incorporate interactive and collaborative features in order to create a richer, more interesting, and more useful experience for their users.

wheel of retailing
A classic distribution theory that suggests that retail firms and retail categories become more upscale as they go through their life cycles.

whistle-blowers
Employees who report their employer's illegal or unethical behavior to either the authorities or the media.

wholesalers
Distributors that buy products from producers and sell them to other businesses or nonfinal users such as hospitals, nonprofits, and the government.

World Bank
An international cooperative of 187 member countries, working together to reduce poverty in the developing world.

World Trade Organization (WTO)
A permanent global institution to promote international trade and to settle international trade disputes.

World Wide Web
The service that allows computer users to easily access and share information on the Internet in the form of text, graphics, video, apps, and animation.

worm
Malicious computer software that, unlike viruses, can spread on its own without being attached to other files.

Business Now: Change Is the Only Constant

WHAT'S INSIDE

Key Topics in this Chapter: Definitions of business, the history of business, the role of nonprofits, factors of production, five dimensions of the current business environment, the impact of government on business, customer value, e-commerce and the World Wide Web, changing demographics, higher ethical standards, globalization, personal success.

LEARNING OBJECTIVES

With the growth in eReader usage among students, this 6th edition of BUSN features a new numbering system for major headings that we recommend you use instead of page numbers when creating assignments.

1-1   Define business and discuss the role of business in the economy

1-2   Explain the evolution of modern business

1-3   Discuss the role of nonprofit organizations in the economy

1-4   Outline the core factors of production and how they affect the economy

1-5   Describe today's business environment and discuss each key dimension

1-6   Explain how current business trends might affect your career choices

MULTIMEDIA

PPT—THE HIGHLIGHTS

Slide 3   Trends in a Twitter-Ready Format
Slide 7   The History of Business: Putting It All in Context
Slide 8   The Business of Doing Good
Slide 20   Technological Environment
Slide 28   Business and YOU: Making It Personal

VIDEO

PowerPoint Clip from *Peet's Coffee and Tea*
Run time 2:06 minutes
On April 1, 1966, Alfred Peet opened his first coffee store on the corner of Walnut and Vine Streets in Berkeley, California, sparking the coffee revolution in the United States. Along with quality coffee, Peet's is known for its commitment to customer relationships fostered in its stores and through the Peetnik's customer loyalty program.

The Peet's home-delivery program started in response to requests from customers who had moved out of the San Francisco Bay area. In 2003, Peet's established the Peetniks program, an automatic replenishment program that evolved into a customer-loyalty program. Through the company website and call center, Peet's seeks to reproduce and reinforce a sense of community among customers. This video segment highlights the importance of customer relationships and shows how Peet's is using the Internet and the Peetniks program to build and extend these relationships.

Source: http://www.peets.com/who_we_are/who_we_are.asp

Ask Your Students:

1. How have customer relationships benefitted Peet's?
2. How does Peet's create a sense of community in a virtual world?

DVD SEGMENT SUMMARY

Holden Outerwear
Run time: 7:04 minutes
Many apparel makers dream of becoming trendsetters in the fashion world, but Holden Outerwear, maker of urban-style snowboarding outfits, is the consummate fashion innovator. Founded in 2002 by entrepreneur and professional snowboarder Mikey LeBlanc, the Portland, Oregon-based garment manufacturer has given a makeover to traditional performance outerwear. Unlike baggy ski-apparel brands that emphasize utility at the expense of looking good, Holden believes technical garments should look cool. Made from authentic denim, wool, and genuine leather, Holden pieces are form-fitting, waterproof, and, most importantly, hip. In 2005, Holden added a highly innovative material to its garment manufacturing process:

CHAPTER 1 OUTLINE

Visit login.cengage.com for additional materials to enhance your lectures!

CHAPTER 1: Business Now: Change Is the Only Constant

KEY TERMS

DISCUSSION QUESTIONS

1. What are some key strategies for developing a competitive edge in today's global market? How important is customer satisfaction?
2. How has the definition of *diversity* changed over time? Can a diverse workforce help a company compete more effectively? How?
3. How has the global free-trade movement impacted business? Who benefits? Who loses? Why?

eco-fabric. LeBlanc invented the natural-fiber waterproof fabric after a long search for the material yielded no results. Today, Holden's earth-friendly outerwear garments are the talk of the industry. Even so, LeBlanc is not one to rest on his laurels. When it comes to hitting the slopes in style, LeBlanc must always be the leader, never the follower.

Ask Your Students:

1. What impact does Mikey LeBlanc's entrepreneurship have on business and society?
2. What factors of production are foundational to Holden's success?

LECTURE EXAMPLE

UPS began more than 100 years ago as a messenger delivery service. Today, it is a global logistics leader with more than 400,000 employees worldwide. But, even a company as solid as UPS had to reassess and strengthen its operations as the world endured the toughest recession since the Great Depression. According to a June 2010 *McKinsey Quarterly* report, the average manufacturer's supply chain touches 35 different countries. When thinking about the increasing significance of global trade and the role that UPS plays in connecting global economies, UPS realized the necessity of strengthening their training, leadership development, and succession planning, to ensure their position in today's fast-changing, global environment.

Sources: Schwartz, Anne. (2011). Leadership development in a global environment: lessons learned from one of the world's largest employers. *Industrial and Commercial Training*, 43, 13–16. Note: Anne Schwartz is the Vice President of Global Learning and Development, UPS, Atlanta, Georgia, USA.

GROUP ACTIVITY

Break into groups of three to five people. Choose a product or service that you all buy on a regular basis. Write a brief description of how the product is positioned in the marketplace relative to its competition. Then work together to figure out *why* you are loyal customers and *how* the competition could dislodge you over the next five years. Write a one-page plan to solidify your position in the marketplace; consider changing everything from the product features to the advertising venues. Share your plan with the class, and gather feedback about how well it might work.

ASSIGNMENTS

Take a moment to jot down 5 things that you love to do. Think broadly (but keep it clean). Your list could include anything from posting pictures on Facebook to listening to your favorite music. Then brainstorm a list of business careers that could encompass two or more of your passions. A position in nightclub marketing, for instance, could include surfing on Facebook and listening to great music. What skills would you need to succeed in each position? Which skills do you have, and which would you need to develop?

BEYOND THE CLASS

A selection of materials is in the Instructor's Manual.

CHAPTER 1—UPDATES TO BUSN THIS YEAR

Page 3—New chapter opening quote

Page 3—Revised information about new business creation in 2009 and 2010

Page 4—New information about new firms generating about 10% of all new jobs in any given year

Page 4—Updated Exhibit 1.1 The Richest Americans 2011

Page 9—Revised information about the economy showing signs of recovery

Page 9—New pull quote

Page 9—*Flex Your Creativity: Build Your Brainpower* box feature replaces *Flex Your Creativity: Use Boredom to Build Your Brain* box feature

Page 10—Updated Exhibit 1.3 2011 Global Brand Champions and the Ones to Watch

Page 10—New examples of companies that lead their industry in customer satisfaction

Page 13—New example of NikeID website allowing customers to create custom Nike products

Page 13—Revised statistics about the population of the U.S.

Page 14—*Say H₂No to "Mystery Chemicals"* box feature replaces *Green Jeans: A Fashion Statement the Really Matters* box feature

Page 14—New Kraft Foods example about increasing spending on Hispanic marketing

Page 14—New company examples of global behemoths

Page 14—Revised information on the current median age in the U.S.

Page 15—New information about employee loyalty hitting a four-year low

Page 16—Revised information about low wages in China compared to the U.S.

Page 16—New information about the European Union's ongoing financial crisis

CHAPTER 1: Business Now: Change Is the Only Constant

Visit login.cengage.com for additional materials to enhance your lectures!

Economics: **The Framework for Business**

WHAT'S INSIDE
Key Topics in this Chapter: Why economics is relevant to your students, macroeconomics vs. microeconomics, global economic crisis, fiscal and monetary policies, capitalism, the four degrees of competition, fundamentals of supply and demand, socialism, communism, mixed economies, GDP, unemployment, phases of the business cycle, inflation, productivity.

LEARNING OBJECTIVES

With the growth in eReader usage among students, this 6th edition of BUSN features a new numbering system for major headings that we recommend you use instead of page numbers when creating assignments.

2-1   Define economics and discuss the evolving global economic crisis

2-2   Analyze the impact of fiscal and monetary policy on the economy

2-3   Explain and evaluate the free market system and supply and demand

2-4   Explain and evaluate planned market systems

2-5   Describe the trend toward mixed market systems

2-6   Discuss key terms and tools to evaluate economic performance

CHAPTER 2 OUTLINE

Economics: Navigating a Crisis
   Global Economic Crisis: How Did This Happen?
   Moving in a Better Direction

Managing the Economy Through Fiscal and Monetary Policy
   Fiscal Policy
   Monetary Policy

Capitalism: The Free Market System
   The Fundamental Rights of Capitalism
   Four Degrees of Competition
   Supply and Demand: Fundamental Principles of a Free Market System

Planned Economies: Socialism and Communism
   Socialism
   Communism

Mixed Economies: The Story of the Future

Evaluating Economic Performance: What's Working?
   Gross Domestic Product
   Employment Level
   The Business Cycle
   Price Levels
   Productivity

The Big Picture

Careers in Economics

MULTIMEDIA

PPT—THE HIGHLIGHTS

Slide 3   Global Economic Crisis: How Did this Happen?
Slide 9   Managing the Economy Through Fiscal & Monetary Policy
Slide 18   Capitalism: The Free Market System
Slide 20   Four Degrees of Competition
Slide 21   Green Guilt

VIDEO

PowerPoint Clip from *Modern Shed*
Run time 1:30 minutes
Modern Shed offers contemporary, customizable prefabricated structures used for a variety of purposes, from backyard offices and studios to residential needs. These environmentally friendly structures are cost-efficient space solutions. Until recently, the focus of Modern Shed's business had been on smaller structures. However, the economic downturn is creating new opportunities for the company.

In this segment, the head of sales and marketing for Modern Shed discusses the impact of the economy on their business. Residential housing prices are driven by land. With the drop in lot prices, anticipated to remain low for the next two to three years, Modern Shed is shifting focus to residential products. While the traditional starter home in the Seattle area would have cost $300,000,

with lower land prices, Modern Shed can offer a starter housing solution for under $200,000.

Ask Your Students:

1. What factors affect demand for Modern Shed residential solutions?
2. Is Modern Shed's business plan consistent with what you'd expect for a period of economic contraction? Why or why not?

DVD SEGMENT SUMMARY

Nederlander
Run time: 9:45 minutes
Nederlander is one of the most respected concert management companies in the United States. Headquartered in Los Angeles, the company owns and operates such award-winning venues as the Greek Theatre, Santa Barbara Bowl, and the San Jose Civic. One of few family-run businesses in all of entertainment, Nederlander takes pride in its ability to book big acts in its small to mid-sized venues. Artists rocking out Nederlander stages range from Pearl Jam and Jimmy Buffett to Dave Matthews and 30 Seconds to Mars. While bands get most of the attention, the behind-the-scenes planning for Nederlander shows falls to 60 full-time employees, who staff the company's marketing, talent buying, finance, and development departments. Hundreds

of seasonal workers join in each year to provide support for concert events and concessions. While many businesses view international expansion as the key to growth, Nederlander prefers its regional approach. Today's global entertainment world is full of flash-in-the-pan promoters, but Nederlander has delivered a century's worth of great entertainment simply by being the best in its space.

Ask Your Students:

1. Explain the role of capitalism in the 100-year growth of Nederlander Concerts.
2. Why is Nederlander able to charge higher prices for small theatre performances when audiences could pay less at stadium concerts?

Visit login.cengage.com for additional materials to enhance your lectures!

CHAPTER 2

KEY TERMS

LECTURE EXAMPLE

Federal Reserve Chairman Ben S. Bernanke, at the Montana Economic Development Summit 2007, Butte, Montana, May 1, 2007, stated: "Trade benefits advanced countries like the United States, but open trade is, if anything, even more important for developing nations. Trade and globalization are lifting hundreds of millions of people out of poverty, especially in Asia, but also in parts of Africa and Latin America. As a source of economic growth and development in poor countries, trade is proving far more effective than traditional development aid. The transition economies of Central and Eastern Europe have also benefited greatly from trade, especially trade with the rest of the European Union."

Sources: "Benefits of Free Trade". National Center for Policy Analysis. Retrieved 11-6-12 - "And among developed nations, the Harvard study found GDP among those with open policies during the same 20 year period grew an average of 2.3 percent annually—contrasted to growth of only 0.7 percent annually among those with restrictive policies." Retrieved (5/21/2011) http://debatepedia.idebate.org/en/index.php/Arguement:_Free_trade_Improves_the_economic_growth_of_developing_nation.

DISCUSSION QUESTIONS

1. How did the global economic crisis unfold? What steps did the federal government and the Federal Reserve take to mitigate the crisis?
2. What is the difference between fiscal and monetary policy? What role does politics play in shaping these policies?
3. Describe the key principles of socialist and communist economic systems. Does more government control mean less economic opportunity? Why or why not?

GROUP ACTIVITY

In the summer of 2011, President Obama and Congress spent several weeks locked in a fierce debate about whether to raise the federal debt ceiling. As the deadline loomed, it became clear that if the debt ceiling were not raised on time, the government would lack nearly half the cash it needed to pay its short-term bills. Break into groups of no more than five people. Identify the top payees (see page 21 of Chapter 2). Determine which five groups you will pay first and why. Remember to ground your thinking in business and economics rather than politics and political thinking. Share your recommendations with the class. Prepare for a passionate, even contentious discussion, and remember to be respectful of different viewpoints.

ASSIGNMENTS

Interview a local business owner who has weathered a recession. How did the recession affect the business? What strategies seemed to work particularly well? What (if anything) would the owner do differently next time? Why?

BEYOND THE CLASS

A selection of materials is in the Instructor's Manual.

CHAPTER 2—UPDATES TO BUSN THIS YEAR

Page 19—New chapter opening quote

Page 20—Revised Exhibit 2.1 House Price Index and surrounding text

Pages 20–21—New information about RealtyTrac's foreclosure rate

Page 21—New information about the average national unemployment rate

Page 22—New national debt numbers for the U.S.

Page 22—Revised Exhibit 2.2 Federal Government Revenue and Expenses

Page 23—*PreOccupied with the 99%!* box feature replaces *Recession Generation: How will the recession affect your life?* box feature

Page 24—Revised information about the M1 & M2 money supply

Page 24—*From Disruptive Demographics Trends to Economic Aftershocks* box feature replaces *How much money would make you happy?* box feature

Page 28—*Pay as You Throw* box feature replaces *Green Guilt* box feature

Page 32—New examples about Hyundai and Nike being foreign-owned companies, but their production is domestic and included in the GDP

Page 32—Revised U.S. GDP statistics and unemployment rate for January 2012

Page 34—New inflation rate for 2011

For more coverage of the debt ceiling, see the Debtpocalypse Now case in the Case Connection section of the Instructor's Manual (Chapter 2 End-of-Chapter Solutions)

CHAPTER 2: Economics: The Framework for Business

Visit login.cengage.com for additional materials to enhance your lectures!

The World Marketplace: Business Without Borders

WHAT'S INSIDE
Key Topics in this Chapter: U.S. business opportunities in a global market, benefits of global trade, competitive advantage, measuring the impact of international trade, exchange rates, global strategies and their risks, trade barriers, reasoning behind trade restrictions, advances toward free trade.

LEARNING OBJECTIVES

With the growth in eReader usage among students, this 6th edition of BUSN features a new numbering system for major headings that we recommend you use instead of page numbers when creating assignments.

3-1 Discuss business opportunities in the world economy

3-2 Explain the key reasons for international trade

3-3 Describe the tools for measuring international trade

3-4 Analyze strategies for reaching global markets

3-5 Discuss barriers to international trade and strategies to surmount them

3-6 Describe the free-trade movement and discuss key benefits and criticisms

CHAPTER 3 OUTLINE

An Unprecedented Opportunity

Key Reasons for International Trade
Competitive Advantage

Global Trade: Taking Measure
Balance of Trade
Balance of Payments
Exchange Rates
Countertrade

Seizing the Opportunity: Strategies for Reaching Global Markets
Foreign Outsourcing and Importing
Exporting
Foreign Licensing and Foreign Franchising
Foreign Direct Investment

Barriers to International Trade
Sociocultural Differences
Economic Differences
Political and Legal Differences

Free Trade: The Movement Gains Momentum
GATT and the World Trade Organization
The World Bank
The International Monetary Fund
Trading Blocs and Common Markets

The Big Picture

Careers in World Markets

PPT—THE HIGHLIGHTS

Slide 7 Global Trade Recovery
Slide 10 Key Reasons for International Trade: Competitive Advantage
Slide 16 Strategies for Reaching Global Markets
Slide 18 Chrysler and Fiat
Slide 25 Barriers to International Trade: Political and Legal Differences

VIDEO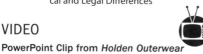

PowerPoint Clip from *Holden Outerwear*
Run time 2:30 minutes
Holden Outerwear manufactures and sells coats, jackets, and pants for snowboarding and cold weather sports, as well as street clothing. Based in Portland, Oregon, Holden is owned by professional snowboarder Mikey LeBlanc and designer Scott Zergebel. The company is known for its unique design aesthetic as well as its commitment to eco-friendly fabrics and processes.

Founder LeBlanc intended Holden to be a global company from the start. Designs are influenced by global travels and sold around the world. In this segment, LeBlanc discusses reasons for outsourcing. Holden chooses to outsource production to China to reduce costs and the price to the customer. Because many of the pieces for the finished goods are produced in Asia, and because the quality of

work for a technical garment is higher, using factories in China is good business strategy.

Source: http://www.facebook.com/pages/holden-outerwear/108716275829688?sk=info

Ask Your Students:

1. What is Holden's strategy for reaching global markets?
2. What are the benefits of this strategy?

DVD SEGMENT SUMMARY

Fossil
Run time: 7:43 minutes
Since launching in 1984, Fossil has grown into a global company and a world-class brand in the fashion accessory industry. The core of the company is its watch division, which sells more than 500 styles in its line. Fossil boasts of having "a watch for every wrist," yet it also sells popular sunglasses, belts, purses, and other related goods—all marked with the brand's fashion-forward design and packaging. After becoming the number-one fashion watch in U.S. department stores, Fossil went international and began selling in the German market. Today, Fossil products are manufactured and sold in more than 70 countries around the world. With sales on the rise, new designs and products on the horizon, and a strong stable of

international partners, Fossil is on its way to achieving its chief global goal: to be the top fashion accessory brand in the world.

Ask Your Students:

1. What strategy is Fossil using to transform itself into a global company?
2. Why did Fossil locate its manufacturing and operations in Hong Kong?

Visit login.cengage.com for additional materials to enhance your lectures!

CHAPTER 3: The World Marketplace: Business Without Borders

KEY TERMS

LECTURE EXAMPLE

Famous Global Marketing Mistakes:

* The Dairy Association's huge success with the campaign "Got Milk?" prompted them to expand advertising to Mexico. It was soon brought to their attention that the Spanish translation read, "Are you lactating?"

* Coors put its slogan "Turn It Loose" into Spanish, where it was read as "Suffer from Diarrhea."

* When Gerber started selling baby food in Africa, they used the same packaging as in the U.S., with the smiling baby on the label. Later they learned that in Africa, companies routinely put pictures on the labels of what's inside the package, since many people can't read.

Source: Firoz, N. & Ramin, T. (Sep 2004). Understanding cultural variables is critical to success in international business. *International Journal of Management.*

DISCUSSION QUESTIONS

1. Why do companies tend to thrive in global markets when their country of origin enjoys a comparative advantage in their industry?

2. Why is outsourcing such an attractive way for firms to tap into foreign markets? What are the risks of foreign outsourcing?

3. How has NAFTA impacted the United States? Overall, do you believe that it was a positive move for the U.S.? Why or why not?

GROUP ACTIVITY

Similar to Coca-Cola and Nike, Hollywood megastars represent global brands in their own right. But their fans might be surprised to learn that many have leveraged their reputation in foreign markets (most often Japan) by creating ads—sometimes downright cheesy ads—to hawk products that they would never endorse in the domestic market. Use the Internet to uncover foreign advertising that features Cameron Diaz, Pierce Brosnan, Jodie Foster, Arnold Schwarzenegger, and Brad Pitt. Do you believe that demand for American stars in foreign advertising will continue? Why or why not? Will the Internet encourage or discourage this trend?

ASSIGNMENTS

Take a look at *Fortune* magazine's most recent list of the 500 largest global companies. What are the top three industries on the list? What three countries appear most frequently? What firms have fallen off the list, and who are the new arrivals? Does a particular industry or country seem to be on the move? Consider what the answers to these questions tell you about today's global economy. How would you expect the answers to change over the next decade? Why? How would your answers change if you also looked at *BusinessWeek's* list over the past few years of the top global brands?

BEYOND THE CLASS

A selection of materials is in the Instructor's Manual.

CHAPTER 3—UPDATES TO BUSN THIS YEAR

Page 37—Revised information about the world GDP growth in 2010 and 2011

Page 37—Updated statistics about the world population

Page 38—Revised numbers of cell phone users in China and India

Page 38—New pull quote

Page 39—Facing Facts: Facebook around the World box feature replaces *Unimpressive Scores* box feature

Page 39—New pull quote

Page 40—New information about consumers showing an interest in traditional and regional foods

Page 40—New statistics about the global trade volume in 2011

Page 42—New example of Amazon.com outsourcing customer service calls

Page 44—Updated information about Hyundai's share of the car market

Page 44—*Working hard versus hardly working….* box feature replaces *To Spend or Not to Spend box* feature

Page 45—Updated information in *Veggie Surprise, Anyone* box feature

Page 46—*Desert Snow?* box feature replaces *Global Greening: The Ultimate Group Project* box feature

Page 46—New information about the 2012 "Doing Business" report

Pages 47–48—Revised information about the worldwide piracy rates

Page 48—New pull quote

Page 49—New pull quote

Page 50—New paragraph on the economic crisis in European Union countries

Page 50—*A Pricey Post-Euro Wake-up Call* box feature replaces *Just Because They Can* box feature

CHAPTER 3: The World Marketplace: Business Without Borders

Visit login.cengage.com for additional materials to enhance your lectures!

Business Ethics and Social Responsibility:
Doing Well by Doing Good

WHAT'S INSIDE
Key Topics in this Chapter: Universal ethical standards, framework for reaching ethical decision making, code of ethics, whistleblowers, social responsibility, responsibility to stakeholders, responsibility to consumers, Sarbanes-Oxley Act of 2002, corporate philanthropy, environmental responsibility, ethics in global business, social audits.

LEARNING OBJECTIVES

With the growth in eReader usage among students, this 6th edition of BUSN features a new numbering system for major headings that we recommend you use instead of page numbers when creating assignments.

4-1   Define ethics and explain the concept of universal ethical standards

4-2   Describe business ethics and ethical dilemmas

4-3   Discuss how ethics relates to both the individual and the organization

4-4   Define social responsibility and examine the impact on stakeholder groups

4-5   Explain the role of social responsibility in the global arena

4-6   Describe how companies evaluate their efforts to be socially responsible

MULTIMEDIA

PPT—THE HIGHLIGHTS

Slide 3   Ethics & Social Responsibility: A Close Relationship
Slide 6   Business Ethics: Not an Oxymoron
Slide 16   The Spectrum of Social Responsibility
Slide 21   Amazon: Who Owns the Books
Slide 29   Corporations Tracking Emissions

VIDEO

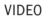

PowerPoint Clip from *Scholfield Honda*
Run time: 2:14 minutes
Dedicated to the environment, Honda is a leader in the development of alternative fuel and hybrid technologies. In 1998, Honda introduced the natural gas Civic in California and New York to address air-quality issues. Today, Scholfield Honda offers this natural gas Civic, the Honda Civic GX, to its customers in Wichita, Kansas. Committed to green initiatives and to alternative fuel sources, Scholfield Honda's alternative fuel manager saw an opportunity to market this Civic in the Midwest. This opportunity was created less by environmental issues and more by rising fuel prices. After learning of the Greensburg Green Town project, dealership owner Roger Scholfield donated a Civic GX

Natural Gas Vehicle to the city of Greensburg, Kansas. Currently, the dealership targets fleet markets and sells primarily to municipalities who can support their own filling stations.

Source: http://www.scholfieldhonda.com/dealership/greenzone.htm

Ask Your Students:

1.   How is Scholfield Honda practicing social responsibility?
2.   What are the benefits of this hybrid technology to stakeholders?

DVD SEGMENT SUMMARY

Theo Chocolate
Run time: 6:43 minutes
When Joe Whinney was a teen, he volunteered for a conservation program that explored cocoa bean farms in the rainforests of Central America. The experience proved to be life changing. Whinney had always loved chocolate, but now, after having seen cacao trees firsthand, he dreamed of building the first organic fair-trade chocolate factory in the United States. Propelled by a love of chocolate and the environment, the Philadelphia native pioneered the import of organic cocoa beans to the United States. In 2006,

CHAPTER 4 OUTLINE

Business Ethics and Social Responsibility: Doing Well by Doing Good

Ethics and Social Responsibility: A Close Relationship
Defining Ethics: Murkier Than You'd Think
Universal Ethical Standards: A Reasonable Goal or Wishful Thinking?

Business Ethics: Not an Oxymoron

Ethics: Multiple Touchpoints
Ethics and the Individual: The Power of One
Ethics and the Organization: It Takes a Village
Creating and Maintaining an Ethical Organization

Defining Social Responsibility: Making the World a Better Place
The Stakeholder Approach: Responsibility to Whom?

Ethics and Social Responsibility in the Global Arena: A House of Mirrors?

Monitoring Ethics and Social Responsibility: Who Is Minding the Store?

The Big Picture

Careers in Business Ethics and Social Responsibility

KEY TERMS

BEYOND THE CLASS

A selection of materials is in the Instructor's Manual.

Whinney's Theo Chocolate Company became the first and only sustainable chocolate maker in the nation. Unlike chocolate manufacturers that deliver sweets in high volume, Theo produces its award winning chocolate in small batches. Moreover, the company's bean-to-bar production method uses cocoa beans harvested without harm to farmers or the environment. The result is a creamy, delectable milk chocolate bar that is as good for the ecosystem as it is for the palate.

Ask Your Students:

1. What business practices at Theo Chocolate illustrate the concept of sustainable development?

2. What does the term "fair trade" mean to the leaders at Theo, and what happens if fair trade goals conflict with the company's goal to be profitable?

LECTURE EXAMPLE

The disaster in the Gulf of Mexico is only the most recent example of the consequences of negligent social responsibility. BP Oil Company executives are alleged to have disregarded safety concerns, which were occurring on the *Deepwater Horizon*, in their effort to maximize shareholders' wealth. BP CEO Tony Hayward often repeated that he was "personally devastated" by the gulf spill. When called to account before the House Energy and Commerce committee, Hayward was shamed publicly.

Source: Spitzer, Randy. (October 2010). Is Social Responsibility Good? *Journal for Quality and Participation, 33,* 3 13–17.

DISCUSSION QUESTIONS

1. Do you believe that employers should respond to employee needs for work-life balance? Why or why not? What are the tradeoffs?

2. Define the concept of planned obsolescence. Is this strategy ethically unsound? Why or why not?

3. Define sustainable development. What are three examples of successful companies that have pursued sustainable development programs?

GROUP ACTIVITY

Break into groups of about five students. Work with your team to develop a corporate philanthropy concept for each of the businesses listed below. Choose ideas that are likely to help the business serve the community, build employee morale, *and* build long-term profitability. Keep in mind that the best programs feature a close link between the firm's product or customers and the needs of the community. To find the most creative ideas, spend a few moments brainstorming with your teammates about each business before you finalize your plan.

- A city newspaper
- A hip-hop music label
- A computer repair service
- A local hot dog stand
- A leading brand of frozen pizza
- A national department store chain

ASSIGNMENTS

Find a small business in your community that takes social responsibility seriously. (Your local chamber of commerce can probably help you identify a candidate.) Interview the owner to learn more about the firm's programs. Did the owner actively choose how to contribute, or did he or she simply respond to opportunities that arose on an ad hoc basis? How does the firm balance the need for short-term profitability with the need for social responsibility? What other options are available for small firms to contribute to your community without undermining their bottom line?

CHAPTER 4—UPDATES TO BUSN THIS YEAR

Page 53—New chapter opening quote

Page 53—Exhibit 4.1, new example of legal and unethical action

Page 54—New examples of free choice

Page 57—New information about business leaders having a heightened commitment to ethics

Page 60—New fun fact

Pages 60–61—New example about a business making a mistake and apologizing to customers

Page 62—Updated information about The Giving USA foundation growth in corporate donations

Page 62—New example of a company launching an international volunteer program

Pages 62–63—New examples of companies participating in corporate responsibility

Page 62—*iHurt—Working Conditions for Employees at Apple Contractors in China May be Painfully Bad* box feature replaces *Just Because They Can…* box feature

Page 63—*Should your tap water go to the dogs?* box feature replaces *Singing the Blues about Going Green* box feature

Page 63—New example of McDonald's sustainability program

Page 64—New pull quote

Page 64—Revised score for India's perceived corruption

Page 65—Revised information in *Going Green—It's Not Just Governments* box feature

Page 65—New fun fact

CHAPTER 4: Business Ethics and Social Responsibility: Doing Well by Doing Good

Visit login.cengage.com for additional materials to enhance your lectures!

Business Communication: Creating and Delivering Messages that Matter

WHAT'S INSIDE

Key Topics in this Chapter: The invisible advantage of effective communication, communication barriers, effective nonverbal communication, active listening, listening do's and don'ts, analyzing the audience, communication channels, tools for high-impact messages and presentations, PowerPoint, handling nerves, handling hostility delivery techniques.

LEARNING OBJECTIVES

With the growth in eReader usage among students, this 6th edition of BUSN features a new numbering system for major headings that we recommend you use instead of page numbers when creating assignments.

5-1	Explain the importance of excellent business communication
5-2	Describe the key elements of nonverbal communication
5-3	Compare, contrast, and choose effective communication channels
5-4	Choose the right words for effective communication
5-5	Write more effective business memos, letters, and emails
5-6	Create and deliver successful verbal presentations

MULTIMEDIA

PPT—THE HIGHLIGHTS

Slide 3 Excellent Communication Skills: Your Invisible Advantage
Slide 9 Nonverbal Communication: Beyond the Words
Slide 10 Active Listening: The Great Divider
Slide 14 Choose the Right Channel: An Array of Options
Slide 30 Ten Tips for Dynamic Delivery

VIDEO

PowerPoint Clip from *Effective On-the-Job Presentation Skills*
Run time 1:48 minutes
Most people get at least a little nervous when they have to speak to a group of people. In fact, the *Book of Lists* asserts that public speaking ranks as the number-one fear for the majority of people. However, the right preparation and rehearsal can help manage stage fright and ensure an effective presentation.

This segment features practical strategies for dealing with nerves, as well as tips to guide presenters in preparing, delivering, and concluding their presentations. Before a presentation, speakers should know their subject and rehearse with visual aids. Tips for the actual presentation include greeting the audience, maintaining eye contact, speaking slowly with no "ums" or "you knows," and discussing each visual aid. After the presentation, speakers are encouraged to take questions, reiterate main points in their answers, distribute handouts, and end with a summary and thanks.

Ask Your Students:

1. What are some effective strategies for dealing with stage fright?
2. What do you notice about the visual aids used by the presenter in this video?

DVD SEGMENT SUMMARY

Plant Fantasies
Run time: 7:14 minutes
Can companies really Twitter their way to profits? Is Facebook replacing face-to-face meetings? Do handwritten business letters have any place in the digital age? If New York's Plant Fantasies is any indication, reports on the death of traditional business communication have been greatly exaggerated. The urban landscaping company began in 1987 and quickly developed a reputation as the gardener of choice for New York City's top real estate moguls. Although the company's growth occurred side-by-side with the rise of the Internet, founder Teresa Carleo has maintained a preference for traditional face-to-face meetings and phone calls.

CHAPTER 5 OUTLINE

Business Communication: Creating and Delivering Messages That Matter

Excellent Communication Skills: Your Invisible Advantage
    Communication Barriers: "That's Not What I Meant!"

Nonverbal Communication: Beyond the Words
    Active Listening: The Great Divider

Choose the Right Channel: A Rich Array of Options
    Consider the Audience: It's Not about You!

Pick the Right Words: Is That Car Pre-Loved or Just Plain Used?!
    Analyze Your Audience
    Be Concise
    Avoid Slang
    Avoid Bias
    Use the Active Voice Whenever Possible

Write High-Impact Messages: Breaking through the Clutter
    Strike the Right Tone
    Don't Make Grammar Goofs
    Use Block Paragraphs
    Use Headings and Bulleted Lists Wherever Appropriate

Create and Deliver Successful Verbal Presentations: Hook 'Em and Reel 'Em In!
    Opening
    Body
    Close
    Questions
    Visual Aids
    Handling Nerves
    Handling Hostility
    Incorporating Humor
    A Spot on the Back Wall?
    Delivery

The Big Picture

Careers in Business Communication

Visit **login.cengage.com** for additional materials to enhance your lectures!

CHAPTER 5: Business Communication: Creating and Delivering Messages that Matter

KEY TERMS

According to Carleo, the key to effective communication is to match the right methods with the right business needs. Some tasks at Plant Fantasies focus on the labor of gardening, while other situations involve professional collaborations with landscape architects and clients. Each situation has its own requirements. In the end, good business communication is about using time wisely and making positive connections with people.

Ask Your Students:

1. Which communication channels are most common at Plant Fantasies?
2. Using the concept of channel richness, explain why leaders at Plant Fantasies place a high value on face-to-face communication.

LECTURE EXAMPLE

Effective communication is critical in business. Weak written or spoken delivery can result in even important information being ignored or overlooked. Additionally, effective nonverbal communication is also essential. And ensuring that the nonverbal message is congruent with the verbal message being delivered is crucial. One study from UCLA found that up to 93 percent of a person's message was conveyed nonverbally. However, what may be appropriate nonverbal communication in one area of the world may be seen as rude or ignorant in another area.

For a brief summary of nonverbal communication, see: http://humanresources.about.com/od/interpersonalcommunicatio1/a/nonverbal_com.htm

For examples of differences in global nonverbals, see: http://soc302.tripod.com/soc_302rocks/id6.html

DISCUSSION QUESTIONS

1. Why is nonverbal communication so important? How can you tell when nonverbal communication is effective?
2. Why is active, effective listening difficult for many people? What are five strategies for improving listening skills within the American culture?
3. What are your options for creating an effective opening "hook" for a verbal presentation? Why is humor not always the best approach?

GROUP ACTIVITY

Imagine that you're working as a video game developer at the Chicago office of Electronic Arts (EA). Your boss recently offered you an excellent opportunity to transfer to the EA development studio in Tokyo, Japan. You are certain that this new position will build your successful career even more quickly, and you're eager to make the move. While you don't speak more than a few words of Japanese, you're not too concerned, since you plan to enroll in an intensive web-based language program before you leave. However, you *are* worried that you'll make some major gaffes in your nonverbal communication. Break into teams of four or five students. Use the Internet to research differences in nonverbal communication between the United States and Japan, and compile a list. Spend one group meeting using those approaches to communicate with each other. How did it work? Discuss what was comfortable and what was not. Develop some strategies for helping to make foreign students and businesspeople feel more comfortable with American nonverbal communication.

ASSIGNMENTS

Spend a day at school communicating with your friends without using any gestures at all in your conversations. How did it feel? Were you able to connect as effectively with your friends? Did your lack of gestures evoke any feedback from them? Overall, how much do you think gestures add to your communication? Does it depend on what you're trying to communicate? Why or why not?

BEYOND THE CLASS

A selection of materials is in the Instructor's Manual.

CHAPTER 5—UPDATES TO BUSN THIS YEAR

Page 70—*Dress for Success—Redefined!* box feature replaces *A New Look at Dressing for Success* box feature

Page 71—*Social Media Kaleidoscope* box feature replaces *Same Scene, Different Takes* box feature

Page 73—New pull quote

Page 74—*Say What??!!* box feature replaces *Huh?!!* box feature

Page 74—New pull quote

Page 75—*Minding your Manners in the Digital World* box feature replaces *There's English and Then There's English* box feature

Page 77—New pull quote

Page 78—New pull quote

CHAPTER 5: Business Communication: Creating and Delivering Messages that Matter

Visit login.cengage.com for additional materials to enhance your lectures!

Business Formation: Choosing the Form that Fits

WHAT'S INSIDE
Key Topics in this Chapter: Sole proprietorships, general partnerships, corporations, limited liability companies, stockholders, S corporations, statutory close corporations, non-profit corporations, mergers and acquisitions, forming and managing an LLC, franchising.

LEARNING OBJECTIVES

With the growth in eReader usage among students, this 6th edition of BUSN features a new numbering system for major headings that we recommend you use instead of page numbers when creating assignments.

6-1   Describe the characteristics of the four basic forms of business ownership

6-2   Discuss the advantages and disadvantages of a sole proprietorship

6-3   Evaluate the pros and cons of the partnership as a form of ownership

6-4   Explain why corporations have become the dominant form of business ownership

6-5   Explain why limited liability companies are becoming an increasingly popular form of ownership

6-6   Evaluate the advantages and disadvantages of franchising

MULTIMEDIA

PPT—THE HIGHLIGHTS

Slide 3   Business Ownership Options: The Big Four
Slide 4   Net Income by Form of Ownership
Slide 5   Corporate Profit and Revenue
Slide 17   Corporate Restructuring: Mergers & Acquisitions
Slide 25   Franchising in Foreign Markets

VIDEO

PowerPoint Clip from *Murray's Cheese*
Run time: 2:34 minutes
The mission of Murray's Cheese is to bring great cheese to everyone. Opened in 1940 as a neighborhood cheese shop in New York, Murrays expanded to sell cheese and specialty food items to midtown commuters in New York in 2002. The company has a wholesale business and has been shipping cheese around the country for over a decade. But a new partnership with Kroger is offering unprecedented opportunity for growth. Through Kroger, mini-Murray shops are bringing their unique in-store experience to communities across the country. The Murray's passion for cheese, customer service, and tastings create a unique experience within Kroger stores. In this segment, the vice president of Murray's Cheese discusses

the benefits and potential challenges of the partnership.

Source: http://www.murrayscheese.com/kroger.asp

Ask Your Students:

1. Why would a retail giant like Kroger pursue a partnership with a small New York cheese shop?
2. What are the benefits of the partnership to Murray's?

DVD SEGMENT SUMMARY

Jordan's Furniture
Run time: 15:12 minutes
Jordan's Furniture is a unique business. The company's history stretches back to 1918, when Samuel Tatelman opened a small furniture store in Waltham, Massachusetts. The business passed to grandsons Barry and Eliot, who targeted the business towards 18- to 34-year-olds and made the stores virtual amusement parks. For instance, the 110,000-square-foot store in Natick, Massachusetts, evokes the spirit of Bourbon Street in New Orleans, complete with Mardi Gras festivities. Other amusements include an IMAX theater and a Motion Odyssey 3D Movie Ride for children of all ages. In 1999, Warren Buffett bought Jordan's Furniture, but the brothers stayed on to direct the

CHAPTER 6 OUTLINE

Business Formation: Choosing the Form that Fits

Business Ownership Options: The Big Four

Advantages and Disadvantages of Sole Proprietorships
   Advantages
   Disadvantages

Partnerships: Two Heads (and Bankrolls) Can Be Better Than One
   Formation of General Partnerships
   Advantages of General Partnerships
   Disadvantages of General Partnerships
   Limited Partnerships
   Limited Liability Partnerships

Corporations: The Advantages and Disadvantages of Being an Artificial Person
   Forming a C Corporation
   Ownership of C Corporations
   The Role of the Board of Directors
   Advantages of C Corporations
   Disadvantages of C Corporations
   Other Types of Corporations: Same but Different Corporate Restructuring
   Corporate Restructuring

The Limited Liability Company: The New Kid on the Block
   Forming and Managing an LLC
   Advantages of LLCs
   Limitations and Disadvantages of LLCs

Franchising: Proven Methods for a Price
   Franchising in Today's Economy
   Advantages of Franchising
   Disadvantages of Franchising
   Entering into a Franchise Agreement

The Big Picture

Careers in Business

Visit login.cengage.com for additional materials to enhance your lectures!

CHAPTER 6: Business Formation: Choosing the Form that Fits

KEY TERMS

BEYOND THE CLASS

A selection of materials is in the Instructor's Manual.

chain's ongoing expansion. Barry left in 2006, but Eliot's sons followed family tradition and joined the company. Today, Jordan's Furniture is a profitable retail operation employing more than 1,200 people. It serves thousands of shoppers daily, and its sales average of $950 per square foot is considerably higher than that of the typical furniture store. But then, Jordan's Furniture is hardly a typical store.

Ask Your Students:

1. Jordan's Furniture founder Samuel Tatelman began by selling furniture out of his own truck. What form of ownership does this represent?
2. What advantages did Tatelman gain by incorporating his furniture business back in 1928?

LECTURE EXAMPLE

What started as a summer nanny job for Joseph Keely in 2000 has grown into a national franchise chain. Incorporated in 2001, the College Nannies & Tutors organization has since expanded on Keeley's initial award-winning business to become the nation's largest nanny and tutor resource. A decade later, through local franchise ownership, CNT has helped over 54,000 families in 26 states by providing quality childcare solutions and customized tutoring for their college-bound children. With aggressive growth plans in place, the CNT team is well positioned to fulfill its mission of Building Stronger Families® nationwide.

Retrieved (05/20/2011): http://www.collegenannies.com

DISCUSSION QUESTIONS

1. Why do so many entrepreneurs initially set up their businesses as sole proprietorships? Why do many successful entrepreneurs eventually decide to convert their sole proprietorships to some other form of ownership such as a corporation or LLC?
2. How does a merger differ from an acquisition? What is the difference between a horizontal merger or acquisition and a vertical merger or acquisition? Give an example to illustrate each type of combination.
3. What is a business format franchise? What are the benefits and problems of franchising arrangements from the perspective of the franchisor? What are the benefits and problems of franchising arrangements from the perspective of the franchisee?

GROUP ACTIVITY

As homework, ask your students to research the costs and benefits of becoming a franchisee for a specific franchise. (Basic information on costs and benefits is usually available at the franchise websites and also at websites such as Entrepreneur.com.) Students should come to class prepared to discuss the following questions:

1. From the student's perspective, what do they like about the franchise? Has the franchise been "in the news" for any reason (good or bad) recently?
2. What is the franchise fee for the franchise? What other start-up costs would a franchisee incur? What are the royalties and other ongoing fees that franchisees must pay?
3. Does the franchisor offer any help with financing? If so, what type?
4. What types of training and support does the franchisor offer?

Divide the class into small groups of three to five students. Have students in each group discuss the franchises they have researched, and select the one they view as the best investment opportunity. Each group should provide a brief oral report giving the reasons for its recommendation.

ASSIGNMENTS

Do research on the Internet to determine the forms and fees involved in forming a corporation. What type of information is required in the articles of incorporation? What is the corporate income tax rate for your state? How do the corporate fees and taxes in your state compare to those of other states in your region?

CHAPTER 6—UPDATES TO BUSN THIS YEAR

Page 83—New chapter opening quote

Page 84—Revised Exhibit 6.1 Total Number of Business by Form of Ownership and surrounding text

Page 84—Revised Exhibit 6.2 Total Net Income by Form of Ownership and surrounding text

Page 86—New pull quote

Page 89—Revised Exhibit 6.3 Stock Ownership in Selected Major U.S. Corporations

Page 90—New pull quote

Page 92—Stockholders "Say on Pay" and Boards of Directors Listen box feature replaces *Financial Reform Gives Stockers a "Say on Pay"* box feature

Page 94—*Lowering Apple's Tax Bite: Double Irish with a Dutch Sandwich* box feature replaces *GE's "Taxing" Situation: Double or Nothing?* box feature

Page 95—Updated study information conducted by Global Insights about franchise establishments in the U.S.

Page 95—Updated franchise numbers in foreign countries

Page 97—Updated Exhibit 6.7 Franchisee Costs for Selected Franchises

Page 98—New pull quote

Page 98—*Franchise Consultants: Would You Like Fries with That Franchise?* box feature replaces *Some Franchisees Are Quite Happy When They Don't Earn a Profit*

CHAPTER 6: Business Formation: Choosing the Form that Fits

Visit login.cengage.com for additional materials to enhance your lectures!

Small Business and Entrepreneurship:
Economic Rocket Fuel

WHAT'S INSIDE

Key Topics in this Chapter: Entrepreneurs, advantages of business ownership, common entrepreneurial characteristics, funding options, opportunities vs. threats, pros and cons of various launch options, tools for business success, SBA, economic impact of small business, global entrepreneurship.

LEARNING OBJECTIVES

With the growth in eReader usage among students, this 6th edition of BUSN features a new numbering system for major headings that we recommend you use instead of page numbers when creating assignments.

7-1 Explain the key reasons to launch a small business

7-2 Describe the typical entrepreneurial mindset and characteristics

7-3 Discuss funding options for small business

7-4 Analyze the opportunities and threats that small businesses face

7-5 Discuss ways to become a new business owner and tools to facilitate success

7-6 Explain the size, scope, and economic contributions of small business

MULTIMEDIA

PPT—THE HIGHLIGHTS

Slide 5   The Entrepreneur: A Distinctive Profile
Slide 11   Peer-to-Peer Lending
Slide 12   Small Business Sustainability
Slide 17   The Business Plan
Slide 20   Small Business and The Economy: An Outsized Impact

VIDEO

PowerPoint Clip from *Living Social Escapes*
Run time: 2:22 minutes
The mission of LivingSocial Escapes is to add surprise to every calendar. The company offers daily deals on total travel experiences that can be shared with friends. In this segment, Maya, the entrepreneurial founder of Urban Escapes and national director of LivingSocial Escapes, talks about founding her company. From her own love of adventure and the desire to escape the city on weekends, Maya discovered a passion for providing trip experiences for friends and groups. With an initial investment of $4,000, Maya started and grew Urban Escapes, which was eventually acquired by LivingSocial. While Maya brought the entrepreneurial vision for the company, co-owner Bram brought the structure and organization

to make her business concept function as reality.

Source: http://escapes.livingsocial.com/about

Ask Your Students:

1. What motivated Maya to start Urban Escapes?
2. What entrepreneurial characteristics do you see in Maya?

DVD SEGMENT SUMMARY

Taza Chocolate
Run time: 8:24 minutes
Taza Chocolate is an up-and-coming bean-to-bar chocolate manufacturer located in Somerville, Massachusetts. A seller of premium-quality bars and confections, Taza earns top culinary kudos for delivering stone-ground organic chocolate made in the Mexican tradition. Larry Slotnick, Taza's co-founder and director of sales, helped launch the company in 2006 by biking door-to-door and selling bars to mom-and-pop shops around Boston and San Francisco. Today, the company's discs, bars, and chocolate-covered nuts appear in specialty and natural-foods stores in more than 40 states and a handful of European countries. While most Americans consume chocolate that is mass-produced in the familiar smooth

Visit login.cengage.com for additional materials to enhance your lectures!

CHAPTER 7: Small Business and Entrepreneurship: Economic Rocket Fuel

KEY TERMS

European-style, Taza produces Mexican-style chocolate that is bold and coarse in texture—a difference instantly recognizable to the palate. In addition, the company's organic marketing emphasizes the healthful benefits of Taza's all-natural ingredients harvested through sustainable business practices—a hit with eco-minded consumers. While green marketing helps Slotnick earn new trials, it is Taza's irresistible chocolaty goodness that keeps people coming back for more.

Ask Your Students:

1. What is a market niche, and how does it apply to Taza's business model?
2. Identify Larry Slotnick's entrepreneurial characteristics, and offer examples from the video.

LECTURE EXAMPLE

"Small businesses are one of the main engines for economic growth and job creation, and their increasing optimism as we enter 2011 represents an incredibly positive development," said Raj Seshadri, the head of small-business banking at Citibank, the retail-banking arm of Citigroup Inc. Ms. Seshadri told Dow Jones Newswires that optimism from business owners was typically the first step to a recovery.

Source: *The Wall Street Journal* (Online) ISSN: 1538-6732
Date: 02/18/2011.

DISCUSSION QUESTIONS

1. What role does failure sometimes play in entrepreneurial success? What can an entrepreneur gain from failure?
2. Beyond personal resources, what are other funding options for small businesses? Why don't more entrepreneurs tap into these resources?

3. How could you convince family and friends to support your new business launch? What kind of assurances would they need? What could you do to keep the funding relationships professional?

GROUP ACTIVITY

Take a moment to write down three to five things that you find frustrating about daily life on a fairly regular basis. Be honest, and use real problems. Then break into groups of three to five students and exchange papers. Take about three minutes to choose one problem on the list that you received, and to develop a product or service idea that could solve that problem. Then, together with your team, review each person's idea, and choose the one with the most potential. Working together, further develop the idea into a business concept. Create a logo and a slogan for your business, and present your idea to the class, along with the problem that your business will solve.

ASSIGNMENTS

A huge number of successful businesses—such as Apple, The Cheesecake Factory, and eBay—were built around the personal passions of their founders. Consider your own personal passions. What do you love to do? Can you shape any of your interests into a business opportunity? Why or why not? Be sure to think big. For instance, if you love hanging out with friends and listening to music, a club-promotion business might make sense for you. Write a one- to two-page paper outlining the *specific* steps you would need to take over the next few years to make your "dream business" real.

BEYOND THE CLASS

A selection of materials is in the Instructor's Manual.

CHAPTER 7—UPDATES TO BUSN THIS YEAR

Page 101—New information about entrepreneurship in the U.S. over the past few years

Page 102—New pull quote

Page 102—*App-surd? Or not so much?* box feature replaces *Opportunity Lost* box feature

Page 103—New pull quote

Page 103—New section on Energy

Page 104—New pull quote

Page 105—*Elevating Hoodies* box feature replaces roach *Coaches Minus the Roaches* box feature

Page 105—Revised statistic about entrepreneurs funding their business with personal resources

Page 106—Revised information about angel funding

Page 106—Revised statistics about venture capital spending

Page 107—New pull quote

Page 107—*Nutty Market Niches* box feature replaces *Small Business Sustainability* box feature

Page 108—Revised statistics in the Bigger Regulatory Burden section

Page 110—New fun fact

Pages 110–111—Revised statistics from the U.S. Small Business Administration

Page 111—New examples in the *Accidental Inventions* box feature

Page 111—Revised statistics in the Creating New Jobs section

Page 112—New information about GEM and evaluating entrepreneurship levels globally

Page 112—New pull quote

Page 112—Revised Exhibit 7.4 Entrepreneurship Rates

Visit login.cengage.com for additional materials to enhance your lectures!

Accounting: Decision Making by the Numbers

WHAT'S INSIDE
Key Topics in this Chapter: The importance of accounting and key users, the accounting profession, financial accounting, GAAP, FASB, accounting ethics, balance sheets, income statements, statement of cash flows, auditor's reports, Sarbanes-Oxley Act, interpreting financial statements, managerial accounting, cost concepts, budgeting.

LEARNING OBJECTIVES

With the growth in eReader usage among students, this 6th edition of BUSN features a new numbering system for major headings that we recommend you use instead of page numbers when creating assignments.

8–1   Define accounting and describe how accounting information is used by a variety of stakeholders

8–2   Identify the purposes and goals of generally accepted accounting principles

8–3   Describe the key elements of the major financial statements

8–4   Describe several methods stakeholders can use to obtain useful insights from a company's financial statements

8–5   Explain the role of managerial accounting and describe the various cost concepts identified by managerial accountants

8–6   Explain how the budget process can help managers plan, motivate, and evaluate their organization's performance

CHAPTER 8 OUTLINE

Accounting: Decision Making by the Numbers

Accounting: Who Needs It—and Who Does It?
    Accounting: Who Uses It?
    Accounting: Who Does It?

Financial Accounting: Intended for Those on the Outside Looking In
    Role of the Financial Standards Accounting Board
    Ethics in Accounting

Financial Statements: Read All About Us
    The Balance Sheet: What We Own and How We Got It
    The Income Statement: So, How Did We Do?
    The Statement of Cash Flows: Show Me the Money
    Other Statements: What Happened to the Owners' Stake?

Interpreting Financial Statements: Digging Beneath the Surface
    The Independent Auditor's Report: Getting a Stamp of Approval
    Checking Out the Notes to Financial Statements: What's in the Fine Print?
    Looking for Trends in Comparative Statements

Inside Intelligence: The Role of Managerial Accounting
    Cost Concepts: A Cost for All Reasons
    Assigning Costs to Products: As (Not So) Simple as ABC?

Budgeting: Planning for Accountability
    Preparing the Budget: Top-Down or Bottom-Up?
    Developing the Key Budget Components: One Step at a Time
    Being Flexible: Clearing Up Problems with Static

The Big Picture

Careers in Accounting

MULTIMEDIA

PPT—THE HIGHLIGHTS

Slide 3   Accounting: Who Needs It?
Slide 7   He Madoff with How Much?
Slide 19   The Independent Auditor's Report: A Necessary Stamp of Approval
Slide 24   Inside Intelligence: The Role of Managerial Accounting
Slide 34   Preparing the Budget: Top-Down or Bottom-Up?

VIDEO

PowerPoint Clip from *Pizzeria Uno*
Run time: 2:39 minutes
The original Uno's, opened in Chicago in 1943, created the first Chicago-style deep dish pizza. In the mid-1990s, Uno's expanded its concept to encompass a broader variety of dishes. Today, there are over 160 Uno Chicago Grill restaurants found in 24 states, the District of Columbia, Puerto Rico, South Korea, the United Arab Emirates, Honduras, Kuwait, and Saudi Arabia.

    This video highlights the accounting practices of Uno's, including the use of technology to manage cost accounting at the store level, the role of the management team in accounting, the importance of and strategies for cost control, and cash flow. Because the restaurant business is a cash business, Uno's can use working capital from vendors to fund their operations.

Source: http://unos.com/about.php

Ask Your Students:

1. What accounting procedures does Uno's use at the store level to help manage its cost structure?
2. What role does the management team play in accounting for Uno's?

DVD SEGMENT SUMMARY

The Little Guys
Run time: 6:15 minutes
When David and Evie Wexler realized they had strong opinions on how to improve the home electronics store where they worked, the couple decided to launch their own business. They named it The Little Guys. Today, with annual sales of over $10 million, The Little Guys is proof that the Wexlers' ideas

Visit login.cengage.com for additional materials to enhance your lectures!

CHAPTER 8: Accounting: Decision Making by the Numbers

CHAPTER 8

CHAPTER PREP

KEY TERMS

accounting, 115

financial accounting, 116

generally accepted accounting principles (GAAP), 116

Financial Accounting Standards Board (FASB), 116

balance sheet, 118

accounting equation, 118

assets, 118

liabilities, 119

owners' equity, 119

income statement, 121

revenue, 121

accrual-basis accounting, 121

expenses, 121

net income, 121

statement of cash flows, 122

horizontal analysis, 126

managerial (or management) accounting, 126

cost, 126

out-of-pocket cost, 127

implicit cost, 127

fixed costs, 127

variable costs, 127

direct cost, 127

indirect costs, 127

activity-based costing (ABC), 127

budgeting, 128

operating budgets, 129

financial budgets, 130

master budget, 130

ASSIGNMENTS

The Financial Accounting Standards Board (FASB) is currently working with the International Accounting Standards Board to make U.S. financial accounting standards more consistent with international standards. Use the Internet to do some research about how these standards currently differ and how convergence of the two sets of standards would likely affect the practice of financial accounting in the United States.

---

were right. The company's success as a trusted home theater expert is owed, in part, to sound accounting practices. With the help of QuickBooks computer software and a trusted outside accountant, Evie Wexler learned to effectively control her company's overhead costs while carefully monitoring monthly sales trends. The company's cash flow has remained positive with the help of good financial reports and smart inventory decisions. While the Wexlers have achieved personal success from the skillful financial management of their business, they aren't resting on their laurels. Instead, they look forward to making The Little Guys even bigger.

Ask Your Students:

1. Do you think a fairly small company like The Little Guys still needs a professional accountant after its owners have had so much experience running a successful business? Why or why not?

2. Do you think The Little Guys is doing a good job of managing its cash flow? If so, why, and if not, how can the company improve this function?

LECTURE EXAMPLE

Archival analysis of U.S. Department of Labor data indicates that: (1) professional accounting work requires no less creativity than do three competing professions and a diverse sample of U.S. occupations, and (2) greater creativity may be required in financial than in auditing and taxation accounting work. This study further concluded that while creativity matters to accounting work—more to some areas of accounting practice than others— accountancy education and work may attract or reward entrants with less-than-desirable levels of creativity, perhaps due to the common belief that creativity is unneeded in, or even deleterious to, professional accountancy work.

Source: Bryant, S. M., Stone, D., & Wier, B. (2011) An Exploration of Accountants, Accounting Work, and Creativity. *Behavioral Research in Accounting*; 2011, 23, 1, 45–64.

DISCUSSION QUESTIONS

1. Why is it important to look at the independent auditor's opinion of a company's financial statements? How did the Sarbanes-Oxley Act change the audit process? What does it mean when an auditor renders a qualified opinion?

---

2. What are the key differences between financial accounting and management accounting?

3. How do management accountants view cost? How do implicit costs differ from explicit costs? Give some examples to illustrate the difference.

GROUP ACTIVITY

Pick out several publicly traded corporations, taking care to include some that you know are doing very well financially and others that are struggling. Print out the most recent comparative financial statements for each company. (Links to these statements are available on most financial websites.) Break the class into small groups and give each group the financial statements for one of the corporations. Tell the group to work together to find out what has happened over the past two years to the firm's total liabilities and stockholder's equity, revenues, expenses, net income, and cash position, and discuss what these figures tell them about the company's financial performance. Have each team report its findings to the class, and let the class interpret the results.

BEYOND THE CLASS

A selection of materials is in the Instructor's Manual.

CHAPTER 8—UPDATES TO BUSN THIS YEAR

Page 115—New chapter opening quote

Page 116—New pull quote

Page 117—*Accounting Fraud, The Not-So-Usual Suspects: Friends, Neighbors, Co-Workers, Bosses, and Relatives* box feature replaces *He Madoff with How Much?* box feature

Page 118—*Is There an Easier Way to Do Accounting?* box feature replaces *Accounting Fraud: As American as Wiener Schnitzel?* box feature

Page 122—New pull quote

Page 124—New Exhibit 8.4 An External Auditor's Opinion

Page 125—*Lions and Tigers and Bears, Oh My! Management's Discussion and Analysis* box feature replaces *GAAP ♥ IFRS?* box feature

Page 129—New *Accounting Trend: Cloud-Based Accounting* box feature replaces *New Accounting Trend: Stretching a Single into a Triple* box feature

Page 131—Revised statistics in Careers in Accounting box feature

CHAPTER 8: Accounting: Decision Making by the Numbers

Visit login.cengage.com for additional materials to enhance your lectures!

Finance: Acquiring and Using Funds to Maximize Value

WHAT'S INSIDE

Key Topics in this Chapter: Determining what motivates financial decisions, shareholder value, risk and return, evaluating and planning financial needs, ratio analysis, budgeted financial statements and cash budget, short-term financing, long-term funds, pros and cons of debt financing and equity financing, financial leverage, managing cash, managing accounts receivable, managing inventories, capital budgeting, time value of money.

LEARNING OBJECTIVES

With the growth in eReader usage among students, this 6th edition of BUSN features a new numbering system for major headings that we recommend you use instead of page numbers when creating assignments.

9-1 Identify the goal of financial management and explain the issues financial managers confront as they seek to achieve this goal

9-2 Describe the tools financial managers use to evaluate their company's current financial condition and then develop financial plans

9-3 Evaluate the major sources of funds available to meet a firm's short-term and long-term financial needs

9-4 Identify the key issues involved in determining a firm's capital structure

9-5 Describe how financial managers acquire and manage current assets

9-6 Explain how financial managers evaluate capital budgeting proposals to identify the best long-term investment options for their company

CHAPTER 9 OUTLINE

Finance: Acquiring and Using Funds to Maximize Value

What Motivates Financial Decisions?
  Shareholder Value and Social Responsibility: Does Good Behavior Pay Off?
  Risk and Return: A Fundamental Tradeoff in Financial Management

Identifying Financial Needs: Evaluation and Planning
  Using Ratio Analysis to Identify Current Strengths and Weaknesses
  Planning Tools: Creating a Road Map to the Future
  Basic Planning Tools: Budgeted Financial Statements and the Cash Budget

Finding Funds: What Are the Options?
  Sources of Short-Term Financing: Meeting Needs for Cash
  Sources of Long-term Funds: Providing a Strong Financial Base

Leverage and Capital Structure: How Much Debt Is Too Much Debt?
  Pros and Cons of Debt Financing
  Pros and Cons of Equity Financing
  Financial Leverage: Using Debt to Magnify Gains (And Losses)

Acquiring and Managing Current Assets
  Managing Cash: Is It Possible to Have Too Much Money?
  Managing Accounts Receivable: Pay Me Now or Pay Me Later
  Managing Inventories: Taking Stock of the Situation

Capital Budgeting: In It for the Long Haul
  Evaluating Capital Budgeting Proposals
  Accounting for the Time Value of Money
  The Risk-Return Tradeoff Revisited
  Net Present Value: A Decision Rule for Capital Budgeting

The Big Picture

Careers in Financial Management

MULTIMEDIA

PPT—THE HIGHLIGHTS

Slide 3 What Motivates Financial Decisions?
Slide 13 Planning Tools: Creating a Road Map to the Future
Slide 15 Basic Planning Tools
Slide 19 Sources of Long-term Funds
Slide 23 Financial Leverage: Using Debt to Magnify Gains (and Losses)

VIDEO

PowerPoint Clip from Pizzeria Uno
Run time: 2:30 minutes
The original Uno's, opened in Chicago in 1943, created the first Chicago-style deep dish pizza. In the mid-1990s, Uno's expanded its concept to encompass a broader variety of dishes. Today, there are over 160 Uno Chicago Grill restaurants found in 24 states, the District of Columbia, Puerto Rico, South Korea, the United Arab Emirates, Honduras, Kuwait, and Saudi Arabia.

This video highlights Uno's strategies for managing the balance sheet to create shareholder value. Uno's uses debt as a tool for building equity value. This segment touches on topics including shareholder value, debt

and equity, return on equity, capital investments, and profitability ratios. In a capital-intensive industry with profit margins of three to five cents per dollar, strategic financial management plays a critical role in Uno's profitability and continued growth.

Source: http://unos.com/about.php

Ask Your Students:

1. How do financial managers at Uno's maximize shareholder value?
2. How does debt help build equity value for Uno's?

DVD SEGMENT SUMMARY

Nederlander
Run time: 11:33 minutes
Launched in 1912 with the purchase of a single opera house, Nederlander has grown into a premier concert-management firm, operating venues such as the award-winning Los Angeles Greek Theatre, Santa Barbara Bowl, and the San Jose Civic. One of few family-run businesses in all of entertainment, Nederlander takes pride in its ability to host big acts like Pearl Jam and Flogging Molly

Visit login.cengage.com for additional materials to enhance your lectures!

CHAPTER 9: Finance: Acquiring and Using Funds to Maximize Value

KEY TERMS

financial capital, 133

finance, 133

risk, 134

risk-return tradeoff, 134

financial ratio analysis, 134

liquid asset, 135

liquidity ratios, 135

asset management ratios, 136

financial leverage, 136

leverage ratios, 136

profitability ratios, 136

budgeted income statement, 137

budgeted balance sheet, 137

cash budget, 138

trade credit, 138

spontaneous financing, 140

factor, 140

line of credit, 140

revolving credit agreement, 140

commercial paper, 140

retained earnings, 141

covenants, 142

equity financing, 142

debt financing, 142

capital structure, 142

Dodd-Frank Act, 145

cash equivalents, 145

U.S. Treasury bills (T-bills), 145

money market mutual funds, 145

capital budgeting, 147

time value of money, 147

certificate of deposit (CD), 147

present value, 147

net present value (NPV), 148

in its small West Coast venues. According to CEO Adam Friedman, Nederlander's success is owed to management's ability to maintain control over fixed and variable costs, which appear on numerous financial reports throughout the year. On the revenue side of the equation, Nederlander makes money from concert promotion and other events hosted at amphitheaters. While every employee contributes to Nederlander's bottom line, Friedman and the Finance Department have an important role in tracking financials and communicating the company's return on investment to owners. While everyone agrees that concerts are cool, show business is like any business: if the finances don't add up, the show is over.

Ask Your Students:

1. How does Nederlander plan, manage, and measure financial progress?
2. How does Nederlander earn revenues? What are Nederlander's costs?

LECTURE EXAMPLE

Heated discussions continue regarding the appropriate balance of maximizing shareholders' wealth and corporate social responsible. Some researchers suggest that the debates have taken place within the wrong context and that social responsibility is a phenomenon both external and internal to organizations, as it lies on the cusp of organizational culture and social expectations. Some believe CSR is seen as a deviant behavior at times, but it should become a common organizational practice. Many argue that ideas of socially responsible behaviors should be incorporated into the existing set of social expectations and corporate norms. The pressure for this shift in social expectations could come from the investors themselves.

Sources: Ekaterina S. Ralston, (2010) "Deviance or norm? Exploring corporate social responsibility," *European Business Review*, Vol. 22 Iss: 4, pp. 397–410

DISCUSSION QUESTIONS

1. What are the major challenges financial managers face when they try to find the best sources and uses of funds?
2. Is it possible for a firm to have too much money? Explain.
3. What is financial leverage? How, and under what conditions, can financial leverage benefit a company? How, and under what conditions, can it harm a company?

GROUP ACTIVITY

Select 4 or 5 companies in the same basic market or industry, and print their most recent financial statements before class. Break the class into small groups, give each the financial statements for one of the firms, and have them work together to compute basic financial ratios for that firm. (The formulas for several common ratios are given in Exhibit 9.1. If you have a large class, you can assign the same company to more than one group and have the groups compute different ratios.) Then have each group report their results. Compare the ratios reported by each group. In cases where ratios differ significantly among the firms, discuss the implications of these differences.

ASSIGNMENTS

Visit the sites of at LendingClub.com and Prosper.com to find out more about peer-to-peer (P2P) lending. How do these sites match small lenders and borrowers? How are the sites similar, and how do they differ? Do some additional research to find out what others are saying about the pros and cons of these sites. Would you be willing to participate in this type of arrangement as a borrower? Would you participate as a lender? Why or why not?

BEYOND THE CLASS

A selection of materials is in the Instructor's Manual.

CHAPTER 9—UPDATES TO BUSN THIS YEAR

Page 133—New chapter opening quote

Page 139—*Strong Profits = Private Equity + EcoValueScreen* box feature replaces *For a Socially Responsible Firm in Need of Funds, There's No Need to Fear* box feature

Page 141—New example about Berkshire Hathaway

Page 143—*Liking Facebook's IPO: Too Early for Thumbs Down?* box feature replaces *Is Too Big to Fail a Thing of the Past?* box feature

Page 144—New pull quote

Page 146—*Robin Hood? Big Customers Help Themselves by Paying Accounts Receivable Later* box feature replaces *T-Bills Why Lots of Investor Interest Means Earning Zero Interest* box feature

Page 148—Revised Exhibit 9.4 How a Present Value of $10,000 Grows

Page 148—*Apple's "Walking Around Money": What Do You Do with $100 Billion in Cash?* box feature replaces *Are Minsky Moments Inevitable?* box feature

Page 149—Revised statistics in the Careers in Financial Management box feature

CHAPTER 9: Finance: Acquiring and Using Funds to Maximize Value

Visit login.cengage.com for additional materials to enhance your lectures!

Financial Markets: **Allocating Financial Resources**

WHAT'S INSIDE
Key Topics in this Chapter: Types of financial markets, regulation of financial markets, common stock, preferred stock, bonds, primary securities markets, secondary securities markets, tips for personal investing, mutual funds, tracking investment performance, stock indices, interpreting stock quotes on financial websites.

LEARNING OBJECTIVES

With the growth in eReader usage among students, this 6th edition of BUSN features a new numbering system for major headings that we recommend you use instead of page numbers when creating assignments.

10-1 Explain the role of financial markets in the U.S. economy and identify the key players in these markets

10-2 Identify the key laws that govern the way financial markets operate and explain the impact of each law

10-3 Describe and compare the major types of securities that are traded in securities markets

10-4 Explain how securities are issued in the primary market and traded on secondary markets.

10-5 Compare several strategies that investors use to invest in securities

10-6 Interpret the information provided in the stock quotes available on financial websites

MULTIMEDIA

PPT—THE HIGHLIGHTS

Slide 8	Investing in Financial Securities
Slide 10	Common Stock
Slide 18	Trading Securities: The Secondary Market
Slide 22	Personal Investing
Slide 29	Stock Indices: Tracking the Trends

VIDEO

PowerPoint Clip from Developing an Investment Plan
Run time: 2:32 minutes
Establishing a strategic personal investing plan requires careful analysis of short- and long-term objectives, of personal tolerance for risk, and of current assets. Most people are not comfortable with high levels of risk, but no investment strategy is risk-free. To meet personal goals, investors need to find the balance between risk and return that works for them. An investment portfolio that includes high-quality, blue chip stocks, combined with growth opportunities and international investments, diversifies investments and reduces risk.

This segment highlights investing options in terms of the risk involved and features an investment professional from Smith Barney who offers a basic strategy for personal financial planning. An investment professional as well as a home-based investing group are featured as options for seeking direction and support in the investing process.

Ask Your Students:

1. What questions should you ask in the process of creating a financial plan?
2. What is diversification, and why is it important in an investment plan?

DVD SEGMENT SUMMARY

J.P. Morgan Chase Bank
Run time: 6:32
J.P. Morgan Chase is a global financial holding company formed from a merger of two financial institutions: Chase (formerly Chase Manhattan Corp.) and J.P. Morgan. Additional acquisitions since the year 2000 have made Chase the second-largest branch network, with operations in 60 countries and assets estimated at $2 trillion. In addition to providing personal banking services, Chase is an important partner to small businesses. From the moment a small firm opens an

CHAPTER 10 OUTLINE

The Role of Financial Markets and Their Key Players
    Depository Institutions
    Nondepository Financial Institutions

Regulation of Financial Markets to Protect Investors and Improve Stability
    Financial Regulations: Early Efforts
    Deregulation during the 1980s and 1990s
    Recent Developments: Re-regulation in the Aftermath of Financial Turmoil

Investing in Securities: What Are the Options?
    Common Stock: Back to Basics
    Preferred Stock: Getting Preferential Treatment
    Bonds: Earning Your Interest
    Convertible Securities: The Big Switch
    Mutual Funds and ETFs: Diversification Made Easy
    Exchange Traded Funds: Real Basket Cases

Issuing and Trading Securities: The Primary and Secondary Markets
    The Primary Securities Market: Where Securities Are Issued
    Secondary Securities Markets: Let's Make a Deal

Personal Investing
    Choosing a Broker: Gaining Access to the Markets
    Buying Securities: Let's Make a Deal
    Strategies for Investing in Securities

Keeping Tabs on the Market
    Stock Indices: Tracking the Trends
    Tracking the Performance of Specific Securities

The Big Picture

Careers in Financial Markets

BEYOND THE CLASS

A selection of materials is in the Instructor's Manual.

Visit login.cengage.com for additional materials to enhance your lectures!

CHAPTER 10: Financial Markets: Allocating Financial Resources

KEY TERMS

account with Chase, a trusted partnership forms between the business owner and Chase's account manager. Chase employees learn the client's industry, and they work to offer strategic solutions from lock-boxes and electronic transfers to loans and new lines of credit. Whether the goal is to build a new warehouse or fund the manufacture of new products, Chase has the funds that businesses need to achieve success.

Ask Your Students:

1. In what ways can Chase Bank be an important partner to small businesses?
2. According to the video, how does Chase help businesses manage collection of payments?

LECTURE EXAMPLE

The online discount broker Zecco.com recently launched the first Facebook app with a stock-trading platform that allows stock trading, live quotes, charts, and market-discussion groups on Facebook. You can actually enter buy and sell orders for stocks from within Facebook. Zecco has named this Facebook app "Wall Street." Accessing these trading tools is free but requires a Zecco account. This app has also integrated the social aspect of Facebook by allowing customers to share their stock picks and trading ideas with Facebook's "Like" buttons if they so choose. For those with trading buddies on Facebook, you can track and follow how your friends are viewing the market.

Found at: http://marketheist.com/2011/05/30/online-broker-zecco-launch.

DISCUSSION QUESTIONS

1. What are the major types of depository institutions and what roles do they play in financial markets? How do institutional investors differ from depository institutions?
2. How have recent financial disruptions changed the ways that financial markets are regulated?
3. What investment strategy do you personally favor? What types of investments fit best with your strategy?

GROUP ACTIVITY

Prior to the day of the group activity, ask each student to identify a stock they might want to invest in and to write up a brief report explaining why they think the stock would be a good investment. On the day of the project, divide the class into small groups. Give the students about 10 minutes to compare notes on their stocks and to select one stock to recommend as an investment. (Optional: Offer bonus points to each group in proportion to the performance of their stock over a specified time period.) Record the recommendation of each group, and record the current market price. Over the next few weeks, have students periodically check the price, volume, and market capitalization of their stocks and update the performance in class. At the end of the time period, compute the percentage capital gain (or loss) that each group would have earned if they had bought their stock on the day the group made its selection.

ASSIGNMENTS

The Dodd-Frank Act established the Financial Stability Oversight Council to identify emerging risks to the financial sector and propose new rules to the Federal Reserve that would reduce risky behavior. Use the Internet to find out more about the structure and responsibilities of this council. Who are the key players on the FSOC and who is its chairperson? What recommendations has the council made to the Federal Reserve over the past two years? What is the rationale for these recommendations?

CHAPTER 10—UPDATES TO BUSN THIS YEAR

Page 151—New chapter opening quote

Page 151—New statistics about total bank assets, including credit unions

Page 152—New information about savings and loans in regards to mortgage financing

Page 152—*Woof! Dividends and Dogs of the Dow* box feature replaces *Congress Decides It's Time to Trim the Hedges* box feature

Page 155—New pull quote

Page 156—New information about companies issuing century bonds

Page 156—*QE? Queen Elizabeth? Quod Est? Quantitative Easing?* box feature replaces *Could Your Best Investment Be a Piece of Junk?* box feature

Page 160—New information about NYSE & NASDAQ

Page 160—New pull quote

Page 161—*Affinity Fraud: I'm Your Friend. I'm Your Neighbor. I'm a Con Man* box feature replaces *Symbolic Logic: Do You LUV this HOG's DNA?* box feature

Page 165—New Exhibit 10.3 Yahoo! Finance Quote for a Stock and surrounding text

Page 167—New information about annual income for brokers in the Careers in Financial Markets box feature

CHAPTER 10: Financial Markets: Allocating Financial Resources

Visit login.cengage.com for additional materials to enhance your lectures!

Marketing: Building Profitable Customer Connections

WHAT'S INSIDE

Key Topics in this Chapter: Type of marketing utility, marketing tactics, four U.S. marketing eras, CRM, value, customer satisfaction and loyalty, marketing plans, market segmentation, target markets, B2C vs. B2B, marketing mix, global considerations, marketing environment, consumer behavior, marketing research, social responsibility, marketing technology.

LEARNING OBJECTIVES

With the growth in eReader usage among students, this 6th edition of BUSN features a new numbering system for major headings that we recommend you use instead of page numbers when creating assignments.

11-1   Discuss the objectives, the process, and the scope of marketing

11-2   Identify the role of the customer in marketing

11-3   Explain each element of marketing strategy

11-4   Describe the consumer and business decision-making process

11-5   Discuss the key elements of marketing research

11-6   Explain the roles of social responsibility and technology in marketing

MULTIMEDIA

PPT—THE HIGHLIGHTS

Slide 4   Marketing: Getting Value by Giving Value

Slide 5   The Scope of Marketing: It's Everywhere

Slide 6   The Evolution of Marketing: From the Product to the Customer

Slide 15   Facebook Changes the Marketing Environment

Slide 26   Consumer Decision Process

VIDEO

PowerPoint Clip from VANS Downtown Showdown
Run time 2:28 minutes
In 1966, Paul Van Doren and three partners opened up their first shoe store in Anaheim, California. Today, VANS is about more than shoes. VANS is a global lifestyle brand, integrally connected with the worlds of street fashion, action sports, art, and music. VANS spreads its culture through a targeted media mix aimed at its primary demographic.

VANS invests heavily in event marketing, supported by cause marketing. The Warped Tour offers consumers an onsite experience that spreads the Southern California action sports lifestyle of VANS. In this segment, the VANS marketing team talks about building relationships through event marketing and giving back through cause marketing. VANS

looks for ways to be socially responsible in ways that matter to their core markets and partners.

Sources: http://www.vans.net.au/wawcs0130206/tn-history.html, http://www.vans.com

Ask Your Students:

1.   How does VANS perform customer relationship management?
2.   Why does VANS invest so heavily in event marketing?

DVD SEGMENT SUMMARY

Flight 001
Run time: 6:50 minutes
While seated on a flight from New York to Paris in 1998, garment-industry veterans Brad John and John Sencion hatched an idea for a one-stop travel shop targeted to fashion-forward globetrotters like themselves. They called it Flight 001 and began selling guidebooks, luggage, electronic gadgets, passport covers, and other consumer travel products. As the partners embark on their second decade together, Flight 001 is being hailed as of the most exciting businesses in the industry. In addition to selling Flight 001 brand merchandise, the New York-based retailer has become famous for its unique atmospherics: Flight 001 stores are shaped like airplane fuselages. According to John and Sencion, the company's popularity has grown without paid advertising. Instead, co-marketing

CHAPTER 11 OUTLINE

Marketing: Building Profitable Customer Connections

Marketing: Getting Value by Giving Value
   The Scope of Marketing: It's Everywhere!
   The Evolution of Marketing: From the Product to the Customer

The Customer: Front and Center
   Value
   Customer Satisfaction
   Customer Loyalty

Marketing Strategy: Where Are You Going, and How Will You Get There?
   Target Market
   Consumer Markets Versus Business Markets
   Consumer Market Segmentation
   Business Market Segmentation
   The Marketing Mix
   The Global Marketing Mix
   The Marketing Environment
   The Global Marketing Environment

Customer Behavior: Decisions, Decisions, Decisions!
   Consumer Behavior
   Business Buyer Behavior

Marketing Research: So What Do They REALLY Think?
   Types of Data
   Primary Research Tools
   An International Perspective

Social Responsibility and Technology: A Major Marketing Shift
   Marketing and Society: It's Not Just About You!
   Technology and Marketing: Power to the People!

The Big Picture

Careers in Marketing

BEYOND THE CLASS

A selection of materials is in the Instructor's Manual.

Visit login.cengage.com for additional materials to enhance your lectures!

CHAPTER 11: Marketing: Building Profitable Customer Connections

KEY TERMS

partnerships with companies like MINI Cooper and Yves Behar have delivered results for the retailer. The company also appears frequently in top fashion magazines, and even on the *Rachel Ray Show*. With more than a decade of growth behind them, Flight 001's founders see nothing but clear skies ahead.

Ask Your Students:

1. How important are Flight 001's strategic alliances to its marketing?
2. What other companies or industries would be a good fit with Flight 001?

LECTURE EXAMPLE

Marketers now realize that simply satisfying customers may not be enough to ensure loyalty. Rather, they should strive for customer delight, defined as a combination of joy and surprise. Yet, only in the past decade have customer delight and especially its proposed opposite, outrage or disgust, been given much attention in the literature.

Source: Alexander, Wayne. (Jan 2010). Customer delight: A review. *Academy of Marketing Studies Journal*, 14, 1, 39–54.

DISCUSSION QUESTIONS

1. How has marketing evolved over time? How have current events, economics, and culture influenced thinking about marketing?
2. What are the different ways to segment a consumer market? Does it make sense to use more than just a single segmentation variable? Why or why not?
3. What are the five key dimensions of the marketing environment? How can marketers stay abreast of changes in each area?

GROUP ACTIVITY

Break into groups of five to seven students and consider this scenario: You and your teammates are partners in the ownership of a medium-sized fast-food chain in the Midwest. You own 41 outlets, most of them in small towns. The mainstays of your menu are hamburgers and seasoned French fries, a couple of sandwiches, various chips, soft-serve ice cream, and sodas. Your most important customers are men aged 18 to 34 (they account for about 20% of your customers and about 55% of your sales), but since restaurant options are limited in most of the towns where you operate, you serve customers across a wide demographic range. Sales in the past two years have been dropping at an accelerating rate. You think the issue may be a national focus on low-carb diets—not a great fit with your local focus on sandwiches, french fries, and ice cream. Eager to rejuvenate the business, you are about to meet with your partners to discuss potential solutions.

Spend about 10 minutes brainstorming possible strategies with your team. Be sure to consider all of the possibilities, including doing nothing ("This will all blow over . . ."). Then, choose your best option, and identify the potential risks and benefits (e.g., If you made changes to attract new customers, would you alienate your current core customers?). How does your solution compare to ideas from other teams? What are the ethical implications of your approach?

ASSIGNMENTS

Select a specific product or service that you know and love. (It could be in any category, as long as it's clean and legal.) Describe and analyze each area of the marketing mix. What works well? What could be better? If you were the marketing manager for this product or service, how would you change the marketing mix to add more value and to create stronger, more profitable relationships with your customers? From a customer perspective, how would those changes affect your decision-making process?

CHAPTER 11—UPDATES TO BUSN THIS YEAR

CHAPTER 11: Marketing: Building Profitable Customer Connections

Visit login.cengage.com for additional materials to enhance your lectures!

Product and Promotion: Creating and Communicating Value

WHAT'S INSIDE

Key Topics in this Chapter: Definitions of products and services, product layers, consumer and business product categories, quality, product lines, product mix, cannibalization, branding, licensing, packaging, six stages of new product development, product life cycle, the power of promotion, integrated marketing communication, developing a positioning statement, international considerations, emerging and traditional promotional tools, personal selling, developing the right promotional mix.

LEARNING OBJECTIVES

With the growth in eReader usage among students, this 6th edition of BUSN features a new numbering system for major headings that we recommend you use instead of page numbers when creating assignments.

12-1   Explain "product" and identify product classifications

12-2   Describe product differentiation and the key elements of product planning

12-3   Discuss innovation and the product life cycle

12-4   Analyze and explain promotion and integrated marketing communications

12-5   Discuss development of the promotional message

12-6   Discuss the promotional mix and the various promotional tools

CHAPTER 12 OUTLINE

MULTIMEDIA

PPT—THE HIGHLIGHTS

Slide 3   Product: It's Probably More Than You Thought
Slide 6   Product Layers: Peeling the Onion
Slide 21   Internet vs. TV Watching
Slide 27   The Promotional Mix: Communicating the BIG IDEA
Slide 32   Starbucks Samples

VIDEO

PowerPoint Clip from Ogden Publications, Integrated Marketing Communications
Run time: 2:36 minutes
Ogden Publications is North America's largest publisher serving the sustainable living, rural lifestyle, farm memorabilia, and classic motorcycle communities. Key brands include *Mother Earth News, Natural Home, Utne Reader, Capper's,* and *Grit.* Ogden Publications also provides insurance and financial services. The variety of unique titles offered by Ogden, each with its own individual brand, creates a marketing challenge.

In this segment, Ogden marketers discuss the challenge of integrating their marketing communications. Marketing works with editorial teams to develop products, event strategies, and public relations.

They drive readership through direct mail, email, insert cards, and card decks as well as newsstands. Individual marketing teams focus efforts on circulation, merchandising and events, creative services, and public relations.

Source: http://www.ogdenpubs.com/

Ask Your Students:

1.   How does Ogden Publications define integrated marketing communications?
2.   What challenges does Ogden face in developing integrated marketing communications?

DVD SEGMENT SUMMARY

L.L. Bean
Run time: 8:09 minutes
From a tiny mail-order company begun 100 years ago, L.L. Bean has grown into a well-known retail firm with net sales of over $1.5 billion annually. It encompasses stores in more than 10 states, continues to distribute its ever-popular catalog, and boasts a thriving online store. The Freeport, Maine-based retailer sells approximately 20,000 high-quality items, including outdoor apparel, camping gear, and luggage. While advertising has always been a priority, the

Visit login.cengage.com for additional materials to enhance your lectures!

CHAPTER 12: Product and Promotion: Creating and Communicating Value

KEY TERMS

CHAPTER 12—UPDATES TO BUSN THIS YEAR

Page 190—Revised Exhibit 12.2

Page 191—Revised Exhibits 12.3 and 12.4

Page 193—New *Oops!* box feature

Page 195—Revised *Wacky Labels* box feature

Page 203—Revised Exhibit 12.9

Page 207—New box feature Examples, statistics, and quotes revised throughout Chapter 12. For details, see online instructor materials at login.cengage.com.

company's marketing communications are more sophisticated now than when L.L. Bean publicized his first waterproof boot using a homemade brochure. The retailer uses marketing databases to manage mailing lists, and the L.L. Bean website garners significant sales. Internet advertising is also a promising tool. Banner ads at popular sites lead customers to the L.L. Bean online store, and the company's Facebook, Twitter, and YouTube accounts attract the social networking generation. When all promotion tools work together properly, the L.L. Bean brand stays on everyone's mind.

Ask Your Students:

1. Does L.L. Bean sell goods, services, or both? Explain.
2. Of the many promotional tools discussed in the video, which one is the most important to L.L. Bean's marketing promotion, and why?

LECTURE EXAMPLE

The study results show that social media usage by small business owners to promote their company and product or service increased from 12% to 24% in just the last year, and almost one out of five actively uses social media as part of his or her marketing strategy.

- 75% have a company page on a social networking site.
- 69% post status updates or articles of interest on social media sites.
- 57% build a network through a site such as LinkedIn.
- 54% monitor feedback about the business.
- 39% maintain a blog.
- 26% tweet about areas of expertise.
- 16% use Twitter as a service channel.

Source: "The State of Small Business Report," sponsored by Network Solutions, LLC and the University of Maryland's Robert H. Smith School of Business.

Retrieved (05/20/2011): http://www.socialmediaexaminer.com/3-new-studies-prove-social-media-marketing-growth/

DISCUSSION QUESTIONS

1. Would it ever make sense for a firm to offer a new product line that they know would cannibalize an existing line? Explain your answer.
2. What are the key risks and the potential rewards of product placement in both movies and television? Do you think this promotional tool will continue to grow? Why or why not?

3. Given that each type of media offers strengths and drawbacks, what factors should you consider in developing a media plan for a specific product?

GROUP ACTIVITY

Break into groups of three to five students and spend a few moments talking as a group about the meaning of product quality. Does the definition of quality change depending on the type of business? Does the definition of quality change across cultures? Define what quality means specifically for each of the following categories:

- A visit to the dentist
- A computer
- A motorcycle
- A haircut
- A pair of blue jeans
- A cup of coffee
- A stereo system

How can marketers in each category demonstrate product quality to potential customers before they make the purchase?

ASSIGNMENTS

Imagine for a moment that you've been hired as the marketing director for an alternative music radio station that will launch in one month, targeting a core group of men and women ages 18 to 24. The owner of the station—your boss—has already worked with the advertising agency to develop a creative concept for the station: "A New Voice for a New Day." He has asked you to develop the "ideal" media plan for launching the station. (For this initial draft, you may ignore budget concerns.) Your challenge is to develop a highly innovative, carefully targeted plan for the first six months of operation, keeping in mind that too much exposure will turn away the alternative music crowd, but too little exposure will yield too few listeners. Assume that advertising will begin two weeks before the day of the launch. Where will you advertise? Can you think of creative ways to use media to emphasize your promotional message? Will you use emerging media vehicles such as text messaging or podcasting? How will you time your advertising? Last but not least, what other promotional tactics would you recommend to supplement your advertising plan? Share the results with your classmates.

BEYOND THE CLASS

A selection of materials is in the Instructor's Manual.

CHAPTER 12: Product and Promotion: Creating and Communicating Value

Visit login.cengage.com for additional materials to enhance your lectures!

Distribution and Pricing: Right Product, Right Person, Right Place, Right Price

WHAT'S INSIDE

Key Topics in this Chapter: : Distribution strategy, distribution channels, the role of distributors, retailers vs. wholesalers, wholesaling options, multichannel retailing, wheel of retailing theory, supply chain management, modes of transportation, pricing strategy, breakeven analysis, profit margin.

LEARNING OBJECTIVES

With the growth in eReader usage among students, this 6th edition of BUSN features a new numbering system for major headings that we recommend you use instead of page numbers when creating assignments.

13-1 Define distribution and differentiate between channels of distribution and physical distribution

13-2 Describe the various types of wholesale distributors

13-3 Discuss strategies and trends in store and nonstore retailing

13-4 Explain the key factors in physical distribution

13-5 Outline core pricing objectives and strategies

13-6 Discuss pricing in practice, including the role of consumer perceptions

CHAPTER 13 OUTLINE

Distribution: Getting Your Product to Your Customer
    The Role of Distributors: Adding Value

Wholesalers: Sorting Out the Options
    Merchant Wholesalers
    Agents and Brokers

Retailers: The Consumer Connection
    Store Retailers
    Nonstore Retailers

Physical Distribution: Planes, Trains, and Much, Much More…
    Transportation Decisions
    Proactive Supply Chain Management

Pricing Objectives and Strategies: A High-Stakes Game
    Building Profitability
    Boosting Volume
    Matching the Competition
    Creating Prestige

Pricing in Practice: A Real-World Approach
    Breakeven Analysis
    Fixed Margin Pricing

Consumer Pricing Perceptions: The Strategic Wild Card

The Big Picture

Careers in Distribution and Pricing

MULTIMEDIA

PPT—THE HIGHLIGHTS

Slide 5   Distribution: Getting Your Product to Your Customer
Slide 7   Reducing Transactions Through Marketing Intermediaries
Slide 18 Elements of the Supply Chain
Slide 20 Modes of Transportation
Slide 27 Applying Breakeven Analysis

VIDEO

PowerPoint Clip from Blu Dot Styles Marketing Strategy
Run time: 2:31 minutes
Blu Dot furniture was founded in 1997 by three college friends who shared a passion for art, architecture, and design. When they began to furnish their first homes, they discovered that they didn't like the stuff they could afford and couldn't afford the stuff they liked. Today, the goal of Blu Dot is to bring good design to as many people as possible by creating products that are useful, affordable, and desirable.

Affordability and design are the keys to Blu Dot's position in the furniture market space. They begin design with a retail price point in mind that is based on costs plus mark up as well as an analysis of the competition. Blu Dot now offers a second line

of furniture with the same design values at a lower price point in an attempt to reach more market segments.

Source: http://www.bludot.com/about-bludot-dir/our-story

Ask Your Students:

1. What is Blu Dot's approach to pricing?
2. What is Blu Dot's strategy for reaching new market segments?

DVD SEGMENT SUMMARY

Netflix
Run time: 10:41 minutes
When DVD technology first hit the market, software engineer Reed Hastings decided to conduct a test. He mailed numerous discs to himself to see whether they would ship safely by United States Postal Service. Hastings liked the result, and today the computer whiz's DVD mail-delivery business, Netflix, is the top movie-rental service in the world. Prior to Netflix, the movie-rental business was slow and inconvenient. Today, consumers browse films online and receive their favorite new releases, old classics, and popular television series overnight—with no late fees. Netflix's growth has been explosive. In 1999, the Silicon Valley company offered approximately 4,000 titles on DVD. Now Netflix boasts more than 100,000 DVD titles, as well as 12,000

KEY TERMS

on-demand programs. Innovative distribution is the key to Netflix's success: delivering 2 million DVDs daily to customers would be impossible without the retailer's strategically located distribution centers, automated disc handling, and convenient online ordering.

Ask Your Students:

1. How does technology enable Netflix to process and ship nearly two million DVD movie rentals daily?
2. Why is Netflix able to manage so many DVDs without the use of many large storage warehouses?

LECTURE EXAMPLE

"CHARGE WHAT THE MARKET WILL BEAR" summarizes the pricing strategy of many businesses. They believe that pricing means finding out what the value of their offering is, relative to alternatives for their customers, and then charging as high a price as they can. If they think their offering is superior, they include in their pricing the full premium that they think the superiority earns. But pursuing pricing in that way is usually shortsighted. First, it neglects other potential means of profiting from delivering superior value that may result in greater overall profitability to a supplier. Second, it weakens customer relations rather than strengthening them, which a more progressive and comprehensive approach to value-based pricing can accomplish.

Source: Anderson, J.C., Wouters, M. & van Rossum, W. (2010). Why the highest price isn't the best price: How to practice value-based pricing that boosts profits and promotes better relationships with customers. *MIT Sloan Management Review*.

DISCUSSION QUESTIONS

1. Do you think that the movement toward multichannel retailing will continue to grow? Why or why not?
2. Who benefits most from collaborative supply chain relationships? Explain your answer.
3. How does a breakeven analysis help marketers determine the best price for their products? What other factors should companies consider? Why?

GROUP ACTIVITY

Today's retailers have gone to extraordinary lengths to create a shopping experience based on more than just the products they sell and the services they offer. Clothing purveyor Abercrombie & Fitch, for instance, adorns its stores with oversized posters of sexy, half-dressed models and sprays its signature scent throughout the store. Break into groups of three to five students. With your teammates, visit a retailer you all like and check out the look and feel of the store. Notice background music, lighting, colors, decorations, signs, layout, and the appearance of the salespeople. Then, develop recommendations for how your store could improve the shopping experience for you and other college students. If possible, share your recommendations with management of the store.

ASSIGNMENTS

As you market yourself to employers, the salary you demand is essentially your personal price. Keeping that in mind, what pricing strategy should you follow (penetration, skimming, or competitive)? Why? Issues to consider:

- Who is your target market?
- How would you position your price to this market?
- What are the psychological pricing considerations?
- What are the image considerations?
- What are the promotional considerations?

Be creative as you prepare your strategy—a novel approach could give you an edge in a competitive job market. Explain your pricing strategy to your classmates and your teacher, and solicit their constructive feedback.

BEYOND THE CLASS

A selection of materials is in the Instructor's Manual.

CHAPTER 13—UPDATES TO BUSN THIS YEAR

Page 211—New chapter opening quote

Page 212—New examples of form utility, time utility, ownership utility, and information utility

Page 213—*Who's the real hog in the food distribution system?* box feature replaces *Go Green, Go Local!* box feature

Page 215—New fun fact

Page 215—New examples of intensive distribution, selective distribution, exclusive distribution

Page 215—Revised stats about online retailing

Page 215—Revised information about the NRF/ American Express Customers' Choice survey

Page 216—Revised number of catalogs Victoria's Secret mails annually

Page 216—New pull quote

Page 216—New vending example

Page 217—Revised information about Gap distributing products to eight different countries

Page 219—*Hide and Seek Pricing* box feature replaces *Right Is Always Right, But Sometimes Left Is Wrong* box feature

Page 221—Revised *Putting iTunes on the Spot* box feature

Page 223—Revised salary information for logistics professionals

Management, Motivation, and Leadership:
Bringing Business to Life

WHAT'S INSIDE
Key Topics in this Chapter: The critical role of managers, motivation theories and real-world practice, strategic planning, tactical planning, operational planning, contingency planning, defining a mission, SWOT analysis, creating an organizational chart, modern organization models, leadership style, control process.

LEARNING OBJECTIVES

With the growth in eReader usage among students, this 6th edition of BUSN features a new numbering system for major headings that we recommend you use instead of page numbers when creating assignments.

14-1 Discuss the role of management and its importance to organizational success

14-2 Explain key theories and current practices of motivation

14-3 Outline the categories of business planning and explain strategic planning

14-4 Discuss the organizing function of management

14-5 Explain the role of managerial leadership and the key leadership styles

14-6 Describe the management control process

CHAPTER 14 OUTLINE

Bringing Resources to Life
  Management Hierarchy: Levels of Responsibility
  Management Skills: Having What It Takes to Get the Job Done

Motivation: Lighting the Fire
  Theories of Motivation
  Motivation Today

Planning: Figuring Out Where to Go and How to Get There
  Strategic Planning: Setting the Agenda

Organizing: Fitting Together the Puzzle Pieces
  Key Organizing Considerations
  Organization Models

Leadership: Directing and Inspiring
  Leadership Style

Controlling: Making Sure It All Works

The Big Picture

Careers in Management

MULTIMEDIA

PPT—THE HIGHLIGHTS

Slide 5 Bringing Resources to Life
Slide 18 Planning: Figuring Out Where to Go and How to Get There
Slide 20 Contingency Planning
Slide 34 Leadership: Directing and Inspiring
Slide 37 Controlling: Making Sure It Works

VIDEO

PowerPoint Clip from Camp Bow Wow: Leadership
Run time: 2:28 minutes
In 2000, Camp Bow Wow opened its first doggy day and overnight camp in Denver, Colorado. Since the company started franchising in 2003, Camp Bow Wow has awarded over 200 franchises in 40 states, plus one in Canada. For Camp Bow Wow, it's all about the dogs. Founder Heidi Ganahl's goal is to be a full-service provider for all aspects of dog care.

Heidi Ganahl's leadership is characterized by a passion for animals, humility, authenticity, and a personal approach to problems and people. In this segment, Heidi talks about balancing visionary and goal-oriented leadership with relationships with friends and family in the business. A franchise owner talks about Heidi's strengths in negotiating relationships by focusing on the right things and setting clear expectations, while giving latitude and allowing for input.

Source: http://www.campbowwowusa.com/corporate-info/about-us

Ask Your Students:

1. What types of management skills can you identify in this video?
2. How would you describe Heidi's leadership style?

DVD SEGMENT SUMMARY

L.L. Bean
Run time: 8:35 minutes
Since its launch in 1912, outdoor retailer L.L. Bean has grown into a successful retail business with sales of more than $1.5 billion annually. *BusinessWeek* even ranked the company tops on its 2010 Customer Service Champs list. What motivates L.L. Bean workers to achieve excellence? For one thing, employees share the purpose and values of the company's founders and managers, so they feel like part of a large family. Unlike other mail-order companies that micromanage employees, L.L. Bean empowers representatives to make decisions on behalf of the company and to advocate better ways of doing business. Generous wages, benefits, and

Visit login.cengage.com for additional materials to enhance your lectures!

CHAPTER 14: Management, Motivation, and Leadership: Bringing Business to Life

KEY TERMS

profit-sharing extras foster a sense of equity among employees. The result is a highly productive workforce comprising employees who remain for decades. According to company leaders, the retailer's people-oriented policies are a reflection of the company's founder: L.L. Bean loved the outdoors and expressed genuine concern for people.

Ask Your Students:

1. Which level of management at L.L. Bean acts as "the face of the company" to customers?
2. How does managerial planning take place across different levels of the L.L. Bean hierarchy?

LECTURE EXAMPLE

According to self-determination theory (SDT, Ryan and Deci 2000) of motivation, in order to create and maintain an innovative, proactive, and happy workforce, businesses ought to adopt organizational designs that cultivate employees' autonomous (versus controlled) work motivation. This is because numerous SDT-based studies have found that autonomous (versus controlled) motivation is associated with higher (versus lower) levels of creativity, cognitive flexibility, persistence, and psychological well-being. It further predicts that autonomous-versus-controlled work motivation will affect various outcome variables, such as employees' willingness to acquire new knowledge and skills, their attributional tendency for their performance, and their proactivity at work.

Source: Lan, Guo. (2007). Self-determination theory of motivation and performance management systems. Washington State University, 2007, 228 pages; AAT 3301979.

DISCUSSION QUESTIONS

1. Review the definition of management at the beginning of the chapter and briefly define each of the four functions. What are the key challenges in carrying out these functions in today's hyper-competitive marketplace?
2. What are the characteristics of effective leaders? What leadership style do most effective leaders use?
3. If an employee falls short of meeting his or her goals, what factors should a manager consider before engaging in disciplinary action? Explain your answer.

GROUP ACTIVITY

Before you begin this project, gather plenty of newspapers and enough masking tape so that each group of three to five students has its own roll. The purpose is for each group of students to use the newspaper and tape to build the best possible tower in 15 minutes. As a class, determine the potential criteria for "best" tower (e.g., tallest, widest, wackiest), and vote on three to five standards to use for the project. Then break into small groups. Earmark one student per group to be the observer, and let the building begin!

Ask the observer from each group to present the tower and to comment on the group process. Did a leader emerge? What style did the leader use? What seemed to motivate the group to perform? How much time did the group spend planning their approach versus actually building the tower? How did the group resolve conflict?

ASSIGNMENTS

Spend a moment thinking about all the teachers you've had over the past several years. What motivational techniques did your favorite teacher use? Your least favorite teacher? How did the teacher's approach to motivation affect your performance? Using the motivational techniques you've learned in this chapter, design a motivational plan for this business class.

BEYOND THE CLASS

A selection of materials is in the Instructor's Manual.

CHAPTER 14—UPDATES TO BUSN THIS YEAR

Page 225—New chapter opening quote

Page 226—Revised *The Power of One* box feature

Page 227—Revised *Oops! What Were They Thinking?* box feature

Page 228—New example of a company that uses self-actualization for motivation

Pages 229–230—New examples of companies that are part of the 100 Best Companies to Work for

Page 231—Revised Exhibit 14.5 Examples of Mission Statements

Page 231—New examples of companies with contingency plans

Page 232—Revised *Slackers? Not so much* box feature

Page 234—*Should you work fewer hours?* box feature replaces *Laughing All the Way* box feature

Page 237—New pull quote

CHAPTER 14: Management, Motivation, and Leadership: Bringing Business to Life

Visit login.cengage.com for additional materials to enhance your lectures!

Human Resource Management: Building a Top-Quality Workforce

WHAT'S INSIDE

Key Topics in this Chapter: The importance of a quality workforce, challenges facing today's HR managers, HR perception problems and solutions, HR planning process, effective recruitment and selection, training and development for a competitive edge, evaluations and feedback, employee benefits, potential HR legal issues, affirmative action, sexual harassment.

LEARNING OBJECTIVES

With the growth in eReader usage among students, this 6th edition of BUSN features a new numbering system for major headings that we recommend you use instead of page numbers when creating assignments.

15–1 Explain the importance of human resources to business success

15–2 Discuss key human resource issues in today's economy

15–3 Outline challenges and opportunities that the human resources function faces

15–4 Discuss human resource planning and core human resources responsibilities

15–5 Explain the key federal legislation that affects human resources

CHAPTER 15 OUTLINE

MULTIMEDIA

PPT—THE HIGHLIGHTS

Slide 3 Human Resource Management
Slide 11 Selection: Making the Right Choice
Slide 25 Benefits: From Birthday Cakes to Death Benefits
Slide 30 Separation: Breaking Up Is Hard to Do
Slide 31 Legal Issues: Human Resource and the Long Arm of the Law

VIDEO

PowerPoint Clip from Barcelona Restaurant Group: Managing Human Resources
Run time: 2:35 minutes
Restaurants in the Barcelona Restaurant Group are trendy tapas and wine bars. Quality service, excellent food, and a fun atmosphere are keys to Barcelona's success. Barcelona management demands quality customer service. To achieve this, they are continually hiring and firing servers and managers. In the transient restaurant business, with a high burnout rate, Barcelona experiences 60 to 70 percent turnover in its management.

Hiring effective, high-energy managers is critical for Barcelona. In this segment, Barcelona's COO discusses his three-step selection process for floor managers. He begins with a brief interview and then gives candidates $100 to "shop" one or two Barcelona restaurants. Candidates write an essay about their restaurant experience. The third step of the selection process involves an experience actually working the floor in the restaurant.

Ask Your Students:

1. What role does human resources play in the success of Barcelona Restaurant Group?
2. What is the function of the initial interview for a management position at Barcelona?

DVD SEGMENT SUMMARY

PepsiCo
Run time: 6:56 minutes
How does a company with a massive international presence, conducting business in multiple time zones and languages, manage its employees? Strategic human resources. At PepsiCo, human resource management is about finding strategies that contribute to company expansion and innovation. Human resource leaders integrate fully with the broader PepsiCo organization, partnering with each division of the business to produce real results. In conventional companies, human

Visit login.cengage.com for additional materials to enhance your lectures!

CHAPTER 15: Human Resource Management: Building a Top-Quality Workforce

KEY TERMS

BEYOND THE CLASS

A selection of materials is in the Instructor's Manual.

resource personnel rarely leave their offices. But PepsiCo believes it's important for HR managers to promote employee training, mentoring, and career planning across all company departments. That's why PepsiCo sends senior human resource personnel to work along side sales reps, warehouse managers, distribution workers, and other employees. At PepsiCo, the human resource function goes beyond the basics to deliver measurable hard-line results—a necessity for any company in today's business environment.

Ask Your Students:

1. What challenges do human resource organizations face in today's competitive business environment? How is PepsiCo meeting those challenges?
2. *Human resources management* refers to an integrated personnel/human resource function. Describe the components of the HRM planning process and how each one contributes to PepsiCo's corporate development and growth.

LECTURE EXAMPLE

Human resources, already involved in ensuring legal compliance in many business functions, sits at the center of organizational efforts to create diverse and inclusive environments, and thus holds a strategic position at the forefront on workplace issues and concerns arising from religious diversity. One concern stems from religious discrimination, one of the types of employment discrimination that can lead to lawsuits.

Some studies have shown that some of the accommodations that are most meaningful to employees, such as providing personal days for religious observance, are not yet offered by many organizations.

Source: Schramm, Jennifer. (Jan 2009). Human resources gets religion. *HR Magazine*, 54, 1, 96.

DISCUSSION QUESTIONS

1. How has management's attitude toward human resources changed in the past

couple of decades? What factors have influenced this change?
2. Why do interviews tend to be ineffective at determining whether a candidate will perform well on the job? How can managers improve the interview process?
3. Looking ahead, do you believe that job flexibility options—from flextime, to telecommuting, to job sharing—will continue to grow at American businesses? Explain your answer.

GROUP ACTIVITY

Before beginning the project, students should take a couple of minutes to write down their three most positive qualities. Next, ask five *other* students to name what they see as your single best quality. Remember that while you might not know each other well, you surely know each other better than an interviewer would upon first meeting, and interviewers often make decisions based on first impressions. Then reconvene as a class and check your lists. Did most of you find consistency between the qualities you see in yourselves and qualities others see in you? What were some of the surprises?

ASSIGNMENTS

Looking back at your own job history (or interviewing someone you know well about his or her job history), identify a firm that does a poor job of training its employees. Design the ideal training program for this company. Be sure to outline the key elements of orientation, job-specific training for at least three different positions, and management development. Include recommended timing for each type of training (e.g., skills training updates every six months, management development once a year). How would your training program improve profitability for the company?

CHAPTER 15—UPDATES TO BUSN THIS YEAR

Page 241—New chapter opening quote

Page 241—Revised information about Southwest Airline's profits

Page 241—Revised information about the average CEO salary

Page 242—Revised *Humble Beginnings* box feature

Page 242—New pull quote

Page 242—Revised information about CEO pay tied to the stock market

Page 243—New pull quote

Page 246—New pull quote

Page 246—Revised statistic about how many candidates for a job are vetted by companies

Page 246—Revised statistic about how many contingent workers account for U.S. employment

Page 250—Revised information about minimum wage

Page 250—New example of less traditional benefits companies offer

Page 251—Revised information about the number of Americans telecommuting

Page 251—Revised *Wacky Benefits* box feature

Page 252—Revised *Commuting at Zero Gallons per Mile* box feature

Page 253—New fun fact

Page 254—Revised statistics about sexual harassment charges over the past decade

CHAPTER 15: Human Resource Management: Building a Top-Quality Workforce

Visit login.cengage.com for additional materials to enhance your lectures!

Managing Information and Technology:
Finding New Ways to Learn and Link

WHAT'S INSIDE

Key Topics in this Chapter: Dramatic changes in the basic elements of computer technology, Internet2, cloud computing, decision making with information technology, the impact of information technology on e-commerce, Web 2.0, B2B e-commerce, solutions to the challenges sparked by rapid technological advances, ethical and legal concerns.

LEARNING OBJECTIVES

With the growth in eReader usage among students, this 6th edition of BUSN features a new numbering system for major headings that we recommend you use instead of page numbers when creating assignments.

16–1 Explain the basic elements of computer technology—including hardware, software, and networks—and describe key trends in each area

16–2 Discuss the reasons for the increasing popularity of cloud computing

16–3 Describe how data becomes information and how decision support systems can provide high-quality information that helps managers make better decisions

16–4 Explain how Internet-based technologies have changed business-to-consumer and business-to-business commerce

16–5 Describe the problems posed by the rapid changes in Internet-based technologies, and explain ways to deal with these problems

CHAPTER 16 OUTLINE

Information Technology: Explosive Change
    Hardware and Software
    Networks
    The Role of the IT Department

Cloud Computing: The Sky's the Limit!

Information Technology and Decision Making: A Crucial Aid
    Data and Information
    Characteristics of Good Information
    Using Information Technology to Improve Decision Making
    Expert Systems

Information Technology and the World of e-Commerce
    Using Information Technology in the B2C Market
    Using Information Technology in the B2B Market

Challenges and Concerns Arising from New Technologies
    Malware
    Spyware
    Computer Viruses
    Spam, Phishing, and Pharming
    Hackers: Break-ins in Cyberspace
    Ethical and Legal Issues

The Big Picture

Careers in Information Technology

MULTIMEDIA

PPT—THE HIGHLIGHTS

Slide 8   The Role of the IT Department
Slide 9   The Web is Dead, You Say? That's App-surd
Slide 10   Cloud Computing: The Sky's the Limit
Slide 12   Information Technology and Decision Making: A Crucial Aid
Slide 21   Using Information Technology in the B2C Market

VIDEO

PowerPoint Clip from Method: Technology-Driven Marketing
Run time: 2:02 minutes
In 2001, two childhood friends, Adam Lowry and Eric Ryan, came up with an idea to revolutionize the cleaning world. Today, Method provides stylish, eco-friendly household products made with non-toxic ingredients that clean well and smell great. Method launched nationally in Target stores in 2002 and has grown to become a leader in the eco-friendly cleaning market.

    The Method website plays a key role in marketing and selling the brand. Method's site provides e-commerce opportunities, product information, and an interactive community for loyal and enthusiastic Method advocates. Through the website, marketers track consumer patterns and behaviors.

    Additionally, Method advocates provide valuable insights about the site. These advocates connect through profiles, blogs, and forums. All of this consumer participation helps establish Method as an ownable brand.

Source: http://methodhome.com/methodology/our-story/method-firsts

Ask Your Students:

1. How does information technology aid in decision making at Method?
2. How do e-commerce capabilities benefit Method?

DVD SEGMENT SUMMARY

RogueSheep
Run time: 6:03 minutes
That 25-cent postcard in the gift shop may soon become a thing of the past. RogueSheep's new postcard application for iPhone, "Postage," is giving the traditional postcard a run for its money. Unlike standard postcards, Postage allows users to send a digital card to family and friends quickly and efficiently. For $4.99, iPhone users can purchase the app, choose from more than

ASSIGNMENTS

Do some Internet research to identify and learn about three or four examples of successful recent viral marketing campaigns. Describe the basic approach taken by each campaign. Which viral campaign did you personally find the most effective? Why?

BEYOND THE CLASS

A selection of materials is in the Instructor's Manual.

KEY TERMS

60 postcard designs, and insert personal photos and greetings. The process is done in minutes. RogueSheep launched in Seattle when Christopher Parrish, Daniel Guenther, Matt Joss, and Jeff Argast banded together to create graphics and publishing applications. The company offers consulting services and custom applications, but the company's best-known product is Postage for iPhone. In prior decades, a firm like RogueSheep would have been content living in the shadow of Microsoft or Adobe. But in the era of Web 2.0 and mobile computing, any small hot-handed developer has the potential to make it big.

Ask Your Students:

1. Is RogueSheep in the business of making hardware or software? Explain the difference.
2. How is RogueSheep using viral marketing to promote its products?

LECTURE EXAMPLE

Cloud computing is associated with serious risks to privacy and consumer rights, and current privacy laws do little to assist either providers or customers. Consumers using cloud computing products need to be cautious. Providers of cloud computing products would do well to familiarize themselves with applicable consumer protection and privacy laws—a very difficult task where they are marketing, or otherwise making available, their products globally and thereby exposing themselves to the diverse laws of multiple countries. The continuing tension between the law's focus on geographical locations and the ubiquitous nature of cloud computing may represent the largest obstacle to a widespread adoption of cloud computing.

Source: Svantesson, Dan & Clarke, Roger. (July 2010). Privacy and consumer risks in cloud computing. *Computer Law & Security Review*, 26, 4, 391–397.

DISCUSSION QUESTIONS

1. What is the difference between data and information? What are the characteristics of high-quality information?
2. What are the characteristics of the Web 2.0 approach to B2C e-commerce? Describe a real-world website you are familiar with that does a particularly good job of using this approach.
3. Explain why cloud computing is likely to revolutionize the way firms acquire and use information technology resources. What issues and concerns might limit the acceptance of cloud computing?

GROUP ACTIVITY

This project is designed to make students more aware of the Web 2.0 approach to B2C e-commerce. Before the project select several commercial websites that cater to college-age students and note their URLs. Break the class into small groups and assign students in each group the responsibility of visiting the website for one of the companies as homework. Tell the students to evaluate the extent to which their site makes use of Web 2.0 concepts. Give the groups 10 to 15 minutes at the beginning of the next class session to compare notes. Ask each group to prepare a list of "likes and dislikes" for the site and come up with suggestions to make it more effective. After the discussion period, have each group provide a brief summary of their ideas to the class.

CHAPTER 16—UPDATES TO BUSN THIS YEAR

Page 257—New chapter opening quote

Page 257—Revised information about flash memory, iPad2 computing power

Page 258—Revised Exhibit 16.1 Growth in Broadband Internet Access and surrounding text

Page 259—*Reply All: Instant Panic and Regret with the Rare Happy Ending* box feature replaces *The Web Is Dead, You Say? That's App-surd!* box feature

Page 260—New information about fundamental change in IT in regards to cloud computing

Page 261—New pull quote

Page 262—New example about data mining

Page 264—Revised magazine advertising revenue

Page 265—Revised information about number of PayPal accounts

Page 265—Revised information about RFID range

Page 265—New pull quote

Page 266—New RFID example

Page 266—*Use Two-Factor Authentication on Your Gmail Account So You're Not "Mugged" in London* box feature replaces *A Crowd Pleasing Approach to Finance*

Page 267—New fun fact

Page 268—New information about strong passwords

Page 269—Information about encryption and protective sleeves

Page 269—*Multitasking Makes You Stupid* box feature replaces *Information Overload: Too Much of a Good Thing* box feature

Pages 269–270—Revised statistics on piracy around the world

Page 271—Revised information about salaries in the Careers in Information Technology box feature

CHAPTER 16: Managing Information and Technology: Finding New Ways to Learn and Link

Visit login.cengage.com for additional materials to enhance your lectures!

Operations Management: Putting It All Together

WHAT'S INSIDE

Key Topics in this Chapter: The role of operations management, efficiency to effectiveness, goods vs. services, what operations managers do, process selection and facility layout, strategies for inventory control, project scheduling tools, managing value chains, servicescape, operations technology, quality improvement, Baldrige National Quality Program, Six Sigma, and lean and green production.

LEARNING OBJECTIVES

With the growth in eReader usage among students, this 6th edition of BUSN features a new numbering system for major headings that we recommend you use instead of page numbers when creating assignments.

17-1 Define operations management and describe how the role of operations management has changed over the past fifty years

17-2 Discuss the key responsibilities of operations managers

17-3 Describe how operations managers deal with the special challenges posed by the provision of services

17-4 Explain how changes in technology have revolutionized operations management

17-5 Describe the strategies operations managers have used to improve the quality of goods and services

17-6 Explain how lean and green practices can help both the organization and the environment

CHAPTER 17 OUTLINE

MULTIMEDIA

PPT—THE HIGHLIGHTS

Slide 8 What Do Operations Managers Do?
Slide 11 Inventory Control: Knowing When to Hold 'Em
Slide 18 Automation: The Rise of the Machine
Slide 24 Waking Up the Need for Quality
Slide 33 Lean Thinking in The Service Sector

VIDEO

PowerPoint Clip from Theo Chocolate, Strategy Formulation and Execution
Run time: 2:24 minutes
Theo Chocolate is the only organic, fair trade, bean-to-bar chocolate factory in the United States. Founder Joseph Whinney pioneered the supply of organic cocoa beans into the United States and produced Theo's first chocolate run in 2006. The company emphasizes quality and unites delicious award-winning chocolate with a commitment to changing the way the cocoa industry does business.

   Theo is the only organic, fair trade chocolate with a vertically integrated supply chain. Theo controls the entire supply chain, working directly with farmers, importing the beans, and making the chocolate in its own facility. Controlling this chain of relationships and the manufacturing process ensures quality. Theo's factory tour business is a valuable marketing vehicle that makes it possible to share the Theo story and values with new customers.

Source: http://www.theochocolate.com

Ask Your Students:

1. Describe Theo's supply chain.
2. How does Theo's supply chain benefit the business?

DVD SEGMENT SUMMARY

Washburn Guitar
Run time: 11:00 minutes
Washburn Guitar has been making high-quality instruments since 1883. Over the past decade, the Chicago-based manufacturer enhanced its quality reputation by recruiting expert production specialist Gil Vasquez. In addition to establishing high standards, Vasquez has overseen the acquisition of high-end guitar maker Parker Guitars. At the heart of Washburn's enduring success is a rich

Visit login.cengage.com for additional materials to enhance your lectures!

CHAPTER 17: Operations Management: Putting It All Together

KEY TERMS

operations management, 273

efficiency, 273

effectiveness, 273

goods, 273

services, 273

process, 275

inventory, 277

critical path method (CPM), 277

immediate predecessors, 277

critical path, 277

value chain, 279

vertical integration, 279

outsourcing, 279

offshoring, 279

enterprise resource planning (ERP), 280

servicescape, 280

automation, 281

robot, 281

computer-aided design (CAD) software, 282

computer-aided engineering (CAE) software, 282

computer-aided manufacturing (CAM) software, 282

computer-aided design/computer-aided manufacturing (CAD/CAM), 282

computer-integrated manufacturing (CIM), 283

total quality management (TQM), 285

poka-yokes, 285

Six Sigma, 285

Baldrige National Quality Program, 285

ISO 9000, 285

lean production, 286

just-in-time (JIT) production, 286

ISO 14000, 288

guitar-making tradition maintained by highly skilled craftsmen. The production process starts with Washburn's AutoCAD engineers—computer specialists who develop drawings and prototypes. Once a design for a new guitar is approved, individual parts move through various stations of the Washburn facility. The end-to-end process involves woodcutting, body-and-neck assembly, sanding and painting, and components assembly. From the drafting board to the final inspection, Washburn technicians ensure that Vasquez's high standards are met. The result is a line of masterfully crafted guitars like the DD75 Maya Pro signature model—rock-steady instruments guaranteed to thrill musicians and audiences worldwide.

Ask Your Students:

1. What factors influence Washburn's process selection and facility layout?
2. What role does technology have in the art of guitar making?

LECTURE EXAMPLE

Researchers and scholars are finding that employees are perhaps even more critical than equipment and processes in Lean Manufacturing Systems. Flexible machines are expensive and lead to high fixed costs. Use of manual operations can make productions systems both flexible and adaptable. JIT requires a work culture that allows the worker to become a participant in decision making, and thus putting trust and responsibility in the hands of the workers is necessary.

Source: Upadhye, N., Deshmukh, S.G., Garg, S. (Jan 2010). Lean manufacturing for sustainable development. *Global Business and Management Research: An International Journal*, 2, 1, 125–138.

DISCUSSION QUESTIONS

1. How have the goals and strategies of operations management changed over the past fifty years? What are some of the key factors that have precipitated these changes?
2. How can an emphasis on quality improve a firm's effectiveness? How can it improve the firm's efficiency? What are some of the key ways firms can use to improve quality?
3. What is a servicescape? Why is it important for a service provider to pay attention to this concept?

GROUP ACTIVITY

This project consists of two stages. Break the class into groups of three to five students. In the first stage, ask each group to brainstorm and come up with a list of three or four companies that they believe practice environmentally responsible production methods. (At this stage, the lists will be based purely on perception.) List the choices of each group and allow the class to vote on the four or five companies that are candidates for the class's "Green Star." In the second stage, assign each group the responsibility for finding information on the Internet about the actual green practices of one of the firms on the list. (If you have a large class, you can assign the same company to more than one group.) Have the groups report back to the class with their findings. Were real practices consistent with prior perceptions? Discuss the findings in class and choose one or more firms to receive the coveted "Green Star."

ASSIGNMENTS

Think about your own recent encounters with service providers such as restaurants, theaters, car repair facilities, and banks. Identify and describe one service experience that met or exceeded your expectations, and another that left you dissatisfied. What characteristics stood out in each case? How could the service provider that disappointed you improve its performance?

BEYOND THE CLASS

A selection of materials is in the Instructor's Manual.

CHAPTER 17—UPDATES TO BUSN THIS YEAR

Page 273—Revised percentage of workers in nonfarm labor force and service sectors

Page 274—New pull quote

Page 276—New pull quote

Page 282—New pull quote

Page 282—*Wall-E and R2D2: Robots Lower Hospital Costs* box feature replaces *A New Dimension in Production Technology* box feature

Page 284—*Apple Stores: Predicted to Fail, Have Highest Sales in Retail* box feature replaces *Oops! What Were They Thinking?* box feature

Page 285—New pull quote

Page 285—Revised cost of a Baldrige program consultation

Page 286—Revised information about worldwide organizations earning ISO 9001 certificates

Page 286—*Just-in-Time: Not too small. Not too big. Just Right* box feature replaces *Six Sigma Belts Quality Concerns* box feature

Page 287—New example of lean production

Page 287—*LED Light Bulbs: Don't Change, Go Green!* box feature replaces *The Greening of Supply Chains* box feature

CHAPTER 17: Operations Management: Putting It All Together

Visit login.cengage.com for additional materials to enhance your lectures!

Personal Finance

WHAT'S INSIDE

Key Topics in this Appendix: Budgets, assessing your revenues and expenses, spending habits, savings accounts, building credit, credit card laws and regulations, abusing credit, investments, different investment options, acquiring financial assets, building a portfolio, and retirement planning.

LEARNING OBJECTIVES

With the growth in eReader usage among students, this 6th edition of BUSN features a new numbering system for major headings that we recommend you use instead of page numbers when creating assignments.

A-1 Apply the principles of budgeting to your personal finances

A-2 Identify strategies to help build a sufficient savings

A-3 Explain the importance of using credit wisely

A-4 Discuss key wealth-building principles and the financial instruments that may be part of a wealth-building strategy

APPENDIX OUTLINE

Your Budget
How Do I Get Started?
Assessing Revenues: Where Does My Money Come From?
Assessing Expenses: Where Does It All Go?

Your Savings: Building a Safety Net

Your Credit: Handle with Care
Credit Cards: Boon or Bane?
Protection for Consumers: New Laws and Regulations
Using Credit Cards Wisely: The Need for Discipline

Your Investments: Building for the Future
Building Wealth: The Key Is Consistency—and an Early Start!
Financial Securities: What Are My Investment Options?
Acquiring Financial Assets: The Role of a Broker Building a Portfolio: A Few Words about Diversification Risk, and Return But What Is My Best Investment? (Hint: Look in the Mirror!)
Investing for the Long Term: Planning for Your Retirement

The Big Picture

MULTIMEDIA

PPT—THE HIGHLIGHTS

Slide 6 Understanding Your Spending Habits: Know Thyself
Slide 7 Your Savings: Building a Safety Net
Slide 10 Credit Cards: Boon or Bane?
Slide 14 Building Wealth: The Key Is Consistency
Slide 20 Investing for the Long Term: Planning for Your Retirement

VIDEO

PowerPoint Clip from Money
Run time: 2:13 minutes
Money exerts an influence on almost every area of our lives. The ability to manage money, in terms of both our personal and professional lives, is critical to achieving success. Money gives us a standardized system for determining worth and an acceptable medium for exchange of goods and services. Money as a medium of exchange allows us to store and transfer value. Every decision we make to spend, save, or invest is based on an understanding of money. This segment focuses on the function of money to measure value and to store value over time. It also touches on the implications of devalued currency and the inflationary spending mindset that can result.

Ask Your Students:

1. When you are preparing a budget to determine your personal spending, what is the primary function of your money?

2. Whether you are saving or investing part of your paycheck, what is the primary function of your money?

DVD SEGMENT SUMMARY

Edward Jones
Run time: 7:17 minutes
Edward Jones is one of the largest investment firms in the United States, with more than four thousand branch offices and three million investors coast to coast. Unlike other brokerage firms, Edward Jones exclusively targets individual investors and small business owners. The company meets the needs of clients through a philosophy of one-on-one personalized service, which is carried out by investment representatives at thousands of branch offices around the country. At Edward Jones, every client's financial situation is considered to be unique. As a result, financial advisors work to understand customers' life goals before making investment recommendations. In general, the financial goals of younger customers differ from those of clients nearing retirement age. Nevertheless, all Edward Jones customers seek a combination of financial growth and safety. With that in mind, the financial advisors at Edward Jones have a single focus each day: find the investment strategy that's right for the individual.

Ask Your Students:

1. Do the financial advisors at Edward Jones recommend that clients wait until they have significant savings before investing? Explain.

Visit login.cengage.com for additional materials to enhance your lectures!

APPENDIX: Personal Finance

2. How does retirement planning for a 40-year-old differ from the investment planning of twenty-something college graduates?

LECTURE EXAMPLE

College students are relying on student loans and credit card debt more than ever before. A variety of forces are impacting their reliance, including tightening credit, a sluggish economy, and the continuing rise in the price of college. To pay for the escalating cost of college, students are required to carry greater amounts of debt. In 2009, two-thirds of college students borrowed to pay for college, carrying an average debt load of $23,186 by the time of graduation (Chaker, 2009).

Source: Ross, C. A. & Pinto, M. B. (Dec 2010). College students and credit card use: An analysis of financially at-risk students. *College Student Journal*, 44, no 4, 823-35; A. Chaker, Students Borrow More than Ever for College. *The Wall Street Journal*, September 4, 2009, http://online.wsj.com/article/SB10001424052970204731804574388682129316614.html.

DISCUSSION QUESTIONS

1. What is a credit score, and why is it important? What are some key factors that influence an individual's score? How would you interpret a credit score of 500? 820?
2. What is common stock? What are the two types of return on this type of security and how do they differ? Why is common stock considered to be a relatively risky investment?
3. How are 401(k), 403(b), and 457 retirement plans similar and how do they differ? How do Roth plans differ from traditional plans? What are the key advantages of these plans compared to IRAs?

GROUP ACTIVITY

Assign each student the responsibility of researching a specific online brokerage site, such as Charles Schwab, Scottrade, E*Trade, TD Ameritrade, Wells Trade, or Options-House. (You can assign the same brokerage firm to several students.) Tell them to find out the fees and commissions charged by their broker, the minimum initial deposit, the types of investment products offered, and the investment research tools available on the site. Students should check the broker's own website to obtain basic information but should also look at reviews and rankings of brokerage firms provided by financial websites such as Kiplinger or Smart Money. At the beginning of the next class session, break the class into groups. (Put students who researched the same brokerage firm into different groups.) Have the groups compare their findings and choose the brokerage firm that represents the best overall value. End the project by having a discussion of each group's findings.

ASSIGNMENTS

Go to website such as Creditcards.com or Creditcardguide.com (http://www.creditcardguide.com/), and click on the link to student credit cards. Look at the list of recommended cards. Which card would you most like to hold? What is the initial APR on this card—and how long does the introductory rate apply? What is the regular APR? Does the card have an annual fee? What type of "perks" does it offer? How good does your credit have to be to qualify for this card?

BEYOND THE CLASS

A selection of materials is in the Instructor's Manual.

PERSONAL FINANCE APPENDIX— UPDATES TO BUSN THIS YEAR

Page 291—New chapter opening quote

Page 292—New pull quote

Page 292–293—Revised information about FDIC deposits

Page 293—New example of mortgage rates related to different credit scores

Page 294—New fun fact

Page 298—Revised stats from the BLS on monthly earnings for high school and college graduates, also unemployment rates

Page 298—*What Are the Best Personal Finance Apps for Smartphones?* box feature replaces *Do You Really Need a Broker to Buy Stocks?* box feature

Page 299—Revised information about contributions on traditional and Roth IRAs

APPENDIX: Personal Finance

Visit login.cengage.com for additional materials to enhance your lectures!

Labor Unions and Collective Bargaining

WHAT'S INSIDE

Key Topics in this Appendix: Labor unions, organization of unions, U.S. labor laws, collective bargaining, distributive bargaining, interest-based bargaining, strikes, lockouts, picketing, boycotting, mediation, arbitration, unions and compensation, job security, productivity, and challenges that unions face.

LEARNING OBJECTIVES

With the growth in eReader usage among students, this 6th edition of BUSN features a new numbering system for major headings that we recommend you use instead of page numbers when creating assignments.

A1-1   Describe how unions in the United States are organized

A1-2   Discuss the key provisions of the laws that govern labor–management relations

A1-3   Explain how labor contracts are negotiated and administered

A1-4   Evaluate the impact that unions have had on their members' welfare and the economy, and explain the challenges that today's unions face

APPENDIX 1 OUTLINE

The Basic Structure of Unions

Labor Laws in the United States

Collective Bargaining: Reaching an Agreement
    Subjects of Bargaining: What It's All About
    Approaches to Collective Bargaining
    Dealing with Impasse
    Administering a Collective Bargaining Agreement

The State of the Unions: Achievements, Problems, and Challenges
    Unions and Compensation
    Unions and Job Security
    Unions and Productivity
    The Challenge of Declining Union Membership

The Big Picture

MULTIMEDIA

PPT—THE HIGHLIGHTS

Slide 6   The Basic Structure of Unions
Slide 12   Right-to-Work Laws
Slide 15   Collective Bargaining: Reaching an Agreement
Slide 17   Approaches to Collective Bargaining
Slide 26   The Challenges of Declining Union Membership

VIDEO

PowerPoint Clip from Boston Ballet/ Boston Musician's Association
Run time: 2:16 minutes
Chartered in 1897, the Boston Musicians' Association (BMA) is a labor union representing over 1,600 professional musicians in the Boston metro area and beyond. The union works to ensure that musicians have fair wages and economic security, through collective bargaining agreements, wage scales, guaranteed contracts, instrument insurance and a pension fund. BMA musicians perform in a variety of venues, including the orchestra for the Boston Ballet. Founded in 1963, Boston Ballet was the first professional repertory ballet company in New England.

In this segment, ballet Music Director and conductor Jonathan McPhee, an orchestra musician, and a BMA representative discuss the relationship between the union and management. McPhee speaks as management about why it is in his interest to maintain a positive relationship with the union.

Sources: http://www.bostonmusicians.org/union, http://www.bostonballet.org/about/history.html

Ask Your Students:

1. How does the Music Director, as ballet management, view the union?
2. How does the union benefit Boston Ballet musicians?

DVD SEGMENT SUMMARY

Writers Guild of America
Run time: 14:03 minutes
As U.S. manufacturing jobs move overseas, unions are busy recruiting new groups of American workers who aren't yet unionized. For the Writers Guild of America (WGA), labor organizing focuses on the nation's entertainment writers, those talented behind-the-scenes workers who craft magical banter for movies and television shows. Mona Mangan, executive director for the Guild's eastern territory, says that WGA began with a mission to help writers get public credit for their work. Today the union addresses a broader range of financial and contractual matters. The Guild made headlines in 2007 when television writers organized a strike to get a share of revenues from foreign market productions and videocassette sales—a move that left late-night TV hosts starved for witty one-liners. Despite widespread public opposition to union tactics like mandatory membership

Visit login.cengage.com for additional materials to enhance your lectures!

ONLINE APPENDIX 1: Labor Unions and Collective Bargaining

KEY TERMS

and collective bargaining, the Writers Guild of America sees itself as an important vehicle for the unionization of the entertainment industry.

Ask Your Students:

1. Should union members in nonessential industries like entertainment have the right to strike when their actions may put others out of work as well?
2. Do you think a labor dispute outcome that leaves both sides partly satisfied is a good outcome? Why or why not?

LECTURE EXAMPLE

"Organized labor now has the opportunity to embrace the rhetoric of the Thirteenth Amendment to continue its advocacy of all workers, including immigrant workers, in this century. Commentator James Pope, while discussing the right to strike and other traditional labor rights, suggested that organized labor arguing without the help of the Thirteenth Amendment is like the gun lobby arguing without the help of the Second Amendment. As organized labor continues to partner with immigrant rights groups and continues to actively take on a role of representing workers against abusive government action, the Thirteenth Amendment provides labor with the moral basis for its action. The Amendment called for the ending of state-sanctioned abuses of worker rights, citizenship rights, civil rights, and labor rights. Now more than ever, unions need to be in the forefront of that fight."

Source: Ontiveros, Maria Lina. (Mar 2008). Out of the shadows and into the spotlight: Immigrants and organized labor. *WorkingUSA*, 11, 1, 157–164.

DISCUSSION QUESTIONS

1. Which factors have contributed to the dramatic decline in union membership over the past quarter century? Do you think unions will be able to reverse this trend? Why or why not?
2. What is the difference between distributive bargaining and interest-based bargaining? Under what conditions is interest-based bargaining likely to be most effective?
3. How are mediation and arbitration similar? What is the key difference between them?

GROUP ACTIVITY

This activity involves role-playing and requires a bit of preparation. As homework prior to the activity, tell students to review that material in the appendix on the benefits of unions and the criticisms leveled against them. Suggest that they also do additional research on the Internet about the pros and cons of union representation. On the day of the activity, divide the class into groups of six to nine students. Then randomly subdivide the groups so that two or three students in each group play union organizers, two or three play anti-union company management, and the remaining students play the role of workers who are to vote in a union-certification election. Let the "union reps" and "managers" each present their case for and against union representation, then have the "workers" vote. At the end of the project compare results from each group. Did most votes have pro or anti-union outcomes? Ask the workers in each group to briefly explain why they voted the way they did.

ASSIGNMENTS

Visit the website of the Federal Mediation and Conciliation Service (http://www.fmcs.gov/internet/index.asp) and learn about this service. Describe the basic functions and services the FMCS performs and identify the qualifications required to become a federal mediator.

BEYOND THE CLASS

A selection of materials is in the Instructor's Manual.

LABOR UNIONS ONLINE APPENDIX—UPDATES TO BUSN THIS YEAR

Page A1-3—New chapter opening quote

Page A1-5—Revised Exhibit A1.2 Right-to-Work Laws and surrounding text

Page A1-8—Revised Exhibit A1.3 Trends in Work Stoppages: 1970–2011

Page A1-8—Revised Exhibit A1.4 Union vs. Nonunion Median Weekly Earnings in Selected Industries (2011) and surrounding text

Page A1-8—Revised statistics about union worker benefits

Page A1-9—Revised statistics about public employee unions

Page A1-9—Revised stats on number of employees in private industry belonging to unions

Page A1-10—States and Cities Attack Public-Sector Union Costs box feature replaces The Un-Union Option box feature

ONLINE APPENDIX 1: Labor Unions and Collective Bargaining

Visit login.cengage.com for additional materials to enhance your lectures!

Business Law

WHAT'S INSIDE
Key Topics in this Appendix: Constitutional law, statutory law, administrative law, case law, civil law, criminal law, contracts, breach of contract, sales of transferring ownership, titles, principal–agent relationships, bankruptcy, intellectual property, patents, trademarks, and copyrights.

LEARNING OBJECTIVES

With the growth in eReader usage among students, this 6th edition of BUSN features a new numbering system for major headings that we recommend you use instead of page numbers when creating assignments.

A2–1 Explain the purposes of laws and identify the major sources of law in the United States

A2–2 Describe the characteristics of a contract and explain how the terms of contracts are enforced

A2–3 Describe how both title and risk pass from the seller to the buyer when a sale occurs

A2–4 Provide an overview of the legal principles governing agency, intellectual property, and bankruptcy

MULTIMEDIA

PPT—THE HIGHLIGHTS

Slide 3 The Purpose and Origin of Laws
Slide 8 Difference Between Civil and Criminal Law Cases
Slide 9 Contracts: The Ties that Bind
Slide 13 Principle-Agent Relationships
Slide 16 Intellectual Property

VIDEO

PowerPoint Clip from Intellectual Property: Permissions in Cyberspace
Run time: 2:29 minutes
While we generally think of property that is protected by law in terms of land, buildings, and physical goods, the law also recognizes intellectual property—for example, the right of an inventor, innovator, writer, or artist to own their creations and prevent others from copying or using these creations without their permission. While a website might not carry a patent, trademark, or copyright, ethically and legally, web content may still be considered protected intellectual property. In this segment, a programmer is using a frame to present content from deep within another site. The manager and programmer discuss the legalities and ethics of presenting content from another site as part of their site. The programmer feels that content on the Internet should be free. The manager makes the point that permission may be needed to link to the site in this manner.

Ask Your Students:

1. What legal issue is presented in this video?
2. What is required in order to frame this web content legally and ethically?

DVD SEGMENT SUMMARY

Real World Legal—Pharzime
Run time: 8:57 minutes
At Pharzime, an opportunity to extend the company's epilepsy drug to patients with depression has the company buzzing with excitement. Gensol received U.S. Food and Drug Administration (FDA) approval as an epilepsy medication, but it has not yet undergone a "double blind" study to verify benefits for patients with bipolar disorder. Pharzime's four-year patent has the company positioned for unprecedented new sales of Gensol, and executives worry that a lengthy review by the FDA could erase Pharzime's opportunity. The vice president of market planning, who supports the immediate "off label" sale of Gensol, advises a Regulatory Affairs executive that the company should bypass the FDA's burdensome review process. Meanwhile, in Pharzime's sales department, a veteran sales leader meets with a new hire to discuss Gensol's sales potential, and sticky questions arise about Pharzime's marketing approach and the potential pitfalls of Gensol's off-label use.

APPENDIX 2 OUTLINE

Visit login.cengage.com for additional materials to enhance your lectures!

ONLINE APPENDIX 2: Business Law

KEY TERMS

Ask Your Students:

1 Why is business law important to this case?

2. Which source of law discussed in the appendix allows the U.S. Food & Drug Administration to regulate medicines manufactured by Pharzime?

LECTURE EXAMPLE

Protecting the rights of intellectual property owners is, therefore, a critical task of the federal government in the current environment, where the distribution of illegitimate goods can be achieved on scales like never before. While owners of intellectual property can protect their rights by pursuing civil remedies, the threat of civil sanctions is often insufficient to deter infringing activities. By 2000, U.S. companies had lost over $1 trillion from intellectual property theft, and that number is reportedly growing by $250 billion every year. Intellectual property theft may also compromise the safety of the general public due to the use of counterfeit materials in pharmaceuticals, auto parts, and many other goods.

Source: Cormier, J.W., Kozell, R., McCurdy, J.L. (Spring 2009). Intellectual property crimes: Twenty-fourth annual survey of white-collar crime. *American Criminal Law Review*, 46, 2, 761–713.

DISCUSSION QUESTIONS

1. What are the major differences between civil law and criminal law?

2. What is the Uniform Commercial Code? How does this code benefit businesses?

3. What is the purpose of a copyright? What would happen if copyrights protection were not available? How would this affect the incentives of authors, songwriters, and playwrights?

GROUP ACTIVITY

This project is designed to illustrate to your students how closely trademarks are linked to their companies in the eyes of the public. Find 10 to 12 reproductions of trademarks used by well-known companies. (A good source is newspaper or magazine ads.) Remove or hide any specific mention of the actual names of the companies or products from the images. Divide the class into small groups. Display the trademarks one at a time, giving the students a minute or so of work within their group to identify the corresponding company. Have each group write down their guesses and hand them in. Discuss the results—which trademarks were most strongly identified with their companies? (To create a higher level of interest and motivation, you might offer a few bonus points to any group(s) correctly identifying a certain percentage of the companies.)

ASSIGNMENTS

Use the Internet to find out more about Chapter 7 bankruptcies. How does a debtor file for a voluntary bankruptcy? How do creditors file an involuntary bankruptcy? What is the purpose of the "means test" and how is it applied? What role does the trustee play? Which assets are protected from creditors' claims in your state? Which debts can be discharged under Chapter 7, and which debts remain intact?

BEYOND THE CLASS

A selection of materials is in the Instructor's Manual.

BUSINESS LAW ONLINE APPENDIX—UPDATES TO BUSN THIS YEAR

Page A2-9—*Smokism: Is it Illegal to Not Hire Smokers* box feature replaces *Happy Birthday to You...but If You Sing It We'll Sue!* box feature

Page A2-10—New example of trademarks

Page A2-11—Revised BLS salaries for lawyers

ONLINE APPENDIX 2: Business Law

Visit login.cengage.com for additional materials to enhance your lectures!